Part of the Shaker Community of Enfield, Grafton County, New Hampshire, with the
Great Stone House in the center, about 1904. (HABS NH–190, LC HABS NH, 5–
ENFI.V, 1–1)

HISTORIC AMERICA

Buildings, Structures, and Sites

Spiral stairs of the Shaker Centre Family Trustees' Office, Pleasant Hill, Mercer County, Kentucky. Photograph by Jack E. Boucher, 1963 (HABS KY–81, LC HABS KY, 84–SHAKT, 7–13)

HISTORIC AMERICA

Buildings, Structures, and Sites

Recorded by The Historic American Buildings Survey and the Historic American Engineering Record

Checklist compiled by Alicia Stamm
Historic American Buildings Survey/
Historic American Engineering Record
National Park Service
U.S. Department of the Interior

Essays edited by C. Ford Peatross
Library of Congress

Library of Congress   Washington   1983

Published for the Fiftieth Anniversary of the Historic American Buildings Survey, *Historic America* marks fifty years of cooperation among the American Institute of Architects, the Historic American Buildings Survey of the National Park Service, and the Library of Congress. This book was prepared by the staffs of the Historic American Buildings Survey/Historic American Engineering Record Division of the National Park Service and the Prints and Photographs Division of the Library of Congress.

Book design is by David Haddock, a member of the Typography and Design Division of the Government Printing Office.

Library of Congress Cataloging in Publication Data
Main entry under title:

Historic America : buildings, structures, and sites

    Includes bibliographical references and index.
    1. Architecture—United States. 2. Historic buildings—United States. 3. Historic sites—United States. I. Stamm, Alicia. II. Peatross, C. Ford. III. Historic American Buildings Survey. IV. Historic American Engineering Record. V. Library of Congress.
NA705.H53 1983   973   83–14422
ISBN 0–8444–0431–4

For sale by the Superintendent of Documents
U.S. Government Printing Office
Washington, D.C. 20402

Contents

IN APPRECIATION   *vii*

FOREWORD   *ix*

ACKNOWLEDGMENTS   *xi*

LIST OF CONTRIBUTORS   *xiii*

Using the HABS/HAER Collections at
the Library of Congress   *3*
   MARY M. ISON

The Historic American Buildings Survey: Its
Beginnings   *7*
   CHARLES E. PETERSON

The Survey in Louisiana in the 1930s   *23*
   SAMUEL WILSON, JR

Documenting a City: Philadelphia   *41*
   GEORGE B. TATUM

Cape May, New Jersey: Preservation of
a Victorian Town   *57*
   CAROLYN PITTS

Main Street: Its Revitalization   *71*
   CAROLE RIFKIND

Documenting Early American Technology: Covered
Bridges   *89*
   RICHARD SANDERS ALLEN

Recording a Room: The Kitchen   *107*
   RODRIS ROTH

Fittings and Fixtures: Miscellaneous Americana
in Survey Photographs   *127*
   DENYS PETER MYERS

America's Cast-Iron Heritage   *159*
   MARGOT GAYLE

Vernacular Construction in the Survey   *183*
   CARL LOUNSBURY

Recording the Work of an Architect:
Frank Lloyd Wright   *197*
   DAVID G. DELONG

Contents

HABS at an Awkward Age: The 1960s and 1970s *211*
ROBERT BRUEGMANN

A Rich Vein in the Mother Lode: HABS
in the Library of Congress *241*
C. FORD PEATROSS

Recording Historic Buildings: New Philosophies,
New Techniques, New Technologies *225*
JOHN BURNS

Future Directions for the Historic American Buildings
Survey *279*
ROBERT J. KAPSCH

The Checklist of Buildings, Structures, and Sites *287*

Using the Checklist *289*
ALICIA STAMM

Alabama *293*	Kentucky *409*	Ohio *555*
Alaska *319*	Louisiana *413*	Oklahoma *563*
Arizona *319*	Maine *417*	Oregon *564*
Arkansas *324*	Maryland *421*	Pennsylvania *567*
California *324*	Massachusetts *446*	Puerto Rico *597*
Canal Zone *349*	Michigan *470*	Rhode Island *598*
Colorado *349*	Minnesota *473*	South Carolina *606*
Connecticut *350*	Mississippi *474*	South Dakota *614*
Delaware *357*	Missouri *479*	Tennessee *615*
District of Columbia *363*	Montana *487*	Texas *619*
Florida *372*	Nebraska *488*	Utah *631*
Georgia *378*	Nevada *489*	Vermont *635*
Hawaii *387*	New Hampshire *490*	Virgin Islands *638*
Idaho *388*	New Jersey *494*	Virginia *641*
Illinois *389*	New Mexico *513*	Washington *667*
Indiana *398*	New York *516*	West Virginia *670*
Iowa *404*	North Carolina *544*	Wisconsin *675*
Kansas *408*	North Dakota *554*	Wyoming *678*

Index to County by City *681*

In Appreciation

This volume is dedicated to those who
founded the Historic American Buildings Survey
fifty years ago

Charles E. Peterson

Who invented the Survey, justified its initial
funding, and recruited its original staff

Arthur E. Demaray

Whose quick understanding and warm support
encouraged the wholehearted commitment of the
National Park Service

Leicester B. Holland

Who established an efficient and reliable
repository in the Library of Congress

Edward C. Kemper

Who arranged the immediate and comprehensive
participation of the American Institute of Architects

Thomas C. Vint

Who fought for the Survey in Washington and
across the country for twenty-three years

William Graves Perry

Who convened the national advisory board
and lent it his personal prestige

Foreword

In 1933, when the National Park Service, the American Institute of Architects, and the Library of Congress first joined together to create the Historic American Buildings Survey, this nation was in the midst of its greatest economic crisis. Franklin Delano Roosevelt's administration, promising a "New Deal" to a people buffeted as well by the winds of social and political change, launched many public works programs to offer immediate relief to thousands of unemployed Americans. These efforts produced many things of lasting value, including improvements to our great system of national parks, vast public works construction projects, and creative efforts as various as the Federal Writers' Program, the Federal Theatre Project, and the Index of American Design. Of all these programs begun in the 1930s, however, only the Historic American Buildings Survey continues today.

It was natural that a troubled nation should look toward its past in such a time, and there can be no more tangible evidence of a people's aspirations and accomplishments than its material culture. As we saw examples of our characteristic buildings, both great and humble, slip out of memory without record, we recognized a collective loss. From the Atlantic to the Pacific, we began to look at what our immigrant civilization had built in little more than three

centuries, and at what native American cultures had produced still earlier.

The Historic American Buildings Survey was our first national attempt to preserve this heritage through graphic and written records of our built environment. Perhaps the Survey's major innovation, however, was a standard format designed to facilitate the study and use of its records. This concern for public accessibility combined with the Survey's scope to make the collection democratic in both intent and content. At first, the Survey put unemployed architects to work; since, it has trained generations of architectural students, historians, photographers, and others in historic principles of design and construction. From the beginning it has provided a resource for writers, researchers, and scholars in many fields. Countless publications have drawn upon its images and records, copies of which are now widely available in this country and abroad. The National Park Service, the American Institute of Architects, and the Library of Congress are all justifiably proud of their participation in this rewarding effort.

The idea which led to all of this began in the National Park Service, in the mind of the chief of the Eastern Division of its Branch of Plans and Design, a man then in his twenties. In the fall of 1933 Charles E. Peterson recognized the opportunity to employ jobless architects to record a vanishing architectural patrimony. He seized upon the moment and convinced his superior, Arthur E. Demaray, of the feasibility of such a program. With that support he enlisted the cooperation of the American Institute of Architects (AIA), through Edward C. Kemper, and the Library of Congress, with the help of Leicester B. Holland. Besides securing initial funding, Peterson recruited the original staff to produce the Survey's records. Meanwhile, Holland, chief of the Library's Fine Arts Division and chairman of the American Institute of Architects Committee on Preservation of Historic Buildings, adapted an existing system at the Library of Congress to receive and arrange those records for public use.

Work began late in 1933 under the direction of Thomas C. Vint, and a national advisory committee was convened in January 1934 by William Graves Perry, head of the firm noted for its architectural work at Colonial Williamsburg. The tripartite agreement among the National Park Service, the American Institute of Architects, and the Library of Congress, under which the Survey has since operated, became effective on July 23 of the same year. The program received its legislative mandate through the Historic Sites, Buildings, and Antiquities Act of 1935, reaffirmed by the Historic Preservation Act of 1980. To this day, the original partners continue in a productive and unparalleled cooperative venture that includes both the public and the private sector.

In May 1981 representatives from the Park Service, the AIA, and the Library met to discuss how they might mark a half century of effort. To most of those present it was evident that no commemorative publication could be more appropriate or useful than a complete listing of the HABS records. The last HABS national catalog, published in 1941, was woefully out of date, even taking into account its supplement of 1959. The state catalog series was incomplete, and no thorough published account of the thousands of sites and structures documented since 1960 existed. It was also felt that a group of essays showing the range and effect of the Survey's recording activities and the potential its records offered for study and analysis would provide a useful complement to such an inventory.

We hope that this checklist and commentary expand still further the usefulness of a great collection, making more people aware of its existence and its possibilities. Just as the Historic American Buildings Survey and its companion program, the Historic American Engineering Record, will continue to provide a training ground for students and historians of architecture, the records these agencies create will serve as evidence of our built heritage and as a resource for those who would draw from it. We invite you to use and enjoy the rich store of information that has been created during the past half century.

Russell E. Dickenson
Director, National Park Service

Robert Broshar, F.A.I.A.
President, American Institute of Architects

Daniel J. Boorstin
The Librarian of Congress

Acknowledgments

This publication would be noteworthy under any circumstances, but when one considers that it was produced in less than twenty months—and as a cooperative venture—its timely appearance is the more remarkable. Many people gave tirelessly in order to make it happen, and we take this opportunity to thank them. They included the professional and support staff at the National Park Service (NPS), particularly in the offices of the Historic American Buildings Survey and the Historic American Engineering Record (HABS/HAER), at the American Institute of Architects, and at the Library of Congress, where the Prints and Photographs Division worked hand in hand with the Publishing Office, which coordinated the entire effort. The interns who helped to create the checklist and the authors of the essays deserve special thanks for their hard and excellent work accomplished under a demanding schedule.

Between May and July of 1981, staff from the National Park Service, the Library of Congress, and the American Institute of Architects and others met and determined the particular sort of publication that would best mark the fiftieth anniversary of the Historic American Buildings Survey. Participants in those meetings included Mary Lou Grier, Deputy Director of the National Park Service; Jerry Rogers, Associate Director of the National Park Service; Ernest Connally, former Associate Director of the National Park Service; Robert Kapsch, Alicia Stamm, Kenneth

Anderson, John Burns, Isabel Hill, Allen Chambers, Carolyn Pitts, Pat Cejka, Jan Cigliano, and others from the Historic American Buildings Survey/Historic American Engineering Record staff; John Peterson and John Ritterhoff from the NPS Data Systems Division; Maurice Payne, Michael Cohn, Richard van Os Keuls, John McCune, and Bruce Judd of the American Institute of Architects; and Alan Fern, Oliver Jensen, Dana J. Pratt, Evelyn Sinclair, C. Ford Peatross, and Mary M. Ison of the Library of Congress. Russell Keune of the National Trust for Historic Preservation, former HABS Chief James Massey, and HABS founder Charles Peterson also took part. Almost without exception the participants agreed that a comprehensive inventory of the sites and structures recorded by the Survey was the most urgent need that could be met for the celebration of the fiftieth anniversary. It was suggested that such a listing would be more useful if accompanied by a group of essays illuminating the nature and uses of the HABS records. It was also decided that sites and structures documented by the Survey's sister program, the Historic American Engineering Record, should be included in the inventory.

After these early meetings, the HABS/HAER Division began investigating what had to be done to develop a useful inventory and what resources would be required. The first feasibility study was undertaken in the autumn of 1981 by intern Anne Bisceglia under the direction of HABS/HAER archivist Alicia Stamm and with technical assistance from John Peterson and Robert Kapsch. It focused on one state—Massachusetts—and yielded much valuable information, demonstrating some difficulties and problems that could be resolved. An improved approach was tested on five states in the spring of 1982.

By May 1982 it was apparent that HABS/HAER would have to undertake a crash program to develop a computerized inventory by the fall of 1982 so that a book could be published by November 1983. Appropriated funds were not available, and National Park Service Associate Director Jerry Rogers and Division Chief Robert Kapsch decided to hire student interns to work over the summer and to use special contracts and funds donated to the HABS/HAER Division, an approach approved by National Park Service Deputy Director Mary Lou Grier. Alicia Stamm was selected as program leader.

In a very short time, ten summer interns were hired and trained, thousands of index cards recording existing HABS/HAER data were reproduced, thousands of data input sheets were duplicated for data entry use, and contracts were negotiated and equipment and supplies procured. Besides the obvious task of entering thousands of HABS/HAER records into the computer system, HABS and HAER numbers had to be checked and corrected, property names had to verified, standard codes had to be developed and assigned, and numerous other tasks had to be completed.

Special thanks go to the ten interns on the team Alicia Stamm had assembled by June 1982. Anne Bisceglia, Kristin Cleaver, Kevin Darken, Janet Gwaltney, Martha Hagedorn, Daithi Houlihan, Lisa Mausolf, Katherine Penovich, Sharman Roberts, and Michael Sullivan and Susan McCown of the HABS staff worked together to make computer entries identifying HABS/HAER records for almost seventeen thousand sites and structures in the United States and its territories and possessions. The first data entry was made on June 22, 1982, and the monumental task was completed by September 30, 1982. This achievement would not have been possible without the help of the Mini Computers Branch of the Data Systems Division of the National Park Service. We gratefully acknowledge the contributions of Glenn Schumaker, John Peterson, Shirley Huffman, Sheila Smith, Keith Carr, and Mae Williams. In addition, the firm Automated Sciences Group provided data input services under contract to the National Park Service. Of particular assistance from that staff were Theodore Ferguson, Brenda Young, and Scott McGilvrey.

Meanwhile, Ford Peatross at the Library of Congress brought together a roster of fifteen authors for the illustrated essays. All had made use of the Survey's work or participated in it, each in a different way, and they seemed pleased to have an opportunity to acknowledge the collection's potential. Charles E. Peterson, Richard Allen, and Samuel Wilson were familiar with certain aspects of the Survey since its beginnings. Peterson knew its history and mission. Allen recognized the Survey's particular role in documenting—and encouraging others to record—the covered bridge, and Wilson had participated in the Survey's substantial work in his own state, Louisiana. George Tatum's intimate knowledge of the city of Philadelphia recommended him for an essay on that city. A narrowing focus tightened still further with Rodris Roth's analysis of a room, the kitchen, and with Peter Myers's delightful examination of miscellaneous details in Survey photographs. Carl Lounsbury, Margot Gayle, and David De Long looked at the collection from the vantage point of their own particular specialities in construction, materials, and design. Carolyn Pitts and Carole Rifkind drew upon their knowledge of the active role which the Survey has played in the revitalization of historic districts. John Burns, Robert Bruegmann, and Robert Kapsch, all familiar with the recording process, examined its nature, problems, and potential. The editor discussed the interrelationship of HABS with kindred architectural resources at the Library of Congress.

The publishing of the book was undertaken by the Publishing Office of the Library of Congress, under the direction of Dana J. Pratt. Evelyn Sinclair coordinated the publication of both essays and checklist, and Johanna Craig supervised the book's production according to an unrelenting timetable. Michael Seyfrit, on special contract, wrote the program that allowed the magnetic tape of the checklist provided by the Park Service to be adapted for use in setting the type for the book.

Many other offices and individuals at the Library of Congress contributed to this effort. In the Prints and Photographs Division, former chief Oliver Jensen, Robert Lisbeth, Carol Johnson, Doris Lee, Roberta Phillips, Kermit Klouser, and Gail Markowitz assisted in various ways. Mary Ison provided reference assistance to many of the authors, carefully reviewed the checklist, and provided the introductory essay on the use of the collection. Marita Stamey and the staff of the Photoduplication Service provided photographic prints for the book's illustrations.

Without these contributions, this book would not have been possible. We thank each of those who participated in this special effort to commemorate fifty years of the Historic American Buildings Survey. *Historic America* is your invitation to this nation's rich history in architecture, design, and engineering, a built heritage to take pride in, to learn from, to preserve, and to explore.

Robert J. Kapsch, *Chief*
Historic American Buildings Survey/
Historic American Engineering Record

Renata V. Shaw, *Acting Chief*
Prints and Photographs Division
Library of Congress

List of Contributors

RICHARD SANDERS ALLEN is an engineering historian, retired from the New York State Education Department, Albany, New York 12230. Since 1937 he has researched early American bridge building, later embracing other fields, such as American iron manufacture, coastal fortifications, commercial aviation of 1920–40, and the aircraft used in the Spanish Civil War of 1936–39. Among his books are *Covered Bridges of the Northeast* (Brattleboro, Vt., 1957; rev. ed., 1974), *Covered Bridges of the South* (Brattleboro, Vt., 1970), *Covered Bridges of the Middle West* (Brattleboro, Vt., 1970), and *Revolution in the Sky* (Brattleboro, Vt., 1974).

ROBERT BRUEGMANN is Associate Professor in the History of Architecture and Art Department, University of Illinois at Chicago, Chicago, Illinois 60680. He is the author of *Benicia, Portrait of an Early California Town* (San Francisco, 1980), a forthcoming book on the Chicago architectural firm Holabird and Roche/Holabird and Root, and numerous articles and exhibition catalog essays on European and American modern architecture. He worked for the Historic American Buildings Survey and the Historic American Engineering Record in the 1970s.

JOHN A. BURNS, A.I.A., is an architect with the Historic American Buildings Survey/Historic American Engineering Record, National Park Service, U.S. Department of the Interior, Washington, D.C. 20240. He specializes in architectural documentation and has lectured and published on the architectural technology of the late nineteenth and early twentieth century especially. With his wife, Deborah Burns, an architectural historian, he wrote "The Bauhaus As You've Never Seen It," *AIA Journal* (July 1981), about the restoration of the Bauhaus building in Dessau, East Germany. For the U.S. Department of Housing and Urban Development, he wrote *Energy Conserving Features Inherent in Older Homes* (Washington, 1982). His architectural photographs have been published in numerous periodicals and shown at the AIA's Octagon House in the exhibit "Le Corbusier in Paris" in 1975.

DAVID G. DE LONG is Associate Professor of Architecture and Chairman of the Division of Historic Preservation at Columbia University, New York, New York 10027. His publications include *The Architecture of Bruce Goff; Buildings and Projects, 1916–1974* (New York and London, 1977) and fourteen volumes of *Historic American Buildings* (New York and London, 1979–80), compiled from the Historic American Buildings Survey materials for New York, Texas, and California.

MARGOT GAYLE is a preservationist and a writer. She is president and founder of Friends of Cast Iron Architecture, a national organization devoted to the preservation of architectural and decorative ironwork. She is author of *Cast Iron Architecture in New York* (New York, 1974) and coauthor of *Metals in America's Historic Buildings* (Washington, 1980). She provided historical introductions to reprints of two classic foundry trade catalogs: *Badger's Illustrated Catalogue of Cast Iron Architecture* (New York, 1981) and *Victorian Ironwork: The Wickersham Catalogue of 1857* (Philadelphia, 1977). Mrs. Gayle has lectured on cast-iron architecture in many parts of the country and written on the subject for several magazines, including a regular column on "Changing New York" in the New York *Daily News* Sunday magazine. As a preservationist, she has helped save many buildings in the SOHO Cast-Iron Historic District in Manhattan and elsewhere. She has worked with the Planning Commission of New York City and as a staff writer for CBS.

MARY M. ISON is a Reference Specialist for the Architecture, Design, and Engineering Collections in the Prints and Photographs Division of the Library of Congress, Washington, D.C. 20540. She is responsible for reference services for the Historic American Buildings Survey/Historic American Engineering Record and related collections, and she edits the quarterly *COPAR* (Cooperative Preservation of Architectural Records) *Newsletter*. She has published articles and book reviews in the Special Libraries Association's *Picturescope* and the *Quarterly Journal of the Library of Congress* and has spoken about the Library's architectural collections before various groups.

ROBERT J. KAPSCH is Chief of the Historic American Buildings Survey/Historic American Engineering Record Division of the National Park Service, U.S. Department of the Interior, Washington, D.C. 20240. A veteran of nineteen years of service in a variety of management positions at several building-related federal agencies in Washington, he is a graduate engineer with degrees in management, American studies, and engineering and architecture. He has published a number of articles on architectural and engineering documentation as well as on other aspects of architectural and engineering practice.

CARL LOUNSBURY is an architectural historian in the Architectural Research Department of the Colonial Williamsburg Foundation, Williamsburg, Virginia 23187. His background is in American studies. He has conducted fieldwork in vernacular architecture in North Carolina and Virginia and is a participant in the Friends of Friendless Farmbuildings as well as a member of the board of directors of the Vernacular Architecture Forum. His publications include *The Architecture of Southport* (Southport, N.C., 1979), "The Development of Domestic Architecture in the Albemarle Region" in *Carolina Dwelling: Towards Preservation of Place* (Raleigh, N.C., 1978), edited by Doug Swaim, and "The Building Process in Antebellum North Carolina" in the *North Carolina Historical Review* (1983). He is coauthor with Charlotte Brown and Catherine Bishir of the forthcoming book *Architects and Builders in North Carolina*.

DENYS PETER MYERS is an architectural historian on the staff of the Historic American Buildings Survey/Historic American Engineering Record, National Park Service, U.S. Department of the Interior, Washington, D.C. 20240. He is the author of *Maine Catalog: The Historic Architecture of Maine* (Augusta, Maine, 1974) and *Gaslighting in America—A Guide for Historic Preservation* (Washington, 1978) and a contributor to *Maine Forms of American Architecture* (Camden, Maine, 1976), edited by Deborah Thompson, and the *Macmillan Encyclopedia of Architects* (New York and London, 1982), as well as to a number of scholarly journals. A former art museum director in Ohio, Oklahoma, and Iowa and assistant director of the Baltimore Museum of Art, he taught at Johns Hopkins University and the Catholic University of America before joining HABS/HAER in 1966. His special field of interest is material culture of the nineteenth century.

C. FORD PEATROSS is Curator of the Architecture, Design, and Engineering Collections in the Prints and Photographs Division of the Library of Congress, Washington, D.C. 20540. With a background in business administration and the history of art, he is particularly interested in the history of architecture and its documentation. He has spoken before many groups concerning the Cooperative Preservation of Architectural Records (COPAR) and serves on the Historic Resources Committee of the American Institute of Architects, the Executive Committee of the International Confederation of Architectural Museums, and the Advisory Board of the Art and Architecture Thesaurus Project. His publications include the exhibition catalog *William Nichols, Architect* (University, Ala., 1979), "Architectural Collections in the Library of Congress," *Quarterly Journal of the Library of Congress* (July 1977), reprinted in *Graphic Sampler* (Washington, 1979), and contributions to the *Macmillan Encyclopedia of Architects* (New York and London, 1982) and the quarterly *COPAR Newsletter*.

CHARLES E. PETERSON, F.A.I.A., is a registered architect practicing out of Society Hill, Philadelphia 19106. After graduating from the University of Minnesota in 1928 and qualifying in the California examination for National Park Service Landscape Architect, he entered on duty at the San Francisco field headquarters. Transferred to the East to pioneer new historical and architectural programs, he was in charge of routine planning from the Acadia Park (Maine) to the Great Smokies (North Carolina to Tennessee) and Hot Springs (Arkansas). His last government posts were as Resident Architect of the Independence Park (Philadelphia, 1950–56) and Supervising Architect, Historic Structures (in the East, 1956–62). He has fought on the bloody barricades of local preservation wars, at the same time advising private, public, and educational projects from Hawaii and Easter Island to Turkey and Morocco. He works on neglected historical subjects and has published many articles, his subjects ranging from the early French buildings along the Middle Mississippi to builder-architect Robert Smith (1722–1777) of Dalkeith, Scotland, and Philadelphia and the invention of the structural I-beam. He edited *Building Early America* (Radnor, Pa., 1976) and was the editor of the "American Notes" of the *Journal of the Society of Architectural Historians* from 1950 to 1967.

CAROLYN PITTS is the Senior Architectural Historian of the Historic American Buildings Survey/Historic American Engineering Record, National Park Service, U.S. Department of the Interior, Washington, D.C. 20240. She wrote *The Cape May Handbook* (Philadelphia, 1977) and the descriptions for *Sculpture of a City: Philadelphia's Treasures in Bronze and Stone* (New York, 1974), for which she also did the archival work. She was Executive Assistant, Division of Education, at the Philadelphia Museum of Art, held a Fulbright Lectureship in Istanbul, Turkey, and taught at St. Joseph's College, Temple University, and Beaver College before joining HABS/HAER.

CAROLE RIFKIND is a free-lance writer and consultant who lives in New York City. Her fields of interest are architecture, urban development, and travel. She is coauthor with Carol Levine of *Mansions, Mills, and Main Streets* (New York, 1975) and author of *Main Street: Face of Urban America* (New York, 1975) and *A Field Guide to American Architecture* (New York, 1980). She has written articles for the *New York Times, Travel and Leisure, American Arts,* and other publications.

RODRIS ROTH is a Curator at the Smithsonian Institution's National Museum of American History. She has written on a variety of topics, including tea drinking in eighteenth-century America, the Colonial Revival, and patented furniture. She has worked on a number of exhibitions at the Smithsonian, including the "Hall of Everyday Life in the American Past," "1876: A Centennial Exhibition," and the special display "Going to Housekeeping."

ALICIA STAMM is Archivist for the Historic American Buildings Survey/Historic American Engineering Record collections at the National Park Service, U.S. Department of the Interior, Washington, D.C. 20240. These collections, begun in 1933, document over seventeen thousand sites of national architectural and engineering significance. She formerly worked as a manuscripts assistant in the Archives of American Art, Smithsonian Institution. She contributed to the *Archives of American Art Exhibition Card Catalog* (Boston, 1978). Her educational background is in art history and museum administration.

GEORGE TATUM is a resident of Old Lyme, Connecticut, where he devotes his time to teaching an occasional course, writing and lecturing about architectural history and gardens, and tending his own garden. His preparation for these activities included thirty years of teaching, first at the University of Pennsylvania and later at the University of Delaware. More recently, he has been a visiting professor at Williams College and at Columbia University in the Graduate School of Architecture and Planning. At various times during his professional career, Dr. Tatum has served as president of the Society of Architectural Historians, as a member and chairman of the Advisory Board of the Historic American Buildings Survey, and as a member and chairman of the Commission of the National Collection of Fine Arts (now the National Museum of American Art). In 1961 he was elected an honorary member of the American Institute of Architects for his contribution as an architectural historian. His works include *Penn's Great Town: 250 Years of Philadelphia Architecture in Prints and Drawings* (Philadelphia, 1961) and *Philadelphia Georgian: The City House of Samuel Powel and Some of Its Eighteenth-Century Neighbors* (Middletown, Conn., 1976).

SAMUEL WILSON, JR., F.A.I.A., is a practicing architect and architectural historian at Koch and Wilson, Architects, New Orleans, Louisiana 70130. He was made a Fellow of the American Institute of Architects in 1955. His firm has done numerous restoration projects in Louisiana and Mississippi and as far away as Corpus Christi, Texas, and Edenton, North Carolina. He has published numerous articles on Louisiana and Gulf Coast architecture and over the past forty years has lectured on Louisiana architecture at the Tulane University School of Architecture, his alma mater, and at other universities and historical associations. He edited *Impressions Respecting New Orleans by Benjamin Henry Boneval Latrobe* (New York, 1951). He has served on the board and as president of the Friends of the Cabildo, Associates of the Louisiana State Museum, and has contributed articles to their published series, New Orleans Architecture. He has also contributed to *Frenchmen and French Ways in the Mississippi Valley* (Urbana, Ill., 1969) and *The Spanish in the Mississippi Valley, 1762–1804* (Urbana, Ill., 1974), edited by John Francis McDermott.

HISTORIC AMERICA

Buildings, Structures, and Sites

Using the HABS/HAER Collections
at the Library of Congress

by

MARY M. ISON

For fifty years the photographs, measured drawings, and written histories of buildings made for the Historic American Buildings Survey have delighted and served readers in the Prints and Photographs Reading Room of the Library of Congress. With its sister collection, the Historic American Engineering Record, established in 1969 to record engineering sites, it is one of the division's most popular collections. The use of these two surveys is equaled only by use of the Library's extensive visual holdings of the Civil War and the now popular depression-era pictures taken by the Farm Security Administration/Office of War Information.

First among the attractions of the two surveys is that all materials in them are in the public domain. The Library's Photoduplication Service can provide, at reasonable costs and in a variety of kinds of reproduction, copies of all types of documentation in the surveys, and these copies can be used in any way desired. Second, the materials are created in standardized sizes and formats, ensuring a uniformity throughout the collection which allows for convenient and easy use. Third, a variety of card catalogs, indexes, lists, printed catalogs, books, and microfiche and microfilm publications allow for easy use both by persons able to visit the collections and those who by necessity must use them from a distance.

The HABS/HAER collections were conceived by their founders as records to be used by the public in a variety of ways. The agreements which established the surveys are signed by the U.S. Department of the Interior, which administers them, the Library of Congress, which houses and serves the collections created through the surveys to the public, and the advisory groups for each survey—the American Institute of Architects for HABS and the American Society of Civil Engineers for HAER. They state that the records created will be housed at the Library of Congress where proper care, preservation, and reference service can be ensured. The Library's commitment to this charge, as well as the continuing popularity of the surveys, has resulted in reference and cataloging systems unparal-

HABS/HAER documents are filed in easy-to-use formats and sizes. Measured drawings are available in both large, seventeen-by-twenty-four-inch copies and reduced, eight-by-ten-inch photocopies. Black-and-white photographs are mounted on eight-by-ten-inch mounts and filed in ring binders with corresponding captions and written histories. The general arrangement is by geographic area, with additional access by subject and name of architect or engineer. In the Prints and Photographs Division Reading Room all types and sizes of HABS/HAER documents are available for use.

Readers who are unable to visit the collections at the Library of Congress will find that microformat publications of the HABS collections can be extremely helpful in making full use of the Survey. HABS measured drawings were published by the Library of Congress on microfilm in 1974 and the photographs and written histories by Somerset House on microfiche in 1980. Many libraries throughout the country have bought these publications, facilitating use of the Survey nationwide.

leled in other Prints and Photographs Division holdings. Readers with a wide variety of concerns therefore find the collections a great resource not only because of the material they include but because of its availability.

The HABS and HAER reference collections are housed in the Prints and Photographs Reading Room of the Library of Congress. All readers are welcome to visit the collection at that site and examine the records and finding aids in person. The records are arranged by geographic order: state, county name, city or vicinity, and building name or the order in which the building was recorded within the given vicinity. Captioned black-and-white photographs, primarily five-by-seven-inches in size, are mounted on eight-by-ten-inch mounts in ring binders. When a written history is included, it is typed on eight-by-ten-inch paper and filed in the ring binder behind the photographs for the structure. Measured drawings are filed either in a reduced format (eight by ten inches) in the ring binders with the other documentation for a building, or, and this more likely, in a seventeen-by-twenty-four-inch format in separate binders, these also arranged by geographic place. A duplicate set of drawings in an eight-by-ten-inch reduction format is filed by HABS and HAER survey number, a unique number for each building assigned by the U.S. Department of the Interior as a building's documentation is being created.

With the exception noted above, the HABS and HAER survey numbers are not used by the Library as filing numbers. Instead, each building is assigned a unique call number based on its geographic designation. Not all buildings are recorded with all three forms of documentation but all forms can be retrieved by using this one call number. This number also serves as the negative number for individual photographs. A card catalog providing a card for each building or site and giving the amount of documenta-

tion and applicable call numbers for the available records also follows the geographic arrangement. This arrangement serves readers well, as it enables records for areas of the country, for several or individual states, for portions of states, or for individual structures to be pulled with ease. In many cases the card catalog need not even be consulted. For example, if a reader wishes to examine log buildings in eastern Pennsylvania, the cards in the card catalog may not specify the building material. The reader might find appropriate sites more readily by determining the counties in eastern Pennsylvania and calling for all the materials in those counties.

The primary access by geographic location is supplemented by a card index to records by subject, vertical files of reduced-size measured drawings arranged by building type and survey number, and a card index by name of architect, engineer, or firm. Thus a reader interested in measured drawings of banks can be given a file of reduced-size drawings in which to browse, and photographs of the buildings shown in the drawings can be found through the geographic card catalog. A reader interested in the work of a particular architect or engineer can check the biographical card index to determine which of his designs are included in the Survey.

Many people are excited by the possibilities offered by the resources of the HABS/HAER surveys and the Library receives a steady stream of readers who make trips to Washington specifically to use these collections. It has always been the intention of those responsible for the surveys, however, that they be accessible to people throughout the entire country. This was made clear by the printing in 1938, only five years after the Historic American Buildings Survey was created, of the first published catalog to the HABS collection at the Library of Congress. A second national catalog followed in 1941 and a supplement to that publication was published in 1959. After 1959 it was decided that the size of the survey prohibited future national catalogs, and a program of publishing building lists by state and region was begun. This publishing program has been adopted also by the Historic American Engineering Record, with the first national catalog to that collection published in 1976, only eight years after the Record was established.

The checklist of buildings in this volume is the first attempt to list all buildings and sites in both surveys and is the first national catalog to the HABS collections since the publication of the 1941 catalog and its 1959 supplement. It is intended to serve as a major guide to persons unable to visit the collections in Washington.

There are, however, several additional aids for long distance use. First, the Library can provide a list of publications about the surveys, including all published catalogs. Second, a list of publications which reproduce substantial portions of the HABS collection is also available. Of great importance on the latter list are two publications in microformat. A microfilm of all HABS measured drawings at the Library of Congress as of 1974 may be ordered from the Photoduplication Service of the Library of Congress. A microfiche edition of all photographs and written histories in the Library's cataloged collections as of January 1979 is available from the publisher, Somerset House, Teaneck, New Jersey. These microform publications are being bought not only by libraries throughout the country but by individuals who purchase them to view on machines at their area libraries. Both of these lists include ordering information for the publications cited.

The reader who must use the collection from a distance can write the Prints and Photographs Division to request an information packet on the Architecture, Design, and Engineering Collections that includes written information on the HABS and HAER collections. Included is the list of HABS

and HAER catalogs and other publications, the bibliography of publications which reproduce portions of the Historic American Buildings Survey, a price list for all types of reproductions of documentation in the two collections, a list of subjects for which building lists have been compiled by the Library staff, and basic information on both surveys as well as the general architectural and engineering collections in the Prints and Photographs Division.

Copies of all HABS and HAER materials which have been transferred to the Library are available through the Library's Photoduplication Service. Current price information is available from that service as well as from the Prints and Photographs Division. Readers making requests for copies should provide names and locations of the buildings in which they are interested and specify the type of documentation desired. The Library will cite the amount of documentation available and provide an order form with building identification numbers and a price quotation. This order form is returned by the reader with the proper payment to the Photoduplication Service, the office which actually makes the copies and sends them to the reader. Limited photocopying facilities are available in the Prints and Photographs Reading Room.

Preservationists, historians, students, genealogists, authors, architects, engineers, and others interested in buildings and history are welcome to use the great resources of the HABS/ HAER collections. Through printed catalogs to the surveys, the publication of the collections in both print and microform, and the provision of excellent reference facilities where the collections are physically housed, the Library of Congress and the U.S. Department of the Interior have attempted to make the wealth of these surveys available to the American public for which they were created. We invite you to use this material and to share the delights and rewards it offers.

Copies of all HABS/HAER materials at the Library of Congress can be obtained through the Library's Photoduplication Service. Lists of prices, price quotations for specific documents, and other information for ordering copies of materials in the collections can be obtained from the Library by mail or in person. Readers able to visit the Library can call upon the experienced reference staff to advise on duplication options and prices.

The Historic American Buildings Survey:
Its Beginnings

by

CHARLES E. PETERSON

The Historic American Buildings Survey did not begin in a bureaucratic routine. It was founded a half century ago by a handful of public servants in a burst of idealism and energy. Distinction was achieved through the immediate and generous help of outside friends who agreed that it would be fine to build a treasury of American architectural information. Under the conditions that prevail today, it probably could not have been started.

Looking back over a half century, one sees that the years have taken their toll and the people who created the Survey have mostly gone to their reward. Their written records have been hustled off to oblivion by efficiency experts. A large and forgetful bureaucracy has grown up and HABS has been able to survive only by good luck as it staggers from one Interior Department reorganization to another. If it had not made so many friends in the early days, the Survey would probably have expired long ago—like the other New Deal programs of the 1930s.

As a survivor of those days, I am often called upon to describe the beginnings of HABS and to recall some of the people who built quality, character, and interest into the vast collection of records so splendidly housed today in the new Madison Building of the Library of Congress. And so popular with Americans who care about our historic architecture.[1] My recollections of places and persons are vivid but somewhat colored by a variety of prejudices. I hope the reader will forgive the personal character of these notes.

My own background was out-of-doors in the West, like that of most of the pioneers in the National Park Service. Work for pay in the field of history began for me on a field trip in January of 1930 to the eighteenth-century Mission San Cayetano del Tumacacori in the desert near Nogales, Arizona. All of us professionals in the Service were at that time headquartered in San Francisco. But in September of that year I was to unpack my bags in the "Vest House" on Duke of Gloucester Street in Williamsburg and—except for World War II—I have been continuously involved ever since with elderly structures and their problems. I found myself in an unnamed but distinctive profession

Figure 1 Branch of Plans and Design drafting room in the Navy Building on Constitution Avenue, Washington, about 1934. HABS sprang from this office as a program by architects for architects. Here was designed the seventh floor of the old Interior Building on Rawlins Square to which HABS was later moved. T.T. Waterman is seated at the drafting board in the foreground.

Figure 2 Arthur E. Demaray, native of Minnesota, came as a draftsman from the U.S. Geological Survey and eventually served as director of the U.S. National Park Service. One of the most intelligent and alert executives of the Service, he was the first to endorse HABS and speed it to success. Photograph by Abbie Rowe. Courtesy National Park Service.

Figure 3 Thomas T. Waterman, brilliant investigator of early American architecture and author of many books and articles. His understanding of buildings and their graphic analysis, especially of floor plans, helped HABS to establish and maintain high standards from the beginning.

that has been called "the geriatrics of the building business."

After three unforgettable years in Virginia I was ordered to remove to Washington. Then, on a Sunday afternoon in November of 1933—in an apartment at 2501 Calvert Street (now demolished)—I wrote a proposal for what very soon became the Historic American Buildings Survey. The pencilled sheets have been preserved as a souvenir of those exciting times.[2] The following day I discussed the draft with Arthur E. Demaray, associate director of the Park Service (fig. 2). Quick and imaginative, he thought it could fly as a relief project for architects unemployed in the Great Depression. President Roosevelt was then shaking the national capital with ambitious new programs, and nothing seemed too bold to try.

Within two weeks a tidy sum of nearly half a million dollars was set aside by the Civil Works Administration, then inhabiting the Walker-Johnson building on New York Avenue (now demolished).[3] HABS had picked up the support of Secretary of the Interior Harold I. Ickes and of Harry Hopkins and Louis Howe, close advisers to the president. Very little overhead or equipment was required and work could start in record time. It did.[4]

For a national program, the money and personnel had first to be set out in quotas by states. Some midnight work in the drafting room—architect Alston G. Gutterson (Al was recently from Montana) assisting on the slide rule—turned the trick. The first and principal staff members were quickly recruited. Architect and historian Thomas T. Waterman (Tom was lately of the Williamsburg Restoration but at the time unemployed and studying in England), John P. O'Neill (formerly of Notre Dame University and recently returned from an archaeological dig in Latin America) and Dudley C. Bayliss (teaching at Fargo, North Dakota) were ready for action. Frederick D. Nichols (of Colorado and about to be graduat-

ing from Yale) joined them. All were architects (figs. 3, 4, 5).

Then new in the East, the Park Service was pretty much unknown in the field of historic conservation. Professional support needed to be rounded up. Leicester B. Holland, architectural scholar of Philadelphia and Washington, was at that time wearing two convenient hats (fig. 7). At the Library of Congress he was head of the Division of Fine Arts. He also was a Fellow of the American Institute of Architects (AIA) and chairman of its national historic buildings committee. There was a vice chairman of the AIA committee too—Edward W. Donn of Washington—but no other members I can recall. Holland joined us with ready enthusiasm and he helped design the format of the HABS records so as to make them both convenient to file and yet readily available to users in his reading room and to those ordering copies by mail.

Edward C. Kemper, executive secretary of the AIA, an exceptionally adroit and cooperative administrator, saw the possibilities and quickly obtained the unanimous approval of his national board. He telegraphed the local Institute chapters across the country, which brought forth the best talent in the profession. Special pains were taken to recognize those who had already achieved success and recognition in the historic field. Richard Koch of New Orleans, Charles Morse Stotz, Jr., of Pittsburgh, and Frank Chouteau Brown of Boston stood out from the start.

In accordance with the initial proposal, a national advisory board was promptly assembled. My own nominations were architects Leicester B. Holland, William G. Perry of Boston, Albert Simons of Charleston, and John Gaw Meem of Santa Fe as well as historian Herbert E. Bolton, the great Spanish colonial scholar of the University of California at Berkeley. Arthur Demaray nominated Harlean James of the American Civic and Planning Association and Waldo G. Leland of the American Council of Learned Societies to give the program a good Washington front. They became lifelong supporters. Secretary Ickes added Thomas E. Tallmadge, Chicago architect-author, and I. T. Frary of Cleveland, an architectural historian. It was a blue ribbon group.

In those same months, the Park Service (its name had been unexpectedly but temporarily changed to the Office of Parks, Buildings, and Reservations) was then being loaded with new responsibilities all over the East. Its chief of design and construction, Thomas C. Vint, was directed to move his headquarters from San Francisco to Washington. He complied with orders— though reluctantly—and took over personally the direction of all the bureau's planning, landscape, and architectural operations. They included HABS, and for the next twenty-seven years Tom Vint was the Survey's ardent in-house champion (fig. 10).

The tiny headquarters staff of HABS had to work in a continuous frenzy in order to cope with fast-changing rules and the almost continual reorganization of the New Deal emergency programs. But within a few weeks HABS found it possible to put up a fine exhibition of measured drawings and photographs at the National Museum in Washington. The quality was excellent and the press favorable. All across the country occupants of old buildings were surprised to learn that their homes and offices were of interest to the Library of Congress.

The *Washington Evening Star* selected for its report on April 5, 1934, four photographs which showed the variety of building art being investigated. There was a sun-dried pueblo church, a Richard Koch shot of a French landmark in New Orleans, a Dutch windmill near what is now the O'Hare airport in Chicago, and a collapsing tavern near the mouth of the Wabash River (fig. 6). That diversity reflected the broad concept of the program, which called for a general canvass of structures erected between the earli-

est times and 1860. There was in those days a general consensus that Victorian buildings were ugly and not worth serious study or any effort to save them. Indeed, Greek Revival was only then coming up for attention and the two first works on that subject, I remember, were avant-garde curiosities. Now, a half century later, the pendulum of taste has swung the other way. To many enthusiasts, anything with a few feet of jigsaw on one end is antique and therefore venerated as a national monument.

It seems worth remembering that HABS was a program designed by architects for architects. Several years were yet to pass before the founding, by a splinter group from the College Art Association, of a block of dissidents which first called itself the American Society of Architectural Historians. And it was some sixteen years before David Finley of the National Gallery in Washington rallied the conservation group subsequently called the National Trust for Historic Preservation. Today we live in an age of expensive interdisciplinary teams undreamed of fifty years ago.

In the 1930s the historical wing of the architectural profession was mainly concerned with investigating Georgian buildings that could serve as good models for new buildings. Beginning a half century earlier with a renewal of interest in what was called Early American design, prospective homeowners as far away as Kansas City and San Francisco had got the urge to live in red brick Georgian houses. Their architects were glad to accommodate and in the East they began to make measured drawings of old floor plans, facades, and interior details. These appeared in periodicals and books and even penetrated the offices of giants like McKim, Mead and White, who obliged millionaires with large wooden Colonial houses in fashionable resorts. This taste spread generally and eventually, in 1926, engulfed John D. Rockefeller, Jr., in the restoration of Colonial Williamsburg.

That spectular project was at first

Figure 4 John P. O'Neill, from a passport photograph taken in Merida, Mexico, while he was on a Carnegie dig in 1933. He was one of the first appointees to HABS and served to 1937 as manager during the hectic early days of the unemployment relief program.

Figure 5 Frederick D. Nichols, native of Trinidad, Colorado, was recruited for HABS as he was graduated in architecture from Yale in 1934. Nichols stayed with the program until the U.S. Navy claimed him for World War II. He became Langhorne Professor of Architecture at the University of Virginia and writer of architectural history, especially of Thomas Jefferson's buildings.

Historic American Buildings Exhibit Opens

the province of the architects Perry, Shaw and Hepburn. The Boston firm, setting up shop in Virginia, naturally stirred memories of the Civil War disasters of the nineteenth-century, and some locals grumbled that their town was being "Yankeefied." But the architects, of whom William Graves Perry was certainly the genius, took their opportunity seriously. They began the graphic analysis of the distinctive Tidewater eighteenth-century style with the brilliant success still to be seen in their earliest work. It ranged all the way from wooden smokehouses in backyards to the great reconstructed Governor's Palace.

Careful study of the numerous antique structures still standing across the Tidewater country gave the architects a mastery of the local style. The relationship between structures and measurements projected on paper became a highly developed subject. The drafting rooms were full of adventure and excitement and every junior architect was working on a book of his own. Though not a Rockefeller employee, I was working nearby (Jamestown to

Figure 6   Washington Evening Star, April 5, 1934. HABS has been a popular subject for the American press, which has by invitation exploited both photographs and drawings. The *Washington Star* for November 29, 1933, carried the first HABS picture story, and one of the latest may be found in the magazine *Historic Preservation* for January-February 1983, titled "Racing against Oblivion," by Andy Leon Harney. The Survey has always encouraged authors to use its records and in some instances priority has been given to subjects relating to proposed publications. Survey activities and materials have also been used to attract support for buildings threatened by urban renewal and other forces.

Figure 7   Leicester B. Holland of Philadelphia was a key man from the beginning as he established HABS as a permanent feature of the Library of Congress. A pioneer aviator and man of many interests, including classical archaeology, he resigned from the Library of Congress when its Fine Arts Division was reorganized in the 1940s and later taught architecture at the University of Miami, Ohio.

Yorktown) and knew them all. Williamsburg society, both professional and civilian, floated on an evening tide of corn whiskey and there were few secrets. Those were great years; a fine time to be alive and learning.

Compiling documents of early architecture for publication, as we have seen, had already been under way for decades. In England a large collection had been made under the guidance of the Royal Institute of British Architects[5] and in New York the Architects' Emergency Committee had produced drawings to illustrate two fine volumes called *Great Georgian Houses of America* (1933, 1937). HABS was bigger and wider in scope. But its great innovation was ready availability at moderate cost.

While HABS was producing records of other peoples' buildings, the Park Service was taking over care of a wide variety of structures belonging to the nation. These buildings needed repairs and restoration, and it was made the policy to translate in-house measured drawings into HABS format so they could be preserved at the Library of Congress. If such drawings stay with the architects they get lost sooner or later. The Moore House, a small frame revolutionary war landmark at Yorktown, Virginia, became a part of the Colonial National Monument. Its restoration had begun in 1931. The

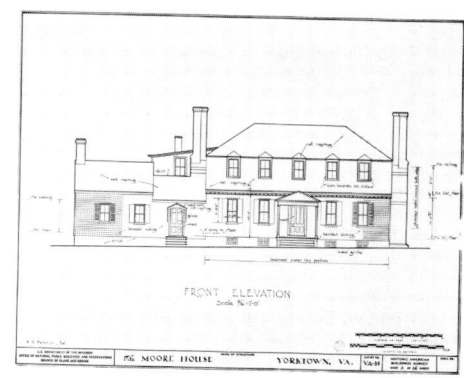

Figure 8 The preparation of measured scale drawings depicting existing conditions is usually the first step undertaken in planning any restoration. The Moore House on the York River below Yorktown, Virginia, was a feature at the town's Sesquicentennial Celebration in 1931. This sheet was redrawn four years later by Walter G. Peter, Jr., of Washington, D.C., for a report published in 1981. It shows (left) the nineteenth-century wing removed during restoration. In the early years in the East such records were generally made for HABS. The West just didn't bother. Front elevation. (HABS VA−80, sheet 5 of 16 sheets)

Figure 9 In order to understand an architectural fabric it is customary to collect early views for comparative examination. Here we have an 1864 watercolor by McIlvaine showing the original framing of the Moore House exposed by Civil War shooting. Such old views are often photographed for the HABS collections. (HABS VA−80, LC HABS VA, 100-York.V, 1−10)

Figure 10 Thomas C. Vint, born in Salt Lake City, grew up in Los Angeles and graduated in landscape architecture from the University of California, Berkeley. In 1926 he became head of general planning for the landscape and architectural program of the Western Field Headquarters in San Francisco. Transferred to the East during the New Deal, he was a champion of HABS from the beginning and fought its in-house battles until his retirement in 1961. (Brooks, Photographers)

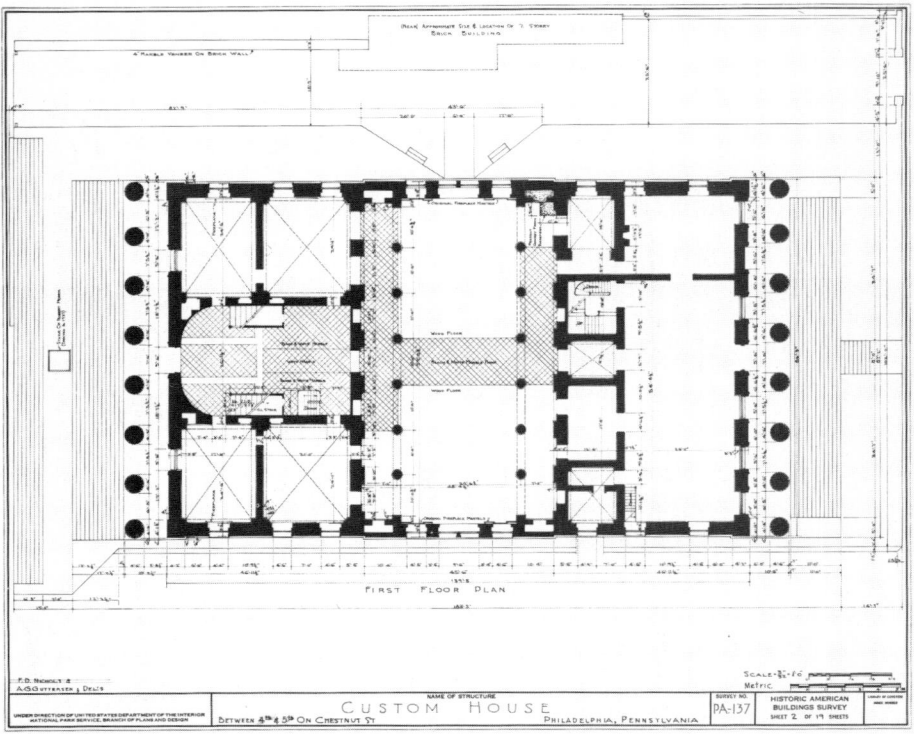

Figure 11 The Old Custom House (now known as the Second Bank of the United States) in Philadelphia became redundant and was taken over by the Park Service in the late 1930s to save it. Measured drawings were made in preparation for a restoration funded by the Carl Schurz Foundation. William Strickland originally won the job in an architectural competition; the handsome, marble structure was built 1819–24. It is now a museum in the Independence National Historical Park. Plan, first floor, measured drawing by F.D. Nichols and A.G. Gutterson, 1939. (HABS PA–137, sheet 2 of 19 sheets)

architects' plans were afterward specially redrawn on HABS sheets for my 1935 report titled *The Physical History of the Moore House, 1931–34.* That publication (not in print until 1981) set a precedent that was later followed, though not consistently (figs. 8, 9).

HABS had originally been started under the authority of the National Industrial Recovery Act. When that was overturned in the courts, the Survey was specifically legitimized by the Historic Sites and Buildings Act of 1935. In the meantime the relationship of the Park Service to the American Institute of Architects and the Library of Congress had been reaffirmed by the

Tripartite Agreement of 1934. Five years later it was agreed that the Survey was worth continuing and four field offices (Boston, Washington, St. Louis, and San Francisco) were set up substantially with well organized architectural teams and a station wagon each. I took over direction of the Mississippi Valley office, which encompassed the region from Iowa to Louisiana and Kentucky to Kansas.

The spectacular achievement of HABS was marked by the publication of a national catalog in 1938. In letterpress, abundantly illustrated by drawings and photographs, it announced to the American community the availability of the collections. A second and much enlarged edition appeared three years later, the fateful year that ended in Pearl Harbor.[6]

When the Independence Park project began at Philadelphia in 1950, the great postwar building boom was going on, and experienced draftsmen were unavailable. At that juncture, it was found possible to employ students during their summer recess, following the successful example of the U.S. Army Corps of Engineers. We could soon demonstrate that carefully selected students under carefully selected supervisors could be trained to examine old structures intelligently and to produce excellent drawings of them. Once that was established our new student summer programs under the "Mission 66" program spread to such places as the Adams Mansion at Quincy and the village of Harpers Ferry, West Virginia, where a major restoration program was planned (fig. 13).

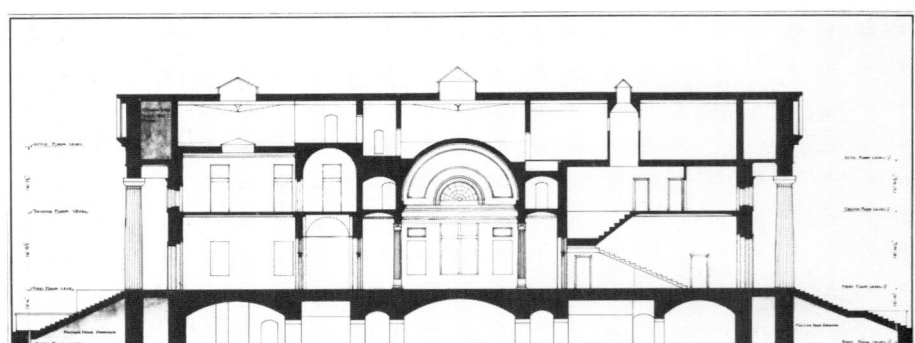

Figure 12 Custom House, Philadelphia, Philadelphia County, Pennsylvania. Longitudinal section, measured drawing by A.G. Gutterson, 1939. (HABS PA–137, sheet 5 of 19 sheets)

As an inducement to serious students we promised to coach them in drafting, have outside lecturers on local history, and generally make the subject worthwhile and interesting. This appealed to the school faculties and we got cooperation in recruiting. Among the first schools to offer promising students were the University of Illinois, the Rhode Island School of Design, and the University of Florida.

It should be clear by now that the potentialities of HABS are vast, indeed. Even the excavated substructures of demolished historic buildings can be studied and recorded profitably. Unfortunately, archaeology in this country has now become the almost

exclusive domain of anthropologists, most of whom don't understand buildings. The contributions of HABS architects at seventeenth-century Jamestown, Virginia, have been almost forgotten, as have the spectacular revelations at Mannsfield near Fredericksburg on the Rappahannock. Those records were intended to be emulated but have been generally overlooked (figs. 14-17).

On the other hand, HABS successfully pioneered historical photogrammetry in this century by contracting with Prof. Perry E. Borchers of Ohio State University (OSU) for sheets of "measured" drawings. I am still proud of his first product, done in

Figure 13 John Brown's Fort, Harpers Ferry, West Virginia. In the exciting days which led up to the Civil War, the fanatic John Brown holed up in the fire engine house at Harpers Ferry. Now immortal in history and legend, the structure was moved several times (including once to Chicago). Most of the buildings shown in this photograph by W.G. Russell of Baltimore have now been restored by the Park Service. The basic drawings were prepared by summer teams of architectural students. Prints and Photographs Division. (LC–USZ62–19351)

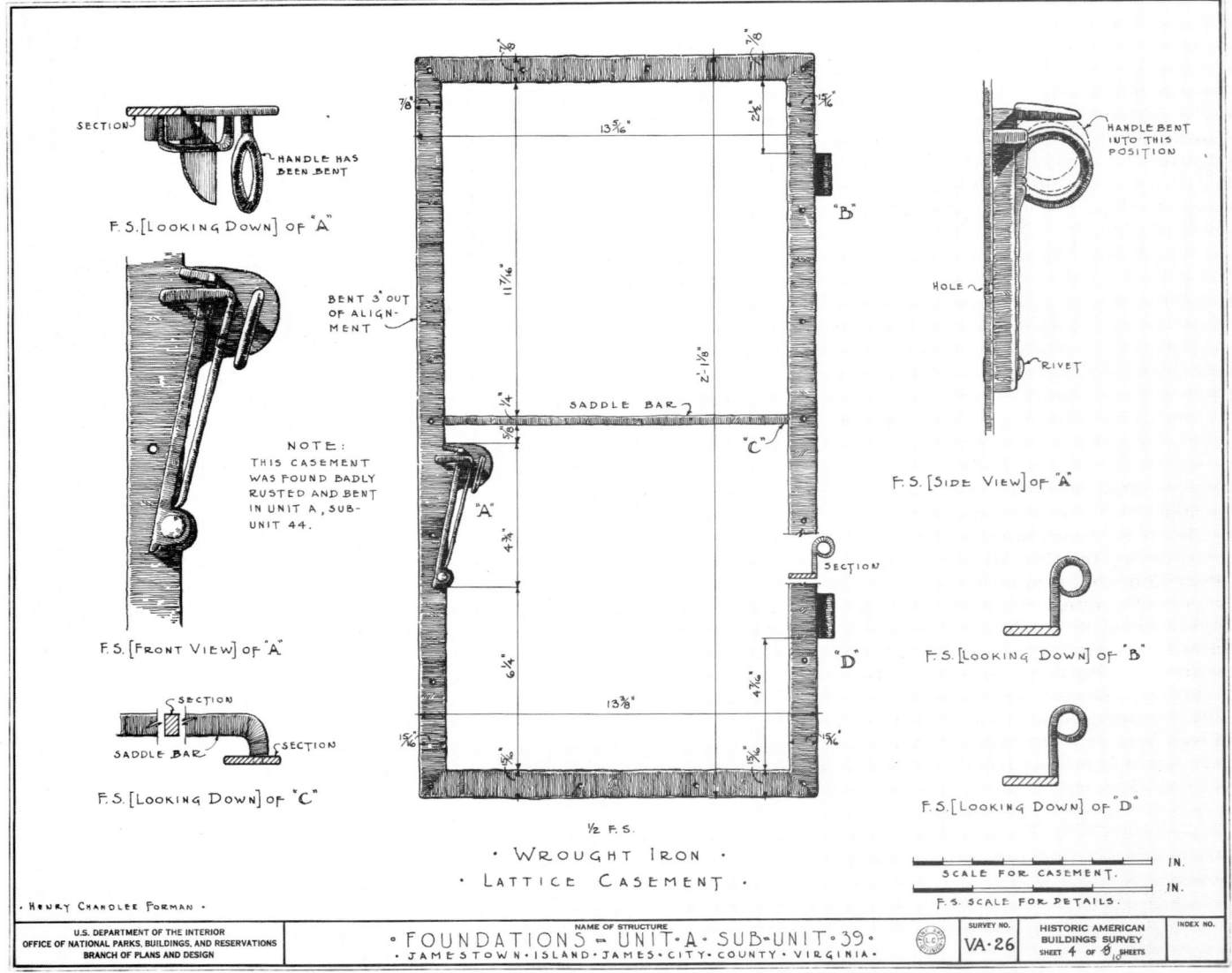

U.S. DEPARTMENT OF THE INTERIOR
OFFICE OF NATIONAL PARKS, BUILDINGS, AND RESERVATIONS
BRANCH OF PLANS AND DESIGN

NAME OF STRUCTURE
° F O U N D A T I O N S ━ U N I T · A · S U B - U N I T · 3 9 ·
· J A M E S T O W N · I S L A N D · J A M E S · C I T Y · C O U N T Y · V I R G I N I A ·

SURVEY NO.
VA · 26

HISTORIC AMERICAN
BUILDINGS SURVEY
SHEET 4 OF 9 SHEETS

INDEX NO.

Figure 14 The first Park Service archaeologists at seventeenth-century Jamestown were Indian mound diggers from the Middle West. A battle of professional prerogatives was soon raging and the echoes have hardly died down even yet. Henry Chandlee Forman of Maryland served as captain of the architectural teams which recorded the substructures excavated, along with a selection of architectural specimens. Here we have a casement window frame of wrought iron probably fabricated in England. It seems to be a unique survival in this country. Measured drawing by Henry Chandlee Forman, 1935. (HABS VA–26, sheet 4 of 9 sheets)

1957—the Plum Street Temple in Cincinnati (fig. 27). It was soon followed by OSU recording in Philadelphia, New York City, and other places.

Our success with a few examples of engineering and industrial structures led to the establishment of the Historic American Engineering Record (HAER), which brings to the fore a whole new set of history buffs. With the leadership of such enthusiasts as Robert Vogel of the Smithsonian and other less visible supporters, HAER, we hope, will have a splendid future. The historical relics of American leadership in technology are even more fragile than its architecture. "Industrial archaeology" as a public interest did not arrive a minute too soon.

Not everything new was good. Among the disastrous programs of a recent administration was an attempt to add social engineering to the summer student program. It was the kind of expensive failure that should not be repeated.

Alternative means of building up the collections were explored. In some areas, student measured drawings done in HABS format were purchased or donated, and extensive work was done at North Carolina State University and the University of Florida. One of the more unusual cooperative pro-

Figure 15 Fragments excavated at Jamestown. The two tiles are typical features of fireplace surrounds. They are of a yellow clay coated with a white tin enamel wash and decorated by hand in cobalt blue. These are standard Dutch designs outlined with charcoal dust to guide the painter. The glass "quarries" set in lead cames are typical of the period. Drawn by John Zaharov, recently of the Williamsburg restoration, known as "The Terrible Russian." Measured drawing, 1939. (HABS VA–26, sheet 9 of 9 sheets)

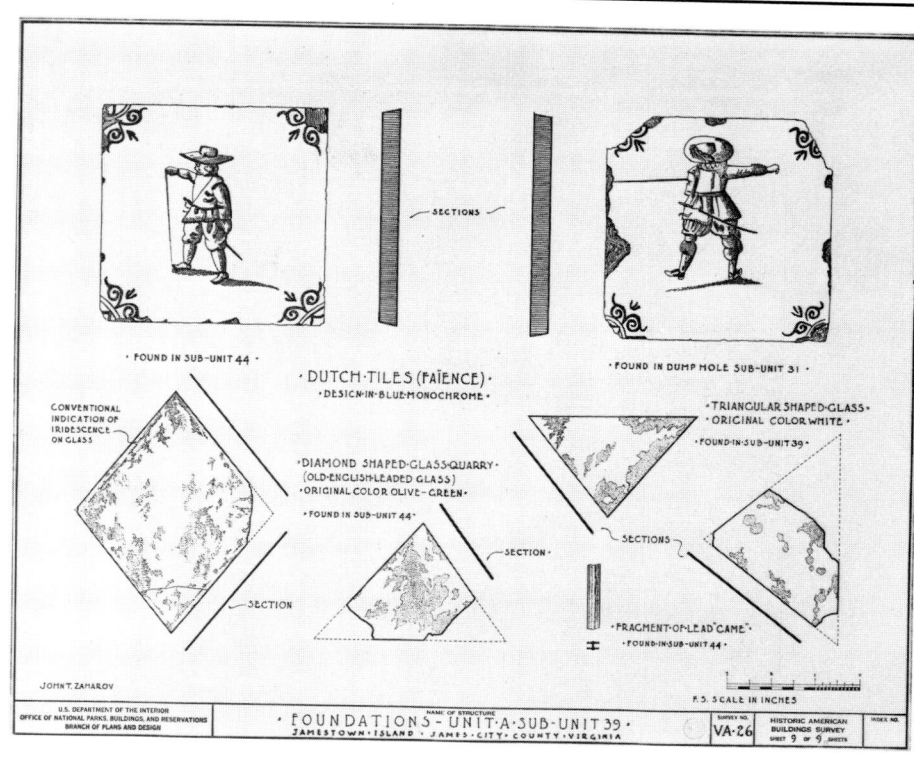

Figure 16 Mannsfield, a great sandstone plantation house on the Rappahannock River below Fredericksburg, Virginia, was burned during the Civil War while occupied by Louisiana troops (not Yankees). The ruins lay within reach of the CCC camps working in the National Military Park and were excavated under the direction of Stuart Barnette, who made this drawing, 1935–36. Barnette was a graduate of the Naval Academy at Annapolis and later became a professor of architecture at Cornell University. (HABS VA–122, sheet 1 of 25 sheets)

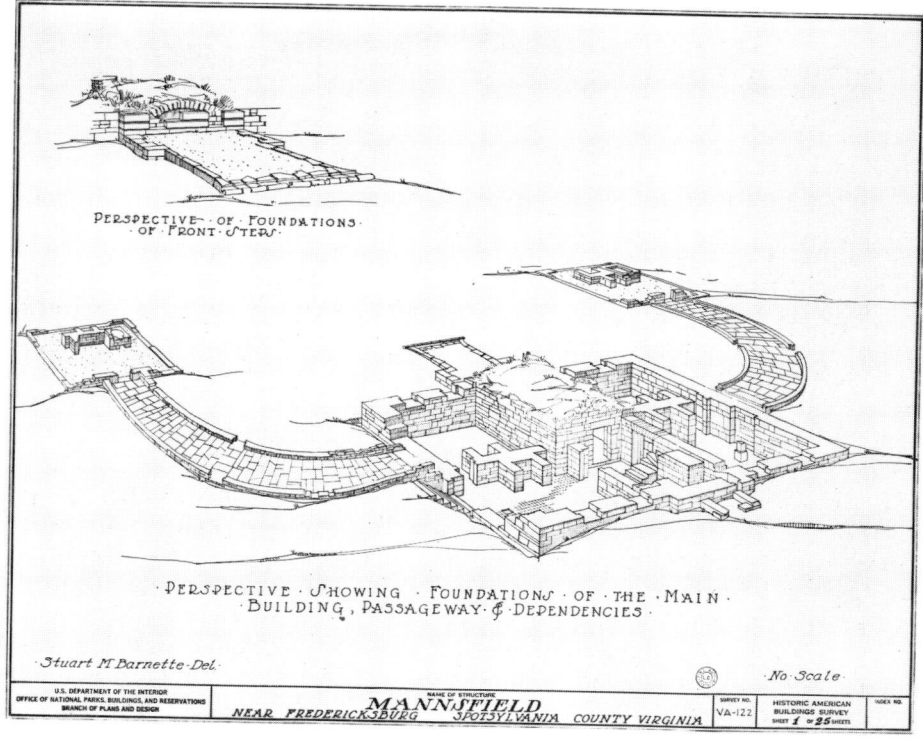

Figure 17 Mannsfield hardware. The wrought-iron hinges numbered 4 and 10 would have supported wooden doors where they were inserted in the rails and secured with wooden wedges. Known as "mortice hinges" they were a refinement this writer years later learned to identify. The cast-iron hinge (no. 78) was a nineteenth-century type designed to lift doors clear of carpets. (HABS VA–122, sheet 16 of 25 sheets)

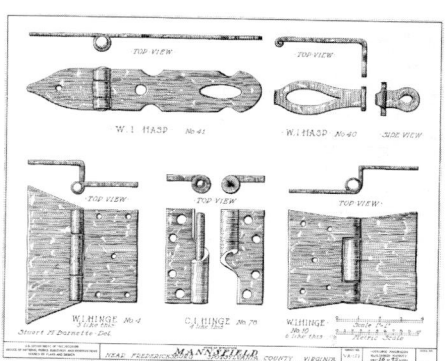

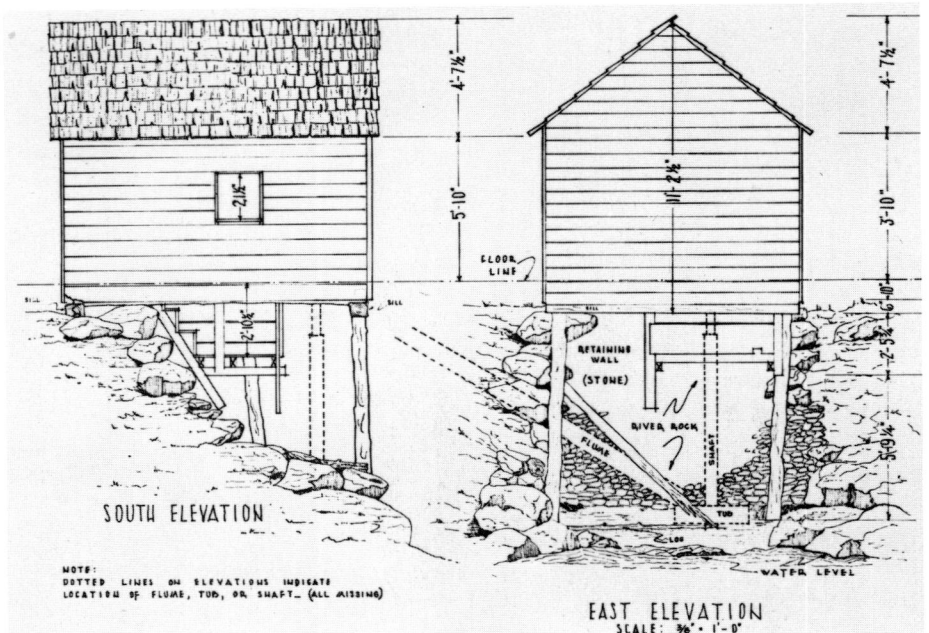

SOUTH ELEVATION

NOTE:
DOTTED LINES ON ELEVATIONS INDICATE
LOCATION OF FLUME, TUB, OR SHAFT. (ALL MISSING)

EAST ELEVATION
SCALE: 3/8" = 1'-0"

Figure 18 The tub mill is still found on remote streams in the southern Appalachians. It was a primitive, homemade turbine which probably harkens back to ancient times. In 1957 Sam Henry, formerly of Pigeon Forge, Tennessee, was commissioned to go back and record examples of this mountaineer technology. Shown here is a view of the Alfred Reagan mill on Roaring Fork, Tennessee. Measured drawing, 1957. (HABS TENN–165, sheet 2 of 4 sheets)

Figure 19 Grinding parts of the Alfred Reagan tub mill. Drawing by Samuel E. Henry, 1957. (HABS TENN–165, sheet 4 of 4 sheets)

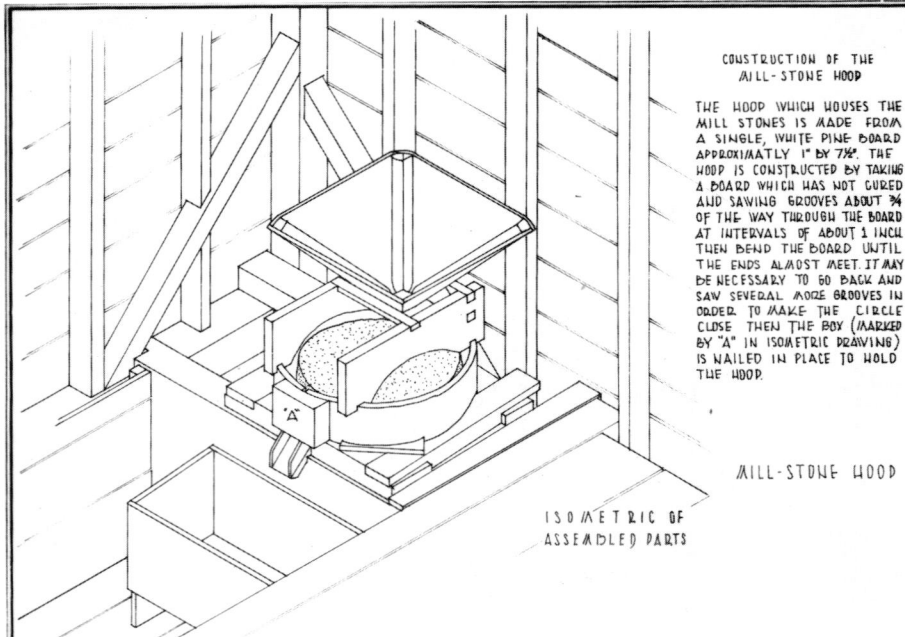

jects was our American field party working in the Virgin Islands with the Royal Academy of Arts of Copenhagen in 1961. The making of measured drawings had been a regular part of architectural education in Denmark. Annually the academy dispatched parties of students to interesting places—in this case to the Caribbean, where Danish colonists of the eighteenth and nineteenth century left a rich collection of colorful architecture (fig. 21).

Special funding under the Park Service's "Mission 66" program made it possible to take a very wide view of the United States, and an attempt was again made to program work in areas previously bypassed. For some time there had been loose talk in some circles about "completing HABS." One of our first steps was to obtain a blank county map of the country, in which there are some three thousand counties.[7] We then selected Chester County, Pennsylvania, for an example (fig. 22). The historical society there had an impressive dossier on each of its favorite historical structures and together we picked out 100 of them to be photographed and written up on standard data sheets. This was done and the accomplishment was celebrated by a dinner party at West Chester at which a large set of salon prints were displayed, opening up a public showing.

Figure 20 The homemade tub or turbine wheel carved from a log and set up at "Junglebrook" near Gatlinburg in the Great Smoky Mountains Park. Drawing by Samuel E. Henry, 1958. (HABS TENN–165, sheet 4 of 6 sheets)

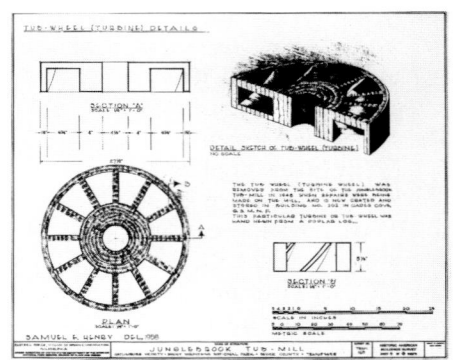

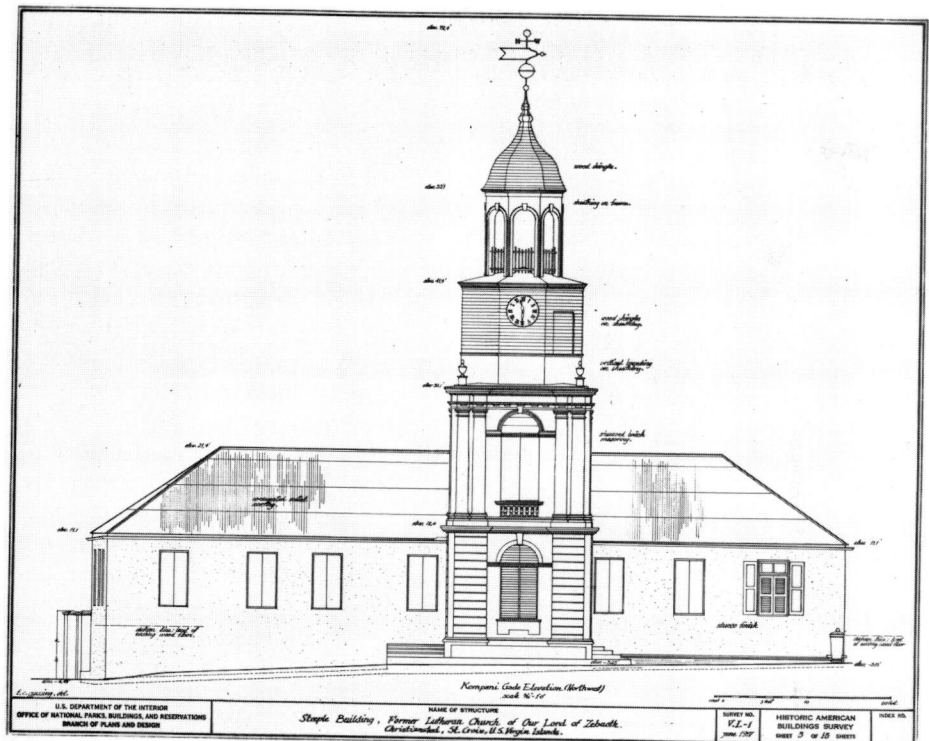

Figure 21 The Steeple Building (formerly the Lutheran Church of Our Lord of Zeboath), one of the permanent landmarks of Christiansted, the eighteenth-century Danish colonial metropolis of St. Croix in the Virgin Islands. This coral stone stuccoed structure was drawn by National Park Service Resident Architect Frederick C. Gjessing, himself a graduate of the Royal Academy in Copenhagen, in 1957. (HABS VI–1, sheet 5 of 15 sheets)

Figure 22 The Pim Hexagonal School. Now moved to the Caln Township Municipal Park, Chester County, Pennsylvania. This curious stone structure, built in 1841, still had many of its original features but some were in disarray when teams arrived to record them. Ned Goode, contract photographer, captured the building's cupola in this shot taken in 1961. The historical writeup was by Curator Bart Anderson. In cooperation with the Chester County Historical Society, 100 buildings in that county were selected for photography. (HABS PA–5136–4, LC HABS PA, 15–THORN, 1–4)

Afterward it was pointed out that if this were done for all the American counties, we would have a new collection of three hundred thousand structures represented by 1.5 million photographs. Talk about "completing HABS" soon died down and the Survey was afterward referred to as an "open-end archive."

As outside requests for recording increased, it was possible to get local assistance in kind to make our funds go farther. An early example was Dartmouth College, which offered us a headquarters for our Middle Connecticut Valley season.

During the establishment of the Cape Cod Seashore National Park, HABS became a great help in public relations. Some of the local residents worried that the Smoky Joes would tear down all the historic landmarks in an attempt to return the area to a pris-

Figure 23 Liberty Hall, Frankfort, Kentucky. This fine house constructed by Virginia bricklayers in the closing years of the eighteenth century went through many changes, especially in the original rear wing shown here. In the twentieth century private owners began to restore the house by removing later intrusions one at a time, making the evolution of the various parts hard to follow. During recent work by the Kentucky Colonial Dames, HABS drawings by L. H. Tehman dated 1934 were important to understanding the structure. (HABS KY–20–2, sheet 7 of 15 sheets)

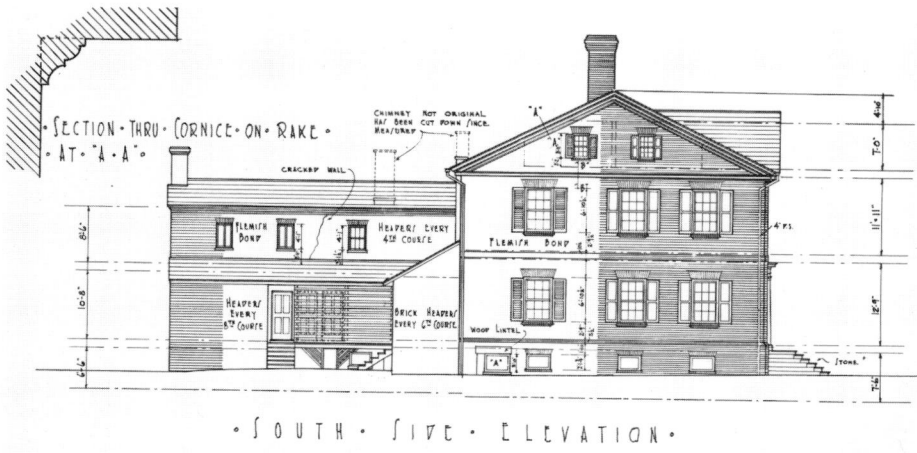

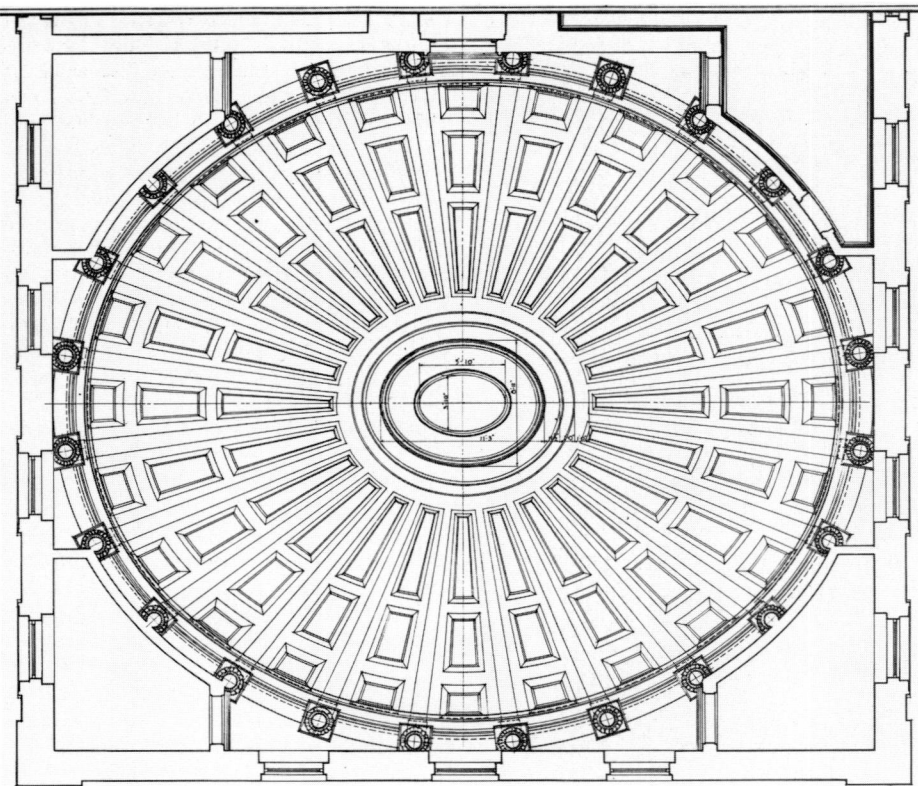

Figure 24 Old St. Louis Courthouse. This great stone structure, built over a twenty-five year period, was the climax of the Greek Revival style west of the Mississippi. It became part of the Jefferson National Expansion Memorial on the Mississippi riverfront and one of the few buildings to escape demolition. In preparation for restoration, a large set of measured drawings was made by Park Service architects. The wooden ceiling of this second floor courtroom was hung from a pioneer example of wrought iron triangular truss. Drawing by staffer Frank R. Leslie, 1940. (HABS MO−31−8, sheet 46 of 49 sheets)

Figure 25 Fort Marion, St. Augustine, Florida, under the care of the National Park Service. Now called the Castillo San Marcos, this picturesque structure was built of the local coquina rock and exhibits the classic features of bastions (with *guerites* or watchhouses), moat, and drawbridge. It guards the entrance to the harbor of this picturesque Spanish town dating from the sixteenth century. Drawing by J. Erwin Page, 1936. (HABS FLA−17, sheet 1 of 9 sheets)

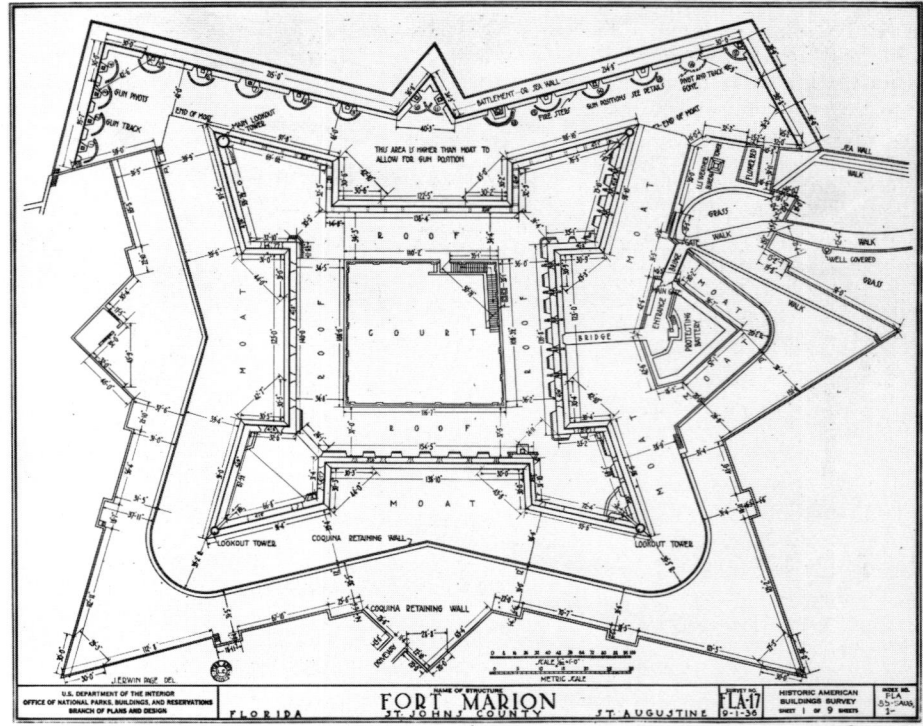

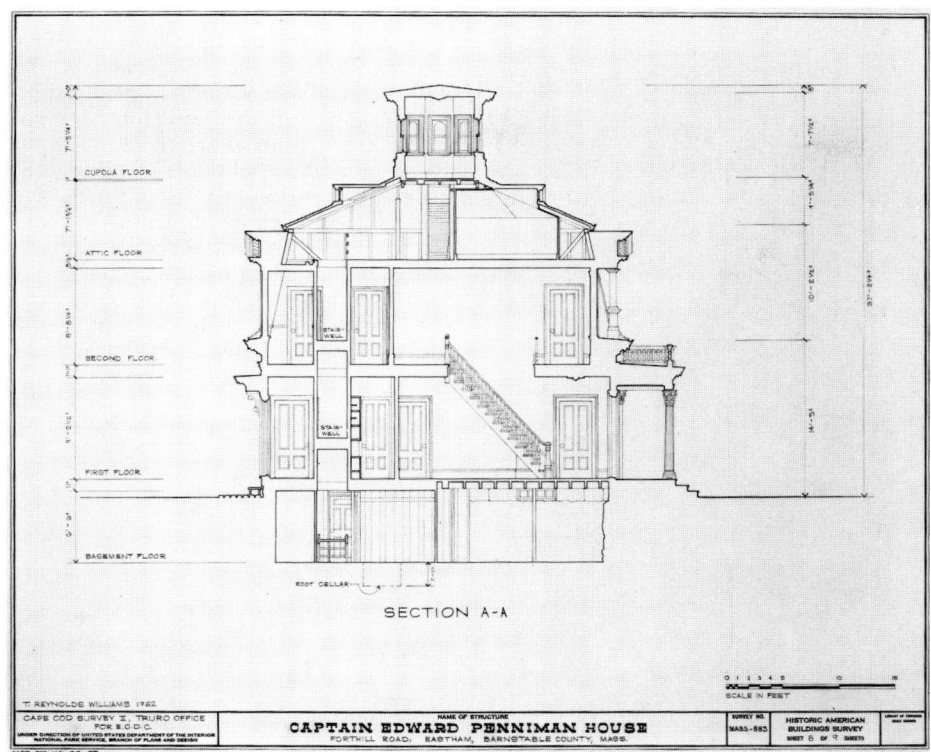

Figure 26 Captain Edward Penniman House, Fort Hill Road, Eastham, Barnstable County, Massachusetts. The work of HABS summer teams on Cape Cod from 1959 through the 1960s led the National Park Service to establish policies for the classification, protection, and documentation of historic buildings in national recreation areas. HABS recorded structures like this Victorian sea captain's house and examples of the widely imitated "Cape Cod cottage." Sectional elevation by Reynolds Williams, 1962. (HABS MASS−693, sheet 8 of 9 sheets)

Figure 27 The Plum Street (or Isaac M. Wise) Temple, Cincinnati, Ohio. Much of the elaborate ornament on this oriental fantasy would have been impracticable to record by conventional methods. But Professor of Architecture Perry E. Borchers, pioneer architectural photogrammetrist at Ohio State University, developed successful procedures by which draftsmen delineated architecture on plotting machines from photographic glass plates made under carefully controlled field conditions. Drawing by George F. Erssey, 1957. (HABS O−643, sheet 1 of 2 sheets)

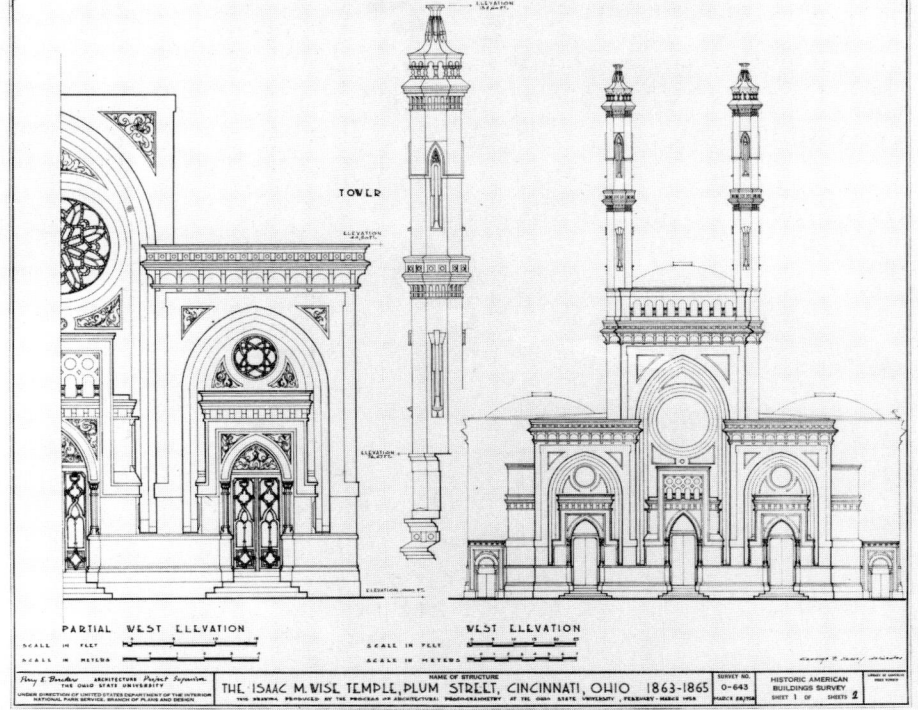

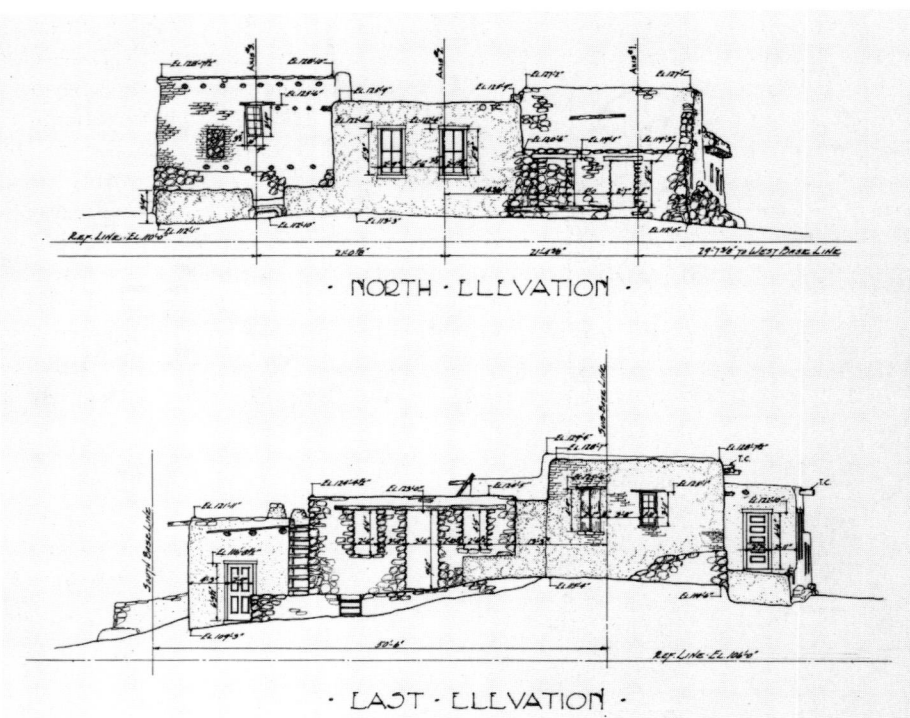

· NORTH · ELEVATION ·

· LAST · ELEVATION ·

Figure 28 Acoma Pueblo, New Mexico. In 1934 a team of architects went south from Denver to the Indian country to record structures where there were no local architects. Clusters of primitive houses like these are difficult to record because there are few if any right angles that can be easily handled on a standard drawing board. More recently, some of the pueblos have been covered by photogrammetry done from the air, making more accurate drawings possible. Measured drawing by Paul Atwood, Stanley Kent, and A. G. Longfellow, 1934. (HABS NM−6, sheet 59 of 85 sheets)

Figure 29 Iolani Palace, Honolulu, Hawaii. This great brick structure was built for Kalakaua, last of the Hawaiian kings, in 1879−81. The all-around iron porches (called *lanais*) were cast in San Francisco and the whole finished with a dazzling coat of sanded paint. There were three architects: T. J. Baker, C. J. Wall, and Isaac Moore. (See Charles E. Peterson, "The Iolani Palaces and the Barracks," *Journal of the Society of Architectural Historians* 22: 96−102.) Drawing by E. Davis Chauviere of the Columbia University School of Architecture team, 1966. (HABS HA−1, sheet 6 of 22 sheets)

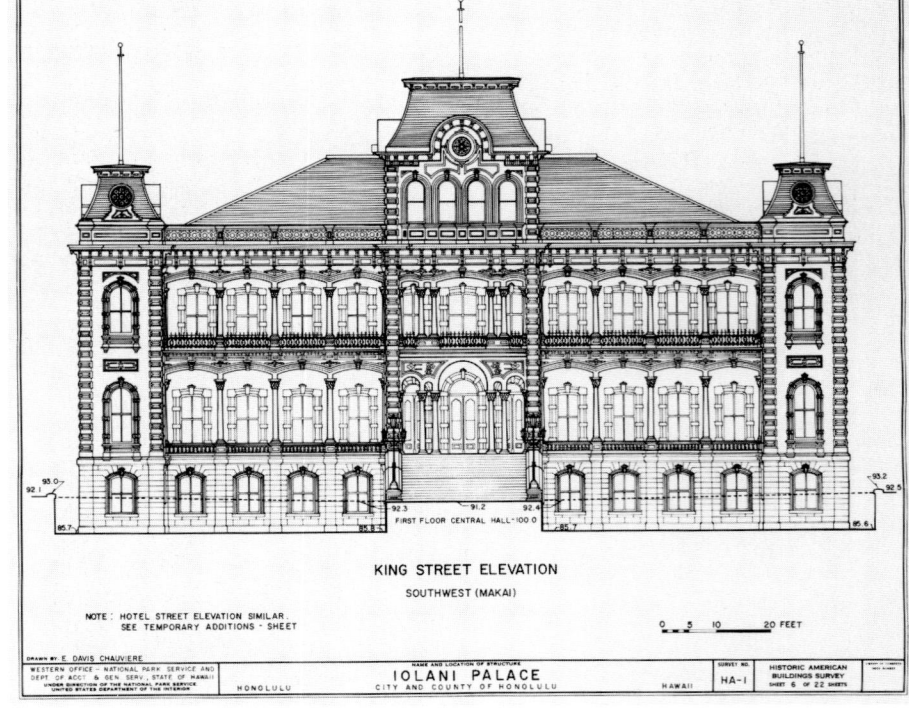

KING STREET ELEVATION

SOUTHWEST (MAKAI)

tine wilderness. Two seasons of HABS teamwork under Ernest A. Connally of the University of Illinois helped relieve the tensions on the Cape (fig. 26).

I am also proud of two summers' work under a contract with Columbia University, where I taught from 1964 to 1978. No HABS records at all had been made in distant Hawaii, an area with which I had some familiarity. Working with state and local experts, teams under Profs. Melvin M. Rotsch of Texas A & M and Woodrow W. Wilkins of the University of Miami made a fine set of records (fig. 29). Good photographic coverage of the Honolulu landmarks—as well as a scattering of those in the outer islands—was added by photographer Jack E. Boucher.

When the Park Service historical architects were all under one roof, the HABS summer programs were deliberately contrived to enlist new talent for careers in the Service. Every effort was made to locate bright students not yet brainwashed by the stern idealogues of the International Style. By encouraging the best of the summer talent to throw in with the Park Service's conservation program, we gradually assembled a notable group. Since that effort was dropped, nearly a whole generation of such students has been missing or remains as yet unidentified.

I am sometimes asked about the future of HABS, and I must say it now looks rather dim. The Survey's advisory board was surreptitiously dropped five years ago. Within the Park Service the architectural profession has been fragmented, dispersed, and suppressed. Management—whatever that is—rides the wave. Attempts to "reprofessionalize" the Service seem to get nowhere. Overhead, the weight of the highly political Interior Department is felt as suffocating. In its preoccupation with the raw resources of the West, the department, under recent administrations, leaves the impression that the national parks as an ideal are only for juveniles and that the historic treasures of the nation are for the crazies. A general jailbreak may be the only solution.

But if its natural friends outside the federal government are encouraged to participate—as they were in the beginning—there will be no end to the usefulness and growth of the Historic American Buildings Survey.

Notes

1. A different version of this narrative may be found as an introduction to Richard J. Webster, *Philadelphia Preserved: Catalog of the Historic American Buildings Survey* (Philadelphia: Temple University Press, 1976). An account full of interesting particulars is in Charles B. Hosmer, Jr., *Preservation Comes of Age*, vol. 1 (Charlottesville, 1981), pp. 548–62.

2. The proposal was published in full in "American Notes," *Journal of the Society of Architectural Historians* 16 (October 1956):29–31.

3. Our office at that time was in Room 3065 Navy Building on Constitution Avenue (now demolished).

4. The first press announcement appeared in the *Washington Post*, November 29, 1933.

5. In 1935 these were resting in large wooden packing boxes in the attic of 66 Portland Place, London, without any plan to make them available. They are now under government care in the National Buildings Record in Fortress House, London.

6. John P. O'Neill, comp. and ed., *Historic American Buildings Survey Catalog of the Measured Drawings and Photographs of the Survey in the Library of Congress, January 1, 1938* (Washington, 1938), introduction by Leicester B. Holland. At that time, 2,200 structures were represented by 14,500 sheets of drawings and photographic negatives of 3,800 structures.

7. My first valuable assistant in that period was Agnes Addison Gilchrist of Mount Vernon, New York, author of the first biography of William Strickland (1950) and a president of the Society of Architectural Historians. She literally worked herself into a hospital.

The Survey in Louisiana in the 1930s

by

SAMUEL WILSON, Jr.

The financial crash of 1929 and the Great Depression that followed brought building activity in Louisiana, as in the rest of the nation, practically to a standstill. Huey P. Long had been elected governor of the state in 1928 and soon had the architectural firm of Weiss, Dreyfous and Seiferth designing a new state capitol (fig. 2). Numerous other state buildings were being planned and built as well. Nevertheless, there was little or no work for many established architects, for recent graduates of Tulane University's School of Architecture, or for many draftsmen.

Following the election of Franklin D. Roosevelt as president in 1932 and his inauguration on March 4, 1933, his program for economic recovery began to be implemented. Among the many projects initiated to relieve unemployment were several in the cultural and artistic spheres and one to give jobs to "starving architects," the Historic American Buildings Survey, developed largely through the efforts of

Charles E. Peterson of the National Park Service. As the HABS program was planned as a three-party agreement among the National Park Service, the Library of Congress, and the American Institute of Architects, the local chapter of the Institute was asked to set up the program in Louisiana to document historic buildings in that state.

Moise H. Goldstein, F.A.I.A., who served for many years as Gulf States regional director on the national board of the Institute, presented the proposal to the chapter and nominated Richard Koch as district officer in Louisiana (fig. 3). Koch accepted the position with enthusiasm, not only because of the slowness of work in his firm, Armstrong and Koch, but largely because of his interest in the historic architecture of his native state and his appreciation of it. He had been graduated from Tulane University in 1910 and after two years of study in Paris and several years in New York and New England offices, had begun his own practice in New Orleans in partnership with Charles R. Armstrong in 1916.

Armstrong and Koch were pioneers in restoration and adaptive reuse of buildings of historic and architectural importance in Louisiana. They restored Shadows-on-the-Teche (fig. 4) in New Iberia for Weeks Hall in 1922 and Oak Alley Plantation at Vacherie in 1926 for Mr. and Mrs.

Figure 1 Watercolor of the "Three Sisters" at Rampart and Bienville streets, New Orleans. This is one of many such watercolors made by A. Boyd Cruise for HABS to record the color and character of buildings. Although not then generally part of the HABS program, these drawings give an added dimension to HABS recording. Architectural Drawings Collection, Prints and Photographs Division (LC–USZ62–83606)

Figure 2 Louisiana State Capitol, Baton Rouge. Weiss, Dreyfous and Seiferth, architects. Several of the draftsmen who had worked on the plans of this building in the early 1930s became part of the HABS team in Louisiana. Photograph, 1932. Gottscho-Schleisner Collection, Prints and Photographs Division. Commercial use by permission only. (LC–G612–18959)

Figure 3 Advisory committee of the Vieux Carré Survey, ca. 1965. Standing left to right: Richard Koch, HABS district officer; Boyd Cruise, HABS artist and draftsman and executive director of the Vieux Carré Survey; Gen. L. Kemper Williams, founder of the Historic New Orleans Collection; Samuel Wilson, Jr., HABS draftsman; Bernard Lemann, professor of architecture, Tulane University; John W. Lawrence, dean, School of Architecture, Tulane University; Edith Long, senior archivist, Vieux Carré Survey; Leonard V. Huber, author and business and civic leader. Courtesy Historic New Orleans Collection.

Andrew Stewart. They restored the Victor David House on St. Peter Street for Le Petit Salon, a ladies club, also in 1926 and built a new building adjacent to it, in a traditional style, for Le Petit Théâtre du Vieux Carré that same year. No better choice than Richard Koch could have been made to organize and direct the Historic American Buildings Survey in Louisiana.

There had been earlier recording efforts made in Louisiana and practically from its beginnings in 1907 the Tulane University School of Architecture encouraged the study and recording of Louisiana's historic architecture. In the 1913–1914 *Year Book* of the Department of Architecture, some of a set of measured drawings of the "Old Hurst Residence" made by four students were reproduced, drawings which are now deposited in the Southeastern Architectural Archive in the Tulane University Library. In 1922 this house, built in 1832, was taken down and reerected on a suburban site by Armstrong and Koch, architects, who made use of these early measured drawings. Tulane students continued to produce measured drawings of old buildings and architectural details, as well as historical studies, for which the S. S. Labouisse Prize is awarded annually. Unfortunately, only a few of these draw-

ings have been preserved at Tulane. One such drawing was published in the *Western Architect* in March 1928—a wrought iron gate at 613 Royal Street by A. A. Callender. It was titled "Tulane Series No. 4," but neither this nor any other drawings of such a series have been found at Tulane (fig. 5). These early documentation efforts, however, provided the training which enabled the Survey in Louisiana to produce such high quality results.

Work for the Survey began in January 1934 in offices at 614 Audubon Building, on the same floor as the offices of Armstrong and Koch. From the office of Moise H. Goldstein came F. Monroe Labouisse and this writer, Tulane graduates in 1932 and 1931 respectively. Among those from other local offices in which there was little or no work was Douglass V. Freret, a 1925 Tulane graduate with a master's degree from Cornell in 1926, who came from the office of Favrot and Livaudais. From the office of Weiss, Dreyfous and Seiferth, where they had completed the drawings for the new Louisiana State Capitol in Baton Rouge (fig. 2), were G. E. Dupont, H. H. Dowling, Horace Trepagnier, and W. Byron Proctor. Others in this first few months of the Survey were David C. E. Geier, Allison Owen, Jr., Robert G. Crump,

Ulisse M. Nolan, and Myrthé Stauffer, all Tulane graduates, Louis Sarrazin, Jr., apprentice and office boy in the Armstrong and Koch office, and Walter McKinstry, who had worked similarly in the Goldstein office. Others included F. P. Dufrechou, Charles J. Phillips, and O. Couloheras. All were excellent draftsmen and in the first year produced an extraordinary number of beautiful measured drawings that set a standard that was followed in the years to come. Helen Niver was employed as secretary, doing the necessary typing and keeping the records of the day-to-day activity. Richard Koch kept a close watch over all the work in the office and insisted on the highest standards of quality in all the drawings.

Koch selected the buildings to be measured and drawn, basing his choice on the importance of the building, architecturally and historically, its availability, its danger of destruction, and his own personal interest and preference. Measuring began first on the Beauregard House at 1113 Chartres Street in New Orleans, with a field party under the direction of Douglass V. Freret consisting of Allison Owen, Jr., Gaston E. Dupont, this writer, Myrthé Stauffer, Horace Trepagnier, and F. Monroe Labouisse (fig. 6). By the end of June 1934, sixteen sheets of drawings had been produced by Freret, Foster, Geier, Owen, and Proctor.

This important raised house with a four-column portico was built in 1826, and, for a brief period after the Civil War, Confederate General P. G. T. Beauregard lived in it. In 1925 the house was sold and slated to be demolished and replaced by a warehouse. A group of patriotic and historically minded citizens succeeded in purchasing it but were unable to finance its restoration. In the 1940s it was leased to Frances Parkinson Keyes, the novelist, who began the work of restoration under Richard Koch's direction and making use of the HABS drawings of the 1930s. In 1955 she acquired the house from Beauregard House, Inc., for the Keyes Foundation, which

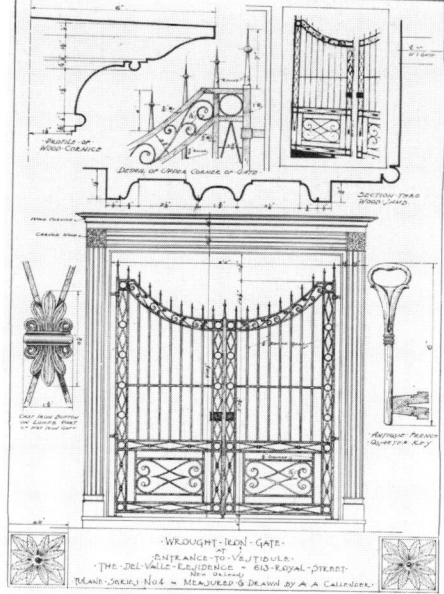

Figure 4 Shadows-on-the-Teche, New Iberia, Louisiana, built in the 1830s and restored in 1922 for Weeks Hall, Armstrong and Koch, architects. Bequeathed by Weeks Hall to the National Trust for Historic Preservation and again restored and recorded for HABS in 1961, Richard Koch and Samuel Wilson, Jr., architects. Photograph by Frances Benjamin Johnston. Carnegie Survey of the Architecture of the South, Prints and Photographs Division. (LC–J7–LA–1366)

Figure 5 Measured drawing of wrought iron gate at 613 Royal Street, New Orleans, a pre-HABS recording by A. A. Callender, Tulane University architecture student, published in the *Western Architect*, March 1928. Although many such drawings were made through the years, few have been retained at Tulane. The present status of this drawing is unknown.

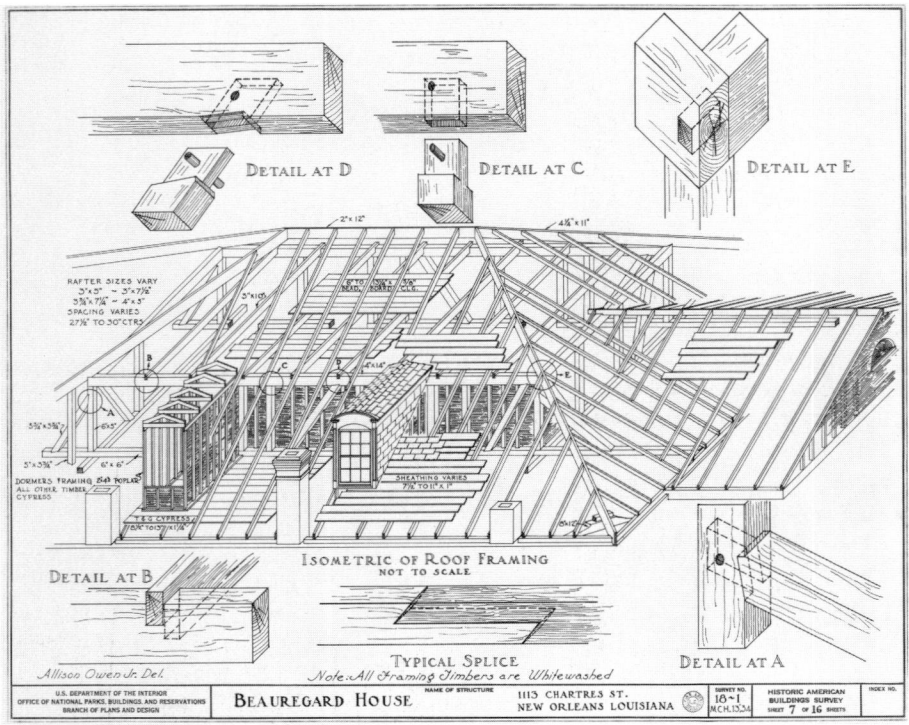

Figure 6 Isometric drawing of roof construction details. Beauregard House, 1113 Chartres Street, New Orleans, the first project recorded by the Survey in Louisiana. Drawing by Allison Owen, Jr., March 13, 1934. (HABS LA–18–1, sheet 7 of 16 sheets)

Figure 7 Main stairway, old Ursuline Convent, New Orleans. The only building surviving substantially intact from the period of French domination in Louisiana, this convent, also known as the Archbishopric, was recorded by HABS in 1934. It was designed in 1745 by Ignace François Broutin. This stairway was reused from an earlier convent (1727–34) near the site, according to a manuscript *toisé* of the building dated 1749, now in the Library of Congress. Original plans of both convent buildings are in the Archives nationales, Paris. Photograph by Richard Koch, 1934. (HABS LA–18–2, LC HABS LA, 36–NEWOR, 2–16)

still owns and operates it as a historic house museum. Frances Keyes wrote several of her well-known novels here, including two which used the house as the setting. In 1954 she purchased the adjacent corner property and restored the garden that had formerly existed there. This restoration was based on a drawing of 1865 found in the Notarial Archives by HABS researchers in the 1930s. Mrs. Keyes died at Beauregard House on July 3, 1970. The HABS drawings, photographs, and historical data concerning the house were published as one of a series in the *Architectural Forum* in November 1935.

The second project undertaken in Louisiana was documenting the old Ursuline Convent at 1114 Chartres Street, opposite Beauregard House. Thirty-one sheets of drawings were produced to document this National Historic Landmark, the only building known to survive almost intact from Louisiana's French colonial period. At the time the building was generally known as the Archbishopric, and this became the name of the HABS project. The field party consisted of this writer and Gaston E. Dupont, who also made all but one of the drawings. I had made measured drawings and done some research on the building as a student project at Tulane in 1929 and I did most of the research for this HABS project. It had been believed for well over a century that this was the building that had been built by Royal French Engineers between 1727 and 1734 to house the Ursuline nuns who came to New Orleans in 1727 and had occupied this site until the early 1820s. My interest in architectural history was stimulated by HABS, and I received an Edward W. Langley Scholarship from the American Institute of Architects in 1938 to do research and study on the origins of Louisiana architecture in Europe. In Paris in the Archives nationales, I found drawings and other documentation clearly proving that the former Archbishopric was actually the second convent erected on the site for the Ursuline nuns. It was designed by

Ignace François Broutin in 1745 and completed in the early 1750s. Research in the Library of Congress revealed that the great staircase of the earlier convent was reused in the later building. It is still in place in the building, which has recently been renovated to house the archives of the Roman Catholic Archdiocese of New Orleans (fig. 7).

Koch appreciated the importance of careful documentation of buildings that were to be included in the Survey and expanded the staff to include several researchers. They worked in parish conveyance offices to trace chains of titles and in the New Orleans Notarial Archives, where they found countless building contracts and examined early and mid-nineteenth-century watercolor drawings of building plans, elevations, and perspectives in more than a hundred plan books on file in that office (fig. 11). Many of these were meticulously copied by the artist Boyd Cruise (figs. 8, 21), who also made many of the HABS sheets of hardware, cast ironwork, plaster ornaments, and other decorative details. Cruise also made many watercolor sketches in the field to record the color and character of buildings included in the Survey (fig. 1). Additional research was done in New Orleans in the newspaper files and other resources of the New Orleans Public Library, the library of the Louisiana State Museum (fig. 13), the City Archives, then located in the attic of the old City Hall on Lafayette Square, the Howard Memorial Library at Lee Circle, the Tilton Library of Tulane University (fig. 9), and many courthouses throughout the state.

Photography had become one of Koch's hobbies, and he personally took practically all the photographs included in the HABS collection. He used an old camera that produced four-by-five-inch negatives, and he often spent Saturdays and Sundays on photographic expeditions in the city and in the country. He had made a trip around the state in 1927 with the noted architectural photographer Robert W. Tebbs, from whom he gained much

knowledge of photography. Most of Koch's photographs were developed and printed by the local photographer Dan S. Leyrer, who also made a number of enlargements that were used in a HABS exhibition at the old Arts and Crafts Club.

Koch was particularly interested in the plantations of Louisiana, an interest probably stemming from his earlier work on the Shadows and Oak Alley. I accompanied him on extensive tours of the state in 1934 and 1935 to inventory and photograph many of these buildings for the Survey. On some of these trips we were joined by A. Hays Town, district officer for HABS in Mississippi, an old friend who had

Figure 8 Cast-iron column detail from the gallery of the Le Pretre House, 710 Dauphine Street, New Orleans. Boyd Cruise made many such measured drawings of ornamental cast iron as well as other decorative elements during his many years with HABS. U. J. Theriot assisted in this 1940 drawing. (HABS LA—53, sheet 21 of 26)

once worked in the Armstrong and Koch office. With Hays, we also visited many Mississippi plantations and country houses.

In the first year of the Survey, the dovecote or pigeonnier and dollhouse (fig. 16) at Angelina Plantation were measured and drawn. Not long afterward, these interesting little plantation outbuildings were demolished. In that same year, 1934, the Réné Beauregard House at Chalmette (figs. 15, 17), on the site of the 1815 Battle of New Orleans, was recorded on nine HABS sheets by Charles J. Phillips. The house was later badly damaged by vandals and by neglect so that when it was eventually acquired by the National Park Service and restored as a visitors' center for the Chalmette

National Historical Park, the HABS drawings were an invaluable aid in its restoration.

Woodlawn Plantation (fig. 18) near Napoleonville was selected as a project, and a field party consisting of F. P. Dufrechou, R. G. Foster, David Geier, W. B. Proctor, and this writer spent many a cold winter day in December 1934 measuring every detail of that abandoned derelict, then stored with hay and later demolished. We could not find accommodations any closer than Donaldsonville, where we obtained rooms in the town's old-fashioned hotel. Twenty sheets of drawings of this important plantation house resulted from this expedition (fig. 19).

Some projects were undertaken on an emergency basis as a building

Figure 9 Plan of New Orleans in 1808 by Joseph Pilié, a manuscript map in the Tulane University Library, recording the name and location of all property owners in the city at that time. Such historical documents are an important source in providing HABS documentation and data. (HABS LA–1100, LC HABS LA, 36–NEWOR, 25)

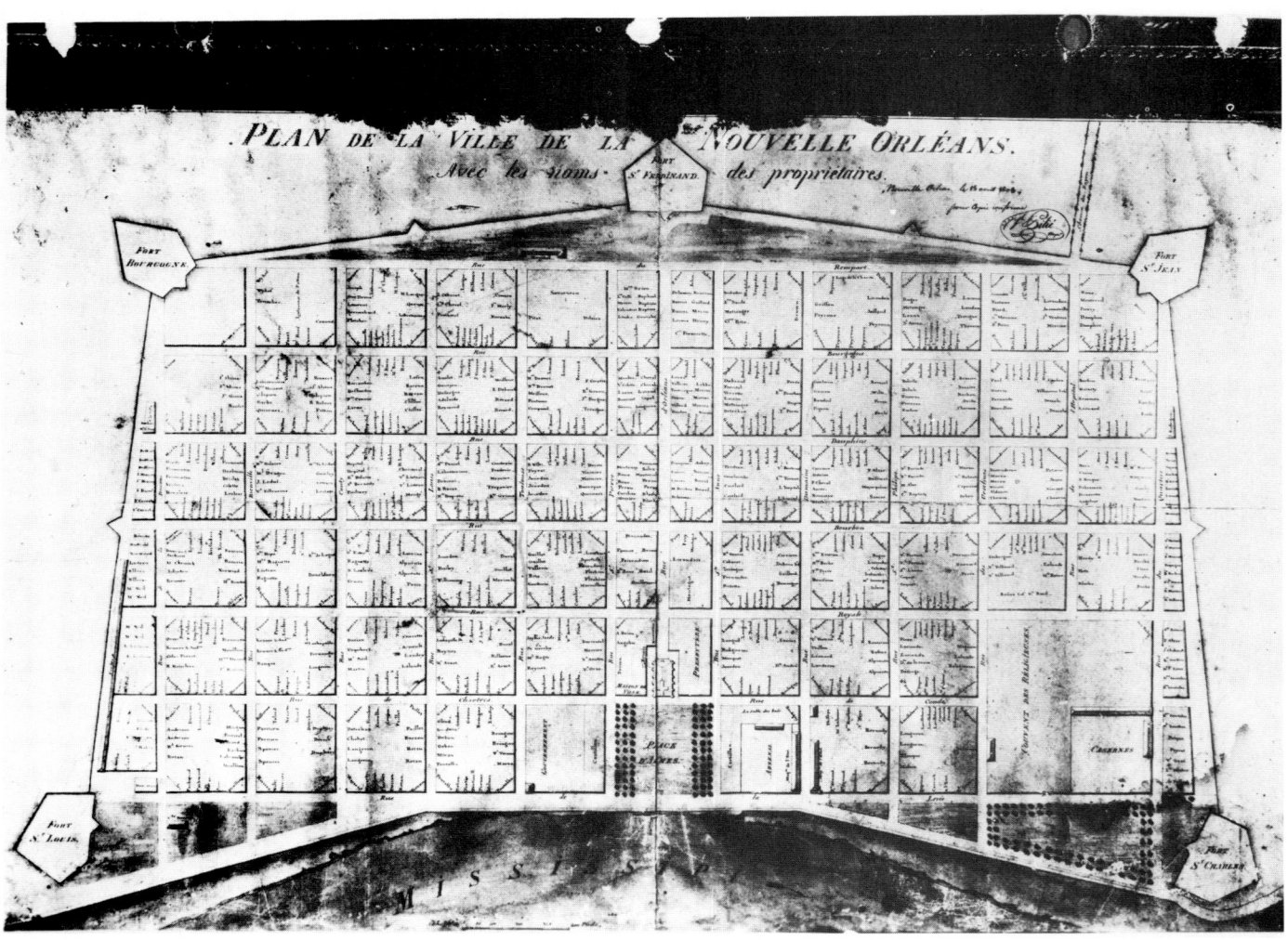

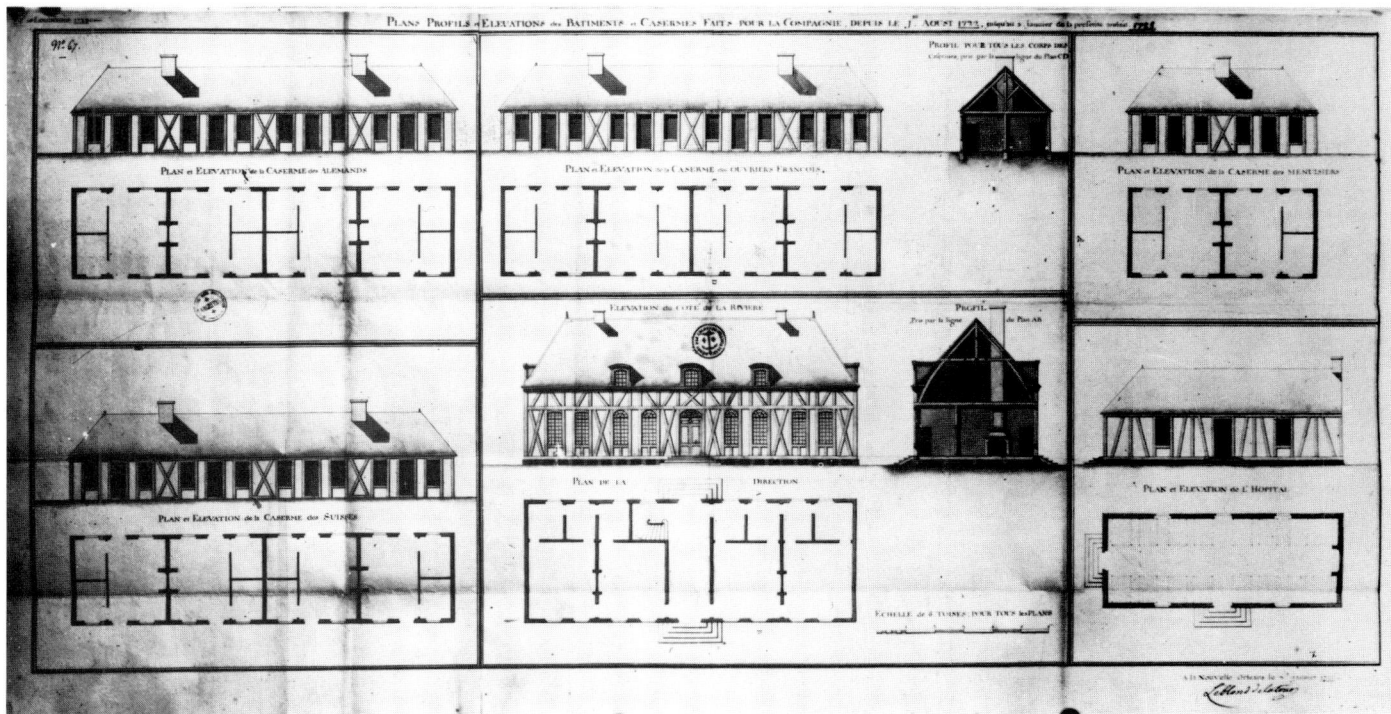

Figure 10   Drawing signed by Le Blond de la Tour, engineer-in-chief of Louisiana, dated January 3, 1723, showing some of the first buildings erected in New Orleans for the Company of the Indies. The *colombage* or timber frame construction shown here continued in use in Louisiana into the latter half of the nineteenth century. This is one of many such architectural drawings I located in the Archives nationales, Paris, in 1938. (HABS LA−1100, LC HABS LA, 36−NEWOR, 25)

Figure 11   Old house at 722 Toulouse Street, New Orleans, as depicted in an 1852 watercolor drawing in the Notarial Archives. This is a meticulously accurate copy made by Boyd Cruise for HABS. Hundreds of such nineteenth-century drawings exist in this archive, an invaluable HABS research source. This building, which now houses the archives of the Historic New Orleans Collection, was restored on the basis of this drawing in 1978, Koch and Wilson architects. (HABS LA−33, LC HABS LA, 36−NEWOR, 15−19)

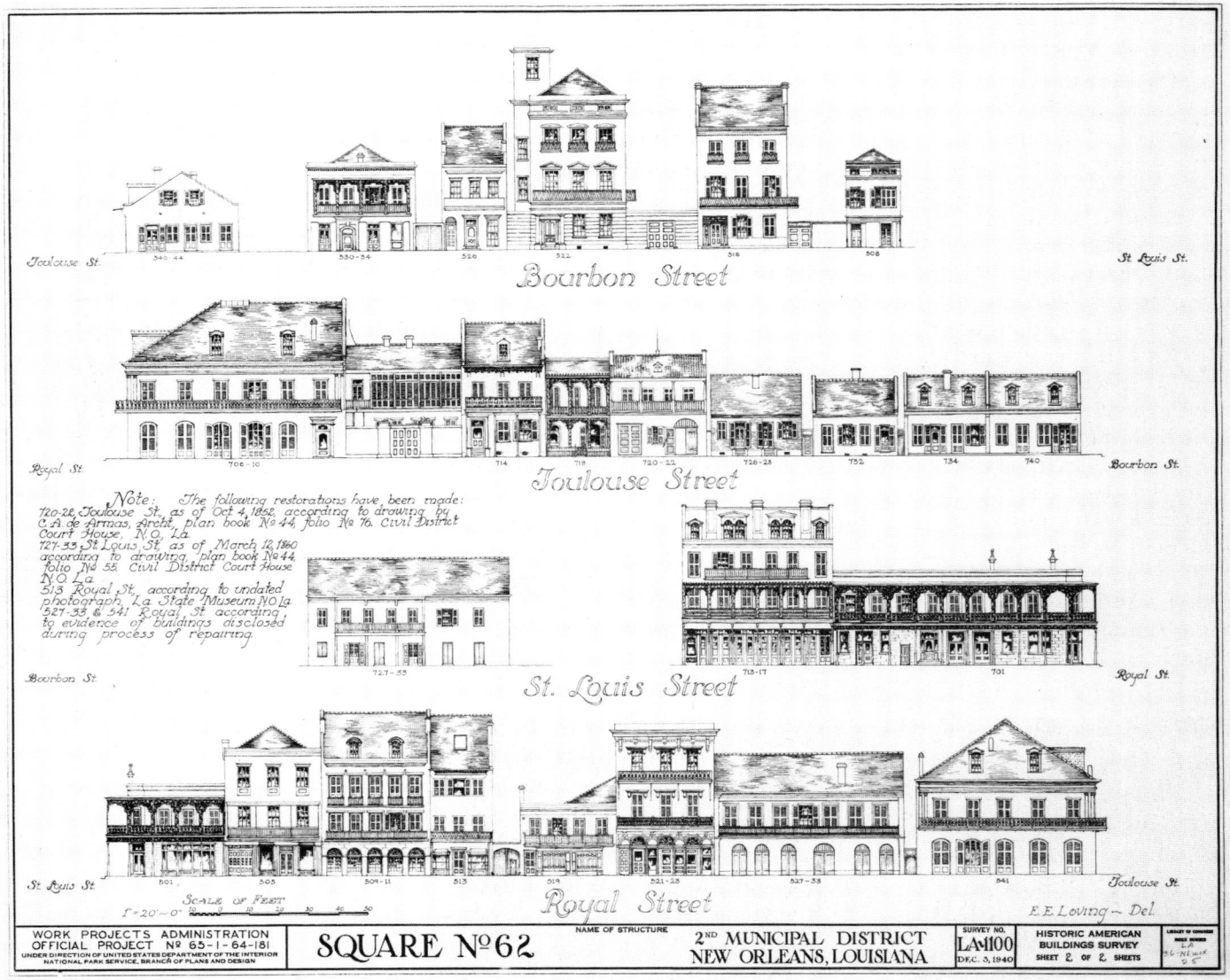

Figure 12 Sketch elevations of the buildings on the four sides of Square No. 62 of the New Orleans Vieux Carré by E. E. Loving, 1940, to show the relationship of buildings to each other in the streetscape. Several buildings are shown as restored according to old photographs and archival drawings. This sort of neighborhood survey has been developed further by HABS in the last twenty years and has been made an important element of the Vieux Carré Survey. (HABS LA−1100, sheet 2 of 2 sheets)

was threatened with immediate demolition. Such was the case with the Central Congregational Church (fig. 20). A contract for the demolition of this handsome Greek Revival church with a tall spire had already been let when permission to record it was obtained from the demolisher. In March 1935 a field party consisting of F. P. Dufrechou, Louis Sarrazin, Jr., Charles Phillips, David Geier, and this writer began the task. We only just finished as the building was falling down around us and the demolisher ordered us to leave. Six sheets of drawings and four of Koch's photographs record this interesting building.

Another such last minute project was the Troxler cottage at 919 St. Philip Street in New Orleans. This was a small eighteenth-century house in ruinous condition and practically unknown. It was not until the last year of the Survey, in the summer of 1940, that it was learned that it was to be demolished. Georgia B. Drennan and Chester H.

Wicker led a field party that also included C. R. Coleman, H. S. Kenison, U. J. Theriot, and Boyd Cruise. The building was promptly measured and drawn up on four sheets of drawings, perhaps the last project completed by this New Orleans team (fig. 21).

The Louisiana State Bank, the last design of Benjamin Henry Latrobe and now a National Historic Landmark, was among the important buildings measured in the first weeks of the Survey and drawn during the first year (fig. 24). The field party consisted of Peter F. Donnes, Jr., H. H. Dowling, Charles Phillips, Jr., and Walter McKinstry. Eighteen sheets of drawings were produced by Dowling and Phillips and by Douglass V. Freret. Drawings from field notes were often made by others who were not actually on the field party. Later visits, however, were often made to a building to verify details and moulding profiles. Koch checked these personally and insisted on the greatest possible accuracy.

Figure 13 Elevation drawing of the high altar of St. Patrick's Church by James Gallier, architect for the completion of this great Gothic Revival church in 1839. Original architects' drawings were among the many historical documents studied by HABS in Louisiana. From the collections of the Louisiana State Museum. (HABS LA–1111, LC HABS LA, 36–NEWOR, 59–12)

Figure 14 A 1963 photograph by Dan Leyrer for HABS of the high altar of St. Patrick's Church, New Orleans. Fig. 13 is the architect's original drawing for this altar. The church celebrates its 150th anniversary in 1983 and is in the process of restoration. (HABS LA–1111, LC HABS LA, 36–NEWOR, 59–4)

Figure 15 Chimney arch in attic of Réné Beauregard House, Chalmette, Louisiana. The flues of two chimneys were brought together by this arch to emerge from the roof as one. The arch was destroyed by vandals, who also did extensive damage to the house. The HABS drawings and photographs were of great assistance when the house was restored in 1958 for the National Park Service as the visitors' center of the Chalmette National Historical Park on the site of the 1815 battle of New Orleans. Samuel Wilson, Jr., architect. Photograph by Richard Koch, 1934. (HABS LA−18−7, LC HABS LA, 44−CHALM, 1−10)

Research and writing for the Louisiana State Bank project were done mostly by this writer. As a result, I became so interested in Latrobe that I later became acquainted with the Latrobe family in Baltimore, edited and published Latrobe's New Orleans Journals in 1951, and, that same year, married Ellen Elizabeth Latrobe in Latrobe's Baltimore Cathedral. In December 1936 the HABS drawings and historical data of the Louisiana State Bank were published in the short-lived *Southern Architectural Review*.

During the course of the first two years of the project, which came under the Works Progress Administration in Louisiana, many of the original teams returned to private employment and some transferred to other WPA projects. One of these was for the development of the New Orleans City Park, a project in which Koch himself was particularly interested. A drafting room was set up in the Casino Building in the park under the supervision of David Geier. I worked with Koch in the

Audubon Building offices and in association with the firm of Weiss, Dreyfous and Seiferth in designing the City Park Stadium, various park buildings, gardens, pools, bridges, roads, and so forth. We used HABS drawings in the design and detailing of many of these park buildings and indeed of Koch's own house. I remained in Koch's office, eventually becoming a partner, continuing with him until his death on September 20, 1971.

About 1936, after the dissolution of the Armstrong and Koch partnership, Koch removed his office from the Audubon Building to the Queen and Crescent Building. Offices for the Survey were then obtained in the Stern Building at 348 Baronne Street, and the work continued under Koch's direction and the office supervision of Robert G. Foster, then Chester H. Wicker, and finally Georgia Bertha Drennan. After a few years in the Stern Building, Koch secured offices for the Survey in the second floor of the old Arts and Crafts Club, then located at 712 Royal

Figure 16 Dollhouse at Angelina Plantation at Mt. Airey, Louisiana, recorded together with a brick, hexagonal dovecote or pigeonnier, by a HABS field party in 1934. Both of these unusual plantation outbuildings were demolished shortly afterward. Photograph by Richard Koch, 1934. (HABS LA−18−14, LC HABS LA, 48−MOTAI.V, 1A−3)

Figure 17 Front elevation of Réné Beau-regard House, Chalmette, Louisiana, by Charles J. Phillips, 1934. (See fig. 15.) (HABS LA 18—7, sheet 4 of 9 sheets)

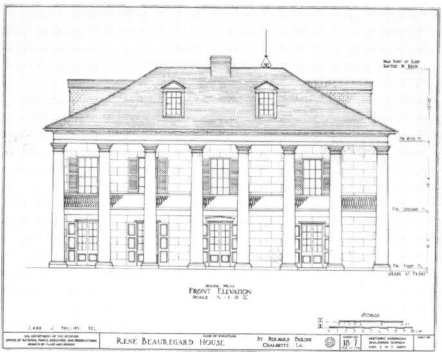

Figure 18 Woodlawn Plantation, near Napoleonville, Louisiana, the house design-ed for W. W. Pugh in the 1850s by Henry Howard, architect. It was in ruinous condi-tion when recorded by HABS in 1934 and was subsequently demolished. This photo-graph was part of the Carnegie Survey of the Architecture of the South by the noted photographer Frances Benjamin Johnston in the 1930s and complements the HABS collection. Richard Koch, HABS district officer, accompanied her on visits to Loui-siana plantations. (LC—J7—LA—1404)

Figure 19 Front elevation of Woodlawn Plantation by Louis Sarrazin, Jr., one of the measured drawings made by HABS in 1934, shortly before this important example of the work of architect Henry Howard was demolished. Nearby Madewood Plantation, built by the same architect in 1846 for Thomas Pugh, brother of the builder of Woodlawn, was not recorded in measured drawings but only in photographs, as it was not in danger of destruction. Madewood has been carefully restored by its present owners, Mr. and Mrs. Harold K. Marshall. (HABS LA—20, sheet 5 of 20 sheets)

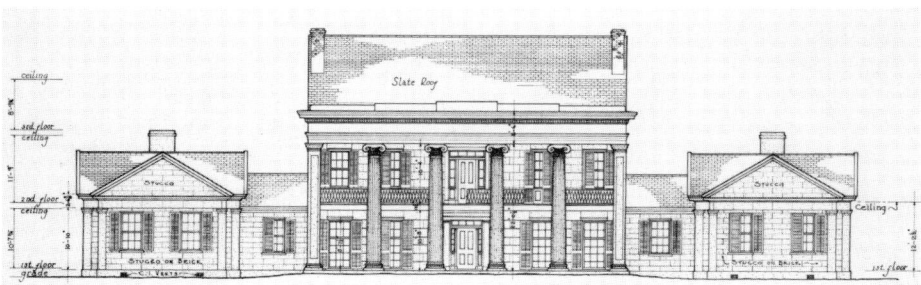

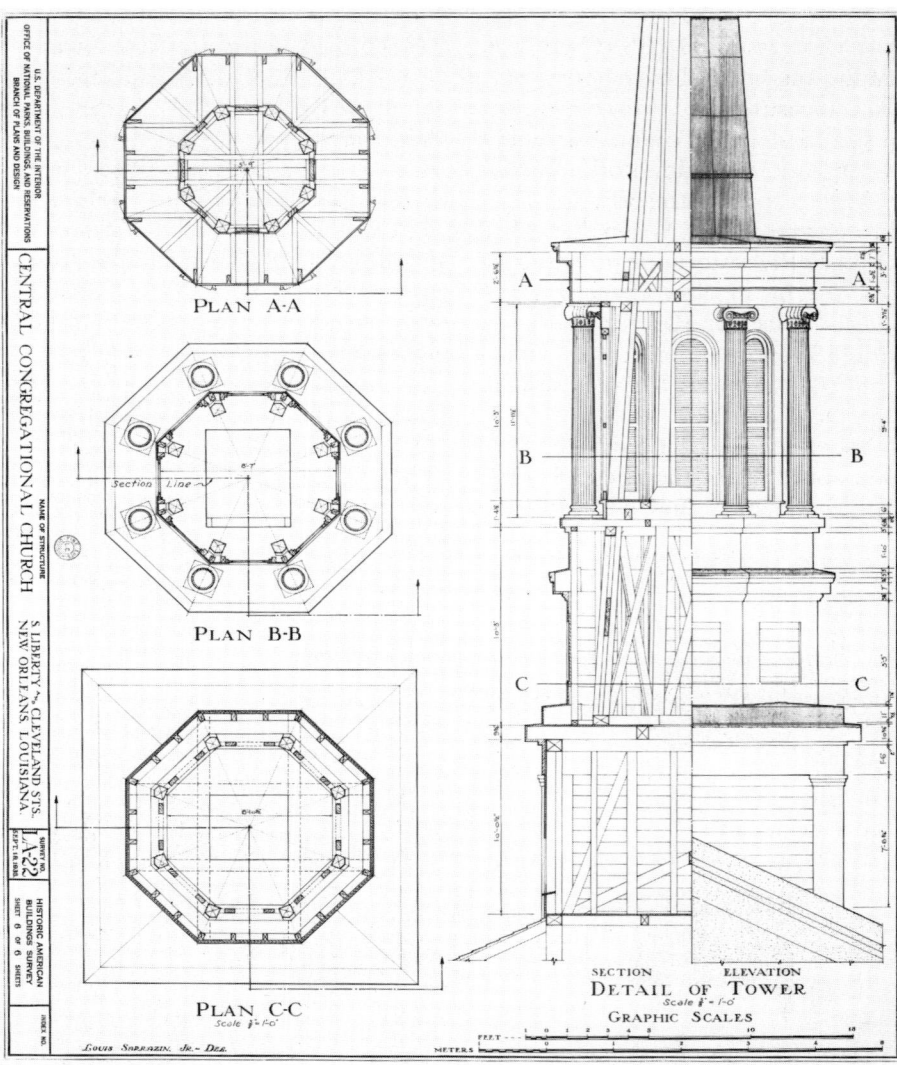

Figure 20 Details of the tower of the Central Congregational Church, New Orleans, as recorded by HABS as the building was being demolished in 1935. Measured drawing by Louis Sarrazin, Jr. (HABS LA–22, sheet 6 of 6 sheets)

Street, through the generosity of the owner of the building, Sarah Henderson. Though no longer officially part of the HABS staff, I remained interested in the work of the Survey and participated in research in the courthouse archives and accompanied Koch on photographic expeditions. The Louisiana project continued through 1940 when the approach of World War II brought an end to the Works Progress Administration.

As the work of the HABS office in New Orleans was drawing to an end in 1940, a team was sent to Louisiana from the HABS central unit at the St. Louis National Park's office to record a number of significant buildings that had not yet been documented. This unit, with F. Ray Leimkuehler as architect-in-charge, consisted of A. H. Felder, J. P. Marlow, and W. Van Valkenburgh. During 1940 this team recorded Homeplace Plantation at Hahnville, Louisiana (figs. 23, 22), Uncle Sam Plantation at Convent (fig. 25), demolished soon after, Chrétien Point Plantation (figs. 26, 27), and the Lastraps house (fig. 28) near Opelousas, Louisiana, later destroyed by fire. Many of Koch's photographs of these buildings taken during the 1930s are included in the Survey records in the Library of Congress. The work of the St. Louis Central Unit was done under a Public Works Administration program.

In 1965 a student team under James C. Massey, HABS director in Washington, and led by Woodrow W. Wilkins measured and drew the Lanoix House at 514–518 Toulouse Street in New Orleans and added other drawings from records in the office of Richard Koch and myself. When that office undertook the restoration of Shadows-on-the-Teche in New Iberia for the National Trust for Historic Preservation in 1961, the building was drawn up on HABS sheets for inclusion in the Survey.

When the HABS Louisiana office closed about 1940, the research files, index cards, and other records were deposited in the library of the Louisiana State Museum in New Orleans. Most of this material consisted of chains of title to properties in the Vieux Carré and other areas, filed by square and municipal district number. This material had been compiled by HABS researchers from records in the Parish Conveyance Office and the Notarial Archives. Koch felt that this title information was essential to determining the true history of a building.

In 1961 the Vieux Carré Survey was started as a project of the Louisiana Landmarks Society and sponsored by the Tulane University School of Architecture, financed by grants from

Figure 21 Wrought iron hardware from the Troxler cottage, measured and drawn by H. S. Kenison and Boyd Cruise. This small house was an unusual example of French colonial construction techniques with all of its original eighteenth-century hardware. It was demolished soon after being recorded by HABS in 1940. (HABS LA–196, sheet 4 of 4 sheets)

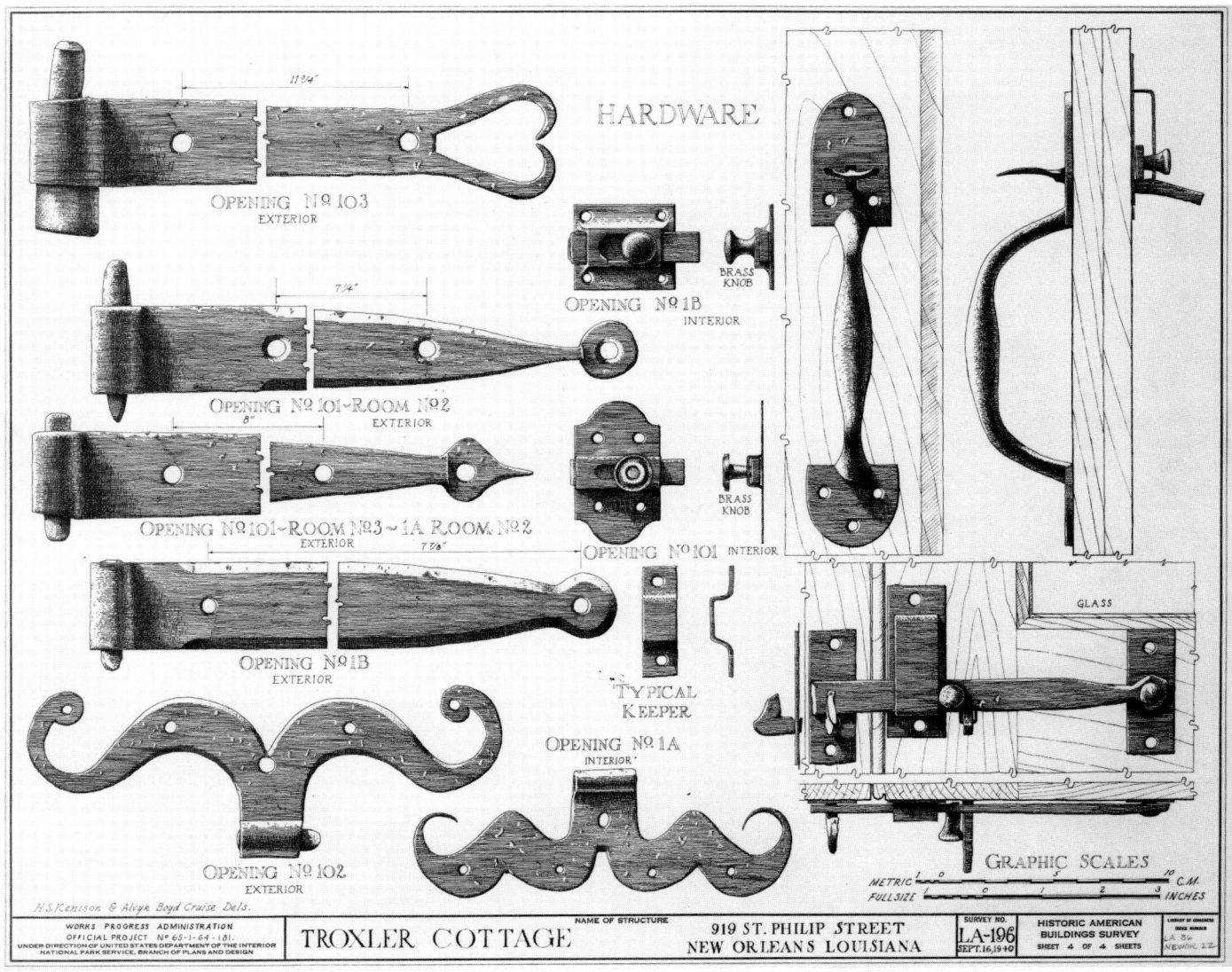

35

Figure 22 King post roof construction of the huge roof of the barn at Homeplace Plantation, now destroyed. Photograph by Lester Jones, 1940. (HABS LA−155, LC HABS LA, 45−HAHN.V, 1B−3)

Figure 23 Barn at Homeplace Plantation at Hahnville, Louisiana, a splendid vernacular structure, recorded by a Survey team from St. Louis as its great spreading roof was almost gone. The late eighteenth-century plantation house adjacent was also recorded and has been preserved, but the barn no longer stands. Photograph by Lester Jones, 1940. (HABS LA−155, LC HABS LA, 45−HAHN.V, 1B−2)

Figure 24 Elevation and cross section of the Louisiana State Bank, New Orleans, the last design of Benjamin Henry Latrobe, now a National Historic Landmark. HABS research on this building was the beginning of my involvement with the Latrobe family, which led to editing Latrobe's New Orleans journals and marriage to Latrobe's great-great grandaughter Ellen Elizabeth Latrobe in 1951. Drawing by Douglass V. Freret. (HABS LA 18−8, sheet 4 of 18 sheets)

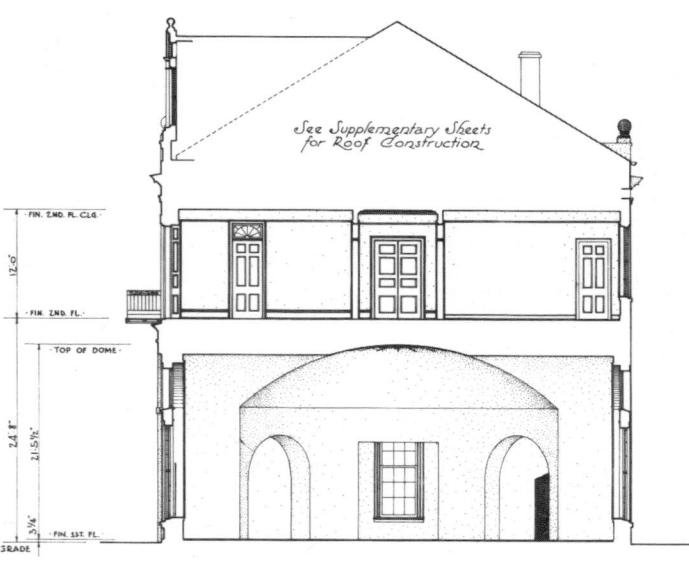

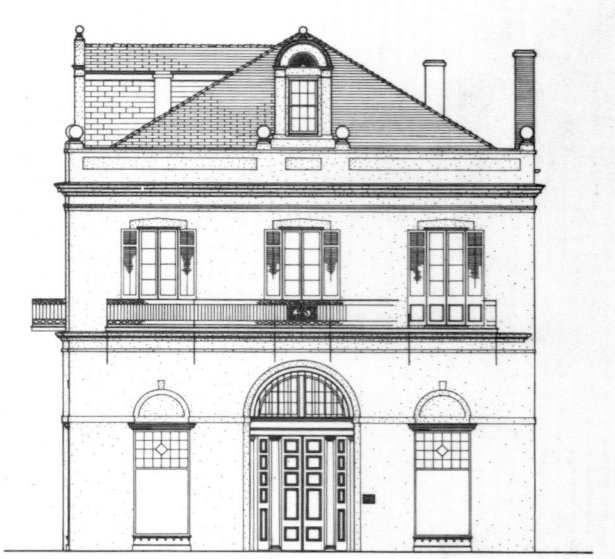

Figure 25 Bird's-eye perspective of Uncle Sam Plantation, Convent, Louisiana, a valuable HABS record showing the relationship of the various plantation buildings to one another and to the river. Soon after being recorded by HABS in 1940, the entire group of buildings was demolished because of a projected relocation of the levee in front of it. Drawing by Joseph P. Harlow. (HABS LA−74)

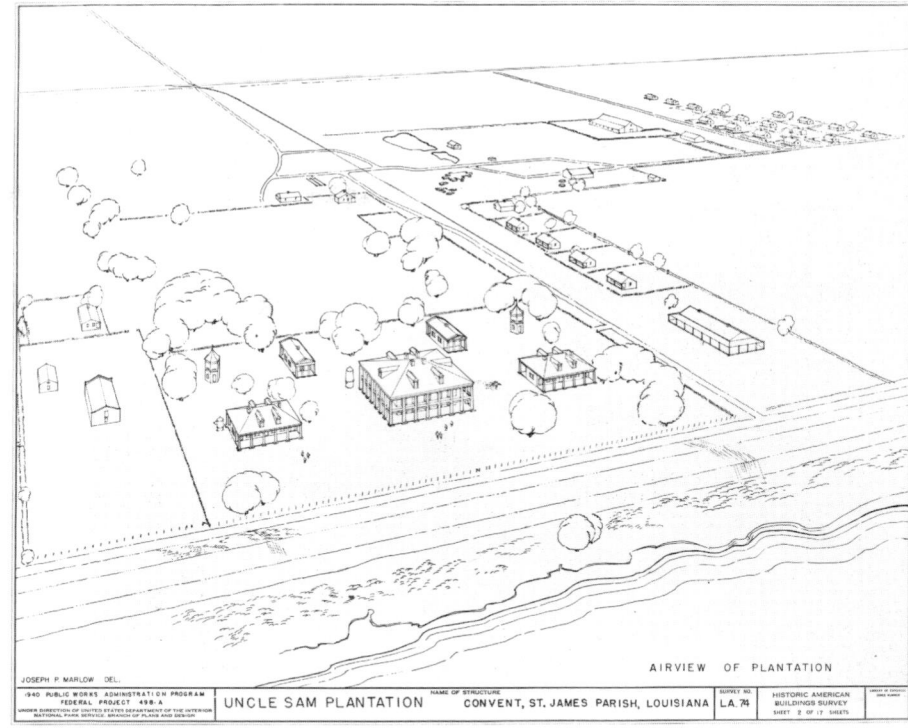

Figure 26 Chretien Point Plantation house, Sunset, St. Landry Parish, Louisiana as photographed by Lester Jones for HABS in 1940. Compare the building as actually built with the 1831 contract drawings, fig. 27. (HABS LA−64, LC HABS LA, 49− SUN.V, 1−2)

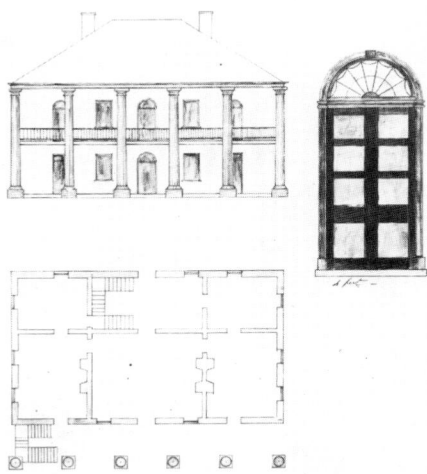

Figure 27 Original contract drawings for Chretien Point Plantation house located by HABS when the house was recorded in 1940 and reproduced together with the building contract in J. Frazer Smith, *White Pillars* (1941). (HABS LA−64, LC HABS LA, 49−SUN. V, 1)

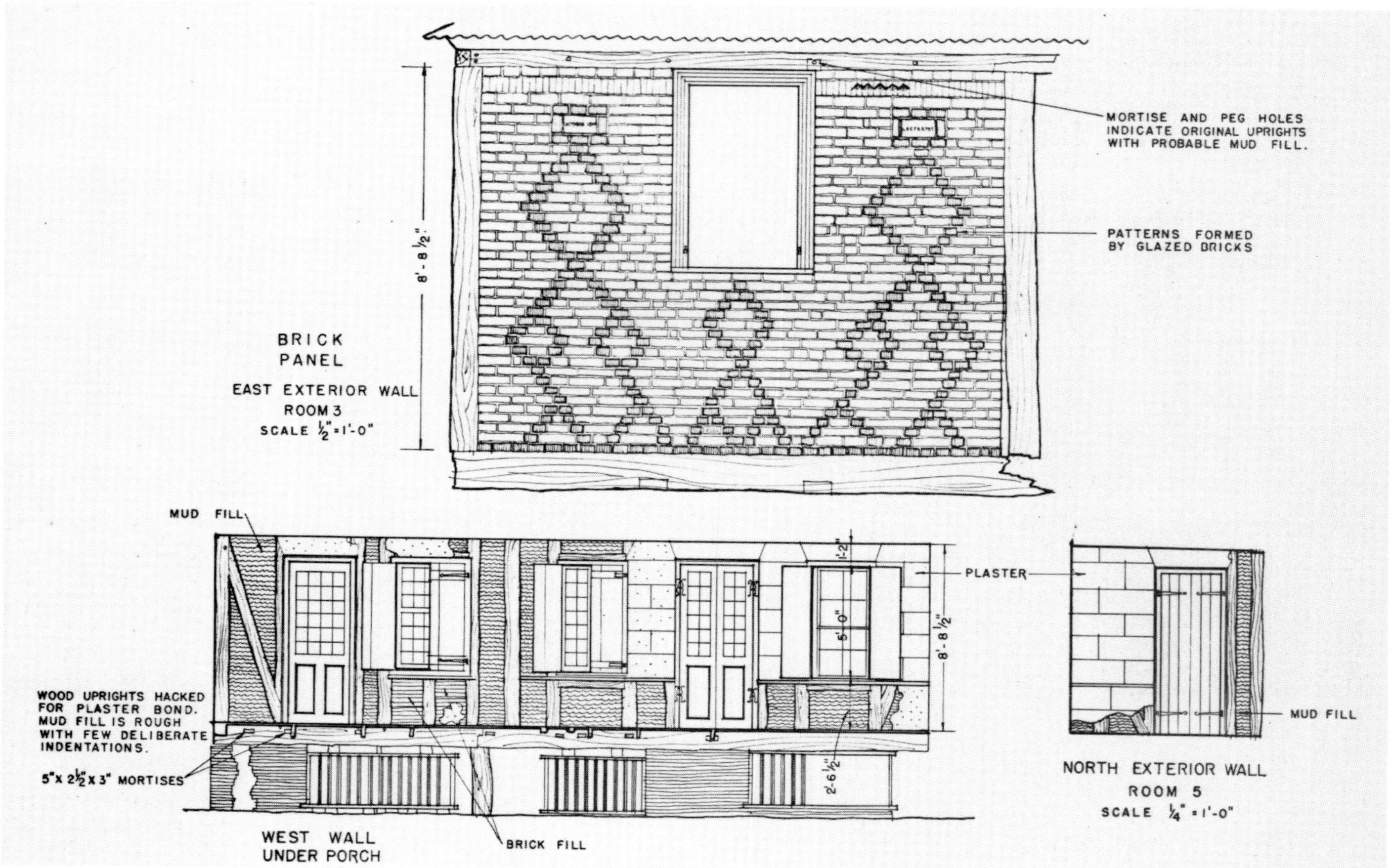

MORTISE AND PEG HOLES
INDICATE ORIGINAL UPRIGHTS
WITH PROBABLE MUD FILL.

PATTERNS FORMED
BY GLAZED BRICKS

8'-8½"

BRICK
PANEL
EAST EXTERIOR WALL
ROOM 3
SCALE ½"=1'-0"

MUD FILL

PLASTER

8'-8½"

WOOD UPRIGHTS HACKED
FOR PLASTER BOND.
MUD FILL IS ROUGH
WITH FEW DELIBERATE
INDENTATIONS.

5"x 2½x 3" MORTISES

5'-0"

1'-2"

2'-6½"

WEST WALL
UNDER PORCH

BRICK FILL

MUD FILL

NORTH EXTERIOR WALL
ROOM 5
SCALE ¼"=1'-0"

Figure 28 The Lastrapes house, near Opelousas, Louisiana, an excellent example of "brick-between-posts" construction common in Louisiana from its French colonial days. The patterned brickwork in the rear wall, dated 1801, is unique and probably reflects an American influence from the East Coast. The house was destroyed by fire some years after it was recorded by HABS in 1940. Drawing by Joseph P. Marlow. (HABS LA−89, sheet 3 of 6 sheets)

Figure 29 Afton Villa, near St. Francisville, Louisiana, one of the most important mid-nineteenth-century Gothic Revival houses in Louisiana, destroyed by fire. One of the many great buildings now lost that are preserved in HABS records. (HABS LA−58, LC HABS LA, 63−SAIFR.V, 1−1)

the Edward Schleider Foundation. The Vieux Carré Survey was intended to document every property in the historic district in New Orleans with prints, photographs, and written data. The HABS records proved to be an invaluable aid in this documentation, and they were transferred from the Museum library to the Vieux Carré Survey office, which was established in the historic Merieult House at 533 Royal Street through the generosity of Gen. and Mrs. L. Kemper Williams. The Vieux Carré Survey records have since been deposited in the Historic New Orleans Collection of the Kemper and Leila Williams Foundation, where the material is available to researchers. The Collection staff continues to add material and provides reference service. The Vieux Carré Survey might be considered as an outgrowth of the Historic American Buildings Survey. Boyd Cruise, who had been part of the HABS program through the years, served as director of the Vieux Carré Survey. Richard Koch and I served on the advisory committee of this important project (fig. 3).

Drawings, photographs, and research data of the Historic American Buildings Survey have been used frequently in restoration projects. Among these were the restoration of the Cabildo, the Arsenal, and the Jackson and Creole Houses of the Louisiana State Museum, in New Orleans; Live Oak Plantation at Bains, Louisiana; and the Courthouse at Clinton (fig. 30). HABS has preserved the images of great buildings since lost, like Afton Villa (fig. 29) at St. Francisville, and continues to record important structures, even as they are demolished (fig. 31). The New Orleans Sugar Exchange, built 1883−84 by architect James Freret, would not even have been considered for recording in the 1930s, yet by 1963 its architectural significance could be recognized. Through its past and ongoing recording of the state's architectural legacy, HABS in Louisiana can be considered to be one of the most significant projects of lasting benefit of the Works Progress Administration.

Figure 31 Demolition in 1963 of the New Orleans Sugar Exchange, designed by James Freret, architect, in 1883. Buildings of this period were outside the range of the 1930s project but are now included in continuing HABS documentation. Photograph by Dan Leyrer. (HABS LA−1110, LC HABS LA, 36−NEWOR, 58−3)

Documenting a City:
Philadelphia

by

GEORGE B. TATUM

hiladelphia was the subject for one of the first major Historic American Buildings Survey monographs devoted to a single city. *Philadelphia Preserved*[1] appeared in 1976, and the principal considerations that lay behind its publication are not far to seek.

During the eighteenth century, colonial prominence (fig. 2) and a central location on the Atlantic seaboard had made Philadelphia a logical site for many of the events leading up to the American Revolution and to the subsequent establishment of the new republic. And if later economic leadership—and with it architectural preeminence—seemed to pass to New York and Chicago, Philadelphia remained a railroad and mercantile center of importance (fig. 3), the site of the Centennial Exhibition (fig. 4), and,

late in the nineteenth century, the home of a group of architects who produced collegiate and domestic designs of remarkable sensitivity and distinction (fig. 5).

Though Quaker Philadelphia has traditionally treated its architectural heritage with indifference, almost from the beginning there were those who sought to produce a visual record of the ever-changing city. Names like Birch, Childs, Breton, and Kennedy are well known to print collectors and historians. And even before the end of the nineteenth century a few talented draftsmen undertook to make detailed drawings of some of Philadelphia's most impressive structures (fig. 6). But any kind of detailed architectural record had to await the Great Depression, which freed architects and draftsmen to take part in what came to be known as the Old Philadelphia Survey. Others have told in greater detail how the hundreds of drawings thus produced in Philadelphia and several other American cities were later incorporated into the Historic American Buildings Survey that took shape during the 1930s. Here need only be noted the extent and quality of these early drawings (fig. 7), which, on balance, set a standard of excellence that has seldom been equaled—and almost never surpassed—by later contributors to the program.

Figure 1 Guard box. Built ca. 1873; restored 1973; moved to present site in front of Philadelphia Museum of Art, 1973. As is true of most mid-Victorian structures, this one incorporates elements of several styles, but its pointed openings are unmistakably Gothic, considered at the time to be the most "rural" of past modes and presumably therefore selected as appropriate to the original site in Fairmount Park. Photograph by Jack Boucher, 1973. (HABS PA−1652−A−1, LC HABS PA, 51−PHILA, 289−1)

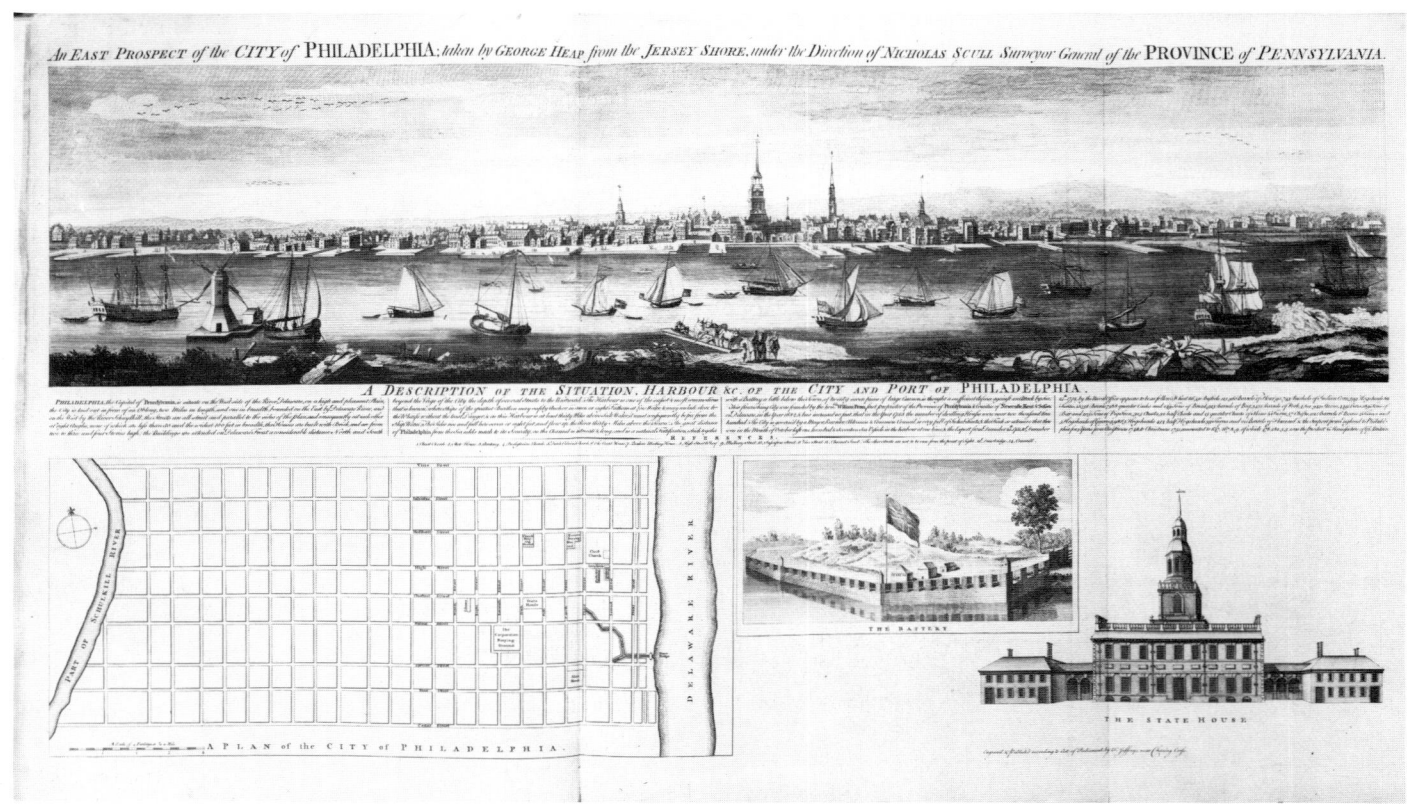

Figure 2 East Prospect of the City of Philadelphia. Adapted by Thomas Jeffreys in 1756 from the larger version drawn originally by George Heap and published in London two years earlier. One of the most ambitious of colonial prints, the East Prospect was undertaken at the instigation of Thomas Penn, proprietor of Pennsylvania, and intended to compete with William Burgis's views of Boston and New York. To enliven the Philadelphia skyline, Heap exaggerated the principal spires of the city; in descending order of height there are: Christ Church, the Second (Arch Street) Presbyterian Church (demolished), the State House, and the German Reformed Church (demolished). Engraving by Thomas Jeffreys, London, 1756. Popular and Applied Graphic Arts Collection, Prints and Photographs Division. (LC–USZ62–3282)

Following the Second World War, continuing efforts to preserve the older portions of the city and the subsequent location there of the Eastern Office of Design and Construction of the National Park Service focused renewed attention on Philadelphia. This, in turn, helped bring into being the Philadelphia Historical Commission, one of the earliest and most successful agencies of its kind, and one that both augmented the efforts of HABS and helped provide funds to support its activities. Predictably, the financial support from private and public groups that has always figured importantly in deciding where HABS teams would work and what they would record had also a bearing on the development of the Philadelphia survey—a fact worth remembering when occasionally the detailed attention given an individual structure or a site like Fort Mifflin (figs. 8, 9) seems to threaten the balance of the whole. And if the city's history and its distinguished architecture did not provide sufficient reason

to record Philadelphia's architectural past, throughout the 1960s and early 1970s there was always the approaching bicentennial of American independence to be reckoned with.

Like the cities of which they are a part, most buildings are of interest to different people for a variety of reasons. When they used the word *historic*, early preservationists usually meant a building associated with some person or event important for the history of the region. Not claims of architectural merit for the structure itself but the belief (later found to be erroneous) that it was somehow associated with the Penn family explains the preservation of the Letitia Street (or Court) House, which was moved in 1883 to its present site in Philadelphia's Fairmount Park and which is now valued as the earliest urban structure to survive from the first decades of the city.

And precisely because Philadelphia was among the first American cities to be recorded, the early photographs of the Letitia Street House, like those made

Figure 3 Broad Street Station of the Pennsylvania Railroad. North portion (at the extreme right) built 1880–82 from designs of Wilson Brothers & Co. Enlarged 1892–94 from designs of Furness, Evans & Co. Demolished 1952–53. Joseph M. Wilson was a civil engineer for the Pennsylvania Railroad who had achieved prominence as one of the designers of two of the principal, but temporary, buildings of the Centennial Exhibition of 1876, and Frank Furness is now recognized as one of the most talented and original American architects active during the last quarter of the nineteenth century. When built, the Broad Street Station was the world's largest passenger terminal, and its more than three hundred feet made the roof of the train shed the greatest permanent span yet achieved. The extensive additions begun in 1892 included terra-cotta decorations designed by the Austrian-born sculptor Karl Bitter. Photograph by William H. Rau, 1894. Courtesy of the Pennsylvania Railroad. (HABS PA–1527)

Figure 4 British Building (St. George's House). Built 1875 for the Centennial Exhibition of 1876 from designs of Thomas Harris, London. Demolished 1963. Except for Memorial Hall, Horticultural Hall (demolished 1955), the Ohio Building, and the British Building, the more than two hundred structures that served the Centennial Exhibition were either demolished or moved to other sites and there adapted to a variety of purposes. The British donated their building to the City of Philadelphia, where it may have helped foster the later American fashion for half-timbered houses. Photograph by T.F. Dillon, 1961. (HABS PA–1080, LC HABS PA, 51–PHILA, 265–2)

Figure 5 Museum, University of Pennsylvania. Begun 1893 from the collaborative designs of Cope & Stewardson, Wilson Eyre, Jr., and Frank Miles Day & Bro. The portion of the University Museum pictured here represents less than a third of the gigantic complex originally planned. Such eclectic references as the Japanese gateway, the Moorish courtyard with its reflecting pool, and the distinctive Lombard masonry and characteristic entrance are so skillfully and imaginatively blended that their designers are considered by many to constitute a distinctive Philadelphia School. Photograph by Jack E. Boucher, 1973. (HABS PA–1646)

43

Figure 6 Woodford, Fairmount Park, front elevation. As first built about 1756, Woodford seems to have been a one-story country house. To this David Franks, crown agent for Philadelphia and a noted Tory, added a second story complete with central pavilion and Venetian (Palladian) window, both prominent features of the mid-Georgian style in the colonies, in about 1772. Franks may also have had something to do with the bold enframement of the front door and the beautifully carved overmantel in the parlor, though these features have traditionally been assigned to the time of Woodford's first owner, Judge William Coleman. Drawing by Charles L. Hillman and John McClintock, 1897. Courtesy Free Library of Philadelphia. (HABS PA–1307, LC HABS PA, 51–PHILA, 13–28)

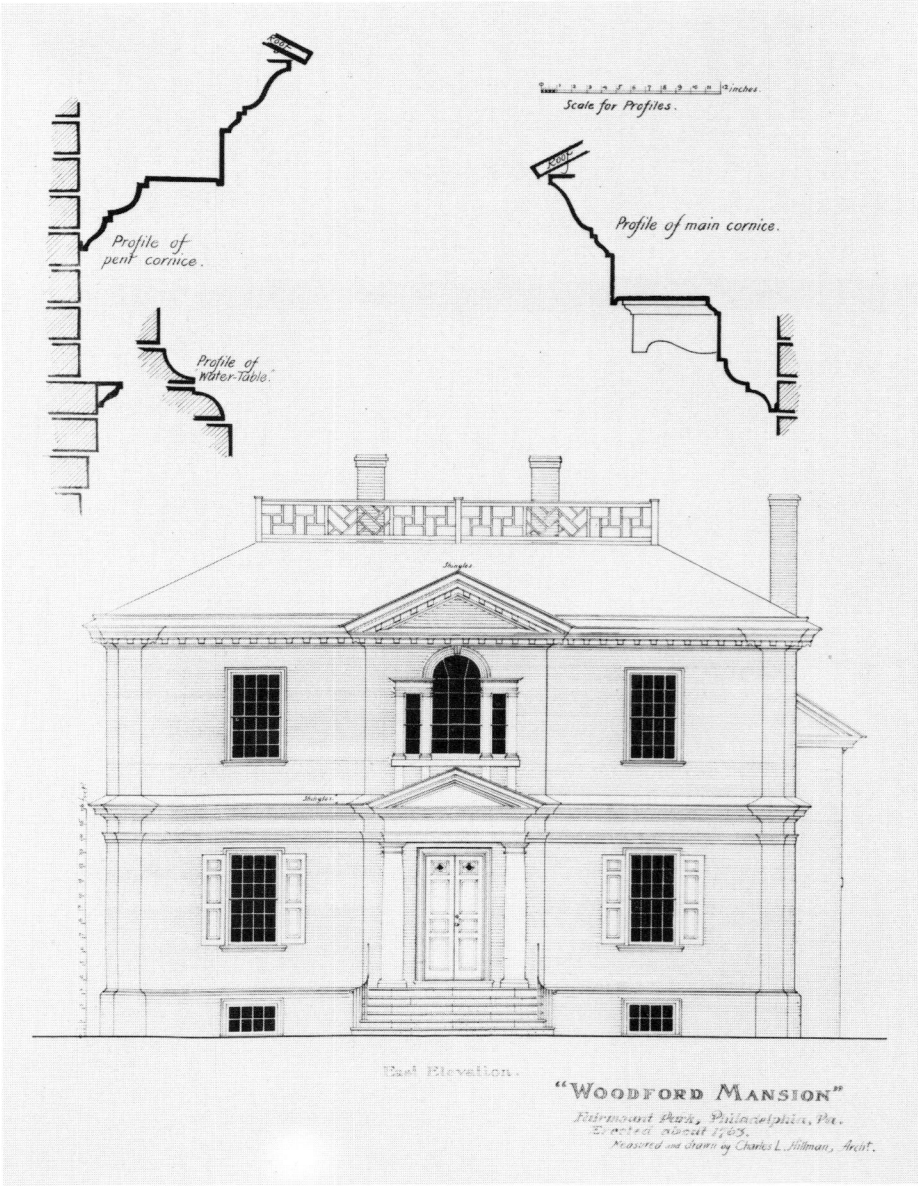

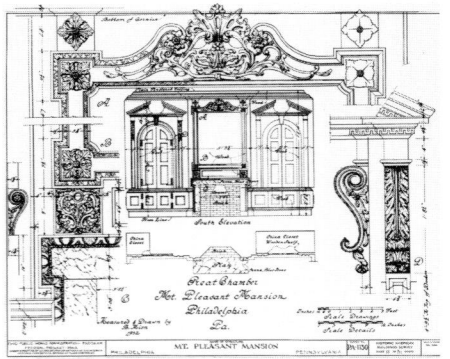

Figure 7 Mount Pleasant, Fairmount Park. Begun 1761. Details of carving in the so-called Great Chamber. Accurate drawings provide the best way to study the Rococo decoration characteristic of the highest quality interiors and furnishings produced in Philadelphia during the middle years of the eighteenth century. Although English books like those of Abraham Swan or Batty Langley may have served to inspire them, most Philadelphia craftsmen knew their trade so well they had no need to follow closely another's design. Drawing by B. Mion, 1932. (HABS PA–1130, sheet 11 of 31 sheets)

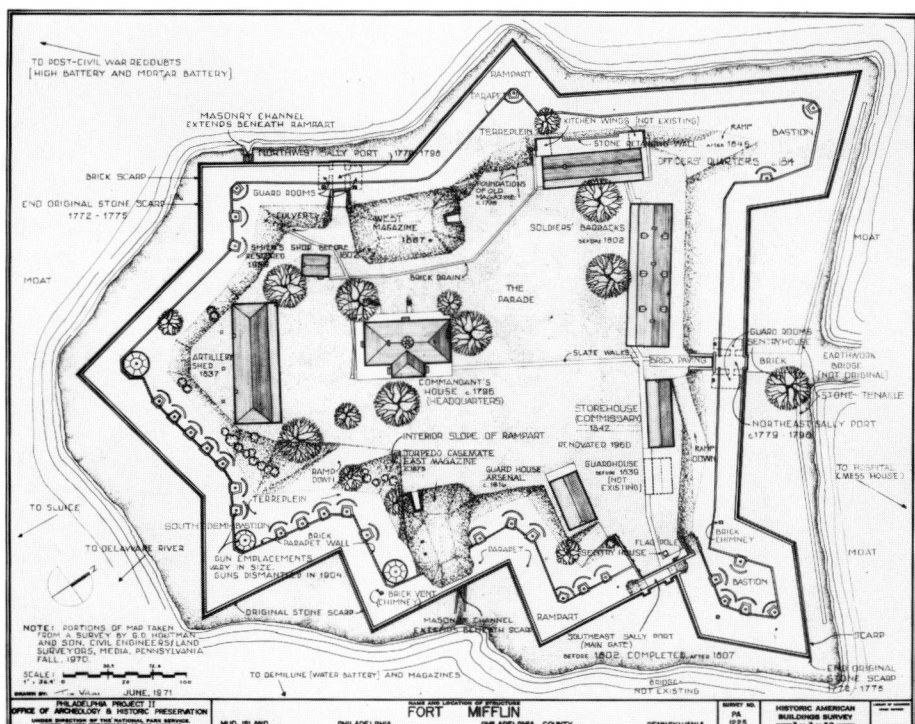

Figure 8 Fort Mifflin. Plan of fortifications and related structures as measured and drawn by HABS teams, 1971. Begun ca. 1772 with numerous additions, some as late as the 1880s. Drawing by Tim Wolosz. (HABS PA–1225, sheet 3 of 50 sheets)

Figure 9 Fort Mifflin, "with the Operations for reducing it," as drawn by Maj. John André, November 15, 1777. Mud Island, the site of Fort Mifflin, lies off the west bank of the Delaware River, 0.76 miles below the confluence of the Schuylkill and Delaware rivers. Though of limited architectural significance in their own right, the fortifications on Mud Island threatened the British supply lines, and so they were probably represented in more eighteenth-century views and maps than any other Philadelphia subject. After a week-long siege, the British forced the evacuation of the island on the night of November 15, 1777. In recording Fort Mifflin, HABS teams could draw on the information provided by such earlier representations as that of Major André. Courtesy Henry E. Huntington Library. (HABS PA–1225, LC HABS PA, 51–PHILA, 111–3)

for HABS elsewhere during the 1930s, are apt to be comparatively poor by modern standards. Too late to be of much value as historical documents, they lack the accuracy and quality we have come to expect in professional work of more recent date. Fortunately, the American Revolution Bicentennial helped spur efforts to correct this deficiency, and many of the later photographs of Jack Boucher, Cortlandt Hubbard, and others are outstanding both as architectural records and as works of art in their own right. Some, in fact, like those of the Arch Street Presbyterian Church (fig. 10), reveal aspects of Philadelphia architecture often neglected or overlooked, even by those who know the city well. Unfortunately for those who would examine them, many of the best of these more recent photographs remain in the files of the Park Service, awaiting transmittal to the Library of Congress and incorporation there in the permanent files of the Survey.

In the wake of World War II, the declining emphasis on draftsmanship in architectural education and the improvements in photography, which led increasingly to the substitution of the photograph for the measured drawing throughout HABS, were also evident in the recording of Philadelphia. But here, too, may be found abundant evidence that the photograph can never entirely supplant the drawing. More than any other feature, it is the plan of the Woodlands that illustrates the extent to which Philadelphia led in the introduction of the new approach to architecture popularized in England by the brothers Adam (fig. 11). In its accomplished use of curvilinear forms the Woodlands went far beyond anything produced in Boston or Charleston at so early a date. And surely no more eloquent testimony could be found of the continuing English bias held in America in general and by Philadelphia and the Hamilton family in particular.

Those who first recorded Philadelphia's architectural past were at no pains to hide their predilection for the eighteenth century, a point of view that during the 1950s contributed to the demolition of numerous nineteenth-

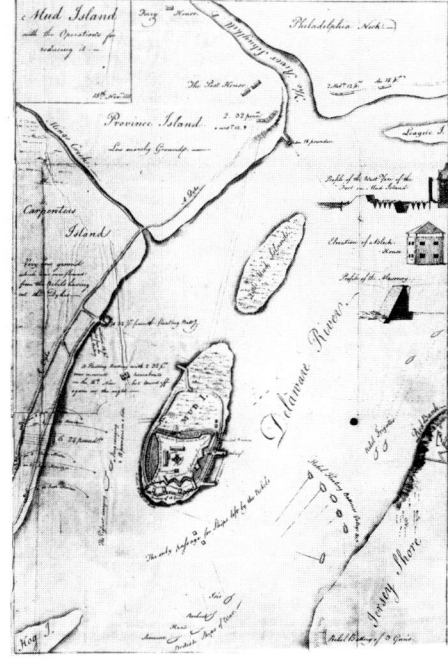

Figure 10 West Arch Street Presbyterian Church. Built 1853–55 from designs of Joseph C. Hoxie. Though eclipsed in size by the nearby Roman Catholic Cathedral of Saints Peter and Paul (1846–64) and much less familiar to the general public than either the Academy of Music (1855–57) or the Athenaeum (1845–47), Hoxie's design compares favorably with those Philadelphia landmarks or indeed with most other examples of the renewed interest in the forms of the Italian Renaissance that characterizes many of the most ambitious American buildings erected between about 1845 and the Civil War. Photograph by Cortlandt V. D. Hubbard, 1976. (HABS PA–1696, LC HABS PA, 51–PHILA, 280–5)

century structures in the name of "redevelopment" or simply of "good taste." Not all in the Park Service shared this attitude toward the more recent past, and even if they could not halt the destruction of such a forerunner of the American skyscraper as the Jayne Building (fig. 24), they could record its structural system as revealed during demolition (fig. 12). As time passes, photographs of this kind should prove of increasing value, as should the drawings of interior details of other lost structures, features not likely to have been recorded except by HABS (fig. 13).

By helping to call attention to the merits of nineteenth-century designers, HABS doubtless played a part in the preservation of such controversial structures as John McArthur's City Hall, which as late as 1956 no less percep-

tive a critic than Louis Mumford dismissed as "an architectural nightmare" but which is now proudly accepted as the premier symbol of Philadelphia as well as the major example of the Second Empire style anywhere (fig. 14). And much the same might be said of the work of Frank Furness, a Philadelphian who designed little outside of his native city. Despite the protests of architectural historians, both inside the Park Service and outside it, such notable buildings by Furness as the Broad Street Station and the Guarantee and Provident banks have been swept away at the urging of antiquarians and those advocating "urban renewal." But lacking funds to build a replacement, the Pennsylvania Academy was obliged to keep its building (fig. 15). Now happily restored to something approaching its original grandeur, the Academy

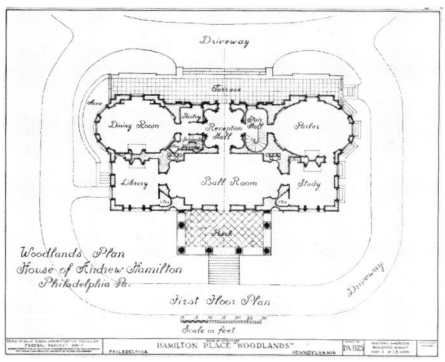

Figure 11 The Woodlands, West Philadelphia. Built (or extensively remodeled) ca. 1788 for William Hamilton, whose admiration for things English came close to supporting a charge of treason at the time of the Revolution. Because many of the elements of the Woodlands appear too close to those in designs of Robert Adam to be entirely coincidental, it seems likely that Hamilton obtained the plans for his new house while in England. Colossal porticoes had been used on English country houses since the 1720s, but that on the south front of the Woodlands, overlooking the Schuylkill River, was the first domestic example of this important feature in Philadelphia. Although rooms for special purposes became increasingly common in American houses following the Revolution, the designations that appear on this plan of the Woodlands owe more to modern practice than to that current when the house was built. First-floor plan by L. G. Park, 1932. (HABS PA–1125, sheet 1 of 15 sheets)

is today widely hailed as one of the most successful American structures to survive from the Victorian period as well as one of the most satisfying of Furness's designs.

If in retrospect it seems that the worth of a building like that of the Pennsylvania Academy should have been recognized more promptly, the same cannot so readily be said of the designs of such contemporaries of Furness as Willis Hale, Angus Wade, or Thomas Lonsdale. Fortunately, HABS has often made it a practice in Philadelphia, as elsewhere, to record structures that are currently out of favor, especially those faced with imminent demolition (fig. 16). Certainly the designs of men like Lonsdale loomed large in the cityscape of their day; perhaps later generations will discover in

Figure 12 Rear view of the Jayne Building, January 2, 1958. Begun 1849 from designs of William Johnston; completed under direction of Thomas U. Walter. Demolished 1957–58. Details of construction, revealed in the course of demolition, confirmed that the Jayne Building had little in common with the skeleton form of the modern skyscraper. On the exterior, conventional brick walls were all load bearing, while within, iron was used only for the columns that supported wooden joists at regular intervals. Photograph by George A. Eisenman, 1958. (HABS PA–188, LC HABS PA, 51–PHILA, 237–14)

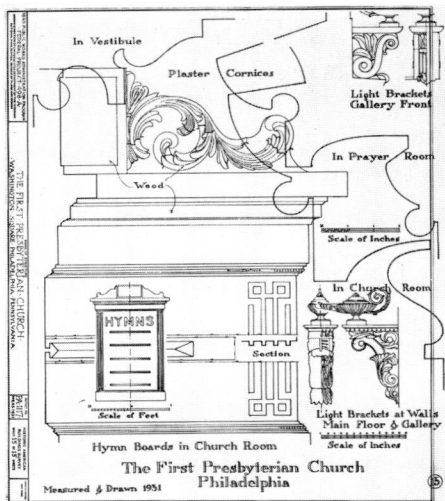

Figure 13 Interior details of the Washington Square (First) Presbyterian Church, measured 1931. Built 1820–22 from the designs of John Haviland. Since it stood until 1939, when it was demolished to make way for a parking lot, there are numerous photographs of the exterior of the Washington Square Presbyterian Church. Not so well known is the extent to which Greek motifs inspired the interior details shown in this and other of the drawings made in 1931. Trained for the profession in England and the author of the first book published in America to include the Greek orders, Haviland helped establish Philadelphia as a leader in the emerging interest in Greek architectural forms notable among architects of American buildings erected during the second quarter of the nineteenth century. (HABS PA–1117, sheet 15 of 15 sheets)

Figure 14 Philadelphia City Hall. Begun 1872 from designs of John McArthur, Jr., who had been awarded first place in the competition of 1869. After 1874 McArthur had an experienced consultant in the person of Thomas U. Walter, whose influence should perhaps be seen in the upper stages of the tower. These are of cast iron, a material used to advantage for the dome of the U.S. Capitol, for which Walter had earlier provided the design and supervised the construction. Even before it was topped out in 1894 the tower of City Hall had been surpassed in height by the Washington Monument and the Eiffel Tower, but for a decade it remained the tallest occupied structure in the United States and may still be said to be the highest building supported entirely by load-bearing walls without the aid of a steel frame. Photograph by Jack E. Boucher, 1963. (HABS PA–1530)

them virtues more recent ones have largely overlooked.

However that may be, to the first recorders of Philadelphia buildings it must have seemed that a city— like an individual—is entitled to be remembered by its most noteworthy achievements. They made no apologies for concentrating their attention on the major structures to survive from the eighteenth century. In this, they chose wisely. Christ Church, Mount Pleasant, or the Powel House still command our attention, both for their intrinsic beauty and for the clues to life in colonial Philadelphia they provide. Nor can his-

torians safely disregard structures of this caliber that no longer stand. In the case of Chalkley Hall (fig. 17), for example, the colossal pilasters that define the corners are usually considered a distinguishing feature of Middle Georgian architecture in New England and one which is otherwise all but unknown in the central colonies at the same period.

Just as early in the twentieth century collectors and museum directors sought colonial interiors to serve as background for the furnishings being assembled in numerous museums around the country, the first delinea-

Figure 16 American Life Insurance Company (Manhattan Building). Built 1888 from designs of Thomas P. Lonsdale and promptly altered on the exterior by Will Decker, who has sometimes erroneously been listed as the original architect. Demolished 1961. Aside from references to the first building for Temple University (1894) and to the east portion of the Spring Garden Institute (1898), little additional information on Lonsdale's professional career seems to have come to light. Photograph by Ned Goode, 1960. (HABS PA−1064, LC HABS PA, 51−PHILA, 257−2)

Figure 17 Chalkley Hall, North Philadelphia. Thomas Chalkley, who has been described as a "Quaker missionary-merchant," began his country house in 1723. A half-century later Chalkley's son-in-law turned this early dwelling into the lateral wing of the more pretentious mansion he had built of cream-colored sandstone reputedly brought from England as ballast. When encroaching industry rendered its area of Frankford no longer suitable for residential use, Chalkley Hall was first abandoned and then finally demolished in 1954. At that time the Metropolitan Museum acquired some of the architectural details, but authorities in Philadelphia showed little interest in preserving all or part of what by any standard must be counted one of the city's most important Colonial mansions. Southwest elevation, measured (1937) and drawn (1938) by Daniel McGlynn and George Stanford. (HABS PA−110, sheet 6 of 24 sheets)

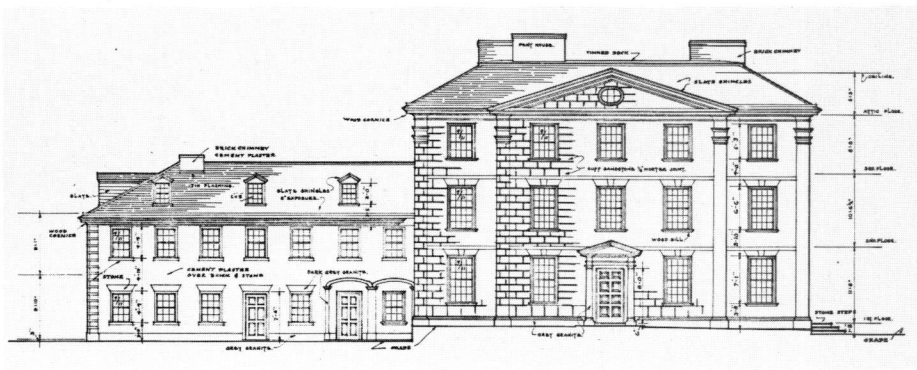

tors of Philadelphia architecture were apt to place special emphasis on the architectural details that their training equipped them so superbly to record. With the 1940s and 1950s, attention gradually shifted from individual rooms and specific details to entire buildings, which might on occasion be moved to prevent demolition or to create appealing village museums such as those at Cooperstown, Deerfield, or Old Sturbridge. By the 1960s and 1970s, horizons of the historians and preservationists had expand-

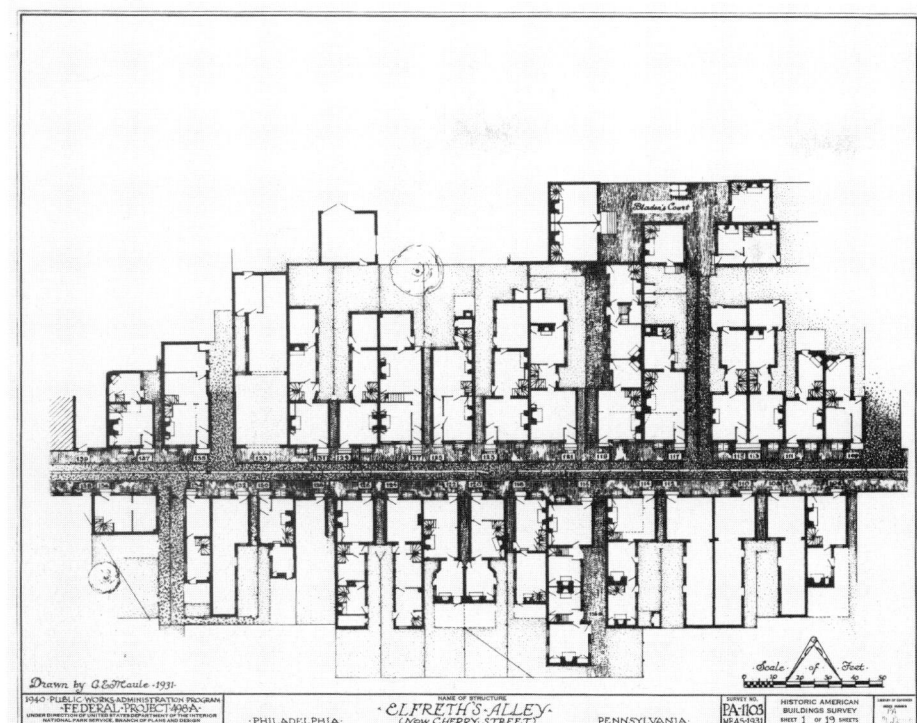

Figure 18 Plan of Elfreth's Alley. Measured and drawn by G.E. Maule, 1931. (HABS PA−1103, sheet 1 of 19 sheets)

Figure 19 West portion of north side of Elfreth's Alley. The large blocks into which Thomas Holme divided his 1683 plan of Philadelphia were early cut up by numerous courts and small alleys. This six-foot wide passage between Front and Second streets was opened about 1703 and since the middle of the eighteenth century has been known by the name of one of its principal owners, Jeremiah Elfreth. The first residents of the alley seem to have been largely engaged in occupations associated with the Delaware River, which flows nearby. Those after the Revolution were oriented more toward such domestic trades as carpentry or cabinetmaking. When viewed in combination with major country seats like Woodford or Chalkley Hall, the simple artisans' houses of Elfreth's Alley help complete the picture of life in colonial Philadelphia. Drawn by L.B. MacLeod, 1931. (HABS PA−1103, sheet 2 of 19 sheets)

ed still further to encompass whole streets or neighborhoods, and not a few of the older towns and cities could claim a "historic district" listed on the National Register. In these, the integrity of the whole counted for more than the merit of the individual structure, which was often fairly commonplace when judged by the standards of its own time. Philadelphia's Elfreth's Alley is one of the most acclaimed of these historic neighborhoods (figs. 18, 19). Its importance was recognized well before such a concept gained wide acceptance elsewhere.

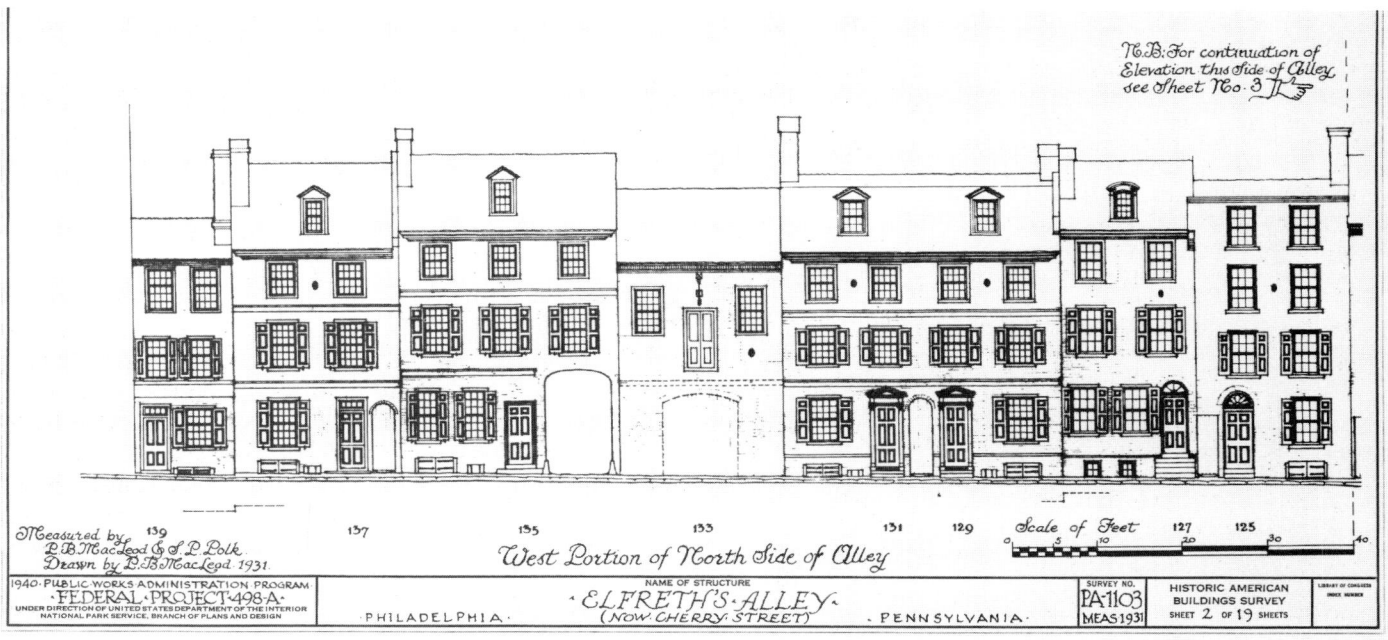

Figure 20 LaTour Warehouse. Built 1817–18; demolished 1967. Name and scale (21 by 50 feet) serve as reminders that a domestic model lies behind the form of buildings such as this. Thus we speak of meeting*houses,* play*houses,* counting*houses,* and work*houses,* as well as ware*houses.* In the first decades of the nineteenth century, it was still hard to imagine traversing any great distance except by boat. As the name implies, South Water Street, where John LaTour built his warehouse, is near the Delaware River. Photograph by Cervin Robinson, 1958. (HABS PA–1656, LC HABS PA, 51–PHILA, 254–2)

no architectural survey of Philadelphia could be considered adequate that did not include one of the guard boxes that speak so eloquently of the Victorian era and of the Centennial which they served (fig. 1). Elsewhere in the HABS record of the city the diligent searcher may find a privy—with six private compartments—that once stood behind John Notman's Athenaeum, a cast-iron sidewalk, and even one of the White Towers that served as the architectural symbol of an early purveyor of that peculiarly American commodity, fast food.

Since zoning by use is a comparatively modern development, one could expect to find a number of commercial structures intermixed with residential ones in an area such as Elfreth's Alley. On occasion a shop might be located in a portion of its owner's house. At other times what was essentially a domestic design would be adapted for commercial purposes, as in the case of the LaTour Warehouse that once stood on Water Street (fig. 20). Though usually lacking many of the more obvious esthetic qualities valued by modern recorders of Philadelphia architecture, such commercial structures— especially those of the nineteenth century (fig. 21)—have come to hold increasing interest for historians of urban life as well as for students of building technology. For the latter, Christ Church merits attention not so much for the elaboration of its Early Georgian design as for the technical knowledge that permitted its builders to erect what may well have been the tallest Colonial steeple of its day (fig. 22). And from this aspect of Christ Church it is only a short step to concern for a variety of structures that only a few years ago we should probably not have considered architecture at all. Prominent among these would be the bridges that loomed large in the life of Philadelphia, since its planners carefully chose for it a site between two rivers (fig. 23).

The limitations of the HABS survey of Philadelphia— or of any city— are principally those imposed by time,

Perhaps we should see the modern concern for the neighborhood in all its aspects as part of a reaction to earlier generations' exclusive interest in important structures built by and for important people. According to this later view, elitism in any form is to be avoided, and folk objects and vernacular artifacts are taken as subjects for serious concern. Luckily for those whose interests lie in this latter area, HABS has usually shown a refreshing willingness to record what all too many of us are apt to take for granted or to dismiss as of little consequence. Surely

funding, and, above all, the nature of the project. A record of Strickland Kneass's Chestnut Street span would undoubtedly be welcomed by anyone studying the bridges of Philadelphia. But a full treatment of the subject must inevitably include such notable predecessors as the "Permanent Bridge" (begun 1798; burned 1875), so called because its piers were sunk more deeply than any before them; Louis Wernwag's "Colossus" (begun 1809; burned 1838), the greatest span ever achieved in wood or stone; and Charles Ellet's "Wire Bridge" (opened 1842; demolished 1874), often regarded as the first suspension bridge opened to general traffic. And then there is the present Benjamin Franklin Bridge over the Delaware, considered the longest suspension bridge in the world when it was begun in 1920. To date, the Benjamin Franklin Bridge has not been included in the survey of Philadelphia,

presumably because HABS has traditionally omitted most twentieth-century structures, and the earler bridges over the Schuylkill could be neither photographed nor drawn because they had disappeared long before the Survey was begun.

Happily, these deficiencies are not necessarily either permanent or inevitable. Historians are making less and less distinction between the past and the present, recognizing that the present is moment by moment becoming the past. Once the records of earlier centuries are more complete, HABS teams will undoubtedly turn their attention to structures of more recent date. At the same time, the computerization of HABS records that appears to offer such promise for architecture buffs everywhere should appeal especially to students of Philadelphia architecture. Well before another half century has passed, with little more than a touch

Figure 21 Business block, Chestnut Street between Third and Strawberry Streets. Built for the most part between 1851 and 1856 from designs of such leading Philadelphia architects as Samuel Sloan, Joseph C. Hoxie, and Stephen D. Button. A remarkably homogeneous group of commercial structures that illustrate various ways in which fashionable Italian Renaissance forms—then popular for their conservative elegance, versatility, and economy—could be adapted to the needs of multistory buildings. Photograph by Jack E. Boucher, 1972. (HABS PA—1402)

Figure 22 Interior steeple of Christ Church. Built to the design of master carpenter Robert Smith. Rebuilt after fire of 1908. A lottery (in which Benjamin Franklin had a part) helped raise the large sum necessary to complete so ambitious a structure. After 1754 the frequent ringing of the peal of bells at Christ Church made Philadelphia appear to one eighteenth-century visitor "almost. . . an Imperial or Popish city." Photograph by George Eisenman, 1965. (HABS PA– 1071)

Figure 23 Bridge over the Schuylkill River at Chestnut Street. Built 1861–66 from designs of Strickland Kneass, architect and engineer. Demolished 1957–58. As the third iron-arch bridge in the United States, the Chestnut Street Bridge is said to have marked a notable advance in the evolution of tubular-arch construction. Although the pointed arch may have inherent structural advantages, Gothic as a style probably appealed to engineers like Kneass because of the way in which medieval builders permitted their structural systems to function as elements of design. Photograph by Theodore F. Dillon, 1957. (HABS PA–1054, LC HABS PA, 51–PHILA, 253–2)

Figure 24 The Jayne Building. Engraved at J.M. Butler's establishment, ca. 1855. The appearance of the owner's name in three places on this print is evidence that despite its size (21½ by 15⅛ inches), it was intended primarily as a "trade card" or advertisement. The building, begun in 1849 from designs of William Johnston and completed under the direction of Thomas U. Walter, was said at the time of its completion to be the most expensive commercial structure in the country. The mortar and pestle that decorate the corners of the front parapet of the Jayne Building are reminders that the funds for its construction came largely from the sale of patent medicine, specifically Jayne's Expectorant. Undoubtedly its eight stories made this one of the tallest buildings of its day, but of even greater interest to historians is the way the architect suppressed the lintels in order to express the verticality of his design, a solution similar to that for which Louis Sullivan was widely hailed nearly half a century later. Since the first architect died when Dr. Jayne's new building was scarcely above its foundations, it may be that his successor deserves more credit for the final design than has commonly been supposed. Color lithograph, Popular and Applied Graphic Arts Collection, Prints and Photographs Division. See also fig. 12.

of the finger they may be able to integrate HABS architectural records with the incomparable collections of prints and drawings owned by the Historical Society of Pennsylvania and the other great libraries and archives of the city. What tantalizing possibilities such a prospect holds!

Note

1. Richard J. Webster, *Philadelphia Preserved*, with an introduction by Charles E. Peterson (Philadelphia: Temple University Press, 1976). In this context should also be mentioned Nancy B. Schwartz, *District of Columbia Catalog* (Charlottesville: University Press of Virginia for the Columbia Historical Society, 1974) and the modest but useful list of buildings in J. William Rudd, *Chicago and Nearby Illinois Areas* (Park Forest: Prairie School Press, 1966).

Cape May, New Jersey: Preservation of a Victorian Town

by

CAROLYN PITTS

Over the past thirty years, Cape May, New Jersey, has undergone a metamorphosis. Existing in a state of genteel seediness, the town suffered widespread destruction when hit by a hurricane in 1962 but then rose to become a bustling tourist mecca. Many guests now come to Cape May to admire one of the largest ensembles of late Victorian frame seaside structures left in the United States. When the summer people disperse, architecture buffs take over, lengthening the short three-month season. They bring economic health to a once-depressed and almost forgotten town.

In the wake of the spring hurricane of 1962, President John F. Kennedy declared the New Jersey coast a disaster area. The federal government offered a 3.5 million-dollar grant from the Urban Renewal Administration(URA) of

Figure 1 Chalfonte Hotel, Howard and Sewell Streets. The Chalfonte, built in 1876, is the oldest and most ornate large hotel in Cape May. It was originally a four-story boardinghouse, 150 feet long by 40 feet wide, with gas light and running water, but the central block was extended several times. The side porch on Sewell Street was built in 1879. The original owner was Colonel Henry W. Sawyer, a Civil War hero. The contractor was a local Cape May craftsman, Charles Shaw. Photograph by Jack E. Boucher. (HABS NJ−743)

the Housing and Home Finance Agency (HHFA), today the Department of Housing and Urban Development (HUD), under the Planning Assistance program authorized by Section 701 of the Housing Act of 1954. At a time when urban renewal was infamous for heavy demolition and displacement, the unusual and innovative master plan for Cape May mandated a complete assessment of the town's historic resources with the understanding that one of the basic steps to recovery would be the use of the existing building stock. The legislation for such urban renewal activity, as amended in the Housing Act of 1961, laid the groundwork for the federal preservation laws of the 1960s.

When town government and the planning firm of Kendree and Shepherd insisted that a historic evaluation be built into the master plan, Cape May discovered that its collection of over six hundred hotels, cottages, and churches was a textbook sampling of nineteenth-century architectural styles. One city council member remarked, "Our philosophy was that if we could offer the public something more to see than just the beach and bathing in two months during the summertime, perhaps we could extend the tourist season from early April until late October." Most of the five thousand year-round residents had no idea that they were the custodians of such a rich heritage.

Figure 2 Cape May strand and the Atlantic Hotel. Lithograph, ca. 1830. From the collection of Carolyn Pitts.

Figure 3 A photograph of the beach at Cape May, ca. 1908. The largest single structure visible on the beachfront is the Stockton Hotel, demolished in 1912. From the collection of Carolyn Pitts.

In the years since the hurricane there has been a great variety of activity— for renewal, preservation, and rehabilitation—some of it excellent, some of it poor. It is safe to say today that had it not been for federal and state guidance and grants and loans, the quality of preservation would have been far less impressive. Four events made the difference: the HUD project, the placing of a large part of the town on the National Register of Historic Places (without owner consent or even the city government's knowledge, however) in 1971, the designation of the entire town as a National Historic Landmark in 1976, and the Historic American Buildings Survey activity during the summers of 1973, 1974, and 1977. The culmination of these efforts was the *Cape May Handbook* (Philadelphia: Athenaeum of Philadelphia, 1977), a rehabilitation guide and historic study.

Cape May began gradually to appreciate what it had. Much of the town had survived because of benign neglect. When the Urban Renewal fund was granted, great care had to be exercised not to succumb to the "level-it-and-rebuild" mentality so prevalent in the 1960s. It was difficult to convince Cape May that the structures they had were, as a district, worth the trouble to restore. Wood rots and salt air is hard on paint. There was a rash of plastic siding in consequence. Proper maintenance of wooden structures was basically a problem in educating property owners.

A number of serious preservation battles began in Cape May after the town was nominated to the National Register in 1970. Because owner consent was not required for nomination at that time—as it is today—the historic district nomination was processed without the knowledge of public officials or many town residents. The mayor, the city council, and developers considered the nomination an impossible obstacle to development. The town was then polarized—pro-preservation residents against supporters of "progressive development"—and the fight became national news. The delicate balance between opposing forces encouraged preparations to document what might be destroyed. In 1973 it seemed wise to structure a recording team of student architects and historians to work using the HABS format to establish what really did exist and to help protect it. There was no immediate source of funding for such work in August 1972 when the Windsor Hotel, one of the coast's finest wood-frame beach front hotels, was slated for demolition because it did not meet New Jersey's fire code standards (figs. 5, 6). An emergency volunteer team came from the University of Pennsylvania and produced a set of measured drawings of exterior elevations and floor plans that were used by the preservation group to convince local and state building inspectors that the hotel was important to the historic fabric of the town. The HABS drawings were used to revise the state codes for historic structures. The presence of the ad hoc team in 1972 made a great difference.

Funding for a full HABS team in the summer of 1973 was obtained from the National Endowment for the Humanities (NEH) and the Barra Foundation of Philadelphia. In 1974, NEH again funded the project, and the 1977 effort was supported by the National Endowment for the Arts and the Atlantic Richfield Foundation, with additional support from the Philadelphia Athenaeum.

It isn't often obvious, but one of the most valuable contributions HABS teams have made in Cape May and elsewhere is working with local property owners and educating residents

while recording. During the three summers when HABS team members were in the town, we encountered every sort of reaction from harassment (a local religious group objected to bearded young men) to cooperation (the volunteer fire company lent us their hook-and-ladder truck under their supervision). Historians and architects worked in tandem, often helping each other—discovering new material in the county courthouse basement or walking on a roof looking at construction changes. First the townspeople were curious, then enthusiastic. In September 1977 the National

Figure 4 The elaborate fretwork on the houses in the 600 block of Columbia Avenue is typical of the many cottages in the historic district of Cape May. Most of the houses in this block were designed by the Philadelphia architect Stephen Decatur Button in the 1870s. Photograph by Carolyn Pitts, 1974.

Figure 5 The Windsor Hotel, Beach Drive and Windsor Street, was built in 1878–79 by Stephen Decatur Button in the Second Empire style, for the owner Thomas Whitney. This plate shows the hotel in its heyday, when the beach was wide enough for carriages. *New Jersey Atlas,* 1886. (HABS NJ–749)

Figure 6 Windsor Hotel, ca. 1975. The old frame building deteriorated as it reached its hundredth birthday and badly needed refurbishing. It was declared a fire hazard by the state. And, on May 18, 1979, the hotel burned to the ground. The Congress Hall on the adjacent lot to the right of this picture still stands as a reminder of the flourishing resort hotels that once lined the beachfront. Photograph by Carolyn Pitts, 1972. (HABS NJ–749)

Landmark ceremony drew hundreds of citizens and dignitaries. A luncheon at the Chalfonte Hotel gave HABS the opportunity to present certificates to owners whose buildings had been recorded.

Occasionally HABS records become invaluable when disaster strikes. Cape May's frame buildings have always been vulnerable to fire. Three great fires in 1856, 1867, and 1878 took a heavy toll on earlier building stock, and on May 18, 1979, fire destroyed the Windsor Hotel on the beach front. HABS measured drawings and photographs provide the best remaining record of what it was (figs. 5, 6).

Although HABS documentation material was superior in itself, one of the primary concerns of both historians and architects was to put it to good use locally. Nonresidents often appreciated Cape May more than the people who lived there. The logical way to remedy this situation was to create a handbook that would include information on what architecture existed, on how it related to nineteenth-century buildings elsewhere, and about how to properly preserve existing structures. Such a guide, if successful, would forever silence the plaint, "But we didn't have any idea it had any value." The

Figure 7 George Allen House, 720 Washington Street. Designed in 1863 by Samuel Sloan, this large and elegant American bracketed villa is one of the most significant nineteenth-century seaside structures in New Jersey. A veranda surrounds the house. The walk-through windows are nine feet high, and the brackets in the eaves measure five feet high and four feet deep. This imposing structure is in a style popularized in Sloan's books on architecture. It is one of the few remaining large estates in Cape May. Photograph by Jack E. Boucher, 1977. (HABS NJ–845)

Figure 8 The octagon cottage designed by Orson Squire Fowler. First published in 1848, Fowler's book on architecture advocated modern improvements he thought were healthful and convenient. Hot and cold running water, indoor flush toilets, filtered drinking water, and dumbwaiters were recommended. The great advantages afforded by the octagon shape were that it admitted more light, was easier to heat and cool, saved steps, and yet was 70 percent larger than a square house with the same perimeter. From Fowler, *A Home for All; or, the Gravel Wall and Octagon Mode of Building* (New York: Flower and Wells, 1853), fig. 20, p. 111.

Figure 9 Josiah Schellenger Cottage, 1286 Washington Street. The octagon style flourished around the time of the Civil War and many octagonal structures survive today. Cape May's one example, constructed in 1875, was probably designed according to Orson Squire Fowler's text. Photograph by Jack E. Boucher. (HABS NJ–747)

Figure 10 Fryer's Cottage (Cook's Villa), 9 Perry Street. Designed by Frank Furness and George Hewitt in 1871, this house was rebuilt in 1879 to the original specifications after the devastating fire of 1878. It is basically a Second Empire house, with Stick style ornament in the overlay and in the simple diagonal brackets. The Chinese ceramic fret tiles, which are set into the porch railing, are unique to this house. It is believed that the tiles were from a pavilion at the 1876 Centennial Exposition in Philadelphia. Photograph by Jack E. Boucher. (HABS NJ–860)

Figure 11 Evan Morris House, 19 Ocean Street. One of a number of picturesque houses on Ocean Street, the Morris House was built in 1887–88 from plans ordered from a pattern book—a mail-order builder's guide published by Robert W. Shoppell. The house has been slightly modified but is essentially unchanged. Photograph by Carolyn Pitts, 1974.

DESIGN No. 346.   PERSPECTIVE VIEW

DESCRIPTION OF DESIGN NUMBER 346

SIZE OF STRUCTURE: Front, 31 ft. Side, 46 ft.

SIZE OF ROOMS: See floor plans.

HEIGHT OF STORIES: Cellar, 7 ft.; First Story, 10 ft.; Second Story, 9 ft.; Third Story, 8 ft.

MATERIALS: Foundation, stone and brick; First Story, clapboards; Second Story, shingles; Roof, slate.

COST: $4,500, complete, except mantels, kitchen range and heater.

[See page 147 for information about details, specifications, bill of quantities and working plans of this design.]

NOTES

The cost is figured from prices of material and labor in the neighborhood of New York City, June, 1886. In other localities and at different dates the cost will be somewhat modified. The publishers will be glad to acquaint the intending builder with this modified cost at any time.

This design can be reversed, enlarged, reduced or altered to suit special wants. The specifications can be altered, also, to employ different materials that may be best or cheapest in any locality.

SPECIAL FEATURES.—Square hall, with platform staircase.

Sliding doors between hall and parlor and between sitting-room and dining-room.

Four bed-rooms, a bath-room, ample hall and large closets in the second story.

Three good bed-rooms in the third story.

Cellar under the whole house.

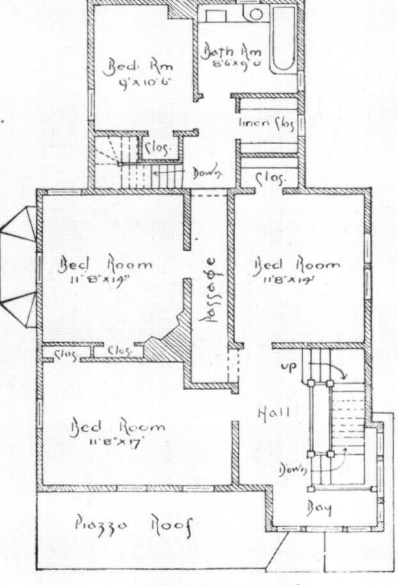

FIRST FLOOR. NO. 346

SECOND FLOOR. NO. 346

Figure 12   Shoppell's Modern Houses, vol. 1, no. 3 (July 1886), design no. 346. The stated cost of building this house was "$4,500 complete, except mantels, kitchen range and heater." (LC–USZ62–63043)

Figure 13 Dr. Thomas Roger Wales House, 1000 Lafayette Street. This house, built in 1856, was originally designed after the pattern book by J. C. Sidney, *American Cottage and Villa Architecture* (New York: Appleton, 1850). In the 1890s, the estate was given to the City of Cape May and turned into a country club and golf course. Photograph by Atlantic Studios, Cape May, ca. 1920, from the collection of Carolyn Pitts.

Figure 14 The Cape May Golf Club failed in the 1940s and the Fraternal Order of Moose acquired the Thomas Roger Wales House. Empty since 1978, the Wales House is now at the center of a preservation battle to save the structure itself and the open space surrounding it from destruction and dense development. Collection of Carolyn Pitts.

Figure 15 Jackson's Club House, 635 Columbia Avenue. This elaborate villa was designed for Colonel Robert R. Lear by the Philadelphia architect Stephen Decatur Button in 1872. The house was deeded the same year to Charles Jackson, who managed it as a gentlemen's club. It also housed a gambling casino and a bordello. Contemporary newspaper accounts referred to the new villa as the "finest in that neighborhood . . . and the cost when completed will be about $20,000." It is one of the greatest houses of this style extant. Photograph by Jack E. Boucher. (HABS NJ–748)

Figure 16 John B. McCreary House, 34 Gurney Street. This notable Gothic Revival frame villa with a massive four-story corner tower has recently been refurbished and painted in darker nineteenth-century colors. It is a popular boardinghouse today. Built for John B. McCreary, a wealthy Philadelphia coal baron, in 1869–70 to designs by architect Stephen Decatur Button, it has elaborate trim. Contemporary newspaper accounts called it "a beautiful and costly marine residence." Photograph by Jack E. Boucher. (HABS NJ–855)

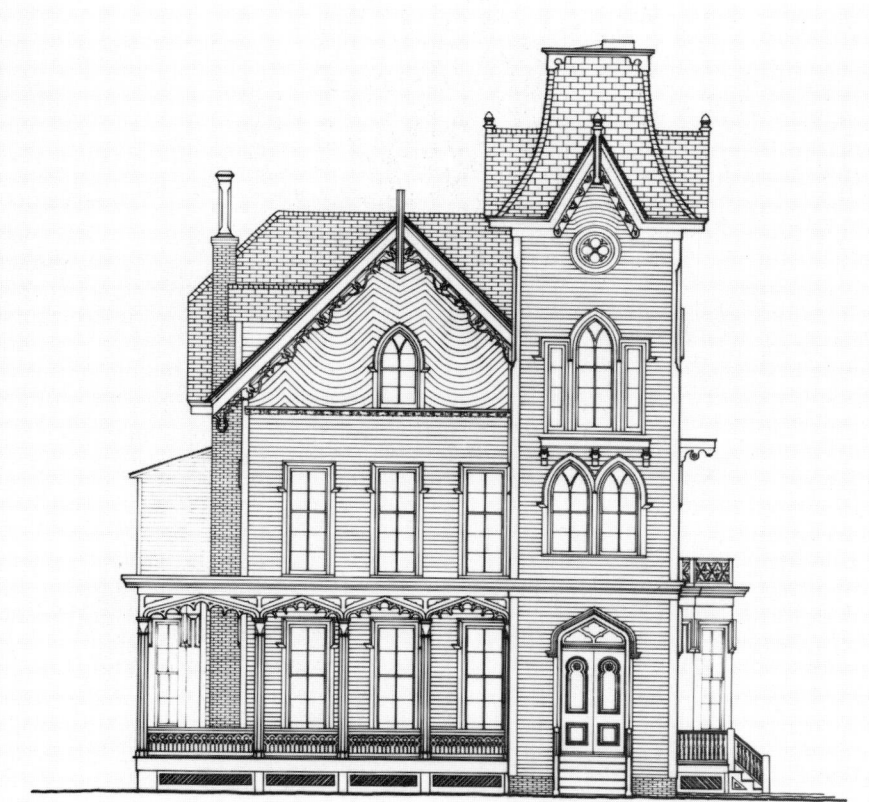

Figure 17 John B. McCreary House, 34 Gurney Street. East elevation. Measured and drawn in 1973. M. M. Thomas, delineator. (HABS NJ–855)

Figure 18 Chalfonte Hotel. The Sewell Street wing was added in 1879 and forty more rooms constructed in 1888. The old frame hotel escaped the great fire of 1878 that destroyed forty city blocks and, with its ornate scrollwork, it is one of the great surviving examples of High Victorian picturesque eclecticism. Photograph by Jack E. Boucher. (HABS NJ-743)

Figure 19 Chalfonte Hotel. Side porch on Sewell Street. Photograph by Jack E. Boucher. (HABS NJ-743)

Figure 20 Chalfonte Hotel. Howard Street facade. Southwest elevation. Measured and drawn in 1974. Perry Benson, delineator. (HABS NJ-743)

Figure 21   Dr. Emlen Physick Estate, 1048 Washington Street. Attributed to Frank
Furness, the Philadelphia architect, this house, constructed in 1878–79, is designed in
the Stick style. The bold design, tapering chimneys, steeply gabled roofs, tall proportions,
structural framing overlay, and irregular silhouette are typical of Furness's work. The
local papers in 1878 were full of comments on the "unusual character" of the new house
that had been designed as a year-round residence. This photograph, taken about 1890,
shows the large estate that originally had gardens and numerous outbuildings. It is
relatively intact today. Photograph from the collection of Carolyn Pitts. (HABS NJ–746)

Figure 22 Dr. Emlen Physick Estate, 1048 Washington Street. By 1970 the estate was in serious disrepair. The exterior has remained largely as it was originally designed, although the interior has been modified several times. In 1970, the house was leased from the city by the Mid-Atlantic Center for the Arts. Collection of Carolyn Pitts.

handbook produced was funded by the Atlantic Richfield Foundation and the National Endowment for the Arts and sponsored by the Philadelphia Athenaeum and HABS. The Arts Endowment further sponsored a series of lectures on such topics as proper rehabilitation and deed research, at the conclusion of which one could receive a free handbook. The goal was to preserve the town's architectural heritage forever and to promote intelligent and sensitive rehabilitation.

Some of the more rewarding aspects of HABS and property-owners working together were the outstanding discoveries made. A great summer cottage, the George Allen House (1863), was verified as the work of nationally known architect Samuel Sloan (fig. 7). The team documented a small octagon (1875), right out of Orson Squire Fowler's work on the "octagon mode of building" (fig. 8). They recorded Fryer's Cottage (1879), having discovered that the architects were Frank Furness and George Hewitt (fig. 10). And it was established that the Evan Morris House (fig. 11) is based on design no. 346 from *Shoppell's Modern Houses*, a popular architectural pattern book at the end of the nineteenth century (fig. 12).

Figure 23 Dr. Emlen Physick Estate, 1048 Washington Street. North elevation. Measured and drawn in 1973. Hugh McCauley, delineator. (HABS NJ–746)

Cape May still has its problems. Intense real estate development on the beachfront is still going on, now controlled to a certain extent by the zoning board and the Historic District Commission, although at this time the HDC acts only in an advisory capacity. The old Cape May Golf Club, abandoned and in shabby condition, is vulnerable to demolition (figs. 13, 14). The citizens of the town are now fully aware of what it means to monitor new development and unsympathetic restoration, however, and many appear at public meetings to voice opinions.

There is still no year-round industry or any generous patron-philanthropist for the town, so preservation must be funded on a small-scale step-by-step basis. The longer tourist season makes more funds available. In the last several years, a Vintage Home Owners Association, made up largely of the young people who run the very popular bed-and-breakfast inns, has been active, forming a sophisticated restoration constituency. They have made much use of the HABS measured drawings and the *Cape May Handbook* directives on correct siding, trim, and, most noticeably, Victorian paint colors—which have turned the once

ubiquitous white-and-green-shuttered houses into a great variety of handsomely painted cottages. Cape May today is alive and getting better. Local pride in the cultural significance of the town's building stock is now firmly established. Cape May is not a outdoor museum but is part of our environment, healthy economically, providing shelter and delight.

Figure 24 Dr. Emlen Physick Estate, 1048 Washington Street. The estate today has been painted and refurnished and operates as a museum and art center. The carriage house is maintained by the Cape May County Art League and houses art classes and an exhibition gallery. The Physick House was the object of an intense preservation effort in the early 1970s and is perhaps the most conspicuous example of the new local interest in historic architecture. Photograph by Jack E. Boucher. (HABS NJ–746)

MAIN STREET, SPRINGFIELD, MASS.

Main Street:
Its Revitalization

by

CAROLE RIFKIND

The Historic American Buildings Survey began both as a way to give unemployed architects work during the dire construction slump of the depression and as a way to foster awareness of a rapidly disappearing architectural heritage.

Figure 1 Main Street, Springfield, Massachusetts. This photograph, a copyright deposit submitted in 1908 by William Henry Jackson's Detroit Publishing Company, is characteristic of hundreds produced by that great publisher of souvenir brochures and postcards. Main Street's symbolic significance in the period preceding World War I is demonstrated by its prominence in such photographic imagery. Pride in place is obvious; it would not be surprising to find on the back of a postcard with this picture the typical inscription, "Wish you were here." Jackson, pioneer photographer of the western frontier, joined the Detroit Company in 1897 as part-owner and chief photographer, and he himself photographed townscape and landscape all over the United States. He also trained a team of other photographers whose combined output probably exceeded one hundred thousand images. A substantial portion of these can be consulted today together with the HABS records in the Prints and Photographs Division of the Library of Congress, where they provide an extraordinarily detailed visual archive of the American environment over the period of a generation. Lot 9150, Prints and Photographs Division. (LC–USZ62–83630)

The first Survey selections reflected the interests and prejudices of the 1930s, when American architectural history as a discipline for study was in its infancy. We can see today that there was a bias toward early domestic architecture, in particular the notably grand, regional, unique, or quaint examples. Although utilitarian structures such as barns, mills, bridges, and the like were covered by HABS, commercial buildings were rarely represented. Only commercial structures with a unique character, such as the iron-fronted Haughwout Building in New York City, were recorded (Gayle, fig. 29).

The commercial streetfront as an ensemble, the uniquely American Main Street that foreigners have so frequently commented on, was not represented in HABS research at that time. Only in special instances—as, for example in New Orleans (Wilson, fig. 12) and Philadelphia (Tatum, figs. 18, 19)—was the focus on streets rather than individual structures. Photographers like William Henry Jackson (fig. 1) and Walker Evans (fig. 2), by contrast, had recognized Main Street as a subject rich in meaning and detail.

The National Historic Preservation Act of 1966 reinvigorated HABS. In giving the federal government a leadership role in the area of historic preservation, this

Figure 2 Main Street architecture, Selma, Alabama, December 1935, a photograph by Walker Evans for the Farm Security Administration. Under the direction of Roy Stryker, a pioneer in the didactic use of photography, the Farm Security Administration (FSA) produced more than half a million images of American life between 1935 and 1942, in an effort to garner favorable publicity for the agency's often controversial programs. Main Street was a recurrent theme, documented by a team of brilliant photographers, of whom Walker Evans was perhaps most gifted. Evans was particularly sensitive to architecture and the expressive qualities of building elements and materials. FSA/OWI Collection, Prints and Photographs Division. (LC–USF342–1146–A)

legislation pointed to an approach in which the Survey could spark and sustain state and local preservation efforts. Thus, with local cosponsorship and with growing appreciation for the effectiveness of historic preservation as a tool for downtown revitalization, HABS has conducted projects focusing on a number of main streets over the past decade.

This attention to Main Street has deep significance, for the Main Street image, though powerful and evocative, has been tarnished by persistent connotations of sameness, obsolescence, and provincialism. Even the briefest overview of a half-dozen projects corrects this impression. Instead, we can see that there is extraordinary geographic, economic, ethnic, and

cultural diversity; creative energy and optimism; and resourcefulness and faith in material progress. The clearer perception of these characteristics helps us to better appreciate—and more effectively use—a vital and valuable urban tradition.

Certainly, Main Street in Madison, Indiana—selected as the typical American town by our propaganda office during World War II—suggests the stereotype at its best. The town, platted in 1812 on a low and narrow plain between the Ohio River and limestone bluffs which tower five hundred feet above it, flourished as an entry point to the Northwest Territory for a steady stream of steamboat travelers in years before the Civil War (figs. 3–6). Today, similarly styled brick and cast-iron commercial buildings have a charm and homogeneity that lend the street something of the quality of a movie set. The town was left a quiet backwater by the railroads; and it suffered hard times in the automobile age before its recent rediscovery.

The oldest of HABS main streets is South El Paso Street, which connects downtown El Paso to Juarez, on the Mexican border (figs. 7–10). The town began at the site of a river ford on the trail of Spanish missionaries almost four centuries ago, spread as a settlement on the north-south trade route, and was shaped by the real estate dealings of venturesome entrepreneurs from Kentucky. South El Paso Street enjoyed several generations of prosperity in the glory years of railroad growth after

1880, but today its appearance reflects struggle, the constant struggle for economic success by continuing waves of Mexican immigrants.

A frontier Main Street with a different kind of history is First Street in Benecia. A California town whose origins are in New England, Benecia had ambitions to serve as state capital, a position it held only briefly before Sacramento captured that prize in 1854 (figs. 11–14). The most important fact in Benecia's existence has been its site. Because it is located on San Francisco Bay, it was selected as the seat of an important government arsenal, a time in which the waterfront earned a somewhat dubious reputation. Since the arsenal closed in 1964, the waterfront has been redeveloped as an industrial

Figure 3 View of the City of Madison, Indiana. In the nineteenth century a veritable explosion of illustrated books and journals spread reassurances that there were civilized conditions to be found on the frontier, thus helping to fan the western expansion. Woodcut engraving from *Gleason's Pictorial Magazine,* July 1854. Lot 4389A, Prints and Photographs Division.

MADISON, INDIANA.

This city, represented below, is well situated on a bend of the Ohio river, above the reach of the highest floods. It is handsomely built, the houses being mostly of brick. It is a place of much enterprise and success in business. Large manufacturing operations are carried on here by steam power. The advantages which this place possesses must secure for it, as the resources of the State are more developed, a steady increase of prosperity and wealth, and insure its commercial influence.

Figure 4 Commercial building (Foster Building), 102–104 1/2 East Main Street, Madison, Jefferson County, Indiana. Photograph by Jack E. Boucher, September 1971. (HABS IND–86, LC HABS IND, 39–MAD, 10–3)

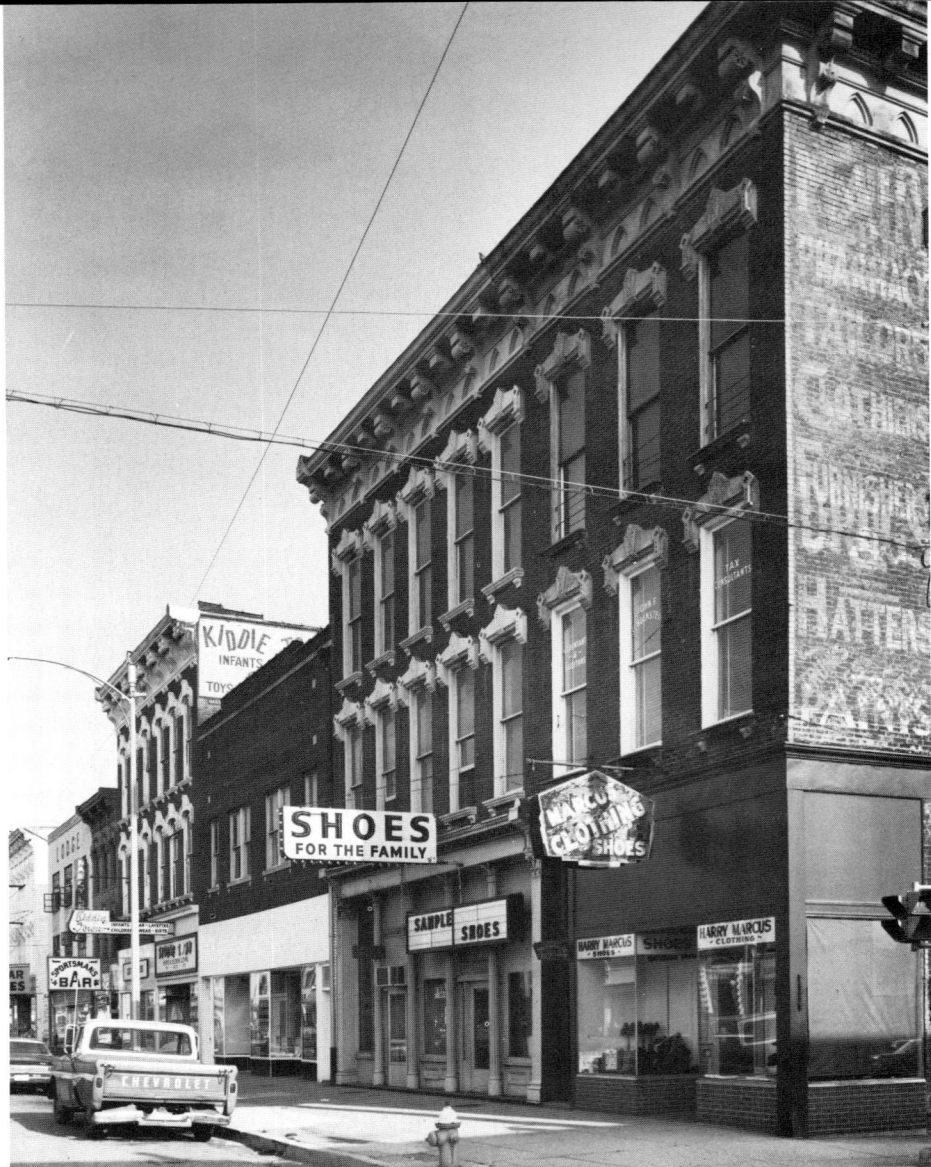

Figure 5 Cornice section, elevation detail, commercial building (Foster Building), Main and West Streets, Madison, Jefferson County, Indiana. The lintels, cornice, and eaves elements of the Foster Building were executed in the Eastlake style, fashionable in the 1870s and reflective of the contemporary love affair with machine production. Note the vigorous articulation of the brackets, with their abruptly reversed curves, and the tooled quality of the cornice, with chamfering, embossing, and other linear embellishments. Elaborations such as these, which were at first made possible by technological advances in mechanized carpentry, were subsequently translated into cast iron, as in this example. Measured drawing by John G. Albers, 1971. (HABS IND–86, sheet 2 of 3 sheets)

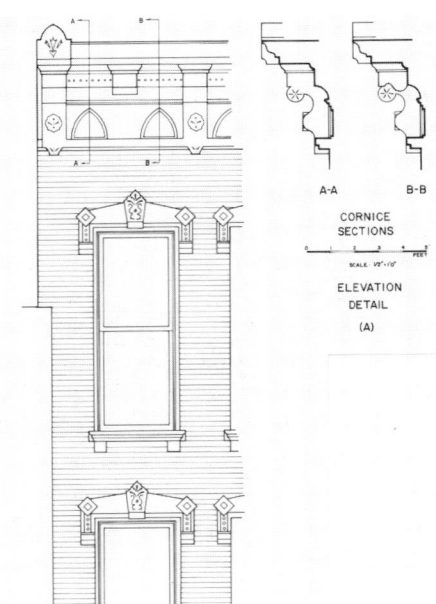

park, and the town has faced looming suburbanization within the Oakland-San Francisco metropolitan area.

Main Street, Idaho City, is at the center of a pleasant mountain town about an hour's drive from the state capital (figs. 15–18). Today, it has a placid population of around three hundred, many of whom are retirees. But when Idaho City flourished in the 1860s as a gold mine camp, the population was six thousand. Local historians fondly remember its gamblers, highwaymen, thieves, and robbers. The town was built up with one-story wood or brick storefronts. Although most of the Boise Basin boom towns are dead and gone, Idaho City retains enough early structures to evoke a strong sense of its golden days.

Guthrie, Oklahoma, was another boom town, a town which marked the closing of the frontier. Its main street—Oklahoma Avenue—was born on a day in April 1889 when it was chosen as the starting line for the race to stake out the newly opened Indian Territory for settlement (figs. 19–23). Like Benecia, Guthrie was temporarily a state capital, holding that position long enough to transform its frame and canvas-tent main street into an impressive ensemble of masonry civic and commercial buildings. Guthrie was somnolent for almost three-quarters of a century, but Sun Belt prosperity coupled with historical consciousness are now setting development in motion once again.

There are also some impressive

structures on Atlanta's Auburn Avenue, standing out among their more utilitarian neighbors (figs. 24–28). It was on Auburn Avenue that black economic success earned the area the name of "Sweet Auburn" and black political success sparked the civil rights movement of the 1960s. The Odd Fellows Building and Auditorium served as a focal point for social cohesiveness. The Herndon Building and Atlanta Life were headquarters for numerous black entrepreneurs. From the pulpit of Ebenezer Baptist Church on Auburn Avenue, Martin Luther King sounded the call for desegregation. Ironically, the success of the civil rights movement, which allowed blacks to enter the economic mainstream, has contributed to the decline of Sweet Auburn Avenue.

Each main street project undertaken by the Historic American Buildings Survey has been different and each has had a different impact—perhaps as different as the main streets

themselves. In Madison, for example, the Survey had both local and national implications. The project was conducted in the summer of 1971, cosponsored by Historic Madison, Inc., an organization founded by local business and civic leaders in 1960, and the Historic Landmarks Foundation of Indiana, a state agency. The research embarked upon helped to sustain strong local historic awareness and assisted the nomination of Madison to the National Register of Historic Places. In 1977 Madison's Main Street was one of three selected by the National Trust for Historic Preservation to serve as a national demonstration project for the coordinated revitalization of a commercial area through historic preservation, physical enhancement, and improved marketing. The following year, another HABS team recorded several commercial buildings that were under consideration for rehabilitation as part of the Main Street project.

Guthrie was documented by HABS

Figure 6 Mulberry Street block, Madison, Jefferson County, Indiana. This street facade has a homogeneity which results from the similarity of scale and height but also a diversity which traces the transition from Greek Revival to Italianate forms that occurred during the Victorian period. Faithfully recorded details report on the changes, which proceed in an orderly manner from right to left: numbers 307 and 305 have the modest cornices and simpler lintels common through the 1830s. The windows of numbers 303 and 301 respectively have flat-headed Italianate lintels on consoles and segmentally arched ones defined by keystones and "ears," the first type popular in the 1850s and the second after the mid-1860s. A common heavily projecting and articulated cornice unites both. Measured drawing, 1971, by H. T. Moriarity. (HABS IND–83, sheet 3 of 8 sheets)

(301)   (303)   (305)   (307)

Figure 7 East elevation, Merrick Building, North El Paso Street, El Paso, El Paso County, Texas. Compare this view with that of the same building in 1888 (fig. 8). Measured drawing by Ann Louise Barr, Dwight H. Burns, and Paul D. Dolinsky, 1980. (HABS TX−330, sheet 4 of 4 sheets)

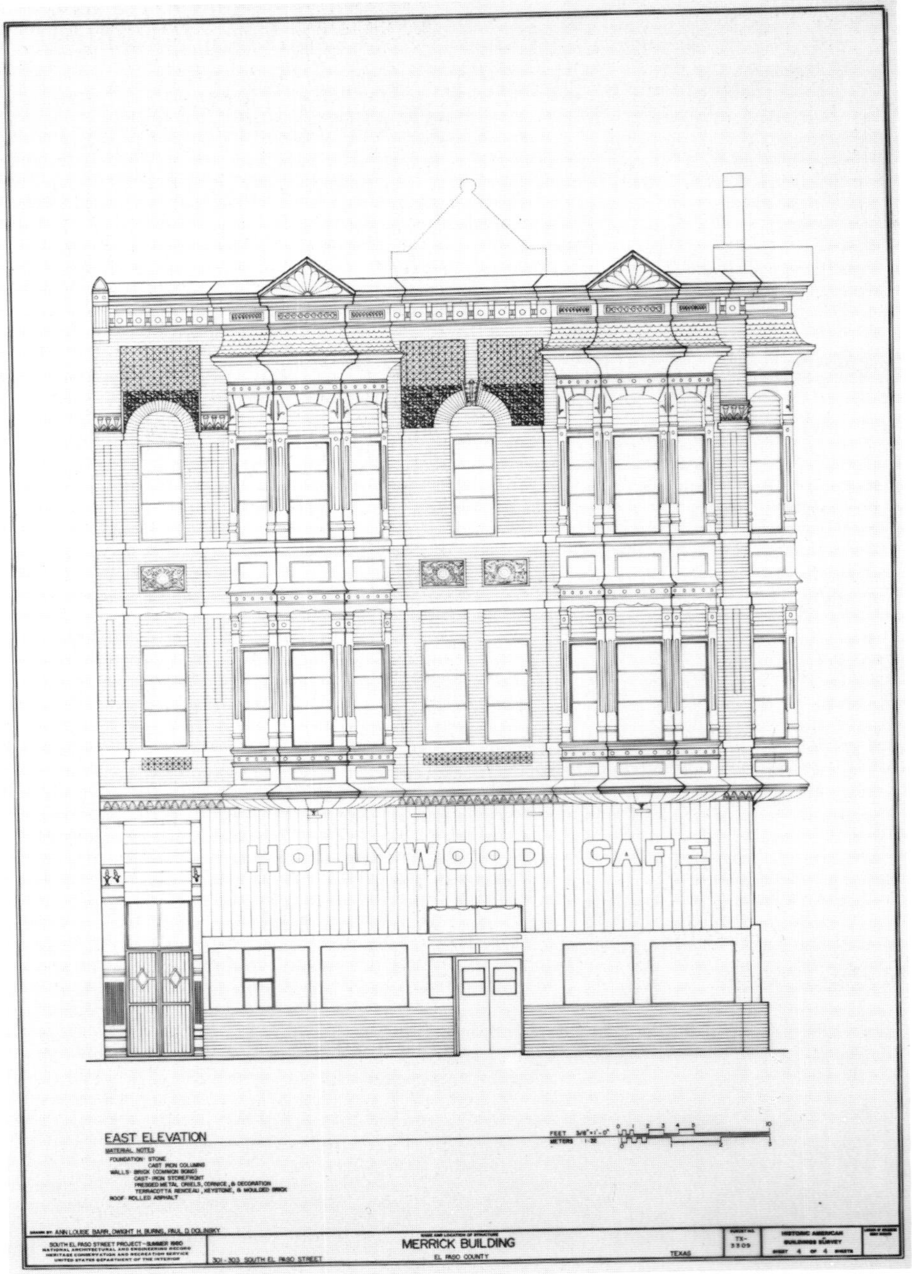

Figure 8 Bird's-eye view of El Paso, from Mesa Garden, and vignette of El Paso Street. Engraved view from the souvenir brochure *El Paso, Texas, and Paso del Norte, Mexico* (Columbus, Ohio: Ward Brothers, 1887). Souvenir Brochure Files, Prints and Photographs Division. (LC−USZ62−83628)

Figure 9 Alhambra (Palace) Theater, 209 South El Paso Street, El Paso, El Paso County, Texas. HABS documentation of South El Paso Street reflects a significant set of business conditions: alternating cycles of prosperity and depression, the trend toward specialization in a low-cost entertainment and retail-goods market, and modernization attempted in the 1950s to hold onto an eroding retail base. Photograph by David Kaminsky, July 1980. (HABS TX—3307—5, LC HABS TEX, 71—ELPA, 4/5—1)

Figure 10 Colón Theater, 507—509 South El Paso Street, El Paso, El Paso County, Texas. Photograph by David Kaminsky, 1980. (HABS TX—3307—22, LC HABS TEX, 71—ELPA, 4/22—1)

in 1973. The project gave a much-needed boost to local historical awareness as the "Eighty-Niners," the pioneer generation whose reenactments had kept memories of early days vivid, were fast dwindling. It was sponsored by the Oklahoma Historical Society, a state agency that operates the Oklahoma Territorial Museum. A subsequent development was the formation of the Logan County Historical Society, whose programs have included the administration of Urban Development Action Grants for downtown improvements totaling $800,000. One business leader regards the Logan County Historical Society as the most influential organization in town after city and county government. Guthrie, only a thirty-five-minute drive from Oklahoma City, is increasingly attractive to

developers, and several million dollars of rehabilitation is now under way in the downtown business district.

Major reinvestment is also taking place in Benecia, allowing construction of several hundred condominium units and a large marina. Local citizens did not favor nomination to the National Register but an architectural review commission has been established there to ensure that the character of new construction is compatible with the historic ambience of the town.

As recently as ten or fifteen years ago, the historic quality and value of South El Paso Street or Auburn Avenue would not have been apparent to most people. Today, however, we are much more aware of the significance of areas such as these and much more sensitive to the long-neglected need to

Figure 11 This nineteenth-century souvenir view of Benicia, copied by HABS, reveals that the character of its architecture is reminiscent of New England. A number of its early structures were shipped in parts from the East. Lithograph published by W.W. Elliott, Oakland, California, 1885. Courtesy California State Library. (HABS CA−2079−2, LC HABS CAL, 48−BENI, 5−2)

Figure 12 Benicia, California, 1853. A U.S. military post. Lithograph after Charles Koppel. Lot 4309A, Prints and Photographs Division. (LC−USZ62−1135)

Figure 13 Benicia, Solano County, California. Photograph by Sirlin Studios, 1977. (HABS CA−2079−11, LC HABS CAL, 48−BENI, 5−11)

Figure 14 South elevation, north elevation, and main entrance detail of the Benicia State Capitol, First and West G Streets, Benicia, Solano County, California. Measured drawing by James Cook, 1976. (HABS CA−1188, sheet 4 of 5 sheets)

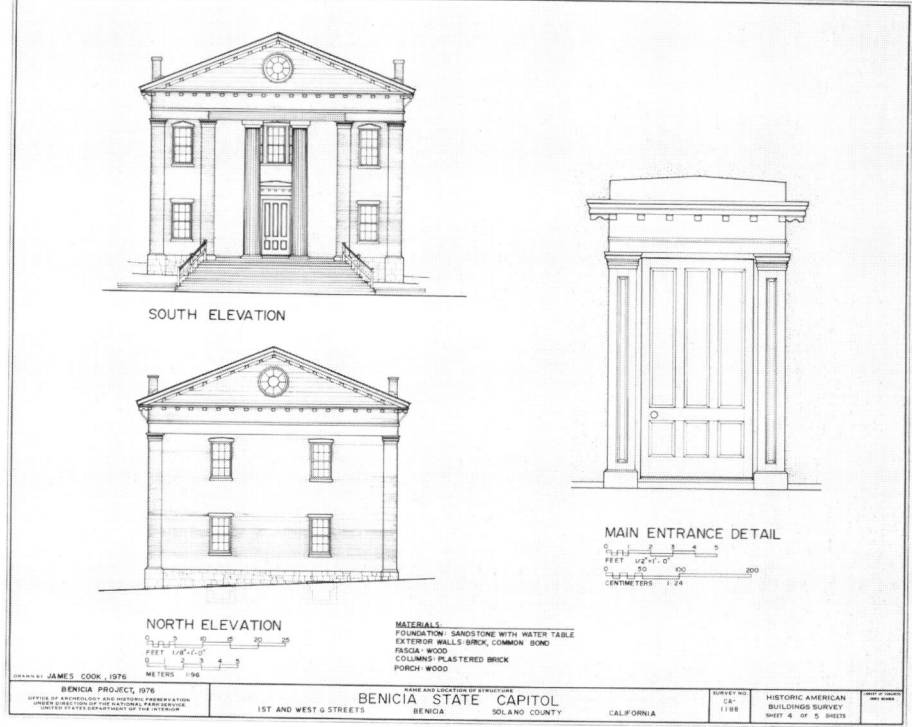

79

Figure 15 Post office block (Boise Basin Museum), 313 Main Street, Idaho City, Boise County, Idaho. Settled in the 1860s gold rush, Idaho City was twice rebuilt after disastrous fires. The *Idaho Mountaineer* reported 16 July 1865: "The city is being rebuilt once more and everything looks gay. Saloons, billiard salons, gambling houses, dry goods establishments, barber shops, and everything else has opened up in grander style and upon larger scale than before." The places mentioned were important gathering places for the exchange of news and sociability. Courtesy Idaho Historical Society. (HABS ID−14−10, LC HABS ID, 8−IDCI, 9−10)

Figure 16 Post office block (Boise Basin Museum), 313 Main Street, Idaho City, Boise County, Idaho. Photograph by Duane Garrett, 1976. (HABS ID−15−1, LC HABS ID, 8−IDCI, 10−1)

Figure 17 East elevation, Boise Basin Mercantile Company Block (Boise Basin Museum), 313 Main Street, Idaho City, Boise County, Idaho. Measured drawing, by Jack W. Schafer, 1976. (HABS ID−13, sheet 4 of 4 sheets)

study the cultural and historic traditions of minority groups. Thus, in Atlanta and in El Paso, HABS researchers have ventured into relatively uncharted areas. Similarly, as "urban action" projects, these surveys went considerably beyond traditional parameters in calling attention to opportunities to capitalize on historic resources in planning for economic development.

Sweet Auburn is a designated Preservation District associated with the Martin Luther King Historic Site, a property of the National Park Service that is currently under development. It is anticipated that the area will become an important visitors' attraction and a major spur to local economic development. The survey undertaken there by HABS in 1979 reflected close coordination between a range of public and private institutions, including the Georgia State Historic Preservation Office, the City of Atlanta Bureau of Cultural Affairs, Office of Economic Development and Urban Design Commission, and the Auburn Area Revitalization Committee. The detailed study of the market potential of Auburn Avenue and recommendations for specific strategies to enhance economic development that were part of the

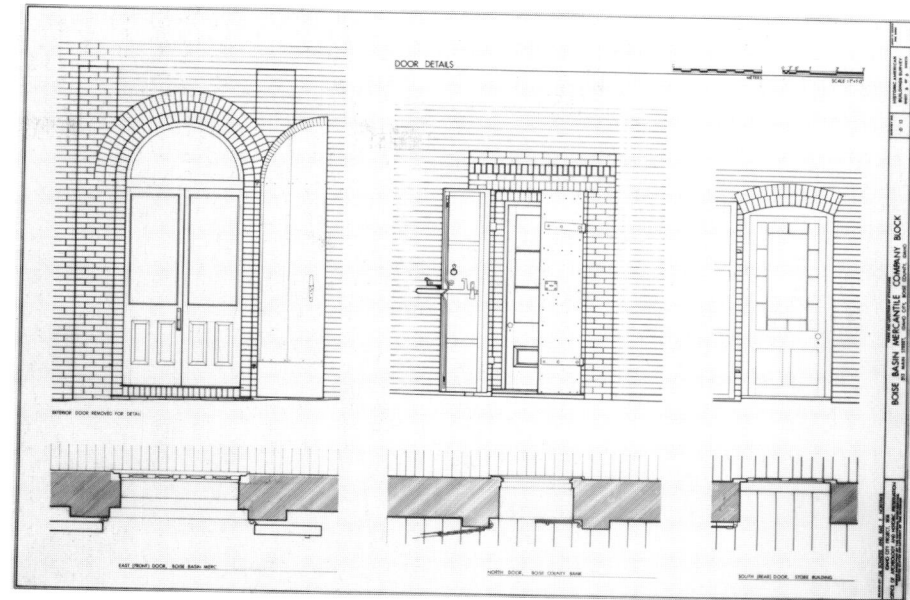

HABS report have affected the direction of local economic planning.

The El Paso project also suggested possibilities for architectural rehabilitation and commercial revitalization. Conducted in the summer of 1980, the project was cosponsored by the City of El Paso and the Texas Historical Commission, which anticipated that a historic district nomination to the National Register would be made. Since then, however, a strong private-sector

Figure 18 Door details, Boise Basin Mercantile Company Block (Boise Basin Museum), 313 Main Street, Idaho City, Boise County, Idaho. Measured drawing by J. W. Schafer and Rae F. Noritake, 1976. (HABS ID–13, sheet 6 of 6 sheets)

Figure 19 The opening of Oklahoma. The tent city of Guthrie, five days after the first homesteading run, 27 April 1889. Linocut by Milburn & Cross in *Cosmopolitan*, September 1889. Lot 4388I, Prints and Photographs Division. (LC–USZ62–31965)

Figure 20 Oklahoma Avenue, West, Guthrie, Logan County, Oklahoma. Copyright 1908, Wittemann Brothers, the Albertype Company. Souvenir Brochure File, Prints and Photographs Division. (LC–USZ62–83626)

Figure 21 Gray Brothers Block, Guthrie, Logan County, Oklahoma. The exuberant Romanesque Revival style of this office-and-shop complex mirrors the frontier optimism of Guthrie's territorial days. Fig. 20 shows the structure at left about 1900. Measured drawing by Julian Smith, 1973. (HABS OK–12, sheet 6 of 6 sheets)

NORTH ELEVATION

CROSS SECTION FACING SOUTH

SCALE IN FEET   1/8" = 1'-0"

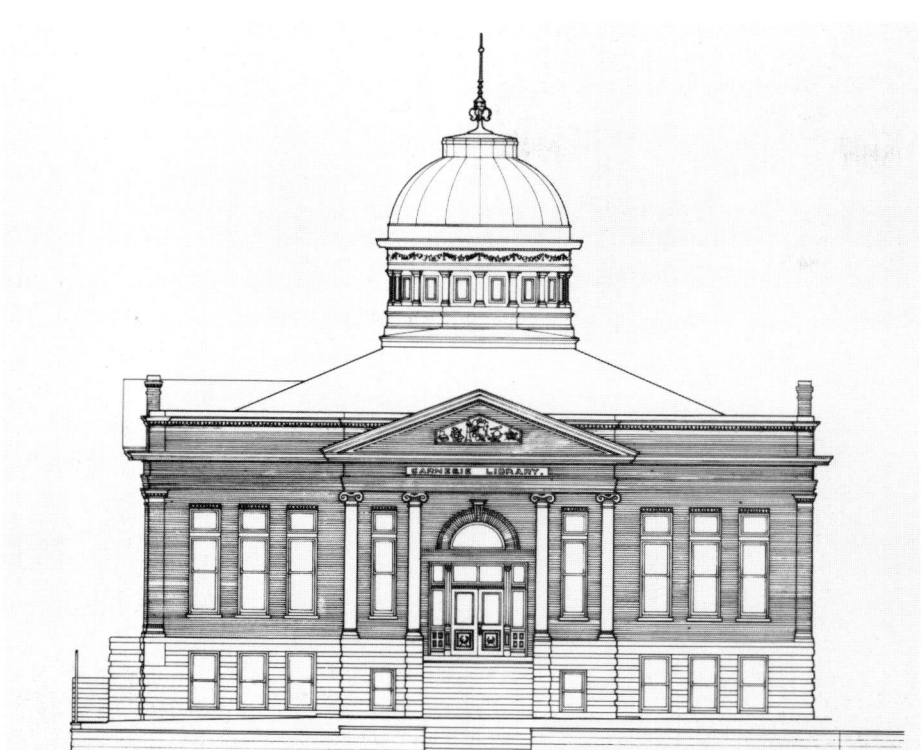

Figure 22 South elevation, Carnegie Library, 402 East Oklahoma Avenue, Guthrie, Logan County, Oklahoma. Measured drawing by Julian Smith, 1973. (HABS OK—14, sheet 5 of 8 sheets)

Figure 23 Carnegie Library, 402 East Oklahoma Avenue, Guthrie, Logan County, Oklahoma. Copyright 1908, Wittemann Brothers, the Albertype Company. Unusually elaborate for a library—especially one paid for by Andrew Carnegie, who had strict ideas concerning which features were appropriate—this structure also reflects Guthrie's aspiration to serve as Oklahoma's capital. Souvenir Brochure File, Prints and Photographs Division. (LC—USZ62—83627)

Figure 24 Commercial street, Sweet Auburn district, Atlanta, Fulton County, Georgia, ca. 1900. View by W. E. B. DuBois, scholar and leader of the black civil rights movement who settled in Atlanta in 1897. DuBois established the South's first department of sociology at Atlanta University and used the Sweet Auburn neighborhood for field study. Many of the photographs taken during the course of his work were exhibited at the Paris Exposition of 1900. Number 303, DuBois Collection, Prints and Photographs Division. (LC—USZ62—83631)

effort to revitalize one section of the street only, as part of an ambitious redevelopment in the downtown, has, for the time being at least, slowed momentum for historic redevelopment of the study area.

Some may question the appropriateness and efficacy of HABS intervention in local community development. It would certainly be improvident to ignore opportunities to extend and deepen HABS research on these grounds, however. Architectural and historical analysis of main streets inevitably provides evidence of economic development patterns as well, and there are likely to be many occasions when the old adage that experience is the best teacher will prove itself again on Main Street.

For example, HABS projects develop a rich trove of information that can be mined for much-needed research in the history of retail commerce. The history of financing, public improvements, and business leadership are surely other rich fields for investigation. Contemporary planners would benefit from some sharper insights into Main Street's historical responses to changing times. Guthrie, for obvious reasons, had to diversify its concentration of lawyers and realtors. Idaho City was forced to reduce its number of general stores. Madison made an effort to capture the local retail trade.

Similarly, the adaptation of architectural form in previous times may provide useful guidelines for contemporary building rehabilitation and urban design. On Auburn Avenue there is a long history of low-cost renovation. In Madison, there has traditionally been a flair for using locally manufactured building products. In Benecia today, as in times past, new construction shows sensitivity to existing scale and building form.

Main street projects have been effective training programs for future preservationists. Consider the example of Tom Moriarity, in 1971 an architectural student on the Madison project. After he was graduated from the University of Texas in 1974, Moriarity worked at the Historic Sites and Restoration Branch of the state parks agency in Texas until 1975, when he was hired by Historic Madison, Inc., as its first director. Later, he returned to Madison to help coordinate historic preservation, physical improvements, and

commercial revitalization as part of the National Main Street Demonstration Project. With several years of experience in Madison, Moriarity went to work in the National Trust's Main Street Center in Washington, D.C., a resource service which has shared its growing expertise with hundreds of communities across the country.

HABS team members have assumed important professional positions in many other niches of historic preservation. For example, John Hnedak, a student architect on the Guthrie project in 1973, is now historian in the northeast regional office of the National Park Service. Darlene Roth, a member of the Sweet Auburn team, is president of The History Group, Inc., a private firm that consults on preservation-related projects. Most HABS team members are not primarily preservationists but archi-

Figure 25 North elevation, Herndon Building, Auburn Avenue, Atlanta, Fulton County, Georgia. Constructed in 1924 directly across from the Odd Fellows complex, the Herndon Building was the project of Alonzo Herndon. Acting both as designer and contractor, Herndon used black labor and recycled building materials. Measured drawing by Michael D. Clark and Willie J. Graham, 1979. (HABS GA−1170−C, sheet 17 of 18 sheets)

Figure 27 Detail, south entrance, Odd Fellows Building and Auditorium, 228–250 Auburn Avenue, Atlanta, Fulton County, Georgia. Photograph by David J. Kaminsky, July 1979. (HABS GA–1170–B–13, LC HABS GA, 61–ATLA, 1B–13)

Figure 26 Odd Fellows Building and Auditorium, 228–250 Auburn Avenue, Atlanta, Fulton County, Georgia. *Atlanta's Sweet Auburn* is a report by the National Architectural and Engineering Record (as HABS was known in the late 1970s). It explains the social significance of the Odd Fellows Building: "Benjamin Jefferson Davis was the leader of the program to construct the Auburn Avenue Odd Fellows Complex. Davis was a member of the lodge and editor of the Atlanta *Independent,* which began as an Odd Fellow's voice and became a local black newspaper. Davis saw the complex as a way to counteract the 'ignorant and irresponsible' image conveyed in the 'low' saloons and entertainment spots on Decatur Street, two blocks south of Auburn Avenue." Photograph by David J. Kaminsky, July 1979. (HABS GA–1170–B–3, LC HABS GA, 61–ATLA, 1B–3)

tects and historians, whose education and professional outlook are substantially enriched by HABS field experience.

By no means are the educational advantages of HAS projects limited to HABS team members. When one considers the heavy volume of tourism associated with these main streets, it is clear that the educational benefits are very broadly distributed indeed.

In downtown Madison, for example, one can visit the Judge Jeremiah Sullivan house museum, a fine example of Northwest Territory Federal-style architecture. Dr. William Hutchings's Office and Hospital there is like

an eighty-year-old time capsule of medical practice. The splendid Victorian Shrewsbury House, designed by an outstanding local architect, and the James Lanier house, memorialized because of Lanier's contribution to the Union cause during the Civil War, attract many visitors. Under development is the Schroder Saddle Tree Factory, a unique early industrial site. Walking tour brochures are distributed by Historic Madison, Inc., and the Madison Area Chamber of Commerce. There are Open House Days and a variety of cultural programs that use the historic Main Street ambience to good advantage.

In Guthrie, the Chamber of Commerce provides a town map with a detailed, fact-filled itinerary that suggests forty-two historic sites to visit. In Benecia, the HABS study spurred the publication of an excellent book by Robert Bruegmann, *Benecia, Portrait of an Early California Town: An Architectural History* (San Francisco: 101 Productions, 1980). The number of inns, restaurants, art galleries, and antique shops that now fill First Street testify to the fact that Benecia has been rediscovered. In Atlanta, the National Park Service estimates potential annual visitors at a half-million or more. Even with its small population, Idaho City manages to operate its old post office as a museum. And on South El Paso Street, where fortune is now at a very low ebb, economic study suggests that historic resources such as foreign flavor, personalized merchandising, and pleasant pedestrian scale may bring tourists and promote economic growth in the area.

Main streets cannot be frozen in time, but neither should they be abandoned heedlessly in the cloudy waters of "progress." There will always be thorny issues that arise in relation to economic development, physical growth, and the management of change in historic areas. The close scrutiny of a HABS project can illuminate characteristics which are particular, unique, and significant and that are essential to the preservation of the sense of place on Main Street.

Figure 28 First Congregational Church, Sweet Auburn neighborhood, Atlanta, Fulton County, Georgia. This, another turn-of-the-century image by W. E. B. DuBois, takes pride in showing not only the neat surroundings of the First Congregational Church but a prosperous black family seated on the porch of the adjacent house. The second oldest church of its kind in the country, First Congregational was established in 1867 by members of the American Missionary Association. These missionaries arrived in Atlanta at the close of the Civil War to work among and educate the newly freed blacks. Number 359, DuBois Collection, Prints and Photographs Division. (LC—USZ62—83629)

Documenting Early American Technology: Covered Bridges

by

RICHARD SANDERS ALLEN

As late as fifty years ago, little attention was paid to the subject of bridge building, bridge architecture, or bridge sites. Covered wooden bridges were not accorded the nostalgia and veneration they receive today. In most areas they were simply means of crossing a stream. Early iron bridges went even more unnoticed.

Literature on the history of bridges in America was sparse and spotty, to be found for the most part in local histories from which state and national accounts were laboriously pieced together. Yet the covered bridge figured prominently in the development of American architecture in the nineteenth century. These economical, expedient, and artfully designed wooden structures—"barns over rivers" —which we now observe much as we would examine the skeletons of mastodons, signaled the coming together of several key elements in this country in the nineteenth century: rapid geographic expansion, exploitation of great forests, use of inventive mechanics, and the prevalence of a spirit of enterprise. At their most ambitious these bridges were as brash and heroic as the young nation which fostered them, as can be seen in an 1824 engraving of the great bridge across the Schuylkill at Philadelphia, framed by architect Robert Mills's handsome neoclassical propylaea (fig. 2), or a photograph of a remarkable tripartite bridge spanning the Muskingum and Licking rivers near Zanesville, Ohio (fig. 3). The technological discoveries which they embodied were far-reaching. By 1859 Parisian engineers rebuilding the venerable Pont au Change were making use of the lattice truss system first patented by American inventor Ithiel Town (fig. 4).

Unlike the related histories of early American canals and railroads, the annals of the country's bridge-building and bridge-builders were seemingly lost. Unique and historic bridges stood, but they were taken for granted. No tears

Figure 1   The Fitchburg Railroad used the Montague City bridge in Massachusetts as a crossing for their Turners Falls Branch line, built in 1870. Tolls were collected from horse-and-buggy traffic on the bridge floor below, while iron horses snorted across on the roof. Lit only by two small openings in each span, it was a dark, scary tunnel of noise when a train passed over. A Dr. Watson's horse is reported to have dropped dead of fright in this dark interior. The laminated arches were added in 1901 to support the railroad's heavier rolling stock. When the raging waters of the Connecticut River demolished the structure in March 1936, it was the longest covered wooden bridge in the United States. Photograph by Arthur C. Haskell, 1934. (HABS MASS–101, LC HABS MASS 6, MONT, 1–3)

Figure 2   One of the best-known of early American covered wooden bridges was erected in 1812–14 over the Schuylkill River above Philadelphia. The contractor-builder was German-born Lewis Wernwag, assisted by American architect Robert Mills in the capacity of consulting engineer. With elaborately embellished portals, the immense, 340-foot arched span was quickly dubbed "The Colossus," and was likened by actress Fanny Kemble to "a white scarf thrown across the river." The bridge was destroyed by fire on September 1, 1838. Aquatint by Akrell after a drawing by Baron Axel Klinckowström illustrating his *Bref om de Förenta Staterne* (Stockholm, 1824). Lot 4384G, Prints and Photographs Division. (LC–USZ62–1078)

Figure 3   Zanesville stands at the confluence of the Muskingum and Licking Rivers, on the Old National Road aross Ohio. Here a unique crossing was devised to span both rivers, a multispanned wooden arch structure in the form of a *Y*. The bridge was completed in 1832 by Catharinus P. Buckingham, a twenty-four-year-old West Point graduate, and it was not replaced until 1901. Confused motorists who use the Y Bridge's concrete successor today are still occasionally directed to "go to the middle of the bridge and turn right!" Photograph by Lauck Bros., 1900. Prints and Photographs Division. (LC–USZ62–24696)

Figure 4 In their 1858–59 rebuilding of the stone Pont au Change over the River Seine in Paris, French engineers needed a temporary access to piers and pile drivers. They chose the wooden lattice bridge truss design first patented in 1820 by the American architect Ithiel Town. Photograph by Collard, Paris, 1859. Lot 8500, Prints and Photographs Division. (LC–USZ62–80180)

were shed or protest mounted as they disappeared from the landscape. Considered unsightly, narrow, and dangerous to automobile traffic (fig. 5), their replacements, often just as narrow and dangerous, were hailed as part of the progress of American transportation.

People's eyes began to be opened, however, by wholesale destruction such as that caused by the great Vermont flood of 1927. In that flood, an estimated two hundred covered wooden bridges in the Green Mountain State were destroyed in the space of forty-eight hours. Fires, both accidental and deliberately set, and gross overloading contributed to the passing of many other outstanding examples of American bridge-building know-how. Then came wholesale replacement projects, such as those of Pennsylvania and Ohio, in which dozens of "inadequate" stream crossings were renewed with spans of steel and concrete (fig. 6). The money was available during the boom times of the late 1920s. Later, in the 1930s, funding for such replacements came from the Works Progress Administration.

Gradually, the situation came to be looked upon with alarm by civil engineers, historians, and budding

preservationists endowed with a sense of what constitutes an available engineering heritage, but the wheels of change rolled inexorably on.

Here and there were individuals who made a point of photographing and recording the major dimensions of old bridges, particularly the covered wooden spans, which possessed special romantic appeal. Not until 1933, however, was any national project launched that would serve, even in a small way, to record the images of the vanishing number of covered bridges in the United States.

That year saw the beginning of the Historic American Buildings Survey, which, assembling an archive of early American architecture, surveyed and recorded thousands of structures: public, private, domestic, and industrial. Architectural interest and merit, together with historical associations, were the first criteria. An early report states that "dependencies such as barns and smokehouses—even covered bridges— were recorded."

The first bridge projects were of necessity limited to spans in the immediate vicinity of the unemployed architects enlisted by the American Institute of Architects. These resulted ultimately in photographs of forty-five

Figure 5 Locally maintained and still standing over Schoharie Creek at North Blenheim, New York, this two-lane covered bridge dates from 1855. It was built under the direction of Nicholas M. Powers, who devised a unique plan of hanging the wooden truss superstructure on a single arch (see figs. 24 and 25). Its clear span of 210 feet (only two feet longer than a similar bridge in California) gives Blenheim Bridge the true title of "the longest existing single-span covered bridge in the world." The admonitory sign was typical of American wooden bridges. Photograph by Nelson E. Baldwin, 1936. (HABS NY 359, LC HABS NY, 48–BLEN, 1–2)

Figure 6 Documentation by casual photographers has enhanced the HABS/HAER collection. This fine arched truss, built in 1840 by contractor J. W. Slee, spanned Paint Creek between Bainbridge and Bourneville, Ohio. It was dismantled in 1933 through no fault of the wooden workmanship but because of an undermined stone abutment. Photograph, dated 1933, from a collection documenting covered bridges in Ohio, Indiana, Wisconsin, Michigan, Illinois, and Virginia that was transferred from the National Park Service to the Library of Congress. Lot 11,185−2, Prints and Photographs Division. (LC−USZ62−80215)

Figure 7 Long the connecting link between the Connecticut River towns of Orford, New Hampshire, and Fairlee, Vermont, this two-span covered bridge had a roof length of 438 feet. It was damaged by flood waters in March 1936 and was closed awaiting demolition when measured and photographed by HABS. Because of the legal delineation of the interstate boundary, all but a few feet of the bridge was in New Hampshire. Photograph by L. C. Durette, 1936. (HABS NH−29, LC HABS NH, 5−ORF, 2−2)

covered wooden crossings, representative of nineteen states. On the face of it, considering that at the time there were probably over four thousand covered bridges still standing in the United States, this may seem a puny contribution. By luck, the scattered representation turned out to be well-chosen.

Perhaps more important, the initial historic buildings survey included detailed architectural drawings of thirty-one of the covered bridges photographed. Professionally prepared and drawn, these were and continue to be a major source of accurate historical and technical data. They can be consulted not only for clues to engineering history but for the building of small-scale models and the creation of full-scale replicas.

Documentation of covered bridges in New England, where the American popular imagination traditionally locates them, is especially good. Three interesting examples were recorded in New Hampshire in the 1930s. The earliest of these lay between Orford, New Hampshire, and Fairlee, Vermont. Originally built about 1850, recorded

in 1936, and destroyed by 1937, this dramatic timber lattice truss spanned 438 feet supported only by a solitary central stone pier between abutments of the same material (figs. 7–9). Also destroyed soon after being recorded in 1935 was the Contoocook River covered bridge at Contoocook, in the town of Hopkinton, a bridge which dated from 1853 (figs. 10, 11). Col. Stephen H. Long of the U.S. Army engineers, a native of Hopkinton, had taken out the first of his several bridge patents in 1830. This example of a Long Truss was built by his local agents, the Childs Brothers. Last of these New Hampshire examples, and again lost, was the "New Bridge" or "Henniker Bridge," erected west of Hopkinton in 1863 (figs. 12–14). A special combination of lattice type trusses with arches, it replaced a predecessor carried away by a freshet in the spring of 1852 and was itself taken down after damage suffered in the flood of 1936.

The HABS photographs of covered bridges include a number that appear nowhere but in this collection. Four spans which stood in remote Alabama and Mississippi are among

Figure 8 The interior of the Orford-Fairlee Bridge over the Connecticut River shows the heavy truss design. Here the lattices were of massive square timbers rather than the usual plank found in the original patented Town Truss. This improvement on the basic design is credited to Bela J. Fletcher of Claremont, New Hampshire, the probable builder of this bridge. Photograph by L. C. Durette, 1936. (HABS NH–29, LC HABS NH, 5–ORF, 2–3)

Figure 9 Details from a measured drawing of a covered bridge spanning the Connecticut River at Orford in Grafton County, New Hampshire. Drawing by John C. Fletcher. (HABS NH–29, sheet 1 of 5 sheets)

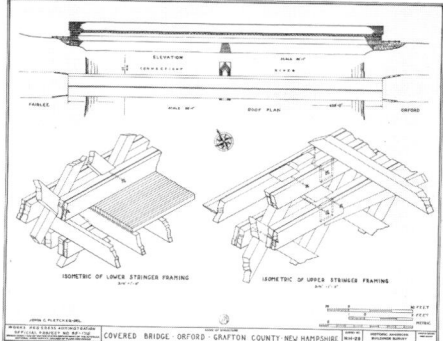

Figure 10 At Contoocook, New Hampshire, spanning the Contoocook River, stood a covered bridge built on the plan patented in 1830 by Col. Stephen H. Long of the U.S. Army Engineers. Because of heavy pedestrian traffic, this structure had two sidewalks and was flanked by a covered wooden railroad bridge that served a branch of the Boston & Maine Railroad. The Childs brothers, who, like Colonel Long, were natives of nearby Hopkinton, erected the Contoocook Bridge in 1853. It served the village for over eighty years. Photograph by Clement Moran, 1935. (HABS NH—21, LC HABS NH, 7—CONT, 1—1)

Figure 11 A measured drawing shows the inside-end elevation and a section of the center bay of the Contoocook Covered Bridge spanning the Contoocook River at the village of Contoocook in Merrimack County, New Hampshire. Drawing by J. C. Fletcher. (HABS NH—21, sheet 4 of 6 sheets)

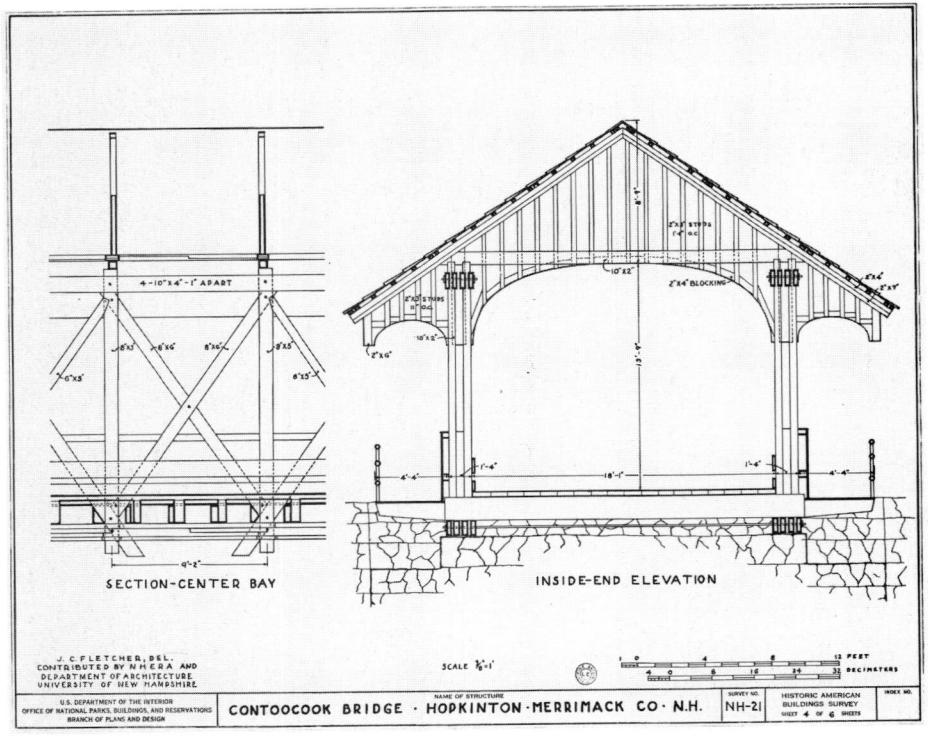

Figure 12 Since this New Hampshire crossing was on the road to Henniker, it was sometimes called the "Henniker Bridge," but it was also known as "New Bridge," because its construction followed that of other covered spans in the Town of Hopkinton. It spanned the Contoocook River west of Hopkinton Village. Aided by a HABS plan (fig. 14), researchers have recently shown the bridge to have been on the design of U.S. patent no. 38,653, issued to John C. Briggs of Concord, New Hampshire, on May 26, 1863. Briggs erected this rare example of the design in the same year. Photograph by L. C. Durette, 1936. (HABS NH−30, LC HABS NH, 7−HOP, 2−1)

Figure 13 The interior of John Briggs's Henniker Bridge shows his patented combination of several tried-and-true truss components: laminated arches, inclined posts, and timber lattices. Tightly packed planking, set on edge, makes the floor a smooth passageway. Signs in the rafters (see also fig. 8) advertised such nostrums as "Flint's Powders" and "Kendall's Spavin Cure." Photograph by L. C. Durette, 1936. (HABS NH−30, LC HABS NH, 7−HOP, 2−3)

Figure 14 A measured drawing shows the plan, side elevation, and a longitudinal section of the covered bridge spanning the Contoocook River called the Henniker Bridge or the New Bridge. Drawing by John C. Fletcher. (HABS NH−30, sheet 1 of 4 sheets)

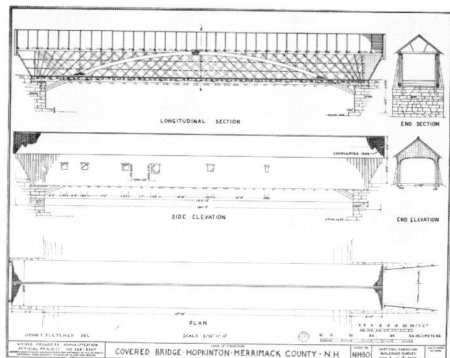

Figure 15 At the time that his lattice truss bridge patent was granted in 1820, Connecticut architect Ithiel Town was professionally engaged in the South. His lattice "mode," as he called it, proved popular in adjacent states. Town's Clarendon Bridge, near Fayetteville, North Carolina, was one of the earliest to use his patented truss. Another example, pictured here, although left to the ravages of weather, survived as late as 1936, spanning Cripple Deer Creek near Allsboro, Alabama. Photograph by Alex Bush, 1936. (HABS ALA−361, LC HABS ALA, 17−ALBO.V, 1−2)

Figure 16 A number of covered bridges were recorded by HABS only in the nick of time—even after roofs and siding had been removed in the process of demolition. Such was the case in 1934 with the crossing of the Licking River at Butler, Kentucky, a long Burr arch truss structure of three spans. Using native white pine and oak timbers, two contractors from Ohio, J. J. Newman, and F. B. Erwin, erected it in 1871. Photograph by Theodore Webb, 1934. (HABS KY 20−11, LC HABS KY, 96−BUT, 1−2)

these (fig. 15), as is a very long roofed structure which spanned the Licking River at Butler in Pendleton County, Kentucky (fig. 16). The Butler bridge, uncovered at the time of recording, demonstrates on a small scale how arched truss units could be repeated indefinitely. Such a capability made possible contemporary American engineering feats like the High Bridge across the Appomattox on the South Side Railway between Petersburg and Lynchburg, Virginia, which stretched 2,400 feet in length and stood 128 feet above the level of the stream (fig. 17).

The three main record types created by HABS each serve a purpose. In addition to photographs, historical data are often included, such as a transcript of the contract for the bridge across the Licking River in Kentucky. The type of information gathered in the 1930s, however, cannot compare with the extensive reports often found in more recent projects. For Bartram's Covered Bridge, which spans Crum Creek between Chester and Delaware County in Pennsylvania, the HABS report written in 1958 fills five pages. Bridge histories prepared since 1969 by the Historic American Engineering Record (HAER) are usually even more extensive.

The third type of record, the sheets of measured architectural drawings produced by HABS—and which, especially in the 1930s, served

as the Survey's primary tool—constitute the finest sources of their type. Here the researcher, engineer, and would-be modeler can find authentic details of major American wooden covered bridge truss types, with exact measurements. Isometric views and cutaway drawings show precisely how timbers were fastened and joined (figs. 9, 23, 25). Reproducible copies of the HABS sheets of drawings show the structural framework of covered bridges and other representative bridge types used in America. The following examples are well documented by HABS measured drawings. They include three

Figure 17 During the Civil War, wooden arch trusses of the deck variety carried the railroad high above the valley at Appomattox, Virginia. Partially destroyed during the conflict, the viaduct's missing spans were replaced by spindly trestlework, like that described by Abraham Lincoln as being composed of "beanpoles and cornstalks." Photograph by T. H. O'Sullivan, 1865. Brady-Handy Collection, Prints and Photographs Division. (LC−B8184−4152)

Figure 18 With two covered sidewalks, the Mahoning River Bridge at Newton Falls, Ohio, was a favorite gathering place for Sunday strollers. Built on a truss plan and composed of wooden timbers with vertical rods of iron, it marked the transition between American wooden and iron bridges. The plan was devised in 1840 by a Massachusetts housewright, William Howe, whose more famous nephew invented the sewing machine. Photograph by Carl Waite, 1936. (HABS OH−270, LC HABS OH 78−NEWT, 1−1)

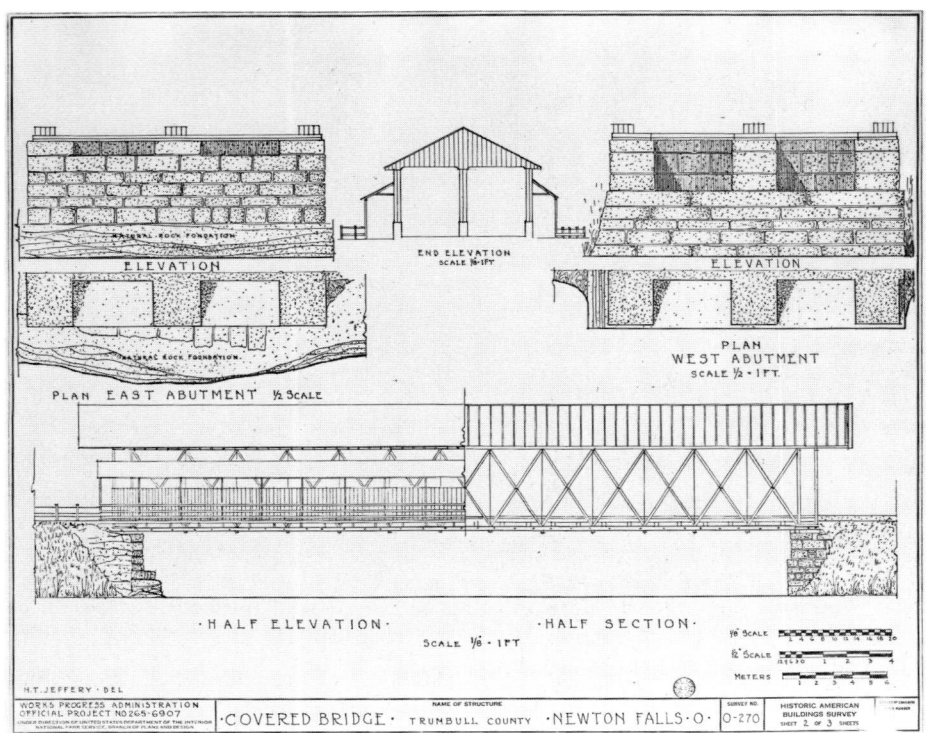

Figure 19 A covered bridge spanning the Mahoning River at Newton Falls in Trumbull County, Ohio. Drawing by H. T. Jeffery, 1936. (HABS OH−270, sheet 2 of 3 sheets)

Figure 20 A covered bridge spanning Darby Creek in Union County, Ohio, near North Lewisburg. Drawing by Charles H. Uthe, 1934. (HABS OH−22−13, sheet 1 of 3 sheets)

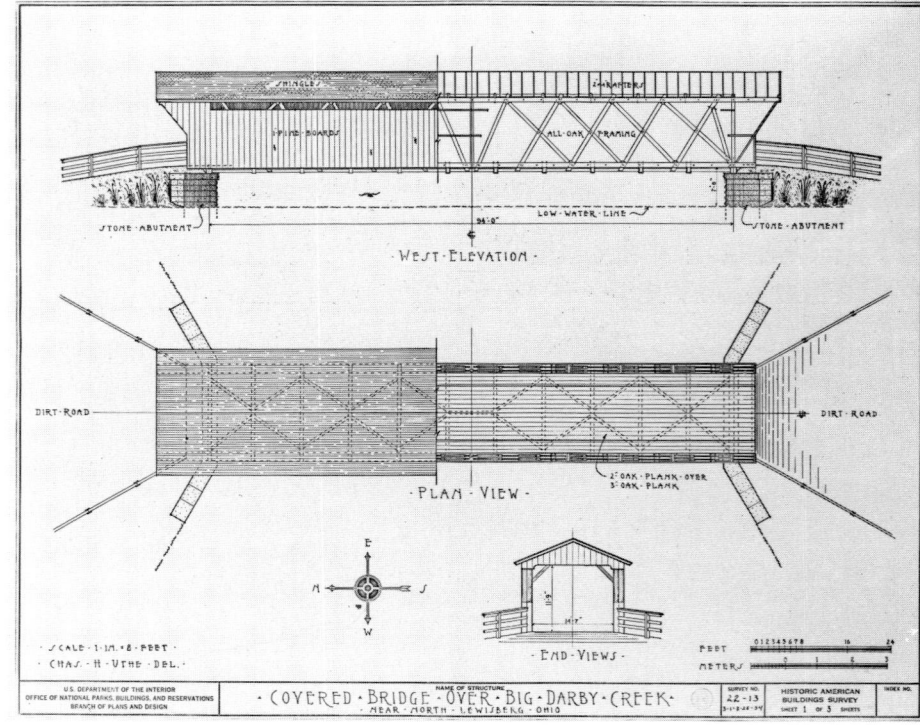

Figure 21 A covered bridge spanning Seven Mile Creek in Butler County, Ohio, in the vicinity of Collinsville. Measured and drawn by Cliff Kernen, 1936. (HABS OH−623, sheet 1 of 2 sheets)

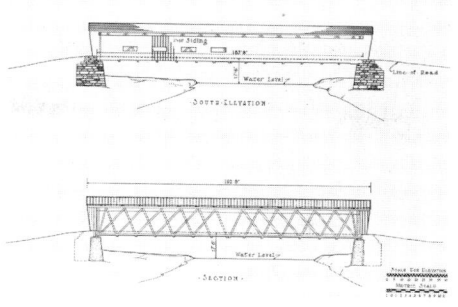

Figure 22 Perrine's Bridge at Rifton, New York, has spanned the Wallkill for 138 years, but only HABS research has disclosed the name of its builder: Rosencrans Wood. It is a fine example of the arch-and-kingpost design first used by Connecticut bridge-builder Theodore Burr in 1804. Hundreds of Burr Truss covered wooden bridges such as this were erected from Maine to Missouri (see also figs. 6 & 16). Photograph by E. P. MacFarland, 1934. (HABS NY−4−204, LC HABS NY, 56−RIF. V, 1−2)

Figure 23 A measured drawing of Perrine's Bridge, 1934, by T. R. Kilbourne. (HABS NY−4−204, sheet 1 of 1 sheet)

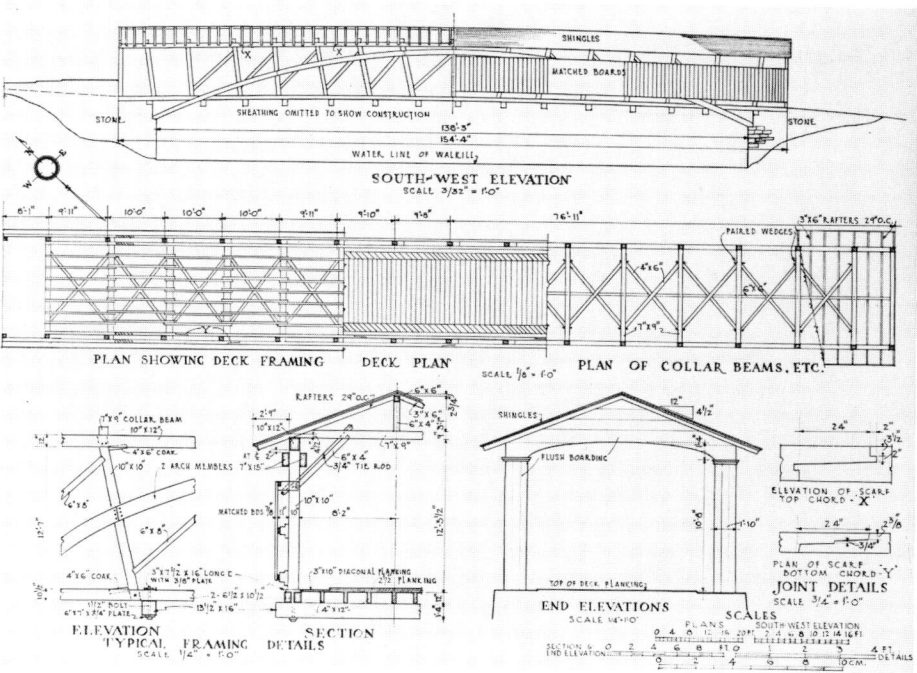

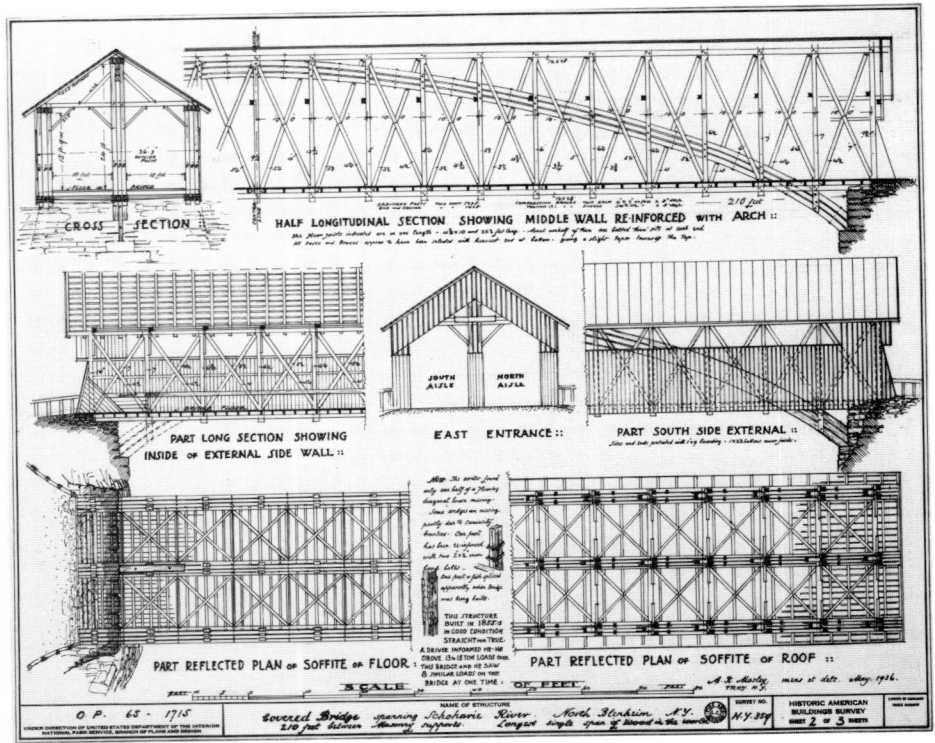

Figure 24   Measured drawing of the covered bridge spanning Schoharie Creek at North Blenheim, New York, by A. K. Mosley, 1936. (HABS NY−359, sheet 2 of 3 sheets)

Figure 25   Details captured in a measured drawing of the covered bridge over the Schoharie Creek, North Blenheim, New York. Drawing by A. K. Mosley. (HABS NY−359, sheet 3 of 3 sheets)

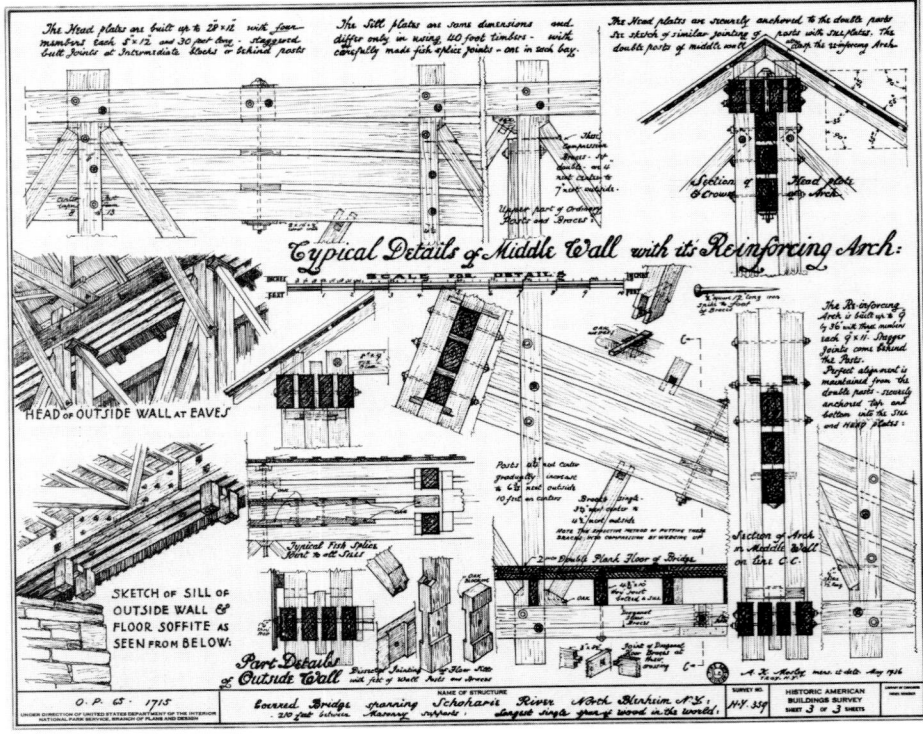

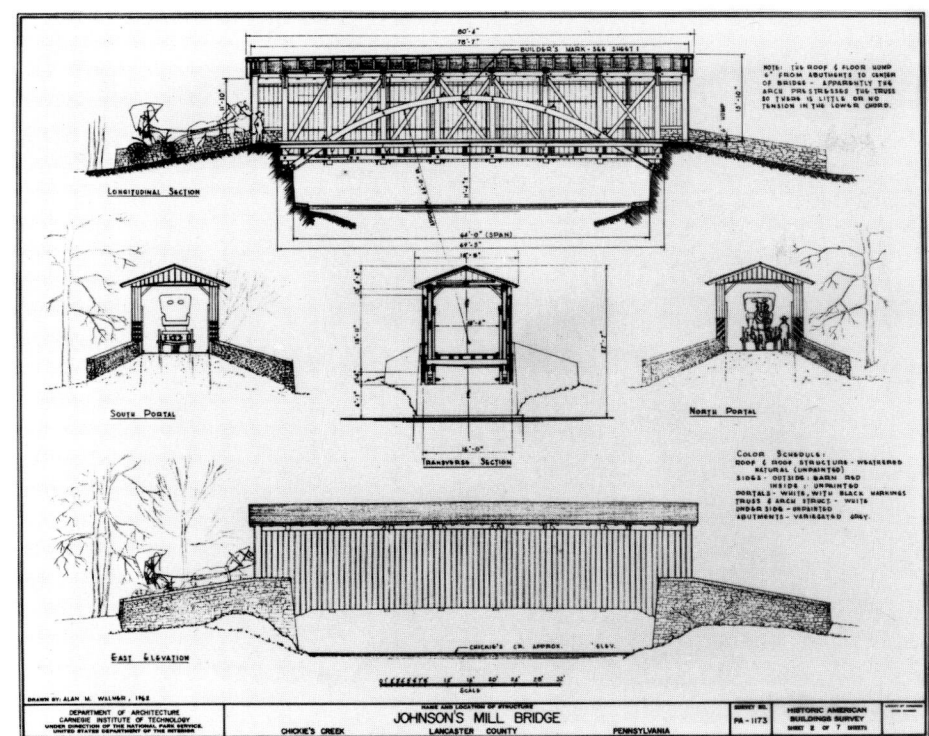

Figure 26 Johnson's Mill Bridge, spanning Chickie's Creek, Lancaster County, Pennsylvania. Drawn by Alan M. Walker, 1968. (HABS PA – 1173, sheet 2 of 7 sheets)

Figure 27 Measured drawing of Waterford Covered Bridge in Erie County, Pennsylvania. Drawing by R. Pierce, 1936. (HABS PA – 535, sheet 1 of 1 sheet)

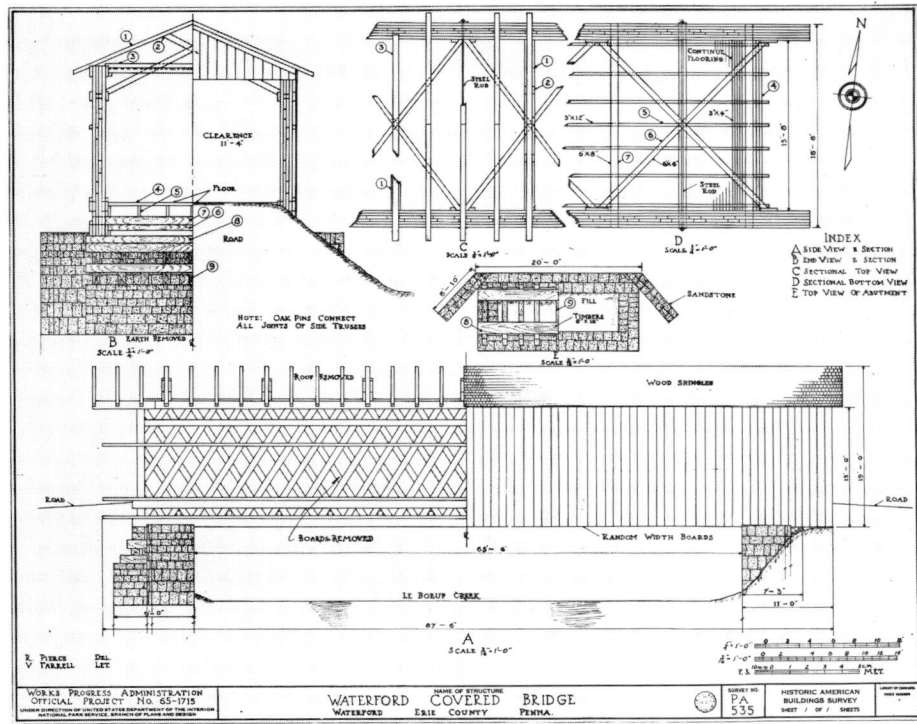

Figure 28 This bridge had five spans of Howe wood-and-iron trusses, with huge auxiliary laminated arches, stretching 754 feet across the Connecticut River at Montague City, Massachusetts. Primarily a railroad bridge, with the trains trundling across on the flat decked roof, the Montague City structure also carried vehicular traffic between the trusses. It had right-angle entrances at either end, like rat holes in a wainscot. Photograph by Arthur C. Haskell, 1934. (HABS MASS–101, LC HABS MASS, 6–MONT 1–2)

covered bridges in Ohio, two in New York, two in Pennsylvania, and one in Massachusetts.

In Ohio, HABS has recorded an unusual two-lane or "double-barreled" bridge with two outside sidewalks (figs. 18, 19). It was designed to handle heavy urban traffic across the Mahoning River at Newton Falls in Trumbull County. Devised and patented in 1840 by William Howe of Massachusetts (uncle of Elias Howe, the inventor of the sewing machine), this type had iron rods as an integral part of its design and marked the transition between American wooden and iron bridges. The truss plan was promoted in Ohio by Howe's brother-in-law, Amasa Stone, a Cleveland financier and railroad magnate.

A second Ohio bridge still stands over Big Darby Creek in Union County. It used the patented design of Reuben L. Partridge (fig. 20). For fifty years Partridge, who came to Ohio from New York State, dominated bridge building

in the west-central Ohio region. A third Ohio example is a 183-foot single-span bridge which stood over Seven Mile Creek near Collinsville in Butler County (fig. 21). Typical of the patent bridge truss devised in 1869 by Robert W. Smith of Tippecanoe City, it was built throughout the Midwest by his Toledo-based firm.

In Ulster County, New York, HABS recorded Perrine's Bridge, an early example of the arched type of construction first patented by Theodore Burr of Connecticut in 1804 (figs. 22, 23). This type soon found wide favor with builders in New York, Pennsylvania, and Virginia, and such arched bridges later dominated construction in Indiana for several decades. Over Schoharie Creek in Schoharie County, New York, the Blenheim bridge, recorded by HABS in 1936, remains unique among American covered bridges (figs. 5, 24, 25). A two-lane span with a single central supporting arch, it was erected in

1854–55 by Vermonter Nicholas M. Powers. Its 210-foot clear span makes it today the world's longest single-span covered wooden bridge.

For Johnson's Mill Bridge over Chickies Creek, Lancaster County, Pennsylvania, the HABS collection has an unusually fine set of seven measured drawings illustrating many aspects of this 64-foot single-span Burr Truss covered bridge of 1866 (fig. 26). The drawings include cutaways that show the stone parapets, typical of the abutments found with many Pennsylvania bridges. Truss details are those used in later bridges of the Burr type down to the last mortice-and-tenon joint, nut, bolt, and washer.

Pennsylvania's Waterford Covered Bridge, in Erie County, represents a typical Town lattice-type covered bridge, in the details of both its substructure and superstructure (fig. 27). Invented and patented in 1820 by Ithiel Town of New Haven, Connecticut, this wholly American bridge truss was composed of easily obtainable latticed planks. Much less difficult to erect than an arch bridge, the lattice-type bridge was built in all the Eastern seaboard states from Maine to Mississippi. The architect-patentee received a good income from royalties paid for the use of this invention, which was also used abroad (fig. 4).

The Montague City Covered Bridge across the Connecticut River in Franklin County, Massachusetts, was the longest in America at the time of its loss in the flood waters of March 1936. Although the exterior and interior photographs made for HABS by Arthur Haskell in 1934 are better than usual for this period (figs. 1, 28), they can but partially reveal the bridge's construction. Only measured drawings could have fully explained William Howe's wood-and-iron truss plan, with its addition of auxiliary arches in five spans covering 754 feet (fig. 29). This structure served vehicular traffic inside and a single-track railroad on its roof. One can imagine the fright of a skittish horse when caught on the

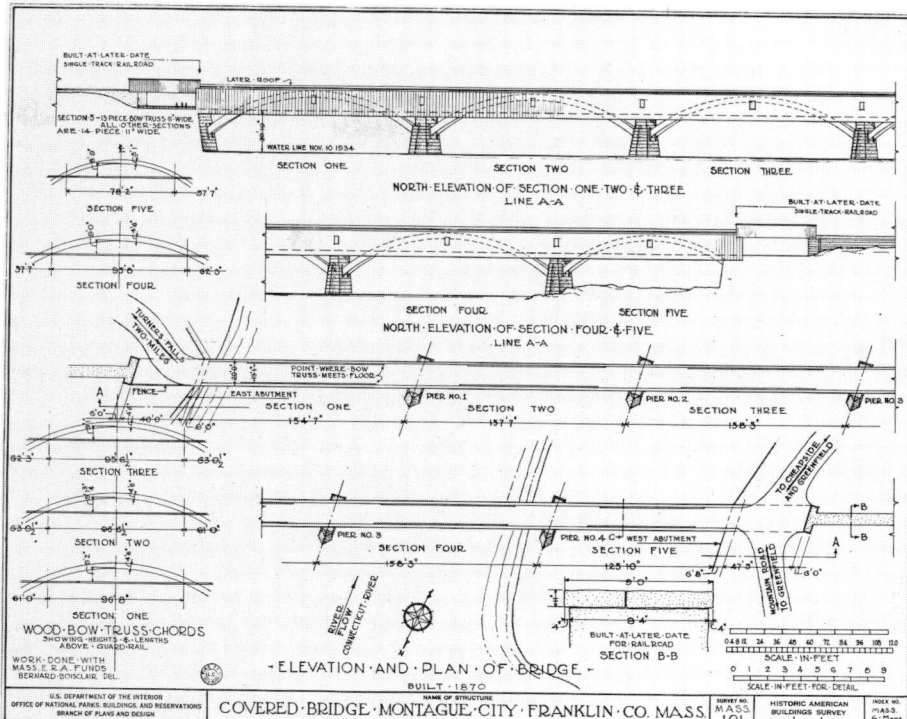

bridge as a train came rumbling across overhead.

Though small and little-known, the nucleus of covered bridge photographs and drawings from the early 1930s in the HABS collection was widely appreciated from its beginnings by a handful of engineering historians and later by the growing number of people who became interested in covered bridges as a hobby. Since the original HABS activities in the 1930s, the National Park Service has continued to make records of historic structures that come under its care. The Historic American Engineering Record, established in 1969, now covers the field of historic bridges: wooden, wire, iron, stone, and concrete.

A joint project of the National Park Service, the Library of Congress, and the American Society of Civil Engineers, HAER continues to provide documentation on engineering landmarks and significant structures, including numerous bridges throughout the nation, so that even if the structures themselves are destroyed, permanent records will remain. HAER does more than take

Figure 29 Measured drawing for the covered bridge at Montague City in Franklin County, Massachusetts. Drawing by Bernard Boisclair. (HABS MASS–101, sheet 1 of 4 sheets)

Figure 30 Documentation has improved in the past half a century. The HABS files on the 1859 Suspension Bridge over the Kaskaskia River at Carlyle, Illinois, contained little more than this 1936 photograph and a historical note that "Griffith D. Smith of Pennsylvania" was its builder. Photograph by Clark Bullard, 1936. (HABS ILL–225, LC HABS ILL, 14–CARL, 1–3)

103

Figure 31 The exhaustive coverage given in 1969–71 to John Roebling's Delaware River Aqueduct between Lackawaxen, Pennsylvania, and Minisink Ford, New York, includes forty-nine pages of data and photographs, plus field notes. This unusual canal-into-highway structure is the oldest existing suspension bridge in the United States. Photograph by David Plowden. (HAER PA–1, LC HAER PA, 52–LACK, 1–7)

photographs and prepare original measured drawings. Today a bridge nominated for inclusion in the Record may become the subject of extensive historical reports, technical analysis, photogrammetric stereopairs, and, in some cases, even motion pictures. Thus today's complete files are usually much richer than those created in the 1930s. When we compare the single photograph and three data pages prepared by HABS in 1936 for the 1859 wire suspension span across the Kaskaskia River at Carlyle, Illinois (fig. 30), to HAER's 1969–71 records for the Delaware and Hudson Canal Aqueduct (fig. 31) at Lackawaxen, Pennsylvania, of 1847–48, the difference becomes clear. The latter, documenting the earliest surviving work by John Roebling and probably the oldest suspension bridge in the United States, include field notes (1968), four sheets of drawings (1969), fourteen photo-

graphic copies of historical documents and photographs, three aerial (1971) and sixteen ground-level photographs (1969), and twelve pages of written historical information (1971).

Between 1969 and 1976, nearly a hundred historic bridges in ten states—including thirteen of the covered wooden variety—were added to the structures illustrated with technical information at the Library of Congress. Others have been researched and photographed since 1976 and still more await nomination to the National Register of Historic Places. The gathering of information and the work of evaluation is a tremendous and continuing process, involving research, travel, people with expertise, and, of course, the necessary allocation of funds. Many significant American bridges await thorough HABS/HAER documentation, especially the metal trusses that evolved from wooden trusses in the mid-nineteeth century. Thousands of these structures are threatened by massive federal programs to improve the primary and secondary road systems in America.

Begun itself a half century ago, the HABS and HAER effort has yielded photographs, measured drawings, and related documentation of bridges and other engineering and industrial structures. These records remain continuously available both in the Library of Congress and through copies in hundreds of research collections in this country and abroad. They provide a great resource for the growing number of historians, engineers, architects, and preservationists and for the general public interested in this nation's technological achievements.

Recording a Room:
The Kitchen

by

RODRIS ROTH

The fireplace remains a symbol of the kitchen even though the cook stove long ago replaced it. Of considerable width, depth, and height, and often having a bake oven in the back wall, the fireplace of the 1600s was modified in the 1700s, its dimensions reduced and the oven moved next to it. One of the most important innovations in the history of the kitchen was the cook stove, which evolved in the 1830s and 1840s. Mass produced, it contained and controlled the heat source. Furthermore, the height of its cooking surface meant less bending and lifting for the cook.

Figure 1 The open hearth reigns in this nineteenth-century kitchen. A semi-cylindrical roasting oven has been placed before the fire, however, to supplement it in cooking. One woman prepares a fowl for roasting while the other rolls out pastry for the top crust of a pie. Various utensils have been hung on the walls, placed on shelves and tables, and stored on the floor. The basket on the floor in front, filled with food, is as accurately portrayed as the rest of the room, but it serves as well as a traditional artistic device symbolizing the earth's bountiful harvest. The illustration is the frontispiece in Esther A. Howland, *The New England Economical Housekeeper, and Family Receipt Book* (Worcester: Published by S. A. Howland, 1845). (LC–USZ62–83637)

As the stove became generally available in the nineteenth century, it took over the fireplace to make use of the flue. Sometimes a stove was placed in the fireplace recess, but more often it stood in front of the opening, hiding the fireplace, which was then usually closed up. With the advent of the stove, fireplaces were no longer required for either cooking or heating. The great hulking chimney stack with many flues became obsolete. Beginning about 1850, newly built houses had only a single narrow chimney or stovepipe in the kitchen to vent a wood or coal stove.

With the introduction of gas and electricity, the stove could be located practically anywhere and the chimney was completely eliminated. Gas ranges were in general use by 1900 and electric stoves about four decades later. Although the pipe connection fixed the location of a gas stove once it was decided on, an electric stove could be moved about and plugged in wherever there was an electric outlet. Another major change in the kitchen, the result of scientific studies of the work process, was the widespread appearance in the 1940s of the continuous work surface, which used cabinets and equipment of standardized size as components and linked stove, sink, and refrigerator.

The Historic American Buildings Survey records all

Figure 2 Kitchen mantel, Morris Goodwin House, vicinity of Salem, New Jersey. The focus of this kitchen—and many others in America— remained the fireplace, even though the hearth was no longer used in cooking. Its replacement, the cast-iron cooking range, was connected to it to make use of the flue. With the introduction of the electric stove, which could be plugged in anywhere, the connection became symbolic. Photograph by George Neuschafer, 1941. (HABS NJ−690, LC HABS NJ, 17−SAL.V, 6−8)

these types of kitchen arrangements and more with plans, elevations, sections, details, data sheets, and photographs. Photographs and drawings show detached kitchens and other outbuildings, such as ice, smoke, and milk houses, along with a few covered walkways, well covers, root cellars, pantries, cupboards, and wine cellars. Included in the survey are examples dating from the seventeenth to the twentieth century. Some are associated with simple cabins and others with modest dwellings, palatial mansions, or historic house museums. They are located in both rural and urban areas in all parts of the country, from New Jersey to Oregon and Wyoming to South Carolina.

Although the evolution of the kitchen can be traced in the HABS collections, the material does not lend itself to an in-depth examination of the room. Sources such as advertisements, directories, housekeeping manuals, cookbooks, women's magazines, architectural books, houseware catalogs, and trade journals prove far more fruitful—and direct—for a study of the kitchen. They provide specifications, names, dates, materials, and locations, information seldom found in the HABS collections. In addition, they often provide a clue to contemporary attitudes and give contemporary comments and opinions. Indeed, Siegfried Giedion used such materials in writing *Mechanization Takes Command:*

Figure 3 Mantel in kitchen, Smith House, Smithville, Alabama. As long as it stands, a fireplace may continue to serve its original functions of cooking and heating. Although nothing is known about this scene, the casual array of boxes, jars, tins, bags, and a scale lining the mantel shelf suggests that the fireplace here was still being used with some regularity in 1934. Photograph by W. N. Manning, 1934. (HABS ALA 16−544, LC HABS ALA, 34−SHOR.V, 2−7)

Figure 4 Interior—south wall—of the kitchen, Maj. John Bradford House, Kingston, Massachusetts. A popular image of colonial America is the New England fireplace of cavernous dimensions in a low-ceilinged room with exposed beams, paneled walls, and wide floor boards. It is a valid image that is documented here. Starting about the second quarter of the eighteenth century, the brick bake oven was built adjacent to the kitchen fireplace rather than within it. Photograph by Arthur C. Haskell, 1935. (HABS MASS 2–78, LC HABS MASS, 12–KING, 1–7)

Figure 5 Detail of fireplace in kitchen no. 2, San Ygnacio Ranch, San Ygnacio, Texas. This cooking fireplace, a corner type with a raised hearth, is related to a kind common in Mexico. This is not surprising since the San Ygnacio Ranch is located on the Mexican border. Photograph by Arthur W. Stewart, 1936. (HABS TEX 3–112, LC HABS TEX, 253–SANYG, 1–16)

A Contribution to Anonymous History (New York: Oxford University Press, 1948), still the best, most interesting, and most thought-provoking study of the kitchen.

Recording the kitchen was not the purpose of HABS. The Survey's purpose was—and is—to record architecture. This determined what to photograph and draw—which building, rooms within the building, and features within the room were selected. A further purpose of the Survey was to record buildings before they disappeared. Consequently, HABS concentrated its initial resources on early structures, and understandably so. The result in regard to kitchens was a great number of fireplaces being recorded because they were an architectural

feature in early houses. As a bonus, some views might include a stove, sink, or other piece of kitchen equipment because it was in front of the mantel or next to a door or another architectural element. These accidental glimpses not only show us kitchens but also how some people lived in old houses, introduced new technology, and modified their surroundings. There is much not shown, however. Whether the house was lived in by choice or necessity, whether it was a single-family dwelling or divided into apartments, and whether there were more kitchen appliances and what they were are questions not answered by HABS.

Thus some cautions about using

Figure 6 Interior of the Santana Sanchez house, Acoma Pueblo, Acoma, New Mexico. Acoma Pueblo is described as the "oldest continuously occupied settlement" in the United States. In addition to indoor corner fireplaces such as this one, which have raised hearths for cooking and heating, there are a few outdoor bake ovens of semispherical shape built against the pueblo walls. Photograph by M. James Slack, 1934. (LC HABS NM, 31–ACOMP, 1–37)

Figure 7 Kitchen in the Van Cortlandt Mansion, Bronx, New York. Many fireplaces were recorded by HABS, but the utensils for hearth cooking are seldom seen in HABS photographs. In this view, an exhibit technique once common in historic houses and museums is used to display kettles and other implements of various sizes and shapes, and materials are displayed left, right, and center. Photograph by Arnold Moses, 1937. (HABS NY−455, LC HABS NY, 3−BRONX, 5−8)

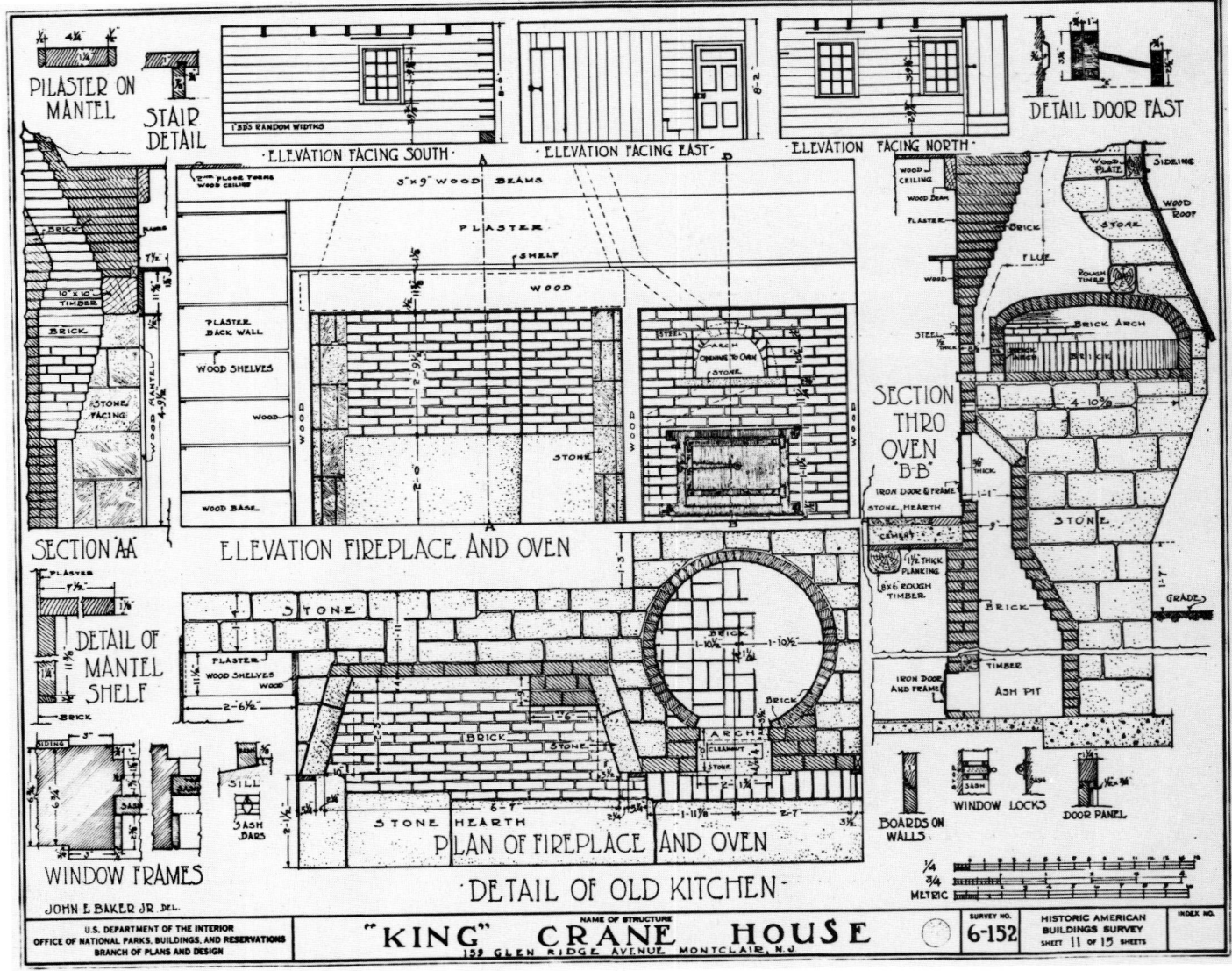

Figure 8 Detail of the old kitchen, Israel Crane house, Montclair, New Jersey. The HABS drawings of ovens and fireplaces are an important resource. This example is one of fifteen sheets recording in plans, elevations, and details the Crane house, which was built in 1797 and remodeled in 1840. Although the door or cover is missing from the oven here, drawings of many other ovens record examples in wood and metal, attached and loose. Drawing by John E. Baker, Jr., 1935. (HABS NJ 6−152, sheet 11 of 15 sheets)

Figure 9 First floor plan, Israel Crane house, Montclair, New Jersey. The original kitchen for the Israel Crane house was detached. Its fireplace and oven were the subject of a detail sheet (fig. 8) and were also noted on the floor plan. In contrast, the coal stove, gas range, and sink in the attached kitchen were not shown in elevation but appear only on the floor plan. Drawing by Anthony DeCastro, 1935. (HABS NJ 6−152, sheet 6 of 15 sheets)

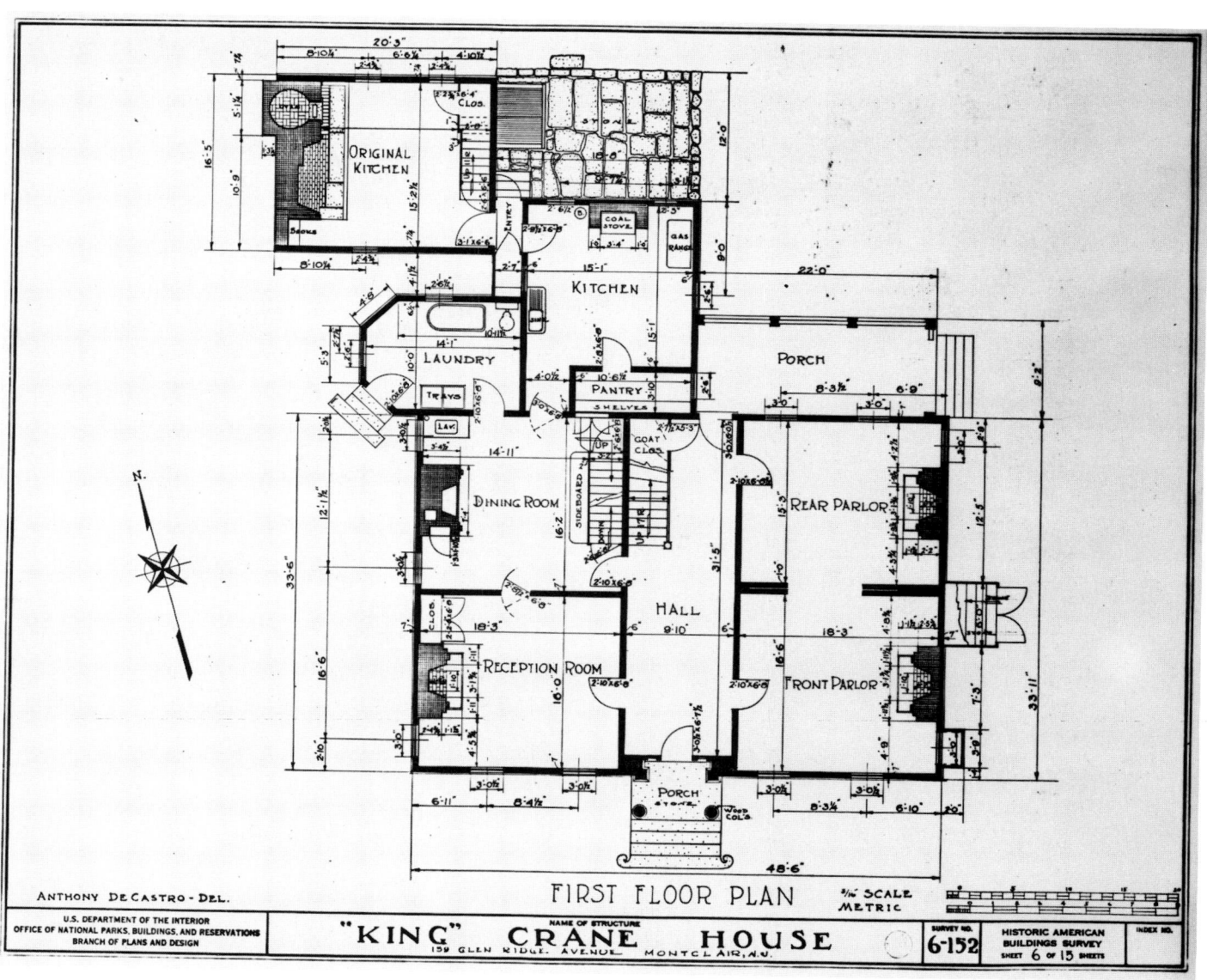

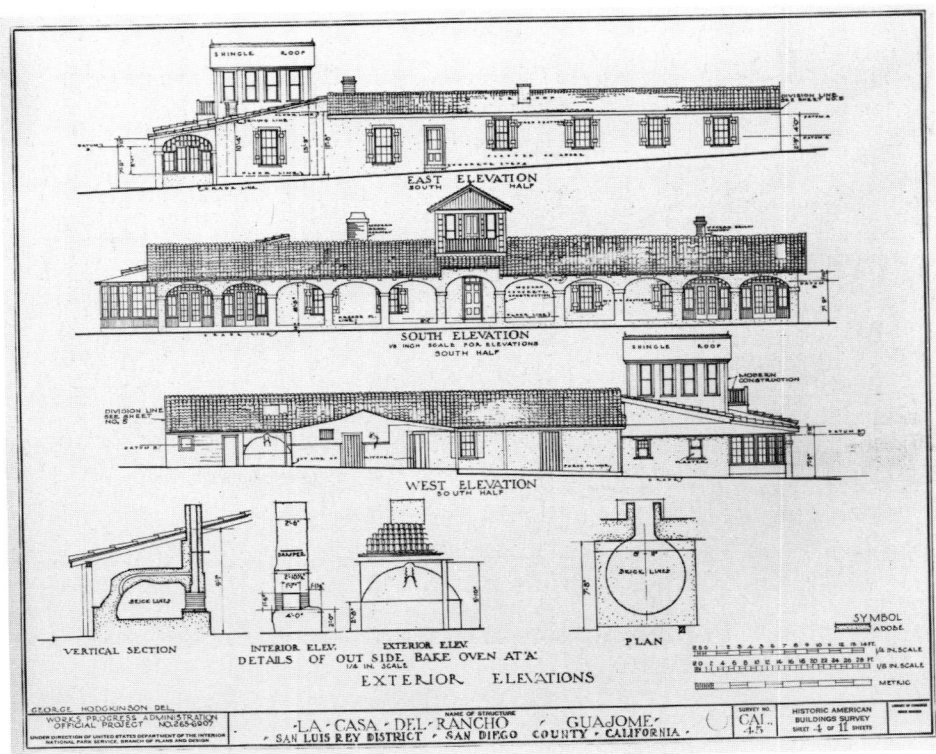

Figure 10 Exterior elevations, La Casa del Rancho Guajome, California. Built outside against the bakery's west wall, the oven of La Casa del Rancho Guajome is accented on top by the secondary flue as shown in the vertical section. The interior elevation provides a view of the oven's square opening, located between the pantry and "old kitchen." These and the other rooms of the house surrounded a square open court. Drawing by George Hodgkinson, 1937. (HABS CAL–43, sheet 4 of 11 sheets)

Figure 11 Ice house, old slave kitchen, and well house, Pitts Folly, Uniontown, Alabama. Detached kitchens are usually associated with the warm southern climate, and rightfully so. Along with outbuildings such as ice and smoke houses, wells and cisterns, and root cellars, they are a vivid reminder of the various tasks and people once required for the storage, preparation, and serving of food on plantations. Photograph by Alex Bush, 1935. (HABS ALA–267, LC HABS ALA, 53–UNITO, 1C–2)

Figure 12 Walkway from home to old kitchen, Old Carlisle Home, vicinity of Marion, Alabama. A detached kitchen necessitated the carrying of food between it and the house. A symbol of this traffic is the covered walkway. The one shown linked an Italian villa-style brick house and its kitchen. Photograph by Alex Bush, 1937. (HABS ALA−765, LC HABS ALA, 53−MARI, 5A−3)

Figure 13 Full-size Rumford Roaster details, Captain Barnes house, Portsmouth, New Hampshire. An oval brass nameplate identified the Rumford Roaster. It carried the name Joseph Howe. Howe was listed in the Boston directories from 1789 to 1818 as a tinplate worker at No. 7 Marshall's Lane, the address given on the Barnes house roaster. The inset nameplate shows the Cutter house roaster was made by tinplate workers Cate and Badger of Portsmouth, New Hampshire. Drawing by John C. Fletcher, 1936. (HABS NH−26, sheet 56 of 65 sheets)

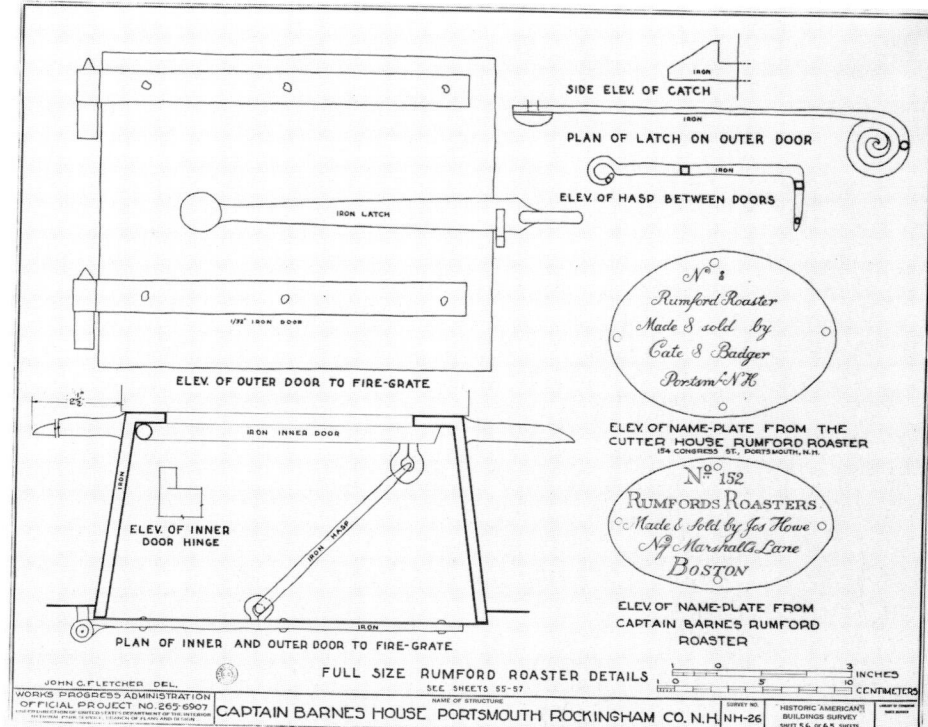

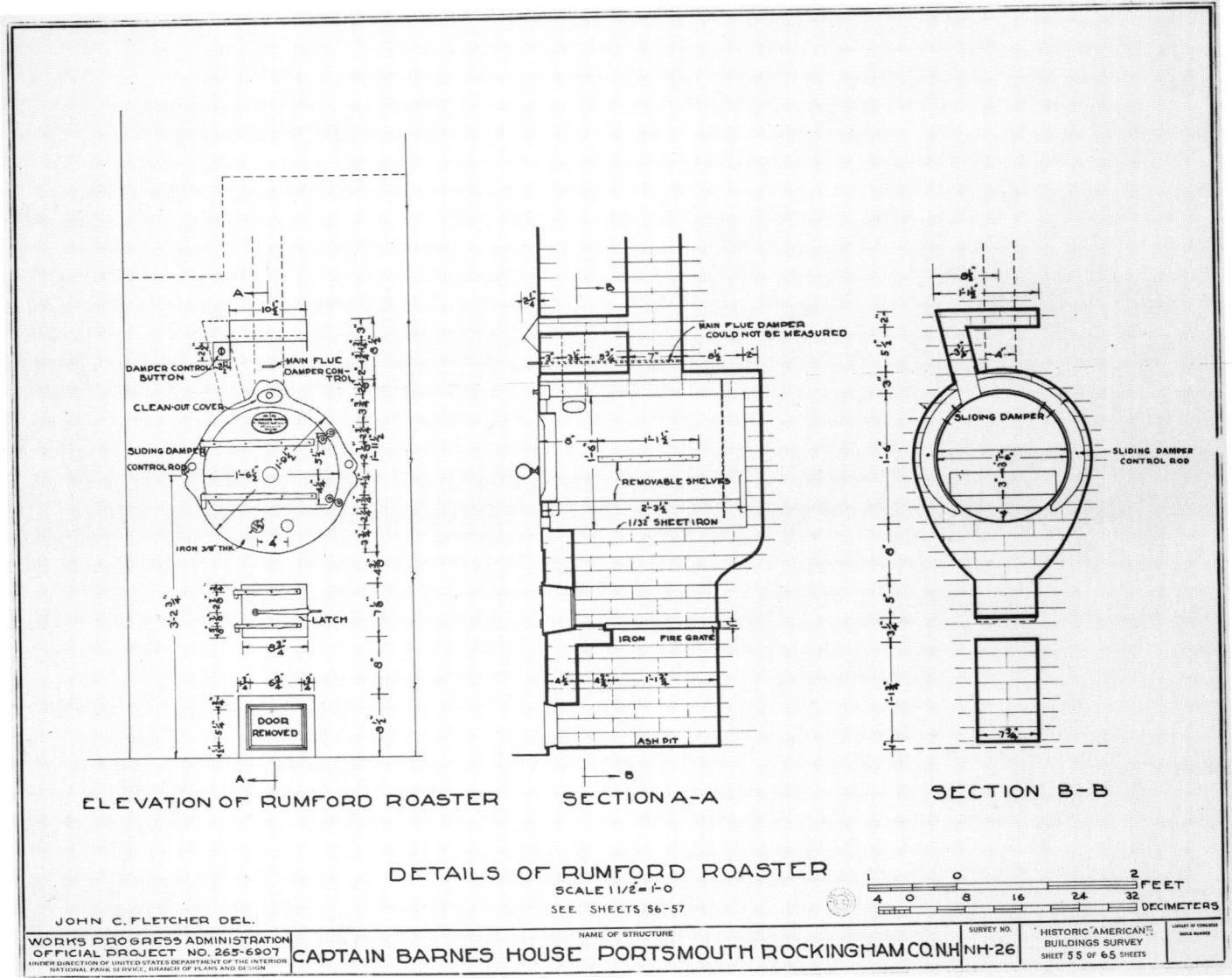

Figure 14 Details of Rumford Roaster, Captain Barnes house, Portsmouth, New Hampshire. The Rumford Roaster, a "Contrivance for roasting Meat," was described by its inventor as "a hollow cylinder of sheet iron . . . closed at one end, and set in a horizontal position in a mass of brick-work" so that "the flame of a small fire" might "heat it equally and expeditiously." Drawing by John C. Fletcher, 1936. (HABS NH–26, sheet 55 of 65 sheets)

Figure 15 Kitchen, Captain Barnes house, Portsmouth, New Hampshire. An improvement over the fireplace, the Rumford Roaster was itself displaced by the stove, as in the Barnes house kitchen. Its round door (on the left) goes almost unnoticed because two large ranges dominate the picture, one in front of another that is set partially in the fireplace. Photograph by L. C. Durette, 1936. (HABS NH−26, LC HABS NH, 8−PORT, 124−15)

Figure 16   The oven is ready, its door ajar, as the mistress of the kitchen prepares another pan of dough to be baked. Staples are stored in an adjacent pantry. Although a stove has replaced the open hearth, the same kind of shelf remains above it, and, as in kitchens of thirty years earlier, it still holds a clock and lamps. Lighting devices were brought to the kitchen for cleaning and refueling—in mid-century with whale oil and here in 1879 with kerosene. "B. F. Barton & Co.'s Peerless Yeast Powder." Engraved by D. Van Vleck. Trademark registered by B. F. Barton, September 23, 1879. Popular and Applied Graphic Art Collections, Prints and Photographs Division. (LC–USZ62–83638)

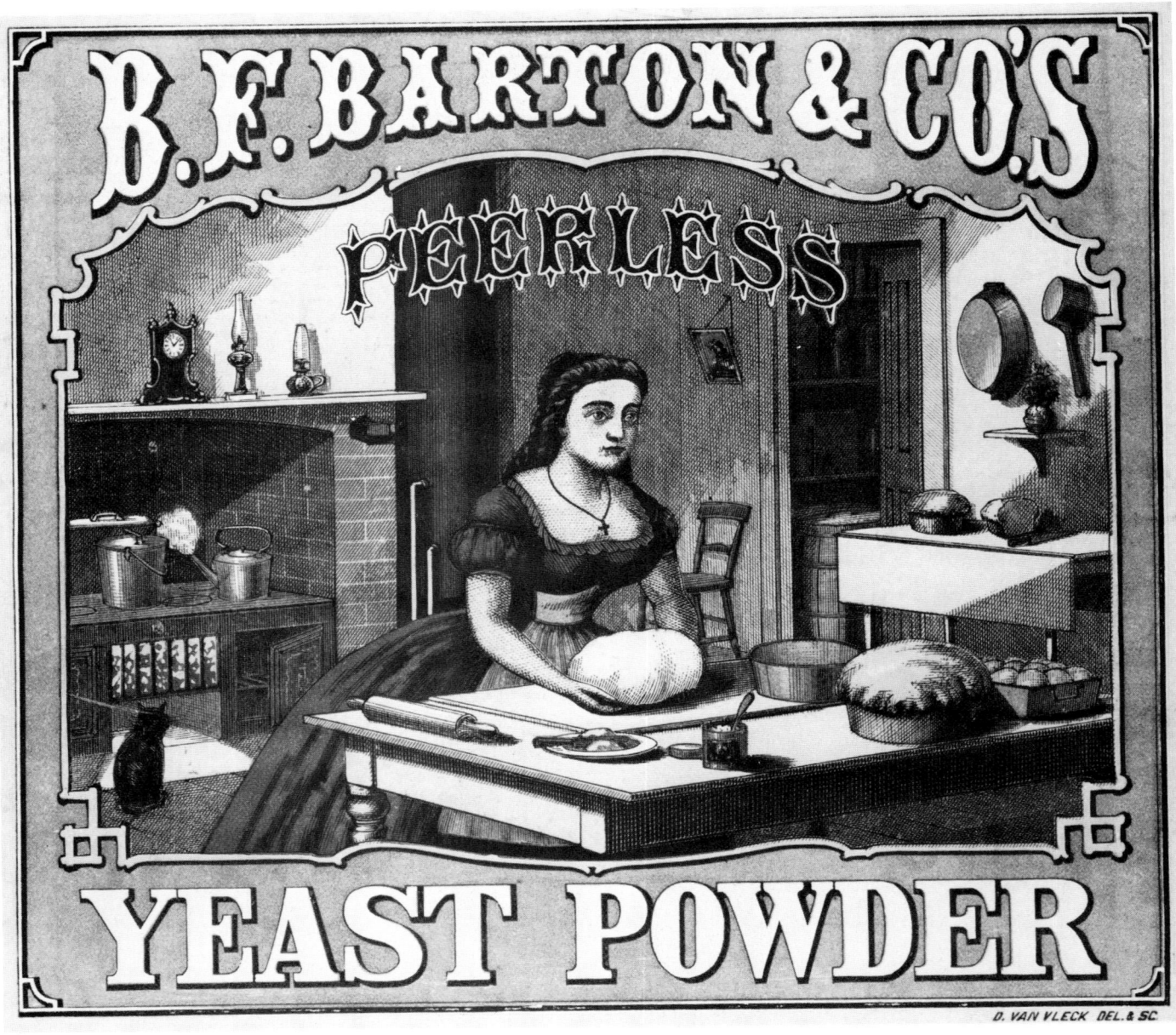

Figure 17 Detail of a kitchen stove, William A. Farnsworth Homestead, Rockland, Maine. Looking like a buffet or sideboard, this cast-iron range, a model no. 7 by George W. Walker and Co., Boston, is a form seen in advertisements and pictures beginning about 1875. As in this instance, the range was sometimes connected to a "bath boiler," which stored water hot from having been piped through the range. Photograph by Cervin Robinson, 1960. (HABS ME−77, LC HABS ME, 7−ROCLA, 1−8)

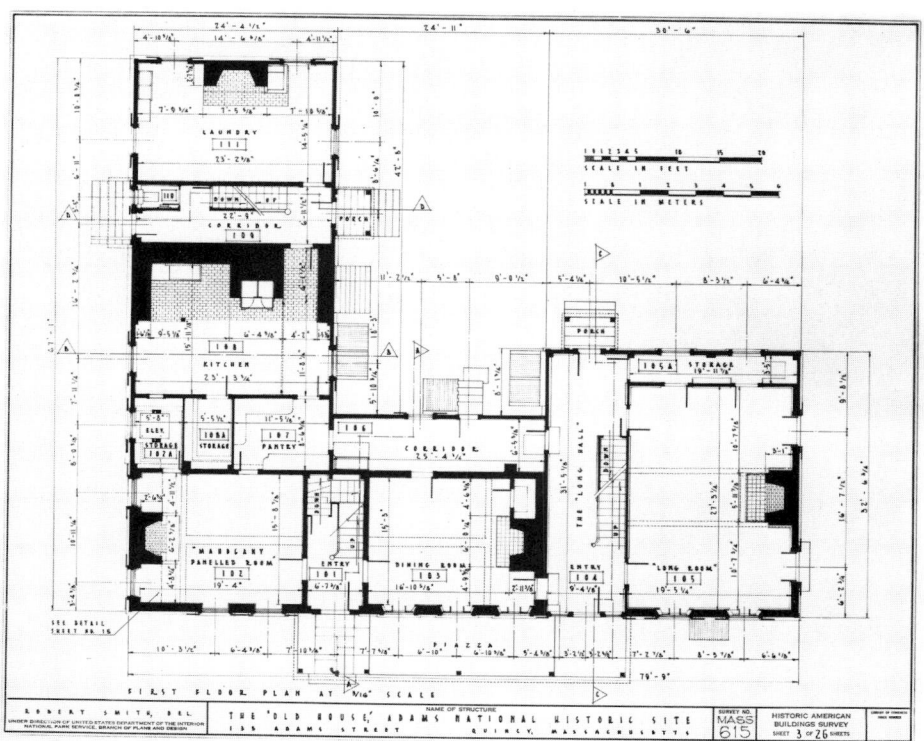

Figure 18 First floor plan, the Adams Mansion or "Old House," Adams National Historic Site, Quincy, Massachusetts. Placed in a specially built brick pier or fireplace, the buffetlike range with its high and low "hot closets," or warming chambers, was an imposing piece of equipment. In the Adams family house, it was the only stove noted on the kitchen floor plan. The elevation provides a different picture (fig. 19). Drawing by Robert Smith, 1955−56. (HABS MASS−615, sheet 3 of 26 sheets)

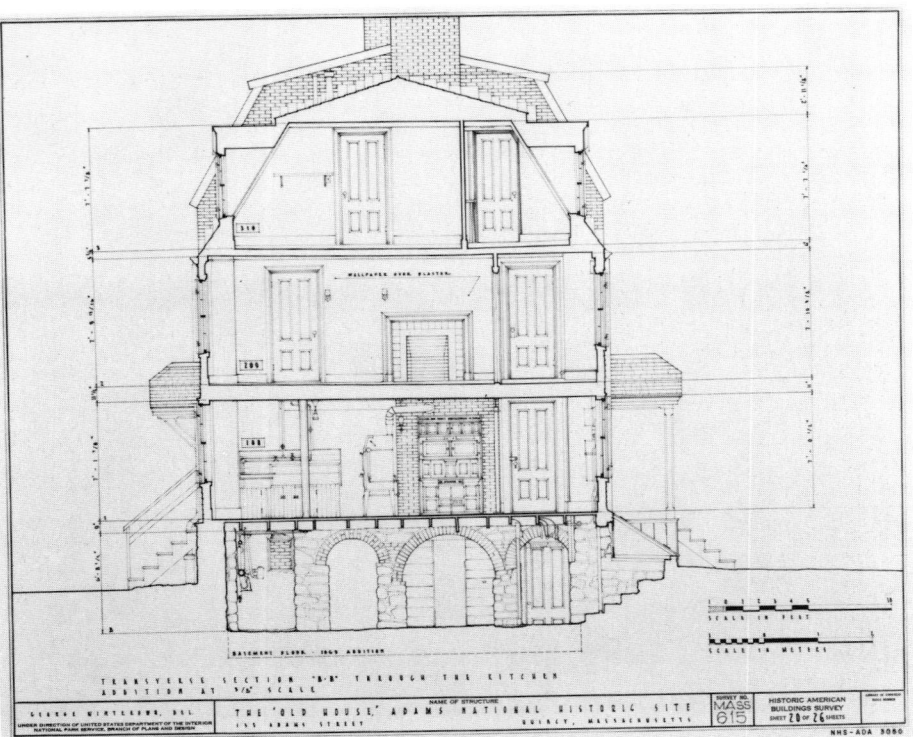

Figure 19 Transverse Section "B-B" through the kitchen, the Adams Mansion or "Old House," Adams National Historic Site, Quincy, Massachusetts. In the Adams Mansion, the cast-iron range shared the kitchen, we learn from the elevation, with a cook stove of the early 1900s, its console raised on tall legs and the oven placed adjacent to the cooking top. Sink, drainboard, and enclosed cupboard are also recorded, expanding our view of the kitchen. Drawing by George Winterowd, 1955–56. (HABS MASS–615, sheet 20 of 26 sheets)

Figure 20 Southeast room—kitchen; Limerick, near Cordsville, South Carolina. The stove continues to be superimposed on the fireplace as long as a fireplace is available and the stove is fueled by wood or coal, which require venting. Furthermore, by adding a cook stove plus pots and pans a room can easily become a kitchen regardless of its original use. Photograph by Frederick D. Nichols, 1940. (HABS SC–8, LC HABS SC, 8–CORD.V, 1–9)

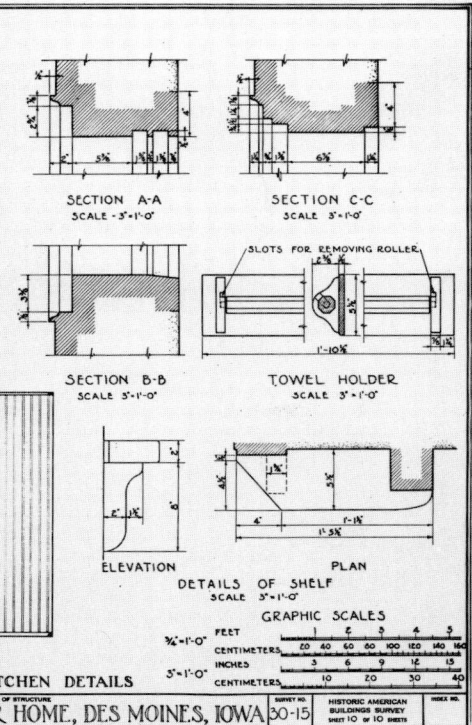

SECTION A-A
SCALE 3"=1'-0"
SECTION C-C
SCALE 3"=1'-0"
SLOTS FOR REMOVING ROLLER
SECTION B-B
SCALE 3"=1'-0"
TOWEL HOLDER
SCALE 3"=1'-0"
ELEVATION
PLAN
DETAILS OF SHELF
SCALE 3"=1'-0"
GRAPHIC SCALES
FEET
CENTIMETERS
INCHES
CENTIMETERS
ITCHEN DETAILS
R HOME, DES MOINES, IOWA
30-15
HISTORIC AMERICAN BUILDINGS SURVEY
SHEET 10 OF 10 SHEETS

Figure 21 Kitchen details, the Barlow Granger home, Des Moines, Iowa. As the cooking stove became generally available during the middle of the nineteenth century, there was no longer a need for a fireplace in a newly built house. A narrow single chimney became evidence of a kitchen. This room in the Barlow Granger home dating from the late 1800s contains another characteristic kitchen piece, the sink. Drawing by B. E. Landes, 1934. (HABS IO 30–15, sheet 10 of 10 sheets)

Figure 22 Detail of stove and chimney in south room, Dakota Street or Jean Chipp Cabin, South Pass City, Wyoming. A ubiquitous sight in kitchens well into the 1900s was the cast-iron cook stove with its connecting stovepipe and simple chimney. (This one recorded in the Dakota Street Cabin is a No. 816 "Prize Novelty" by Abram Cox Stove Company.) Just as common were the cupboard in the corner and table beneath the window seen in the log cabin's kitchen and eating room. Photograph by Jack E. Boucher, 1974. (HABS WYO–33, LC HABS WYO, 7–SOPAC, 6–4)

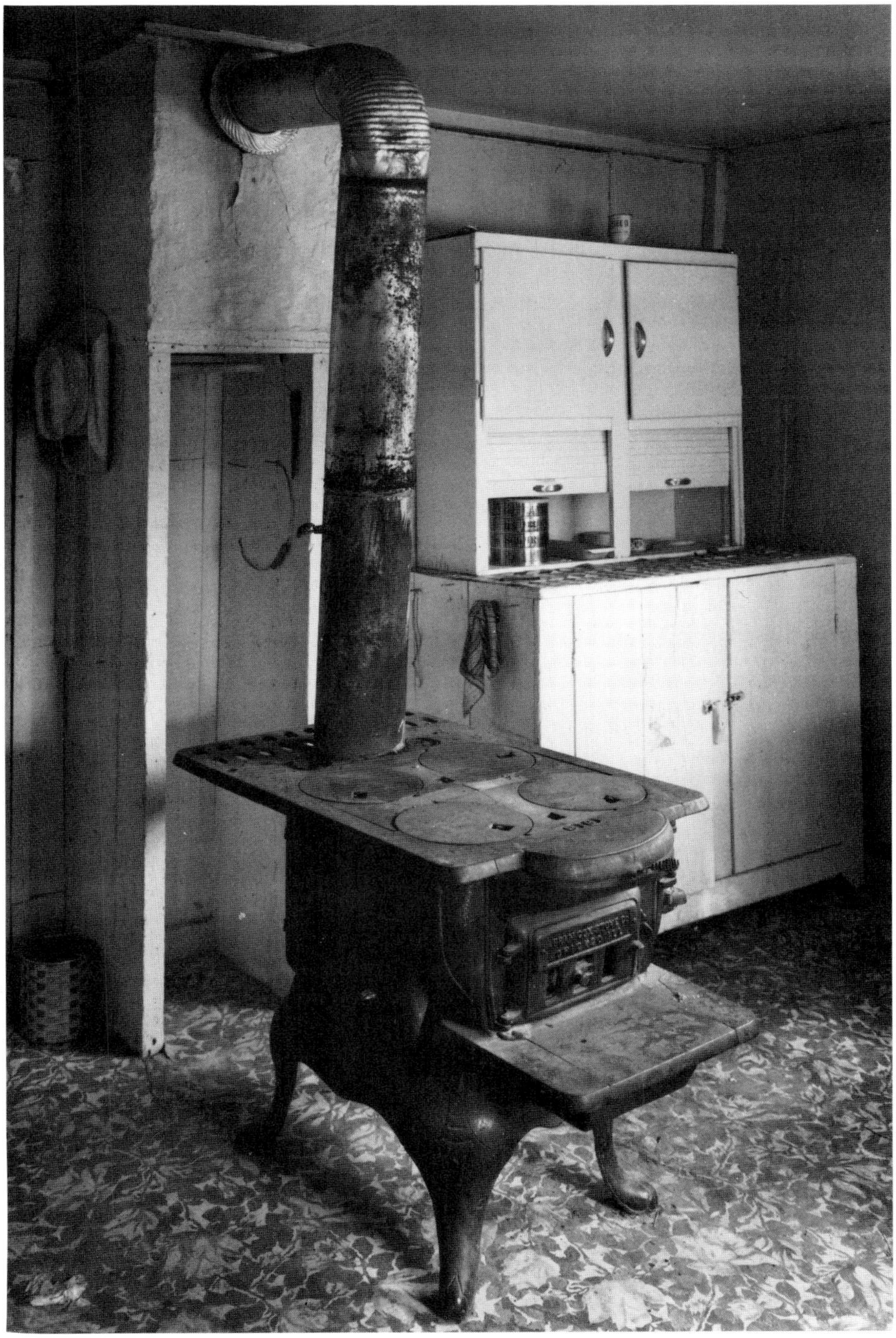

Figure 23 Kitchen from the west, Beekman house, Jacksonville, Oregon. Representing the late 1800s, this kitchen is a restoration in a historic house museum. Its verisimilitude is striking at first glance and reflects quite a different approach to presenting the past from that of a kitchen simply displaying a variety of wares associated with cooking. Photograph by Jack E. Boucher, 1971. (HABS ORE−60, LC HABS ORE, 15−JACVI, 49−7)

Figure 24 "An Electric Kitchen." Contemporary pictures of kitchens do not necessarily show the newest equipment, arrangements, or techniques. They do, however, record the room as seen by someone familiar with it and reveal prevailing attitudes and practices, especially when they show people using the room. This kitchen is specifically identified as "sketched from one in operation," which suggests the newness and novelty of electricity as a fuel in 1894. In fact, it had just been introduced into the kitchen. Although today's appliances may appear more streamlined, their arrangement remains about the same. Illustration by William Mayer, in *The Woman's Book: Dealing Practically with the Modern Conditions of Home-Life, Self-Support, Education, Opportunities, and Every-day Problems*, vol. 1 (New York: Charles Scribner's Sons, 1894).

Figure 25 Typical kitchen, Henry B. Babson estate (stable and service buildings), Riverside, Illinois. Part of the Babson estate designed in 1915 by the firm of Purcell and Elmslie, the service buildings were converted to residences in the 1930s. The cupboards may date from the remodeling and the material on the doors over the counter appears to be even more recent, but these seem compatible with the original windows and sink that distinguish this kitchen. Copy of a photograph, ca. 1956. (HABS ILL–1068, LC HABS ILL, 16-RIVSI, 1A–12)

Figure 26 Kitchen, Oxon Hill Manor, Oxon Hill, Maryland. Oxon Hill Manor is a Neo-Georgian country mansion designed in 1928 by Jules Henri de Sibour for career diplomat Sumner Welles. Planned to be run by a staff, the kitchen retains most of its original fixtures. The cupboards held kitchen wares. The china, crystal, and silver were stored in a separate pantry. Photograph by Jack E. Boucher, 1971. (HABS MD–301, LC HABS MD, 17– OXHI, 1–10)

Figure 27 Kitchen, Brown-Wagner house, Brownsville, Texas. Although the Brown-Wagner house was built in 1894, the kitchen dates from about the 1940s, judging from the equipment. Presumably, it was remodeled. At that time, the cabinet, counter, and sink that formed a continuous work surface, the semicircular shelves framing the window, and the "table top" stove were popular and readily available. Photograph by Bill Engdahl of Hedrich-Blessing, Photographers, 1979. (HABS TX–3271, LC HABS TEX, 31–BROWN, 3–11)

the collections are in order. The information gathered varies from structure to structure. Sometimes it is copious, and other times it is skimpy. Even if construction dates are provided, some of what is seen in any photograph may be more recent. Whatever was in view of the camera was recorded. Room function may have changed. In some houses, for instance, the original kitchen had become a living room by the time the house was surveyed. Yet often a room's compass point location was recorded but no indication was given of the room's use at the time it was documented, with all that that might have told us about shifts in per-

ceptions and customs. Alterations and additions may not have been noted or even recognized at the time the building was recorded. Later users of the collections can easily be led astray. It is well to remember that with HABS materials one is dealing with raw and often incomplete data, and considerable expertise is required in identifying and using it.

Occasionally, kitchens were recorded for their own sake, of course, as were other rooms. I examined virtually all the HABS photographs for this brief foray into the kitchen. I found approximately fifteen photographs specifically of kitchens, six of stoves, and eight of the fireplace-and-stove combinations. There were about one hundred photographs of kitchen fireplaces, however. The preponderance of fireplaces is explained in part by the interest in recording early buildings before they disappeared and in part by its symbolic import. As buildings of more recent date are surveyed, the opportunities to include kitchens increases.

The careful renderings of bake ovens and fireplaces, although not unique to HABS, constitute a useful group of material readily available in one place for the study of these important kitchen features. For instance, size and shape can be compared, regional characteristics charted, and construction variations examined, helping us to understand cooking routines and, in turn, living patterns. As usual, with any of the HABS pictures, one must be alert for remodeling, repairs, and restoration of the object recorded.

Floor plans and elevations are another resource for the study of kitchens. One must check all the drawings and photographs of a given structure, however, as equipment shown on a floor plan may not be recorded on the elevation, or vice versa. In any event, HABS drawings can tell us about the size and location of fireplaces and ovens and the placement of more recent equipment. They reveal the orientation of the kitchen and its relation to the rest of the house, providing insights into, say, concepts of space and social customs.

Finding measured drawings of a Rumford Roaster was serendipitous. Once seen, there is no mistaking the "new Contrivance for roasting Meat" invented in the late 1700s by the American-born Sir Benjamin Thompson, Count Rumford (figs. 13, 14). All one ordinarily sees of the built-in roaster is the circle iron frame with its door, repeating the roaster's shape and punctuated with shiny brass knobs, buttons, fasteners, and an oval name plate.

How the roaster was constructed and installed can be better understood thanks to the HABS drawings. They add to the limited information available on the roaster beyond Rumford's own writings.

There is a revival of interest in the kitchen among historians, curators, and the public. The recent emphasis on history "from the ground up" has helped to focus attention on the household. The women's history movement has been a potent force, too, in turning our attention to some of the fundamental issues of housekeeping and the role of women. Curators of historic houses and museums, of course, have long been exploring home life. As the guardians of material culture, displaying the kitchen and its contents, they have fostered the study of household technology. All of this helps us to look anew at the past and at our sources for its study. The HABS material presents a fragmented picture of the kitchen because it focuses on architectural highlights. Nevertheless, as more is learned about household technology and as our understanding of daily life expands, various facets of the HABS collection may prove to be useful resources for studying the past.

Figure 28 East wall of drawing room, 271 Meeting Street, Charleston, South Carolina. The purpose of this picture—and indeed of the Historic American Buildings Survey—is to record the architectural setting, not the kitchen. This is clear from the title of the photograph and accompanying instruction, "Note pseudo-door at right for purpose of symmetry." Nevertheless, in recording this room the HABS team, as in many other instances, inadvertently recorded the kitchen too. Photograph by C. O. Green, 1940. (HABS SC–217, LC HABS SC, 10–CHAR, 12–1)

Fittings and Fixtures: Miscellaneous Americana in Survey Photographs

by

DENYS PETER MYERS

It takes more than a week to give even a fleeting glance to the thousands of photographs in the Historic American Buildings Survey Collection in the Prints and Photographs Division of the Library of Congress. Anyone who looks through the entire HABS photograph collection, however hastily, is almost certain to be lured astray into fascinating byways unconnected with the principal subject of his or her research. Delightful surprises, as well as occasional disappointments, wait there for the researcher even faintly interested in Americana.

My primary purpose in looking through the multitudinous loose-leaf binders containing HABS photographs was to find illustrations of nineteenth-century lighting fixtures in their original settings. In all, I noted almost three hundred pictures of lighting fixtures—as distinct from movable lighting devices—but every so often other fixtures, such as plumbing, heating, and hardware, were of such interest that they fairly begged for attention. Occasionally, decorative features were so outstanding that I could not pass them by. And although I was not specifically seeking them, photographs that illustrated such widely diverse subjects as Victorian domestic furniture and wheeled vehicles turned out to be so beguiling that they compelled my notice.

To begin with the most unexpected surprise of all, I must mention a particularly fine nineteenth-century carriage recorded by the Survey. A 1937 interior photograph of the carriage shed of the Morris House, a property of the New Haven Colony Historical Society now known as the Pardee-Morris House, shows a resplendent "Scroll-Back Quarter Caleche Coach," illustrated as no. 109 in the

Figure 1 Stair hall, Wickham-Valentine House, Richmond, Virginia. The Wickham-Valentine House, now a part of the Valentine Museum, was built in 1812. Recent research by Pamela J. Scott and Edward F. Zimmer has demonstrated that the house, long attributed to Robert Mills, was in fact designed by Alexander Parris (Zimmer and Scott, "Alexander Parris, B. Henry Latrobe, and the John Wickham House in Richmond, Virginia," *Journal of the Society of Architectural Historians* 41:202–11). In 1854 the house was lavishly redecorated in the mid-century Neo-Rococo style. Two splendid gas chandeliers installed in 1854 remain, one in the parlor and one in the hall. Both are probably by Cornelius and Baker of Philadelphia. The hall chandelier is two-tiered, with a three-light section lighting the upper hall. Photograph by Frederick Doveton Nichols, 1940. (HABS VA, 44–RICH, 5–4)

Figure 2 Carriage shed, Morris House, New Haven, New Haven County, Connecticut. The Morris House was given to the New Haven Colony Historical Society by a member of the Pardee family. The carriage shed was added in the 1930s. The coach bears two labels of Lawrence, Bradley & Pardee and is illustrated in that firm's catalog. Curiously, another New Haven coachmaker, G. & D. Cook & Company, used the same wood engraving to illustrate the "Hamilton Coach" in their 1860 catalog. The Cook coach was priced at $1,200. The extant model has silver-plated hardware and space for two footmen behind. It is as elaborate a carriage as was ever made in America. A decade earlier the coachman's box would probably have been concealed by a lavishly trimmed hammercloth like the one on the Saltonstall coach in the Smithsonian Institution, but by the 1860s hammercloths were obsolescent. The quarter caleche is now on loan to the Eli Whitney Museum in New Haven. Photograph by James Rainey, 1937. (LC HABS CONN, 5– NEWHA, 8A–1)

1862 catalog of the New Haven coachmaker Lawrence, Bradley & Pardee (fig. 2). It sold for $800 to $1,000 in an age when laborers were paid $1 a day.

Other wheeled contrivances in HABS photographs that are of interest include an ancient wheelbarrow at the Major Isaac Foster House at Manchester, Massachusetts, a wooden hand truck at the Swetland Store in Wyoming, Pennsylvania, a later hand truck at the Union Pacific Station in

Cheyenne, Wyoming, and a Concord stagecoach in a HABS copy of a nineteenth-century photograph of Chugwater, Wyoming (fig. 4). Nor should one forget the handsome sleigh at Springwood, President Franklin Delano Roosevelt's house, in Hyde Park, New York. The most impressive of all nineteenth-century wheeled contrivances—the steam locomotive—is well represented by six iron horses in the roundhouse of the Virginia and Truckee Railroad in Carson City, Nevada (figs. 5, 6).

In interior views, HABS photographs record eye-catching decorative features of buildings. I found, for instance, a few examples of etched-glass door panels, of which those in the Governor Henry Lippitt House in Providence, Rhode Island, were the most outstanding (fig. 7). Other details, such as wallpapers or carpets—for which the color was lost in black-and-white photographs—were not frequently captured. One wallpaper at least should be mentioned, however, as it is a rare example called "Décor Chasse et Pêche" or "Renaissance," first issued by S. Lapeyre in 1847 and later by Jules Desfossé. It adorns the parlor

(147)

G. & D. COOK & CO.

No. 104.

HAMILTON COACH.

Figure 3 An illustration of the Hamilton Coach from the G. & D. Cook & Company catalog originally published in 1860. From *G. & D. Cook & Co.'s Illustrated Catalogue of Carriages and Special Business Advertiser* (1860; reprint, New York: Dover Publications, 1970).

Figure 4 Manager's house and original station-hotel, destroyed in 1918, of the Cheyenne-Black Hills Stage Line, Chugwater, Platte County, Wyoming, now part of the Swan Land and Cattle Company. This station was in the first division of the Cheyenne-Black Hills Stage and Express Line, and the team of four appears ready to pull out a Concord-type coach driven by one George Lathrop, accompanied by an unidentified sharpshooter and a female passenger holding an anxious white puppy. Copy of an 1884 photograph. (HABS WYO–71, LC HABS WYO, 16–CHUGW, 1–3)

Figure 5 Two-horse sleigh with coachman and footman in livery and an unidentified woman riding in it, presumably at Springwood, Hyde Park, Dutchess County, New York. This historical photograph was incidentally copied together with other family photographs when a HABS team recorded the Franklin Delano Roosevelt House in the summer of 1941. The site is now the Franklin D. Roosevelt National Historic Site. (HABS NY–4, LC HABS NY, 14–HYP, 5–)

Figure 6 Virginia and Truckee Railroad Roundhouse, Carson City, Ormsby County, Nevada. The Virginia and Truckee Railroad operated nineteenth-century steam locomotives and wooden passenger coaches until it ceased operations in 1950. The roundhouse was constructed between 1872 and 1874. The Virginia and Truckee ran between Virginia City, Nevada, and Truckee, California. It was one of the most famous short line railroads in the world during the 1870s when it carried the immense wealth of silver produced by the Comstock Lode. The antique rolling stock has starred in numerous motion pictures. HABS photograph, 1939. (LC HABS NEV, 13–CARCI, 6–3)

Figure 7 Dining room door detail, Governor Henry Lippitt House, Providence, Providence County, Rhode Island. The splendidly finished Lippitt House was designed by Henry Childs and erected between 1862 and 1865. It retains its original fittings and much of its original furniture. The black walnut and curly maple dining room doors contain lavishly ornamented etched-glass panels and are fitted with silver-plated hardware. Deer, a favorite motif in mid-nineteenth-century dining rooms, appear on the carved black walnut built-in sideboard and on the bronze gas chandelier as well as on the glass door panels. One of Sir Edwin Landseer's paintings may have been the source for this etched-glass vignette. His *Monarch of the Glen* and *Stag at Bay* were two of the most frequently reproduced paintings of the last century. Photograph by Laurence E. Tilley, 1958. (LC HABS RI, 4−PROV, 136−28)

Figure 8 South wall of the library, Thomas Jefferson Southard House, Richmond, Sagadahoc County, Maine. An Italianate mansion, the Southard House was built in 1855. The elaborately appointed parlor is papered in a splendid sharp blue, golden brown, white, and gold paper on a soft gray field. One of the most spectacular French panel sets, this pattern was designed in 1846 by an artist named Wagner and first issued by S. Lapeyre in 1847. It was reissued by Jules Desfossé in 1859−60. Another set survives in a house in Portland, Maine. The Southard parlor is further enriched by a lavishly carved white marble mantelpiece and an ormolu chandelier by the Philadelphia gas fixture firm of Cornelius and Baker. The house is now the St. Alexander Nevsky Foundation, a Russian Orthodox geriatric home established by a Romanov princess. Photograph by Dwight R. Sturgis, 1971. (LC HABS ME, 12−RICH, 2−9)

Figure 9 Interior detail, tin sheathing on walls and ceiling, of the Sig Sautelle Circus Training House (also known as the George Satterly House), Homer, Cortland County, New York. This octagonal structure was built in 1902 for George Satterly (1850–1928), a circus owner. Satterly's family occupied the first two floors, and the third floor was a training area for acrobats. Satterly adopted the stage name Signor Sautelle—evidently pronounced sig-nor, as his friends called him Sig. He started his circus in 1875 and eventually sold his enterprise to a Barnum affiliate in 1904. The training house had become a restaurant by 1964. Photograph by Jack E. Boucher, 1966. (LC HABS NY, 12–HOM, 2–4)

Figure 10 Parlor (seen from the entrance vestibule, looking northeast) of the Francis J. Dewes House, Chicago, Cook County, Illinois. The parlor of this beer baron's mansion is almost manic in its ostentation. The swirling Neo-Rococo forms are far more heavy than their eighteenth-century prototypes. The Watteauesque ceiling painting is the most charming feature of the room. There are unintentionally comic touches, such as the putto in the center of the picture who seems about to make an impolite gesture and the resigned expression of the caryatid at the left. The room was intended to overwhelm—and it succeeds. Photograph by Harold Allen, 1964. (LC HABS ILL, 16–CHIG, 45–3)

Figure 11 Window latch, central room, first floor, north wall, Stephen Girard Country House, Philadelphia, Philadelphia County, Pennsylvania. Casement windows are rare in eighteenth- and early nineteenth-century American buildings. This window latch is of a distinctly European type. Possibly Stephen Girard's French antecedents explain his preference for casements rather than double-hung sash. Photograph by Jack E. Boucher, 1962. (LC HABS PA, 51−PHILA, 226−21)

Figure 12 Classroom doorknob, Fremont School, Salt Lake City, Salt Lake County, Utah. The Fremont School was designed by Henry Monheim and built in 1890. A *Salt Lake Tribune* article published on January 1, 1891, stated: "The finest structure ever erected in this city for educational purposes is the fourteenth district school building built the past year." Elaborately ornamented brass hardware cast by the *cire perdu* (lost wax) process was standard from the 1870s until after the turn of the century. Similar hardware patterns were stock items in the mail order catalogs of Sears Roebuck and Montgomery Ward. Photograph by P. Kent Fairbanks, 1967. (LC HABS UTAH, 18−SALCI, 7−9)

Figure 13 Fire alarm panel of 1894, City Hall and Opera House, Bozeman, Gallatin County, Montana. The Bozeman City Hall and Opera House was built in 1887−90 to house the general city offices, city jail, and fire station on the first floor, a civic auditorium or opera house on the second floor, and rental offices on both floors. The building was designed by Byron Vreeland, a local architect who died in 1889. Architect George Hancock altered the original design and supervised the completion of the building. In 1916 the name of the Opera House was changed to Municipal Theater. The building was demolished in 1966. The presence of a fire station in the multipurpose structure accounts for the fire alarm panel. It was thoroughly up-to-date equipment when it was installed in 1894. Photograph by Al Huntsman, 1965. (LC HABS MONT, 16−BOZ, 1−12)

Figure 14 Carriage block on Government Street, Mobile, Mobile County, Alabama. Such elaborate stone mounting blocks are rare examples of street furniture. It is not clear whether this one was erected at private or municipal expense. The style of the carving suggests a date in the third quarter of the last century. The height of the platform indicates that the block was designed for mounting horses rather than carriages. Photograph by W. N. Manning, 1934. (LC HABS ALA, 49−MOBI, 37A−1)

of the Thomas Jefferson Southard House of 1855, recently a Russian Orthodox home for the aged, in Richmond, Maine (fig. 8). Numerous churches of the 1840s and 1850s and meeting halls, such as the Masonic Temple of 1878 in Belfast, Maine, contain architectural frescoes executed in illusionistic grisaille. Both ceilings and walls of the "Sig" Sawtelle Circus Training House (also known as the George Satterly House) in Homer, New York, are sheathed in stamped metal, one of the least usual of all wall treatments (fig. 9). At the other end of the decorative gamut is the parlor of the Francis J. Dewes House of 1894–96 in Chicago, later the Swedish Engineers' Society. That parlor is one of the very few—perhaps the only—examples in America of a kind of Wilhelmine Baroque-Rococo style (fig. 10). It was a style more characteristic of Norddeutscher-Lloyd Line ships of the 1890s than of residential interiors in the United States. A Hungarian-born architect, Arthur Hercz, who was trained in Vienna, confected it for the brewer Francis Dewes.

Hardware, an often overlooked incidental to architecture, can also be studied in the photographs. Curiously, only a single window latch appears ever to have been photographed by the Survey. That lone example is a rare casement latch dating from around 1800 in the Stephen Girard Country House in Philadelphia (fig. 11). Door hardware, however, does appear with fair frequency, as in the knob, escutcheon plate, and latch plate of an Eastlake pattern in the Fremont School of 1890 in Salt Lake City (fig. 12). Among other curious and rare miscellaneous bits of hardware is an hourglass holder, probably dating from about 1730, in the Rocky Hill Meeting House at Amesbury, Massachusetts. A fire alarm signal panel of 1894 was photographed in the City Hall and Opera House at Bozeman, Montana (fig. 13). And a fine set of old scales appears in photographs of the Elisha Atherton Coray Mill in Exeter Township, Pennsylvania. A considerable amount of early cast-iron street furniture and other exterior ironwork was photographed in Boston and Chicago, and even more was recorded in Mobile, Alabama. Oddly enough, the photographic representation of ironwork in New Orleans is decidedly skimpy, but HABS measured drawings remedy the deficiency. A highly unusual piece of street furniture, an elaborate masonry mounting block, stands on Government Street in Mobile, Alabama (fig. 14).

The HABS photographs provide some data on nineteenth-century plumbing fixtures, although opportunities were missed because such material was not considered interesting until

Figure 15 Bathroom, David Davis Mansion, Bloomington, McLean County, Illinois. The house was built in 1870–72 from plans by Alfred H. Piquenard for Judge David Davis. Davis was a legal and political associate of Abraham Lincoln, a member of the U.S. Supreme Court (1862–77), and a U.S. senator (1877–83). George McIntosh was the plumbing contractor. The painted china wash basin set in marble and the metal-lined wood-encased bathtub are typical of their period. Water pumped manually from the basement to an attic tank and distributed by gravity supplied the extant original faucets of the washstand, tub, and shower. The house is now a museum of nineteenth-century living. Illinois State Historical Library photograph. (LC HABS ILL, 57–BLOOM, 2–7)

Figure 16 Shower stall, Ivinson Mansion (now the Laramie Plains Museum), Laramie, Albany County, Wyoming. Edward Ivinson, mayor of Laramie and unsuccessful candidate for governor of Wyoming in 1892, was a prosperous banker. His mansion was built in 1892 from plans by the Salt Lake City architect E. Waring. House and furniture cost $40,000, a considerable sum in 1892. The shower, which sprays inward from all pipes, was purchased in Chicago and was the most up-to-date plumbing equipment available. Photograph by Jack E. Boucher, 1974. (LC HABS WYO, 1–LARAM, 2–22)

relatively recently. The change in shower baths from the rather primitive contraption in the unspoiled mid-Victorian bathroom of the David Davis Mansion of 1872 in Bloomington, Illinois, to the complex gadget of 1892 in the Ivinson Mansion (Laramie Plains Museum) at Laramie, Wyoming, is well illustrated in two revealing photographs (figs. 15, 16). Other examples of past plumbing may be seen in the bathroom of the Welch-Ross House in Cambridge, Massachusetts. The kitchen of the General Dodge House, in Council Bluffs, Iowa, has a marble sink. The molded china commode set on a marble base in the James Whitcomb Riley House combines ornament with use (fig. 17).

Heating devices, both movable and fixed, are well represented in HABS photographs. Kitchen ranges, like the splendid example in the William A. Farnsworth Homestead in Rockland, Maine, are numerous and the subject of a separate study here by Rodris Roth.

Movable heating stoves are illustrated by examples such as the elegant Gothic parlor stove of 1851 in the Dr. Alfred Paige House built in Bethel, Vermont, in 1833 (fig. 18). The very fine parlor stove in the King House, photographed in 1932 in Virginia City, Nevada, and the stove dated 1883 by the Chicago Stove Works in St. Andrew's Episcopal Church in Atlantic City, Wyoming, are other examples of stoves not for cooking (figs. 19, 20). Steam or hot water radiators are stunningly represented by the grille-shielded example surmounted by an étagère in the dining room dating from 1864 at Lynd-

hurst at Tarrytown, New York, as well as less grandly but more typically by a late nineteenth-century cast-iron radiator in the Townsend House of 1835 in Windsor, Vermont (figs. 21, 22).

Because mantelpieces were almost invariably included among interior views, fireplaces of all periods are abundantly represented. An unusually attractive cast-iron fire frame was photographed in the Nettie Thompson House in Georgetown, Ohio (fig. 23). I was surprised to come upon a photograph of a cast-iron mantelpiece with églomisé glass spandrel panels in the Houseman Residence of 1850, demol-

Figure 17 Original vitreous bathroom fixture, James Whitcomb Riley House, Indianapolis, Marion County, Indiana. The Riley House was completed by 1872. Water was originally pumped from cisterns in the backyard to attic tanks. The bathroom fixtures are original. The water closet is china with a molded leaf pattern and is set on a marble slab within the carpeted floor. The seat and tank, which has a crystal chain pull, are cherry. The lavatory has an oval china basin, a marble top and backsplash set on a cherry cabinet with raised molded panels outlining a door, and a tier of three drawers. The taps are brass. The copper-lined bathtub is enclosed in tongue-and-groove cherry wainscoting, and the whole room has similar wainscoting below red wallpaper with a floral pattern. The ceiling paper is white. The red carpet has a pattern of yellow and blue. Photograph by Jack E. Boucher, 1970. (LC HABS IND, 49-IND, 8-18)

Figure 18 Stove in the northeast bedroom on the second floor of the Dr. Alfred Paige House, Bethel, Windsor County, Vermont. The Dr. Alfred Paige House reflects the continuous ownership of one family through four generations. The house was built in 1833, but during the 1850s a notable cast-iron stove made in Troy, New York, and patented in 1851 replaced the fireplace in the northeast bedroom. Mark Twain, in the chapter titled "The House Beautiful" in his *Life on the Mississippi* referred to a "Polished air-tight stove (new and deadly invention), with pipe passing through a board which closes up the discarded good old fireplace." By 1883, when that was written, Mark Twain thought of fireplaces with nostalgia, but pragmatic Vermonters, coping with their winters, did not share his sentiment. This highly ornamental Gothic stove was probably designed for a parlor, not a bedroom. The urn finial is a water vase to humidify the atmosphere. The Paige House now has central heating as well as two first-floor soapstone fireplaces and another cast-iron stove in a plain, severe style made by R. and J. Wainwright of Middlebury, Vermont. That stove dates from the building of the house. Photograph by Jack E. Boucher, 1959. (LC HABS VT, 14—BETH, 1—8)

ished in 1934 in Montgomery, Alabama, that proved to be identical with a pair of mantelpieces in my own former home, built in 1859 at 17 Clinton Street in Cambridge, Massachusetts (fig. 24). Among the great number of notable mantelpieces recorded, one that particularly struck my fancy was the grand example with a glass mosaic overmantel in the Magerstadt House of 1906–8, in Chicago (fig. 25).

Interior photographs taken by the Survey during the 1930s often yield unexpected information about the past. They reveal survivals such as the carpets in the King House in Virginia City, Nevada, or painted window shades like those in the Blakely Plantation near Vicksburg, Mississippi, and in Malmaison near Carrollton, Mississippi. Since the 1930s, such furnishings have altogether vanished or become exceedingly rare.

The early HABS photographs are invaluable, too, for establishing the original condition of subsequently restored properties. For example, Sturdivant Hall, a fine 1853 house in Selma, Alabama, has been supposedly improved by having its soft pine hall floor replaced by elaborate marble and its original gilded gas chandeliers replaced by crystal fixtures of an eighteenth-century type. The double parlors the crystal fixtures now illuminate have been painted anachronistic Wedgewood blue with white trim! It is most unfortunate that similarly mistreated Natchez, Mississippi, interiors were not photographed during the 1930s while they were still pristine.

Early HABS photographs frequently show lighting fixtures that had survived from the nineteenth century. The gas candles in the Decatur House hall in Washington, D.C., appear in a photograph that shows Victorian frescoes dating from around 1870 when the Beale family bought the house (fig. 26). The frescoes are now obliterated. Many restored houses, for example, the Richardson-Owens-Thomas House of 1816–19 in Savannah, Georgia, once had mid-nineteenth-century gas fixtures. The original condition of fixtures that were later electrified may also often be ascertained from photographs, as, for instance, in those of the Shrewsbury House in Madison, Indiana.

With increasing frequency, copies of nineteenth-century interior photographs are included in HABS records. These provide documentation of furnishings and fixtures that is not otherwise readily obtainable. Citing even a few of these will show their varied subject matter. Copies of photographs dating from 1869 show the interior of St. John's Episcopal Church in Washington, D.C., before James Renwick's enlargement in 1883 altered the east end. Photographs of Chicago's Rookery Building before Frank Lloyd Wright's alterations show the original main stairway (fig. 28). The original lighting fixtures and stenciled ornamentation of the United States Branch Mint in San Francisco are visible in early photographs, too (fig. 29). Old photographs of the now-demolished Valentine-Fuller House of 1848 in Cambridge, Massachusetts, show furniture purchased in 1865 as well as gas fixtures probably by Henry N. Hooper and Company (fig. 30). Photographs dating from the turn of the century of the James Whitcomb Riley House, built about 1866–72 in Indianapolis, show only minor differences from present conditions. This distinguishes the Riley house from house museums where modern canons of taste have been, however subconsciously, imposed (figs. 31, 32). Among the copied photographs, those showing the Stanford-Lathrop Memorial Home in Sacramento, California, as it was refurnished by the Leland Stanfords around 1872 are outstanding for the data they supply.

Let us now consider lighting fixtures, which started out to be the subject of my inquiry. Gas lighting got an early start in the United States with the establishment of a chartered gas company in Baltimore in 1817. By 1840 there were 11 gas companies in America, and by the end of 1850, 51 compa-

Figure 19 Stove, King House, Virginia City, Storey County, Nevada. This Jewel Stove appears to date from the last quarter of the nineteenth century. Its ornately scrolled design includes mica windows—colloquially called isinglass—in its door. Those windows restored some of the missing cheerfulness of the "discarded good old fireplace" by making the fire visible. The long stovepipe helped to radiate heat. Photograph by Robert W. Kerrigan, 1937. (HABS NEV, 15–VIRG, 28–4)

Figure 20 Stove in St. Andrew's Episcopal Church, Atlantic City, Fremont County, Wyoming Atlantic City was founded in 1868 to serve the South Pass mining district. The population soon rose to 2,000, but by 1870 it had dropped to 325. This Ajax Stove in the Episcopal church was made by the Chicago Stove Works in 1883. It is of the simplest possible kind and could be used for either heating or cooking. It may be assumed that in the boom-and-bust economy of the mining area St. Andrew's wardens and vestry were not willing to risk indebtedness for a fancier stove. This stove differs little in general appearance from plain box stoves of the 1830s. Photograph by Jack E. Boucher, 1974. (LC HABS WYO, 7–ATCI, 5–4)

nies had been chartered. By 1863, there were 433 gas companies in the United States and 23 in Canada. By 1876, every American community larger than a village had its own gas company, and many country estates in places too small to support a gas company had private gas plants.

After Edison established the first central power station, the Pearl Street Station in New York, in 1882, electric lighting made slow progress because the Welsbach burner, or gas mantle, first manufactured commercially in 1887, made incandescent gas lighting competitive with electric lighting. The older open-flame burners were rendered obsolete not only by electric bulbs but also by Welsbach's mantles, which permitted gas to retain its lead as an illuminant into the present century.

Except for those in a very few colonial churches, I found no eighteenth-century chandeliers in their original settings. Almost all had been installed during restorations or refurnishings. There were, however, a few fine early nineteenth-century fixtures recorded in situ, the most notable of which hung in the Greek Revival ballroom of the Croghan House, built about 1835 in Pittsburgh (fig. 33). It was later installed in the University of Pittsburgh's Cathedral of Learning. The splendid Empire chandelier was probably imported, not an American artifact. The prism-hung chandelier in the eighteenth-century west parlor of Belmont Hall in Smyrna, Delaware, however, is almost certainly American and appears to date from about 1835–45 (fig. 34). A similar example hangs in Andrew Jackson's back parlor at The Hermitage in Davidson County, Tennessee, and yet another, fitted for oil lamps instead of candles, in the William B. Sappington House near Arrow Rock, Missouri. A fine example with six gas burners hung in the now-vanished Nolting House in Richmond, Virginia. This type, with ormolu finish and tiers of diminishing rings of prisms surrounding the stem, went out of fashion before gas became very common.

In my quest for illustrations of lighting fixtures, I found that places of worship yielded the most information of any building type except dwellings. The large brass chandelier in St. Paul's Episcopal Church of 1707 in Wickford, Rhode Island, appears to be original, as does the fine pair in Trinity church, built in Newport in 1726. The splendid set of five chandeliers in the Touro Synagogue of 1763 in Newport, Rhode Island, are likewise original. The great glass chandelier, now discretely electrified, in the First Baptist Meeting House of 1775 in Providence, Rhode Island, is original and was formerly flanked by four eight-light gas chandeliers dating from around 1850. The grand glass chandelier in the United Church of 1815 in New Haven is also original and is not electrified. All of these chandeliers (except the First Baptist Meeting House gas fixtures) were imported.

Numerous large and handsome

Figure 21 Radiator in the dining room at Lyndhurst, Tarrytown, Westchester County, New York. Lyndhurst was designed by Alexander Jackson Davis for William Paulding and built in 1838. In 1864–65 Davis greatly enlarged the house for George Merritt, making Lyndhurst one of the grandest Gothic Revival houses in America. Steam heating had become fairly common in superior dwellings by 1865 when the new dining room at Lyndhurst was completed. The radiator is Gold's Patent Steam Heating Apparatus manufactured by Hills & Benton of Brooklyn, New York, and New Haven, Connecticut. The étagère surmounting the radiator is not part of the apparatus. A marble-topped ornamental cast-iron grille conceals the radiator itself. Photograph by Jack E. Boucher, 1971. (HABS NY, 60–TARY, 1A–63)

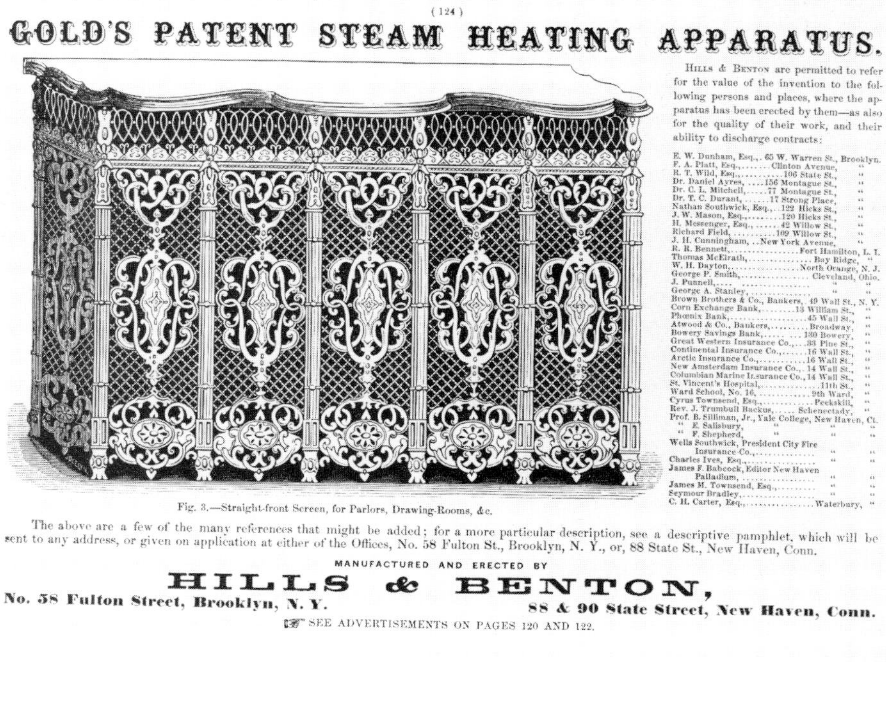

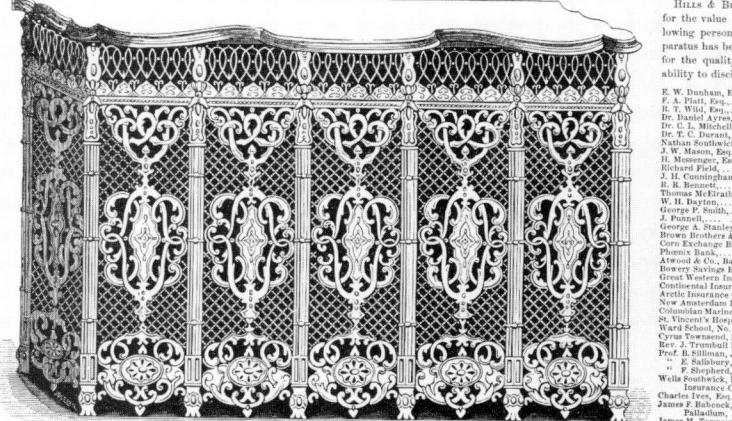

Figure 22 An advertisement for Gold's Patent Steam Heating Apparatus in *G. & D. Cook & Co.'s Illustrated Catalogue of Carriages and Special Business Advertiser* (1860; reprint, New York: Dover Publications, 1970)

(124)

GOLD'S PATENT STEAM HEATING APPARATUS.

Hills & Benton are permitted to refer for the value of the invention to the following persons and places, where the apparatus has been erected by them—as also for the quality of their work, and their ability to discharge contracts:

E. W. Dunham, Esq., 65 W. Warren St., Brooklyn.
F. A. Platt, Esq., Clinton Avenue, "
R. T. Wild, Esq., 106 State St., "
Dr. Daniel Ayres, 156 Montague St., "
Dr. C. L. Mitchell, 77 Montague St., "
Dr. T. C. Durant, 17 Strong Place, "
Nathan Southwick, Esq., 122 Hicks St., "
J. W. Mason, Esq., 120 Hicks St., "
H. Messenger, Esq., 42 Willow St., "
Richard Field, 109 Willow St., "
J. H. Cunningham, New York Avenue, "
R. R. Bennett, Fort Hamilton, L. I.
Thomas McElrath, Bay Ridge, "
W. H. Dayton, North Orange, N. J.
George P. Smith, Cleveland, Ohio.
J. Funnell, "
George A. Stanley, "
Brown Brothers & Co., Bankers, 49 Wall St., N. Y.
Corn Exchange Bank, 13 William St., "
Phoenix Bank, 45 Wall St., "
Atwood & Co., Bankers, Broadway, "
Bowery Savings Bank, 130 Bowery, "
Great Western Insurance Co., 38 Pine St., "
Continental Insurance Co., 16 Wall St., "
Arctic Insurance Co., 16 Wall St., "
New American Insurance Co., 14 Wall St., "
Columbian Marine Insurance Co., 14 Wall St., "
St. Vincent's Hospital, 11th St., "
Ward School, No. 16, 9th Ward, "
Cyrus Townsend, Esq., Peekskill, "
Rev. J. Trumbull Backus, Schenectady, "
Prof. B. Silliman, Jr., Yale College, New Haven, Ct.
" E. Salisbury, "
" F. Shepherd, "
Wells Southwick, President City Fire Insurance Co., "
Charles Ives, Esq., "
James F. Babcock, Editor New Haven Palladium, "
James M. Townsend, Esq., "
Seymour Bradley, "
C. H. Carter, Esq., Waterbury, "

Fig. 3.—Straight-front Screen, for Parlors, Drawing-Rooms, &c.

The above are a few of the many references that might be added; for a more particular description, see a descriptive pamphlet, which will be sent to any address, or given on application at either of the Offices, No. 58 Fulton St., Brooklyn, N. Y., or, 88 State St., New Haven, Conn.

MANUFACTURED AND ERECTED BY
HILLS & BENTON,
No. 58 Fulton Street, Brooklyn, N. Y.   88 & 90 State Street, New Haven, Conn.
☞ SEE ADVERTISEMENTS ON PAGES 120 AND 122.

Figure 23 Mantelpiece in the Nettie Thompson House, Georgetown, Brown County, Ohio. The Nettie Thompson House was built in 1848 in the Greek Revival style. The cast-iron frame within the wooden mantelpiece displays Greek anthemion and palmette motifs. The hearth and fireboard, however, are thoroughly eclectic, combining Baroque and Rococo motifs with the figurine of an American Indian in high relief. The Neo-Classical frame itself is handsomely consistent in design. Photograph by E. F. Schrand and A. Hofmann, 1936. (LC HABS OHIO, 8–GEOTO. V, 1–6)

Figure 24 Housman residence, Montgomery, Montgomery County, Alabama. The Housman residence was built in 1850. Cast-iron mantelpieces with églomisé glass spandrels were quite popular during the 1850s. Identical examples of this design, patented by Hiram Tucker of Cambridge, Mass., on April 2, 1850, existed in the Woolley House in Lexington, Kentucky, as well as in the 1859 house at 17 Clinton Street in Cambridge, Massachusetts. There is a more elaborate Neo-Rococo example, probably by the James L. Jackson Foundry in New York City, in the Benjamin Titcomb-Harriet Beecher Stowe House in Brunswick, Maine. The latter house was extensively remodeled during the 1850s. Photograph by W. N. Manning, 1934. (LC HABS ALA, 51–MONG, 15–3)

Figure 25 Entrance hall mantel in the Ernest J. Magerstadt House, Chicago, Cook County, Illinois. The Magerstadt House was completed in 1908 from plans by George W. Maher. It is an outstanding example of that architect's work and was designated a Chicago Architectural Landmark in 1960. The mantelpiece in the entrance hall, with its glass mosaic panel, is one of the most beautiful features of the distinguished Art Nouveau interior. Photograph by Cervin Robinson, 1963. (LC HABS ILL, 16–CHIG, 26–4)

Figure 26 Entrance hall, Decatur House, Washington, D.C. The house designed in 1818 by Benjamin Henry Latrobe for Stephen Decatur in Washington is a distinguished town house of the federal period. In 1870 the house was acquired by Gen. Edward Beale, who modernized it by adding mid-Victorian decorative elements. Many of the Beale period interior embellishments were obliterated after 1960 by the National Trust for Historic Preservation to which Mrs. Truxton Beale left the property. Photograph by John O. Brostrup, 1937. (LC HABS DC, WASH, 28–14)

Figure 27 Rookery Building lobby, Chicago, Cook County, Illinois. The Rookery Building was erected in 1886–88 from plans by Burnham and Root. A copy of an 1893 photograph shows the lobby in its original state with much ornamental cast-iron work before Frank Lloyd Wright's alterations of 1905. "In every detail of The Rookery the subtlety of Root's creative imagination is apparent, but nowhere is his genius more obvious than in the glass-and-iron vault over the court. It is the finest example of its kind in the United States." So stated Carl W. Condit in *American Building Art: The Nineteenth Century* (New York: Oxford University Press, 1960), p. 55. Photograph, 1893, courtesy of the Chicago Historical Society.

Figure 29 Engine room, U.S. Branch Mint, San Francisco, San Francisco County, California. The U.S. Branch Mint in San Francisco was designed by Alfred Bult Mullett and built in 1869–74. It was so well constructed that it survived the 1906 San Francisco earthquake and fire. It served as the central depot for all the gold and silver produced in the Pacific Coast area until it ceased functioning as a mint in 1937. The room containing the majestic steam engine was handsomely fitted up with a tessellated marble floor and fine bronze gas chandeliers. The engine housing was supported by Tuscan columns on paneled plinths—a blending of Roman classicism with nineteenth-century engineering. Copy of a Runnels & Stateler photograph taken about 1882–85. (LC HABS CAL, 38–SANFRA, 5–21)

Figure 28 (opposite) Rookery Building main lobby in 1963, Chicago, Cook County, Illinois. The court lobby of the Rookery Building was remodeled by Frank Lloyd Wright in 1905. Wright removed most of John Wellborn Root's original iron ornament and replaced it with simple geometric designs. The staircase was enclosed in white marble. Rectangular marble urns and rectangular light fixtures were also designed by Wright. Elaborate gilded arabesques ornament many of the remodeled surfaces. Additional changes were made in 1944 from plans by Magnus Gunderson. Photograph by Cervin Robinson, 1963. (LC HABS ILL, 16–CHIG, 31–7)

Figure 30   Drawing room, Valentine-Fuller House, Cambridge, Middlesex County, Massachusetts. The Valentine-Fuller House with attached carriage house and stable was erected in 1848. House and grounds together made a particularly fine intact example of a mid-nineteenth-century suburban estate. It was demolished in 1937. When Robert O. Fuller bought the property from Charles Valentine in 1865, Fuller ordered the drawing room furniture. The draperies dated from 1865, but the Oriental rug was added atop the carpet during the 1880s. The two gas chandeliers in this large room appear to have been by the Boston firm of Henry N. Hooper. The plaster work and door trim are Greek Revival, but the exterior of the house was Italianate with very wide bracketed eaves. Copy of an 1890 photograph. (LC HABS MASS, 9–CAMB, 10–8)

Figure 32 Dining room of the James Whitcomb Riley House, Indianapolis, Marion County, Indiana, in 1970. The red-on-red floral wallpaper in this view harmonizes well with the original carpet. The molded plaster ceiling centerpiece out of camera range above the chandelier represents apples and leaves. The apples are painted red. Photograph by Jack E. Boucher, 1970. (LC HABS IND, 49–IND, 8–13)

Figure 33 Ballroom chandelier, Croghan House, Pittsburgh, Allegheny County, Pennsylvania. The now-demolished Croghan House was built in the late 1830s on the outskirts of Pittsburgh for weekend entertaining, as its original name, Picnic House, suggests. It originally consisted of a ballroom with oval anteroom and three bedrooms above a high basement containing servants' quarters. The ballroom and its anteroom, now preserved in the University of Pittsburgh, are among the most lavishly enriched Greek Revival interiors ever executed in an American residence. The magnificent chandelier is a trifle overscaled for the size of the ballroom. Photograph by Charles M. Stotz, 1934. (LC HABS PA 2–PITBU, 3–9)

Figure 31 (opposite) Dining room of the James Whitcomb Riley House, Indianapolis, Marion County, Indiana, around 1900. Comparison of the picture taken around 1900 with a photograph taken in 1970 shows almost no change in the Riley House dining room (see fig. 32). The same furniture and carpet are there, and even the shades of the gas chandelier and the smoke bells above them have survived intact. Only the upholstery of the chairs and the wallpaper have been replaced. The carpet is dark red with a light red arabesque design. The embossed paper wainscot is dark brown. The built-in cherry buffet in the framed recess of the south wall has a white marble top. The fireplace on the opposite wall has a round-arched brown-veined Vermont marble mantelpiece surmounted by a cherry framed mirror. Other interiors of the James Whitcomb Riley House are shown in figs. 17, 51, 52. (LC HABS IND, 49–IND, 8–12)

Figure 36 (opposite)   Chandelier in First Parish Church (Unitarian), Kennebunk, York County, Maine. The First Parish Church was commenced in 1772, enlarged in 1803, and subdivided horizontally in 1838. Brass ormolu chandeliers with ornamental chains were very popular in America during the 1840s and early 1850s. The Neo-Rococo arms and grape-patterned chains are typical. Many chandeliers of this style were made for gas. This one supports six oil lamps. The shades of these lamps date from after 1880, and the lamps themselves appear to be replacements of earlier ones. Photograph by Jack E. Boucher, 1965.

Figure 34   West parlor of Belmont Hall, Smyrna, Kent County, Delaware. Belmont Hall was built in 1753 and enlarged in 1771. It was extensively rebuilt after fire damage in 1882. The west parlor dates from 1771, but the chandelier is at least sixty years later in date. Tiered prism-hung chandeliers of this general pattern were common in America from around 1830 until about 1850 or later. Some held candles; others held oil lamps; and still others were piped for gas. Photograph by Cortlandt VanDyke Hubbard, 1960. (LC HABS DEL, 1–SMYR V, 3–10)

Figure 35   Interior of the Dutch Reformed Church, Millstone, Somerset County, New Jersey. This church was built in 1828. The large Neo-Grec three-tiered chandelier supports a total of eighteen oil lamps and dates from the late 1860s or the 1870s. There are also three-lamp wall brackets *en suite* with the chandelier. The Neo-Grec style had reached its apogee in America by the centennial year, 1876. The stamped metal sheathing of the walls and ceiling appears to date from around the turn of the century. Photograph by Nathaniel R. Ewen, 1937. (LC HABS NJ, 18–MIL, 2–3)

Figure 37 Main staircase of the General Grenville M. Dodge House, Council Bluffs, Pottawattamie County, Iowa. In 1866 Gen. Grenville Mellen Dodge was made chief engineer of the Union Pacific Railroad. In 1869–70 he built his brick mansard-roofed house, modifying plans by the Chicago architect William W. Boyington. The fourteen-room mansion cost $35,000, a considerable sum for the time. The gas standard on the newel post of the main staircase is ornamented with polychromed ceramic elements in the Anglo-Japanese style. The gas fitting for the house was done by an Omaha firm. The house is now subdivided into apartments. Anonymous photograph, after 1916. (LC HABS IOWA, 78–COUB, 1–4)

Figure 38 Main stairs, Morse-Libby House, Portland, Cumberland County, Maine. The Morse-Libby House was built in 1859–63 from plans by the New Haven architect Henry Austin. The first owner, Ruggles Sylvester Morse, was a hotel entrepreneur. The interiors of this towered Italianate villa were sumptuously ornamented by Giuseppe Guidicini—now often miscalled Giovanni Guidirini—a New York artist. The most elaborate form of gas standard was the bronze statue. Here a pair of them both ornaments and illuminates the newel posts of the flying staircase in the Morse-Libby House hall. The house is now known as Victoria Mansion—a museum. See fig. 47 for another interior view of this splendid dwelling. Anonymous photograph, 1936. (LC HABS ME, 3–PORT, 15–3)

chandeliers fitted for oil lamps existed in churches when HABS photographs were taken during the 1930s. Among the excellent examples are the two-tiered chandelier in the Presbyterian Church at Pisgah, Kentucky, and that in the Zion church near Columbia, Tennessee. The latter blends Eastlake and Néo-Grec details in an eclectic mélange. An even grander post-Civil-War oil chandelier is the three-tiered example that a HABS photographer found hanging in the Dutch Reformed Church in Millstone, New Jersey (fig. 35). Among later recordings, two of the handsomest church chandeliers are the examples from about 1845–50, each with eight lamps (now electrified), in the First Parish Church, Unitarian, in Kennebunk, Maine. Four matching four-light gas chandeliers, similar in style to the Kennebunk examples, are suspended by brackets from the side galleries of the Beneficent Congregational Church in Providence, Rhode Island. Small gas chandeliers suspended from the wall by brackets were called *toilets*, as they were intended to hang beside dressing tables to illuminate their looking glasses. A very fine six-light gas chandelier, now fitted with electric candles instead of glass-shaded bulbs, is in the Oliver Hazard Perry house, built about 1845 in Southport, Connecticut. It belongs to the same Neo-Rococo type with ornamental chains as the Kennebunk and Providence examples. By the mid-1850s, the chains common to such chandeliers were considered passé.

The only examples found in the Survey of reflector chandeliers, a type once widely used after the Civil War in places of public assembly, were those in churches. In the Methodist Church in Forkland, Alabama, and in the

Figure 39 Second floor drawing room mirror, Emerson and Holmes Building, Macon, Bibb County, Georgia. The Emerson and Holmes Building was built in 1854 as an unusually fine set of dentist's offices for a Dr. Emerson from New Hampshire. The third floor contained living quarters. The two-tiered ten-light gas chandelier still had most of its original globes when a HABS photographer caught its reflection. The building was still used for dental offices in 1936. Photograph by L. D. Andrew, 1936. (LC HABS GA, 11–MACO, 13–4)

Figure 40 Province Street steps, Boston, Suffolk County, Massachusetts. The Greek Revival palmette motifs in the wrought-iron archway supporting this gas street lantern suggest a date in the 1830s. The steps connect Bosworth Street, which runs a short block from Tremont Street, with a formerly narrow lane called Province Street. Gas street lighting first came to Boston in the 1820s. Photograph by Arthur C. Haskell, 1934. (LC HABS MASS, 13–BOST, 38A–1)

Figure 42 Detail of columns, Reid-Jones-Carpenter House, Augusta, Richmond County, Georgia. The Corinthian portico of the Greek Revival Reid-Jones-Carpenter House is lighted by at least one gas bracket affixed to the inner face of a fluted column. This unusual arrangement is made even more uncommon by the form of the bracket, which was certainly designed for interior use. Exterior gas lights require more protection from wind than that provided by the open glass shade of this bracket in the form of an angel. Photograph by Lawrence Bradley, 1936. (HABS GA−227, LC HABS GA, 122−AUG, 13−3)

Figure 41 Lamp post in front of Christ Episcopal Church, Mobile, Mobile County, Alabama. This cast-iron lamp post probably dates from around 1855, when the City of Mobile received numerous requests for the placement of posts on designated corners. The crossbar served to support the lamplighter's ladder. The post is a standard design, but the lantern shielding the gas light is more ornamental than most. Possibly the lantern was provided by the wardens and vestry of Christ Church, not by the city. Photograph by E. W. Russell, 1937. (LC HABS ALA, 49−MOBI, 33C−2)

Figure 43 Gas machine in the cellar of the Isaac Kinsey House, Milton vicinity, Wayne County, Indiana. Beechwood, the Isaac Kinsey House, was built during 1871−73 from plans by the Richmond, Indiana, architect Joel Stover. This rare private gas machine had a small furnace for the distillation of gas from coal. Counterweights attached to the drum had to be cranked upward to effect a constant pressure of gas to as many as thirty burners throughout the house. See fig. 44 for another gas machine. Photograph by Jack E. Boucher, 1975. (LC HABS IND, 1−MILT V, 1−19)

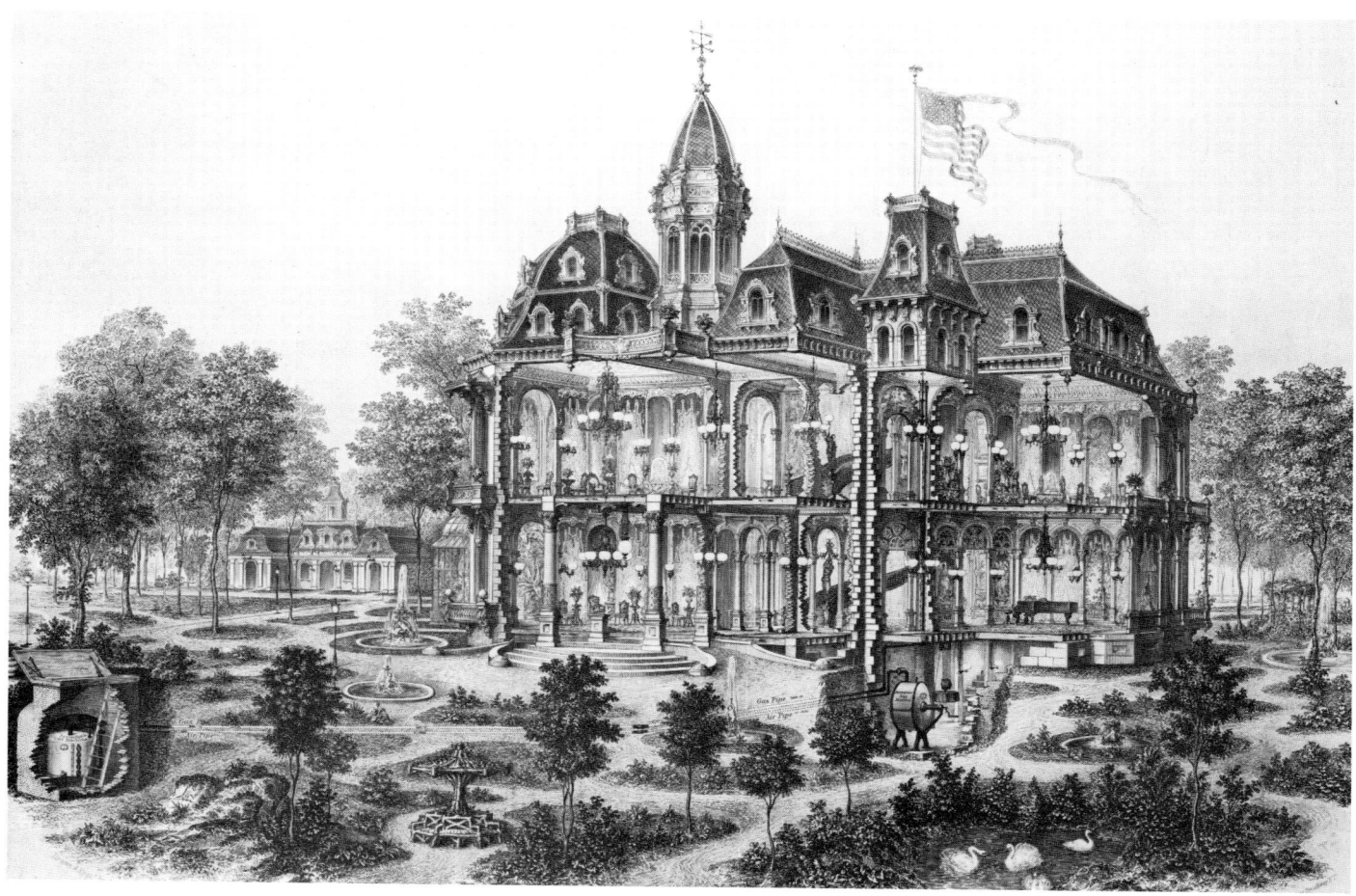

Figure 44 Advertisement for a Springfield Gas Machine around 1868. The Springfield Gas Machine generated gas from gasoline in an evaporating tank placed underground at a distance from the building to be lighted. An air pump driven by a weight suspended from the cellar ceiling forced air through a pipe leading to the generating tank, and a second pipe conveyed the gas from the tank to the house. The extraordinary mansion in this advertisement appears to contain only parlors. Engraving by John Keim, published by Hay Brothers. (LC–USZ62–44118)

Congregational Church in Rocky Hill, Connecticut, hung typical examples. The Congregational Church chandelier was photographed from above. Reflector fixtures used mirror-lined shades to throw light down where it was needed. The Oahe Congregational Mission in Pierre, South Dakota, had a three-light oil chandelier in which the turn-of-the-century lamps were designed on a new principle to project their light downward.

Gas standards—that is, fixtures rising from the floor or a flat raised surface to support one or more burners—appear in photographs of church interiors more frequently than elsewhere. The St. Thomas Reformed Church of 1846 at Charlotte Amalie in the Virgin Islands was lighted by gas standards on the pew ends. The First Parish Church in Castleton, Vermont, has a pair of two-light pulpit standards now

electrified. And Trinity Church in Southport, Connecticut, contains a striking pair of brass chancel candelabra similar to those designed for gas. The Alexander House, a dwelling of the Federal period located in Springfield, Massachusetts, has an extremely rare pair of gas mantelpiece standards. Most standards in private houses appear on newel posts. The newel post standard in the General Dodge House in Council Bluffs, Iowa, is an example in the Anglo-Japanese taste. A splendid pair of bronze figurines, each supporting a gas light, stand atop the carved Santo Domingo mahogany newel posts of the flying staircase in the Morse-Libby House of 1859–63 in Portland, Maine (figs. 37, 38).

Until 1959, only one gas fixture was itself specifically photographed by the Survey. The rest appear only incidentally with ceiling centerpieces or in general interior views. Thus, the battered and bent three-light gaselier of the 1850s, captioned "Typical Original Gas-Fired Chandelier," photographed on March 10, 1934, in the weedy yard of the James Vance House in San Antonio, Texas, by Marvin Eickenroht is unique among the early HABS photographs. An August 2, 1936, photograph captioned "Mirror in Drawing Room Second Floor," which shows the reflection of a fine two-tiered gaselier with original shades in the Emerson and Holmes Building, den-

tal offices of 1854 in Macon, Georgia, typifies the prevailing myopia of the 1930s toward gas fixtures (fig. 39). Photographer Jack E. Boucher's picture of the very large Gothic gaselier in the 1857 National Guard's Hall in Philadelphia, taken in April 1959, is among the earliest photographs expressly intended to show chandeliers and marks a change of emphasis in recording.

There are relatively few exterior gaslights represented in the Survey. Certainly the gas lantern supported by a wrought-iron archway over the

Figure 45 Gas chandelier in the southeast room of the Charles Dana House, Woodstock, Windsor County, Vermont. The Charles Dana House, now a historical society museum, was built in 1807. This fanciful gas chandelier was probably installed in 1856, when gas came to Woodstock, or shortly thereafter. Its style is typical of the late 1850s. If it had been electrified to take smaller bulbs, the effect would have been better. The shades are original. Photograph by Jack E. Boucher, 1959. (LC HABS VT, 14−WOOD, 6−10)

Figure 46 Gas chandelier in the northeast room of the Hardaway-Wilson House, Mobile, Mobile County, Alabama. Georgia Cottage, the Hardaway-Wilson House, was built in 1840. Electricity was installed by the present owner in 1935. The house had never been piped for gas, and this chandelier is not original to the house. It was acquired locally from a demolished property and is typical of the 1850s in its Neo-Rococo design. The shades date from around 1890−1900. Photograph by Jack E. Boucher, 1963. (LC HABS ALA, 49−MOBI, 133−7)

Figure 47 Music room in the Morse-Libby House, Portland, Cumberland County, Maine. The gilt bronze gas chandeliers in the Morse-Libby House of 1859–63 are exceptionally fine. Most, including the music room chandelier, retain their original shades. The shades on the gas brackets flanking the mantel mirror are later. Wide-based shades came in after 1876 and were common by 1880. They allowed a greater flow of air to the flame and thus greatly reduced flickering.

This view of the music room shows the original carpet as well as the lavishly carved white marble mantelpiece with dancing figures, the rich plaster cornice, and some of Giuseppe Guidicini's decorative painting. See fig. 38 for another interior of this magnificent mansion. Anonymous photograph, 1936. (LC HABS ME, 3–PORT, 15–7)

Figure 48 Northwest double parlor in the Stanford-Lathrop Memorial Home, Sacramento, Sacramento County, California. The Stanford-Lathrop Memorial Home was built in 1857–58 from plans by Seth Babson (1828–1907), a Sacramento architect who was born in Maine. In 1861 the original owner, Shelton C. Fogus, sold the property to Governor Leland Stanford. In 1871–72 Stanford vastly enlarged the house. The Stanfords moved to San Francisco in 1874, and in 1900 Stanford's widow gave the house to the Roman Catholic Bishop of Sacramento for an orphanage. The double parlor is part of the original, 1857–58 structure. Its contents date from 1872. The carpet is sewn together from unusually wide strips. Most carpet strips were only twenty-seven inches wide. The gas chandeliers may possibly date from 1857–58. See also figure 49. From a copy of a photograph taken around 1872. (HABS CAL, 34–SAC, 9–10)

Figure 50 Chandelier in the J. Stuart Wells House, Binghamton, Broome County, New York. J. Stuart Wells was the leading building contractor of Binghamton. His nineteen-room house was built in 1867–70 from plans by Isaac G. Perry. The Neo-Grec plaster centerpiece above this four-light bronze gas chandelier accords well with the same stylistic expression in the fixture itself. Griffins like those perched at the springing of the branches were a favorite motif on Neo-Grec chandeliers. The style flourished in America from around 1865 until the late 1870s. The shades on this fixture date from the 1880s. Photograph by Jack E. Boucher, 1966. (LC HABS NY, 4–BING, 6–7)

Figure 49 West parlor and dining room in the Stanford-Lathrop Memorial Home, Sacramento, Sacramento County, California. These rooms are in the newer portion of the house dating from 1871–72. The *San Francisco Chronicle* for February 7, 1872, reported that the house contained "forty-four rooms, all most elaborately and luxuriously furnished and fitted up. Good taste and cultured imagination have been exhausted in furnishing the establishment. Magnificent and costly furniture in every room; lace curtains of the finest fabric; carpets that receive with noiseless tread the footfall." The Neo-Renaissance bronze stands with putti supporting lidded urns may well have exhausted "cultured imagination." The table in the foreground was certainly "magnificent and costly." The sculpture in the niche and the circular photographs of Bertel Thorvaldsen's once-famous bas reliefs *Day* and *Night* certified the culture of their owner. Geometric medallion-patterned carpets like those seen here were popular in the 1860s and early 1870s. These both silenced footfalls and visually dominated the rooms. The chandelier with the patent center slide was made by the New York firm of Mitchell, Vance and Company. The brass crowns on the shades were an extra luxury. This house is now run by the Sisters of Social Service as a home for girls and is open by request. Many Stanford pieces are still in place. From a copy of a photograph taken around 1872. (LC HABS CAL, 34–SAC, 9–12)

Figure 51 Riley's bedroom in the James Whitcomb Riley House, Indianapolis, Marion County, Indiana. The James Whitcomb Riley House was completed by 1872 for John R. Nickum. Nickum died in 1902. Riley resided in the house from 1893 until his death in 1916 as a paying guest of Nickum and his heirs. The house is now a museum operated by the James Whitcomb Riley Memorial Association.

Riley's bedroom has a tan carpet with a multicolored geometric pattern. The wallpaper has white "snowflake geometric" designs on a light brown ground. The frieze above the picture molding has gilded swags on a tan ground. The ceiling is tan. The mantelpiece is a dark Vermont marble. The massive walnut bedstead and marble-topped bureau date from the 1850s or early 1860s. Glass bells suspended over the gas chandelier protect the ceiling from smoke. See also figs. 17, 31, 32, 52. From a copy of a photograph taken around 1900. (LC HABS IND, 49−IND, 8−14)

Province Street steps in Boston is one of the most memorable examples (fig. 40). Somewhat more typical is a gas lantern bracketed out from a wall in the courtyard of the Cabildo in New Orleans. Several standard street lamps were recorded, one standing in front of Christ Episcopal Church in Mobile among the most handsome (fig. 41). A greatly enlarged version of this type, the Harbor Beacon in Savannah, Georgia, is certainly a splendid extant example. The gas bracket on the inner face of a portico column at the Reid-Jones-Carpenter House of 1849 in Augusta, Georgia, is a great rarity (fig. 42). It may have produced an effect similar to that admired at the Second Bank of the United States in Philadelphia on February 14, 1838, by the diarist Philip Hone, who wrote: "The portico . . . appeared more beautiful . . . than usual, from the effect of the gaslight. Each of the fluted columns had a jet of light from the inner side so placed as not to be seen from the street . . . which . . .produced an effect strikingly beautiful."

By 1873, when the Isaac Kinsey House was completed near Milton, Indiana, city and town gas was widely available, but village and country houses had to rely on private gas machines. The only gas machine recorded in the Survey is the exceedingly rare example in the Kinsey House cellar (fig. 43). Its undated label reads: "30 light combination/ gas machine/ manufactured by/ Detroit Heating & Lighting Co/ Detroit Mich."

Domestic gas lighting is well represented in the Survey. Examples range from the simple to the elaborate and from early to late. The gaselier with rope and tassel motif in the southwest room of the 1807 Charles Dana House

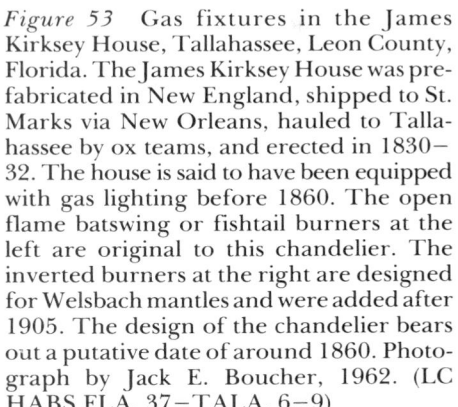

Figure 53 Gas fixtures in the James Kirksey House, Tallahassee, Leon County, Florida. The James Kirksey House was prefabricated in New England, shipped to St. Marks via New Orleans, hauled to Tallahassee by ox teams, and erected in 1830–32. The house is said to have been equipped with gas lighting before 1860. The open flame batswing or fishtail burners at the left are original to this chandelier. The inverted burners at the right are designed for Welsbach mantles and were added after 1905. The design of the chandelier bears out a putative date of around 1860. Photograph by Jack E. Boucher, 1962. (LC HABS FLA, 37–TALA, 6–9)

Figure 52 Gas fixture in Holstein's bedroom in the James Whitcomb Riley House, Indianapolis, Marion County, Indiana. John R. Nickum's son-in-law, Charles L. Holstein, was a U.S. district attorney. Until his death in 1901 he occupied the southeast corner bed-sitting room in the house. The chandelier in that room was originally all gaslighted. The electrical elements were added early in the present century. Although James Whitcomb Riley never owned the house that now bears his name, his fame as a popular poet and journalist has eclipsed the memory of the Nickum and Holstein families who were his hosts. Photograph by Jack E. Boucher, 1970. (LC HABS IND, 49–IND, 8–16)

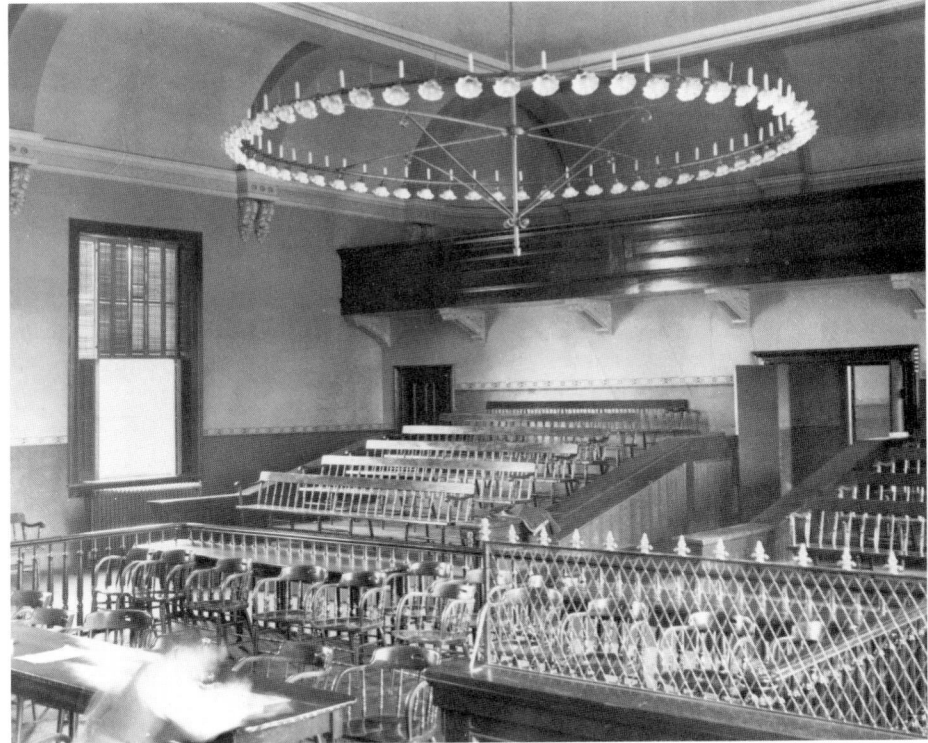

Figure 54 Main courtroom, Courthouse, Charles Town, Jefferson County, West Virginia. Originally built in 1801, the Jefferson County Courthouse was partially destroyed during the Civil War and restored and enlarged around 1867. The main courtroom is on the second floor, which was added at that time. The extraordinary chandelier in the form of a corona dates from around 1900 and combines over fifty gas candles with a like number of white-shaded electric bulbs. Photograph by Edward M. Craig, 1936. (LC HABS W-VA, 19–CHART, 3–11)

Figure 55 Basement women's lounge in the Paramount Theatre, Oakland, Alameda County, California. The Paramount Theatre was built in 1930–31 from plans by Timothy L. Pflueger. It is one of the finest remaining examples of Art Deco design in the United States. It was one of the first depression-era buildings to incorporate and integrate the work of numerous creative artists into its architecture and is particularly noteworthy for its successful orchestration of the various artistic disciplines into an original and harmonious whole. The corners of this women's lounge contain floor-to-ceiling concave quarter-round amber-back-lit etched glass panels, creating an unusual spatial effect. A large silvered plaster bas-relief, representing a female nude blowing a slender horn and sitting precariously on a goat prancing over a stylized cloud and shooting star, is centered on the east wall opposite the entrance. A recessed shallow silvered dome occupies the center of the ceiling and contains a very large-scaled plaster centerpiece of stylized foliation from which depends a two-tiered frosted glass lobe-edged light fixture accented by radiating metal spokes. The theater was restored in 1973 and is now a National Historic Landmark. Photograph by Gabriel Moulin Studios, 1932. (LC HABS CAL, 1–OAK, 9–25)

in Woodstock, Vermont, dates from the 1850s and is an unusually fanciful example of a basically simple type (fig. 45). The relatively large Neo-Rococo gaselier in the northeast room of the Hardaway-Wilson House of 1840 in Mobile is also typical of the 1850s, but the shades are about forty years later in date (fig. 46). Similarly elaborate fixtures of the 1850s survived in the Elk's Club in Montgomery, Alabama. The Wickham-Valentine House in Richmond, Virginia, has superb examples in the parlor and hall (fig. 1). Gas fixtures of the 1860s are splendidly represented in the Governor Henry Lippitt House in Providence, Rhode Island, and by equally lavish and generally more graceful examples in the Morse-Libby House in Portland, Maine (fig. 47).

Glass gas chandeliers normally hung in parlors, but almost never in dining rooms. A particularly fine example of this "crystal" type with cut glass shades hangs in the Wayne-Gordon House in Savannah, Georgia. The double parlor of the Stanford-Lathrop Memorial Home of 1857 in Sacramento, California, had a handsome pair of six-light crystal fixtures that apparently dated from a remodeling finished in 1872 (fig. 48). The west parlor had a center-slide chandelier, whose central Argand burner could be lowered, executed by Mitchell, Vance and Company of New York (fig. 49). Such fixtures were used principally over library and dining room tables. The Néo-Grec chandelier in the first-floor southeast room of the J. Stuart Wells House of 1870 in Binghamton, New York, is highly characteristic of a style that flourished from around 1865 until the late 1870s (fig. 50).

The use of glass and porcelain smoke bells suspended above gas jets was primarily confined to hall fixtures (called pendants) like that in the James B. Weeks House in Kingston, New York. Occasionally smoke bells were used with chandeliers like the example with original shades dating from the 1850s in the Dearing House in Tuscaloosa, Alabama. The James Whitcomb Riley House in Indianapolis has smoke bells above the chandeliers in the dining room and in Riley's bedroom (fig. 51). The Riley House remains as it was when six electric lights were added to the original Eastlake gas fixture in Charles L. Holstein's bedroom (fig. 52).

The gradual progress electric light made against gas was slowed by the incandescent Welsbach burner which was first advertised in 1890. In 1905 an inverted Welsbach burner was introduced. Both the old and new types of gas burner are present in a partially converted chandelier in the James Kirksey House in Tallahassee, Florida

(fig. 53). Before 1900, combination gas and electric fixtures became fairly common, and so-called gas candles were then a favored form of burner. The extraordinary corona in the Court House in Charles Town, West Virginia, combines gas candles with electric lights and thus heralds the approaching end of the gaslight era (fig. 54).

Artistically significant lighting fixtures by no means vanished with the conclusion of the gaslight era. Unquestionably some of the most striking lighting effects of this century were achieved in the Art Deco Paramount Theatre built in 1930−31 in Oakland, California. There the potentialities of indirect lighting were ingeniously exploited throughout the theater. The women's lounge in the basement has a particularly handsome ceiling fixture of frosted glass (fig. 55). Such lighting devices and all other important architectural details continue to be documented by the Historic American Buildings Survey.

America's Cast-Iron Heritage

by

MARGOT GAYLE

Cast iron was a gift of the eighteenth century to the nineteenth, and one of vast potential. The expansion of the world's modern cities was aided by it, as were the development of land and sea transportation and the creation of new systems of manufacture and production on an unprecedented scale. Cast iron also made beautiful architecture and landscape decoration democratically available at modest prices. It was strong, durable, and easily handled. As the nineteenth century opened, the age enjoyed a heritage made possible by this gift of eighteenth-century technology and invention. In the same sense, steel may be said to have been the gift of the nineteenth century to the twentieth.

Cast iron is a high carbon alloy, steel a low carbon alloy, and wrought iron an alloy with so little carbon that it is very close to pure iron. Other materials may also be included in these alloys by nature or added by man, but the carbon content is crucial. Each of these iron alloys has markedly different characteristics.

The alloy cast iron can be melted and then cast with the aid of patterns and cores, or by lost wax methods, into almost any shape that man can devise. It will hold that shape forever unless remelted. It has tremendous strength in compression but virtually no elasticity, and hence it is brittle and has little tensile strength. Wrought iron cannot be cast but it can be forged, hammered, and rolled. Steel unites the properties of strength in compression and in tension. It can be rolled, extruded, and cast, although the last presents difficulties.

In 1747 Abraham Darby of Shropshire, England, separated iron from its ore by substituting coke for scarce and costly charcoal, and when he was able to substitute coal for coke a few years later the future availability of cast iron was assured. There was no shortage of raw material, for iron is estimated to constitute one-twentieth of the earth's surface. After 1750 cast iron was no longer scarce, while wrought iron could be produced only with considerable labor and experience in small quantities by the process known as "puddling" and steel remained a distant dream. Darby's celebrated breakthrough became a principal factor in making the Industrial Revolution possible.

In England early railroad rails and steam boilers were cast iron. As sail gave way to steam, powerful engines required large-scale cast-iron components, which in the United States were produced in foundries along the east coast by sand casting in deep pits. Operations like the

For a description of the illustration, see p. 160.

159

Figure 1 Color lithograph by Sarony, Major & Knapp, the frontispiece in *Illustrations of Iron Architecture* (New York: Baker & Godwin, 1865), the catalog of Daniel D. Badger's Architectural Iron Works of New York. Only five copies of this beautifully illustrated publication are known, including one in the Library of Congress Prints and Photographs Division. None of its illustrations better show the full range of activities than this wonderfully imaginative, evocative pastiche of the factory in action. It reveals a beehive of activity, the artist having concentrated on the galleries, the foundry floor, and the basement beneath it, depicting in one scene the numerous processes that took place in various portions of what was actually a sprawling foundry. On the top balconies are typical post-and-lintel assemblies, probably representing shop-fitting of raw parts. One post is being raised to the right balcony on a gin pole and tackle, and a similar operation is

seen on the middle balcony at the left, where a large lathe is in action and a drilling machine is being diligently cranked. The pattern shop occupies the middle right balcony. At the back, a patternmaker at his bench is engaged in hand work, which most patternmaking at that time involved. The big lathes are for wood turning, most of the balance of the work on patterns. The lathe in the foreground has elaborate gears propelled by a flat drive belt. In the background a workman uses a hammer, and other hammers are raised throughout the foundry. Eight chimneys belch smoke above the roof.

In the foreground architects are discussing their working drawings with foundry representatives and clients. In this happiest of all foundries, there are ladies in Victorian garb participating, looking over plans or strolling down the stairs, one with a parasol, tranquil amid all the hammering, grinding, assembling, and transporting of iron pieces.

On the basement level, a foundry with two cupola furnaces is seen in the space on the left. A stiff-leg crane is maneuvering the ladle of molten metal and pouring it into a flask containing a sand mold. Another part of a mold, the "drag," lies open on the floor. The horse and cart appear to be taking out a load of sand much used and ready to be discarded. Behind them, a workbench supports a large shear for cutting small bar stock or wire, basic to fence production. To the right, wrought iron is being produced by the puddling process in three reverberatory furnaces. Two workmen strike blows to a wrought iron part which a third man holds in position on the anvil. Although the company's stock in trade was cast-iron elements, wrought iron was produced for special structural uses, such as in bridges or girders reinforced with tension rods. (LC–USZ62–80408)

Novelty Iron Works on the banks of Manhattan's East River became well known to the maritime trade.

Cast iron proved a boon to the growing young nation, and the small ironworks which were set up throughout colonial America rapidly expanded after the Revolution removed the manufacturing restrictions of the mother country. The Historic American Buildings Survey has recorded cold blast charcoal furnaces like those in use in colonial times (fig. 2), and its sister agency, the Historic American Engi-

neering Record, has documented later examples (fig. 3).

The ancient sand-casting process for creating objects large and small from molten lead, brass, bronze, and iron continued its usefulness for cast-iron architectural and industrial elements. Occasionally the lost wax process for casting metals has been used to produce small precision components, usually for machinery, although we think of it most often in connection with making fine bronzes or jewelry.

In primitive sand casting, a bed of damp sand on the foundry floor received the imprint of a form or pattern that was pressed into it. Ornamental touches were easily added by also pressing a length of rope, a bit of lettering, a coat of arms or a trademark, or some other appropriate design into the molded sand. Molten metal was poured into the resulting impressions in the sand and on cooling retained the shape of the temporary mold, at which time the sand could be brushed away to be used again. This method has enjoyed a variety of uses, whether for medieval iron graveslabs and firebacks or flat plate stoves and modern manhole covers. From Louisiana firebacks (fig. 4) to kitchen stoves (Roth, fig. 17) and Philadelphia sidewalks (fig. 5), HABS has recorded a variety of examples of sand-cast ironwork.

More useful and capable of producing more sophisticated castings is the flask system, wherein the damp refractory sand is packed into a two-part box called a "flask." A pattern—usually carved of pine or mahogany and shaped like the casting that will be the end result—is embedded in the center of the flask, and sand is rammed around it. After the "cope" or top half of the flask has been lifted to allow the pattern to be withdrawn, leaving a perfect impression, it is replaced and molten metal is poured into the cavity through small channels poked in the sand. This system makes possible a casting with a front and a back of different designs, like those found in the exterior railing of the Dakota Apartments or in the gallery railing of the U.S. Sub-Treasury Building in New York City, in a Brooklyn row house, on the stoop of a house in Schenectady, or on the veranda of the rectory of St. John's Church in Troy, New York (figs. 6, 7).

We have seen that cast iron can be shaped into many forms, either plain and utilitarian or complex and ornamental. Perhaps the most familiar use of cast iron, combining its decorative and structural properties, has been in the porticoes, porches, and verandas of the type seen in the Albany rectory but more characteristic of the American South. The Col. Robert Henry Short House in New Orleans provides a handsome example of two common residential uses of cast iron (fig. 8). Its two-story portico and cornstalk fence have cast filigreed shadows on house and lawn since 1859. Architect William Strickland made extensive interior use of similar cast-iron elements in his Tennessee Capitol, most conspicuously in its library, where the balconies, bookcases, lamp standards, and even the ceiling panels are of iron

(fig. 9). In 1851 Thomas Ustick Walter used the material almost exclusively to render the Library of Congress room in the Capitol fireproof (Peatross, fig. 5), ordering his castings from the Janes, Beebe Ironworks in the Bronx, New York. The same ironworks was soon thereafter to supply the iron plates for the Capitol dome under the name of Janes, Kirtland & Co. Cast iron remained a popular material for library construction during the next half century and was used extensively for the bookstacks of the new Library of Congress building, finished in 1897, and Georgetown University's Riggs Memorial Library (fig. 10), completed in 1889, both works of the architectural firm of Smithmeyer & Pelz.

It was for exterior use, however, that cast iron proved most popular. The economy, durability, and maleability of iron recommended its widespread use in ornamental enclosures for parks, pleasure grounds, yards, and, not infrequently, cemeteries. If ever a metal was appropriate to the spirit of a period it was cast iron—with its endless capacity for ornament—in the

Figure 2 Bear Spring furnace, five miles east of Dover, Tennessee. Although not built until 1873, this abandoned charcoal blast furnace in Stewart County is of a classic type, its thirty-seven-foot limestone stack typical of earlier usage. Photograph of south front by Jack Boucher, November 1971. (HABS TENN–36, LC HABS TENN, 81-DOVE.V, 1–2)

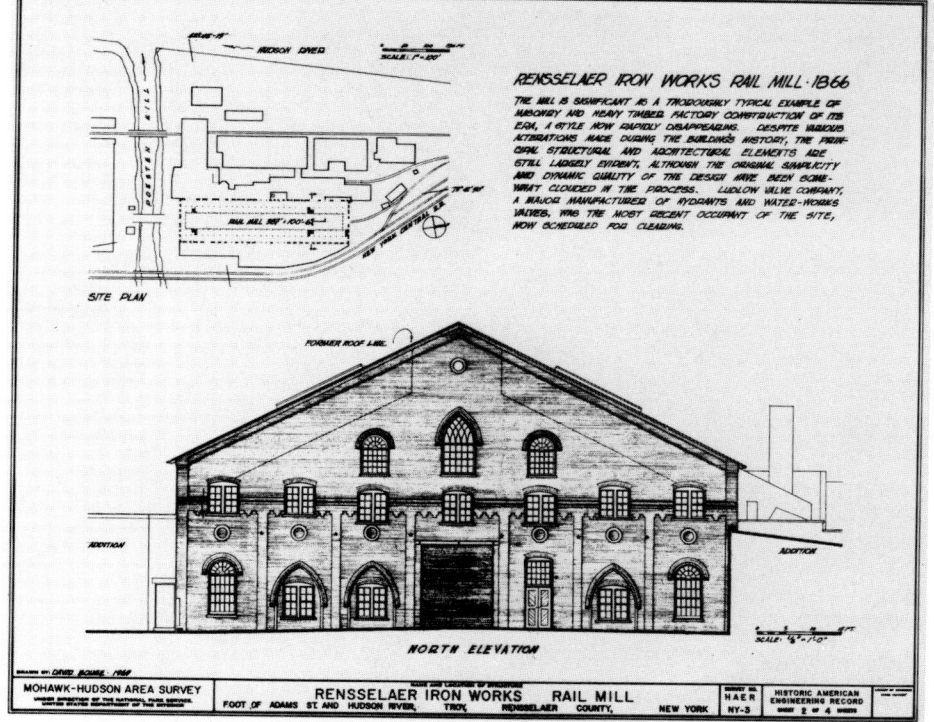

Figure 3 Rennselaer Iron Works rail mill, site plan, and north elevation by David Bouse, 1969. HAER's survey of New York's Mohawk-Hudson area recorded many notable nineteenth-century industrial structures, including this rail mill, recorded shortly before its demolition. Other iron foundries represented in the HAER collection are the famous Tredegar Works in Richmond, Virginia, and the Columbus Works in Columbus, Georgia, both of which served as major arsenals of the Confederacy. (HAER NY–3, sheet 2 of 4 sheets)

Figure 4 Flatbed sand-cast fireback panels are evident in this September 1934 photograph by architect Richard Koch, then in charge of HABS in Louisiana. Recorded in the David Olivier house at 4111 Chartres Street in New Orleans, dated ca. 1820 and since demolished, the iron plates bear a sunburst design. (HABS LA–70, LC HABS LA, 36–NEWOR, 49–7)

Figure 5 Iron paving blocks represent an extraordinary use of cast iron recorded by HABS in Philadelphia. The hexagonal flat pavers had an embossed geometric design and were laid in a considerable length of midtown sidewalk, alongside North Seventh Street. It is said that they have since been relaid at a museum house in Germantown. Photograph by Jack Boucher, May 1972. (HABS PA–1723–4, LC HABS PA, 51– PHILA, 291–4)

Victorian Age. HABS has recorded the beautiful rustic cast-iron fence protecting the Johnstone family plot in the cemetery of the Chapel of the Cross near Madison, Mississippi (fig. 11). Intertwining oak branches are combined with leaves and acorns beneath berried juniper for picturesque effect. Tall iron fences often guarded entire cemeteries, such as Boston's Mount Auburn and Brooklyn's Greenwood (Peatross, fig. 14), as well as private plots. Nineteenth-century landscape designers could not fail to exploit the possibilities of cast iron. Cast-iron figures and other elements populated public parks and private grounds throughout the century. Elegant Woodruff Place, laid out in 1872 in Indianapolis, Indiana, was conceived as such a suburban-dweller's dream, a bourgeois Versailles both enclosed and embellished by the versatile material.

Cast iron was a very democratic material in that it enabled families of modest means to have neat iron fences around their yards, pretty railings on their stoops, an attractive bench on the lawn, and even a useful umbrella holder and hatrack of iron in the hall. Upstairs all the children might have iron beds. Of course there would be iron tea kettles and skillets on the iron cookstove in the kitchen.

A more affluent family might have in addition lacelike iron cresting along the ridgeline of the roof of their house or accentuating its pavilions, peaks, and parapets. Charming iron balconies at the windows, elaborate urns for flowers in the yards, a cast-iron

Figure 6 The flask-casting method makes possible a form with a different design on front and back. This example is from the iron fence at the sidewalk's edge around the celebrated Dakota Apartments, built on New York's Upper West Side overlooking Central Park in 1883. Manufactured by the Hecla Iron Works in Brooklyn, this ornament presents the stern face of Neptune. The back shows Neptune's long locks surmounted by a crown. Sea monsters guard him. Photograph by Jack Boucher, 1965. (HABS NY–5467, LC HABS NY, 31–NEYO, 74–6)

watchdog beside iron-railed steps, and even a bubbling iron fountain topped by a cherub struggling to hold a spouting iron fish were likely domestic appurtenances of the well-to-do.

Cast iron figured in the daily life of Americans in many ways. Nineteenth-century city dwellers found it all around them in the form of street furniture, both useful and ornamental. Myriad hitching posts once punctuated the streetscape. HABS fortunately recorded a nice sampling of these posts and other vanishing artifacts in a 1930s survey of ironwork in Mobile, Alabama (fig. 13), including lamp posts (Myers, fig. 41). The remarkable lighting fixtures which once adorned the terraces of Strickland's Tennessee Capitol would have been worthy of any European capitol (fig. 14). Even the figures are of iron. To achieve sufficient height, the old harbor beacon in Savannah, Georgia, used several iron sections rising from a polygonal base to a foliate top from which the beacon itself seemingly blossoms (fig. 15). The serviceable cast-iron column was sometimes called upon to support another once-common main street fixture, the bank clock. A handsome example of the sidewalk variety survives at the corner of Main and South First Street in Salt Lake City, where it has kept time for over a century (fig. 16).

The versatile cast-iron column is a form which can best exploit one of the material's most outstanding qualities, its load-bearing capacity. This ferrous alloy is so strong that it can be used sparingly and economically in thin-walled shapes like pipes and hollow columns. From the nineteenth century until this day, cast-iron pipe has provided towns and cities with services necessary for urban expansion, carrying water and gas for illumination, cooking, heating, and industry. HABS documentation of a multiplicity of cast-iron artifacts has focused on the nineteenth century, from early surveys of miscellaneous ironwork in cities as widely separated as Mobile and Chicago to more recent documenta-

tion of iron front buildings, reflecting the increased appreciation of a unique nineteenth-century building type. Cast-iron columns, used throughout the western world in building construction, are best seen in these buildings. They revolutionized nineteenth-century construction. It has been said that there are more iron columns in SoHo in lower Manhattan than there were stone columns in the whole of the antique world. HABS has recorded examples throughout the United States.

The U.S. Customhouse in Galveston, Texas, is a handsome example of the sophisticated mid-century use of cast iron by the Office of the Supervising Architect of the U.S. Treasury. Ammi B. Young's column designs, the subject of handsome published lithographs, were key elements in a neo-Palladian structure which brought something of the nobility of Vicenza to a remote American port city. Interior cast-iron columns proved equally serviceable substitutes for their stone counterparts and allowed the architects of the capitol buildings required by the rapidly

Figure 7 Sculptor John Frazee's Sub-Treasury railing was copied by others. Versions of it can be seen in New York City and elsewhere in the state, the two-story iron veranda of St. John's Rectory in Troy among them. Built in 1863 and demolished in 1936, it demonstrates various ornamental uses of cast iron. Measured drawing by A. H. Mosley, 1934. (HABS NY–358, sheet 1 of 1 sheet)

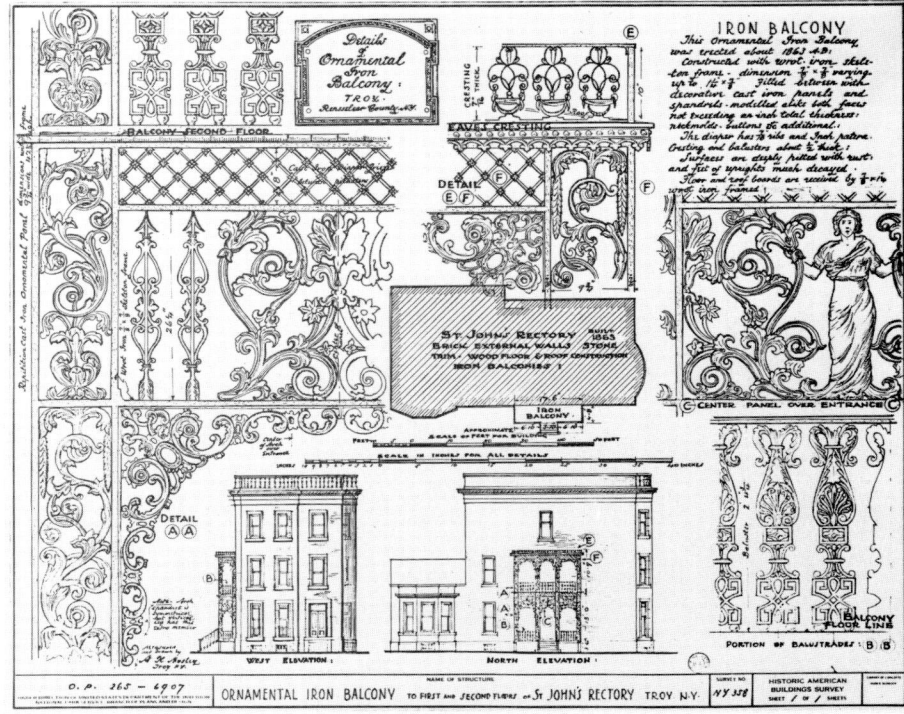

Figure 8 The Short-Moran House (Colonel Short's Villa), 1448 Fourth Street at Prytania, New Orleans, Louisiana, was begun in the summer of 1859 by architect Henry Howard. The house is notable both for its lace-like iron galleries and for its imposing length of cast-iron fence, the latter in the famous cornstalk pattern. The name Wood & Miltenberger, the New Orleans agent of the Philadelphia ornamental ironworks Wood & Perot, is embossed at the base of the fence posts. New Orleans, romantically identified with lovely iron verandahs in both the French Quarter and the Garden District, has had gallant preservation champions in the late Richard Koch and in Samuel Wilson, Jr., architects who deeply appreciated cast-iron architecture and over the years battled for its preservation. Wilson provided the following paragraph from the New Orleans *Daily Picayune* of July 7, 1852: "One of the most admirable innovations upon the old system of building tall, staring structures for business purposes is the plan, which we are glad to see is generally coming into use, of erecting galleries and verandahs of ornamental iron work." Obviously, houses as well as commercial structures benefited from this trend, which changed the face of many Southern cities. Photograph by Dan Leyrer, August 1963. (HABS LA–1112, LC HABS LA, 36–NEWOR, 60–2)

Figure 9 Libraries in public buildings and institutions sought in every way to reduce fire hazards in the nineteenth century, and cast-iron interior construction provided one answer. William Strickland's Tennessee Capitol, built at Nashville, 1845–59, was filled with charming ironwork cast by the Wood & Perot foundry, installed about 1858 and still intact. Two high galleries of iron bookstacks cover most of one wall and are reached by a cast-iron spiral stairway with perforated treads and risers and an extremely lacy railing highlighted by animal heads. Equally elaborate but quite different railings guard the narrow walkway along the galleries. Enwreathed foliate designs feature a row of iron rondels into each of which is cast a profile portrait of a famous philosopher or statesman. The galleries have ornate soffits and are held to the wall by elaborate acanthus brackets five feet in length. Because the original legislative reference collection has long since outgrown this library room in the capitol, the space now serves as a legislative meeting room. Measured drawing by George D. Nevins, 1934. (HABS TENN 19–15, sheet 18 of 23 sheets)

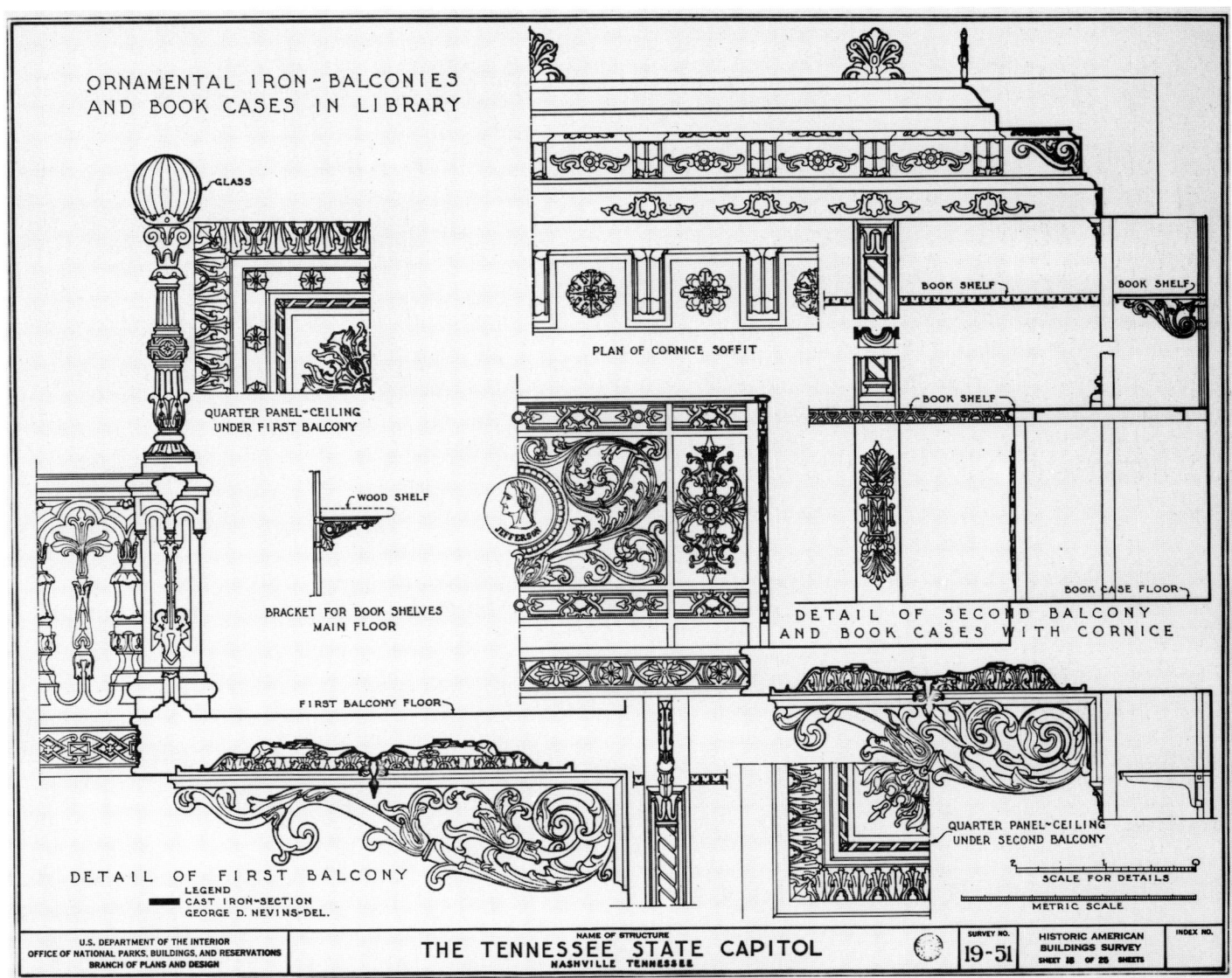

Figure 10 Completed in 1889, the Riggs Memorial Library forms one part of Georgetown University's Healy Building, begun in 1877 by the architectural firm of Smithmeyer & Pelz, which was also responsible for the 1897 Library of Congress building. Bookstacks in both structures made extensive use of cast-iron elements. The Riggs Library has cast-iron piers, some iron flooring, iron railings, and many levels of iron stacks. Photograph by Jack Boucher, November 1969. (HABS DC–248, LC HABS DC GEO, 118–24)

growing states to compete with one another in the creation of grand public spaces. Elijah Myers specialized in designs for state capitols and county courthouses from Illinois to Texas. Characteristic of his ornate Victorian interiors is the stairhall of the Michigan Capitol at Lansing (figs. 17,18, 19).

The greatest tests of the structural possibilities of cast-iron columns are found in industrial structures. Both the gasholder of the Petersburg, Virginia, Gas Light Company (fig. 20) and the Harlem (New York) Fire Watchtower (fig. 21) demonstrate how a minimum of cast-iron columns could be used to achieve both great height and stability. Such skeletal structures led the way for the iron and later steel framing which made possible the peculiarly American achievement, the skyscraper.

The history of the development of iron framing begins in England. Carl Condit observed in his *American Building Art, the Nineteenth Century,* "the decisive step in the direction of iron

framing was the application of the material to columns" in England. Perhaps the first appearance of iron columns was in St. Ann's, Liverpool, in 1770. By 1779 the iron bridge had been placed across the Severn River at Coalbrookdale, a totally cast-iron monument that still stands for use by pedestrians. The Prince of Wales in ceremonies in July 1979 saluted its bicentennial and its restoration. Other cast-iron bridges followed, as well as aqueducts with cast-iron troughs to carry canals across streams. Recurring fires in English cotton mills drove owners to seek fireproofing. Iron columns began to replace wooden and masonry supports toward the close of the eighteenth century, and Charles Bage's spinning mill was built in Shropshire with both slender cruciform cast-iron columns and cast-iron beams in 1796. It is acknowledged to be the first metal-framed multistory building in the world, and it still serves as a working industrial structure.

Our friend William Strickland is

regarded as the first architect to have employed iron columns in this country. In 1822 he supported "three rows of boxes resting on cast iron columns secured with iron sockets" in Philadelphia's Chestnut Street Theater, now gone. Five years later in the same city he used eighty-eight slender cast-iron columns quite differently to support the double-decked piazzas on both wings of the U.S. Naval Asylum. This structure still stands, an excellent candidate for a HABS recording project. The British-American architect John Haviland was also much interested in the innovative possibilities of cast iron, and in 1830 he veneered the front of a two-story bank in Pottsville, Pennsylvania, with flat cast-iron plates painted to resemble stone. This non-load-bearing system for iron building fronts, popular in the Philadelphia area, continued to be used for several more decades (fig. 28). The development of the load-bearing iron front was, however, to prove far more significant in the use of cast iron for the construction of entire buildings. Before looking at applications of these developments in commercial buildings, a glance at the increasing use of cast-iron elements in other nineteenth century structures is in order.

Perhaps the simplest and most

Figure 11 The ornamental possibilities of cast iron are usefully compared to those of wrought iron in this January 1934 measured drawing by Jay T. Liddle, Jr., and A. N. Town showing details of three iron fences guarding the cemetery lots of the Mannsdale, Mississippi, Chapel of the Cross. Detail B shows the Sutton family's fence, entirely of wrought iron with the possible exception of the palmette at the upper left. Detail C depicts the wrought iron gate capped by cast-iron decorations which opened to the Wiggins family plot. And detail A represents the dramatically more sculptural and organic forms of the entirely cast-iron fence erected by the Johnstone family. (HABS MISS 17–3, sheet 6 of 6 sheets)

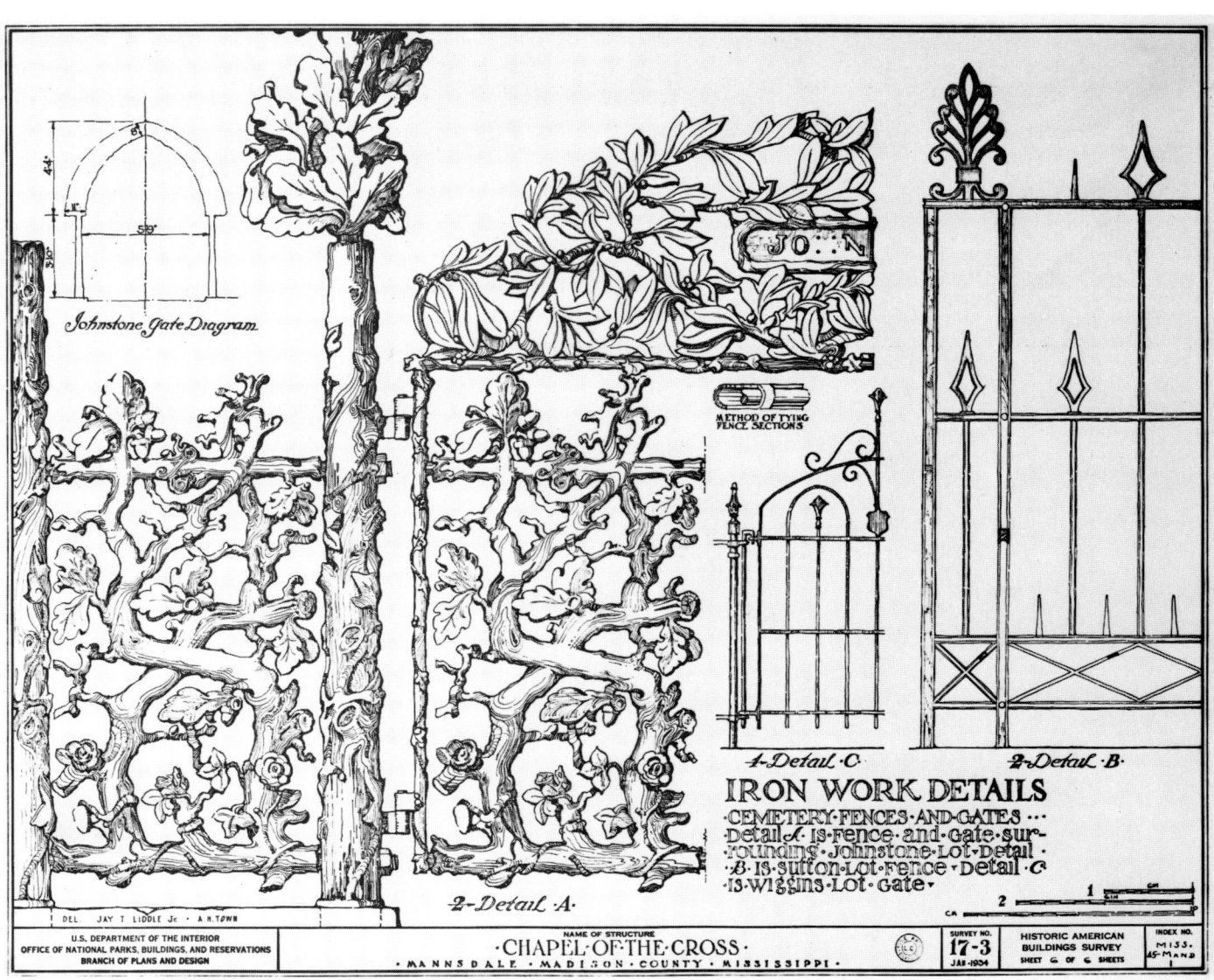

Figure 12 Along with fences, many other outdoor amenities were produced in cast iron, such as the embellishments for the malls of Woodruff Place, a subdivision laid out in 1872 in Indianapolis and recorded by HABS almost a century later. In the landscaped and planted malls were placed a variety of cast-iron adornments that included large iron urns or flower planters ornamented with cherubs and floral patterns. There were iron benches, iron statues (usually Grecian ladies on pedestals), ornamental lamp standards, and a series of iron fountains both large and small. Jordan L. Mott cast these popular Victorian pieces in his Bronx foundry and advertised them in folio catalogs illustrated with large wood engravings of his products. A number of these original nineteenth-century catalogs are available in the Case Book Collection of the Prints and Photographs Division of the Library of Congress as a supplement to the HABS collection. This illustration is a HABS photographic copy of a lithograph by Braden & Burford, ca. 1888, depicting the entrance to Woodruff Place, whose three esplanades were improved and ornamented between 1872 and 1877 at a cost of $250,000. (HABS IND–67, LC HABS IND, 49–IND, 22–1)

Figure 13 The 1935 HABS survey of iron street furniture in Mobile, Alabama, includes drawings of two gas lamp posts standing at that time as well as these iron posts for hitching horses. The four cast-iron posts are hollow and variously ornamented with acanthus, horses' and lions' heads, finials, and flutes. The single wrought iron example is solid with simple facets. Gateposts, fencing, and porch railings are also recorded in the Mobile survey, carried out in a city where to walk the streets is to study a textbook of beautiful and utilitarian urban cast-iron work. (HABS ALA–36, sheet 1 of 2 sheets)

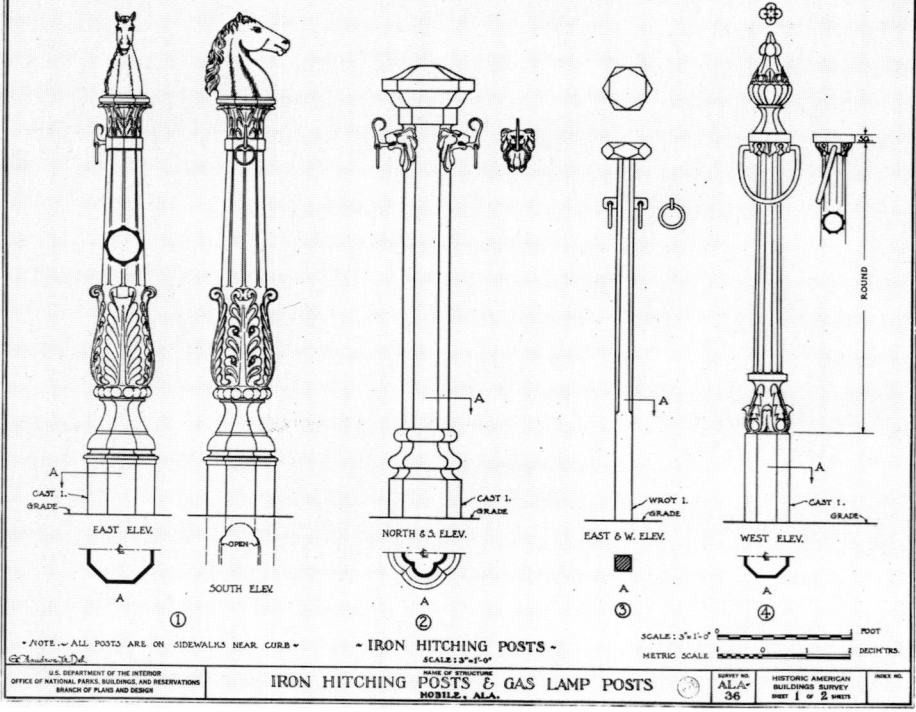

Figure 15 HABS recorded Savannah's old harbor beacon in 1934. Produced in the ironworks of Wood & Perot, the very tall and graceful cast-iron standard was erected in 1858, and although it no longer serves as a beacon to mariners it is still well maintained. (HABS GA–232, LC HABS GA, 26–SAV, 23–1)

Figure 14 Although HABS made record photographs of the Tennessee Capitol in 1934 and 1940, the remarkable iron lamp standards which flanked the south or principal entrance steps had already suffered the loss of their handsome capitals and lanterns. Their original form is preserved in the Ordway Collection in the Prints and Photographs Division of the Library of Congress, which includes this 1862 image by a staff photographer for Mathew Brady. Three graceful, classically draped, life-size cast-iron figures encircle each lampstand's base. The ten-foot fluted column is surmounted by an ornamental lantern. A wartime barricade blocks the steps, where it is said cannon were at one time set up. (HABS TENN 19–51, LC–B811–2627)

Figure 16 Utah provided an example of the cast-iron post clock. A Main Street landmark in Salt Lake City since about 1870, the Zion's First National City Bank clock reputedly had works which were first driven by a water wheel, later hand wound, then battery run, and finally fully electrified. Swags of metal drapery hang from its four large faces, draped through corner rings held by lion masks. This example is very like a Seth Thomas clock that for years stood on Lexington Avenue opposite Bloomingdale's store in Manhattan and is also reminiscent of a jeweler's clock still standing in downtown St. Louis. (HABS U–38, LC HABS UTAH, 18–SALCI, 12A–1)

DETAILS
or
EXTERIOR COLUMNS, etc.
(Scale ¼ size.)

TOP VIEW
of A

FRONT VIEW of A

Drawing No. 6.

DAUGHTER IRON   PURLIN

SECTION of UPPER CORNICE AT VERANDA.

A

COLUMNS of SECOND STORY

VIEW and SECTION from ABOVE

COLUMNS of THIRD STORY

DETAIL showing CONNECTION of DORIC and IONIC ORDER by SECTIONS.

COLUMNS of LOWER STORY

Designed by A.B. Young, Archt.

Figure 17 This handsome 1856 lithograph of a design by Ammi B. Young was one of nine printed by A. Kollner of Philadelphia and included in volume 29 of *Plans of Public Buildings in Course of Construction under the Direction of the Secretary of the Treasury*. The publication illustrates a three-story pseudoperipteral scheme for the U.S. Customhouse at Galveston, Texas, quite different from the two-story structure with closed corner pavilions completed six years later (fig. 18). According to Young's design, seen here but later superseded, the customhouse would have followed classical principles in the proper superimposition of the Doric, Ionic, and Corinthian orders. The sectional views demonstrate how iron and wooden members were to be joined. Prints and Photographs Division. (LC–USZ62–58021)

Figure 19 State capitols, especially those built between 1850 and 1880, display noble tall iron columns in profusion. The Michigan Capitol at Lansing by Elijah E. Myers was no exception, constructed over a period of six years and completed in 1878. Here we see the cast-iron staircase leading up from the main floor, with tall paired columns on paneled bases. Similar iron columns are to be met throughout the structure's spacious main level. Other iron elements include the rotunda balustrade and the framing and exterior columns of the dome above it. The extensive HABS report written by Harley J. McKee in 1965 states that the prevailing interior colors are brown and yellow and warm dark red, together with certain deep blue-greens. Also notable are the wall and ceiling frescoes and the great brass chandelier, originally piped for gas. (HABS MICH–230)

Figure 18 This July 1936 HABS photograph by Harry L. Starnes shows the handsome use of forty-eight cast-iron columns on the exterior of the U.S. Customhouse in Galveston, Texas, as it was completed in 1861 to designs by Cluskey and Moore, contracted by Blandell and Emerson of Boston. Corinthian above and Ionic below, the columns form in-antis porticoes on the structure's longer north and south fronts while that on the west projects. Inside the brick structure are more iron columns, iron staircases, and apparently some early "Cooper Beams." Supervising Architect of the Treasury Ammi B. Young was an enthusiastic supporter of the innovative metal and often combined cast columns with wrought iron beams such as Peter Cooper had by 1854 succeeded in rolling in his Trenton, New Jersey, foundry. This customhouse has survived Galveston's disastrous storm in 1900, Hurricane Carla in 1961, and then a gas explosion in 1979 that knocked out the unadorned east wall, since repaired. When the structure was threatened with demolition, a federal judge who had presided in its courtroom led the local demands that it be saved. (HABS TEX–259, LC HABS TEX, 89–GALV, 12–1)

Figure 20 A highly utilitarian use of almost fragile-looking cast-iron columns can be seen in the six pairs of three-tiered, fluted cast-iron columns which form the metal frame of the gasholder erected in 1851–52 by the Petersburg Gaslight Company in Petersburg, Virginia. These are stabilized at the top by a ring of perforated horizontal cast-iron members which complete the framework. The paired columns held vertical rails that guided the inverted tank as it rose and fell within the water-filled pit which sealed in the gas, then used by customers primarily for illumination. Recorded by HAER in 1970–71, this rare survivor stands now like a piece of delicate sculpture. Photograph by Jack Boucher, 1971. (HAER VA–14)

common use of cast iron for domestic exteriors was for window and, less frequently, doorway lintels. Characteristic is the row house built in Georgetown, in the District of Columbia, in 1859 by Francis Wheatley, where bold iron windowheads punctuate the brick front, combined with stylistically similar doorways and cornices in other materials (fig. 22). It is likely that the Wheatley lintels were stock items ordered from a dealer or catalog, whereas the more elaborate tripartite Gothic lintels of Ingelside in Lexington, Kentucky, were made in the owner's foundry to the designs of architect John McMurtry (fig. 23). Even the ornate crocketed spires of this handsome villa, completed in 1852, were cast of iron. Even more sophisticated are the traceried Gothic elements which make up the tomb of President James Monroe in the Hollywood cemetery in Richmond, Virginia (fig. 24). Erected in 1859 to the design of Albert Lybrock, an Alsatian emigrant, the structure is entirely of iron and was ordered from

the Philadelphia works of Wood and Perot, despite the fact that Richmond was itself a center for the material's manufacture. Perhaps the ultimate combination of traceried Gothic elements in iron is to be found in the spectacular central rotunda of the old Louisiana Capitol at Baton Rouge as rebuilt by architect William A. Freret in 1880. Combining the form of an English chapter house with iron tracery filled with brightly colored glass, Freret created one of nineteenth-century America's most delightful and dramatic interiors (fig. 25).

The commercial uses of cast iron in this country, from storefronts to entire buildings, expanded yearly in both type and volume. Main street merchants could choose from a whole array of storefronts when building new structures or updating existing ones. Through a mid-century addition of a cast-iron front with large plate glass windows, an old red brick Greek Revival hotel in Athens, Georgia, was transformed into a flourishing commercial block (fig. 26). An iron storefront did many things for a commercial building. It opened up the facade to glazing, which allowed daylight to flood in. It permitted merchandise to be displayed in clear view of the passersby. It took up very little floor space. Such iron fronts became such a pervasive all-purpose type of iron architecture that virtually every little foundry in the country offered columns, piers, and colonettes made either from standard patterns or to custom designs. Seldom were these iron members called on to carry part of a building's floor load. For the most part they simply held up from two to five upper stories of a front wall built of wood, brick, stone, iron, or pressed metal.

The cast-iron front constituted an almost uniquely American development. It was an industrialized architecture in which mass-produced iron parts, many of them identical and interchangeable, could readily be delivered to nearby construction sites or shipped great distances. Looking back,

Figure 21 Iron fire lookout tower in Harlem's Marcus Garvey Park. This cast-iron structure was built in 1857 by Julius Kroehl from a design by James Bogardus, who had already built two even taller towers for the city's volunteer fire department. In the 1850s Bogardus had also erected two high shot towers along the same lines, adding brick curtain walls to prevent the wind from blowing hot shot out. These towers were in effect miniskyscrapers. As pioneer cast iron scholar Turpin Bannister wrote in 1957, they were probably the most prophetic of Bogardus's many inventions. Photograph, 1975. (HAER NY–104)

Figure 22 HABS records illustrate a variety of ways that cast iron was used in the decoration and construction of domestic buildings. This example, the town house of Francis Wheatley, was built in Georgetown, D.C., in 1859. It makes use of cast iron in a number of ways, for window lintels and sills, balcony and stair rails. Had the lintels been individually carved out of stone, their cost might have been prohibitive. Identical iron lintels were made from sand molds for which only one carved wooden pattern was required, making them relatively inexpensive. Widely used, such iron lintels can still be seen on both residential and commercial buildings in the older sections of most American cities and towns. Photograph by J. Alexander, June 1969. (HABS DC–186, LC HABS DC GEO, 109–1)

Figure 23 Joseph Bruen, who owned an iron and brass foundry in Lexington, Kentucky, commissioned architect John McMurtry to design this Gothic Revival house on Gibson Avenue. It was completed in 1852, and it is not surprising that its tripartite windows had iron lintels and sills and that the cornices, roof, and crocketed spirelets of this picturesque home were also of iron, made at the Bruen Foundry. Photograph by Lester Jones, June 1, 1940. (HABS KY–57, LC HABS KY, 34–LEX, 6–1)

Figure 24 Without question the most hand-some cast-iron tomb structure in the nation is that marking the final resting place of President James Monroe in the Hollywood Cemetery, Richmond, Virginia. On a bluff overlooking the winding James River, this masterpiece of cast-iron craftsmanship was designed in the Gothic style by Albert Lybrock of Richmond and produced by the famous Wood & Perot Foundry of Philadelphia. It was dedicated in 1859 with high military honors after Monroe's body had been moved to his native Virginia from the Marble Cemetery in New York City. The former president had died at the home of his daughter in New York in 1831. Photograph by Edward F. Heite, April 1969. (HABS VA–843, LC HABS VA, 44–RICH, 92–4)

Figure 25 The most romantic of all the state capitols may well be that designed by architect James Dakin for Louisiana, at Baton Rouge. The crenellated Gothic castle of 1850 overlooks the Mississippi River. Its interior was burned out during the hostilities of the Civil War and was rehabilitated after thirty years by New Orleans architect William A. Freret. His genius in the use of cast iron can be seen to best effect in the capitol rotunda, with its sweeping iron staircase and central clustered piers which rise ninety feet before breaking out into a great umbrella of traceried ribs filled with colored glass. Photograph by David J. Kaminsky, 1978. (HABS LA–1132–17, LC HABS LA, 17–BATRO, 6–17)

Figure 26   HABS district officer Harold Bush-Brown recorded this red brick Greek Revival structure, formerly a hotel, in 1936 in Athens, Georgia. A high stoop once led to its main entrance above the ground floor, where stores were later inserted at street level. This transformation had been made possible by that popular American institution, the cast-iron storefront. Here we see the most basic post and lintel framing with cast-iron piers and horizontal members which carry the weight of the wall above. Cast iron being very poor for supporting weight, wrought iron beams were used as soon as they were successfully rolled in this country in the 1850s. Later, steel was the indicated metal, but use of cast-iron supports and columns persisted in storefronts well into the twentieth century because they were economical and handled the job so well. Photograph by L. D. Andrew, August 13, 1936. (HABS GA–1122, LC HABS GA, 30–LATH, 12–1)

Figure 28 Shortly after the fire of July 9, 1850, swept Philadelphia's waterfront, a row of stores was erected at 238–48 Delaware Avenue in the "Burnt District" for John Brock Sons & Co. Joseph C. Hoxie and Stephan Decatur Button were the architects and they designed a two-tier storefront with pleasingly ornamented cast-iron arches glazed with wide windows for lighting the interior as well as for the display of merchandise. The upper three floors were of the Haviland system, veneered with plates of iron giving the appearance of rusticated ashlar masonry. The first stores were occupied by October 1850. Three foundries are stated in the HABS report to have provided cast-iron elements, perhaps to help achieve such remarkable speed. Only the two center stores (at 242–244 North Delaware Avenue) remained and were in use as a warehouse when HABS recorded them in 1970, when they were regarded as the oldest iron-front buildings in the country. Their fate was already sealed by highway development plans when fire raced through the empty structures September 26, 1977. Quick action by Richard Tyler of the Philadelphia Historical Commission secured funds for disassembly of the iron parts and for their storage, and some of these are now re-erected in the Smithsonian Institution. Photograph by Jack Boucher, 1973. (HABS PA–1395, HABS LC PA, 51–PHILA, 278–1)

Figure 29 Often referred to as the Parthenon of iron-front buildings, E. V. Haughwout's store at 490 Broadway, at the corner of Broome Street in Manhattan, has attracted attention from the day it was built in 1856. It was recorded for HABS in 1968 by historian Diana Waite, with photographs by Cervin Robinson. Here we see the original color lithograph of the structure published by the manufacturer of its iron elements, Daniel B. Badger, as plate III in his 1865 catalog, *Illustrations of Iron Architecture*. The complex castings, which in style echo a Venetian palace, demonstrate the virtuosity of his firm. Now a city landmark, the Haughwout Building seemed doomed in 1968 when the proposed Broome Street Expressway received official endorsement. Urbanists Jane Jacobs and James Marston Fitch, among others, came to its defense. It is now included in the SoHo Historic District. Case Collection, Prints and Photographs Division. (LC–USZ62–80409)

Figure 27 (opposite) The Edgar Laing Stores, northwest corner of Washington and Murray Streets, New York, New York. This structure, actually a group of five stores, was erected in only two months in 1849 by James Bogardus, a pioneer in the early use of cast iron for building purposes and a brilliant inventor. By the late 1850s Bogardus had commissions in Philadelphia, Baltimore, Washington, Chicago, San Francisco, and Havana. When the stores were demolished in 1971, the process was recorded by HABS to supplement measured drawings and photographs made in 1965–66. The structure was the earliest example of cast iron front architecture then remaining in the country. Thieves subsequently stole and sold for scrap the iron components of the Laing Stores as they lay enclosed by a chain link fence, stacked, cleaned, primed, and numbered for future reerection. Photograph by John Feulner, March 1966. (HABS NY–5469, LC HABS NY, 31–NEYO, 76–3)

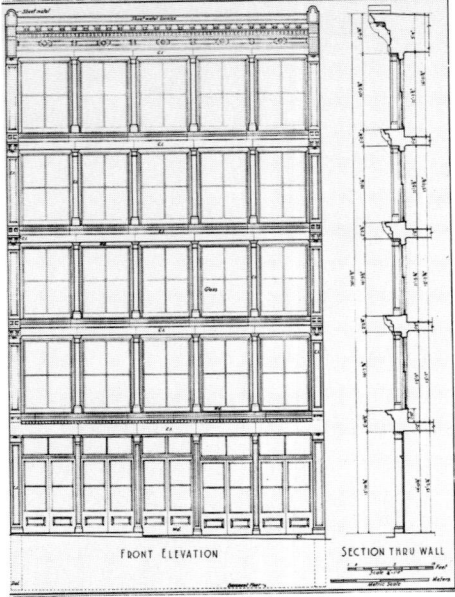

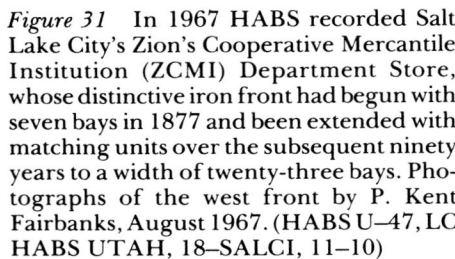

Figure 30 As the time approached around 1940 for the clearance of some forty blocks of old warehouses along the St. Louis waterfront for the creation of the Jefferson National Expansion Memorial Park, now familiar to most because of Eero Saarinen's dramatic stainless steel arch, HABS recorded the iron front of the Thomas Gantt Building. Frank R. Leslie's measured drawing shows the spare iron-and-glass front at 219 Chestnut Street, a simple grid with the slenderest of columns between floor to ceiling windows and a sheet metal cornice. (HABS MO–1138, sheet 2 of 9 sheets)

Figure 31 In 1967 HABS recorded Salt Lake City's Zion's Cooperative Mercantile Institution (ZCMI) Department Store, whose distinctive iron front had begun with seven bays in 1877 and been extended with matching units over the subsequent ninety years to a width of twenty-three bays. Photographs of the west front by P. Kent Fairbanks, August 1967. (HABS U–47, LC HABS UTAH, 18–SALCI, 11–10)

cast iron seems to have held more interest for the practical businessman who wanted a good-looking store or corporate headquarters at an affordable price—and often wanted it built with all speed possible—than for most of the architects to the Establishment.

Architects argued about what they regarded as aesthetic and moral problems posed by cast iron as a building material. Some said it was dishonest because it was cast in shapes that had originated in masonry. Others pleaded for designers to create a new architecture appropriate for the material. In fact, this happened by natural processes as builders and architects became more familiar with the potential of cast iron. A fragile looking, very nearly all-glass building facade became recognizable as an iron front. Quite simply, such a front—often five or six stores tall—could not have supported itself had its slender pillars been fashioned of stone, brick, or wood. They had to be of metal and, in the nineteenth century, before aluminum and steel, that could only be cast iron.

It remained for James Bogardus, a New York inventor of note, to erect in 1848 the first self-supporting multistory iron front combining pillars, cross beams, and infill spandrel panels for the refurbishing of Dr. John Milhau's old pharmacy on lower Broadway in Manhattan. He promoted the idea for making buildings entirely of iron, as he did his own factory in 1849. In 1850 he secured a patent for the fastening of iron parts and for iron roofing and flooring systems. Businessman Edgar Laing persuaded Bogardus to build a row of four-story iron-front stores on his downtown coalyard at the corner of Washington and Murray Streets in New York. Constructed in two months early in 1849, the Laing Stores survived until urban renewal dictated their removal in 1971 (fig. 27).

Protests at the destruction of this historic example that held within it the seeds of the skyscraper led to its being carefully dismantled and stored. Recognizing its significance and the uncertainty of its future, HABS recorded the structure in 1965, and additional photographs were made in 1971 as it was being taken down. Those images reveal how a sophisticated early iron front was joined to a building of conventional warehouse construction, with brick bearing walls and heavy wooden floor construction. HABS has recorded a great variety of iron-front buildings throughout the United States, ranging from what has been called the Parthenon of such structures, New York's E. V. Haughwout Store at 490 Broadway, a commercial palace in the Venetian style whose complex castings were the pride of Daniel Badger's architectural ironworks (fig. 29), to the far simpler Thomas Gantt Building in St. Louis, Missouri, whose broad planes

of glass and minimal metal structure prophesied the future of the American tall building (fig. 30). The cast-iron front of Salt Lake City's Zion's Cooperative Mercantile Institution (ZCMI) Department Store evolved over a period of more than ninety years, and was recently taken down, repaired—including the recasting of many elements—repainted, and reerected as a more or less freestanding screen a few feet in front of the new store building behind it (fig. 31). The Hart Block in Louisville, Kentucky, on the other hand, represents a sophisticated composition using a large Néo-Grec cast-iron vocabulary (fig. 32). Windows on each floor differ from those of floors above, alternating segmentally arched windows with square-headed windows. All are separated by very delicate ironwork in the form of freestanding colonettes, both paired and single. The rich diversity which these fronts contribute to our cities has at last been recognized, and the wholesale destruction of cast-iron districts—such as the forty blocks cleared along the St. Louis waterfront before World War II—has been arrested.

Even in the years that buildings with cast-iron exteriors were proliferating, architects primarily in Chicago and New York were putting up increasingly taller buildings with interior frames of cast-iron columns and wrought iron beams, and eventually with steel beams when they became affordable. In Chicago HABS has recorded two such structures. Burnham and Root's eleven-story Rookery, built between 1886 and 1888, was named for a site where flocks of pigeons had gathered. Its frame of cast-iron pillars and wrought iron beams wraps around a central light court, the lower two floors of which form a lobby covered by an iron-and-glass ceiling supported by perforated cast-iron members (Myers, fig. 27). The richly detailed cast iron of its lobby was originally designed by John Root and produced in Brooklyn's famous Hecla Iron

Works. Hecla partner William H. Winslow was sent to Chicago in 1885 as a young man, to plan the work for the lobby. He settled there and formed his own nationally known ornamental iron business. He is perhaps best known as a friend and patron of the young Frank Lloyd Wright, who called on Winslow to produce his own brand of ornament in iron, including the 1905 remodeling of the Rookery lobby (Myers, fig. 28). Just south of the Loop at 431 South Dearborn Street stands William LeBaron Jenney's sixteen-story Manhattan Building, for a time the world's tallest building. It is a monument to Jenney; to his engineer, Louis E. Ritter, who was responsible for its framing system; and to the cast-iron column. Its skeleton consists of hundreds of cast-iron pillars and wrought iron beams and girders resting on heavy foundations of concrete and iron rails.

The all-iron structure represents the ultimate use of this material, and several quite different examples have been recorded by HABS. The Watervliet Arsenal building is one of a kind. Almost totally of iron, it was designed on the eve of the Civil War for the storage of gun carriages at Watervliet, near Albany, New York (fig. 33). It is an outstanding case of early prefabrication, yet is surprisingly ornamental. Erected in the summer of 1859, its iron sections had been designed and cast in the big iron foundry of Badger's Architectural Ironworks over the winter and were ready to ship up the Hudson when the ice melted in the spring. The foundation was prepared and waiting and the iron parts could be immediately assembled and bolted together at the site.

The arsenal was surveyed by HAER staff especially trained to recognize and record this nation's technological triumphs. Iron bridges are another example of technology recorded. None are more picturesque than the bowstring truss bridges based on Squire Whipple's inspired design, patented April 24, 1841. The truss bridge

Figure 32 In Kentucky's old Louisville Restoration Area, near the Ohio River, stand several iron-front buildings that have received new recognition in recent years. The most remarkable of these is the Hart Building, an ornate five-story former hardware warehouse at 728 West Main Street. Windows on each floor differ from those of the floor above, segmental arched windows alternating with square-headed ones. All are separated by very delicate ironwork in the form of free-standing colonnettes, some paired and some single. The front is organized into three units, each defined by a handsome perforated arch spanning four bays. The mode is Neo-Grec and one is reminded of Richard Morris Hunt's very original 1874 iron front in New York City's SoHo district. Old photographs show a large metal pediment, since blown away in a storm, which read "Hart Block 1884." Its history is further revealed on the base of the street-level iron plasters where the words "Charles E. Meyer, Architect" and "Merz Architectural Iron Works" are embossed. (HABS KY–120, sheet 3 of 3 sheets)

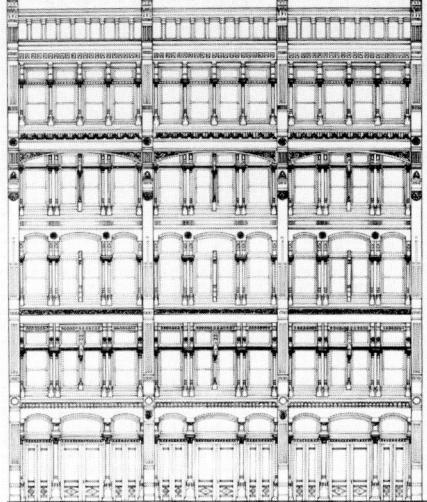

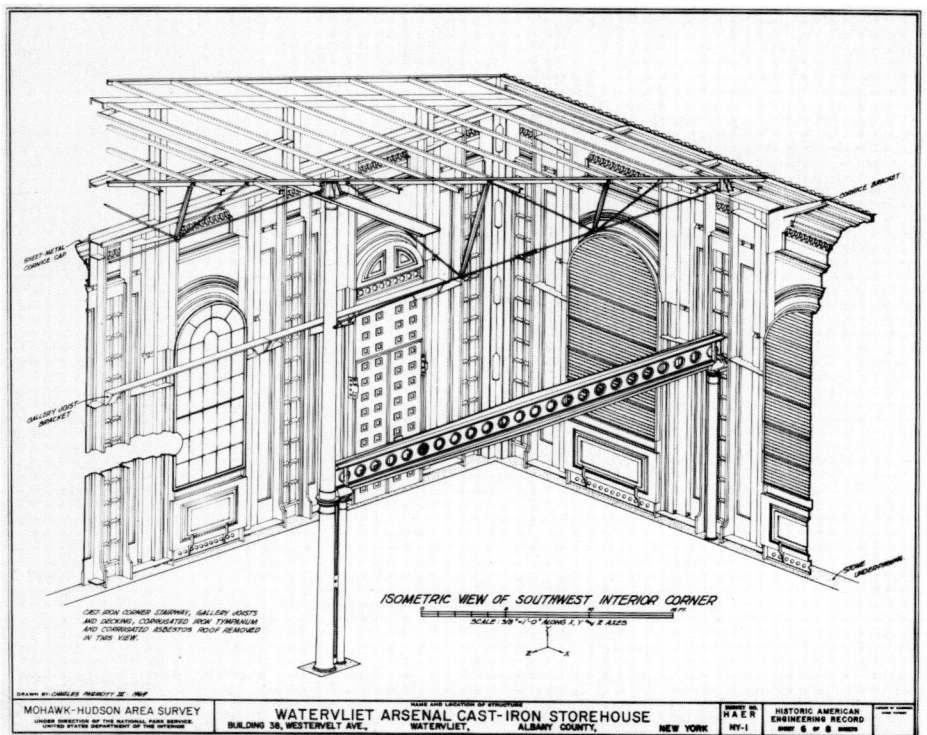

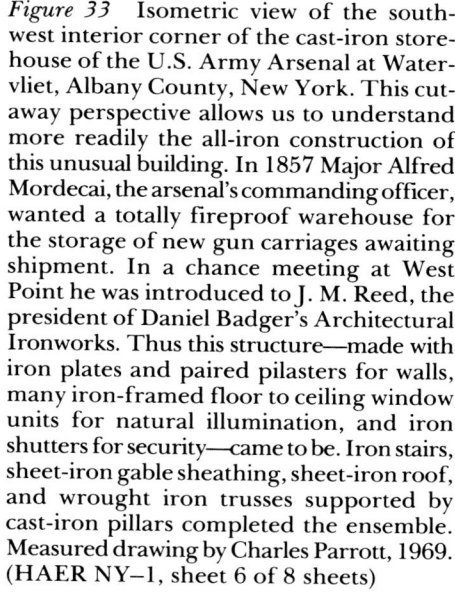

Figure 33 Isometric view of the southwest interior corner of the cast-iron storehouse of the U.S. Army Arsenal at Watervliet, Albany County, New York. This cutaway perspective allows us to understand more readily the all-iron construction of this unusual building. In 1857 Major Alfred Mordecai, the arsenal's commanding officer, wanted a totally fireproof warehouse for the storage of new gun carriages awaiting shipment. In a chance meeting at West Point he was introduced to J. M. Reed, the president of Daniel Badger's Architectural Ironworks. Thus this structure—made with iron plates and paired pilasters for walls, many iron-framed floor to ceiling window units for natural illumination, and iron shutters for security—came to be. Iron stairs, sheet-iron gable sheathing, sheet-iron roof, and wrought iron trusses supported by cast-iron pillars completed the ensemble. Measured drawing by Charles Parrott, 1969. (HAER NY–1, sheet 6 of 8 sheets)

Figure 34 North elevation and site map, Whipple cast-iron and wrought iron bowstring truss bridge, near Albany, Albany County, New York. Another important use of iron was in nineteenth-century American bridges. Squire Whipple's patented truss of 1841 was among the more popular of many innovative designs for iron crossings. Measured drawing by David Bouse, 1969. (HAER NY–4, sheet 2 of 5 sheets)

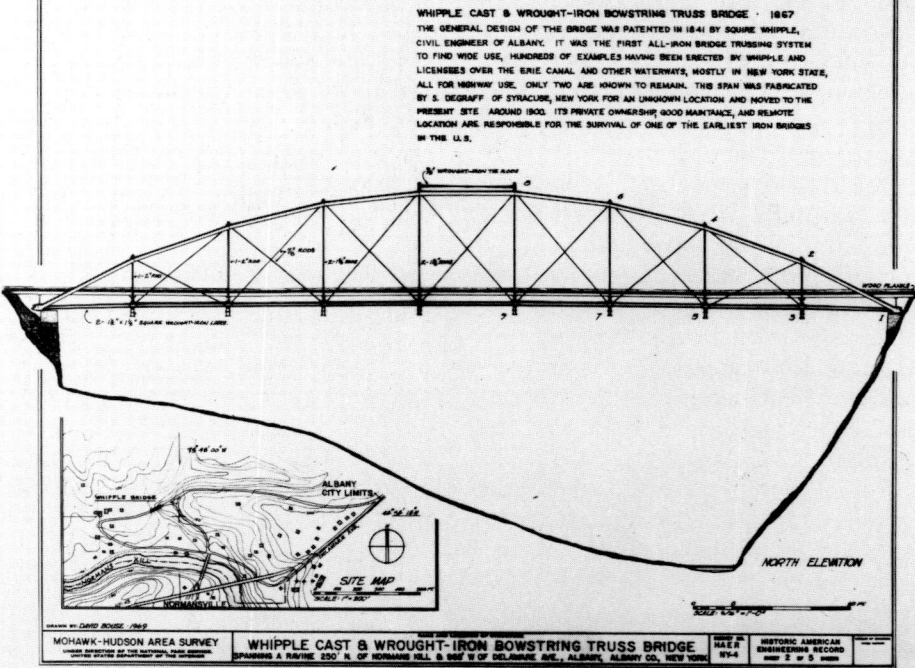

is a small work of art, so directly conceived with a top arched chord of cast iron tied at the base with square wrought iron tie rods and floored with wooden planks. Whipple, a civil engineer in Albany, was meeting the need for the road crossings over the new Erie Canal. Although scores of these bowstring truss bridges were built over the canal and other New York waterways by Whipple and his licensees, very few survive today. The one recorded in 1969 by HAER was originally constructed in 1867; it was moved about 1900 to carry a private road over a ravine near Albany (fig. 34).

The final all cast-iron structure we shall mention, Maine's Portland Breakwater Lighthouse, does not figure largely in any great cycle of technological evolution (fig. 35). It is simply quite lovely, representing the dignity and durability of which one of the most versatile of American building materials is capable. First built in 1855 and rebuilt in 1875, this iron essay in Corinthian architecture was abandoned in 1943. Its 1962 HABS record includes photocopies of the original architectural drawings discovered in the district office of the U.S. Coast Guard, its owner. It is one more example of the role played by the Historic American Buildings Survey in recognizing and recording the role of cast iron during and since the nineteenth century. Continuing survey projects by HABS, together with those of the Historic American Engineering Record, enlarge our understanding of the forms and technology of America's remarkable cast-iron age.

Figure 35 Portland Breakwater Lighthouse, northeast end of the breakwater, Portland Harbor, South Portland, Cumberland County, Maine. Built in 1855, this handsome small structure is of iron backed with brick and follows that ever popular model, the Choragic Monument of Lysicrates. Denys Peter Myers has pointed out, however, that the engaged iron columns are of a Roman rather than a Greek Corinthian order. Photograph by Gerda Peterich, September 1962. (HABS ME–112, LC HABS ME, 3–PORTS, 1–2)

Vernacular Construction
in the Survey

by

CARL LOUNSBURY

In December 1933 the Washington office of the newly established Historic American Buildings Survey issued general instructions to its district officers in the field which outlined the vast scope of this new federal program. The project directors contemplated "measuring and recording the complete field of Early American Architecture from the earliest aboriginal structures to the latest buildings of the Greek Revival period." From the outset they envisioned a survey which included "structures of all types, from the smallest utilitarian structures to the largest and most monumental. Barns, bridges, mills, toll houses, jails, and in short buildings of every description" were to be covered so that "a complete picture of the culture of the time as reflected in the buildings of the period may be put on record." Recognizing these goals to be extremely ambitious, the directors established a set of priorities which

gave precedent to "buildings of architectural or historical interest, or buildings of unusual type, or buildings exhibiting features of plan or design which have not been restored or remodeled and which are in imminent danger of destruction or material alteration."[1]

With their instructions to record common utilitarian structures, the HABS directors considered the vernacular buildings of the American landscape to be an integral part of the country's architectural heritage. Although the term *vernacular architecture* has been expanded in recent years to encompass a broad range of building forms, from nineteenth-century pattern book houses to the modern commercial strip, it has customarily been applied to traditional farmhouses and agricultural buildings. The Survey's treatment of the rural buildings of this latter, more restricted definition forms the subject here considered.

In contrast to academic architecture, the vernacular buildings of the rural landscape were erected by their owners to accommodate particular needs and activities without benefit of formal plans. Although the functional aspects of such buildings dominated the plans, these buildings were in general not devoid of some aesthetic considerations in execution. Built according to local custom with native materials, farmhouses, barns, and associated agricultural

Figure 1 Towles House, Lancaster County, Virginia. Through the use of local materials and the development of house types which best suited social and economic conditions of a particular area, vernacular building in the American colonies by the mid-eighteenth century had formed distinctive regional characteristics. Comparing the Chesapeake area farmhouse here with a farmhouse in New England (fig. 3) and one in the mid-Atlantic region (fig. 4) reveals regional differences. Photograph by F. D. Nichols, 1940. (LC HABS VA, 52–BERT.V, 1–11)

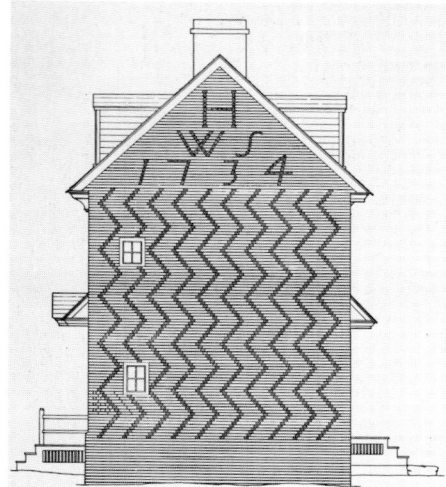

Figure 2 Hancock House, Hancock Bridge, New Jersey. Although the primary concern of vernacular builders was to provide functional structures, they could also provide aesthetically pleasing buildings through the decorative treatment of materials. The gable-end patterning of glazed headers as shown here in the Hancock House was characteristic of brickwork in the mid-Atlantic colonies in the eighteenth century for embellishment of otherwise relatively plain and stark walls. Drawing by E. Ray Coutch, 1935. (HABS NJ 6–54, sheet 19 of 19 sheets)

Figure 3 Benjamin Abbot Farmhouse, Andover, Massachusetts. Photograph by Arthur C. Haskell, 1934. (LC HABS MASS, 5–ANDO, 1–3)

buildings "took such form as best served their owner's occupations and household habits."[2]

The recording of vernacular buildings by HABS has proceeded in an uneven fashion over the past fifty years. The number and variety of structures that have been inventoried as well as the quality of the fieldwork have varied greatly over time and from state to state. Collectively, the product of fifty years in the field appears impressive, yet, if studied regionally or by building type, the HABS collection has several weaknesses. In states like New Jersey and Massachusetts which have had active survey programs since the 1930s, the voluminous photographs and measured drawings of barns, mills, and farmhouses provide the historian of vernacular architecture with a rich source of material. In other areas, early HABS teams fortunately recorded many derelict rural buildings threatened with decay and destruction which otherwise would have vanished unnoticed. Well over half of the two dozen eighteenth-century farmhouses that Thomas T. Waterman investigated in the Albemarle region of northeastern North Carolina are now destroyed and but for his exemplary HABS fieldwork in the summer of 1940 would have been lost altogether. But, although the

HABS files may contain a number of important buildings which have since been altered or demolished, those scholars interested in traditional house types and agricultural buildings in states such as New Hampshire, Arkansas, and North Dakota will be disappointed by the paucity of information to be had. The recording of vernacular buildings for HABS has scarcely begun in many states, particularly those beyond the East Coast. The mid-to-late nineteenth-century farmhouses of the upper Midwest, many of them exemplary of ethnic building practices, still await more detailed investigation by HABS.

Much of the early fieldwork concentrated on recording buildings designed with some academic pretensions, embellished with abundant stylistic details. This was natural considering the priorities established by the Washington office and the architectural training of some of the members of the field teams. Outside peripheral antiquarian interests in old houses in regions like New England and the Chesapeake, the recording of simple farm buildings for their architectural qualities had little precedent when HABS fieldwork began.

In Massachusetts and Virginia, two states which had strong HABS programs during the depression, most of

Figure 4 Phillips house, Camden County, New Jersey. Photograph by Nathaniel Ewan, 1936. (LC HABS NJ 4–DELA.V, 1–1)

Figure 5 White House, Perquimans County, North Carolina. The HABS collections often contain documentary information on buildings that have been destroyed in the last fifty years. The White House is one such example. Without Thomas T. Waterman's fieldwork in this area of northeastern North Carolina, many important eighteenth-century buildings would have disappeared unrecorded. Photograph by Thomas T. Waterman, July 1940. (LC HABS NC, 72–HERF.V, 10–1)

Figure 6 The Buttonwoods barn, near Newcastle, Delaware. Although HABS documentation of agricultural buildings has been limited, those that have been recorded range from substantial brick and stone barns in the Delaware Valley to log outbuildings in Kentucky (fig. 7), fanciful icehouses in New Jersey (fig. 8), and mule-driven cotton gins in the South (fig. 9). Photograph by W. S. Stewart, 1936. (LC HABS DEL, 2–NEWCA.V, 3B–2)

Figure 7 Hikes Place, log outbuilding, Jefferson County, Kentucky. Photograph by Lester Jones, 1940. (LC HABS KY, 56–BEUCH.V, 1B–1)

Figure 8 Githens Ice House, Burlington County, New Jersey. Photograph by Nathaniel Ewan, 1936. (LC HABS NY, 3–EARTO, 2B–1)

the fieldwork covered buildings which were perceived to be the earliest and which had some connections with important historical figures and events. Thus in Massachusetts there was an attempt to record houses and structures associated with Pilgrim and Puritan settlements of the seventeenth century. In this effort HABS photographed and measured what was considered the distinctive vernacular house type of New England, the clapboard-covered frame house characterized by a center chimney and steep roof line. In Virginia, surveyors perceived the most important period of architectural development as one that neatly led up

to and coincided with the American Revolution. Eighteenth-century plantation houses set dramatically along the main rivers became the principal objects of the HABS teams. The fact that the Carters, Lees, and other families associated with the Revolution built and lived in these plantation houses left little doubt that they would receive full attention.

This work in Massachusetts and Virginia was important but naturally forced the Survey to devote little time to the smaller and more characteristic buildings of these states. The early work also tended to reinforce notions about building in these states which were misleading. In Virginia, the early attention devoted to the brick mansion houses wrongly led many architectural historians to assume that brick building was more prevalent than it actually was in the eighteenth century.

In a review of the comprehensive HABS catalog published in 1941, Turpin C. Bannister praised the intention of the program but wisely pointed out several deficiencies in the scope of the Survey. Among them, he noted an uneven coverage both geographically and chronologically in many states and found "little assurance, as yet, that one consults a typical cross section" of house types in the Survey.[3] It is this randomness of the recording process inherent in a national survey that has limited the usefulness of HABS materials in the study of traditional buildings. The study of vernacular architecture must proceed with a systematic and careful investigation of a large sample of buildings in a given area in order to distinguish common house types, materials, and structural systems. Unlike the study of academic architecture where emphasis is placed on the analysis of individual buildings of exceptional character, the study of vernacular forms depends on the recognition of the repetitive and commonplace. Too few buildings in a survey may distort the overall picture.

By covering large numbers of buildings within a concentrated area,

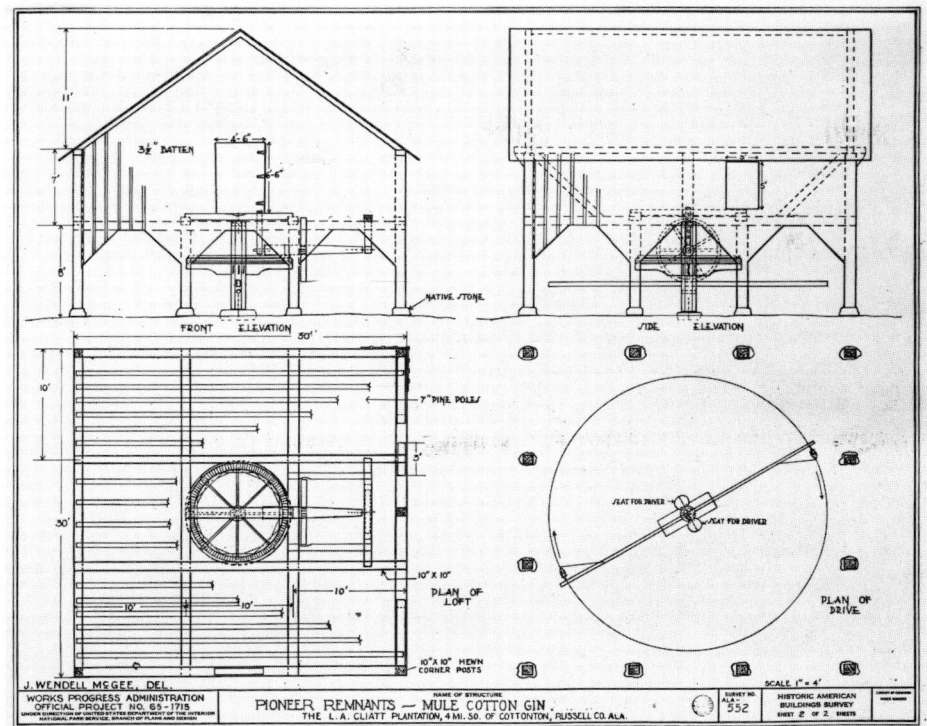

Figure 9 Cliatt Plantation cotton gin, Russell County, Alabama. Drawing by Wendell McGee, 1936. (HABS ALA 552, sheet 2 of 2 sheets)

Figure 10 Magnolia Grove, Greensboro, Alabama. Site plans are invaluable sources for understanding the layout of farm buildings. The plan of Magnolia Grove in Greensboro, Alabama, clearly illustrates the arrangement of the main house, domestic outbuildings, and slave quarters. Drawing by Kirby Stinger, 1936. (HABS ALA 219, sheet 1 of 8 sheets)

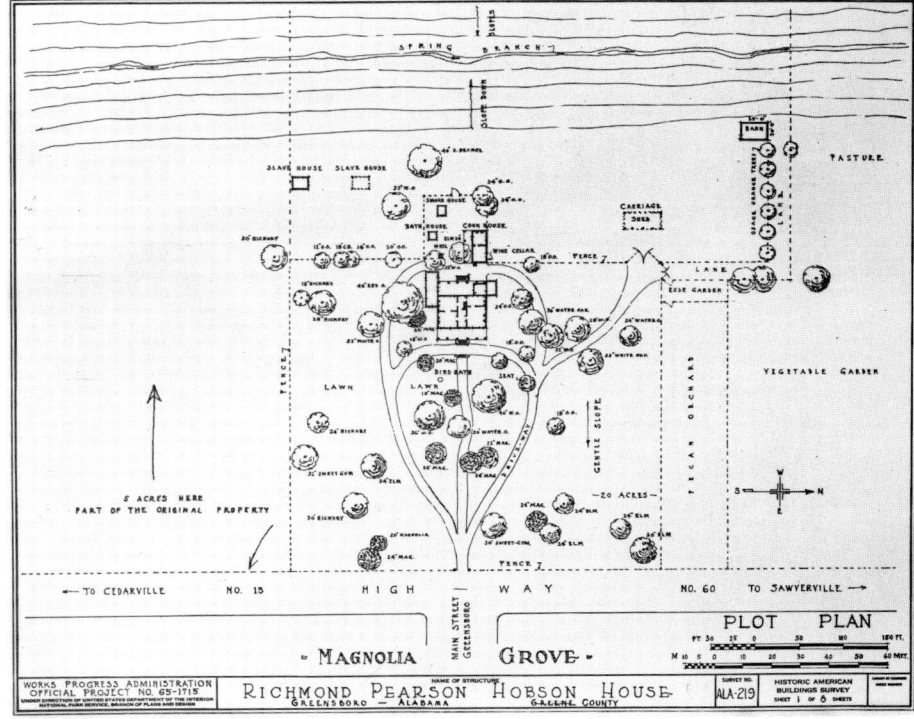

Figure 11 Thornhill main house, Greene County, Alabama. The HABS team which visited Thornhill in Greene County, Alabama, in the 1930s was careful to record not only the main house but also the full complement of mid-nineteenth-century agricultural and domestic outbuildings as well. With the rapid disappearance of outbuildings whose functions have become redundant in the twentieth century, the detailed attention given to outbuildings at sites such as Thornhill during the depression provides historians with an important source for the study of the appearance and routine of antebellum farmsteads. Photograph by W. N. Manning, 1936. (HABS ALA, 32–WATSO, 1–1)

Figure 12 Thornhill slave quarters. Photograph by Alex Bush, 1934. (LC HABS ALA, 32–WATSO, 1E–3)

Figure 13 Interior of Thornhill slave quarters. Photograph by Alex Bush, 1934. (LC HABS ALA, 32–WATSO, 1D–2)

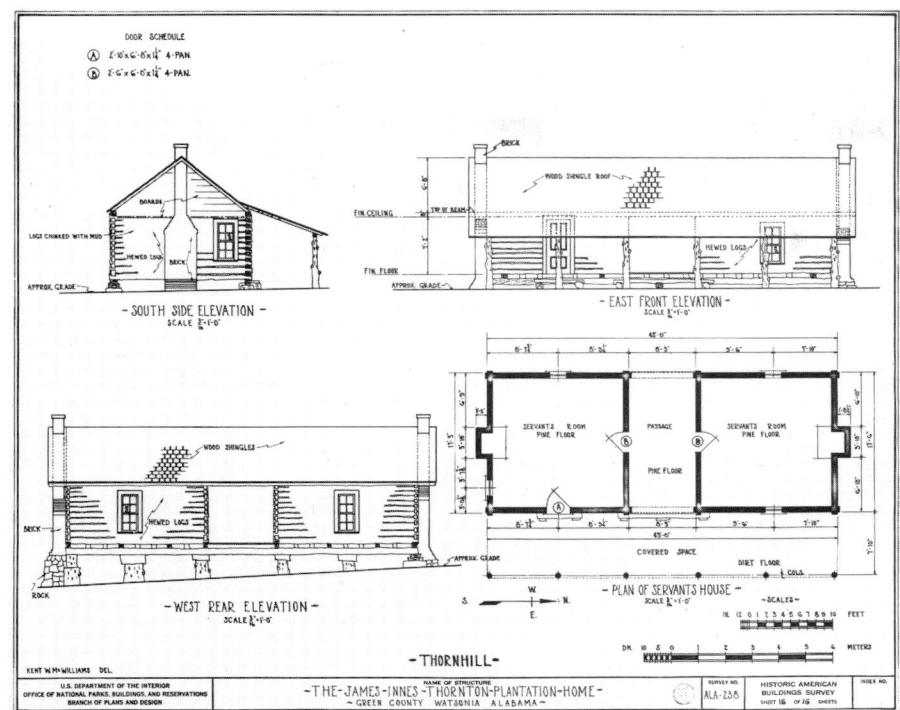

Figure 14 Thornhill slave house. Drawing by Kent McWilliams, 1934–35. (HABS ALA–238, sheet 16 of 16 sheets)

Figure 15 Traditional worm-and-post fence on the Crenshaw settlement near Greenville, Alabama. Fences, an important element in the rural landscape, vary in construction, materials, and use. Photograph by W. N. Manning, 1935. (LC HABS ALA, 7–   , 2B–1)

Figure 16 From the seventeenth through the early twentieth century, many buildings in the South were erected with roughly finished materials in an impermanent fashion. This cabin in Berkeley County, South Carolina, features wooden block foundations, wooden shutters in place of glass lights, large board shakes, and a stick-and-mud chimney. Photograph by Albert Simons, 1935. (LC HABS SC, 8–CRO.V, 1–1)

comprehensive field surveys make it possible to detect patterns in vernacular building. The small Theophilus White house in Perquimans County, North Carolina, has few architectural details or historical associations which would cause it to merit attention on its own. Little can be made of room use or the building's social context if it is viewed in isolation. Only when this simple house type is examined in conjunction with large numbers of structures in surrounding areas does its significance begin to emerge. Comprehensive surveys produce the social cross section of house types which can then be compared and contrasted with vernacular buildings nearby and with those of other regions. Intensive fieldwork in Perquimans County has made it possible to identify the Theophilus White

house as a prevalent house type of the eighteenth century tobacco-growing society of the greater Chesapeake.[4] This recognition in turn has allowed historians to describe the social and economic activities for which this building form was designed.[5] The work of interpreting vernacular architecture begins for the historian, folklorist, or geographer only after the general pattern of building in an area has been established. Since HABS fieldwork has only occasionally reached the point where it has canvassed a typical cross section of building types within a region, it has not been regarded as an essential tool in vernacular studies.

If not essential, the HABS collection can nonetheless be useful to vernacular studies in a number of ways. During the 1930s HABS teams in Ala-

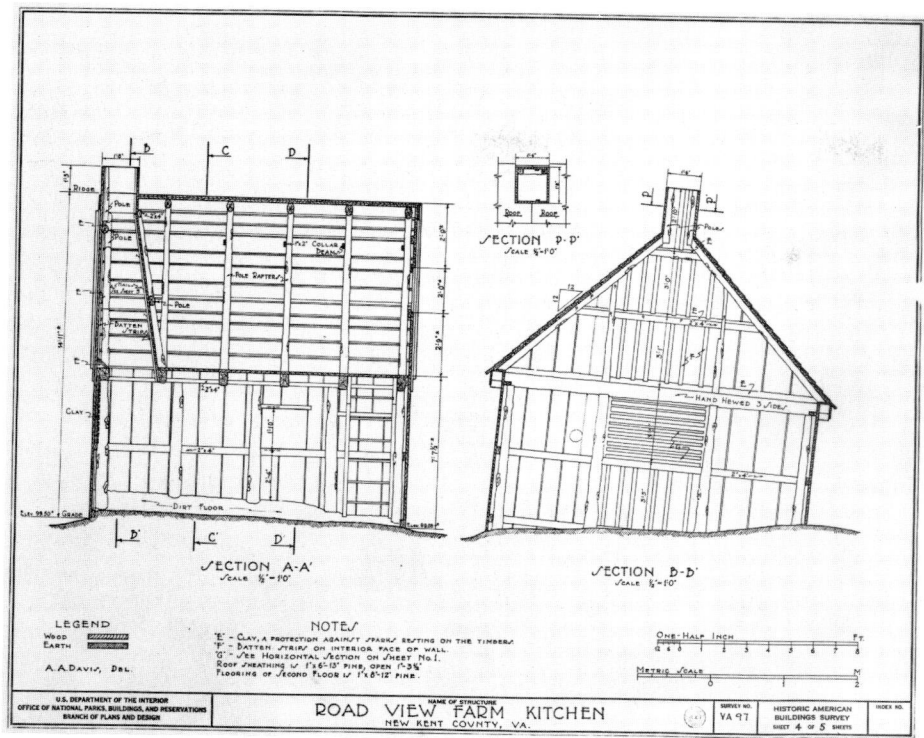

Figure 17 Kitchen, Road View Farm, section, New Kent County, Virginia. The mud-and-stick chimney, once a common impermanent building feature through much of the South, has rapidly disappeared in the second half of the twentieth century. The HABS collection fortunately has several recorded examples, including the Road View Farm kitchen in New Kent County, Virginia, and a log house in Sampson County, North Carolina (fig. 18). Drawing by A. A. Davis, 1936. (HABS VA–97, sheet 4 of 5 sheets)

Figure 18 Log house in Sampson County, North Carolina. (LC HABS NC, 82–KER.V, 1–2)

bama recorded scores of great antebellum mansions erected by the prosperous cotton planters in the quarter century preceding the Civil War. In Alabama, unlike most states, the surveyors did not neglect the complement of domestic and agricultural buildings which surrounded the main houses. More kitchens, slave quarters, and log outbuildings were photographed and measured than in any other state. Detailed site plans showing the relationship of the main house to its subordinate buildings were frequently made. These are invaluable to social historians studying the spatial arrangements of slavery, since the plans clearly outline the division of the plantation into realms of shared and exclusive space among masters, overseers, and slaves. The early photographs often reveal how tenants in the first third of the twentieth century continued traditional folkways in many matters such as the maintenance of swept yards enclosed with worm and paled fences.

Many of the slave houses and outbuildings were constructed with flimsy materials in an impermanent manner and have not survived the last fifty years. HABS recorded dozens of such buildings erected with stick-and-clay chimneys, dirt floors, shake roofs, and wood block foundations in Alabama and, to a lesser degree, in other southern states. These features, once characteristic of the lowest level of vernacular building, have grown increasingly rare since the 1930s. When Albert Simons photographed the small frame house near Cross in Berkeley County, South Carolina, in 1935, tenant houses with the same roughly worked materials could be found along almost any road in the state. Now features such as the clay-and-stick chimney have virtually disappeared. In North Carolina less than a handful of these rude chimneys survive. Combined with the photographs taken for the Farm Security Administration during the depression, the HABS collection provides one of the best documentary sources for the study of impermanent construction in the South.

Since many traditional structures possess few stylistic details which can aid in determining periods of construction,

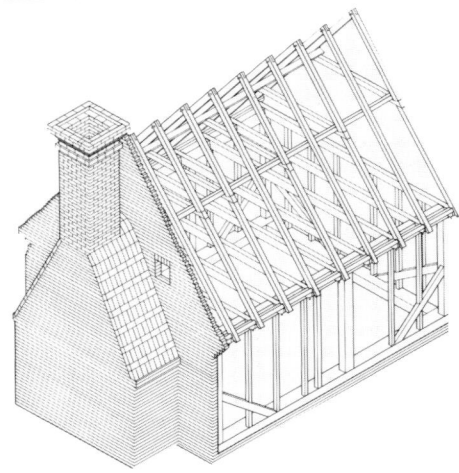

Figure 19 Isometric of framing and brick end, Pear Valley, Northampton County, Virginia. Building technology has been a matter of great concern in the study of vernacular architecture. Structural details of a building often aid in determining its age, help distinguish subsequent changes, or reveal the origins of its builders. (HABS VA–960, sheet 5 of 5 sheets)

Figure 20 Gristmill, framing detail, New Kent County, Virginia. Photograph by John O. Bostrup, 1937. (LC HABS VA, 64–PROFO.V, 1–13)

a firm understanding of building technology has been an important concern in vernacular studies. An analysis of construction details, hardware, and materials can offer clues to the age of a building as well as leading to answers to broader questions about the relationship between traditional and industrialized building practices. A random sampling of HABS files reveals that the documentation of structural systems and details by field teams has increased over the last twenty-five years. In Mississippi, for example, the drawings of Mount Locust, a late eighteenth-century frame house that was expanded several times in the nineteenth century, demonstrate a sensitive concern for construction methods. The sections and exploded isometric drawings provide clear illustrations of the different building periods as evidenced in the wall-framing system. This attention to detail can also be found in material compiled by Survey members in New Jersey during the 1930s. In recording more than two hundred eighteenth- and early nineteenth-century farmhouses, surveyors carefully documented locks, hinges, and kitchen

hardware. By leafing through these drawings along with those of Pennsylvania, one can obtain a thorough introduction to the decorative and functional ironwork of the mid-Atlantic colonies. Such knowledge facilitates the dating, interpretation, and understanding of regional building types and techniques.

The serious study of vernacular architecture is relatively new. Twenty years ago comprehensive survey techniques and the classification of comparable building examples had scarcely begun. Even today, traditional farmhouses in many parts of the country await much-needed fieldwork. If HABS is to play an important role in vernacular studies, it must encourage contributions from public and private organizations which oversee local field surveys. State surveys, now being conducted under the auspices of the National Register program, could upgrade their recording procedures to the quality of HABS standards and, by sharing their material, augment HABS coverage of vernacular buildings. Such a cooperative arrangement was established in the 1970s among the

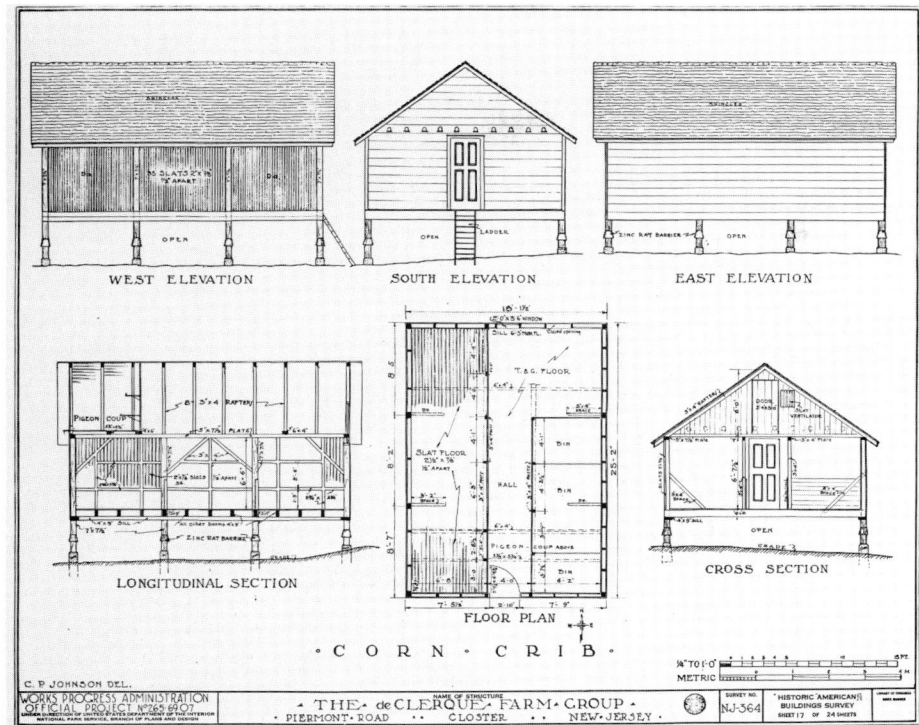

Figure 21 De Clerque Farm corn crib, Closter, New Jersey. Drawing by C. P. Johnson, 1936–37. (HABS NJ–364, sheet 17 of 24 sheets)

Figure 22 Mt. Locust, Jefferson County, Mississippi. Many early HABS teams failed to document evidence of previous changes made to a building but merely recorded the building as it existed at the time they were recording it. In recent years, greater attention has been paid to noting any structural changes that a building might have undergone. Careful notation of structural changes can be seen in the details of Mt. Locust. Drawing by H. A. Judd and Calvin Hooker, 1955. (HABS MISS 159–A, sheet 3 of 9 sheets)

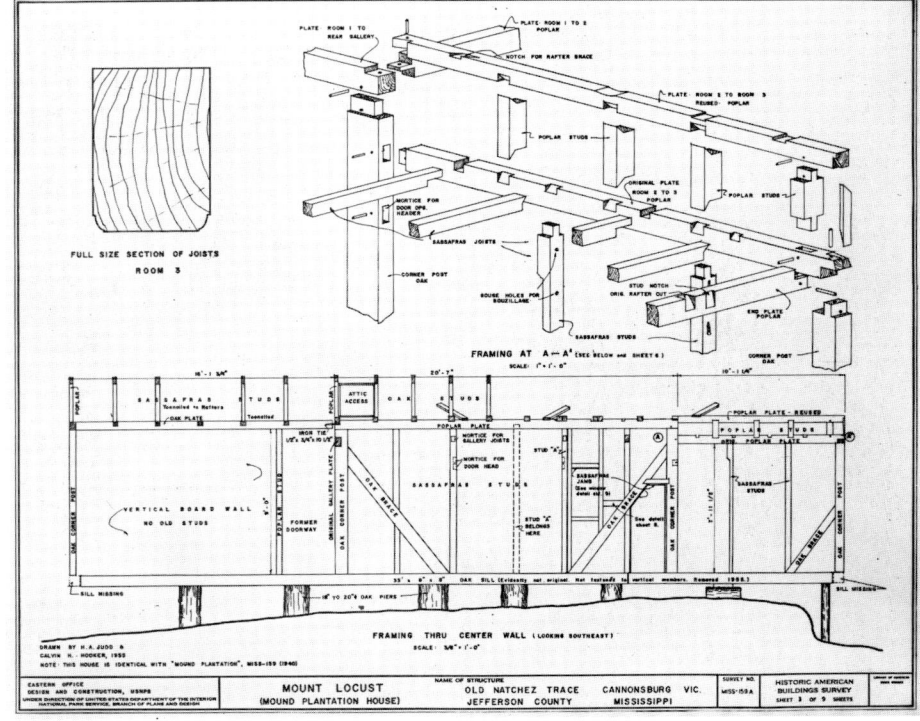

Figure 23 Reuben Matlack Blacksmith Shop, Burlington County, New Jersey. From blacksmith forges such as the one in the Matlack shop in Burlington County, New Jersey, a wealth of hardware was produced that can now be found throughout many of the buildings in the Delaware Valley. In the 1930s HABS teams made a practice of recording hardware details such as those found in the Blue Anchor Tavern (fig. 24). Photograph by Nathaniel Ewan, 1936. (LC HABS NJ, 3–MAPSH, 1A–3)

Figure 24 Blue Anchor Tavern hardware, Blue Anchor, New Jersey. Drawing by Edwin Mason, 1935. (HABS NJ 6–131, sheet 12 of 13 sheets)

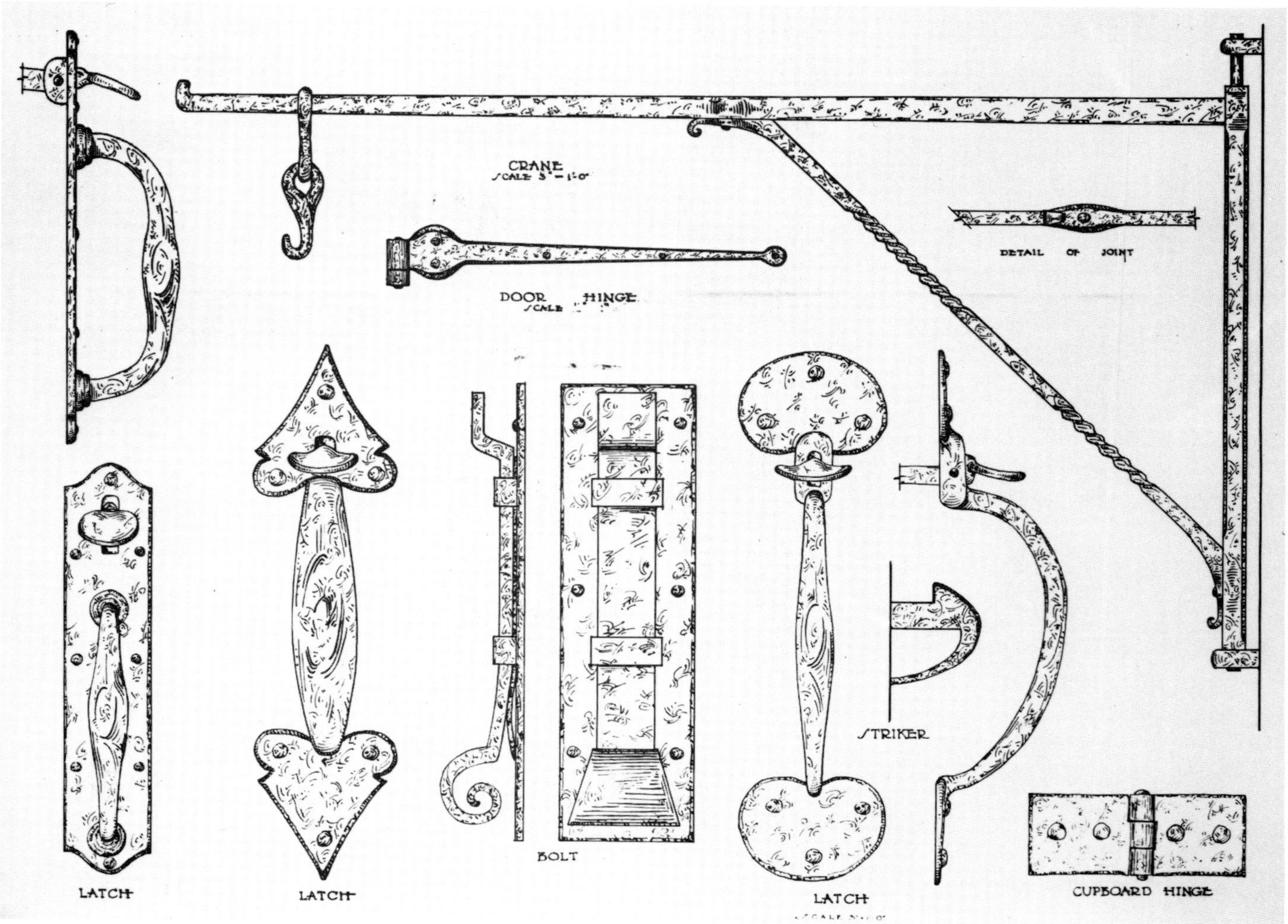

CRANE
SCALE 3" = 1'-0"

DETAIL OF JOINT

DOOR HINGE
SCALE

BOLT

STRIKER

LATCH

LATCH

LATCH
SCALE

CUPBOARD HINGE

St. Mary's City Commission, the Maryland Historical Trust, and the Historic American Buildings Survey. The St. Mary's City Commission conducted a survey of southern Maryland, documenting with HABS drawings, photographs, and archival research scores of rural buildings dating from the mid-nineteenth century or earlier. HABS received the original drawings and the local and state organizations retained copies. Similarly, past neglect of agricultural buildings has led the Colonial Williamsburg Foundation and a private group of concerned field surveyors to record threatened farm buildings in the Chesapeake region.[6] Under cooperative agreements, materials gathered by organizations such as these can be deposited with HABS. With proper encouragement HABS has the opportunity to become, in its next fifty years, an essential collection for the study of vernacular building in America.

Notes

1. National Park Service, U.S. Department of the Interior, *Historic American Buildings Survey Bulletin,* no. 3, December 20, 1933.

2. Cary Carson, "The 'Virginia House' in Maryland," *Maryland Historical Magazine* 69 (Summer 1974): 185.

3. *Journal of the Society of Architectural Historians* 2 (January 1942): 42.

4. Dru Gatewood Haley and Raymond A. Winslow, Jr., *Historic Architecture of Perquimans County, North Carolina* (Hertford, N.C.: Town of Hertford, 1982).

5. See Dell Upton, "Early Vernacular Architecture in Southeastern Virginia" (Ph.D. diss., Brown University, 1979).

6. For a description of the work of Friends of Friendless Farm Buildings, see Orlando Ridout V, "The Chesapeake Farm Buildings Survey," in *Perspectives in Vernacular Architecture,* ed. Camille Wells (Annapolis: Vernacular Architecture Forum, 1982), pp. 137-49.

Recording the Work of an Architect: Frank Lloyd Wright

by

DAVID G. DE LONG

Studies of individual genius are fundamental to history. During the past decade, architectural historians have focused increasingly on Frank Lloyd Wright (1867–1959), and the astonishing number of books and articles now appearing have led at least one historian to characterize their production as a veritable cottage industry.[1] Such attention seems deserved, however, for the sort of ideas that architectural historians rightfully seek are abundant in Wright's work, and the clarification of these ideas through scholarly analysis is of real importance to the field. Probably no American architect has claimed the term genius more aggressively than Wright, nor have any yet appeared that deserve it more.

In accord with its underlying objectives, the Historic American Buildings Survey does not constitute a major archive of any single architect. Yet the manner in which individual architects are represented in the Survey can be informative. Thus a review of materials relating to Wright helps define his place in American architecture, for it illustrates selected examples in an appropriate geographical and chronological sequence, balanced by the work of his contemporaries as well as his precursors and followers.[2] Moreover, the neutrality of the Survey's presentation can reveal unique qualities to the discerning eye. Wright and his assistants produced drawings that were understandably sympathetic to the designs themselves, for, as most architects, they adjusted conventions and varied drawing techniques to enhance and even exaggerate significant aspects of their proposals. During the early years of the Historic American Buildings Survey, drawing conventions were sometimes similarly adjusted, but at that time Wright's work was not regarded as sufficiently historic to merit inclusion. During the postwar years, when selected examples by Wright were recorded, drawing conventions specified by the Survey were imposed without compromise, reducing buildings throughout the Survey to a common denominator.

A comparison of two plans for the same building illustrates the dilemma. For the famous Wasmuth edition of 1910, Wright supplied a plan of Unity Temple, 1906–7, that subtly revealed the complex levels and screening elements defining its revolutionary space (fig. 2). Partly this was achieved through intelligent complication of ordinary methods of representation. By contrast, the standardized plan in the Survey omits clear reference to split levels or to

Figure 1 Upper tower, Schiller Building, Chicago, 1891–92, by the firm of Adler and Sullivan, which employed the young Frank Lloyd Wright. Photograph (exterior detail) by Richard Nickel, 1961. (HABS ILL–1058, LC HABS ILL, 16–CHIG, 60–1)

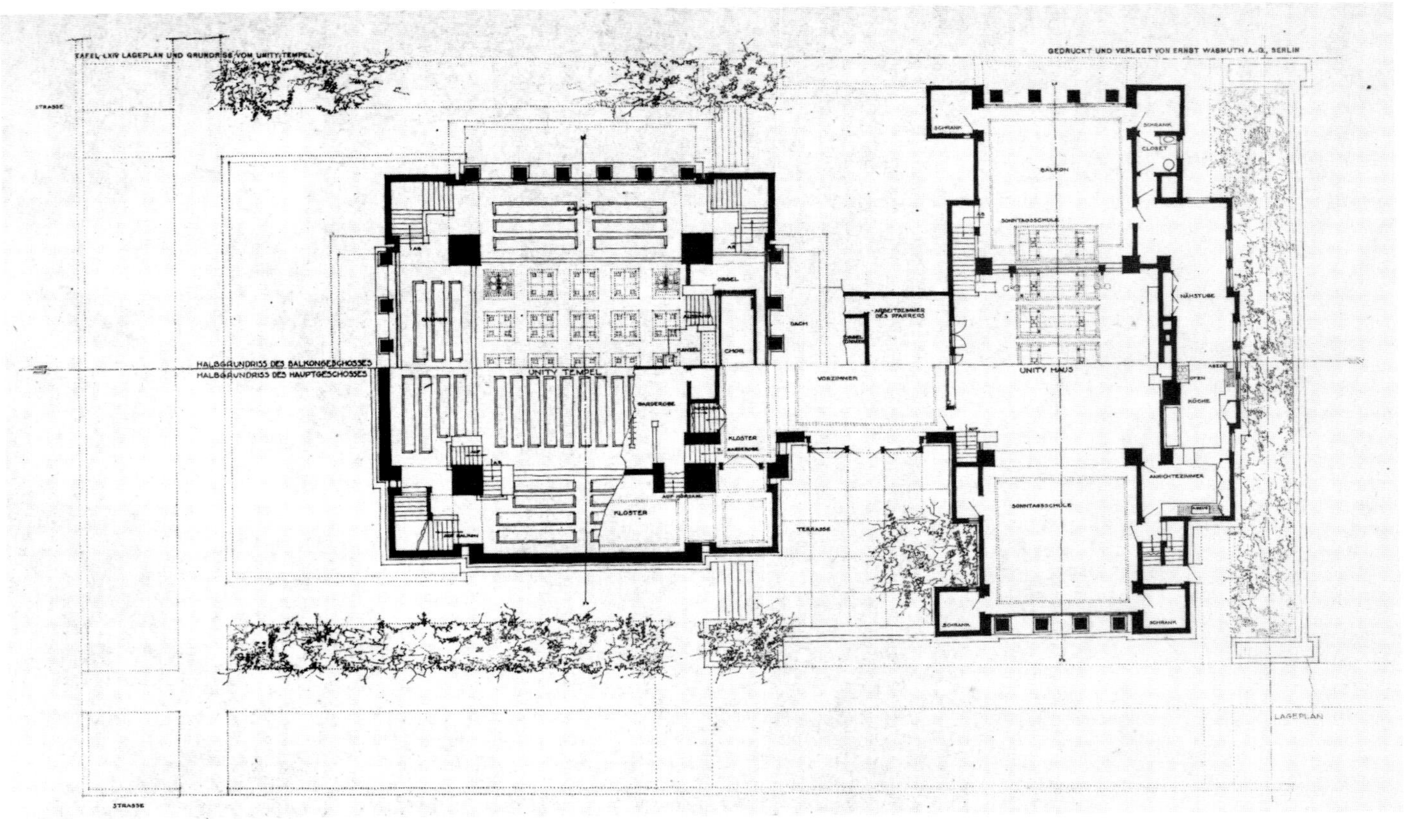

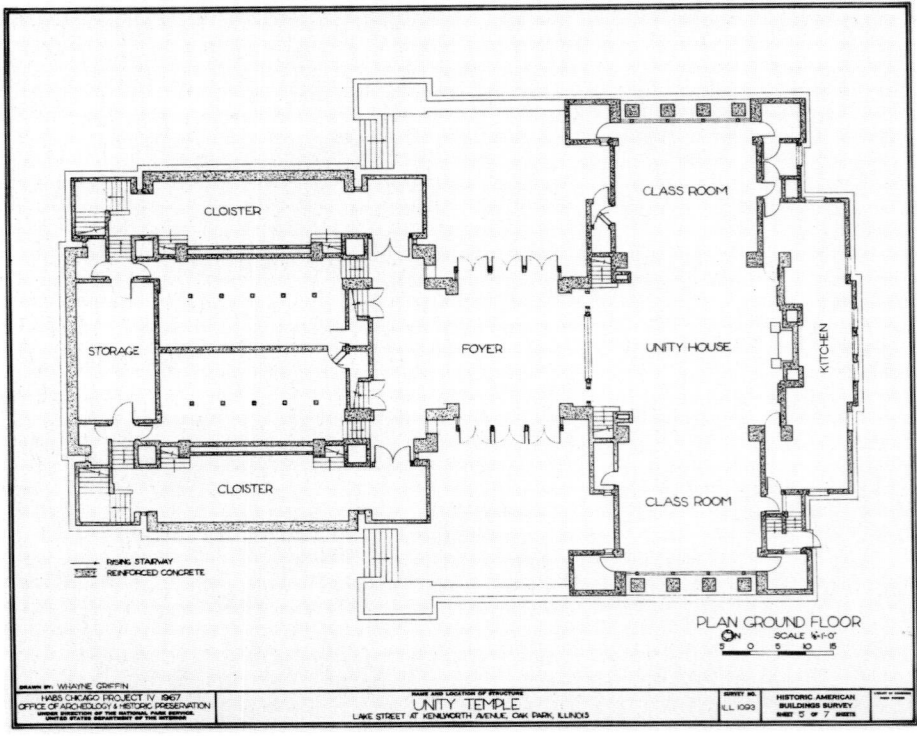

Figure 2 Frank Lloyd Wright, Unity Temple, Oak Park, Illinois, 1906-7. Plan by Frank Lloyd Wright in *Ausgeführte Bauten und Entwürfe von Frank Lloyd Wright* (Berlin: Ernst Wasmuth, 1910). Delineated to express unique features of the building, Wright's plan contrasts with the more mechanical representations in the Historic American Buildings Survey. (LC USZ62–80181)

Figure 3 Frank Lloyd Wright, Unity Temple, Oak Park, Illinois, 1906-7. Plan of lower levels. Somewhat confusingly, though in accord with the standardized convention specified by the Historic American Buildings Survey, the foyer here is shown adjacent to the level below the sanctuary, obscuring the sense of spatial connection Wright effected. Drawn by Whayne Griffin, 1967. For Wright's solution, see fig. 2. (HABS ILL–1093, sheet 5 of 7 sheets)

patterns of walls, piers, windows, and skylights. The building is accurately recorded, yet to render the walls of the sanctuary without their essential openings, to show the foyer with the lower level of the sanctuary (fig. 3) rather than the main floor, and to portray the building without reference to its site is to detract from the very meaning of that which is being shown. Comparisons between elevations and sections reveal similar differences, and in every case it can be argued that however insensitive such drawings are to the buildings themselves, the standardized conventions specified by the Survey facilitate orderly study. Photographs of Wright's buildings in the Survey are also meant to record rather than enhance, and many are equally unappealing. That any work can survive such cold portrayal is a testament to its strength.

The selection of Wright's buildings in the Survey is somewhat uneven, with an emphasis on the earlier work. Yet each of his major periods is represented by at least one example, as will be shown.[3] Between 1887 and 1893, while working for Dankmar Adler (1844–1900) and Louis H. Sullivan (1856–1924), Wright apparently designed around 25 buildings, of which some 20 were built.[4] The HABS materials include three independent commissions of 1892—the Blossom, Harlan, and McArthur houses—as well as two designs from the Adler and Sullivan office that are sometimes credited to Wright: Sullivan's house in Mississippi, 1890, and the Charnley house, 1891.[5] Whatever Wright's role in these two designs, themes apparent in his later and fully independent work can be sensed. The T-shaped plan of the Sullivan house, for instance, seems premonitory of Wright's River Forest Golf Club, 1895.

Other recorded examples by Adler and Sullivan in which Wright's role is assumed to have been more restricted suggest origins of certain attitudes and motifs that Wright later developed on his own. Thus the detail of Adler and

Sullivan's Schiller Building, 1891–92, can be compared to an entrance detail of Wright's Francis Apartments, 1895–96 (figs. 1, 4). Wright's involvement with both may explain their similarities. Yet Wright's belief in ornament as essential to meaningful architecture

Figure 4 Frank Lloyd Wright, Francis Apartments, Chicago, 1895-96. This entrance court detail illustrates ornamental themes that are seen also in the Schiller Building and elsewhere in the Francis Apartments. Photograph by Harold Allen, 1965. (HABS ILL–1076, LC HABS ILL, 16–CHIG, 74-1)

Figure 6 Adler and Sullivan, Hammond Library, Chicago, 1882. Interior detail. Photograph by Cervin Robinson, 1963. (HABS ILL–1017, LC HABS ILL, 16–CHIG, 19–3)

Figure 5 Frank Lloyd Wright, Francis Apartments, Chicago, 1895–96. View toward the entrance court. Like Sullivan, Wright used bands of geometric ornament to emphasize selected areas of a building. Here, patterns derived from intersecting circles give special prominence to the entrance level of an apartment building. Photograph by Harold Allen, 1965. (HABS ILL–1076, LC HABS ILL, 16–CHIG, 74–5)

and his early use of geometric ornamental bands to emphasize selected wall areas (fig. 5) derive clearly from Sullivan. Earlier examples by Adler and Sullivan document Sullivan's own development of ornamental as well as other architectural themes and suggest a fuller genealogy of Wright's work.[6] Details of the exposed truss in the Hammond Library, 1882 (fig. 6), parallel many contemporary examples, such as those seen in work by Frank Furness (1839–1912), for whom Sullivan worked briefly in 1873. Both interior and exterior details by Wright also suggest a sympathy to nineteenth-century French rationalism, as did comparable work by Furness (fig. 7). Such ties were more than coincidental: Sullivan had studied in Paris at the École des Beaux-Arts and so had Furness's teacher, Richard Morris Hunt (1827–1895).[7]

Wright's design ability developed rapidly between 1893 and 1901, when he achieved results of profound significance. During these first eight years of independent practice he designed over 50 buildings, of which more than 35 were built. Five are included in the Survey: in addition to the Francis Apartments, they are the Winslow house, 1893; Francisco Terrace, 1895; the E. C. Waller Apartments, 1895; and the Heller house, 1897. Missing are key examples of 1900 and 1901, as are major examples of the next three years, such as the now-threatened Ward W. Willits house, 1902. Yet even the few included demonstrate his early talent, as apparent in the Winslow house, his first independent commission after leaving Adler and Sullivan's office. The plans (fig. 20) are not unconventional in themselves and contain such elements as a formal entrance hall with related alcove and fireplace (fig. 8), often combined by other architects in these years. Similar entrance halls recorded in Chicago include the Lathrop house, 1891–93, by Charles F. McKim (1847–1909), William R. Mead (1846–1928), and Stanford White (1853–1906) and the Dewes

house by Adolf Cudell and Arthur Hercz, 1894–96. Distinct differences can be seen, however, in the architects' handling of these similar spaces. The earlier, assured manner of classical elements in the Lathrop House (fig. 9) reflects the skill of its New York architects, acknowledged leaders of the Academic Reaction, just as the slightly later and highly decorative combination of classical elements in the Dewes

Figure 7 Adler and Sullivan, Hammond Library, Chicago, 1882. Exterior. Sullivan's earlier and less original ornament recalls comparable work by Frank Furness, for whom Sullivan worked briefly in 1873. Photograph by Cervin Robinson, 1963. (HABS ILL–1017, LC HABS ILL, 16–CHIG, 19–1)

Figure 9   McKim, Mead and White, Bryan Lathrop house, Chicago, 1891–93. Entrance hall. Photograph by Harold Allen, 1964. (HABS ILL–1037, LC HABS ILL, 16–CHIG, 40–3)

Figure 8   Frank Lloyd Wright, William H. Winslow house, River Forest, Illinois, 1893. Entrance hall. Photograph by Richard Nickel, 1965. (HABS ILL–1061, LC HABS ILL, 16–RIVFO, 1–7)

Figure 11 Frank Lloyd Wright, Frederick C. Robie house, Chicago, 1908–10. Interior view of windows. Patterned windows show Wright's advanced skill at abstract composition. Photograph by Cervin Robinson, 1963. (HABS ILL–1005, LC HABS ILL, 16–CHIG, 33–8)

Figure 10 Cudell and Hercz, Francis J. Dewes house, Chicago, 1894–96. Entrance hall. A comparison of Wright's first interiors with work by sometimes prominent contemporaries shows significant differences. Photograph by Harold Allen, 1964. (HABS ILL–1043, LC HABS ILL, 16–CHIG, 45–7)

Figure 12 Frank Lloyd Wright, Emil Bach house, Chicago, 1915. Exterior detail. Photograph by Richard Nickel, 1967. (HABS ILL–1088, LC HABS ILL, 16–CHIG, 83–2)

Figure 13 Frank Lloyd Wright, F.C. Bogk house, Milwaukee, 1916–17. Exterior view. Selected details of Wright's mature work before World War I underline his contribution to the development of modern architecture in Europe. Photograph by Jack E. Boucher, 1969. (HABS WIS–252, LC HABS WIS, 40–MILWA, 15–1)

house (fig. 10) illustrates a local and more exuberant expression of talent. Both define space as conventionally as do the plans of which they are a part. In the Winslow house, classical elements are treated more abstractly, visually reduced in scale by the continuous entablature that emphasizes a wholly different conception of interior space. Moreover, for Wright the fireplace and its related elements of intimate enclosure came to symbolize aspects of family and place that gave it special prominence in his designs.[8] Even at this early date, Wright was moving in a different direction.

Some of Wright's most significant achievements were realized during the years of his early maturity between 1901 and 1910, when he designed more than 135 buildings, of which some 90 were built. In these the promise of earlier work is fulfilled, and in many he had the welcomed opportunity to design all components of a building, including such elements as furniture, lighting fixtures, and patterned windows. Drawings and photographs for the Robie house, 1908–10 (figs. 11, 19) illustrate these significant components of Wright's vision, and suggest

the fully integrated effect he sought. Eleven buildings from this period are represented in the HABS materials, including, beside Unity Temple and the Robie house, the Darwin D. Martin house, 1904; the E-Z Polish Factory, 1905; alterations to the Rookery Building lobby, 1905; the W. A. Glasner house, 1905; the Boynton house, 1908; the May house, 1909; the Steffens house, 1909; and the Park Inn and City National Bank, 1909–10. Several are accompanied by pages of written information, and although these vary greatly in quality, some yield facts of real use. For the Martin house, this information lists drawings and other archival materials accessible in Buffalo. For the Robie house, it includes a copy of the builder's ledger sheets. Both sets of data sheets include names of contractors, references to property records, and a basic bibliography, as do most of the newer data sheets in the archive.

From 1910 through 1914, when his private life was in a state of tumultuous upheaval, Wright designed around 50 buildings, of which about 20 were actually constructed.[9] The HABS materials include one example:

Figure 14 Frank Lloyd Wright, Hollyhock House (for Aline Barnsdall), Los Angeles, 1917–21. Exterior view. A transitional building in Wright's career. Photograph by Marvin Rand, 1965. (HABS CAL–356, LC HABS CAL, 19–LOSAN, 28–1)

Figure 15 Frank Lloyd Wright, Loren B. Pope house, Falls Church, Virginia, 1940. Exterior view. Photograph by Jack E. Boucher, 1964. (HABS VA–638, HABS VA, 30–FALCH, 2–4)

Figure 16 Frank Lloyd Wright, Loren B. Pope house, Falls Church, Virginia, 1940. Living room detail. Moved to its present location at Woodlawn Plantation in 1964, this small house is typical of many Wright designed during the last decades of his career. Photograph by Jack E. Boucher, 1964. (HABS VA–638, LC HABS VA, 30–FALCH, 2–6)

Figure 17 Purcell and Elmslie, Babson stable and service building, Riverside, Illinois, 1915–16. Inner court from east. Photograph by Richard Nickel, 1967. (HABS ILL–1068, LC HABS ILL, 16–RIVSI, 1A–4)

the Ziegler house, 1910. Its construction unsupervised by Wright and undistinctive except for its Kentucky location, the Ziegler house does little to suggest advances signaled by such examples as Taliesin, 1911; the Coonley playhouse, 1912; and Midway Gardens, 1913–14. The first two have been radically altered, however, and the last demolished.

From 1915 through 1927, while Wright sought stability in his private life, he designed about 75 buildings of which some 35 or 40 were built. The four recorded in the HABS materials are the Bach house, 1915; the Bogk house, 1916–17; Hollyhock House, 1917–21; and Residence "A" at Hollyhock House, 1920–21. The Bach and Bogk houses show Wright's tendency in these years to design abstractly cubic forms, a tendency that infused details with sharpened clarity (figs. 12, 13). Hollyhock House (fig. 14) reflects a determined move from his earlier vocabulary, a shift stimulated by new clients and distant sites, and one that led to such exceptional projects as San Marcos-in-the-Desert, 1927. Data sheets compiled for Hollyhock House in 1965 offered clear explanations of its complex construction that have only recently been published.[10]

Some of Wright's most important works were realized during the last thirty years of his life, when he received a volume of commissions more commensurate with his talent. He designed more than 100 buildings between 1928 and the beginning of American involvement in World War II, of which some 50 were built, and from 1941 until his death in 1959 he designed close to 400, of which more than 150 were built. These included major examples of public and institutional buildings, partly fulfilling a potential that had too infrequently been tapped. Although Wright's larger designs of the period are not yet included in the Survey, three small houses are: the Pope house, 1940; the Walter house, 1949–50; and the Trier house, 1958–59. These lack the impressive scale of his grander commissions, but they do illustrate attitudes that consistently informed his career. Thus his concern for appropriately expressive ornament shows in the Pope house (figs. 15, 16) as clearly as in the Francis Apartments (figs. 4, 5), though in the later example pattern was more a function of light than mass.[11]

It is perhaps in the indication of Wright's legacy that the Survey more appropriately excels. More than thirty architects have so far been identified as members of the Prairie School; all practiced in the Chicago area in the early decades of the twentieth century and all were heavily indebted to Wright.[12] Twelve of them are represented in the Survey. As the documents show, these architects focused on the more observable features of Wright's work as a point of departure. The vocabulary they reinforced came to have a reassuring consistency. Produced without benefit of genius, such examples suggest how abstract principles can be reduced to a repeatable formula that characterizes a stylistic manner. The results could be appealing, as in the Babson stable and service buildings by William Gray Purcell (1880–1965) and George Elmslie (1871–1952), 1915–16 (figs. 17, 18).

Figure 19 Frank Lloyd Wright, Frederick C. Robie House, Chicago, 1908–10. Elevations of chairs and andirons. Measured drawings of Wright's furniture are essential in documenting his work. Drawing by David T. Van Zanten, 1963. (HABS ILL–1005, sheet 12 of 14 sheets)

Figure 18 Purcell and Elmslie, Babson stable and service building, Riverside, Illinois, 1915–16. Detail. Prairie School architects were clearly dependent on Wright in terms of spatial composition as well as ornamental details. Photograph by Richard Nickel, 1967. (HABS ILL–1068, LC HABS ILL, 16–RIVSI, 1A–5)

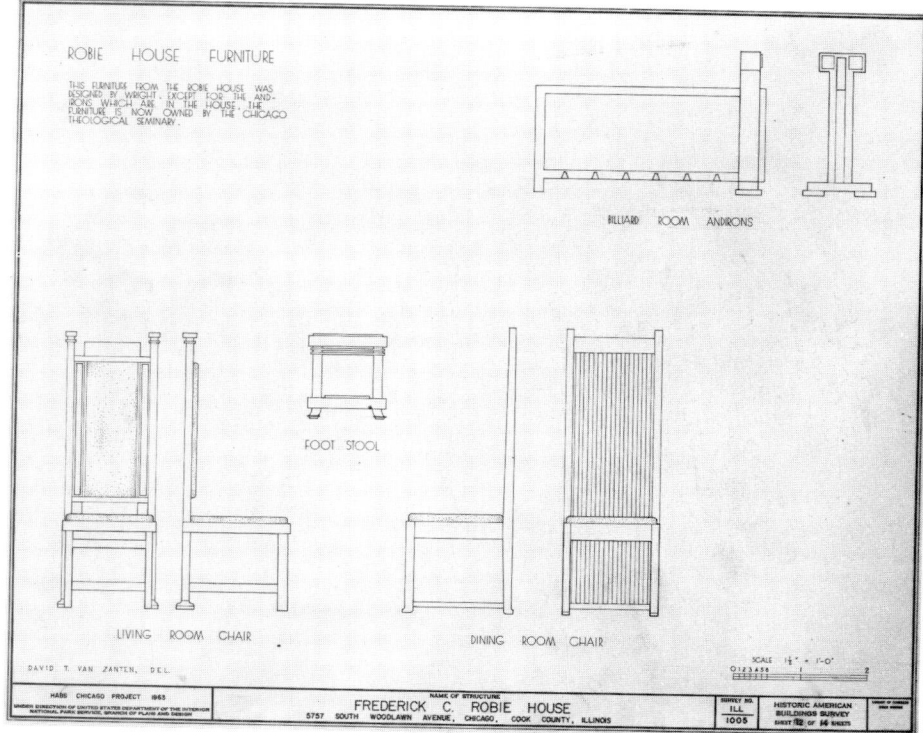

ROBIE   HOUSE   FURNITURE

THIS FURNITURE FROM THE ROBIE HOUSE WAS
DESIGNED BY WRIGHT, EXCEPT FOR THE AND-
IRONS WHICH ARE IN THE HOUSE. THE
FURNITURE IS NOW OWNED BY THE CHICAGO
THEOLOGICAL SEMINARY.

BILLIARD   ROOM   ANDIRONS

FOOT   STOOL

LIVING   ROOM   CHAIR

DINING   ROOM   CHAIR

SCALE

DAVID T. VAN ZANTEN, DEL.

HABS CHICAGO PROJECT 1963
UNDER DIRECTION OF UNITED STATES DEPARTMENT OF THE INTERIOR
NATIONAL PARK SERVICE, BRANCH OF PLANS AND DESIGN

NAME OF STRUCTURE
FREDERICK C. ROBIE HOUSE
5757 SOUTH WOODLAWN AVENUE, CHICAGO, COOK COUNTY, ILLINOIS

SURVEY NO.
ILL
1005

HISTORIC AMERICAN
BUILDINGS SURVEY
SHEET 12 OF 14 SHEETS

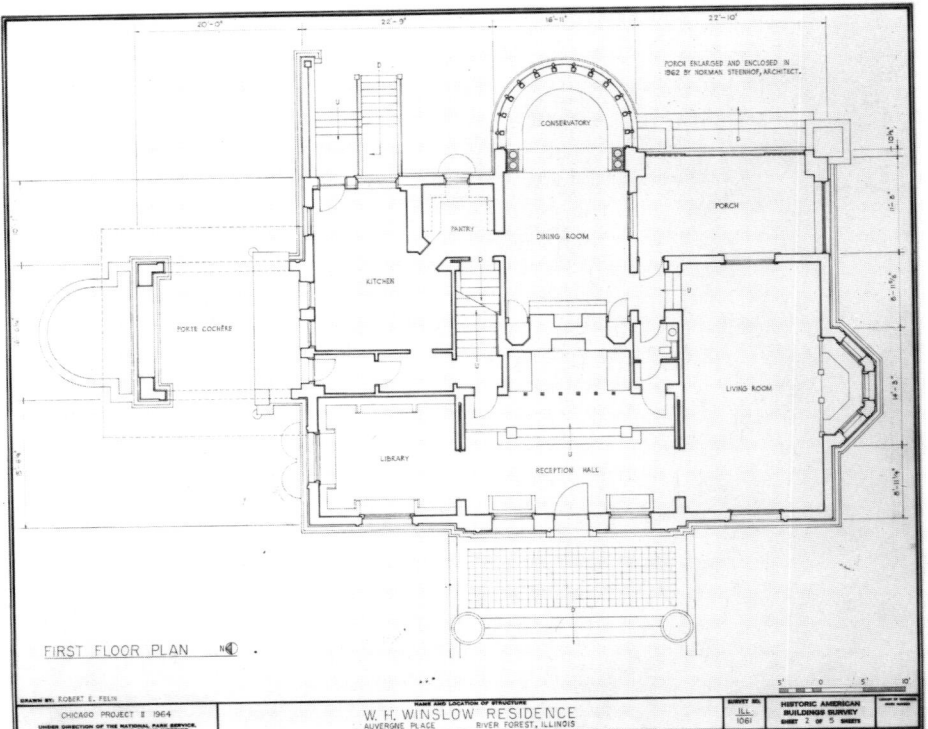

Figure 20 Frank Lloyd Wright, William H. Winslow house, River Forest, Illinois, 1893. Plan of first floor. Drawing by Robert E. Felin, 1964. (HABS ILL–1061, sheet 2 of 5 sheets)

Figure 21 Hotel lobby, Texas (Kingsville?). At a more anonymous level, Wright's influence can be sensed in such details as the column capitals, light fixtures, and patterned windows in this hotel lobby. Wittemann Collection, Prints and Photographs Division. (LC–USZ62–83868)

Wright's influence, coupled with that of his immediate colleagues, was not restricted to the Chicago area or to known architects, as documents in the Library of Congress show. An anonymous hotel lobby in Texas (fig. 21) illustrates one of many examples. To chart such influence is essential in the measure of genius, and in this regard the Historic American Buildings Survey collections will surely prove a major resource.

Notes

1. Henry-Russell Hitchcock, during a conversation in 1981. I am grateful to C. Ford Peatross, Mary Ison, and others at the Library of Congress for their unwavering support and valued assistance in the preparation of this essay as well as in all other research projects that I have undertaken in Washington. Their dedication to furthering scholarship deserves much praise.

2. The primary archive of Wright materials is maintained at Taliesin West by the Frank Lloyd Wright Foundation under the direction of Olgivanna Lloyd Wright. Bruce Brooks Pfeiffer serves as historian and archivist. Soon to be published by Garland is Patrick J. Meehan, *Frank Lloyd Wright: A Research Guide to Archival Sources* (New York, announced for 1983). Published information is listed in Robert L. Sweeney, *Frank Lloyd Wright; an Annotated Bibliography* (Los Angeles, 1978).

3. Figures are based on the Historic American Buildings Survey inventory forms as well as the materials of the Survey proper deposited in the Prints and Photographs Division of the Library of Congress.

4. Chronological lists of Wright's designs are included in Henry-Russell Hitchcock, *In the Nature of Materials, 1887–1941: The Buildings of Frank Lloyd Wright* (New York, 1942; reprint ed., 1973); Olgivanna Lloyd Wright, *Frank Lloyd Wright: His Life, His Work, His Words* (New York, 1966); and Alberto Izzo and Camillo Gubitosi, *Frank Lloyd Wright; Three-Quarters of a Century of Drawings* (New York, 1981). Executed designs are listed in William Allin Storrer, *The Architecture of Frank Lloyd Wright: A Complete Catalog*, 2d ed. (Cambridge, Mass., 1978). A geographical guide to Wright's buildings is contained in Frank Lloyd Wright, *Frank Lloyd Wright: Writings and Buildings*, selected by Edgar Kaufmann, jr., and Ben Raeburn (New York, 1960). The approximate totals mentioned in this essay are based on these sources; discrepancies in dates and differences in numbers reflect different approaches.

5. Sullivan's work is discussed in Hugh Morrison, *Louis Sullivan, Prophet of Modern Architecture* (New York, 1935).

6. The evolution of Sullivan's ornament is analyzed in Paul E. Sprague, "The Architectural Ornament of Louis Sullivan and his Chief Draftsmen" (Ph.D. diss., Princeton University, 1968).

7. Links between Sullivan, Furness, and France are discussed in James F. O'Gorman, *The Architecture of Frank Furness* (Philadelphia, 1973), pp. 30–38.

8. The meaning of fireplaces—and more particularly of inglenooks—in Wright's work is discussed in Edgar Kaufmann, jr., "Precedent and Progress in the Work of Frank Lloyd Wright," *Journal of the Society of Architectural Historians* 39 (May 1980): 145–49.

9. Wright's personal life is discussed in Robert C. Twombly, *Frank Lloyd Wright; An Interpretative Biography* (New York, 1973).

10. Kathryn Smith, "Frank Lloyd Wright, Hollyhock House, and Olive Hill, 1914–1924," *Journal of the Society of Architectural Historians* 38 (March 1979): 15–33.

11. The relocation in 1964 of the Loren Pope house, or Pope-Leighey house as it was later called, is the subject of a special issue of *Historic Preservation*, vol. 21 (April–September 1969).

12. The major study of this work is H. Allen Brooks, *The Prairie School; Frank Lloyd Wright and His Midwest Contemporaries* (Toronto, 1972).

Association Wood Construction Details

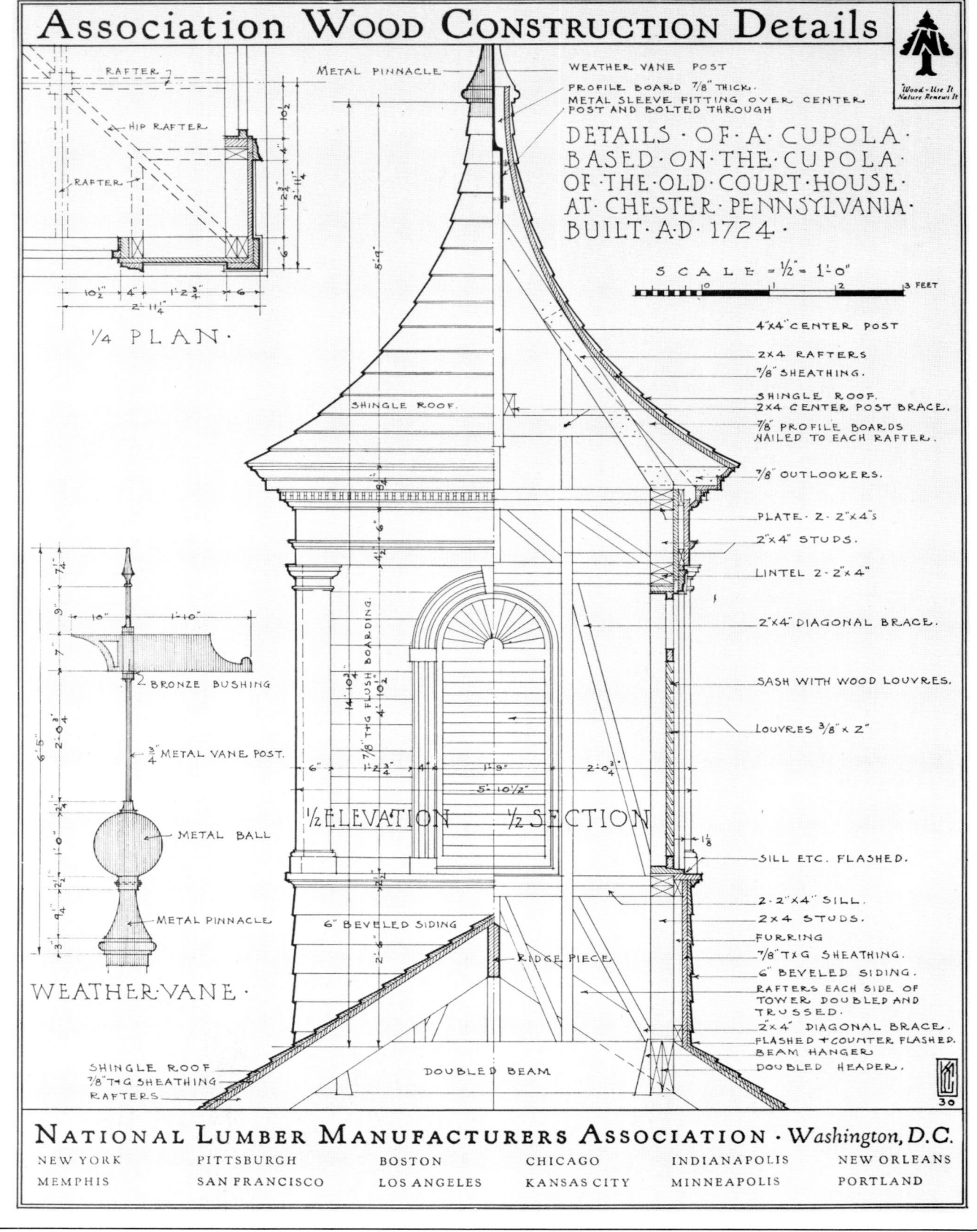

**DETAILS · OF · A · CUPOLA ·
BASED · ON · THE · CUPOLA ·
OF · THE · OLD · COURT · HOUSE ·
AT · CHESTER · PENNSYLVANIA ·
BUILT · A·D· 1724 ·**

SCALE = ½" = 1'-0"

3 FEET

¼ PLAN·

RAFTER

HIP RAFTER

RAFTER

METAL PINNACLE

WEATHER VANE POST
PROFILE BOARD ⅞" THICK.
METAL SLEEVE FITTING OVER CENTER
POST AND BOLTED THROUGH

SHINGLE ROOF.

4"x4" CENTER POST

2"x4" RAFTERS

⅞" SHEATHING.

SHINGLE ROOF.
2"x4" CENTER POST BRACE.
⅞" PROFILE BOARDS
NAILED TO EACH RAFTER.

⅞" OUTLOOKERS.

PLATE · 2 · 2"x4"S

2"x4" STUDS.

LINTEL 2 - 2"x4"

2"x4" DIAGONAL BRACE.

SASH WITH WOOD LOUVRES.

LOUVRES ⅜" x 2"

SILL ETC. FLASHED.

2 · 2"x4" SILL.

2x4 STUDS.

FURRING

⅞" T&G SHEATHING.

6" BEVELED SIDING.

RAFTERS EACH SIDE OF
TOWER DOUBLED AND
TRUSSED.

2"x4" DIAGONAL BRACE.

FLASHED + COUNTER FLASHED.
BEAM HANGER
DOUBLED HEADER.

½ ELEVATION   ½ SECTION

BRONZE BUSHING

¾" METAL VANE POST.

METAL BALL

METAL PINNACLE

WEATHER·VANE·

6" BEVELED SIDING

RIDGE PIECE

DOUBLED BEAM

SHINGLE ROOF
⅞" T&G SHEATHING
RAFTERS

30

NATIONAL LUMBER MANUFACTURERS ASSOCIATION · Washington, D.C.

| NEW YORK | PITTSBURGH | BOSTON | CHICAGO | INDIANAPOLIS | NEW ORLEANS |
| MEMPHIS | SAN FRANCISCO | LOS ANGELES | KANSAS CITY | MINNEAPOLIS | PORTLAND |

"Wood - Use It
Nature Renews It"

HABS at an Awkward Age: The 1960s and 1970s

by

ROBERT BRUEGMANN

At age fifty the Historic American Buildings Survey may be on the verge of outgrowing a difficult adolescence. Born into a world in which architects were still interested in fanlight details for new Colonial houses, HABS found itself after the Second World War in an age of steel and glass high-rise buildings. Despite a good many problems in the 1960s and 1970s, HABS has survived that period, and there are signs that it may enjoy a vigorous future. What follows are some observations on HABS in its awkward age.[1]

What HABS achieved in the 1930s was remarkable. In a few short years, a group of dedicated professionals turned out an astonishing quantity of useful and attractive drawings.[2] For the subsequent history of the Survey, however, one thing that did not happen is perhaps most interesting.

What did not happen was a debate about the purpose or the technical means of recording historic buildings. This was taken for granted because the measured drawing was already so familiar to almost every architect.

What the HABS founders had in mind were drawings like those published in the White Pine monograph series in the 1920s. These crisp drawings of early American frame buildings were only the best known examples of this kind of recording activity (fig. 1). Indeed, the late 1920s and early 1930s saw a large number of projects at a local level very similar to what would later be proposed for HABS at the national level. So common had this kind of recording activity become, that John O'Neill, Park Service coordinator of HABS, could write in a report of 1930: "This report assumes that the basic principle, the techniques and the utility of measured records of architectural monuments are already established through many years of experience in many countries."[3]

The White Pine and other survey drawings had two major direct precedents. One was the builder's guides or "pattern books" published in Britain and America in the eighteenth and nineteenth centuries. Written to illustrate "correct" construction techniques and ornamental details, these books contained engraved plates as illustrations. They

Figure 1 Wood construction details from an advertisement for the National Lumber Manufacturers Association, in the White Pine series, 1931. This design was adapted from an eighteenth-century cupola in Chester, Pennsylvania, to provide practicing architects with wood details appropriate for new work. It clearly shows how much the study and adaptation of old buildings were part of current architectural practice in the years immediately before the birth of the Survey. (LC–USZ62–83829)

Figure 2 Joseph Conrad Farm (Miller's Farm), Mt. Pleasant vicinity, Pennsylvania Township, Berks County, Pennsylvania. Although many HABS drawings of the 1960s and 1970s are somewhat mechanical and dull, these decades did see the unexpected development of a kind of virtuoso fine-line drafting. This drawing of the Conrad Farm barn by Perry Benson is one of the most extraordinary examples. (HABS PA–260–B, sheet 4 of 5 of 10 sheets)

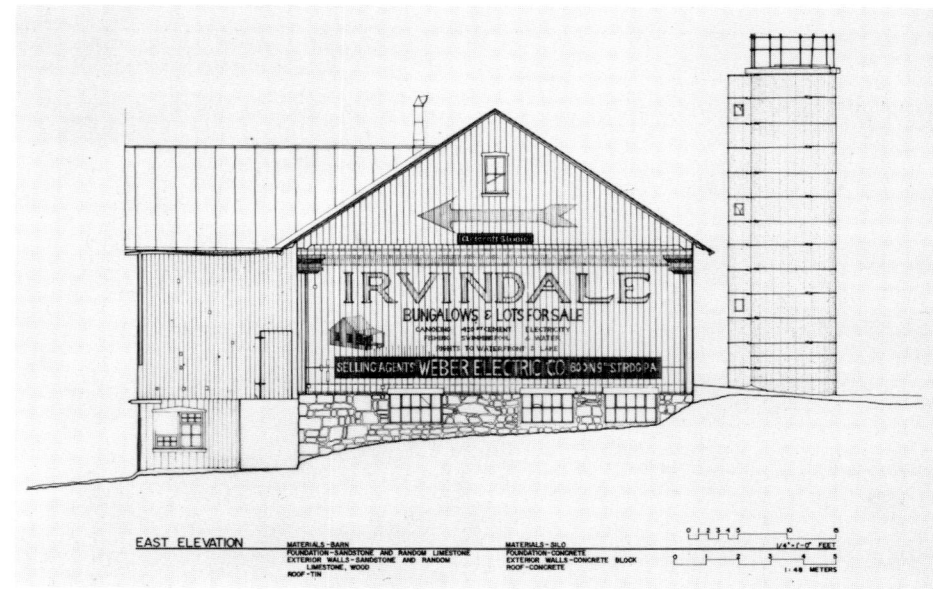

Figure 3 "Fragments antiques à Rome." The classic nineteenth-century volume of historical drawings shows the elaborate compositions and use of shading that gave drawings of the period an extremely painterly quality. This kind of composition, although often simplified, was the model for most American early twentieth-century measured drawings, and suggestions of it survive today, especially in the title sheets of some HABS drawing sets. Reconstruction drawing by G. Ancelet, from H. d'Espouy, *Monuments antiques relevés et restaurés par les architectes pensionnaires de l'Académie de France à Rome* (Paris, 1890). (LC–USZ62–83828)

were extensively used by the carpenters and masons who designed and built America's Colonial buildings. The other major precedent was the archaeology project of the École des Beaux-Arts in Paris, the foremost architectural school of the time and the dominant influence on American architectural education. The product of this classroom exercise was a series of intricate sheets with plans, elevations, details, ornamental text, and decorative devices appropriate to the structure being measured (figs. 3, 4).

Two crucial, but often overlooked aspects of this kind of drawing must be considered to understand the founders' intentions. First, the measuring and drawing of a Corinthian capital or chair rail molding was thought to have much the same value for architects as the copying of masterpieces in the museum by art students. Repeated over and over, the details and propor-

tions became second nature just as the major and minor scales would be to music students.

Second, measured drawings, besides their stated purpose of recording, almost always carried implicit polemical content. For example, the extensive sheets of drawings of the monuments of classical antiquity prepared by Renaissance architects were part of an attempt to break with medieval traditions and to reinstitute supposedly correct architectural principles based on an exhaustive comparative study of the remains of the best ancient buildings. Likewise in this country in the early years of the twentieth century, the study of Colonial architecture was thought to be a way of returning to simplicity and order after the unrestrained exuberance of the late nineteenth century. This was definitely the spirit in which HABS was founded, although by the 1930s the range had

Figure 4 "Un Puits dans le cloître de St.-Jean d'Angers." This elaborate sheet, containing a plan, two elevations, and a perspective of a well in a church at Angers, France, is an excellent example of the virtuoso treatment of measured drawings that American students learned at the École de Beaux-Arts and brought back to schools of architecture in this country. It is obvious that the design of the sheet was at least as important as the information conveyed. Drawing by Albert G. Nash, an American student of Pascal at the École des Beaux-Arts, Paris. Architectural Drawings Collection, Prints and Photographs Division. (LC–USZ62–83825)

Figure 5 Charles E. Peterson, a founder of the Historic American Buildings Survey, was responsible for the program's original directives. Photograph by Bachrach.

Figure 6 Capt. Thomas Bennett House, Fairhaven, Bristol County, Massachusetts. This plan of the Bennett house garden was drawn in 1943-44 by Frank Chouteau Brown, longtime head of the Survey's New England operations. Brown apparently took measurements provided by others and created a fanciful composition with a plan in the center bordered on two sides by sections in one case extending beyond the sheet's border lines. This sheet shows the kind of freedom enjoyed by HABS draftsmen in the 1930s. A drawing of the same subject in the 1970s would probably have been clearer but less interesting in appearance. (HABS MASS–608, sheet 15 of 15 sheets)

been broadened to include buildings from the seventeenth through the early nineteenth centuries.

Indeed it seems clear that the HABS pioneers and many architects thought of the drawings done by the Historic American Buildings Survey as a kind of pattern book. Professional architectural magazines, notably *Architectural Forum,* started to reproduce HABS drawings to provide details for practicing architects exactly in the same way the White Pine series had done (fig. 7). In fact it is often difficult, leafing through the pages of these magazines, to distinguish at first glance between working drawings for new buildings of the period and HABS measured drawings.

The program set out by Charles E. Peterson in his memo was a logical and comprehensive one. He wrote that the buildings recorded should provide "an almost complete resume of the builder's art," including not only houses and churches but bridges, forts, shops, log cabins, ghost towns, pueblos, and others. Altogether it was an extremely forward-looking list for the time. His

intention was to create a complete taxonomy of American building types and styles, illustrated by the best preserved and most intact examples.[4]

Despite the temporary nature of the program, the Survey's founders had great ambitions. They fully believed they could achieve a comprehensive record. John O'Neill estimated in 1938 that there were some fourteen thousand prime important structures that should be recorded and that already seventy-five hundred had been recorded in photographs and twenty-eight hundred in drawings. The early HABS staff members planned to do a major book in which HABS drawings would document the whole development of American architecture.[5] In addition to the buildings that were measured, an inventory was set up that would record many more structures. According to the 1935 instruction sheets, "Specifications for the Measurement and Recording of Historic American Buildings and Structural Remains," "it is proposed to continue the indexing of historic American architecture until a complete catalog of all important

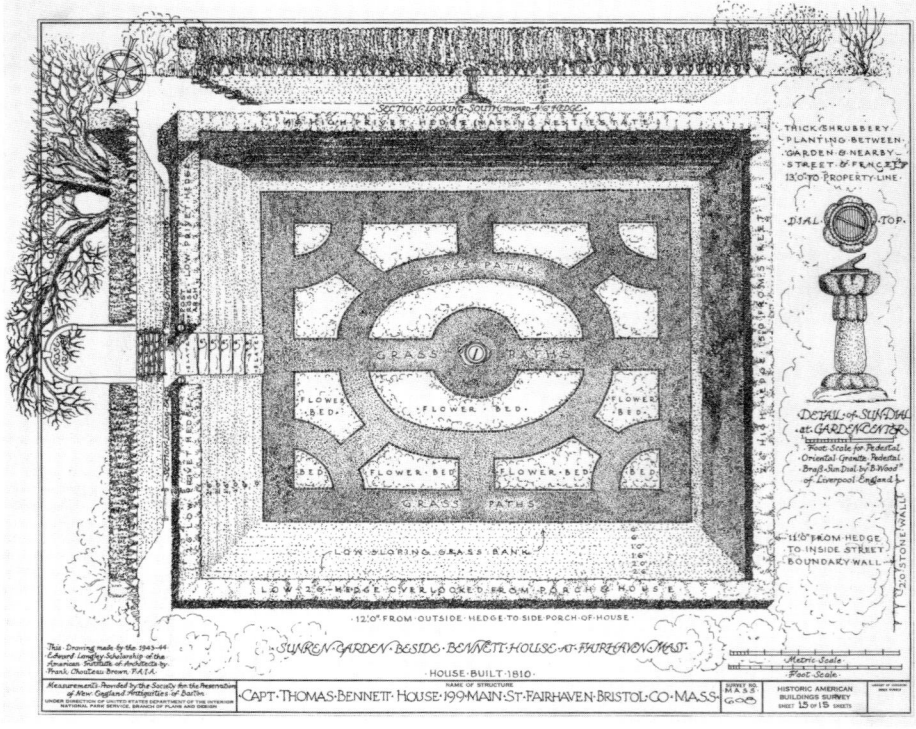

structures is available in the Library of Congress." It was a very bold and comprehensive vision.

Set up as a strictly temporary relief measure, the Survey operated in a somewhat irregular fashion with a variety of funding sources through the 1930s, but by the time America entered World War II it had become largely inoperative. After the war the kind of recording HABS started was continued by Peterson at the Park Service's Independence Hall in Philadelphia, but it was not until 1957 that HABS itself was reinstituted. It was a real tribute to its founders that HABS was revived, apparently the only survivor among all of the federal government's federal relief programs.

When the Survey did resume operations, it took up almost exactly where it had left off in the 1930s. The only really substantial change in the operation was the use of student draftsmen instead of unemployed architects on the recording teams. The rest of the world had changed dramatically, however.

First, the total number of buildings considered historic skyrocketed as first the late nineteenth and then the early twentieth century were considered worthy of serious attention. To keep up with changing ideas about architectural history, the cut-off date for recording was moved from 1860 to 1900 and finally to a sliding scale that would include buildings more than fifty years old. The number of potential structures increased correspondingly, creating instant problems.

As early as the 1950s HABS already estimated that there were over three million historic structures. In 1975 the Survey's chief estimated that, at an average cost of $2,000–3,500 per structure, it would take over a hundred years at the current pace just to measure the twelve thousand buildings on the National Register, only a fraction of the country's historic buildings. Since then both the drawing cost and the number of buildings on the Register have continued to rise

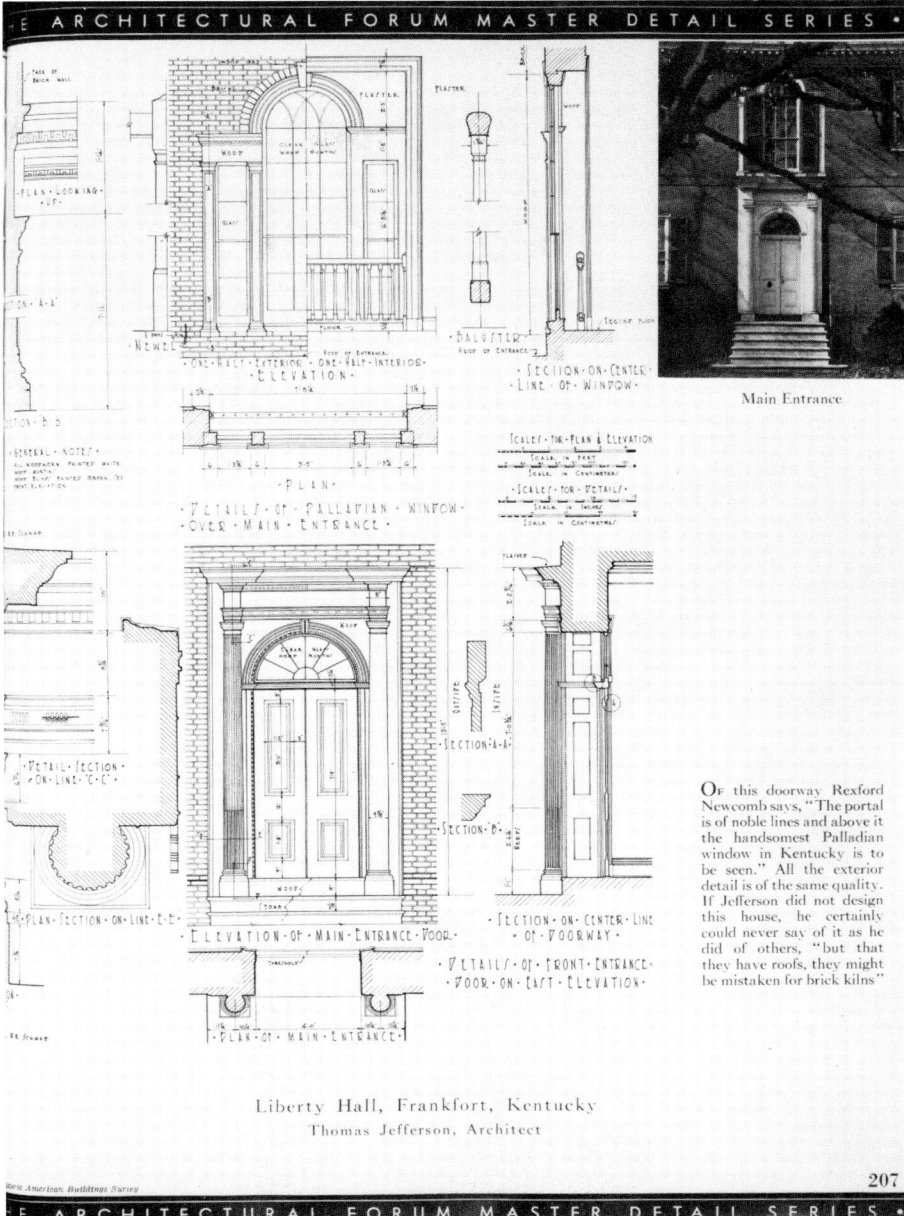

Liberty Hall, Frankfort, Kentucky
Thomas Jefferson, Architect

Of this doorway Rexford Newcomb says, "The portal is of noble lines and above it the handsomest Palladian window in Kentucky is to be seen." All the exterior detail is of the same quality. If Jefferson did not design this house, he certainly could never say of it as he did of others, "but that they have roofs, they might be mistaken for brick kilns"

much faster than the HABS budget, even in the era when that budget was increasing.[6] As if all this were not enough, HABS was challenged as never before by the volume of demolition unleashed by urban renewal, highway construction, and the reconstruction of large areas of America's cities.

In the face of these dramatic changes, HABS did, over the next two decades, try to bring itself into line with the demands of the postwar years. This is most immediately noticeable in

Figure 7 A page from *Architectural Forum*, September 1934, shows HABS details and a photograph of the main entrance of Liberty Hall, Frankfort, Kentucky. The reproduction of these drawings in the professional architectural literature shows how closely HABS was tied to actual practice in the 1930s. This close tie was broken as European Modernism increased in popularity after World War II. Courtesy Billboard Publications, Inc. (LC–USZ62–83826)

Figure 8 North elevation, Boscobel, Garrison, Putnam County, New York. Drawing by Steven E. Bauer, 1977. (HABS NY–5667)

moldings were replaced by steel spandrel panels and neoprene window gaskets. No longer could HABS rely on previous training to ensure high quality and uniformity.

HABS instituted a number of new procedures to deal with this situation. To some extent they worked, and the drawings of the 1960s and 1970s are, for the most part, clear and uniform in treatment. The same policies had the unfortunate side effect of making many of them dry and academic. In the 1930s the instruction sheets sent out to teams were quite modest and only laid down the most basic procedures. Even these were often disregarded. One of the most common practices of the 1930s was the reconstruction drawing. Despite instructions to avoid conjectural restorations, there were a surprising number of sheets based on fuzzy old photographs or, in some cases, on nothing more than old sketches and written descriptions. This was probably done because many of the draftsmen felt so familiar with the construction and details of that period that they felt these drawings could be completely plausible even if not necessarily correct.

After the war, on the other hand, practice became much more codified. Graphic techniques were standardized. Mechanical lettering replaced hand lettering, and polyester was substituted for

HABS drawings. By the 1960s these had become cut off from the world of architectural practice. By then students in schools of architecture no longer learned how to draw Corinthian capitals with shades and shadows. Spare hard-line drawings with stenciled letters replaced the more elaborate rendered plans and perspectives with watercolor washes and elegant hand lettering. For the average student draftsman the whole art of the measured drawing became virtually unknown as fanlights and egg-and-dart

Figure 9 Boscobel (the Dyckman-Cruger House), Garrison, Putnam County, New York. Drawn by John C. Merrill, Paul Lutfer Wood, and William Sterzbach, Columbia University, 1932.

paper. The instruction booklets became more specific. Harley J. McKee's *Recording Historic Buildings*, which appeared in 1950, was intended as a summary of HABS procedures. All of these things made HABS records more uniform and probably more accurate, but this was done at the expense of the spontaneity and invention which made the 1930s sheets so compelling. Comparing some sheets prepared for Boscobel Plantation in the early 1930s, before HABS was inaugurated, with sheets made by Columbia University students for HABS in 1977 to show currently existing conditions immediately demonstrates how mechanical the new sheets can be. Even begging for a moment the question of why these sheets were needed at all, it is apparent that the information is there but the grace of the old drawings has disappeared (figs. 8, 9).

If in the 1930s the two-fold goal of producing beautiful drawings and creating meticulous records was sometimes accomplished by slighting the latter aspect, many of the drawings of the 1960s and 1970s err decidedly on the other side. The late 1970s did see one curious attempt to resolve this problem. Perhaps to compensate for the loss of the tapestry-like ornamental appearance that occurred when many of the notes, measurements, molding profiles, and other details were left off drawings, a new interest in virtuoso, fine-line drafting developed. Used primarily for elevations, it turned into a highly developed style as good examples from previous years were sent out to each new set of summer teams (figs. 2, 10). Unfortunately, where earlier drawings had been done primarily with heavy line weights so they could be easily reproduced, the HABS drawings of the 1970s with their exquisite four-aught pen lines—and occasionally even diluted ink—often could not be reproduced at small scale without losing most of the detail, and it was only in reproduction that most people ever saw them.

Much more serious were the con-

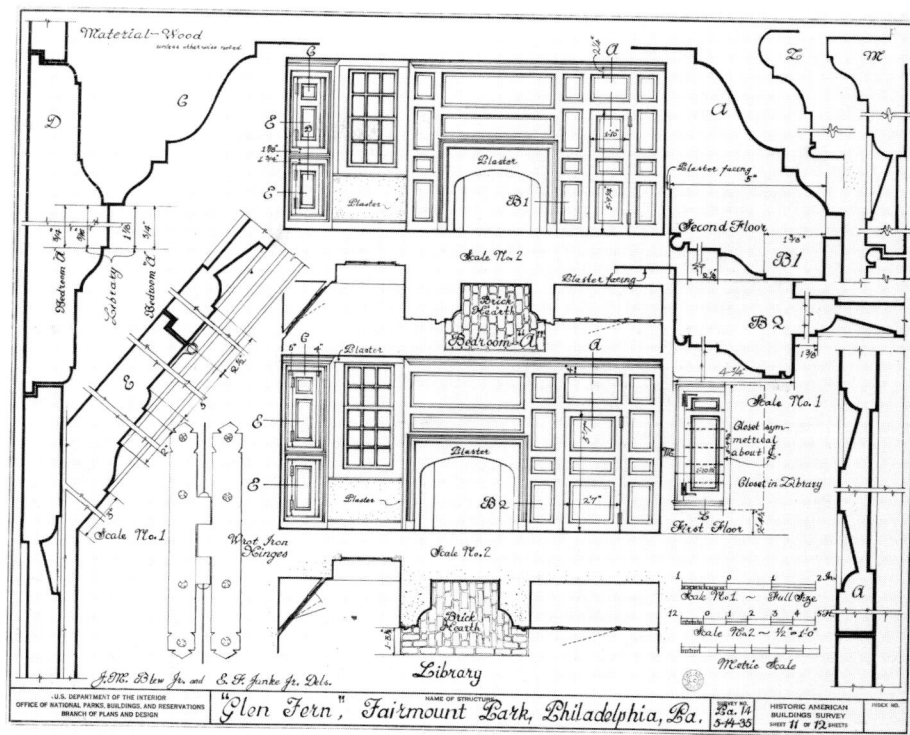

ceptual problems brought about by the expanded activities of the Survey. In the 1930s HABS drawings proved a perfect vehicle for recording small buildings in detail, showing the small variations which differentiated one period from the next and one region from another. When the scale of the building increased dramatically, HABS did introduce a larger sheet size, but this did not solve the basic problems. For an eighteenth-century house, five or six drawings, including a full set of elevations, plans, and sections as well as a few details, could record a building quite well. With a six-story late nineteenth-century Romanesque-style courthouse taking up a city block, many more sheets were needed just to record the architectural features, forgetting for a moment the structural, electrical, heating, and ventilating systems as well as the sculptural and painted decorations that would have to be documented to give an adequate idea of such a structure. The standard drawing set that once satisfied most of the uses to which HABS drawings might be put was no longer adequate.

Figure 10 Glen Fern, Fairmount Park, Philadelphia, Pennsylvania. This sheet was reproduced in the 1935 "Specifications for the Measurement and Recording of Historic American Buildings and Structural Remains" and clearly shows the ornamental tapestrylike appearance created by the inclusion of numerous moulding profiles, details, and notes. Measured drawing by J. M. Blew, Jr., and E. F. Janke, Jr. (HABS PA–14, sheet 11 of 12 sheets)

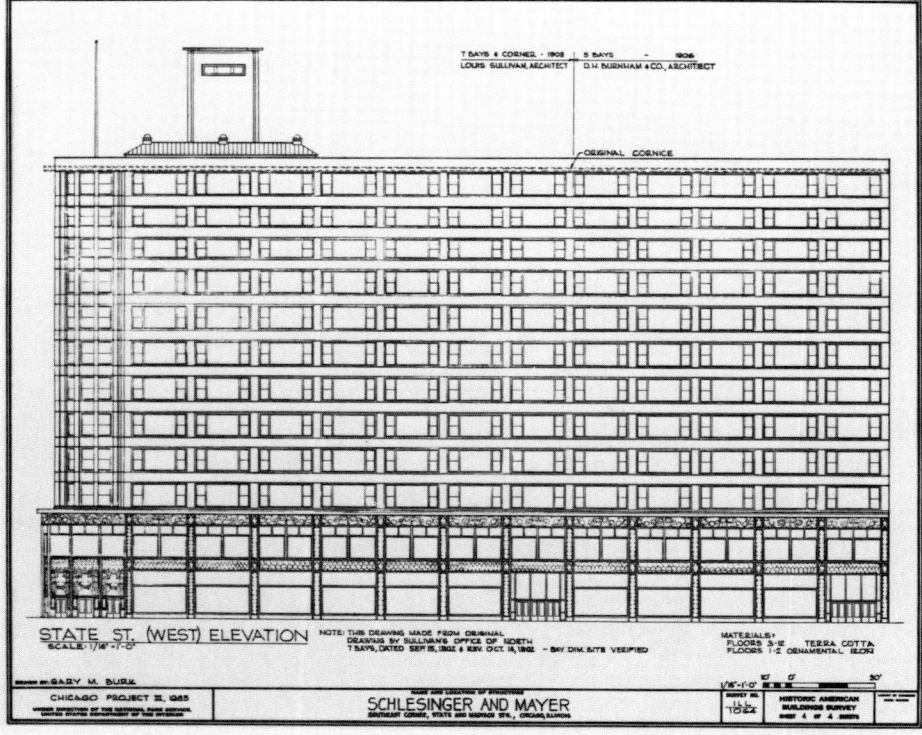

Figure 11 Schlesinger and Mayer, Chicago, Illinois. This elevation illustrates typical problems the Historic American Buildings Survey encountered in recording large late nineteenth-and early twentieth-century buildings. According to a note on the sheet, this drawing was redrawn from a Sullivan drawing of 1902 with the bay dimensions verified on the site. It would have been cheaper and more useful to have photocopied the original drawing. Researchers would then have had an authentic document. Here—because the HABS team decided to alter the drawing to make it reflect conditions in 1965 but did not do this consistently and did not make enough notes to explain what they did— the result is a drawing that shows neither Sullivan's original intention nor the condition of the building at a given time in the past. Measured drawing by Gary M. Burk. (HABS ILL–1064, sheet 4 of 4 sheets)

The attempt to record these larger, later structures ultimately led to more difficult problems still. Some of the most spectacular HABS drawings of the last two decades record in great detail the lavish ornament of great Second Empire and High Victorian Gothic piles that dot the American landscape. Many of their ornamental features were not handmade but were purchased by the square foot from lumber yards or supply stores. How ironic that these mass-produced details were now measured by hand and redrawn with the same loving care earlier given to the original creations of artisans and local craftsmen. Even more ironic, perhaps, is the spectacle of the HABS format— created by early twentieth-century architects who hated late nineteenth-century architecture and used their drawings as a means of propaganda against it—being used to record mansard roofs, cast-iron facades, and polychrome brick details.

A good example of the limitations of the HABS format can be found in the drawings of Louis Sullivan's famous Carson-Pirie-Scott Store (labeled on the drawings only with the store's original name, Schlesinger and Mayer, and not with the name by which it is now universally known) (fig. 11). Although the historical portion of this survey, by Larry J. Homolka, succeeds in being quite useful, despite the straitjacket outline imposed on the material, the drawings have little value. They were primarily traced from original Sullivan drawings but partially and inaccurately altered to show conditions in 1965. Because the draftsmen were obviously torn between reflecting the original intentions of the architect and showing the building as it then existed, they succeeded in doing neither. Instead the drawings show only a portion of the building, omitting without any note a large portion of the store on Wabash Avenue. They fail to distinguish between the dates of the various parts. Most damaging of all, even a casual glance at the building will reveal that the pier between the seven-bay Sullivan section of 1903 and the five-bay Burnham addition of 1906 is twice as wide as the others. No draftsman who was as interested in the actual building as he was in the drawing could have made such an error. What he did was simply extend Sullivan's drawing five more bays without even checking it against the actual building.

More subtle but equally misleading is the fact that the HABS drawings manage to show the structure as a simple rectangular solid with a completely open regular grid of columns in uninterrupted interior spaces punctuated by a regular grid of columns, the whole sheathed in a thin skin of smooth, flat terra-cotta. In other words, the drawings edit the building to make it conform to Modernist notions about it and fail to show it as it was and is: a complex, highly decorated structure with a large number of partitions, display installations, and other architectural features on the interior. How much less expensive and more useful this project would have been if the original drawings had simply been photocopied and the draftsmen sent to do something else.

Despite all the surface changes in the drawings, the one thing that did not change at HABS was the assumption that the HABS drawing was the primary vehicle for recording historic buildings. I feel that it has been this emphasis on the end product rather than on the purpose that has created difficulties. Large building complexes, for instance, had been recorded in the 1930s on magnificent sheets containing a wealth of information (fig. 14). As the use of complex sheets with notes declined, HABS relied more on simple site plans and street elevations (fig. 15). These often give little sense of the neighborhood, and for historical information the user must consult the historical reports. Even used in conjunction with historical reports, however, the format is limiting. It would be very difficult, for example, to record with a standard drawing set a brownstone district in New York or a planned suburban residential community. What is interesting in these cases is not a single building or even a row of buildings but the hundreds of variations on a more-or-less standard theme, the distribution of various building types throughout given eras in the past, and the modification of building types over the years. In cases like this, the drawings should take a distinctly secondary role and an extensive set of photographs, photographic copies of old views, insurance maps, and other maps, and a detailed historical report should be assembled, giving a much more useful package than a standard drawing set.

To its credit, HABS made a major effort to improve the historical portion of the Survey. In the 1930s, because the primary function of the Survey was to make drawings, because buildings surveyed were largely designed by anonymous builders, because few records existed for many Colonial structures, and because the founders and original employees of HABS were architects rather than trained historians, historical research took a distinctly

minor position. In his 1933 memo, Charles Peterson wrote: "It is anticipated that the historical data incident to the buildings studied may be secured through local and state institutions and societies. Only the briefest resume of facts is necessary in each case and it does not seem necessary to build up an overhead for the purpose of getting data which is ordinarily obtainable gratis." After 1957 HABS did start routinely to employ historians on its summer teams, but since the teams needed to start measuring as soon as they arrived, the historians might not discover until too late that a full set of original drawings already existed for a building being measured, or that the building was not, as previously thought, the home of the local hero, or that indeed—in rare instances—HABS had already drawn it, or that the historical data were not housed at the remote site in Utah where the historian had been sent but at the National Archives in Washington.

The growing rift between the architect and historian also had an influence on HABS. The records produced

Figure 12 Framing joint comparison detail, Leiter I Building with Home Insurance Building, Chicago, Illinois. An interesting sheet that could have been of great value, this was unfortunately not done from the building itself but from drawings at the Chicago Art Institute. Moreover, the notes do not explain exactly what drawings were used. This is important to know if one is to judge the degree of misinterpretation one might expect to find in the drawing. In the end, the viewer has no way of knowing either how closely this follows original drawings or whether they actually reflected conditions in the building. Measured drawing by Charles Gregersen, 1965. (HABS ILL–1021, sheet 6 of 6 sheets)

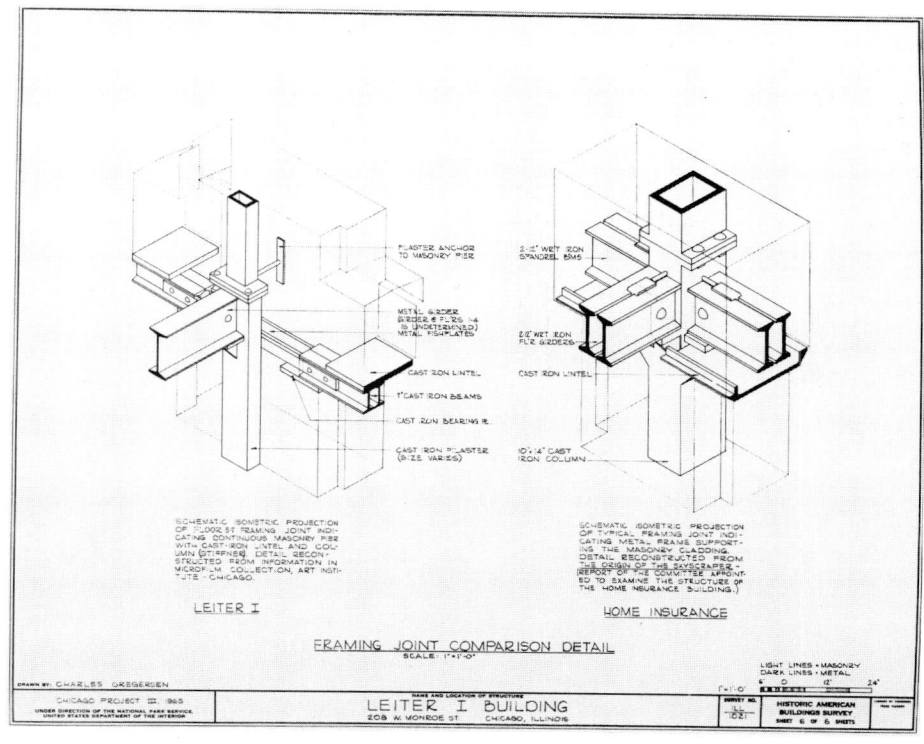

Robert Bruegmann

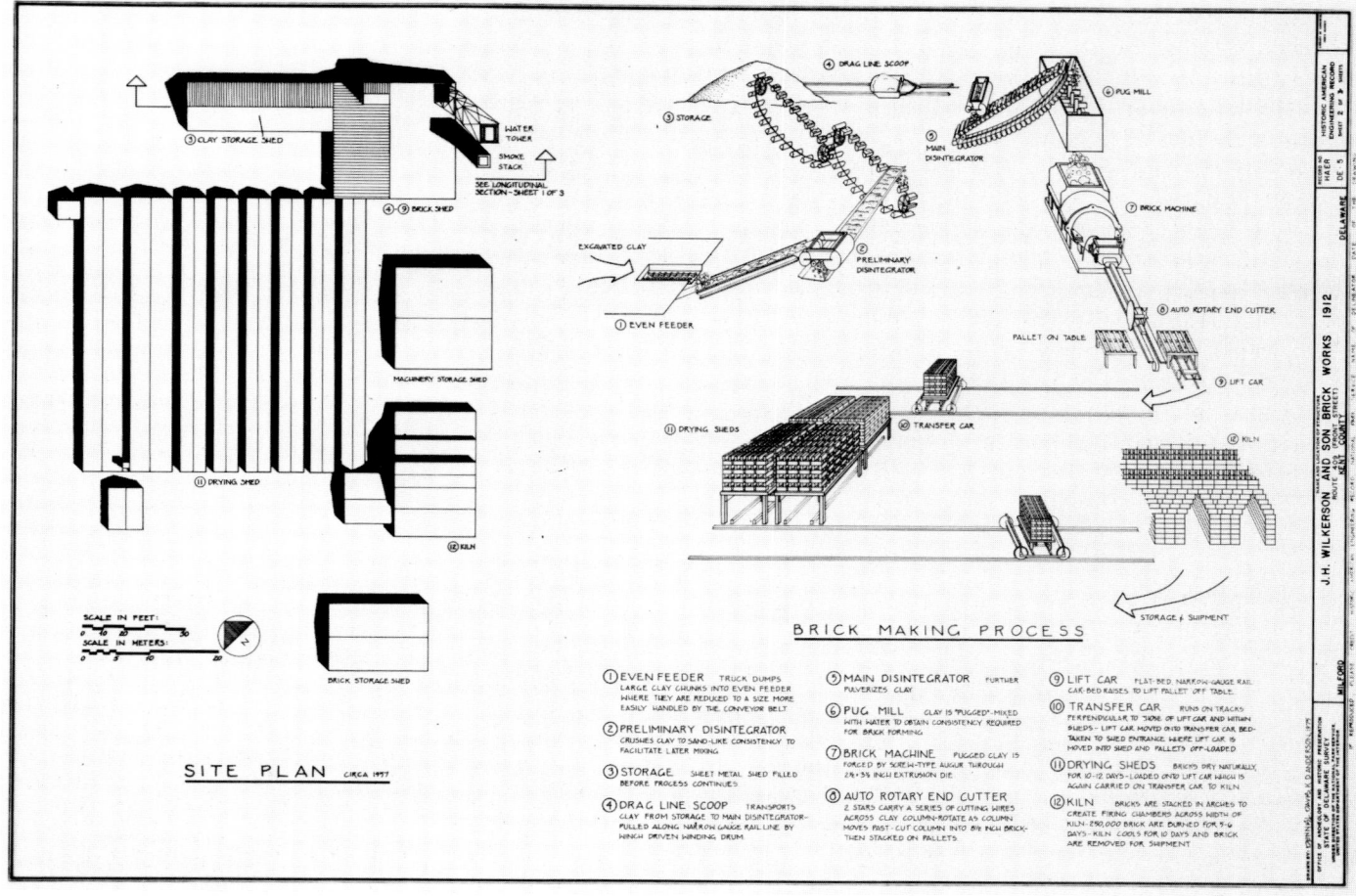

Figure 13 J. H. Wilkerson and Son Brick Works, Milford, Kent County, Delaware. Recognizing that the manufacturing or other processes that took place in the building were often more important than the structure itself, the Historic American Engineering Record pioneered a variety of inventive new recording methods. This drawing, showing the brickmaking process, goes well beyond traditional HABS practice. From its inception in 1969, HAER has been forced to do a good deal of experimentation to find formats that fit its own needs. (HAER DE–5, sheet 2 of 3 sheets)

by HABS in the 1930s were of considerable importance in the rapidly developing field of American architectural history. Many of the most prominent historians were practicing architects closely affiliated with HABS. William G. Perry and Frank Chouteau Brown in Boston, Albert Simons in Charleston, Charles M. Stotz in Pittsburgh, Samuel Wilson, Jr., in New Orleans, Thomas Tallmadge and Earl Reed in Chicago, and Thomas Tileston Waterman in Virginia were all widely known for their research as well as their contributions to HABS.

The same cannot be said for the situation after 1957. By this time a new generation of architectural historians had emerged, and many of its most important members, like Henry-Russell Hitchcock, were not part of the network of historic architects that had created HABS. Many, in fact, were confirmed Modernists, hostile to the most basic principles that guided HABS. They were, moreover, no longer primarily interested in the anonymous craftsmen of the American colonies but in the great architects and complexes of the nineteenth and early twentieth century. There was usually not enough material in the HABS files to be really useful to the authors of major monographs on architects such as H. H. Richardson, Frank Lloyd Wright, or Louis Sullivan, and when it came to studying the works of enormous firms like McKim, Mead and White or Graham, Anderson, Probst and White, HABS couldn't even begin to provide a comprehensive record.

Part of the problem was that as the collection grew, access to the material became increasingly difficult. The Library of Congress shelflist system and other indexes were quite innova-

220

tive when they were devised. The 1941 published catalog and the 1959 supplement also served their purpose. After 1959, however, it was decided, because of the size of the comprehensive catalog, that state catalogs should be issued. Some of these proved to be quite interesting. In many ways the most satisfactory of all was Richard Perrin's *Wisconsin Architecture* (Washington: National Park Service, 1965), the only catalog that reproduces enough drawings for someone to get a good idea of both the buildings and drawings (fig. 16). Perrin's publication is limited to single examples of early,

mostly rural architecture, however. When the much more complex task of producing a catalog that included later buildings, large ensembles, and whole districts was attempted, the limitations of HABS documents created problems. In the most successful of these—for example Richard Webster's *Philadelphia Preserved*—what is the most useful comes not from the HABS materials themselves but from the author's essays and original research.

The state catalog system never really worked, however, because it created a patchwork quilt of information constantly falling further out-of-date.

Figure 14 Watervliet Shakers—South Family, Albany vicinity, Albany County, New York. When large complexes were recorded in the 1930s, the sheets usually contained enough notes and other information to make them nearly sufficient in themselves as descriptions of the complexes. One can learn a great deal about this Shaker property simply by studying this single sheet, drawn in 1937. (HABS NY–3272, sheet 1 of 1 sheet)

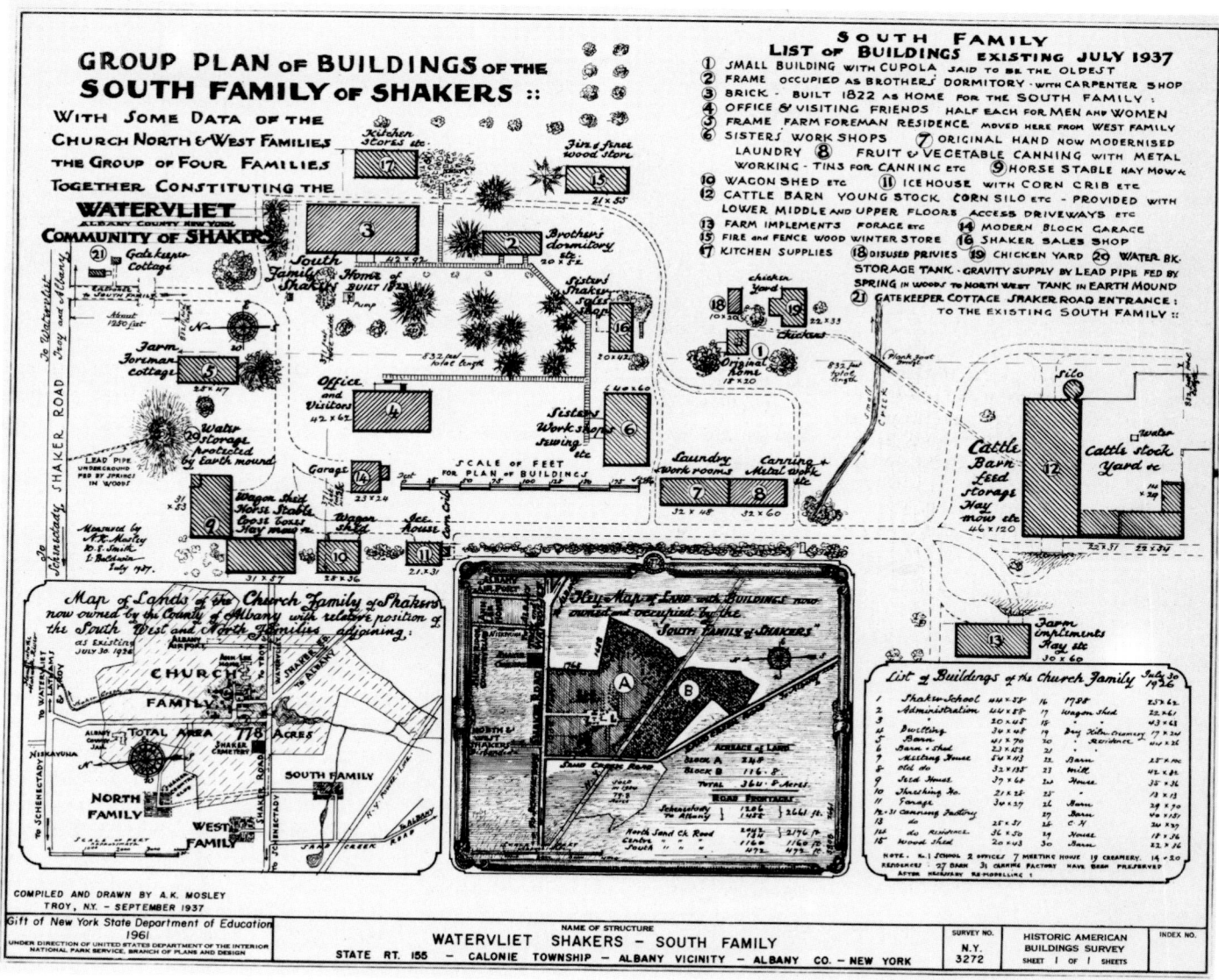

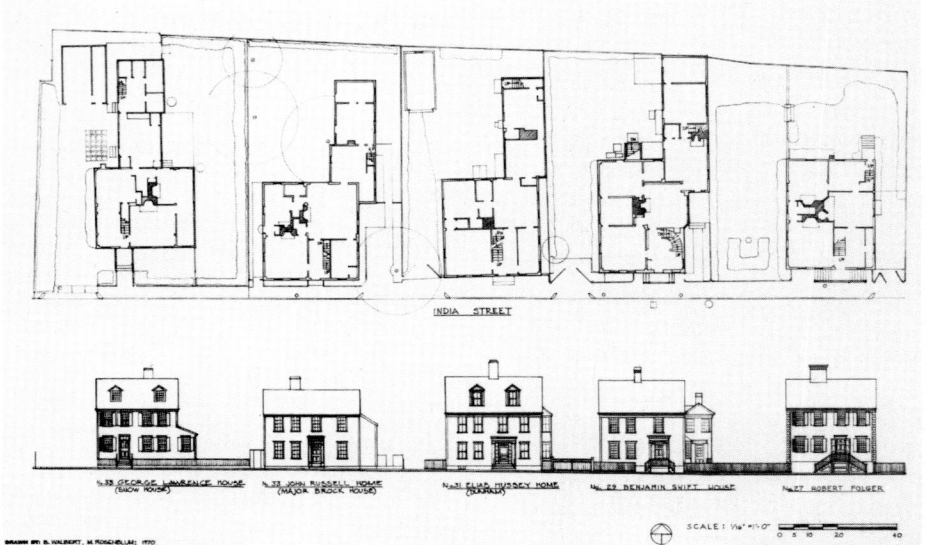

Figure 15 Neighborhood study, India Street, Nantucket, Massachusetts. One of the most comprehensive recording projects ever initiated using the HABS format has been under way for a number of years in Nantucket. Although this sheet is labeled "Neighborhood Study," in itself it gives very little information about the neighborhood. The viewer has no idea whether these are typical or extraordinary houses, when they were built, why they sit the way they do on their lots, or even what the rooms were used for. In the best cases, all is explained in accompanying historical reports. The style of drawing and the type and amount of information conveyed here contrast markedly with the sheets prepared in the 1930s. Measured drawing by E. Walbert and M. Rosenblum, 1970. (HABS MASS 1013, sheet 4 of 7 sheets)

Likewise the ambitious but somewhat ad hoc system of indexing worked out at the Library of Congress had definite limits. Clearly the only satisfactory solution was computerization, which is now under way.

Of all the problems facing HABS in its awkward years, the greatest was one of purpose. In the 1930s the goal was clear: to record the best examples of early American architecture. The means were well known to all HABS employees and there was likewise relatively little debate about which buildings should be recorded. The selection was largely left to the local chapters of the American Institute of Architects and to the regional HABS directors. In most cases these men already knew quite well the most important buildings in their area and, except at a few exceptional sites, the total number of intact examples was fairly limited. To create a comprehensive national inventory and then to photograph the major structures and document by recorded drawings the outstanding ones was a completely logical goal. HABS had made substantial progress along those lines by the end of the 1930s.

When the scale of preservation activity in general and the HABS operation itself increased dramatically after 1957, this concept was effectively lost. A new inventory form was devised and championed by Earl Reed, one of the program's early stalwarts. By the postwar years, however, there was no one left to work on the inventory. It appears that the AIA, which had spearheaded the earlier inventory project, had lost interest. The apparatus of the local advisors with wide discretionary powers had disappeared.

HABS itself certainly did not have the manpower. The inventory form was finally abandoned in 1972, its function supposedly to be taken over by the National Register and state surveys then under way. But among them the Register, the National Landmarks program, the National Trust, and state preservation offices have not created a national inventory. Instead there is an unfinished, often contradictory hodgepodge of inventories, surveys, and protection laws.

Compounding the difficulties HABS faced was the fact that funding levels dropped so low that the agency was obliged to go to outside sources to secure partial or full funding for most of its summer projects. Despite the Survey's justifiable pride in its ability to create partnerships with other agencies and with the private sector, this practice has intensified some of the program's basic problems. It is not difficult to see how the priorities of local sponsors might differ from those of the program as a whole. Some of the buildings recorded in the last few years are so insignificant that they hardly seem worthy of the immortality conferred by a single photograph let alone a full set of measured drawings.

For all of the reasons cited above, HABS might well have appeared a hopeless invalid a few years ago. The Survey, however, has managed to survive for fifty years, has given a small army of young architects and historians an invaluable educational experience, has produced some extraordinary drawings, and has won a large and loyal following unmatched by almost any other government agency. The HABS "alumni" today constitute an extraordinarily interesting group and include many of the pillars of the preservation movement. The importance of the camaraderie developed on these teams over the years cannot be overestimated. Moreover, drawings of historic architecture are once again of potential interest to practicing architects in a way they have not been for decades. The early HABS drawings and even many of more recent date now seem at least as important as period pieces of their own era as they are as documents about the buildings they record. In fact, one of the most appealing things about HABS today is its antique quality. Despite all the surface changes, it is still very much a product of the 1930s and is interesting in much the same way as one of the rare surviving rooms of architectural plaster casts at a museum. After years of neglect these casts are suddenly back in vogue not primarily as records of antique buildings or sculpture but as objects illuminating the era when they were made and admired. Admittedly this is probably not reason sufficient to galvanize the Park Service or Congress into

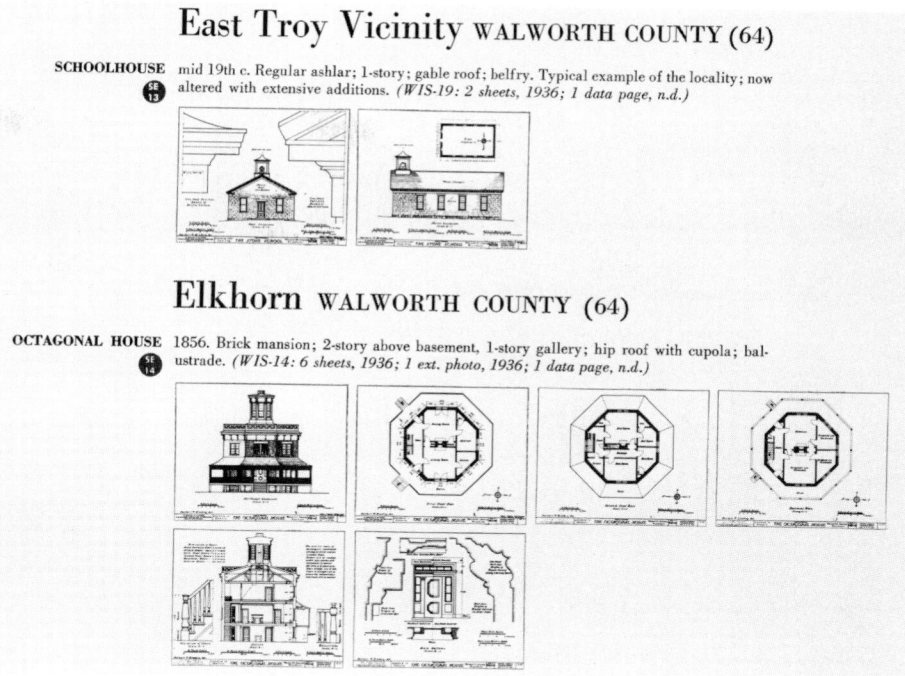

East Troy Vicinity WALWORTH COUNTY (64)

SCHOOLHOUSE mid 19th c. Regular ashlar; 1-story; gable roof; belfry. Typical example of the locality; now altered with extensive additions. *(WIS-19: 2 sheets, 1936; 1 data page, n.d.)*

Elkhorn WALWORTH COUNTY (64)

OCTAGONAL HOUSE 1856. Brick mansion; 2-story above basement, 1-story gallery; hip roof with cupola; balustrade. *(WIS-14: 6 sheets, 1936; 1 ext. photo, 1936; 1 data page, n.d.)*

tripling the budget of the Historic American Buildings Survey, but it does give the collection an even greater significance than it seemed to have several decades ago.

Figure 16 Perhaps the most successful of all the state catalogs, Richard Perrin's catalog of the Historic American Buildings Survey in Wisconsin is virtually the only one that allows the reader to get a good idea of what each structure is like as well as what information is to be found on each sheet. From Richard W. E. Perrin, *Wisconsin Architecture* (Washington, 1965). (LC–USZ62–83827)

Notes

1. This paper is based primarily on my own experiences with HABS and HAER in Indiana and California in the 1970s and research in the documents in the Prints and Photographs Division of the Library of Congress. I am grateful to Ford Peatross and Mary Ison at the Library of Congress, John Burns, Al Chambers, and Carolyn Pitts at HABS, my colleague Joan Draper at the University of Illinois at Chicago, and HABS alumnus Jack Schafer of San Francisco, who read the manuscript and made valuable comments.

2. See, for example, Charles Peterson's accounts: "Thirty Years of HABS," *Journal of the American Institute of Architects,* November 1963, pp. 83-85, "Our National Archives of Historic Architecture," *Octagon,* July 1936, pp. 12-15, and "HABS in and out of Philadelphia," in Richard J. Webster, *Philadelphia Preserved* (Philadelphia: Tem-

ple University Press, 1976), pp. xxi-xlvi, as well as his essay in this volume.

3. John P. O'Neill, *Historic American Buildings Survey: A Brief Summary of the First Five Years* (Washington, 1938), p.1.

4. Charles Peterson's memo was reproduced in "The Historic American Buildings Survey Continued," *Journal of the Society of Architectural Historians* 16, no. 3 (October 1957): 30. This wording was used in all of the instruction sheets sent out in the 1930s.

5. HABS, *Bulletin* 54, 1936, gives details of the projected book. The projections by O'Neill are found in an unlabeled, undated manuscript apparently from the 1950s in the Prints and Photographs Division, Library of Congress.

6. From minutes of the HABS advisory board, 1975. Manuscript in the Prints and Photographs Division, Library of Congress.

Recording Historic Buildings:
New Philosophies, New Techniques, New Technologies

by

JOHN A. BURNS

Charles Peterson's memorandum of November 13, 1933, proposing the establishment of the Historic American Buildings Survey, included a recommendation that the Survey not document structures built after 1860. Aside from being a logical end point, the date determined the type and style of buildings that would dominate the Survey's early recording efforts. The recommendation implied that buildings should be at least seventy-three years old to be considered historic. It eliminated from consideration the huge number of buildings constructed in the last part of the nineteenth century.

Given these limitations, the body of buildings to be studied was relatively small, with a limited number of building types and materials of construction—in other words, manageable. The format designed for the documentation was correspondingly simple and straightforward. The drawing sheet size was roughly 60'-0" × 80'-0"

Figure 1 Fort Sam Houston—Officers' Quarters (Building 101), 1905–6, San Antonio, Bexar County, Texas. South side. The military has long used standardized designs for its buildings, adapting them to local conditions. This house is a typical configuration for officers' quarters, with an enlarged, two-story porch added to adapt it to a warm climate. Photograph by David J. Kaminsky, 1980. (HABS TX–3303–18–11)

at the common scale of ¼" = 1'-0", which allowed most pre-1860 buildings to fit comfortably within the borders. The drawing format was also horizontal: the need to document tall buildings was outside the scope of early HABS work.

Fifty years later, one finds a different set of circumstances. The labor-intensive nature of hand measuring and drafting, ideal for relief employment, is expensive. Following National Register criteria, buildings now come of age historically in just fifty years, so that now HABS is documenting buildings younger than itself. Census figures show that 25 percent of our extant building stock predates 1930, and probably only 5 percent predates 1860. Changes such as these have forced reassessment and adjustment in HABS methodology for documentation and will continue to do so. Expected changes in methodology over the next decade will be governed by the resources available to produce documentation, the actual building stock that has become historic in the last fifty years, and the available research materials on these buildings.

Given the greatly increased universe of buildings HABS is mandated to survey with only limited resources, it will, of necessity, become far more selective in recording historic buildings. Congress has directed that the Department of

Figure 2 Fort Sheridan—Field Officers' Quarters (Building No. 28), 1905, Lake County, Illinois. North facade. The same basic design for officers' quarters as seen at Fort Sam Houston (fig. 1), is found in Illinois. Field photograph by Sally Kress Tompkins, 1979. (HABS IL–1113)

the Interior set national standards for architectural and engineering documentation. These HABS/HAER standards will be issued in 1983, the fiftieth anniversary year of the Historic American Buildings Survey. Two points that the standards will incorporate are worth noting. First, the kind and amount of documentation should be appropriate to the nature and significance of the building. Second, the documentation should concentrate on the features of a building which give it its significance. Measured drawings, for instance, are recommended only for nationally significant buildings. Fewer "complete" sets of drawings will be produced; photographs will be substituted for drawings whenever possible. The drawings that are produced will have more information packed into them: more given dimensions and annotations and denser sheet composition,

similar to the drawings of the 1930s. The drawings will concentrate on features that cannot be adequately described in words or photographed. Fewer measured drawings will mean an increased dependence on photographs for graphic documentation. Sizing aids such as measuring sticks in photographs will be more common and so will rectified photographs.

Buildings constructed between 1860—the 1933 HABS cut-off date—and 1933—the current HABS cut-off date—will be the primary target for documentation in the next decade. These seven decades were a period of tremendous change in America and in the architectural profession. Early American buildings were designed and constructed based on empirical knowledge and traditions that have evolved over centuries. Structural systems were simple and mechanical systems rudimentary in all but the most

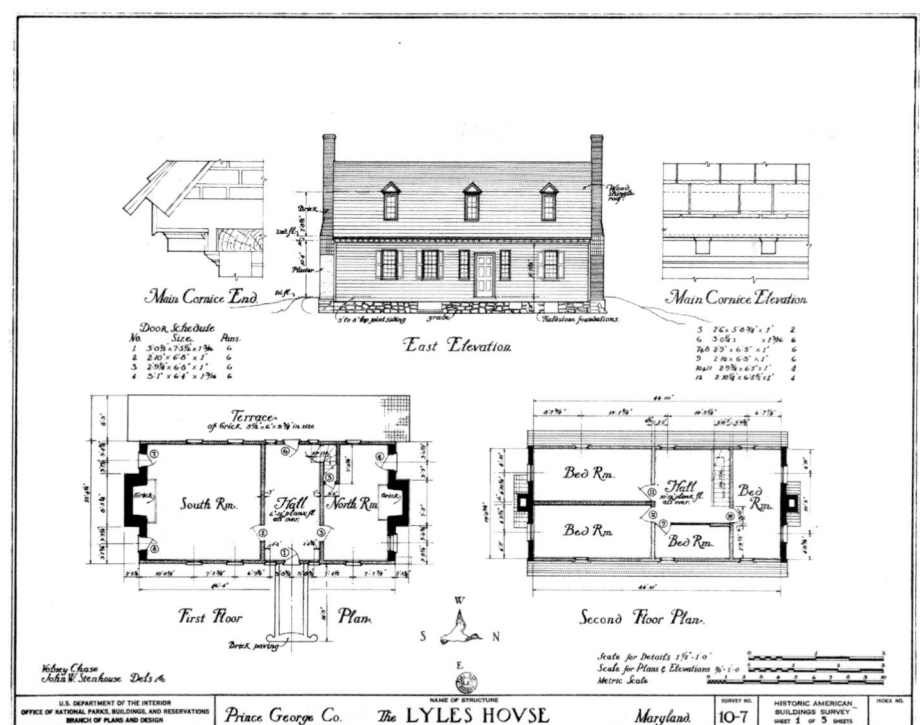

Figure 3 Lyles House, built in 1704, State Route 224, Broad Creek, Prince Georges County, Maryland. Early American homes, small and simply constructed, were easily accommodated within the original HABS drawing format. In this case, both floor plans, the main elevation, and two details are all composed on a single sheet. Drawing by Volney Chase and John W. Stenhouse, 1934. (HABS MD–10–7, sheet 1 of 5 sheets)

Figure 4 Allegheny County Courthouse and Jail, 1884–88, Pittsburgh, Allegheny County, Pennsylvania. The original 19″ x 24″ HABS drawing format was not well-suited for documenting the large public and commercial buildings which became common in the late nineteenth century. A second format, 24″ x 36″ in size, was introduced in the late 1960s after several projects documenting early skyscrapers in Chicago proved the futility of using the smaller sheets to record large buildings. Grant Street elevation. Drawing by Fitch, Kantrowitz, Ketterer, Schinhofen, & Tomlinson, 1963. (HABS PA–610, sheet 10 of 35 sheets)

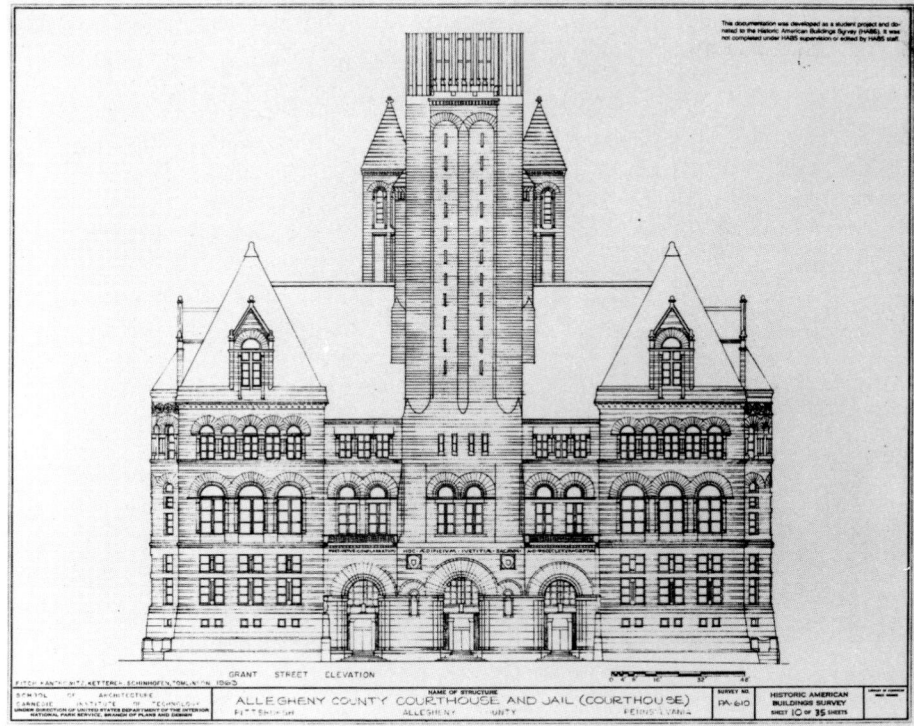

Figure 5 Philadelphia Saving Fund Society, 1930–32, Philadelphia, Philadelphia County, Pennsylvania. The PSFS building is one of the very few buildings named a National Historic Landmark for architecture before it was fifty years old. The dearth of HABS records for the building is offset by the fact that the bank has kept excellent records on it, a fairly common occurrence for twentieth-century buildings. Photocopy of rendering by D. E. Sutton, ca. 1930. (HABS PA–1533)

Figure 6 Drayton Hall, 1738–42, Charleston vicinity, Charleston County, South Carolina. Drayton Hall was an appropriate building to document with measured drawings. First, it is a National Historic Landmark. Second, no original drawings existed. Finally, the National Trust for Historic Preservation, the owner, needed drawings to be able to carry out restoration and maintenance work. Section B–B. Drawing by Belmont Freeman, 1974. (HABS SC–377, sheet 11/14 of 15 sheets)

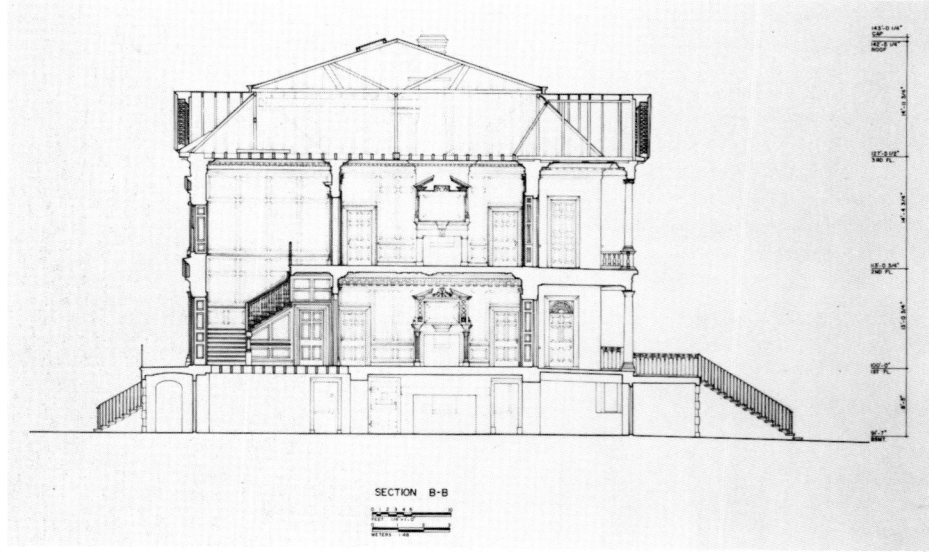

Figure 7 Scoville Building, 1885, Chicago, Cook County, Illinois. This measured drawing of a secondary elevation shows little information in relation to its cost. The decorative elements, although designed by Louis Sullivan, repeat elements included in the drawing for the north elevation. There are no given dimensions or annotations of existing conditions. West elevation, drawn by Christopher R. Hellwig, 1974. (HABS IL–1114, sheet 3 of 8 sheets)

Figure 8 Scoville Building, 1885, Chicago, Cook County, Illinois. The perspective-corrected photograph of the west elevation shows as much information as the measured drawing plus information on existing conditions, all at a significantly lower cost. West elevation. Photograph by Lester B. Knight & Associates, Inc., 1974. (HABS IL–1114)

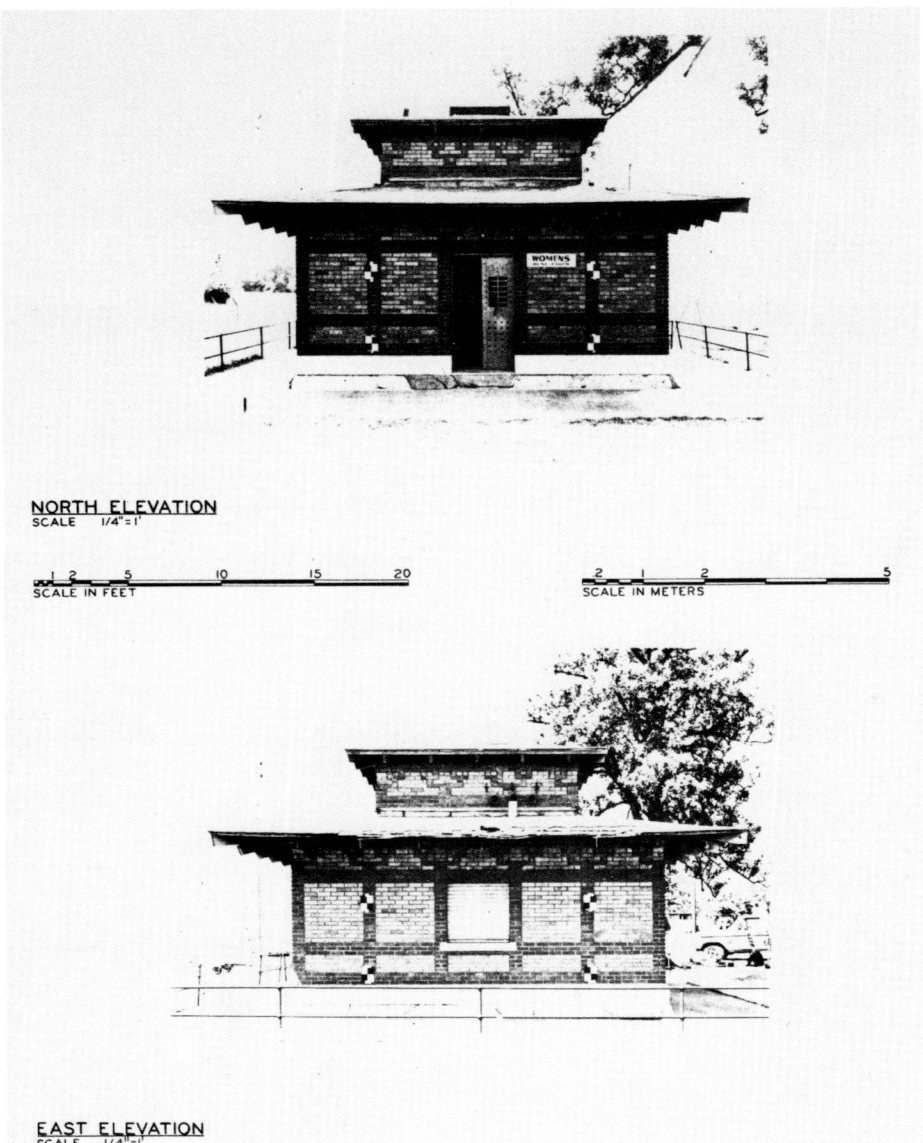

NORTH ELEVATION
SCALE 1/4"=1'

SCALE IN FEET

SCALE IN METERS

EAST ELEVATION
SCALE 1/4"=1'

Figure 9 Waterloo Water Works-Well House 4, 1914, Waterloo, Blackhawk County, Iowa. These are the first rectified photographs made into HABS drawings. The targets define a 4' x 12' grid on each front. The photos are scalable but only in the plane on which the targets are placed. The projecting eaves and monitor cannot be scaled accurately because they are not in the same plane. This is not an ideal building for rectified photography. North and east elevations. Photograph by Hans Muessig, 1978. (HABS IA–125, sheet 4 of 5 sheets)

Figure 10 Specifications by Arthur B. Heaton for the country home of Gilbert Grosvenor. The original specifications for a historic building offer not just information about the specific building but insights about historic construction technology and practice, the cost and availability of materials, and trade and craft practices. Since the architect's specifications are a virtual instruction manual for assembling a building, they are an invaluable source of information. Arthur B. Heaton Collection, Prints and Photographs Division.

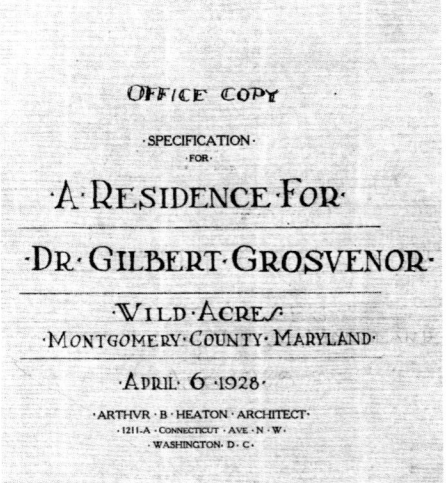

OFFICE COPY

·SPECIFICATION·
·FOR·

·A·RESIDENCE·FOR·

·DR·GILBERT·GROSVENOR·

·WILD·ACRES·
·MONTGOMERY·COUNTY·MARYLAND·

·APRIL·6·1928·

·ARTHVR·B·HEATON·ARCHITECT·
·1211-A·CONNECTICUT·AVE·N·W·
·WASHINGTON·D·C·

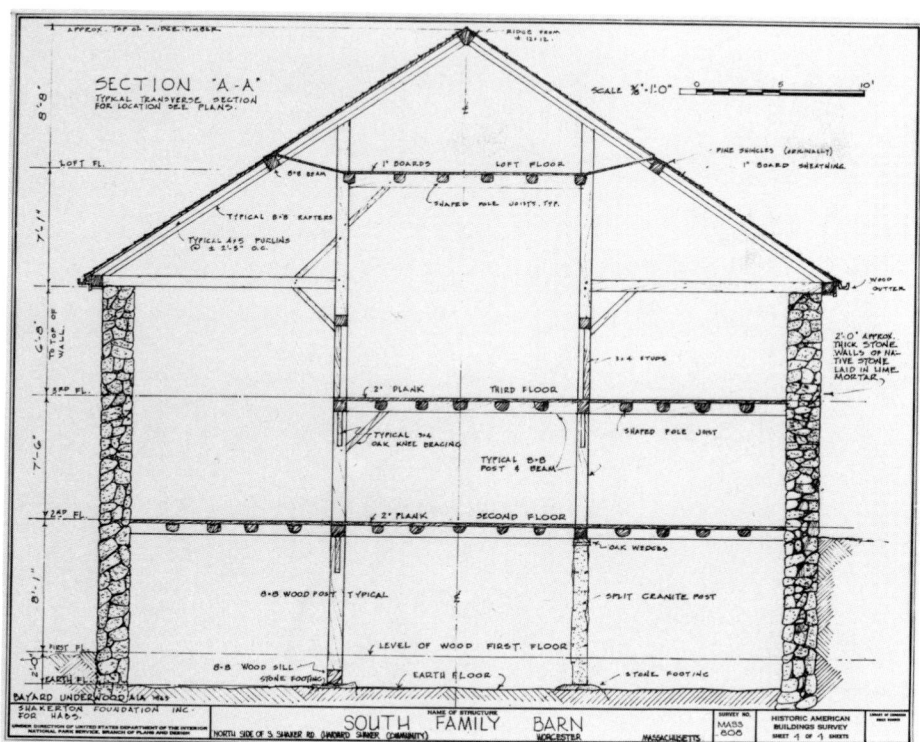

Figure 11 Shaker South Family Barn, 1835, Harvard, Worcester County, Massachusetts. This Shaker barn used post-and-beam construction typical of the early nineteenth century. It was, however, a simple skeletal frame and a precursor to the iron skeletal frames made famous in Chicago in the latter part of the century. Section A–A. Drawing by Bayard Underwood, 1963. (HABS MA–808, sheet 4 of 4 sheets)

Figure 12 Edgar Laing Stores, 1849. Washington and Murray Streets, New York, New York County, New York. The cast-iron facade of the Laing Stores represented a new technology of construction. An exploded drawing is used to explain how the prefabricated, repetitive components fit together. The dismantling of the building allowed access to these structural details. Isometric of basement details and isometric of first-floor details. Drawing by James D. Tobin, 1971. (HABS NY–5469, sheet 12 of 17 sheets)

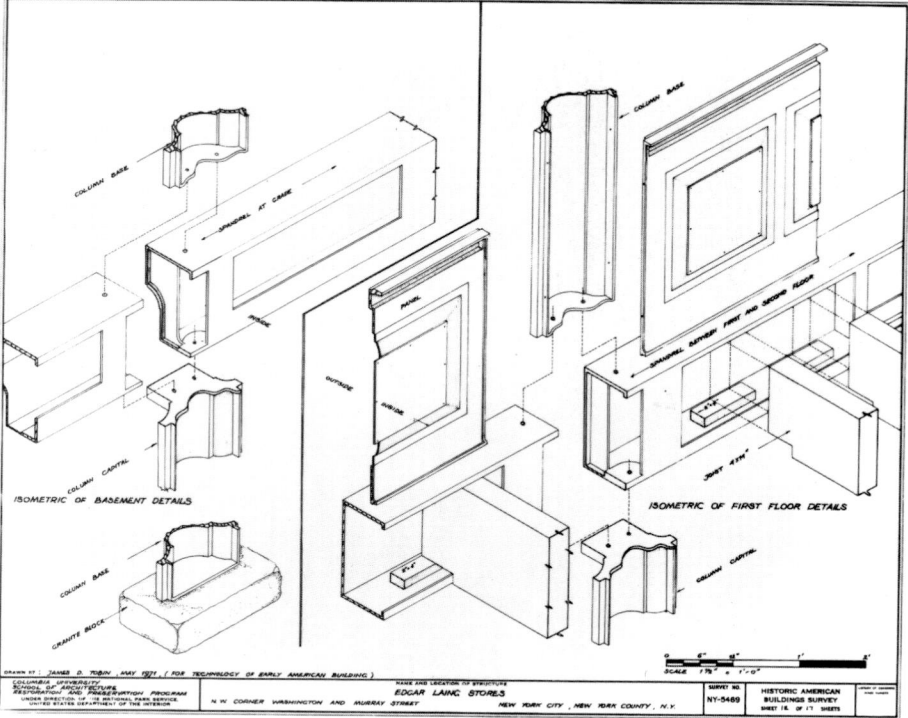

ADDENDUM TO
AUDITORIUM BUILDING
{ROOSEVELT UNIVERSITY}

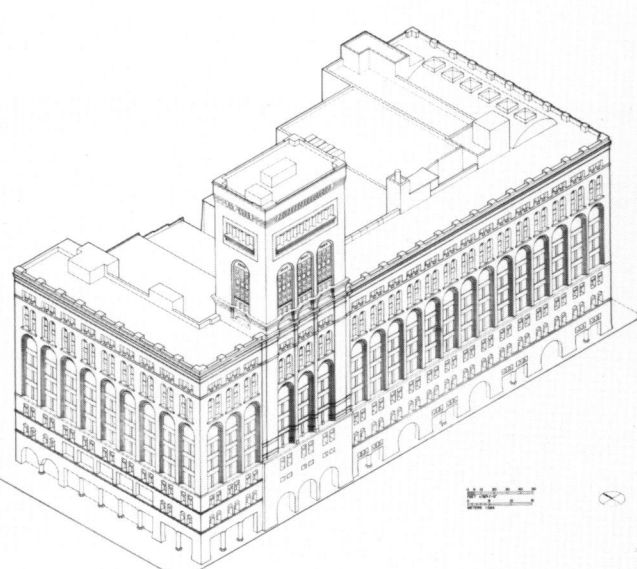

THE RESEARCH AND DOCUMENTATION OF THE ENGINEERING SYSTEMS OF THE AUDITORIUM BUILDING WERE UNDERTAKEN BY THE NATIONAL ARCHITECTURAL AND ENGINEERING RECORD (NAER) IN COOPERATION WITH ROOSEVELT UNIVERSITY AND WITH FINANCIAL SUPPORT FROM THE GRAHAM FOUNDATION OF CHICAGO AND THE STATE OF ILLINOIS DEPARTMENT OF CONSERVATION. NAER'S PARTICIPATION WAS A JOINT EFFORT OF THE HISTORIC AMERICAN ENGINEERING RECORD (HAER) AND THE HISTORIC AMERICAN BUILDINGS SURVEY (HABS). THE RECORDS WILL BE FILED IN THE LIBRARY OF CONGRESS AS AN ADDENDUM TO THE 1963 HABS RECORDS FOR THE BUILDING. THE RESEARCH WAS COMPLETED IN THE SUMMER OF 1979 WITH HAER ARCHITECT DONALD F. STEVENSON, AIA, PROJECT DIRECTOR; RITA GORAWARA (TEXAS A & M UNIVERSITY), PROJECT SUPERVISOR; TOBIN KENDRICK (MONTANA STATE UNIVERSITY), ARCHITECTURAL TECHNICIAN; AND HAER PHOTOGRAPHER JET LOWE. THE DOCUMENTATION WAS COMPLETED IN THE SUMMER OF 1980 WITH HABS ARCHITECT JOHN A. BURNS, AIA, PROJECT DIRECTOR; RITA GORAWARA, AIA (ASSOCIATE), PROJECT SUPERVISOR; CHARLES E. GREGERSEN, AIA, PROJECT HISTORIAN; LAURA L. HOCHULI (UNIVERSITY OF WISCONSIN-MILWAUKEE), FOREMAN; AND CATHY L. BERLOW (UNIVERSITY OF FLORIDA), J. MICHAEL PALMER (UNIVERSITY OF PENNSYLVANIA), WILLIAM PERCIVAL (ILLINOIS INSTITUTE OF TECHNOLOGY), AND AUGUST VENTURA (COOPER UNION), ARCHITECTURAL TECHNICIANS.

THE AUDITORIUM BUILDING, NOW ROOSEVELT UNIVERSITY, WAS THE LARGEST STRUCTURE OF ITS KIND IN AMERICA AT THE TIME OF ITS COMPLETION IN 1890. DESIGNED BY DANKMAR ADLER (1844-1900) AND LOUIS H. SULLIVAN (1856-1924), THE 4,237 SEAT THEATER, HOTEL, AND OFFICE BUILDING EARNED A NATIONAL REPUTATION FOR THEIR FIRM.

THE COMPLEXITY OF A STRUCTURE CONTAINING THREE UNRELATED FUNCTIONS ON A SMALL SITE CREATED DESIGN PROBLEMS OF SPACE AND ACCESS FOR THE ARCHITECTS AND ENGINEERS. THE COMBINATION OF THESE FACTORS WITH THE DESIRE OF THE PROMOTERS TO HAVE THE LATEST CONVENIENCES AND MOST LUXURIOUS SURROUNDINGS REQUIRED STATE OF THE ART STRUCTURAL SYSTEMS AND ASSOCIATED BUILDING TECHNOLOGY. THE RESULT IS A BUILDING THAT IN ITS STRUCTURAL, HEATING, VENTILATING, COOLING, LIGHTING, ELECTRICAL, HYDRAULIC, AND SANITARY SYSTEMS REVEALS ALL THE VIRTUES AND LIMITATIONS OF THE AVAILABLE TECHNOLOGY OF THAT TIME.

THE HYDRAULIC MACHINERY OF THE AUDITORIUM STAGE IS BASED ON THE DESIGN OF BUDAPEST'S ASPHALEIA STAGE. THE TWO FLOORS BELOW THE STAGE FLOOR CONTAIN THE HYDRAULIC MACHINERY WHICH IS REQUIRED TO OPERATE THE SYSTEM OF 14 LIFTS AND TRAPS. A SECTION OF THE STAGE FLOOR, 46 FT. BY 36 FT., HAS FOUR LIFTS WHICH CAN BE ELEVATED OR DEPRESSED. EACH LIFT, 46 FT. LONG BY 9 FT. WIDE, CAN BE ELEVATED 13 FT., SUNK 7 FT. BELOW STAGE LEVEL, OR BE MOVED LATERALLY ACROSS THE WIDTH OF THE STAGE. PIERCING EACH LIFT IS A TRAP MEASURING 26 FT. BY 4 FT. THESE SMALLER TRAPS CAN BE LOWERED 19 FT. BELOW STAGE LEVEL. THEY IN TURN EACH CARRY AN AUXILIARY TRAP 4 FT. BY 6 FT. THAT CAN BE OPERATED INDEPENDENTLY OR IN CONJUNCTION WITH THE OTHER TRAPS. THE AUXILIARY TRAPS HAVE A VERTICAL MOVEMENT OF 19 FT. PLUS THAT OF THE LARGER LIFT WHICH CARRIES IT. IN ADDITION TO THE ABOVE 12 TRAPS ARE TWO STAR TRAPS, BOTH WITH A TRAVEL OF 9 FT. LOCATED ON THE 8TH FLOOR ARE WATER TANKS PROVIDING THE PRESSURE NECESSARY TO OPERATE THE HYDRAULIC MACHINERY.

THE FOUNDATION OF THE TOWER IS ONE LARGE FOOTING APPROXIMATELY 67 FT. BY 100 FT. THIS FOOTING (AS WELL AS THE BUILDING'S OTHER FOOTINGS) CONSISTS OF TWO LAYERS OF 12 INCH TIMBERS LAID PERPENDICULAR TO EACH OTHER IN PREPARED BEDS OF GRAVEL. ABOVE THE TIMBERS IS A STEPPED GRILLAGE OF RAILROAD RAILS, STEEL BEAMS, OR BOTH EMBEDDED IN CONCRETE. THIS GRILLAGE IS TOPPED WITH DIMENSION STONE OR RUBBLE PIERS.

ALONG CONGRESS STREET IS A ROW OF LIGHTLY LOADED COLUMNS. THEIR SETTLEMENT WAS ANTICIPATED TO BE LESS THAN THE REST OF THE STRUCTURE SINCE THEY CARRY LOADS OF ONLY ONE STORY. TO ALLOW FOR FUTURE ADJUSTMENT, SCREWJACKS WITH A RUN OF SIX INCHES WERE INSERTED AT THE TOPS OF THESE COLUMNS.

VAULTS UNDER MICHIGAN AVE. SIDEWALK

EARLY REPAIR

BRICK VAULTS UNDER ALLEY

BEGINNING OF AUDITORIUM SLOPE

ORCHESTRA PIT

TUNNEL TO CONGRESS HOTEL

TUNNEL TO POWER PLANT

EDGE OF PIER

SEE DETAIL BELOW

1932 REPAIR

℄ OF TOWER FOUNDATIONS

COLUMNS WITH SCREWJACKS AT TOP TO ALLOW FOR ADJUSTMENT IN SETTLEMENT.

BASEMENT - STRUCTURE

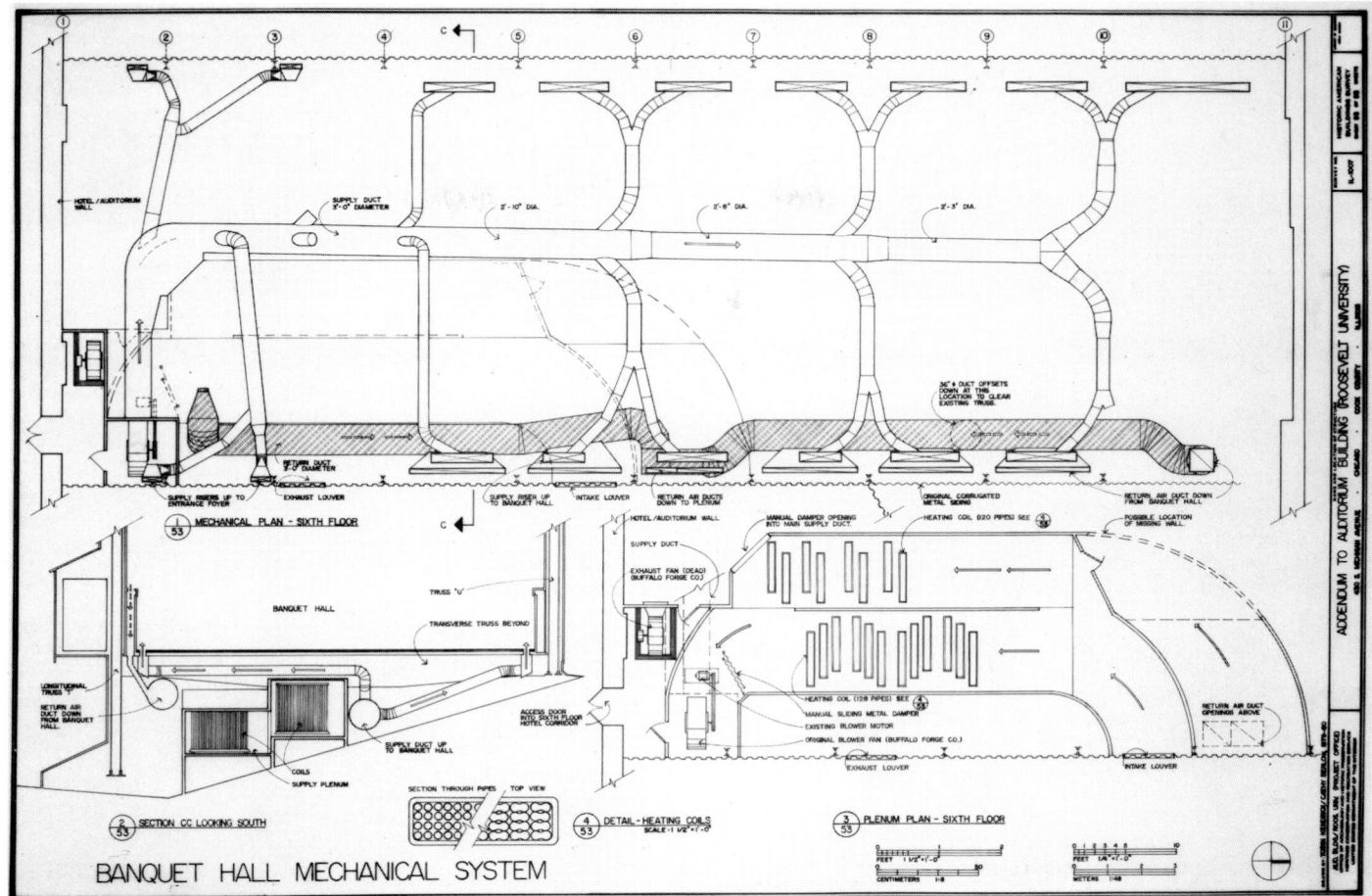

Figure 13 (opposite, top)   Addendum to Auditorium Building (Roosevelt University), 1887–90, Chicago, Cook County, Illinois. Although the Auditorium Building was recorded by HABS in 1963, the seven sheets of drawings did not assess the overall significance of the building. They included a title sheet, one floor plan, one elevation, one section, and three sheets of decorative details. This 1981 axonometric drawing, one of a set of fifty-three, shows the two elevations not drawn in 1963, the volumetric massing of the building, and a roof plan. The one drawing thus provides several different types of information. Buildings the size and complexity of the Auditorium Building demand a sophisticated assessment of their significance. Title sheet. Drawing by Willie Graham and David T. Marsh, 1981. (HABS IL–1007, sheet 1 of 53 sheets)

Figure 14 (opposite, bottom)   Addendum to Auditorium Building (Roosevelt University), 1887–90, Chicago, Cook County, Illinois. A drawing is the only adequate means of explaining the foundation design of the Auditorium Building. The architects, Adler and Sullivan, devised a system of spread footings to carry both linear (bearing walls) and point (columns) loadings with widely varying loads, everything from vaults under the sidewalks to a seventeen-story masonry tower. Basement-structure, drawn by Laura L. Hochuli, 1980. (HABS IL–1007, sheet 13 of 53 sheets)

Figure 15 (above)   Addendum to Auditorium Building (Roosevelt University), 1887–90, Chicago, Cook County, Illinois. The heating system of the Banquet Hall represented the most sophisticated technology of the 1890s and remained in use until 1980, when it was upgraded and air conditioning was added. The original system was recorded before the modifications were made. Banquet Hall mechanical system. Drawing by Tobin Kendrick and Cathy Berlow, 1979–80. (HABS IL–1007, sheet 53 of 53 sheets)

Figure 18 (opposite) Fort Mifflin, 1771 and later, Philadelphia, Philadelphia County, Pennsylvania. Plan drawn by Henry Belin, 1839. This photographic copy is one of the many maps, drawings, and photographs relating to Fort Mifflin in collections from England to California. Rather than copy all of the material, HABS prepared a catalog of graphic material with 143 entries. Bibliographic citations were given for each item. Some of the most informative drawings were then copied for the HABS collection. The result is a thorough but not overly duplicative record of the fort's history. (HABS PA–1225, LC HABS PA, 51–PHILA, 111–10)

Figure 16 Pan American World Airways Clipper System Terminal Building, Miami, Dade County, Florida. Aerial view showing the east (water) front facing Biscayne Bay. Hangars are to the right of the building, which was completed in 1933 to the designs of the firm of Delano & Aldrich as a combined marine/air terminal. Buildings of the twentieth century, often designed for unprecedented functions, increasingly qualify for HABS documentation. This structure is now the Miami City Hall and was recorded as part of a special HABS survey of that building type. Copy of a photograph, ca. 1940, by Pan Am. Courtesy of the Archives, Pan American World Airways.

Figure 17 Connor Hotel, 1907, Joplin, Jasper County, Missouri. This photograph is part of a series documenting the construction of the hotel. It offers rather startling evidence that the exterior walls are not load bearing. The reason the third floor masonry was put in last is not known. Photographer unknown. (HABS MO–1202, LC HABS MO, 49–JOPL, 1–20)

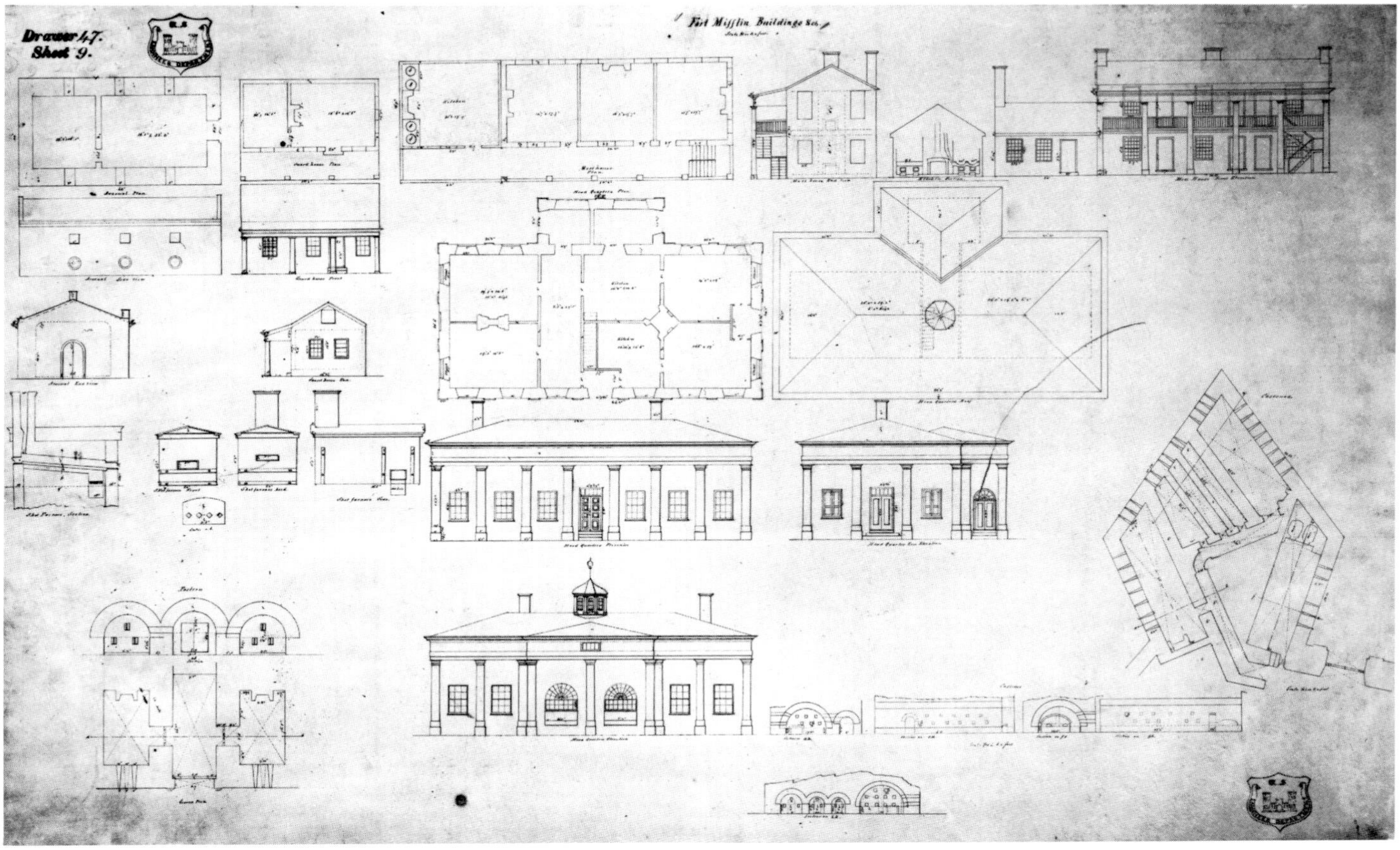

Figure 19 St. Mary's Seminary, 1876–78, Baltimore, Maryland. Because St. Mary's Seminary was threatened by imminent demolition, photogrammetry was the only practical means to record it, given the time and money available. Control points noted on each stereopair relate them to one another. Drawings have not been made, but the forty-five stereopairs contain the information needed to produce them. Photograph by Perry Borchers, 1974. (Stereopair B1974–801R)

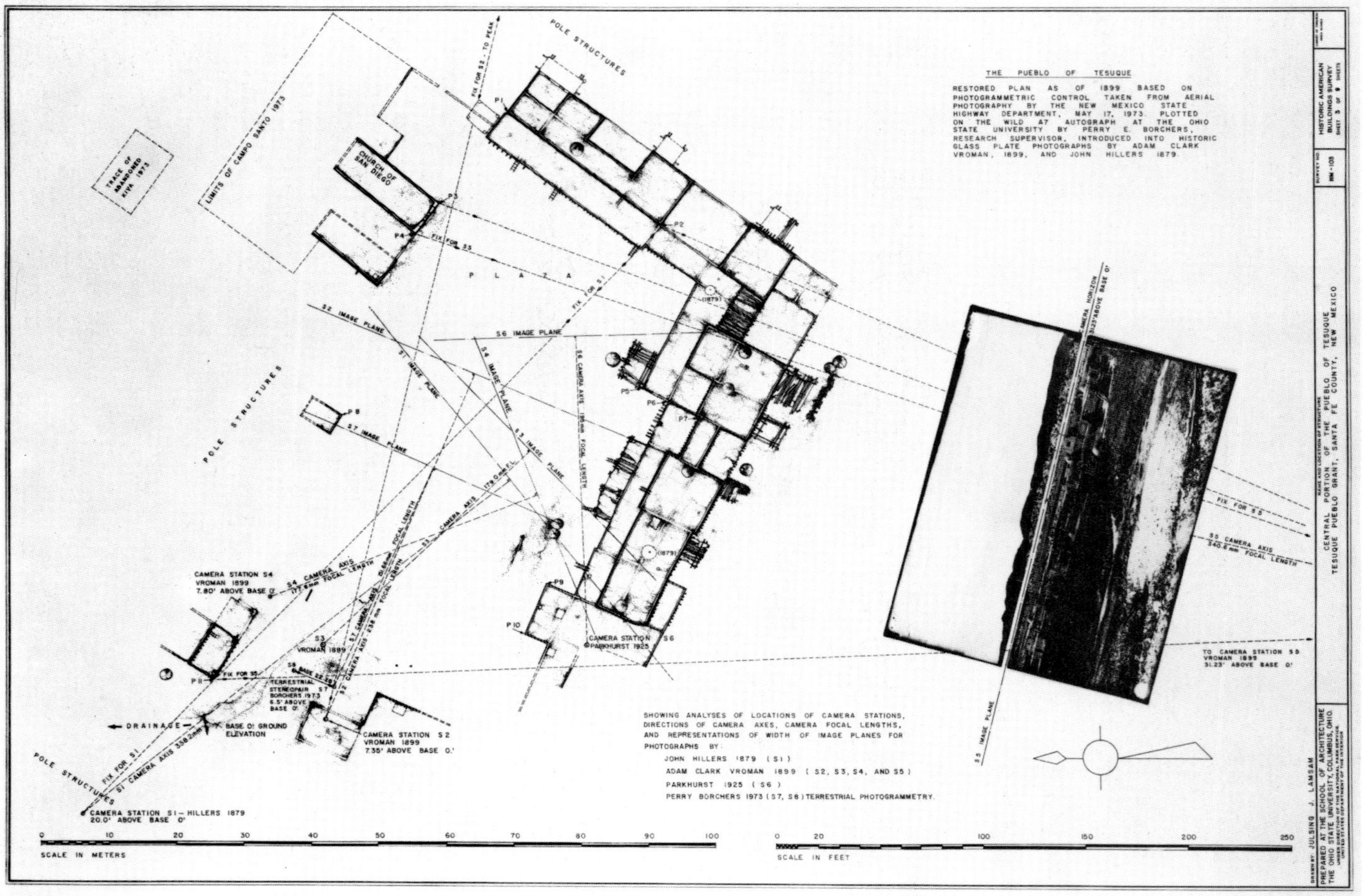

Figure 20 Central portion of the Pueblo of Tesuque, Santa Fe County, New Mexico. Using glass-plate aerial stereopairs from 1973, reverse perspective analysis was used to plot the camera stations, axis, and focal lengths for historic photographs from 1879, 1899, and 1925. Using known dimensions from the 1973 photogrammetric studies, measured drawings could then be prepared for the three earlier views. This drawing shows the location of the earlier views superimposed on the 1973 plan of the site. Measured drawing plotted by Perry E. Borchers; drawn by Julsing Lamsan, 1973. (HABS NM–103, sheet 3 of 9 sheets)

NORTH ELEVATION

FEET 3/16"=1'-0"   0   5   10   15   20
METERS 1·64   0 1 2 3 4 5 6

MATERIALS   FOUNDATION - RANDOM RUBBLE
EXTERIOR WALLS - RANDOM RUBBLE COVERED WITH STUCCO
WING - FRAME COVERED WITH STUCCO
ROOFING - WOOD SHINGLES

Figure 21 Lundale Farm-House (Samuel Townsend House), late eighteenth-early nineteenth century, Pughtown vicinity, Chester County, Pennsylvania. North elevation. The owner of this house granted an easement to the National Trust for Historic Preservation. Drawings were needed as the legal record of the condition of the house at the time the easement was granted. The window spacing and alignment were irregular on this facade, so a rectified photograph was used to locate each window precisely. Drawing by Susan M. Dornbusch, 1978. (HABS PA–1308, sheet 6/6 of 7 sheets)

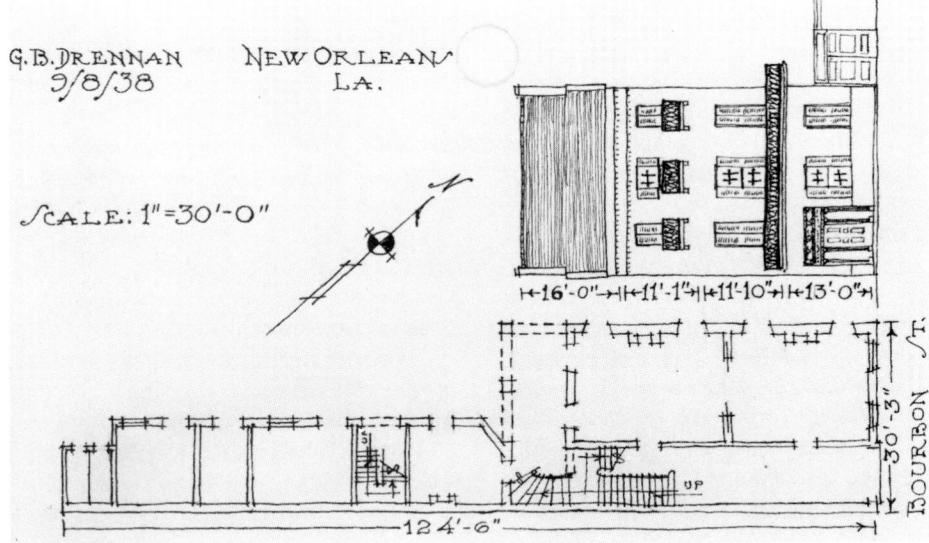

Figure 22 Lundale Farm-House (Samuel Townsend House). North (rear) elevation. This field photograph was enlarged to the same scale as the drawing from a perspective-corrected field photograph. The result is a rudimentary form of rectified photography that proved to be more accurate than hand measurements in locating the windows precisely. Note, however, that the cornice is slightly distorted because it is in front of the image plane and that the roof ridge and chimneys are quite distorted because they are so far beyond the image plane. Field photograph by John A. Burns, 1975. (HABS PA–1308)

Figure 23 Vieux Carré Squares Historic District, Lafcadio Hearn Domicile, 516 Bourbon Street, New Orleans, Louisiana. Sketch plans such as this one are meant to be a supplement to photographs and data, not a replacement for measured drawings. They are quite useful in presenting room arrangments and openings, particularly in irregular structures, when the significance of a building does not warrant measured drawings. Photographs are often keyed to these plans. Sketch plan, drawn by G. B. Brennan, 1938.

Figure 24 Drayton Hall, Charleston vicinity, Charleston County, South Carolina. In addition to the standard HABS format records transmitted to the Library of Congress, field photographs such as this one are often included as unofficial supplemental documentation. In this 1974 photograph, we see a HABS team member holding a measuring rod beside the interior timber framing of the structure's roof. (HABS SC–377)

important buildings. The years following 1860 brought the widespread acceptance of balloon and platform framing, iron and steel structural systems, elevators, electricity, and the automobile. Architects went from being craftsmen to being designers; engineering developed as a profession. Buildings became less and less empirically designed and more and more scientifically designed. Their designs were based on proven knowledge of the strength and characteristics of materials and on mathematical formulas. These scientifically designed buildings cannot be evaluated using the same criteria as those used for empirically designed buildings. Therein lies the big difference for architectural documentation in the 1980s.

The present demands a new philosophical approach to assessing significance in historic buildings. Buildings will be studied with a holistic rather than a stylistic or art-historical approach. There will be more emphasis on the physical history of a building, its design, how it was constructed, and how it has been used. Implicit in this development is the need for trained professionals capable of assessing significance in both stylistic and technological terms. Researchers will need to be able to evaluate the multiplicity of records available concerning the history of post-1860 buildings. Historical studies of buildings types similar to the narrowly distributed HABS Shaker catalog (*Shaker Built: A Catalog of Shaker Architectural Records from the Historic American Buildings Survey*, edited by John C. Poppeliers and Deborah E. Stephens, published in 1974) and an unpublished study of theaters should be developed. Existing HABS records, supplemented as gaps in the HABS collection are identified, provide the resources for such studies. Special emphasis should be placed on building types dependent on technology, such as airports and gas stations, which are replaced long before they are old enough to be considered historic. Concurrent with studies of building types should be

studies of building components that have had a major impact on architecture, such as balloon framing, heating, ventilating, and air conditioning (HVAC) systems, and standardized construction.

Better records and improved recordkeeping as well as increased public awareness of the importance of architectural records will make research easier. Broader research can be carried out on the physical history of buildings using original drawings and specifications, tax records, building permits, insurance records, trade journals, manufacturers catalogs, and city directories. Historic photographs are an especially important source of information for the period 1860–1933. HABS should develop indexes and other reference tools for material in other collections that is not copied for the record but which might be useful to later researchers. Such aids will help avoid duplication of effort .

New technologies will provide more cost-effective means of assembling information in architectural documentation. Advances in photography and photographic sciences and computers will be most influential. Computer-generated finding aids such as the HABS/HAER checklist in this publication and other indexes will simplify access to existing records. For instance, users will be able to search the HABS/HAER data base by state, county, vicinity, name, date, function, architect, or engineer. In another example, computers have been used by the Jet Propulsion Laboratory to enhance photographs from the space program in order to retrieve more information than is visible to the naked eye. The technique works as well on terrestrial photographs as on celestial and has already been used to enhance historic photographs.

Photogrammetry will be used far more extensively, particularly the preparation of stereopairs and control data, which will be plotted and drawn only as necessary. Since plotting and drawing is the most expensive part of photogrammetry, this will allow more buildings to be documented for a given expenditure while still retaining the capability to produce measured drawings. A photogrammetric technique called reverse perspective analysis can be used to prepare drawings for buildings that have been demolished, but for which photographs remain and a few dimensions can be determined. Rectified photography, although less versatile than stereo photogrammetry because its accuracy is limited to one plane, can be used to record room elevations or flat facades.

Changes in the number and nature of the buildings being recorded and the available personnel and appropriations to accomplish that recording will determine future HABS documentation efforts. HABS has traditionally relied on three forms of documentation—hand-measured architectural drawings, large-format photographs, and written historical and descriptive data in outline format—no matter what the relative significance of the building. There are alternatives, all of which have been used by the Survey. Sketch plans are simple page-size drawings which show the room arrangement and

location of openings but no detail. Architectural data forms are one-page, fill-in-the-blank forms ideal for less significant buildings. Field photographs are generally 35-millimeter black-and-white photographs that contain valuable information simply by virtue of being more numerous than the more expensive large-format photographs can be.

Evolutionary change in HABS methodology will continue to occur. Suggestions for assessment and adjustment from within the program, from users of the collection, and from others are a welcome part of that process.

A Rich Vein in the Mother Lode:
HABS in the Library of Congress

by

C. FORD PEATROSS

Since its creation fifty years ago the Historic American Buildings Survey has become one of the largest, best-known, and most widely used and copied of the special collections in the Library of Congress. Its popularity has influenced the collecting policies for the Library's general and specialized collections, where the increase of materials relating to the history and development of American architecture and engineering has mirrored the growth of the HABS and HAER collections. Within the Library's Prints and Photographs Division (begun in 1897 as the Prints Division, reorganized as the Fine Arts Division in 1929, and reorganized again under its current name in 1945), custodian of the HABS/HAER collections, the organization and subject access to supplemental materials in documentary photography and popular and applied graphic arts have reflected the needs of HABS users.

Figure 1 Frances Benjamin Johnston, preeminent photographer of American garden and estate architecture and historic buildings, and the single greatest individual contributor to the collections of architectural photographs at the Library of Congress. Her work is included in both the Pictorial Archives of Early American Architecture and the Carnegie Survey of the Architecture of the South. She donated tens of thousands of negatives, prints, and lantern slides over a period of twenty years. (LC–USZ62–80299)

In its acquisitions the Library has attempted since the 1930s to build upon the strengths of the HABS collections and to counter certain unavoidable weaknesses in them. A great collection of collections has thus been assembled. Together with the HABS/HAER records for almost seventeen thousand sites and structures in the United States and its territories and possessions, one can consult superb supplementary collections of books and serials, catalogs, maps, manuscripts, prints, photographs, and drawings. Information concerning related holdings throughout the country is also available. Extensive documentation on architecture all over the world has been assembled, facilitating comparative study.

Perhaps no other nation enjoys such remarkable resources for the study of its architecture, yet researchers have only started to plumb their depths. With the publication of this catalog and the creation of an automated data base, a new chapter is begun. To better understand the possibilities for the future, however, we must start with an examination of the origins of the Library's interest and acquisitions in architecture in the century before HABS.

The rich architectural collections of the Library of Congress can be said to have begun with the acquisition by Congress in 1815 of the library of Thomas Jefferson, the

Figure 2 Monticello, near Charlottesville, Albemarle County, Virginia, the plantation house designed and repeatedly modified between 1769 and 1809 according to the tastes of its owner, Thomas Jefferson, third president of the United States. It was under this roof, in the rooms seen facing right in this view, that the great architectural collections of the Library of Congress began. West front. Photograph by Robert W. Tebbs, November 1937. Tebbs was active from 1917 to 1942 and worked under the firm name of Tebbs & Knell during the 1920s. This print is from one of twelve hundred of his photographic negatives, representing buildings in twenty-three states. The collection was purchased by the Interior Department and deposited with the Library of Congress as a supplement to the HABS collection in 1962. Tebbs Collection, Prints and Photographs Division. (LC–T3–1137017)

young nation's third president. That library naturally reflected the tastes and interests of a man whom the marquis de Chastellux in 1784 described as "the first American who has consulted the Fine Arts to know how he should shelter himself from the weather" (figs. 2, 3). With Mr. Jefferson's library, the Congress began the expansion of a small reference collection to an intellectual storehouse which reflected his omnivorous genius. The fine arts, and architecture in particular, have since remained a focus of the collecting policies of the Library of Congress. The dramatic growth of the Library's collections has prompted equally dramatic increases in its physical size. From a series of rooms in the Capitol (figs. 4, 5) to the present group of three buildings (figs. 6, 7) adjacent to that structure, the Library has grown and required its own architecture.

After the arrival in Washington of Jefferson's library, three events in the late 1860s marked major increases in the Library's holdings. First came the transfer of the library of the Smithsonian Institution in 1866. This collection, according to Joseph Henry, secretary of the Smithsonian and responsible for the transfer, was sufficient to make the Library of Congress

"worthy of the name of the National Library" (fig. 8). Next came the acquisition by act of Congress in 1867 of the magnificent collection of Americana assembled by Peter Force, which included an architectural drawing, Force's own competitive design for the Washington Monument (fig. 9). Third, and most important, was Librarian Ainsworth Rand Spofford's successful attempt to consolidate responsibility for administering the U.S. Copyright Law within the Library of Congress, ensuring that his institution would receive deposit copies of everything from books to photographs and architectural drawings. In the 1860s the Library began to acquire as well a limited number of photographs of architectural subjects for reference purposes (fig. 10). From these beginnings in the third quarter of the nineteenth century grew collections of architectural documents now totaling over a million items.

Naturally the Library had received architectural publications between 1815 and the 1860s. Architects had frequently provided the illustrations for general periodicals; in fact, Charles Bulfinch, later architect of the Capitol, was responsible for some of the earliest of these (fig. 11). In general, however, it was not until the twentieth century that the Library made a special effort to acquire original architectural drawings, including early drawings related to such popular periodical illustrations (fig. 12). With the Copyright Law of 1870 the Library not only began to receive new deposits but also acquired those deposits which had been made in the U. S. district courts since early in the nineteenth century. Both nineteenth-century American life and architectural aspirations are handsomely documented in the thousands of individually published prints which came into the Library's collections with these retrospective deposits. In an 1825 engraving depicting the never-realized dream of British architect Whitman Stidwell's plan for Robert Dale Owen's well-ordered utopian community at New Harmony, Indiana (fig. 13), or in the picturesque layout for such an influential work as Greenwood Cemetery (fig. 14), begun near New York in 1839, peculiarly American visions are preserved.

Over seventy thousand photographs in various formats had been deposited for copyright by 1896, as were over six thousand designs, models, and drawings. Together these constitute a remarkable survey of American architecture of the period. For example, one can trace the work of a single architect throughout his career, even in varying locales. The dramatic change in the scale and appearance of Napoleon LeBrun's buildings from 1842 until 1909 can be seen in three different types of copyright deposits. First, a stereograph deposited in 1861 by the photographer, McAllister & Brother, as part of a series depicting Philadelphia's churches, shows one of LeBrun's first independent works, the Seventh Presbyterian Church built in Philadelphia in 1842 (fig. 15). A photograph deposited by the trustees of New York's Masonic Hall and Asylum Fund in 1870, and one of the last to be entered for copyright in a district court, shows LeBrun's perspective rendering for an elaborate Second Empire structure (fig. 16). Last, a large photograph deposited by photographer Irving Underhill in 1909 shows the towering Venetian campanile added to LeBrun's Metropolitan Life Insurance Building by his sons, who continued his practice (fig. 17). Similarly, copyright records preserve the Philadelphia work of architect John McArthur, Jr. It is unusual that the architect deposited the original drawing—rather than a copy—of his unsuccessful 1873 entry for the main building of the Centennial Exposition (fig. 18). The following year he registered a photographic copy of his perspective rendering for Philadelphia's New City Buildings, for which he was successful in winning the commission (fig. 19). McArthur himself, together with chief assistant architect Thomas Ustick Walter and building

superintendent William C. McPherson, can be seen posing before the same building while it was still under construction in an 1874 stereograph deposited by photographer James Cremer (fig. 20). Whether viewed as an object of civic pride, as Pittsburgh's Smithfield Street Bridge must have been soon after its completion by engineer Gustave Lindenthal in 1883 (fig. 21), or illustrated for commercial promotion, as were countless buildings and details in handsome manufacturers catalogs (fig. 22), much of nineteenth-century American architecture is revealed in the Library's contemporary copyright deposits.

Even while such copyright material was streaming in, the Library was also building its small reference collection of photographs of foreign architectural monuments to one exhaustive in geographical and chronological scope. Primarily through gift, purchase, transfer, and exchange, the Library was at the turn of the century adding an average of five thousand photographs of architecture, sculpture, and painting to its collections each year. The emphasis was primarily on sites in the Mediterranean countries, the Near East, Europe, and the British Isles. In 1893, for example, Sultan Abdul-Hamid II of Turkey presented a fifty-one-volume photographic survey of his country to "the National Library of the United States of Amer-

Figure 3 Perspective view of the east and north fronts of the United States Capitol, Washington, D. C., as B. Henry Latrobe proposed to complete it, 1806. The drawing is dedicated to President Jefferson, who had appointed Latrobe surveyor of public buildings for the United States in 1803, beginning six years of official collaboration. Neither Latrobe nor Jefferson lived to see the completion of the central domed section of the Capitol, which the latter envisioned as "the first temple dedicated to the sovereignty of the people, embellishing with Athenian taste the course of a nation looking far beyond the range of Athenian destinies." This handsome watercolor rendering was presented to the Library of Congress in 1975 by William Morrow Roosevelt of Whitemarsh, Pennsylvania, who had inherited it from his grandfather, Nicholas Latrobe Roosevelt. It joined over two hundred other works by Latrobe in the Architectural Drawings Collection in the Prints and Photographs Division. (LC–USZ62–37195)

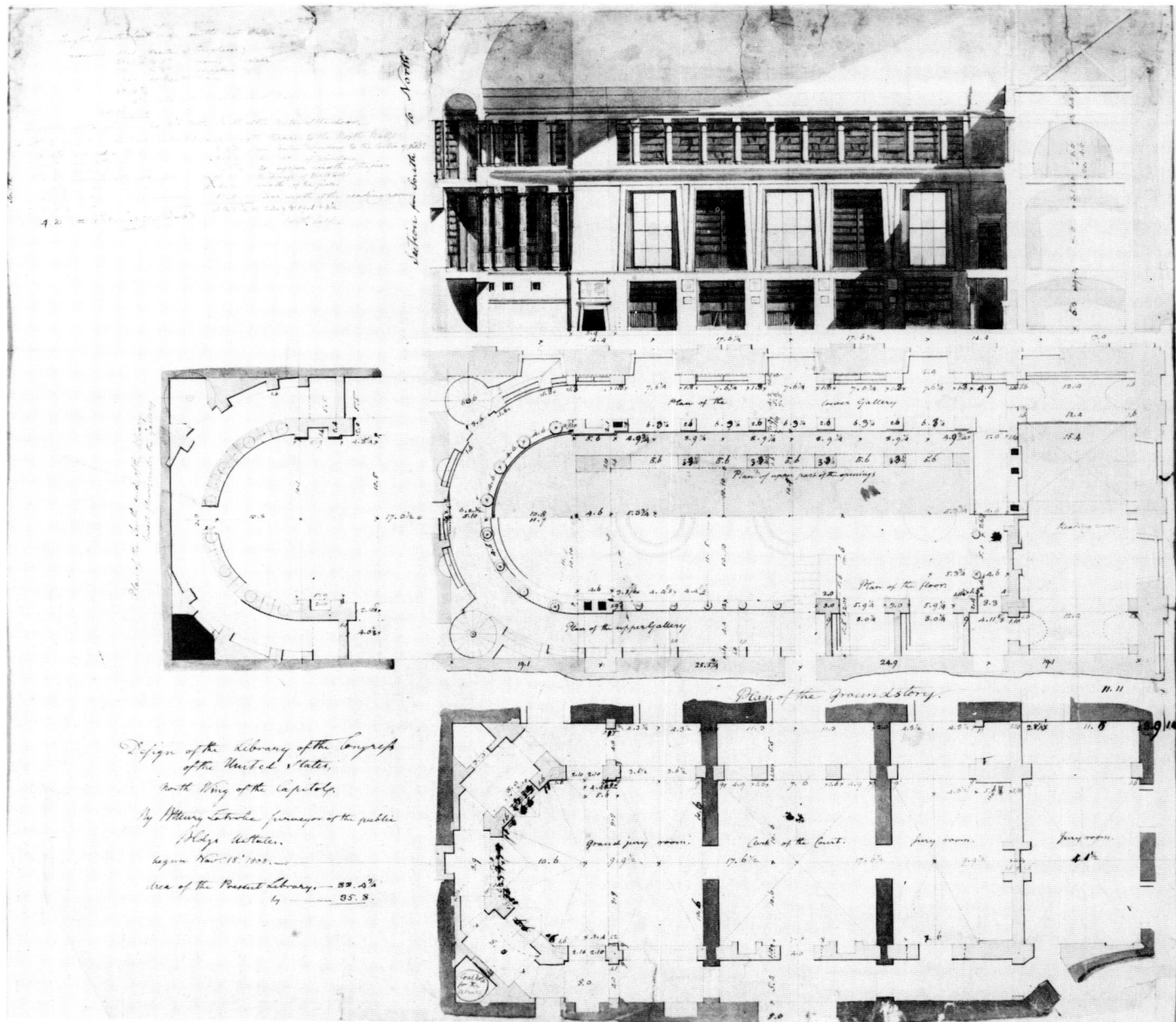

Figure 4 B. Henry Latrobe's proposed Egyptian scheme for the first Library of Congress in the United States Capitol, ca. 1807–9. Never fully executed, this nevertheless indicates the original scale of the Library's relatively small collection, destroyed when the British burned the Capitol in 1814. The architect's choice of Egyptian Revival details may represent their first appearance in this country. Architectural Drawings Collection, Prints and Photographs Division. (LC–USZ62–26147)

ica" (fig. 23). In 1914 the Library purchased 732 large contact photoprints made from negatives taken of sites in Germany, Greece, and the Near East for the Königliche Preussische Messbildanstalt, perhaps the first attempt at a photogrammetric architectural survey (fig. 24). Today the majority of the images thus secured are filed in series by size, country, city, town or site, and building name. In the largest of these geographic files, one can today consult over fifty thousand foreign views. Typical of the type of reference prints in these extensive foreign geographical collections are those acquired from the noted firm of Bonfils. An example shows an Egyptian temple built at Dendur by the Romans (fig. 25). A comparison with a copyright deposit photograph of New York's monumental but short-lived Egyptian Revival prison known as the "Tombs" just before its demolition, shows the assimilation of ancient architectural forms for modern purposes (fig. 26). Many institutions formed collections of such architectural views, purchased from commercial publishers, for they both furnished an excellent record of the world's historical architecture and provided inspiration for contemporary designers.

In certain subjects the Library's holdings are particularly strong, as in its photographs of the many fairs, expositions, and other architectural ensembles commissioned for special events in the late nineteenth and early twentieth centuries. Groups of photographs of these exuberant but transient sites and structures came into the Library both in sets copyrighted by commercial publishers and collections presented because of some official government participation or support. They preserve daring and often amusing essays in various historical and modern vocabularies, both foreign (fig. 27) and native (fig. 29). At their best they could be brilliant and innovative, expressing the finest in contemporary American design (figs. 30, 31).

The Library of Congress first

began to systematically collect photographs documenting early American architecture and design in the late 1920s when Leicester B. Holland of Philadelphia, himself and architect and later chairman of the committee on the preservation of historic buildings of the American Institute of Architects, came to Washington to head its Fine Arts Division (Peterson, fig. 7). The first major acquisition which he secured in this area was through his friend Frances Benjamin Johnston, preeminent recorder of American gardens and estate architecture (fig. 1). In 1929 Johnston deposited over five thousand of her negatives with the Library for, in her own words, "the purpose of creating a national foundation for the study of early American architecture and of garden design."[1]

Even in her early journalistic work,

Figure 5 Following a second destructive fire on Christmas Eve, 1851, architect Thomas Ustick Walter was commissioned to design enlarged and fireproof quarters for the Library of Congress in the Capitol. Entirely of cast iron, this remarkable suite of rooms was not fully completed until after 1865 but served until the Library's removal to its own building in 1897. Architectural Drawings Collection, Prints and Photographs Division. (LC– USZ62–6001)

Figure 6 Construction of steel and mahogany cases to house the collections of the Prints Division of the Library of Congress, ca. 1905. Created in 1897 with the completion of the new building of the Library of Congress, designed by Smithmeyer & Pelz, the Prints Division (later the Fine Arts Division and currently the Prints and Photographs Division) commanded new quarters almost as large as the entire Library of Congress had enjoyed in the Capitol. Photograph, ca. 1905. Prints and Photographs Division. (LC–USZ62–3865)

Figure 7 Model of the James Madison Memorial Building of the Library of Congress, where the Prints and Photographs Division now occupies new third-floor quarters. The third building of the Library of Congress was designed by the New York firm of Dewitt, Poor and Shelton in collaboration with the office of the Architect of the Capitol and constructed from 1968 to 1980. Architect of the Capitol Collection, Prints and Photographs Division. (LC–USA7–34860)

Figure 8 "North West Elevation for No. 1 Design," one of several Italianate villas illustrated in Charles Frederick Anderson's *American Villa Architecture* (New York: G. P. Putnam & Co., 1853), one of the architectural volumes that came to the Library of Congress with the transfer of the Smithsonian Institution Library in 1866. According to Joseph Henry, Secretary of the Smithsonian, his institution's deposit helped to make the Library of Congress a truly national library. Although the Library came to possess two copies of this work with the 1944 transfer of the great architectural library of the supervising architect of the treasury, it is otherwise recorded in no other American library, nor in the latest edition of Henry-Russell Hitchcock's *Architectural Books Published in America before 1895*. Case Collection, Prints and Photographs Division. (LC–USZ62–80403)

Figure 9 Original drawing, 1837, of a proposed plan for the Washington Monument by Peter Force, Washington publisher, politician, and avid collector of Americana. One of the Library's principal acquisitions after the Jefferson and Smithsonian libraries was the purchase by an 1867 act of Congress of the Peter Force Library, which included among more than 22,500 volumes eighteenth-century American newspapers, incunabala, early American imprints, manuscripts, rare maps, and atlases, Force's own unsuccessful entry in the Washington Monument competition. This modified Egyptian pyramid would have taken up a considerably larger portion of both the mall and the Washington Monument Committee's budget than Robert Mills's winning design for the obelisk which stands today. Force's drawing is probably one of the first original architectural drawings to have come into the Library's collections. Architectural Drawings Collection, Prints and Photographs Division. (LC–USZ62–46017)

Figure 10 West front of the United States Capitol, with the new cast-iron dome under construction, 1859. In the foreground is the Tiber Creek or Washington City Canal, filled in around 1870, and the octagonal greenhouse designed by Thomas U. Walter for the Botanic Garden, which was then administered for Congress by its Joint Committee on the Library. It was also in the 1860s that the Library first began to acquire such architectural photographs for public reference, beginning with images of the principal public buildings of the capital. This particular example is a vintage salt print from the personal photographic album of Montgomery B. Meigs, who had been in charge of construction on the Capitol from 1853 until 1858. The album was presented to the Library by William H. Boswell of Washington, D. C., in 1980. Prints and Photographs Division. (LC–USZ62–80394)

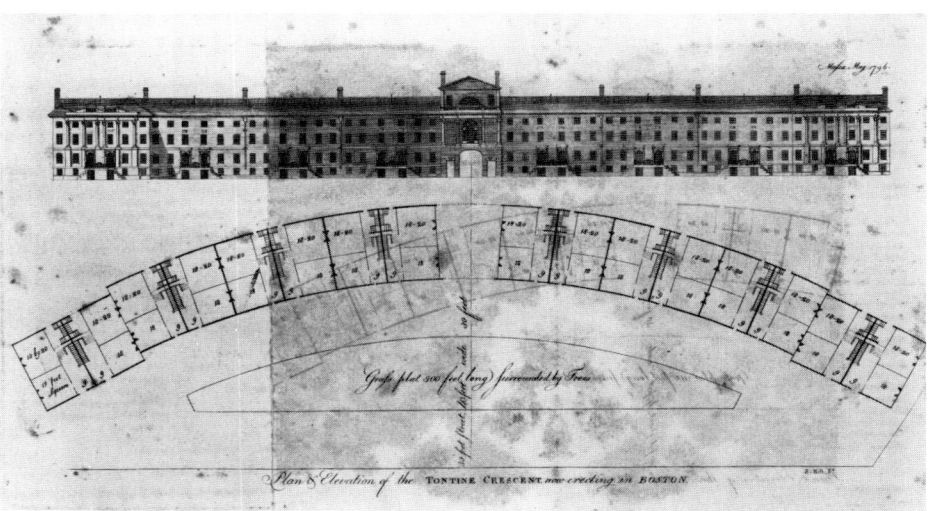

Figure 11 Engraving by S. Hill of the "plan and elevation of the Tontine Crescent, now erecting in Boston," published in volume two (1794) of the *Massachusetts Magazine*. The architect of this sophisticated bit of urban design, demolished about 1858, was Charles Bulfinch, who doubtless furnished the drawing on which this engraving was based. Similar serial publications, in which architectural illustrations appeared with increasing frequency, would have been found in the Library's collections before the 1860s. General Collections, Library of Congress. (LC–USZ62–31136)

Figure 12 Charles Bulfinch's original drawing for the central pavilion of the Tontine Crescent, probably one of a set from which S. Hill's engraving (fig. 11) was produced. It was not far removed in time or quality from the monumental English town planning of the Wood family in Bath, and its centerpiece featured an archway and pedestrian passages connecting two streets, with a first floor given over to the Boston Library Society and a second to the Massachusetts Historical Society. In the 1930s, as a complement to HABS, the Library made a concerted effort to form a representative collection of original early American architectural drawings, and this is one of many Bulfinch drawings deposited in 1935 by the Massachusetts Institute of Technology. Architectural Drawings Collection, Prints and Photographs Division. (LC–USZ62–32386)

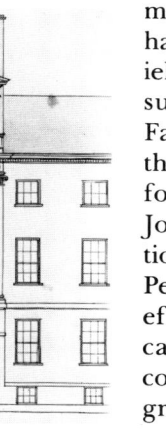

Johnston had shown a predilection for architectural themes (fig. 32), and her eye had captured subjects ranging from the Oriental composition of the Gamble House and garden in Pasadena (fig. 33) to the formal parterres of Whitemarsh Hall near Philadelphia (fig. 34). Through Miss Johnston's generosity the Library eventually fell heir to tens of thousands of her negatives and prints of American houses and their gardens and interiors. Those redolent images preserve a time and a way of life difficult for HABS to recapture, and they have therefore become a rich documentary complement to that collection. Indeed, without Frances Benjamin Johnston's pioneering efforts and generosity, the Historic American Buildings Survey would probably not be what it is today.

In 1927, two years before her first major gift to the Library, Johnston had been commissioned by Mrs. Daniel B. Devore to do an architectural survey of the Fredericksburg and Falmouth, Virginia, area (fig. 35). In these photographs, which were used for a popular traveling exhibition, Johnston's subjects presaged the directions laid out for HABS by Charles Peterson in 1933, for she made a special effort to record characteristic American building types and forms of construction. These included both grand and rudimentary structures,

from great plantation and town houses to frontier cabins and their barns, sheds, mills, and fences. From 1930 through the early 1940s the Library continued where Devore had left off, creating what has come to be known as the Carnegie Survey of the Architecture of the South. During that time, through grants from the Carnegie Corporation administered by the Library of Congress, Frances Benjamin Johnston traveled through Virginia, Maryland, North Carolina, South Carolina, Georgia, Florida, Alabama, Mississippi, and Louisiana. She made almost eight thousand photographs in which the vanishing architectural heritage of that region has been preserved.

In 1930 Holland also began the Pictorial Archives of Early American Architecture. Through newspapers, professional and trade association journals, and even radio talks, he solicited gifts of architectural negatives from donors across the country. Within ten years, over ten thousand negatives had been assembled in this collection, and reference prints of a substantial portion of them had been made, again with funds given by the Carnegie Corporation (fig. 36). The Pictorial Archives was soon overshadowed by the Historic American Buildings Survey, which featured standardized measured drawings and written information in addition to photographs and was broader in range and more uniform in quality. It is doubtful whether the Library of Congress could have accepted, assimilated, and served the HABS records in such a timely way, however, without its four years of experience with the Pictorial Archives, which might be considered a parent to HABS. The former required a program for cataloging a large collection of photographic negatives and prints in different formats, from multiple sources, and representing buildings and sites in many locations and not consistently fully identified. Thus, when HABS began in 1933 as an emergency relief project, a system which allowed the immediate cataloging and public use of its records was already in place, for it had been tested and proven with the Pictorial Archives.

It is still amazing to consider that between November 1933 and March 1934 HABS put 772 architects to work across the country and produced over five thousand sheets of measured drawings of 880 sites and structures. Within weeks after the Survey began, an exhibition was held in Washington to display already completed records. Independent of the Survey, measured drawings were made of Philadelphia's Christ Church in September of the same year, but they too eventually made their way into the HABS collection (fig. 37). By 1941 the Library had received over twenty-three thousand measured drawings and twenty-five thousand photographs, representing over six thousand sites. In 1947 alone the Library received orders for over fourteen thousand copies of HABS records. Libraries and historical socie-

Figure 13 "A bird's eye view of one of the new communities at Harmony, in the state of Indiana, North America." With its assumption of responsibility for administering U.S. copyright regulations in 1870, the Library acquired the retrospective deposits in the U.S. district courts. Included among these were thousands of popular prints like this 1825 lithograph published by the firm of Ingrey & Madeley. It shows Robert Dale Owen's ambitious plan for a complete, self-contained Utopian community of two thousand inhabitants. Never realized according to British architect Stedman Whitwell's plan, it nevertheless links early American urban planning to the development of late nineteenth-century industrial towns like Pullman, near Chicago, Illinois. Pullman and many earlier communities built by Utopian and religious sects have been extensively documented by HABS. Lithograph by Ingrey & Madeley. Popular and Applied Graphic Arts Collection, Prints and Photographs Division. (LC–USZ62–1045)

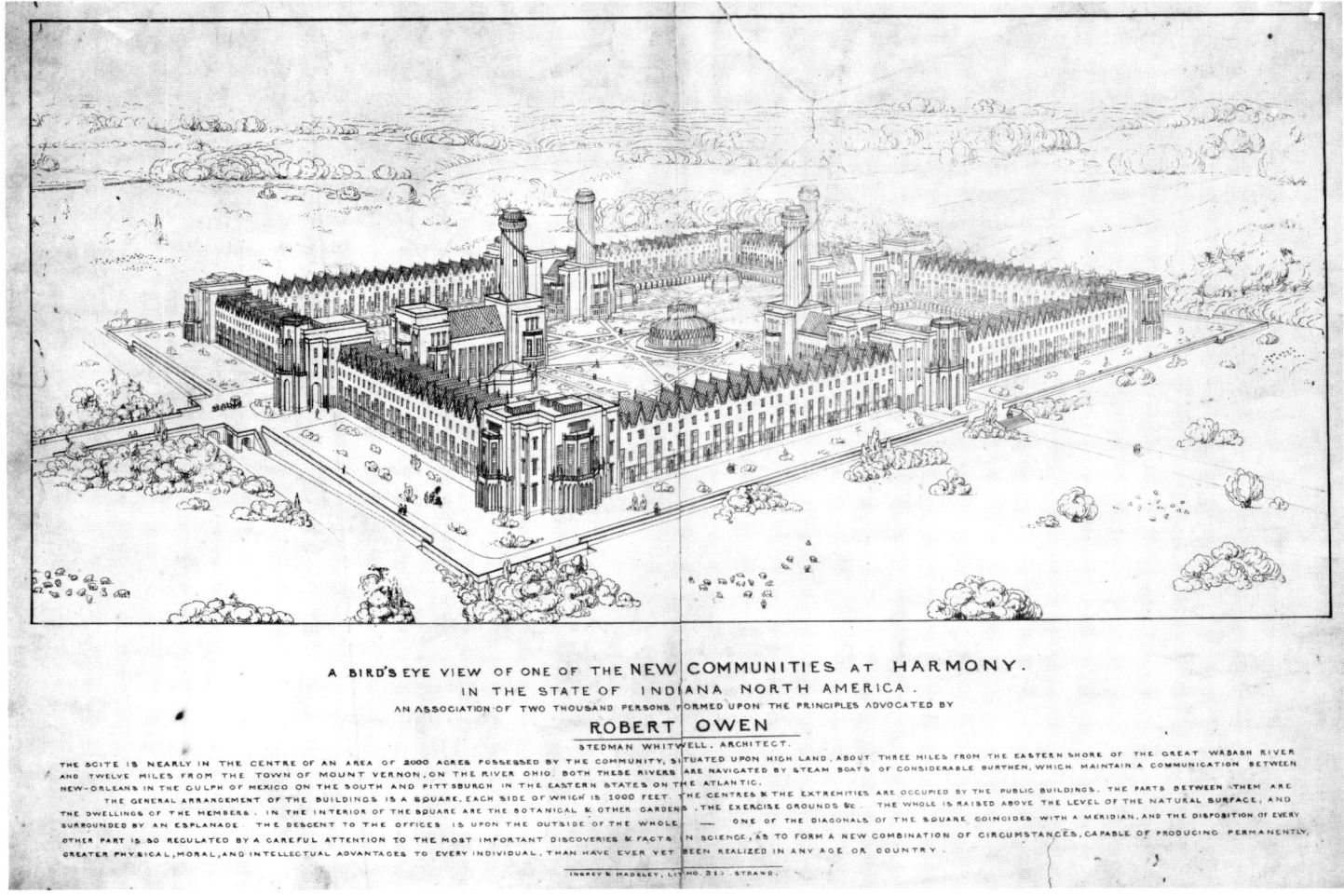

A BIRD'S EYE VIEW OF ONE OF THE NEW COMMUNITIES AT HARMONY.
IN THE STATE OF INDIANA NORTH AMERICA.
AN ASSOCIATION OF TWO THOUSAND PERSONS FORMED UPON THE PRINCIPLES ADVOCATED BY

ROBERT OWEN
STEDMAN WHITWELL, ARCHITECT.

THE SCITE IS NEARLY IN THE CENTRE OF AN AREA OF 2000 ACRES POSSESSED BY THE COMMUNITY, SITUATED UPON HIGH LAND, ABOUT THREE MILES FROM THE EASTERN SHORE OF THE GREAT WABASH RIVER AND TWELVE MILES FROM THE TOWN OF MOUNT VERNON, ON THE RIVER OHIO. BOTH THESE RIVERS ARE NAVIGATED BY STEAM BOATS OF CONSIDERABLE BURTHEN, WHICH MAINTAIN A COMMUNICATION BETWEEN NEW-ORLEANS IN THE GULPH OF MEXICO ON THE SOUTH AND PITTSBURGH IN THE EASTERN STATES ON THE ATLANTIC. THE GENERAL ARRANGEMENT OF THE BUILDINGS IS A SQUARE, EACH SIDE OF WHICH IS 1000 FEET. THE CENTRES & THE EXTREMITIES ARE OCCUPIED BY THE PUBLIC BUILDINGS. THE PARTS BETWEEN THEM ARE THE DWELLINGS OF THE MEMBERS. IN THE INTERIOR OF THE SQUARE ARE THE BOTANICAL & OTHER GARDENS, THE EXERCISE GROUNDS &c. THE WHOLE IS RAISED ABOVE THE LEVEL OF THE NATURAL SURFACE, AND SURROUNDED BY AN ESPLANADE. THE DESCENT TO THE OFFICES IS UPON THE OUTSIDE OF THE WHOLE. — ONE OF THE DIAGONALS OF THE SQUARE COINCIDES WITH A MERIDIAN, AND THE DISPOSITION OF EVERY OTHER PART IS SO REGULATED BY A CAREFUL ATTENTION TO THE MOST IMPORTANT DISCOVERIES & FACTS IN SCIENCE, AS TO FORM A NEW COMBINATION OF CIRCUMSTANCES, CAPABLE OF PRODUCING PERMANENTLY, GREATER PHYSICAL, MORAL, AND INTELLECTUAL ADVANTAGES TO EVERY INDIVIDUAL, THAN HAVE EVER YET BEEN REALIZED IN ANY AGE OR COUNTRY.

INGREY & MADELEY, LITHO. 311, STRAND.

Figure 14 Greenwood Cemetery, near New York, 1852. Maj. David B. Douglass is said to have furnished the elaborate master plan for this 478-acre necropolis in 1839. Community planning extended beyond this life for nineteenth-century Americans. Indeed, the picturesque planning promoted by A. J. Downing and Frederick Law Olmsted was on occasion adopted with perhaps greater zeal for the dead than for the living. This handsome bird's-eye view was also a copyright deposit transferred to the Library from the U.S. district court in the Southern District of New York, where it had been deposited in 1852. Color lithograph by J. Bachman. Popular and Applied Graphic Arts Collection, Prints and Photographs Division. (LC–USZ62– 19372)

ties in this country and abroad have purchased copies in microform. Now we look toward the technological advances offered by machine-readable catalogs and videodisk images to further increase accessibility of the collections.

Although the Prints and Photographs Division relinquished custody of the Library's fine arts books, its specialists remain partially responsible for this significant reference collection. The volumes in the Library's architecture classification alone number over seventy thousand and form part of the nation's largest architectural library. Books which are especially rare, valuable, or otherwise notable are kept as

part of the growing Case Collection of the Prints and Photographs Division or in the Rare Book and Special Collections Division, which has recently announced a special program to rebuild Thomas Jefferson's architectural library, many volumes of which were lost in the fire of 1851. In the Prints and Photographs Division an effort is being made to fill gaps in the Library's holdings of certain specialized architectural publications, ranging from architectural club yearbooks to manufacturers catalogs. Another category includes publications usually described as "builder's guides" or "pattern books," which were so influential in eighteenth- and nineteenth-

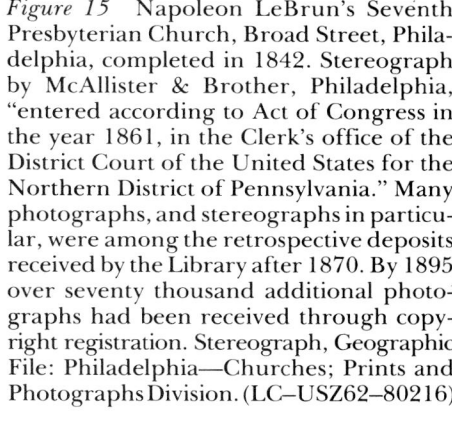

Figure 15 Napoleon LeBrun's Seventh Presbyterian Church, Broad Street, Philadelphia, completed in 1842. Stereograph by McAllister & Brother, Philadelphia, "entered according to Act of Congress in the year 1861, in the Clerk's office of the District Court of the United States for the Northern District of Pennsylvania." Many photographs, and stereographs in particular, were among the retrospective deposits received by the Library after 1870. By 1895 over seventy thousand additional photographs had been received through copyright registration. Stereograph, Geographic File: Philadelphia—Churches; Prints and Photographs Division. (LC–USZ62–80216)

century America. In the form of model house plan books they continue to be popular today. Recent acquisitions include the first edition of Owen Biddle's *Young Carpenter's Assistant* (Philadelphia, 1805). It includes an engraved elevation of the spire of Philadelphia's Christ Church, which allowed the Gibbsian spire to serve as a model for countless other church spires in this country (fig. 38). Similarly, more recent publications which demonstrate the early influence of Frank Lloyd Wright on American domestic architecture have been purchased (figs. 39, 40).

Although published materials constitute a valuable adjunct to the HABS collection, collections of unique items provide documentation unavailable elsewhere. The Survey greatly expanded the Library's documentation of architecture in the American Southwest, including both Indian sites and

Figure 16 Napoleon LeBrun's perspective elevation for a Masonic Hall in New York City, deposited for copyright by the Trustees of the Masonic Hall and Asylum Fund in the clerk's office of the district court of the Southern District of New York in 1870. This photoprint of LeBrun's original rendering demonstrates that architectural designs were also subject to copyright protection. Only a few months later this would have been entered at the Library of Congress rather than the office of the district court. Photographic reproduction, Architectural Drawings Collection, Prints and Photographs Division. (LC–USZ62–80183)

C. Ford Peatross

Figure 17 Napoleon LeBrun & Sons, Metropolitan Life Insurance Building, Madison Square, New York, New York. The skyscraper tower was designed by LeBrun's sons and not completed until 1909, eight years after his death. This remarkable translation of a Venetian campanile represents a dramatic change in scale from LeBrun's Seventh Presbyterian Church built sixty-five years earlier. The image was copyrighted in the year the tower was completed by the great architectural photographer Irving Underhill, whose hundreds of deposits of photographs of New York buildings constitute an independent archive of that city's history. Miscellaneous Oversize Photographs, Prints and Photographs Division. (LC–USZ62–80185)

Figure 18 (opposite, top) Original perspective rendering for an entry by John McArthur, Jr., architect, and Joseph M. Wilson, civil engineer, for the main exhibition building of the 1876 Centennial Exposition at Philadelphia. Winner of the third prize in a two-stage competition, the drawing was deposited for copyright in 1873. The principal feature of the brick and iron structure was its five-hundred-foot central tower, which would have been the highest structure in the world at that time. Architectural Drawings Collection, Prints and Photographs Division. (LC–USZ62–80186)

Figure 19 (opposite, bottom) Perspective elevation for the "New City Buildings, Penn Square, Philadelphia," by John McArthur, Jr., architect. In this case McArthur in 1874 registered a photocopy rather than his original rendering, providing us with a record of the design of his greatest achieved work as well as his greatest attempted one. A comparison with a recent HABS photograph of the massive structure, which still dominates downtown Philadelphia (Tatum, fig. 14), shows a number of alterations in its final execution. Photographic reproduction (by F. A. Wenderoth). Architectural Drawings Collection, Prints and Photographs Division. (LC–USZ62–80184)

JOHN McARTHUR JR. } ARCHITECTS.
JOS. M. WILSON, C. E. } ARCHITECTS.

Figure 20 Architect John McArthur, Jr., chief assistant architect Thomas Ustick Walter, and building superintendent William C. McPherson standing before the subbasement of Philadelphia's "New City Building," August 1874. This stereograph by James Cremer is from the series "Views of Construction of the New City Buildings, Philadelphia," deposited for copyright in 1874. Geographic File: Philadelphia—Buildings—Miscellaneous (full stereo); Prints and Photographs Division. (LC–USZ62–53924)

Figure 21 Copyright deposit photograph, 1883, of the recently completed Smithfield Street Bridge spanning the Monongahela River and connecting central and south Pittsburgh, Pennsylvania. Major new structures were often the subject of copyrighted photographs and this lenticular truss bridge designed by engineer Gustave Lindenthal must have been the pride of Pittsburgh with its twin 360-foot spans and impressive entrance porticoes. The porticoes were taken down before HAER recorded Lindenthal's bridge, which was itself a replacement for John Roebling's first road bridge and second completed structure, a multi-span wire suspension bridge completed on the same site in 1846. Roebling's bridge had replaced a timber structure first erected in 1816. Miscellaneous Oversize Photographs, Prints and Photographs Division. (LC–USZ62–80393)

Figure 22 *Catalogue* (1886) of the Dearborn Foundry Co., Chicago, Illinois, "Manufacturers of architectural iron work, iron columns, lintels, wrought iron beams and girders, lamp posts, boiler fronts and machinery castings." Color lithograph frontispiece drawn by E. A. May, Jr., for the publication deposited for copyright in 1884, 1885, and 1886. Many such catalogs for building materials have come into the Library's collection through copyright deposit and reveal much about the sources of nineteenth-century American architecture. Lot 11451, Prints and Photographs Division. (LC–USZ62–83917)

Figure 23 This late nineteenth-century aerial view of Constantinople is captioned "Vue du quartier Nouri Asmanie et Heidi Kemi." It is one of 2,250 beautiful gold-toned albumen photoprints by Abdullah Frères contained in the fifty-one volume photographic survey of Turkey presented to the Library of Congress in 1893 by the Turkish Sultan Abdul-Hamid II. Since the late nineteenth century, the Library of Congress has acquired tens of thousands of photographs of world architecture by gift, purchase, exchange, and special commission. Lot 9521, Abdul-Hamid II Collection, Prints and Photographs Division. (LC–USZ62–78322)

Figure 24 Rathaus, Cologne, Germany, its handsome Renaissance portico of 1569–71 designed by Wilhelm Vernickel. Taken not long after the 1881 restoration of the structure, this is one of 732 record photographs of architectural monuments in Germany, Greece, and Turkey made 1882–1907 under the direction of the Königliche Preussische Messbildanstalt of Berlin and purchased by the Library of Congress in 1914. These standardized images, measuring 40 by 40 cm, were meant to serve as source material for measured drawings, much as photogrammetric stereopairs are used today by HABS (Burns, fig. 19). Messbild Collection, Prints and Photographs Division. (LC–USZ62–80392)

Figure 25 This handsome Egyptian temple and pylon represent an early revival of ancient forms, for they were erected at Dendur under Roman rule and patronage. Ancient architecture provided inspiration for many American architects, at first from printed sources and after the middle of the nineteenth century increasingly through photographs. Reference collections of such prints were formed at the Library of Congress and similar institutions or could be purchased privately. This handsome albumen print is by the firm of Bonfils, one of the great recorders of the architectural monuments of the Near East. Fortunately Bonfils did not attach the firm's name to all the great monuments it surveyed, and the graffiti evident here was scrubbed away in time for later views. Geographic File— Egypt; Prints and Photographs Division. (LC– USZ62–80418)

Figure 26 The old and new Tombs, the prison of the City of New York, in 1901, just after the erection of the new prison on the site of the old, here awaiting complete demolition. The old prison had been erected 1835–38 to the designs of John Haviland, whose innovative penal plans were the subject of international interest. Its ancient Egyptian models proved more lasting than this substantial granite edifice erected in Manhattan, where a building's life is more often measured in decades than in centuries. The new Tombs fared little better; it was demolished in 1947. Photograph by Irving Underhill. Geographic File: New York City—Buildings; Prints and Photographs Division. (LC–USZ62–83919)

Figure 27 Egyptian entranceway at the California Mid-Winter Fair of 1894, copyright deposit photograph by J. W. Tober, San Francisco. This bold pastiche combines and superimposes details from several different Egyptian sites and periods. Even shorter-lived than buildings in Manhattan and still more exuberant in their borrowings from historical architecture, the fantastic structures erected for America's numerous fairs and expositions are recorded in photographs, often equally impressive in scale and imagination, that have come to the Library both through copyright deposit and gift. Gifts were often presentation sets resulting from congressional support. Specific Subject File: Fairs and Expositions—California; Prints and Photographs Division. (LC–USZ62–80419)

Figure 28 Admiral Dewey Arch, Fifth Avenue, New York, New York; 1899 copyright deposit photograph by William Bechtel. American triumphal architecture, although unusual, could be bold and extravagant. This magnificent ensemble created by Charles R. Lamb may represent its pinnacle. Geographic File: New York City—Miscellaneous Buildings; Prints and Photographs Division. (LC–USZ62–80417)

Figure 29 Photographic reproduction of the original drawing for the front elevation of the main or Administration Building of the Jamestown Exposition, deposited for copyright in 1906 by the Jamestown Official Photograph Corporation, Norfolk, Virginia. Egypt and Rome are rejected here in favor of American, indeed Jeffersonian, prototypes. This pastiche shows a swollen version of Monticello, which has intercepted the dome and portico of Jefferson's University of Virginia Library and its ranges, with Colonial Revival quoining and Beaux-Art cartouches added for good measure. Geographic File: Virginia—Jamestown—Jamestown Exposition; Prints and Photographs Division. (LC–USZ62–80348)

Figure 30 Travel and Transport Group "Century of Progress," 1933 copyright deposit photograph for a publicity poster. At Chicago's Century of Progress Exposition of 1933–34, designed 1929–32, a group of eight architects headed by Harvey Wiley Corbett and directed by Nathaniel Owings and Louis Skidmore turned their backs on historical precedents in favor of a distinctly American modern architecture. Engineered by E. H. Bennett, the Travel and Transport building was the first notable American building constructed using the suspension principles usually reserved for bridges. Geographic File: Illinois—Chicago—Century of Progress Exposition; Prints and Photographs Division. (LC–USZ62–80357)

outstanding examples of Spanish colonial influence, as in the mission church of San Xavier del Bac (fig. 41). The HABS record has been expanded in parallel collections. Because the Library possessed limited records concerning the architecture of neighboring Latin America, it created the Archives of Hispanic Culture during the early 1940s with funds from the Rockefeller Foundation. Photographs of architecture, painting, and sculpture in Latin America were collected and commissioned. Used in conjunction with HABS, the materials assembled provide an excellent basis for comparative study (fig. 42). Further, in 1950 the hundreds of historical photographs of American Spanish Colonial architecture collected by historian Prentice Duell were given to the Library, as was two years later a large collection of photographs of Span-

ish architecture assembled by Georgiana Goddard King.

A number of large collections of documentary photographs, all rich in architectural subject matter, either came into the Library during the 1940s and early 1950s or were first made generally accessible during that period. In 1944, for instance, the now-famous Farm Security Administration/Office of War Information (FSA/OWI) collection was transferred to the Library of Congress from the Department of Agriculture. In the Prints and Photographs Division, some seventy-five thousand FSA/OWI reference prints were arranged by geographic region and subject in a way that made them convenient to use in tandem with HABS materials. Thousands of these photographs, taken throughout the United States between 1935 and 1942,

Figure 31 Night view of the Travel and Transport Group, Century of Progress International Exposition, Chicago. Exposition buildings were among the first to use electric light as a critical design element, as seen in this photograph from an album presented to one of the exposition's supporters, Harry H. Blum, and acquired by the Library in 1982. Beginning in the 1920s, deposits of copyrighted architectural photographs began to diminish, and gifts and purchases became necessary to fill this gap. Prints and Photographs Division. (LC–USZ62–80782)

show buildings and the life in and around them. Even techniques of construction, both traditional and modern, are recorded (fig. 43).

The tens of thousands of copyright deposit photographs received by the Library—most before 1920—constituted a collection in and of themselves. Since the 1940s, a substantial portion of the copyright photographs have been progressively sorted and filed according to size, subject, and geographic location, making them an excellent companion to the HABS photographs. After their receipt in 1948, over four thousand photoprints in the Ordway Collection were similarly arranged by subject and location, pro-

viding access to the many images of historic buildings recorded during the Civil War and further represented in the Library's negatives by Mathew B. Brady. From the early 1950s, HABS users at the Library have thus found available to them additional views of American buildings ranging from a 1906 copyrighted view of "the only remaining sod school house in Decatur County, Kansas" by an obscure local photographer (fig. 44) to Brady's marvelous image showing Westover, one of America's greatest houses, without its distracting additions (fig. 45).

The huge collections of two of this country's most successful publishers of souvenir views, brochures, and

Figure 32 Student carpenters at work on a staircase, Hampton Institute, Hampton, Virginia. Photograph by Frances Benjamin Johnston, 1895. Miss Johnston proved sensitive to architecture even in her early work as a photojournalist. Such documentation complements the Library's other photographs of the building trades and professions. Master Photographs Collection, Prints and Photographs Division. (LC–USZ62–38595)

Figure 33 Balcony and garden of the David B. Gamble bungalow, Pasadena, California, built in 1908 by Charles Sumner and Henry Mather Greene. This 1917 photograph by Frances Benjamin Johnston came to the Library with her deposit of architectural and garden photographs, including over five thousand negatives, "for the purpose of creating a nucleus for a national foundation for the study of early American architecture and of garden design." Frances Benjamin Johnston Collection, National File: California—Pasadena—Gamble Bungalow; Prints and Photographs Division. (LC–USZ62–80347)

Figure 34 The formal gardens of the Edward Stotesbury estate, Whitemarsh Hall, near Philadelphia. Copyright deposit photograph by Frances Benjamin Johnston, 1922. Both the gardens and the small palace which overlooked them, designed by Horace Trumbauer, have since vanished, reinforcing the importance of Miss Johnston's record. Frances Benjamin Johnston Collection, National File: Pennsylvania—Philadelphia—Whitemarsh Hall; Prints and Photographs Division. (LC–USZ62–54552)

Figure 35 Staircase, Kenmore, Fredericksburg, Spotsylvania County, Virginia, built by Fielding Lewis after 1752 for his bride Betty Washington. Thomas Waterman has attributed the interior plasterwork—"the most beautiful in America"—to the "Gibbs Modern" style of John Ariss, ca. 1770. This 1927 photograph by Frances Benjamin Johnston was one in an architectural survey of Fredericksburg and Falmouth commissioned by Mrs. Daniel B. Devore. This project prompted the Carnegie Survey of the Architecture of the South and was subsequently absorbed into it. Under grants from the Carnegie Corporation administered by the Library of Congress, Johnston continued her photographic survey in Virginia through 1934. Thereafter, until 1943, she expanded the survey to include Maryland, North Carolina, South Carolina, Georgia, Florida, Alabama, Mississippi, and Louisiana, producing a total of almost eight thousand large-format negatives. For this effort Frances Benjamin Johnston was made an honorary member of the American Institute of Architects in 1945, the first woman to receive honorary membership. Carnegie Survey of the Architecture of the South, Prints and Photographs Division. (LC–J7–VA–2899)

Figure 36 (opposite) Congregational Church, Avon, Hartford County, Connecticut, built 1818–19 by David Hoadley. Photograph donated in June 1930 by Albert E. Robinson of New York City, the seventh of what came to be thousands of original negatives in the Library's Pictorial Archives of Early American Architecture. Established by a $5,000 grant from the Carnegie Corporation in 1930, the Pictorial Archives was conceived to establish a "national repository for photographic negatives of early American architecture, to preserve and make available to students of history . . . records of our rapidly disappearing ancestral homes." The collection sought to include a wide range of characteristic American building types but naturally was limited to the subjects and locations popular for architectural photographers up until the early 1930s. This handsome Federal church in New England is typical of those biases. Although comprising only photographs, the Pictorial Archives both provided model for HABS and indicated the Library as its logical repository. In fact, HABS was at first considered a part of the Pictorial Archives, which by 1938 included almost ten thousand negatives by such varied photographers as John Mead Howells, Frances Benjamin Johnston, Delos Smith, Thomas Tileston Waterman, and Francis M. Wigmore. Reference prints were cataloged and organized according to state, county, and city or vicinity. HABS, however, with its more truly national scope and standardized format, soon outpaced its parent collection. Prints and Photographs Division. (LC–PAEAA CONN, 2–AVOE, 1–1)

Figure 37 North elevation of Christ Church, Philadelphia, Philadelphia County, Pennsylvania. Measured drawing by J. Spence, Jr., under the supervision of Horace Wells Sellers, September 1933. This drawing, dated only a few months before HABS officially began, was apparently commissioned by the Old Christ Church Preservation Trust. Subsequently it became part of the HABS collection, as have many drawings prepared to HABS standards by others. Begun in 1727 with a spire added in 1754, Philadelphia's Christ Church has been described as the most advanced and the most completely English church in the colonies. Prints and Photographs Division. (HABS PA–1071, sheet 9 of 19 sheets)

Figure 38 "Elevation of the Steeple of Christ Church in Second Street, which for the justness of its proportions, simplicity and symmetry of its parts is allowed by good judges to be equal if not superior in beauty to any Steeple of the spire kind, either in Europe or America. It was erected in the year 1755 by Robert Smith." Plate 44 in Owen Biddle's book *The Young Carpenter's Assistant; or, A System of Architecture, Adapted to the Style of Building in the United States* (Philadelphia: Benjamin Johnson, 1805). Such builders' guides or pattern books, as they are sometimes called, constitute a useful supplement to the HABS collection. Case Collection, Prints and Photographs Division. (LC–USZ62–80425)

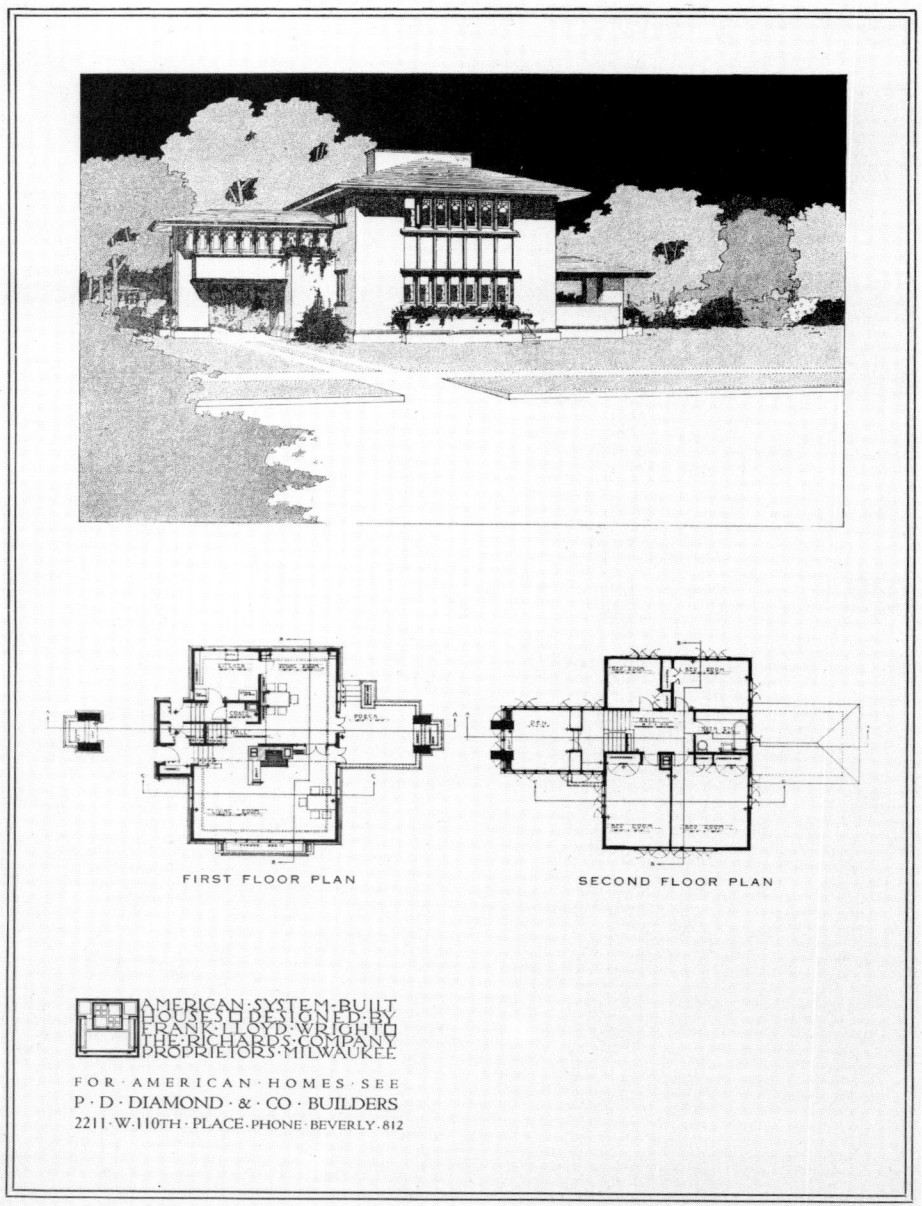

FIRST FLOOR PLAN   SECOND FLOOR PLAN

AMERICAN·SYSTEM·BUILT
HOUSES·DESIGNED·BY
FRANK·LLOYD·WRIGHT·TO
THE·RICHARDS·COMPANY
PROPRIETORS·MILWAUKEE

FOR·AMERICAN·HOMES·SEE
P·D·DIAMOND·&·CO·BUILDERS
2211·W·110TH·PLACE·PHONE·BEVERLY·812

Figure 39 One of three "American System Built Houses" designed by Frank Lloyd Wright for the Richards Company of Milwaukee, published in *Home Suggestions* (Chicago: Burhans, Ellinwood & Co., 1917). Such model home publications were the outgrowth of nineteenth-century builders' guides and continue to be popular. This volume demonstrates a Chicago real estate firm's early promotion of houses designed by Wright together with other more conventional models. Case Collection, Prints and Photographs Division. (LC–USZ62–80426)

postcards—the Detroit Publishing Company and the Wittemann Brothers (Albertype) Company—were received in 1949 and 1953, respectively. Each collection added over twenty thousand reference prints to the geographic and subject reference files in the Prints and Photographs Division. Made up primarily of views of cities, towns, buildings, parks, and resorts (figs. 46, 47), the Detroit and Wittemann materials constitute a remarkable record of American buildings and landscape from about 1890 through 1930.

The most recent comparable acquisition is the Gottscho-Schleisner collection. Comprising over twenty-three thousand architectural negatives dating primarily from the 1930s through 1968, this record group includes more recent buildings and sites, helping to round out the Library's representation of American buildings of the last fifty years. Many designers and building types characteristic of this period are included, from Manhattan skyscrapers (fig. 49) to Miami hotels, from the work of John Russell Pope to that of Raymond Loewy and Morris Lapidus. Especially valuable are the collection's images of commercial and domestic interiors, subjects again difficult or impossible for documentary surveys like HABS to recapture (fig. 48).

Records of various American building types have been a focus of the Library's architectural acquisitions in the 1970s and 1980s. Several distinguished collections document buildings which share a common function but are geographically and chronologically diverse. The Seagram County Court House Archives, given in 1980, surveys over eleven hundred county courthouses in forty-eight states (fig. 50). From 1974 until 1976, Joseph E. Seagram & Sons commissioned twenty-four photographers to produce over eight thousand images. These photographs were cataloged under the Library's supervision according to a system modeled on HABS cataloging. The American Fire House Survey, similarly organized, documents over three hundred fire stations in thirty states (fig. 52). Received in 1982, the survey materials were created in 1978–79 by two Harvard students supported by a National Endowment for the Arts (NEA) Youthgrant and sponsored by the Library of Congress.

Hundreds of smaller or less comprehensive collections complement the HABS records received by the Library. The development of two other building types, theaters and service stations, can be observed in the collections of two individuals, one a recorder and the other a creator. Anthony F. Dumas's great passion was the American stage, and from 1916 until 1939 he traveled the major vaudeville and motion picture circuits, taking the time to produce 248 pen-and-ink drawings of the theaters he visited. Carl E. Petersen, on the other hand, was responsible for the design of thousands of service stations and other structures related to the automobile all over the United States from 1916 until 1965. As head of design for the Gulf (1916–23) and Pure (1925–57) oil companies he oversaw the development of the ubiquitous but now rapidly disappearing architectural forms which served the American automobile and transformed the face of our land. Following World War II, almost half of the estimated two hundred thousand stations in the United States were scheduled for rebuilding or replacement, a process documented in Petersen's drawings (fig. 52, 53).

The Library's holdings of the papers of architects and designers, found in both the Manuscript and Prints and Photographs Divisions, form an important supplement to the HABS collection, for they provide the evidence of the process whose result the Survey records. Four of these collections demonstrate their usefulness in different ways. Fifty years of experimentation in a wide variety of building types and styles can be observed in the collection of Arthur B. Heaton of Washington, D. C. For a 1936 hamburger restaurant on Pennsylvania Avenue, Heaton produced fourteen very different designs, only to be informed by the Fine Arts Commission that his cupola to house the establishment's trademark, a blue bell, was inappropriate to the location (fig. 54). Architect and historian Thomas Tileston Waterman, at one time staff architect for HABS (Peterson, fig. 3), was both a creator and recorder of buildings, and his drawings reveal both activities (fig. 55). Historian Alfred Marie's tracings of eighteenth-century French estate plans (fig. 56) might

appear unrelated to American architecture, but not when compared with Nathaniel Owings's master plan for Washington, D. C., based on similar principles (fig. 57).

This vital dialogue between documentary and original materials enlivens and enriches the study of architecture at the Library of Congress. To further stimulate and aid such research, the Library has since 1980 attempted to increase access to architectural

Figure 40 Design submitted by Pittsburgh architect B. Haldane Douglas in a 1916 model house competition sponsored by the Cleveland chapter of the American Institute of Architects. The entries were published in *The Average Man's Home* (Cleveland, Ohio: Complete Building Show Co., 1916). The influence of Frank Lloyd Wright is evident throughout Douglas's design, demonstrating Wright's early and widespread appeal. General Collections, Library of Congress. (LC–USZ62–80427)

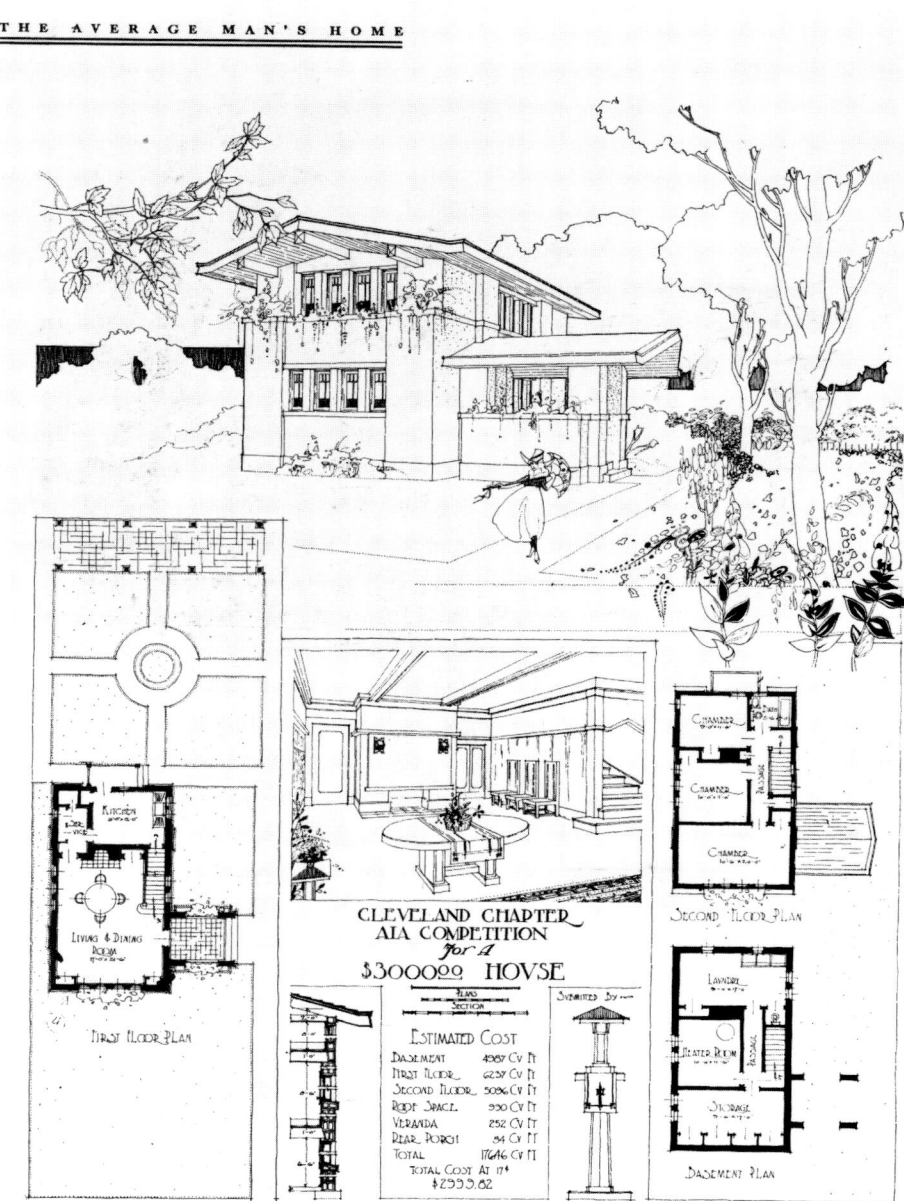

Figure 42 (below)   Side entrance, Iglesia de la Campania, Arequipa, Peru. The Spanish Colonial forms seen in the Southwest are linked to those throughout the New World. Although holding photographic documentation of the architecture of many civilizations, the Library lacked material on Latin America. From 1940 until 1944, aided by the Rockefeller Foundation, it therefore created a photographic reference collection of Latin American art and architecture known as the Archives of Hispanic Culture, which offers excellent material for comparative studies of Spanish influence. Prints and Photographs Division. (LC–USH5–1296)

Figure 41 (above)   South front and main entrance, Mission of San Xavier del Bac, Tucson vicinity, Arizona. HABS has recorded in great detail many examples of Spanish Colonial architecture in the American Southwest. These data have been supplemented at the Library of Congress by a number of collections of historical photographs of the same subjects. The most notable among these is the Prentice Duell Collection, presented to the Library in 1952, which includes hundreds of rare early views and details of Spanish missions. Photograph by Donald W. Dickensheets, March 1940. (HABS ARIZ–13, LC HABS ARIZ, 10–TUCSO.V, 3–19)

Figure 45 North or land front of Westover, the plantation house built about 1730 by William Byrd II near the James River in Charles County, Virginia. Photograph, July 1862. The original appearance of this, perhaps the finest country house erected in colonial America, is best seen in a view taken before the addition of flanking wings and other alterations. The Library's collection of photographs by Mathew B. Brady was enlarged in 1948 by the presentation of approximately forty-five hundred reference prints collected in the nineteenth century by Gen. Albert Ordway. Many early views of historic structures in this collection have been filed by subject and location, making them a useful adjunct to the collections created by HABS, which has recently completed measured drawings of Westover. Lot 41, Brady-Handy Collection. (LC–USZ62–80404)

Figure 44 "The only remaining sod school house in Decatur County, Kansas." Copyright deposit photograph by Joseph H. King, 1907. American photographers have sought to record many structures of the type we now call vernacular. (See Carl Lounsbury, "Vernacular Architecture in the Survey.") Little attempt had been made until the 1940s to organize the thousands of copyright deposit photographs received by the Library since 1870. When organizing and cataloging began, the influence of the already large use of the HABS collections was evident. Thus this photograph was cataloged by building type and geographic location. Specific Subject File: Dwellings—U.S.—Kansas; Prints and Photographs Division (LC–USZ62–16456)

Figure 43 (opposite) "Chamisal, New Mexico. Spanish-American women replastering an adobe house. This is done once a year." Photograph by Russell Lee for the Farm Security Administration, July 1940. The photographs of American life taken between 1935 and 1942 by the now famous photographers of the Farm Security Administration include thousands of images of American buildings, building materials, and building techniques. The FSA/OWI photographs and the HABS records have been among the Library's most popular photodocumentary collections for almost four decades. FSA/OWI Collection, Prints and Photographs Division. (LC–USF34–37082–D)

ORIENTAL
FISH POND.

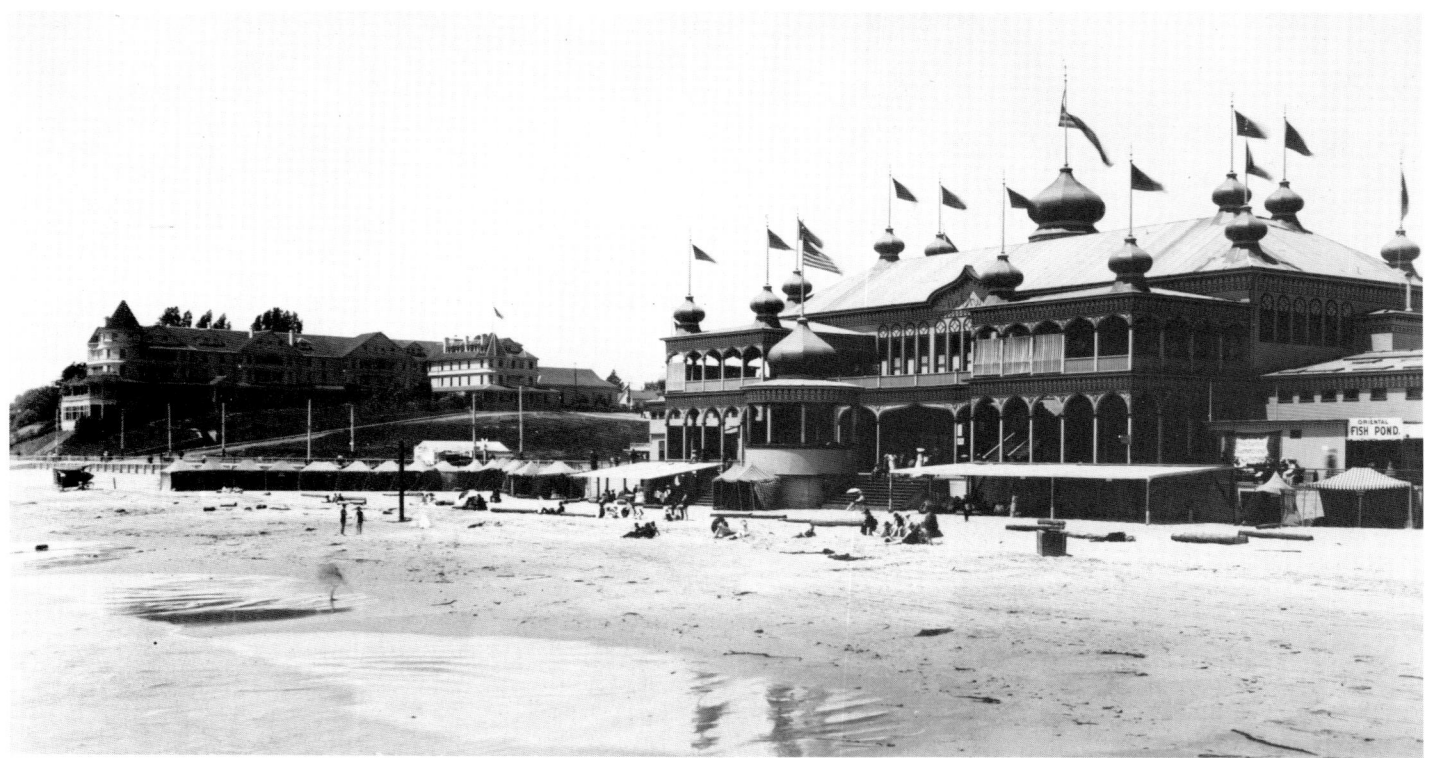

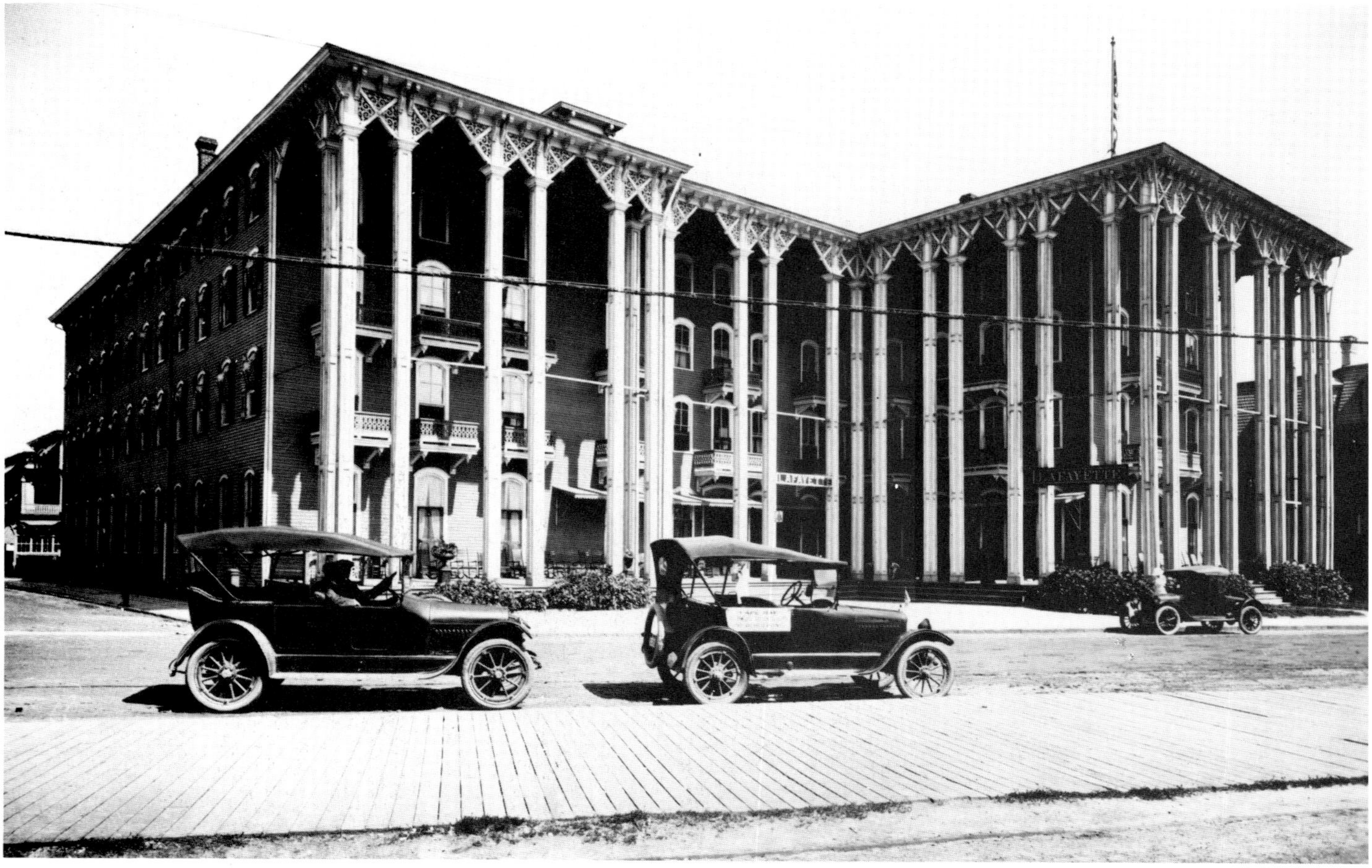
LAFAYETTE
LAFAYETTE

Figure 48 Interior, Mrs. William E. Clow, Jr., house, Lake Forest, Illinois. Photograph by Samuel Gottscho, June 1934. The Gottscho-Schleisner Collection preserves the appearance of the transitory interiors of buildings, houses, and apartments designed by many of America's most notable architects and decorators, including features difficult or impossible for surveys like HABS to recapture. This elegant but icy enfilade by David Adler offered its owners refuge from the Great Depression. Gottscho-Schleisner Collection, Prints and Photographs Division. Commercial use by permission only. (LC–G612–21930)

Figure 46 (opposite, top) Casino and Sea Beach Hotel, Santa Cruz, California. Photograph by the Detroit Photographic Company, copyright 1904. America's great resorts were a favorite subject of William Henry Jackson's Detroit Publishing Company, for many years one of our largest producers of postcards and souvenir views. Adding to prints deposited for copyright before 1924, the State Historical Society of Colorado transferred to the Library of Congress over eighteen thousand of the company's original glass plate negatives in 1949. Prints and Photographs Division. (LC–USZ62–62507)

Figure 47 (opposite, bottom) Hotel Lafayette, Cape May, New Jersey. Photograph by the Albertype Company. Similar in scope to the Detroit Collection is the Wittemann or Albertype Company Collection. It includes over twenty-five thousand photoprints and fifty thousand photo-gelatin reproductions presented to the Library in 1953 by the souvenir booklet-publishing firm known under both names and based in Brooklyn, New York. Both the Detroit and the Wittemann collections are especially rich in their records of the resort, park, and main street architecture of turn-of-the-century America (Rifkind, fig. 1). Like HABS, they have been organized by the Library in a manner which allows access according to geographic location and building type or name. Specific Subject File: Hotels and Taverns—New Jersey—Cape May; Prints and Photographs Division. (LC–USZ62–62456)

Figure 49 (opposite) New York City's seventy-story RCA Building nearing completion. Reinhard & Hofmeister; Corbett, Harrison & MacMurray; Hood & Fouilhoux, principal architects; Raymond Hood, principal designer. Photograph by Samuel Gottscho, 1936. The central element of Rockefeller Center, one of the twentieth century's handsomest and most successful urban developments, was for a time the world's largest commercial structure, with 2.7 million square feet of floor area. The Library recently acquired over twenty-three thousand architectural negatives by Samuel Gottscho and his son-in-law William Schleisner of Jamaica, New York. Gottscho-Schleisner Collection, Prints and Photographs Division. Commercial use by permission only.(LC–USZ62–80405)

Figure 50 Exterior and entrance to the Woodbury County Court House, Sioux City, Iowa. Photograph by Bob Thall, ca. 1975. Built in 1913 to the designs of William L. Steele and Purcell & Elmslie, with architectural sculpture by Alfonso Iannelli, the simple but powerful massing and rich decoration of this structure offer eloquent testimony to the genius of the original architectural vocabulary which we have come to call the Prairie Style. This is one of over eleven hundred county courthouses in the United States represented in the Seagram County Court House Archives. As an American Revolution Bicentennial project, Joseph E. Seagram & Sons, Inc., commissioned twenty-four photographers to travel throughout the United States. From 1974 to 1976 they produced over eight thousand images showing this peculiarly American building type in all its variety of scale, form, and material. The entire collection of photographic negatives, master and reference photoprints, and historical information was organized and cataloged under the direction of the Library of Congress according to a system modeled after that used for HABS and was presented to the Library in 1980. HABS began a more modest survey of building types in the 1960s, documenting the nation's great motion picture palaces, and it recently completed a similar but much more comprehensive project on city halls. Seagram County Court House Archives, Prints and Photographs Division. Copyright © Seagram County Court House Archives. (LC–S35–BT91–6)

Figure 51 Four theaters—the Allen, the Ohio, Loew's State, and B. F. Keith's—lined Cleveland's equivalent of the Great White Way. Original drawing by Alfred F. Dumas, ca. 1925. The great passion of Dumas, a restorer of paintings at New York's Metropolitan Museum of Art, was the American vaudeville theater, which was quickly joined and eventually overwhelmed by the motion picture palace. HABS made a special effort in the 1960s and 1970s to document these rapidly vanishing monuments of cinematic splendor. Dumas, however, recorded hundreds of them in their heyday through simple pen-and-ink drawings apparently executed as he waited for the next show to begin. In 1979 the Library acquired almost three hundred of these drawings, dating from 1908 to 1935, through purchase and gift from Alfred Dumas's family. They are arranged by state, city, and building name. Dumas Collection, Prints and Photographs Division. (LC–USZ62–80407)

records nationwide. This work has been through the quarterly publication of the *COPAR* (Cooperative Preservation of Architectural Records) *Newsletter,* the building of a national union index to architectural records in many different kinds of repositories, and the encouragement of the preservation and reporting of architectural documentation at the local and regional level. This, of course, supplements the written reports of the HABS collection, which have from the beginning made reference to the nature and location of primary source material.

Little could Thomas Jefferson have dreamed what his fine but modest library would grow into. The sites and structures represented in the Library's collections reflect the course of a nation which has in many ways exceeded "Athenian destinies."[2] Technological change, cultural diversity, and aspirations and achievements, both individ-

Figure 52 Albany, New York, Hook and Ladder Unit Number 4, built in 1910 by architect Marcus T. Reynolds. Photograph by Teresa Beyer, 1978. Local and regional architectural styles are often mirrored in structures like fire houses. This example shows the Dutch influence typical in Albany. It is one of over three hundred fire stations recorded as part of the American Fire House Survey, a documentary collection created 1978–79 under an NEH Youth Grant to two Harvard students, Rebecca Zurier and Teresa Beyer, who were sponsored by the Library of Congress. The project also resulted in the publication of a book on the subject by Rebecca Zurier, *The American Fire House, An Architectural and Social History* (New York: Abbeyville Press, 1982). The mounted and captioned photographs and files of historical information produced by this survey are organized by geographic location and building name. American Fire House Survey, Prints and Photographs Division. (LC–F5–2–2–b–4)

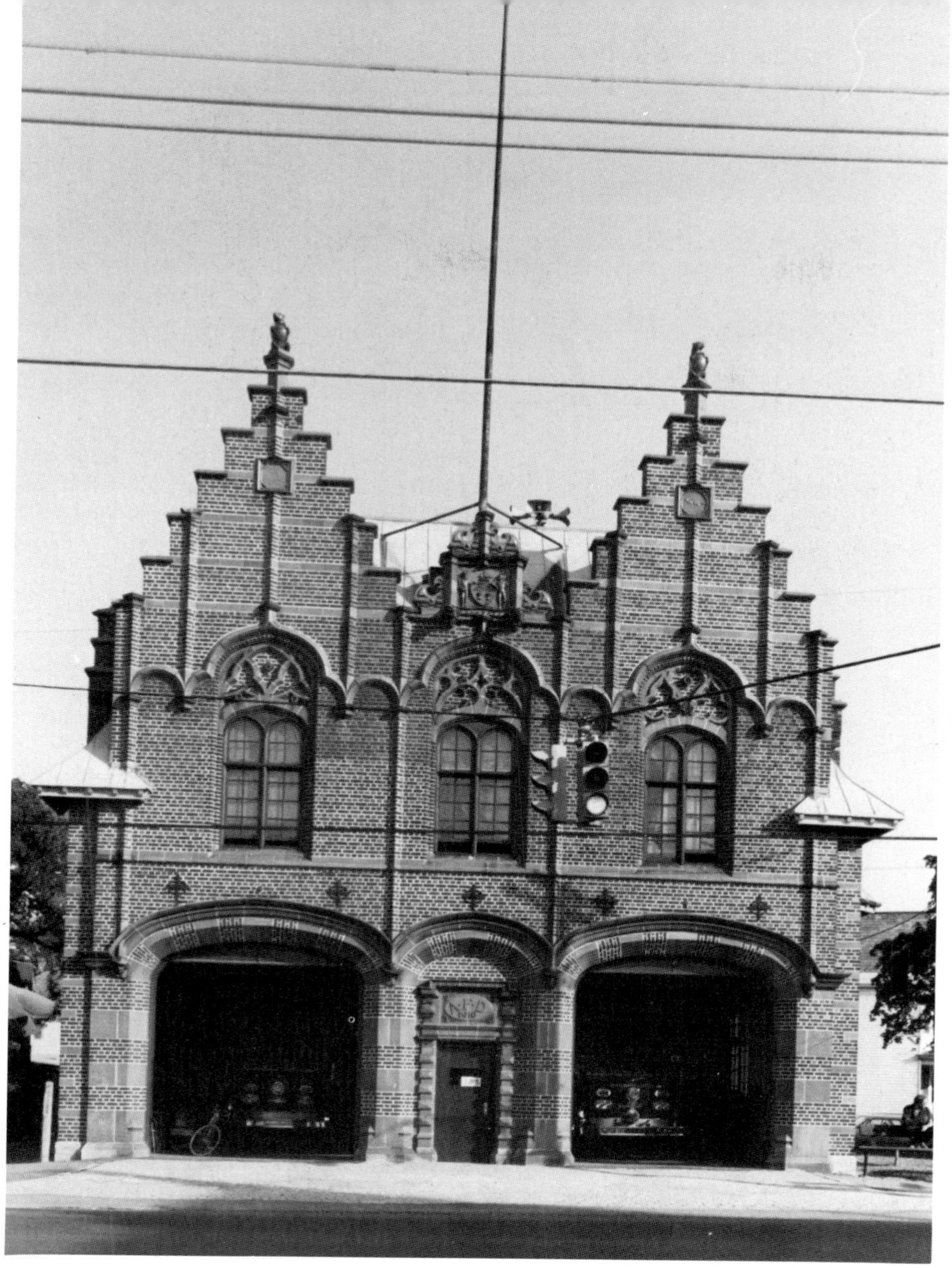

Figure 53 Original drawing by Carl E. Petersen, ca. 1945, showing how to remodel an early automobile service station into a larger and more modern version. For over fifty years the full-service gas station has been part of the daily lives of millions of Americans, yet these familiar structures have undergone frequent transformations and are rapidly disappearing altogether from the landscape. Carl E. Petersen designed buildings for Gulf Oil and Pure Oil. His book entitled *The Station Ahead* describes service station planning and construction. Although not a trained architect, he gave form to thousands of structures throughout the United States from 1914 through the 1950s, when he planned the first truck plazas for the rapidly growing interstate highway system. His drawings, given to the Library in 1980, preserve the development of the various building forms he created to serve an automobile culture. Petersen Collection, Prints and Photographs Division. (LC–USZ62–80406)

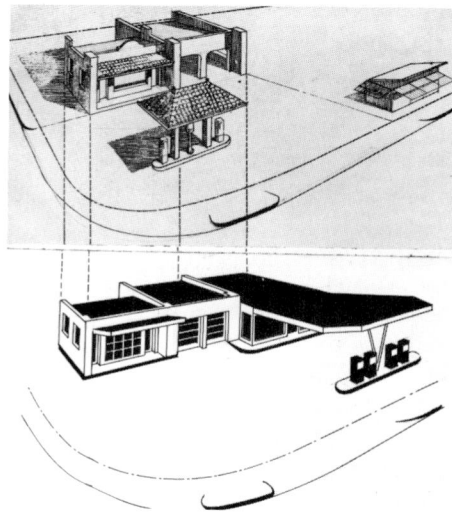

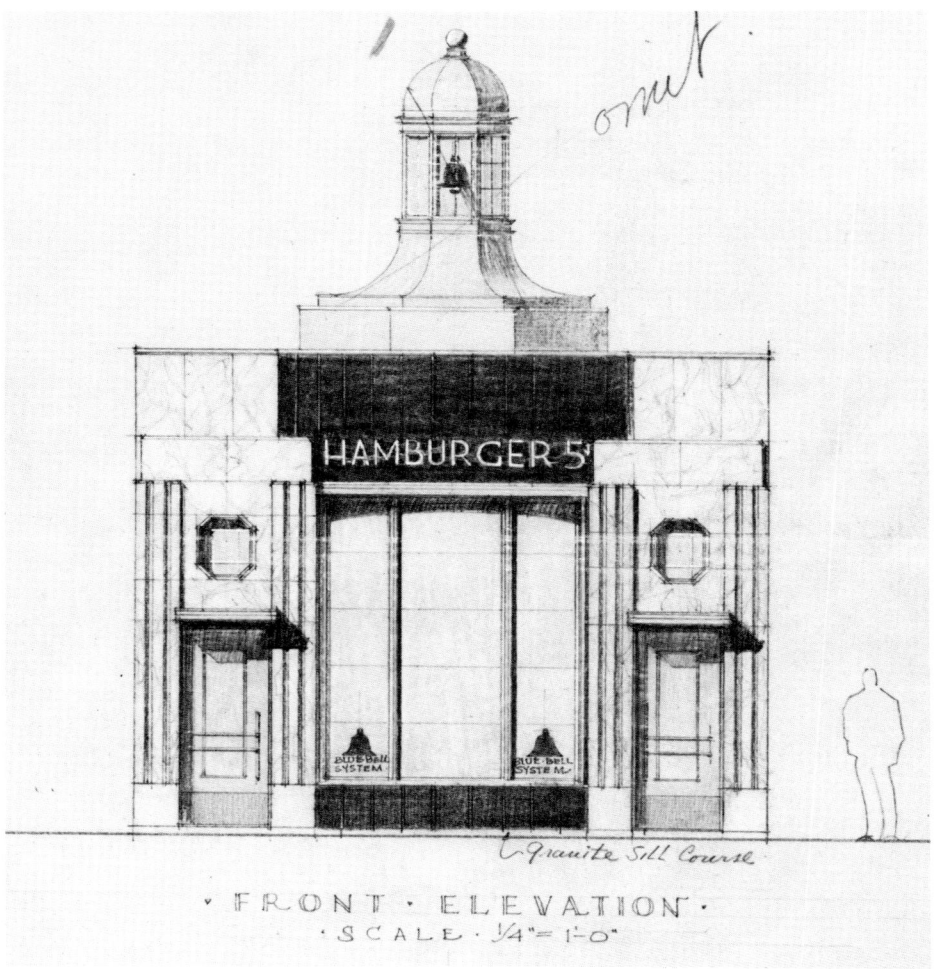

Figure 54 Original drawing for a "Blue Bell System" hamburger restaurant designed in 1936 by architect Arthur B. Heaton for a location on Pennsylvania Avenue, Washington, D.C. It is one of seven varying designs by Heaton for what was at the time a relatively new building form. One of these proclaims, "Food for All, Hamburgers 5¢." This final version was submitted to the capital's Fine Arts Commission and was partially rejected. The cupola meant to house the blue bell was deemed "inappropriate." Here it has been struck through with the word "omit" written to its side. Heaton's files, dating from the 1890s through the 1940s, were presented to the Library in 1981 by Leon Chatelain III. They contain original correspondence, specifications, material and fixture catalogs, and thousands of working drawings, including full-scale details. These records reveal the practice of architecture over half a century and thus constitute an excellent supplement to the documentary records in HABS. Prints and Photographs Division. (LC–USZ62–80423)

Figure 55 Measured drawing of the principal front, plan, and "carcase" framing of the floor of the great room of the Tebbs House at Dumfries, Prince William County, Virginia. Although not as grand as Westover (fig. 45), this fine early Georgian house built by Maj. Fouchee Tebbs makes an interesting comparison. Without the measured drawing made by Thomas Tileston Waterman in 1932, before the destruction of the house in 1933, such comparison would be impossible. Waterman, historical architect for Perry, Shaw and Hepburn at Colonial Williamsburg, staff architect for the HABS during the 1930s, and author of a number of books on American architecture, directed his family to give his papers to supplement the HABS materials in the Library of Congress. Many of his photographs were presented in 1953, and additional photographs, drawings, and the notebook containing this drawing came to the Library in 1980. Architectural Drawings Collection, Prints and Photographs Division. (LC–USZ62–80424)

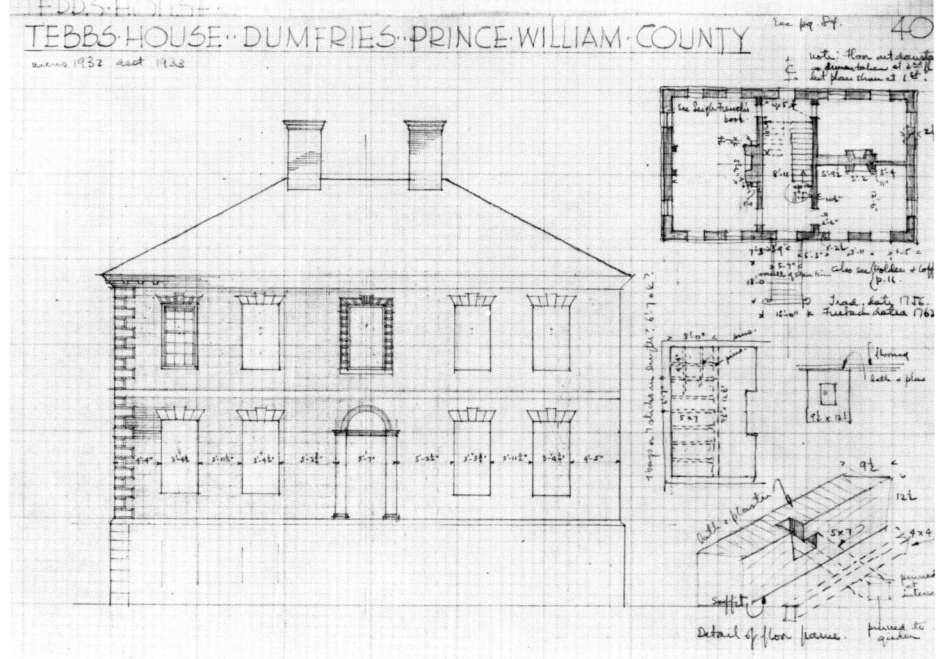

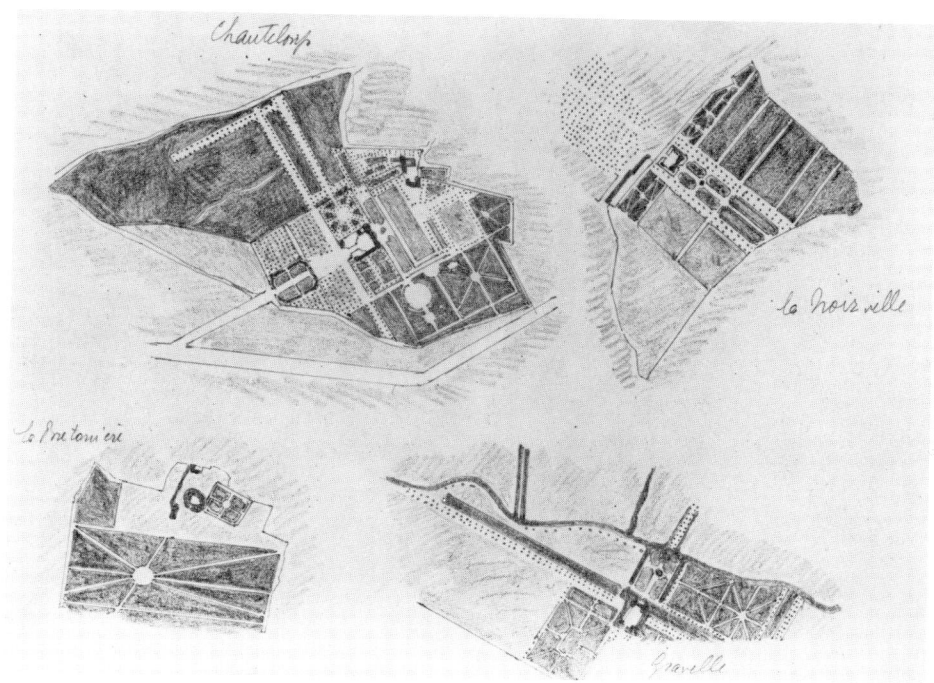

Figure 56 Colored tracing by Alfred Marie of original manuscript maps in the Archives nationales, Paris, France. The original maps are part of a survey commissioned after 1774 by Daniel Trudaine and Jean Rodolphe Perronnet to record the plans of eighteenth-century parks and formal gardens located along the "grandes routes" of France. This drawing shows four French estates: Chanteloup, la Noirville, Gravelle, and la Pretanière. Over two thousand such tracings, including many of original drawings for seventeenth- and eighteenth-century royal building projects, were purchased for the Library in the early 1950s by the Société Mansart, headed by historian Fiske Kimball. American planning has relied heavily on French precedent, from Pierre L'Enfant's original scheme for Washington through the "City Beautiful" movement at the beginning of this century to the present. Architectural Drawings Collection, Prints and Photographs Division. (LC–USZ62–80422)

Figure 57 Architect and planner Nathaniel Owings, partner in the firm of Skidmore, Owings and Merrill and 1982 recipient of the Gold Medal of the American Institute of Architects, standing before his plan for Washington, D.C. Owings here played a large role in reinforcing and further developing many of the principles proven in France and transported to this country almost two centuries earlier. Several presidents called upon his talents from the 1960s until he resigned as chairman of the Pennsylvania Avenue Development Corporation in 1982. Both Owings and his partner Louis Skidmore have deposited their papers in the Library of Congress, where they join those of William Thornton, Robert Mills, Montgomery C. Meigs, Frederick Law Olmsted, Charles Follen McKim, Cass Gilbert, and Ludwig Mies van der Rohe, among others. Access to these records, and to the papers of architects and firms across the United States, supplements the documentation in HABS. Photograph by Stone and Steccati. Owings Collection, Prints and Photographs Division.

Figure 58 "*Some* of the Buildings Built or Designed by me. Add to this a lot of the smaller bldgs. for railroad co's, manufacturers, private enterprises, &c. &c.—small churches—clubs &c., the Supreme Court," by Cass Gilbert, August 1924. Such architectural fantasies are usually referred to as "architects' dreams," only this one was to a large extent true. Even a decade before the end of his career Gilbert had completed enough buildings to populate this imaginary city of considerable size, proving that early twentieth-century America could be a promised land for an ambitious, enterprising, and talented architect. From left to right are listed his Kill van Kull Bridge; National Bank, Minneapolis; Texas University; U. S. Army Supply Base, Brooklyn; Federal Reserve Bank, Minneapolis; Union Club, New York City; Atlantic Refining Company Building; proposed Girard Trust Company Building, Philadelphia; West Street Building, New York City; Bridgeport, Connecticut, Savings Bank; Hotchkiss Tower; U. S. Custom House, New York City; National State Bank, Newark; First Division Monument; Arkansas Capitol, Little Rock; Detroit Public Library; U. S. Treasury Annex, Washington; Oberlin College Auditorium, Finney Memorial Chapel, Allen Memorial Art Museum, Memorial Tower; proposed International Building; St. Louis Public Library; Endicott Buiding, St. Paul; Kinnery Building; Woolworth Building, New York City; New York Life Insurance Company Building; Festival Hall and cascades, Louisiana Purchase Exposition, St. Louis; Scott Fountain, Duluth; Union Central Life Insurance, Cincinnati; Soldiers and Sailors Memorial, Detroit; Waterbury City Hall; Broadway-Chambers Building, New York City; Herald Square Building; United States Chamber of Commerce, Washington; Chase Offices, Waterbury, Connecticut; Essex County Court House, Newark; Minnesota Capitol, St. Paul; Hudson River Bridge; New Haven Public Library; Dayton Avenue Church, St. Paul; Austin Nichols Warehouse; St. Louis Art Museum; Scovill Manufacturing Tower; Brazer Building, Boston; University of Minnesota; West Virginia Capitol, Charleston; Prudential Life Insurance Company Building. This is one of over four hundred handsome and revealing sketches, drawings, and watercolors given to the Library of Congress by Gilbert's granddaughter, Mrs. Walter A. Bastedo. Architectural Drawings Collection, Prints and Photographs Division. (LC–USZ62–80421)

ual and corporate, can all be seen in our architecture. The opportunities which this rich land has afforded its formgivers have rarely been matched in any time or place. Cass Gilbert's graphic inventory of his works is imaginary only in their juxtaposition (fig. 58). The building-up and the tearing-down will take place as long as we breathe; indeed it is one of the surest measures of our vitality. Samuel Gottscho's dramatic 1936 image fixes a moment in the ongoing transforma-

tion of Manhattan's skyline (fig. 59), a process that has continued since before the creation of this republic. It reflects the forces and talents at work throughout this land. The Historic American Buildings Survey and the Historic American Engineering Record should be as busy recording these achievements during the next half-century as they have been in the past fifty years. The collections of the Library of Congress reveal that their work has only begun.

Figure 59 Manhattan skyline. Photograph by Samuel Gottscho, 1931. Few images are more symbolic of the constantly changing face of American architecture than the profile of its greatest city, the dream and reality of many architects, builders, and planners. Gottscho-Schleisner Collection, Prints and Photographs Division. Commercial use by permission only. (LC– USZ62– 83914)

Notes

1. *Annual Report of the Librarian of Congress* (Washington: Library of Congress, 1930), p. 229.
2. Jefferson to B. Henry Latrobe, July 12, 1812, quoted in *The Eye of Thomas Jefferson,* ed. William Howard Adams (Washington: National Gallery of Art, 1976).

LAND FRONT PORCH

Future Directions for the Historic American Buildings Survey

by

ROBERT J. KAPSCH

The Historic American Buildings Survey (HABS) has been documenting the architectural heritage of the United States since 1933. The subjects documented, the techniques used, the types of data collected, the purposes to which the documentation has been put, and the delivery of that documentation to the HABS user have all changed during the first fifty years. These changes have occurred because the needs of the architectural and academic communities for HABS documentation have changed, as have the opportunities to undertake such documentation. We expect HABS documentation to continue to evolve.

Certain administrative, legal, and regulatory mechanisms that will stimulate change have already been set in motion and we can begin to project with some certainty future directions for HABS. On March 25, 1982, for example, the deputy director of the National Park Service (NPS) sent a memorandum to regional directors stating the following: "I encourage you to use every practical opportunity to record the major historic structures of the

National Park Service to the standards of the Historic American Buildings Survey (HABS) or the Historic American Engineering Record (HAER)." This directive was the result of several disastrous events that affected Park Service properties.

In January 1982, fire broke out at Franklin D. Roosevelt's birthplace, a Park Service property in Hyde Park, New York. Damage—particularly water damage—was extensive. The HABS measured drawings produced in 1941 by HABS architects Daniel M. C. Hopping and Frank Chouteau Brown and fifty-seven interior HABS photographs greatly assisted NPS architects planning the restoration of this historic building. The Hyde Park fire came soon after fire destroyed Marshall Hall, an eighteenth-century manor house in Maryland owned by the National Park Service. Fortunately, measurements for HABS drawings for this structure had been completed by the time of the fire. These measurements will be used to prepare HABS drawings for this structure, thus leaving a permanent record (figs. 3, 4).

Besides demonstrating the fragility of some historic resources, these and other fires have pointed out the need for HABS documentation of NPS historic buildings. The emphasis on Survey recording of NPS buildings reaffirms

279

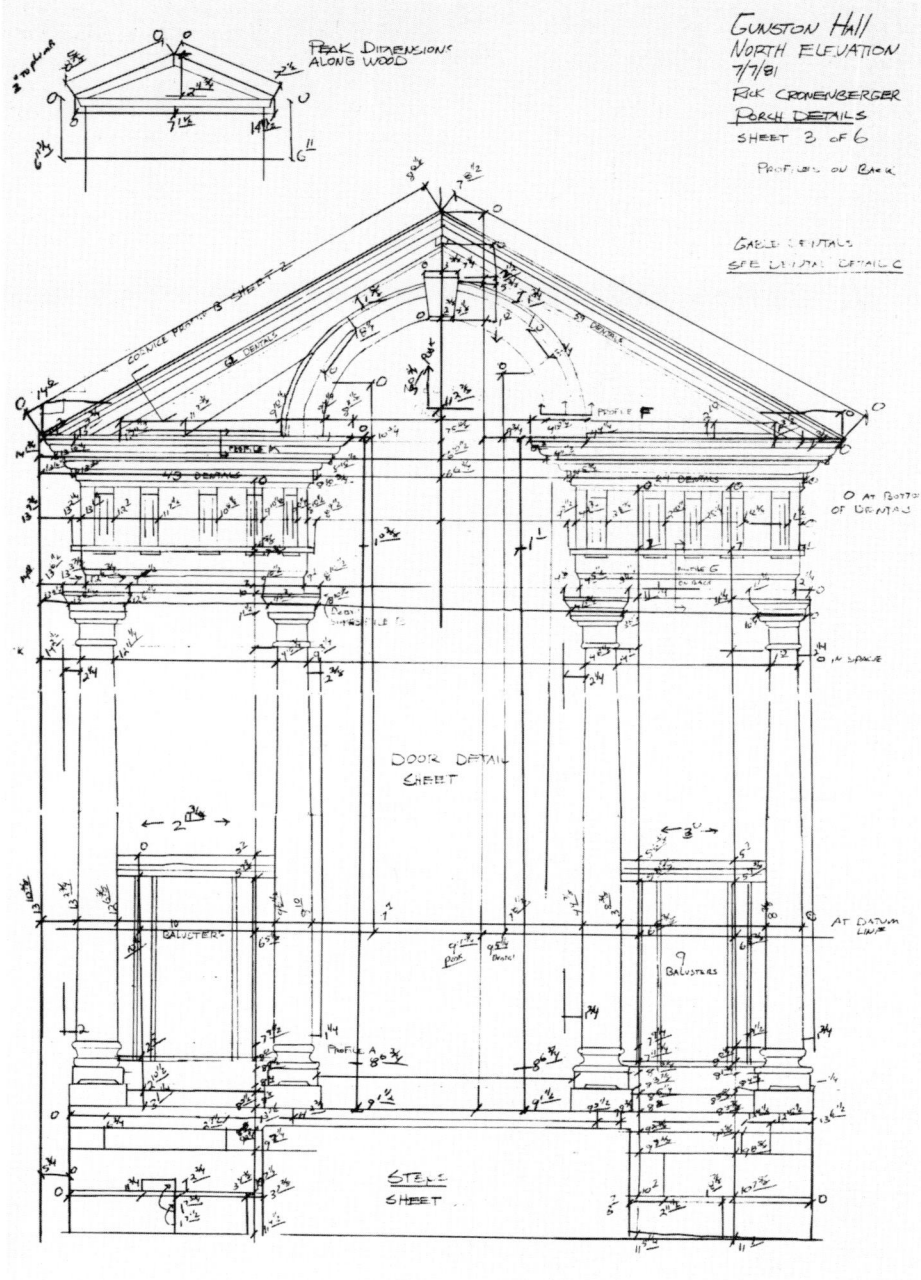

Figure 2 Measured drawings are developed from measurements recorded in field notebooks. From the information in the notebooks, the accuracy of the final drawing can be judged. Gunston Hall, north elevation, by Richard Cronenberger, 1981. (HABS field notebook, sheet 3 of 6 sheets)

and HAER staff have undertaken a number of new recording projects in the last year. Surveys have been done for the Dorchester Heights Monument in Boston, the Elizabeth Cady Stanton House in Seneca Falls, New York, and the Frederick Law Olmsted House in Brookline, Massachusetts, and an inventory project was undertaken in Lake Clark, Alaska. HABS and HAER documentation projects for other NPS historic properties are expected to increase greatly in the next several years.

HABS and HAER programs are not being limited to the recording of National Park Service buildings. Park Service Director Russell Dickenson has also encouraged HABS and HAER to record national historic landmarks. This goal is being met in a number of ways. Gunston Hall, Virginia (fig. 1), is one example where private funds have been provided to support a HABS recording team. The focus on recording nationally significant buildings reflects the National Park Service's goal of making the HABS collection even more national in scope. This goal is being met in a number of ways. A recent agreement entered into by HABS/HAER with the U.S. Department of the Army provided HABS and HAER with more than one million dollars to do an inventory of over eighty army installations, recording to HABS/HAER standards all the nationally significant buildings on those installations.

Besides the change in emphasis to encourage the recording of nationally significant buildings, newer buildings are now being documented by HABS. Today HABS follows a fifty-year minimum age requirement in selecting historic buildings for documentation. In the 1930s, few buildings constructed after 1860 were documented. Later, HABS became involved in documenting buildings built between 1880 and 1930. The Adler and Sullivan Auditorium Building is one example (fig. 6).

In the 1970s, HABS became increasingly concerned with documenting not only the architecture of build-

a Park Service management goal for cultural resources—to make available to the architectural community, the academic community, and the general public detailed, accurate information on the historic buildings entrusted to the Park Service's care.

To reorient HABS and HAER documentation projects to focus on Park Service historic buildings, HABS

EAST ELEVATION
(SOUTH PORTION)
FOR FULL SIZE DETAILS OF THIS ELEVATION
SEE SHEETS #11,13,14,15,16,17,18 & 19

Figure 3 In 1940, HABS documented Franklin Roosevelt's birthplace in Hyde Park, New York. In 1982, fire and the water used to extinguish it damaged the central portion of this mansion. HABS drawings and photographs, made over forty years earlier, were used in making the restoration plans. This and other fires in historic properties demonstrated the need for HABS and HAER documentation. Drawing by Daniel M. C. Hopping, 1941. (HABS NY—4355, sheet 8 of 35 sheets)

ings but the engineering systems of certain structures as well. Beginning in the late nineteenth century, American buildings increasingly incorporated within their fabric features such as elevators, electrical power systems, heating, and air conditioning and ventilation systems. Simultaneously, more sophisticated structural systems began to be used in American buildings. To document such buildings adequately, it is necessary to document the engineering features as well as the architectural. Joint HABS/HAER projects are essential. The Adler and Sullivan Auditorium Building project, undertaken

Figure 4 Fire at Hyde Park, New York, January 23, 1982. Courtesy of Wide World Photos.

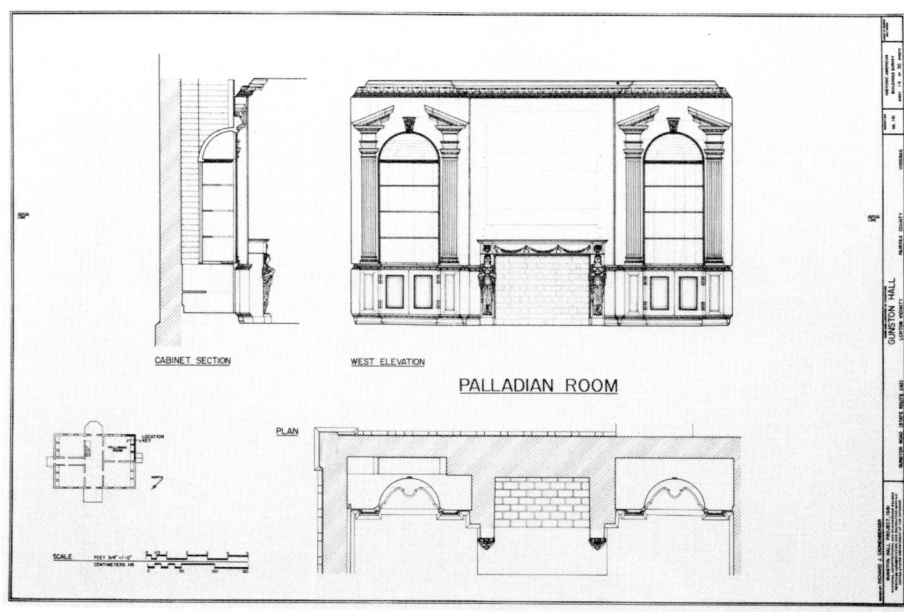

Figure 5 Palladian Room, Gunston Hall, Fairfax County, Virginia. The Palladian Room is considered William Buckland's masterpiece. With the return of the Historic American Buildings Survey and the Historic American Engineering Record to the National Park Service in 1981, more attention was given to the documentation of nationally significant buildings, such as Gunston Hall, a National Historic Landmark. Drawing by Richard Cronenberger. (HABS VA–141, sheet 14 of 30 sheets)

in the summers of 1980 and 1981 under the supervision of HAER architect Donald Stevenson and HABS architect John Burns, with architect Rita Gorawara as field supervisor, is an example of the increase of such projects. The architectural features of this landmark building had been recorded in 1962 by HABS. The purpose of the 1980–81 project was to record the innovative structural and mechanical features of the Auditorium Building.

The techniques of recording are a second aspect of the HABS program that is changing. Although more reliance has been placed on photorecording—particularly formal photography and rectified photography—today than in the 1930s, photogrammetry has never become a standard recording technique for the HABS program. When used in HABS recording efforts, photogrammetry has always been done by contractors and only for buildings where hand measurement is difficult or impossible to do. There are several reasons for this. First, the cost of equipment is high—the stereoscopic camera alone costs thousands of dollars—and HABS has always been a sparsely funded program. Most funds, in fact, are used to pay summer team salaries. Second, HABS recording projects have served to train over one thousand

architects, historians, and photographers—many of whom have entered the field of historic preservation as a result of their HABS experience. Photogrammetry, if used on a large scale, might diminish the training value of HABS summer projects.

Yet HABS must develop photogrammetric capability in the years ahead, particularly for emergency recording projects where there is not time for traditional, hand-measurement techniques. The acquisition of a stereoscopic camera is a necessary first step. This camera would produce stereopairs that could be deposited in the Library of Congress for later use in the production of measured drawings, if these were needed. I expect HABS to gain this type of capability in the very near future.

A third aspect of change is in the presentation of data collected on HABS recording projects. The Historic Preservation Amendment of 1980 (Public Law 96-515) calls upon the secretary of the interior to develop and promulgate standards for architectural and engineering recording. These standards, the first such formal standards for HABS and HAER, allowed the programs to review this documentation in light of the needs of HABS/ HAER users.

Surveys of users were conducted to find out how they were using HABS or HAER documentation and what they needed from it. The results were surprising. It was found that the HABS collection is used more than any other collection in the Prints and Photographs Division of the Library of Congress, and its use continues to grow dramatically. It is extensively used by preservationists, architects, and engineers facing real-life preservation problems, as well as by academics, researchers, and the general public.

One of the uses of the HABS collections has been in book and magazine publishing, and HABS documentation had changed to favor this particular user group. HABS measured drawings once contained substantial line dimensions, assisting architects and engineers who needed exact measurements. Because these were visually distracting, most were eliminated over the last several decades so that drawings were suitable for publication (figs. 8, 9). The measuring stick, used to establish critical dimensions, was contained in many of the HABS photographs in the 1930s, but it was eliminated in later HABS shots. This resulted in photographs without intrusions but which contained less information for those interested in the details of the building under study.

In the HABS and HAER standards now being developed, an attempt at balance will be made. Although a return to the extensive line dimensions contained on the 1930s measured drawings may not be desirable, additional line dimensions are proposed for future HABS drawings. Measuring sticks may be used in some but not all of the photographic views of a building. Further, these standards propose

Figure 6 With the passage of time, more and newer buildings are being documented by the Historic American Buildings Survey. Adler and Sullivan's Auditorium Building would probably have been considered too new when HABS first started in 1933. Documented in 1980–81, it was one of the first examples of a joint Historic American Buildings Survey and Historic American Engineering Record project. Besides architectural features, innovative structural and mechanical aspects of this building were documented. Drawing by August Ventura, 1980. (HABS IL–1007, sheet 44 of 53 sheets)

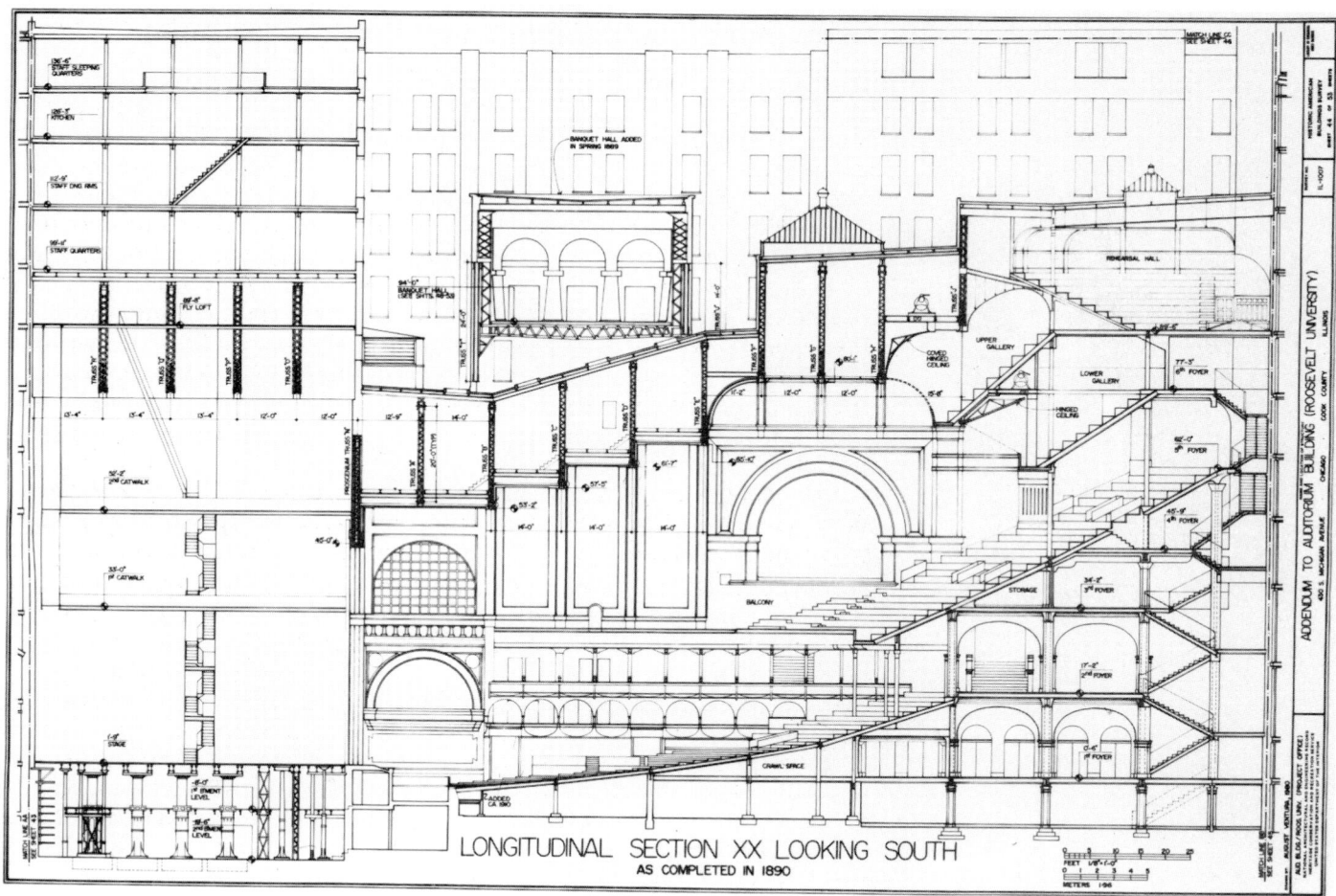

LONGITUDINAL SECTION XX LOOKING SOUTH
AS COMPLETED IN 1890

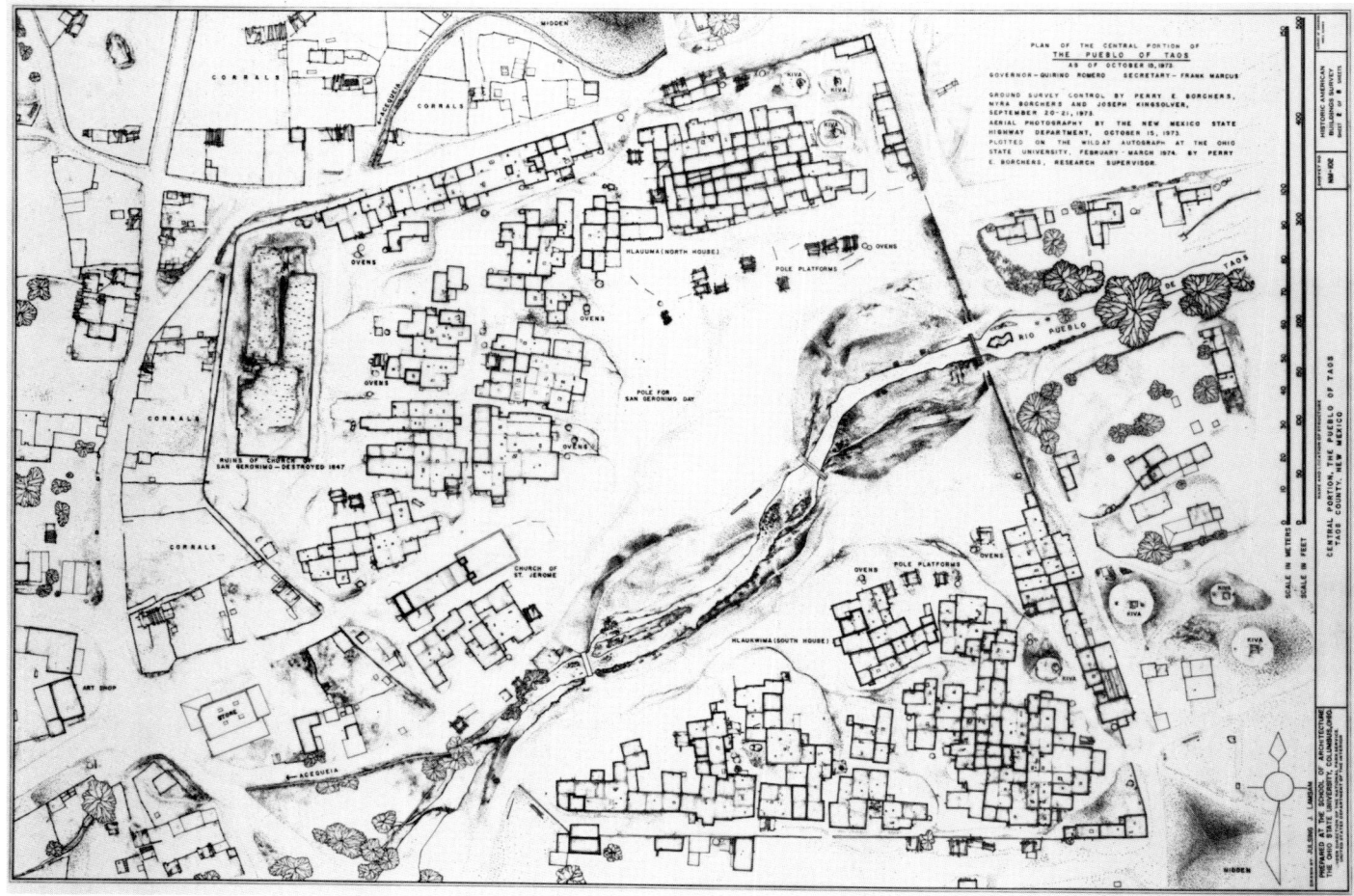

Figure 7 A measured drawing developed from photogrammetric studies shows the Pueblo of Taos, Taos County, New Mexico. Although HABS has used photogrammetry in the past through contracts with private firms, funds have not been available for the purchase of equipment that could make photogrammetry a regular part of the HABS program. Drawing by J. J. Lansam. (HABS NM–102, sheet 2 of 8 sheets)

establishing a series of levels, so that buildings judged especially significant, such as national historic landmarks, will receive more extensive documentation than less significant buildings.

In addition, both HABS and HAER will make more forms of documentation available to the user. Traditionally, the HABS/HAER user had only measured drawings, formal photographs, and written data from which to work on comprehensively documented buildings. Field notebooks, which recorded building dimensions and served as the basis for HABS measured drawings, were sometimes discarded once the HABS measured drawings were completed (fig. 9). Now these field notebooks are always transmitted to the Library of Congress where the HABS user can consult them. They frequently contain information pertaining to a building above and beyond

what is included on the measured drawings. More importantly, the field notebooks can be used to validate the accuracy of the measured drawings, since the notebooks contain primary visual data. In the development of a HABS or HAER project, hundreds of 35-mm black-and-white photographs may be taken. These field photographs are used in making measured drawings. In the past, such photographs were discarded because they were not archivally stable. Yet they contained much valuable information. In the future, where practical, these field photographs will be transmitted to the Library of Congress, where they too will be made available to HABS and HAER users. Although field photographs will not meet normal HABS/HAER standards of archival stability, they will provide years of service to HABS/HAER users.

Figure 8 Elevations of Glouchester, Natchez, Adams County, Mississippi, done in 1934, show numerous dimension lines that provide essential information to users of the drawing. Drawing by Thomas J. Biggs, Edward M. Nelson, and Jay T. Liddle. (HABS MISS 17–5, sheet 5 of 6 sheets)

Figure 9 A drawing of Berkeley, Charles City vicinity, Virginia, done in 1980 shows how dimension lines are absent in more recent HABS documents. Drawing by Susan B. Gallagher. (HABS VA–363, sheet 10 of 16 sheets)

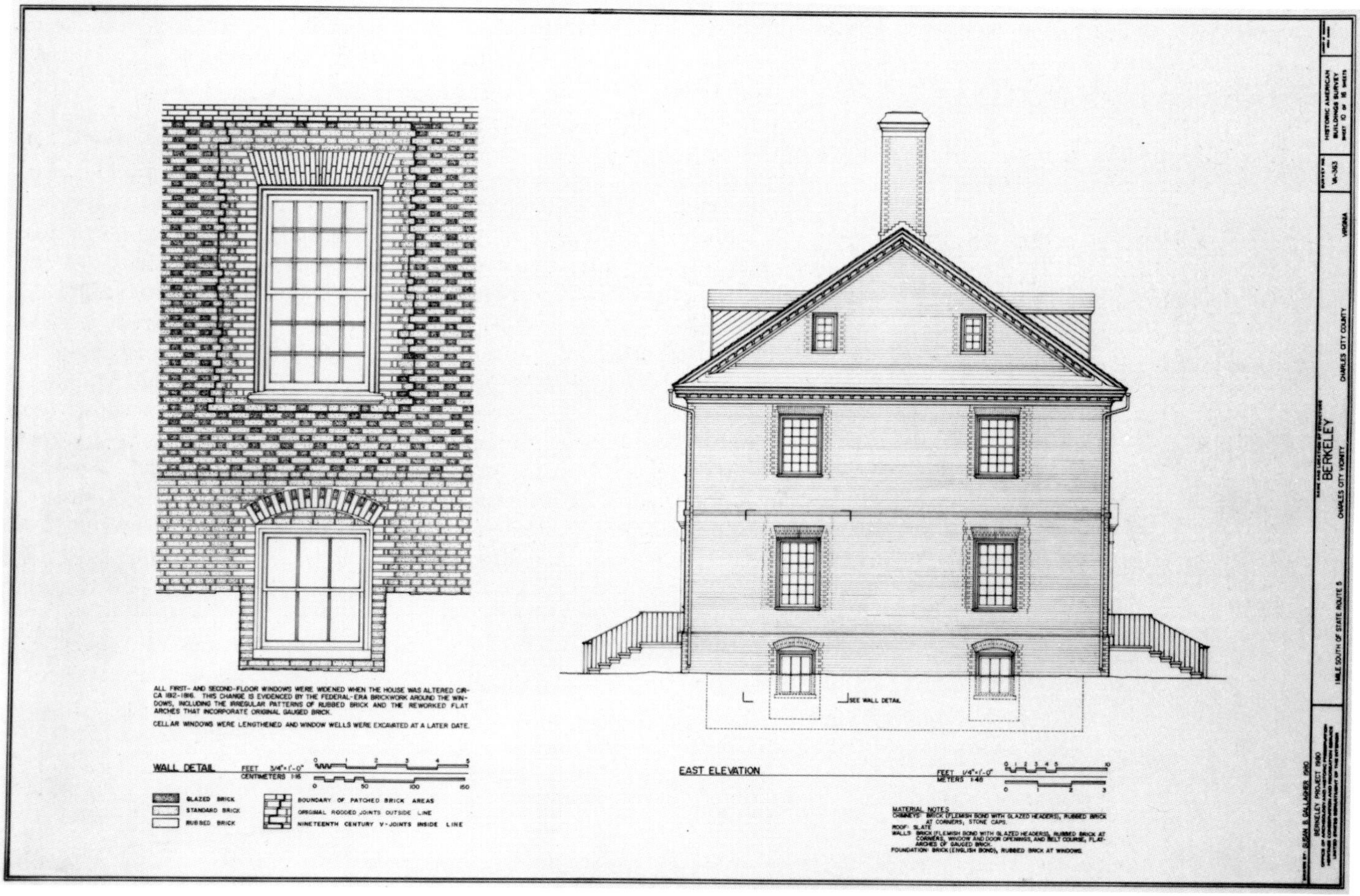

Figure 10 A barn in one of the many new national parks in Alaska will not be preserved but it has been recorded by HABS. Photograph by Jet Lowe.

A fourth aspect of change in the Survey is the development of HABS documentation intended to meet special purposes. In Alaska, for example, HABS recording projects are being used to permanently record historic vernacular buildings that cannot be preserved. Frequently, there is not sufficient preservation funding available to preserve every log cabin within a given park. In these cases, it is an appropriate preservation strategy to record what remains and allow the structure to return to its natural state. HABS is also investigating the use of HABS documentation for assessing the condition of historic buildings, particularly for studies over long periods of time to detect long-term degradation processes affecting a structure.

A fifth aspect of change in the program is in the delivery of HABS and HAER documentation to the user. The HABS and HAER collections are maintained in a single location— the Library of Congress in Washington, D.C. Copies could be made available of all items within the HABS collection, but the cost of reproduction was naturally high for any but the most narrow of studies. Generally, if an individual wanted to use the collections, he had to travel to Washington, D.C.

In 1982 the firm of Chadwyck-Healey, Ltd., published on microfiche all HABS photographs and data pages transmitted to the Library of Congress through 1979. Approximately eighty-five thousand images were thus made available to HABS users for purchase that same year. Coupled with a Library of Congress microfilm of HABS measured drawings, the HABS microfiche set makes the collections available at institutions throughout the United States for the fiftieth anniversary of the Historic American Buildings Survey. In conjunction with the anniversary, HABS/HAER is also offering its office file copies of photographs to state archives that agree to maintain the integrity of the collection and make it available to the public.

These developments—publications in microfiche and microfilm and the establishment of statewide HABS archives—will greatly increase the use of HABS documents. To use these collections effectively, however, requires an index. It is this need that *Historic America* is designed to meet.

The checklist in this book is the result of a HABS/HAER project to establish a computer data base containing information in the HABS/HAER catalogs. The results of the project, which was begun in 1982, provide the HABS user with the first comprehensive index to the HABS collections. But this is only the first product of the data base that was developed. In the future, the data base will be available to be queried—through computer terminals in the Prints and Photographs Division of the Library of Congress and in Park Service offices—by HABS users who want answers for specific questions. The data base developed contains much more information than published here. It will be used to develop specialized lists, such as updated state HABS listings and HAER indexes. It will also be used by HABS/HAER management to identify gaps in the HABS and HAER collections. This information will be used to develop priorities for future recording programs.

HABS and its sister program HAER continue to change. In the future, expected changes will not be random but will be designed to meet users' needs and respond to opportunities facing these programs.

The Checklist
of Buildings, Structures, and Sites

Using the Checklist

by

ALICIA STAMM

Since 1933 the goal of the Historic American Buildings Survey (HABS) has been not only to document our nation's significant historic architecture but also to make this documentation available to the largest possible audience. It is to assist in this latter purpose that a comprehensive listing of sites and structures recorded by HABS over the last fifty years is presented here. The checklist encompasses the collections of both HABS and the Historic American Engineering Record (HAER), which was formed in 1969 to document nationally significant engineering sites. The collections include architectural measured drawings, large-format photographs, and written historical data. The checklist is not a complete catalog but a basic list generated from a complete, computerized data base that will be amended and updated on a regular basis

to reflect the changing scope of the collections and needs of their users.

This checklist is the first comprehensive guide to both the HABS and HAER collections and reflects documentation received and processed by both offices of the National Park Service as of January 1, 1982. The HABS and HAER collections are combined in one list because they complement each other and in fact often overlap. Before 1969, HABS documented many sites and structures that were of interest because of technological or engineering features rather than architectural ones. For every entry in the checklist, either a HABS or a HAER number is given, and sometimes both appear, when material related to a structure was obtained through both surveys.

The need for a single listing of the collections has been great. A comprehensive catalog of the HABS collection has not been compiled since 1941. A supplement to that complete catalog was published in 1959. Together these two volumes list 7,888 buildings, fewer than half the number included in this checklist. A catalog for the HAER collection was published in 1976. Information on more recent acquisitions to the collections has been available only through some state catalogs and card catalogs maintained at the National Park Service and Library of Congress in Washington, D.C. The present checklist includes 16,738 entries for fifty states and three territories of the United States. It is hoped that this single volume will serve architects, engineers, planners, university students and faculty, other professionals, and the general public across the country in giving them access to the drawings, photographs, and written data that make up the HABS and HAER collections.

Arrangement

The arrangement of the checklist follows the geographic arrangement of the records held at the Library of Congress. The checklist is arranged alphabetically first by state (or territory), second by county (or, in the case of Louisiana, by parish), and third by city or nearest vicinity. Independent cities, however, do not have a county entry and are arranged alphabetically at the beginning of the state. If a rural structure is not in the vicinity of a city or town, it appears alphabetically at the beginning of the appropriate county listing. Individual entries are then arranged alphabetically within a geographic location by the historic name of the structure or by the most prominent name of the structure as listed at the Library of Congress. Since many structures have more than one name, secondary names are given following the main entry. Each secondary name is also listed in its alphabetical sequence as a cross-reference entry that will refer the reader back to the main entry. If a structure does not have a historic name, its street address followed by the building type becomes the name, for example "301 Elm Street (House)" or "5000 Main Street (Commercial Building)." If a building is in a rural location and there is no specific address available, it is listed simply by building type, for example, "Maryland, Harford County, Stockton vicinity, Farm House."

Structures that are located within a historic district or a complex are listed following the main entry giving the district or complex name. In the case of a designated historic district, the structure name appears as a secondary name to the main entry—for example, the "Ufford, E. L., Building" appears under the "Strand Historic District" under Galveston, Galveston County, Texas. Complexes represent smaller groupings of related buildings, and for these both the name of the complex and the names of individual buildings are listed as part of a main entry, as in "Pennsylvania, Philadelphia County, Philadelphia, Fort Mifflin, Commissary" or "Massachusetts, Barnstable County, Barnstable, Lombard Farm, Barn." When documentation is available on only a portion of a structure or on an architectural detail only, a notation appears in parentheses following the proper name of the house to indicate this. An example is "Cooper, Thomas, House (Doorway)."

The building name (or names) is followed by the address. The address is not repeated if it is listed as the name of the structure in the main entry. If a structure has been moved, a parenthetical note follows the address stating that the structure has been either "moved to" or "moved from" another address and gives the appropriate two-letter state abbreviation and city or town. Moved structures are not cross-referenced but are entered twice, once under each location. If a structure has been moved within a city, however, it appears only once, with the alternate street address following either "moved to" or "moved from."

After the address, the HABS number or HAER number (or sometimes both) is given, followed by symbols indicating the types of documentation existing for the structure—drawings, photographs, or data—and the location of the documentation—either at the HABS/HAER office or at the Library of Congress.

Alphabetizing

Structures are listed alphabetically by the building name, for instance, "Chesterfield Blacksmith Shop." Personal names that have become part of a building name are listed with the last name first, then the first name, and then the descriptive building type, as in "Eddy, Zachariah, Law Office." If there is a rank or title attached to a name, it is entered following the surname but preceding the Christian name, and the name is alphabetized accordingly, for example, "Potter, Capt. John, House."

When an address is the name of the building, the entry is alphabetized by the street name. If the street name is numerical, it is spelled out in full, as in "1919 Twenty-first Street (House)," and alphabetized accordingly ("Twenty-first" coming under T). If a street name is preceded by "North," "South," "East," or "West," it is alphabetized first by that designation.

Descriptive adjectives—such as "Old," "Stone," or "Brick"—follow the name of the building, as in "Courthouse, Old," "House, Brick," or "Barn, Stone." Articles also follow the name of the structure, except when the name is a foreign one, for example, "Friends School, The" and "El Polvrin."

Sample Entry and Abbreviations

The elements of the sample entry and the abbreviations used are explained in the box on page 291 in sequence as they appear in the checklist.

Future Needs

This checklist of the HABS and HAER collections is meant to fulfill not only the current, urgent need for a single comprehensive list that is published and widely distributed but future needs as well. The checklist was completed from catalogs and data currently existing in the HABS/HAER office and at the Library of Congress. Data were entered into an automated computer system that will continue in use as the basis for future cataloging. The use of a computer system offers great advantages for the future management of the collections. It also has, however, some slight disadvantages. For instance, exceptions must be treated in a standard manner. Thus, territories appear as states, parishes as counties, and boroughs or townships as cities or towns in this published checklist. Certain proper names of structures had to be abbreviated to fit within the number of characters allotted for them in the computer record.

Much of the information contained in the collections has not been updated since the 1930s and 1940s when the records were first created. Since it was not possible to make on-site visits to documented structures, we ask you, the researcher, to inform us of changes. Using the automated data base, HABS/HAER staff will revise and amend information to improve and refine the collections, making their future as promising as their past has been valuable. Incorrect or outdated information found in the checklist should be reported to the Historic American Buildings Survey/Historic American Engineering Record, National Park Service, Department of the Interior, Washington, D.C. 20240.

1 ⟶ **Rhode Island**

2 ⟶ KENT COUNTY

3 ⟶ *West Warwick*
4 ⟶ **Lippitt Mill**
5 ⟶ 825 Main St.
6 ⟶ {HABS RI-338
{HAER RI-4

7 8 9 10 11

s pd L H

1. State
2. County
3. City
4. Name of building, structure, or site
5. Address
6. HABS or HAER number

HABS = Historic American Buildings Survey

HAER = Historic American Engineering Record

Each number is preceded by the Postal Service two-letter abbreviation for the state where the building, structure, or site is located, here RI for Rhode Island.

Documentation

7. s = sheets of measured drawings
8. p = photographs
9. d = data pages

Location

10. L = Library of Congress
11. H = HABS/HAER Office, National Park Service

The Checklist
of Buildings, Structures, and Sites

Alabama

AUTAUGA COUNTY

Mulberry vic.

Ivy Creek Methodist Church
State Hwy. 14
HABS AL-724   pd   L

Prattville

Coe-Swift-Fay House; see Fay, Thomas
    Avery, House

Continental Gin Company; see Pratt,
    Daniel, Cotton Gin Factory Complex

Fay, Thomas Avery, House (Coe-Swift-Fay
    House)
203 Washington St.
HABS AL-653   p   L

Pratt, Daniel, Cotton Gin Factory Complex
    (Continental Gin Company)
Autauga Creek
HABS AL-685
HAER AL-5   p   L

Pratt, Daniel, House
Autauga Creek
HABS AL-686   p   L

Smith Racing Stables
County Rd. 75
HABS AL-669   p   L

Prattville vic.

Buena Vista; see
    Montgomery-Jones-Whitaker House
Golson, John B., House; see Pope-Golson
    House
Montgomery-Jones-Whitaker House
    (Buena Vista)
County Rd. 4 (Reynolds Mill Rd.)
HABS AL-695   p   L
Pope-Alexander-Golson House; see
    Pope-Golson House
Pope-Golson House (Golson, John B.,
    House; Pope-Alexander-Golson House)
815 Shadow Ln. (moved from original
    location)
HABS AL-654   p   L

BALDWIN COUNTY

Blakely

Reingard Double House
(moved to AL, Mobile)
HABS AL-25   s pd   L

Gulf Shores vic.

Fort Morgan
Mobile Point
HABS AL-101   p   L

Point Clear

Battle House (Gunnison House)
U.S. Hwy. 98 (State Hwy. 42)
HABS AL-120   pd   L
Gunnison House; see Battle House

Stockton

House, Old; see McMillan House
Kitchen-McMillan House; see McMillan
    House
McMillan House (Kitchen-McMillan
    House; House, Old)
County Rd. 21
HABS AL-118   p   L

Tensaw

Atkinson-Till House
State Hwy. 59
HABS AL-116   p   L
Tunstall House (Woolf House)
State Hwy. 59
HABS AL-115   p   L
Woolf House; see Tunstall House

BARBOUR COUNTY

Eufaula

Alabama National Bank; see Eastern Bank
    of Alabama

Alexander-McDonald-Smartt House; see McDonald-Smartt House

Baptist Church (St. Luke's African Methodist Episcopal Church)
234 S. Van Buren St.
HABS AL-590　　　　p　L

Cato, Lewis Llewellyn, House
823 W. Barbour St.
HABS AL-554　　　　p　L

Cowan-Ramser House
441 E. Barbour St.
HABS AL-519　　　　p　L

East Alabama National Bank; see Eastern Bank of Alabama

Eastern Bank of Alabama (East Alabama National Bank; McNab Bank Building; Alabama National Bank)
201 Broad St.
HABS AL-592　　　　p　L

Ferrell's Gardens; see Irwinton Inn

Hart-Milton House
211 Eufaula St.
HABS AL-591　　　　p　L

Irwinton Inn (Tavern, The; Marshburn House; Pease Tavern; Ferrell's Gardens)
105 Riverside Dr.
HABS AL-516　　　　pd　L

Marshburn House; see Irwinton Inn

McDonald-Smartt House
(Alexander-McDonald-Smartt House)
315 N. Randolph St.
HABS AL-517　　　　pd　L

McNab Bank Building; see Eastern Bank of Alabama

Pease Tavern; see Irwinton Inn

St. Luke's African Methodist Episcopal Church; see Baptist Church

Tavern, The; see Irwinton Inn

Thomas-Wills House; see Wellborn, Dr. Levi Thomas, House

Wellborn, Dr. Levi Thomas, House
(Thomas-Wills House)
Broad St. (moved from 134 Livingston St.)
HABS AL-520　　　　p　L

BULLOCK COUNTY

High Ridge vic.

Berry House (Berry-Braswell House; Braswell, E. B., House)
County Rd. 14 (see AL, Orion vic.)
HABS AL-595　　　　p　L

Berry-Braswell House; see Berry House
Braswell, E. B., House; see Berry House

Chancey, John, House
(see Al, Orion vic.)
HABS AL-572　　　　p　L

Howe-Roughton House
County Rd. 14
HABS AL-561　　　　p　L

Peachburg

Seale, Arnold, House; see Seale-Mosley House

Seale-Mosley House (Seale, Arnold, House)
County Rd. 40 (moved from original location)
HABS AL-546　　　　p　L

Peachburg vic.

Atkinson, Octavia House
(Cunningham-Atkinson House)
(moved to AL, Mobile)(see AL, Union Springs)
HABS AL-539　　　　p　L

Cunningham-Atkinson House; see Atkinson, Octavia House

Evergreen Bower; see Walker, Col. Luther, House

Frazier, Sen. Thomas Sidney, House
(Walker-Frazier-Adams House)
County Rd. 40 (see AL, Union Springs vic.)
HABS AL-538　　　　p　L

Mulberry; see Walker, Col. Luther, House

Walker, Col. Luther, House (Evergreen Bower; Walker-Adams House; Mulberry)
County Rd. 40 (see AL, Union Springs vic.)
HABS AL-598　　　　p　L

Walker-Adams House; see Walker, Col. Luther, House

Walker-Frazier-Adams House; see Frazier, Sen. Thomas Sidney, House

Union Springs

Atkinson, Octavia, House
(Cunningham-Atkinson House)
(moved to AL, Mobile)(see AL, Peachburg vic.)
HABS AL-539　　　　p　L

Cunningham-Atkinson House; see Atkinson, Octavia, House

Foster, Mrs. Hugh, House
(Foster-Bryan-Brown House; Laurel Hill)
201 Kennon St.
HABS AL-599　　　　p　L

Foster-Bryan-Brown House; see Foster, Mrs. Hugh, House

Laurel Hill; see Foster, Mrs. Hugh, House

Union Springs vic.

Evergreen Bower; see Walker, Col. Luther, House

Frazier, Sen. Thomas Sidney, House
(Walker-Frazier-Adams House)
County Rd. 40 (see AL, Peachburg vic.)
HABS AL-538　　　　p　L

Mulberry; see Walker, Col. Luther, House

Walker, Col. Luther, House (Evergreen Bower; Walker-Adams House; Mulberry)
County Rd. 40 (see AL, Peachburg vic.)
HABS AL-598　　　　p　L

Walker-Adams House; see Walker, Col. Luther, House

Walker-Frazier-Adams House; see Frazier, Sen. Thomas Sidney, House

BUTLER COUNTY

Greenville

Beeland, Judge Henry, House; see Beeland-Stanley House

Beeland, Leavy, House; see Beeland, Leroy, House

Beeland, Leroy, House
(Dunklin-Beeland-Kendrick House; Beeland, Leavy, House)
504 Ft. Dale Rd.
HABS AL-693　　　　p　L

Beeland, R. A., House; see Dunklin, Major James, House

Beeland-Stanley House (Beeland, Judge Henry, House)
218 E. Commerce St.
HABS AL-692　　　　p　L

Burnett-Dunklin-Smith House; see Smith, Earl, House

Dunkin-Smith House; see Smith, Earl, House

Dunklin, Major James, House
(Dunklin-Beeland House; Beeland, R. A., House)
111 Herbert St.
HABS AL-688　　　　p　L

Dunklin-Beeland House; see Dunklin, Major James, House

Dunklin-Beeland-Kendrick House; see Beeland, Leroy, House

Magnolia Cemetery, Grave House; see Pine Crest Cemetery, Grave House

Pine Crest Cemetery, Grave House
(Magnolia Cemetery, Grave House)
W. Commerce St.
HABS AL-689-A　　　　p　L

Smith, Earl, House (Dunkin-Smith House; Waller House; Burnett-Dunklin-Smith House)
Commerce & Pine Sts.
HABS AL-691　　　　p　L

Waller House; see Smith, Earl, House

Greenville vic.

Crenshaw, Judge Anderson, House
(Crenshaw, Nolan, House)
County Rd. 54 (see AL, Manningham vic.)
HABS AL-690-B　　　　p　L

Crenshaw, Nolan, House; see Crenshaw, Judge Anderson, House

Crenshaw, Walter H., Plantation (House); see Crenshaw, Will, Plantation (House)

Crenshaw, Will, Plantation (House)
(Crenshaw, Walter H., Plantation (House))
County Rd. 54 (see AL, Manningham vic.)
HABS AL-690　　　　p　L

Fort Dale Cemetery, Grave Houses
State Hwy. 185
HABS AL-689-B　　　　p　L

Grave House
County Rd. 54 (see AL, Manningham vic.)
HABS AL-689-C　　　　p　L

Hartley, Joseph, House; see Tavern & Stage Inn

Palings, The; see Tavern & Stage Inn

Stagecoach Inn; see Tavern & Stage Inn

Tavern & Stage Inn (Hartley, Joseph, House; Stagecoach Inn; Palings, The)
County Rd. 58
HABS AL-694   p   L

Womack, T. Augustus (Gus) House
County Rd. 54 (see AL, Ridgeville vic.)
HABS AL-690-C   p   L

Womack-Crenshaw House
County Rd. 54 (see AL, Ridgeville vic.)
HABS AL-690-A   p   L

Manningham vic.

Crenshaw, Judge Anderson, House
(Crenshaw, Nolan, House)
County Rd. 54 (see AL, Greenville vic.)
HABS AL-690-B   p   L

Crenshaw, Nolan, House; see Crenshaw, Judge Anderson, House

Crenshaw, Walter, Plantation (House); see Crenshaw, Will, Plantation (House)

Crenshaw, Will, Plantation (House)
(Crenshaw, Walter, Plantation (House))
County Rd. 54 (see AL, Greenville vic.)
HABS AL-690   p   L

Grave House
County Rd. 54 (see AL, Greenville vic.)
HABS AL-689-C   p   L

Ridgeville

Womack, T. Augustus (Gus), House
County Rd. 54 (see AL, Greenville vic.)
HABS AL-690-C   p   L

Womack-Crenshaw House
County Rd. 54 (see AL, Greenville vic.)
HABS AL-690-A   p   L

CALHOUN COUNTY

Alexandria

Green-Woodruff House
Alexandria-Jacksonville Rd.
HABS AL-468   p   L

Anniston vic.

Aderholdt's Mill; see Mill with Water Wheel

Mill with Water Wheel (Aderholdt's Mill; Water Mill)
Aderholdt's Mill Rd. (see AL, Jacksonville vic.)
HABS AL-421   p   L

Water Mill; see Mill with Water Wheel

Jacksonville

Arnold-Rowan House
(Snow-Arnold-Rowan House)
201 Murphy St.
HABS AL-450   p   L

Crow Building; see Tavern, Old

Daugette, Dr. E. W., House (Magnolias, The; Walker-Daugette House)
601 N. Pelham Rd.
HABS AL-415   p d   L

Greenleaf, W. I., House
(Williams-Greenleaf House)
Pelham Rd.
HABS AL-417   p   L

Greenleaf's Store; see Tavern, Old

Hope House (Hotel, Old)
N. Pelham Rd. & Clinton Sts.
HABS AL-481   p   L

Hotel, Old; see Hope House

Magnolias, The; see Daugette, Dr. E. W., House

Martin, Thomas House
(McCampbell-Martin House)
N. Pelham Rd.
HABS AL-480   p   L

McCampbell-Martin House; see Martin, Thomas House

Nisbet-Weaver House; see Weaver House

Presbyterian Church
N. Chinabee & E. Clinton Sts.
HABS AL-419   s p d   L

Snow-Arnold-Rowan House; see Arnold-Rowan House

Tavern, Old (Greenleaf's Store; Crow Building)
E. Clinton & E. Square Sts.
HABS AL-416   s p d   L

Walker-Daugette House; see Daugette, Dr. E. W., House

Weaver House (Nisbet-Weaver House)
420 E. Ladiga St.
HABS AL-420   p   L

Williams-Greenleaf House; see Greenleaf, W. I., House

Wood-Crook-Treadway House; see Wood-Treadway House

Wood-Treadway House
(Wood-Crook-Treadway House)
517 N. Pelham Rd.
HABS AL-418   p   L

Jacksonville vic.

Aderholdt's Mill; see Mill with Water Wheel

Mill with Water Wheel (Aderholdt's Mill; Water Mill)
Aderholdt's Mill Rd. (see AL, Anniston vic.)
HABS AL-421   p   L

Water Mill; see Mill with Water Wheel

Oxford

Boiling Spring; see Freeman-Caver-Christian House

Caver-Christian House; see Freeman-Caver-Christian House

Freeman-Caver-Christian House (Boiling Spring; Caver-Christian House)
Upper Friendship Rd.
HABS AL-470   p   L

Snow, Dudley, House
704 Snow St.
HABS AL-465   p   L

Oxford vic.

Borders-Blackman House
DeArmanville-Choccolocco Rd.
HABS AL-471   p   L

Weaver

Kelly House
Peachburg Rd.
HABS AL-467   p   L

Weaver, D. F., House (Weaver-Rowe House)
Weaver Rd.
HABS AL-464   p   L

Weaver-Rowe House; see Weaver, D. F., House

Weaver vic.

Glover, Doctor, House (Lenlock; Glover-Pollack House)
Weaver Rd.
HABS AL-466   p   L

Glover-Pollack House; see Glover, Doctor, House

Lenlock; see Glover, Doctor, House

White Plains

Cobb, Tom, House; see Cook-Johnson House

Cook-Johnson House (Cobb, Tom, House)
HABS AL-469   p   L

CHAMBERS COUNTY

Lafayette

Andrews House (Andrews-Allen House)
S. Lafayette St. (U.S. Rt. 431)
HABS AL-553   p   L

Andrews-Allen House; see Andrews House

Goodman-Towers-Tatum House; see Tatum, A. A., House

McLemore, Betty, House
(McNamee-Kinsey-McLemore House)
342 N. Lafayette St.
HABS AL-530   p   L

McNamee-Kinsey-McLemore House; see McLemore, Betty, House

Tatum, A. A., House
(Goodman-Towers-Tatum House)
226 N. Lafayette St.
HABS AL-535   p   L

Oak Bowery

Bullard, Gen. Robert Lee, House
(Dowdell-Mathews-Bullard House)
U.S. Rt. 431 (State Rt. 37)
HABS AL-506   s p d   L

Dowdell-Mathews-Bullard House; see Bullard, Gen. Robert Lee, House

CLARKE COUNTY

Grove Hill vic.

Figures-York House; see
Vickers-Chapman-Gordon House
Vickers-Chapman-Gordon House
(Figures-York House)
State Hwy. 69
HABS AL-110   p   L

Suggsville

Wilson, Albert, House
County Rd. 35
HABS AL-109   p   L

CLEBURNE COUNTY

Edwardsville

Cleburne County Courthouse
U.S. Rt. 78
HABS AL-775   s   L

COLBERT COUNTY

Allsboro vic.

Big Bear Creek Covered Bridge
Spanning Big Bear Creek on County Rd. 7
HABS AL-361-A   p   L
Cripple Deer Creek Covered Bridge
Spanning Cripple Deer Creek on County
Rd. 1
HABS AL-361   p   L

Brick vic.

**Mt. Pleasant Cumberland Presbyterian
Meetinghouse;** see Presbyterian Church
Presbyterian Church (Mt. Pleasant
Cumberland Presbyterian Meetinghouse)
Mt. Pleasant Rd. (see AL, Leighton vic.)
HABS AL-382   p   L

Cherokee vic.

Barton Hall; see Cunningham Plantation
Buzzard Roost Covered Bridge
Old Memphis Rd. (Gaines Trace Rd.)
HABS AL-361-B   p   L
Cunningham Plantation (Barton Hall)
Old Memphis Rd. (Gaines Trace Rd.)
HABS AL-337   s p d   L

Leighton

Leckey, Hugh C., House
State Hwy. 20 & County Rd. 48
HABS AL-863   p   H
Oaks, The (Ricks, Abraham, House)
Ricks Ln.
HABS AL-362   pd   L
Ricks, Abraham, House; see Oaks, The

Leighton vic.

**Mt. Pleasant Cumberland Presbyterian
Meetinghouse;** see Presbyterian Church
Presbyterian Church (Mt. Pleasant
Cumberland Presbyterian Meetinghouse)
Mt. Pleasant Rd. (see AL, Brick vic.)
HABS AL-382   p   L

Vinson, Drury, House
County Rd. 63 (see AL, Tuscumbia vic.)
HABS AL-381   p   L

Sheffield

Barner House; see Bonner House
Bonner House (Barner House;
Winter-Barner House)
2708 Tenth Ave.
HABS AL-323   p   L
Jackson, Andrew, House; see Winston,
Anthony, House
Winston, Anthony, House (Jackson,
Andrew, House)
Eighth St. & 14th Ave. (see AL, Tuscumbia
vic.)
HABS AL-316-A   p   L
Winter-Barner House; see Bonner House

Sheffield vic.

House (Kernachan House)
County Rd. 40 (River Rd.)
HABS AL-862   p   H
Kernachan House; see House

Spring Valley vic.

Belmont (Thornton, Henry P., Plantation)
U.S. Hwy. 43 (see AL, Tuscumbia vic.)
HABS AL-388   s p   L
Thornton, Henry P., Plantation; see
Belmont

Tuscumbia

**107 & 109 East Fifth Street (Commercial
Buildings);** see Morgan House
Aycock, Tom, House
205 W. Jefferson St.
HABS AL-350   p   L
Barber's House (306 West Fifth Street
(House))
HABS AL-351   p   L
Bell-Prout-Edwards House; see Edwards
House
Carriage Factory (Young's Carriage Shop;
Post Office; Keller, Helen, Library)
Main & E. Fourth Sts.
HABS AL-315   s pd   L
Carroll, G. W., House (Carroll-Johnson
House)
801 E. North Commons
HABS AL-322   pd   L
Carroll House; see Minor House
Carroll-Johnson House; see Carroll, G. W.,
House
Christian-Lindsay House; see Lindsay, Gov.
Robert, House
City Clerk's Office; see First Methodist
Church, Old
City Fire Station; see First Methodist
Church, Old
Commercial Row
Fifth St.
HABS AL-360   p   L

Coons-Steele-Armistead House; see
Goodloe, Judith, House
Edwards House (Bell-Prout-Edwards
House)
Dickson & E. Second Sts.
HABS AL-354   p   L
First Methodist Church, Old (City Clerk's
Office; City Fire Station)
Dickson & E. Seventh Sts.
HABS AL-313   p   L
First Presbyterian Church
E. Fourth & N. Broad Sts.
HABS AL-314   s pd   L
Garmon, Kate, House; see Johnson, John,
House
Goodloe, Judith, House
(Coons-Steele-Armistead House)
406 N. Main St.
HABS AL-356   pd   L
Gresham House (Stonecroft)
608 E. Fifth St.
HABS AL-319   p   L
Houston-Abernathy-Minor House; see
Newson-Minor House
Ivy Green; see Keller, Helen, House
Johnson, John, House (Garmon, Kate,
House)
Broad St.
HABS AL-357   p   L
Jones-Winston-Rand House; see Rand,
Carl, House
Keller, Helen, House (Ivy Green; Rose &
Honeysuckle House)
300 W. North Commons
HABS AL-317   pd   L
Keller, Helen, Library; see Carriage
Factory
Lindsay, Gov. Robert, House
(Christian-Lindsay House; Tennessee
Valley Country Club)
U.S. Hwy. 72
HABS AL-312   p   L
Locust Hill; see Rather, John Daniel, House
Minor House (Carroll House)
HABS AL-384   d   L
Minor House; see Newson-Minor House
Morgan House (107 & 109 East Fifth Street
(Commercial Buildings))
HABS AL-321   p   L
Newson-Minor House (Minor House;
Houston-Abernathy-Minor House)
204 N. Main St.
HABS AL-355   p   L
Post Office; see Carriage Factory
Rand, Carl, House (Jones-Winston-Rand
House)
501 E. Third St.
HABS AL-352   p   L
Rand, Dr. R. A., House (Violet Hall)
402 N. Commons St.
HABS AL-353   pd   L

Rather, John Daniel, House (Locust Hill)
209 S. Cave St.
HABS AL-318   p   L
Rose & Honeysuckle House; see Keller, Helen, House
Stein House; see Stine House
Stine House (Young-Stine House; Stein House)
407 W. Second St.
HABS AL-349   pd   L
Stonecroft; see Gresham House
Tennessee Valley Country Club; see Lindsay, Gov. Robert, House
Violet Hall; see Rand, Dr. R. A., House
306 West Fifth Street (House); see Barber's House
Winston, William, House
North Commons St,
HABS AL-316   p   L
Young's Carriage Shop; see Carriage Factory
Young-Stine House; see Stine House

Tuscumbia vic.
Belmont (Thornton, Henry P., Plantation)
U.S. Hwy. 43 (see AL, Spring Valley vic.)
HABS AL-388   s p   L
Goodloe, Colonel, House
HABS AL-380   p   L
Thornton, Henry P., Plantation; see Belmont
Vinson, Drury, House
County Rd. 63 (see AL, Leighton vic.)
HABS AL-381   p   L
Winston, Anthony, House
Eighth St. & Fourteenth Ave. (see AL, Sheffield)
HABS AL-316-A   p   L

COVINGTON COUNTY

Andalusia vic.
Camp Chapel; see Methodist Church
Methodist Church (Camp Chapel)
Camp Blue Lake (moved from AL, Forkland)
HABS AL-256   p   L

CRENSHAW COUNTY

Luverne vic.
Grave Houses
Local Cemetery
HABS AL-689-D   p   L

Mount Ida vic.
Carlton-Autrey House; see Jenkins-Carlton-Autrey House
Jenkins-Carlton-Autrey House (Carlton-Autrey House)
County Rd. 52 (see AL, Alpine vic.)
HABS AL-449   p   L

DALLAS COUNTY

Cahaba
Barker-Kirkpatrick House; see Kirkpatrick House
Bell House (Fambro-Troy House)
First North & Oak Sts.
HABS AL-731   p   L
Crocheron House (Remains) (Crocheron-Matthews House (Remains))
Second North St.
HABS AL-728   p   L
Crocheron-Matthews House (Remains); see Crocheron House (Remains)
Duke, Captain, House; see Evans, Grace, House
Evans, Grace, House (Duke, Captain, House)
Alabama River vic.
HABS AL-729   p   L
Fambro-Troy House; see Bell House
First State Capitol Marker; see Monument
Gayle, Col. Rees D., House
Oak & First South Sts.
HABS AL-732   p   L
Kirkpatrick House (Barker-Kirkpatrick House)
Oak St.
HABS AL-727   p   L
Methodist Church
Walnut St.
HABS AL-726   s pd   L
Monument (First State Capitol Marker)
HABS AL-725   p   L
St. Luke's Episcopal Church
(moved to AL, Martin's Station/Orrville vic.)
HABS AL-734   s pd   L

Martin's Station
St. Luke's Episcopal Church
(moved from AL, Cahaba)(see AL, Orrville vic.)
HABS AL-734   s pd   L

Orrville
Craig-Wilson House
County Rd. 2
HABS AL-738   p   L
Dunaway, Ben Ellis, House (Orrville Male Academy)
State Hwy. 22
HABS AL-737   p   L
Kelley-Bland-Ward House
County Rd. 2 vic.
HABS AL-755   p   L
Milhous-Albritton House; see Mill-Albritton House
Mill-Albritton House (Milhous-Albritton House)
State Hwy. 22
HABS AL-736   p   L
Molette Houses
County Rds. 33 & 31 vic.
HABS AL-753   p   L

Orrville Male Academy; see Dunaway, Ben Ellis, House
Smith-Sutton House
State Hwy. 22
HABS AL-735   p   L

Orrville vic.
Bland House (Bland-Chestnut House)
County Rd. 11 vic.
HABS AL-749   p   L
Bland-Chestnut House; see Bland House
Cochran House (Cochran-Crumpton House; McCreary House; Crumptonia)
County Rd. 21
HABS AL-750   p   L
Cochran-Crumpton House; see Cochran House
Crumptonia; see Cochran House
McCreary House; see Cochran House
McMillan, Lewis, House
County Rd. 31
HABS AL-752   p   L
Moseley-Seal House; see Seal House
Seal House (Moseley-Seal House)
County Rd. 33 vic.
HABS AL-751   p   L
St. Luke's Episcopal Church
(moved from AL, Cahaba)(see AL, Martin's Station)
HABS AL-734   s pd   L

Selma
Beel-Bennett House (Burns-Bell House; Bell House)
412 Lauderdale Ave.
HABS AL-707   p   L
Bell House; see Beel-Bennett House
Blake, Samuel R., House; see McKee, Harvey L., House
Brantley Hotel; see St. James Hotel
504 Broad Street (House); see Pitts, L. B., House
Burns-Bell House; see Beel-Bennett House
Dawson-Vaughan House
704 Tremont St.
HABS AL-711   p   L
First Christian Church Property (House) (207 Franklin Street (House))
HABS AL-710   p   L
Franklin, H. F., House; see White-Franklin House
207 Franklin Street (House); see First Christian Church Property (House)
819 Jefferson Davis Avenue (House); see White-Franklin House
Jones, C., House (433 Lauderdale Avenue (House))
HABS AL-706   p   L
King-Welch House
607 Union St.
HABS AL-703   p   L

Kirkpatrick, Doctor, House (601
Washington Street (House))
HABS AL-709   p   L
433 Lauderdale Avenue (House); see Jones,
C., House
Mabry, A. T., House (Mabry-Jones House)
629 Tremont St.
HABS AL-705   p   L
Mabry-Jones House; see Mabry, A. T.,
House
Marks House; see Plattenburg House
Marks-Plattenburg House; see Plattenburg
House
McKee, Harvey L., House (Blake, Samuel
R., House; Suttle House)
911 Mabry St.
HABS AL-701   p   L
Morgan, Sen. John T., House; see
Morgan-Agee House
Morgan-Agee House
(Wetmore-Morgan-Agee House;
Morgan, Sen. John T., House)
719 Tremont St.
HABS AL-712   p   L
Pitts, L. B., House (504 Broad Street
(House))
HABS AL-708   p   L
Planters' Hotel; see St. James Hotel
Plattenburg House (Marks-Plattenburg
House; Marks House)
1009 N. Lapsley St.
HABS AL-702   p   L
St. James Hotel (Brantley Hotel; Planters'
Hotel; Troupe House; Warehouse)
1200 Water Ave.
HABS AL-713   p   L
Sturdivant Hall; see
Watts-Parkman-Gillman House
Sturdivant House; see
Watts-Parkman-Gillman House
Suttle House; see McKee, Harvey L., House
Troupe House; see St. James Hotel
Warehouse; see St. James Hotel
601 Washington Street (House); see
Kirkpatrick, Doctor, House
Watts-Parkman-Gillman House (Sturdivant
House; Sturdivant Hall)
713 Mabry St.
HABS AL-700   p   L
Wetmore-Morgan-Agee House; see
Morgan-Agee House
White-Franklin House (Franklin, H. F.,
House; 819 Jefferson Davis Avenue
(House))
HABS AL-704   p   L

Selma vic.

Harper, Doctor, House
(Harrison-Hunter-Harper House; Oaks,
The)
State Hwy. 219 & County Rd. 344
HABS AL-754   p   L
Harrison-Hunter-Harper House; see
Harper, Doctor, House

Kenan, Dan, House
Summerfield Rd. (County Rd. 37)
HABS AL-739   p   L
Oaks, The; see Harper, Doctor, House

Summerfield

Blacksmith Shop
Centenary & Main Sts.
HABS AL-763   p   L
Boys' Methodist College (Summerfield
College, Boys' Dormitory; Centenary
Institute, Boys' Dormitory)
Centenary & Main Sts.
HABS AL-746   p   L
Centenary Institute, Boys' Dormitory; see
Boys' Methodist College
Centenary Institute, Dr. Hudson Building;
see Summerfield College, Dr. Hudson
Building
Centenary Institute, Dr. Jackson Building;
see Summerfield College, Dr. Jackson
Building
Centenary Institute, Main Building; see
Summerfield College, Main Building
Centenary Institute, Music Building; see
Summerfield College, Music Building
Childers-Tate House
Centenary St.
HABS AL-730   p   L
Hudson Summer House (Moore-Hudson
House)
County Rd. 37
HABS AL-744   p   L
King House (Mitchell-King House;
Mitchell House)
Centenary St.
HABS AL-758   p   L
Main Street (Bank Building)
HABS AL-757   p   L
Methodist Church; see Methodist Episcopal
Church
Methodist Episcopal Church (Methodist
Church)
College St.
HABS AL-748   p   L
Methodist Orphans' Home; see
Summerfield College, Main Building
Mitchell House; see King House
Mitchell-King House; see King House
Moore House (Swift-Moore-Cottingham
House)
Persimmon St.
HABS AL-747   p   L
Moore-Hudson House; see Hudson
Summer House
Sturdivant-Moore-Hartley House
Centenary & Main Sts.
HABS AL-745   p   L
Summerfield College, Boys' Dormitory; see
Boys' Methodist College

Summerfield College, Dr. Hudson Building
(Centenary Institute, Dr. Hudson
Building)
College St.
HABS AL-742   p   L
Summerfield College, Dr. Jackson Building
(Centenary Institute, Dr. Jackson
Building)
Main & College Sts.
HABS AL-743   p   L
Summerfield College, Main Building
(Centenary Institute, Main Building;
Methodist Orphans' Home)
Main & College Sts.
HABS AL-741   p   L
Summerfield College, Music Building
(Centenary Institute, Music Building)
Main & College Sts.
HABS AL-740   s p d   L
Swift-Moore-Cottingham House; see
Moore House

ELMORE COUNTY

Elmore vic.

Fitzpatrick, Gov. Benjamin, House (Oak
Grove)
State Rt. 14 vic.
HABS AL-697   p   L
Oak Grove; see Fitzpatrick, Gov. Benjamin,
House

Robinson Springs

Methodist Church (Robinson Springs
United Methodist Church)
State Rt. 143
HABS AL-682   p   L
Methodist Parsonage, Old
State Rt. 143
HABS AL-698   p   L
Robinson Springs United Methodist
Church; see Methodist Church

Wetumpka

Airey, J. Bruce, House (Seaman-Airey
House)
1202 W. Tuskeena St.
HABS AL-659   p   L
Baptist Church (First Baptist Church)
205 W. Bridge St.
HABS AL-657   p   L
Bateman, Florence Golson, House; see
Bates-Jesse House
Bates-Jesse House (Northrup-Bateman
House; Bateman, Florence Golson,
House; Bates-Jesse-Ensken House)
311 Government St.
HABS AL-660   p   L
Bates-Jesse-Ensken House; see Bates-Jesse
House
Bradford House (Bradford-Stowe House)
401 W. Main St.
HABS AL-664   p   L
Bradford-Stowe House; see Bradford House

Cantelow, Laura, House (207 West
Tuskeena Street (House); Fitzpatrick,
Kelly, Birthplace)
HABS AL-663   p   L

First Baptist Church; see Baptist Church

Fitzpatrick, Kelly, Birthplace; see
Cantelow, Laura, House

Fitzpatrick, Kelly House
(Trimble-Fitzpatrick House)
Autauga St.
HABS AL-658   pd   L

McQueen-McCullars House; see Tavern,
Old

Methodist Church; see Wetumpka
Methodist Church

Northrup-Bateman House; see Bates-Jesse
House

Presbyterian Church; see Wetumpka
Presbyterian Church

Seaman-Airey House; see Airey, J. Bruce,
House

Smoot, E. L., House
705 Mansion St.
HABS AL-661   p   L

Tavern, Old (McQueen-McCullars House)
Broad & W. Bridge Sts.
HABS AL-662   p   L

Trimble-Fitzpatrick House; see Fitzpatrick,
Kelly House

207 West Tuskeena Street (House); see
Cantelow, Laura, House

Wetumpka Methodist Church (Methodist
Church)
306 W. Tuskeena St.
HABS AL-655   p   L

Wetumpka Presbyterian Church
(Presbyterian Church)
W. Bridge & N. Bridge Sts.
HABS AL-656   pd   L

Wetumpka vic.

Bullard, John, House
(Bullard-Brannon-Owen House;
Sugarberry Hill; Henderson House;
Tennessee Place)
Harrogate Springs Rd. vic.
HABS AL-665   pd   L

Bullard-Brannon-Owen House; see Bullard,
John, House

Henderson House; see Bullard, John, House

Sugarberry Hill; see Bullard, John, House

Tennessee Place; see Bullard, John, House

FAYETTE COUNTY

Fayette vic.

McCaleb-Hollingsworth Mill (McCaleb's
Old Mill)
Mill Creek (see AL, Herrick)
HABS AL-390   p   L

McCaleb's Old Mill; see
McCaleb-Hollingsworth Mill

Herrick

McCaleb's Old Mill; see
McCaleb-Hollingsworth House

McCaleb-Hollingsworth House (McCaleb's
Old Mill)
Mill Creek (see AL, Fayette vic.)
HABS AL-390   p   L

GREENE COUNTY

Boligee

Beth Salem Presbyterian Church
County Rd. 1
HABS AL-282   pd   L

Boligee vic.

Boligee Hill (Myrtlewood; Hays House)
U.S. Rt. 11 (see AL, Eutaw vic.)
HABS AL-209   pd   L

Gould House; see Hill of Howth

Hays House; see Boligee Hill

Hill of Howth (McKee-Gould House;
Gould House)
County Rd. 19
HABS AL-208   pd   L

McKee-Gould House; see Hill of Howth

Myrtlewood; see Boligee Hill

Weston (House, Smokehouse &
Schoolhouse)
U.S. Rt. 11 & County Rd. 19 vic.
HABS AL-272   p   L

Clinton

George Washington Lodge Number 24; see
Masonic Temple

Masonic Temple (George Washington
Lodge Number 24; Store)
State Rts. 14 & 39 (moved from AL, Erie)
HABS AL-229   pd   L

Store; see Masonic Temple

Erie

George Washington Lodge Number 24; see
Masonic Temple

Masonic Temple (George Washington
Lodge Number 24; Store)
(moved to AL, Clinton)
HABS AL-229   pd   L

Store; see Masonic Temple

Eutaw

Alexander-Webb House; see
Webb-Alexander House

Anthony, David Rinehart, House; see
Wynne House

Banks, J. O., House & Smokehouse
(Shawver-Coleman-Banks House &
Smokehouse)
Springfield Ave. & Pickens St.
HABS AL-246   pd   L

Clark-Malone House
243 Wilson St.
HABS AL-240   pd   L

Clark-Smith House; see Smith, A. W.,
House

Dunlap, C. W., House
(Wilson-Herndon-Dunlap House)
237 Wilson Ave.
HABS AL-270   p   L

Eutaw Female Academy (Eutaw Female
College; Mesopotamia Female Seminary;
Mesopotamia Academy; Miles College,
Dormitory)
Main St. & Wilson Ave. (moved from
original site)
HABS AL-243   pd   L

Eutaw Female College; see Eutaw Female
Academy

First Presbyterian Church
Main St. & Wilson Ave.
HABS AL-252   pd   L

Greene County Courthouse
Main & Boligee Sts., Prairie & Monroe
Aves.
HABS AL-218   pd   L

Kirksey, Dr. H. A., House; see Kirkwood

Kirkwood (Kirksey, Dr. H. A., House)
Mesopotomia St. & Kirkwood Dr.,
HABS AL-210   pd   L

Law Office, Old
Main St.
HABS AL-273   p   L

Mesopotamia Academy; see Eutaw Female
Academy

Mesopotamia Female Seminary; see Eutaw
Female Academy

Miles College, Dormitory; see Eutaw
Female Academy

Perkins-Spencer House (Spencer-Perkins
House)
Spencer St.
HABS AL-241   pd   L

Reese-Lucius House
242 Wilson Ave.
HABS AL-242   pd   L

Shawver-Coleman-Banks House &
Smokehouse; see Banks, J. O., House &
Smokehouse

Smith, A. W., House (Clark-Smith House)
220 Main St.
HABS AL-251   pd   L

Spencer-Perkins House; see
Perkins-Spencer House

Webb-Alexander House (Alexander-Webb
House)
309 Main St.
HABS AL-245   pd   L

White-McGiffert House & Office
Mesopotamia St.
HABS AL-269   p   L

Wilson-Herndon-Dunlap House; see
Dunlap, C. W., House

Winn House; see Wynne House

Wynne House (Anthony, David Rinehart,
House; Winn House)
307 Wilson Ave.
HABS AL-244   pd   L

Eutaw vic.

Boligee Hill (Myrtlewood; Hays House)
U.S. Rt. 11 vic. (see AL, Boligee Vic.)
HABS AL-209   p d   L
Hays House; see Boligee Hill
Myrtlewood; see Boligee Hill

Forkland

Brewer, H. B., House
     (Lewis-Parker-Gilmore House)
County Rd. 4
HABS AL-258   p   L
Episcopal Church (St. John's Episcopal
     Church; St. John's-in-the-Prairies)
County Rd. 4 (moved from original
     location)
HABS AL-255   p   L
Glover, Virginia, House
County Rds. 19 & 4
HABS AL-253   p   L
Glover, William, House; see Tavern, The
Inn, Old; see Tavern, The
Levy-Glover Store (Store)
County Rds. 19 & 4
HABS AL-254   p   L
Lewis-Parker-Gilmore House; see Brewer,
     H. B., House
Methodist Church
County Rd. 19 (moved to AL, Andalusia
     vic.)
HABS AL-256   p   L
Methodist Parsonage
County Rd. 4
HABS AL-256-A   p   L
St. John's Episcopal Church; see Episcopal
     Church
St. John's-in-the-Prairies; see Episcopal
     Church
Store; see Levy-Glover Store
Tavern, The (Glover, William, House; Inn,
     Old)
County Rd. 19
HABS AL-259   p   L

Forkland vic.

Fair Hill; see Perrin-Willis House
Glen Alpine; see McAlpine House
Glover-Legare House; see Rosemount

McAlpine House (Glen Alpine)
F. A. S. Rd. 1306 (see AL, Watsonia)
HABS AL-281   p   L

Perrin-Willis House (Fair Hill)
County Rd. 19 (see AL, Watsonia)
HABS AL-280   p   L

Rosemount (Glover-Legare House)
County Rd. 19
HABS AL-212   s pd   L

Strawberry Hill Plantation (Walton,
     William, House)
U.S. Rt. 43
HABS AL-271   pd   L

Thornhill Plantation (Thornton Plantation
     House)
County Rd. 19 (see AL, Watsonia)
HABS AL-238   s pd   L
Thornton Plantation House; see Thornhill
     Plantation
Walton, William, House; see Strawberry
     Hill Plantation

Watsonia

Fair Hill; see Perrin-Willis House
Glen Alpine; see McAlpine House
McAlpine House (Glen Alpine)
F. A. S. Rd. 1306 (see AL, Forkland vic.)
HABS AL-281   p   L
Perrin-Willis House (Fair Hill)
County Rd. 19 (see AL, Forkland vic.)
HABS AL-280   p   L
Thornhill Plantation (Thornton Plantation
     House)
County Rd. 19 (see AL, Forkland vic.)
HABS AL-238   s pd   L
Thornton Plantation House; see Thornhill
     Plantation

HALE COUNTY

Gallion

Gracey-Spencer Mansion & Outbuildings;
     see Waldwic, House & Outbuildings
Spencer House & Outbuildings; see
     Waldwic, House & Outbuildings
Waldwic, House & Outbuildings
     (Gracey-Spencer Mansion &
     Outbuildings; Spencer House &
     Outbuildings)
State Rt. 69
HABS AL-260   p   L

Greensboro

Carson, Doctor, House; see Seay, Gov.
     Thomas, House
Derrick House (Drake-Northrup House;
     Stickney-Northrup House)
603 E. Main St.
HABS AL-250   p   L
Drake-Northrup House; see Derrick House
Erwin, Cadwallader, House; see Glencairn
Gayle, Gov., House; see Southern
     University, Chancellor's House
Gayle-Hobson-Tunstall House
1801 W. Main St.
HABS AL-232   pd   L
Gayle-Locke House
University Ave. (College St.)
HABS AL-278   p   L
Glencairn (Erwin, Cadwallader, House)
Tuscaloosa St.
HABS AL-266   pd   L

Greenwood; see Pickens, W. C., House

Hannah, Dr. Robert C., House
Church & South Sts.
HABS AL-275   p   L

Hobson, Adm. Richmond Pearson, House;
     see Magnolia Grove
Jackson House (Jackson-Locke House)
Demopolis St.
HABS AL-287   p   L
Jackson-Locke House; see Jackson House
Japonica Path; see Knight House
Johndston-Torbert House; see Torbert,
     Judge W. E., House
Knight House (Norris-Smaw House;
     Japonica Path; Smaw House; Withers,
     Louise, House)
512 Main St.
HABS AL-220   pd   L
Lewis-Murphy-Stewart House; see Webb
     House
Magnolia Grove (Hobson, Adm. Richmond
     Pearson, House)
1002 Hobson St.
HABS AL-219   s pd   L
Magnolia Hall; see McCrary-Otts House
McCrary-Otts House (Magnolia Hall; Otts,
     J. W., House)
805 Otts St.
HABS AL-265   s pd   L
Methodist Hospital; see Southern
     University, Chancellor's House
Moore, Col. Sydenham, House; see Pickens,
     W. C., House
Multa Flora; see Webb House
Norris-Smaw House; see Knight House
Otts, J. W., House; see McCrary-Otts
     House
Otts, Lee, House; see
     Shackelford-McCrary-Otts House
Pickens, W. C., House (Greenwood; Moore,
     Col. Sydenham, House; Rothenberg, E.
     G., House)
2201 Main St.
HABS AL-235   p   L
Rothenberg, E. G., House; see Pickens, W.
     C., House
Seay, Gov. Thomas, House (Vaughn, J. A.,
     House; Carson, Doctor, House)
E. Main & Whelan Sts.
HABS AL-234   pd   L

Shackelford-McCrary-Otts House (Otts,
     Lee, House)
901 Centreville St.
HABS AL-274   pd   L

Smaw House; see Knight House

Southern University, Chancellor's House
     (Methodist Hospital; Gayle, Gov.,
     House)
College St.
HABS AL-277   p   L

Southern University, Old
University Ave. (College St.)
HABS AL-221   pd   L

Stickney-Northrup House; see Derrick
     House

Torbert, Judge W. E., House
(Johndston-Torbert House)
1101 South St.
HABS AL-286   p   L
Vaughn, J. A., House; see Seay, Gov.
Thomas, House
Webb House (Multa Flora;
Lewis-Murphy-Stewart House)
520 Main St.
HABS AL-289   pd   L
Withers, Louise, House; see Knight House

Greensboro vic.

Cedarwood (Stickney, Joseph Blodgett,
House)
(moved to AL, Woodland)(see AL,
Moundville vic.)
HABS AL-843   s   L H
Stickney, Joseph Blodgett, House; see
Cedarwood
Tinker House (Columns)
HABS AL-220-A   pd   L

Moundville vic.

Cedarwood (Stickney, Joseph Blodgett,
House)
(moved to AL, Woodland)(see AL,
Greensboro vic.)
HABS AL-843   s   H
Stickney, Joseph Blodgett, House; see
Cedarwood
Whatley, J. W., House (Woodland)
State Rt. 69
HABS AL-279   p   L
Woodland; see Whatley, J. W., House

Newbern

Baptist Church
State Rt. 61
HABS AL-237   pd   L
Presbyterian Church
State Rt. 61
HABS AL-288   pd   L
Walthalia; see Walthall House
Walthall House (Walthalia)
State Rt. 61
HABS AL-215   pd   L

Prairieville

Episcopal Church (St. Andrew's Episcopal
Church)
U.S. Rt. 80
HABS AL-291   p   L
St. Andrew's Episcopal Church; see
Episcopal Church

Sawyerville vic.

Pickens, Gov. Samuel, House (Umbria;
Sledge House)
State Rt. 14
HABS AL-236   s pd   L
Sledge House; see Pickens, Gov. Samuel,
House
Umbria; see Pickens, Gov. Samuel, House

HENRY COUNTY

Abbeville

Oates-Danzey House
W. Washington & Trawick Sts.
HABS AL-523   p   L

Columbia vic.

Dunwoody, S. M., House
Abbeville Hwy. (see AL, Forkland vic.)
HABS AL-579   p   L

Haleburg vic.

Fluker, Col. Baldwin M., House
Abbie Ridge Rd. (see AL, Shorterville)
HABS AL-566   p   L

Shorterville

Chitley House
River Rd. (County Rd. 97)
HABS AL-575   p   L
Fluker, Col. Baldwin M., House
Abbie Ridge Rd.
HABS AL-566   p   L
Irwin-McAllister House
Ft. Gaines Hwy.
HABS AL-524   p   L
Smith, Bartlett, House
River Rd. (County Rd. 97)(see AL,
Haleburg vic.)
HABS AL-544   p   L

Shorterville vic.

Smith, Bartlett, House
River Rd. (County Rd. 97)
HABS AL-544   p   L

HOUSTON COUNTY

Columbia

Bowden, Sam, Hotel; see Bowden, Tom,
House
Bowden, Tom, House (Bowden, Sam,
Hotel)
Greenwood St.
HABS AL-580   p   L
McGriff, T. P., House; see Taylor, J. B.,
House
Taylor, J. B., House (McGriff, T. P., House;
Taylor-McGriff House)
Washington St.
HABS AL-565   p   L
Taylor-McGriff House; see Taylor, J. B.,
House
Teague-Regell House
South & Washington Sts.
HABS AL-567   p   L

Forkland vic.

Dunwoody, S. M., House
Abbeville Hwy. (see AL, Columbia vic.)
HABS AL-579   p   L

Gordon

Britt-Williams-Borders House
Greenwood St.
HABS AL-568   p   L

Gordon vic.

Nunnley-Bowden House
State Rt. 95
HABS AL-569   p   L

JACKSON COUNTY

Bridgeport

Bridgeport Swing Span Bridge
Tennessee River
HAER AL-7   pd   H

JEFFERSON COUNTY

Birmingham

Arlington (Mudd-Munger House; Munger
House)
331 Cotton Ave., SW
HABS AL-424   pd   L
Hanover Circle
HABS AL-873   d   H
Mill, The Old
2780 Mountain Brook Pwy.
HABS AL-872   d   H
Mudd-Munger House; see Arlington
Munger House; see Arlington
Sloss-Sheffield Steel & Iron Company,
Furnaces
HAER AL-3   s pd   L H
Smith House; see Walker House
Walker House (Smith House;
Walker-Smith House)
300 Center St.
HABS AL-425   pd   L
Walker-Smith House; see Walker House
Worthington, Benjamin Pinckney, House
Sixth Ave South
HABS AL-426   p   L

Woodward

Woodward Iron Company
Opossum Creek vic.
HAER AL-4   d   H

LAMAR COUNTY

Crews Depot

Bankhead, George, House
(Bankhead-Crews House)
Old Military Rd.
HABS AL-397   p   L
Bankhead-Crews House; see Bankhead,
George, House

Sulligent

Bankhead, James Greer, House (Forest
Home)
U.S. Rt. 278
HABS AL-391   p   L
Forest Home; see Bankhead, James Greer,
House

LAUDERDALE COUNTY

Center Star vic.

Cunningham House (first); see
Taylor-Cunningham House (first)
Cunningham House (second); see
Taylor-Cunningham House (second)
Cunningham, Jonathan B., House; see
Taylor-Cunningham House (second)
Taylor-Cunningham House (first)
(Cunningham House (first))
Bellevue Rd. (see AL, Rogersville vic.)
HABS AL-377-A   p   L
Taylor-Cunningham House (second)
(Cunningham House (second);
Cunningham, Jonathan B., House)
Bellevue Rd. (see AL, Rogersville vic.)
HABS AL-377-B   pd   L

Florence

Ashcraft House (Irvine, James Bennington,
House)
461 N. Pine St.
HABS AL-358   pd   L
Coulter-McFarland House; see McFarland,
Mary, House
Courtview (Foster-Rogers House; Rogers
Hall)
505 N. Court St., Univ. of N. Alabama
Campus
HABS AL-329   s pd   L
First Presbyterian Church
E. Mobile St.
HABS AL-328   pd   L H
Foster-Rogers House; see Courtview
Hawkins-Sample House (Sample, Mattie,
House)
219 Hermitage Dr.
HABS AL-326   pd   L
Irvine House (Simpson-Irvine House)
459 N. Court St.
HABS AL-332   pd   L H
Irvine, James Bennington, House; see
Ashcraft House
Lambeth House (Pope's Tavern)
203 Hermitage Dr.
HABS AL-334   pd   L
Mapleton; see McFarland, Mary, House
McFarland, Mary, House (Mapleton;
Coulter-McFarland House)
420 S. Pine St.
HABS AL-376   p   L
Patton, Gov. Robert, House; see
Sweetwater
Patton-Perry House; see Perry House
Perry House (Patton-Perry House)
N. Pine & Tuscaloosa Sts.
HABS AL-359   pd   L
Pope's Tavern; see Lambeth House
Rogers Hall; see Courtview
Sample, Mattie, House; see
Hawkins-Sample House
Simpson, John, House; see Simpson, Will,
House

Simpson, Will, House (Simpson, John,
House)
112 S. Pine St.
HABS AL-330   pd   L
Simpson-Irvine House; see Irvine House
Sweetwater (Patton, Gov. Robert, House)
Sweetwater Ave. & Florence Blvd.
HABS AL-333   p   L

Florence vic.

Forks of Cypress, The (Jackson Plantation
House)
Jackson Rd. vic.
HABS AL-375   s pd   L
Hood, James, House (Woodlawn;
Woodland)
County Rd. 14 & Savannah Hwy.
HABS AL-331   pd   L
Jackson Plantation House; see Forks of
Cypress, The
Woodland; see Hood, James, House
Woodlawn; see Hood, James, House

Rogersville vic.

Cunningham House (first); see
Taylor-Cunningham House (first)
Cunningham House (second); see
Taylor-Cunningham House (second)
Cunningham, Jonathan B., House; see
Taylor-Cunningham House (second)
Taylor-Cunningham House (first)
(Cunningham House (first))
Bellevue Rd. (see AL, Center Star vic.)
HABS AL-377-A   p   L
Taylor-Cunningham House (second)
(Cunningham House (second);
Cunningham, Jonathan B., House)
Bellevue Rd. (see AL, Center Star vic.)
HABS AL-377-B   pd   L
Weaver, Adam, Log House
U.S. Hwy. 72
HABS AL-374   pd   L

LAWRENCE COUNTY

Courtland

Baker-Campbell House; see Campbell
House
Campbell House (Baker-Campbell House;
Tennessee Street (House))
State Hwy. 20
HABS AL-383   s p   L
Tennessee Street (House); see Campbell
House

Courtland vic.

Bride's Hill
County Rd. 43
HABS AL-865   p   H

Rocky Hill (Saunders, Col. James Edmonds,
House)
State Hwy. 20
HABS AL-311   pd   L

Saunders, Col. James Edmonds, House; see
Rocky Hill

Moulton

Lawrence County Courthouse
Courthouse Square
HABS AL-310   s pd   L H

Town Creek vic.

Goode, Freeman, House; see
Saunders-Goode-Hall House
Hall House; see Saunders-Goode-Hall
House
Saunders-Goode-Hall House (Hall House;
Goode, Freeman, House)
State Hwy. 101
HABS AL-324   pd   L

Wheeler Station

Home Sweet Home; see Wheeler, Gen.
Joseph, House (& Later House)
Pond Spring; see Wheeler, Gen. Joseph,
House (& Later House)
**Wheeler, Gen. Joseph, House (& Later
House)** (Home Sweet Home; Pond
Spring)
State Hwy. 20
HABS AL-347   s pd   L

LEE COUNTY

Auburn

Cauthen House (Perry-Cauthen House)
E. Drake Ave.
HABS AL-551   p   L
Drake-Samford House
449 N. Gay St.
HABS AL-503   p   L
Holliday-Carey House
(Kidd-Holliday-Carey House)
360 N. College St.
HABS AL-540   s pd   L
Jones Hotel; see McElhaney House
Kidd-Holliday-Carey House; see
Holliday-Carey House
McElhaney Hotel; see McElhaney House
McElhaney House (McElhaney Hotel;
Jones Hotel)
135 N. College St.
HABS AL-550   p   L
Meadows House
342 N. College St.
HABS AL-582   p   L
Perry-Cauthen House; see Cauthen House

Auburn vic.

Casey Homestead; see Frazier-Brown
House
Frazier-Brown House (Noble Hall; Casey
Homestead)
Shelton Mill Rd.
HABS AL-502   s p   L
Moore-Whatley House
Moore's Mill Rd.
HABS AL-501   s pd   L

Noble Hall; see Frazier-Brown House

Chewacla

Chewacla Limeworks
Limekiln Rd. (see AL, Opelika vic.)
HABS AL-509   p L

Gold Hill

Ellington, James, House (Gold Hill)
Oak Bowery Rd. vic.
HABS AL-581   p L
Gold Hill; see Ellington, James, House

Loachapoka

Baptist Church
Stage Rd.
HABS AL-512   s pd L

Loachapoka vic.

Hammack Plantation House
Waverly Rd.
HABS AL-513   s pd L

Mount Jefferson

Methodist Church (abandoned) (Mount
    Jefferson Methodist Church)
U.S. Rt. 431 (see AL, Opelika vic.)
HABS AL-505   p L
Mount Jefferson Methodist Church; see
    Methodist Church (abandoned)
Tucker-Fincher House
    (Wheat-Tucker-Fincher House)
U.S. Rt. 431 (see AL, Opelika vic.)
HABS AL-878   p L
Wheat-Tucker-Fincher House; see
    Tucker-Fincher House

Notasulga vic.

Le Sueur's Mill
Ropes Creek
HABS AL-537   p L

Opelika vic.

Chewacla Limeworks
Limekiln Rd. (see AL, Chewacla)
HABS AL-509   p L
Methodist Church (abandoned) (Mount
    Jefferson Methodist Church)
U.S. Rt. 431 (see AL, Mount Jefferson)
HABS AL-505   p L
Moffitt's Mill
County Rd. 12
HABS AL-507   s pd L
Mount Jefferson Methodist Church; see
    Methodist Church (abandoned)
Spring Villa
County Rd. 36 (Spring Villa Rd.)
HABS AL-508   s pd L
Tucker-Fincher House
    (Wheat-Tucker-Fincher House)
U.S. Rt. 431 (see AL, Mount Jefferson)
HABS AL-878   p L
Wheat-Tucker-Fincher House; see
    Tucker-Fincher House

LIMESTONE COUNTY

Athens

Athens Agricultural School Building; see
    Donnell, Father Robert, House
Athens College, Founder's Hall (Athens
    College, Main Building; Athens Female
    College, Main Building)
Beaty St.
HABS AL-301   s pd L
Athens College, Main Building; see Athens
    College, Founder's Hall
Athens Female College, Main Building; see
    Athens College, Founder's Hall
Beaty-Mason House (Mason, J. G. & Mary,
    House)
211 S. Beaty St.
HABS AL-306   s pd L
Cedars, Thee
E. Pryor St.
HABS AL-368   p L
Coman Hall; see
    Jones-Coman-Westmoreland House
Donnell, Father Robert, House (Athens
    Agricultural School Building)
601 S. Clinton St.
HABS AL-367   p L
Houston, Gov. George S., House
101 Houston St.
HABS AL-341   pd L
Jones-Coman-Westmoreland House
    (Westmoreland House; Coman Hall)
517 S. Clinton St.
HABS AL-338   pd L
Mason, J. G. & Mary, House; see
    Beaty-Mason House
Masonic Hall, Old
Monroe & E. Hobbs Sts.
HABS AL-305   s pd L
Pettus House (Sloss-Pettus House)
N. Beaty & Hobbs Sts.
HABS AL-340   p L
Pryor, Frances Snow, House & Office
405 N. Jefferson St.
HABS AL-304   s pd L
Richardson, Dr. R. H., House
401 S. Clinton St.
HABS AL-370   p L
Sloss-Pettus House; see Pettus House

Vasser House; see Vining-Wood-Vasser
    House

Vining-Wood-Vasser House (Vasser House)
301 E. Washington St.
HABS AL-379   p L

Walker, Judge William Harrison, House
309 E. Clinton St.
HABS AL-371   p L

Westmoreland House; see
    Jones-Coman-Westmoreland House

Athens vic.

Cotton Hill; see Rowe, Jack, House

Rowe, Jack, House (Cotton Hill)
Brown's Ferry Rd. vic. (see AL, Mooresville)
HABS AL-343   pd L

Belle Mina

Belle Mina; see Bibb, Gov. Thomas, House
Bibb, Gov. Thomas, House (Belle Mina)
County Rd. 71
HABS AL-303   s pd L

Mooresville

Cotton Hill (Rowe, Jack, House)
Brown's Ferry Rd. vic. (see AL, Athens
    Vic.)
HABS AL-343   pd L
High Street (Old Tavern)
HABS AL-308   s pd L
Hundley House (Hundley-Minor House)
Market St.
HABS AL-369   p L
Hundley-Minor House; see Hundley House
Peebles-Zeitler-McCrary House; see
    Zeitler, Henry, House
Rowe, Jack, House; see Cotton Hill
Zeitler, Henry, House
    (Peebles-Zeitler-McCrary House)
High St.
HABS AL-302   p L

LOWNDES COUNTY

Benton

Masonic Hall
Second & Church Sts.
HABS AL-756   p L

Burkville vic.

Magnolia Crest; see Stone-McCarty House
Stone-McCarty House (Magnolia Crest)
County Rd. 40
HABS AL-652   p L

Lowndesboro

Boxwood; see Reese, Mary, House
Cottage, The; see Lewis, Dixon H., House
Episcopal Church; see St. Paul's Episcopal
    Church
Gordon, F. J., House; see Williams-Bragg
    House
Hagood House; see Haygood House
Haygood House (Hagood House;
    Meadowlawn; Thomas-Hagood House)
State Hwy. 97 (County Rd. 29)
HABS AL-678   p L
Homestead, Old; see Lewis, Francis, House
Howard House (Lewis-Cilley-Howard
    House)
State Hwy. 97 (County Rd. 29)
HABS AL-679   p L
James, E. L., House; see Lewis, Dixon H.,
    House

Lewis, Dixon H., House (Cottage, The;
James, E. L., House; Lewis-Jones House;
Lewis-Hall-James House)
State Hwy. 97 (County Rd. 29)
HABS AL-670   p   L

Lewis, Francis, House (Homestead, Old)
State Hwy. 97 (County Rd. 29)
HABS AL-671   p   L

Lewis-Cilley-Howard House; see Howard
House

Lewis-Hall-James House; see Lewis, Dixon
H., House

Lewis-Jones House; see Lewis, Dixon H.,
House

**Lowndesboro Female Institute, President's
House;** see Reese, Mary, House

Meadowlawn; see Haygood House

Meadows-Powell House; see Powell House

Methodist Church, Old (Negro Methodist
Church; St. James United Methodist
Church)
State Hwy. 97 (County Rd. 29)
HABS AL-651   p   L

Mockingbird Place; see Powell House

Negro Methodist Church; see Methodist
Church, Old

Powell House (Mockingbird Place;
Meadows-Powell House)
State Hwy. 97 (County Rd. 29)
HABS AL-681   p   L

Presbyterian Church
State Hwy. 97 (County Rd. 29)
HABS AL-687   p   L

Red Church, The; see St. Paul's Episcopal
Church

Reese, Mary, House (Boxwood;
Lowndesboro Female Institute,
President's House)
State Hwy. 97 (County Rd. 29)
HABS AL-677   p   L

St. James United Methodist Church; see
Methodist Church, Old

St. Paul's Episcopal Church (Episcopal
Church; Red Church, The)
State Hwy. 97 (County Rd. 29)
HABS AL-674   p   L

Thomas-Hagood House; see Haygood
House

Tyson, Archibald, House
State Hwy. 97 (County Rd. 29)
HABS AL-672   p   L

Williams-Bragg House (Gordon, F. J.,
House)
State Hwy. 97 (County Rd. 29)
HABS AL-673   p   L

Lowndesboro vic.

Dicksonia; see Turner-Dickson House

Meadows, A. W., House; see
Wooten-Meadows House

Rosewood; see Wooten-Meadows House

Turner-Dickson House (Dicksonia)
State Hwy. 97 (County Rd. 29)
HABS AL-676   pd   L

Wooten-Meadows House (Rosewood;
Meadows, A. W., House)
State Hwy. 97 (County Rd. 29)
HABS AL-680   p   L

MACON COUNTY

Tuskegee

Band Cottage; see Foundry & Blacksmith
Shop

Callaway, C. J., House; see
Hunter-Callaway House

Carr, W. B., House (301 Maple Street
(House); Martin House)
HABS AL-536   p   L

Carver Museum (Tuskegee Institute
National Historic Site)
Tuskegee Institute Campus
HABS AL-876   s   H

Cobb House (Foster-Cobb-Laslie House)
504 E. Main St.
HABS AL-541   s pd   L

Dowdell, Rev. Lewis Flournoy, House; see
Rush-Thornton House

First Methodist Church
S. Main & Oaks Sts
HABS AL-874   d   L

Foster-Cobb-Laslie House; see Cobb House

Foundry & Blacksmith Shop (Band
Cottage)
Tuskegee Institute Campus
HABS AL-868   s   H

Grey Columns (Tuskegee Institute National
Historic Site)
Tuskegee Institute Campus
HABS AL-875   s   H

Grey Columns; see Varner-Alexander
House

Harris-Wadsworth House
615 W. Main St.
HABS AL-533   p   L

Hunter-Callaway House (Callaway, C. J.,
House)
811 N. Maple St.
HABS AL-559   p   L

Johnston-Abercrombie-Lamar House; see
Lamar, G. Y., House

Lamar, G. Y., House
(Johnston-Abercrombie-Lamar House;
Vason, Doctor, House)
U.S. Hwy. 29 (State Hwy. 15)
HABS AL-532   p   L

301 Maple Street (House); see Carr, W. B.,
House

Martin House; see Carr, W. B., House

Oaks, The (Tuskegee Institute National
Historic Site)
Tuskegee Institute Campus
HABS AL-877   s   H

Rush-Thornton House (Thornton House;
Dowdell, Rev. Lewis Flournoy, House)
U.S. Hwy. 29
HABS AL-585   p   L

Tate-Thompson House; see Thompson, G.
C., House

Thompson, G. C., House (Tate-Thompson
House)
302 N. Main St.
HABS AL-542   s pd   L

Thornton House; see Rush-Thornton
House

Tuskegee Institute National Historic Site;
see Carver Museum

Tuskegee Institute National Historic Site;
see Grey Columns

Tuskegee Institute National Historic Site;
see Oaks, The

Varner-Alexander House (Grey Columns)
State Hwy. 126 (Old Montgomery Hwy.)
HABS AL-543   s pd   L

Vason, Doctor, House; see Lamar, G. Y.,
House

Tuskegee vic.

Alexander-Hurt-Whatley House (Hurt,
Judge W. H., House)
County Rd. 10 (Old Columbus Hwy.)
HABS AL-560   s pd   L

Cox House; see Plantation House, Frame

Hurt, Judge W. H., House; see
Alexander-Hurt-Whatley House

Plantation House, Frame (Cox House;
Stagecoach Inn)
County Rd. 26
HABS AL-534   p   L

Stagecoach Inn; see Plantation House,
Frame

MADISON COUNTY

Huntsville

Beirne House; see Bibb-Bradley-Beirne
House

Bibb, Gov. Thomas, House; see
Bibb-Bradley-Beirne House

Bibb-Bradley-Beirne House (Beirne House;
Bibb-Newman House; Bibb, Gov.
Thomas, House)
303 Williams St.
HABS AL-403   pd   L

Bibb-Newman House; see
Bibb-Bradley-Beirne House

Boswell, C. S., House; see Boswell-McClung
House

Boswell-McClung House (Boswell, C. S.,
House; McClung-Watkins House)
415 McClung St.
HABS AL-478   p   L

Brandon-Read-Burritt House; see Burritt
House

Burritt House (Brandon-Read-Burritt
House)
303 Eustis Ave.
HABS AL-474   pd   L

Cabiness House (Roach-Cabiness House)
603 Randolph St.
HABS AL-431   s pd   L

Chase, Henry B., House (McDowell-Chase House)
517 Adams Ave.
HABS AL-409   pd   L
Clarke-Fackler House; see Pynchon House
Clay, J. Withers, House (Huntsville Female Seminary, Steward's House; Lewis-Clay-Anderson House)
513 Eustis Ave.
HABS AL-408   pd   L
Cox-White House; see White, Thomas W., House
Dillworth, W. P., House; see Robinson-Dillworth House
Fearn-Garth House
517 Franklin St.
HABS AL-414   s pd   L
First National Bank (Huntsville Branch, State Bank of Alabama)
Jefferson St. & Fountain Rd.
HABS AL-405   s pd   L
Greenlawn (Otie House)
U.S. Hwy. 431 (Memorial Pkwy.)
HABS AL-476   p   L
Hamlet House (Windham, William, House)
413 E. Holmes St.
HABS AL-413   p   L
Horton-McCracken House; see McCracken House
Huntsville Branch, State Bank of Alabama; see First National Bank
Huntsville Female Seminary, Steward's House; see Clay, J. Withers, House
Lewis-Clay-Anderson House; see Clay, J. Withers, House
Madison County Courthouse
Courthouse Square
HABS AL-437   s pd   L
Mastin, Gus, House (Meridian Pike (House))
HABS AL-436   p   L
McClung-Watkins House; see Boswell-McClung House
McCracken House (Horton-McCracken House)
Meridian Pike
HABS AL-410   pd   L
McDowell-Chase House; see Chase, Henry B., House
Meridian Pike (House); see Mastin, Gus, House
Morgan-Neal House; see Neal House
Neal House (Morgan-Neal House)
558 Franklin St.
HABS AL-412   pd   L
Oaklawn; see Robinson-Dillworth House
Oaks Place (Steele-Fowler House)
808 Maysville Rd.
HABS AL-402   s pd   L
Otie House; see Greenlawn

Perkins-Orgain-Winston House (Scruggs House)
401 Lincoln St.
HABS AL-473   pd   L
Pope, Col. Leroy, House; see Pope-Spragins House
Pope-Spragins House (Pope, Col. Leroy, House; Poplar Grove)
407 Echols Ave.
HABS AL-406   s pd   L
Poplar Grove; see Pope-Spragins House
Pynchon House (Clarke-Fackler House)
518 Adams Ave.
HABS AL-430   s pd   L
Roach-Cabiness House; see Cabiness House
Robinson, John, House; see Robinson-Dillworth House
Robinson-Dillworth House (Dillworth, W. P., House; Robinson, John, House; Oaklawn)
2709 Meridian Pike
HABS AL-411   s pd   L
Scruggs House; see Perkins-Orgain-Winston House
Steele-Fowler House; see Oaks Place
Wade, David, House
Bob Wade Ln.
HABS AL-477   p   L
Weeden, Miss Howard, House
300 Gates Ave.
HABS AL-404   s pd   L
White, Thomas W., House (Cox-White House)
461 Eustis Ave.
HABS AL-475   p   L
Windham, William, House; see Hamlet House

New Market

Five Oaks (Laxon, W. L. Jr., House)
Winchester Pike
HABS AL-407   p   L
Laxon, W. L. Jr., House; see Five Oaks

MARENGO COUNTY

Dayton

Bruce House; see Walton-Bruce House

Jones, Leroy King, House; see Magnolia Grove

Magnolia Grove (Jones, Leroy King, House)
State Hwy. 25
HABS AL-153   p   L

Methodist Church
State Hwy. 25
HABS AL-149   p   L

Walton-Bruce House (Bruce House)
State Hwy. 25
HABS AL-140   p   L

Demopolis

Bluff Hall (Lyon-Smith House)
407 N. Commissioners Ave.
HABS AL-213   pd   L
Gaineswood (Whitfield-Kirven House)
805 S. Cedar St.
HABS AL-211   s pd   L
Glover Family Mausoleum
Riverview Cemetery
HABS AL-212-A   s p   L
Lyon Hall; see Lyon House
Lyon House (Lyon Hall; Lyon-Lamar House)
102 S. Main St.
HABS AL-239   pd   L
Lyon-Lamar House; see Lyon House
Lyon-Smith House; see Bluff Hall
Whitfield-Kirven House; see Gaineswood

Dixon Mills vic.

Pearson House (Wright-Pearson House)
County Rd. 6
HABS AL-145   p   L
Wright-Pearson House; see Pearson House

Faunsdale vic.

Cedar Grove (Walker, Charles, House)
Uniontown Rd.
HABS AL-200   p   L
Norwood Plantation
County Rd. 54
HABS AL-261   p   L
Walker, Charles, House; see Cedar Grove

Jefferson

Grant, Basil, House; see Grant, Charles Brasfiels, House
Grant, Charles Brasfiels, House (Grant, Basil, House)
State Hwy. 28
HABS AL-144   p   L

Jefferson vic.

Allen, W. G., House (Evergreen)
State Hwy. 28
HABS AL-142   p   L
Evergreen; see Allen, W. G., House

Linden

Baptist Church; see Marengo County Courthouse, Old
Marengo County Courthouse, Old (Baptist Church)
Cahaba Ave. & Mobile St.
HABS AL-143   p   L

MARION COUNTY

Bexar

Apothecary (Moorman, Dr. A. L., Office)
County Rd. 13
HABS AL-389   p   L
Moorman, Dr. A. L., Office; see Apothecary

MOBILE COUNTY

Chastang

Chestang, Zeno, House
U.S. Hwy. 43, Chestang Landing
HABS AL-187   p   L

Citronelle

Jones House; see Pullman House
Pullman Hotel; see Pullman House
Pullman House (Pullman Hotel; Jones
    House)
104 Center St.
HABS AL-163   pd   L

Dauphin Island

Fort Gaines
Pelican Point
HABS AL-102   pd   L H

Dawes

Vogtner Farm (House & Smokehouse)
Jeff Hamilton Rd. vic.
HABS AL-188   p   L

Mobile

Anderson, Decatur C., House; see 251
    North Conception Street (House)
Ashalnd (Ruins); see Wilson, Augusta
    Evans, House (Ruins)
Atkinson, Octavia, House; see
    Cunningham-Atkinson House
Ayers House (Private School; Robert,
    Madame Paul, House)
57 S. Hamilton St.
HABS AL-49   s pd   L
Azalea Grove (Dawson, John C., House;
    McKeon House; Palmetto Hall)
55 S. McGregor Ave.
HABS AL-54   pd   L
Barker, P. D., House (109 Saint Anthony
    Street (House); Spanish Dwelling, The;
    Creole House)
HABS AL-21-D   p   L
Barnwell-Mitchell House; see Kennedy,
    Joshua, House
Barton Academy
Government St.
HABS AL-32   s pd   L
Bates-Henderson House; see Henderson,
    Doctor, House
Batre-Bernheimer-Saad House (Batre-Saad
    House; Bernheimer House)
155 Monroe St.
HABS AL-801   pd   L
Batre-Hamilton House; see Broun, W. M.,
    House
Batre-Saad House; see
    Batre-Bernheimer-Saad House
Battle-Ross House (Ironwork); see Ross,
    William H., House (Ironwork)
Beal-Gaillard House; see Gaillard, S. P.,
    House
Beck House; see Goelet-Randlette-Beck
    House

Beehive Church (Franklin Street Methodist
    Episcopal Church; Franklin Street
    Baptist Church)
Franklin & Saint Michael Sts.
HABS AL-26   pd   L
Bernheimer House; see
    Batre-Bernheimer-Saad House
**Bestor, Daniel Perrin Jr., House
    (Ironwork)**
208 Government St.
HABS AL-9-X   p   L
Bishop's House & Gates; see Ketchum,
    William H., House & Gates (Ironwork)
Bloodgood's Row
306, 308 & 310 Monroe St.
HABS AL-818   pd   L
Bowers, Lloyd, Double House; see
    Huger-Douglas Houses
Bragg, Judge John, House (Bragg-Mitchell
    House)
1906 Spring Hill Ave.
HABS AL-30   pd   L
Bragg-Mitchell House; see Bragg, Judge
    John, House
Briarwood (Sewall, Judge Kiah B., House)
Dauphin Way & Mobile St.
HABS AL-69   pd   L
Brisk & Jacobson Store (Daniels, Elgin &
    Company)
51 Dauphin St.
HABS AL-790   pd   L
Brooks House (Ironwork) (108 North
    Conception Street (House, Ironwork))
HABS AL-7-B   s p   L
Broun, W. M., House (Batre-Hamilton
    House)
320 Avalon St. (see AL, Spring Hill)
HABS AL-58   pd   L
Brown, Milton S., House
108 S. Conception St.
HABS AL-78   p   L
Brown Place; see Bunker, Robert S., House
Bunker, Robert S., House (Moreland
    House; Brown Place)
157 Monroe St. (moved to 201 S. Warren
    St.)
HABS AL-802   pd   L
Bunker-DuMont House; see DuMont
    House
Burgess-Maschmeyer House
1209 Government St.
HABS AL-847   p   L
Bush-Mohr House (Ironwork); see Mohr,
    Dr. Charles, House (Ironwork)
Butt-Kling House (Iron Gate) (Kling
    House)
254 N. Jackson St.
HABS AL-7-WG   p   L

Calef House (Staples, N. A., House;
    Calef-Staples House)
1614 Old Shell Rd.
HABS AL-51   s pd   L

Calef-Staples House; see Calef House

Calvert-Webster House
265 N. Conception St.
HABS AL-55   pd   L
Carolina Hill; see Dawson, William A.,
    House
Carriage Block
Government St.
HABS AL-36-A   p   L
**Carriage Block, Iron Hitching Posts &
    Lamp Posts**
Various Mobile locations
HABS AL-36   s pd   L
Cathedral of the Immaculate Conception
S. Claiborne St.
HABS AL-35   pd   L
Catholic High School; see McGill Institute
Chamberlain-Rapier Double House; see
    Girard Double House
Chandler, Daniel, House; see McGill
    Institute
Christ Episcopal Church
Church & Saint Emanuel Sts.
HABS AL-31   s pd   L
Church Street Block Study (Ravesies,
    Frederick P., House; Delamier House;
    Hamilton-Gaillard House; 405 Church
    Street (House))
401-407 Church St.
HABS AL-803   pd   L
Church Street Cemetery (Ironwork)
    (Mobile Cemetery, Old (Ironwork))
Church & Bayou Sts.
HABS AL-845   s p   L
**6 Church Street (Commercial Building,
    Doorway)**
HABS AL-66-A   p   L
301 Church Street (House) (Three Sisters
    House)
HABS AL-24   s pd   L
405 Church Street (House); see Church
    Street Block Study
City Hall (Southern Market)
111 S. Royal St.
HABS AL-5   s pd   L
City Hospital, Old (Mobile City Hospital)
900-950 Saint Anthony St.
HABS AL-13   s pd   L

Clarke House; see Smith-Clarke House

Clarke Houses; see Robinson, Cornelius,
    Twin Houses

Clitherall House; see Horst, Henry, House

Cluis, Frederick V., House (Cluis-Rubira
    House)
156 Saint Anthony St.
HABS AL-804   pd   L

Cluis-Rubira House; see Cluis, Frederick
    V., House

Coley Building; see Townsend-Foreman
    Building

Commercial Building; see Pollock Building

Conti House; see Rider House

308-310 Conti Street (Double House)
(Durand House)
HABS AL-59　　　　pd　L

Convent of the Visitation (Visitation Convent)
2300 Spring Hill Ave.
HABS AL-73　　　　p　L

Convent of the Visitation, East Wing; see Convent of the Visitation, Section A

Convent of the Visitation, Gates & Wall
Spring Hill Ave.
HABS AL-73-A　　　　p　L

Convent of the Visitation, Section A
(Convent of the Visitation, East Wing)
Spring Hill Ave.
HABS AL-73-B　　　　p　L

Convent of the Visitation, Section B
(Convent of the Visitation, South Wing)
Spring Hill Ave.
HABS AL-73-C　　　　p　L

Convent of the Visitation, South Wing; see Convent of the Visitation, Section B

Convent of the Visitation, Water Wheel
Spring Hill Ave.
HABS AL-73-D　　　　p　L

Cotton Warehouse, Old; see Magnolia Cotton Warehouse

Craft, John, House & Servants' Quarters; see Sanford-Staylor House & Servants' Quarters

Creole House; see Barker, P. D., House

Creole House; see Hammond-Willoughby House

Creole House; see 256 Saint Louis Street (House)

Creole House; see Tarloon House

Cunningham-Atkinson House (Atkinson, Octavia, House)
Wilson Rd. (moved from AL, Union Springs vic.)
HABS AL-539　　　　p　L

Daniels, Elgin & Company; see Brisk & Jacobson Store

Dargan-Waring House; see Waring House

Dargan-Waring House, Gates; see Waring House, Gates

Dargan-Waring House, Privy; see Waring House, Privy

Dargan-Waring House, Slave Quarters; see Waring House, Slave Quarters

Dargan-Waring House, Stables; see Waring House, Stables

Dargan-Wraing House, Lodge; see Waring House, Texas

12 Dauphin Street (Commercial Building)
HABS AL-61-C　　　　p　L

2 Dauphin Street (Commercial Building)
HABS AL-61-B　　　　p　L

56 Dauphin Street (Commercial Building)
HABS AL-61-D　　　　p　L

715 Dauphin Street (Commercial Building)
HABS AL-61-A　　　　p　L

Dawson, James, Creole House; see Tarloon House

Dawson, John C., House; see Azalea Grove

Dawson, William A., House (Carolina Hill; Perdue House)
76 S. McGregor Ave. (see AL, Spring Hill)
HABS AL-10　　　s pd　L

Delamier House; see Church Street Block Study

Denniston House & Slave Quarters; see Oakleigh, House & Slave Quarters

Double House, French-type; see Girard Double House

Double House, French-type; see Reingard Double House

Douglas-Huger Houses; see Huger-Douglas Houses

DuMont House (Bunker-DuMont House; Noble, Annie B., House)
157 Church St.
HABS AL-28　　　　pd　L

Durand House; see 308-310 Conti Street (Double House)

Elkus, Isaac, House (Ironwork); see 50 South Franklin Street (House, Ironwork)

Ellis-Lyons House; see Lyons House

Emanuel, Jonathan, House (Shrine House)
251 Government St.
HABS AL-3　　　s pd　L

Eslava House; see Marshall-Eslava-Sledge House

Eslava, Miguel Jr., House; see McMahon, J. J., House

Exchange Alley (Commercial Building, Doorways)
HABS AL-66　　　　p　L

Finch House (Ironwork); see 301 North Joachim Street (House, Ironwork)

Finnigan, Capt. Owen, House (Ironwork)
752 Government St.
HABS AL-9-Z　　　　p　L

Foote, Charles K., House (Ironwork); see Trammell House (Ironwork)

Ford House; see Hall House

Forsyth, John, House; see Tardy-Thorp House

Fort Conde, Charlotte House; see Kirkbride, Jonathan, House

Four Sisters House; see Tardy-Thorp House

Franklin Street Baptist Church; see Beehive Church

Franklin Street Methodist Episcopal Church; see Beehive Church

Frascatti
Conception St.
HABS AL-71　　　　pd　L

French Creole House; see McMahon, J. J., House

French Creole, House; see 652 Saint Francis Street (House)

Gaillard, S. P., House (Beal-Gaillard House)
111 Myrtlewood Lane (see AL, Spring Hill)
HABS AL-107　　　　p　L

Garconniere; see Waring House, Texas

Gas Lamps; see Lampposts

Gates-Daves House
1570-1572 Dauphin St.
HABS AL-799　　　　pd　L

Gazzam, Audley H., House & Servants' Quarters
1255 Government St.
HABS AL-53　　　　pd　L

Gee, Gideon, House (Gee-Barrow, House)
253 Monroe St. (moved to 251 Saint Anthony St.)
HABS AL-825　　　　pd　L

Gee-Barrow, House; see Gee, Gideon, House

George, Elizabeth, House (Ironwork)
159 Monroe St.
HABS AL-9-K　　　　p　L

Georgia Cottage; see Hardaway-Evans-Wilson-Sledge House

Gibbons-Torry House, Gate & Privy (Torry, C. J., House, Gate & Privy)
60 S. Conception St.
HABS AL-43　　　　pd　L

Gibbs House; see Wilson-Gibbs House

Gilmore-Gaines-Quigley House (Ironwork); see Quigley, Albert, House (Ironwork)

Girard Double House (Double House, French-type; Chamberlain-Rapier Double House)
56-58 S. Conception St.
HABS AL-12　　　s pd　L

Gliddon, John S., House
400 Saint Anthony St.
HABS AL-18　　　s pd　L

Goelet-Randlette-Beck House (Beck House; Randlette House; Randlette-Beck-Bedlin House)
1005 Augusta St.
HABS AL-855　　　　p　L

Goldsby, J. W., House & Iron Fence
452 Government St.
HABS AL-9-W　　　　p　L

Goldsmith, Meyer, House (Griffin-Goldsmith House)
408 Conti St.
HABS AL-76　　　　pd　L

Gonzales, Margaret, House (Ironwork)
(352 State Street (House, Ironwork))
HABS AL-9-E　　　　p　L

Gordon House; see Tacon-Gordon House

Government St. Methodist Episcopal Church, South (Government Street United Methodist Church)
901 Government St.
HABS AL-853　　　　p　L

110 Government Street (Commercial Building)
HABS AL-62-D　　　　p　L

112-114 Government Street (Commercial Building)
HABS AL-62-E   p   L

158 Government Street (Commercial Building)
HABS AL-62-H   p   L

51-69 Government Street (Commercial Building)
HABS AL-62-G   p   L

66 Government Street (Commercial Building)
HABS AL-62-F   p   L

67-69 Government Street (Commercial Building)
HABS AL-67   pd   L

71-93 Government Street (Commercial Building)
HABS AL-66-D   p   L

9 Government Street (Commercial Building)
HABS AL-62-A   p   L

453 Government Street (Iron Gate & Fence)
HABS AL-7-XXV   p   L

201 Government Street (Iron Gate)
(moved to Spring Hill Ave. & Riviere du Chin Rd.)
HABS AL-9-BA-7   p   L

605 Government Street (Iron Gate)
HABS AL-8-U   p   L

250 Government Street (Ironwork)
HABS AL-7-D   s p   L

Government Street Presbyterian Church
Government & Jackson Sts.
HABS AL-1   s pd   L

Government Street United Methodist Church; see Government St. Methodist Episcopal Church, South

Griffin-Goldsmith House; see Goldsmith, Meyer, House

Guesnard-Craft House
Jackson & Conti Sts.
HABS AL-806   pd   L

Gulf City Hotel; see Southern Hotel

Gulf, Mobile & Ohio R.R., Passenger Terminal
Beauregard St. & Telegraph Rd.
HABS AL-796   pd   L H

Hall House (Ford House; Hall-Ford House)
165 Saint Emanuel St.
HABS AL-46   s pd   L

Hall-Ford House; see Hall House

Hall-Horst House; see Horst, Henry, House

Hamilton-Gaillard House; see Church Street Block Study

Hammond-Willoughby House (Creole House)
Saint Michael & Hamilton Sts.
HABS AL-44   pd   L

Hanlein House; see 652 Saint Francis Street (House)

Hannah Houses; see Robinson, Cornelius, Twin Houses

Hardaway-Evans-Wilson-Sledge House (Georgia Cottage)
2564 Spring Hill Ave.
HABS AL-826   pd   L

Hazard-Semmes House; see Semmes, Judge Oliver J., House

Hellen-Croom House
1001 Augusta St.
HABS AL-808   pd   L

Henderson, Doctor, House (Bates-Henderson House)
12 N. Jackson St.
HABS AL-22-A   p   L

Hitching Posts, Iron
Various Mobile locations
HABS AL-36-B   s p   L

Home Industry Foundry (Hunley Building)
250 N. Water St.
HABS AL-809   pd   L

Horst, Henry, House (Hall-Horst House; Clitherall House)
110 Saint Emanuel St.
HABS AL-23   pd   L

Horst, Martin, House
407 Conti St.
HABS AL-776   s d   L

Horta-Semmes House & Fence (Semmes, Adm. Raphael, House & Fence)
802 Government St.
HABS AL-56   s pd   L

Huger, Charles L., House (Ironwork)
154 S. Conception St.
HABS AL-9-BA-5   p   L

Huger-Douglas Houses (Bowers, Lloyd, Double House; Douglas-Huger Houses)
109-111 S. Conception St.
HABS AL-60   pd   L

Hunley Building; see Home Industry Foundry

Iron Lace; see Richards, Charles G., House

Jacobson House; see 351 Saint Michael Street (House)

James, Thomas S., Double House; see Ottenstein, Augustine, House

Jordan House; see Rider House

Kennedy, Joshua, House (Barnwell-Mitchell House)
607 Government St.
HABS AL-800   pd   L

Ketchum, Dr. George, House; see Silver-Ketchum House

Ketchum, William H., House & Gates (Ironwork) (Bishop's House & Gates)
400 Government St.
HABS AL-9-U   p   L

Kilduff-Ray House
200 George St.
HABS AL-849   p   L

Kirkbride, Jonathan, House (Fort Conde, Charlotte House)
104 Theatre St.
HABS AL-14   s pd   L

Kling House; see Butt-Kling House (Iron Gate)

LaClede Hotel
150-160 Government St.
HABS AL-811   pd   L

Lampposts (Street Lamps; Gas Lamps)
Various Mobile locations
HABS AL-36-C   s pd   L

Larrouil House; see Larrouil-Arresijac House

Larrouil-Arresijac House (Larrouil House)
252 S. Claiborne St.
HABS AL-812   pd   L

LeLoupe House; see Weldon-LeLoupe House

LeVert, Madame, House & Office
151 & 153 Government St.
HABS AL-29   s pd   L

Lodge, The; see Waring House, Texas

Ludlow House
1113 Church St.
HABS AL-41   pd   L

Lyons House (Ellis-Lyons House)
168 S. Royal St.
HABS AL-40   pd   L

Lyons, Patrick, House (Ironwork)
300 State St.
HABS AL-9-S   p   L

Macy, Robert C., House; see Macy-Adams House

Macy-Adams House (Macy, Robert C., House)
1569 Dauphin St.
HABS AL-813   pd   L

Magnolia Cemetery (Ironwork)
Virginia St.
HABS AL-7-JP   p   L

Magnolia Cotton Warehouse (Cotton Warehouse, Old; Warrant Warehouse Company)
Lipscomb & Magnolia Sts.
HABS AL-74   p   L

Marine Hospital & Gates; see U.S. Marine Hospital & Gates

Marshall-Eslava-Sledge House (Eslava House)
152 Tuthill Ln. (see AL, Spring Hill)
HABS AL-6   s pd   L

Marx, Isaac, House (Tuthill House)
113 Church St. (moved to 307 University Blvd.)
HABS AL-778   s d   L

Mastin, Dr. Claude, House; see Phillipi-Mastin House

Maybrick House; see McGill Institute

McDowell, Withers, Company; see 50-52 North Commercial Street (Commercial Bldg.)

McGill Institute (Chandler, Daniel, House; Maybrick House; Catholic High School)
252 Government St.
HABS AL-77   s p   L

McGowin-Creary House
1151 Government St.
HABS AL-852   p   L

McKeon House; see Azalea Grove

McMahon, J. J., House (Eslava, Miguel Jr.,
     House; French Creole House)
456 Saint Francis St.
HABS AL-21-A   pd   L

McMillan House (Ironwork)
256 N. Joachim St.
HABS AL-9-B   p   L

McMillan, Richard, House; see Richards,
     Charles G., House

Middle Bay Light; see Mobile Light
     Number 6639

Middleton-Boulo House; see
     Middleton-Creole House

Middleton-Creole House (Middleton-Boulo
     House)
13 N. Cedar St.
HABS AL-42   pd   L

Miller, James P., House; see
     Miller-O'Donnell House

Miller-O'Donnell House (Miller, James P.,
     House)
1102 S. Broad St.
HABS AL-814   pd   L

Mobile & Ohio Railroad Office Building
409 N. Royal St.
HABS AL-794   s pd   L

Mobile Cemetery, Old (Ironwork); see
     Church Street Cemetery (Ironwork)

Mobile City Hospital; see City Hospital,
     Old

Mobile Light Number 6639 (Middle Bay
     Light)
Mobile Bay
HABS AL-780   s   d   L

Mohr, Dr. Charles, House (Ironwork)
     (Bush-Mohr House (Ironwork))
254 Saint Anthony St.
HABS AL-9-J   p   L

350 Monroe Street (House, Ironwork)
HABS AL-7-X   p   L

Moreland House; see Bunker, Robert S.,
     House

**8-10 NMorth Jackson Street (Double
     House);** see Reingard Double House

Noble, Annie B., House; see DuMont
     House

**104 North Commerce Street (Commercial
     Building)**
HABS AL-63-J   p   L

**114 North Commerce Street (Commercial
     Building)**
HABS AL-63-K   p   L

**117 North Commerce Street (Commercial
     Building)**
HABS AL-63-L   p   L

**15 North Commerce Street (Commercial
     Building)**
HABS AL-63-D   p   L

**150 North Commerce Street (Commercial
     Building)**
HABS AL-63-M   p   L

**16 North Commerce Street (Commercial
     Building)**
HABS AL-63-G   p   L

**50-52 North Commerce Street
     (Commercial Building)**
HABS AL-784   s   d   L

**7 North Commerce Street (Commercial
     Building)**
HABS AL-791   pd   L

**8 North Commerce Street (Commercial
     Building)**
HABS AL-63-A   p   L

**9 North Commerce Street (Commercial
     Building)**
HABS AL-63-F   p   L

**50-52 North Commercial Street
     (Commercial Bldg.)** (McDowell,
     Withers, Company)
HABS AL-784   s   d   L

**203 North Conception Street (Commercial
     Building)**
HABS AL-8-C   s p   L

251 North Conception Street (House)
     (Anderson, Decatur C., House)
HABS AL-52   pd   L

**108 North Conception Street (House,
     Ironwork);** see Brooks House (Ironwork)

8 North Hamilton Street (House) (Riley,
     James, House)
HABS AL-50   pd   L

**256 North Jackson Street (House,
     Ironwork)** (Riley, Tom, House
     (Ironwork))
HABS AL-9-Q   p   L

**301 North Joachim Street (House,
     Ironwork)** (Finch House (Ironwork))
HABS AL-9-F   p   L

**364 North Royal Street (Commercial
     Building)**
HABS AL-793   pd   H

**106 North Water Street (Commercial
     Building)**
HABS AL-65-E   p   L

**108 North Water Street (Commercial
     Building)**
HABS AL-65-C   p   L

**110 North Water Street (Commercial
     Building)**
HABS AL-65-D   p   L

**112 North Water Street (Commercial
     Building)**
HABS AL-65-B   p   L

**116 North Water Street (Commercial
     Building)**
HABS AL-65-A   p   L

**19-21 North Water Street (Commercial
     Building)**
HABS AL-65-F   p   L

**3 North Water Street (Commercial
     Building)**
HABS AL-795   pd   L

**4 North Water Street (Commercial
     Building)**
HABS AL-65-N   p   L

**55 North Water Street (Commercial
     Building)** (Partin Paper Company)
HABS AL-65-M   p   L

Number 5 Fire Station; see Washington
     Fire Engine Company Number 8

Oakleigh, House & Slave Quarters
     (Denniston House & Slave Quarters)
350 Oakleigh Place
HABS AL-47   s pd   L

Odd Fellows Hall; see Second American
     Theater

Ottenstein, Augustine, House (James,
     Thomas S., Double House)
207-209 N. Jackson St.
HABS AL-27   s pd   L

Palmetto Hall; see Azalea Grove

Parmly, Dr. Ludolph, Houses
303-305-307 Conception St.
HABS AL-815   s pd   L

Partin Paper Company; see 55 North Water
     Street (Commercial Building)

Perdue House; see Dawson, William A.,
     House

Phillipi-Mastin House (Mastin, Dr. Claude,
     House; Pinto, Antoine, House)
53 N. Jackson St.
HABS AL-816   pd   L

Phoenix Fire Company Number 6
154 S. Franklin St. (moved to 203 S.
     Claiborne St)
HABS AL-7-Z   p   L

Pinto, Antoine, House; see Phillipi-Mastin
     House

Planters & Merchants Insurance Company
60 Saint Michael St.
HABS AL-777   s   d   L

Pollock Building (Commercial Building)
51 S. Royal St.
HABS AL-48   pd   L

Pomeroy Family Tomb
Magnolia Cemetery, Virginia St.
HABS AL-785   s   d   L

Portier, Bishop Michael, House
307 Conti St.
HABS AL-37   s pd   L

Private School; see Ayers House

Protestant Orphans' Asylum
911 Dauphin St.
HABS AL-33   pd   L

Quigley, Albert, House (Ironwork)
     (Gilmore-Gaines-Quigley House
     (Ironwork))
751 Government St.
HABS AL-9-C   pd   L

Quigley Twin House (Ironwork)
258 Congress St.
HABS AL-9-D   p   L

Randlette House; see
     Goelet-Randlette-Beck House

Randlette-Beck-Bedlin House; see
Goelet-Randlette-Beck House

Ravesies, Frederick P., House; see Church
Street Block Study

Redwood, R. H., House (Ironwork)
260 Saint Louis St.
HABS AL-9-T   p   L

Reingard Double House (8-10 NMorth
Jackson Street (Double House); Double
House, French-type)
(moved from AL, Blakely)
HABS AL-25   s p d   L

**Revault-Maupin-Shawhan House
(Ironwork);** see Revault-Shawhan House
(Ironwork)

Revault-Shawhan House (Ironwork)
(Shawhan, Narcissa M., House
(Ironwork); Revault-Maupin-Shawhan
House (Ironwork))
254 N. Conception St.
HABS AL-9-G   p   L

Richards, Charles G., House (McMillan,
Richard, House; Iron Lace)
256 Joachim St.
HABS AL-810   pd   L

Rider House (Conti House; Jordan House)
303 Conti St.
HABS AL-38   s pd   L

Riley, James, House; see 8 North Hamilton
Street (House)

Riley, Tom, House (Ironwork); see 256
North Jackson Street (House, Ironwork)

Robert, Madame Paul, House; see Ayers
House

Roberts, James F., Houses; see Robinson,
Cornelius, Twin Houses

Robinson, Cornelius, Twin Houses (Clarke
Houses; Hannah Houses; Roberts, James
F., Houses)
157-159 N. Conception St.
HABS AL-807   pd   L

Ross, William H., House (Ironwork)
(Battle-Ross House (Ironwork))
602 Government St.
HABS AL-9-V   p   L

109 Saint Anthony Street (House); see
Barker, P. D., House

Saint Anthony Street (Iron Fence)
HABS AL-9-A   p   L

652 Saint Francis Street (House) (Hanlein
House; French Creole, House)
HABS AL-21-B   p   L

256 Saint Francis Street (House, Ironwork)
HABS AL-7-R   p   L

251 Saint Joseph Street (Iron Fence &
Gate)
HABS AL-8-TC   p   L

253 Saint Joseph Street (Iron Gate)
HABS AL-8-TM   p   L

256 Saint Louis Street (House) (Creole
House)
HABS AL-45   pd   L

154 Saint Louis Street (House, Iron Gate)
HABS AL-9-B   s pd   L

155 Saint Louis Street (House, Iron Gate)
HABS AL-7-C   s p   L

Saint Michael Street (Alley)
HABS AL-64-H   p   L

10 Saint Michael Street (Commercial
Building)
HABS AL-64-B   p   L

56-58 Saint Michael Street (Commercial
Building)
HABS AL-64-C   p   L

57 Saint Michael Street (Commercial
Building)
HABS AL-64-D   p   L

67 Saint Michael Street (Commercial
Building)
HABS AL-64-E   p   L

7 Saint Michael Street (Commercial
Building)
HABS AL-792   pd   L

78 Saint Michael Street (Commercial
Building)
HABS AL-64-G   p   L

74-76 Saint Michael Street (Commercial
Buildings)
HABS AL-64-F   p   L

351 Saint Michael Street (House)
(Jacobson House; Vanroy-Barnwell
House)
HABS AL-39   pd   L

**Sanford-Staylor House & Servants'
Quarters** (Staylor, William, House &
Servants' Quarters; Craft, John, House &
Servants' Quarters)
451-453 Saint William St.
HABS AL-22   pd   L

Sanford-Thompson House (Thompson
House)
1621 Spring Hill Ave.
HABS AL-817   pd   L

Schieffelin-Sledge House (Gate & Fence)
(Sledge House (Gate & Fence))
54 S. Jackson St.
HABS AL-72   p   L

Schley-Rutherford House
1263 Selma St.
HABS AL-857   p   L

Seamen's Bethel
75 Church St. (moved to 307 University
Blvd.)
HABS AL-779   s d   L

Second American Theater (Odd Fellows
Hall)
17 S. Royal St.
HABS AL-16   p   L

Semmes, Adm. Raphael, House & Fence;
see Horta-Semmes House & Fence

Semmes, Judge Oliver J., House
(Hazard-Semmes House; Zimlich,
Andrew, House)
2828 Dauphin Way
HABS AL-57   pd   L

Sewall, Judge Kiah B., House; see
Briarwood

Shawhan, Narcissa M., House (Ironwork);
see Revault-Shawhan House (Ironwork)

Shippers Exchange Saloon
50 S. Commerce St.
HABS AL-789   pd   L

Shrine House; see Emanuel, Jonathan,
House

Silver-Ketchum House (Ketchum, Dr.
George, House)
257 Saint Francis St.
HABS AL-798   pd   L

Slatter Family Tomb
Magnolia Cemetery, Virginia St.
HABS AL-860   p   L

Sledge House (Gate & Fence); see
Schieffelin-Sledge House (Gate & Fence)

Smith, Sidney, House (Iron Gate &
Balcony)
203 Government St.
HABS AL-9-BA-8   p   L

Smith-Clarke House (Clarke House)
161 Saint Anthony St.
HABS AL-15   s pd   L

12 South Commerce Street (Commercial
Building)
HABS AL-63-E   p   L

55 South Commerce Street (Commercial
Building)
HABS AL-63-B   p   L

58 South Commerce Street (Commercial
Building)
HABS AL-63-C   p   L

207 South Conception Street (House)
HABS AL-8-SR   p   L

215 South Conception Street (Iron Fence
& Gate)
HABS AL-8-X   p   L

456 South Conception Street (Iron Fence
& Gate)
(moved to 1802 Old Govt. & 3333 Riviere
du Chin)
HABS AL-8-CX   p   L

50 South Franklin Street (House,
Ironwork) (Elkus, Isaac, House
(Ironwork))
HABS AL-7-Y   p   L

204 South Joachim Street (House)
HABS AL-786   s pd   L

208 South Joachim Street (House)
HABS AL-787   s pd   L

23 South Royal Street (Commercial
Building)
HABS AL-66-E   p   L

12 South Water Street (Commercial
Building)
HABS AL-65-G   p   L

16 South Water Street (Commercial
Building)
HABS AL-65-P   p   L

4 South Water Street (Commercial Building)
HABS AL-65-H   p   L
54 South Water Street (Commercial Building)
HABS AL-65-R   p   L
64 South Water Street (Commercial Building)
HABS AL-65-J   p   L
Southern Hotel (Gulf City Hotel)
53-65 Water St.
HABS AL-11   s pd   L
Southern Market; see City Hall
Spanish Dwelling, The; see Barker, P. D., House
Spring Hill College
Old Shell Rd. (see AL, Spring Hill)
HABS AL-34   d   L
Spring Hill College, Administration Building; see Spring Hill College, Main Building
Spring Hill College, First Building; see Spring Hill College, Original Building
Spring Hill College, Infirmary
Old Shell Rd.
HABS AL-34-C   p   L
Spring Hill College, Main Building (Spring Hill College, Administration Building)
Old Shell Rd.
HABS AL-34-B   s p   L
Spring Hill College, Original Building (Spring Hill College, First Building)
Old Shell Rd.
HABS AL-34-A   p   L
Spring Hill College, Sodality Chapel
Old Shell Rd.
HABS AL-34-D   p   L
Staples, N. A., House; see Calef House
304 State Street (House, Ironwork) (Tate House (Ironwork))
HABS AL-9-P   p   L
350 State Street (House, Ironwork) (Walsh House)
HABS AL-9-N   p   L
352 State Street (House, Ironwork); see Gonzales, Margaret, House (Ironwork)
Staylor, William, House & Servants' Quarters; see Sanford-Staylor House & Servants' Quarters
Street Lamps; see Lampposts
Tacon-Gordon House (Gordon House)
1216 Government St.
HABS AL-848   p   L
Tardy, Balthasar, House; see Tardy-Thorp House
Tardy-Thorp House (Four Sisters House; Tardy, Balthasar, House; Forsyth, John, House)
112 S. Conception St.
HABS AL-17   pd   L

Tarloon House (Dawson, James, Creole House; Creole House)
101 N. Hamilton St.
HABS AL-21   pd   L
Tate House (Ironwork); see 304 State Street (House, Ironwork)
Texas House; see Waring House, Texas
Thompson House; see Sanford-Thompson House
Three Sisters House; see 301 Church Street (House)
Torry, C. J., House, Gate & Privy; see Gibbons-Torry House, Gate & Privy
Toulmin, Gen. Theopolis, House (moved to 307 Univ. Blvd.)(see AL, Toulminville)
HABS AL-106   pd   L
Townsend-Foreman Building (Coley Building)
56 Saint Francis St.
HABS AL-805   pd   L
Trammell House (Ironwork) (Foote, Charles K., House (Ironwork))
255 N. Conception St.
HABS AL-9-H   p   L
Trinity Episcopal Church
Jackson St. (moved to 1900 Dauphin St.)
HABS AL-879   p   L
Tuthill House; see Marx, Isaac, House
U.S. Custom House & Post Office, Old
Royal & Saint Francis Sts.
HABS AL-830   pd   H
U.S. Marine Hospital & Gates (Marine Hospital & Gates)
800 Saint Anthony St.
HABS AL-781   s pd   L
U.S. Post Office Building
Saint Joseph & Saint Michael Sts.
HABS AL-797   pd   L
Vanroy-Barnwell House; see 351 Saint Michael Street (House)
Vincent-Walsh House (Walsh, Richard, House)
1664 Spring Hill Ave.
HABS AL-70   pd   L
Visitation Convent; see Convent of the Visitation
Walsh House; see 350 State Street (House, Ironwork)
Walsh, Richard, House; see Vincent-Walsh House
Waring House (Dargan-Waring House)
351 Government St.
HABS AL-19   s pd   L
Waring House, Gates (Dargan-Waring House, Gates)
351 Government St.
HABS AL-19-A   s p   L
Waring House, Privy (Dargan-Waring House, Privy)
351 Government St.
HABS AL-19-C   s p   L

Waring House, Slave Quarters (Dargan-Waring House, Slave Quarters)
351 Government St. (now S. Claiborne St.)
HABS AL-19-B   s p   L
Waring House, Stables (Dargan-Waring House, Stables)
108 S. Claiborne St.
HABS AL-19-E   s p   L
Waring House, Texas (Dargan-Wraing House, Lodge; Garconniere; Lodge, The; Texas House)
110 S. Claiborne St.
HABS AL-19-D   s p   L
Warrant Warehouse Company; see Magnolia Cotton Warehouse
Washington Fire Engine Company Number 8 (Number 5 Fire Station)
7 N. Lawrence St.
HABS AL-2   s pd   L
Weldon, John, House; see Weldon-LeLoupe House
Weldon-LeLoupe House (LeLoupe House; Weldon, John, House)
107 Saint Emanuel St.
HABS AL-20   pd   L
Wilson, Augusta Evans, House (Ruins) (Ashalnd (Ruins))
Lanier Ave.
HABS AL-68   pd   L
Wilson-Gibbs House (Gibbs House)
1012 Palmetto St.
HABS AL-856   p   L
Worker's House
457 Eslava St.
HABS AL-821   pd   L
Zimlich, Andrew, House; see Semmes, Judge Oliver J., House

Mon Louis Island

Boat Repair Yard, Old
Fowl River
HABS AL-189   p   L

Mount Vernon

Beasley House; see Cooper-Beasley House
Cooper-Beasley House (Beasley House)
County Rd. 96 (Old Saint Stephens Rd.)
HABS AL-117   pd   L
Curry, L. B., House (Rogers-Curry House)
County Rd. 96 (Old Saint Stephens Rd.)
HABS AL-124   p   L
Fall, Nelias, House
County Rd. 96 (Old Saint Stephens Rd.)
HABS AL-162   pd   L
Mount Vernon Arsenal (Mount Vernon Barracks)
County Rd. 96 (Old Saint Stephens Rd.)
HABS AL-105   pd   L
Mount Vernon Arsenal, Administration Building
Old Saint Stephens Rd. (County Rd. 96)
HABS AL-105-C   p   L

Mount Vernon Arsenal, Baracks Building
(Mount Vernon Arsenal, Subaltern's Quarters)
Old Saint Stephens Rd. (County Rd. 96)
HABS AL-105-E   p   L

Mount Vernon Arsenal, Center Building
Old Saint Stephens Rd. (County Rd. 96)
HABS AL-105-G   p   L

Mount Vernon Arsenal, Gates
Old Saint Stephens Rd. (County Rd. 96)
HABS AL-105-A   p   L

Mount Vernon Arsenal, Inner Wall
Old Saint Stephens Rd. (County Rd. 96)
HABS AL-105-B   p   L

Mount Vernon Arsenal, Laboratory & Office (Mount Vernon Arsenal, Old Officers' Qtrs.)
Old Saint Stephens Rd. (County Rd. 96)
HABS AL-105-H   p   L

Mount Vernon Arsenal, Officers' Quarters; see Mount Vernon Arsenal, Workshop

Mount Vernon Arsenal, Old Barracks Building
Old Saint Stephens Rd. (County Rd. 96)
HABS AL-105-D   p   L

Mount Vernon Arsenal, Old Mess Hall
Old Saint Stephens Rd. (County Rd. 96)
HABS AL-105-M   p   L

Mount Vernon Arsenal, Old Officers' Qtrs.; see Mount Vernon Arsenal, Laboratory & Office

Mount Vernon Arsenal, Paymaster's Office
Old Saint Stephens Rd. (County Rd. 96)
HABS AL-105-J   p   L

Mount Vernon Arsenal, Stables (Mount VernonArsenal, Old Barn)
Old Saint Stephens Rd. (County Rd. 96)
HABS AL-105-K   p   L

Mount Vernon Arsenal, Subaltern's Quarters; see Mount Vernon Arsenal, Baracks Building

Mount Vernon Arsenal, Workshop (Mount Vernon Arsenal, Officers' Quarters)
Old Saint Stephens Rd. (County Rd. 96)
HABS AL-105-F   p   L

Mount Vernon Arsenal, Workshop & Old Officers Qtrs.
Old Saint Stephens Rd. (County Rd. 96)
HABS AL-105-L   p   L

Mount Vernon Barracks; see Mount Vernon Arsenal

Mount VernonArsenal, Old Barn; see Mount Vernon Arsenal, Stables

Rogers-Curry House; see Curry, L. B., House

Schoolhouse, Indian
County Rd. 96 (Old Saint Stephens Rd.)
HABS AL-125   p   L

Spring Hill

Batre-Hamilton House; see Broun, W. M., House

Beal-Gaillard House; see Gaillard, S. P., House

Broun, W. M., House (Batre-Hamilton House)
320 Avalon St. (see AL, Mobile)
HABS AL-58   pd   L

Carolina Hill; see Dawson, William A., House

Dawson, William A., House (Carolina Hill; Perdue House)
76 S. McGregor Ave. (see AL, Mobile)
HABS AL-10   s pd   L

Eslava House; see Marshall-Eslava-Sledge House

Gaillard, S. P., House (Beal-Gaillard House)
111 Myrtlewood Lane (see AL, Mobile)
HABS AL-107   p   L

Marshall-Eslava-Sledge House (Eslava House)
152 Tuthill Ln. (see AL, Mobile)
HABS AL-6   s pd   L

Perdue House; see Dawson, William A., House

Spring Hill College
Old Shell Rd. (see AL, Mobile)
HABS AL-34   s pd   L

Toulminville

Toulmin, Gen. Theopolis, House
(moved to 307 University Blvd.)(see AL, Mobile)
HABS AL-106   pd   L

MONROE COUNTY

Burnt Corn vic.

Watkins House
State Hwy. 30
HABS AL-112   pd   L

Claiborne

Deer's Store
U.S. Hwy. 84 (State Hwy. 12)
HABS AL-104   s pd   L

Dellet, James, House
U.S. Hwy. 84 (State Hwy. 12)
HABS AL-121   d   L

Masonic Hall (Masonic Temple)
(moved to AL, Perdue Hill)
HABS AL-103   s pd   L

Masonic Temple; see Masonic Hall

Franklin vic.

Gin House (Mule Gin, Old)
State Hwy. 41 (moved from AL, Goode Plantation)
HABS AL-141   p   L

Mule Gin, Old; see Gin House

Monroeville vic.

Andrews, W. T., House (Pioneer House)
State Hwy. 21-47
HABS AL-122   p   L

Pioneer House; see Andrews, W. T., House

Mount Pleasant

Ferrell, Judge, House
Old Federal Rd. (Chrysler vic.)
HABS AL-114   p   L

Perdue Hill

Daniels, John, House; see House, Old Frame

House, Old Frame (Daniels, John, House)
U.S. Hwy. 84 (State Hwy. 12)
HABS AL-123   p   L

Masonic Hall (Masonic Temple)
U.S. Hwy. 84 (moved from AL, Claiborne)
HABS AL-103   s pd   L

Masonic Temple; see Masonic Hall

MONTGOMERY COUNTY

Montgomery

Alabama State Capitol (First Confederate Capitol)
Dexter Ave.
HABS AL-601   s pd   L

Arrington House; see Bibb-Goldthwaithe-Arrington House

Ball, Charles P., House; see Seibels-Ball-Lanier House

Barnes School for Boys; see Figh-Pickett House

Bibb-Goldthwaithe-Arrington House (Arrington House)
203 Church St.
HABS AL-611   pd   L

Branch, E. W., House; see Ray-Branch House

Davis, Jefferson, House; see First White House of the Confederacy

Elks Club; see Murphy, John, House

Figh-Pickett House (Barnes School for Boys; Pickett House)
14 Clayton St.
HABS AL-626   p   L

First Confederate Capitol; see Alabama State Capitol

First White House of the Confederacy (Davis, Jefferson, House)
625 Washington St. (moved from Bibb & Lee Sts.)
HABS AL-624   s pd   L

Fitzpatrick-Saffold House (Saffold House)
442 S. McDonough St.
HABS AL-617   s pd   L

Garrett-Hatchett House (Hatchett House)
313 Catoma St.
HABS AL-630   s pd   L

Gerald-Bethea House (St. Mary's of Loretta Academy; Loretta Academy)
203 S. Lawrence St.
HABS AL-604   s pd   L

Gilmer-Shorter-Lomax House (Lomax House)
235 S. Court St.
HABS AL-607   pd   L

Graves, Gov. Bibb, House; see
Taylor-Ponder-Graves House

Harris-Smith House (Smith House)
Church & Catoma Sts.
HABS AL-610   p   L

Hatchett House; see Garrett-Hatchett
House

Hilliard, Henry, House; see
Hilliard-Nicrosi-Diffly House

Hilliard-Nicrosi-Diffly House (Hilliard,
Henry, House)
Jackson St.
HABS AL-613   d   L

Housman House; see Oliver-Housman
House

Kenneworth-Moffatt House (Moffatt
House)
405 S. Hull St.
HABS AL-614   p   L

Lomax House; see Gilmer-Shorter-Lomax
House

Loretta Academy; see Gerald-Bethea House

McBryde-Screws-Tyson House (Tyson,
John C., House)
423 Mildred St.
HABS AL-608   p   L

Moffatt House; see Kenneworth-Moffatt
House

Murphy, John, House (Elks Club)
22 Bibb St.
HABS AL-603   s pd L

Oliver-Housman House (Housman House)
Wilkerson & Montgomery Sts.
HABS AL-635   s pd L

Owens-Teague House (Teague House)
440 S. Perry St.
HABS AL-606   s pd L

Pickett House; see Figh-Pickett House

Pollard, Col. Charles Teed, House
(Mansion)
117 Jefferson St.
HABS AL-605   s pd L

Ray House; see Ray-Branch House

Ray-Branch House (Branch, E. W., House;
Ray House)
730 S. Court St.
HABS AL-609   p   L

Saffold House; see Fitzpatrick-Saffold
House

Sayre-Troy House (Troy House)
Adams & Jefferson St.
HABS AL-641   pd   L

Seibels-Ball-Lanier House (Ball, Charles P.,
House)
407 Adams Ave.
HABS AL-612   pd   L

Smith House; see Harris-Smith House

St. John's Episcopal Church
113 Madison Ave.
HABS AL-643   pd   L

St. Mary's of Loretta Academy; see
Gerald-Bethea House

Stone-Young Plantation House; see
Stone-Young-Baggett House

Stone-Young-Baggett House (Stone-Young
Plantation House)
County Rd. 54 (Old Selma Rd.)
HABS AL-650   s pd L

Taylor-Ponder-Graves House (Graves, Gov.
Bibb, House)
511 S. McDonough St.
HABS AL-644   p   L

Teague House; see Owens-Teague House

Troy House; see Sayre-Troy House

Tyson, John C., House; see
McBryde-Screws-Tyson House

Union Station
Water St.
HAER AL-2   p   H

Union Station, Train Shed
Water St.
HAER AL-1   pd   H

Winter Building
2 Dexter Ave.
HABS AL-602   s pd L

MORGAN COUNTY

Decatur

Hinds House; see Rhea-Burleson-McEntire
House

McEntire House; see
Rhea-Burleson-McEntire House

Rhea-Burleson-McEntire House (McEntire
House; Hinds House)
120 Sycamore St.
HABS AL-364   p   L

State Bank Building, Old; see State Bank of
Alabama, Decatur Branch

State Bank of Alabama, Decatur Branch
(State Bank Building, Old)
Bank St. & Wilson Ave.
HABS AL-348   s pd L

Somerville

Morgan County Courthouse, Old
Bluff City Rd.
HABS AL-861   p   H

Rather-Rice-Gilchrist House
Bluff City Rd. vic.
HABS AL-864   p   H

PERRY COUNTY

Marion

Edwards, W. H., House
Edwards Rd.
HABS AL-824   p   L

Elmcrest; see Moore, Judge John, House

Ford House & Kitchen; see Lowrey-Ford
House & Kitchen

Hanna, Doctor, House; see
Whitsett-Hurt-Hanna House

King, Judge Porter, House
1001 Washington St.
HABS AL-772   pd   L

Lowrey-Ford House & Kitchen (Ford
House & Kitchen)
Washington St. (County Rd. 45)
HABS AL-822   p   L

Marion Female Seminary (Perry County
High School, Old)
Monroe & Centreville Sts.
HABS AL-771   pd   L

Moore, Gov. Andrew Barry, House
State Hwy. 14
HABS AL-767   pd   L

Moore, Judge John, House (Elmcrest)
H. G. Williams Circle
HABS AL-770   pd   L

Perry County Courthouse, Old
Washington, Pickens, Jefferson & Green Sts.
HABS AL-766   s pd L

Perry County High School, Old; see
Marion Female Seminary

Siloam Baptist Church
Washington & Early Sts.
HABS AL-774   pd   L

Whitsett-Hurt-Hanna House (Hanna,
Doctor, House)
110 W. Lafayette St.
HABS AL-773   pd   L

Marion vic.

Carlisle, Edwin Kenworth, House; see
Kenworthy Hall

Carlisle Hall; see Kenworthy Hall

Coke-Crenshaw House; see
Jones-Cocke-Crenshaw House

Jones-Cocke-Crenshaw House (Tuthill
House; Coke-Crenshaw House)
Washington St. (County Rd. 45)
HABS AL-823   p   L

Kenworthy Hall (Carlisle Hall; Carlisle,
Edwin Kenworth, House)
State Hwy. 14 (Greensboro Rd.)
HABS AL-765   pd   L

Osborne-Jones House
County Rd. 45 (Washington St.)
HABS AL-788   p   L

Tuthill House; see Jones-Cocke-Crenshaw
House

Uniontown

Davidson House; see Westwood

Masonic Hall
Water Ave. & North St.
HABS AL-768   p   L

Pitts' Folly, House & Outbuildings
State Hwy. 21
HABS AL-267   pd   L

Westwood (Davidson House)
Water Ave. (State Hwy. 61)
HABS AL-769   p   L

313

PICKENS COUNTY

Aliceville

Hughes, Benjamin, House & Outbuildings;
see Ingleside, House & Outbuildings
Ingleside, House & Outbuildings (Hughes, Benjamin, House & Outbuildings)
Second St. (State Hwy. 14)
HABS AL-395   p   L

Aliceville vic.

Hughes, Dr. William, House & Outbuildings
Hughes Creek vic.
HABS AL-396   p   L

Carrollton

First United Methodist Church; see Methodist Episcopal Church
Methodist Episcopal Church (First United Methodist Church)
Tuscaloosa St. (State Hwy. 86)
HABS AL-394   p   L
Pettus, Edmund Winston, House
State Rd. 17
HABS AL-372   p   L
Phoenix Hotel
Phoenix St.
HABS AL-393   p   L

Memphis

Boykin, Will, House
State Rt. 32 & County Rt. 1 vic.
HABS AL-870   s pd   L
Charity House
State Rt. 32 & County Rt. 1 vic.
HABS AL-871   s pd   L
Memphis, Town of
HABS AL-869   pd   L

Pickensville

Baptist Church
Bonner Mill Rd.
HABS AL-342   p   L
Ferguson-Long House (Long, Gus, House)
Chopitoulas St. (State Hwy. 14)
HABS AL-386   p   L
Long, Gus, House; see Ferguson-Long House
Methodist Church
Ferguson St.
HABS AL-387   p   L
Peterson Building; see Store
Sander's House; see Saunders, Henry Williams, House
Saunders, Henry Williams, House (Williams, Henry, House; Sander's House)
Bonner Mill Rd. & Ferguson St.
HABS AL-392   p   L
Store (Peterson Building)
State Hwys. 14 & 86
HABS AL-309   p   L

Wilkins, Doctor, House
State Hwys. 14 & 86 vic.
HABS AL-378   p   L
Williams, Henry, House; see Saunders, Henry Williams, House

PIKE COUNTY

Orion

Alabama College, Old; see Orion Male & Female Institute
Baptist Church
U.S. Hwy. 231
HABS AL-562   p   L
Chancey House; see Hanchey-Pennington House
Chancey, John, House
U.S. Hwy. 231 (see AL, High Ridge vic.)
HABS AL-572   p   L
Hanchey-Pennington House (Chancey House; Pennington House)
U.S. Hwy. 231
HABS AL-563   p   L
Henderson House; see McCullough-Henderson House
McCullough-Henderson House (Henderson House)
U.S. Hwy. 231
HABS AL-596   p   L
Orion Academy; see Orion Male & Female Institute
Orion Male & Female Institute (Alabama College, Old; Orion Academy)
U.S. Hwy. 231
HABS AL-574   p   L
Pennington House; see Hanchey-Pennington House
Siler, Solomon, House
U.S. Hwy. 231
HABS AL-597   p   L

Orion vic.

Berry House (Berry-Braswell House; Braswell, E. B., House)
County Rd. 14 (see AL, High Ridge vic.)
HABS AL-595   p   L
Berry-Braswell House; see Berry House
Braswell, E. B., House; see Berry House

RANDOLPH COUNTY

Woodland

Cedarwood (Stickney, Joseph Blodgett, House)
State Rd. 69 (moved from AL, Moundville vic.)
HABS AL-843   s   H
Stickney, Joseph Blodgett, House; see Cedarwood

RUSSELL COUNTY

Cottonton

Cotton Gin & Well Sweep (Mule Cotton Gin; Well Sweep)
Cliatt Plantation, State Rt. 165
HABS AL-552   s pd   L
Mule Cotton Gin; see Cotton Gin & Well Sweep
Well Sweep; see Cotton Gin & Well Sweep

Crawford

Tuskabatchee Masonic Lodge Number 863
U.S. Hwy. 80 & County Rd. 79
HABS AL-515   p   L

Fort Mitchell

Crowell, Col. John, House; see Crowell-Cantey-Alexander House
Crowell-Alexander House; see Crowell-Cantey-Alexander House
Crowell-Cantey-Alexander House (Crowell, Col. John, House; Crowell-Alexander House)
State Rd. 165
HABS AL-578   p   L
Johnson, Enoch, House; see Post Office, Old
Post Office, Old (Johnson, Enoch, House)
HABS AL-594   p   L

Glenville

Elmoreland; see Mitchell, Col. Americus, House
Glenville Plantation; see Mitchell, Col. Americus, House
Mitchell, Col. Americus, House (Elmoreland; Glenville Plantation)
U.S. Hwy. 431 (see AL, Pittsview vic.)
HABS AL-570   s pd   L

Pittsview vic.

Elmoreland; see Mitchell, Col. Americus, House
Glennville Plantation; see Mitchell, Col. Americus, House
Mitchell, Col. Americus, House (Elmoreland; Glennville Plantation)
U.S. Hwy. 431 (see AL, Glenville)
HABS AL-570   s pd   L
Quarles, W. T., House; see Richardson-Quarles-Comer House
Richardson-Quarles-Comer House (Quarles, W. T., House)
U.S. Hwy. 431 vic.
HABS AL-514   p   L

Seale

Dudley's Hotel
Railroad & Main Sts.
HABS AL-531   p   L

Seale vic.

Bass-Perry House (Magnolia Green; Mott, J. F., House; Perry-Mott House)
U.S. Hwy. 431
HABS AL-588   p   L

Magnolia Green; see Bass-Perry House

Mott, J. F., House; see Bass-Perry House

Perry-Mott House; see Bass-Perry House

Vilula

Birds' Nest, The (Martin House; Vilula Tea Garden, The)
U.S. Rt. 43
HABS AL-545   p   L

Martin House; see Birds' Nest, The

Vilula Tea Garden, The; see Birds' Nest, The

SHELBY COUNTY

Harpersville vic.

Chancellor, William, House
Chancellor Crossroads
HABS AL-435   pd   L

Eastis House; see Rock House, The

Rock House, The (Eastis House)
U.S. Rt. 280 (State Rt. 38)
HABS AL-447   pd   L

Helena vic.

Cotton Press (Remains) (Mule Cotton Press (Remains))
Dunham Plantation, County Rd. 17
HABS AL-422   s   L

Mule Cotton Press (Remains); see Cotton Press (Remains)

Montevallo

Alabama Women's College, Reynolds Hall; see Montevallo Male Institute

King, Edmund, House (University of Montevallo, Guest House)
Highland & Bloch Sts.
HABS AL-438   pd   L

Montevallo Male Institute (University of Montevallo, Reynolds Hall; Alabama Women's College, Reynolds Hall)
Highland St.
HABS AL-427   pd   L

University of Montevallo, Guest House; see King, Edmund, House

University of Montevallo, Reynolds Hall; see Montevallo Male Institute

SUMTER COUNTY

Brewersville

Brewersville Methodist Church
State Rd. 28 (see AL, Coatopa vic.)
HABS AL-295   p   L

Henson House
State Rt. 28 (see AL, Coatopa vic.)
HABS AL-293   p   L

Patton, Joe, House; see Patton-Scales House

Patton-Scales House (Patton, Joe, House)
State Rt. 28 (see AL, Coatopa vic.)
HABS AL-292   p   L

Coatopa vic.

Brewersville Methodist Church
State Rt. 28 (see AL, Brewersville)
HABS AL-295   p   L

Henson House
State Rt. 28 (see AL, Brewersville)
HABS AL-293   p   L

Lee Haven
County Rd. 21 (see AL, Livingston)
HABS AL-290   pd   L

Patton, Joe, House; see Patton-Scales House

Patton-Scales House (Patton, Joe, House)
State Rt. 28 (see AL, Brewersville)
HABS AL-292   p   L

Livingston

Arrington-Chapman House (Livingston Hotel; Inn, Old)
207 W. Main St.
HABS AL-285   p   L

Episcopal Church; see St. James' Episcopal Church

Harris-Ennis-White House (White, T. V., House)
W. Main St.
HABS AL-264   p   L

Inn, Old; see Arrington-Chapman House

Lakewood (Parker, J. L., House)
U.S. Hwy. 11 (Washington St.)
HABS AL-284   p   L

Lee Haven
County Rd. 21 (see AL, Coatopa vic.)
HABS AL-290   pd   L

Little, W. G., House
W. Main & Spring Sts.
HABS AL-262   p   L

Livingston Hotel; see Arrington-Chapman House

McMahon House; see Pleasant Ridge

Parker, J. L., House; see Lakewood

Pleasant Ridge (McMahon House)
100 W. Main St.
HABS AL-263   p   L

Sherard, John H., House (Southerland, R. H., House)
State Rd. 28
HABS AL-283   p   L

Southerland, R. H., House; see Sherard, John H., House

St. James' Episcopal Church (Episcopal Church)
Spring & Monroe Sts.
HABS AL-294   p   L

White, T. V., House; see Harris-Ennis-White House

Livingston vic.

Lee, Col. J. M., House; see Oak Manor

Oak Manor (Lee, Col. J. M., House)
State Rd. 28
HABS AL-257   p   L

TALLADEGA COUNTY

Alpine

Alpine (Welch, Nathaniel, House & Outbuildings)
County Rd. 46
HABS AL-433   p   L

Welch, Nathaniel, House & Outbuildings; see Alpine

Alpine vic.

Carlton-Autrey House; see Jenkins-Carlton-Autrey House

Jenkins-Carlton-Autrey House (Carlton-Autrey House)
County Rd. 52 (see AL, Mount Ida vic.)
HABS AL-449   p   L

Lawler House (Orange Vale; Lawler-Whiting-Bliss House; Whitney House)
County Rd. 11 (see AL, Talladega vic.)
HABS AL-443   pd   L

Lawler-Whiting-Bliss House; see Lawler House

Mallory House; see Sellwood

Morris, John, House; see Morris-Holmes House

Morris-Holmes House (Morris, John, House)
State Rt. 76 (see AL, Winterboro)
HABS AL-459   p   L

Mount Ida (Reynolds House; Rendalia)
County Rd. 11 (see AL, Sylacauga vic.)
HABS AL-442   pd   L

Orange Vale; see Lawler House

Rendalia; see Mount Ida

Reynolds House; see Mount Ida

Riser House; see Wewoka

Riser House, Grist Mill; see Wewoka, Grist Mill

Sellwood (Mallory House)
State Rt. 76 (see AL, Sylacauga vic.)
HABS AL-448   p   L

Wewoka (Riser House)
Riser Mill Rd. (see AL, Sylacauga vic.)
HABS AL-429   p   L

Wewoka, Grist Mill (Riser House, Grist Mill)
Riser Mill Rd. (see AL, Sylacauga vic.)
HABS AL-429-N   L

Whitney House; see Lawler House

Eastaboga vic.

Covered Bridge (Peg Bridge, The Old)
Spanning Choccolocco Creek on County Rd. 93
HABS AL-445   p   L

Peg Bridge, The Old; see Covered Bridge

Munford

Academy, Old; see Spence House
Spence House (Academy, Old)
State Rd. 21
HABS AL-463   p L

Sylacauga

Fluker, Baldwin, House
Talladega Hwy.
HABS AL-454   pd L

Sylacauga vic.

Bledsoe-Cook House (Cook House)
State Rd. 21
HABS AL-439   pd L
Bledsoe-Kelly House; see Mountain Spring
Cook House; see Bledsoe-Cook House
Gantts' Quarry
Quarry Rd.
HAER AL-4   d H
Kelly House; see Mountain Spring
Mallory House; see Sellwood
Mount Ida (Reynolds House; Rendalia)
County Rd. 11 (see AL, Alpine vic.)
HABS AL-442   pd L
Mountain Spring (Bledsoe-Kelly House; Kelly House)
State Rd. 21
HABS AL-428   p L
Rendalia; see Mount Ida
Reynolds House; see Mount Ida
Riser House; see Wewoka
Riser House, Grist Mill; see Wewoka, Grist Mill
Sellwood (Mallory House)
State Rt. 76 (see AL, Alpine vic.)
HABS AL-448   p L
Wewoka (Riser House)
Riser Mill Rd. (see AL, Alpine vic.)
HABS AL-429   p L
Wewoka, Grist Mill (Riser House, Grist Mill)
Riser Mill Rd. (see AL, Alpine vic.)
HABS AL-429-N   p L

Talladega

Alabama Institute for Deaf & Blind; see East Alabama Masonic Female Institute
Cedarwood; see King Plantation
Chambers House (Huey-Stone-Chambers House)
301 N. East St.
HABS AL-457   pd L
East Alabama Masonic Female Institute (Alabama Institute for Deaf & Blind; Manning Hall; Masonic Female Institute)
205 E. South St.
HABS AL-446   s pd L
Huey-Stone-Chambers House; see Chambers House
Isbell, James, House (Isbell-Hicks House; Usrey Funeral Home)
108 E. North St.
HABS AL-455   pd L

Isbell-Hicks House; see Isbell, James, House
King Plantation (Cedarwood)
Frank St.
HABS AL-462   p L
Manning Hall; see East Alabama Masonic Female Institute
Masonic Female Institute; see East Alabama Masonic Female Institute
Plowman, T. L., House (Plowman-Elliott House)
511 S. East St.
HABS AL-456   pd L
Plowman-Elliott House; see Plowman, T. L., House
Usrey Funeral Home; see Isbell, James, House

Talladega vic.

Burt House (Curry-Burt-Smelley House; Curry House)
State Rd. 21
HABS AL-472   p L
Curry House; see Burt House
Curry-Burt-Smelley House; see Burt House
Hardie-Lewis House; see Thornhill
Lawler House (Orange Vale; Lawler-Whiting-Bliss House; Whitney House)
County Rd. 11 (see AL, Alpine vic.)
HABS AL-443   pd L
Lawler-Whiting-Bliss House; see Lawler House
Mardis House (Mardis-Batchelor House)
U.S. Hwy. 231
HABS AL-460   p L
Mardis-Batchelor House; see Mardis House
Marker of Jackson Trace
U.S. Hwy. 231
HABS AL-460-A   p L
Orange Vale; see Lawler House
Thornhill (Hardie-Lewis House; Welch, Tom, House)
State Rd. 21
HABS AL-441   pd L
Welch, Tom, House; see Thornhill
Whitney House; see Lawler House

Winterboro

Morriss, John, House; see Morriss-Holmes House
Morriss-Holmes House (Morriss, John, House)
State Rt. 76 (see AL, Alpine vic.)
HABS AL-459   p L

TALLAPOOSA COUNTY

Dadeville

Dennis Hotel; see United States Hotel
Lane House (Mitchell-Lane House; Little Huntington)
311 W. Columbus St.
HABS AL-510   p L

Little Huntington; see Lane House
Mitchell-Lane House; see Lane House
Post Office & Hotel; see United States Hotel
United States Hotel (Dennis Hotel; Post Office & Hotel)
N. Broadnax & E. Green Sts.
HABS AL-511   p L

Dadeville vic.

Black House; see Black-Gilling House
Black-Gilling House (Gregory House; Black House)
County Rd. 44 (see AL, Dudleyville)
HABS AL-548   p L
Gardner, William A., House
Lafayette Hwy. (County Rd. 75)
HABS AL-529   p L
Gregory House; see Black-Gilling House

Dudleyville vic.

Balck-Gilling House (Gregory House; Black House)
County Rd. 44 (see AL, Dadeville vic.)
HABS AL-548   p L
Black House; see Balck-Gilling House
Gregory House; see Balck-Gilling House

TUSCALOOSA COUNTY

Bucksville

Tannehill Furnace (Ruins)
Mud Creek vic.
HABS AL-276   p L

Tuscaloosa

Alabama State Capitol, Old (Capitol, Old)
Broad St.
HABS AL-867   p H
Battle, Alfred, House; see Battle-Friedman House
Battle-Friedman House (Battle, Alfred, House)
Greensboro Ave.
HABS AL-226   pd L
Capitol, Old; see Alabama State Capitol, Old
Christ Episcopal Church
605 Twenty-fifth Ave.
HABS AL-249-A   pd L H
Cochrane, Judge William C., House (Stillman Institute)
3600 Fifteenth St.
HABS AL-217   pd L
Collier, Governor, House; see Collier-Whitt-Boone House
Collier-Whitt-Boone House (Collier, Governor, House)
905 Twenty-first Ave.
HABS AL-268   p L
Deal, Doctor, House; see Dearing-Bagby House
Dearing House; see Dearing-Swaim House

Dearing-Bagby House (Deal, Doctor, House; Governor's Mansion; University Club)
421 Queen City Ave.
HABS AL-230   pd   L

Dearing-Swaim House (Spence House; Dearing House)
2111 Fourteenth St.
HABS AL-228   pd   L

Drish, Dr. John R., House
2300 Seventeenth St.
HABS AL-201   s pd   L H

Duffies Tavern (Tavern, Old)
2800 Twenty-eighth Ave.
HABS AL-224   pd   L

Eddins House (Price-Eddins-Rosenau House)
919 Greensboro Ave.
HABS AL-204   s pd   L

Foster House; see Foster-Shirley House
Foster-Shirley House (Foster House)
1600 Dearing Place
HABS AL-216   pd   L

Gluck House (Martin-Comegys-Cluck House)
2021 Seventh St.
HABS AL-225   s pd   L

Gorgas House; see University of Alabama, Gorgas House
Governor's Mansion; see Dearing-Bagby House
Guild, Dr. Lafayette, House; see Ormond-Litte House
Janus Place; see Scott-Moody House
Jemison, Sen. Robert, House; see Jemison-Van de Graaf-Burchfield House
Jemison-Van de Graaf-Burchfield House (Jemison, Sen. Robert, House)
1305 Greensboro Ave.
HABS AL-205   pd   L

Martin-Comegys-Cluck House; see Gluck House
Martin-Marlowe House; see Martin-Randolph-Marlowe House
Martin-Randolph-Marlowe House (Martin-Marlowe House)
816 Twenty-second Ave.
HABS AL-223   pd   L

Masonic Club House; see Prince, Thomas, House
Moody House; see Scott-Moody House
Ormond-Litte House (Guild, Dr. Lafayette, House)
325 Queen City Ave.
HABS AL-202   s pd   L

Peck, Samuel M., House (Snow-Peck House)
Eighteenth St. & Thirtieth Ave.
HABS AL-222   pd   L

Presbyterian School; see Snow, E. N. C., House
Price-Eddins-Rosenau House; see Eddins House

Prince, Thomas, House (Students' Masonic Building; Masonic Club House)
University Blvd.
HABS AL-248   pd   L

Scott, David, House; see Scott-Moody House
Scott-Moody House (Janus Place; Moody House; Scott, David, House)
1925 Eighth St.
HABS AL-227   pd   L

Snow, E. N. C., House (Wesleyan Female Academy; Presbyterian School)
2414 Eighth St.
HABS AL-206   pd   L

Snow-Peck House; see Peck, Samuel M., House
Spence House; see Dearing-Swaim House
Stillman Institute; see Cochrane, Judge William C., House
Students' Masonic Building; see Prince, Thomas, House
Tavern, Old; see Duffies Tavern
University Club; see Dearing-Bagby House
University of Alabama, Gorgas House (Gorgas House)
Ninth Ave. & Capstone Dr.
HABS AL-203   s pd   L

University of Alabama, Observatory
Stadium Dr. & Fifth St.
HABS AL-231   pd   L

University of Alabama, President's House
University Blvd.
HABS AL-207   s pd   L

Wesleyan Female Academy; see Snow, E. N. C., House

WASHINGTON COUNTY

Mc Intosh

Andrews Chapel
U.S. Hwy. 43 (State Hwy. 13)
HABS AL-866   s   H

St. Stephens

Masonic Lodge; see Washington County Courthouse, Old
Masonic Temple; see Washington County Courthouse, Old
Washington County Courthouse, Old (Masonic Lodge; Masonic Temple)
County Rd. 34
HABS AL-111   pd   L

WILCOX COUNTY

Allenton

Fitzgerald House; see Tavern, Old
Grace, Joshua B., House & Outbuildings (Grace-Chestnut House)
County Rd. 24
HABS AL-190   pd   L

Grace-Chestnut House; see Grace, Joshua B., House & Outbuildings

Tavern, Old (Fitzgerald House)
County Rd. 24
HABS AL-191   pd   L

Camden

Bagby House (Bagby-Liddell House)
Broad St.
HABS AL-133   p   L

Bagby-Liddell House; see Bagby House
Baptist Church
Broad St. (State Rd. 28)
HABS AL-169   p   L

Beck, Franklin King, House
312 Clifton St.
HABS AL-132   p   L

Black, Doctor, Store Number 1; see Bloch, Dr. Morris, Store Number 1
Black Store Number 2; see Broad Street (Store)
Bloch, Dr. Morris, Store Number 1 (Water Street (Store); Black, Doctor, Store Number 1)
HABS AL-175-A   p   L

Bloch House; see Block House
Block House (Bloch House; 101 Hill Street (House))
HABS AL-171   p   L

Broad Street (Store) (Sperlin, R. L., Store)
HABS AL-175-B   p   L

Broad Street (Store) (Black Store Number 2; McMillan Store)
HABS AL-175-C   p   L

Camden High School; see Female Academy, Old
Coster House (Kester, Henry, House)
Broad & Hill Sts.
HABS AL-184   p   L

Dale Lodge Number 25; see Masonic Temple
Dunn, Thomas, House (Dunn-Bonner House)
Broad St.
HABS AL-176   pd   L

Dunn-Bonner House; see Dunn, Thomas, House
Episcopal Church; see St. Mary's Episcopal Church

Fail-McIntosh House; see McIntosh House

Female Academy, Old (Wilcox Female Institute; Camden High School)
Broad St. (State Rt. 28)
HABS AL-170   p   L

Handley-Felts House; see Hanley House

Hanley House (Handley-Felts House)
209 Caldwell St.
HABS AL-128   pd   L

Harris House; see McDowell House
101 Hill Street (House); see Block House

Jones, Eustis, House (Jones-Liddell House)
Broad St.
HABS AL-178   p   L

Jones, Gen. R. C., House (Jones-McIntosh House)
Broad St.
HABS AL-180   pd   L
Jones Law Office; see Law Office
Jones-Liddell House; see Jones, Eustis, House
Jones-McIntosh House; see Jones, Gen. R. C., House
Kester, Henry, House; see Coster House
Kilpatrick, Col. John Young, House & Outbuildings
Bridgeport Rd. (County Rd. 37)
HABS AL-168   p   L
Law Office (Miller, Gov. Benjamin M., Law Office)
Planters & Water Sts.
HABS AL-173-A   p   L
Law Office (Jones Law Office)
Court & Water Sts.
HABS AL-173-C   p   L
Law Office (Moore, Dr. W. W., Office)
Court St.
HABS AL-173-B   p   L
Law Office; see Newspaper Plant, Old
Liberty Hall; see McDowell House
Masonic Lodge Number 25; see Masonic Temple
Masonic Temple (Masonic Lodge Number 25; Dale Lodge Number 25)
Broad St. (State Rd. 28)
HABS AL-131   p   L
Matheson-Moore-McLeod House; see Moore, S. D., House
McDowell House (Liberty Hall; Harris House)
State Rd. 221
HABS AL-164   p   L
McIntosh House (Fail-McIntosh House)
Fail St.
HABS AL-151   pd   L
McMillan House (McMillan-Moore-Gibbs House)
Broad St. (State Rd. 28)
HABS AL-182   pd   L
McMillan Store; see Broad Street (Store)
McMillan-Moore-Gibbs House; see McMillan House
McWilliams House (Sterrett-McWilliams House)
400 Clifton St.
HABS AL-134   p   L
Miller, Gov. Benjamin M., Law Office; see Law Office
Moore, Dr. W. W., Office; see Law Office
Moore, S. D., House
(Matheson-Moore-McLeod House)
310 Broad St.
HABS AL-127   pd   L
Newson House (Newson-Sharp House)
State Rd. 10
HABS AL-113   pd   L
Newson-Sharp House; see Newson House

Newspaper Plant, Old (Law Office)
Planters St.
HABS AL-174   p   L
Presbyterian Church
Broad St. (State Rd. 28)
HABS AL-185   pd   L
Sperlin, R. L., Store; see Broad Street (Store)
St. Mary's Episcopal Church (Episcopal Church)
302 Clifton St.
HABS AL-135   p   L
Sterrett-McWilliams House; see McWilliams House
Water Street (Store); see Bloch, Dr. Morris, Store Number 1
Wilcox County Courthouse
Broad, Claiborne, Court & Water Sts.
HABS AL-172   p   L
Wilcox Female Institute; see Female Academy, Old
Wilcox Hotel
Broad St. (State Rt. 28)
HABS AL-136   p   L

Camden vic.

Burford House
County Rd. 33 vic.
HABS AL-129   p   L
Capell House
State Rt. 41 (see AL, Capell)
HABS AL-166   p   L
Clifton Ferry Landing & Store (Cook Store)
Clifton Ferry Access Rd. (see AL, Clifton Ferry)
HABS AL-167-A   p   L
Clifton House
Clifton Ferry Access Rd. (see AL, Clifton Ferry)
HABS AL-167   p   L
Cook Store; see Clifton Ferry Landing & Store
Countryside; see Tait, Robert, Plantation
Dawson, Col. E. N., House
County Rd. 31
HABS AL-126   pd   L
Dry Forks Plantation (Tait, James Charles, House)
County Rd. 12 (see AL, Coy vic.)
HABS AL-137   p   L
Ervin House; see Tait, Robert, Plantation
Miller, Dr. George, House; see Miller-Smith House
Miller-Smith House (Miller, Dr. George, House)
State Rd. 28 (see AL, Canton Bend)
HABS AL-179   pd   L
Star, P. E., House; see Tait, Felix, Plantation
Tait, Felix, Plantation (Tait-Starr House; White Columns; Star, P. E., House)
County Rd. 23
HABS AL-138   p   L

Tait, James Charles, House; see Dry Forks Plantation
Tait, Robert, Plantation (Tait-Ervin House; Ervin House; Countryside)
County Rd. 33
HABS AL-139   p   L
Tait-Ervin House; see Tait, Robert, Plantation
Tait-Starr House; see Tait, Felix, Plantation
White Columns; see Tait, Felix, Plantation

Canton Bend

Bethea, Ervett, House; see Bethea-Strother House
Bethea-Strother House (Bethea, Ervett, House)
State Rd. 28
HABS AL-186   pd   L
Henderson, William, Store (Strother Store)
State Rd. 28
HABS AL-194   pd   L
Miller, Dr. George, House; see Miller-Smith House
Miller-Smith House (Miller, Dr. George, House)
State Rd. 28 (see AL, Camden vic.)
HABS AL-179   pd   L
Strother Store; see Henderson, William, Store

Canton Bend vic.

Matthews, William T., House; see Tait, Frank, House
Matthews-Tait House; see Tait, Frank, House
Tait, Frank, House (Matthews-Tait House; Youpon; Matthews, William T., House)
County Rd. 19
HABS AL-130   p   L
Youpon; see Tait, Frank, House

Capell

Capell House
State Rt. 41 (see AL, Camden vic.)
HABS AL-166   p   L

Clifton Ferry

Clifton Ferry Landing & Store (Cook Store)
Clifton Ferry Access Rd. (see AL, Camden vic.)
HABS AL-167-A   p   L
Clifton House
Clifton Ferry Access Rd. (see AL, Camden vic.)
HABS AL-167   p   L
Cook Store; see Clifton Ferry Landing & Store

Coy vic.

Dry Forks Plantation (Tait, James Charles, House)
County Rd. 12 (see AL, Camden vic.)
HABS AL-137   p   L

Tait, James Charles, House; see Dry Forks Plantation

Millers Ferry

Henderson House & Smokehouse; see Sellers-Henderson House & Smokehouse

Sellers House & Smokehouse; see Sellers-Henderson House & Smokehouse

Sellers-Henderson House & Smokehouse (Henderson House & Smokehouse; Sellers House & Smokehouse)
State Rt. 28
HABS AL-147   pd   L

Millers Ferry vic.

Matthews House & Plantation Store; see Rosemary, House & Plantation Store

Matthews-Cade House & Plantation Store; see Rosemary, House & Plantation Store

Rosemary, House & Plantation Store (Matthews House & Plantation Store; Matthews-Cade House & Plantation Store)
State Rt. 28 vic.
HABS AL-150   pd   L

Oak Hill

Fox, Dr. Daniel J., House; see Fox-Harris-Jones House

Fox-Harris-Jones House (Fox, Dr. Daniel J., House)
State Rd. 21
HABS AL-148   pd   L
Ramsey House; see Ramsey-Jones-Bonner House

Ramsey-Jones-Bonner House (Ramsey House)
State Rt. 10
HABS AL-108   pd   L

Pine Apple

Hawthorne, Col. Joseph R., House
Broad St. (County Rd. 59)
HABS AL-119   pd   L

Alaska

CORDOVA-MC CARTHY COUNTY

Mc Carthy

Kennecott Mines
HAER AK-1   d   L

HAINES COUNTY

Haines vic.

Dalton Trail Post (Pleasant Camp)
Mile 40, Haines Hwy.
HABS AK-4   pd   L

Pleasant Camp; see Dalton Trail Post

KETCHIKAN GATEWAY COUNTY

Ketchikan vic.

Totem Bight Community House
N. Tongass Hwy.
HABS AK-3   pd   H

KODIAK ISLAND COUNTY

Kodiak

Erskine House
Main St. & Marine Way
HABS AK-2   s   L

SITKA COUNTY

Sitka

St. Michael's Cathedral
Lincoln St.
HABS AK-1   s d   L

Arizona

APACHE COUNTY

Chinle vic.

Canyon de Chelly National Monument; see Mummy Cave

Mummy Cave (Canyon de Chelly National Monument)
Navajo Indian Reservation
HABS AZ-72   s   L

Ganado

Hubbell, J. L., Trading Post (Hubbell Trading Post National Historic Site)
State Rt. 3 (Navajo Indian Reservation)
HABS AZ-59   s   L

Hubbell, J. L. Trading Post, House (Hubbell Trading Post National Historic Site)
State Rt. 3 (Navajo Indian Reservation)
HABS AZ-60   s   L

Hubbell, J. L., Trading Post, Stone House (Hubbell Trading Post National Historic Site)
State Rt. 3 (Navajo Indian Reservation)
HABS AZ-64   s   L

Hubbell, J. L., Trading Post, Two-Story Barn (Hubbell Trading Post National Historic Site)
State Rt. 3 (Navajo Indian Reservation)
HABS AZ-61   s   L

Hubbell, J. L., Trading Post, Unfinished Shed (Hubbell Trading Post National Historic Site)
State Rt. 3 (Navajo Indian Reservation)
HABS AZ-62   s   L

Hubbell Trading Post National Historic Site; see Hubbell, J. L. Trading Post, House

Hubbell Trading Post National Historic Site; see Hubbell, J. L., Trading Post

Hubbell Trading Post National Historic Site; see Hubbell, J. L., Trading Post, Stone House

Hubbell Trading Post National Historic Site; see Hubbell, J. L., Trading Post, Two-Story Barn

Hubbell Trading Post National Historic Site; see Hubbell, J. L., Trading Post, Unfinished Shed

COCHISE COUNTY

Bowie vic.

Fort Bowie, Cavalry Barracks (Fort Bowie National Historic Site)
HABS AZ-63-A   s   L
Fort Bowie, Commanding Officer's Quarters (Fort Bowie National Historic Site)
HABS AZ-63-D   s   L
Fort Bowie, Corrals (Fort Bowie National Historic Site)
HABS AZ-63-B   s   L
Fort Bowie, Guardhouse (Fort Bowie National Historic Site)
HABS AZ-63-E   s   L
Fort Bowie, Infantry Barracks (Fort Bowie National Historic Site)
HABS AZ-63-C   s   L
Fort Bowie, Magazine (Fort Bowie National Historic Site)
HABS AZ-63-I   s   L
Fort Bowie National Historic Site; see Fort Bowie (Ruins)
Fort Bowie National Historic Site; see Fort Bowie, Cavalry Barracks

Fort Bowie National Historic Site; see Fort
   Bowie, Commanding Officer's Quarters
Fort Bowie National Historic Site; see Fort
   Bowie, Corrals
Fort Bowie National Historic Site; see Fort
   Bowie, Guardhouse
Fort Bowie National Historic Site; see Fort
   Bowie, Infantry Barracks
Fort Bowie National Historic Site; see Fort
   Bowie, Magazine
Fort Bowie National Historic Site; see Fort
   Bowie, New Hospital
Fort Bowie National Historic Site; see Fort
   Bowie, Schoolhouse
Fort Bowie National Historic Site; see Fort
   Bowie, Sutler's Store
Fort Bowie, New Hospital (Fort Bowie
   National Historic Site)
HABS AZ-63-G   s   L
Fort Bowie (Ruins) (Fort Bowie National
   Historic Site)
HABS AZ-63   s p   L
Fort Bowie, Schoolhouse (Fort Bowie
   National Historic Site)
HABS AZ-63-F   s   L
Fort Bowie, Sutler's Store (Fort Bowie
   National Historic Site)
HABS AZ-63-H   s   L

Fairbank

Fairbank Commercial Company Building
HABS AZ-76   p   L
Fairbank Hotel
HABS AZ-75   p   L

Fairbank vic.

San Pablo de Quiburi Mission (Ruins); see
   Santa Ana de Quiburi Mission (Ruins)
Santa Ana de Quiburi Mission (Ruins)
   (San Pablo de Quiburi Mission (Ruins))
San Pedro River vic.
HABS AZ-16   pd   L

Tombstone

Allen Street (Commercial Building) (Shop
   Number 3)
HABS AZ-9   pd   L
Allen Street (Commercial Building)
HABS AZ-78   p   L
Allen Street (Commercial Building) (Shop
   Number 2)
HABS AZ-9-B   s pd   L
Allen Street (Commercial Building, Door)
   (Shop Number 1 (Door))
HABS AZ-9-A   p   L
Bird Cage Theatre
Allen St.
HABS AZ-10   s pd   L
Can Can Saloon
Fourth & Allen Sts.
HABS AZ-82   p   L
Cashman, Nellie, House
Toughnut & Sixth Sts.
HABS AZ-80   p   L

City Hall
Fremont St.
HABS AZ-86   p   L
City Hall, Old
Fremont St.
HABS AZ-48   p   L
Cochise County Courthouse
Toughnut & Third Sts.
HABS AZ-83   p   L
Crystal Palace Saloon
Allen & Fifth Sts.
HABS AZ-7   s pd   L
Episcopal Church
Third & Safford Sts.
HABS AZ-84   p   L
Fifth Street (Commercial Building)
HABS AZ-79   p   L
Fire Station
Toughnut St.
HABS AZ-85   p   L
**Fremont Street (Commercial Buildings,
   Ruins)**
HABS AZ-49   p   L
Rose Tree Inn
Toughnut & Fourth Sts.
HABS AZ-81   p   L
Shop Number 1 (Door); see Allen Street
   (Commercial Building, Door)
Shop Number 2; see Allen Street
   (Commercial Building)
Shop Number 3; see Allen Street
   (Commercial Building)
**South Third Street (Fence, Fenceposts &
   Gate)**
HABS AZ-77   p   L
Third & Allen Streets (Bank)
HABS AZ-87   p   L

Willcox

House & Fence
HABS AZ-55   p   L

COCONINO COUNTY

Grand Canyon N. P.

El Tovar Hotel
HABS AZ-74   p   H
Power Plant
HAER AZ-2   p   H
Railroad Depot
HAER AZ-1   p   H
Water Reclamation Plant
HAER AZ-3   pd   H

Page vic.

Glen Canyon National Recreation Area;
   see Lee's Ferry
Glen Canyon National Recreation Area;
   see Lee's Ferry, Chicken House
Glen Canyon National Recreation Area;
   see Lee's Ferry, Fort
Glen Canyon National Recreation Area;
   see Lee's Ferry, Old Spencer Cabin

Glen Canyon National Recreation Area;
   see Lee's Ferry, Post Office
Glen Canyon National Recreation Area;
   see Lee's Ferry, Root Cellar
Lee's Ferry (Glen Canyon National
   Recreation Area)
U.S. Rt. Alt. 89
HABS AZ-58   L
Lee's Ferry, Chicken House (Glen Canyon
   National Recreation Area)
U.S. Rt. Alt. 89
HABS AZ-58-C   s   L
Lee's Ferry, Fort (Glen Canyon National
   Recreation Area)
U.S. Rt. Alt. 89
HABS AZ-58-A   s   L
Lee's Ferry, Old Spencer Cabin (Lee's
   Ferry, Silt Cabin; Spencer Building; Glen
   Canyon National Recreation Area)
U.S. Rt. Alt. 89
HABS AZ-58-E   L
Lee's Ferry, Post Office (Glen Canyon
   National Recreation Area)
U.S. Rt. Alt. 89
HABS AZ-58-B   s   L
Lee's Ferry, Root Cellar (Glen Canyon
   National Recreation Area)
U.S. Rt. Alt. 89
HABS AZ-58-D   s   L
Lee's Ferry, Silt Cabin; see Lee's Ferry, Old
   Spencer Cabin
Spencer Building; see Lee's Ferry, Old
   Spencer Cabin

Walpi

Pueblo of the First Mesa; see Pueblo of
   Walpi
Pueblo of Walpi (Pueblo of the First Mesa)
Hopi Reservation
HABS AZ-69   s   H

MARICOPA COUNTY

Phoenix

606 1/2-608 Monroe Street (House)
HABS AZ-38   p   L
Anderson House
505 N. Seventh St.
HABS AZ-30   p   L
725 East Washington Street (House)
HABS AZ-35   p   L
Evans House
Washington St. & Eleventh Ave.
HABS AZ-31   p   L
Ford Hotel
Washington St. & Second Ave.
HABS AZ-32   p   L
Messinger House
Wood St. & Ninth Ave.
HABS AZ-36   p   L
3320 North Central Avenue (House)
HABS AZ-33   p   L
3502 North Central Avenue (House)
HABS AZ-34   p   L

Rosens House
139 N. Sixth St.
HABS AZ-37   p   L

Sweatnan House
Adams St. & Eighteenth Ave.
HABS AZ-39   p   L

Wickenburg

Center Street (House)
HABS AZ-52   p   L

South Flont Street (House)
HABS AZ-53   p   L

South Flont Street (House)
HABS AZ-54   p   L

MOHAVE COUNTY

Moccasin vic.

Pipe Spring Fort (Pipe Spring National
     Monument; Windsor Castle)
HABS AZ-18   s pd   L

Pipe Spring National Monument; see Pipe
     Spring Fort

Windsor Castle; see Pipe Spring Fort

NAVAJO COUNTY

Kayenta vic.

Cliff Dwelling of Keet Seel (Navajo
     National Monument)
Tsegi Canyon (Navajo Indian Reservation)
HABS AZ-70   s   L H

Navajo National Monument; see Cliff
     Dwelling of Keet Seel

PIMA COUNTY

Arivaca

Arivaca Ranch
HABS AZ-88   p   L

Double House
HABS AZ-20   p   L

House
HABS AZ-22   p   L

House
HABS AZ-21   p   L

House & Addition
HABS AZ-23   p   L

Houses
HABS AZ-24   p   L

Santa Gertrudes de Arivaca Mission
     (Ruins)
HABS AZ-8   s pd   L

Tucson

479 & 481 South Convent Avenue (House);
     see Barrio Libre

168 1/2 West Kennedy Street (House,
     Addition); see Barrio Libre

Adobe Brick Kilns (Ruins)
HABS AZ-90   p   L

Ahloy House; see Barrio Libre

Aragon, Albert, House
402 Second St.
HABS AZ-89   p   L

Aros House; see Barrio Libre

Barrio Historico; see Barrio Libre

Barrio Libre (Barrio Historico; Palafox
     House)
575-585 S. Meyer Ave.
HABS AZ-73-38   s pd   L

Barrio Libre (Barrio Historico; Romero
     House)
469-471 S. Convent Ave.
HABS AZ-73-41   pd   L

Barrio Libre (Barrio Historico; Valencia
     House)
432-436 S. Convent Ave.
HABS AZ-73-48   s pd   L

Barrio Libre (Barrio Historico; Terrazas
     House)
418 S. Convent Ave.
HABS AZ-73-47   pd   L

Barrio Libre (Barrio Historico; Garcia
     House)
496-498 S. Convent Ave.
HABS AZ-73-19   s pd   L

Barrio Libre (Barrio Historico; 400 West
     Simpson Street (Commercial Building);
     Elysian Grove Market)
HABS AZ-73-46   p   L

Barrio Libre (Barrio Historico; 74 West
     Kennedy Street (House))
HABS AZ-73-21   s p   L

Barrio Libre (Barrio Historico; 530-576
     South Eighth Avenue (House))
HABS AZ-73-24   s pd   L

Barrio Libre (Barrio Historico;
     Wherehouse, The)
551-557 S. Meyer Ave.
HABS AZ-73-29   s pd   L

Barrio Libre (Barrio Historico; 367-371
     South Meyer Avenue (House))
HABS AZ-73-51   d   L

Barrio Libre (Barrio Historico; 471-473
     South Convent Avenue (House))
HABS AZ-73-52   pd   L

Barrio Libre (Barrio Historico; 447-451
     South Main Avenue (House))
HABS AZ-73-53   s pd   L

Barrio Libre (Barrio Historico; Bustamante,
     Antonio, House)
485-489 S. Meyer Ave. & 186 W. Kennedy
     St.
HABS AZ-73-5   s pd   L

Barrio Libre (Barrio Historico; Bustamante,
     Ramon, House)
505 S. Meyer Ave.
HABS AZ-73-6   s pd   L

Barrio Libre (Barrio Historico; Fimbres
     House Number 2)
521-525 S. Meyer Ave.
HABS AZ-73-18   s pd   L

Barrio Libre (Barrio Historico; 147 West
     Kennedy Street (House))
HABS AZ-73-22   s p   L

Barrio Libre (Barrio Historico; 527-529
     South Meyer Avenue (House))
HABS AZ-73-28   s pd   L

Barrio Libre (Barrio Historico; Aros House)
145 W. Kennedy St.
HABS AZ-73-2   s pd   L

Barrio Libre (Barrio Historico; Bojorquez
     House)
459 S. Convent Ave.
HABS AZ-73-4   pd   L

Barrio Libre (Barrio Historico; 363 South
     Meyer Avenue (House))
HABS AZ-73-27   s p   L

Barrio Libre (Barrio Historico; Ahloy
     House)
492-494 S. Convent Ave.
HABS AZ-73-1   s pd   L

Barrio Libre (Barrio Historico; Bernal
     House)
571 S. Meyer Ave.
HABS AZ-73-3   s p   L

Barrio Libre (Barrio Historico)
W. Kennedy, & W. 17th Sts., Meyer &
     Convent Aves.
HABS AZ-73   s pd   L

Barrio Libre (Barrio Historico; Lopez
     House)
517 S. Convent Ave.
HABS AZ-73-26   s pd   L

Barrio Libre (Barrio Historico; 520-526
     South Meyer Avenue (Apartments))
HABS AZ-73-34   pd   L

Barrio Libre (Barrio Historico; 614 South
     Meyer Avenue (Building))
HABS AZ-73-36   pd   L

Barrio Libre (Barrio Historico; 486-490
     South Meyer Avenue (Building); Lucky's
     Market)
HABS AZ-73-31   s pd   L

Barrio Libre (Barrio Historico; 488-498
     South Meyer Avenue (Apartments))
HABS AZ-73-32   pd   L

Barrio Libre (Barrio Historico; 508-518
     South Meyer Avenue (Apartments))
HABS AZ-73-33   pd   L

Barrio Libre (Barrio Historico; 441-447
     South Convent Avenue (House))
HABS AZ-73-7   s pd   L

Barrio Libre (Barrio Historico; 451 South
     Convent Avenue (House))
HABS AZ-73-8   s pd   L

Barrio Libre (Barrio Historico; Prince
     Chapel, African M. E. Church)
S. Convent Ave. & W. Seventeenth St.
HABS AZ-73-40   s pd   L

Barrio Libre (Barrio Historico; 558-564
     South Meyer Avenue (Apartments))
HABS AZ-73-35   pd   L

Barrio Libre (Barrio Historico; 500-502
     South Convent Avenue (House))
HABS AZ-73-12   s pd   L

Barrio Libre (Barrio Historico; 168 1/2 West Kennedy Street (House, Addition); Bustamante, Antonio, Addition)
HABS AZ-73-14   s pd   L

Barrio Libre (Barrio Historico; Munoz House)
499-501 S. Meyer Ave.
HABS AZ-73-37   s pd   L

Barrio Libre (Barrio Historico; Escalante House)
482-484 S. Convent Ave.
HABS AZ-73-16   s pd   L

Barrio Libre (Barrio Historico; 209-219 West Seventeenth Street (Apartments))
HABS AZ-73-43   pd   L

Barrio Libre (Barrio Historico; 141-147 West Simpson Street (Building))
HABS AZ-73-45   p   L

Barrio Libre (Barrio Historico; Wishing Shrine)
S. Main Ave.
HABS AZ-73-50   p   L

Barrio Libre (Barrio Historico; 519-527 South Convent Avenue (Apartments))
HABS AZ-73-10   s pd   L

Barrio Libre (Barrio Historico; 440-446 South Convent Avenue (House))
HABS AZ-73-11   s pd   L

Barrio Libre (Barrio Historico; 510-512 South Convent Avenue (House))
HABS AZ-73-13   s pd   L

Barrio Libre (Barrio Historico; 29-33 West Kennedy Street (House))
HABS AZ-73-20   p   L

Barrio Libre (Barrio Historico; Diaz House)
483 S. Convent Ave.
HABS AZ-73-15   pd   L

Barrio Libre (Barrio Historico; Fimbres House Number 1)
509-513 S. Meyer Ave.
HABS AZ-73-17   s pd   L

Barrio Libre (Barrio Historico; Preciado House)
148-150 W. Kennedy St.
HABS AZ-73-39   s pd   L

Barrio Libre (Barrio Historico; 477 South Meyer Avenue (House); 155-159 West Kennedy Street (House))
HABS AZ-73-23   s pd   L

Barrio Libre (Barrio Historico; Lee Lung Sing Market)
600 S. Meyer Ave.
HABS AZ-73-25   s pd   L

Barrio Libre (Barrio Historico; Rubio House)
140 W. Kennedy St.
HABS AZ-73-42   s pd   L

Barrio Libre (Barrio Historico; 609-619 South Meyer Avenue (Apartments))
HABS AZ-73-30   s p   L

Barrio Libre (Barrio Historico; 139 West Simpson Street (Building))
HABS AZ-73-44   p   L

Barrio Libre (Barrio Historico; 479 & 481 South Convent Avenue (House))
HABS AZ-73-9   s pd   L

Barrio Libre (Barrio Historico; Villa House)
504-506 S. Convent Ave.
HABS AZ-73-49   s pd   L

Bechtold House
Fifth & Main Sts.
HABS AZ-92   p   L

Bernal House; see Barrio Libre

Bojorquez House; see Barrio Libre

Bustamante, Antonio, Addition; see Barrio Libre

Bustamante, Antonio, House; see Barrio Libre

Bustamante, Ramon, House; see Barrio Libre

Carrillo, Leopoldo, House (Priests' House)
1005 Mission Ave.
HABS AZ-5   s pd   L

Church of San Augustine
HABS AZ-15   pd   L

Courthouse Plaza (Row Houses)
HABS AZ-131   s   L

Diaz House; see Barrio Libre

47 East Alameda Street (House)
HABS AZ-93   p   L

Elysian Grove Market; see Barrio Libre

Escalante House; see Barrio Libre

Feldman House
First Ave. & Second St.
HABS AZ-94   p   L

Fickett, Fred W., House
105 W. Franklin St.
HABS AZ-95   p   L

Fimbres House Number 1; see Barrio Libre

Fimbres House Number 2; see Barrio Libre

Garcia House; see Barrio Libre

Hoff House
W. Franklin St.
HABS AZ-96   p   L

House, Adobe
Paseo Redondo
HABS AZ-91   p   L

Lee Lung Sing Market; see Barrio Libre

Lopez House; see Barrio Libre

Lucky's Market; see Barrio Libre

45-51 Mittenburg Street (House)
HABS AZ-97   p   L

Munoz House; see Barrio Libre

299 North Court Street (House)
HABS AZ-98   p   L

293 North Meyer Street (House)
HABS AZ-99   p   L

124 North Stone Street (House)
HABS AZ-100   p   L

Odermott, Dr., House
304 N. Church St.
HABS AZ-102   p   L

Palafox House; see Barrio Libre

385 Perry Street (House)
HABS AZ-101   p   L

Police Station
S. Main St.
HABS AZ-50   p   L

Preciado House; see Barrio Libre

Priests' House; see Carrillo, Leopoldo, House

Prince Chapel, African M. E. Church; see Barrio Libre

Robinson, Ballantyne, House
Military Plaza (141 S. Fifth Ave.)
HABS AZ-6   s pd   L

Romero House; see Barrio Libre

Rubio House; see Barrio Libre

San Cosme del Tucson Mission (Ruins)
Menlo Park
HABS AZ-12   pd   L

519-527 South Convent Avenue (Apartments); see Barrio Libre

440-446 South Convent Avenue (House); see Barrio Libre

441-447 South Convent Avenue (House); see Barrio Libre

451 South Convent Avenue (House); see Barrio Libre

471-473 South Convent Avenue (House); see Barrio Libre

500-502 South Convent Avenue (House); see Barrio Libre

510-512 South Convent Avenue (House); see Barrio Libre

68 South Convent Street (House)
HABS AZ-103   p   L

530-576 South Eighth Avenue (House); see Barrio Libre

447-451 South Main Avenue (House); see Barrio Libre

212 South Main Street (House)
HABS AZ-105   p   L

315 South Main Street (House)
HABS AZ-104   p   L

820 South Main Street (House)
HABS AZ-106   p   L

488-498 South Meyer Avenue (Apartments); see Barrio Libre

508-518 South Meyer Avenue (Apartments); see Barrio Libre

520-526 South Meyer Avenue (Apartments); see Barrio Libre

558-564 South Meyer Avenue (Apartments); see Barrio Libre

609-619 South Meyer Avenue (Apartments); see Barrio Libre

486-490 South Meyer Avenue (Building); see Barrio Libre

614 South Meyer Avenue (Building); see Barrio Libre

363 South Meyer Avenue (House); see Barrio Libre

367-371 South Meyer Avenue (House); see Barrio Libre

477 South Meyer Avenue (House); see
Barrio Libre
527-529 South Meyer Avenue (House); see
Barrio Libre
443 South Meyer Street (House, Doorway)
HABS AZ-107   p   L
421 South Sixth Avenue (House)
HABS AZ-108   p   L
St. John the Evangelist Church
3522 S. Seventh Ave.
HABS AZ-51   p   L
Terrazas House; see Barrio Libre
University of Arizona, Old Main
University of Arizona Campus
HABS AZ-110   p   L
Valencia House; see Barrio Libre
Villa House; see Barrio Libre
195 West Alameda Street (House)
HABS AZ-109   p   L
147 West Kennedy Street (House); see
Barrio Libre
155-159 West Kennedy Street (House); see
Barrio Libre
29-33 West Kennedy Street (House); see
Barrio Libre
74 West Kennedy Street (House); see
Barrio Libre
209-219 West Seventeenth Street
(Apartments); see Barrio Libre
139 West Simpson Street (Building); see
Barrio Libre
141-147 West Simpson Street (Building);
see Barrio Libre
400 West Simpson Street (Commercial
Building); see Barrio Libre
Wherehouse, The; see Barrio Libre
Wishing Shrine; see Barrio Libre

Tucson vic.
Fort Lowell
Fort Lowell Rd. vic.
HABS AZ-17   s p d   L
Fort Lowell, Officers' Quarters
Fort Lowell Rd. vic.
HABS AZ-17-A   s p   L
Fort Lowell, Post Hospital (Ruins)
Fort Lowell Rd. vic.
HABS AZ-17-C   p d   L
Fort Lowell, Summer Kitchen
Fort Lowell Rd. vic.
HABS AZ-17-B   s p   L
Indian Mission Village of Bac, House
Number 1
HABS AZ-111-A   p   L
Indian Mission Village of Bac, House
Number 2
HABS AZ-111-B   p   L
Indian Mission Village of Bac, House
Number 3
HABS AZ-111-C   p   L
Indian Mission Village of Bac, House
Number 4
HABS AZ-111-D   p   L

Indian Mission Village of Bac, House
Number 5
HABS AZ-111-E   p   L
Indian Mission Village of Bac, House
Number 6
HABS AZ-111-F   p   L
Leon Ranch House
Silver Bell Rd.
HABS AZ-4   s p   L
San Xavier del Bac Mission
Mission Rd.
HABS AZ-13   s p d   L

PINAL COUNTY

Coolidge vic.
Casa Grande National Monument; see Casa
Grande (Ruins)
Casa Grande (Ruins) (Casa Grande
National Monument)
HABS AZ-14   p d   L

Florence
Collingwood Hotel, Old; see Post Office,
Adobe
Collingwood House
HABS AZ-115   p   L
Convent, Old; see Ranch House, Adobe
House
Courthouse vic.
HABS AZ-116   p   L
House
Church vic.
HABS AZ-120   p   L
House
High School vic.
HABS AZ-118   p   L
Land Office
HABS AZ-27   p   L
Main Street (House)
HABS AZ-114   p   L
Pinal County Courthouse
HABS AZ-130   p   L
Post Office, Adobe (Collingwood Hotel,
Old)
HABS AZ-119   p   L
Ranch House, Adobe (Convent, Old)
HABS AZ-117   p   L

Poston vic.
Blacksmith's Ramada
Gila River vic.
HABS AZ-113   p   L
Double House, Indian
Gila River vic.
HABS AZ-121   p   L
Farmhouse Group, Indian
Gila River vic.
HABS AZ-123   p   L
Farmhouse, Indian Wattle-and-Daub
Gila River vic.
HABS AZ-122   p   L

Farmhouse, Indian Wattle-and-Daub (with
Ramada)
Gila River vic.
HABS AZ-124   p   L

Sacaton
House, Indian
Vah Ki vic.
HABS AZ-43   p   L

Sacaton vic.
Farmhouse, Indian Framed Adobe
HABS AZ-42   p   L
House, Indian
HABS AZ-44   p   L
House, Indian, with Bow Roof
HABS AZ-45   p   L
House, Indian, with Shelter
HABS AZ-46   p   L
House, Indian, with Veranda
HABS AZ-47   p   L

SANTA CRUZ COUNTY

Nogales vic.
Kitchen, Pete, Ranch House
Portrero Creek vic.
HABS AZ-125   p   L
San Cayetano de Calabasas (Mission,
Ruins)
Santa Cruz River vic.
HABS AZ-2   s p d   L
San Gabriel de Guevavi (Mission, Ruins)
(San Miguel de Guevavi (Mission,
Ruins); San Rafael de Guevavi (Mission,
Ruins); Santos Angeles (Mission, Ruins))
Santa Cruz River vic.
HABS AZ-1   s p d   L
San Miguel de Guevavi (Mission, Ruins);
see San Gabriel de Guevavi (Mission,
Ruins)
San Rafael de Guevavi (Mission, Ruins);
see San Gabriel de Guevavi (Mission,
Ruins)
Santos Angeles (Mission, Ruins); see San
Gabriel de Guevavi (Mission, Ruins)

Patagonia
Commercial Hotel
State Rt. 82 vic.
HABS AZ-127   p   L

Patagonia vic.
Fort Crittenden (Ruins)
HABS AZ-126   p   L

Tubac
House, Mexican
HABS AZ-128   p   L
Santa Gertrudes de Tubac (Church)
HABS AZ-129   p   L

Tubac vic.

San Jose de Tumacacori (Mission, Ruins)
(Tumacacori National Monument)
HABS AZ-3   s pd L

Tumacacori National Monument; see San
Jose de Tumacacori (Mission, Ruins)

YAVAPAI COUNTY

Camp Verde

Camp Verde, Officer's House
HABS AZ-26   p   L

Camp Verde, Officer's House
HABS AZ-25   p   L

Prescott

Capitol, Old (Governor's Mansion)
W. Gurley St.
HABS AZ-40   p   L
Governor's Mansion; see Capitol, Old

Prescott vic.

Miller, S. C., House
Miller's Valley
HABS AZ-41   p   L

Arkansas

Arkansas, Historical Map
HABS AR-23   s   L

BENTON COUNTY

Pea Ridge vic.
Elkhorn Tavern
Telegraph Rd.
HABS AR-23   s   L

CRAWFORD COUNTY

Van Buren
Drennen, Col. John, House
HABS AR-21   p   L

HEMPSTEAD COUNTY

Blevins
Log Cabin Tavern
State Hwy.
HABS AR-32-10   s pd   L

Washington
Baptist Church
State Hwy. 4
HABS AR-32-5   s pd   L

Confederate State Capitol (Courthouse &
State House, Old)
Old Military Rd.
HABS AR-32-3   s pd   L
Courthouse & State House, Old; see
Confederate State Capitol

Jones, Dan W., House
HABS AR-32-7   s pd L
Royston, Grandison D., House
State Hwy. 4
HABS AR-32-11   s pd L
Stuart, A. O., House
HABS AR-32-6   s pd L
Tavern, Old
Military Rd.
HABS AR-32-4   s pd L
Thomas, John T., House
Old Military Rd.
HABS AR-32-8   s pd L

Washington vic.
Holt, Milton T., House
Old Military Rd.
HABS AR-32-9   s pd   L

JOHNSON COUNTY

Clarksville vic.
Stage Coach Inn, Old
HABS AR-17   p   L

MISSISSIPPI COUNTY

Wilson
Wilson Cabin
HABS AR-22   p   L

PULASKI COUNTY

Little Rock
Crittenden, Robert, House; see Henderliter
Place, The

Henderliter Place, The (Crittenden,
Robert, House)
Second & Cumberland Sts.
HABS AR-32-2   s pd L
McHenry House
Hwy. 70 vic.
HABS AR-13   s pd L
Pike, Albert, House
411 E. Seventh St.
HABS AR-20   p   L
State Capitol Building, Old
Markham & Center Sts.
HABS AR-32-1   s pd L
Trapmall Hall
423 E. Capitol Ave.
HABS AR-19   p   L
U.S. Arsenal Building
City Park
HABS AR-32-12   s pd L

SEBASTIAN COUNTY

Fort Smith
Fort Smith, Commissary Building (Fort
Smith National Historic Site)
100 S. Garrison Ave.
HABS AR-16   s pd L
Fort Smith National Historic Site; see Fort
Smith, Commissary Building

WASHINGTON COUNTY

Fayetteville vic.
Yell, Archibald, House
HABS AR-18   p   L

California

ALAMEDA COUNTY

Berkeley
Peralta Hall (St. Joseph's Academy)
HABS CA-1655   p   L

St. Joseph's Academy; see Peralta Hall

Fremont
Mission San Jose Guadalupe
Mission & Washington Blvds.
HABS CA-1132   pd L

Fremont (Niles)

Rancho Arroya de la Alameda Adobe
(Vallejo, Jose de Jesus, Adobe)
Niles Blvd. & Nursery Ave.
HABS CA-1194   p   L

Vallejo Flour Mill
Niles Canyon
HABS CA-1660   p   L
Vallejo, Jose de Jesus, Adobe; see Rancho
    Arroya de la Alameda Adobe

Fremont (Warm Spring)

Cohen, A. A., House (Rancho Agua
    Caliente; Hidden Valley Ranch)
State Hwy. 9
HABS CA-1656   p   L
Hidden Valley Ranch; see Cohen, A. A.,
    House
Higuera, Abelardo, Adobe
Wabana St.
HABS CA-1666   p   L
Higuera, Fulgencio, Adobe (Rancho Agua
    Caliente)
HABS CA-1665   p   L
Indian Cemetery
Washington Blvd.
HABS CA-1658   p   L
Rancho Agua Caliente; see Cohen, A. A.,
    House
Rancho Agua Caliente; see Higuera,
    Fulgencio, Adobe

Hayward

Brewery
HABS CA-1325   p   L

Oakland

716 Castro Street (House)
HABS CA-2058   p   L
Galinda Hotel
Eighth & Franklin Sts.
HABS CA-1898   p   H
Greek Orthodox Church of the Assumption
920 Bush St.
HABS CA-2055   pd   L
Mahoney, Thomas, House
69 Eighth St.
HABS CA-2056   p   L
Moss, J. Mora, House
Broadway & McArthur Blvd.
HABS CA-1897   s pd   L H
Paramount Theatre
2025 Broadway
HABS CA-1976   pd   L
Pardee, Gov., House
672 Eleventh St.
HABS CA-1899   pd   L
Quinn, William H., House
1425 Castro St.
HABS CA-2057   p   L
Southern Pacific Ferry Slips; see Southern
    Pacific Mole & Pier
Southern Pacific Mole & Pier (Southern
    Pacific Ferry Slips)
Seventh St.
HABS CA-1888   pd   L
White, James, House
702 Eleventh St.
HABS CA-2054   pd   L

Pleasanton

Kottinger, John W., Adobe
Ray St.
HABS CA-1859   p   L

San Leandro

Estudillo House
1291 Carpenter St.
HABS CA-1662   p   L
Peralta, Ignacio, House
561 Lafayette
HABS CA-1896   pd   L

Tracy vic.

Mountain House
Mountain House & Livermore Altamont
    Pass Rds.
HABS CA-1199   p   L

Union City

Apple Schmidt House; see Smith, Henry C.,
    House
Smith, Henry C., House (Apple Schmidt
    House)
HABS CA-1659   p   L

ALPINE COUNTY

Pasadena

Busch Estate
160 S. San Rafael
HABS CA-2191   pd   H

AMADOR COUNTY

Amador City

Amador Hotel
Hwy. 49
HABS CA-1346   p   L
Commercial Buildings
Hwy. 49
HABS CA-1349   p   L
House, Brick (Mine House Hotel)
Hwy. 49
HABS CA-1350   p   L
Imperial Hotel
Hwy. 49
HABS CA-1348   p   L
Mine House Hotel; see House, Brick

Buena Vista

Buena Vista Stone Store
Lancha Plana & Jackson-Stockton Rds.
HABS CA-1508   p   L

Butte City

Benoist-Ginocchio Store (Walls)
Hwy. 49
HABS CA-1506-1   p   L

Drytown

Drytown Hall
HABS CA-1155   p   L
Masonic Temple
HABS CA-1515   p   L

Fiddletown

St. Charles Hotel
HABS CA-1154   p   L

Jackson

Brown, Armstead C., House (House, Brick)
HABS CA-1277   p   L
Hotel
Marcucci & Broadway
HABS CA-1283   p   L
House, Brick; see Brown, Armstead C.,
    House
National Hotel
Main & Waxer Sts.
HABS CA-1520   p   L
Native Daughters of the Golden West
    Building
HABS CA-1509   p   L
Serbian Church
HABS CA-1870   p   L
Toll House
HABS CA-1519   p   L
Wells Fargo Express Office
HABS CA-1156   p   L

Jackson Gate

Chichizola Store
Jackson Gate Rd.
HABS CA-1513   p   L

Michigan Bar

Heath's Store
HABS CA-1516   p   L

Oleta

Barn, Frame
HABS CA-1352   p   L

Pine Grove

House, First
HABS CA-1514   p   L

Plymouth

House
HABS CA-1351   p   L

Round Top

Kirkwood Inn & Round Top Post Office
U.S. Hwy. 88
HABS CA-1197   p   L

Volcano

Adams Express Company Building
Main & Consolation Sts.
HABS CA-1518   p   L
Cannon, Old Abe
HABS CA-1507   p   L
Cigar Emporium; see Store, Stone
Cobblestone Art Gallery; see Store, Stone
Main Street (Commercial Buildings, Stone
    Walls)
HABS CA-1504   p   L
Masonic & I. O. O. F. Building
Main St.
HABS CA-1345   p   L
Sibley's Brewery; see Wine Shop

St. George Hotel
Main & National Sts.
HABS CA-1285   p   L

Store, Stone (Cigar Emporium;
    Cobblestone Art Gallery)
Main St.
HABS CA-1505   p   L

Volcano, General View
HABS CA-1510   p   L

Wine Shop (Sibley's Brewery)
HABS CA-1517   p   L

BUTTE COUNTY

Bidwell Bar

Suspension Bridge & Stone Toll House
Curry-Bidwell Bar State Park
HABS CA-1476   p   L

Cherokee

Brewery (Ruins)
HABS CA-1702   p   L

Wells Fargo & Company Vault (Ruins)
HABS CA-1680   p   L

Chico

Bidwell Mansion
585 Espianade St.
HABS CA-1317   s   d   H

CALAVERAS COUNTY

Albany Flat

Romaggi, James, Fandango House
Hwy. 49
HABS CA-1204   p   L

Altaville

Gravestones
North Branch Cemetery
HABS CA-1487   p   L

**Pache, P. F. & Company (Commercial
    Building); see Prince & Garibaldi Store**

Prince & Garibaldi Store (Pache, P. F. &
    Company (Commercial Building))
Hwys. 4 & 49
HABS CA-1205   p   L

Angeles Camp

Angels Camp, General View
Main Street
HABS CA-1499   p   L

Angels Camp

Fox House
HABS CA-1493   p   L

Hotel Angels
Main St.
HABS CA-1547   p   L

House
Hwy. 49
HABS CA-1275   p   L

House, Stone (Pierano, Joseph, House &
    Store)
HABS CA-1276   p   L

**Pierano, Joseph, House & Store; see House,
    Stone**

Scribner's Store
HABS CA-1491   p   L

Utica Mine
HABS CA-1492   p   L

Angels Camp vic.

Burch, John, House
HABS CA-1278   p   L

Mine Building
Salt Springs Valley
HABS CA-1209   p   L

Campo Seco

Eperson, Robert, Building
Main St.
HABS CA-1115   p   L

Messenger, Capt., House
Comanche Reservoir
HABS CA-1206   p   L

Carson Hill

House
HABS CA-1273   p   L

Oneta Brothers General Merchandise
    (Stores, Frame & Stone)
HABS CA-1490   p   L

**Stores, Frame & Stone; see Oneta Brothers
    General Merchandise**

Clear View

House, First; see Noce, John, House

Noce, John, House (Whiskey Slide; House,
    First)
HABS CA-1489   p   L

Whiskey Slide; see Noce, John, House

Copperopolis

Congregational Church (I. O. O. F. Hall)
HABS CA-1123   p   L

I. O. O. F. Hall; see Congregational Church

Copperopolis vic.

Stage Station
Tullock Reservoir
HABS CA-1480   p   L

Eldoradotown

Raggio Adobe
HABS CA-1587   p   L

Rodesino Adobe
HABS CA-1586   p   L

Felix

Felix Post Office & School (Stage Stop,
    Old; Tower Ranch)
HABS CA-1118   s   pd   L H

Pedroli Ranch House (Williams, Andrew,
    Ranch)
HABS CA-1208   p   L

**Stage Stop, Old; see Felix Post Office &
    School**

**Tower Ranch; see Felix Post Office &
    School**

Tower Ranch Barn
HABS CA-1207   p   L

Tower Ranch House
HABS CA-1117   p   L

**Williams, Andrew, Ranch; see Pedroli
    Ranch House**

Felix vic.

**House (Ruins); see Stone Creek Settlement
    (Ruins)**

Mine Building (Williams, Andrew, Ranch)
HABS CA-1209   p   L

Stone Creek Settlement (Ruins) (House
    (Ruins))
Salt Springs Valley
HABS CA-1122   p   L

**Williams, Andrew, Ranch; see Mine
    Building**

Fourth Crossing

**Foreman's Ranch Hotel; see Reddick, John,
    House**

Reddick, John, House (Foreman's Ranch
    Hotel)
Hwy. 49
HABS CA-1129   p   L

Glencoe

Store, Frame
HABS CA-1488   p   L

Happy Valley

Building, Stone (North Star Mine Building)
HABS CA-1497   p   L

**North Star Mine Building; see Building,
    Stone**

Jesus Maria

Commercial Buildings & Houses, Frame
HABS CA-1483   p   L

Melones vic.

Barn
HABS CA-1274   p   L

Mokelumne Hill

Brewery (Ruins); see Stone Ruins

**Calaveras County Branch Library; see
    Store & Post Office**

Church, Frame (Congregational Church)
HABS CA-1285   p   L

Congregational Church; see Church, Frame

I. O. O. F. Hall
Main St.
HABS CA-1281   p   L

Leger Hotel
Main St.
HABS CA-1874   p   L

Stone Ruins (Brewery (Ruins))
HABS CA-1280   p   L

Store & Post Office (Calaveras County
    Branch Library)
Main St.
HABS CA-1875   p   L

Store (Ruins)
HABS CA-1279   p   L

Murphy's

Compere, Victorene, Store
Main St.
HABS CA-1108   p   L

Michaelson House (Michelson, Albert, House)
Main St.
HABS CA-1211   p   L

Michelson, Albert, House; see Michaelson House

Mitchler Hotel (Murphy's Hotel)
Main St.
HABS CA-1109   p   L

Murphy's Hotel; see Mitchler Hotel

Old Timers Museum; see Traver's, Peter L., Store & Wells Fargo Bldg.

School
HABS CA-1110   p   L

St. Patrick's Catholic Church
HABS CA-1112   p   L

Traver's, Peter L., Store & Wells Fargo Bldg. (Old Timers Museum)
HABS CA-1485   p   L

Pilot Hill

Bayley, A. J., Road House
HABS CA-1383   pd   L

Poverty Flat

Commercial Building, Stone (Ruins)
HABS CA-1479   p   L

Roaring Camp

Roaring Camp Buildings, Frame
HABS CA-1484   p   L

San Andreas

Aqostini Building; see Banque, J., Store

Banque, J., Store (Aqostini Building)
Main St.
HABS CA-1210   p   L

Calaveras Bar; see Friedburger Building

Friedburger Building (Calaveras Bar)
HABS CA-1478   p   L

I. O. O. F. Hall
Main St.
HABS CA-1496   p   L

Metropolitan Hotel
HABS CA-1495   p   L

San Andreas, General View
Main St.
HABS CA-1494   p   L

Store, Adobe
HABS CA-1481   p   L

Theatre, Old
HABS CA-1482   p   L

COLUSA COUNTY

Colusa

Colusa Bridge
Spanning Sacramento River
HAER CA-7   pd   L

Colusa County Courthouse
HABS CA-1806   p   L

Hall of Records & County Jail
HABS CA-1807   p   L

CONTRA COSTA COUNTY

Alamo

Henry Hotel (Wolf Store)
Mt. Diablo Rd. & Hwy. 21
HABS CA-1657   p   L

Wolf Store; see Henry Hotel

Brentwood vic.

Los Medanos Rancho; see Marsh, John, House

Marsh, John, House (Los Medanos Rancho)
Marsh Creek Rd.
HABS CA-1500   pd   L

Concord

Pacneco, Fernando, Adobe
3119 Grant St.
HABS CA-173   p   L

Pancheco, Salvio, Adobe
2030 Adobe St.
HABS CA-1847   p   L

Danville

O'Neill, Eugene, House (O'Neill, Eugene, National Historic Site; Tao House)
Kuss Rd.
HABS CA-2078   p   H

O'Neill, Eugene, National Historic Site; see O'Neill, Eugene, House

Tao House; see O'Neill, Eugene, House

Martinez

Martinez, Vicente, Adobe
Pleasant Hill & Franklin Canyon Rds.
HABS CA-1913   s pd   L

Muir, John, House (Muir, John, National Historic Site; Strentzel, John, House)
Alhambra Blvd.
HABS CA-1890   s pd   L

Muir, John, National Historic Site; see Muir, John, House

Strentzel, John, House; see Muir, John, House

Moraga Valley

Moraqa, Jose Joaquin, Adobe
HABS CA-1860   p   L

San Pablo

Castro-Alvarado Adobe (Racho San Pablo)
2748 San Pablo Ave.
HABS CA-1654   p   L

Racho San Pablo; see Castro-Alvarado Adobe

EL DORADO COUNTY

Coloma

Barn
HABS CA-1377   p   L

Chinese Store (Ruins) (Wilder, Jonas, Store)
Main St.
HABS CA-1380   p   L

House
HABS CA-1378   p   L

Marshall, James W., Cabin
Marshall Monument Rd.
HABS CA-1309   p   L

Meyer House; see Sierra Nevada Hotel

Meyer's Dance Hall & Saloon
Shingle Spring Rd.
HABS CA-1381   p   L

Orleans Hotel; see Post Office

Post Office (Orleans Hotel)
Main St.
HABS CA-1376   p   L

Sierra Nevada Hotel (Meyer House)
HABS CA-1503   p   L

Wilder, Jonas, Store; see Chinese Store (Ruins)

Coloma vic.

Meyer Hotel; see Sutter's Sawmill

Sutter's Sawmill (Meyer Hotel)
Marshall Gold Discovery State Historic Park
HABS CA-1301   p   L

El Dorado

Commercial Buildings, False Front
HABS CA-1355   L

Main Street (Store, Ruins)
HABS CA-1367   p   L

Kelsey

Allen's, Tom, Saloon; see Marshall, James W., House

Marshall, James W., Blacksmith Shop
HABS CA-1696   p   L

Marshall, James W., House (Allen's, Tom, Saloon)
HABS CA-1308   p   L

Kyburz

Kyburz Hotel (Yarnold's, Dick, Toll House; Mountain Retreat)
U.S. Hwy. 50
HABS CA-1708   p   L

Mountain Retreat; see Kyburz Hotel

Yarnold's, Dick, Toll House; see Kyburz Hotel

Millerton

Fort Miller Blockhouse
Lake Millerton
HABS CA-1324   p   L

Nashville

Barn, Log
HABS CA-1354   p   L

House
HABS CA-1353   p   L

Pilot Hill
Hotel
HABS CA-1382   p   L

Placerville
Bedford Inn
HABS CA-1364   p   L
Bedford Street (House)
HABS CA-1370   p   L
Bedford Street (House)
HABS CA-1375   p   L
2934 Bedford Street (House)
HABS CA-1371   p   L
50 Benham Street (House)
HABS CA-1368   p   L
Building Adjoining Community Church
Main St.
HABS CA-1366   p   L
**California Automobile Association
    Building;** see Main Street (Commercial
    Buildings)
Coloma Road (House)
HABS CA-1374   p   L
Community Church; see El Dorado County
    Federated Church
El Dorado County Courthouse (Ruins)
Main St.
HABS CA-1675   p   L
El Dorado County Federated Church
    (Community Church)
Main St.
HABS CA-1365   p   L
House, Brick & Stone
HABS CA-1373   p   L
Main Street (Commercial Buildings)
HABS CA-1673   p   L
Main Street (Commercial Buildings)
    (California Automobile Association
    Building)
HABS CA-1362
HAER 3   p   L
136 Main Street (House)
HABS CA-1372   p   L
**Pony Express Courier Bldg., (Strong Box &
    Cradle)**
HABS CA-1707   p   L
Thompson, Judge, House
32 Cedar Ravine
HABS CA-1369   p   L
Zeisz, J., Building
HABS CA-1363   p   L

Shingle Springs
Phelps Store
U.S. Hwy. 50
HABS CA-1357   p   L

Strawberry
Strawberry House
Placerville Rd.
HABS CA-1682   p   L

Tragedy Springs
Carved Tree Marker
HABS CA-1502   L

FRESNO COUNTY

Millerton
Fort Miller
Lake Millerton
HABS CA-170   p   L
Fort Miller Bakery
Lake Millerton
HABS CA-1329   p   L
Fort Miller Ford
Lake Millerton
HABS CA-1330   p   L
Fort Miller Hospital
Lake Millerton
HABS CA-1327   p   L
Fort Miller Mess Hall
Lake Millerton
HABS CA-1328   p   L
Fort Miller Officer's Quarters
Lake Millerton
HABS CA-1326   p   L

Millerton vic.
Camp Barbour Blockhouse
HABS CA-1306   p   L

GLENN COUNTY

Willows
Glenn County Courthouse
526 Sycamore St.
HABS CA-1804   p   L

HUMBOLDT COUNTY

Arcata
Fourteenth & J Streets (House)
HABS CA-1457   p   L
Nixon House
1022 Tenth St.
HABS CA-1458   p   L

Bridgeville
Bridgeville, General View
HABS CA-1456   p   L

Eureka
Carson House (Ingomar Club)
Second & M Sts.
HABS CA-1911   pd   L
Fort Humboldt
HABS CA-1643   p   L
314 H Street (House)
HABS CA-1461   p   L
Hanna House; see Hustes House
Hustes House (Hanna House)
916 Second St.
HABS CA-1462   p   L
Ingomar Club; see Carson House

Lindsay House
HABS CA-1459   p   L
Stokes House
HABS CA-1460   p   L

Garberville vic.
Moody Bridge
Spanning South Fork Eel River
HAER CA-4   pd   L

Mad River
Erickson Ranch House
HABS CA-1454   p   L
Erickson Ranch Log Cabin
HABS CA-1455   p   L

IMPERIAL COUNTY

Winterhaven
Fort Yuma
Yuma Indian Reservation
HABS CA-415   d   H
Fort Yuma Old Barracks
Yuma Indian Reservation
HABS CA-414   s   L
Fort Yuma Old Indian Girls' Dormitory
Yuma Indian Reservation
HABS CA-416   s   L
Fort Yuma Old Officers' Kitchen Cottage
Yuma Indian Reservation
HABS CA-413   s   L
Fort Yuma Old Officers' Quarters
Yuma Indian Reservaiton
HABS CA-412   s   L

INYO COUNTY

Keeler
Main Street (Commercial Buildings)
HABS CA-1678   p   L

KERN COUNTY

Lebec vic.
Fort Tejon
Hwy. 99
HABS CA-39   s d L
Fort Tejon Barracks Number One
Hwy. 99
HABS CA-39-A   s p L
Fort Tejon Barracks Number Two
Hwy. 99
HABS CA-39-B   p   L
Fort Tejon Officers' Quarters
Hwy. 99
HABS CA-39-C   s p L
Fort Tejon Smokehouse
Hwy. 99
HABS CA-39-E   s p L
Fort Tejon Soldiers' Quarters
Hwy. 99
HABS CA-39-D   s p L

LASSEN COUNTY

Susanville vic.
Fort Defiance (Roop's Fort)
HABS CA-1310   p   L
Roop's Fort; see Fort Defiance

LOS ANGELES COUNTY

Baldwin Park
Baldwin Park City Hall; see Central School
Central School (Baldwin Park City Hall)
14403 E. Pacific Ave.
HABS CA-2016   p   L

Bell
Casa del Rancho San Antonio (Lugo,
     Vicente, House)
6360 E. Gage
HABS CA-36   s p d   L
Lugo, Vicente, House; see Casa del Rancho
     San Antonio

Beverly Hills
Doheny Mansion (Greystone)
501 Doheny Rd.
HABS CA-2193   p d   H
Green Acres; see Lloyd, Harold, Estate
Greystone; see Doheny Mansion
Lloyd, Harold, Estate (Green Acres)
HABS CA-2192   p d   H

Calabasas
Leonis, Miguel, Adobe
23537 Calabasas Rd.
HABS CA-342   p d   L

Calabasas vic.
Los Virgenes Rancho; see Reyes House
Reyes House (Los Virgenes Rancho)
State Hwy. 101
HABS CA-329   s p d   L

Elizabeth Lake vic.
Gorman, Maj., Stage Station
San Francisquito Rd.
HABS CA-330   s p d   L

Glendale
Casa Adobe de San Rafael (Sanchez,
     Thomas, House)
1340 Dorothy Dr.
HABS CA-323   s p d   L
Sanchez, Thomas, House; see Casa Adobe
     de San Rafael

Inglewood
Academy Theater
3141 W. Manchester Blvd.
HABS CA-2020   p   L
Casa del Rancho Aguaja de la Centinela
7634 Midfield Rd.
HABS CA-312   s p d   L
Freeman, Daniel, House
HABS CA-2115   p   H

Long Beach
Casa de los Alamitos (Nieto, Don Manuel,
     House)
E. Anaheim Rd.
HABS CA-310   s d   L
Casa de los Cerritos (Temple, Don Juan,
     House)
4600 American Ave.
HABS CA-37-12   s p d   L
Nieto, Don Manuel, House; see Casa de los
     Alamitos
Temple, Don Juan, House; see Casa de los
     Cerritos

Los Angeles
Angels Flight
Third & Hill Sts.
HABS CA-337   p d   L
Barn, Adobe; see El Escorpion Rancho
Barnsdall, Aline, House; see Hollyhock
     House
Barnsdall Park Residence A (Studio
     Residence A)
4800 Hollywood Blvd.
HABS CA-357   p d   L
Bolton Hall (Tujunga City Hall)
10110 Commerce Ave.
HABS CA-340   p d   L
Bradbury Building
304 S. Broadway
HABS CA-334   s p d   L H
Broadway Department Store; see Coulter's
     Department Store
Bullocks-Wilshire Department Store
3050 Wilshire Blvd.
HABS CA-1941   s d   H
Bunker Hill District
Temple, Fifth, Hill, & Fiqueroa Sts.
HABS CA-344   p d   L
Carl's Market; see Union Market
Casa Avila (Francisco, Don, Adobe)
14 Olvera St.
HABS CA-37-2   s p d   L
Casa Pelanconi (Covacichi, Guiseppe,
     Building)
33-35 Olvera St.
HABS CA-37-3   s p d   L
Cathedral of St. Vibiana
Second & Main Sts.
HABS CA-343   p d   L
Coca-Cola Bottling Company
1334 S. Central Ave.
HABS CA-2022   p   L
Commercial Buildings
462 S. Cochran Ave. & 5515-5525 W. Sixth
     St.
HABS CA-2042   p   L
Coulter's Department Store (Broadway
     Department Store)
5600 Wilshire Blvd.
HABS CA-2023   p   L
Covacichi, Guiseppe, Building; see Casa
     Pelanconi

Dark Room, The
5370 Wilshire Blvd.
HABS CA-2024   p   L
Diamond Bar Ranch; see Vejar, Ricardo,
     Casa de
Dodge.Walter Luther, House
950 N. Kings Rd.
HABS CA-355   s p d   L H
Domiquez-Wilshire Building; see Hiss
     Tower
Drum Barracks Officers' Quarters
     (Wilmington Federal Army Post Officers'
     Quarters)
1053-1955 Cary Ave.
HABS CA-353   p d   L
523 East Third Street (House)
HABS CA-350   p d   L
Eastern Outfitting Company
849-851 S. Broadway
HABS CA-2025   p   L
El Alisal (Lummis, Charles, House)
200 East Ave.
HABS CA-339   p d   L
El Escorpion Rancho (Barn, Adobe)
400 Muirfield Rd.
HABS CA-326   s p d   L
Ennis House
2607 Glensower Ave.
HABS CA-1942   s d   H
First Masonic Temple; see Masonic Temple
     Number 42 F. & A. M.
Francisco, Don, Adobe; see Casa Avila
Freeman, Samuel, House
1962 Glencoe Way
HABS CA-1989   s p d   H
Garnier Block
415 N. Los Angeles St.
HABS CA-321   p d   L
Heath House; see Lovell House
Hiss Tower (Domiquez-Wilshire Building)
5400-5420 Wilshire Blvd.
HABS CA-2027   p   L
Hollyhock House (Barnsdall, Aline, House)
4800 Hollywood Blvd.
HABS CA-356   p d   L
**Iqlesia de Nuestra Senora la Reina de los
     Angeles;** see Plaza Church
Jefferson, Thomas, High School
1319 E. Forty-First St.
HABS CA-2026   p   L
KEHE Radio Studios
133-141 N. Vermont Ave.
HABS CA-2028   p   L
Leimert Park Theater
3341 W. Forty-Third Pl.
HABS CA-2029   p   L
**Los Angeles Department of Water & Power
     Office**
5928 S. Vermont Ave.
HABS CA-2030   d   H
Los Angeles Public Library
630 W. Fifth St.
HABS CA-1937   s p d   H

Lovell House (Heath House)
4616 Dundee Dr.
HABS CA-1936   s d   H

Lugo, Don Vicente, Casa de (St. Vincent's
   College)
516-522 1/2 N. Los Angeles St.
HABS CA-319   s pd   L

Lummis, Charles, House; see El Alisal

Masonic Temple Number 42 F. & A. M.
   (First Masonic Temple)
416 1/2 N. Main St.
HABS CA-32   s pd   L

May Company Department Store
6067 Wilshire Blvd.
HABS CA-2031   p   L

Medical Square
2200 W. Third St.
HABS CA-2032   p   L

Merced Theatre
420-422 N. Main St.
HABS CA-327   s pd   L

Merle Norman Building
2525 Main St.
HABS CA-2043   p   L

Pan Pacific Auditorium
1600 Beverly Blvd.
HABS CA-2033   p   L

Pico Hotel (Pico House, Old)
430 N. Main St.
HABS CA-317   s pd   L

Pico House, Old; see Pico Hotel

Plaza Church (Iglesia de Nuestra Senora la
   Reina de los Angeles)
535 N. Main St.
HABS CA-37-1   s pd   L

Plaza Fire House
126 Plaza St.
HABS CA-338   pd   L

Rancho La Brea Adobe
6301 W. Third St.
HABS CA-354   pd   L

Rancho Rincon de los Bueyes; see Rocha,
   Antonio Jose, House

Rees & Wirsching Building
223-227 N. Los Angeles St.
HABS CA-318   pd   L

Richfield Oil Building
555 S. Flower St.
HABS CA-1987   s pd   H

Rocha, Antonio Jose, House (Rancho
   Rincon de los Bueyes)
Cadillac & Shenandoah Sts.
HABS CA-311   s pd   L

**Sawtelle Veterans' Admin. Ctr.
   Domiciliary No. Six**
Wilshire & Sawtelle
HABS CA-336   pd   L

**Sawtelle Veterans' Administration Center
   Chapels**
Wilshire & Sawtelle Blvds.
HABS CA-335   d   L

Schindler, Rudolph M., House
833 N. Kings Rd.
HABS CA-1939   s d   H

**Sears, Roebuck & Company Department
   Store Building**
4548 W. Pico Blvd.
HABS CA-2034   pd   H

Security First National Bank Building
5207-5209 Wilshire Blvd.
HABS CA-2039   p   L

Seliq Commercial Building
269-273 Western Ave.
HABS CA-2041   p   L

Skinner House
1530 Easterly Terrace
HABS CA-2035   p   L

Smith, Nelson K., House
191 S. Hudson Ave.
HABS CA-2036   p   L

221 South Bunker Hill Avenue (House)
HABS CA-348   pd   L

**237-241 South Bunker Hill Avenue
   (House)**
HABS CA-347   pd   L

238 South Bunker Hill Avenue (House)
HABS CA-352   pd   L

251 South Bunker Hill Avenue (House)
HABS CA-351   pd   L

245 South Grand Avenue (House)
HABS CA-349   pd   L

221 South Olive Street (House)
HABS CA-346   pd   L

Sowden House
5121 Franklin Ave.
HABS CA-1940   s pd   H

St. Vincent's College; see Lugo, Don
   Vicente, Casa de

Storer House
8161 Hollywood Blvd.
HABS CA-1944   s d   H

Story, W. P., Building, (Garage Entrance)
610 S. Broadway
HABS CA-2040   p   L

Studio Residence A; see Barnsdall Park
   Residence A

Sunset Towers Apartments
8358 Sunset Blvd.
HABS CA-2037   p   L

Tujunga City Hall; see Bolton Hall

Union Market (Carl's Market)
1530-1536 W. Sixth St.
HABS CA-2021   p   L

Val D'Amour Apartments
854 Oxford Ave.
HABS CA-2038   p   L

Vejar, Ricardo, Casa de (Diamond Bar
   Ranch)
Valley Blvd.
HABS CA-37-10   s pd   L

605 West Third Street (House)
HABS CA-345   pd   L

**Wilmington Federal Army Post Officers'
   Quarters;** see Drum Barracks Officers'
   Quarters

Lynwood

Lynwood Pacific Electric Railway Depot
11453 Long Beach Blvd.
HABS CA-2074   pd   L

Pasadena

El Molino Viejo
1120 Old Mill Rd.
HABS CA-34   s pd   L

Gamble, David B., House
4 Westmoreland
HABS CA-1981
HAER .   d   H

Irwin, Theodore, House
240 N. Grand Ave.
HABS CA-1985   s d   H

Neighborhood Church
S. Pasadena Ave. & W. California Blvd.
HABS CA-2116   p   H

Tilt, J. E., House
455 Bradford
HABS CA-2190   pd   H

Pomona

Palomares, Yqnaclo, Casa de
1569 N. Park Ave.
HABS CA-37-25   s pd   L

San Dimas vic.

Carrion, Saturnino, Casa de
Mountain Meadows Rd.
HABS CA-315   s pd   L

San Fernando

Celis, Eulogio de, House; see Pico, Andres,
   House

Harrington, M. R., House; see Pico,
   Andres, House

Lopez, Geronimo, Casa de
1102 Pico St.
HABS CA-341   pd   L

**Mission San Fernando Rey de Espana
   Church**
1551 San Fernando Rd.
HABS CA-325-B   s pd   L

**Mission San Fernando Rey de Espana
   Fountains**
15151 San Fernando Rd.
HABS CA-325-C   s p   L

**Mission San Fernando Rey de Espana
   Monastery**
15151 San Fernando Rd.
HABS CA-37-5   s pd   L

Pico, Andres, House (Celis, Eulogio de,
   House; Harrington, M. R., House)
10940 Sepulveda Blvd.
HABS CA-324   s pd   L

San Gabriel

Casa Viejo de Lopez
330 N. Santa Anita Ave.
HABS CA-316   s pd   L

Grape Vine Adobe; see Padillo Adobe
Las Tunas Rancho; see Purcell House
Mission San Gabriel Arcangel
W. Mission Dr. & Junipero Serra St.
HABS CA-37-8   s p d   L
Mission San Gabriel Arcangel Industrial Shop Ruins
W. Mission Dr. & Junipero Serra St.
HABS CA-37-8-A   s p   L
Mission San Gabriel Arcangel Mill
W. Mission Dr. & Junipero Serra St.
HABS CA-37-8-B   p   L
Padillo Adobe (Grape Vine Adobe)
Mission Dr.
HABS CA-328   s p d   L
Purcell House (Las Tunas Rancho)
308 Mission
HABS CA-35   s p d   L

San Marino
Blanco, Miquel, Casa de
2625 Huntington Dr.
HABS CA-322   s p d   L

Santa Catalina Isl.
Mount Ida; see Wrigley, William, House
Wrigley, William, House (Mount Ida)
HABS CA-2189   s p d   H

Santa Monica
Horatio West Court Apartments
140 Hollister
HABS CA-1984   s p d   H

South Pasadena
Adobe Flores; see Perez, Jose, Casa de
Miltimore House
1301 S. Chelton Way
HABS CA-1988   s d   H
Perez, Jose, Casa de (Adobe Flores)
1804 Foothill Blvd.
HABS CA-33   s p d   L

Whittier
Haceienda del Rancho Paso; see Pico, Pio, Casa de
Pico, Pio, Casa de (Haceienda del Rancho Paso)
Whittier Blvd. & Guirado St.
HABS CA-37-24   s   L

MARIN COUNTY

Angel Island
Fort McDowell
Angel Island
HABS CA-1841   p   L

Bolinas
Booth, F. E. Company Pier
Point Reyes National Seashore
HABS CA-2073   p d   L

Olema vic.
Lime Kiln
State Hwy. 1
HABS CA-1437   p   L

San Rafael
Marin County Courthouse
Fourth & A Sts.
HABS CA-1955   s p d   H
Mission San Rafael Archangel
HABS CA-1131   p   L

MARIPOSA COUNTY

Agua Fria
Agua Fria, General View
HABS CA-154   p   L

Bagby
Bagby, General View (Benton Hills)
HABS CA-1703-1   p   L
Benton Hills; see Bagby, General View
Railroad Station
HABS CA-1650   s   L

Bear Valley
Bear House Hotel; see Oso House Hotel
Fremont Cottage
HABS CA-1861   p   L
Oso House Hotel (Bear House Hotel)
HABS CA-1106   p   L
Wells Fargo Building
HABS CA-1704   p   L

Coulterville
Bruschi Building (Bruschi Warehouse)
Main St.
HABS CA-1531   p   L
Bruschi Stores
Main St.
HABS CA-1532   p   L
Bruschi Warehouse; see Bruschi Building
Coulter's Hotel & Wagoner's Store
Main St.
HABS CA-1533   p   L
Coulterville, General View
HABS CA-1336   p   L
Coulterville, General View
Main St.
HABS CA-1107   p   L

Hornitos
Fandango Dance Hall
HABS CA-1530   p   L
Ghirardelli's Store (Ruins)
HABS CA-1526   p   L
Hornitos Hotel
HABS CA-1102   p   L
House, Adobe
HABS CA-1101   p   L
Jail
HABS CA-1522-1   p   L
Masonic Hall
HABS CA-1523   p   L
Native Sons of the Golden West Building (Wells Fargo Building)
HABS CA-1521   p   L
Plaza
HABS CA-1103   p   L
Principal Street & Plaza
HABS CA-1104   p   L
Wells Fargo Building; see Native Sons of the Golden West Building

Indian Gulch
Solari Hotel
HABS CA-1525   p   L

Mariposa
Fremont's Store & Assay Office
HABS CA-1528   p   L
Gazette Building
Mariposa County Fairgrounds
HABS CA-1534   p   L
Mariposa County Courthouse
HABS CA-1105-2   p   L

Mormon Bar
Chinese Adobe Building
HABS CA-1529   p   L

Mount Bullion
Marre Store
HABS CA-1527   p   L

Mount Ophir
Trabucco Store (Ruins)
HABS CA-1524-1   p   L

Wawona
Wawona Hotel
Yosemite National Park
HABS CA-1805   p   L

Yosemite Natl. Park
Cedar Cottage
HABS CA-1645   s   L
Sentinel Hotel
HABS CA-1644   s p   L H
Yosemite Chapel
HABS CA-1649   s   L

MENDOCINO COUNTY

Albion
Albion, General View
Albion River vic.
HABS CA-1468   p   L
Lumber Mill
Albion River
HABS CA-1469   p   L

Elk
Elk, General View
HABS CA-1471   p   L

Fort Bragg vic.
School
HABS CA-1465   p   L

Mendocino
Main Street (Commercial Buildings)
HABS CA-1467   p   L
Masonic Temple
Lansing & Ukiah Sts.
HABS CA-1801   p   H

Residence Street (Houses)
HABS CA-1464   p   L
Ukiah Street (Houses)
HABS CA-1466   p   L

Navaro River
Fishing Resort
HABS CA-1470   p   L

Westport
Westport, General View
HABS CA-1463   p   L

MERCED COUNTY

Los Banos vic.
San Luis Gonzaga Adobe
State Hwy. 152
HABS CA-1891   s pd   L

MONO COUNTY

Bodie
Bodie Bank
Main St.
HABS CA-1926   p   H
Bodie, General View
Bodie State Historic Park
HABS CA-1918   pd   L
Bodie Jail
Bodie State Historic Park
HABS CA-1925   p   H
Bodie Railroad Station
Bodie State Historic Park
HABS CA-1928   p   H
Bodie Schoolhouse
Green & Mono Sts.
HABS CA-1934   p   H
Boone Store
Main & Green Sts.
HABS CA-1932   p   H
Cain, D. V., House
Green & Fuller Sts.
HABS CA-1921   s pd   L
Cain, J. S., House
Bodie State Historic Park
HABS CA-1920   s pd   L
House, Miner's
HABS CA-2200   p   L
Johl House
Main St.
HABS CA-1922
HAER 3   s pd   L
Methodist Church
Green & Fuller Sts.
HABS CA-1924   s pd   L
Miners' Union Hall
Main St.
HABS CA-1919   s pd   L
Murphy House
Prospect & Union St.
HABS CA-1935   p   H

Parr House
Main St.
HABS CA-1931   p   H
U.S. Land Office Building (Wheaton &
   Hollis Hotel & Bodie Store)
Main & Green Sts.
HABS CA-1933   p   H
Wheaton & Hollis Hotel & Bodie Store; see
   U.S. Land Office Building

San Pedro Valley
Sanchez, Francisco, Adobe
Linda Mar Blvd. & Adobe Dr.
HABS CA-156   s pd   L

MONTEREY COUNTY

Carmel
Misson San Carlos Borromeo del Carmelo
Rio Rd. & Lausen Dr.
HABS CA-136   p   L

Jolon vic.
Mission San Antonio de Padua
Hunter Liggett Military Reservation
HABS CA-38-3   s pd   L
Roth Ranch
HABS CA-1433   p   L

Monterey
Abrego, Don Jose, Casa
Abrego & Webster Sts.
HABS CA-139   p   L
Alvarado, Casa
570 Dutra St.
HABS CA-135   p   L
Alvarado-La Porte Adobe (Wall)
Alvarado & Pearl
HABS CA-1646   p   L
Amesti, Jose, Casa
516 Polk St.
HABS CA-143   s pd   L
Bonifacio, Casa (Gonzales, Jose Rafael,
   House; Rose, Sherman, Cottage)
785 Mesa Rd. (moved from Alvarado St.)
HABS CA-153   p   L
Boronda, Don Manuel de, Casa
Boronda St.
HABS CA-1821   p   L
Brown-Underwood Adobe
Pacific & Madison Sts.
HABS CA-129   p   L
Bushton, Capt. William, House (House,
   First Frame)
Munras & Webster Sts.
HABS CA-1535   p   L
Casa de la Torre; see Federal Court, First
Casa de la Torre; see Torre, Jose, Casa
Casa del Oro (House of Gold)
Scott & Oliver Sts.
HABS CA-132   p   L
Castro, Gen. Jose, Headquarters
Tyler & Pearl Sts.
HABS CA-142   p   L

Colton Hall & Jail
Pacific St.
HABS CA-130   s   L
Convent of St. Catherine at Monterey
Main & Franklin Sts.
HABS CA-1169   p   L
Cooper, Capt. John, House (Molera House)
508 Muras St.
HABS CA-125   p   L
Cooper House (Stone Wall)
508 Munras St.
HABS CA-1647   p   L
Custom House
Custom House Plaza
HABS CA-133   s pd   L
Diaz Store; see Escolle Store
Dickenson, Duncan, House (House, First
   Brick)
351 Decatur St.
HABS CA-145   p   L
Doud, Frances, House
177 Van Buren St.
HABS CA-1648   p   L
Escolle House; see Stokes House
Escolle Store (Diaz Store)
Munras & Polk Sts.
HABS CA-1184   p   L
Federal Court, First (Casa de la Torre;
   Gree Adobe, The)
599 Polk St.
HABS CA-122   p   L
Finon-Fleischer House
410 Monroe St.
HABS CA-1893   pd   L
Fremont, Gen., House
539 Hartnell St.
HABS CA-121   p   L
French Consulate, First
404 Camino El Estero (moved from
   Fremont St.)
HABS CA-1202   p   L
French Hotel; see Stevenson, Robert Louis,
   House
Garcia, Francisco, House (Molera, Andrew
   J., House)
Van Buren & Jackson Sts.
HABS CA-148   p   L
Gonzales, Jose Rafael, House; see
   Bonifacio, Casa
Gordon, Samuel, House (Roach, Phillip,
   House)
526 Pierce St.
HABS CA-150   p   L
Gree Adobe, The; see Federal Court, First
Gutierrez, Don Joaquin, House
590 Calle Princeipal
HABS CA-1201   p   L
Hall of Records; see House of the Four
   Winds

House, First Brick; see Dickenson, Duncan,
   House
House, First Frame; see Bushton, Capt.
   William, House

House of Gold; see Casa del Oro

House of the Four Winds (La Casa de Los Ventanos; Hall of Records)
540 Calle Principal
HABS CA-126   p   L

Jimeno, Don Manuel, Adobe
Main St.
HABS CA-1895   p   L

La Casa de Los Ventanos; see House of the Four Winds

Lara-Soto House; see Soto, Jesus, Casa

Larkin House
464 Calle Principal
HABS CA-128   s p d   L

Merritt House
386 Pacific St.
HABS CA-147   p   L

Molera, Andrew J., House; see Garcia, Francisco, House

Molera House; see Cooper, Capt. John, House

Oliver House; see Torre, Jose, Casa

Pacheco, Don Francisco, Casa
Abrego & Webster Sts.
HABS CA-140   p   L

Pacific House
200-222 Calle Principal
HABS CA-124   p   L

Roach, Phillip, House; see Gordon, Samuel, House

Rose, Sherman, Cottage; see Bonifacio, Casa

Royal Presidio Chapel of San Carlos Boromeo (San Carlos Church)
550 Church St.
HABS CA-38-6   s p d   L

Sambert, Adolph, Casa
HABS CA-1536   p   H

San Carlos Church; see Royal Presidio Chapel of San Carlos Boromeo

Serrano, Casa
412 Pacific St.
HABS CA-152   p   L

Sherman, Gen., Quarters (Sherman-Halleck Quarters)
464 Calle Principal
HABS CA-127   p   L

Sherman-Halleck Quarters; see Sherman, Gen., Quarters

Soberanes Adobe
336 Pacific St.
HABS CA-1892   d   L

Soto, Jesus, Casa (Lara-Soto House)
460 Pierce St.
HABS CA-151   p   L

Stevenson, Robert Louis, House (French Hotel)
530 Houston St.
HABS CA-141   p   L

Stokes House (Escolle House)
500 Hartnell St.
HABS CA-123   p   L

Theatre, First in California
Scott & Pacific Sts.
HABS CA-131   p   L H

Torre, Jose, Casa (Oliver House; Casa de la Torre)
502 Pierce St.
HABS CA-149   p   L

U.S. Post Office
497 Alvarado St.
HABS CA-1203   p   H

Washington Hotel
Washington & Pearl Sts.
HABS CA-1894   p   L

Whaling Station
391 Decatur St.
HABS CA-144   p   L

Monterey vic.

Lighthouse
Point Pinos
HABS CA-1264   p   L

Salinas

El Colegio de San Jose, Academic Building (Hartnell College)
Rancho El Alisal
HABS CA-1171   p   L

El Colegio de San Jose, Dormitory (Hartnell College)
Rancho El Alisal
HABS CA-1172   p   L

Hartnell College; see El Colegio de San Jose, Academic Building

Hartnell College; see El Colegio de San Jose, Dormitory

Salinas vic.

Sherwood Ranch (Sobranes, Feliciano & Mariano, Ranch)
Natividad Rd.
HABS CA-1121   s p d   L

Sherwood Ranch, Barns
Natividad Rd.
HABS CA-1121-D   s   L

Sherwood Ranch, Center Adobe
Natividad Rd.
HABS CA-1121-A   s p   L

Sherwood Ranch, Main Frame Building
Natividad Rd.
HABS CA-1121-C   s p   L

Sherwood Ranch, Northeast Adobe
Natividad Rd.
HABS CA-1121-B   s p   L

Sobranes, Feliciano & Mariano, Ranch; see Sherwood Ranch

Soledad

Mission Nuestra Senora de la Soledad
HABS CA-1130   p   L

NAPA COUNTY

Calistoga vic.

Bale's, Dr. Edward Turner, Grist Mill
Hwy. 29
HABS CA-166   p   L

Napa

Behlow Building
Second & Brown Sts.
HABS CA-1982   s   L

Migliavacca Building
First & Brown Sts.
HABS CA-1983   s   L

NEVADA COUNTY

Bridgeport

Covered Bridge
Pleasant Valley Rd. & Yuba River
HABS CA-1401   p   L

Grass Valley

Farmhouse, Frame; see Taylor-Barker House

Finney-Watt House (Watt House)
506 Linden St.
HABS CA-1391   p   L

Iron Stove
HABS CA-1667   p   L

Montez, Lola, House
248 Mill St.
HABS CA-1642   p   L

Morateur's Hotel & Store
Mill St.
HABS CA-1539   L

Mount St. Mary's Academy
Church & Chapel St.
HABS CA-1799   p   L

Stores A & B, Brick
Mill St.
HABS CA-1692   p   L

Taylor-Barker House (Farmhouse, Frame)
653 Linden St.
HABS CA-1392   p   L

Thomas House
220 N. School St.
HABS CA-1393   p   L

Watt House; see Finney-Watt House

Nevada City

Broad & North Pine Streets (Store)
HABS CA-1394   p   L

Commercial Buildings
HABS CA-1538   p   L

Fire House Number 2
Broad St.
HABS CA-1395   p   L

Nevada City, General View
HABS CA-1802   p   L

Nevada County Courthouse
HABS CA-1803   p   L

North Bloomfield

Houses, Frame
HABS CA-1537   p   L

Red Dog

Wells Fargo Building
HABS CA-1717   p   L

Rough And Ready
Rough and Ready Hotel
HABS CA-1540   p   L

San Juan
Capwell & Furth Store (Store, Brick)
Main St.
HABS CA-1397   p   L
House
HABS CA-1396   p   L
Main Street (Brick Buildings)
HABS CA-1398   p   L
Main Street (Frame Buildings)
HABS CA-1697   p   L
Masonic Hall & Wells Fargo Building
Main St.
HABS CA-1698   p   L
Methodist Episcopal Church
Flume St.
HABS CA-1399   p   L
Store, Brick; see Capwell & Furth Store

San Juan Capistrano
Mission San Juan Capistrano
Olive St. & Hwy. 101
HABS CA-331   s pd   L

Sweetland
Hotel & Store
HABS CA-1400   p   L

ORANGE COUNTY

Anaheim
German House, Old; see Sheffield House
Pioneer House of the Mother Colony
414 N. West St. (moved from N. Los
   Angeles St.)
HABS CA-320   s pd   L
Sheffield House (German House, Old)
506 Los Angeles St.
HABS CA-37   s pd   L

Newport Beach
Lovell Beach House
1242 W. Ocean Front
HABS CA-1986   s pd   H

San Juan Capistrano
Mission San Juan Capistrano, Barracks; see
   Mission San Juan Capistrano, Guest
   House
Mission San Juan Capistrano, Fountains
Olive St. & Hwy. 101
HABS CA-331-C   p   L
Mission San Juan Capistrano, Guest House
   (Mission San Juan Capistrano, Barracks)
Olive St. & Hwy. 101
HABS CA-331-F   s p   L
**Mission San Juan Capistrano, Industrial
   Shops**
Olive St. & Hwy. 101
HABS CA-331-G   s p   L

**Mission San Juan Capistrano, Living
   Quarters**
Olive St. & Hwy. 101
HABS CA-331-E   s p   L
**Mission San Juan Capistrano, Serra's
   Church**
Olive St. & Hwy. 101
HABS CA-331-B   s p   L
**Mission San Juan Capistrano, Stone
   Church**
Olive St. & Hwy. 101
HABS CA-331-A   s p   L
**Misson San Juan Capistrano, Padres'
   Campanerio**
Olive St. & Hwy. 101
HABS CA-331-D   s p   L

PLACER COUNTY

Auburn
Auburn, Chinese Section, General View
HABS CA-1388   p   L
Auburn, General View
HABS CA-1385   p   L
City Hall, Old Town (Ruins)
HABS CA-1390   p   L
Commercial Buildings
HABS CA-1387   p   L
Fire House & Commercial Buildings
Grass Valley & Sacramento Rds.
HABS CA-1384   p   L
Lincoln Way & Maple Street (Commercial
   Building)
HABS CA-1386   p   L
Stone, Henry, House
Nevada St.
HABS CA-1389   p   L

RIVERSIDE COUNTY

Prado vic.
Bandini, Don Juan, House; see Cota House
Cota House (Bandini, Don Juan, House)
HABS CA-332   s pd   L

SACRAMENTO COUNTY

Folsom
Assay Office; see Wells Fargo & Company
   Building
House
HABS CA-1361   p   L
Methodist Episcopal Church
HABS CA-1359   p   L
Trinity Episcopal Church
HABS CA-1360   p   L
Wells Fargo & Company Building (Assay
   Office)
HABS CA-1358   p   L

Locke
Town of Locke, Boat House
River Rd.
HABS CA-2071-AA   d   L
Town of Locke, Christian Center
Key St.
HABS CA-2071-CC   d   L
Town of Locke, Commercial Building
13931 River Rd.
HABS CA-2071-C   d   L
Town of Locke, Commercial Building
13963 River Rd.
HABS CA-2071-I   d   L
Town of Locke, Commercial Building
13952 Main St.
HABS CA-2071-K   d   L
Town of Locke, Commercial Building
13959 Main St.
HABS CA-2071-Y   d   L
Town of Locke, Commercial Building
13947 River Rd.
HABS CA-2071-F   d   L
Town of Locke, Commercial Building
13943 River Rd.
HABS CA-2071-E   d   L
Town of Locke, Commercial Building
13927 River Rd.
HABS CA-2071-B   d   L
Town of Locke, Commercial Building
13955 River Rd.
HABS CA-2071-H   d   L
**Town of Locke, Commercial-Residential
   Structure**
13935 Main St.
HABS CA-2071-S   d   L
**Town of Locke, Dai Loy Gambling
   Museum**
13951 Main St.
HABS CA-2071-W   d   L
Town of Locke, General View
HABS CA-2071   s d   L
Town of Locke, House
Main & Levee Rds.
HABS CA-2071-Z   d   L
Town of Locke, House
13919 Main St.
HABS CA-2071-O   d   L
Town of Locke, House
Key St.
HABS CA-2071-BB   d   L
Town of Locke, House
13915 Main St.
HABS CA-2071-N   d   L
Town of Locke, House
13927 Main St.
HABS CA-2071-Q   d   L
Town of Locke, House
13936 Main St.
HABS CA-2071-L   d   L
Town of Locke, Jan Ying Association
13947 Main St.
HABS CA-2071-V   d   L

Town of Locke, Joe Shoong Chinese
School
13920 Main St.
HABS CA-2071-M   d L

Town of Locke, Residential Building
River & Levee Rds.
HABS CA-2071-G   d L

Town of Locke, Residential Building
13931 Main St.
HABS CA-2071-R   d L

Town of Locke, Residential Building
13939 Main St.
HABS CA-2071-T   d L

Town of Locke, Residential Structure
13955 Main St.
HABS CA-2071-X   d L

Town of Locke, Restaurant
13943 Main St.
HABS CA-2071-U   d L

Town of Locke, Star Theatre
13939 River Rd.
HABS CA-2071-D   d L

Town of Locke, The Tules
River Rd.
HABS CA-2071-J   d L

Town of Locke, Warehouse
13923 Main St.
HABS CA-2071-P   d L

Town of Locke, Yuen Chong Market
13923 River Rd.
HABS CA-2071-A   d L

Sacramento

Adams & Company Building
1014 Second St.
HABS CA-1883   s pd L

Apollo Building
228-230 K St.
HABS CA-1716   s pd L

Aschenauer Building
1022 Third St.
HABS CA-1715   s pd L

Bank Exchange Building
1030 Second St.
HABS CA-186   p H

Bee Building
1016-1020 Third St.
HABS CA-1714   s pd L

Big Four Building
220-226 K St.
HABS CA-1170   s pd L

Blake-Waters Assay Office
222 J St.
HABS CA-1711   s pd L

Booth Building
1019-1021 Front St.
HABS CA-182   pd H

Brannon Building
HABS CA-181   p H

Cavert Building
HABS CA-1254   p H

Cienfugo Building
1119 Second St.
HABS CA-1256   pd L

City Market
118 J St.
HABS CA-199   pd L

Collicott Drug Store (Haines Building)
129 J St.
HABS CA-171   pd L

Cornwall, P. B., Building (Smith Building)
1011-1013 Second St.
HABS CA-1257   pd L

Crocker Art Gallery
216 O St.
HABS CA-1885   s pd L

Democratic State Journal Building
Second & K Sts.
HABS CA-1251   pd L

Diana Saloon
205 J St.
HABS CA-1706   s pd L

Dingley Spice Mill
115 I St.
HABS CA-167   pd H

Ebner's Hotel
116 K St.
HABS CA-1252   pd L

Eureka Swimming Baths
908-910 Second St.
HABS CA-177   pd L

Fashion Saloon
209 J St.
HABS CA-1261   d L

Figg, E. P., Building
224 J St.
HABS CA-1713   s pd L

Fratt, Francis William, Building
1103-1109 Second St.
HABS CA-1255   pd L

Governor's Mansion
H & Sixteenth Sts.
HABS CA-1886   pd L

Gregory-Barnes Store
126 J St.
HABS CA-197   pd L

Haines Building; see Collicott Drug Store

Halls, Luhrs & Company Building
912-916 Second St.
HABS CA-176   pd L

Hastigs, B. F., Bank Building
128-132 J St.
HABS CA-1884   pd L

Heywood Building
1001-1009 Second St.
HABS CA-1258   pd L

Howard House
109-111 K St.
HABS CA-184   pd L

J Street (Commercial Buildings)
HABS CA-1683   pd L

125 K Street (House); see Union Hotel
(Annex)

Lady Adams Building
113-115 K St.
HABS CA-190   s pd L

Latham Building
221-225 J St.
HABS CA-1710   s pd L

Leggett Ale House
1023 Front St.
HABS CA-183   pd L

Mechanics Exchange Hotel
116-122 I St.
HABS CA-178   pd L

Morse Building
1025-1031 Second St.
HABS CA-1259   pd L

Our House Saloon
926 Second St.
HABS CA-175   pd L

Pioneer Hall & Bakery
120-124 J St.
HABS CA-198   pd L

Pioneer Telegraph Building
1015 Second St.
HABS CA-191   s pd L

Rialto Building
225-230 J St.
HABS CA-192   s H

Rivett-Fuller Building
128 K St.
HABS CA-1250   pd L

Sacramento Engine Company No. 3
1112 Second St.
HABS CA-1249   pd L

Sacramento, General View
HABS CA-1671   p L

Sacramento, General View, 1865
HABS CA-1677   p L

Sacramento, Historic View, l850 Flood
HABS CA-1705   p L

Sacramento, Historic View, l852 Fire
HABS CA-1669   p L

Sazerac Building
131 J St.
HABS CA-172   pd L

Smith Building; see Cornwall, P. B.,
Building

Stanford Brothers Store
1203 Front St.
HABS CA-1253   pd L

Stanford-Lathrop Memorial Home
800 N. St.
HABS CA-1709   pd L

Stein Building
218 J St.
HABS CA-1712   s pd L

Sutter's Fort
L & Twenty-Seventh Sts.
HABS CA-1294   p L

Union Hotel
1024-1028 Second St.
HABS CA-187   pd L

Union Hotel (Annex) (125 K Street
(House))
HABS CA-185   pd L

U.S. Post Office, Old
K & Seventh Sts.
HABS CA-1914   pd   L
Vernon-Brannan House
112-114 J St.
HABS CA-179   pd   L
Wormser, I. & S., Building
128 J St.
HABS CA-196   pd   L

SAN BENITO COUNTY

San Juan Bautista
Anza, Juan de, House
Third & Franklin Sts.
HABS CA-38-5   s p   L
Castro, Gen. Jose, House
Mission Plaza
HABS CA-1120   p   L H
Mexican Barracks; see Plaza Hotel
Mission San Juan Bautista
Second St.
HABS CA-38-4   s pd L
Mission San Juan Bautista, Church
Second St.
HABS CA-38-4-A   s p   L
Mission San Juan Bautista, Garden
Second St.
HABS CA-38-4-C   p   L
Mission San Juan Bautista, Monastery
Second St.
HABS CA-38-4-B   p   L
Mission San Juan Bautista, Rectory
Second St.
HABS CA-38-4-D   p   L
Plaza Hotel (Mexican Barracks)
Second St.
HABS CA-1954   s p   H
Zanetta House
HABS CA-1501   p   H

SAN BERNARDINO COUNTY

Chino vic.
Slaughter House (Yorba, Antonio, House)
Prado Rd.
HABS CA-333   L
Yorba, Antonio, House; see Slaughter House

SAN DIEGO COUNTY

Carlsbad vic.
Rancho Agua Hedionda, Casa del
HABS CA-410   pd   L

Coronado
Graham Memorial Presbyterian Church
C & Tenth Sts.
HABS CA-2195   d   H
Hotel Del Coronado
1500 Orange Ave.
HABS CA-1958   s pd L

Julian
Julian Library; see Witch Creek School
Witch Creek School (Julian Library)
Fourth & Washington Sts.
HABS CA-1972   p   H

La Jolla
Bishop's School
7607 La Jolla Blvd.
HABS CA-1968   pd   H
La Jolla Women's Club
715 Silverado St.
HABS CA-1957   s pd L
Neptune Cottage; see Red Rest & Red Roost Cottages
Pueblo Ribera Court
230 Granville St.
HABS CA-1943   pd   H
Red Rest & Red Roost Cottages (Neptune Cottage)
1179 & 1187 Coast Blvd.
HABS CA-1973   pd   H

National City
Granger Music Hall
1700 Fourth St.
HABS CA-1998   s pd H
Kimball Block Row Houses
906-940 A St.
HABS CA-1969   pd   H
Kimball, Frank, House
21 W. Plaza Blvd.
HABS CA-2166   pd   H
St. Matthew's Episcopal Church
521 E. Eighth St.
HABS CA-1959   s pd L

Oak Grove
Butterfield Stage Station
HABS CA-49   pd   L H

Oceanside
Mission San Luis Rey de Francia
Mission Rd.
HABS CA-42   s pd L
Rancho Santa Margarita y Los Flores, Casa del
U.S. Hwy. 101
HABS CA-48   pd   L

Pala
Asistencia of San Antonio de Pala
Mission Rd.
HABS CA-44   s pd L

Point Loma
Point Loma Lighthouse No. 355
Cabrillo National Monument
HABS CA-41   pd   L

San Diego
Albatross Cottages
2353-3415 Albatross
HABS CA-2165   pd   H
Albatross Cottages, Lee Cottage
3353 Albatross
HABS CA-2165-A   pd   H

Albatross Cottages, Teats Cottage
3415 Albatross
HABS CA-2165-D   d   H
Albatross Cottages, Teats Cottage
3407 Albatross
HABS CA-2165-C   pd   H
Albatross Cottges, Lee Cottage
3367 Albatross
HABS CA-2165-B   pd   H
Backesto Block
Fifth Ave. & Market St.
HABS CA-427   pd   L
Balboa Park, Botanical Garden
HABS CA-1970-B   p   H
Balboa Park, California Tower
HABS CA-1970-A   pd   H
Bank of Commerce Building
835 Fifth Ave.
HABS CA-1961   s pd L
Cossitt, Mary, House
3526 Seventh Ave.
HABS CA-2163   pd   H
Davis, William Heath, House
227 Eleventh Ave.
HABS CA-423   s pd L
Fraternal Spirtualist Church; see Temple Beth Israel
Grand Hotel (Horton Hotel)
332 F St.
HABS CA-1974   s pd H
Greely Building; see Nesmith-Greely Building
Horton Hotel; see Grand Hotel
I. O. O. F. Building
526 Market St.
HABS CA-429   pd   L
Johnson-Taylor Ranch House
Rancho Penasquitos
HABS CA-2072   s pd H
Klauber, Melville, House
3060 Sixth Ave.
HABS CA-1962   s pd L
Lee, Alice, House
3578 Seventh Ave.
HABS CA-2161   pd   H
Long-Waterman House
2408 First Ave.
HABS CA-1964   s pd H
Marston, Arthur, House
3575 Seventh Ave.
HABS CA-2164   pd   H
Marston, George W., House
3525 Seventh Ave.
HABS CA-1960   s pd L
McGurck Block
Fifth & Market Sts.
HABS CA-428   pd   L
Mission San Diego de Alcala
Misson Valley Rd.
HABS CA-321   s pd L
Nesmith-Greely Building (Greely Building)
825 Fifth Ave.
HABS CA-1971   s pd L

Santa Fe Railroad Station
1050 Kettner Blvd.
HABS CA-1965   pd   H

Shepard, Jesse, House; see Villa Montezuma

Sherman-Gilbert House
139 Fir St.
HABS CA-1967   pd   H

Spreckles Building & Theater
123 Broadway
HABS CA-1966   pd   H

Teats, Katherine, House
3560 Seventh Ave.
HABS CA-2162   pd   H

Temple Beth Israel (Fraternal Spirtualist Church)
1502 Second Ave.
HABS CA-1999   s pd   L

Villa Montezuma (Shepard, Jesse, House)
1925 K St.
HABS CA-432   pd   L

Whaley House
2482 San Diego Ave.
HABS CA-422   pd   L

San Diego (Old Town)

Bandini, Don Juan, Home
Mason & Calhoun Sts.
HABS CA-46   s pd   L

Casa de la Bandera; see Machado, Casa de

Derby, George, House (Pendleton, George, House)
4017 Harney St.
HABS CA-430   pd   L

Estudillo, Jose Antonio, House (Ramona's Marriage Place)
Mason St. & San Diego Ave.
HABS CA-45   s pd   L

Lopez, La Casa de
Twiggs St.
HABS CA-47   s pd   L

Machado, Casa de (Casa de la Bandera)
2745 San Diego Ave.
HABS CA-411   pd   L

Pendleton, George, House; see Derby, George, House

Ramona's Marriage Place; see Estudillo, Jose Antonio, House

San Luis Rey (Vista)

Rancho Guajome, La Casa de
HABS CA-43   pd   L

Spring Valley

Bancroft House
9050 Memory Lane
HABS CA-431   pd   L

Warner Springs

Kimbie-Wilson House
HABS CA-426   p   H

Warner Springs vic.

Warner Ranch, Barn, Trading Post
HABS CA-425   s pd   L H

Warner Ranch, Ranch House
HABS CA-424   pd   L

SAN FRANCISCO COUNTY

Fort Mason

Building Quarters Number 17; see Fort Mason, Barracks

Fort Mason, Barracks (Building Quarters Number 17)
HABS CA-1179   p   L

Fort Mason, Barracks Number 19
HABS CA-1181   p   L

Fort Mason, N C O Quarters Number 13
HABS CA-1177   p   L

Fort Mason NCO Quarters, Number 12
HABS CA-1178   p   L

Fort Mason, Quarters Number 3
HABS CA-1879   p   L

Fort Mason, Quarters Number 4
HABS CA-1880   p   L

Fort Mason, W O & N C O Quarters Number 14
HABS CA-1176   p   L

Fort Mason, W O Quarters Number 16
HABS CA-1180   p   L

San Francisco

Abandoned Ships, Historic View, 1849-1850
Yerba Beuna Cove
HABS CA-1557   p   L

Admission Day Celebration, Historic View, 1850 (San Francisco, Historic View, 1850)
Montgomery & California Sts.
HABS CA-1159   p   L

Alcatraz, Military Buildings
Alcatraz Island
HABS CA-1792   p   L

Anderson-Christofam Marine Shipyard
HAER CA-14   p   H

Appraiser's Building (Custom House, Old)
Sansome St.
HABS CA-1231   p   L

Bank Building
California & Liedesdorff Sts.
HABS CA-1728   pd   L

Battery Street, Historic View
HABS CA-1723   p   L

Blackstone House
Blackstone Court
HABS CA-1224   p   L

Bolton & Barron Building
Montgomery & Merchant Sts.
HABS CA-1232   p   L

Booth, Edwin, House
35 Calhoun St.
HABS CA-1242   p   L

Broderick Engine Company Number 1, Historic View
Sacramento & Kearny Sts.
HABS CA-1166   p   L

California & Sansome Streets, Historic View, 1872
HABS CA-1167   p   L

City Hall
Civic Center
HABS CA-1881   pd   L

City of Paris Dry Goods Company (Spring Valley Water Company Building)
Geary & Stockton Sts.
HABS CA-2019   s pd   L

Clay Street Bank, Historic View
35 Clay St.
HABS CA-1744   p   L

Cliff House Fire, Historic View
Point Lobos
HABS CA-1736   p   L

Cunningham's Wharf, Historic View
Commercial St.
HABS CA-1743   p   L

Custom House, Old; see Appraiser's Building

Dakin, Capt., House
Taylor & Vallejo Sts.
HABS CA-1240   p   L

Eagle Cafe (McComrick Steamship Office)
2566 Powell St. (moved to Pier 39)
HABS CA-2046   pd   L

Engine 15 Firehouse
California St.
HABS CA-1882   s pd   L

Express Building, Historic View
California & Montgomery Sts.
HABS CA-1769   p   L

Ferry Building
Embarcadero & Market St.
HABS CA-1910   pd   L

Fleischhacker Pool & Bath House
Sloat Blvd. & Great Hwy.
HABS CA-2075   pd   L

Flood, James Clair, Mansion (Pacific Union Club)
1000 California St.
HABS CA-1230   p   L

Folsom & Second Streets, Historic View
HABS CA-1718   p   L

Fort Gunnybags, Historic View; see Sacramento Block, Historic View

Fort Mason
Van Ness, Bay & Laguna Sts.
HABS CA-1119   p   L

Fort Mason, Officers' Club (Fort Mason, Quarters Number 1)
HABS CA-1877   p   L

Fort Mason, Quarters Number 1; see Fort Mason, Officers' Club

Fort Mason, Quarters Number 2
HABS CA-1878   p   L

Fort Point (Fort Point National Historic Site; Fort Winfield Scott)
U.S. Hwy. 101
HABS CA-1239   p   L

Fort Point National Historic Site; see Fort Point

Fort Winfield Scott; see Fort Point

Fortman House
Gougn & Eddy Sts.
HABS CA-1161   p   L

Fremont Hotel, Historic View
Telegraph Hill
HABS CA-1726   p   L

Fremont House, Historic View
Black Point
HABS CA-1175   p   L

Haas-Lilienthal House
2007 Franklin St.
HABS CA-1160   pd   L H

Hibernia Savings & Loan Soc. Bldgs., Historic View
Montgomery & Post Sts.
HABS CA-1735   p   L

Hindu Society (Vedanta Society)
First & Webster Sts.
HABS CA-1286   p   H

Hotaling Building
451 Jackson St.
HABS CA-1475   pd   L

Humphrey House
986 Chestnut St.
HABS CA-155   p   L

Jackson Square (Commercial Building)
441 Jackson St.
HABS CA-1902   p   H

Jackson Square (Commercial Building)
463-473 Jackson St.
HABS CA-1900   p   H

Jackson Square (Commercial Building)
415-431 Jackson St.
HABS CA-1903   p   H

Jackson Square (Commercial Building)
445 Jackson St.
HABS CA-1901   p   H

King, James, of William Banking House, Historic View
Montgomery & Commercial Sts.
HABS CA-1822   p   L

Leese, Jacob, House, Historic View
Grant Ave.
HABS CA-1869   p   L

Lick House, Historic View
Montgomery & Sutter Sts.
HABS CA-1727   p   L

Lincoln School, Historic View
Fifth St.
HABS CA-1868   p   L

Maguires Music Hall, Historic View
Pine St.
HABS CA-1724   p   L

Market Street, Historic View
HABS CA-1722   p   L

Market Street, Historic View
HABS CA-1796   p   L

Masonic Hall, Old, Historic View
Montgomery St.
HABS CA-1747   p   L

Masonic Temple Center, Historic View
Post & Montgomery Sts.
HABS CA-1739   p   L

McComrick Steamship Office; see Eagle Cafe

McCoy Label Company; see U.S. Sub-Treasury & Mint

Mercantile Library Building, Historic View
Bush & Sansome Sts.
HABS CA-1163   p   L

Metroplitan Theater, Historic View
Montgomery & Jackson Sts.
HABS CA-1745   p   L

Mexican Custom House, Historic View
Portsmouth Sq.
HABS CA-1293   p   L

Miners' Exchange Bank, Historic View; see Wright's Historic View

Mission Delores; see Mission San Francisco de Asis

Mission San Francisco de Asis (Mission Delores)
Mission & Sixteenth Sts.
HABS CA-113   s pd   L

Montgomery & Post Streets, Historic View
HABS CA-1823   p   L

Montgomery Block
28 Montgomery St.
HABS CA-1228   s pd   L

Montgomery Street (Commercial Building)
HABS CA-1474   p   L

802 Montgomery Street (Commerical Building)
HABS CA-1472   p   L

Montgomery Street, Historic View
HABS CA-1165   p   L

Montgomery Street, Historic View
HABS CA-1797   p   L

Neveda National Bank, Historic View
Montgomery & Pine Sts.
HABS CA-1164   p   L

Niantic Hotel, Historic View
Clay & Sansome Sts.
HABS CA-1719   p   L

North Beach, Historic View, 1865
HABS CA-1733   p   L

North Point Pier Bulkhead Buildings
Embarcadero, Kearney & Powell Sts.
HABS CA-2047   pd   L

O'Brien House
1045 Green St.
HABS CA-1236   p   L

Occidental Hotel, Historic View
Montgomery & Bush Sts.
HABS CA-1162   p   L

Octagon House
2645 Gough St.
HABS CA-1223   pd   L

Pacific Union Club; see Flood, James Clair, Mansion

Palace of Fine Arts
Baker St.
HABS CA-1909   pd   L

Palmer, Silas, House
Van Ness & Washington Sts.
HABS CA-1289   p   L

Parrott's Granite Block, Historic View
California & Montgomery Sts.
HABS CA-1770   p   L

Phelps House
329 Divisadero St.
HABS CA-1904   pd   L

Pier 16 & Bulkhead Building
Howard St.
HAER CA-5   pd   L

Portmouth Square, Historic View
HABS CA-1725   p   L

Portmouth Square, Historic View
HABS CA-1555   p   L

Post Office, First, Historic View
Stockton & Washington Sts.
HABS CA-1791   p   L

Post Office, Old, Historic View
Kearney & Clay Sts.
HABS CA-1751   p   L

Post Office, Second, Historic View
Clay & Pike Sts.
HABS CA-1225   p   L

Presidio, Chapel of Our Lady
Moraga Ave.
HABS CA-1217   L

Presidio, Commandancia (Presidio, Officer's Club)
Moraga Ave.
HABS CA-1100   p   L

Presidio, Gen. Pershing's House
Moraga Ave.
HABS CA-1215   p   L

Presidio of San Francisco
U.S. 101 & I-480
HABS CA-1114   p   H

Presidio, Officer's Club; see Presidio, Commandancia

Presidio, Officers' Quarters
Funston Ave.
HABS CA-1214   p   L

Presidio, Old Station Hospital
Funston Ave. & Lincoln Blvd.
HABS CA-1216   p   L

Presidio, Powder Magazine
Graham St.
HABS CA-1213   p   L

Railroad House, Historic View
48 Commercial St.
HABS CA-1720   p   L

Reservoir Keeper's House
Bay & Hyde Sts.
HABS CA-1234   p   L

Roos Brothers Store, Historic View
Post & Kearny Sts.
HABS CA-1721   p   L

Russ Building, Historic View
Montgomery & Pine Sts.
HABS CA-1754   p   L

Russian Hill (Houses), Historic View
Green St.
HABS CA-1737   p   L

Sacramento Block, Historic View (Fort Gunnybags, Historic View)
Sacramento St. & Battery St.
HABS CA-1746   p   L

Sacramento Street, Historic View
HABS CA-1780   p   L

Sacramento Street, Historic View
HABS CA-2199   p   L

3397-3399 Sacramento Street (House)
HABS CA-2044   L

Sailors' Home, Historic View; see U.S. Marine Hospital, Historic View

San Francisco & San Jose Railroad Building
Montgomery & Post Sts.
HABS CA-1729   p   L

San Francisco Daily Morning Call, Historic View
Clay & Montgomery Sts.
HABS CA-1753   p   L

San Francisco Fire Dept., Pumping Station Number 2
Van Ness Ave.
HAER CA-1   p   H

San Francisco, Historic View, 1837
HABS CA-1866   p   L

San Francisco, Historic View, 1846
HABS CA-1732   p   L

San Francisco, Historic View, 1848
HABS CA-1760   p   L

San Francisco, Historic View, 1849
HABS CA-1758   p   L

San Francisco, Historic View, 1849
HABS CA-1782   p   L

San Francisco, Historic View, 1849
HABS CA-1759   p   L

San Francisco, Historic View, 1850
HABS CA-1776   p   L

San Francisco, Historic View, 1851
HABS CA-1756   p   L

San Francisco, Historic View, 1851 Fire
HABS CA-1730   p   L

San Francisco, Historic View, 1852 Plat Map
HABS CA-1222   p   L

San Francisco, Historic View, 1853
HABS CA-1761   p   L

San Francisco, Historic View, 1853 Plat Map
HABS CA-1221   p   L

San Francisco, Historic View, 1856
HABS CA-1814   p   L

San Francisco, Historic View, 1856
HABS CA-1762   p   L

San Francisco, Historic View, 1859 Plat Map
HABS CA-1220   p   L

San Francisco, Historic View, 1868
HABS CA-1734   p   L

San Francisco, Historic View, 1875
HABS CA-1767   p   L

San Francisco, Historic View, 1906
HABS CA-1764   p   L

San Francisco, Historic View, 1906 Fire
HABS CA-1817   p   L

San Francisco, Historic View, 1906 Fire
Market St.
HABS CA-1778   p   L

San Francisco, Historic View, 1906 Fire
HABS CA-1819   p   L

San Francisco, Historic View, 1906 Fire
HABS CA-1798   p   L

San Francisco, Historic View, 1906 Fire
HABS CA-1818   p   L

San Francisco, Historic View, 1906 Fire
California & Sansome Sts.
HABS CA-1820   p   L

San Francisco, Historic View, l850; see Admission Day Celebration, Historic View, l850

San Francisco, Historic View, l880
HABS CA-1781   p   L

Sansome Street, Historic View, 1850
HABS CA-1227   p   L

Sea Wall Warehouse
1501 Sansome St.
HABS CA-2194   p   H

Spreckels Mansion
2080 Washington St.
HABS CA-1906   pd   L

Spring Valley Water Company Building; see City of Paris Dry Goods Company

St. Francis Church, Historic View
610 Vallejo St.
HABS CA-1219   p   L

St. Mary's Church
660 California St.
HABS CA-1237   p   L

St. Patrick's Church
756 Mission St.
HABS CA-1233   p   L

St. Rose's Church
N. Brannan & Fifth Sts.
HABS CA-1311   p   L

Stevenson-Osbourne House
Hyde & Lombard Sts.
HABS CA-1229   p   L

Stockton Street, Historic View
HABS CA-1815   p   L

Sutro, Adolph, House
Pt. Lobos & Forty-Eighth Ave.
HABS CA-1238   p   L

Telegraph Hill, Historic View
HABS CA-1247   p   L

Telegraph Hill, Historic View
Greenwich St.
HABS CA-1248   p   L

Telegraph Hill (House)
1301 Montgomery St.
HABS CA-1241   p   L

Telegraph Hill (Houses)
Montgomery & Union Sts.
HABS CA-1245   p   L

Telegraph Hill (Houses)
Filbert St.
HABS CA-1246   p   L

Telegraph Hill (Houses)
Union St.
HABS CA-1226   p   L

Telegraph Hill (Houses)
Alta St.
HABS CA-1243   p   L

Telegraph Hill (Houses)
Napier La.
HABS CA-1244   p   L

Trocadero Inn
Twenty-second Ave.
HABS CA-119   s pd   L H

Union Depot & Ferry House, Historic View
Market St.
HABS CA-1749   p   L

U.S. Branch Mint
Mission & Fifth Sts.
HABS CA-160   s pd   L

U.S. Custom House, Old, Historic View
Battery & Washington Sts.
HABS CA-1556   p   L

U.S. Marine Hospital, Historic View (Sailors' Home, Historic View)
Spear & Harrison Sts.
HABS CA-1741   p   L

U.S. Sub-Treasury & Mint (McCoy Label Company)
608 Commercial St.
HABS CA-1218   p   L

2213-2217 Van Ness Avenue, Historic View, (Houses)
HABS CA-1235   p   L

Vedanta Society; see Hindu Society

Warner's Cobweb Palace, Historic View
HABS CA-1740   p   L

Wells Fargo & Company Building, Historic View
114 Montgomery St.
HABS CA-1768   p   L

Wells Fargo Bank, Historic View
Sansome & California Sts.
HABS CA-1771   p   L

Whittier Mansion
2090 Jackson St.
HABS CA-1907   pd   L

Wright's Historic View (Miners' Exchange Bank, Historic View)
Montgomery & Jackson Sts.
HABS CA-1731   p   L

Yerba Buena Island, Naval Buildings
HABS CA-1793   p   L

Yerba Buena Lighthouse Buildings
Yerba Buena Island
HABS CA-1554   p   L

San Fransisco
Holy Cross Parish Hall
Eddy St. (moved from Market & Second
  Sts.)
HABS CA-1908   pd   L

SAN JOAQUIN COUNTY

Alba
Farmhouse
HABS CA-12   p   L

Corral Hollows
House, Frame
HABS CA-1619   p   H
Outbuilding
HABS CA-1613   p   H

Escalon
Jones House
HABS CA-117   p   L

French Camp
Noble, Col., Store
HABS CA-1617   p   H

Lathrop
Main Street (Commercial Buildings)
HABS CA-1595   p   H

Lockeford
Harmony Grove Methodist Church
Locke Rd.
HABS CA-1614   p   H

Lodi
Commercial Buildings
HABS CA-1598   p   H

Stockton
Avon Theatre
Main & California Sts.
HABS CA-1593   p   H
Barnhart House
Magnolia & Hunter Sts.
HABS CA-1621   p   H
Budd, Gov. James H., Mansion
HABS CA-1627   p   H
Carson House
HABS CA-1612   p   H
Christian Church
HABS CA-1615   p   H
Clark, Dr. Asa, House
Oak & Hunter Sts.
HABS CA-1581   p   H
Columbia House (Green Dragon)
Channel & San Joaquin Sts.
HABS CA-1580   p   H
Commercial Hotel
Main St.
HABS CA-1629   p   H
Creanor, Judge, House
Fremont & Commercial Sts.
HABS CA-1616   p   H
Eureka Firehouse
HABS CA-1638   p   H

First Baptist Church
HABS CA-1583   p   H
Forty-Nine Drug Store; see Holden Store
Globe Iron Works
HABS CA-1605   p   H
Green Dragon; see Columbia House
Hart & Thrift Building
HABS CA-1600   p   H
Hazelton Library; see Stewart, Frank,
  Library
Holden Store (Forty-Nine Drug Store)
El Dorado & Main Sts.
HABS CA-1634   p   H
I. O. O. F. Building
El Dorado & Main Sts.
HABS CA-1625   p   H
Keyes House
California & Market Sts.
HABS CA-1609   p   H
Mansion House
HABS CA-1603   p   H
Masonic Temple & R. P. Parker Store
Hunter St.
HABS CA-1604   p   H
McKee Block (Sterling Corner)
Main & Hunter Sts.
HABS CA-1602   p   H
Philadephia House
HABS CA-1607   p   H
San Joaquin County Courthouse
HABS CA-1632   p   H
San Joaquin County Courthouse
Main & Hunter Sts.
HABS CA-1639   p   H
San Joaquin Firehouse
Weber Ave. & California St.
HABS CA-1640   p   H
Simpson, Andrew, House
Oak & El Dorado Sts.
HABS CA-1626   p   H
Smith, Capt., House
HABS CA-1618   p   H
St. Mary's Cathedral Church
HABS CA-1624   p   H
Sterling Corner; see McKee Block
Stewart, Frank, Library (Hazelton Library)
Market & Hunter Sts.
HABS CA-1631   p   H
Stockton, Historic View
HABS CA-1601   p   H
Terry, Judge Daniel S., House
Fremont & Center Sts.
HABS CA-1582   p   H
Trahearne, Washington, House
El Dorado & Park Sts.
HABS CA-1596   p   H
Weber, Capt. Charles M., House
HABS CA-1641   p   H

Stockton vic.
Tone, Jack, House
Jack Tone Rd.
HABS CA-1620   p   H

Woodbridge
Arizona State Home for Insane
HABS CA-1636   p   H
I. O. O. F. Building
HABS CA-1590   p   H
Woodbridge College
HABS CA-1635   p   H
Woods Hotel
HABS CA-1610   p   H
Woods, Jeremiah, Cottage
HABS CA-1611   p   H

SAN LUIS OBISPO COUNTY

Nipomo vic.
Dana, William G., House
Guadalupe Rd.
HABS CA-23   s pd   L

San Luis Obispo
Mission San Luis Obispo de Tolosa
782 Monterey St.
HABS CA-210   s d   L
Mission San Luis Obispo de Tolosa,
  Church
782 Monterey St.
HABS CA-210-A   s p   L
Mission San Luis Obispo de Tolosa,
  Monastery
782 Monterey St.
HABS CA-210-B   s p   L

San Miguel vic.
Caledonia Inn
Hwy. 101
HABS CA-1300   p   L H
Mission San Miguel Archangel
Hwy. 101
HABS CA-38-2   s pd   L H

Santa Margarita vic.
Mission Chapel of Santa Margarita; see
  Santa Margarita Asistencia
Santa Margarita Asistencia (Mission
  Chapel of Santa Margarita)
HABS CA-1182   p   H

SAN MATEO COUNTY

Atherton
Linden Tower Gates
Middlefield Rd. & James Pl.
HABS CA-2118   L
Watkins-Cartan House
25 Isabella Ave.
HABS CA-1990   s pd   H

Belmont
Ralston Hall (Ralston-Sharon House)
Ralston Ave.
HABS CA-1674   d   L
Ralston-Sharon House; see Ralston Hall

Burlingame
Southern Pacific Railroad Station
Burlingame Ave. & California St.
HABS CA-2120   H

Half Moon Bay

Alarcitas Livery Stable; see Vasquez Stable
Community Methodist Church
Johnston & Miramontes Sts.
HABS CA-2121   p   H
Johnston, James, House
Higgins Rd.
HABS CA-2122   p   H
Johnston, William, House
306 Higgins Rd.
HABS CA-2123   p   H
Vasquez, Pablo, Hosue
270 N. Main St.
HABS CA-2124   p   H
Vasquez Stable (Alarcitas Livery Stable)
200 Main St.
HABS CA-2124-A   p   H

Hillsborough

Carolan
565 Remillard Dr.
HABS CA-2196   pd   H
Clark House
945 Tournament Dr.
HABS CA-2126   p   H
Grant-Blyth House (Villa Rose)
HABS CA-2125   p   H
Villa Rose; see Grant-Blyth House

Menlo Park

Atalaya; see Meyer, J. Henry, House
Church of the Nativity
210 Oak Grove Ave.
HABS CA-1995   s pd   H
Meyer, J. Henry, House (Atalaya)
2212 Santa Cruz
HABS CA-2127   p   H
Payne-Douglass House
Menlo Park School & College
HABS CA-2128   pd   H
San Francisco & San Jose Railroad Station
(Southern Pacific Railroad Station)
1100 Merrill St.
HABS CA-1994   s pd   H
Southern Pacific Railroad Station; see San
Francisco & San Jose Railroad Station

Millbrae

Southern Pacific Depot
21 E. Millbrae Ave.
HABS CA-2059   p   L

Pescadero

Ano Nuevo Ranch, House (Steele Brothers
Dairies)
Ano Nuevo State Preserve
HABS CA-2129-F   p   H
Cascade Ranch (Steele Brothers Dairies)
Cabrillo Hwy.
HABS CA-2129-B   pd   H
Cascade Ranch, Dairy (Steele Brothers
Dairies)
Cabrillo Hwy.
HABS CA-2129-A   H

Cloverdale Ranch, Barn (Steele Brothers
Dairies)
Cabrillo Hwy.
HABS CA-2129-C   p   H
Congregational Church
San Gregorio St.
HABS CA-163   H
Dickerson Barn (Steele Brothers Dairies)
Ano Nuevo State Preserve
HABS CA-2129-E   p   H
Garretson Schoolhouse
2307 Pescadero Rd.
HABS CA-2132   p   H
Graham, Issac, House (White House)
Ano Nuevo State Preserve
HABS CA-2130   p   H
I. O. O. F. Hall
110 San Gregorio St.
HABS CA-2134   p   H
McCormick, James, House
San Gregorio St.
HABS CA-2131   p   H
Methodist Episcopal Church
108 San Gregorio St.
HABS CA-162   p   H
Moore, Thomas W., House
114 San Gregorio St.
HABS CA-2136   H
Ramsey-Steele Ranch Complex (Steele
Brothers Dairies)
Cabrillo Hwy.
HABS CA-2129-D   p   H
108-114 San Gregorio Street (House)
HABS CA-1996   s d   H
St. Anthony's Roman Catholic Church
North St.
HABS CA-2133   p   H
Steele Brothers Dairies; see Ano Nuevo
Ranch, House
Steele Brothers Dairies; see Cascade Ranch
Steele Brothers Dairies; see Cascade
Ranch, Dairy
Steele Brothers Dairies; see Cloverdale
Ranch, Barn
Steele Brothers Dairies; see Dickerson Barn
Steele Brothers Dairies; see Ramsey-Steele
Ranch Complex
Steele Brothers Dairies, Barn
Ano Nuevo State Preserve
HABS CA-2129-G   p   H
Steele Brothers Dairies, House
Ano Nuevo State Preserve
HABS CA-2129-I   p   H
Steele Brothers Dairies, House
Ano Nuevo State Preserve
HABS CA-2129-H   p   H
Weeks, Bartlett V., House
172 Goulson St.
HABS CA-2137   p   H
Weeks, Braddock, House
Pascadero Rd.
HABS CA-2138   p   H

Wells Fargo & Company Building
HABS CA-1701   p   H
White House; see Graham, Issac, House
Woodhams House
112 San Gregorio St.
HABS CA-2135   p   H

Pescadero vic.

Pigeon Point Lighthouse
State Hwy. 1
HABS CA-1997   s pd   H

Portola Valley

Alpine Beer Garden; see Buelna's
Roadhouse
Buelna's Roadhouse (Alpine Beer Garden)
3915 Alpine Rd.
HABS CA-2139   p   H
Lady of Wayside Church
930 Portola Rd.
HABS CA-2140   p   H
Portola Valley School
775 Portola Rd.
HABS CA-1992   s pd   H

Redwood City

Bank of San Mateo County
2000-2002 Broadway
HABS CA-1991   s pd   H
Diller-Chamberlain Store (Pioneer Store)
726 Main St.
HABS CA-2141   pd   H
Fitzpatrick Building
2010 Broadway
HABS CA-2142   p   H
Pioneer Store; see Diller-Chamberlain
Store
San Mateo County Courthouse
Middlefield, Hamilton, Broadway &
Marshall Sts.
HABS CA-2143   pd   H

San Gregorio

Bell Hotel; see San Gregorio House
San Gregorio House (Bell Hotel)
San Gregorio Rd.
HABS CA-1993   s pd   H

San Mateo

St. Matthew's Episcopal Church
El Camino Real & Baldwin St.
HABS CA-2144   p   H

Woodside

Bourn-Roth Estate; see Filoli
Filoli (Bourn-Roth Estate)
Canada Rd.
HABS CA-2117   d   H
Fleischacker House; see Green Gables
Green Gables (Fleischacker House)
329 Albion Ave.
HABS CA-2147   p   H
LaQuesta Wind Cellar
240 La Questa Rd.
HABS CA-2145   p   H

Woodside Store
Kings Mountain & Trip Rds.
HABS CA-2146   p   H

SANTA BARBARA COUNTY

Buellton

Cuesta, La Casa de Eduardo de la
Hwy. 101
HABS CA-27   s pd   L

Buellton vic.

Cuesta, La Case de Cota de la
Lompoc Rd.
HABS CA-28   s pd   L

Coyote

Laguna Seca Rancho (Rancho del Refugio de la Laguna Seca)
Hwy. 101
HABS CA-2003   pd   L

Rancho del Refugio de la Laguna Seca; see Laguna Seca Rancho

Guadalupe

Guadalupe Rancho Adobes, Adobe Number 1
114 Third Ave.
HABS CA-29-A   s p   L

Guadalupe Rancho Adobes, Adobe Number 2
120 Third Ave.
HABS CA-29-B   s p   L

Guadelupe Rancho Adobes
114 & 120 Third Ave.
HABS CA-29   pd   L

Lompoc vic.

Mission La Purisima Conception
HABS CA-211   pd   L

Point Arguello Coast Guard Rescue Station
HAER CA-6   s pd   L

Milpitas

Alviso, Jose Maria, Adobe
Piedmont & Calaveras Rds.
HABS CA-1663   p   H

Montecito

Ortega House
29 Sheffield Dr.
HABS CA-314   s pd   L

Santa Barbara

Adobe, Historic
715 Santa Barbara St.
HABS CA-249   p   H

Birabent Adobe
820 Santa Barbara St.
HABS CA-247   p   H

Caneda Adobe
121 E. Canon Perdido St.
HABS CA-242   pd   L

Carillo, La Case de Toaquin
11 E. Carrillo St.
HABS CA-25   s pd   L H

Covarrubias Adobe
715 Santa Barbara St.
HABS CA-26   s pd   L H

East de la Guerra Street (Commercial Building)
HABS CA-245   p   H

El Cuartel
122 E. Canon Perdido St.
HABS CA-37-36   s pd   L

Fernald, Charles, House
412 W. Montecito St. (moved fr. 422 Santa Barbara)
HABS CA-240   pd   L

Guerra, La Casa de la
11-19 E. de la Guerra St.
HABS CA-313   s pd   L

Hunt-Stambach House
404 W. Montecito St. (moved from Victoria St.)
HABS CA-241   d   L

Knox Brick House
914 Anacape St.
HABS CA-244   pd   L

Miranda House
806 Anacapa St.
HABS CA-37-35   s pd   L

Mission Santa Barbara
Laguna St. & Mission Canyon Rd.
HABS CA-21   s pd   L

Orena, Gaspar, House
E. de la Guerra St.
HABS CA-246   H

Pico, Buena Ventura, Adobe
920 Anacapa St.
HABS CA-243   pd   L

Trussel House
327 Castillo St.
HABS CA-248   p   H

Trussell-Winchester Adobe
412 W. Montecito St.
HABS CA-239   pd   L

Vhay, Mrs. A. L. M., House
835 Leguna St.
HABS CA-37-37   pd   L

Yorbe-Abadie House
de la Guerra Plaza
HABS CA-37-33   s pd   L

Solvang

Mission Santa Ynez
State Hwy. 150
HABS CA-24   pd   L

Mission Santa Ynez, Church
State Hwy. 150
HABS CA-24-A   s p   L

Mission Santa Ynez, Monastery
State Hwy. 150
HABS CA-24-B   s p   L

Mission Santa Ynez, Tannery
State Hwy. 150
HABS CA-24-C   s p   L

SANTA CLARA COUNTY

Coyote

Laguna Seca Rancho, Barn
U.S. Hwy. 101
HABS CA-2003-B   L

Laguna Seca Rancho, Office
U.S. Hwy. 101
HABS CA-2003-C   s   L

Laguna Seca Rancho, Stone Building
U.S. Hwy. 101
HABS CA-2003-A   s p   L

Coyote vic.

Stevens Ranch Complex
State Rt. 101
HABS CA-2018   pd   L

Twin Oaks Dairy
Metcalfe Rd.
HABS CA-2017   pd   L

Cupertino

Collins School (Cupertino de Oro Club)
20441 Homestead Ave.
HABS CA-2091   pd   L

Cupertino de Oro Club; see Collins School

House, Old; see Woodhills

Maryknoll Seminary
23000 Cristo Rey Dr.
HABS CA-2092   pd   L

Picchetti Winery
13100 Montebello Rd.
HABS CA-2012   s pd   L

Woodhills (House, Old)
Prospect Rd.
HABS CA-2007   s pd   L

Gilroy

Christian Church (Latin American Assemblies of God)
160 Fifth St.
HABS CA-2060   s pd   L

Eschenburg-Silva Cow Barn
3665 Pacheco Pass Rd.
HABS CA-2096   s pd   L

Gilroy Free Public Library (Gilroy Historical Museum)
195 Fifth St.
HABS CA-2093   d   L

Gilroy Historical Museum; see Gilroy Free Public Library

Hoenck House
9480 Murray Ave.
HABS CA-2095   pd   L

Latin American Assemblies of God; see Christian Church

Lilly's Auto Camp
8877 Monterey Hwy.
HABS CA-2094   s pd   L

Live Oak Creamery
88 Martin St.
HABS CA-2065   s pd   L

Willson House
1980 Pacheco Rd.
HABS CA-2097   pd   H

Gilroy vic.

Norris, Frank, Memorial
Redwood Retreat Rd.
HABS CA-1544   p   H

Stevenson, Robert Louis, House
Redwood Retreat Rd.
HABS CA-1545   p   H

Los Altos

Christ Episcopal Church (Foothills
   Congregational Church)
461 Orange Ave.
HABS CA-2013   s pd   L

Foothills Congregational Church; see
   Christ Episcopal Church

Los Altos Hills

Lynn, Martha, Tank House
12899 Viscano Pl.
HABS CA-2066   s pd   L

Los Gatos

Forbes Mill Addition
Church & E. Main Sts.
HABS CA-2062   s pd   L

Young's Home in the Heart of the Hills; see
   Yung See San Fong (House)

Yung See San Fong (House) (Young's
   Home in the Heart of the Hills)
16660 Cypress Way
HABS CA-2070   pd   L

Menlo Park

Y. W. C. A. Hostess House
Santa Cruz Ave. (moved to CA, Palo Alto)
HABS CA-1670   p   H

Milpitas vic.

Higuera, Jose, Adobe
Rancho Higuera Rd.
HABS CA-1664   p   H

Monta Vista vic.

Woelffel Cannery
10120 Imperial Ave.
HABS CA-2099   pd   L

Morgan Hill

Fountain Oaks
15835 Carey Ave.
HABS CA-2100   pd   L

Foutain Oaks, Guest House
15835 Carey Ave.
HABS CA-2100-A   pd   L

Morgan Hill House; see Villa Miramonte

Villa Miramonte (Morgan Hill House)
17860 N. Monterey Rd.
HABS CA-2101   p   L

Morgan Hill vic.

Machado School
Sycamore Ave.
HABS CA-2102   p   L

Malaguerra Winery
Burnett Rd.
HABS CA-2004   s pd   L

New Almaden

Adobe House
Almaden Rd.
HABS CA-1623   p   H

Almaden Club House; see Casa Grande

Almaden Mine, Office & Shop Buildings;
   see New Almaden Quicksilver Mine

Carson House
21570 Almaden Rd.
HABS CA-115   s pd   L H

Casa Grande (Almaden Club House)
21350 Almaden Rd.
HABS CA-1116   pd   L

El Adobe Viejo
Almaden Rd.
HABS CA-1622   p   L H

Guadalupe Mine, Church & School
HABS CA-157   p   H

Guadalupe Mine, Miner's Cabins
HABS CA-120   p   H

Laird Adobe
Almaden Rd.
HABS CA-134   p   H

Mine Hill School
New Almaden Quicksilver Mine County
   Park
HABS CA-1125   s pd   L

New Almaden Quicksilver Mine (Almaden
   Mine, Office & Shop Buildings)
New Almaden Quicksilver Mine County
   Park
HABS CA-114   s pd   L

Shannon Farmhouse
14475 Shannon Rd.
HABS CA-1124   p   H

West, Dr., House
HABS CA-1183   p   H

Palo Alto

Channing Market; see Emperger Grocer

Courtyard Building; see 520-526 Ramona
   Street (Commercial Building)

de Lemos, Pedro, Building; see 520-526
   Ramona Street (Commercial Building)

Emperger Grocer (Channing Market)
532 Channing Ave.
HABS CA-2103   s pd   L

General Petroleum Gasoline Station; see
   Violet Ray Gasoline Station

Kennedy, John G., House
423 Chaucer St.
HABS CA-2076   s pd   L

**520-526 Ramona Street (Commercial
   Building)** (de Lemos, Pedro, Building;
   Courtyard Building)
533-539 Ramona St.
HABS CA-2067   s pd   L

Violet Ray Gasoline Station (General
   Petroleum Gasoline Station)
799 Alma St.
HABS CA-2069   s pd   L

Palto Alto

Y. W. C. A. Hostess House
University Ave. (moved from CA, Menlo
   Park)
HABS CA-1670   p   H

San Jose

Allen, Horace, Gasoline Station
505 E. San Carlos St.
HABS CA-2105   s pd   L

Blanchard House
HABS CA-1787   p   L

1147 Chapman Street (House)
HABS CA-2109   p   L

Col, Peter E., House
1163 Martin Ave.
HABS CA-2008   s pd   L

**College Park Association of Friends'
   Meetinghouse** (Friends' Meetinghouse)
1041 Morse St.
HABS CA-2061   s pd   L

Fredericksburg Resort
HABS CA-1786   p   H

Friends' Meetinghouse; see College Park
   Association of Friends' Meetinghouse

Gates, Howard B., House
62 S. Thirteenth St.
HABS CA-2077   s pd   L

Greenawalt, David, Farm (Greenawalt,
   David, Tank House)
14611 Almaden Expwy.
HABS CA-2009   s pd   L

Greenawalt, David, Farm, Tank House
14611 Almaden Expwy.
HABS CA-2009-A   p   L

Greenawalt, David, Tank House; see
   Greenawalt, David, Farm

Hanchett Residence Park
1225-1257 Martin Ave.
HABS CA-2010   s pd   L

Horn, Emily, House
2341 N. First St.
HABS CA-2108   pd   L

Kennedy House
HABS CA-1789   p   H

Kirk-Farrington House
1615 Dry Creek Rd.
HABS CA-2090   H

Lick Observatory
Mt. Hamilton
HABS CA-2110   pd   L

Masonic Temple
262-272 S. First St.
HABS CA-2045   p   L

O'Brien Court
1076-1092 O'Brien Court
HABS CA-2106   s pd   L

Pina House
3260 Alameda St.
HABS CA-1846   p   H

Winchester House (Winchester Mystery
   House)
525 S. Winchester Blvd.
HABS CA-2107   pd   L

Winchester Mystery House; see Winchester House

San Martin

Krohn, John, Tank House
13000 Foothill Ave.
HABS CA-2111   s pd   L

Santa Clara

Durand-Kirkman House
623 Cabrillo Ave.
HABS CA-2176   p   H

Harrison Street Block (Houses)
1009-1091 Harrison St.
HABS CA-2063   s pd   L

Landrum, Andrew, House
1217 Santa Clara St.
HABS CA-2064   s pd   L

Larder House
1065 Alviso St.
HABS CA-2112   p   L

Mission Santa Clara de Asis
University of Santa Clara
HABS CA-1133   p   H

Santa Clara Verein
1082 Alviso St.
HABS CA-2068   s pd   L

Santa Clara vic.

Lick, James, Mill
Montague Rd.
HABS CA-2011   pd   L

Lick, James, Mill, Granary
Montague Rd.
HABS CA-2011-B   s p   L

Lick, James, Mill, House
Montague Rd.
HABS CA-2011-A   p   L

Lick, James, Mill, Office
Montague Rd.
HABS CA-2011-C   p   L

Saratoga

Casa Tierra
15231 Quito Rd.
HABS CA-2113   pd   L

Dyer, H. P., House
16055 Sanborn Rd.
HABS CA-2050   pd   L

Saratoga Foothill Club
20399 Park Pl.
HABS CA-2014   pd   L

Welch-Hurst
15800 Sanborn Rd.
HABS CA-2006   s pd   L

Saratoga vic.

Phelan, James Duval, House; see Villa Montalvo

Villa Montalvo (Phelan, James Duval, House)
Montalvo Rd.
HABS CA-2048   pd   L

Stanford

Dunn-Bacon House
565 Mayfield Ave.
HABS CA-2175   p   H

Escondite Cottage
Escondido Rd.
HABS CA-2168   p   H

Frenchman's Library
860 Escondido Rd.
HABS CA-2169   p   H

Frenchman's Tower
Old Page Mill Rd.
HABS CA-2170   p   H

Griffin-Drell House
570 Alvarado Rd.
HABS CA-2173   p   H

Hoover, Lou Henry, House
Stanford University
HABS CA-2177   p   H

Palo Alto Winery
HABS CA-2171   p   H

Salvatierra Street (House)
HABS CA-2174   p   H

Stanford University
HABS CA-2172   p   H

Stanford University, Memorial Church
HABS CA-2172-A   p   H

SANTA CRUZ COUNTY

Glen Canyon

Covered Bridge
HABS CA-1551   p   H

Covered Bridge
HABS CA-1551   p   H

Santa Cruz

Covered Bridge
Spanning San Lorenzo River
HABS CA-1549   p   H

Hall of Records
Fron & Cooper Sts.
HABS CA-1548   p   H

Mission Santa Cruz
Emmet & School Sts.
HABS CA-1552   p   H

Santa Cruz, General View
HABS CA-1550   p   H

Soquel

Congregational Church
HABS CA-1192   p   H

SHASTA COUNTY

Lassen Volcanic vic.

Building Number 1; see Park Headquarters
Building Number 178; see Loomis Seismograph Station
Building Number 21; see Service Station
Building Number 284; see Warner Valley Hay Barn

Building Number 287; see Warner Valley Cook's Cabin
Building Number 37; see Summit Lake Ranger Station
Building Number 41; see Naturalist's Residence
Building Number 43; see Loomis Museum, Auditorium
Building Number 44; see Comfort Station
Building Number 49; see Manzanita Ranger Residence, Storage & Workshop
Building Number 50; see Manzanita Kiosk
Building Number 58; see Warner Valley Ranger Station

Comfort Station (Lassen Volcanic National Park; Building Number 44)
HABS CA-2114-G   p   H

Lassen Volcanic National Park
HABS CA-2114   H

Lassen Volcanic National Park; see Comfort Station

Lassen Volcanic National Park; see Loomis Museum, Auditorium

Lassen Volcanic National Park; see Loomis Seismograph Station

Lassen Volcanic National Park; see Lost Creek Flume

Lassen Volcanic National Park; see Manzanita Kiosk

Lassen Volcanic National Park; see Manzanita Ranger Residence, Storage & Workshop

Lassen Volcanic National Park; see Naturalist's Residence

Lassen Volcanic National Park; see Park Headquarters

Lassen Volcanic National Park; see Service Station

Lassen Volcanic National Park; see Summit Lake Ranger Station

Lassen Volcanic National Park; see Warner Valley Cook's Cabin

Lassen Volcanic National Park; see Warner Valley Hay Barn

Lassen Volcanic National Park; see Warner Valley Ranger Station

Loomis Museum, Auditorium (Lassen Volcanic National Park; Building Number 43)
HABS CA-2114-F   p   H

Loomis Seismograph Station (Lassen Volcanic National Park; Building Number 178)
HABS CA-2114-K   p   H

Lost Creek Flume (Lassen Volcanic National Park)
HABS CA-2114-A   p   H

Manzanita Kiosk (Lassen Volcanic National Park; Building Number 50)
HABS CA-2114-I   p   H

Manzanita Ranger Residence, Storage & Workshop (Lassen Volcanic National Park; Building Number 49)
HABS CA-2114-H   p   H

Naturalist's Residence (Lassen Volcanic National Park; Building Number 41)
HABS CA-2114-E   p   H

Park Headquarters (Lassen Volcanic National Park; Building Number 1)
HABS CA-2114-B   p   H

Service Station (Lassen Volcanic National Park; Building Number 21)
HABS CA-2114-C   p   H

Summit Lake Ranger Station (Lassen Volcanic National Park; Building Number 37)
HABS CA-2114-D   p   H

Warner Valley Cook's Cabin (Lassen Volcanic National Park; Building Number 287)
HABS CA-2114-M   p   H

Warner Valley Hay Barn (Lassen Volcanic National Park; Building Number 284)
HABS CA-2114-L   p   H

Warner Valley Ranger Station (Lassen Volcanic National Park; Building Number 58)
HABS CA-2114-J   p   H

Red Bluff vic.

Battle Creek Hydroelectric System (Coleman Power House; Inskip Power House; South Power House; Volta Power House)
Battle Creek & Tributaries
HAER CA-2   s pd   L

Coleman Power House; see Battle Creek Hydroelectric System

Inskip Power House; see Battle Creek Hydroelectric System

South Power House; see Battle Creek Hydroelectric System

Volta Power House; see Battle Creek Hydroelectric System

Shasta

Bystle House
Trinity & High Sts.
HABS CA-1445   p   L

Foster House
HABS CA-1443   p   L

Main Street (Commercial Buildings)
HABS CA-1305   p   L H

Masonic Hall & Store (Ruins) (Western Star Lodge Number 2)
HABS CA-1303   p   H

Shasta County Courthouse (Ruins)
HABS CA-1297   p   L H

Shurtleff, Dr., House
HABS CA-1444   p   L

Western Star Lodge Number 2; see Masonic Hall & Store (Ruins)

SIERRA COUNTY

Downieville

Catholic Church
Sierra City Rd.
HABS CA-1405   p   L

Courthouse, House
HABS CA-1417   L

Downie, Maj., House
HABS CA 1407   p   L

Downieville Courthouse (Pioneer Museum Building)
HABS CA-1402   p   L H

Downieville, General View
HABS CA-1291   L

Downieville, General View
Main St.
HABS CA-1290   p   L

Elmwood Cottage; see Sierra City Road (Houses)

I. O. O. F. Hall
HABS CA-1403   p   L

Main Street (Commercial Buildings)
HABS CA-1290   L

Miner's Drug Store; see Wells Fargo Building

Pioneer Museum Building; see Downieville Courthouse

Sierra City Road (Church)
HABS CA-1404   p   L

Sierra City Road (Frame Houses & Church)
HABS CA-1410   p   L

Sierra City Road (House)
HABS CA-1412   p   L

Sierra City Road (House)
HABS CA-1414   L

Sierra City Road (Houses) (Elmwood Cottage)
HABS CA-1408   p   L

Sierra City Road (Frame Houses & Church)
HABS CA-1410   L

St. Charles Hotel
HABS CA-1406   L

Wells Fargo Building (Miner's Drug Store)
HABS CA-1292   p   H

Downieville vic.

Hydraulic Mine
HABS CA-1420   p   L

Goodyear's Bar

Goodyear's Bar, General View
HABS CA-1679   p   H

Sierra City

Bush, August C., Building; see Wells Fargo and Company Building

Main Street (Commercial Buildings)
HABS CA-1422   p   L

Main Street (Commercial Buildings)
HABS CA-1477   p   L

Main Street (House)
HABS CA-1423   p   L

Main Street (House)
HABS CA-1425   L

Mine, Old
HABS CA-1421   p   L

Wells Fargo and Company Building (Bush, August C., Building)
HABS CA-1426   p   L

Sierraville

Sierraville, General View
HABS CA-1676   p   H

SISKIYOU COUNTY

Callahan

Callahan Ranch Hotel & Farrington Hotel
HABS CA-1189   p   H

Sawyers Bar

Catholic Church
HABS CA-1190   p   H

SOLANO COUNTY

Benicia

Benicia Arsenal, Barracks (Building Number 45)
HABS CA-1826   s pd   L

Benicia Arsenal, Barracks
HABS CA-1774   L

Benicia Arsenal, Building Number 1; see Benicia Arsenal, Hospital

Benicia Arsenal, Building Number 14; see Benicia Arsenal, Powder Magazine Number 5

Benicia Arsenal, Building Number 39; see Benicia Arsenal, Guard and Engine House

Benicia Arsenal, Building Number 74
HABS CA-1775   p   L

Benicia Arsenal, Buildings Number 33, 34, 35; see Benicia Arsenal, Enlisted Men's Quarters

Benicia Arsenal, Commanding Officer's Quarters (Quarters Number 1, Building Number 28)
HABS CA-1843   s pd   L

Benicia Arsenal, Dock
HABS CA-1834   L

Benicia Arsenal, Duplex Officer's Quarters (Officer's Quarters No. 3 & 4, Buildings No. 25 & 26)
HABS CA-1947   s pd   L

Benicia Arsenal, Enlisted Men's Quarters (Benicia Arsenal, Buildings Number 33, 34, 35)
HABS CA-1949   L

Benicia Arsenal, Guard and Engine House (Benicia Arsenal, Building Number 39)
HABS CA-1832   pd   L

Benicia Arsenal, Gun Yard
HABS CA-1842   p   L

Benicia Arsenal, Hospital (Benicia Arsenal,
  Building Number 1)
HABS CA-1945   s pd   L

Benicia Arsenal, Lieutenant's Quarters
  (Officer's Quarters Number 2, Building
  Number 27)
HABS CA-1825   s pd   L

Benicia Arsenal, Main Gateway
HABS CA-1844   p   L

Benicia Arsenal, Office Building (Building
  Number 47)
M St. vic.
HABS CA-1827   s pd   L

Benicia Arsenal, Powder Magazine
  Number 2 (Building Number 10)
HABS CA-1948   s pd   L

Benicia Arsenal, Powder Magazine
  Number 5 (Benicia Arsenal, Building
  Number 14)
I-680 vic.
HABS CA-1839   pd   L

Benicia Arsenal, Shop Buildings (Buildings
  Numbers 55, 56, 57)
Tyler St., Benicia Industrial Park
HABS CA-1833   s pd   L

Benicia Arsenal, Shops Storehouse
  (Building Number 49)
HABS CA-1838   pd   L

Benicia Arsenal, Stables (Building Number
  51)
HABS CA-1979   p   L

Benicia Arsenal, Storehouse (Building
  Number 48)
HABS CA-1978   L

Benicia Arsenal, Storehouse (Clocktower
  Building, Number 29)
Comandant's Lane, Benicia Industrial Park
HABS CA-1828   s pd   L

Benicia Arsenal, Storehouses and Engine
  House (Camel Barns; Bldgs. Nos. 7, 8, 9)
HABS CA-1946   L

Benicia, General View
HABS CA-2079   p   L

Benicia State Capitol (California State
  Capitol)
First & G Sts.
HABS CA-1188   p   L

Bldgs. Nos. 7, 8, 9; see Benicia Arsenal,
  Storehouses and Engine House

Building Number 10; see Benicia Arsenal,
  Powder Magazine Number 2

Building Number 45; see Benicia Arsenal,
  Barracks

Building Number 47; see Benicia Arsenal,
  Office Building

Building Number 48; see Benicia Arsenal,
  Storehouse

Building Number 49; see Benicia Arsenal,
  Shops Storehouse

Building Number 51; see Benicia Arsenal,
  Stables

Buildings Numbers 55, 56, 57; see Benicia
  Arsenal, Shop Buildings

California Hotel (California House)
First & H Sts.
HABS CA-1187   p   L

California House; see California Hotel

California State Capitol; see Benicia State
  Capitol

Camel Barns; see Benicia Arsenal,
  Storehouses and Engine House

Carr House
165 E. D St.
HABS CA-2052   s pd   L

City Hotel (Golden Horseshoe)
415 First St.
HABS CA-2080   pd   L

Clocktower Building, Number 29; see
  Benicia Arsenal, Storehouse

Crooks House
285 W. G St.
HABS CA-2081   pd   L

Fairview Hotel (Washington House Hotel)
333 First St.
HABS CA-2088   pd   L

Fischer-Hanlon House
G St. between First and W. Second Sts.
HABS CA-1889   pd   L

Fish House; see Riddell Fish House

Frisbie-Walsh House
235 E. L St.
HABS CA-2087   pd   L

Golden Horseshoe; see City Hotel

Masonic Temple
110 W. J St.
HABS CA-1887   pd   L

Officer's Quarters No. 3 & 4, Buildings No.
  25 & 26; see Benicia Arsenal, Duplex
  Officer's Quarters

Officer's Quarters Number 2, Building
  Number 27; see Benicia Arsenal,
  Lieutenant's Quarters

Quarters Number 1, Building Number 28;
  see Benicia Arsenal, Commanding
  Officer's Quarters

Riddell Fish House (Fish House)
245 W. K St.
HABS CA-2082   pd   L

Solano House; see Union Hotel

Southern Pacific Passenger Depot
SE First & A Sts. (moved from CA, Banta)
HABS CA-2085   pd   L

St. Catherine's Academy
Solano Square
HABS CA-1542   p   L

St. Dominic's Catholic Church
475 E. I St.
HABS CA-2083   pd   L

St. Paul's Episcopal Church, Rectory
122 E. J St. (moved from CT, Torrington)
HABS CA-2084   pd   L

St. Paul's Episcopal Church, Rectory
122 E. J St. (moved from CT, Torrington)
HABS CA-2084   p   L

Union Hotel (Solano House)
401-05 First St.
HABS CA-2086   pd   L

Von Pfister, Semple, Store
D St. vic.
HABS CA-1912   pd   L

Washington House Hotel; see Fairview
  Hotel

Wingfield, Bishop J. H. D., House
36 Wingfield Way
HABS CA-2089   pd   L

Mare Island

Building 47; see Mare Island Naval
  Shipyard

Commandant's Office and Administration
  Building; see Mare Island Naval
  Shipyard

Magazine A1; see Mare Island Naval
  Shipyard

Mare Island Naval Shipyard (St. Peter's
  Chapel)
HABS CA-1543-C   H

Mare Island Naval Shipyard (Smithy, Bldg.
  No. 46)
HABS CA-1543-D   H

Mare Island Naval Shipyard (Building 47)
HABS CA-1543-A   p   H

Mare Island Naval Shipyard
  (Commandant's Office and
  Administration Building)
HABS CA-1824   p   L

Mare Island Naval Shipyard (Magazine
  A1)
HABS CA-1543-B   p   H

Mare Island Naval Shipyard (Naval
  Buildings, Old)
HABS CA-1543
HAER CA-3   s pd   L

Naval Buildings, Old; see Mare Island
  Naval Shipyard

Smithy, Bldg. No. 46; see Mare Island
  Naval Shipyard

St. Peter's Chapel; see Mare Island Naval
  Shipyard

Vacaville

Pena Adobe
Pena Adobe Rd.
HABS CA-1198   s pd   L H

SONOMA COUNTY

Fort Ross

Barracks; see Fort Ross

Block House; see Fort Ross

Fort Ross (Block House)
HABS CA-1314   L

Fort Ross
HABS CA-1312   p   L H

Fort Ross (Barracks)
HABS CA-1315   L

Fort Ross (Russian Chapel)
HABS CA-110   s p   L H

Russian Chapel; see Fort Ross

Petaluma vic.
Adobe
NE of Petaluma on Pacific Duck Farm
HABS CA-38-9   s p   L
Vallejo, Adobe
HABS CA-38-1   s p   L

Santa Rosa
Carrillo Adobe
HABS CA-1442   s pd   L
Fountain Grove, Barn
Mendocino Ave. at US 101
HABS CA-1915   p   L H
Fountain Grove, House
HABS CA-1917   p   H
Santa Rosa Post Office and Federal Building
401 Fifth St. (moved to Seventh St.)
HABS CA-2051   pd   L

Santa Rosa vic.
Fountain Grove, Winery
HABS CA-1916   p   H

Sonoma
Alder Adobe; see Ray House
Blue Wing Inn (Sonoma House)
HABS CA-1438   p   L
Lachryma Montis; see Vallejo, Gen., House
Mexican Army Barracks; see Sonoma Barracks
Mission San Francisco Solano De Sonoma
First and Spain Sts.
HABS CA-1138   L H
Ray House (Alder Adobe; Ray-Adler House)
HABS CA-1439   p   L
Ray-Adler House; see Ray House
Sonoma Barracks (Mexican Army Barracks)
HABS CA-1560   p   H
Sonoma House; see Blue Wing Inn
Sonoma Plaza, Bear Flag Flagstaff
HABS CA-1436   L
Temelec Hall
20750 Arnold Ave.
HABS CA-1563   pd   L
Vallejo Chalet
HABS CA-1441   p   L
Vallejo, Gen., House (Lachryma Montis)
N. Third St. W.
HABS CA-1440   s pd   L

STANISLAUS COUNTY

Knights Ferry
Covered Bridge
Tulloch Mill, Stanislaus River
HABS CA-158   p   L
Dent House
Ellen St.
HABS CA-1193   p   L

Fire House
HABS CA-161   p   L
Jail
Main St.
HABS CA-164   p   L
Knights Ferry, General View
HABS CA-169   p   L
Miller House
Sonora Hwy.
HABS CA-18   s p   L
Schell House
HABS CA-118   p   L
Tulloch Mill
Stanislaus River
HABS CA-137   p   L
Tulloch Mill, Crib Dam
HABS CA-168   p   L
Tulloch Mill, Power House
HABS CA-159   s p   L
Tulloch Mill, Warehouse
HABS CA-165   s p   L

TEHAMA COUNTY

Red Bluff vic.
Battle Creek Hydroelectric System
(Coleman Power House; Inskip Power House; South Power House; Volta Power House)
Battle Creek & Tributaries
HAER CA-2   s pd   L
Coleman Power House; see Battle Creek Hydroelectric System
Inskip Power House; see Battle Creek Hydroelectric System
South Power House; see Battle Creek Hydroelectric System
Volta Power House; see Battle Creek Hydroelectric System

TRINITY COUNTY

Carrville
Gold Dredge
HABS CA-1186   p   H

Weaverville
Blacksmith Shop
HABS CA-1185   p   H
Brewery, Old
Main st.
HABS CA-1449   p   L
Chinese Joss House
State Historical Park
HABS CA-1452   s pd   L
Cole, John, Building; see I. O. O. F. Lodge Number 55 Hall
Fire Engine, Old
HABS CA-1453   p   L
I. O. O. F. Lodge Number 55 Hall (Cole, John, Building)
HABS CA-1448   p   L

Jumper House
HABS CA-1451   p   L
Native Sons of the Golden West Building
HABS CA-1668   p   H
Store
HABS CA-1450   p   L
Trinity County Courthouse
Main & Court Sts.
HABS CA-1447   p   L
Weaverville, General View
HABS CA-2197   p   L

TULARE COUNTY

Tulare
Commercial Buildings
HABS CA-1794   p   H

TUOLUMNE COUNTY

Big Oak Flat
I. O. O. F. Hall
HABS CA-1578   p   H

Chinese Camp
Bruschi Store
HABS CA-1569   p   H

Columbia
Building, Brick
HABS CA-1695   p   L
City Hotel
Main St. (Columbia State Historical Park)
HABS CA-1146   p   L H
Columbia, General View
Columbia State Historical Park
HABS CA-1873   p   H
Grave Stones, Mountain View Cemetery
Bigler St.
HABS CA-37-11-A   p   L
Grave Stones, St. Anne's Cemetery
HABS CA-38-11-B   p   L
I. O. O. F. Building
State& Broadway Sts. (Columbia State Hist. Park)
HABS CA-1693   p   H
Livery Stable
HABS CA-1872   p   H
Main Street (Commercial Building)
Columbia State Historical Park
HABS CA-1147   p   L
Main Street (Commercial Buildings)
HABS CA-1299   p   H
Mills, D. O., Bank; see Mills, D. O., Building
Mills, D. O., Building (Mills, D. O., Bank)
HABS CA-1573   p   H
Pioneer Saloon
HABS CA-1145   p   L
Solari's Building
Columbia State Historical Park
HABS CA-1144   p   L

Springfield Brewery; see Tuolumne, Engine House, Number 1

St. Anne's Church
Church St.
HABS CA-1142   s p   L H

Sun Ling Store
N. Main St. (Columbia State Historical Park)
HABS CA-2000   p   H

Trading Post, Old
Main & State Sts.
HABS CA-1143   p   L H

Tuolumne, Engine House, Number 1 (Springfield Brewery)
Columbia State Historical Park
HABS CA-1871   p   H

Wells Fargo and Company Building
Main & Washington Sts. (Columbia State Hist. Park)
HABS CA-174   s p   L H

Dragon Gulch

Gilman, Tom, Cabin
HABS CA-1200   p   H

Groveland vic.

Harte, Bret, House (Tennessee's Cabin)
HABS CA-1568   p   H

Tennessee's Cabin; see Harte, Bret, House

Jackass Hill

Gillis Cabin; see Twain, Mark, Cabin

Twain, Mark, Cabin (Gillis Cabin)
HABS CA-1296   p   H

Montezuma

Hotel and Store
HABS CA-1574   p   L

Priests

Priest's Hotel
HABS CA-1572   p   H

Quartz Mountain

Quartz Mountain, General View
HABS CA-1196   p   H

Shaw's Flat

Mississippi House and Post Office
Shaw Flat & Mt. Beow Rds.
HABS CA-1579   p   H

Sonora

Cady House
Dodge and Norlin Sts.
HABS CA-116   s pd   L H

City Hotel
HABS CA-1566   p   L H

Commercial Building (Iron Doors)
HABS CA-1699   p   H

Dodge & Stuart Streets (House)
HABS CA-1139   p   L

Dorsey House
HABS CA-1134   p   L

Gem Cafe; see Store Building

Grave Stones, Jewish Cemetery
Yaney Ave. between Vigilance and Seco Sts.
HABS CA-38-11-A   p   L

Gunn, Dr. Lewis, Adobe; see Italia Hotel

House, Second
Dodge and Stewart Sts.
HABS CA-1140   p   L

Italia Hotel (Gunn, Dr. Lewis, Adobe)
Washington St.
HABS CA-1135   p   L

Jewish Cemetery
Yaney Ave.
HABS CA-38-7   s p   L

Leonard, Thomas, House
HABS CA-1512   p   L

McCormick House
HABS CA-1111   p   L

Methodist Church
HABS CA-1567   p   H

Post Office, First
HABS CA-1575   p   L

Sonora, General View
HABS CA-1195   p   H

St. James Episcopal Church
Washington & Theall Sts.
HABS CA-1141   p   L

St. Patrick's Church
Dodge & Norlin Sts.
HABS CA-189   p   L

Stockton Record Building
HABS CA-1690   p   H

Store Building (Gem Cafe)
Washington St.
HABS CA-1688   p   L

Sugg House (Sugg-McDonald House)
37 Theall St.
HABS CA-1137   p   L

Sugg-McDonald House; see Sugg House

Union Democrat Building
HABS CA-1691   p   H

1100 Washington Street (House)
HABS CA-1136   p   L

Sonora vic.

Dam, Stone
HABS CA-188   p   L

Kiln, Lime
HABS CA-195   p   L

Springfield

House
HABS CA-1148   p   L

Methodist Church; see School

School (Methodist Church)
Horseshoe Bend and Springfield Rd.
HABS CA-1149   p   L

Stent

Stent, General View
HABS CA-1577   p   H

Tuttletown

Swerer's Store; see Tuttletown Hotel

Tuttletown Hotel (Swerer's Store)
HABS CA-1272   p   L H

Tuttletown vic.

Farmhouse
HABS CA-1271   p   L

Woods Crossing

Farm Buildings
HABS CA-1570   p   H

VENTURA COUNTY

Marysville

D Street (Commerical Buildings)
HABS CA-1808   p   H

Piru vic.

Camulos, Del Rancho, La Casa
State Hwy. 12
HABS CA-38   s pd   L

Ventura

Mission San Buenaventura
E. Main St. & S. Figueroa St.
HABS CA-22   s pd   L

YUBA COUNTY

Bear River

Bear River Hotel and Wells Fargo Office
HABS CA-1689   p   H

Brown's Valley vic.

Oregon House (Stage Station, Old)
HABS CA-1428   p   L

Stage Station, Old; see Oregon House

Dobbins

Hotel
HABS CA-1427   p   L

Marysville

Aaron, Mary, Museum; see Miller-Aaron House

C Street & Sixth Street (Houses)
HABS CA-1430   p   L

C Street (House)
HABS CA-1432   p   L

C Street (House)
HABS CA-1431   p   L

Marysville Grammar School
HABS CA-1812   p   H

Marysville High School
HABS CA-1811   p   H

Miller-Aaron House (Aaron, Mary, Museum)
704 D St.
HABS CA-1113   p   L

O'Brian, James, House
O'Brian Rd.
HABS CA-1809   p   H

Presbyterian Church
Fifth & D Sts.
HABS CA-1429   p   L

Yuba County Courthouse
Sixth & D Sts.
HABS CA-1810   p   H

Yuba County Hall of Records
HABS CA-1813   p   H

Timbuctoo
Main Street (Commercial Buildings)
HABS CA-1546   p   H

Wells Fargo Express Office
N. Hwy. 20, Marysville & Grass Valley
HABS CA-1295   p   L H

Canal Zone

Colon vic.
Fort San Lorenzo
Chagres River
HABS CZ-1   s   L

Colorado

BENT COUNTY

La Junta
Bent's Old Fort National Historic Site; see Fort Bent, Old
Fort Bent, Old (Bent's Old Fort National Historic Site)
HABS CO-22   s   L

CLEAR CREEK COUNTY

Silver Plume
Silver Plume School
Main St.
HABS CO-23   s d   L H

DENVER COUNTY

Denver
1650 Blake Street (Commercial Building)
HABS CO-31   pd   L
Cory Hotel; see Plymouth Place
Denver Mint
Colfax & Delaware Sts.
HABS CO-49   pd   H
1611 Market Street (Commercial Building)
HABS CO-30   pd   L
1615-1617 Market Street (Commercial Building)
HABS CO-28   pd   L
1623 Market Street (Commercial Building)
HABS CO-29   pd   L
Milwaukee Brewery Company; see Tivoli-Union Brewery
Plymouth Place (Cory Hotel)
1560-1572 Broadway
HABS CO-24   s pd   L
Skyline Urban Renewal Area
HABS CO-50   p   H

Tears-McFarlane Garage
1200 Williams St.
HABS CO-27   pd   L
Tivoli-Union Brewery (Milwaukee Brewery Company)
Thirty-First St.
HABS CO-26
HAER CO-1   p   H
U.S. Post Office & Federal Building
Eighteenth & Stouts Sts.
HABS CO-51   p   H

Denver vic.
South Platte Canyon Road Bridge
HAER CO-7   s   H
Wells Fargo Butterfield Stage Station
HABS CO-36-C-2   s d   L

EAGLE COUNTY

Wolcott
Bocco House (Wolcott Stage Station)
NW Junction-U.S. Hwy. 6 & 131
HABS CO-33   s pd   L
Wolcott Stage Station; see Bocco House

GARFIELD COUNTY

Glenwood Springs
Hot Springs Lodge
HABS CO-52   p   H
Rifle vic.
Havemeyer-Willcox Canal System
HAER CO-3   s pd   L H

GILPIN COUNTY

Central City
Opera House
HABS CO-36-C-3   p   L

Teller House
HABS CO-36-C-4   p   L

GUNNISON COUNTY

Gunnison vic.
Cooper 2BR Ranch, Barn
Curecanti Recreation Area
HABS CO-25-A   p   L
Cooper 2BR Ranch, Bunkhouse
Curecanti Recreation Area
HABS CO-25-B   p   L

JEFFERSON COUNTY

Mount Vernon
Steele, Gov., House
HABS CO-36-C-1   s d   L

Waterton
South Platte River, Foothills Project
HAER CO-9   pd   H

LAS ANIMAS COUNTY

Segundo
Penitente Morada
HABS CO-58   p   L

Tijeras
Santa Nina de Atoche
Tijeras Plaza
HABS CO-54   p   L

Trinidad
Benitez, Frederico, House
612 E. Main St.
HABS CO-55   p   L

Weston vic.

Guadaloupe Mission Church
Medina Plaza
HABS CO-57   p   L
Vigil Plaza, Church
HABS CO-56   p   L

SAN JUAN COUNTY

Silverton
Miscellaneous Structures
HABS CO-53   p   H

SAN MIGUEL COUNTY

Ophir vic.

Ames Hydroelectric Plant; see Telluride
    Power Company

Telluride Power Company (Ames
    Hydroelectric Plant)
HAER CO-2   p   H

SUMMIT COUNTY

Kokomo
Masonic Temple
HABS CO-21   p   L

WELD COUNTY

Greeley
Lincoln Schools (Structure Number 2)
Eleventh St. & Fourth Ave.
HABS CO-32   pd   L

Connecticut

FAIRFIELD COUNTY

Bridgeport

Armstrong Mill Historic District (3-31/2
    Armstrong Place (House))
HABS CT-344   p   L
3-31/2 Armstrong Place (House); see
    Armstrong Mill Historic District
Barna House; see Knapp, George S., House
Harr-Al-Wheeler House
HABS CT-350   p   H
Knapp, George S., House (Barna House)
2414 North Ave.
HABS CT-343   p   L
Victorian Cottage
Boston Post Rd.
HABS CT-106   pd   L

Cos Cob

Bush-Holley House
39 Strickland Rd.
HABS CT-279   s pd   L H

Darien

Clock-Turner House
1830 Boston Post Rd.
HABS CT-17   s pd   L
Hubbard House; see Parsons, Lt. William,
    House
Mather, Deacon Joseph, House; see
    Mather, Stephen Tyng, House
Mather, Stephen Tyng, House (Mather,
    Deacon Joseph, House)
19 Stephen Mather Rd.
HABS CT-289   pd   L
Parsons, Lt. William, House (Hubbard
    House)
(moved from MA, Northampton)
HABS MA-188   s d   L

Easton

Dillon, Jane, House
Rock House Rd.
HABS CT-73   pd   L
Trup, Rudolph, House
Rock House Rd.
HABS CT-72   s pd   L

Fairfield

Bronson, Frederic, Windmill
Bronson Rd.
HABS CT-325   s p   H
Burr, Thaddeus, Homestead
491 Old Post Rd.
HABS CT-3-17   pd   L
Congregational Parsonage; see Sherman,
    Judge Roger M., House
Fairfield Academy, Old
Boston Post Rd.
HABS CT-28   s pd   L
Ogden, David, House
1520 Bronson Rd.
HABS CT-56   s pd   L
Powder House
Center St.
HABS CT-40   pd   L
Sherman, Judge Roger M., House
    (Congregational Parsonage)
500 Old Post Rd.
HABS CT-60   s pd   L
Sherwood, Hull, House
762 Mill Hill Rd.
HABS CT-58   s pd   L
Sturges, Benjamin, House (Trubee-Knapp
    House)
Rowland Rd.
HABS CT-54   pd   L
Trubee-Knapp House; see Sturges,
    Benjamin, House

Greenwich

Mead, Abraham D., House
Field Pt. Park vic.
HABS CT-38   pd   L

New Canaan

Rogers, John, Studio
10 Cherry St.
HABS CT-351   p   H

New Canaan vic.

Fauntleroy House
Ponus Ridge
HABS CT-43   s pd   L

North Greenwich

Field-Carpenter House
Old Bedford Rd.
HABS CT-352   s d   H

Norwalk

Lockwood-Mathews House
Veterans' Memorial Park, SE
HABS CT-265   s pd   L H
Sherman, Taylor, House
89 Main St.
HABS CT-77   pd   L

Redding

Bartlett, Rev. Nathaniel, Parsonage; see
    Sanford, Jonathan B., House
Sanford, Jonathan B., House (Bartlett, Rev.
    Nathaniel, Parsonage)
Georgetown Rd.
HABS CT-74   pd   L

Ridgefield

Hawley, Rev. Thomas, House
Main St. & Branchville Rd.
HABS CT-46   s p   L
Remington, Frederick, House
HABS CT-353   p   H

Silvermine

Buttery Sawmill
Silvermine Brook
HABS CT-63   pd   L

South Norwalk

**South Main Street, Block 43 (Commercial
    Buildings)**
HABS CT-349   s p   H

Southport

Bulkley, Capt. Ward, House
298 Harbor Rd.
HABS CT-330   p   L
Bulkley, Moses, House
176 Main St.
HABS CT-299   pd   L
Bulkley, William, House
824 Harbor Rd.
HABS CT-309   pd   L

Connecticut Bank, Mill River Branch
227 Main St.
HABS CT-319   pd   L

Jelliff, C. O., Company
354 Pequot Rd.
HABS CT-291   pd   L

Jelliff, Francis, House
212 Center St.
HABS CT-290   s p   L

Jennings, Nehemiah, Block
668-70 Main St.
HABS CT-294   p   L

Meeker, Wakeman B., House
25 Westway Rd.
HABS CT-318   pd   L

New York, New Haven & Hartford RR Freight House
Station St.
HABS CT-292   p   L

New York, New Haven & Hartford RR Station
Railroad Pl.
HABS CT-293   pd   L

Nichols, Allen, House
494 Harbor Rd.
HABS CT-336   p   L

Osborn, John, House
Kings Highway
HABS CT-20   pd   L

Pequot Library
720 Pequot Rd.
HABS CT-314   s pd   L

Pequot School
214 Main St.
HABS CT-320   pd   L

Perry, Austin, House
712 Harbor Rd.
HABS CT-300   pd   L

Perry, Charles, House
564 Harbor Rd.
HABS CT-306   pd   L

Perry, Francis D., House (Trinity Church Rectory)
678 Pequot Rd.
HABS CT-317   pd   L

Perry, Gurdon, House
780 Harbor Rd.
HABS CT-328   p   L

Perry, Henry, House
45 Westway Rd.
HABS CT-305   pd   L

Perry, John Hoyt, House
134 Center St.
HABS CT-334   p   L

Perry, Oliver H., House
750 Harbor Rd.
HABS CT-302   pd   L

Pike, Julius, House
62 Center St.
HABS CT-337   p   L

Pomeroy, Benjamin, Carriage House
658 Pequot Rd.
HABS CT-310   pd   L

Pomeroy, Benjamin, House
658 Pequot Rd.
HABS CT-298   pd   L

Sheffield, Paschal, House
104 Old South Rd.
HABS CT-303   pd   L

Sherwood, Oliver T., House
683 Pequot Rd.
HABS CT-295   pd   L

Sherwood, Simon C., House
67 Westway Rd.
HABS CT-296   pd   L

Sherwood-Banks House
98 Banks Pl.
HABS CT-316   p   L

Southport Congregational Church
523 Pequot Rd.
HABS CT-311   pd   L

Southport Harbor, Mill River
Southport Harbor
HABS CT-331   s p   L H

Southport Savings Bank
226 Main St.
HABS CT-315   s pd   L

46 Station Street (House)
HABS CT-327   p   L

Sturges, Barnabas, House
534 Harbor Rd.
HABS CT-332   p   L

Sturges, Henry, House
608 Harbor Rd.
HABS CT-335   p   L

Thorp, Capt. Walter, House
198 Oxford Rd.
HABS CT-307   pd   L

Trinity Church (P. E.)
651 Pequot Rd.
HABS CT-312   s pd   L

Trinity Church Rectory; see Perry, Francis D., House

Trinity Parish Chapel (P. E.)
651 Pequot Rd.
HABS CT-313   s pd   L

Wakeman, Capt. William Webb, House
478 Harbor Rd.
HABS CT-301   pd   L

Wakeman Memorial
648 Harbor Rd.
HABS CT-321   pd   L

Wakeman, Zalmon, House
418 Harbor Rd.
HABS CT-297   pd   L

Waugh House
249 Old South Rd.
HABS CT-338   p   L

Stamford

Knap, Samuel, House
Oxen Walk, 984 Stillwater Rd.
HABS CT-354   pd   H

Stanwich vic.

Blockhouse; see Stone House

Ingersoll House; see Stone House

Stone House (Ingersoll House; Blockhouse)
Farms Rd.
HABS CT-37   s p   L

Stratford

Christ Church
Main St.
HABS CT-355   p   H

Cranston House; see McEwen House

Curtis, Freeman L., House
3355 Main St.
HABS CT-12   s pd   L

McEwen House (Cranston House)
HABS CT-215   p   L

Perry-Fairchild Homestead
1128 W. Broad St.
HABS CT-65   s pd   L

Plant House, Old
HABS CT-216   p   L

Walker, Gen. Joseph, House
2175 Elm St.
HABS CT-66   pd   L

Trumbull

Kaatz Ice House
Whitney Ave.
HAER CT-6   pd   H

Westport

Dunn House
Myrtle Ave.
HABS CT-16   pd   L

First Congregational Church of Saugatuck
HABS CT-123   p   L

Jessup House
HABS CT-214   p   L

Prince, William Meade, House (Raymond, Lewis, House)
St. John Place
HABS CT-69   pd   L

Raymond, Lewis, House; see Prince, William Meade, House

Wilton

Congregational Church
HABS CT-194   p   L

Lambert, David, House
Danbury Post Rd.
HABS CT-29   s pd   L

Lambert, David, Servants House
Danbury Post Rd.
HABS CT-30   s pd   L

Wilton Town Hall
HABS CT-31   pd   L

HARTFORD COUNTY

East Granby

Thompson Farmhouse
HABS CT-197   p   L

East Hartford

Minister's Hotel; see Pitkin, Squire Elisha, House

351

Pitkin, Squire Elisha, House (Minister's Hotel)
Roberts Lane
HABS CT-18   pd   L

East Hartland
Congregational Church
HABS CT-195   p   L

East Windsor Hill
Watson-Bancroft House
Main St.
HABS CT-219   p   L
Woods House
HABS CT-218   p   L

Farmington
Cowles, Maj. Gen. Solomon, House
Main St.
HABS CT-3-6   s pd   L
Deming House
HABS CT-115   pd   L
First Church of Christ Congregational Church (Meetinghouse)
HABS CT-224   p   L
Gleason House
23 Main St.
HABS CT-389   p   L
Meetinghouse; see First Church of Christ Congregational Church
Stanley-Whitman House
37 High St.
HABS CT-356   p   H

Glastonbury
Welles, Gideon, House
Main & Hebron Sts.
HABS CT-39   pd   L H

Hartford
Armsmear; see Colt, Samuel, House
Barnard, Henry, House
118 Main St.
HABS CT-358   p   H
Catlin House; see Sigourney, Lydia, House
Colt, Samuel, House (Armsmear)
80 Wethersfield Ave.
HABS CT-357   p   H
22-24 Congress Street (House)
HABS CT-339   p   L
42 Dean Street (House)
HABS CT-341   p   L
50 Dean Street (House)
HABS CT-340   p   L
12-20 Morris Street (Apartments)
HABS CT-342   p   L
Sigourney, Lydia, House (Catlin House)
15 Hurlburt St.
HABS CT-24   s pd   L
296-283 Sigourney Street Residence
HABS CT-346   p   L
State House, Old
Main St. & Central Row
HABS CT-3   s pd   L H

Twain, Mark, Memorial
531 Farmington Ave.
HABS CT-359   p   H

Rocky Hill
Academy Hall
HABS CT-230   s   L
Deming, Capt. Asa, House
Rocky Hill (moved to MA, Wellesley)
HABS CT-13   s pd   L
Rocky Hill Congregational Church
Church & Main Sts.
HABS CT-64   s pd   L

Scantic
House (Doorways)
HABS CT-196   p   L

South Glastonbury
Welles-Shipman House
Station St.
HABS CT-57   pd   L

Suffield
Bissell, Harvey, House
240 Main St.
HABS CT-81   pd   L
Burbank-Hatheway Barns & Carriage House
Main St.
HABS CT-266   pd   L
Burbank-Hatheway House
Main St.
HABS CT-240   pd   L
Burbank-Hatheway Summer or Well House
Main St.
HABS CT-267   pd   L
King, Lt. William, Place
N. Main St.
HABS CT-61   s pd   L

Suffield Center
Gay, Rev. Ebenezer, Manse
Rt. 75
HABS CT-59   pd   L

West Hartford
Webster, Noah, House
227 S. Main St.
HABS CT-16   p   H

West Suffield
Sheldon, Capt. Jonathan, House
Sheldon St.
HABS CT-85   s pd   L

Wethersfield
Belden, Simeon, House
HABS CT-129   p   L
Congregational Church, Old; see First Church of Christ
Deming, Peter, House
HABS CT-110   pd   L
First Church of Christ (Congregational Church, Old)
HABS CT-128   p   L

Fish House; see Warehouse, Old
Hospitality Hall; see Webb, Joseph, House
Warehouse, Old (Fish House)
HABS CT-127   p   L
Webb, Joseph, House (Webb, Joseph, Tavern; Hospitality Hall)
HABS CT-114   pd   L
Webb, Joseph, Tavern; see Webb, Joseph, House
Williams House, Older
HABS CT-390   p   L

Windsor
Chaffee, Hezekiah, House
108 Palisado Ave.
HABS CT-34   pd   L
Ellsworth, Jonathan, House
HABS CT-391   p   L
Fyler, Lt. Walter, House
HABS CT-112   pd   L

Windsor Hill
Moore, Samuel, House
Main St.
HABS CT-42   pd   L

LITCHFIELD COUNTY

Barkhamsted
Mallory Tavern
HABS CT-199   p   L

Colebrook
General Store
HABS CT-201   p   L
Phelphs, Capt. Arah, Inn (Red Lion Inn)
HABS CT-200   p   L
Red Lion Inn; see Phelphs, Capt. Arah, Inn
Rockwell, Capt. Samuel, House
HABS CT-202   p   L
Rockwell, Martin, House
Colebrook Green
HABS CT-203   p   L

Cornwall
Congregational Church
HABS CT-188   p   L

East Canaan
Congregational Church
HABS CT-189   p   L

Falls Village
Hosford House
Beebe Hill Rd.
HABS CT-222   p   L
Matthews, Col., House
HABS CT-179   p   L
Robbins House
HABS CT-178   p   L

Gaylordsville
Gaylord House
HABS CT-176   p   L

Goshen
Birds Eye Norton House
HABS CT-147   p   L

Harwinton
Congregational Church
HABS CT-158   p   L
House on Center Green
HABS CT-221   p   L
Messenger House
HABS CT-159   p   L

Kent
Bacon House; see Mills House
Flanders Arms; see Hall, Lawrence K.,
    House
Hall, Lawrence K., House (Flanders Arms)
HABS CT-186   p   L
House
HABS CT-187   p   L
Mills House (Bacon House)
HABS CT-183   p   L
Roberts House
HABS CT-185   p   L
Tolman House
HABS CT-184   p   L

Lakeville
Holly House
HABS CT-141   p   L

Litchfield
First Congregational Church
HABS CT-177   p   L
Gould House; see Sheldon, Elisha, House
Law School
South St.
HABS CT-381   p   L
Phelps' Tavern
East St.
HABS CT-79   pd   L
Seymour, Ozias, Homestead (St. Michael's
    Episcopal Rectory)
South St.
HABS CT-384   p   L
Sheldon, Elisha, House (Sheldon Tavern;
    Gould House)
HABS CT-220   p   L
Sheldon Tavern; see Sheldon, Elisha, House
St. Michael's Episcopal Rectory; see
    Seymour, Ozias, Homestead
Welch, Gerret P., House
HABS CT-382   p   L
Welch, Maj. David, House
HABS CT-383   p   L

New Preston
Congregational Church
HABS CT-236   s   L

Norfolk
First Congregational Church
Norfolk Green vic.
HABS CT-193   p   L

North Canaan
Herman House
HABS CT-126   p   L

North Cornwall
Adelphi Institute
HABS CT-156   p   L
Church
HABS CT-155   p   L
Long House
HABS CT-157   p   L

North Woodbury
Store at the Four Corners
HABS CT-175   p   L

Sharon
House
Sharon Green vic.
HABS CT-152   p   L
King, George, House
HABS CT-149   p   L
Prindle, Charles, House
HABS CT-150   p   L
Shop & Post Office, Old
Sharon Green vic.
HABS CT-151   p   L

South Canaan
Congregational Church
HABS CT-190   p   L
House Opposite Church
HABS CT-191   p   L
Hunt House (Doorway)
HABS CT-192   p   L

Torrington
St. Paul's Episcopal Church, Rectory
(moved to CA, Benicia, 122 E. J St.)
HABS CT-2084   pd   L

Watertown
First Congregational Church
HABS CT-223   p   L
Green & De Forest Streets (House)
HABS CT-173   p   L

West Goshen
Academy, Old (Library)
HABS CT-148   p   L
Library; see Academy, Old

Winchester Center
Bronson House (Sherwood, George, House)
Winchester Center Green vic.
HABS CT-154   p   L
Greek Doric Church; see Winchester
    Center Congregational Church
Sherwood, George, House; see Bronson
    House
Winchester Center Congregational Church
    (Greek Doric Church)
Winchester Center Green vic.
HABS CT-153   p   L

Winsted
Historical Society; see Rockwell, Solomon,
    House
Rockwell, Solomon, House (Historical
    Society)
Prospect St.
HABS CT-142   p   L

Woodbury
Curtiss House
HABS CT-226   p   L
Glebe House
Hollow Rd.
HABS CT-324   s   H
King Solomon's Lodge (Masonic Temple)
State Rt. 202
HABS CT-44   s p   L
Masonic Temple; see King Solomon's
    Lodge
Minor, Joseph, House
HABS CT-227   p   L
North Congregational Church
Town Square vic.
HABS CT-174   p   L
St. Paul's Church
HABS CT-113   pd   L
Thompson House
HABS CT-228   p   L
Webb, Dr., House
HABS CT-377   p   L

Woodbury vic.
Minor, Samuel, House
W. side of Flanders Rd.
HABS CT-322   s   L

MIDDLESEX COUNTY

Chester
Clark-Holmes Cottage
HABS CT-139   p   L
Mitchell, Abram, House (Pratt, Dr.
    Ambrose, House)
HABS CT-138   p   L
Pratt, Dr. Ambrose, House; see Mitchell,
    Abram, House
Warner, Jonathan, House
Middlesex Turnpike
HABS CT-137   p   L

Clinton
Stanton, Adam, House (Stanton, John A.,
    Memorial)
HABS CT-102   p   L
Stanton, John A., Memorial; see Stanton,
    Adam, House

Durham
Lyman, Thomas, House
HABS CT-233   s   L

East Haddam
Champion, Gen. Epaphroditus, House
    (Terraces, The)
HABS CT-130   p   L

Goodspeed Opera House
Rt. 82 vic.
HABS CT-360   s   H

Hale, Nathan, Schoolhouse
Nathan Hale Park (moved from Village Green)
HABS CT-131   p   L

Terraces, The; see Champion, Gen. Epaphroditus, House

Essex

Dauntless Club; see Hayden, Uriah, House

Hayden, Uriah, House (Ship Tavern, Old; Dauntless Club)
HABS CT-133   p   L

House, Long Yellow
26 West Ave.
HABS CT-135   p   L

Pratt House
HABS CT-134   p   L

Ship Tavern, Old; see Hayden, Uriah, House

Starkey House
Main St.
HABS CT-36   p   L

Killingworth

Healy, Kent, House
Chestnut Hill Rd.
HABS CT-232   s   L

North Congregational Church
HABS CT-105   pd   L

Middlefield

Talcott, Stephen, House
HABS CT-235   s   L

Middletown

Alsop, Richard, House
301 High St.
HABS CT-3-4   s pd   L

Exchange Block (Mansion House Block)
108-150 Main St.
HABS CT-326   pd   L

Mansion House Block; see Exchange Block

Russell, Samuel, House
350 High St.
HABS CT-388   pd   L

Russell, T. Mcdonough, House
High & Washington Sts.
HABS CT-387   pd   L

Moodus

Hurd House
HABS CT-132   p   L

North Plain

Baker, Nathaniel, House
HABS CT-41   s p   L

Old Saybrook

Bushnell House, Older
Boston Post Rd.
HABS CT-368   d   H

Cornfield Point Farm; see Hart, Samuel, Farm House

Dickinson, Capt. George, House
191 N. Cove Rd.
HABS CT-361   pd   H

Eliot, Dr. Samuel, House
500 Main St.
HABS CT-364   d   H

Hart, Gen. William, House
350 Main St.
HABS CT-366   d   H

Hart, Samuel, Farm House (Neck Farm; Cornfield Point Farm; Jarvis Farm)
Moore Park, Forest Glen
HABS CT-365   d   H

Jarvis Farm; see Hart, Samuel, Farm House

Lynde, Judge William, House
33 Old Boston Post Rd.
HABS CT-367   pd   H

Neck Farm; see Hart, Samuel, Farm House

Pratt, Humphrey, Tavern
287 Main St.
HABS CT-369   d   H

Pratt, Timothy, House
325 Main St.
HABS CT-370   d   H

Sill, R. W., House
N. of Ayer's Point Rd.
HABS CT-362   pd   H

St. Mary's-By-The-Sea (Chapel)
Borough of Fenwick
HABS CT-371   d   H

Williams, Capt. Charles, House
48 Cromwell Place
HABS CT-363   pd   H

Portland

Hall, Samuel, House
478 Main St.
HABS CT-51   s pd   L

NEW HAVEN COUNTY

Bethany

Wheeler-Beecher House
Amity Rd.
HABS CT-68   s pd   L

Branford

Academy (Masonic Lodge)
HABS CT-19   s pd   L

Harrison-Linsley House
New Haven Turpike
HABS CT-111   p   L

Masonic Lodge; see Academy

Cheshire

Beach Tavern (Franklin, Ben, Inn; Roxbury School)
Main St.
HABS CT-32   s pd   L

Field, Azabah, House
Main St.
HABS CT-36   s pd   L

Franklin, Ben, Inn; see Beach Tavern

Hitchcock, Col. Rufus, House (Phillips, A. W., House)
46 Church Dr.
HABS CT-385   p   L

Holt, Benjamin, Hall; see Peck, Levi, House

Peck, Levi, House (Holt, Benjamin, Hall)
HABS CT-386   p   L

Phillips, A. W., House; see Hitchcock, Col. Rufus, House

Roxbury School; see Beach Tavern

East Haven

Church, Old Stone (Congregational)
3 High St.
HABS CT-104   pd   L

Hotchkiss, Joseph, House
N. High St.
HABS CT-21   s pd   L

Smith, Jim, House; see Thompson, Stephen, House

Thompson, Stephen, House (Smith, Jim, House)
298 Hemingway Ave.
HABS CT-78   pd   L

Guilford

Acadian House
Union St.
HABS CT-15   s pd   L

Kingsworth, Henry, House; see Starr, Comfort, House

Leete-Griswold House
Petticoat Lane
HABS CT-234   s   L

Starr, Comfort, House (Kingsworth, Henry, House)
138 State St.
HABS CT-82   s pd   L

Hamden

Ford, Moses, House
152 Waite St.
HABS CT-52   s pd   L

Grace Episcopal Church
Dixwell Ave.
HABS CT-67   s pd   L

Whitney, Eli, Armory (Barn)
Whitney Ave.
HAER CT-2-A   s pd   L

Whitney, Eli, Armory (Boarding House)
Whitney Ave.
HAER CT-2-D   s pd   L

Whitney, Eli, Armory (Forge Building)
Mill River
HAER CT-2-B   s pd   L

Whitney, Eli, Armory (Fuel Storage Shed)
Mill River
HAER CT-2-C   s pd   L

Whitney, Eli, Armory Site
W. of Whitney Ave., Armory St. vic.
HAER CT-2   s pd   H

Madison

Field, David, House
HABS CT-33   pd   L

Graves, Deacon John, House (Redfield House; Tuxas Farms)
HABS CT-122   p   L

Redfield House; see Graves, Deacon John, House

Tuxas Farms; see Graves, Deacon John, House

Meriden

Andrews Homestead
Rt. 6A West
HABS CT-323   s   H

Milford

Ford, Col. Stephen, House
W. Main St.
HABS CT-14   pd   L

Montowese

Beach, Benjamin, House (Button House)
U.S. Rt. 5
HABS CT-50   s pd   L

Button House; see Beach, Benjamin, House

New Haven

Atwater-Ciampolini House
321 Whitney Ave.
HABS CT-282   pd   L

Bassett, John E. & Company (Hardware Store)
754 Chapel St.
HABS CT-283   pd   L

Benjamin, Everard, House (Bigelow, H. B., House)
232 Bradley St.
HABS CT-286   pd   L

Bigelow, H. B., House; see Benjamin, Everard, House

Bishop, Timothy, House
Elm St.
HABS CT-276   s pd   L

Bristol, Willis, House
584 Chapel St.
HABS CT-274   s pd   L

Chandler-Bacon House (New Haven Coffee House)
247 Church St.
HABS CT-75   s pd   L

Collins House; see Townshend House

Connecticut Agriculture Experiment Station (Osborne Library)
123 Huntington St.
HABS CT-372   p   H

Cook, John, House (Ballroom)
35 Elm St.
HABS CT-270   s pd   L

Dana, James Dwight, House
24 Hillhouse Ave.
HABS CT-273   p   L

Davies, John M., House
393 Prospect St.
HABS CT-284   pd   L

First Telephone Exchange Building
741 Chapel St.
HABS CT-373   p   H

Grove Street Cemetery Entrance
227 Grove St.
HABS CT-275   s pd   L

Hardware Store; see Bassett, John E. & Company

Hyland-Fiske-Wildman House
Boston St.
HABS CT-117   s p   L

Marsh, Othniel C., House
360 Prospect St.
HABS CT-374   p   H

Morris, John, House (Pardee, William S., House)
Lighthouse Rd. & Morris Ave.
HABS CT-27   s pd   L

New Haven City Hall & Courthouse
Church St.
HABS CT-281   pd   L

New Haven Coffee House; see Chandler-Bacon House

North Church, Old; see United Church

Norton, John Pitkin, House
52 Hillhouse Ave.
HABS CT-287   pd   L

Osborne Library; see Connecticut Agriculture Experiment Station

Pardee, William S., House; see Morris, John, House

Pinto, William, House (Whitney, Eli, House)
275 Orange St.
HABS CT-277   s pd   L

Sachem Street Barn
HABS CT-229   s   L

Skinner-Trowbridge House
46 Hillhouse Ave.
HABS CT-272   s pd   L

Smith, Widow, House
1706 Quinnipiac Ave.
HABS CT-84   s pd   L

Third Congregational Soc., Church of the Redeemer (Trinity Evangelical Lutheran Church)
292 Orange St.
HABS CT-278   s pd   L H

Townsend City Savings Bank
793 Chapel St.
HABS CT-288   pd   L

Townshend House (Collins House)
35 Hillhouse Ave.
HABS CT-107   pd   L

Trinity Evangelical Lutheran Church; see Third Congregational Soc., Church of the Redeemer

United Church (North Church, Old)
Elm & Temple Sts.
HABS CT-3-1   s pd   L

Webster, Noah, House
Temple & Grove Sts. (moved to MI, Dearborn)
HABS CT-3-16   s pd   L

Whitney, Eli, House; see Pinto, William, House

Woodward, Rev. John, House
409 Forbes Ave.
HABS CT-271   s pd   L

Yale University, Connecticut Hall
HABS CT-3-5   s pd   L

Yale University, Dwight Hall
69 High St.
HABS CT-285   pd   L

North Branford

Tolman House (Ruins)
HABS CT-140   p   L

North Branford vic.

Baldwin, George, House (Russell, Lydia, House)
State Rt. 80
HABS CT-48   s pd   L

Russell, Lydia, House; see Baldwin, George, House

North Guilford

North Guilford Congregational Church
HABS CT-231   s   L

Northford Center

Parsonage, Old; see Williams, Rev. Warham, House

Williams, Rev. Warham, House (Parsonage, Old)
HABS CT-53   pd   L

Norwich

Shannon, James B., Mausoleum
St. Mary's Cemetery
HABS CT-264   pd   L

Southbury

Bullet Hill School
U.S. Rts. 6 & 202
HABS CT-45   s p   L

Straitsville

Collins Tavern
HABS CT-379   p   L

Wallingford

Beach, Moses Yale, House
86 N. Main St.
HABS CT-269   s pd   H

Royce, Nehemiah, House
N. Main St.
HABS CT-238   s   L

Waterbury

Hotchkiss Block (Irving Block)
11 E. Main St.
HABS CT-345   pd   L

West Haven

Atwater House; see Hemingway Tavern, Old

Hemingway, Samuel, Tavern; see Hemingway Tavern, Old

Hemingway Tavern, Old (Hemingway, Samuel, Tavern; Atwater House)
262 Main St.
HABS CT-11   s pd   L

Painter, Thomas, House (Smith, Capt. Samuel, House)
255 Main St.
HABS CT-62   s p d   L
Smith, Capt. Samuel, House; see Painter, Thomas, House
Ward-Heitmann House
277 Elm St.
HABS CT-22   s p   L

Whitneyville
Whitneyville Congregational Church
HABS CT-108   p   L

Woodbridge
Clark Tavern
Litchfield Turnpike
HABS CT-76   s p d   L

NEW LONDON COUNTY

Colchester
Champion, Col. Henry, House
HABS CT-143   p   L
Felton House on Green
HABS CT-146   p   L
Hayward House on Green
HABS CT-144   p   L
Lyman & Rapello Viaducts (Warren Truss & Stone Arch. Bridges)
N. Y., New Haven & Hartford Railroad, Old
HAER CT-7   p   H
Warren Truss & Stone Arch. Bridges; see Lyman & Rapello Viaducts
Williams House on Green
HABS CT-145   p   L

Fitchville
Bozrah Town Hall
HABS CT-243   pd   L

Hadlyme
Selden, Col. Samuel, Homestead
Selden's Neck
HABS CT-70   s p d   L

Hamburg Cove
Brockway House, Old; see Johnson, Capt., House
Johnson, Capt., House (Brockway House, Old)
Hamburg Cove
HABS CT-55   s p d   L

Lebanon
Trumbull, Gov. Jonathan, House
(moved from Town St. & Colchester Rd.)
HABS CT-180   p   L
Trumbull, Gov. Jonathan, War Office
HABS CT-181   p   L

Lyme
Cottage
HABS CT-380   p   L

New London
County Courthouse
State & Huntington Sts.
HABS CT-3-2   s p d   L
Hempstead, Stephen, House
HABS CT-208   s p   L
Huguenot House
HABS CT-209   p   L
Latimer, Jonathan, House
HABS CT-211   p   L
New London Railroad Station (Union Railroad Station)
State St. vic.
HABS CT-347   p   H
Shaw, Capt. Nathaniel, Mansion
11 Blinman St.
HABS CT-210   p   L
Thames Shipyard; see Thames Tow Boat Company
Thames Shipyard (Headhouse)
Uncasville
HAER CT-1-A   s p   H
Thames Shipyard (Marine Railway No. 3)
Uncasville
HAER CT-1-B   s d   H
Thames Tow Boat Company (Thames Shipyard)
HAER CT-1   s p d   H
Town Mill, Old
Mill St.
HABS CT-3-18   s p d   L
Union Railroad Station; see New London Railroad Station

North Stonington
House
Post Office vic.
HABS CT-124   p   L
Main St. (House, Front entrance)
HABS CT-125   p   L

Norwich
Christ Church Rectory
118 Washington St.
HABS CT-261   pd   L
Converse, Col., Barn
185 Washington St.
HABS CT-263   pd   L
Converse, Col., House
185 Washington St.
HABS CT-260   pd   L
Dewitt, Capt. Jacob, House (Sigourney, Lydia Huntley, School)
189 Broadway St.
HABS CT-249   pd   L
Donahue-Wood House
24 Maple St.
HABS CT-256   pd   L
Elks Club; see Slater, John Fox, House
Ely House
231 Broadway
HABS CT-225   pd   L

Huntington, Eliza, Memorial Home
99 Washington St.
HABS CT-259   pd   L
Indian Leap Pedestrian Bridge
HAER CT-4   pd   L
Johnson, John, House
171 Broadway
HABS CT-258   pd   L
Learned-Aiken House
157 Washington St.
HABS CT-253   pd   L
Leffingwell, Thomas, Inn
348 Washington St.
HABS CT-245   pd   L
Osgood, Charles, House
151 Washington St.
HABS CT-254   pd   L
Perkins, Hezekiah, House
185 Broadway
HABS CT-262   pd   L
Sigourney, Lydia Huntley, School; see Dewitt, Capt. Jacob, House
Slater, John Fox, House (Elks Club)
352 E. Main St.
HABS CT-252   pd   L
Slater, John Fox, Memorial Museum
108 Crescent St.
HABS CT-251   pd   L
Trinity Episcopal Church
HABS CT-375   s   H
Washington Street Historic District
HABS CT-348   pd   L
Whiting, Capt., House (Y. M. C. A.)
337 E. Main St.
HABS CT-250   pd   L
Woodhull House
167 Broadway
HABS CT-257   pd   L
Y. M. C. A.; see Whiting, Capt., House

Norwichtown
Baldwin, Ebenezer, House, Old
HABS CT-3-19   s pd   L
Bradford-Huntington House
16 Huntingtown Lane
HABS CT-247   pd   L
Carpenter, Gardner, House
55 E. Town St.
HABS CT-244   pd   L
Carpenter, Joseph, Silversmith Shop
71 E. Town St.
HABS CT-248   pd   L
Charlton, Capt. Richard, Cottage
12 Mediterranean Lane
HABS CT-246   pd   L

Old Lyme
Mather, Samuel, House (Parsonage, The)
HABS CT-118   p   L
Parsonage, The; see Mather, Samuel, House

Pawcatuck

Noyes, Capt. Thomas, House
Old Pequot Trail
HABS CT-101   p   L

Preston City

Church, Old
HABS CT-206   p   L
House Opposite the Church
HABS CT-207   p   L

Stonington

Stanton, Robert, House
HABS CT-26   s pd   L

Taftville

Ponemah Mills
Main St.
HABS CT-242   pd   L
Ponemah Mills Workers' Houses
Shetucket & Norwich Aves.
HABS CT-241   pd   L

TOLLAND COUNTY

Bolton *(center)*

White, Asa, Tavern
HABS CT-47   s p   L

W. Stafford Springs

Bradway, Charles P., Machine Works
State Rt. 190, intersection Cooper Lane Rd.
vic.
HABS CT-280   s d   L

WINDHAM COUNTY

Brooklyn

First Ecclesiastical Society; see Unitarian
Church
Putnam, Gen. Israel, Privy
HABS CT-103   p   L
Town Hall (Windham County Courthouse)
HABS CT-120   p   L
Trinity Episcopal Church
HABS CT-205   p   L
Unitarian Church (First Ecclesiastical
Society)
HABS CT-119   p   L
Well House, Old
Maplehurst Farm
HABS CT-204   p   L
Windham County Courthouse; see Town
Hall

Canterbury

**Crandall, Prudence, School for Negro
Girls;** see Payne, Elisha, House
First Congregational Church
HABS CT-162   p   L
House (Palladian Window)
HABS CT-161   p   L
Kinney, David, House (Maple Lane Farm)
Black Hill Rd.
HABS CT-170   p   L
Maple Lane Farm; see Kinney, David,
House
Payne, Elisha, House (Crandall, Prudence,
School for Negro Girls)
HABS CT-163   p   L
Turnpike House (Doorway)
Rt. 14
HABS CT-164   p   L

Eastford vic.

Phoenix Mills
N. bank of Still River
HAER CT-3   s pd   H

Hampton

Ahern House
HABS CT-378   p   L

Plainfield

Academy, Old
HABS CT-171   p   L
Cleveland House
Bradford Hill
HABS CT-169   p   L
First Congregational Church
HABS CT-172   p   L
Main Street (Houses)
HABS CT-168   p   L

South Canterbury

Baldwin, Capt., House
HABS CT-182   p   L
Clark, Capt. John Benjamin, House
HABS CT-160   p   L

Sterling Hill

Douglass House
HABS CT-165   p   L
Dunay Homestead (Doorway)
HABS CT-167   p   L
Gallup, A. J., House
HABS CT-166   p   L

Willimantic

House, Stone
HABS CT-392   p   L

Woodstock

Bowen House
HABS CT-376   p   H

Delaware

KENT COUNTY

Camden

Camden Friends Meetinghouse (Quaker
Meetinghouse)
E. Camden-Wyoming Ave.
HABS DE-5   pd   L
Hunn House; see Spruce Acres
Jenkins, Hunn House; see Spruce Acres
Quaker Meetinghouse; see Camden Friends
Meetinghouse
Spruce Acres (Hunn House; Jenkins, Hunn
House)
110 N. Main St.
HABS DE-4   pd   L

Camden vic.

Brecknock
U.S. Rt. 13
HABS DE-178   d   H

Clayton vic.

Hoffecker House
State Rt. 6
HABS DE-140   pd   L

Cowgill Corner

Octagonal School House (Pleasant Hill
Academy)
Rt. 9
HABS DE-18   pd   L
Pleasant Hill Academy; see Octagonal
School House

Dover

Bradford-Loockerman House
(Loockerman, Vincent, House;
Lookerman, Nicholas, House)
419 S. State St.
HABS DE-142   pd   L

Christ Church (Episcopal) (Old Christ
Church)
Water & S. State Sts.
HABS DE-73   pd   L
Crawford House; see Ridgely, Dr. Henry,
House
Governor's House; see Woodburn
Hillyard, Charles, House; see Woodburn
Loockerman, Vincent, House; see
Bradford-Loockerman House
Lookerman, Nicholas, House; see
Bradford-Loockerman House
Old Christ Church; see Christ Church
(Episcopal)
Parke-Ridgely House (Ridgely House)
7 The Green
HABS DE-144   pd   L
Richardson & Robbins Cannery
Kings Hwy.
HAER DE-3   pd   L

Ridgely, Dr. Henry, House (Crawford House)
6 S. State St.
HABS DE-177   d   H

Ridgely House; see Parke-Ridgely House

Rose Cottage
120 S. State St.
HABS DE-176   d   H

Woodburn (Hillyard, Charles, House; Governor's House)
Kings Hwy.
HABS DE-146   pd   L

Dover vic.

Dickinson, John, Mansion (Dickinson, Samuel, House)
Kitts Hummock Rd.
HABS DE-17   pd   L

Dickinson, Samuel, House; see Dickinson, John, Mansion

Kingston-Upon-Hull (Town Point)
Kitts Hummock Rd.
HABS DE-175   s pd   H

Town Point; see Kingston-Upon-Hull

Frederica

Wooten Store
2 Market St.
HABS DE-174   d   H

Frederica vic.

Barrett's Chapel, Old (Methodist)
Rt. 113
HABS DE-16   pd   L

Harrington vic.

Baynard House
Lewis Rd. (moved to MD-Chesapeake City vic.)
HABS DE-159   s pd   L

Vogl House
State Rd. 277
HABS DE-173   d   H

Kenton vic.

Aspendale (Numbers, Charles, House)
Rt. 300 (Downs Chapel)
HABS DE-143   s pd   L H

Numbers, Charles, House; see Aspendale

Lebanon vic.

Great Geneva
Rt. 10
HABS DE-139   pd   L

Leipsic

Mansion, Ruth, House
Main St.
HABS DE-130   pd   L

Leipsic vic.

Naudain, Andrew, House; see Snowland (Interiors)

Snowland (Interiors) (Naudain, Andrew, House)
Rt. 42
HABS DE-145   pd   L

Wheel of Fortune (House)
Rt. 9
HABS DE-76   pd   L

York Seat Farm
Rt. 9
HABS DE-75   pd   L

Little Creek vic.

Cedar Tree Lane Farm (Maple Lane Farm)
Rt. 8
HABS DE-74   pd   L

Little Creek Friends Meetinghouse (Quaker Meetinghouse)
State Rd. 340
HABS DE-19   pd   L

Maple Lane Farm; see Cedar Tree Lane Farm

Quaker Meetinghouse; see Little Creek Friends Meetinghouse

Magnolia

Lindale, John B., House
24 S. Main St.
HABS DE-172   s pd   H

Lowber, Matthew, House
N. Main St.
HABS DE-182   s d   H

Milford vic.

Douglass House; see Mordington

Mordington (Douglass House)
Canterbury-Milford Rd.
HABS DE-6   pd   L

Wilkerson, J. H., & Sons Brick Works
Rd. 409
HAER DE-5   s pd   L

Smyrna

Belmont Hall (Collins, Thomas, House)
Rt. 13
HABS DE-147   pd   L

Benson, Benjamin, House (Hoffecker, W. O., House)
123 W. Commerce St.
HABS DE-126   pd   L

Clayton House, Old; see Spruance, Enoch, House

Collins, Thomas, House; see Belmont Hall

Cummins-Stockley House (Stockley House)
N. Main St.
HABS DE-124   pd   L

Hoffecker, W. O., House; see Benson, Benjamin, House

Peterson-Mustard House; see Pope-Mustard Mansion

Pierce, Abraham, House (Spruance House)
12 E. Commerce St.
HABS DE-123   pd   L

Pope-Mustard Mansion (Peterson-Mustard House)
204 W. Mount Vernon St.
HABS DE-125   pd   L

Spruance, Enoch, House (Clayton House, Old)
E. Commerce St.
HABS DE-122   pd   L

Spruance House; see Pierce, Abraham, House

Stockley House; see Cummins-Stockley House

Smyrna vic.

Davis-Boyer House
Duck Creek Pkwy.
HABS DE-128   pd   L

England, John, House; see Woodlawn

Lindens, The (Short House)
Rt. 13 A
HABS DE-127   pd   L

Morris-Cummins House; see Woodlawn

Short House; see Lindens, The

Woodlawn (Morris-Cummins House; England, John, House)
Rt. 13
HABS DE-141   pd   L

NEW CASTLE COUNTY

Ashland

Ashland Covered Bridge (Barley Mill Road Covered Bridge)
Red Clay Creek-Barley Mill Rd.
HABS DE-162   pd   L

Barley Mill Road Covered Bridge; see Ashland Covered Bridge

Biddles Corner vic.

Liston Range Rear Light
State Rd. 2
HAER DE-10   s pd   L

Centerville vic.

Center Meeting House
Center Meeting Rd.
HABS DE-53   pd   L

Christiana

Shannon Hotel
1 E. Main St.
HABS DE-190   s d   H

Christiana vic.

Foster, Alexander, Grist Mill
Smalley's Dam Rd.
HABS DE-59   pd   L

Claymont

Block House; see Robinson, Thomas Jr., Kitchen Dependency

Naaman's House; see Robinson, Col. Thomas, House

Robinson, Col. Thomas, House (Robinson House; Naaman's House)
Naaman's Rd. at Philadelphia Pike (Rt.13)
HABS DE-52   pd   L

Robinson House; see Robinson, Col. Thomas, House

Robinson, Thomas Jr., Kitchen Dependency (Block House)
Naaman's Rd. at Philadelphia Pike
HABS DE-51   pd   L

Claymont vic.

Lodge House, Old
Rt. 13
HABS DE-50   pd   L

Collins Beach vic.

Collins-Johnson House; see Collins-Sharp
House

Collins-Sharp House (Vogel House;
Collins-Johnson House)
State Rd. 493 (moved to DE, Odessa)
HABS DE-179   p   H

Vogel House; see Collins-Sharp House

Corner Ketch vic.

Eastburn Farmhouse; see House, Rural
Farmhouse

House, Rural Farmhouse (Eastburn
Farmhouse)
Pleasant Hill Rd.
HABS DE-166   pd   L

Mill Creek Friends Meetinghouse
Landenburg-Wilmington Rd.
HABS DE-161   pd   L

Glasgow

Pencader Presbyterian Church
Rt. 896
HABS DE-58   pd   L

Granogue vic.

Smith's Bridge (Smith's Covered Bridge)
Brandywine Creek at Smith Bridge Rd.
HABS DE-1   s pd   L

Smith's Covered Bridge; see Smith's Bridge

Greenville vic.

Birkenhead Mill; see Du Pont Powder Mill

Brandywine River Powder Mill; see
Eleutherian Mills Historic Site (Hagley
Museum)

Broom, Jacob, House; see Eleutherian Mills
Historic Site (Hagley Museum)

du Pont Family House, First; see
Eleutherian Mills Historic Site (Hagley
Museum)

Du Pont Powder Mill (Birkenhead Mill;
Lynch, Charles, Mill)
Brandywine Creek in Hagley Museum
HABS DE-2   pd   L

**Eleutherian Mills Historic Site (Hagley
Museum)** (du Pont Family House, First;
Brandywine River Powder Mill; Broom,
Jacob, House)
Brandywine River at Barley Mill Rd.
HABS DE-195   s d   H

Lynch, Charles, Mill; see Du Pont Powder
Mill

Hockessin vic.

Mendenhall Mill
Mill Creek Rd.
HABS DE-167   pd   L

North Star Schoolhouse (Public School
Number Thirty)
North Star & Henderson Rds.
HABS DE-163   pd   L

Public School Number Thirty; see North
Star Schoolhouse

Kirkwood vic.

McCoy House
Kirkwood Rd.
HABS DE-191   d   H

Mermaid vic.

Harlan Grist Mill
Mermaid-Stoney Batter Rd.
HABS DE-68   pd   L

Middletown vic.

Hedgelawn
U.S. Route 301
HABS DE-189   d   H

Naudain, Arnold S., House; see Naudain
House

Naudain House (Naudain, Arnold S.,
House; Schee House)
Rt. 896
HABS DE-148   pd   L

Noxontown Mill
State Rd. 38
HAER DE-9   s pd   L

Schee House; see Naudain House

St. Anne's Church, Old; see St. Anne's
Episcopal Church

St. Anne's Episcopal Church (St. Anne's
Church, Old)
Route 896
HABS DE-72   pd   L

Milltown vic.

Delaware Log House; see
Robinson-Murray House

Murray House; see Robinson-Murray
House

Robinson-Murray House (Murray House;
Delaware Log House)
Limestone Rd.
HABS DE-169   pd   L

Montchanin vic.

Kirk's Mill, Old
Brandywine River at Rd. 232
HABS DE-64   pd   L

Mill House Row
Rockland Road
HABS DE-63   pd   L

New Castle

Academy Building, Old
The Green
HABS DE-78   pd   L

Alexander, Archibald, House
26-28 Third St.
HABS DE-105   pd   L

Amstel House
2 E. Fourth St.
HABS DE-9-3   s pd   L

Arsenal, The
The Green
HABS DE-133   pd   L

Aull House (Double Wooden Laird House)
49-51 The Strand
HABS DE-86   pd   L

Bedford, Gunning, House
6 The Strand
HABS DE-99-B   pd   L

Booth, James, House & Office
216 Delaware St.
HABS DE-88   pd   L

Cloud's Row
117-125 Delaware St.
HABS DE-83   pd   L

Colby House (Rosemont House)
110 Delaware St.
HABS DE-82   pd   L

Couper, Samuel, House
14 The Strand
HABS DE-112   pd   L

Deemer House; see Lesley-Travers Mansion

Dorsey House
8 E. Third St.
HABS DE-109   pd   L

Double Wooden Laird House; see Aull
House

Dutch House, Old
32 E. Third St.
HABS DE-93   pd   L

Farmers Bank, Old
4 The Strand
HABS DE-99-A   pd   L

Foster, James W., House
159 E. Third St.
HABS DE-120   pd   L

Gemmill House (Wiley, John, House)
18 E. Third St.
HABS DE-110   pd   L

Glebe Farm; see Glebe House

Glebe House (Glebe Farm)
Sixth St. East of Rt. 9
HABS DE-134   pd   L

Hermitage, The
Rt. 273
HABS DE-106   pd   L

Immanuel Church (Episcopal)
The Green
HABS DE-79   pd   L

Immanuel Church Parish House; see
Thomas, Charles, House

Jefferson Hotel, Old (Strand Hotel, The;
Jefferson House)
Delaware St. & The Strand
HABS DE-98   pd   L

Jefferson House; see Jefferson Hotel, Old

Johns, Chancellor Kensey, House; see
Johns, Kensey, Sr., House

Johns, Kensey, Jr., House
Delaware & Fourth Sts.
HABS DE-119   pd   L

Johns, Kensey, Sr., House (Johns, Chancellor Kensey, House)
2 E. Third St.
HABS DE-116   s pd   L

King, William M., House
100 The Strand
HABS DE-95   pd   L

Lesley-Travers Mansion (Deemer House)
112 W. Sixth St.
HABS DE-181   d   H

McCullough's Row; see 27-33 The Strand, Row Houses

McIntire House (McWilliams, R., House)
8 The Strand
HABS DE-99-C   pd   L

McWilliams, R., House; see McIntire House

Mercer, Hugh, House; see Willis, Rodney, House

Monk Barns (Tenant House)
Rt. 9
HABS DE-85   pd   L

New Castle & Frenchtown Railroad
HAER DE-18   s pd   L

New Castle Courthouse, Old
Delaware St.
HABS DE-80   pd   L

New Castle Presbyterian Church; see Presbyterian Church, Old

New Castle-Frenchtown Railroad Ticket Office
Washington Ave. Crossing (moved to Delaware St.)
HABS DE-104   pd   L

Penn, William, House
206 Delaware St.
HABS DE-101   pd   L

Presbyterian Church, Old (New Castle Presbyterian Church)
Second St.
HABS DE-84   pd   L

Read, George II, House
The Strand
HABS DE-81   pd   L

Rodney, George, House & Office
16 Third St.
HABS DE-118   pd   L

Rosemont House; see Colby House

Stoneham; see Stonum

Stonum (Stoneham)
Ninth & Washington Sts.
HABS DE-91   pd   L

Strand Hotel, The; see Jefferson Hotel, Old

Tenant House; see Monk Barns

27-33 The Strand, Row Houses (McCullough's Row)
HABS DE-97   pd   L

Thomas, Charles, House (Immanuel Church Parish House)
The Strand & Harmony St.
HABS DE-87   pd   L

Tile House
54 The Strand
HABS DE-138   p   L

Town Hall
Second & Delaware Sts.
HABS DE-9-4   s pd   L

Van Dyke, Kensey Johns, House
300 Delaware St.
HABS DE-92   pd   L

Van Dyke, Nicholas Jr., House
400 Delaware St.
HABS DE-9-5   s pd   L

Van Leuvenigh House
2 The Strand West
HABS DE-121   pd   L

Wiley, John, House; see Gemmill House

Willis, Rodney, House (Mercer, Hugh, House)
126 Harmony St.
HABS DE-94   pd   L

New Castle vic.

Buttonwoods, The (Mansion House)
Forrester Ave.
HABS DE-71   pd   L

Eves Place, Old
Delaware Memorial Bridge vic.
HABS DE-70   pd   L

Grantham House
229 Grantham Lane
HABS DE-107   pd   L

Mansion House; see Buttonwoods, The

Maple Shade Mansion
Delaware River
HABS DE-135   pd   L

Porter, Alexander, Mansion Farm
Rt. 9
HABS DE-108   pd   L

Regency House; see Swanwyck
Swanwick; see Swanwyck
Swanwick Manor; see Swanwyck
Swanwyck (Swanwick; Swanwick Manor; Regency House)
65 Landers Lane
HABS DE-48   pd   L

Newark

Curtis Paper Mill (Millford Mills; Nonantum Mills)
Rt. 72
HAER DE-1   pd   L

Millford Mills; see Curtis Paper Mill
Nonantum Mills; see Curtis Paper Mill

Newark vic.

Cooch House; see Cooch, Thomas, House
Cooch, Thomas, House (Cooch House)
961 Old Baltimore Pike
HABS DE-57   pd   L

Eastburn-Jeanes Limekilns
Pike Creek Rd.
HABS DE-165
HAER DE-2   s pd   L

England, John, House (England-Eastburn House; Red Mill Farm)
81 Red Mill Rd.
HABS DE-137   pd   L

England-Eastburn House; see England, John, House

Red Mill Farm; see England, John, House

Welsh Tract Baptist Church
Welsh Tract Church Rd.
HABS DE-56   s pd   L

White Clay Creek Presbyterian Church
Robert Kirkwood Hwy. & Polly Drummond Hill Rd.
HABS DE-160   pd   L

Newport

Galloway House
Johns & Ayre Sts.
HABS DE-132   pd   L

Myers House (Parkin-Myers House)
Market & Johns Sts.
HABS DE-47   pd   L

Parkin-Myers House; see Myers House

Odessa

Appoquinimink Friends Meetinghouse; see Odessa Friends Meetinghouse

Brick Hotel, The (Odessa Inn, Old)
Main St.
HABS DE-113   pd   L

Corbit, William, House; see Corbit-Sharp House

Corbit-Sharp House (Corbit, William, House)
Main St.
HABS DE-90   pd   L

Heller House (Wilson, David, House)
Rt. 299
HABS DE-114   pd   L

Odessa Friends Meetinghouse (Appoquinimink Friends Meetinghouse)
Rt. 299
HABS DE-115   pd   L

Odessa Inn, Old; see Brick Hotel, The
Wilson, David, House; see Heller House
Wilson, David, House; see Wilson-Warner House

Wilson-Warner House (Wilson, David, House)
Main St.
HABS DE-89   pd   L

Odessa vic.

Drawyers Presbyterian Church, Old
Rt. 13
HABS DE-3   s pd   L

Ogletown vic.

England's, John, Grist Mill
81 Red Mill Rd.
HABS DE-136   pd   L

Pea Patch Island

Fort Delaware
HABS DE-194   p   H

Price's Corner vic.

Bird, Thomas, House
(moved to DE-Wilmington)
HABS DE-131   pd   L

Greenbank Mill
Greenbank Rd.
HABS DE-164   pd   L

Rockland vic.

Black Gates (Gate Lodges)
Rockland Rd.
HABS DE-62   pd   L

Gate Lodges; see Black Gates

Smyrna vic.

Allee House (McClements Farm)
Adjoining Bombay Hook Wildlife Refuge
HABS DE-180   p   H

McClements Farm; see Allee House

Stanton

Stanton-Tatnall-Byrnes House
201 Old Mill Lane
HABS DE-168   pd   L

Stanton vic.

Boyce House; see Hale-Byrnes House

Bread & Cheese Island House; see
Hale-Byrnes House

Hale-Byrnes House (Boyce House; Bread &
Cheese Island House)
Rt. 7
HABS DE-60   pd   L

St. James Protestant Episcopal Church
St. James Church Rd. & Old Capital Trail
HABS DE-55   pd   L

Taylor's Bridge

Reedy Island Range Rear Light
Rt. 9
HAER DE-11   s pd   L

Taylor's Bridge vic.

Huguenot House (Naudain, Elias S.,
House)
Rt. 9
HABS DE-77   pd   L

Naudain, Elias S., House; see Huguenot
House

Wilmington

Asbury Methodist Episcopal Church
Third & Walnut Sts.
HABS DE-39   pd   L

Augustine Bridge
Brandywine River, Augustine Cutoff
HAER DE-20   s pd   L

Banning House
809 S. Broom St.
HABS DE-43   pd   L

Brandywine Academy
5 Vandever Ave.
HABS DE-9-1   s pd   L

Brandywine Pumping Station
Sixteenth & Market Sts.
HAER DE-19   pd   L

Brick Arch Viaduct; see Pennsylvania
Railroad Improvements

Bush, Samuel, House
211 N. Walnut St.
HABS DE-38   pd   L

Canby, Samuel, House
1401 N. Market St.
HABS DE-11   s pd   L

Coxe, Thomas A., Houses
107-109 E. Sixth St. (moved to Market St.)
HABS DE-42   pd   L

Customs House, Old
King at Sixth St.
HABS DE-188   p   H

Derrickson House
1801 N. Market St.
HABS DE-34   pd   L

Dingee, Jacob, House (Gray, Joseph,
House)
105 E. Seventh St. (moved to Market St.)
HABS DE-24   pd   L

Dingee, Obadiah, House (Lloyd House)
107 E. Seventh St. (moved to Market St.)
HABS DE-23   pd   L

duPont, Charles I., House
Henry Clay Rd.
HABS DE-66   pd   L

Febiger, Christian, House; see Tatnall,
Edward T., House

German Hall
205 E. Sixth St.
HABS DE-41   pd   L

Gibbons House
1311 N. Market St.
HABS DE-27   pd   L

Grand Opera House (Masonic Hall &
Grand Theater)
818 Market St. Mall
HABS DE-170   p   H

Gray, Joseph, House; see Dingee, Jacob,
House

Harlan & Hollingsworth Company Factory
100 S. West St.
HAER DE-8   pd   L

Holy Trinity Church (Swedes Church, Old)
Seventh & Church St.
HABS DE-9-2   s pd   L

Latimer, Henry, House; see Woodstock

Lea, William, House
1901 N. Market St.
HABS DE-31   pd   L

Lloyd House; see Dingee, Obadiah, House

Lobdell Car Wheel Company
Christina Ave.
HAER DE-15   pd   L

Marot, John, House
1203 & 1205 N. Market St.
HABS DE-29   pd   L

Masonic Hall & Grand Theater; see Grand
Opera House

Mendenhall, Capt. Thomas, House
Front & Walnut Sts.
HABS DE-21   pd   L

Newlin, Ann, Houses
108 & 110 E. Fifth St.
HABS DE-36   pd   L

Newlin, Samuel, Houses
423-425 French St.
HABS DE-37   pd   L

Palmer House
1322 King St.
HABS DE-25   pd   L

Peirce, Robert, House
201-203 N. Walnut
HABS DE-22   pd   L

Pennsylvania Central Wilmington Shop;
see Pennsylvania Railroad Improvements

Pennsylvania Railroad Improvements
(Repair Shop; Wilmington Yards &
Shop; Pennsylvania Central Wilmington
Shop)
Vandever & Bowers Sts.
HAER DE-12-A   pd   H

Pennsylvania Railroad Improvements
(Brick Arch Viaduct)
Liberty St. to Baltimore & Ohio Railroad
HAER DE-12-B   pd   H

Pennsylvania Railroad Improvements
Vandever St. & Baltimore & Ohio Railroad
vic.
HAER DE-12   pd   L H

Pennsylvania Railroad Improvements
(Powerhouse)
Water & Walnut Sts.
HAER DE-12-F   pd   H

Pennsylvania Railroad Improvements
(Pennsylvania Railroad Office Building)
French St. at Christiana River
HAER DE-12-E   s p   H

Pennsylvania Railroad Improvements
(Wilmington Train Station)
Front & French Sts.
HAER DE-12-D   pd   H

Pennsylvania Railroad Improvements
(Swing Bridge)
Penn. R. R. over Brandywine River
HAER DE-12-C   pd   H

Pennsylvania Railroad Office Building; see
Pennsylvania Railroad Improvements

Powerhouse; see Pennsylvania Railroad
Improvements

Price, Joseph, House
1301 N. Market St.
HABS DE-28   s pd   L

Repair Shop; see Pennsylvania Railroad
Improvements

Rhoads, J. E. & Sons
2100 W. Eleventh St.
HAER DE-17   pd   L

Rockford Village
Rockford & Ivy Rds.
HABS DE-187   p   H

Rockford Water Tower
Rockford Park
HAER DE-16   pd   L

Sharp, Jacob, House
213 Lombard St.
HABS DE-40   pd   L
Smith, William, House
1905 N. Market St.
HABS DE-30   pd   L
Starr, Jacob, House (Van Kirk, Michael, House)
1310 N. King St.
HABS DE-26   s pd   L
Strauss, Emma, House
625 French St.
HABS DE-35   pd   L
Swedes Church, Old; see Holy Trinity Church
Swing Bridge; see Pennsylvania Railroad Improvements
Tatnall, Edward T., House (Febiger, Christian, House)
1807 N. Market St.
HABS DE-32   pd   L
Tatnall, Joseph, House
1803 N. Market St.
HABS DE-33   pd   L
Van Kirk, Michael, House; see Starr, Jacob, House
Welde, William, House
102 N. Walnut St.
HABS DE-20   pd   L
Wilmington & Northern Railroad Repair Shop
Beech St.
HAER DE-13   s pd   L
Wilmington Train Station; see Pennsylvania Railroad Improvements
Wilmington Yards & Shop; see Pennsylvania Railroad Improvements
Woodstock (Woodstock-Latimer House; Latimer, Henry, House)
102 Middleboro Rd. in Banning Park
HABS DE-54   pd   L
Woodstock-Latimer House; see Woodstock

Wilmington vic.
Bell Tower Mill; see Walker's Mill
Brick Mill House; see Richardson, John, House
First Bank of the U.S. Iron Gates; see Winterthur Museum Iron Gates
Glynrich; see Richardson, John, House
Glynrich; see Richardson, Richard, House
Jacquett, Peter, House; see Long Hook Farm
Kent Manor Inn; see Long Hook Farm
Latimer House; see Latimeria
Latimeria (Latimer House)
Newport Pike (Maryland Ave.)
HABS DE-44   pd   L
Long Hook Farm (Jacquett, Peter, House; Kent Manor Inn)
1051 S. Market St.
HABS DE-61   pd   L
Mill House Row; see Walker's Bank

Richardson, John, House (Brick Mill House; Glynrich)
Maryland Ave. (Rt. 4)
HABS DE-45   pd   L
Richardson, Richard, House (Glynrich)
Maryland Ave. (Rt. 4)
HABS DE-46   pd   L
Rockwood (Shipley-Bringhurst-Hargraves Museum)
610 Shipley Rd.
HABS DE-186   d   H
Shipley-Bringhurst-Hargraves Museum; see Rockwood
Tussey House
Philadelphia Pike
HABS DE-49   pd   L
Walker's Bank (Mill House Row)
Rising Sun Lane
HABS DE-67   pd   L
Walker's Mill (Bell Tower Mill)
Rising Sun Lane
HABS DE-65   pd   L
Winterthur Museum Iron Gates (First Bank of the U.S. Iron Gates)
Rt. 52
HABS DE-193   p   H

Yorklyn
Garrett Snuff Mill
Rt. 82
HAER DE-14   pd   H

SUSSEX COUNTY

Bethel
Dowd House; see Ship-Carpenter's House
Robins House; see Ship Carpenter's House
Ship Carpenter's House (Robins House)
Main St.
HABS DE-151   pd   L
Ship-Carpenter's House (Dowd House)
Main St.
HABS DE-150   pd   L

Bridgeville
Sudler House
N. Main St.
HABS DE-184   s d   H

Cool Spring vic.
Fisher House; see White Meadow Farm
Martin House; see White Meadow Farm
White Meadow Farm (Fisher House; Martin House)
State Rds. 290 & 262 (moved to DE, Lewes)
HABS DE-157   pd   L

Dagsboro
Prince George's Chapel
Rt. 26
HABS DE-158   pd   L

Georgetown
Judges, The (House)
104 W. Market St.
HABS DE-154   pd   L
Judges, The, Law Office
100 W. Market St.
HABS DE-155   pd   L

Greenwood vic.
Locust Grove (Richards House)
State Rds. 34 & 32
HABS DE-171   pd   L
Richards House; see Locust Grove

Laurel
Collins House; see Rosemont
Mitchell, Gov. Nathaniel, House; see Rosemont
Rosemont (Collins House; Mitchell, Gov. Nathaniel, House)
121 Delaware Ave.
HABS DE-7   pd   L

Laurel vic.
Christ Church, Old (Lightwood, Old; Christ Episcopal Church)
State Rds. 465 & 465-A
HABS DE-8   s pd   L
Christ Episcopal Church; see Christ Church, Old
Lightwood, Old; see Christ Church, Old
Whaley Homestead
Rt. 24
HABS DE-9   pd   L

Lewes
Coleman House
422 Kings Hwy.
HABS DE-15   pd   L
Hall, Col. David, House
107 Kings Hwy.
HABS DE-149   pd   L
Hocker, H. W., Manufacturing Company Factory
224 Front St.
HAER DE-7   pd   L
Maull Homestead; see Maull, Thomas, House
Maull, Thomas, House (Paynter, Samuel, House; Maull Homestead)
542 Pilot Town Rd.
HABS DE-13   pd   L
Metcalf House
202 W. Third St.
HABS DE-12   pd   L
Paynter, Samuel, House; see Maull, Thomas, House
Skellenger House
Pilot Town Rd.
HABS DE-14   pd   L

Milford
Causey House
2 Causey Ave.
HABS DE-183   d   H

Milford Ice & Coal
Maple & Church Sts.
HAER DE-4   s pd L

Millsboro

Houston-White Co. Mill & Basket Factory
Main & Railroad Aves.
HAER DE-6   s pd L

Oak Orchard vic.

White House Farm
Long Neck Rd. vic. at Indian River Bay
HABS DE-10   pd L

Rehoboth Beach vic.

Homestead, The; see Marsh, Peter, House
Marsh, Peter, House (Homestead, The)
10 Dodd's Lane
HABS DE-152   pd L

Seaford vic.

Cannon's Savannah; see Maston House
Maston House (Cannon's Savannah)
Atlanta-Seaford Rd.
HABS DE-192   d L

Woodland

Cannon Hall (Cannon, Jacob, House)
Road 79 at Woodland Ferry
HABS DE-156   pd L

Cannon, Jacob, House; see Cannon Hall

Woodland vic.

Walnut Landing (House)
State Rd. 79
HABS DE-153   pd L

District of Columbia

Washington

600-602 & 1100 G Street (House); see
Southeast Area Survey
101 & 122-124 Carroll Street (House); see
Southeast Area Survey
**1308-1344 & 1501-1523 Vermont Avenue
NW (Houses);** see Logan Circle
**2024 & 2026 G Street NW (Commercial
Buildings)**
HABS DC-403   p H
330 & 706-708 Virginia Avenue (Houses);
see Southeast Area Survey
**132-144 & 900-905 Eleventh Street (Row
Houses);** see Southeast Area Survey
1002, 1006 Eye Street (House); see
Southeast Area Survey
**306-308, 324-326 Virginia Avenue
(Houses);** see Southeast Area Survey
808-810, 812-814, & 1016 K Street (House);
see Southeast Area Survey
Adams Building
816 F St.
HABS DC-214   pd L
Adams-Mason House
1072 Thomas Jefferson St. NW
HABS DC-161   pd L
Adas Israel Congregation Synagogue
Sixth & G Sts. NW (moved to Third & G
Sts. NW)
HABS DC-173   s pd H
Aged Woman's Home; see Female Union
Benevolent Society
American Building
1317 F St. NW
HABS DC-305   p H
**American Institute of Architects
Headquarters;** see Octagon House
American Institute of Architects Library;
see Octagon Stable, The
American Mosaic Company Building
912 I St. NW
HABS DC-387   pd L
**American University, The College of
History** (Hurst Hall)
Massachusetts & Nebraska Aves. NW
HABS DC-399   d H

Anacostia Historic District, Old
Thirteenth & U Sts. SE
HABS DC-408   p H
Anderson, Larz, House (Society of the
Cincinnati Headquarters)
2118 Massachusetts Ave. NW
HABS DC-255   pd L
Apex Liquor Store; see Central National
Bank Building
Argyle Terrace; see Miller House
Armed Forces Medical Museum
Seventh & Independence Ave. SW
HABS DC-306   pd H
Arts & Industries Building; see Smithsonian
Institution
Arts Club of Washington; see Caldwell,
Timothy, House
Atlas Building; see Wardner Building
Australian Embassy; see Wilkins House
1000 B Street SW (House)
HABS DC-15   s p L
Bacon House; see Ringgold-Carroll House
Baker Building
1320-1322 F St.
HABS DC-379   pd L
Bank of Columbia (Georgetown Town
Hall; DC Engine Company Number Five
Firehouse; National Firefighting
Museum)
3210 M St. NW
HABS DC-119   s pd L
Barber Shop
3251 M St. NW
HABS DC-121   pd L
Barney, A. Clifford, House; see Hughs,
Charles Evans, House
Barney, Alice P., Studio; see Barney, Alice
Pike, Studio House
Barney, Alice Pike, Studio House (Barney,
Alice P., Studio)
2306 Massachusetts Ave. NW
HABS DC-256   pd L H
Barney Neighborhood House; see
Duncanson-Cranch House
Barney's Restaurent; see Metropolitan
Hotel

Barrett, James I., House
1400 Twenty-ninth St. NW
HABS DC-180   pd L
Bassin's Restaurant; see Loughran Building
Beale, Joseph, House (Embassy of the Arab
Republic of Egypt)
2301 Massachusetts Ave. NW
HABS DC-257   pd L
Beall's Express Building
1522 Wisconsin Ave. NW
HABS DC-80   p L
Bebb House (Octagonal House)
1830 Phelps Pl. NW
HABS DC-13   s L
Becker's Leather Goods Store; see 1314 F
Street NW (Commercial Building)
**Bell, Alexander Graham, Association for
the Deaf;** see Volta Bureau
Bellevue (Rittenhouse Place; Dunbarton
House)
2715 Q St. NW
HABS DC-434   p L
Berry, Philip T., House
1402 Thirty-first St. NW
HABS DC-253   pd L
Bibb House; see Bronaugh-Bibb-Libby
House
Birch Funeral Home
3034 M St. NW
HABS DC-142   pd L
Birch, W. Taylor, House
3099 Q St. NW
HABS DC-187   pd L
Bliss, Dr. A. C., House
1218 Sixteenth St. NW
HABS DC-398   p H
Bodisco House; see Smith, Clement, House
Bomford's Mill (Wilkins-Rogers Milling
Company)
Potomac & Grace Sts.
HABS DC-143   pd L
Bowen, Anthony, YMCA Building; see
Twelfth Street YMCA Building
Bowie House (Sevier House)
3124 Q St. NW
HABS DC-60   p L

Brickyard Hill House
3134 South St. NW
HABS DC-158   pd   L

Bronaugh-Bibb-Libby House (Bibb House)
1409 Thirty-fifth St. NW
HABS DC-209   pd   L

Brown House
1404 Thirty-fifth St. NW
HABS DC-191   pd   L

Brown House; see Goszler-Meem-Brown
House

Brownley Building
1300-1304 F St. NW
HABS DC-381   pd   L

Brown's Hotel; see Metropolitan Hotel

Bruce, Blanche K., House
909 M St. NW
HABS DC-370   p   H

Buehler House; see Sullivan House

Bunche, Ralph J., House
1510 Jackson St. NE
HABS DC-360   pd   L

Bussard-Newman House
1311 Thirty-fifth St. NW
HABS DC-196   pd   L

458 C Street NW
HABS DC-374   pd   L

Cairo Hotel
1615 Q St. NW
HABS DC-307   p   H

Caldwell, Timothy, House (Arts Club of
Washington)
2017 I St. NW
HABS DC-84   s pd   L

Camaroon Chancery; see Hauge, Christian,
House

Cameron House; see Tayloe, Benjamin
Ogle, House

Canadian Chancery; see Moore, Clarence,
House

Canal Street at Independence Avenue
(Row House); see Southeast Area Survey

Canal Warehouse
3222 M St. NW
HABS DC-144   pd   L

Capital Garage
1320 New York Ave. NW
HABS DC-279   p   H

Capital Traction Company Powerhouse
3142 K St. NW
HABS DC-145   pd   L

Capital Traction Company Union Station
3600 M St. NW
HABS DC-125   pd   L

Capitol-Light Standards
Capitol Grounds, E. of Capitol
HABS DC-77   p   L

Capitol-Shelter
Capitol Grounds, NE of Capitol
HABS DC-75   p   L

Careleton, Joseph, House
1052-54 Potomac St. NW
HABS DC-146   pd   L

Carriage House
314 U St. NW
HABS DC-397   p   H

Carriage House
1313 Thirty-first St. NW
HABS DC-250   pd   L

Carroll House; see Duddington Mansion

Cary, Mary Shadd, House
1421 W St. NW
HABS DC-368   p   H

Central Armature Works
629 D St. NW
HABS DC-308   p   H

Central Heating Plant; see U.S. General
Services Administration Building

Central National Bank Building (Apex
Liquor Store)
633 Pennsylvania Ave. NW
HABS DC-229   pd   L

**Chesapeake & Ohio Canal, Georgetown
Section** (Chesapeake & Ohio Canal
National Historic Park)
E. & W. parallel to M St. NW
HABS DC-147   pd   L H

**Chesapeake & Ohio Canal National
Historic Park;** see Chesapeake & Ohio
Canal, Georgetown Section

Chinese Chancery; see Fahnestock, Gibson,
House

Chinese Legation
Nineteenth & Vernon Sts. NW
HABS DC-425   p   H

Christ Church
620 G St. NE
HABS DC-48   p   H

Christ Church (Episcopal)
3116 O St. NW
HABS DC-243   pd   L

Christian Science Building; see Gray,
Justice Horace, House

City Hall, Old (Court House)
451 Indianna Ave. NW
HABS DC-41   pd   L H

City Tavern
3206-3208 M St. NW
HABS DC-81   pd   L

Cloud, Abner, House
Intersection of Canal Rd. & Reservoir Rd.
NW
HABS DC-99   s pd   L

Columbia Historical Society; see Heurich,
Christian, Mansion

Commandant's House; see U.S. Marine
Corp Commandants House

Concordia United Church of Christ
1920 G St. NW
HABS DC-396   p   H

Congressional Cemetary (Latrobe
Cenotaphs)
Eighteenth & E Sts. SE
HABS DC-424   s   L

Connecticut Avenue & R Street NW
(House) (Golden Parrot Restaurant)
HABS DC-318   p   H

**Convention Center Site, District of
Columbia** (H Street, 900 & 1000 Block;
Ninth Street, 800 & 900 Block; Eleventh
Street, 800 Block; New York Avenue, 900
& 1000 Block)
I St., 900 & 1000 Block, Tenth St., 800 &
900 Block
HABS DC-384   pd   L

Cooke's Row, Villa Number Three
3013 Q St. NW
HABS DC-182   pd   L

Corcoran Art Gallery (U.S. Court of
Claims; Smithsonian Institution,
Renwick Gallery)
Seventeenth St. & Pennsylvania Ave. NW
HABS DC-49   pd   H

Corcoran, Thomas, House
3119 M St. NW
HABS DC-34   p   L

Cordova Apartments
1908 Florida Ave. NW
HABS DC-422   p   H

Corson & Gruman Company; see Ray's
Warehouse & Office

Cosmos Club; see Townsend House

Cosmos Club (Old); see Cutts, Richard,
House

Court House; see City Hall, Old

Cox, Col. John, House
3339 N St. NW
HABS DC-150   p   L

Cramphin, Thomas, Building
3209-3211 M St. NW
HABS DC-118   pd   L

Crandell, Germond, Building
401-407 Seventh St. NW
HABS DC-224   pd   L

Crawford-Cassin House
3017 O St. NW
HABS DC-184   pd   L

Culver, Fredrick B., House
809 E St. NW
HABS DC-220   pd   L

Cutts, Richard, House (Madison, Dolley,
House; Cosmos Club (Old))
1518 H St. NW
HABS DC-58   pd   L

Czechoslovakian Embassy; see Hauge,
Christian, House

D. C. Central Public Library, Old
499 Pennsylvania Ave. NW
HABS DC-372   pd   L

22 D Street SE (House)
HABS DC-17   p

Daly, Carroll, House
1306 Thirty-fifth St. NW
HABS DC-205   pd   L

Dashiell, George W., Building
1203 Pennsylvania Ave. NW
HABS DC-432   pd   L

Dash's Designer; see 1308 F Street NW
(Commercial Building)

Davidson, John, House
1220 Wisconsin Ave. NW
HABS DC-102   pd   L

Davis, James Y., Sons Building
1201-04 Pennsylvania Ave. & 408 Twelfth
    St. NW
HABS DC-312   pd   L

DC Engine Company Number Five
    Firehouse; see Bank of Columbia

D.C. Engine Company Number Two
719 Twelfth St. NW
HABS DC-350   p   H

De La Roche-Jewell Tenant House
1320 Thirtieth St. NW
HABS DC-179   pd   L

Decatur House (National Trust for Historic
    Preservation)
748 Jackson Pl. NW
HABS DC-16   s pd   L

Decatur-Gunther House (Williams, John S.,
    House; Hood House)
2812 N St. NW
HABS DC-29   s pd   L

Deincanson-Cranch House
468-470 N St. SW
HABS DC-394   p   H

Delano, Fredric, House
2244 S St. NW
HABS DC-419   p   H

Devore-Chase House
2000 Twenty-fourth St. NW
HABS DC-288   pd   L

District Building
Fourteenth St. & Pennsylvania Ave.
HABS DC-314   p   H

Dix, General John A., House
456 C St. NW
HABS DC-373   pd   L

Dodge, Francis, Warehouse
1006 Wisconsin Ave. NW
HABS DC-436   pd   L

Dodge, Robert P., House
1534 Twenty-eighth St. NW
HABS DC-246   pd   L

Douglass, Fredrick, House (Douglass,
    Fredrick, National Historic Park)
Fourteenth & W St. SE
HABS DC-97   s pd   L H

Douglass, Fredrick, National Historic Park;
    see Douglass, Fredrick, House

Doxiadas Associates; see Potomac Lodge
    Number Five

Duddington Mansion (Carroll House)
First & Second & E & F Sts. SE
HABS DC-8   s pd   L

3015 Dumbarton Avenue NW (House)
HABS DC-183   pd   L

Dunbarton House; see Bellevue

Duncanson, William, House; see Maples,
    The

Duncanson-Cranch House (Barney
    Neighborhood House)
468-470 N St. SW
HABS DC-128   p   L

Duvall Foundry
1050 Thirtieth St. NW
HABS DC-154   pd   L H

1200 E Street NW (Commercial Building)
    (Service Station and Garage)
HABS DC-420   pd   L

625 E Street NW (Commercial Building)
HABS DC-228   pd   L

1208-1214 E Street NW (Garage)
HABS DC-426   pd   L

2029 E Street NW (House)
HABS DC-136   s   H

514 E Street NW (House)
HABS DC-236   p   L

Eagle House; see Mountz, John, House

Easby House
D St. NW
HABS DC-7   s p   L

Eastern Market
Seventh St. SE
HABS DC-291   p   H

**310 Eighth Street NW (Commercial
    Building)**
HABS DC-310   p   H

**320 Eighth Street NW (Commercial
    Building)**
HABS DC-237   p   H

**308 Eighth Street NW (Commerical
    Building)**
HABS DC-309   p   H

Eleventh Street, 800 Block; see Convention
    Center Site, District of Columbia

**304-306 Eleventh Street SW, (Double
    House)**
HABS DC-56   p   L

Elks Lodge; see Washington Lodge Number
    15, B. P. O. E.

Embassy of Luxembourg; see Stewart,
    Alexander, House

Embassy of the Arab Republic of Egypt;
    see Beale, Joseph, House

**Embassy of the Fed. Repub. of Camaroon
    Chancery;** see Hauge, Christian, House

**Engine Company Number Fifteen,
    Firehouse**
2100 Fourteenth St. SE
HABS DC-92   p   L

Engine Company Number Four, Firehouse
931 R St. NW
HABS DC-87   p   L

Engine Company Number Nine, Firehouse
1624 U St. NW
HABS DC-89   p   L

**Engine Company Number Seventeen,
    Firehouse**
1227 Monroe St. NE
HABS DC-93   p   L

Engine Company Number Six, Firehouse
438 Massachusetts Ave. NW
HABS DC-88   p   L

Engine Company Number Ten, Firehouse
1341 Maryland Ave. NE
HABS DC-90   p   L

**Engine Company Number Twelve,
    Firehouse**
1626 N. Capitol St.
HABS DC-91   p   L

**Engine Company Number Twenty-one,
    Firehouse**
1763 Lanier Place NW
HABS DC-94   p   L

**Engine Company Number Twenty-Two,
    Firehouse**
5760 Georgia Ave. NW
HABS DC-95   p   L

Engine Company Nuumber One, Firehouse
1643 K St. NW
HABS DC-86   p   L

Estes Mill (Ruins)
Rock Creek Park
HABS DC-40   p   L

Evening Star Building
1101 Pennsylvania Ave. NW
HABS DC-316   p   H

Everett, Edward H., House (Turkish
    Embassy)
1606 Twenty-third St. NW
HABS DC-258   pd   L

Evermay
1623 Twenty-eighth St. NW
HABS DC-61   p   L

Executive Mansion; see White House, The
    (West Wing)

Eye Street NW (House)
HABS DC-131   p   L

Eynon Building
3407 M St. NW
HABS DC-124   pd   L

F Street Club; see Ray, Alexander, House

1308 F Street NW (Commercial Building)
    (Dash's Designer)
HABS DC-380   pd   L

1310 F Street NW (Commercial Building)
    (Raleigh's Haberdasher)
HABS DC-377   pd   L

1314 F Street NW (Commercial Building)
    (Becker's Leather Goods Store)
HABS DC-376   pd   L

1901 F Street NW (Commercial Building)
HABS DC-327   p   H

1903 F Street NW (Commercial Building)
HABS DC-328   p   H

814 F Street NW (Commercial Building)
HABS DC-213   pd   L

818 F Street NW (Commercial Building)
HABS DC-215   pd   L

Fahnestock, Gibson, House (Republic of
    China Chancery; Chinese Chancery)
2311 Massachusetts Ave. NW
HABS DC-259   pd   L

Fairbanks, Henry Parker, House; see
  Wilson, Woodrow, House
Female Union Benevolent Society (Lutz,
  John, House; Aged Woman's Home)
1255 Wisconsin Ave. NW
HABS DC-105   pd   L
Fenwick, Teresa, House (Parrot, Thomas,
  House)
3512 P St. NW
HABS DC-83   s pd   L
Findley House
3606 N St. NW
HABS DC-192   pd   L
Firemen's Insurance Company Building
303 Seventh St. NW
HABS DC-235   p   L
First Baptist Church of Georgetown
Twenty-Seventh St. NW
HABS DC-241   pd   L
214 First Street (House); see Southeast
  Area Survey
Fitzhugh, Emma S., House (Philippine
  Embassy)
2253 R St. NW
HABS DC-260   pd   L H
Florida State Society; see Manning,
  Edward C., House
Ford Motor Company Building
451-455 Pennsylvania Ave. NW
HABS DC-375   pd   L
Ford's Theater (Ford's Theater National
  Historic Park)
511 Tenth St. NW
HABS DC-82   s p   H
Ford's Theater National Historic Park; see
  Ford's Theater
Forrest-Marbury House
3350 M St. NW
HABS DC-68   pd   L
**501-511 Fourteenth Street NW
  (Commercial Building)** (Locker Room,
  The)
HABS DC-356   pd   L
Foxhall, Henry, House (McKenny House)
3123 Dumbarton Ave.
HABS DC-66   p   L
Franklin School
Thirteenth & K Sts. NW
HABS DC-289   p   H
French House; see Oak Hill
Friendship House; see Maples, The
Frisco's; see Stone, William J., Building
G Street NW, 1900 Block (Houses)
HABS DC-404   H
Gallaudet College, Gate House
Seventh & Florida Ave. NE
HABS DC-304   p   H
Gallaudet College, President's House
Seventh St. & Florida Ave. NE
HABS DC-303   p   H
Gallaudet College, Chapel Hall
Seventh & Florida Ave. NE
HABS DC-301   p   H

Gallaudet College, General
Seventh & Florida Ave. NE
HABS DC-300   p   H
Gallaudet College, Hall
Seventh & Florida Ave. NE
HABS DC-302   p   H
Gantt-Williams House; see Owens, Isaac,
  House (Doorway)
Gazebo
3233 N St. NW
HABS DC-155   p   L
Georgetown Club, The; see 1530 Wisconsin
  Avenue NW (House)
Georgetown Market, The
3276 M St. NW
HABS DC-123   pd   L
Georgetown Town Hall; see Bank of
  Columbia
Georgetown University, Healy Building
Thirty-seventh & O Sts. NW
HABS DC-248   pd   L
**Georgetown University, Old North
  Building**
Thirty-Seventh & O Sts. NW
HABS DC-170   p   L H
Georgetown Visitation Convent
1500 Thirty-fifth St. NW
HABS DC-211   pd   L
Gilman Drugs
627 Pennsylvania Ave. NW
HABS DC-129   pd   H
Godey Lime Kilns (Ruins)
Junction of Rock Creek & Potomac Pkwy.
HABS DC-102-A
HAER DC-3   s pd   L H
Golden Parrot Restaurant; see Connecticut
  Avenue & R Street NW (House)
Goszler-Manogue House
1307 Thirty-fifth St. NW
HABS DC-193   pd   L
Goszler-Meem-Brown House (Brown
  House)
3412 O St. NW
HABS DC-204   pd   L
Grace Protestant Episcopal Church
1041 Wisconsin Ave. NW
HABS DC-440   s pd   L
Gray, Justice Horace, House (Christian
  Science Building)
1601 Eye St. NW
HABS DC-79   p   L
Greyhound Terminal
New York Ave., Eleventh & Twelfth Sts.
  NW
HABS DC-402   p   H
Grimke, Charlotte Forten, House
1608 R St. NW
HABS DC-366   p   H
Gunston Hall School for Girls
1904 I St. NW
HABS DC-416   p   H
Gutman-Wise Building
3140 M St. NW
HABS DC-117   pd   L

H Street, 900 & 1000 Block; see Convention
  Center Site, District of Columbia
1003 H Street NW (House)
HABS DC-132   p   L
Halcyon House (Stoddert, Benjamin,
  House)
3400 Prospect St. NW
HABS DC-69   pd   L
Hall, John Stoddert, House
2808 N St. NW
HABS DC-156   p   L
Halliday, Henrietta M., House (Irish
  Chancery)
2234 Massachusetts Ave. NW
HABS DC-261   pd   L
Hamburgh House
412 Twentieth St. NW
HABS DC-10-6   s pd   L
Harnedy Row Houses
3617-21 Prospect St. NW
HABS DC-206   pd   L
Harrison, Jane Stone, Building
1205 Pennsylvania Ave. NW
HABS DC-429   pd   L
Hauge, Christian, House (Czechoslovakian
  Embassy; Embassy of the Fed. Repub. of
  Camaroon Chancery; Camaroon
  Chancery)
2349 Massachusetts Ave. NW
HABS DC-262   pd   L
Hayman, David & Company; see 625
  Indiana Avenue NW (Commercial
  Building)
Hedges, Nicholas, House
1069 Thomas Jefferson St. NW
HABS DC-160   pd   L
Herron-Moxley House
1503 Thirty-fifth St. NW
HABS DC-195   pd   L
Heurich, Christian, Mansion (Columbia
  Historical Society)
1307 New Hampshire Ave.
HABS DC-292   s p   H
High Street Bridge (Wisconsin Avenue
  Bridge)
Wisconsin Ave. NW, Spanning C & O
  Canal
HABS DC-30   s   L
Hillyer Place
Connecticut Ave. & R St. NW
HABS DC-294   p   H
Holt, Dr. Henry C., House; see Jackson Hill
Holy Trinity Parish
Thirty-sixth St. btw. N & O Sts. NW
HABS DC-201   pd   L
Honeymoon House; see Law, Thomas,
  House
Hood House; see Decatur-Gunther House
Hooe, James C., House
2230 Massachusetts Ave. NW
HABS DC-263   pd   L
Hooper, Robert King, House; see Lindens,
  The

Hotel Washington
Fifteenth St. & Pennsylvania Ave. NW
HABS DC-317   p   H

House Where Lincoln Died; see Peterson House

Howard, Gen. Oliver O., House (Howard University, Howard Hall)
607 Howard Pl. NW
HABS DC-284   p   H

Howard University, Founders Library
2400 Sixth St. NW
HABS DC-364   pd   L

Howard University, Howard Hall; see Howard, Gen. Oliver O., House

Hughs, Charles Evans, House (Barney, A. Clifford, House; Union of Burma Chancery)
2223 R St. NW
HABS DC-278   p   H

Humble Service Station
Twenty-sixth St. & Pennsylvania Ave. NW
HABS DC-319   p   H

Hurley, John, House
3619 O St. NW
HABS DC-200   pd   L

Hurst Hall; see American University, The College of History

I Street (House)
Btw. Twentieth & Twenty-first Sts. NW
HABS DC-400   p   H

2030 I Street NW (Commercial Building)
HABS DC-337   p   H

625 Indiana Avenue NW (Commercial Building) (Hayman, David & Company)
HABS DC-230   pd   L

Indonesian Embassy; see Walsh-Mclean House

Irish Chancery; see Halliday, Henrietta M., House

Jackson, Albert, House
1694 Thirty-first St. NW
HABS DC-181   pd   L

Jackson Hill (Holt, Dr. Henry C., House; National Zoological Park, Adminstration Building)
Adams Mill Rd. vic.
HABS DC-21   p   H

Jackson (Public) School
R St. & Avon Pl. NW
HABS DC-244   pd   L

Japanese Embassy
2516 Massachusetts Ave. NW
HABS DC-264   pd   L

1063 Jefferson Street NW (House)
HABS DC-159   p   L

Jewell, Capt. Theodore, House
2135 R St. NW
HABS DC-417   p   H

Johnson, Capt. Joseph, House
49 T St. SW, Buzzards Point
HABS DC-10-3   p   L

Kane, Daniel, House
1419 Thirty-sixth St. NW
HABS DC-197   pd   L

Kann, S., Sons & Company
Market Square
HABS DC-365   p   H

Keep Building
801-803 Pennsylvania Ave. NW
HABS DC-320   p   H

Keith-Albee Building
Fifteenth & G Sts. NW
HABS DC-423   p   H

Kelly House
1239 Thirty-seventh St. NW
HABS DC-203   pd   L

Key, Francis Scott, House
3518 M St. NW
HABS DC-23   s p   L

King House
528 Seventeenth St. NW
HABS DC-57   pd   L

Klingle House; see Linnean Hill

Knowles, William, House
1228 Thirtieth St. NW
HABS DC-163   pd   L

Kraemer, Charles, House
1841 Park Rd. NW
HABS DC-283   p   H

817-819 L Street (House); see Southeast Area Survey

L Street NW, 1000 Block (Commercial Building)
HABS DC-433   p   H

Lansburgh, Juilius, Furniture Company, Inc.; see Masonic Temple

Lansburgh's Department Store
E & Eighth Sts. NW
HABS DC-355   pd   H

Latrobe Cenotaphs; see Congressional Cemetary

Law, Thomas, House (Honeymoon House; Tiber Island Center for Cultural & Community Act.)
1252 Sixth St. SW
HABS DC-20   s p   L H

Layhman, Christopher, House; see Old Stone House

Le Droit Building
800-812 F St. NW
HABS DC-212   pd   L

Le Droit Park Area Survey (1922 Third Street NW (Commercial Building))
HABS DC-287-B   p   H

Le Droit Park Area Survey (1901 Sixth Street NW (Commercial Building))
HABS DC-287-C   p   H

Le Droit Park Area Survey (Le Droit Park House)
603-605 U St. NW
HABS DC-287-A   p   H

Le Droit Park Area Survey
Second & Seventh Sts. & Florida Ave. & Elm St. NW
HABS DC-287   p   H

Le Droit Park House; see Le Droit Park Area Survey

Lee, Thomas Simm, House; see 3001-3009 M Street NW (Row Houses)

Lenthall Townhouses
612-614 Nineteenth St. NW-moved to 606-610 21st St
HABS DC-438   p   H

Lewis, Edward Simon, House
456 N St. SW
HABS DC-26   s p   L H

Library of Congress
First St. & Independence Ave. SE
HABS DC-351   p   H

Lihault House (Simms House)
3610 O St. NW
HABS DC-207   pd   L

Lindens, The (Hooper, Robert King, House)
2401 Kalorama Ave. (moved from MA, Danvers)
HABS MA-2-33   s p   L

Linnean Hill (Pierce, Joshua, House; Klingle House)
3545 Williamsburg Lane NW
HABS DC-168   s p   L

Litchfield House
2010 Massachusetts Ave. NW
HABS DC-321   p   H

Litwin, L. & Son; see McCutcheon Building

Lock Keeper's House (Toll Keepers Lodge)
Seventeenth St. & Constitution Ave. NW
HABS DC-36   p   L

Locker Room, The; see 501-511 Fourteenth Street NW (Commercial Building)

Loeb Company Store; see Merchants & Mechanics Savings Bank

Logan Circle (1314 Vermont Avenue NW (House))
HABS DC-339-A   p   H

Logan Circle (1502 Thirteenth Street NW (House))
HABS DC-339-B   p   H

Logan Circle (1500 Thirteenth Street NW (House))
HABS DC-339-C   p   H

Logan Circle
Vermont Ave., R. I. Ave., & Thirteenth St.
HABS DC-339   p   H

Logan Circle (1308-1344 & 1501-1523 Vermont Avenue NW (Houses))
HABS DC-339-D   p   H

Longden House
1555 Thirty-fifth St. NW
HABS DC-194   pd   L

Loughran Building (Bassin's Restaurant)
1347 E St. NW
HABS DC-392   pd   L

Lovell, Joseph, House (Lovell-Blair House)
1651 Pennsylvania Ave. NW
HABS DC-45   pd   L

Lovell-Blair House; see Lovell, Joseph, House

Lowes Palace Theatre
1306 F Street
HABS DC-378   pd   L

Lutz, John, House; see Female Union
   Benevolent Society
2919 M Street NW (House)
HABS DC-64   p   L
2922 M Street NW (House)
HABS DC-112   pd   L
3111-3113 M Street NW (House)
HABS DC-32   p   L
3115-17 M Street NW (House)
HABS DC-33   s pd   L
3001-3009 M Street NW (Row Houses)
   (Lee, Thomas Simm, House)
HABS DC-65   s p   L H
Mackall House, Old; see Mackall Square
Mackall Square (Mackall House, Old)
1633 Twenty-ninth St.
HABS DC-164   p   L H
Madison, Dolley, House; see Cutts,
   Richard, House
Mahorney-Harrington House
1423 Thirty-Sixth St. NW
HABS DC-188   pd   L
Mahorney-O'Brien House
3522 P St. NW
HABS DC-198   pd   L
Mankins, William, House
1411 Thirty-fifth St. NW
HABS DC-190   pd   L
Manning, Edward C., House (Florida State
   Society)
200 E. Capitol St. SE
HABS DC-330   pd   H
Maple Square; see Maples, The
Maples, The (Maple Square; Duncanson,
   William, House; Friendship House)
630 South Carolina Ave. SE
HABS DC-5   s p   L
Marceron, William, Building
1335 Wisconsin Ave. NW
HABS DC-107   pd   L
Marcey-Payne Building
1321 1/2-1325 1/2 Wisconsin Ave. NW
HABS DC-106   pd   L

Marine Barracks; see U.S. Marine Corp
   Commandants House

**809 Marketspace NW (Commercial
   Building)**
Pennsylvania Ave.
HABS DC-222   pd   L

**811 Marketspace NW (Commercial
   Building)**
Pennsylvania Ave.
HABS DC-232   pd   L

Mason, Gen. John, House
Analostan Island or Theodore Roosevelt
   Island
HABS DC-28   s pd   L

Mason, John Thomson, House (Quality
   Hill; Worthington House)
3425 Prospect St. NW
HABS DC-167   pd   L

Masonic Hall; see Masonic Temple
Masonic Temple (Masonic Hall;
   Lansburgh, Juilius, Furniture Company,
   Inc.)
F & Ninth Sts. NW
HABS DC-218   pd   L
Masonic Temple, Old (Naval Lodge
   Number Four)
Virginia Ave. & Fifth St. SE
HABS DC-437   p   L
Maury, John, House
302 C St. NW
HABS DC-10-4   s pd   L
Mayor-Smallwood House
324-326 Virginia Ave.
HABS DC-439   p   L
McCarthy-Sullivan House
3623 O St. NW
HABS DC-199   pd   L
McCleery House
1068 Thirtieth St. NW   .
HABS DC-162   pd   L
McCormick Apartments (National Trust
   for Historic Preservation Hq.)
1785 Massachusetts Ave. NW
HABS DC-265   pd   L
McCutcheon Building (Litwin, L. & Son)
637 Indiana Ave.
HABS DC-413   s   H
McKenny House; see Foxhall, Henry,
   House
McLean, John R., House
1500 I St. NW
HABS DC-24   pd   L
Meigs, Gen. Montgomery, House
1239 Vermont Ave. NW
HAB$ DC-50   pd   L
Memorial Continental Hall (National
   Society of the DAR Headquarters &
   Museum)
1776 D St. NW
HABS DC-282   p   H
Merchants & Mechanics Savings Bank
   (Loeb Company Store)
Seventh & G Sts. NW
HABS DC-239   p   L
Methodist Episcopal Parsonage House
1221 Twenty-eighth St. NW
HABS DC-176   pd   L
Metropolitan Bank Building
605 Fifteenth St. NW
HABS DC-347   p   H
Metropolitan Hotel (Brown's Hotel;
   Barney's Restaurent)
621 Pennsylvania Ave. NW
HABS DC-322   p   H
Metropolitian A. M. E. Church
1500 Block of M St. NW
HABS DC-352   p   H
Michler Place
F St. btw. Seventeenth & Eighteenth Sts.
   NW
HABS DC-340   p   H

Miller, Benjamin, House
1524 Twenty-eighth St. NW
HABS DC-247   pd   L
Miller House (Argyle Terrace)
2201 Massachusetts Ave. NW
HABS DC-275   pd   L
Moore, Clarence, House (Canadian
   Chancery)
1746 Massachusetts Ave. NW
HABS DC-267   pd   L
Moran, Francis B., House (Pakistani
   Chancery)
2315 Massachusetts Ave. NW
HABS DC-268   pd   L
Motion Picture Association; see
   Tuckerman, Lucius, House
Mount Vernon Apartments
922-924 Ninth St. NW
HABS DC-385   pd   L
Mount Vernon Theatre
918 Ninth St. NW
HABS DC-254   s pd   L
Mount Zion United Methodist Church
1334 Twenty-ninth St. NW
HABS DC-242   pd   L
Mountz, John, House (Eagle House)
3016 M St. NW
HABS DC-18   s p   L
Mulliken-Spragins Tenant House
Nat'l Museum of American History,
   Smithsonian Inst.
HABS DC-390   s p   L
Munsey Building
1327-1329 E St. NW
HABS DC-358   s pd   L
2817 N Street NW (House)
HABS DC-157   p   L
3038 N Street NW (House)
HABS DC-412   s   H
National Archives Building
Constitution Ave.
HABS DC-296   p   H
National Bank of Washington (National
   Bank of Washington, Washington
   Branch)
301 Seventh St. NW
HABS DC-223   pd   L
**National Bank of Washington, Georgetown
   Branch;** see Potomac Savings Bank
**National Bank of Washington, Washington
   Branch;** see National Bank of
   Washington
National Firefighting Museum; see Bank of
   Columbia
**National Portrait Gallery, Smithsonian
   Institution;** see Patent Office Building
National Presbyterian Church
Connecticut Ave. & N St. NW
HABS DC-140   p   H
**National Society of the DAR Headquarters
   & Museum;** see Memorial Continental
   Hall

National Trust for Historic Preservation; see Decatur House

National Trust for Historic Preservation Hq.; see McCormick Apartments

National Zoological Park, Adminstration Building; see Jackson Hill

Naval Lodge Number Four; see Masonic Temple, Old

Naval Observatory, Old, Building Two (U.S. Navy Bureau Med. & Surg., Potomac Annex)
Twenty-Third & E Sts. NW, (moved to Mass. Ave.)
HABS DC-341   p   H

Navy Department
Seventh St. & Constitution Ave. NW
HABS DC-324   p   H

Navy Yard, Commandants House (Quarters A)
Eighth & M St. SE
HABS DC-12   s pd L

Navy Yard Main Gate
Eighth & M Sts. SE
HABS DC-100   pd L

Navy Yard Quarters B (Second Officer's House)
E. Side of Drill Field, Washington Navy Yard
HABS DC-101   s pd L

New York Avenue, 900 & 1000 Block; see Convention Center Site, District of Columbia

1810-1820 Nineteenth St. NW (Houses) (Wood, Waddy Houses)
HABS DC-415   p   H

Nineteenth Street Baptist Church
Nineteenth & I Sts.
HABS DC-357   p   H

Ninth Street, 800 & 900 Block; see Convention Center Site, District of Columbia

616 Ninth Street NW (Commercial Building)
HABS DC-234   pd L

618 Ninth Street NW (Commercial Building)
HABS DC-231   pd L

Nordlinger Building
3128 M St. NW
HABS DC-116   pd L

156-158 North Carolina Avenue (Houses); see Southeast Area Survey

Northern Market
Seventh & O Sts. NW
HABS DC-342   p   H

2906 O Street (House)
HABS DC-371   d   H

Oak Hill (French House)
Connecticut Ave.
HABS DC-42   p   L

Oak Hill Cemetery, Chapel
3001 R St. NW
HABS DC-172   s pd L

Oak Hill Cemetery, Gatehouse
3001 R St. NW
HABS DC-249   pd L

Occidental Hotel & Restaurant
1411 Pennsylvania Ave. NW
HABS DC-325   pd L

Occidental Restaurant (Owen House)
1413 Pennsylvania Ave. NW
HABS DC-382   pd L

Octagon House (Tayloe, Col. John, House; American Institute of Architects Headquarters)
1799 New York Ave. NW
HABS DC-25   p   L

Octagon Stable, The (Tayloe, John, House; American Institute of Architects Library)
1799 New York Ave. NW
HABS DC-336   pd L H

Octagonal House; see Bebb House

Old Ebbitt Grill
1427 F St. NW
HABS DC-315   p   H

Old Executive Office Building; see State, War & Navy Building

Old Stone House (Layhman, Christopher, House)
3051 M St. NW
HABS DC-10-2   s pd L H

Owen House; see Occidental Restaurant

Owens, Isaac, House (Doorway) (Gantt-Williams House)
2806 N St. NW
HABS DC-62   p   L

Pakistani Chancery; see Moran, Francis B., House

1841 Park Road NW (House)
HABS DC-395   p   H

Parrot, Thomas, House; see Fenwick, Teresa, House

Patent Office Building (National Portrait Gallery, Smithsonian Institution)
Seventh & G Sts. NW
HABS DC-130   pd   H

Patterson, Edgar, House
1241 Thirtieth St. NW
HABS DC-177   pd L

Patterson House (Washington Club)
15 Dupont Circle NW
HABS DC-270   pd L

1922-1932 Pennsylvania Ave. NW (Commercial Bldg.)
HABS DC-334   p   H

2411 Pennsylvania Avenue NW (House)
HABS DC-27   s p   L

206 Pennsylvania Avenue SE (Commercial Building)
HABS DC-137   p   H

Pension Building
440 G St. NW
HABS DC-76   p   L H

PEPCO Power Station
922 I St. NW
HABS DC-388   pd L

Perry Building
821 Market Space at Ninth St. NW
HABS DC-221   pd L

Peruvian Embassy; see Wilkins House

Peter Houses
2618-2620 K St. NW
HABS DC-70   pd L

Peter, Thomas, House; see Tudor Place

Peterson House (House Where Lincoln Died)
516 Tenth St. NW
HABS DC-165   p   H

Philippine Embassy; see Fitzhugh, Emma S., House

Pierce, Isaac, House
711 Sixth St. SE
HABS DC-14   s p   L

Pierce, Isaac, Mill
Tilden St. & Beach Dr. NW
HABS DC-22   pd L

Pierce, Joshua, House; see Linnean Hill

Potomac Aqueduct
Thirty-sixth St. NW
HABS DC-166   s pd L H

Potomac Lodge Number Five (Doxiadas Associates)
1058 Thomas Jefferson St. NW
HABS DC-153   pd   H

Potomac Savings Bank (National Bank of Washington, Georgetown Branch)
1200 Wisconsin Ave. NW
HABS DC-323   pd L

1008 Potomac Street (House); see Southeast Area Survey

1016-1018 Potomac Street (House); see Southeast Area Survey

1061-1063 Potomac Street NW, Double House
HABS DC-152   p   L

Pullman House (Russian Embassy)
1125 Sixteenth St. NW
HABS DC-270   p   H

Quality Hill; see Mason, John Thomson, House

Quarters A; see Navy Yard, Commandants House

Raleigh's Haberdasher; see 1310 F Street NW (Commercial Building)

Ray, Alexander, House (Steedman-Ray House; F Street Club)
1925 F St. NW
HABS DC-44   p   L

Ray's Warehouse & Office (Corson & Gruman Company)
3260-3262 K St. NW
HABS DC-148   pd L

Reckert House
3232 M St. NW
HABS DC-120   pd L

Reintzel, Anthony, Building
3258 M St. NW
HABS DC-122   d   L

Republic of China Chancery; see
  Fahnestock, Gibson, House
4437 Reservoir Road NW (House)
HABS DC-126   p   L
Rhodes Tavern
601-603 Fifteenth St. NW
HABS DC-326   p   H
Richards, Zalmon, House
1300 Block Corcoran St. NW
HABS DC-343   p   H
**Riggs National Bank, Washington Loan &
  Trust Branch;** see Washington Loan &
  Trust Company
Riggs-Riley House
3038 N St. NW
HABS DC-46   s pd   L
Ringgold-Carroll House (Bacon House)
1801 F St. NW
HABS DC-391   pd   L
Rittenhouse Place; see Bellevue
Robertson, Thomas, House
3116-3118 M St. NW
HABS DC-115   pd   L
Ross & Getty Building
3005-3011 M St. NW
HABS DC-113   pd   L
Ross, Andrew, Tenant House I
1208 Thirtieth St. NW
HABS DC-435   pd   L
Ross, Andrew, Tenant House II
1210 Thirtieth St. NW
HABS DC-175   pd   L
Ruppert, Anton, House
New York Ave.
HABS DC-6   s pd   L
Russian Embassy; see Pullman House
**Scottish Rite Temple, Prince Hall
  Affiliation**
1633 Eleventh St. NW
HABS DC-346   p   H
Second Officer's House; see Navy Yard
  Quarters B
215 Second Street (House); see Southeast
  Area Survey
Service Station and Garage; see 1200 E
  Street NW (Commercial Building)
Seven Buildings
1901-1913 Pennsylvania Ave. NW
HABS DC-59   pd   L
**Seventh & D Streets NW (Commercial
  Building)**
HABS DC-233   pd   L
**Seventh & F Streets NW (Commercial
  Buildings)**
HABS DC-335   p   H
Seventh & G Streets (School); see
  Southeast Area Survey
**415 Seventh Street NW (Commercial
  Building)**
HABS DC-225   pd   L
Sevier House; see Bowie House

Sheridan, Irene, House
2211 Massachusetts Ave. NW
HABS DC-343   p   H
Simms House; see Lihault House
Sims House
2803 M St. NW
HABS DC-111   pd   L
Sixth & G Streets SW (House)
HABS DC-54   p   L
507 Sixth Street NW (Apartment House)
HABS DC-227   pd   L
**1901 Sixth Street NW (Commercial
  Building);** see Le Droit Park Area Survey
513 Sixth Street NW (House)
HABS DC-226   pd   L
306 Sixth Street NW (Houses)
HABS DC-332   p   H
601-603 Sixth Street SW (Row Houses)
HABS DC-55   p   L
Smith, Clement, House (Bodisco House)
3322 O St. NW
HABS DC-251   p   H
**Smith, Clement, House (Doorway)
  (Bodisco House)**
3322 O St. NW
HABS DC-174   p   L
Smith, Col. James, Row Houses
3255-3263 N St. NW
HABS DC-67   p   H
Smith-Morton Row House
3034 P St. NW
HABS DC-185   pd   L
Smithsonian Institution (Arts & Industries
  Building)
900 Jefferson Dr. SW
HABS DC-298   pd   H
Smithsonian Institution Building, Old
Jefferson Dr. btw. Ninth & Twelfth Sts. SW
HABS DC-141   s pd   H
Smithsonian Institution, Renwick Gallery;
  see Corcoran Art Gallery
Society of the Cincinnati Headquarters; see
  Anderson, Larz, House
Soldiers Home, Old; see U.S. Soldiers
  Home
Southeast Area Survey (101 & 122-124
  Carroll Street (House); 1008 Potomac
  Street (House); Canal Street at
  Independence Avenue (Row House);
  1016-1018 Potomac Street (House))
HABS DC-71   p   L
Southeast Area Survey (600-602 & 1100 G
  Street (House); 1002, 1006 Eye Street
  (House); 808-810, 812-814, & 1016 K
  Street (House); 817-819 L Street
  (House))
HABS DC-73   p   L
Southeast Area Survey (132-144 & 900-905
  Eleventh Street (Row Houses); 215
  Second Street (House); Seventh & G
  Streets (School); 214 First Street (House))
Sixth & G Streets (Synagogue)
HABS DC-74   p   L

Southeast Area Survey (330 & 706-708
  Virginia Avenue (Houses); 306-308,
  324-326 Virginia Avenue (Houses);
  156-158 North Carolina Avenue
  (Houses))
HABS DC-72   p   L
St. Elizabeth's Hospital
2700 Martin Luther King Jr. Ave. SE
HABS DC-349   pd   L
**St. Elizabeth's Hospital, B Building (No.
  75)**
2700 Martin Luther King Jr. Ave. SE
HABS DC-349-A   p   L
**St. Elizabeth's Hospital, C Building (No.
  73)**
2700 Martin Luther King Jr. Ave. SE
HABS DC-349-B   p   L
St. Elizabeth's Hospital, I Building (No. 95)
2700 Martin Luther King Jr. Ave. SE
HABS DC-349-C   p   L
St. Elizabeth's Hospital, J Building (No. 60)
2700 Martin Luther King Jr. Ave. SE
HABS DC-349-D   p   L
**St. Elizabeth's Hospital, K Building
  (No.66)**
2700 Martin Luther King Jr. Ave. SE
HABS DC-349-E   p   L
**St. Elizabeth's Hospital, L Building (No.
  64)**
2700 Martin Luther King Jr. Ave. SE
HABS DC-349-F   p   L
**St. Elizabeth's Hospital, M Building
  (No.72)**
2700 Martin Luther King Jr. Ave. SE
HABS DC-349-G   p   L
**St. Elizabeth's Hospital, N Building (No.
  94)**
2700 Martin Luther King Jr. Ave. SE
HABS DC-349-H   p   L
**St. Elizabeth's Hospital, P Building (No.
  100)**
2700 Martin Luther King Jr. Ave. SE
HABS DC-349-I   p   L
**St. Elizabeth's Hospital, Q Building
  (No.68)**
2700 Martin Luther King Jr. Ave. SE
HABS DC-349-J   p   L
**St. Elizabeth's Hospital, R Building (No.
  89)**
2700 Martin Luther King Jr. Ave. SE
HABS DC-349-K   p   L
St. John's Church
Sixteenth & H Sts. NW
HABS DC-19   s pd   L H
St. Luke's Episcopal Church
Fifteenth & Church Sts. NW
HABS DC-359   pd   L
St. Paul's Episcopal Church
Rock Creek Parish
HABS DC-47   s   L
Stanley, Arthur C., House
2370 Massachusetts Ave. NW
HABS DC-271   pd   L

State, War & Navy Building (Old Executive Office Building)
Pennsylvania Ave. & Seventeeth St. NW
HABS DC-290   p   H

Steedman-Ray House; see Ray, Alexander, House

Stewart, Alexander, House (Embassy of Luxembourg)
2200 Massachusetts Ave. NW
HABS DC-272   pd   L

Stoddert, Benjamin, House; see Halcyon House

Stohlman's Confectionary
1254 Wisconsin Ave. NW
HABS DC-104   pd   L

Stone, William J., Building (Frisco's)
1345 E St. NW
HABS DC-430   p   L

Street Furniture, Georgetown
Georgetown Vicinity
HABS DC-252   pd   L

Sulgrave Club; see Wadsworth, Herbert, House

Sullivan House (Buehler House)
3617 O St. NW
HABS DC-189   pd   L

Sullivan, Jeremiah, Building
1331 Thirty-fifth St. NW
HABS DC-202   pd   L

201 T Street NW (House)
HABS DC-407   p   H

Tayloe, Benjamin Ogle, House (Cameron House)
25 Madison Pl. NW
HABS DC-51   pd   L

Tayloe, Col. John, House; see Octagon House

Tayloe, John, House; see Octagon Stable, The

Temperance Fountain
Pennsylvania Ave. & Seventh St. NW
HABS DC-240   p   L

Terrell, Mary Church, House
326 T St. NW
HABS DC-367   p   H

1922 Third Street NW (Commercial Building); see Le Droit Park Area Survey

1908 Third Street NW (House)
HABS DC-406   p   H

1500 Thirteenth Street NW (House); see Logan Circle

1502 Thirteenth Street NW (House); see Logan Circle

2618 Thirtieth Street NW (House)
HABS DC-299   p   H

Thomson, John Strong, Elementary School
1024 Twelfth St. NW
HABS DC-414   p   H

Thoron, Ward, House; see Williamson, William, House (Doorway)

Tiber Island Center for Cultural & Community Act.; see Law, Thomas, House

Toll Keepers Lodge; see Lock Keeper's House

Townsend House (Cosmos Club)
2121 Massachusetts Ave. NW
HABS DC-273   pd   L

Trans Lux Theater
Fourteenth St. btw. H St. & New York Ave.
HABS DC-393   p   H

Trinidad Cable Barns
Fifteenth St. & Benning Rd. NE
HABS DC-297   p   H

Truck Company Number Four, Firehouse
219 M St. NW
HABS DC-96   p   L

True Reformer Building
1200 U St. NW
HABS DC-362   pd   L

Tuckerman, Lucius, House (Motion Picture Association)
1600 I St. NW
HABS DC-78   pd   L H

Tudor Place (Peter, Thomas, House)
1644 Thirty-first St. NW
HABS DC-171   p   H

Turkish Embassy; see Everett, Edward H., House

Twelfth Street YMCA Building (Bowen, Anthony, YMCA Building)
1816 Twelfth St. NW
HABS DC-361   pd   L

723-725 Twentieth Street (House)
HABS DC-127   p   L

1222 Twenty-eighth St. NW (Cottage)
HABS DC-149   p   L

Tyler, Grafton, Double House
1314 Thirtieth St. NW
HABS DC-178   pd   L

Union of Burma Chancery; see Hughs, Charles Evans, House

Union Station
50 Massachusetts Ave. NE
HABS DC-139   p   H

United Clay Products Co., New York Ave. Brickyard
HAER DC-2   d   H

U.S. Capitol
Intersection of N., S., & E. Capitol Sts.
HABS DC-38   p   L H

U.S. Capitol Gatehouse, Fifteenth & Const. Avenue
Moved from West entrance of the Capitol
HABS DC-31   s pd   L H

U.S. Capitol Gatehouse, Nineteenth & Const. Avenue
Moved from West entrance of the Capitol
HABS DC-35   s pd   L H

U.S. Court of Claims; see Corcoran Art Gallery

U.S. Customhouse & Post Office (U.S. Post Office, Georgetown Station)
1221 Thirty-first St. NW
HABS DC-138   s pd   L

U.S. Department of the Interior
Eighteenth & C Sts. NW
HABS DC-410   p   H

U.S. Department of the Treasury
Fifteenth St. & Pennsylvania Ave. NW
HABS DC-348   s p   H

U.S. General Post Office (U.S. Tariff Commission Building)
Btw. Seventh, Eighth, E & F Sts. NW
HABS DC-219   pd   L

U.S. General Services Administration Building (Central Heating Plant)
C & D Sts. SW
HABS DC-383   pd   L

U.S. Marine Corp Commandants House (Commandant's House; Marine Barracks)
801 G St. SE
HABS DC-134   p   H

U.S. Navy Bureau Med. & Surg., Potomac Annex; see Naval Observatory, Old, Building Two

U.S. Post Office, Georgetown Station; see U.S. Customhouse & Post Office

U.S. Soldiers Home (Soldiers Home, Old)
Rock Creek Church Rd. & Upshur St. NW
HABS DC-353   p   H

U.S. Storage Company
418 Tenth St. NW
HABS DC-311   p   H

U.S. Tariff Commission Building; see U.S. General Post Office

Van Ness Mausoleum
Thirtieth & R Sts., Oak Hill Cemetary
HABS DC-169   p   L

1314 Vermont Avenue NW (House); see Logan Circle

Vigilant Firehouse
1066 Wisconsin Ave. NW
HABS DC-98   s pd   L

Volta Bureau (Bell, Alexander Graham, Association for the Deaf)
1537 Thirty-fifth St. NW
HABS DC-245   pd   L

Wadsworth, Herbert, House (Sulgrave Club)
1801 Massachusetts Ave. NW
HABS DC-274   pd   L

Walker, David, House
932 Twenty-seventh St. NW
HABS DC-9   s p   L

Walsh-Mclean House (Indonesian Embassy)
2020 Massachusetts Ave. NW
HABS DC-266   pd   L

Wardman Building
14 K St. NW
HABS DC-409   p   H

Wardner Building (Atlas Building)
527 Ninth St. NW
HABS DC-216   pd   L

Washington Club; see Patterson House

Washington Loan & Trust Company
(Riggs National Bank, Washington Loan
& Trust Branch)
F & Ninth Sts.
HABS DC-217   pd   L

**Washington Loan & Trust Company, West
End Branch**
Seventeenth & G Sts. NW
HABS DC-344   p   H

Washington Lodge Number 15, B. P. O. E.
(Elks Lodge)
919 H St. NW
HABS DC-386   L

Washington Monument (Washington
Monument National Historic Park)
Fifteenth St. Btw. Independence &
Constitution
HABS DC-428   p   H

**Washington Monument National Historic
Park;** see Washington Monument

**Washington Terminal Company Power
Plant**
HAER DC-1   d   H

West Georgetown School
1640 Wisconsin Ave. NW
HABS DC-110   pd   L

West Washington Hotel
1238 Wisconsin Ave. NW
HABS DC-103   pd   L

Westory Building
605 Fourteenth St. NW
HABS DC-329   p   H

Wheat Row
1315, 1317, 1319, 1321 Fourth St. SW
HABS DC-10   s p   L

Wheatley, Francis, House
3060-3066 M St. NW
HABS DC-114   pd   L

Wheatley Row House
1018 Twenty-ninth St. NW
HABS DC-168   pd   L

Wheatley Town House
3043 N St. NW
HABS DC-186   pd   L

White House National Historic Park; see
White House, The (West Wing)

White House, The (West Wing) (Executive
Mansion; White House National Historic
Park)
1600 Pennsylvania Ave.
HABS DC-37   p   L

Whitelaw Apartment House
1839 Thirteenth St. NW
HABS DC-363   pd   L

Wilkins House (Austrailian Embassy;
Peruvian Embassy)
1700 Massachusetts Ave. NW
HABS DC-276   pd   L

Wilkins-Rogers Milling Company; see
Bomford's Mill

Willard Hotel
1401-1409 Pennsylvania Ave. NW
HABS DC-293   pd   H

Williams, John S., House; see
Decatur-Gunther House

Williamson, William, House (Doorway)
(Thoron, Ward, House)
2900 N St. NW
HABS DC-63   p   L

Wilson, Woodrow, House (Fairbanks,
Henry Parker, House)
2340 S St. NW
HABS DC-133   s   L

Winder Building
HABS DC-389   s p   H

Wisconsin Avenue Bridge; see High Street
Bridge

1527-1529 Wisconsin Avenue NW (House)
HABS DC-108   pd   L

1530 Wisconsin Avenue NW (House)
(Georgetown Club, The)
HABS DC-109   pd   L

Wood, Waddy Houses; see 1810-1820
Nineteenth St. NW (Houses)

Wood-Denning Twin Houses
2017-2019 Connecticut Ave. NW
HABS DC-427   p   H

Woodley
300 Cathedral Ave.
HABS DC-52   pd   L

Woodson, Carter G., House
1538 Ninth St. NW
HABS DC-369   p   H

Worthington House; see Mason, John
Thomson, House

Zepp Row House
1407 Thirty-seventh St. NW
HABS DC-208   pd   L

Florida

ALACHUA COUNTY

Cross Creek

Rawlings, Marjorie Kinnan, House
State Rt. 32 vic.
HABS FL-165   s pd   H

Gainesville

Bailey, Maj. James B., House
1121 NW Sixth St.
HABS FL-121   s d   L

Bauknight Building
SW First Ave. & S. Main St.
HABS FL-273   s   L

Gulf Oil Company Service Station
SE First Ave. & SE Second St.
HABS FL-275   s   L

Odd Fellows Home
SE Second St. & SE Eighth St.
HABS FL-285   s   L

BRADFORD COUNTY

Starke

Bradford County Courthouse
W. Call St.
HABS FL-286   s   L

DADE COUNTY

Coral Gables

**Coral Gables Entrances, Streets, Gates &
Squares**
HABS FL-335   p   H

Granada Plaza
HABS FL-333   s   H

Merrick Manor; see Merrick, Rev. Solomon
G., House

Merrick, Rev. Solomon G., House (Merrick
Manor)
HABS FL-334   s   H

Municipal Building (Police & Fire Station)
2801 Salzeda St.
HABS FL-332   s   H

Police & Fire Station; see Municipal
Building

Miami

Barnacle, The; see Munroe, Ralph M.,
House

Black, Sarah Elizabeth, House (Maud
House)
HABS FL-336   s   H

Fort Dallas, Barracks
Lummas Park
HABS FL-15-6   s pd   L

Jackson, Dr. James M., Office & Surgery
HABS FL-337   s   H

Maud House; see Black, Sarah Elizabeth,
House

Miami Beach Art Deco Historic District
HABS FL-322   p   H

Munroe, Ralph M., House (Barnacle, The)
3485 Main Hwy., Coconut Grove
HABS FL-261   s pd   H

Plymouth Congregational Church
Miami Hwy. & Devon Rd.
HABS FL-339   s   H

DUVAL COUNTY

Fort George Island
Jai, Anna, House (Slave Quarters & Driver's Cabin)
HABS FL-15-1   s p d   L

Jacksonville
Adams Building
517-527 W. Bay St.
HABS FL-341   d   H

Ahaveth Chesed Synagogue; see Oriental Greek Orthodox Church

Brewster Hospital & Nurse Training School
915 W. Monroe St.
HABS FL-348   d   H

Daniel, Dr. Richard P., House
1120 Hubbard St.
HABS FL-342   s d   H

Doty, Clarence T., House
510 Lomax St.
HABS FL-343   s d   H

El Modelo Building
501-513 W. Bay St.
HABS FL-345   d   H

LaVilla Boarding House
Houston St.
HABS FL-346   s   H

LaVilla Boarding House (New York Inn)
830 Houston St.
HABS FL-346-A   d   H

LaVilla Boarding House
836 Houston St.
HABS FL-346-C   d   H

LaVilla Boarding House (Turkish Harem)
832-834 Houston St.
HABS FL-346-B   d   H

Love-McGinnis House
2063 Oak St.
HABS FL-347   d   H

Morocco Temple
219 Newnan St.
HABS FL-349   d   H

New York Inn; see LaVilla Boarding House

Oriental Greek Orthodox Church (Ahaveth Chesed Synagogue)
723 Laura St.
HABS FL-350   s d   H

Riverside Baptist Church
2650 Park St.
HABS FL-351   d   H

St. Andrew's Parish Church
317 Florida Ave.
HABS FL-352   d   H

St. James Building
117 W. Duval St.
HABS FL-353   d   H

Turkish Harem; see LaVilla Boarding House

Union Terminal, 1897
1034-1076 W. Bay St.
HABS FL-344   d   H

Worker's Cottage
811 W. Union St.
HABS FL-354   d   H

St. Johns Bluff
Spanish-American War Fort
HABS FL-15-2   s p d   L

ESCAMBIA COUNTY

Pensacola
Axelson, Birger, House
314 S. Florida Blanca St.
HABS FL-321   p   L

Axelson, Gustave, House
318 South Florida Blanca St.
HABS FL-320   p   L

Barkley House
410 S. Florida Blanca St.
HABS FL-148   s p d   L

Barn, The
101 W. Jackson St.
HABS FL-295   p   L

Bateria de San Antonio (Fort San Carlos)
San Carlos & Hovey Rds.
HABS FL-144   s p d   L

Bear Block (Penko Building)
404 S. Palafax St.
HABS FL-201   pd   L

Boysen-Perry House (Scottish Rite Temple; Perry House)
N. Palafax & E. Wright Sts.
HABS FL-149   pd   L

Charbonier, Antonio, House
335 E. Intendencia St.
HABS FL-308   p   L

Christ Church
18 W. Wright St.
HABS FL-288   p   H

Christ Episcopal Church (Pensacola Historical Museum)
405 S. Adams St.
HABS FL-146   pd   H

Christie House
323 E. Romana St.
HABS FL-310   p   H

Dorr House, The
305 S. Adams St.
HABS FL-209   pd   L

411 East Government Street (House)
Seville Square vic.
HABS FL-306   p   L

501 East Government Street (House)
Seville Square vic.
HABS FL-307   p   L

310 East Government Street (Law Offices)
Seville Square vic.
HABS FL-305   p   L

240 East Intendencia Street (Offices)
Seville Square vic.
HABS FL-309   p   L

421 East Zaragoza Street (House)
HABS FL-314   p   L

433 East Zaragoza Street (House)
HABS FL-311   p   L

437 East Zaragoza Street (House)
HABS FL-312   p   L

Fordham House
417 E. Zaragoza St.
HABS FL-315   p   L

Fort Barrancas
San Carlos & Hovey Rds. vic.
HABS FL-143   s p d   L

Fort Redoubt, U.S. Naval Air Station
HABS FL-145   pd   L

Fort San Carlos; see Bateria de San Antonio

Hispanic Museum; see West Florida Museum of History

Information Center (Pensacola-Escambia Development Comm., Offices of)
801 N. Palafax St.
HABS FL-302   p   L

Julee Cottage
214 W. Zaragoza St.
HABS FL-198   s p d   L

Lambert House
412 E. Zaragoza St.
HABS FL-259   s p d   L

Lavalle, Charles, House
203 E. Church St. (moved from 111 W Government St)
HABS FL-199   s p d   L

Lee, William Franklin, House
420 S. Alcaniz St.
HABS FL-317   p   L

Louisville & Nashville Railroad, Marine Terminal
207 E. Main St.
HABS FL-211   pd   L

McClelland House
304 E. Government St.
HABS FL-303   p   L

McKenzie Oerting & Company Building
601 S. Palafax St.
HABS FL-206   pd   L

Merritt-Rule House (Rule House)
619 N. Baylen St.
HABS FL-296   p   L

Moreno Cottage
211 E. Zaragoza St.
HABS FL-204   pd   L

Moreno, Theodore, House
300 E. Government St.
HABS FL-202   s p d   L

1300 North Baylon Street (House)
HABS FL-299   p   L

904 North Baylon Street (House)
HABS FL-301   p   L

919 North Baylon Street (House)
HABS FL-298   p   L

Octagon, The; see U.S. Naval Air Station, Chapel & Armory

Ordnance Workshop; see U.S. Naval Air Station, General Warehouse

Payne House
1125 N. Spring St.
HABS FL-300   p   L

Penko Building; see Bear Block

Pensacola Athletic Club (Rafford Hall)
Baylon & Belmont Sts.
HABS FL-282   s   L

Pensacola Historical Museum; see Christ Episcopal Church

Pensacola Lighthouse
San Carlos Rd.
HABS FL-147   s pd   L

Pensacola-Escambia Development Comm., Offices of; see Information Center

Perry House; see Boysen-Perry House

Perry, Mary Thackeray, House
434 E. Zaragoza St.
HABS FL-203   s pd   L

Piermont-Marple House
18 W. Larva St.
HABS FL-294   p   L

Piney Woods (Sawmill)
Main & Barracks Sts.
HABS FL-316   p   L

Plaza Ferdinand VII
Palafax, Government, Jefferson, & Zaragoza Sts.
HABS FL-207   pd   L

Public Works Center; see U.S. Naval Air Station, Ship Carpenter's Workshop

Quarters Number 8; see U.S. Naval Air Station, Captain's Quarters

Quina, Desiderio, House
206 S. Alcaniz St.
HABS FL-196   s pd   L

Rafford Hall; see Pensacola Athletic Club

Rule House; see Merritt-Rule House

Sawmill; see Piney Woods

Scottish Rite Temple; see Boysen-Perry House

Seville Square
Adams, Government, Alcaniz & Zaragoza Sts.
HABS FL-208   pd   L

Smith House
300 S. Alcaniz St.
HABS FL-319   p   L

St. Michael's Creole Benevolent Association
410 E. Government St.
HABS FL-210   pd   L

Steamboat House
308 E. Government St.
HABS FL-304   p   L

Turner, Charles H., House
823 N. Baylen St.
HABS FL-297   p   L

U.S. Naval Air Sta., U.S. Schools of Photography
HABS FL-257   p   L

U.S. Naval Air Station, Aircraft Repair Shop
HABS FL-250   p   L

U.S. Naval Air Station, Bower's Store
HABS FL-245   p   L

U.S. Naval Air Station, Brig, Building 8
HABS FL-243   pd   L

U.S. Naval Air Station, Buildings 144 & 238
HAER FL-1   pd   L

U.S. Naval Air Station, Captain's Quarters (Quarters Number 8)
HABS FL-219   s pd   L

U.S. Naval Air Station, Carriage House
HABS FL-216   p   L

U.S. Naval Air Station, Chapel & Armory (Octagon, The)
Central Ave.
HABS FL-238   s pd   L

U.S. Naval Air Station, Coal Shed
HABS FL-247   p   L

U.S. Naval Air Station, Commandant's Offices
HABS FL-214   s pd   L

U.S. Naval Air Station, Commandant's Quarters
HABS FL-215   s pd   L

U.S. Naval Air Station, Foundry
HABS FL-248   p   L

U.S. Naval Air Station, General Warehouse (Ordnance Workshop)
West Ave.
HABS FL-213   s pd   L

U.S. Naval Air Station, Marine Barracks
HABS FL-246   p   L

U.S. Naval Air Station, Navy Hospital Wall, Early
HABS FL-258   p   L

U.S. Naval Air Station, Navy Yard Gate
South & West Aves.
HABS FL-142   s pd   L

U.S. Naval Air Station, Plant Maintenance Shop
HABS FL-241   pd   L

U.S. Naval Air Station, Power Plant
HABS FL-249   p   L

U.S. Naval Air Station, Quarters Number 34
HABS FL-251   p   L

U.S. Naval Air Station, Quarters Number 35
HABS FL-252   p   L

U.S. Naval Air Station, Quarters Number 39
HABS FL-253   p   L

U.S. Naval Air Station, Quarters Number 43
HABS FL-254   p   L

U.S. Naval Air Station, Quarters Number 47
HABS FL-256   p   L

U.S. Naval Air Station, Quarters Number 46
HABS FL-255   p   L

U.S. Naval Air Station, Seaplane Hangar
HABS FL-242   pd   L

U.S. Naval Air Station, Senior Officers' Quarters
HABS FL-234   pd   L

U.S. Naval Air Station, Senior Officers' Quarters
HABS FL-244   p   L

U.S. Naval Air Station, Ship Carpenter's Workshop (Public Works Center)
HABS FL-236   s pd   L

U.S. Naval Air Station, Stable
HABS FL-218   p   L

U.S. Naval Air Station, Storehouse Building
HABS FL-237   pd   L

U.S. Naval Air Station, Wet Basin
HABS FL-240   s pd   L

Walton, Dorothy, House
221 E. Zaragoza St. (moved from 137 W. Romana St.)
HABS FL-205   s pd   L

Warehouse
E. Main St.
HABS FL-313   p   L

Weis, C. A. Jr., House
312 W. Blount St.
HABS FL-290   p   L

West Florida Museum of History (Hispanic Museum)
200 E. Zaragoza St.
HABS FL-318   p   L

14 West Gadsden Street (House)
N. Hill vic.
HABS FL-293   p   L

284 West Gonzalez Street (House)
N. Hill vic.
HABS FL-292   p   L

123 West Lloyd Street (House)
N. Hill vic.
HABS FL-291   p   L

Wright, Isaac, House
431 E. Zaragoza St.
HABS FL-200   s pd   L

Yniestra House
1200 N. Palafax St.
HABS FL-289   p   L

FLAGLER COUNTY

St. Augustine vic.

Cherokee Grove
Mantanzas River vic.
HABS FL-235   s   L

FRANKLIN COUNTY

Apalachicola

Raney, David G., House; see Raney House, The

Raney House, The (Raney, David G., House)
Market & F Sts.
HABS FL-150   s p d   L H

Trinity Episcopal Church
Gorrie Square
HABS FL-151   p d   L

GADSDEN COUNTY

Quincy

Bruce, William & Hector, House
U.S. Hwy. 90 (Chattahoochee Hwy.)
HABS FL-152   p d   L

White, Judge P. W., House
212 N. Madison St.
HABS FL-153   p d   L

HAMILTON COUNTY

White Springs

Bath House
Spring St.
HABS FL-277   s   L

HILLSBOROUGH COUNTY

Tampa

Ybor City
HABS FL-324   s p d   H

Tampa, Ybor City

Centro Espanol
1500 Seventh Ave.
HABS FL-331   p   H

Cherokee Club; see El Pasaje

Del Rio, Antonio, Building
1514, 1516, 1518 Eighth Ave.
HABS FL-265   s p d   H

1822 East Fourteenth Street (House)
HABS FL-326   p   H

1504 East Ninth Avenue (Commercial Building)
HABS FL-325   p   H

El Dorado (Scaglione Hotel)
1804 Fourteenth St. (Avenida Republica de Cuba)
HABS FL-264   s d   H

El Pasaje (Cherokee Club)
1318 Ninth & Fourteenth Sts.
HABS FL-271   s p d   H

Gutierrez Building
1603 Seventh Ave.
HABS FL-263   s p d   H

Leibovitz Building
1818 Seventh Ave. (East Broadway)
HABS FL-266   s d   H

Marcos, B. F., Building
1610 E. Seventh Ave.
HABS FL-267   s p d   H

Mayo, E., Building
1518 E. Seventh Ave.
HABS FL-268   s p d   H

1913 North Howard Street (Commercial)
HABS FL-330   p   H

1402 North Nineteenth Street (Commercial)
HABS FL-327   p   H

Scaglione Hotel; see El Dorado

Scozzari Building
1901 Seventh Ave.
HABS FL-269   s p d   H

Simovitz Building
2113 W. Main St.
HABS FL-328   p   H

Warren Building
2117 W. Main St.
HABS FL-329   p   H

Ybor Cigar Factory
1916 Avenida Republica de Cuba
HABS FL-270   s p d   H

JACKSON COUNTY

Marianna

Ely, Francis R., House
242 W. Lafayette St.
HABS FL-154   p d   L

JEFFERSON COUNTY

Capps

May, Asa, House
U.S. Rt. 19
HABS FL-284   s   L

Monticello

Monticello Presbyterian Church
Dogwood & Waukeenia Sts.
HABS FL-155   p d   L

Wirick-Simmons House
Jefferson & Pearl Sts.
HABS FL-156   s   L

LEON COUNTY

Tallahassee

Bank of Florida
Calhoun & Appalachia Pky. (moved from Adams St.)
HABS FL-159   s p d   L

Bethel Baptist Church
224 North Blvd.
HABS FL-287   s   L

Butler, Robert, House
3502 Old Bainbridge Rd.
HABS FL-157   p d   L

Chaires, Benjamin, House; see Columns, The

Columns, The (Chaires, Benjamin, House)
Park & Adams Sts.
HABS FL-158   s p d   L

First Presbyterian Church
Adams & Park Sts.
HABS FL-162   p d   L

Kirksey, James, House
325 N. Calhoun St.
HABS FL-161   p d   L

Randall, Thomas, House
434 North Calhoun St.
HABS FL-160   p d   L

Tallahassee vic.

Goodwood
HABS FL-19   s p d   L

MADISON COUNTY

Madison

Wardlaw-Smith House
Washington St.
HABS FL-163   s p d   L

MANATEE COUNTY

Ellenton

Gamble Mansion
Manatee River vic.
HABS FL-112   s p d   L

MONROE COUNTY

Dry Tortugas

Fort Jefferson (Fort Jefferson National Monument)
HABS FL-44   p d   H

Fort Jefferson, Enlisted Mens' Quarters
HABS FL-44-A   p   H

Fort Jefferson, Hot Shot Furnace
HABS FL-44-B   p   H

Fort Jefferson National Monument; see Fort Jefferson

Fort Jefferson, Officers' Quarters
HABS FL-44-C   p   H

Fort Jefferson, Powder Magazine
HABS FL-44-D   p   H

Key West

Audubon House; see Geiger, John, House

Bartlum, Capt. John, House
730 Eaton St.
HABS FL-185   p d   L

Convent of Mary Immaculate
600 Truman Ave.
HABS FL-184   p d   L

El Patio Apartments; see Gato, Eduardo H., House

Fort Taylor
Whitehead Spit vic.
HABS FL-283   p d   L

Gato, Eduardo H., House (Mercedes
Hospital; El Patio Apartments)
1209 Virginia St.
HABS FL-186   pd   L

Geiger, John, House (Audubon House)
205 Whitehead St.
HABS FL-177   s pd   L

Kemp, Richard Moore, House
601 Caroline St.
HABS FL-180   s pd   L

Key West Post Office (U.S. Custom House;
U.S. Courthouse & Lighthouse Quarters;
Post Office & Customs House, Old)
Front St.
HABS FL-187   pd   L

Lowe, Capt. John Jr., House
620 Southard St.
HABS FL-181   s p   L

**Mallory Steamship Company Ticket
Office;** see Southern Express Company

Memorial to the U.S. Battleship Maine
Key West Cemetery
HABS FL-191   d   L

Mercedes Hospital; see Gato, Eduardo H.,
House

Perky Bat Tower
Airport Rd.
HABS FL-193   pd   L

Porter, Commodore, Apartments; see
Webb-Porter House

Porter, Dr. Joseph Y., II, House; see
Webb-Porter House

Post Office & Customs House, Old; see Key
West Post Office

Roberts, Capt. Richard, House
408 William St.
HABS FL-178   s pd   L

Roberts, George Francis Bartlum, House
412 William St.
HABS FL-183   s pd   L

Roberts, Samuel, House
1025 Fleming St.
HABS FL-182   s pd   L

Sand Key Lighthouse
Sand Key
HABS FL-189   pd   L

Southern Express Company (Mallory
Steamship Company Ticket Office)
Mallory Square
HABS FL-174   s pd   L

**Tift & Company, Ships Chandlery &
Icehouse**
Mallory Square
HABS FL-176   s pd   L

Tift-Hemingway House
907 Whitehead St.
HABS FL-179   s pd   L

U.S. Courthouse & Lighthouse Quarters;
see Key West Post Office

U.S. Custom House; see Key West Post
Office

U.S. Marine Hospital
Emma St.
HABS FL-194   pd   L

U.S. Navy Coal Depot & Storehouse
Front & Whitehead Sts.
HABS FL-190   pd   L

Wall & Company Warehouse
Wall & Exchange Sts.
HABS FL-175   s pd   L

Watlington, Capt. Francis, House
322 Duval St.
HABS FL-192   pd   L

Webb-Porter House (Porter, Dr. Joseph Y.,
II, House; Porter, Commodore,
Apartments)
429 Caroline St.
HABS FL-188   pd   L

NASSAU COUNTY

Fernandina Beach

Custom House & Courthouse; see U.S. Post
Office

Fernandina Depot, Old
100 Atlantic Ave.
HABS FL-280   s   d   H

First Presbyterian Church
19 N. Sixth St.
HABS FL-278   s   d   H

Florida House
Twenty & Twenty-third S. Third St.
HABS FL-356   d   H

Lesesne House
415 Atlantic Ave.
HABS FL-357   d   H

Lewis, C. W., House
27 S. Seventh St.
HABS FL-279   s   d   H

Nassau County Courthouse
Atlantic Ave.
HABS FL-358   pd   H

St. Peter's Parish (Episcopal Church)
Eighth St. & Atlantic Ave.
HABS FL-281   s   d   H

U.S. Post Office (Custom House &
Courthouse)
400 Atlantic Ave.
HABS FL-359   d   H

Villa Las Palmas
315 Alachua Ave.
HABS FL-360   d   H

ORANGE COUNTY

Orlando

Atlantic Coastline Railroad Station
(Orlando Train Station)
1402 Sligh Blvd.
HABS FL-260   s   L

Orlando Train Station; see Atlantic
Coastline Railroad Station

PALM BEACH COUNTY

Manalapan

Vanderbilt, Harold S., House
1100 S. Ocean Blvd.
HABS FL-234   d   L

Palm Beach

Banyans, The; see Brelsford House

Bethesda-By-The-Sea
549 N. Lake Trail
HABS FL-222   pd   L

Bingham-Blossom House
1250 S. Ocean Blvd.
HABS FL-221   pd   L

Bolton, Chester C., House (Casa Apava)
1300 Ocean Blvd.
HABS FL-232   pd   L

Breakers Hotel, Cottage (Spray, The)
S. County Rd.
HABS FL-223   pd   L

Breakers Hotel, The
S. County Rd.
HABS FL-228   pd   L

Brelsford House (Banyans, The)
1 S. Lake Trail
HABS FL-225   pd   L

Casa Apava; see Bolton, Chester C., House

Casa Della Porta; see McAneeny-Howerd
House

Duck's Nest; see Maddock, Henry, House

Everglades Club
HABS FL-226   pd   L

Flagler, Henry M., Mansion (Whitehall)
Whitehall Way
HABS FL-224   s pd   L

Maddock, Henry, House (Duck's Nest)
561 N. Lake Trail
HABS FL-220   pd   L

Mar-A-Lago
1100 S. Ocean Blvd.
HABS FL-195   pd   L

McAneeny-Howerdd House (Casa Della
Porta)
195 Via Del Mar
HABS FL-231   pd   L

Paramount Theatre
Sunrise Ave. & N. County Rd.
HABS FL-230   pd   L

Rasmussen-Donahue House
780 S. Ocean Blvd.
HABS FL-229   pd   L

Seaboard Airline Railway Station
(Seaboard Coast Line Railroad Passenger
Station)
Datura St. & Tamarind Ave.
HABS FL-233   pd   L

**Seaboard Coast Line Railroad Passenger
Station;** see Seaboard Airline Railway
Station

Singer, Paris, Apartment
HABS FL-227   pd   L

Spray, The; see Breakers Hotel, Cottage

Whitehall; see Flagler, Henry M., Mansion

POLK COUNTY

Auburndale

Patterson, Dr. John, House
Northeast Ariana Estates
HABS FL-197   s   L

Lakeland

Esplanade; see Florida Southern College,
Walkway
Florida Southern College
HABS FL-323   d   H
Florida Southern College, Annie Pfeiffer
Chapel
HABS FL-323-A   p   H
Florida Southern College,
Auditorium-Music Building
HABS FL-323-H   p   H
Florida Southern College, Danforth Chapel
HABS FL-323-B   p   H
Florida Southern College, E. T. Rovy
Library
HABS FL-323-D   p   H
Florida Southern College, Ordway Arts
Building
HABS FL-323-G   p   H
Florida Southern College, Polk County
Science Bldg.
HABS FL-323-F   p   H
Florida Southern College, Walkway
(Esplanade)
HABS FL-323-E   p   H
Florida Southern College, Watson Admin.
Building
HABS FL-323-C   p   H

St. Augustine

De Mesa-Sanchez House (Spanish Inn,
Old)
43 Saint George St.
HABS FL-135   s pd   L
Spanish Inn, Old; see De Mesa-Sanchez
House

SEMINOLE COUNTY

Altamonte Springs

Inside-Outside House; see Pierce, Capt.,
House
North J. Bradlee - S. Maxwell McIntire
Cottage
State Rt. 436
HABS FL-361   d   H
Pierce, Capt., House (Inside-Outside
House)
Boston Ave.
HABS FL-274   s   L

ST. JOHNS COUNTY

Rattlesnake Island

Fort Matanzas
HABS FL-15-5   p   H

St. Augustine

Alcazar Hotel
75 King St.
HABS FL-168   pd   H
Arrivas, Don Raimundo, House
44 S. George St.
HABS FL-122   s pd   L
Cannonball House; see Tovar House
Canova-DeMedicis House
46 Bridge St.
HABS FL-127   s pd   L
Casa Monica (Cordova Hotel)
King & Cordova Sts.
HABS FL-169   pd   L
Castillo de San Marcos (Fort Marion;
Spanish Castle San Marco)
HABS FL-17   p   H
Cathedral, The
Saint George & Cathedral Sts.
HABS FL-15-7   s pd   L
City Gate
Orange St.
HABS FL-15-3   s pd   L
City Library (Spanish House; Segui-Smith
House)
Auiles St. & Artillery Lane
HABS FL-13   s pd   L
Cordova Hotel; see Casa Monica
Fatio House; see Ximenez-Fatio House
Fernandez-Llambias House
31 Saint Francis St.
HABS FL-171   pd   L
Flagler Memorial Presbyterian Church
Valencia & Sevilla Sts.
HABS FL-170   pd   L
Flagler Memorial Presbyterian Church,
Parsonage
39 Sevilla St.
HABS FL-172   pd   L
Fornells, Don Pedro, House
62 Spanish St.
HABS FL-137   s pd   L
Fort Marion; see Castillo de San Marcos
Garcia-Dummitt House
279 Saint George St.
HABS FL-129   s pd   L
Gonzalez-Alvarez House (Oldest House,
The)
14 Saint Francis St.
HABS FL-138   s pd   L
Grace Methodist Church (Grace Methodist
Episcopal Church)
Carrera & Cordova Sts.
HABS FL-167   pd   L
Grace Methodist Episcopal Church; see
Grace Methodist Church
Horruytiner, Don Pedro, House
214 Saint George St.
HABS FL-130   s pd   L
Hotel Ponce De Leon
King, Valencia, Sevilla & Cordova Sts.
HABS FL-173   pd   H

Huertas-Canova House (Prince Murat
House)
250 Saint George St.
HABS FL-14   s pd   L
Long-Sanchez House
43 Marine St.
HABS FL-132   s pd   L
Marin, Francisco, House
47 Marine St.
HABS FL-166   pd   L
Minorcan Chapel
39 Saint George St.
HABS FL-134   s pd   L
Oldest House, The; see Gonzalez-Alvarez
House
O'Reilly, Don Miguelde, House
32 Auiles St.
HABS FL-123   s pd   L
Ortega-MacMillan House
224 Saint George St.
HABS FL-124   s pd   L
Papy, Gaspar, House
36 Aviles St.
HABS FL-164   pd   L
Paredes, Don Juan, House
54 Saint George St.
HABS FL-136   pd   L
Perez-Sanchez House
101 Charlotte St.
HABS FL-128   s pd   L
Pomar House
Treasury St.
HABS FL-139   s d   H
Poujoud, Augustus, House (Poujoud-Slater
House)
105-107 Saint George St.
HABS FL-125   s pd   L
Poujoud-Slater House; see Poujoud,
Augustus, House
Prince Murat House; see Huertas-Canova
House
Public Market
Charlotte St.
HABS FL-131   s pd   L
Rodriguez-Avero-Sanchez House
52 Saint George St.
HABS FL-126   s pd   L
Schoolhouse, Old
14 Saint George St.
HABS FL-115   s pd   L
Segui-Smith House; see City Library
Solana, Don Manuel, House
20 Charlotte St.
HABS FL-133   s pd   L
Spanish Castle San Marco; see Castillo de
San Marcos

Spanish House; see City Library

Spanish Treasury, Old (Women's Exchange)
143 Saint George & Treasury Sts.
HABS FL-119   s pd   L

Tovar House (Cannonball House)
22 Saint Francis St.
HABS FL-140   s pd   L

Triay, Antonio J., House
42 Spanish St.
HABS FL-141   s pd   L

Trinity Church (Episcopal)
Saint George & King Sts.
HABS FL-110   s p   L

Women's Exchange; see Spanish Treasury, Old

Ximenez-Fatio House (Fatio House)
22 Auiles St.
HABS FL-116   s pd   L

TAYLOR COUNTY
Hampton Springs vic.
Whiddon Log Cabin
U.S. Rt. 98
HABS FL-276   s   L

Georgia

BALDWIN COUNTY

Milledgeville
Bell, Col. Frank, House
HABS GA-192   pd   L
Cedars, The
Columbia St.
HABS GA-191   L
Conn House
Wilkinson & Green Sts.
HABS GA-132   pd   L
Governor's Mansion, Old
Clark & Green Sts.
HABS GA-156   pd   L
Hotel, Old; see Stetson-Sanford House
Milledgeville State Hospital, Central Building
HABS GA-1156   pd   L
State Capitol, Old
HABS GA-137   pd   L
Stetson-Sanford House (Hotel, Old)
Wilkinson & Hancock Sts.
HABS GA-136   pd   L
Williams-Ferguson House
Liberty & Washington Sts.
HABS GA-134   pd   L
Williams-Orme-Crawford House
211 Liberty St.
HABS GA-133   pd   L

Milledgeville vic.
Boykin Hall (Whitaker House; Hinton Hall)
HABS GA-170   pd   L
Hinton Hall; see Boykin Hall
Johnson-Ennis, Gov., House (Rockwell House)
HABS GA-135   pd   L
Lockerly House; see Tucker, Daniel R., House
Mitchell-McComb House; see Mount Nebo House
Mount Nebo House (Mitchell-McComb House)
Rt. 22
HABS GA-14-4   s pd   L
Rockwell House; see Johnson-Ennis, Gov., House

Tucker, Daniel R., House (Lockerly House; Tucker-Hollinshead-Hatcher House)
HABS GA-1151   pd   L
Tucker-Hollinshead-Hatcher House; see Tucker, Daniel R., House
Westover
Old Eaton Rd.
HABS GA-14-31   s pd   L
Whitaker House; see Boykin Hall

BARROW COUNTY

Hoschton vic.
Cochran Log House
HABS GA-14-23   s pd   L

BIBB COUNTY

Macon
Andrews House
110 Third St.
HABS GA-141   pd   L
Baber House (Clinic Hospital; Lamar-Cobb House)
Walnut St.
HABS GA-190   pd   L
Bibb County Academy; see Callaway House
Birdsey House (Coleman-Solomon-Speer House)
Vineville Ave.
HABS GA-165   pd   L
Callaway House (Macon Hospital; Bibb County Academy)
Pine St.
HABS GA-189   pd   L
Canning House (Holt, Asa, House)
854-56 Mulberry St.
HABS GA-142   pd   L
Chapman-Green House; see Poe House
Christ Church Rectory, Old
211 Walnut St.
HABS GA-1100   pd   L
Clinic Hospital; see Baber House
Coleman House (Cowles-Coleman-O'Neal House; Overlook)
HABS GA-1124   d   L

Coleman-Solomon-Speer House; see Birdsey House
Cowles, Jerry, House (Jones-Walker-Scottish Rite-Masons-Sams House)
4596 Rivoli Dr. (moved from 519 Walnut St.)
HABS GA-14-27   s pd   L
Cowles-Coleman-O'Neal House; see Coleman House
Emerson & Holmes Building
556 Mulberry St.
HABS GA-195   pd   L
Holt, Asa, House; see Canning House
Holt, Thaddeus Goode, House; see Holt-Peeler House
Holt-Peeler House (Holt, Thaddeus Goode, House)
HABS GA-144   pd   L
Jones-Walker-Scottish Rite-Masons-Sams House; see Cowles, Jerry, House
Lamar-Cobb House; see Baber House
Macon Hospital; see Callaway House
Overlook; see Coleman House
Poe House (Chapman-Green House)
Washington Ave. & Poplar St.
HABS GA-139   pd   L
Raines, Cadwalader, House (Raines-Jones-Miller-Carmichael House)
1183 Georgia Ave.
HABS GA-145   pd   L
Raines-Jones-Miller-Carmichael House; see Raines, Cadwalader, House
Slade Houses (State Bank, Old)
453 Walnut St.
HABS GA-168   pd   L
Small, Ralph, House
115 Rogers Ave.
HABS GA-143   pd   L
State Bank, Old; see Slade Houses

BURKE COUNTY

Waynesboro
Munnerlyn House (Waynesboro Inn, The)
HABS GA-2120   pd   L
Waynesboro Inn, The; see Munnerlyn House

CAMDEN COUNTY

Cumberland Island

Carnegie Family Mansion; see Dungeness
Dungeness (Carnegie Family Mansion)
HABS GA-2160   pd   L

Greene, Gen. Nathaniel, Cottage
HABS GA-2161   pd   L

St. Mary's

Orange Hall
HABS GA-14-16   s pd   L

St. Mary's vic.

Santa Maria Mission (Ruins)
HABS GA-14-18   s pd   L

Woodbine vic.

Refuge Plantation
Satilla River
HABS GA-248   pd   L

CHATHAM COUNTY

Savannah

118 & 124 East Harris Street (House)
HABS GA-24   pd   L
312 & 314 Broughton Street (Houses)
HABS GA-240   pd   L
127-129 Abercorn Street (Carriage House)
HABS GA-1200-A   p   H
330 Abercorn Street (Carriage House)
HABS GA-1201-A   p   H
Abercorn Street (Commerical Buildings)
HABS GA-1205   p   H
127-129 Abercorn Street (House)
HABS GA-1200   p   H
330 Abercorn Street (House) (Turner,
    Hamilton, House)
HABS GA-1201   p   H
918 Abercorn Street (House); see Savannah
    Victorian Historic District
Alee Temple; see Mercer-Wilder House
Anderson-Leslie House; see Leslie House
Arnold House, Old
128 State St.
HABS GA-289   pd   L
Battersby-Hartridge-Anderson House
119 E. Charlton St.
HABS GA-254   pd   L
Bay Street (Commerical Buildings)
HABS GA-1202   p   H
Bernard Street (Commerical Buildings)
HABS GA-1206   p   H
Bonticou, Timothy, Double House
419-421 E. Broughton Lane
HABS GA-1176   s pd   H
Bulloch-Stoddard-Cumming House; see
    Cunningham House (Portico)
**Central of Georgia
    Railroad:Administration Bldg.**
W. Broad St.
HABS GA-213-C   p   H

**Central of Georgia Railroad:Brick Arch
    Viaduct**
HABS GA-213
HAER GA-3   d   L
**Central of Georgia Railroad:Brick Arch
    Viaduct**
HABS GA-213-A
HAER GA-4   d   L
Central of Georgia Railroad:Bridge
HABS GA-213-A
HAER GA-4   pd   L
Central of Georgia Railroad:Bridge
HABS GA-213
HAER GA-3   pd   L
Central of Georgia Railroad:Repair Shops
HAER GA-1   d   L
**Central of Georgia Railroad:Station &
    Train Shed**
HAER GA-2   d   L
Central of Georgia Railroad:Train Shed
W. Broad St.
HABS GA-213-B   p   H
Champion-McAlpin-Fowlkes House
230 Barnard St.
HABS GA-288   pd   L
Charlton, Dr., House
220 E. Ogelthorpe
HABS GA-286   pd   L
Chippewa Square Monument
HABS GA-1179   p   H
Christ Church
Bull St. on Johnson Sq.
HABS GA-236-A   pd   L H
Christ Church (Episcopal)
Bull St. on Johnson Sq.
HABS GA-236   L
Clark, William, House (Doorway)
107 Oglethorpe St.
HABS GA-214   pd   L
Cluskey, Charles B., Embankment Stores
HABS GA-1180   s pd   H
Cunningham House (Portico)
    (Bulloch-Stoddard-Cumming House)
101 E. Oglethorpe St.
HABS GA-257   pd   L
Custom House
Bay & Bull Sts.
HABS GA-215   pd   L

Davenport, Isaiah, House
324 E. State St.
HABS GA-14-8   s pd   L H
Denis, Richard, Houses
25-27 Lincoln St.
HABS GA-2143   pd   L
Dent House
Liberty & Bernard Sts.
HABS GA-1210   p   H
1002 Drayton Street (House); see Savannah
    Victorian Historic District
818 Drayton Street (House); see Savannah
    Victorian Historic District

**East & West River Streets (Commerical
    Buildings)**
HABS GA-1203   p   H
19 East Bay Street (Bank)
HABS GA-21-31   pd   L
313 East Bolton Street (House); see
    Savannah Victorian Historic District
321 East Bolton Street (House); see
    Savannah Victorian Historic District
East Broad Street (Commercial Buildings)
HABS GA-1207   p   H
103 East Duffy Lane (House); see
    Savannah Victorian Historic District
201-203 East Duffy Street (House); see
    Savannah Victorian Historic District
404-410 East Duffy Street (House); see
    Savannah Victorian Historic District
525-527-529 East Gwinnett Lane (House);
    see Savannah Victorian Historic District
224 East Henry Street (House); see
    Savannah Victorian Historic District
301-303 East Henry Street (House); see
    Savannah Victorian Historic District
521 East Henry Street (House); see
    Savannah Victorian Historic District
14 East Oglethorpe Street (House)
HABS GA-1212   p   H
18 East Oglethorpe Street (House)
HABS GA-1213   p   H
115 East Park Avenue (House); see
    Savannah Victorian Historic District
103-109 East President Street (House)
HABS GA-1215   p   H
300-306 East Waldburg Street (House); see
    Savannah Victorian Historic District
414-416 East Waldburg Street (House); see
    Savannah Victorian Historic District
**203 East York Street (House, Iron
    Balustrade)**
HABS GA-287   pd   L
Factors Walk (Commercial Buildings)
HABS GA-1209   p   H
Factor's Warehouse
River St. W.
HABS GA-2144   pd   L
First African Baptist Church
Bryant, Montgomery & Saint Julian Sts.
HABS GA-276   pd   L
First Baptist Church
223 Bull St.
HABS GA-1182   p   H

Fort Savannah; see Fort Wayne

Fort Wayne (Fort Savannah)
E. Bay St. vic.
HABS GA-23.   pd   L

Gibbons Block
Congress, Saint Julian, Barnard, Whitaker
Sts.
HABS GA-2130   pd   L

Green, Charles, House; see Green-Meldrim
House

Greene, Nathaniel, Monument
Johnson Sq.
HABS GA-1183   p   H

Green-Meldrim House (Sherman's
    Headquarters; Green, Charles, House)
Bull St.
HABS GA-222   s p d   L H

Habersham House (Pink House)
Reynolds Sq. vic.
HABS GA-238   p d   L

Hampton Lillibridge House Number 1
310 E. Bryan St.
HABS GA-1185   s p d   H

Hampton Lillibridge House Number 2
312 E. Bryan St.
HABS GA-1186   s p   H

Houston-Screven House (Johnston House)
HABS GA-246   p d   L

Independent Presbyterian Church
Bull & Oglethorpe Sts.
HABS GA-237   p d   L H

Johnston House; see Houston-Screven
    House

Le Page House (Entrance)
112 W. Hull St.
HABS GA-259   p d   L

Leslie House (Anderson-Leslie House)
Bull & Oglethorpe Sts.
HABS GA-1173   p   H

Lincoln Street (Commerical Buildings)
HABS GA-1208   p   H

Low House
329 Abercorn St.
HABS GA-210   p d   L

Low, Juliette G., House; see Wayne-Gordon
    House

Lufborrow-Ravennel House
McDonough & Floyd Sts.
HABS GA-2139   p d   L

Mackay House
125 E. Congress St.
HABS GA-2138   p d   L

McDonough Row Troup Trust
412-24 E. Macon St.
HABS GA-1197   p   H

McIntosh, Gen. Lachlan, House
110 E. Oglethorpe
HABS GA-22   p d   L

Mercer-Wilder Carriage House
429 Bull St.
HABS GA-1189-A   p   H

Mercer-Wilder House (Alee Temple)
429 Bull St.
HABS GA-1189   p d   H

Michva Israel Synagogue
Bull St. & Montery Sq.
HABS GA-1190   p   H

Minis, Abram, Carriage House
204 E. Jones St.
HABS GA-281-A   p   H

Minis, Abram, House (Red Cross)
204 E. Jones St.
HABS GA-281   p   H

Minis House
204 Hull St.
HABS GA-14-28   s p d   L

Newspaper Office
17 E. Bay St.
HABS GA-2131   p d   L

Pink House; see Habersham House

Red Cross; see Minis, Abram, House

Reid Servants' & Carriage House
118 E. State St. (rear lot)
HABS GA-2137   p d   L

Remshart, William, Row Houses
108 W. Jones St.
HABS GA-1191   s p d   H

Richardson-Maxwell-Owen-Thomas House
124 Abercorn St.
HABS GA-14-9   s p d   L

Roberts, Hiram, House (Sturges, Oliver,
    House; Sturges-Roberts House)
27 Abercorn St.
HABS GA-25   p d   L

Row Houses
101-129 Gordon St.
HABS GA-2145   p   L

Savannah Cotton Exchange
100 E. Bay St.
HABS GA-1194   p   H

Savannah Vicorian Historict District
Gwinnett, E. Broad, W. Broad St. &
    Anderson La.
HABS GA-1169   s p d   L

Savannah Victorian Historic District (521
    East Henry Street (House))
HABS GA-1169-W   s p d   L

Savannah Victorian Historic District (321
    East Bolton Street (House))
HABS GA-1169-L   s p d   L

Savannah Victorian Historic District
    (300-306 East Waldburg Street (House))
HABS GA-1169-N   s p d   L

Savannah Victorian Historic District
    (301-305 West Duffy Street (House))
HABS GA-1169-G   s p d   L

Savannah Victorian Historic District
    (210-212 West Henry Street (House))
HABS GA-1169-H   s p d   L

Savannah Victorian Historic District (207
    West Waldburg Street (House))
HABS GA-1169-D   s p d   L

Savannah Victorian Historic District
    (525-527-529 East Gwinnett Lane
    (House))
HABS GA-1169-I   s d   L

Savannah Victorian Historic District (818
    Drayton Street (House))
HABS GA-1169-J   s p d   L

Savannah Victorian Historic District
    (301-303 East Henry Street (House))
HABS GA-1169-V   s p d   L

Savannah Victorian Historic District (115
    East Park Avenue (House))
HABS GA-1169-Q   s p d   L

Savannah Victorian Historic District (215
    West Gwinnett Street (House))
HABS GA-1169-A   s p d   L

Savannah Victorian Historic District (103
    East Duffy Lane (House))
HABS GA-1169-R   s d   L

Savannah Victorian Historic District (1002
    Drayton Street (House))
HABS GA-1169-P   s p d   L

Savannah Victorian Historic District (313
    East Bolton Street (House))
HABS GA-1169-K   s p d   L

Savannah Victorian Historic District (918
    Abercorn Street (House))
HABS GA-1169-M   s p d   L

Savannah Victorian Historic District (213
    West Bolton Street (House))
HABS GA-1169-B   s p d   L

Savannah Victorian Historic District (107
    West Duffy Street (House))
HABS GA-1169-F   s p d   L

Savannah Victorian Historic District
    (201-203 East Duffy Street (House))
HABS GA-1169-S   s p d   L

Savannah Victorian Historic District (119
    West Park Avenue (House))
HABS GA-1169-E   s p d   L

Savannah Victorian Historic District
    (217-219 West Bolton Street (House))
HABS GA-1169-C   s p d   L

Savannah Victorian Historic District
    (414-416 East Waldburg Street (House))
HABS GA-1169-O   s p d   L

Savannah Victorian Historic District (224
    East Henry Street (House))
HABS GA-1169-U   s p d   L

Savannah Victorian Historic District
    (404-410 East Duffy Street (House))
HABS GA-1169-T   s p d   L

Scarborough House
W. Broad St.
HABS GA-2127   p d   L

Scarborough, William, House
41 W. Broad St.
HABS GA-2127   s p d   H

Sherman's Headquarters; see
    Green-Meldrim House

Smets House (Iron Balcony)
Jones & Bull Sts.
HABS GA-258   p d   L

Sorrel-Weed House
6 W. Harris St.
HABS GA-2140   p d   L

Spencer-Woodbridge House
22 Habersham St.
HABS GA-2133   p d   L

St. Vincent's Academy
HABS GA-1193   p   H

Sturges, Oliver, House; see Roberts, Hiram,
    House

Sturges-Roberts House; see Roberts,
    Hiram, House

Taylor, William, Store
204 W. Bay St.
HABS GA-1196   s p d   H

Telfair Academy of Arts & Sciences
HABS GA-217   p d   L

Tenement Houses
421-423 E. York St.
HABS GA-2134   p d   L

Tobias House
18 W. Harris St.
HABS GA-256   p d   L

Trinity Church
Saint James Sq.
HABS GA-212   p d   L

Turner, Hamilton, House; see 330 Abercorn
Street (House)

U.S. Bank, Old Branch
HABS GA-291   p d   L

Waring House
127 Oglethorpe St.
HABS GA-2142   p d   L

Wayne-Gordon House (Low, Juliette G.,
House)
10 E. Oglethorpe St.
HABS GA-211   p d   L

213 West Bolton Street (House); see
Savannah Victorian Historic District

217-219 West Bolton Street (House); see
Savannah Victorian Historic District

107 West Duffy Street (House); see
Savannah Victorian Historic District

301-305 West Duffy Street (House); see
Savannah Victorian Historic District

215 West Gwinnett Street (House); see
Savannah Victorian Historic District

210-212 West Henry Street (House); see
Savannah Victorian Historic District

114 West Hull Street (House)
HABS GA-1211   p   H

**115 West Oglethorpe Street (House,
Doorway)**
HABS GA-249   p d   L

119 West Park Avenue (House); see
Savannah Victorian Historic District

211 West Perry Street (House)
HABS GA-1214   p   H

207 West Waldburg Street (House); see
Savannah Victorian Historic District

Wetter House
425 Oglethorpe St.
HABS GA-2136   p d   L

Williamson Street (Commerical Buildings)
HABS GA-1204   p   H

Savannah vic.

Fort Pulaski (Fort Pulaski National
Monument)
Cockspur Island
HABS GA-2158   p   L

Fort Pulaski National Monument; see Fort
Pulaski

Fort Wymberly; see Wormsloe

Harbor Beacon, Old
Harbor
HABS GA-232   p d   L

Hermitage (McAlpin Plantation)
Savannah River vic.
HABS GA-225   s p d   L

McAlpin Plantation; see Hermitage

Wild Heron Plantation
Little Ogeechee River vic.
HABS GA-253   p d   L

Wormsloe (Fort Wymberly)
Isle of Hope, Savannah vic.
HABS GA-2126   p d   L

CLARKE COUNTY

Athens

Camak House
279 Meigs St.
HABS GA-14-67   s p d   L

Cobb House (McKinley-Lumpkin House)
194 Prince Ave.
HABS GA-1116   p d   L

Cobb Institute, Girls' Dormitory
Milledge Ave.
HABS GA-1120   p d   L

Crane, Ross, House (South A. E. Chapter
House)
Pulaski & Washington Sts.
HABS GA-1111   p d   L

Dearing House
HABS GA-1133   p d   L

Delta Tau Delta House; see Lumpkin,
Joseph Henry, House

First Presbyterian Church
HABS GA-1165   p   L

Golding-Gerdine House
129 Dougherty St.
HABS GA-1130   p d   L

Grady, Henry, House; see Taylor, Gen. R.
D. B., House

Grant-Hill-White-Bradshaw House (Hill,
Benjamin J., House)
570 Prince Ave.
HABS GA-120   p d   L

Hamilton-Hunnicutt House
325 Milledge Ave.
HABS GA-1128   p d   L

Hill, Benjamin J., House; see
Grant-Hill-White-Bradshaw House

Hodgson House
87 Oconee St.
HABS GA-1160   p   L

Hotel
480 Broad St.
HABS GA-1122   p d   L

Lumpkin, Joseph Henry, House (Delta Tau
Delta House)
248 Prince St.
HABS GA-1115   p d   L

1234 Lumpkins Street (House)
HABS GA-1166   p   L

Lyle House (Lyle-Hunnicutt House)
320 Lumpkin St.
HABS GA-1129   p d   L

Lyle-Hunnicutt House; see Lyle House

McKinley-Lumpkin House; see Cobb
House

225 Milledge Avenue (House)
HABS GA-1163   p   L

897 Milledge Avenue (House)
HABS GA-1167   p   L

Nicholson House
224 Thomas St.
HABS GA-1134   p d   L

Phi Kappa Literary Society Hall; see
University of Georgia, Phi Kappa Hall

Presbyterian Manse; see Reed House

Reed House (Presbyterian Manse)
185 Hull St.
HABS GA-1112   L

South A. E. Chapter House; see Crane,
Ross, House

Taylor, Gen. R. D. B., House (Grady,
Henry, House)
634 Prince Ave.
HABS GA-1114   p d   L

Thomas, Stevens, House
347 Hancock St. (moved from Pulaski St.)
HABS GA-1113   p d   L

University of Georgia, Demosthenian Hall
HABS GA-14-87   s p d   L

University of Georgia, Demosthenian Hall
HABS GA-14-87   s p   L

University of Georgia, Phi Kappa Hall (Phi
Kappa Literary Society Hall)
Broad & Jackson Sts.
HABS GA-1117   L

Upson House
1000 Prince Ave.
HABS GA-14-66   L

COBB COUNTY

Atlanta vic.

Covered Bridge
Spanning Soap Creek
HABS GA-185   L

Kennesaw Mnt.

Kolb House
HABS GA-299   p   H

Marietta

Bostwick-Fraser-Couper House; see
Fraser-Couper House

Fraser-Couper House
(Bostwick-Fraser-Couper House)
HABS GA-1107   p d   L

COWETA COUNTY

Newnan vic.

Blount House (Gordon-Banks House; Hale
Nui)
(moved from GA, Haddock vic.)
HABS GA-1125   p d   L

Gordon-Banks House; see Blount House
Hale Nui; see Blount House

CRAWFORD COUNTY

Knoxville
Crawford County Courthouse
HABS GA-151   pd   L

DE KALB COUNTY

Panola vic.
Latimer-Felton House
Atlanta vic.
HABS GA-1106   s pd   L

EFFINGHAM COUNTY

Rincon
Jerusalem Church (Lutheran
   Meetinghouse; Salzburger Church)
HABS GA-242   pd   L
Lutheran Meetinghouse; see Jerusalem
   Church
Salzburger Church; see Jerusalem Church

ELBERT COUNTY

Elbert
Blackwell Bridge
Heardmont vic., County Rd. 244
HAER GA-41   s pd   L

Elberton vic.
Perale Cotton Mill & Dam
Elberton vic.
HAER GA-42   s pd   L

Heardmont vic.
Dye-White Farm
County Rd. 244
HABS GA-31   s pd   L

Middleton
Eureka; see Grogan House
Grogan House (Eureka)
NW Side County Rd.
HABS GA-33   s pd   L

Pearl vic.
Allen, Williams, House (Beverly Plantation)
County Rd. 245
HABS GA-34   s pd   L
Beverly Plantation; see Allen, Williams,
   House

Ruckersville
Anderson, W. Frank, Farm
County Rd. 239
HABS GA-35   s pd   L

Ruckersville vic.
Alexander-Cleveland Farm
County Rd. 238
HABS GA-30   s pd   L

Anderson, Reuben J., Farm
County Rd. 239 vic.
HABS GA-32   s pd   L

Savannah
Smith-McGee Bridge
Georgia Rt. 181
HAER GA-39   pd   L

Savannah vic.
Georgia-Carolina Memorial Bridge
State Hwy. 72
HAER GA-38   pd   L

FLOYD COUNTY

Rome
Thornwood
Shorter College vic.
HABS GA-152   pd   L

FULTON COUNTY

Atlanta
Atlanta Library
126 Carnegie Way
HABS GA-1216   p   H
Atlanta University, Stone Hall
HABS GA-1172   p   H
**126-255 Auburn Avenue(Commercial
   Buildings);** see Sweet Auburn Historic
   District, Street Facades
Equitable Building (Trust Company of
   Georgia)
Edgewood Ave. & Pryor St.
HABS GA-2107   p   H
Herndon & Atlantic Life Building; see
   Sweet Auburn Historic District
King, Martin Luther, Birth Home
501 Auburn Ave. NE
HABS GA-1171   p   H
Marietta Bridge
HAER GA-44   p   H
Odd Fellows Building & Auditorium; see
   Sweet Auburn Historic District
Sweet Auburn Historic District (Odd
   Fellows Building & Auditorium)
228-250 Auburn Ave.
HABS GA-1170-B   s pd   L
Sweet Auburn Historic District (Herndon
   & Atlantic Life Building)
229-243 Auburn Ave.
HABS GA-1170-A   s pd   L
Sweet Auburn Historic District
Auburn Ave., Courtland St., I-85
HABS GA-1170   s pd   L
**Sweet Auburn Historic District, Street
   Facades** (126-255 Auburn
   Avenue(Commercial Buildings))
HABS GA-1170-C   s pd   L
Trust Company of Georgia; see Equitable
   Building

Fairburn vic.
Beaver House at Campbellton
HABS GA-1155   pd   L
**Campbell County Courthouse at
   Campbellton, Old**
HABS GA-154   pd   L

Roswell
Barrington Hall
HABS GA-1105   pd   L
Bulloch Hall
HABS GA-14-13   s pd   L
Holly Hill; see Lewis Place
Lewis Place (Holly Hill)
HABS GA-1104   pd   L
Methodist Church, Old
HABS GA-193   pd   L
Mimosa Hall (Phoenix Hall)
HABS GA-1102   pd   L
Phoenix Hall; see Mimosa Hall

GLYNN COUNTY

Broadfield vic.
Elizafield Plantation Sugar Mill Building;
   see Santo Domingo Mission (Ruins)
Santo Domingo Mission (Ruins) (Elizafield
   Plantation Sugar Mill Building)
Altamaha River
HABS GA-2118   s pd   L

Jekyll Island
Horton House (Remains)
Main Rd.
HABS GA-2150   s pd   L
Rockefeller House
HABS GA-2164   s   H

St. Simons Island
Cannons Point, Kitchen Building (Ruins)
   (Fort Frederica National Monument)
Cannons Point
HABS GA-2159   p   L
Couper's Point, °Rest° House (Ruins)
   (Fort Frederica National Monument)
Couper's Point
HABS GA-255   pd   L
Fort Frederica, Barracks (Ruins) (Fort
   Frederica National Monument)
HABS GA-2146   s pd   L
**Fort Frederica, Callwell, John, House
   (Ruins)** (Fort Frederica National
   Monument)
Lot No. 3, North Ward
HABS GA-2147   s pd   L
Fort Frederica, duBignon House (Ruins)
   (Fort Frederica National Monument)
Lot No. 7, South Ward
HABS GA-2152   s pd   L
**Fort Frederica, Foundation in Northeast
   Bastion** (Fort Frederica National
   Monument)
HABS GA-2157   p   L

**Fort Frederica, Hawkins-Davison Houses
(Ruins)** (Fort Frederica National
Monument)
Lots No. 1 & 2, South Ward
HABS GA-2149   s pd   L
**Fort Frederica, Houston House Storage
Bins (Ruins)** (Fort Frederica National
Monument)
Lot No. 3, South Ward
HABS GA-2155   pd   L
Fort Frederica, Humbe House (Ruins)
(Fort Frederica National Monument)
Lot No. 8, South Ward
HABS GA-2153   pd   L
Fort Frederica, King's Magazine (Ruins)
(Fort Frederica National Monument)
HABS GA-2162   s pd   L
**Fort Frederica, Levally, John, House
(Ruins)** (Fort Frederica National
Monument)
Lot No. 9, South Ward
HABS GA-2154   s pd   L
**Fort Frederica, Mackay, Capt. John, House
(Ruins)** (Fort Frederica National
Monument)
Lot No. 6, North Ward
HABS GA-2148   s pd   L
**Fort Frederica, Moore, Francis, House
(Ruins)** (Fort Frederica National
Monument)
Lot No. 20, North Ward
HABS GA-2163   s   L
Fort Frederica National Monument; see
Cannons Point, Kitchen Building (Ruins)
Fort Frederica National Monument; see
Couper's Point, Rest House (Ruins)
Fort Frederica National Monument; see
Fort Frederica, Barracks (Ruins)
Fort Frederica National Monument; see
Fort Frederica, Callwell, John, House
(Ruins)
Fort Frederica National Monument; see
Fort Frederica, Foundation in Northeast
Bastion
Fort Frederica National Monument; see
Fort Frederica, Hawkins-Davison Houses
(Ruins)
Fort Frederica National Monument; see
Fort Frederica, Houston House Storage
Bins (Ruins)
Fort Frederica National Monument; see
Fort Frederica, Humbe House (Ruins)
Fort Frederica National Monument; see
Fort Frederica, King's Magazine (Ruins)
Fort Frederica National Monument; see
Fort Frederica, Levally, John, House
(Ruins)
Fort Frederica National Monument; see
Fort Frederica, Mackay, Capt. John,
House (Ruins)
Fort Frederica National Monument; see
Fort Frederica, Moore, Francis, House
(Ruins)

Fort Frederica National Monument; see
Fort Frederica, Retreat Plantation,
House (Ruins)
Fort Frederica National Monument; see
Fort Frederica, South Storehouse (Ruins)
Fort Frederica National Monument; see
Fort Frederica, Welch House (Ruins)
Fort Frederica National Monument; see
Fort Frederica, duBignon House (Ruins)
**Fort Frederica, Retreat Plantation, House
(Ruins)** (Fort Frederica National
Monument; Orange Grove)
HABS GA-220   pd   L
Fort Frederica, South Storehouse (Ruins)
(Fort Frederica National Monument)
HABS GA-2156   s pd   L
Fort Frederica, Welch House (Ruins) (Fort
Frederica National Monument)
Lot No. 5, South Ward
HABS GA-2151   s pd   L
Orange Grove; see Fort Frederica, Retreat
Plantation, House (Ruins)

GORDON COUNTY

Moss-Kelly House
Lick Creek Rd.
HABS GA-1218   s   H

HALL COUNTY

Gainesville

Chamberlee Building; see Odd Fellows Hall
Odd Fellows Hall (Chamberlee Building)
Sycamore & Summitt Sts.
HABS GA-1168   pd   L

HANCOCK COUNTY

Sparta

Little, Judge, House
Main St.
HABS GA-188   pd   L
Sayre-Shivers House (Turner House)
Broad & Robins Sts.
HABS GA-179   pd   L
Terrell, Dr. William, House; see
Terrell-Stone House
Terrell-Stone House (Terrell, Dr. William,
House)
HABS GA-186   pd   L
Turner House; see Sayre-Shivers House

HARRIS COUNTY

Whitesville vic.

Davidson, John, House
HABS GA-1144   pd   L

HENRY COUNTY

Mc Donough

Lowe-Turner House
88 Keys Ferry St.
HABS GA-270   pd   L

JACKSON COUNTY

Jefferson

Bell House; see Etheridge-Stanton House
Bell-Maddox House
HABS GA-11   pd   L
Etheridge-Stanton House (Bell House)
186 Lee St.
HABS GA-184   pd   L
Harrison Hotel
HABS GA-157   pd   L
Pendergrass Store
HABS GA-16   pd   L
Presbyterian Church
HABS GA-17   pd   L

JEFFERSON COUNTY

Louisville

Slave Market
Public Sq.
HABS GA-14-2   s pd   L

JONES COUNTY

Clinton

Jade-Barron House
HABS GA-155   pd   L
Johnson House
HABS GA-1123   pd   L
Lowther Hall
HABS GA-14-59   s pd   L

Haddock vic.

Blount House (Gordon-Banks House; Hale
Nui)
(moved to GA, Newnan vic.)
HABS GA-1125   pd   L
Gordon-Banks House; see Blount House
Hale Nui; see Blount House

LIBERTY COUNTY

Midway

Midway Congregational Church
HABS GA-14-44   s pd   L

LUMPKIN COUNTY

Dahlenega

Hotel, Old
Main Sq.
HABS GA-180   pd   L
Lumpkin County Courthouse
HABS GA-181   pd   L

MACON COUNTY

Marshallville
Frederick-Wade House
HABS GA-146   pd   L
McCaskill-Rumph House
HABS GA-149   pd   L
Slappey House
HABS GA-147   pd   L

Marshallville vic.
Bryan Place; see Stage Coach Inn
Felton, Billy, Place
HABS GA-169   pd   L
Rumph House
HABS GA-160   pd   L
Stage Coach Inn (Bryan Place)
HABS GA-148   pd   L

MC DUFFIE COUNTY

Cobbham
Few, Ignatius, House
HABS GA-1153   pd   L

MC INTOSH COUNTY

Darien
Ashantilly Plantation
HABS GA-282   pd   L

Darien vic.
Cabin
HABS GA-283   pd   L
Epping House
HABS GA-234   pd   L
Tolomato Mission (Ruins)
HABS GA-271   pd   L

Sapelo Island
Spanish Fort (Ruins)
HABS GA-2129   pd   L

MORGAN COUNTY

Madison
Box Wood; see Kolb-Pou-Newton House
Kolb-Pou-Newton House (Box Wood)
218 S. Second St.
HABS GA-183   pd   L
Thurleston
455 Dixie Hwy.
HABS GA-182   pd   L

MURRAY COUNTY

Spring Place
Vann, Chief James Clement, House
U.S. Rt. 76 & State Rt. 255
HABS GA-174   s pd   L

MUSCOGEE COUNTY

Bibb
Bibb Company (Columbus Plant)
HAER GA-12   s pd   L

Columbus
Alexander-McGehee-Woodall House
1543 Second Ave.
HABS GA-153   pd   ,L
Bradley, W. C., Company
Front Ave.
HAER GA-35   s p   L
Cargill House (Lion House)
1316 Third Ave.
HABS GA-1132   pd   L
City Mills Company
Front Ave.
HAER GA-25   s pd   L
Columbus Iron Works
Front Ave.
HAER GA-28   s pd   L
Columbus Manufacturing Company
Front Ave.
HAER GA-29   pd   L
Columbus Railroad Company:Power Station
Front Ave.
HAER GA-27   pd   L
Cook-Thomas House
HABS GA-111   pd   L
Crawford, Judge, House (Crawford-Jenkins Boarding House)
Thirteenth St.
HABS GA-1142   pd   L
Crawford-Jenkins Boarding House; see Crawford, Judge, House
Dam Sites at Falls of the Chattahoochee River
HAER GA-45   s   H
Downing House (Ironwork)
815 Broadway
HABS GA-1141   pd   L
Eagle & Phenix Mills (Muscogee Mills)
Front Ave.
HABS GA-110
HAER GA-30   s pd   L
Elks' Home; see Fontaine Home
Elms (Estes-Bowers Place)
1846 Buena Vista Rd.
HABS GA-1103   pd   L
Empire Mills Company
Front Ave.
HAER GA-31   s p   L
Estes-Bowers Place; see Elms
Fontaine Home (Elks' Home)
1044 Front Ave.
HABS GA-140   pd   L
Front Avenue Industrial District
HAER GA-33   s   L
Garrard-Slade House; see St. Elmo
Griffin-Mott House
Mott St. & Front Ave.
HABS GA-163   pd   L

Hydroelectric Power Development North Highlands
HAER GA-26   pd   L
Lion House; see Cargill House
Muscogee Manufacturing Company
Front Ave.
HAER GA-23   s pd   L
Muscogee Mills; see Eagle & Phenix Mills
Pease Home
908 Broadway
HABS GA-1135   pd   L
Rankin House (Doorway & Interior)
1440 Second Ave.
HABS GA-112   pd   L
Redd House
HABS GA-138   pd   L
Seaboard Airline Railway, Freight Depot
Front Ave.
HAER GA-21   s pd   L
Sol Loeb Warehouse
Front Ave.
HAER GA-24   s pd   L
St. Elmo (Garrard-Slade House)
2810 Saint Elmo Dr.
HABS GA-129   s pd   L
Swift Mansion
HABS GA-114   pd   L
Water Power Development of Falls of Chattahoochee
Chattahoochee River
HAER GA-22   s pd   L

Columbus vic.
Bass Place (Slave Cabins)
HABS GA-1150   pd   L
Gunby House
HABS GA-119   pd   L

NEWTON COUNTY

Covington
Carr Hill
W. Hill St.
HABS GA-126   pd   L
Downs House
HABS GA-124   pd   L
Spense-Harris House
HABS GA-130   pd   L

Covington vic.
Salem Camp Ground
HABS GA-128   pd   L

Oxford
Emory Church, Old
HABS GA-125   pd   L
Emory College, Few Literary Society Hall
HABS GA-198   pd   L
Emory College, Phi Gamma Literary Society Hall
HABS GA-197   pd   L

OCONEE COUNTY

Watkinsville

Eagle Tavern
Macon Rd.
HABS GA-1127   pd   L

OGLETHORPE COUNTY

Arnoldsville vic.

Daniels Place, Old
HABS GA-1109   pd   L

Lexington

Cox-Chedel-Johnston House
HABS GA-175   pd   L
Cox-Steward-Knox Place (Pigeon House & Farm Bell)
HABS GA-172   pd   L
Gilmer House
HABS GA-178   pd   L
Platt, Judge, House
HABS GA-18   pd   L
Saims-Bacon House
HABS GA-171   pd   L
Willingham-Wadkins House
HABS GA-176   pd   L

PIKE COUNTY

Barnesville vic.

Gachette House
HABS GA-14-121   s pd   L

RICHMOND COUNTY

Augusta

Academy of Richmond County, Old
(Young Men's Library Assoc. & Augusta Museum)
540 Telfair St.
HABS GA-229   pd   L
American Foundry
Augusta Canal
HAER GA-32   s   L
Augusta Canal
HAER GA-5   s pd   L
Augusta Canal Industrial District
HAER GA-36   pd   L
Augusta Lumber Company; see Augusta Machine Works
Augusta Machine Works (Augusta Lumber Company)
Augusta Canal
HAER GA-14   pd   L
Augusta Railway Company: West Power Station
Augusta Canal
HAER GA-20   pd   L
Augusta Water Works
Augusta Canal
HAER GA-16   pd   L

Azalea Cottage
2236 Walton Way
HABS GA-272   pd   L
Bennoch House
119 Eighth St.
HABS GA-230   pd   L
Blanche Mill; see Globe Mill
Broad Street Stores (South Side)
Broad, Fifth & Sixth Sts.
HABS GA-273   pd   L
Chafee House
914 Milledge Rd.
HABS GA-26   pd   L
Chew-Dearing-Battey House
428 Washington St.
HABS GA-260   pd   L
Clanton-Vason-Coleman House
503 Greene St.
HABS GA-224   pd   L
Crescent Grain & Feed Mill (Southern Milling Company)
HAER GA-11   pd   L
Cunningham's Flour Mill
Augusta Canal
HAER GA-17   pd   L
Dartmouth Spinning Company (Sutherland Mill)
Augusta Canal
HAER GA-6   pd   L
Enterprise Manufacturing Company
Augusta Canal
HAER GA-13   s pd   L
Fruitlands
HABS GA-252   pd   L
Georgia Iron Works
Augusta Canal
HAER GA-7   pd   L
Globe Mill (Blanche Mill)
Augusta Canal
HAER GA-9   pd   L
Government House, Old; see Murphey House
Greene Street Historic District
Greene St., Gordon Hwy. to Augusta Canal Bridge
HABS GA-269   pd   L

467 Greene Street (House, Ironwork)
HABS GA-263   pd   L

Harper-Cohen House
2150 Battle Row
HABS GA-221   pd   L

High Gate (Nesbitt House)
820 Milledge Rd.
HABS GA-266   pd   L

Hight & MacMurphey Foundry (Lombard Ironworks & Supply Company)
Augusta Canal
HAER GA-10   pd   L

Jail
Watkins & Elbert St.
HABS GA-264   pd   L

Kilpatrick House
Forrest Hills Rd. (moved from Greene St.)
HABS GA-233   pd   L
King, John P., Manufacturing Company
Augusta Canal
HAER GA-15   s pd   L
Lombard Ironworks & Supply Company; see Hight & MacMurphey Foundry
Lombard Ironworks & Supply Company; see Pendleton & Boardmen Foundry
Mackay's Trading Post; see White House
Meadow Garden (Walton, George, Cottage)
Nelson St.
HABS GA-2100   pd   L
Medical College, Old
598 Telfair St.
HABS GA-14-70   s pd   L
Montrose; see Reid-Jones-Carpenter House
Murphey House (Government House, Old)
Telfair St.
HABS GA-268   pd   L
Nesbitt House; see High Gate
Oertel House
638 Greene St.
HABS GA-297   pd   L
Paragon Mill
Augusta Canal
HAER GA-8   d   L
Pendleton & Boardmen Foundry (Lombard Ironworks & Supply Company)
Augusta Canal
HAER GA-10-A   pd   L
Phinizy Residence
519 Greene St.
HABS GA-223   pd   L
Platt-Fleming-Welker-d'Antignac House
453 Greene St.
HABS GA-262   pd   L
Reid-Jones-Carpenter House (Montrose)
2249 Walton Way
HABS GA-227   pd   L
Richmond County Courthouse
HABS GA-239   pd   L
Russell & Simmons Factory
Augusta Canal
HAER GA-34   pd   L
Shamrock Mill Site
HAER GA-18   d   L
Sibley Manufacturing Company
Augusta Canal
HAER GA-19   s pd   L
Southern Milling Company; see Crescent Grain & Feed Mill

St. Paul's Church (Episcopal)
605 Reynolds St.
HABS GA-241   pd   L
St. Paul's Parish Cemetery Gate & Gravestones
605 Reynolds St.
HABS GA-231   pd   L

Sutherland Mill; see Dartmouth Spinning Company

U.S. Arsenal
Walton Way vic.
HABS GA-251   pd   L

Walton, George, Cottage; see Meadow Garden

Ware-Sibley-Clark House
506 Telfair St.
HABS GA-2128   s pd   L

261 Watkins Street (House)
HABS GA-265   pd   L

White House (Mackay's Trading Post)
1822 Broad St.
HABS GA-14-7   s pd   L

White, Mayor, House
2234 Walton Way
HABS GA-226   pd   L

Women's Club
825 Greene St.
HABS GA-267   pd   L

Young Men's Library Assoc. & Augusta Museum; see Academy of Richmond County, Old

Augusta vic.

Glassock House
Old Savannah Rd.
HABS GA-250   pd   L

Harper House
Wrightsboro Rd.
HABS GA-14-69   s pd   L

SPALDING COUNTY

Griffen

Bailey-Tebeault House
Meriwether St.
HABS GA-1148   pd   L

Drewry House (Eason-Drewry House)
303 N. Thirteenth St.
HABS GA-1147   pd   L

Eason-Drewry House; see Drewry House

Nichols, J. P., House
225 N. Thirteenth St.
HABS GA-1146   pd   L

Griffin

Gibson, Rev. Obediah C., House
W. Tinsley St.
HABS GA-1149   pd   L

STEPHENS COUNTY

Toccoa vic.

Jarrett Manor; see Travelers Rest
Travelers Rest (Jarrett Manor)
HABS GA-14-5   s pd   L

TALBOT COUNTY

Talbotton

Episcopal Church
HABS GA-1139   pd   L

Hill-Leonard House
HABS GA-1108   pd   L

Leonard, Dr., House
Macon Rd.
HABS GA-1118   pd   L

Maxwell House
HABS GA-1140   pd   L

Methodist Church
HABS GA-1126   pd   L

Straus Le Vert Memorial Hall
HABS GA-1136   pd   L

TALIAFERRO COUNTY

Crawfordville

Liberty Hall (Stephens, Alexander, House)
HABS GA-158   pd   L

Stephens, Alexander, House; see Liberty Hall

THOMAS COUNTY

Thomasville

Thomas County Courthouse
HABS GA-216   s   d   H

TROUP COUNTY

La Grange

Beall-Dallis House
206 Broad St.
HABS GA-117   pd   L

Culberson House
207 Broad St.
HABS GA-116   pd   L

Edwards House, Old
203 Broad St.
HABS GA-118   pd   L

Huntley House
302 Broad St.
HABS GA-122   pd   L

Oaks, The; see Todd Place

Render House
Hines St.
HABS GA-14-62   s pd   L

Todd Place (Oaks, The)
1103 Vernon St.
HABS GA-14-99   s pd   L

La Grange vic.

Boddie House
Greenville Rd.
HABS GA-1143   pd   L

Cameron House (Mantel)
HABS GA-121   pd   L

West Point

Booker House
Chattahoochee River vic.
HABS GA-161   pd   L

WALKER COUNTY

La Fayette

Marsh-Warthen House
HABS GA-150   pd   L

Rock Spring

Carter's Quarters
Old Federal Rd.
HABS GA-173   pd   L

WALTON COUNTY

High Shoals

Casulon Plantation
HABS GA-1110   pd   L

Monroe

Birscoe-Selman House
HABS GA-1137   pd   L

Davis House
HABS GA-1138   pd   L

WHEELER COUNTY

Glenwood vic.

Mitchell Plantation (Overseer's Cabin)
Oconee River
HABS GA-290   d   L

WILKES COUNTY

Washington

Bennett House
Robert Toombs Ave.
HABS GA-1158   p   L

Gilbert-Alexander-Wright House
312 N. Alexander Ave.
HABS GA-1145   pd   L

Presbyterian Church
HABS GA-115   pd   L

Toombs, Robert, House
320 E. Robert Toombs Ave.
HABS GA-13   pd   L

Wingfield-Cade-Saunders House
120 Tignall Rd.
HABS GA-19   pd   L

Hawaii

Kualapuu

Meyer, R. W., Sugar Mill, 1878
957 Punchbowl St.
HAER HI-2   s p d   H

HAWAII COUNTY

Kailua Kona

Huliher Palace
Alii Dr.
HABS HI-49   s p d   H

Mokuaikaua Congregational Church
Alii Dr.
HABS HI-50   p d   H

Kohala

Bond House
Iole Valley
HABS HI-48   s p d   H

Puako

Hoku Loa Church
HABS HI-12   s p   H

HONOLULU COUNTY

Honolulu

Academy of Fine Arts
Thomas Square
HABS HI-27   p   H

Aliiolani Hale (Judiciary Building)
463 King St.
HABS HI-18   s p d   H

Bishop Museum, Bishop Hall
Likelike Hwy.
HABS HI-25   p   H

Bishop Museum, Main Building
Likelike Hwy.
HABS HI-26   p   H

Chamberlain House
King & Kawaiahao Sts.
HABS HI-4   s p d   H

Dillingham, Walter F., House; see La Pietra
Governor's House; see Washington Place
Halekoa; see Iolani Barracks
Honolulu, Old
Queen St.
HABS HI-5   s p   H

Iolani Bandstand
Iolani Palace
HABS HI-2   s p d   H

Iolani Barracks (Halekoa)
Richards & Hotel Sts.
HABS HI-3   s p d   H

Iolani Palace
King & Richards Sts.
HABS HI-1   s p d   L H

Izumo Taisha Kyo; see Kukui Shrine
Judiciary Building; see Aliiolani Hale

Kamehameha V, Summer House
Monanalua Gardens
HABS HI-16   p   H

Kapuaiwa Building
426 S. Queen St.
HABS HI-24   p   H

Kawaiahao Church
957 Punchbowl St.
HABS HI-14   s p d   H

Kukui Shrine (Izumo Taisha Kyo)
HABS HI-29   p   H

La Pietra (Dillingham, Walter F., House)
Poni Moi Rd., Diamond Head
HABS HI-30   p d   H

Lunalio's Tomb, Kawaiahao Church
King & Punchbowl Sts.
HABS HI-15   s p d   H

Melchers Building
51 Merchant St.
HABS HI-34   p   H

Mission Group; see Mission House, Frame
Mission Group; see Schoolhouse, Adobe

Mission House, Frame (Mission Group)
553 King St.
HABS HI-21   s p d   H

Mission Printing Office
King & Kawaiahae Sts.
HABS HI-20   s p d   H

Our Lady of Peace Cathedral
1183 Fort St.
HABS HI-28   s p d   H

Post Office, Old
Merchant & Bethel Sts.
HABS HI-7   s p d   H

Punahou School, School Hall
HABS HI-22   p d   H

Queen Emma's Summer Palace
2913 Pali Hwy.
HABS HI-17   s p d   H

Royal Mausoleum
2261 Nuuanu Ave.
HABS HI-23   p d   H

Schoolhouse, Adobe (Mission Group)
Mission & Kawaiahao
HABS HI-19   p d   H

Spalding, Philip, House
Maikiki Heights Dr.
HABS HI-31   p   H

Washington Place (Governor's House)
Beretania & Miller Sts.
HABS HI-6   s p d   H

Pearl Harbor

Headquarters, Commanders, WWII, CINCPACFLT
Marai St.
HABS HI-32   p   H

KAUAI COUNTY

Hanalei

Waioli Church (Waioli Hui'ia Social Hall)
Island of Kauai
HABS HI-52   s p d   H

Waioli Hui'ia Social Hall; see Waioli Church
Waioli Mission House
HABS HI-53   s p d   H

MAUI COUNTY

Lahaina

Baldwin House
Front & Dickenson Sts.
HABS HI-43   p   H

Chee Kung Tong Society Headquarters
858 Front St.
HABS HI-40   p   H

Hale Aloha
600 Laukini St.
HABS HI-10   s p d   H

Hale Paaho (Prison)
Wainee & Prison Rds.
HABS HI-37   p   H

Master's Reading Room
King & Front Sts.
HABS HI-13   s p   H

Maui Courthouse, Old
Wharf & Canal Sts.
HABS HI-9   s p d   H

Pioneer Hotel
Front & Hotel Sts.
HABS HI-41   p   H

Pioneer Mill, Time Clock
Lahainaluna Rd.
HABS HI-38   p   H

U.S. Marine Hospital
1038 Front St.
HABS HI-11   s p d   H

Lahainaluna

Hale Pa'i (Printing Shop)
Lahainaluna Seminary
HABS HI-8   s p d   H

Pioneer Mill, Office
Lahainaluna Rd.
HABS HI-39   p   H

Olowalu

Olowalu Church
HABS HI-35   p   H

Paia

Hamakuapoko Mill (Ruins)
Puunee Sugar Mill vic.
HABS HI-44   p   H

Pukoo
Kaluaaha Congregational Church
Hwy. 45
HABS HI-51   s p d   H

Spreckelsville
Spreckels Sugar Mill
HABS HI-54   p   H

Ulupalakua
Ulupalakua Ranch
HABS HI-47   p   H

Waiakoa
Holy Ghost Roman Catholic Church
HABS HI-45   p   H

Wailuku
Alexander, William & Mary, House (Parsonage)
HABS HI-46   p   H
Bailey House
HABS HI-42   p   H
Kaahumanu Church
HABS HI-36   p   H

Idaho

ADA COUNTY

Boise
Ada Theatre
HABS ID-3   pd   H
Alexander's Building (Alexander's Store)
826 Main St.
HABS ID-4   pd   L H
Alexander's Store; see Alexander's Building
Boise City National Bank (Simplot Building)
805 W. Idaho St.
HABS ID-23   pd   L
Brady, Gov., Mansion
Second & Main Sts.
HABS ID-28   p   H
Christ Chapel
Broadway & Campus Dr.
HABS ID-25   p   H
Churchill's Resturant; see Turnverein Hall
Congregation Beth Israel Synagogue
Eleventh & State Sts.
HABS ID-26   p   H
Eastman Building; see Overland Building
Falk-Bloch Mercantile Company (Falk's ID Department Store)
100 N. Eighth St.
HABS ID-18   pd   L
Falk's ID Department Store; see Falk-Bloch Mercantile Company
Fidelity Building; see Montandon Building
Fort Boise Commanding Officer's Quarters
HABS ID-27   p   H
Idaho Building
216 N. Eighth St.
HABS ID-21   pd   L
Idanha Hotel
Tenth & Main Sts.
HABS ID-29   pd   H
Montandon Building (Fidelity Building)
722 W. Idaho St.
HABS ID-19   pd   L
Moore-Cunningham House
Warm Springs Ave. & Walnut St.
HABS ID-30   p   H
Overland Building (Eastman Building)
Eighth & Main Sts.
HABS ID-17   pd   L

Simplot Building; see Boise City National Bank
St. Alphonsus Hospital
Sixth & State Sts.
HABS ID-31   p   H
Turnverein Hall (Churchill's Resturant)
Sixth & Main St.
HABS ID-32   p   H
Union Block
710-720 W. Idaho St.
HABS ID-20   pd   L
Union Pacific Railroad:Depot
HABS ID-33   p   H
U.S. Assay Office
210 Main St.
HABS ID-10   s pd   H

Snake River Plateau
Murtaugh Bridge
HAER ID-1   pd   H

BOISE COUNTY

Idaho City
Boise Basin Mercantile Company Block
Main & Commercial Sts.
HABS ID-13   s pd   L
Boise Basin Museum; see Post Office Block
Boise County Courthouse
Main & Wall Sts.
HABS ID-11   s pd   L
City Hall; see Idaho City Schoolhouse
Galbraith House
Montgomery St.
HABS ID-7   s pd   L
Idaho City Schoolhouse (City Hall)
School & Main Sts.
HABS ID-6   s pd   L
Idaho World Building
Main & Commercial Sts.
HABS ID-9   s pd   L
Masonic Temple, Idaho Lodge Number 1
Wall St.
HABS ID-5   s pd   L
Miners' Exchange Block
Main & Wall Sts.
HABS ID-14   s pd   L

Pioneer Lodge Number 1
E. Commercial St.
HABS ID-8   s pd   L
Post Office Block (Boise Basin Museum)
Wall & Montgomery Sts.
HABS ID-15   pd   L
St. Joseph's Roman Catholic Church
High & Wallula Sts.
HABS ID-12   s pd   L

IDAHO COUNTY

Kamiah vic.
Cowley, Henry T., House
State Rt. 9
HABS ID-2   s d   L H

KOOTENAI COUNTY

Cataldo
Sacred Heart Mission
HABS ID-1   s pd   L

POWER COUNTY

American Falls
American Falls Power, Light & Water Company
HAER ID-2   s p   H

SHOSHONE COUNTY

Avery
Avery Ranger Station
Saint Joe National Forest
HABS ID-16   d   L

TWIN FALLS COUNTY

Twin Falls
Jerome Bridge (Perrine Bridge)
HAER ID-3   p   H
Perrine Bridge; see Jerome Bridge

Illinois

ADAMS COUNTY

Fall Creek vic.

Fall Creek Bridge Spanning Fall Creek Gorge
Fall Creek Station
HABS IL-267   s p d   L

Payson

Congregational Church
Park Drive & State Rt. 96
HABS IL-265   s p d   L

Quincy

Knoyer Farmhouse
HABS IL-246   p   L

ALEXANDER COUNTY

Cairo

Langan, Peter T., House
HABS IL-218   pd   L
Store Building
509 Commercial Ave.
HABS IL-25-21   s pd   L

Thebes

Thebes Courthouse
HABS IL-25-17   s pd   L

BOONE COUNTY

Belvidere

Dunton House
807 McKinley Ave.
HABS IL-171   s pd   L
Hildrup, Jesse, House
1215 N. State St.
HABS IL-160   s pd   L
Palmer House
HABS IL-173   s p   H
Wheeler House
222 W. Locust St.
HABS IL-172   s pd   L

Belvidere vic.

Newton Farmhouse
Belvidere-Kirkland Rd.
HABS IL-159   s pd   L

Cherry Valley

Hale House
State Rt. 5
HABS IL-161   s p   H

BROWN COUNTY

Elgin

Hinsdell, A. B., House
443 E. Chicago St.
HABS IL-26-10   s pd   L

BUREAU COUNTY

Depue

Hassler Tavern
U.S. Rt. 6
HABS IL-142   s pd   L

La Moille vic.

Smith Farmhouse
U.S. Rt. 34
HABS IL-146   s pd   L

CASS COUNTY

Beardstown

Billings, Horace, House
Lafayette & Third Sts.
HABS IL-26-28   s pd   L
Cass County Courthouse, Old (City Hall)
HABS IL-284   pd   L
City Hall; see Cass County Courthouse, Old
Sturtevant, Christopher C., House
301 Washington St.
HABS IL-26-29   s pd   L

Virginia vic.

Allandale (Cunningham, Andrew, Farm)
HABS IL-261   s pd   L
Cunningham, Andrew, Farm; see Allandale

CHAMPAIGN COUNTY

Homer vic.

Covered Wooden Bridge
Spanning Salt Fork River, State Rt. 49
HABS IL-25-19   s pd   L

CLINTON COUNTY

Carlyle

Suspension Bridge
Spanning Kaskaskia River
HABS IL-225   s pd   L

COOK COUNTY

Brookfield

Brookfield Kindergarten
3601 Forest Ave.
HABS IL-1087   s pd   L

Chicago

Aldine Square
Vincennes Ave.
HABS IL-153   s pd   L
Aldine Square, Smith House (Enterprise Institute)
HABS IL-153-A   p   L
American College of Surgeons; see Nickerson, Samuel M., House

Auditorium Annex (Pick-Congress Hotel)
504 S. Michigan Ave.
HABS IL-1012   pd   L
Auditorium Building (Roosevelt University)
Michigan Ave. & Congress St.
HABS IL-1007   s pd   LH
Ayer Building (McClurg Building; Crown Building)
218 S. Wabash Ave.
HABS IL-1025   pd   L
Ayer, Edward E., House
2 E. Banks St.
HABS IL-1035   pd   L
Bach, Emil, House
7415 N. Sheridan Rd.
HABS IL-1088   s pd   L
Bay State Building & Kranz Building; see Springer Block
Boulevard Recording Studios, Inc.; see Chicago Historical Society
Cable Building
57 E. Jackson Blvd.
HABS IL-1003   s d   L
Cahokia Courthouse
Jackson Park (moved from IL CAHOKIA)
HABS IL-26-31-A   s pd   L
Carpenter, Judge, House(Cast Iron Balcony Railing); see Chicago Ironwork
Carson, Pirie, Scott & Company Department Store; see Schlesinger & Mayer Department Store
Casey Building
173-177 N. Wells St.
HABS IL-1038   pd   L
Cast Iron Fence; see Chicago Ironwork
Cast Iron Fence & Gate; see Chicago Ironwork
Cast Iron Gate; see Chicago Ironwork
Cast Iron Gate & Fence; see Chicago Ironwork
Cast Iron Gatepost & Fence; see Chicago Ironwork
Cast Iron Porch Railing & Fence; see Chicago Ironwork
Cast Iron Stair Railing; see Chicago Ironwork
Cast Iron Stair Railing & Fence; see Chicago Ironwork
Central Cold Storage Warehouse; see Sibley, Hiram, Warehouse
Chapin & Gore Building
63 E. Adams St.
HABS IL-1039   s p   L H
Charnley, James, House
1365 N. Astor St.
HABS IL-1009   s pd   L
Chicago & Western Indiana Railroad:Station
Dearborn St.
HAER IL-6   p   H

Chicago Board of Health; see Chicago Criminal Courts Building

Chicago Criminal Courts Building (Chicago Board of Health)
54 W. Hubbard St.
HABS IL-1036   pd   L

Chicago Historical Society (Boulevard Recording Studios, Inc.)
632 N. Dearborn St.
HABS IL-1010   pd   L

Chicago Home for Girls; see Pontiac Building

Chicago Ironwork (Cast Iron Stair Railing)
66 W. Oak St.
HABS IL-155-M   p   L

Chicago Ironwork (Cast Iron Stair Railing)
923 N. Dearborn St.
HABS IL-155-A   p   L

Chicago Ironwork (Carpenter, Judge, House(Cast Iron Balcony Railing))
945 N. Dearborn St.
HABS IL-155-B   p   L

Chicago Ironwork (Cast Iron Gate)
1150 N. Dearborn St.
HABS IL-155-D   p   L

Chicago Ironwork (Cast Iron Gate & Fence)
1210 N. Dearborn St.
HABS IL-155-H   p   L

Chicago Ironwork (Cast Iron Fence & Gate)
Huron & Wabash Aves.
HABS IL-155-L   p   L

Chicago Ironwork (Cast Iron Fence)
650 Rush St.
HABS IL-155-N   p   L

Chicago Ironwork (Cast Iron Fence & Gate)
701 Rush St.
HABS IL-155-P   p   L

Chicago Ironwork (Cast Iron Gatepost & Fence)
1156 N. Dearborn St.
HABS IL-155-F   p   L

Chicago Ironwork (Cast Iron Fence)
720 N. Rush St.
HABS IL-155-R   p   L

Chicago Ironwork (Cast Iron Fence & Railing)
1133 W. Washington Blvd.
HABS IL-155-U   p   L

Chicago Ironwork (Cast Iron House & Gate; Strong, William M., Estate)
1352 W. Washington Blvd.
HABS IL-155-W   p   L

Chicago Ironwork (Cast Iron Fence Railing)
1153 N. Dearborn St.
HABS IL-155-E   p   L

Chicago Ironwork (Cast Iron Porch Railing & Fence)
1237 N. Dearborn St.
HABS IL-155-I   p   L

Chicago Ironwork (Cast Iron Fence Railing)
1000 N. Dearborn St.
HABS IL-155-C   p   L

Chicago Ironwork (Cast Iron Gate & Fence)
675 Rush St.
HABS IL-155-O   p   L

Chicago Ironwork (Cast Iron Fence)
711 N. Rush St.
HABS IL-155-Q   p   L

Chicago Ironwork (Cast Iron Stair Railing)
1021 S. Wabash Ave.
HABS IL-155-T   p   L

Chicago Ironwork
HABS IL-155   d   L

Chicago Ironwork (Cast Iron Fence)
613 N. Wabash Ave.
HABS IL-155-S   p   L

Chicago Ironwork (Cast Iron Stair Railing)
1149 W. Washington Blvd.
HABS IL-155-V   p   L

Chicago Ironwork (Cast Iron Gate & Fence)
1339 N. Dearborn St.
HABS IL-155-J   p   L

Chicago Ironwork (Cast Iron Stair Railing & Fence)
1159 N. Dearborn St.
HABS IL-155-G   p   L

Chicago Ironwork (Cast Iron Gate)
1362 N. Dearborn St.
HABS IL-155-K   p   L

Chicago Public Library
Michigan, Washington, Randolph Sts. & N. Garland Ct.
HABS IL-1011   pd   L

Chicago School of Architecture Foundation; see Glessner, John J., House

Chicago Stock Exchange Building
30 N. LaSalle St.
HABS IL-1034   s pd   L H

Chicago Water Tower
800 N. Michigan Ave.
HABS IL-1041   p   L

City Club of Chicago (Marshall, John, Law School)
315 S. Plymouth Ct.
HABS IL-1080   pd   L

Clarke, Henry, House (Clarke, Widow, House)
4526 S. Wabash Ave. (moved from Michigan Ave.)
HABS IL-135   s pd   L

Clarke, Widow, House; see Clarke, Henry, House

Cleveland, Grover, Elementary School
3850 N. Albany St.
HABS IL-1079   pd   L

Coleman Funeral Home; see Krause Music Store

Columbian Exposition Store Buildings
E. Fifty-Seventh Blvd. & Stony Island Ave.
HABS IL-1062   pd   L

Crown Building; see Ayer Building

DeKoven, John, Mansion
1150 Dearborn St.
HABS IL-110-A   s d   H

DeKoven, Reginald, House
104 E. Bellevue Place
HABS IL-1042   s pd   L

Dewes, Francis J., House (Swedish Engineers' Society)
503 W. Wrightwood Ave.
HABS IL-1043   pd   L

Edison Shop (Hung-Fa Restaurant)
229 S. Wabash Ave.
HABS IL-1044   pd   L

Enterprise Institute; see Aldine Square, Smith House

Fair Store (Montgomery Ward Store)
126-144 S. State St.
HABS IL-1060   pd   L

Federal Building; see U.S. Post Office, Customs House & Sub-Treasury

Fine Arts Building; see Studebaker Building

First Congregational Church of Austin (Our Lady of Lebanon-Roman Catholic Church)
5701 Midway Park
HABS IL-1067   s pd   L

First Regiment Infantry Armory (First Regiment Infantry Armory Addendum)
1552 S. Michigan Ave.
HABS IL-1069   pd   L H

First Regiment Infantry Armory Addendum; see First Regiment Infantry Armory

Fisher Building
343 Dearborn St.
HABS IL-1082   pd   L

Fortnightly Club of Chicago; see Lathrop, Bryan, House

Francis Apartments
4304 S. Forestville Ave.
HABS IL-1076   pd   L

Fuller Park Community Building
S. Princeton Ave. & Forty-Fifth St.
HABS IL-1083   pd   L

Gage Building; see McCormick, Stanley R., Building

Garden City Warehouse
320 W. Jackson Blvd.
HABS IL-1013   s pd   L

Garrick Theatre; see Schiller Building

Getty Tomb
Graceland Cemetery, N. Clark & W. Irving Park Rd.
HABS IL-1045   pd   L

Giles Building
423-429 S. Wabash Ave.
HABS IL-1014   pd   L

Glessner, John J., House (Chicago School of Architecture Foundation)
1800 Prairie Ave., SW
HABS IL-1015   s pd   L

Government Building; see U.S. Post Office, Customs House & Sub-Treasury

Graham Foundation for Studies in Fine Arts; see Madlener, Albert F., House

Grain Elevator, First
HABS IL-304   p   H

Grand Central Station
Harrison & Wells Sts.
HABS IL-1016   s p d   L

Halsted, Ann, Townhouses
1826-1834 Lincoln Park Ave. W.
HABS IL-1096   s p d   L

Hammond Library
44 N. Ashland Ave.
HABS IL-1017   p d   L

Heath, Ira A., House
3132 S. Prairie Ave.
HABS IL-1066   s p d   L

Heller, Isidore, House
5132 S. Woodlawn Ave.
HABS IL-1046   s p d   L

Holy Family Church (Roman Catholic)
1104-1114 W. Roosevelt Rd.
HABS IL-1048   p d   L

Holy Trinity Russian & Greek Orthodox Church (Holy Trinity Russian Orth., Greek Cath. Church)
1121 N. Leavitt St.
HABS IL-1071   s p d   L

Holy Trinity Russian Orth., Greek Cath. Church; see Holy Trinity Russian & Greek Orthodox Church

Hotel Florence (Hotel Florence Addendum)
11111 S. Forrestville Ave.
HABS IL-1018   s p d   L

Hotel Florence Addendum; see Hotel Florence

Hull House; see University of Illinois, Hull Charles J., House

Hull House (Dining Room); see University of Illinois, Hull, Charles, (Dining Room)

Hung-Fa Restaurant; see Edison Shop

Illinois Central Railroad:Station
Michigan & Roosevelt Sts.
HABS IL-1106   p   H

Immaculata High School (Roman Catholic)
640 W. Irving Park Rd.
HABS IL-1074   p d   L

Irving Apartments (Newberry Library)
Oak & State Sts.
HABS IL-1081   p   H

Jewelers' Building
15-19 S. Wabash Ave.
HABS IL-1049   s p d   L

Jones School
607 S. Plymouth Court
HABS IL-1019   p d   L

Kehilath Anshe Ma'ariv Synagogue (Pilgrim Baptist Church)
3301 S. Indiana Ave.
HABS IL-1054   s p d   L

Kenna, John Francis, Apartments
2214 E. Sixty-Ninth St.
HABS IL-1094   s p d   L

Kimball, W. W., House
1801 S. Prairie Ave.
HABS IL-1077   p d   L

Krause Music Store (Coleman Funeral Home)
4611 N. Lincoln Ave.
HABS IL-1073   p d   L

Lake Street Elevated Railway:Interlocking Tower
Pulaski Rd.
HAER IL-3   p   H

Lakeside Press (Triangle Publications Building)
731 Plymouth Ct.
HABS IL-1020   p d   L

Lathrop, Bryan, House (Fortnightly Club of Chicago)
120 E. Bellevue Place
HABS IL-1037   p d   L

Leiter I Building
200-208 W. Monroe St.
HABS IL-1021   s p d   L

Leiter II Building (Sears, Roebuck & Company Building)
S. State & E. Congress Sts.
HABS IL-1022   p d   L

Madlener, Albert F., House (Graham Foundation for Studies in Fine Arts)
4 W. Burton Place
HABS IL-1023   s p d   L

Magerstadt, Ernest J., House
4930 S. Greenwood Ave.
HABS IL-1024   s p d   L

Malcolm Building
662 N. Clark St.
HABS IL-1050   p d   L

Manhattan Building
431 S. Dearborn St.
HABS IL-1051   p d   L

Marquette Building
140 S. Dearborn St.
HABS IL-1070   s p d   L H

Marshall, John, Law School; see City Club of Chicago

McClurg Building; see Ayer Building

McCormick, Stanley R., Building (Gage Building)
HABS IL-1065   p d   H

Meyer Building
301-311 W. VanBuren St.
HABS IL-1026   p d   L

Midway Airport
HABS IL-305   d   H

Monadnock Block
53 W. Jackson Blvd.
HABS IL-1027   p d   L

Montgomery Ward Store; see Fair Store

Morningstar-Paisley Company; see Schoenhofen Brewing Company, Powerhouse

Newberry Library; see Irving Apartments

Nickerson, Samuel M., House (American College of Surgeons)
40 E. Erie St.
HABS IL-1052   s p d   L

Northwestern Elevated Railway:Interlocking Tower
Wilson Ave.
HAER IL-2   p   H

Occidental Building
107-111 N. Wacker Dr.
HABS IL-1028   p d   L

Old Colony Building
407 S. Dearborn St.
HABS IL-1053   s p d   L

Our Lady of Lebanon-Roman Catholic Church; see First Congregational Church of Austin

Palace Hotel (St. Regis Hotel)
516 N. Clark St.
HABS IL-1057   p d   L

Pick-Congress Hotel; see Auditorium Annex

Pilgrim Baptist Church; see Kehilath Anshe Ma'ariv Synagogue

Plaza Hotel
1553 N. Clark St.
HABS IL-1055   p d   L

Pontiac Building (Chicago Home for Girls)
542 S. Dearborn St.
HABS IL-1102   s p d   L

Pullman Company Administration Building & Shops
1101 S. Cottage Grove Ave.
HABS IL-1091   p d   L

Pullman Industrial Complex
N. of One Hundred Eleventh St.
HAER IL-5   s   H

Quaker Oats Company (Akron Plant)
HAER IL-7   s   H

Reliance Building
32 N. State St.
HABS IL-1029   s p d   L

Republic Building (Strong Building)
209 S. State St.
HABS IL-1004   s p d   L

Robie, Frederick C., House
5757 Woodlawn Ave.
HABS IL-1005   s p d   L

Rookery Building
209 S. LaSalle St.
HABS IL-1030   s p d   L

Roosevelt University; see Auditorium Building

Schiller Building (Garrick Theatre)
64 W. Randolph St.
HABS IL-1058   s p d   L

Schlesinger & Mayer Department Store (Carson, Pirie, Scott & Company Department Store)
S. State & E. Madison Sts.
HABS IL-1064   s p d   L

Schoenhofen Brewing Company, Powerhouse (Morningstar-Paisley Company)
1770 Canalport Ave.
HABS IL-1059   pd   L

Scoville Building
619-631 W. Washington St.
HABS IL-1114   s pd   L

Sears, Roebuck & Company Building; see Leiter II Building

Second Baptist Church
Morgan & Monroe Sts.
HABS IL-26-2   s pd   L

Shedd Park Recreation Building
S. Twenty-Third St. & Lawndale Ave.
HABS IL-1107   s   L

Sheldon, Daniel H., House
723 W. Congress St.
HABS IL-26-1   s pd   L

Shreve Building
100-104 W. Lake St.
HABS IL-1031   pd   L

Sibley, Hiram, Warehouse (Central Cold Storage Warehouse)
315-331 N. Clark St.
HABS IL-1047   pd   L

1017 South Wabash Avenue (House)
HABS IL-184   p   H

Springer Block (Bay State Building & Kranz Building)
126-146 N. State St.
HABS IL-1008   pd   L

St. Gabriel's Church (Roman Catholic)
4522 S. Wallace St.
HABS IL-1032   pd   L

St. Ignatius College (St. Ignatius High School)
1076 Roosevelt Rd.
HABS IL-1056   pd   L

St. Ignatius High School; see St. Ignatius College

St. Patrick's Church
Adams & Desplaines Sts.
HABS IL-1033   s pd   L

St. Regis Hotel; see Palace Hotel

Steffens, Oscar, House
7631 N. Sheridan Rd.
HABS IL-1063   s d   L

Strong Building; see Republic Building

Strong, William M., Estate; see Chicago Ironwork

Studebaker Building (Fine Arts Building)
410 S. Michigan Ave.
HABS IL-1078   p   H

Sullivan, Albert W., House
4575 Lake Park Ave.
HABS IL-1006   pd   L

Swedish Engineers' Society; see Dewes, Francis J., House

Tenement Building E
Langley Ave.
HABS IL-1111   s   H

Triangle Publications Building; see Lakeside Press

Underwriter's Laboratories Building
207-231 E. Ohio St.
HABS IL-1116   pd   H

Union Elevated Railroad: Adams Street Station
Wabash St.
HAER IL-1-C   p   H

Union Elevated Railroad: Clark Street Station
Lake St.
HAER IL-1-E   p   H

Union Elevated Railroad: Quincy Street Station
Wells St.
HAER IL-1-A   p   H

Union Elevated Railroad: Randolph Street Station
Wells St.
HAER IL-1-F   p   H

Union Elevated Railroad: Randolph Street Station
Wabash St.
HAER IL-1-D   p   H

Union Elevated Railroad: State Street Station
Van Buren St.
HAER IL-1-B   p   H

Union Elevated Railroad: Union Loop
HAER IL-1   p   H

University of Illinois, Hull, Charles, (Dining Room) (Hull House (Dining Room))
800 S. Halsted St.
HABS IL-1110-A   d   H

University of Illinois, Hull Charles J., House (Hull House)
800 S. Halsted St.
HABS IL-1110   d   H

U.S. Courthouse; see U.S. Post Office, Customs House & Sub-Treasury

U.S. Marine Hospital (U.S. Public Health Clinic)
4141 N. Clarendon Ave.
HABS IL-1084   pd   L

U.S. Post Office, Customs House & Sub-Treasury (Government Building; Federal Building; U.S. Courthouse)
218 S. Dearborn St.
HABS IL-1040   pd   L

U.S. Public Health Clinic; see U.S. Marine Hospital

Evanston

Carter, Frederick B., Jr., House
1024 Judson St.
HABS IL-1086   s pd   L

Comtock, Hurd, House II
1631 Ashland Ave.
HABS IL-1089   s pd   L

Long, John T., House (Shadrach Bond Mantel)
922 Sheridan Rd.
HABS IL-26-31   s pd   L

Shadrach Bond Mantel
929 Sheridan Rd. (moved from IL Kaskaskia)
HABS IL-26-31-B   s pd   L

Willard, Frances E., House (Women's Christian Temperence Union)
1730 Chicago Ave.
HABS IL-1095   s pd   L

Women's Christian Temperence Union; see Willard, Frances E., House

Glencoe

Albright, Jules, House
Hohfelder Rd.
HABS IL-134   s pd   L

Glasner, W. A., House
850 Sheridan Rd.
HABS IL-1098   s   L

Kenilworth

Kenilworth Club
10 Kenilworth Ave.
HABS IL-1090   s pd   L

Oak Park

Estabrook, T. S., House
200 N. Scoville St.
HABS IL-1085   s pd   L

McCready, Edward W., House
231 N. Euclid St.
HABS IL-1075   s pd   L

Unitarian-Universalist Church; see Unity Temple

Unity Temple (Unitarian-Universalist Church)
875 Lake St.
HABS IL-1093   s pd   L

Wright, Frank Lloyd, House & Studio
428 Forest Ave. & 951 Chicago Ave.
HABS IL-1099   pd   H

River Forest

Drummond, William E., House
559 Edgewood Place
HABS IL-1072   s pd   L

Winslow, William H., House
Auvergne Place
HABS IL-1061   s pd   L

Riverside

Babson Stable & Service Building
283 Gatesby Ln.
HABS IL-1068   s pd   L

Coonley, Avery, House
300 Scottswood Rd.
HABS IL-1100   p   ·   H

Wilmette

Baker, Ralph S., House
1226 Ashland Ave.
HABS IL-1097   s pd   L

Bersbach, Alfred, House
1120 Michigan Ave.
HABS IL-1103   pd   L H

DOUGLAS COUNTY

Genoa vic.
Perkins Farmhouse
Rt. 22
HABS IL-26-30   s pd   L

DU PAGE COUNTY

Addison
Heideman Windmill
Rt. 5
HABS IL-26-4   s pd   L

Bloomingdale vic.
Laudon-Bender Farmhouse
HABS IL-26-7   s pd   L

Elmhurst
Emery House
218 Arlington St.
HABS IL-1101   s pd   H

Fullersburg
Ogden Avenue (House)
HABS IL-170   p   L
Tavern, Old
Ogden Ave.
HABS IL-170   s pd   L
Toll House, Old
HABS IL-170-A   p   L

Fullersburg vic.
Graue Water Mill
York Rd.
HABS IL-26-6   pd   L

Naderville
Hobson Law Office
215 W. Main St.
HABS IL-26-33   s pd   L

Naperville
First Baptist Church
34 Washington Ave.
HABS IL-136   s pd   L
Pre-Emption House
Chicago Ave. & Main St.
HABS IL-26-5   pd   L

Naperville vic.
Hobson Grist Mill (Hobson Mill
   (Monument & Millstones))
DuPage County Pioneer Park
HABS IL-154-A   p   L
Hobson House
HABS IL-154   s pd   L
Hobson Mill (Monument & Millstones); see
   Hobson Grist Mill

Warrenville
Warren, Col., House
Warrenville Rd.
HABS IL-26-8   s pd   L
Warrenville Methodist Church
HABS IL-26-32   s pd   L

EDGAR COUNTY

Paris
Austin, A. B., House
501 Jefferson Ave.
HABS IL-280   s pd   L

EDWARDS COUNTY

Albion
French, George, House
State Rt. 130
HABS IL-25-1   s pd   L
Thompson, F. B., House
State Rt. 130
HABS IL-25-2   s pd   L

FULTON COUNTY

Lewiston
Walker, Maj. Newton, House
Main St.
HABS IL-283   s pd   L

GALLATIN COUNTY

New Haven
Sheridan Tavern
33 Mill St.
HABS IL-25-5   s pd   L

Shawneetown
Bank in Illinois, First; see Marshall, John,
   House
Marshall, John, House (Bank in Illinois,
   First)
HABS IL-25-3   s pd   L
State Bank, Old
Main St. & Rt. 13
HABS IL-25-4   s pd   L

HANCOCK COUNTY

Nauvoo
Babbitt, Almon W., House
Main & Kimball Sts.
HABS IL-26-25   s pd   L
Bangham House
Mulhollen & Seventeenth Sts.
HABS IL-255   p   L
Baumert House
Mulhollen & Fifteenth Sts.
HABS IL-26-27   s pd   L

Browning, Jonathan, House
Main St.
HABS IL-245   s pd   L
Gross, Cooper, House
Knight & Sixteenth Sts.
HABS IL-254   p   L
Kaufman, Adam, House
Corlis & Sidney Sts.
HABS IL-257   p   L
Kimball, Heber C., House
Ninth & Munson Sts.
HABS IL-244   s pd   L
Mansion House (Smith, Joseph, House)
Main & Water Sts.
HABS IL-26-24   s pd   L
Mix, P., House
Kimball & Twenty-First Sts.
HABS IL-256   p   L
Smith, Joseph, House
HABS IL-253   p   L
Smith, Joseph, House; see Mansion House
Woodruff, Wilford, House
Tenth & Hotchkiss Sts.
HABS IL-26-26   s pd   L
Young, Brigham, House
Granger & Kimball Sts.
HABS IL-250   s pd   L

Warsaw
407-413, 421-429 Main Street (Commercial
   Buildings)
HABS IL-249-E   p   L
Adams House & Adjoining Building; see
   Main Street, Historic View
202 Main Street (Commercial Building)
HABS IL-249-B   s pd   L
222 Main Street (Commercial Building)
HABS IL-249-D   s pd   L
421 Main Street (Commercial Building)
HABS IL-249-F   p   L
202-230 Main Street (Commercial
   Buildings)
HABS IL-249-C   pd   L
Main Street, Historic View
HABS IL-249   p   L
Main Street, Historic View (Adams House
   & Adjoining Building)
HABS IL-249-A   p   L
Mussetter House
950 Webster St.
HABS IL-251   p   L

HENDERSON COUNTY

Oquawka
Henderson County Courthouse
Fourth & Warren Sts.
HABS IL-240   s pd   L
Knowles House
Fourth St.
HABS IL-241   pd   L

Oquawka vic.

Eames Covered Bridge
Spanning Henderson Creek
HABS IL-243   s p d   L

Jack's Mill, Covered Bridge
Spanning Henderson Creek
HABS IL-242   s p d   L

HENRY COUNTY

Bishop Hill

Apartment House, Old; see Jansonist
Colony

Apartments, Big Brick; see Jansonist
Colony

Bjorklund Hotel; see Jansonist Colony

Blacksmith & Carpenter Shop; see
Jansonist Colony

Carriage & Wagon Shop; see Jansonist
Colony

Colony Bakery & Brewery, Old; see
Jansonist Colony

Colony Church, Old; see Jansonist Colony

Colony Hospital; see Jansonist Colony

Colony Residence; see Jansonist Colony

Colony School; see Jansonist Colony

Colony Store & Post Office; see Jansonist
Colony

Cooperative Store; see Jansonist Colony

Dairy Building (Butter & Cheese Factory);
see Jansonist Colony

Jansonist Colony (Colony Residence)
HABS IL-169-I   p   H

Jansonist Colony (Cooperative Store)
Main & Christina Sts.
HABS IL-169-L   s   L

Jansonist Colony (Apartments, Big Brick)
Park St.
HABS IL-169-B   p   L

Jansonist Colony (Blacksmith & Carpenter
Shop)
HABS IL-169-D   p   L

Jansonist Colony (Colony Bakery &
Brewery, Old)
HABS IL-169-F   p   L

Jansonist Colony (Colony Hospital)
HABS IL-169-H   p   H

Jansonist Colony (Colony Store & Post
Office)
Main & Bishop Hill Sts.
HABS IL-169-K   s p   L H

Jansonist Colony (Bjorklund Hotel)
HABS IL-169-C   p   L H

Jansonist Colony (Colony School)
Main & Olson Sts.
HABS IL-169-J   p   L H

Jansonist Colony (Apartment House, Old)
Main St.
HABS IL-169-A   p   L

Jansonist Colony
HABS IL-169   s p d   L

Jansonist Colony (Dairy Building (Butter &
Cheese Factory))
HABS IL-169-M   p   L

Jansonist Colony (Street Scene)
HABS IL-169-P   d   L

Jansonist Colony (Carriage & Wagon
Shop)
HABS IL-169-E   p   H

Jansonist Colony (Colony Church, Old)
Bishop Hill & Maiden Lane Sts.
HABS IL-169-G   p   L

Steeple Building
Main & Bishop Hill Sts.
HABS IL-169-N   s p d   L H

Street Scene; see Jansonist Colony

IROQUOIS COUNTY

Onarga vic.

Larch Farm; see Pinkerton, Allan, House

Pinkerton, Allan, House (Larch Farm)
HABS IL-263   p d   L

JACKSON COUNTY

Carbondale vic.

Log Cabin
HABS IL-25-16   s p d   L

JEFFERSON COUNTY

Mount Vernon

Appellate Court Building
Fourteenth & Main Sts.
HABS IL-25-14   s p d   L

JO DAVIESS COUNTY

Galena

Barrows-Coatsworth Building
122 Main St.
HABS IL-1112   p d   L

Buden House
HABS IL-197   p   L

Calderwood, Celia, House
N. Bench St.
HABS IL-178   p d   L

Clarey House
HABS IL-198   p   L

Cottage, Brick
408 S. Dodge St.
HABS IL-151   s p d   L

Custom House & Post Office
HABS IL-306   p   H

Doorways, Dowling, John, House
Main & Diagonal Sts.
HABS IL-178-A   p d   L

Doorways, First Methodist Church
Bench St.
HABS IL-178-C   p d   L

Doorways, Grimm, Heike, House
608 S. Bench St.
HABS IL-178-D   p   L

Doorways, Harmony Lodge of Odd Fellows
Bench St.
HABS IL-178-E   p   L

Doorways, Hempstead, Charles, House
611 S. Bench St.
HABS IL-178-F   p d   L

Doorways, House, Red Brick
Elk & Prospect Sts.
HABS IL-178-B   p d   L

Doorways, Klingel, Peter, House
Bench St.
HABS IL-178-G   p d   L

Doorways, Maxelner, Elizabeth, Cottage
104 S. Bench St.
HABS IL-178-H   s p   L

Doorways of Galena
HABS IL-178   p d   L

Doorways, Porter House
110 N. Bench St.
HABS IL-178-I   s p d   L

Doorways, Ryan House
Bench St.
HABS IL-178-J   p   L

Doorways, Sisters of Mercy Convent
226 N. Bench St.
HABS IL-178-K   s p d   L

Doorways, Telford Shop
Bench St.
HABS IL-178-L   p d   L

Doorways, Warehouse
S. Main St.
HABS IL-178-M   p d   L

Dowling, John, House
120 N. Bench St.
HABS IL-26-14   s p d   L

Dowling, Nicholas, Building
Diagonal & Main Sts.
HABS IL-26-17   s p d   L

Felt, S. M., House (Staircase)
Prospect St.
HABS IL-26-16   p d   L

First Presbyterian Church
Bench St.
HABS IL-177   s p   H

Grace Episcopal Church
S. Prospect St.
HABS IL-150   s p d   L

Grant House, First
121 S. High St.
HABS IL-26-12   s p d   L

Hoge, Joseph, House
512 Park Ave.
HABS IL-26-11   s p d   L

Hunkins House
HABS IL-199   p   L

Market House, Old (Town Hall)
N. Commerce & Troy Sts.
HABS IL-149   s p d   L

Mississippi House (Hotel)
S. Main St.
HABS IL-152   s p d   L

Smith, Gen., House
South & Bench Sts.
HABS IL-26-13   s pd   L
Specht House
HABS IL-196   p   L
Stahl, Frederick, House
605 S. Bench St.
HABS IL-26-18   pd   L
Telford House
Park Ave.
HABS IL-26-20   s pd   L
Town Hall; see Market House, Old
Washburne, Sen. Elihu B., House
908 Third St.
HABS IL-26-19   s pd   L

Galena vic.

Chetlain, Louis, House
HABS IL-26-15   s pd   L
Roberts, James M., House
Rt. 5
HABS IL-26-21   s pd   L

KANE COUNTY

Aurora

**Chicago, Burlington & Quincy
   Roundhouse & Shops**
HAER IL-8   pd   H

Batavia

Burke House
Washington St.
HABS IL-163   s pd   L

Fayville

Keating House
U.S. Hwy. 430
HABS IL-165   s pd   L

Geneva

Unitarian Church, Old
Second & James Sts.
HABS IL-164   s pd   L
Wells, Capt., House
S. Third St.
HABS IL-138   s pd   L

Geneva vic.

Bristol Farmhouse
River Rd.
HABS IL-26-22   s pd   L

St. Charles

Jucket House
110 Third St.
HABS IL-162   s pd   L
Lewis, Dr. Jas. K., House
19 S. Fifth St.
HABS IL-26-9   s pd   L

KENDALL COUNTY

Lisbon

Congregational Church
HABS IL-148   s pd   L H

Plano vic.

Farnsworth, Edith, House
Fox River Rd. & Milbrook Rd.
HABS IL-1005   pd   H

KNOX COUNTY

Knoxville

County Jail
115 Market St.
HABS IL-248-B   p   L
Hall of Records
Main St.
HABS IL-248-A   p   L
Knox County Courthouse, Old
Main St.
HABS IL-248   s pd   L

LA SALLE COUNTY

Mendota

Clark, Warren, House; see Octagon House
Octagon House (Clark, Warren, House)
HABS IL-180   s pd   L H

Ottawa

Hossack, John, House
210 Prospect Ave.
HABS IL-141   s pd   L

LAKE COUNTY

Fort Sheridan

Artillery Barracks, Building Number 84;
   see Fort Sheridan Historic District
**Bachelor Officers Quarters, Open Mess,
   Building 31;** see Fort Sheridan Historic
   District
Bakery, Building Number 34; see Fort
   Sheridan Historic District
Blacksmith Shop, Building Number 77; see
   Fort Sheridan Historic District
Captains' Quarters, Building Number 12;
   see Fort Sheridan Historic District
Cavalry Stable, Building Number 43; see
   Fort Sheridan Historic District
Cold Storage House, Building Number 100;
   see Fort Sheridan Historic District
Company Kitchens, Building Number 108;
   see Fort Sheridan Historic District
Dead House, Building Number 87; see Fort
   Sheridan Historic District
Fire Station, Building Number 79; see Fort
   Sheridan Historic District
Forage Storehouse, Building Number 39;
   see Fort Sheridan Historic District
Fort Sheridan Historic District
   (Non-Commissioned Officer's Quarters,
   Building 46)
Ronan & Lyster Rds.
HABS IL-1113-15   pd   L

Fort Sheridan Historic District (Pumping
   Station, Building Number 29)
Nicholson Rd.
HABS IL-1113-5   pd   L
Fort Sheridan Historic District (Dead
   House, Building Number 87)
Bradley Loop
HABS IL-1113-26   pd   L
Fort Sheridan Historic District
   (Quartermaster Stable, Building Number
   38)
Lyster Rd.
HABS IL-1113-12   pd   L
Fort Sheridan Historic District (Cavalry
   Stable, Building Number 43)
Thorpe & Chapman Rds.
HABS IL-1113-14   pd   L
Fort Sheridan Historic District (Artillery
   Barracks, Building Number 84)
Leonard Wood Ave.
HABS IL-1113-25   pd   L
Fort Sheridan Historic District (Forage
   Storehouse, Building Number 39)
Thorpe Rd.
HABS IL-1113-13   pd   L
Fort Sheridan Historic District (Captains's
   Quarters, Building Number 12)
149 Logan Loop
HABS IL-1113-3   pd   L
Fort Sheridan Historic District (Company
   Kitchens, Building Number 108)
Whistler Rd.
HABS IL-1113-31   pd   L
Fort Sheridan Historic District (Quarter
   Master Stable Guardhouse, Building 37)
Lyster Rd.
HABS IL-1113-11   pd   L
Fort Sheridan Historic District (Bakery,
   Building Number 34)
Lyster Rd.
HABS IL-1113-8   pd   L
Fort Sheridan Historic District (Cold
   Storage House, Building Number 100)
Lyster Rd.
HABS IL-1113-30   pd   L
Fort Sheridan Historic District (Bachelor
   Officers Quarters, Open Mess, Building
   31)
Leonard Wood Ave.
HABS IL-1113-6   pd   L
Fort Sheridan Historic District (Saddlers'
   & Stable Sargeants Building, Number
   78)
Ronan Rd.
HABS IL-1113-23   pd   L
Fort Sheridan Historic District
   (Non-Commissioned Officer's Quarters,
   Building 91)
3612 Lyster Rd.
HABS IL-1113-28   pd   L

Fort Sheridan Historic District (Mess Hall
   & Heating Plant, Building Number 47)
Whistler Rd.
HABS IL-1113-16   pd   L

Fort Sheridan Historic District (Infantry Barracks, Building Number 48)
Leonard Wood Ave.
HABS IL-1113-17   pd   L

Fort Sheridan Historic District (Ordnance Storehouse, Building Number 59)
3588 Lyster Rd.
HABS IL-1113-20   pd   L

Fort Sheridan Historic District (Post Hospital, Building Number 1)
Bradley Loop
HABS IL-1113-1   pd   L

Fort Sheridan Historic District (Quartermaster, Commissary Storehouse, Building 35)
Lyster Rd.
HABS IL-1113-9   pd   L

Fort Sheridan Historic District (Water Tower, Building Number 49)
Leonard Wood Ave.
HABS IL-1113-18   pd   L

Fort Sheridan Historic District (Lieutenant's Quarters, Building Number 22)
165 Scott Loop
HABS IL-1113-4   pd   L

Fort Sheridan Historic District (Lieutenant's Quarters, Building Number 92)
3711 Leonard Wood Ave.
HABS IL-1113-29   pd   L

Fort Sheridan Historic District (Fire Station, Building Number 79)
Whistler & Ronan Rds.
HABS IL-1113-24   pd   L

Fort Sheridan Historic District (Post Commandant's Quarters, Building Number 9)
111 Logan Loop
HABS IL-1113-2   pd   L

Fort Sheridan Historic District (Blacksmith Shop, Building Number 77)
Thorpe Rd.
HABS IL-1113-22   pd   L

Fort Sheridan Historic District (Workshops, Building Number 36)
Lyster Rd.
HABS IL-1113-10   pd   L

Fort Sheridan Historic District
Chicago vic.
HABS IL-1113   pd   L

Fort Sheridan Historic District (Infantry Drill Hall, Building Number 60)
Whistler & Ronan Rds.
HABS IL-1113-21   pd   L

Fort Sheridan Historic District (Magazine, Building Number 57A)
Bartlett Ravine Rd.
HABS IL-1113-19   pd   L

Fort Sheridan Historic District (Gun Shed, Building Number 89)
Ronan Rd.
HABS IL-1113-27   pd   L

Fort Sheridan Historic District (Guardhouse, Building Number 33)
Lyster Rd.
HABS IL-1113-7   pd   L

Guardhouse, Building Number 33; see Fort Sheridan Historic District

Gun Shed, Building Number 89; see Fort Sheridan Historic District

Infantry Barracks, Building Number 48; see Fort Sheridan Historic District

Infantry Drill Hall, Building Number 60; see Fort Sheridan Historic District

Lieutenant's Quarters, Building Number 22; see Fort Sheridan Historic District

Lieutenant's Quarters, Building Number 92; see Fort Sheridan Historic District

Magazine, Building Number 57A; see Fort Sheridan Historic District

Mess Hall & Heating Plant, Building Number 47; see Fort Sheridan Historic District

Non-Commissioned Officer's Quarters, Building 46; see Fort Sheridan Historic District

Non-Commissioned Officer's Quarters, Building 91; see Fort Sheridan Historic District

Ordnance Storehouse, Building Number 59; see Fort Sheridan Historic District

Post Commandant's Quarters, Building Number 9; see Fort Sheridan Historic District

Post Hospital, Building Number 1; see Fort Sheridan Historic District

Pumping Station, Building Number 29; see Fort Sheridan Historic District

Quarter Master Stable Guardhouse, Building 37; see Fort Sheridan Historic District

Quartermaster, Commissary Storehouse, Building 35; see Fort Sheridan Historic District

Quartermaster Stable, Building Number 38; see Fort Sheridan Historic District

Saddlers' & Stable Sargeants Building, Number 78; see Fort Sheridan Historic District

Water Tower, Building Number 49; see Fort Sheridan Historic District

Workshops, Building Number 36; see Fort Sheridan Historic District

Halfday
Tavern
HABS IL-139   s pd   L

Mundelein
Marsh's Settlement, Schoolhouse
Rt. 176
HABS IL-140   s pd   L

Waukegan
Swartout House
414 Sheridan Rd.
HABS IL-26-3   s pd   L

Waukegan vic.
Lighthouse
HABS IL-176   p   L

LEE COUNTY

Lee Center
Adams, Dr., Office
Old Dixon-Chicago Pike
HABS IL-167   s pd   L

Four Bottle Tavern
Old Dixon-Chicago Pike
HABS IL-166   s pd   L

Sublette
Baptist Parsonage, Old
Snyder & Virginia Sts.
HABS IL-168   s pd   L

MACON COUNTY

Decatur
Macon County Courthouse, First
Fairview Park (moved from Main St.)
HABS IL-222   s pd   L

MADISON COUNTY

Alton
Academic Hall, Old; see Shurtleff College, Loomis Hall

Shurtleff College, Loomis Hall (Academic Hall, Old)
HABS IL-25-20   s pd   L

Edwardsville
Wabash Hotel, Old
Main & Union Sts.
HABS IL-236   s pd   L

Warren, Hooper, Print Shop
HABS IL-238   pd   L

Edwardsville vic.
Paddock, Galus, Farm
Springfield Rd.
HABS IL-237   s pd   L

Godfrey
Godfrey Congregational Church
State Rt. 111
HABS IL-25-10   s pd   L

Godfrey Homestead
Delhi Rd.
HABS IL-25-9   s pd   L

MC HENRY COUNTY

Marengo
Rogers, Anson, House & Farm Buildings
U.S. Rt. 20
HABS IL-144   s pd   L

Thompson Store
109 W. Grant Hwy.
HABS IL-143   s pd   L

Woodstock

Kennedy Farmhouse
HABS IL-182   s p   H

MC LEAN COUNTY

Bloomington

Davis, David, Mansion
Monroe & Davis Sts.
HABS IL-302   s pd   L
Major's Hall
117 E. Front St.
HABS IL-239   s pd   L

Normal

Fell, Jesse, House
502 Irving (moved from Broadway & Irving Sts.)
HABS IL-262   pd   L

MENARD COUNTY

Petersburg

Mick Cottage & Summer Kitchens (Ogg-Scott House)
423 N. Seventh St.
HABS IL-1115   pd   L
Ogg-Scott House; see Mick Cottage & Summer Kitchens

MONROE COUNTY

Columbia

Buck Tavern (Grosse Inn)
401 Main St.
HABS IL-232-3   s pd   L
808 East Main Street (House)
HABS IL-232-6   s pd   L
810 East Main Street (House)
HABS IL-232-7   s pd   L
812 East Main Street (House)
HABS IL-232-8   s pd   L
Grosse, Emelie, House (Gundlach House)
HABS IL-232-1   s pd   L
Grosse Inn; see Buck Tavern
Gundlach House; see Grosse, Emelie, House
Habermehl, Jacob, House (Pig's Eye House)
Second & Pine Sts.
HABS IL-232-4   pd   L
Ichmiller, Mary, House
803 E. Main St.
HABS IL-232-9   pd   L
808-812 Main Street (Houses)
HABS IL-232   p   L
Otto, Emil House
Main St.
HABS IL-232-2   s pd   L
Pig's Eye House; see Habermehl, Jacob, House
Schneider, Ed J., House
123 E. Main St.
HABS IL-232-5   s pd   L

Waterloo vic.

Fort Lemen; see Lemen, James, House
Lemen, James, House (Fort Lemen)
State Hwy. 3
HABS IL-230   s pd   L

MORGAN COUNTY

Jacksonville

Clay, Porter, House (Sanders House)
1019 W. State St.
HABS IL-226   pd   L
Duncan, Gov. Joseph, House
4 Duncan Pl.
HABS IL-25-8   s pd   L
Illinois College, Beecher Hall (Prairie College)
HABS IL-25-11   s pd   L
Prairie College; see Illinois College, Beecher Hall
Sanders House; see Clay, Porter, House

OGLE COUNTY

Grand Detour

Paine, Horace, House
Walker & Illinois Sts.
HABS IL-175   s p   L H
Pankhurst House
HABS IL-183   p   L
St. Peter's Episcopal Church
Rock & Main Sts.
HABS IL-174   pd   L

PEORIA COUNTY

Jubilee

Jubilee College
HABS IL-235   s pd   L

Mossville

Methodist Episcopal Church (Presbyterian Church)
HABS IL-282   s pd   L
Presbyterian Church; see Methodist Episcopal Church

PIATT COUNTY

Bement

Bryant House
116 Wilson St.
HABS IL-223   s pd   L

Bement vic.

Lincoln-Douglas Road Marker
HABS IL-1117   p   L

Monticello

Hammerschmidt, Louis, House
817 Charter St.
HABS IL-25-12   s pd   L

PIKE COUNTY

Pittsfield

Worthington House
Franklin & W. Washington Sts.
HABS IL-264   s pd   L

RANDOLPH COUNTY

Eden vic.

Bannister, Oliver, House
HABS IL-297   p   L

Fort Gage

Fort Kaskaskia (Ruins)
HABS IL-287   p   L
Menard, Pierre, House
HABS IL-286   p   L

Kaskaskia

Shandrach Bond Mantel
(moved to IL Evanston 929 Sheridan Rd.)
HABS IL-26-31-B   s pd   L

Prairie Du Rocher

Fort de Chartres
Fort de Chartres State Park
HABS IL-309   p   L
Fort de Chartres:East Barracks Foundation
Fort de Chartres State Park
HABS IL-299   p   L
Fort de Chartres:Foundation of Officers' Quarters
Fort de Chartres State Park
HABS IL-289   p   L
Fort de Chartres:Foundation-Commandant's Quarters
Fort de Chartres State Park
HABS IL-301   p   L
Fort de Chartres:Powder Magazine
Fort de Chartres State Park
HABS IL-288   p   L
Fort de Chartres:West Barracks Foundation
Fort de Chartres State Park
HABS IL-300   L
French (Creole) House
Market St.
HABS IL-234   pd   L

Redbud

Schuck House
HABS IL-294   p   L

Sparta vic.

Fulton House
HABS IL-293   p   L
Glen, Amos, House
HABS IL-292   p   L

Tilden vic.

Boyd, Sammuel, House
HABS IL-298   p   L

ROCK ISLAND COUNTY

Rock Island

Bridge Spanning Mississippi River
HABS IL-1002   p   L
Davenport, Col., House
Arsenal Grounds
HABS IL-158   pd   L
Fort Armstrong
HABS IL-1000   pd   L
Rock Island Arsenal
HABS IL-1001   p   L

SANGAMON COUNTY

Pleasant Plains

Fink, Dr. F. C., House
State Rt. 125
HABS IL-269   pd   L

Springfield

Sangamon County Courthouse; see State
     House, Old
State House, Old (Sangamon County
     Courthouse; Third State Capitol)
HABS IL-224   s pd   L
Third State Capitol; see State House, Old

SCOTT COUNTY

Winchester

Presbyterian Church
W. Cherry & N. Mechanic Sts.
HABS IL-25-15   pd   L

ST. CLAIR COUNTY

Belleville

Hinckley House; see Lincoln Hotel
Lincoln Hotel (Hinckley House)
N. High & E. °A° Sts.
HABS IL-229   s pd   L

Cahokia

Cakohia Courthouse
(moved to IL Chicago Jackson Park)
HABS IL-26-31-A   s pd   L
Church of the Holy Family
State Rt. 157
HABS IL-25-6   s pd   L H
Jarrot, Nicholas, Mansion
State Rt. 157
HABS IL-25-7   s pd   L
Priest's House
State Rt. 157
HABS IL-25-13   s pd   L

Lebanon

McKendree College, Chapel
College Square
HABS IL-228   s pd   L
McKendree College, Old Main Building
College Square
HABS IL-227   s pd   L
Mermaid House
114 E. Saint Louis St.
HABS IL-231   s pd   L

New Baden vic.

Griffen House
HABS IL-296   p   L

STARK COUNTY

Toulon

Hall, Dr., House & Office
301 Franklin St.
HABS IL-247   s pd   L

STEPHENSON COUNTY

Lena vic.

Octagon House, Stone
HABS IL-179   p   L H

TAZEWELL COUNTY

Mackinaw

Pendergast Inn
Market & Monroe Sts.
HABS IL-268   pd   L

Tremont

Jones-Menard House
HABS IL-281   s pd   L

UNION COUNTY

Anna

Stinson Memorial Public Library
Main & High Sts.
HABS IL-1108   s   L

Jonesboro

Jail Building, Old
First & Mississippi Sts.
HABS IL-233   s pd   L

WARREN COUNTY

Monmouth

Johnson House
300 E. Archer Ave.
HABS IL-26-23   s pd   L

WILL COUNTY

Channahon vic.

**Illinois & Michigan Canal, Locks &
     Lockhouse**
HABS IL-157   s pd   L

Plainsfield

Green, Dennison, House
Main St.
HABS IL-147   s pd   L

WINNEBAGO COUNTY

Rockford

Luce House
HABS IL-181   s p   L H

Rockton

First Congregational Church
Union St.
HABS IL-145   s pd   L

Indiana

ADAMS COUNTY

Geneva

Ceylon Covered Bridge
County Rd. 900 S., spanning Wabash River
HABS IN-156   s   H

ALLEN COUNTY

Fort Wayne

Ewing, William G., House
Berry & Ewing Sts.
HABS IN-24-10   s pd   L

Swinney House
Swinney Park & Jefferson St.
HABS IN-24-6   s pd   L

Pleasant Township

Pleasant Township School
Smith & Ferguson Rds.
HABS IN-78   s d   H

BARTHOLOMEW COUNTY

Columbus

Cerealine Manufacturing Company, Mill A
Jackson & Brown Sts.
HAER IN-34   s p   H

Reeves Pulley Company (Reliance Electric
    Company Division)
Seventh & Wilson Sts.
HAER IN-15   s p   H

Reliance Electric Company Division; see
    Reeves Pulley Company

Zaharako's Ice Cream Parlor
329 Washington St.
HABS IN-77   p   H

CARROLL COUNTY

Cutler vic.

Adams Mill Covered Bridge
HAER IN-29   s d   H

CLARK COUNTY

Jeffersonville

Grisamore House
111-113 W. Chestnut
HABS IN-24-18   s pd   L

CLAY COUNTY

Clay City

Fedderham Bridge
State Rt. 59, spanning Eel River
HAER IN-21   p   H

CRAWFORD COUNTY

Alton vic.

Mill Creek Bridge (Modified Pratt Truss
    Bridge)
Mill Creek
HAER IN-23   p   H

Modified Pratt Truss Bridge; see Mill
    Creek Bridge

DAVIESS COUNTY

Washington

Baltimore & Ohio Railroad, Repair Shop;
    see Ohio & Mississippi Railroad, Repair
    Shops, West Shop

Baltimore & Ohio Railroad, Repair Shops;
    see Ohio & Miss. RR, Rpr. Shops,
    Turntable & Roundhouse

Baltimore & Ohio Railroad, Repair Shops;
    see Ohio & Mississippi RR, Repair
    Shops, Office Bldg.

Baltimore & Ohio Railroad, Repair Shops;
    see Ohio & Mississippi RR, Repair
    Shops, Power House

Baltimore & Ohio Railroad, Repair Shops;
    see Ohio & Mississippi RR, Repair
    Shops, Stencil Shop

Baltimore & Ohio Railroad, Repair Shops;
    see Ohio & Mississippi Railroad, Repair
    Shops

Baltimore & Ohio Railroad, Repair Shops;
    see Ohio & Mississippi Railroad, Repair
    Shops, East Shop

**Ohio & Miss. RR, Rpr. Shops, Turntable &
    Roundhouse** (Baltimore & Ohio
    Railroad, Repair Shops; U.S. Railway
    Equipment Company)
Van Trees & Seventeenth Sts.
HAER IN-5-F   p   H

Ohio & Mississippi Railroad, Repair Shops
    (Baltimore & Ohio Railroad, Repair
    Shops; U.S. Railway Equipment
    Company)
Van Trees & Seventeenth Sts.
HAER IN-5-A   p   H

**Ohio & Mississippi Railroad, Repair Shops,
    East Shop** (Baltimore & Ohio Railroad,
    Repair Shops; U.S. Railway Equipment
    Company)
Van Trees & Seventeenth Sts.
HAER IN-5-B   p   H

**Ohio & Mississippi Railroad, Repair Shops,
    West Shop** (Baltimore & Ohio Railroad,
    Repair Shop)
Van Trees & Seventeenth Sts.
HAER IN-5-G   p   H

**Ohio & Mississippi RR, Repair Shops,
    Office Bldg.** (Baltimore & Ohio
    Railroad, Repair Shops; U.S. Railway
    Equipment Company)
Van Trees & Seventeenth Sts.
HAER IN-5-C   p   H

**Ohio & Mississippi RR, Repair Shops,
    Power House** (Baltimore & Ohio
    Railroad, Repair Shops; U.S. Railway
    Equipment Company)
Van Trees & Seventeenth Sts.
HAER IN-5-D   p   H

**Ohio & Mississippi RR, Repair Shops,
    Stencil Shop** (Baltimore & Ohio
    Railroad, Repair Shops; U.S. Railway
    Equipment Company)
Van Trees & Seventeenth Sts.
HAER IN-5-E   p   H

U.S. Railway Equipment Company; see
    Ohio & Miss. RR, Rpr. Shops, Turntable
    & Roundhouse

U.S. Railway Equipment Company; see
    Ohio & Mississippi RR, Repair Shops,
    Office Bldg.

U.S. Railway Equipment Company; see
    Ohio & Mississippi RR, Repair Shops,
    Power House

U.S. Railway Equipment Company; see
    Ohio & Mississippi RR, Repair Shops,
    Stencil Shop

U.S. Railway Equipment Company; see
    Ohio & Mississippi Railroad, Repair
    Shops

U.S. Railway Equipment Company; see
    Ohio & Mississippi Railroad, Repair
    Shops, East Shop

DEARBORN COUNTY

Aurora vic.

Laughery Creek Bridge (Triple Intersection
    Pratt Truss Iron Bridge)
State Rt. 56
HAER IN-16   p   H

**Triple Intersection Pratt Truss Iron
    Bridge;** see Laughery Creek Bridge

DECATUR COUNTY

Greensburg vic.

Barn, Brick
State Rt. 3
HAER IN-43   p   H

DELAWARE COUNTY

Muncie

**Ball State University, Administration
    Building**
University & McKinley Aves.
HABS IN-150   s   H

615 South Hagadorn Street (Office
    Building)
HABS IN-165   s   H

Union Station
630 S. High St.
HABS IN-166   s   H

Muncie vic.

Garner, Job, House
HABS IN-154   s   H

FAYETTE COUNTY

Centerville vic.

Ranck Barn
Willow Grove Rd.
HABS IN-106   d   H

Connersville

Ansted-Higgins Spring Company
Mount & Sixteenth Sts.
HAER IN-9   pd   H

Auburn Automobile Company Factory; see
    Lexington Motor Company Factory

Canal House
111 E. Fourth St.
HABS IN-107   s pd   L

Central Manufacturing Company
Eighteenth St.
HAER IN-10   pd   H

Connersville Blower Company
Columbia Ave. & Mount St.
HAER IN-13   pd   H

Connersville Furniture Company
Illinois Ave.
HAER IN-12   pd   H

Lexington Motor Company Factory
   (Auburn Automobile Company Factory)
Eighteenth St. & Columbia Ave.
HAER IN-11   s p   H

McFarlan Carriage Company
Mount St.
HAER IN-8   pd   H

Munk & Roberts Furniture Company
Western Ave.
HAER IN-14   s pd   H

Roots, P. H. & F. M., Company
Eastern Avenue
HAER IN-3   s pd   H

Connersville vic.

Gray House
County Rd.
HABS IN-108   s pd   L

FLOYD COUNTY

New Albany

Smith, Issac P., House
513 E. Main St.
HABS IN-151   d   H

FRANKLIN COUNTY

Fairfield

Logan Cabin
State Rt. 101
HABS IN-24-19   s pd   L

Metamora

Whitewater Canal Aqueduct
Duck Creek
HABS IN-24-20   s pd   L

FULTON COUNTY

Rochester vic.

Modified Pratt Through-truss Bridge; see
   Tippecanoe River Bridge

Tippecanoe River Bridge (Modified Pratt
   Through-truss Bridge)
State Rt. 25
HAER IN-25   p   H

GRANT COUNTY

Matthews

Cumberland Covered Bridge
HAER IN-32   d   H

HAMILTON COUNTY

Noblesville

Doan House
30 Connor Lane
HABS IN-96   s p   L

Noblesville vic.

Conner, William, House
Hwy. 234
HABS IN-46   p   L

Conner, William, Loom House
State Hwy. 234
HABS IN-47   p   L

Conner, William, Prarie Farm
State Hwy. 234
HABS IN-40   pd   L

Conner, William, Still House
State Hwy. 234
HABS IN-45   p   L

Conner, William, Trading Post
State Hwy. 234
HABS IN-44   p   L

HARRISON COUNTY

Corydon

State Capitol, First
HABS IN-24-26   s p   L

HOWARD COUNTY

Kokomo

Vermont Covered Bridge
Deffenbaugh St.
HAER IN-30   s d   H

HUNTINGTON COUNTY

Huntington

Richardville, Chief, House
U.S. Rt. 24
HABS IN-157   s d   H

JEFFERSON COUNTY

Madison

**102-104 1/2 East Main Street (Commercial
   Building)** (Foster Building)
HABS IN-86   s pd   L

Ben Schroeder Saddle Tree Company
106 Milton St.
HAER IN-26   s pd   H

Bruning Carriage House
722 W. Main St.
HABS IN-122   d   H

Christ Episcopal Church
506 Mulberry St.
HABS IN-123   d   H

Colby-Jeffery House
302 Elm St.
HABS IN-124   d   H

Costigan, Francis, House
408 W. Third St.
HABS IN-87   s pd   L

Devenish-Haigh House
108 E. Third
HABS IN-126   d   H

Eagle Cotton Mill
108 St. Michael's Ave.
HABS IN-94   pd   L

East Main Street Block
217-229 E. Main St.
HABS IN-134   s d   H

710-714 East Main Street (Row Houses)
HABS IN-133   s d   H

Eckert, John, House
510 W. Second St.
HABS IN-126   s d   L

**Fair Play Fire Engine & Hose Company
   No. 1**
405 E. Main St.
HABS IN-90   s d   L

First Baptist Church
416 Vine St.
HABS IN-127   s d   L

First Presbyterian Church
202 Broadway
HABS IN-95   d   H

Foster Building; see 102-104 1/2 East Main
   Street (Commercial Building)

Frevart-Schnaitter House
740 W. Main St.
HABS IN-91   pd   L

Hutchings, Dr. William Davies, Office
718 W. Third St.
HABS IN-81   s pd   L

Jefferson County Jail & Sheriff's House
Courthouse Square
HABS IN-84   s pd   L

Lanier, James E. D., House
511 W. First St.
HABS IN-23   s pd   L H

**Madison & Indianapolis Railroad, Madison
   Incline** (Madison Cut)
W. Main St.
HAER IN-19   p   H

Madison Area Study
HABS IN-88   p   H

Madison Cut; see Madison & Indianapolis
   Railroad, Madison Incline

McNaughton House
   (Sanders-McNaughton)
416 E. Second St.
HABS IN-89   pd   L H

Miller Wagon Manufacturing Shop
805-809 Walnut St.
HABS IN-128   d   H

**Mulberry Street Block (Commercial
   Buildings)**
301-315 Mulberry St.
HABS IN-83   s pd   L

**Pitt., Cinn., Chicago & St. Louis Railway
   Co. Sta.**
614 W. First St.
HABS IN-93   pd   L

Robinson-Schofield House
221 W. Second St.
HABS IN-82   s pd   L

Sanders-McNaughton; see McNaughton House

Second Presbyterian Church
500 West St.
HABS IN-24-15   s pd   L

Shrewsbury, Charles L., House
301 W. First St.
HABS IN-8   s pd   L

Shuh, Jacob, House
718 W. Main St.
HABS IN-92   s d   L

St. Michael's Catholic Church
519 E. Third St.
HABS IN-129   d   H

St. Michael's Rectory
519 E. Third St.
HABS IN-85   s pd   L

Sullivan, Jeremiah, House
304 W. Second St.
HABS IN-9   s pd   L

Talbott, Richard, House
301 W. Second St.
HABS IN-130   s d   L

Walnut Street Fire Company No. 4
808 Walnut St.
HABS IN-131   d   H

Washington Fire Engine Company No. 2
104 W. Third St.
HABS IN-132   d   H

West Main Street Block
201-215 W. Main St.
HABS IN-135   s d   H

Madison vic.

Bachman House
Lonesome Hollow
HABS IN-121   s d   L

JENNINGS COUNTY

Vernon

Madison & Indianapolis Railroad, Stone Overpass
Gains St. & Pike St.
HAER IN-20   p   H

KNOX COUNTY

Vincennes

Brouillette House
509 N. St.
HABS IN-160   pd   H

College of Vincennes; see St. Francis Xavier Cathedral, Old St. Rose Chapel

Grouseland; see Harrison, William Henry, House

Harrison, William Henry, House (Grouseland)
Park & Scott Sts.
HABS IN-24-17   s pd   L

St. Francis Xavier Cathedral
Vigo St.
HABS IN-24-7   s pd   L

St. Francis Xavier Cathedral, Library
Vigo St.
HABS IN-24-7-A   p   L

St. Francis Xavier Cathedral, Old St. Rose Chapel (College of Vincennes)
Vigo St.
HABS IN-24-7-B   p   L

St. Francis Xavier Cathedral, Priests' House
Vigo St.
HABS IN-24-7-C   p   L

LA PORTE COUNTY

Michigan City

Michigan City Lighthouse
Washington Park
HABS IN-99   s d   H

New Carlisle

Brown-Augustine House
U.S. Hwy. 20
HABS IN-21   s   L

Pinola

Ames-Paton House
HABS IN-34   s pd   L

LAGRANGE COUNTY

Mongo

O'Ferrell, John, Store
HABS IN-148   s d   H

LAWRENCE COUNTY

Mitchell

Riley School
Seventh & College Sts.
HABS IN-147   p   H

MADISON COUNTY

Anderson

Anderson Carriage Manufacturing Company
Twenty-fifth & Walton Sts.
HAER IN-37   s p   H

Buckeye Manufacturing Company
Columbia Ave.
HAER IN-35   s p   H

DeTamble Motors Factory; see Speed Changing Pulley Company Factory

Rider-Lewis Motor Car Company
W. Second St. & Sycamore
HAER IN-38   s p   H

Speed Changing Pulley Company Factory (DeTamble Motors Factory; Spring Air Bedding)
Thirty-second St.
HAER IN-36   s p   H

Spring Air Bedding; see Speed Changing Pulley Company Factory

Pendleton vic.

Rogers Log House
Hwy. 36
HABS IN-163   d   H

MARION COUNTY

Indianapolis

Allison, James A., Mansion (Riverdale; Marian College Library)
3200 Coldspring Rd.
HABS IN-68   pd   L

Arsenal Technical High School; see U.S. Arsenal, Arsenal Building

Athenaeum, The; see Das Deutsche Haus

Ayres, L. S., Company, Warehouse Annex; see Elliott's Block

Bates-Hendricks House
1526 S. New Jersey St.
HABS IN-64   pd   L

Brownsville Covered Bridge (Wagon Bridge)
Eagle Creek Park (moved from IN, Brownsville)
HAER IN-27   H

Christ Church (Episcopal)
N. Meridian & E. Wabash Sts.
HABS IN-24-3   s pd   L

Cole Motor Car Company Factory (Service Supply Company, Inc.)
730 E. Washington St.
HABS IN-71   pd   L

Cornelius Printing Company; see Elliott's Block

Courthouse & Post Office
Market St.
HABS IN-164   s   H

Crown Hill Cemetery, Chapel & Vault
Thirty-fourth St.
HABS IN-58   pd   L

Crown Hill Cemetery, Gateway
3402 Blvd. Place
HABS IN-57   pd   L

Crown Hill Cemetery, Office Building
3402 Blvd. Place
HABS IN-56   s pd   L

Das Deutsche Haus (Athenaeum, The)
401 E. Michigan St.
HABS IN-63   pd   L

Despa House
538 Lockerbie St.
HABS IN-55   s d   L

401

Duesenberg Automobile Company Factory
W. Washington & Harding Sts.
HABS IN-70   p   L

Elliott's Block (Ayres, L. S., Company,
     Warehouse Annex; Cornelius Printing
     Company)
14-22 W. Maryland St.
HABS IN-60   s pd   L

Harrison, Benjamin, House
1230 N. Delaware St.
HABS IN-53   s pd   L

Holler, George & Netty, House
324 N. Park Ave.
HABS IN-49   s pd   L

House of the Twin Chimneys (West, John,
     House)
7607 Allisonville Rd.
HABS IN-36   s pd   L

Indiana National Bank Building
3 Virginia Ave.
HABS IN-62   pd   L

**Indiana State Central Hospital for the
     Insane** (Pathological Department
     Building)
3000 W. Washington St.
HABS IN-69   pd   L

Indiana Theatre
134 W. Washington St.
HABS IN-101   pd   L

Indianapolis City Market (Market House)
222 E. Market St.
HABS IN-59
HAER IN-6   s p   L H

Indianapolis City Market; see Market
     House

Macy House
408 N. Delaware St.
HABS IN-24-2   s pd   L

Maennerchor Building
102 W. Michigan St.
HABS IN-100   pd   H

Marian College Library; see Allison, James
     A., Mansion

Market House (Indianapolis City Market)
222 E. Market St.
HAER IN-6   s pd   H

Market House; see Indianapolis City
     Market

Morris-Butler House
1204 N. Park Ave.
HABS IN-52   s pd   L

Nickum, John R., House; see Riley, James
     Whitcomb, House

Pathological Department Building; see
     Indiana State Central Hospital for the
     Insane

Prosser House
1454 E. Tenth St.
HABS IN-35   s pd   L

Riley, James Whitcomb, House (Nickum,
     John R., House)
528 Lockerbie St.
HABS IN-51   s pd   L

Riverdale; see Allison, James A., Mansion

Service Supply Company, Inc.; see Cole
     Motor Car Company Factory

Soldiers' & Sailors' Monument
Monument Plaza
HABS IN-61   pd   L

Sommers, Richard W., House (Tudor Hall)
3650 Coldspring Rd.
HABS IN-73   p   L

Star Service Shop
130 N. Illinois St.
HABS IN-72   pd   L

Staub, Joseph W., House
342 N. College Ave.
HABS IN-50   s pd   L

Tudor Hall; see Sommers, Richard W.,
     House

Union Station
Jackson Place & Illinois St.
HABS IN-65   pd   L

U.S. Arsenal, Arsenal Building (Arsenal
     Technical High School)
1500 E. Michigan St.
HABS IN-66   pd   L

Vinton-Pierce House
1415 N. Meridian St.
HABS IN-24   s   L

Wagon Bridge; see Brownsville Covered
     Bridge

Webber House
621 Lockerbie St.
HABS IN-54   s d   L

West, John, House; see House of the Twin
     Chimneys

Woodruff Place
East, West, & Middle Drives
HABS IN-67   pd   L

MONROE COUNTY

Bloomington
Wylie House
Second & Lincoln Sts.
HABS IN-41   pd   L

MONTGOMERY COUNTY

Alamo vic.
Deer Mill Covered Bridge
HAER IN-28   d   H

Crawfordsville
Montgomery County Jail
Washington & Spring Sts.
HAER IN-17   p   H

Yountsville
Yount Woolen Mill
State Rt. 32
HAER IN-18   p   H

ORANGE COUNTY

Paoli
Gospel Street Bridge
S. Gospel St., spanning Lick Creek
HAER IN-24   p   H

Orange County Courthouse
State Rts. 156 & 37
HABS IN-29   p   L

West Baden
Northwood Institute; see West Baden
     Springs Hotel

West Baden Springs Hotel (Northwood
     Institute)
State Rt. 56
HAER IN-2   s p   H

OWEN COUNTY

Gosport
Gosport Covered Bridge
HAER IN-39   pd   H

Gosport Passenger & Freight Company; see
     New Albany & Salem Railroad

New Albany & Salem Railroad (Gosport
     Passenger & Freight Company)
North St.
HAER IN-4   s pd   H

PARKE COUNTY

Montezuma
Leatherwood Station Covered Bridge
Spanning Leatherwood Creek
HAER IN-40   pd   L

Turkey Run St. Park
Narrows Bridge
HABS IN-159   s   H

PERRY COUNTY

Cannelton
Cannelton Cotton Mill (Indiana Cotton
     Mills)
Front & Fourth Sts.
HAER IN-1   s p   H

**Cannelton Cotton Mill, Superintendent's
     House**
Front & Washington Sts.
HAER IN-1-A   p   H

**Cannelton Cotton Mill, Worker's Housing
     (A)** (Indiana Cotton Mills)
Fourth St.
HAER IN-1-B   p   H

**Cannelton Cotton Mills, Worker's Housing
     (B)** (Indiana Cotton Mills)
Fifth St.
HAER IN-1-C   p   H

Heck, Jacob, Building
HABS IN-162   p   H

Indiana Cotton Mills; see Cannelton Cotton Mill
Indiana Cotton Mills; see Cannelton Cotton Mill, Worker's Housing (A)
Indiana Cotton Mills; see Cannelton Cotton Mills, Worker's Housing (B)

PORTER COUNTY

Chesterton
Bailly, Joseph, House
Howe Rd.
HABS IN-42   d   H

Chesterton vic.
Augsburg Swensk Skola (Burstrom Chapel)
Oak Hill Rd.
HABS IN-48   s pd   L
Burstrom Chapel; see Augsburg Swensk Skola

POSEY COUNTY

New Harmony
Granary; see Rappite Fort
Laboratory, New; see Owen, Dr. David Dale, House
Owen, Dr. David Dale, House (Laboratory, New)
Church St. (State Hwy. 66)
HABS IN-24-4   pd   L
Poet's House (Rappite House)
Granary & West Sts.
HABS IN-37   s pd   L
Rappite Brick House
South St.
HABS IN-22   p   L
Rappite Community House No. 2
Main St.
HABS IN-5   s pd   L
Rappite Community House No. 2 Annex; see Rappite Dye House
Rappite Community House No. 3; see Rappite Tavern
Rappite Community House No. 4
Church St.
HABS IN-32   p   L
Rappite Dye House (Rappite Community House No. 2 Annex)
Main & Granary Sts.
HABS IN-38   s pd   L
Rappite Fort (Granary)
Granary St.
HABS IN-31   p   L
Rappite House
Granary St.
HABS IN-43   pd   L
Rappite House; see Poet's House
Rappite Tavern (Rappite Community House No. 3)
Church St.
HABS IN-39   s pd   L

Rapp-Maclure-Owen House
Church & Main Sts.
HABS IN-161   d   H
Schnee House
Lot 67, Owens Add.
HABS IN-30   p   L
Vondegrift House
Lot 69, Owens Add.
HABS IN-33   p   L

RANDOLPH COUNTY

Ridgeville
Railroad Switching Station
East Rd.
HABS IN-158   s   H

RIPLEY COUNTY

Morris
Nobbe, Marie K., House
State Rd. 46
HABS IN-149   s   H

Versailles vic.
Busching Covered Bridge
HAER IN-33   s d   H

RUSH COUNTY

Rushville
Melodeon Hall
210 N. Morgan St.
HABS IN-97   d   H

Rushville vic.
Kennedy Covered Bridge
State Rt. 44, spanning Flat Rock River
HABS IN-24-1   s d   L

ST. JOSEPH COUNTY

Mishawaka
Kamm Building
111 N. Main St.
HABS IN-139   p   L
Mishawaka Trust & Savings Company
N. Main St. & Lincolnway W.
HABS IN-137   p   L
115 North Main St. (Commercial Building)
HABS IN-141   p   L
North Main Street, 100 Block
HABS IN-136   p   L
107-109 North Main Street (Commercial Building)
HABS IN-138   p   L
113 North Main Street (Commercial Building)
HABS IN-140   p   L
117-119 North Main Street (Commercial Building)
HABS IN-142   p   L

121-125 North Main Street (Commercial Building)
HABS IN-143   p   L
111 West First Street (Commercial Building)
HABS IN-144   d   L

South Bend
Court House, Old
114 S.Lafayette Blvd. (moved from Main St.)
HABS IN-24-12   s pd   L

SWITZERLAND COUNTY

Vevay
DuFour, John Francis, House; see Ferry House
Ferry House (DuFour, John Francis, House; Graham House)
Ohio River vic.
HABS IN-24-16   s pd   L
Graham House; see Ferry House
Methodist Episcopal Church, Ruter Chapel
Main & Union Sts.
HABS IN-27   s   L
Privy (six sided)
Courthouse vic.
HABS IN-80   p   H
Schneck, U. P., House
630 Market St.
HABS IN-28   s   L

TIPPECANOE COUNTY

Lafayette
Lafayette Street Railway Powerhouse
2 South St.
HAER IN-41   pd   L

UNION COUNTY

Brownsville
Brownsville Covered Bridge (Wagon Bridge)
Main St. (moved to IN, Indianapolis)
HAER IN-27   s p   H
Wagon Bridge; see Brownsville Covered Bridge

Liberty vic.
Dunlopsville Covered Bridge
Roseburg Rd.
HAER IN-31   s d   H

VANDERBURG COUNTY

Evansville
Carpenter, Willard, House
413 Carpenter St.
HABS IN-24-11   s pd   L

WABASH COUNTY

North Manchester

North Manchester Public Library
Main St.
HABS IN-152   s   H

WARRICK COUNTY

Newburgh

House, Old Stone; see Roberts, Gaines
 Hardy, House
Roberts, Gaines Hardy, House (House, Old
 Stone)
Wonderland Route
HABS IN-24-13   s pd   L

WASHINGTON COUNTY

Salem

Hay, John, Birthplace (Morrison, John J.,
 House)
College Ave.
HABS IN-25   s   L
Morrison, John J., House; see Hay, John,
 Birthplace

WAYNE COUNTY

Cambridge City

Conklin, Benjamin, House
302 E. Main St.
HABS IN-98   s pd   L

Centerville

Julian, Judge Jacob, House (Morton
 House)
313 W. Main St.
HABS IN-102   d   H
Lantz House
214 W. Main St.
HABS IN-103   s d   H

Mansion House
214 E. Main St.
HABS IN-104   s d   H
Masonic Hall; see Wayne County Warden's
 House & Jail
Morton House; see Julian, Judge Jacob,
 House
Wayne County Warden's House & Jail
 (Masonic Hall)
130 E. Main St.
HABS IN-105   d   H

Fountain City

Coffin, Levi, House
Main Cross & Mill Sts.
HABS IN-79   s   H

Milton vic.

Kinsey, Isaac, House
502 E. Sarver Rd.
HABS IN-109   s pd   L

Mount Auburn

Huddlestone House
Main St.
HABS IN-110   s d   H

Pennville

Coffee Pot Restaurant
U.S. Rt. 40
HABS IN-120   p   H

Richmond

Adams House
Liberty St.
HABS IN-111   d   H
Bethel African Methodist Episcopal
 Church
200 Sixth St.
HABS IN-112   pd   L
City Market House
S. Sixty & A Sts.
HABS IN-24-14   s pd   L

Earlham College Observatory
National Rd.
HABS IN-113   pd   L
Harrison, Thomas, House
514 W. Main St.
HABS IN-146   s pd   L H
Hicksite Friends Meetinghouse (Wayne
 County Museum)
1150 N. A St.
HABS IN-119   pd   L
Raukopf House
240 S. Third St.
HABS IN-118   pd   L
Scott, Andrew, House
126 N. Tenth St.
HABS IN-145   pd   L
Starr Historic District
Sixteenth & E Sts.
HABS IN-114   p   L
Starr Piano Factory & Richmond Gas
 Company
G St. Bridge & Main St. Bridge
HAER IN-42   pd   L
Wayne County Courthouse
Courthouse Square
HABS IN-115   pd   L
Wayne County Museum; see Hicksite
 Friends Meetinghouse
Workers' Cottage Study
Second-Tenth Sts.
HABS IN-116   d   H

WELLS COUNTY

Vera Cruz vic.

Double Intersection Pratt (Whipple) Truss
 Bridge; see Wabash River Bridge
Wabash River Bridge (Double Intersection
 Pratt (Whipple) Truss Bridge)
State Rt. 316
HAER IN-22   p   H

Iowa

BENTON COUNTY

Vinton

Iowa Braille & Sight Saving School; see
 Iowa Institution for the Education of the
 Blind
Iowa Institution for the Education of the
 Blind (Iowa Braille & Sight Saving
 School)
1002 G Ave.
HABS IA-63   pd   H

BLACK HAWK COUNTY

Waterloo

Cedar Park Rest Room; see Waterloo
 Water Works, Well House No. 4

House
HABS IA-101   p   H
Russell, Rensslaer, House
520 W. Third St.
HABS IA-64   pd   H
Waterloo Water Works, Well House No. 4
 (Cedar Park Rest Room)
Fairview & Lafayette Aves.
HABS IA-125   s pd   H

BOONE COUNTY

Boone

City Hall
Eighth & Allen Sts.
HABS IA-105   pd   H

BUCHANAN COUNTY

Ames

Iowa State University, Morrill Building
Morrill Rd.
HABS IA-50   pd   H

Independence

Iowa Hospital for the Insane (State Mental
 Health Institute)
State Rt. 248
HABS IA-54   pd   H
State Mental Health Institute; see Iowa
 Hospital for the Insane

Quasqueton

Cedar Rock; see Walter, Lowell, House

Walter, Lowell, House (Cedar Rock)
Rt. W-38 vic.
HABS IA-130   d L

CEDAR COUNTY

Springdale vic.

Brown, John, House; see Maxson, William,
House
Maxson, William, House (Brown, John,
House)
State Hwy. No. 1
HABS IA-30-16   s p   L

West Branch

Friends Meetinghouse
Downey St., Wapsinonoc Creek vic.
HABS IA-25   s p   H
Hoover, Herbert, Birthplace (Hoover, Jesse,
House)
Penn & Downey Sts.
HABS IA-21   s p   H
Hoover, Jesse, House; see Hoover, Herbert,
Birthplace
Miles House (Rarick House)
HABS IA-141   s   H
Rarick House; see Miles House

CERRO GORDO COUNTY

Mason City

City Fire Department Headquarters
19 First St. SW
HABS IA-26   s pd   H
City National Bank (Van Duyn's Clothing
Store)
4 S. Federal Ave.
HABS IA-79   pd   L
Knights of Columbus Hall
202-204 S. Federal Ave.
HABS IA-127   s pd   H
McFarlane, W. T., Building
123 S. Federal Ave.
HABS IA-128   pd   H
Melson, Joshua G., House
56 River Heights Dr.
HABS IA-95   pd   L
Park Inn Hotel
15 W. State St.
HABS IA-80   pd   L
Rule, Arthur L., House
11 S. Rock Glen
HABS IA-57   pd   H
Van Duyn's Clothing Store; see City
National Bank
Zoller Block (Bijou Theatre)
119-121 South Ave.
HABS IA-129   pd   H

CHEROKEE COUNTY

Cherokee

Hospital for the Insane, Main Building
(State Mental Health Institute)
W. Main St. vic.
HABS IA-51   pd   H
State Mental Health Institute; see Hospital
for the Insane, Main Building

CHICKASAW COUNTY

Nashua vic.

First Congregational Church; see Little
Brown Church in the Vale
Little Brown Church in the Vale (First
Congregational Church)
State Rt. 346
HABS IA-20   s pd   L H

CLAYTON COUNTY

Elkader

Water Mill, Old, Turkey River
N. Main St.
HABS IA-30-37   p   L

CLINTON COUNTY

Clinton

Van Allen, John D. & Son, Store (Von
Mauer, Petersen Harned, Store)
Fifth Ave. S & S. Second St.
HABS IA-22   s p   L
Von Mauer, Petersen Harned, Store; see
Van Allen, John D. & Son, Store
Young, W. J., Machine Shop
HAER IA-5   s   H

CRAWFORD COUNTY

Dow City

Dow, Simeon E., House
S. Prince St.
HABS IA-70   pd   L

DES MOINES COUNTY

Burlington

Carpenter, G. B. P., House
100 Block of Polk Sts. (Prospect Point)
HABS IA-108   pd   L
Hedge Hill (Hedge, Thomas, House)
609 Fifth St.
HABS IA-85   pd   L
Hedge, Thomas, House; see Hedge Hill
House, First Brick in Iowa; see Rorer,
Judge David, House
Mason, Judge Charles, House
931 N. Sixth St.
HABS IA-30   s pd   L H

Rorer, Judge David, House (House, First
Brick in Iowa)
N. Fourth & Columbia Sts.
HABS IA-30   p   L

DICKINSON COUNTY

Spirit Lake

Gardner, Rowland, Log Cabin (Sharp,
Abbie Gardner, Log Cabin)
Monument St., Arnolds Park vic.
HABS IA-30-40   p   L
Sharp, Abbie Gardner, Log Cabin; see
Gardner, Rowland, Log Cabin

DUBUQUE COUNTY

Dubuque

Langworthy, Edward, House
1095 W. Third St.
HABS IA-30-14   s p   L
Shot Tower
Commercial St.
HABS IA-30-8   s p   L

Dubuque vic.

Dubuque, Julien, Monument (Grave)
Mississippi River vic., Julien Dubuque Dr.
HABS IA-30-9   s p   L

Holy Cross vic.

Pin Oak Tavern (Western Hotel)
U.S. Rt. 52
HABS IA-30-10   s p   L
Western Hotel; see Pin Oak Tavern

FAYETTE COUNTY

Clermont vic.

Larrabee, Gov. William, House; see
Montauk
Montauk (Larrabee, Gov. William, House)
U.S. Rt. 18
HABS IA-66   pd   L

FRANKLIN COUNTY

Hampton

Franklin County Courthouse II
Courthouse Square
HABS IA-120   d   H

HAMILTON COUNTY

Webster City

Kendall Young Library
1202 Wilson St.
HABS IA-202   pd   L

HENRY COUNTY

Mount Pleasant

Iowa Insane Hospital (State Mental Health
  Institute)
U.S. Rt. 218
HABS IA-58   p d   H
**Iowa Wesleyan College, Main Building,
  Old** (Mount Pleasant Collegiate
  Institute)
Broad St.
HABS IA-59   p d   H
Iowa Wesleyan College, Pioneer Hall
  (Mount Pleasant Collegiate Institute)
Broad St.
HABS IA-60   p d   H
Mount Pleasant Collegiate Institute; see
  Iowa Wesleyan College, Main Building,
  Old
Mount Pleasant Collegiate Institute; see
  Iowa Wesleyan College, Pioneer Hall
State Mental Health Institute; see Iowa
  Insane Hospital

IOWA COUNTY

Amana

Amana Colonies, General Store & Offices
State Rt. 220
HABS IA-44   p   L
Haas, John, House (Ox Yoke Inn)
State Rt. 220
HABS IA-46   p d   L
Lauer Meetinghouse
State Rt. 220 vic.
HABS IA-30-18   p   L
Main Meetinghouse
State Rt. 220 vic.
HABS IA-84   p d   L
Moershal, W. F., House
State Rt. 220
HABS IA-47   p d   L
Ox Yoke Inn; see Haas, John, House
Pitz Meetinghouse
State Rt. 220 vic.
HABS IA-30-43   p   L

Amana vic.

West Amana Flour Mill
HABS IA-30-45   p   L

JACKSON COUNTY

St. Donatus

Frank, Stephen, House
Davenport Rd.
HABS IA-30-17   s p   L

JASPER COUNTY

Monroe

Kling, H. A., House
416 N. Monroe St.
HABS IA-30-33   p   L

Newton

Marsh Rainbow Arch Bridge
HAER IA-4   p d   H

Vandalia

Pulver, Ferdinand Daniel, House
County Rd. F-70 vic.
HABS IA-30-1   s p   L

JEFFERSON COUNTY

Fairfield

Clarke, Dr. James Frederic, House
500 S. Main St.
HABS IA-23   s p d   L H
Parsons College, Ewing Hall
HABS IA-30   p   L

JOHNSON COUNTY

Iowa City

Capitol, Old (First State Capitol; Third
  Territorial Capitol)
Clinton St. & Iowa Ave.
HABS IA-30-29   p   L
Capitol, Temporary (Second Territorial
  Capitol)
HABS IA-30-28   p   L
First State Capitol; see Capitol, Old
Third Territorial Capitol; see Capitol, Old

LEE COUNTY

Fort Madison

Lee County Courthouse
701 Ave. F
HABS IA-76   p d   L

LINN COUNTY

Cedar Rapids

Hamilton, James E., House
2345 Linden Ave.
HABS IA-86   p   L

LYON COUNTY

Rock Rapids

Bridge, Reinforced Concrete Arch (Melan
  Bridge)
Spanning Dry Creek, SE of Rock Rapids
HABS IA-61   p   H
Melan Bridge; see Bridge, Reinforced
  Concrete Arch

MADISON COUNTY

Winterset

Clark, Caleb, House
814 S. Eighth Ave.
HABS IA-65   s p d   H

Madison County Courthouse
Courthouse Square
HABS IA-83   p d   H
Tidrick, M. R., House
122 S. Fourth St.
HABS IA-139   p   H
Vawter, J. G., House
First & South Sts.
HABS IA-138   s   H

MARION COUNTY

Knoxville vic.

Reichard, John, House
State Rt. 92 vic.
HABS IA-55   s p d   H

Pella

Central College, Temporary Quarters
1107 W. Washington St.
HABS IA-96   p d   L
Earp, Wyatt, House; see Van Spankeren
  House
Roelofsz, Dr. Joost, House (Viersen House)
1008-10 Main St. (Reformation Ave.)
HABS IA-32   p d   L
Van Spankeren House (Earp, Wyatt,
  House)
507 E. Franklin St.
HABS IA-97   p d   L
Viersen House; see Roelofsz, Dr. Joost,
  House

MARSHALL COUNTY

Marietta

Hicksite Friends Meetinghouse
County Rd. E-29
HABS IA-30-13   p   L

Marshalltown

First Church of Christ (Scientist)
W. Main & N. Fifth St.
HABS IA-94   p d   L
Marshall County Courthouse
Square by Center, Main & Church Sts. &
  First Ave.
HABS IA-78   p d   L

MASHAKA COUNTY

Oskaloosa vic.

Nelson, Daniel, Barn
Glendale Rd.
HABS IA-81-A   p   L
Nelson, Daniel, Farm
Glendale Rd.
HABS IA-81   p d   L

MONTGOMERY COUNTY

Red Oak

Montgomery County Courthouse
Courthouse Square
HABS IA-98   pd   L

MUSCATINE COUNTY

Muscatine

Clark, Alexander, Houses
307-309 Chestnut St.
HABS IA-107   pd   H

PAGE COUNTY

Clarinda

**Iowa Hospital for the Insane, Main
    Building** (State Mental Health Institute)
Twelfth St. vic.
HABS IA-52   pd   H
State Mental Health Institute; see Iowa
    Hospital for the Insane, Main Building

POLK COUNTY

Des Moines

Allen-Hubbell House; see Terrace Hill
Bankers' Trust Building; see Equitable Life
    Assurance Company Building
Brindsmaid, S. S., House
Grand Ave. & Thirty-sixth St.
HABS IA-67   p   H
Butler, Earl, House (Open Bible College)
2633 S. Fluer Dr.
HABS IA-89   pd   L
Capitol, Temporary (Second State Capitol)
Site of Soldiers & Sailors Monument
HABS IA-30   p   L
Des Moines Art Center
Greenwood Park
HABS IA-140   pd   H
**Equitable Life Assurance Company
    Building** (Bankers' Trust Building)
605 Locust St.
HABS IA-68   pd   L H
Fleming Building
Walnut & Sixth Sts.
HABS IA-90   pd   L
Fort Des Moines (Log); see House in Des
    Moines, First
Governor's Mansion; see Terrace Hill
Governor's Mansion, Old; see Witmer, W.
    W., House
Granger, Barlow, House
Pioneer Park
HABS IA-30-15   s p   L
House, Bungalow
1506 Thompson Ave.
HABS IA-91   pd   L
House in Des Moines, First (Fort Des
    Moines (Log))
HABS IA-30-34   p   L

**Iowa Girls High School Athletic
    Association;** see Witmer, W. W., House
Open Bible College; see Butler, Earl, House
Polk County Courthouse
Fifth & Court Sts., Courthouse Square
HABS IA-93   pd   L
Post Office Building, First
HABS IA-30-35   p   L
Rollins, Ralph, House (Tudor Style House)
2801 S. Fleur Drive
HABS IA-92   pd   L H
Sakulin, Barney, Log House (Restoration)
Old Fort Des Moines
HABS IA-106   s   H
Terrace Hill (Allen-Hubbell House;
    Governor's Mansion)
2300 Grand Ave.
HABS IA-69   pd   L
Tudor Style House; see Rollins, Ralph,
    House
U.S. Courthouse & Post Office
Fifth St. & Court Ave.
HABS IA-36   pd   H
Witmer, W. W., House (Iowa Girls
    School Athletic Association; Governor's
    Mansion, Old)
2900 Grand Ave.
HABS IA-104   pd   L

Valley Junction vic.

Clegg House
State Hwy. 90, W. Des Moines vic.
HABS IA-30-7   s p   L

POTTAWATTAMIE COUNTY

Council Bluffs

**Iowa Institute for Education of Deaf &
    Dumb** (Iowa State School for the Deaf)
South Ave. & State Rt. 92 vic.
HABS IA-53   pd   H
Iowa State School for the Deaf; see Iowa
    Institute for Education of Deaf & Dumb
Sutherland, D. B., House
HABS IA-103   p   H
Union Pacific Station (Transfer Depot &
    Hotel)
Twenty-first St.
HABS IA-30-6   s p   L

SCOTT COUNTY

Davenport

Grace Episcopal Cathedral (Trinity
    Episcopal Cathedral)
1121 Main St.
HABS IA-114   pd   H
Trinity Episcopal Cathedral; see Grace
    Episcopal Cathedral

Le Claire

Cody, Isaac, House
1034 N. Cody St. (moved to Cody, WY)
HABS IA-56   p   L

STORY COUNTY

Ames

Iowa State University, Farmhouse
Knoll Rd. vic.
HABS IA-123   pd   H
Iowa State University, Main Building, Old
Morrill Rd., site of Beardshear Hall
HABS IA-116   pd   H

Gilbert vic.

Methodist Episcopal Church of Milford
    (Pleasant Grove Community Church)
County Rd. E-23
HABS IA-119   pd   H
Pleasant Grove Community Church; see
    Methodist Episcopal Church of Milford

Sheldahl

First Evangelical Lutheran Church
    (Sheldahl Norwegian Lutheran Church)
County Rd. R-38 & NW 166 Ave.
HABS IA-62   s pd   H
Sheldahl Norwegian Lutheran Church; see
    First Evangelical Lutheran Church

VAN BUREN COUNTY

Bentonsport

Hancock, John, House
Third & Walnut Sts.
HABS IA-30-19   s p   L

Keosauqua

Pearson, Benjamin Franklin, House
Dodge St.
HABS IA-122   p   L

WAPELLO COUNTY

Agency City

Agency House, Old
HABS IA-30-31   p   L

WARREN COUNTY

Carlisle vic.

Covered Bridge (Owens Covered Bridge)
Spanning North River (moved to Lake
    Easter Park)
HABS IA-30-2   s p   L
Owens Covered Bridge; see Covered Bridge

WEBSTER COUNTY

Fort Dodge

Swain-Vincent House
824 S. Third Ave.
HABS IA-38   d   H

WINNESHIEK COUNTY

Decorah

Bucknell, W. S., House
210-13 Winnebago St.
HABS IA-30-4   s p   L

City Stone Mill (Painter-Bernatz Mill)
200 N. Mill St.
HABS IA-30   s p   L

Painter-Bernatz Mill; see City Stone Mill

Festina vic.

St. Anthony's Chapel (The Little Church)
Old Mission vic.
HABS IA-30-12   s p   L

**The Little Church; see St. Anthony's
Chapel**

WOODBURY COUNTY

Sioux City

**Combination Bridge; see Pacific Short Line
Bridge**

Pacific Short Line Bridge (Combination
Bridge)
HAER IA-1   pd   L H

Woodbury County Courthouse
Seventh & Douglas Sts.
HABS IA-82   p   H

Kansas

DICKINSON COUNTY

Abilene

Eisenhower House
(moved from original site)
HABS KS-4   s p   L

DONIPHAN COUNTY

Highland

Highland Junior College, Irvin Hall
Highland Junior College Campus
HABS KS-9   pd   L

DOUGLAS COUNTY

Baldwin

Baker University, Old Castle
Baker University Campus
HABS KS-5   pd   L

Clinton vic.

Barber Schoolhouse
Rt. 442
HABS KS-37   s   L

Lawrence

Babcock Carriage House
HABS KS-31   s   H

Beach, Olive, House
603 Ohio
HABS KS-32   s   H

District School
HABS KS-33   s   H

Lawrence Bible Chapel
HABS KS-35   s   H

Morrow House
1408 Ohio
HABS KS-43   s   H

Pais, Dorothy, House
1008 Ohio
HABS KS-34   s   H

Steen, Elizabeth D., House
HABS KS-44   s   H

Thacher, Solon O., House
1613 Tennessee Ave.
HABS KS-45   s   H

Trinity Episcopal Parish House
1009 Vermont St.
HABS KS-10   pd   L

Zimmerman House
303 Indiana
HABS KS-46   s   H

Stull vic.

Deister Farmhouse
State Rt. 442
HABS KS-36   s   H

Vinland

Presbyterian Church
HABS KS-47   s   H

ELLIS COUNTY

Catherine

Catherine, Town of
HABS KS-38   pd   L

Munjor

Munjor, Town of
HABS KS-39   pd   L

Schoenchen

**St. Anthony's Catholic Church; see St.
Antonius Kirche**

St. Antonius Kirche (St. Anthony's Catholic
Church)
HABS KS-40   pd   L

JEFFERSON COUNTY

Oskaloosa

Jefferson County Courthouse
Town Sq.
HABS KS-19   pd   L

JOHNSON COUNTY

Kansas City vic.

**Manual Training Schl. for Indian
Children, E. Bldg.; see Shawnee
Methodist Mission, East Building**

**Manual Training Schl. for Indian
Children, N. Bldg.; see Shawnee
Methodist Mission, North Building**

**Manual Training Schl. for Indian
Children, W. Bldg.; see Shawnee
Methodist Mission, West Building**

Shawnee Methodist Mission, East Building
(Manual Training Schl. for Indian
Children, E. Bldg.)
Fifty-sixth St. & Mission Rd.
HABS KS-3   pd   L

**Shawnee Methodist Mission, North
Building** (Manual Training Schl. for
Indian Children, N. Bldg.)
Fifty-sixth St. & Mission Rd.
HABS KS-2   pd   L

Shawnee Methodist Mission, West Building
(Manual Training Schl. for Indian
Children, W. Bldg.)
Fifty-sixth St. & Mission Rd.
HABS KS-1   pd   L

Overland Park

Building, Old Stone
11920 W. Ninety-fifth St.
HABS KS-48   s   H

LEAVENWORTH COUNTY

Fort Leavenworth

**Fort Leavenworth, Officers' Quarters; see
Fort Leavenworth, The Rookery**

Fort Leavenworth, The Rookery (Fort
Leavenworth, Officers' Quarters)
12-14 Sumner Place
HABS KS-7   pd   L

20-22 Sumner Place (House)
HABS KS-8   pd   L

Springdale vic.

Covered Bridge
Spanning Stranger Creek
HABS KS-13   pd   L

LYON COUNTY

Miller vic.

Mickel House
HABS KS-16   pd   L

MIAMI COUNTY

Osawatomie

Adair, Samuel, Cabin
John Brown Mem. Park (moved from original site)
HABS KS-18   pd   L

MORRIS COUNTY

Council Grove

Last Chance Store
Chautauqa & Main Sts.
HABS KS-6   pd   L

NEMAHA COUNTY

Albany

Albany Schoolhouse
HABS KS-20   pd   L

PAWNEE COUNTY

Larned

Fort Larned, Bakery & Mess Hall
HABS KS-24   s p   L
Fort Larned, Barracks (East) (Barn) (Fort Larned, Cavalry Barracks (Barn))
HABS KS-22   s p   L

Fort Larned, Barracks (West) (Fort Larned, Infantry Barracks)
HABS KS-21   s p   L
Fort Larned, Blacksmith & Wheelwright Shop
HABS KS-23   s p   L
Fort Larned, Cavalry Barracks (Barn); see Fort Larned, Barracks (East) (Barn)
Fort Larned, Commanding Officer's Quarters
HABS KS-28   s p   L
Fort Larned, Commissary Storehouse & Stables
HABS KS-25   s p   L
Fort Larned, Infantry Barracks; see Fort Larned, Barracks (West)
Fort Larned, Officers' Quarters (North)
HABS KS-29   s p   L
Fort Larned, Officers' Quarters (South)
HABS KS-27   s p   L
Fort Larned, Quartermaster Storehouse
HABS KS-26   s p   L

RILEY COUNTY

Fort Riley

First Territorial Capitol of Kansas
Fort Riley Military Reserve
HABS KS-15   s pd   L

Manhattan

Goodnow, Isaac, House
Claflin Rd.
HABS KS-11   pd   L

RUSH COUNTY

Liebenthal

Liebenthal, Town of
HABS KS-41   pd   L

SHAWNEE COUNTY

Silver Lake vic.

Indian Agency House
U.S. Rt. 1
HABS KS-12   pd   L

WABAUNSEE COUNTY

Wabaunsee

Beecher °Bible & Rifle° Church
HABS KS-14   s pd   L

WYANDOTTE COUNTY

Muncie

Grinter, Moses, House
1420 S. Seventy-eighth St.
HABS KS-17   pd   L

Kentucky

BOONE COUNTY

Burlington vic.

Platt's Landing (Winfield Cottage)
Upper East Bend Bottoms
HABS KY-138   s pd   L
Winfield Cottage; see Platt's Landing

BOURBON COUNTY

Paris

Cane Ridge Meetinghouse
Little Rock Rd.
HABS KY-20-8   s pd   L
Drenan, Tom, House; see Grange, The
Garrard, Gov. James, House; see Mount Lebanon
Grange, The (Drenan, Tom, House)
Maysville Pike (U.S. Rt. 68)
HABS KY-32   pd   L
Johnson's Inn, Old
Georgetown Pike
HABS KY-31   pd   L
Mount Lebanon (Garrard, Gov. James, House)
Peacock Rd.
HABS KY-30   pd   L

BOYLE COUNTY

Danville

Adams House; see Crow's Inn
Barbee House; see Crow's Inn
Boyle County Courthouse
HABS KY-38   p   L
Centre College, Old
HABS KY-34   p   L
Clark Station
Stanford Pike
HABS KY-42   p   L
Cragfont; see Wilson Station
Crow's Inn (Adams House; Barbee House)
Stanford Rd.
HABS KY-36   p   L
Davenport Tavern
W. Main St.
HABS KY-39   pd   L
McDowell, Dr. Ephraim, Apothecary Shop
123 S. Second St.
HABS KY-33-A   p   L
McDowell, Dr. Ephraim, House
125 S. Second St.
HABS KY-33   p   L

McIlvoy Building
W. Main St.
HABS KY-40   pd   L
Mound Cottage
HABS KY-35   p   L
Mount Airy
410 E. Main St.
HABS KY-37   p   L
Wilson Station (Cragfont)
HABS KY-41   p   L

Danville vic.

Crow, William, House
HABS KY-43   p   L

FAYETTE COUNTY

Lexington

Bodley House (Pindell House)
200 N. Market St.
HABS KY-53   pd   L
Botherum (Johnson House)
341 Madison Pl.
HABS KY-54   pd   L
Bradford, John, House
193 N. Mill St.
HABS KY-55   p   L

Bruen, Joseph, House; see Ingelside
Bryan Station (Rogers, Joseph, House)
Bryan Station Pike
HABS KY-161   d   L
Buckner House; see Rose Hill
Gratz, Benjamin, House; see Mount Hope
Hopemount (Morgan, Gen. John Hunt, House)
201 N. Mill St.
HABS KY-60   pd   L
Hunt, Francis Key, House; see Loudoun
Ingelside (Bruen, Joseph, House)
Gibson Ave.
HABS KY-57   pd   L
Johnson House; see Botherum
Loudoun (Hunt, Francis Key, House)
Bryan Ave.
HABS KY-58   pd   L
Morgan, Gen. John Hunt, House; see Hopemount
Morrison College, Transylvania University
W. Third St.
HABS KY-61   pd   L
Mount Hope (Gratz, Benjamin, House)
231 N. Mill St.
HABS KY-56   pd   L
Pindell House; see Bodley House
Rogers, Joseph, House; see Bryan Station
Rose Hill (Buckner House)
461 N. Limestone St.
HABS KY-20-16   s pd   L
Talbert, William, House
Gratz Park
HABS KY-102   pd   H
University of Kentucky, Carnegie Library
HABS KY-158   pd   H
University of Kentucky, Patterson House
HABS KY-157   pd   H
University of Kentucky, White Hall
HABS KY-156   pd   H
535 West Short Street (Old Doorway)
(moved from 655 Price Ave.)
HABS KY-62   p   L

Lexington vic.

Eothan; see Malvern Hill
Malvern Hill (Eothan)
Georgetown Rd.
HABS KY-59   pd   L

FRANKLIN COUNTY

Frankfort

Brown, Orlando, House
202 Wilkinson St.
HABS KY-45   p   L

Church of the Good Shepherd
HABS KY-46   p   L

Liberty Hall
Main & Wilkinson Sts.
HABS KY-20-2   s pd   L

State House, Old
Broadway
HABS KY-20-1   s pd   L
Ziegler, Rev. J. R., House
509 Shelby St.
HABS KY-103   s   L

GREEN COUNTY

Greensburg

Courthouse, Old
Main St.
HABS KY-20-4   s pd   L

HARRISON COUNTY

Cynthiana

Covered Bridge, Wood
Licking River, S. Fork
HABS KY-20-20   s pd   L

HART COUNTY

Munfordville vic.

Buckner, Gen. Bolivar, House; see Glen Lily
Glen Lily (Buckner, Gen. Bolivar, House)
HABS KY-75   p   L

HENDERSON COUNTY

Geneva vic.

Anderson Place; see Indian Valley
Indian Valley (Anderson Place)
HABS KY-29   pd   L

Henderson

Henderson County Courthouse
First & Main Sts.
HABS KY-20-18   s pd   L
Lockett, Beulah & Eva, House
Elm & Jefferson Sts.
HABS KY-28   pd   L
Powell, Gov. Lazarus, House
HABS KY-27   pd   L
St. Paul's Episcopal Church
Third & Main Sts.
HABS KY-26   pd   L

JEFFERSON COUNTY

Buechel vic.

Hikes Place
Rt. 7
HABS KY-70   p   L

Louisville

Atherton Building
466 River City Mall
HABS KY-137   s pd   L
Bainbridge Row; see Palmer, Dr., House

Bank of Louisville Building
322 W. Main St.
HABS KY-20-3   s pd   L
Board of Trade Building (Lithgow Building)
301 W. Main St.
HABS KY-141   pd   H
Brennan House; see Ronald-Brennan House
Bullitt House; see Oxmoor
Caldwell House; see Conrad House
Cave Hill Cemetery
701 Baxter Ave.
HABS KY-142   d   H
City Hall
601 W. Jefferson St.
HABS KY-143   pd   H
Clark, George M., House; see Spring Station
Conrad House (Caldwell House; Hughes, Rose Anna, Presbyterian House)
1402 St. James Court
HABS KY-144   pd   H
Gas Station
HABS KY-154   p   H
Hart Block (Hisderbrand Block)
728 W. Main St.
HABS KY-120   s pd   H
Hisderbrand Block; see Hart Block
Hughes, Rose Anna, Presbyterian House; see Conrad House
Jefferson Community College; see Louisville Presbyterian Theological Seminary
Jefferson County Courthouse
531 W. Jefferson St.
HABS KY-117   s pd   H
Kentucky School for the Blind
1867 Frankfort Ave.
HABS KY-20-19   s pd   L
Kuntz Shotgun House
1401 E. Washington St.
HABS KY-119   s pd   H
Lithgow Building; see Board of Trade Building
Loew's Theater (United Artists Theater; Penthouse Theater)
625 S. Fourth St.
HABS KY-134   pd   H
Louisville, General View
Main St.
HABS KY-150   d   H
Louisville Medical College (University of Louisville, Medical School)
101 W. Chestnut St.
HABS KY-145   pd   H
Louisville Presbyterian Theological Seminary (Jefferson Community College)
109 E. Broadway
HABS KY-146   pd   H
Main Street, 600 & 700 Block (Buildings)
HABS KY-147   pd   H

Oxmoor (Bullitt House)
Shelbyville Pike
HABS KY-67   p L
Palmer, Dr., House (Bainbridge Row)
721 W. Jefferson St.
HABS KY-63   p L
Penthouse Theater; see Loew's Theater
Rathskeller-Seelbach Hotel (Rookwood Room, Seelbach Hotel)
500 S. Fourth St.
HABS KY-148   pd H
Republic Building
427 W. Muhammed Ali Blvd.
HABS KY-140 s pd H
Roman Catholic Cathedral of the Assumption
435 S. Fifth St.
HABS KY-64   p L
Ronald-Brennan House (Brennan House)
631 S. Fifth St.
HABS KY-118 s pd H
Rookwood Room, Seelbach Hotel; see Rathskeller-Seelbach Hotel
Salve-Bullett Mausoleum
Cave Hill Cemetery
HABS KY-121 s pd H
Shelter House; see Waiting House, Rustic
Smith, Ben, Mausoleum
Cave Hill Cemetery
HABS KY-122 s pd H
Spring Bank Farm
7506 Shepherdsville Rd.
HABS KY-149   pd H
Spring Station (Clark, George M., House)
Lexington Rd. & Cannon's Lane
HABS KY-23   pd L
Trinity Methodist Episcopal Church
Third & Guthrie Sts.
HABS KY-65   p L
Tyler Block
319 W. Jefferson St.
HABS KY-151   pd H
Union Station
1000 W. Broadway
HABS KY-152   pd H
United Artists Theater; see Loew's Theater
University of Louisville, Medical School; see Louisville Medical College
Vienna Restaurant
133-135 S. Fourth St.
HABS KY-153   pd H
Waiting House, Rustic (Shelter House)
Cave Hill Cemetery
HABS KY-123 s pd H

Louisville vic.

Croghan House (Locust Grove)
Blankenbaker Lane
HABS KY-66   p L
Farmington (Speed, John, House)
3033 Bardstown Rd.
HABS KY-24   L H
Locust Grove; see Croghan House
Speed, John, House; see Farmington

St. Matthews

Humphrey, Judge Churchill, House; see Ridgeway
Ridgeway (Humphrey, Judge Churchill, House)
Ridgeway & Massie Aves.
HABS KY-68 s pd L H
Taylor, Zachary, House
Blankenbaker Lane
HABS KY-69   pd L H

JOHNSON COUNTY

Fishtrap vic.

Fishtrap United Baptist Church
Paint Creek
HABS KY-135   pd L

KENTON COUNTY

Ludlow

Closson House, Old (Masonic Temple)
Closson Court & Ringold Sts.
HABS KY-20-13 s pd L
Elmwood Hall
246 Forest Ave.
HABS KY-22   s pd L
Masonic Temple; see Closson House, Old

LARUE COUNTY

Hodgenville

Creel Cabin (Lincoln, Abraham, Birthplace National Historic Site)
HABS KY-96   p L
Lincoln, Abraham, Birthplace (Lincoln, Abraham, Birthplace National Historic Site)
HABS KY-95   p L
Lincoln, Abraham, Birthplace National Historic Site; see Creel Cabin
Lincoln, Abraham, Birthplace National Historic Site; see Lincoln, Abraham, Birthplace

LEE COUNTY

Beattyville

Lee County Courthouse
Main St.
HABS KY-139   s pd L

LINCOLN COUNTY

Stanford

Whitley, Col. William, House
Stanford-Crab Orchard Pike
HABS KY-20-7 s pd L

LOGAN COUNTY

South Union

Barn (Center Portion)
HABS KY-104   p H
Shaker Center Family Dairy; see Shaker Centre Family Preservatory
Shaker Centre Family Drying House
U.S. Rt. 68
HABS KY-109   p L
Shaker Centre Family Dwelling House
U.S. Rt. 68
HABS KY-105   p L H
Shaker Centre Family General View
U.S. Rt. 68
HABS KY-107   p L
Shaker Centre Family Ministry's Shop & Dwelling
U.S. Rt. 68
HABS KY-108   p L H
Shaker Centre Family Preservatory (Shaker Center Family Dairy)
U.S. Rt. 68
HABS KY-106   p L H
Shaker Centre Family Washhouse
U.S. Rt. 68
HABS KY-110   p L
Shaker Centre Family Well Structure
U.S. Rt. 68
HABS KY-155   p H
Shaker South Union Hotel; see Shaker South Union Tavern
Shaker South Union Tavern (Shaker South Union Hotel)
Rt. 73
HABS KY-111   p L

MADISON COUNTY

Richmond

Castlewood
U.S. Rt. 25
HABS KY-20-17 s pd L
Woodlawn
HABS KY-98   p L

White Hall

Whitehall
Clay Lane
HABS KY-101   s p H

MASON COUNTY

Maysville

Russell Theater
9 E. Third St.
HABS KY-160   p H

Washington

Collins-Davis House
Main St.
HABS KY-124   s d H
Johnston, Albert Sidney, House; see Wilson, Nathaniel, House

Key, Marshall, House (Taylor, Francis, House)
Main St.
HABS KY-127   s d   H

Main Street (Row Houses)
HABS KY-130   s d   H

Main Street (Stone House)
HABS KY-125   s d   H

Marshall, Thomas, House
U.S. Hwy. 68
HABS KY-20-14   s pd   L

Methodist Episcopal Church, South
Main St.
HABS KY-128   s d   H

Moose House; see Murphy-Lashbrooke House

Murphy-Lashbrooke House (Moose House)
Main St. & Berry Alley
HABS KY-129   s d   H

Taylor, Francis, House; see Key, Marshall, House

Taylor House & Store
Main & Williams Sts.
HABS KY-132   s d   H

Washington Hall
Main St.
HABS KY-131   s d   H

Washington Historic District
HABS KY-133   s   H

Wilson, Nathaniel, House (Johnston, Albert Sidney, House)
Harold St.
HABS KY-126   s d   H

MEADE COUNTY

Brandenburg

Doe Run Hotel (Water Power Mill, Old)
U.S. Rt. 60
HABS KY-25   pd   L

Water Power Mill, Old; see Doe Run Hotel

Grahamton

Textile Mill & Storage Warehouse
U.S. Rt. 60
HABS KY-20-6   s pd   L

MERCER COUNTY

Harrodsburg

Aspen Hall
Beaumont Ave.
HABS KY-47   p   L

Clay Hill
853 Beaumont Ave.
HABS KY-48   p   L

Court View
360 N. Main St.
HABS KY-49   p   L

Hart, Rebecca, Cabin
HABS KY-94   p   L

Mansion, The
Pioneer Memorial State Park
HABS KY-50   p   L

Mud Meetinghouse
Dry Branch Rd.
HABS KY-20-15   s pd   L

Smith, Zachary, House
Hillcrest & S. Greenville Sts.
HABS KY-74   p   L

Taylor, Samuel, House
Chatham Pike
HABS KY-52   s pd   L

Harrodsburg vic.

Marrs Log House
Chatham Pike
HABS KY-51   pd   L

Pleasant Hill

Shaker Blacksmiths' & Carpenters' Shop (Shaker Broom Factory)
Village Rd.
HABS KY-79   p   L

Shaker Broom Factory; see Shaker Blacksmiths' & Carpenters' Shop

Shaker Centre Family Dwelling House (First) (Shaker Farm Deacon's Shop; Shaker First House)
Village Rd.
HABS KY-77   p   L

Shaker Centre Family Dwelling House (Third) (Shaker Church Family House)
Village Rd.
HABS KY-76   p   L

Shaker Centre Family Trustees' Office (Shaker Guest House)
Village Rd.
HABS KY-81   p   L

Shaker Centre Family Washhouse (Shaker Men's Shower House)
Village Rd.
HABS KY-93   p   L

Shaker Church Family House; see Shaker Centre Family Dwelling House (Third)

Shaker Coopers' Shop (Shaker North Workshop)
Village Rd.
HABS KY-83   p   L

Shaker Dr. Pennebaker House; see Shaker West Family Dwelling House (First)

Shaker East Family Brethren's Shop (Shaker South Workshop; Trustees' Office)
Village Rd.
HABS KY-82   p   L

Shaker East Family Broom Shop (Shaker Outbuilding)
Village Rd.
HABS KY-92   p   L

Shaker East Family Dwelling House (Shakertown Inn)
Village Rd.
HABS KY-20-12   s pd   L

Shaker East Family Sisters' Shop (Shaker Silkworm House)
Village Rd.
HABS KY-89   p   L

Shaker East Family Washhouse
Village Rd.
HABS KY-88   p   L

Shaker Farm Deacon's Shop; see Shaker Centre Family Dwelling House (First)

Shaker First House; see Shaker Centre Family Dwelling House (First)

Shaker Guest House; see Shaker Centre Family Trustees' Office

Shaker Meetinghouse (Shakertown Baptist Church)
Village Rd.
HABS KY-78   p   L

Shaker Men's Shower House; see Shaker Centre Family Washhouse

Shaker Ministry's Shop (Second)
Village Rd.
HABS KY-114   p   L

Shaker North Family Home; see Shaker West Family Sisters' Shop

Shaker North Workshop; see Shaker Coopers' Shop

Shaker Old Stone Shop; see Shaker West Family Dwelling House (First)

Shaker Outbuilding; see Shaker East Family Broom Shop

Shaker Pennebaker School for Girls; see Shaker West Family Dwelling House (Second)

Shaker Silkworm House; see Shaker East Family Sisters' Shop

Shaker South Workshop; see Shaker East Family Brethren's Shop

Shaker Water Tower Building
Village Rd.
HABS KY-84   s p   L

Shaker West Family Barn
Village Rd.
HABS KY-87   p   L

Shaker West Family Drying House
Village Rd.
HABS KY-112   p   L

Shaker West Family Dwelling House (First) (Shaker Dr. Pennebaker House; Shaker Old Stone Shop)
Village Rd.
HABS KY-90   p   L

Shaker West Family Dwelling House (Second) (Shaker Pennebaker School for Girls)
Village Rd.
HABS KY-91   p   L

Shaker West Family Preserve House
Village Rd.
HABS KY-85   p   L

Shaker West Family Privy
Village Rd.
HABS KY-115   p   L

Shaker West Family Sisters' Shop (Shaker North Family Home)
Village Rd.
HABS KY-80   p   L
Shaker West Family Washhouse
Village Rd.
HABS KY-116   p   L
Shakertown Baptist Church; see Shaker Meetinghouse
Shakertown Inn; see Shaker East Family Dwelling House
Trustees' Office; see Shaker East Family Brethren's Shop

Talmage

McAfee House
HABS KY-71   s p d   L

MONROE COUNTY

Tompkinsville vic.

Mulkey House, Old (Church)
Hwy. 1446
HABS KY-159   pd   H

NELSON COUNTY

Bardstown

Beckham House; see Wickland
St. Joseph's Cathedral
HABS KY-20-9   s pd   L
Wickland (Beckham House)
U.S. Rt. 55
HABS KY-20-5   s pd   L

Bardstown vic.

Federal Hill; see My Old Kentucky Home
My Old Kentucky Home (Federal Hill)
HABS KY-44   p   L
St. Thomas Catholic Church
U.S. Rt. 31 E.
HABS KY-100   s d   L

PENDLETON COUNTY .

Butler

Covered Bridge, Wood
Spanning Licking River
HABS KY-20-11   s pd   L

POWELL COUNTY

Stanton

Powell County Courthouse
Washington & Court Sts.
HABS KY-136   s p   H

SHELBY COUNTY

Shelbyville

Cross Keys Tavern
U.S. Rt. 60
HABS KY-20-21   s pd   L

Shelbyville vic.

Inn, Old Stone
U.S. Rt. 60
HABS KY-72   p   L

WASHINGTON COUNTY

Springfield

Washington County Courthouse
HABS KY-73   p   L

WOODFORD COUNTY

Pisgah

Pisgah Presbyterian Church & Academy
Pisgah-Georgetown Pike
HABS KY-20-10   s pd   L

Louisiana

ASCENSION COUNTY

Burnside
Burnside Plantation (Houmas, The)
State Hwy. 1
HABS LA-26   s pd   L
Houmas, The; see Burnside Plantation

Geismar vic.
Ashland Plantation; see Belle Helene Plantation
Belle Helene Plantation (Ashland Plantation)
HABS LA-80   s pd   L

ASSUMPTION COUNTY

Napoleonville vic.
Woodlawn Plantation
State Hwy. 77
HABS LA-20   s pd   L

CADDO COUNTY

Shreveport

U.S. Post Office & Courthouse
Marshall & Texas Sts.
HABS LA-1125   p   L

EAST BATON ROUGE COUNTY

Baton Rouge
Blum House
630 Louisiana Ave.
HABS LA-1126   s pd   L
Columbia Theatre (Paramount Theatre)
215 Riverside Mall
HABS LA-1133   s pd   L
Fire Station Number 1; see Laurel Street Station
825-827 Frisco Street (House); see Suburb Gracie
855-865 Frisco Street (House); see Suburb Gracie
1360 Gayso Street (House); see Suburb Gracie
1660 Gracie Street (House); see Suburb Gracie
Grand Theatre
133 S. Twelfth St.
HABS LA-1128   pd   L
Knox Cottage
1029 America St.
HABS LA-1129   s pd   L
Lakes, The; see Suburb Gracie
Laurel Street Station (Fire Station Number 1)
1801 Laurel St.
HABS LA-1127   s pd   L

Louisana State Capitol (Old State Capitol)
N. Blvd., Saint Philip, America & Front Sts.
HABS LA-1132   pd   L
Louisiana State Prison Store (Warden's House)
703 Laurel St.
HABS LA-1140   pd   L
Magnolia Mound
2161 Nicholson Dr.
HABS LA-1130   s pd   L
Old State Capitol; see Louisana State Capitol
Paramount Theatre; see Columbia Theatre
Pentagon Barracks; see U.S. Barracks
Planter's Cabin
7815 Highland Rd.
HABS LA-1135   s pd   L
Post Office (Post Office, Old)
355 N. Blvd.
HABS LA-1131   pd   L
Post Office, Old; see Post Office
Santa Maria Plantation
Perkins Rd.
HABS LA-1137   pd   L
St. James Episcopal Church
208 N. Fourth St.
HABS LA-1136   pd   L
Suburb Gracie (1360 Gayso Street (House))
HABS LA-1138-C   p   L

Suburb Gracie (825-827 Frisco Street
(House))
HABS LA-1138-A   p   L
Suburb Gracie (855-865 Frisco Street
(House))
HABS LA-1138-B   p   L
Suburb Gracie (1660 Gracie Street (House))
HABS LA-1138-D   p   L
Suburb Gracie (Lakes, The)
North, N. Seventeenth, N. Thirteenth &
Fuqua Sts.
HABS LA-1138   s d   L
Tessler Building
342, 346, 348 Lafayette St.
HABS LA-1139   pd   L
U.S. Barracks (Pentagon Barracks)
Riverside Mall, Capitol Ave., Front St.
HABS LA-1134   pd   L
Warden's House; see Louisiana State Prison
Store

EAST FELICIANA COUNTY

Clinton

Braeme House
State Hwy. 36
HABS LA-40   s p d   L
Clinton Courthouse
Saint Helena St.
HABS LA-30   s p d   L
Lawyers' Row
Saint Helena St. & Liberty Rd.
HABS LA-31   s p d   L

IBERIA COUNTY

New Iberia

Shadows on the Teche (Weeks, David,
House)
Main & Weeks Sts.
HABS LA-75   s p d   L
Weeks, David, House; see Shadows on the
Teche

IBERVILLE COUNTY

Bagatelle Plantation
East River Rd. (moved from Saint James
Parish)
HABS LA-1142   s   d   H

Plaquemine

Variety Plantation
State Hwy. 3066
HABS LA-1141   s   H

White Castle vic.
Belle Grove
HABS LA-36   s p d   L

LAFOURCHE COUNTY

Thibadoux
Laurel Valley Plantation Complex
HAER LA-1   pd   L

NATCHITOCHES COUNTY

Bermuda
Bermuda Plantation (Prudhomme Family)
Cane River
HABS LA-2-2   p   L

Melrose
Melrose Plantation (Old Yucca Plantation)
HABS LA-2-69   s p d   L
Old Yucca Plantation; see Melrose
Plantation

Natchitoches
Balcony Building
120 Washington St.
HABS LA-2-3   p   L
Church of the Immaculate Conception
HABS LA-2-4   p   L
Duplex Columns
312 Jefferson St.
HABS LA-2-5   p   L
Episcopal Church (Trinity Church)
HABS LA-2-6   p   L
Lemee House
308-309 Jefferson St.
HABS LA-2-193   s p d   L
Prudhomme-Hughes Building
HABS LA-2-7   p   L
Tauzin House
HABS LA-2-8   p   L
Trinity Church; see Episcopal Church

ORLEANS COUNTY

New Orleans
Antoine's Annex; see Vieux Carre Squares
Antoine's Restaurant; see Vieux Carre
Squares
Antoine's Restaurant (Service Building);
see Vieux Carre Squares
Archbishopric
1114 Chartres St.
HABS LA-18-2   s p d   L
Arsenal
615 Saint Peter St.
HABS LA-18-6   s p d   L
Baker d'Acquin's House; see Vieux Carre
Squares
Beauregard House
1113 Chartres St.
HABS LA-18-1   s p d   L
Boimare-Schloeman Building; see Vieux
Carre Squares
Bosque House
617-619 Chartres St.
HABS LA-81   s   L

Bosworth-Hammond House
1126 Washington Ave.
HABS LA-1143   p   H
701 Bourbon Street (Commercial Building)
HABS LA-1144   pd   H
941 Bourbon Street (Cottage) (Lafayette's
Blacksmith Shop)
HABS LA-24   s p d   L
Brevard, Albert Hamilton, House
1239 First St.
HABS LA-1118   s p d   L
Briggs-Staub House
2603 Prytania St.
HABS LA-1145   pd   H
Cabildo
Jackson Square
HABS LA-18-4   s p d   L H
Cafe Toulousin; see Vieux Carre Squares
Calaboose Building; see Louisiana State
Museum Building
Casa Flinard; see Nichols, Valery, House
Castillon House
Decatur & Saint Peter Sts.
HABS LA-191   d   L
Central Congregational Church
S. Liberty & Cleveland Ave.
HABS LA-22   s p d   L
Chartres Street (Commercial Buildings)
HABS LA-1146   p   H
Church of the Immaculate Conception
132 Baronne St.
HABS LA-1147   pd   H
City Hall (Gallier Hall)
Saint Charles St.
HABS LA-193   p   L
Coffini Cottage; see Vieux Carre Squares
Convent of Notre Dame (St. Joseph's
Orphan Asylum)
835 Josephine St.
HABS LA-1102   pd   L
Convent of the Holy Family
Orleans St.
HABS LA-1124   s   H
**Counting House of William Nott &
Company;** see Vieux Carre Squares
Court of the Lions; see Vieux Carre
Squares
Dabney, Lavinia C., House
2265 Saint Charles Ave.
HABS LA-1113   pd   L
deArmas, Felix, House, Site of; see Vieux
Carre Squares
1107-1133 Decatur Street (Commercial
Buildings); see Ursuline's Row Houses
Duplantier Family Tomb
N. Claiborne St.
HABS LA-1107   s p d   L
Federal Jail; see U.S. Branch Mint
Fernandez-Tissot House (Tivoli)
1400 Moss St.
HABS LA-1117   s p d   L

First Presbyterian Church
South St.
HABS LA-1103   pd   L
Fouche House
619 Bourbon St.
HABS LA-1148   s pd   H
Frostall, Edmund J., House
920 Saint Louis St.
HABS LA-1114   pd   L
Gaillard House
915-917 Saint Ann St.
HABS LA-69   p   H
Gallier Hall; see City Hall
Gally House
536 Chartres St.
HABS LA-29   s pd   L
Gaudet House
Chestnut & Josephine Sts.
HABS LA-1149   p   H
George, Sieur, House; see Skyscraper, First
Girod House
500-506 Chartres St.
HABS LA-18-9   s pd   L
524 Governor Nichols Street (House)
HABS LA-1150   p   L
Grailhe Family Tomb
N. Claiborne St.
HABS LA-1108   s pd   L
Grandchamp's Pharmacie; see Vieux Carre
   Squares
Grinnan, Robert A., House
   (Grinnan-Henderson-Reilly House)
2221 Prytania St.
HABS LA-1120   s pd   L
Grinnan, Robert A., House (Garconniere)
2221 Prytania St.
HABS LA-1121   pd   H
Grinnan-Henderson-Reilly House; see
   Grinnan, Robert A., House
Hearn, Lafcadio, Domicile; see Vieux
   Carre Squares
Herman-Grima House
820 Saint Louis St.
HABS LA-1122   pd   L
**Herman-Grima House (Garconniere &
   Kitchen)**
820 Saint Louis St.
HABS LA-1123   p   L
Holy Rosary Convent; see Michel-Pitot
   House
Jackson House; see Louisiana State
   Museum Building
Jorda, Jayme, House, Site of; see Vieux
   Carre Squares
Jourdan Property, Site of; see Vieux Carre
   Squares
Kohn-Anglade House; see Vieux Carre
   Squares
Kohn-Anglade House (Dependencies); see
   Vieux Carre Squares
Lacoste, Jean, Cottage; see Vieux Carre
   Squares

Lafayette's Blacksmith Shop; see 941
   Bourbon Street (Cottage)
Lanoix, Louis, House
514-516-518 Toulouse St.
HABS LA-1115   s pd   L
LaRionda Cottage
1218-1220 Burgundy St.
HABS LA-192   s pd   L
Latour & Laclotte's Atelier
625-627 Dauphine St.
HABS LA-1151   s pd   H
Lemonnier House; see Skyscraper, First
Louisiana State Bank
403 Royal St.
HABS LA-18-8   s pd   L
Louisiana State Museum Building (Jackson
   House)
Saint Peter St. & Cabildo Ave.
HABS LA-18-10-B   p   L
Louisiana State Museum Building
   (Calaboose Building)
616 Orleans Alley
HABS LA-18-10-A   p   L
Louisiana State Museum Buildings
HABS LA-18-10   s pd   L
Louisiana Sugar Exchange
N. Front & Bienville Sts.
HABS LA-1110   pd   L
Madame John's Legacy
632 Dumaine St.
HABS LA-39   s pd   L H
Marine Hospital
HABS LA-1153   p   H
Meilleur House; see Vieux Carre Squares
Merieult Mansion; see Vieux Carre Squares
Michel-Pitot House (Holy Rosary Convent)
1370 Moss St. (moved to 1440 Moss St.)
HABS LA-1116   s pd   L
Nichols, Valery, House (Casa Flinard)
723 Toulouse St.
HABS LA-33   s pd   L
Nolte, Vincent, House; see Vieux Carre
   Squares
Olivier, David, House (Olivier, David,
   Plantation)
4111 Chartres St.
HABS LA-70   s pd   L
Olivier, David, Plantation; see Olivier,
   David, House
Orleans Ball Room
717 Orleans St.
HABS LA-1155   s pd   H
**Our Lady of Guadaloupe Roman Catholic
   Church;** see St. Anthony's Chapel
1436 Pauger Street (Cottage)
HABS LA-23   s pd   L
Pension de Boulanger, Site of; see Vieux
   Carre Squares
Petit Desert; see Seven Oaks Plantation
Peychaud House (Service Wing); see Vieux
   Carre Squares
Planter's Association Office; see Vieux
   Carre Squares

Poeyfarre House; see Vieux Carre Squares
Poeyfarre Houses; see Vieux Carre Squares
Presbytere
Jackson Square
HABS LA-18-5   s pd   L
Pretre Mansion, Le
716 Dauphine St.
HABS LA-53   s pd   L
Ramsey, James, Commercial Building; see
   Vieux Carre Squares
Robinson-Jordan House
1415 Third St.
HABS LA-1156   pd   H
Roche, Widow, House; see Vieux Carre
   Squares
Rouzan Residence; see Vieux Carre
   Squares
Royal House Hotel; see Vieux Carre
   Squares
Royal Street (Commercial Buildings)
HABS LA-176   p   H
San Antoine Mortuary Chapel; see St.
   Anthony's Chapel
Second District, Square Number 62; see
   Vieux Carre Squares
Seven Oaks Plantation (Petit Desert)
HABS LA-1158   pd   H
Short, Col. Robert Henry, House
1448 Fourth St.
HABS LA-1112   pd   L
Skyscraper, First (George, Sieur, House;
   Lemonnier House)
HABS LA-21   s pd   L
Spanish Comandancia; see Vieux Carre
   Squares
Spanish Custom House
1300 Moss St.
HABS LA-18-3   s pd   L
St. Anthony's Chapel (Our Lady of
   Guadaloupe Roman Catholic Church;
   San Antoine Mortuary Chapel)
411 N. Ramparti St.
HABS LA-1104   pd   L
St. John the Baptist Church
1117-1139 Dryades St.
HABS LA-1105   pd   L
St. Joseph's Orphan Asylum; see Convent of
   Notre Dame
St. Mary's Assumption Church
2030 Constance St.
HABS LA-1106   pd   L
St. Patrick's Roman Catholic Church
724 Camp St.
HABS LA-1111   pd   L
Taney, C. H., House
908 Saint Louis St.
HABS LA-1160   pd   H
Tivoli; see Fernandez-Tissot House
Troxler-Psayla Cottage
919 Saint Philip St.
HABS LA-196   s   L

Ursuline's Row Houses (1107-1133 Decatur
  Street (Commercial Buildings))
HABS LA-1101-41   p   L

U.S. Branch Mint (Federal Jail)
400 Esplanade Ave.
HABS LA-1119   pd   L

U.S. Custom House
423 Canal St.
HABS LA-1109   pd   L

Vieux Carre Squares (Poeyfarre Houses)
734-740 Toulouse St. & 540 Bourbon St.
HABS LA-1100-U   d   L

Vieux Carre Squares (Grandchamp's
  Pharmacie)
501 Royal St.
HABS LA-1100-I   d   L

Vieux Carre Squares (Jourdan Property,
  Site of)
500 Bourbon St.
HABS LA-1100-K   d   L

Vieux Carre Squares (Peychaud House
  (Service Wing))
727 Toulouse St.
HABS LA-41   s   L

Vieux Carre Squares (Poeyfarre House)
532 Bourbon St.
HABS LA-1100-T   d   L

Vieux Carre Squares (Roche, Widow,
  House)
HABS LA-1100-V   d   L

Vieux Carre Squares (Meilleur House)
511-512 Bourbon St.
HABS LA-1100-O   s p   H

Vieux Carre Squares (Merieult Mansion;
  Royal House Hotel)
718 Toulouse St.
HABS LA-1100-P   d   L

Vieux Carre Squares (deArmas, Felix,
  House, Site of)
513 Royal St.
HABS LA-1100-C   d   L

Vieux Carre Squares (Nolte, Vincent,
  House; Court of the Lions)
535-541 Royal St. & 708 Toulouse St.
HABS LA-1100-Q   d   L

Vieux Carre Squares (Rouzan Residence)
522 Bourbon St.
HABS LA-1100-W   d   L H

Vieux Carre Squares (Kohn-Anglade
  House (Dependencies))
508 Bourbon St.
HABS LA-1100-M   d   L

Vieux Carre Squares (Second District,
  Square Number 62)
Royal, Bourbon, Saint Louis, & Toulouse
Sts.
HABS LA-1100   s d   L

Vieux Carre Squares (Baker d'Acquin's
  House)
720-724 Toulouse St.
HABS LA-1100-D   d   L

Vieux Carre Squares (Cafe Toulousin)
732 Toulouse St.
HABS LA-1100-F   d   L

Vieux Carre Squares (Counting House of
  William Nott & Company; Antoine's
  Restaurant (Service Building); Spanish
  Comandancia)
519 Royal St.
HABS LA-1100-H   d   L

Vieux Carre Squares (Jorda, Jayme, House,
  Site of)
521-523 Royal St.
HABS LA-1100-J   d   L

Vieux Carre Squares (Pension de
  Boulanger, Site of)
727-733 Saint Louis St.
HABS LA-1100-R   d   L

Vieux Carre Squares (Planter's Association
  Office)
714 Toulouse St.
HABS LA-1100-S   d   L

Vieux Carre Squares (Lacoste, Jean,
  Cottage)
526 Bourbon St.
HABS LA-1100-N   d   L

Vieux Carre Squares (Antoine's
  Restaurant; Ramsey, James, Commercial
  Building)
713-717 Saint Louis St.
HABS LA-1100-B   d   L

Vieux Carre Squares (Antoine's Annex)
719-723-725 Saint Louis St.
HABS LA-1100-A   d   L

Vieux Carre Squares (Kohn-Anglade
  House; Hearn, Lafcadio, Domicile)
516 Bourbon St.
HABS LA-1100-L   d   L

Vieux Carre Squares (Boimare-Schloeman
  Building)
509-511 Royal St.
HABS LA-1100-E   d   L

Vieux Carre Squares (Coffini Cottage)
726-728 Toulouse St.
HABS LA-1100-G   d   L

New Orleans vic.
Bayou St. John Hotel (Ruins); see Spanish
  Fort (Ruins)
Fort St. John (Ruins); see Spanish Fort
  (Ruins)
Spanish Fort (Ruins) (Fort St. John
  (Ruins); Bayou St. John Hotel (Ruins))
Bayou Saint John at Lake Pontchartrain
HABS LA-18-25   s pd   L

RenNew Orleans

PLAQUEMINES COUNTY

Frank's Island Lighthouse
North East Pass, Mississippi River
HABS LA-19   s pd   L

POINTE COUPEE COUNTY

New Roads vic.
Negro Cabin; see Riche, Fannie, Plantation
Parlange Plantation
State Hwy. 93
HABS LA-34   s pd   L

Riche, Fannie, Plantation
State Hwy. 30
HABS LA-35   s pd   L
Riche, Fannie, Plantation (Negro Cabin)
State Hwy. 30
HABS LA-35-A   s p   L

RAPIDES COUNTY

Alexandria vic.
Baillio, Peter, House (Kent)
Bayou Rapids
HABS LA-2-1   p   L
Kent; see Baillio, Peter, House

ST. BERNARD COUNTY

Mississippi River
Beauregard, Rene, House
HABS LA-18-7   s pd   L

ST. CHARLES COUNTY

Hahnville
Homeplace Plantation
River Rd.
HABS LA-155   s pd   L
Lehmann, Dr., House
HABS LA-194   p   L

Saint Rose
Ormond Plantation
State Hwy. 1
HABS LA-18-13   s pd   L

Saint Rose vic.
Barbara Plantation (Garconniere) (Rose
  Plantation)
HABS LA-18-12   s pd   L
Rose Plantation; see Barbarra Plantation
  (Garconniere)

ST. JAMES COUNTY

Convent vic.
Uncle Sam Plantation
HABS LA-74   s pd   L
Union vic.
Academy, The
HABS LA-1161   p   L

ST. JOHN THE BAPTIST COUNTY

Angelina Plantation (Dove Cote & Doll
  House)
State Hwy. 1
HABS LA-18-14   s pd   L
Lucy
Glendale Plantation
HABS LA-150   p   L

ST. LANDRY COUNTY

Grand Coteau

Convent of the Sacred Heart
HABS LA-54 p L

Petetin's Store
HABS LA-86 p L

Opelousas

Hebrard House
304 Bellevue St.
HABS LA-83 p L

Opelousas vic.

Lastrapes House
HABS LA-89 s pd L

Sunset vic.

Chretien Point Plantation
HABS LA-64 s pd L

Washington

Hinckley House
Dejean St.
HABS LA-1162 s d H

Immaculate Conception Catholic Church
Moundville St.
HABS LA-1163 s d H

Lyons Warehouse
Water & Main Sts.
HABS LA-1164 s H

Magnolia Ridge
Dejean St.
HABS LA-1165 s d H

Nicholson House
Corso St.
HABS LA-1166 s d H

Pierrel, A. S., House
Dejean St.
HABS LA-1167 d H

Schmit Hotel
HABS LA-195 p L

Schulze House
Water St.
HABS LA-1168 s H

Wolff, J., House
Main St.
HABS LA-1169 s d H

WEST FELICIANA COUNTY

Bains

Greenwood Plantation (Ventress)
HABS LA-16 s L

Ventress; see Greenwood Plantation

Saint Francisville

Afton Villa
Hwy. 61
HABS LA-58 pd L

Rosedown Plantation
HABS LA-1101 pd L

Weyanoke vic.

Live Oak Plantation House
HABS LA-17 s pd L

Maine

Factory Island

Cutts, Col. Thomas, House
(moved to ME, Saco, Glen Haven Circle)
HABS ME-7 s pd L

Squam Island

Antoinette, Marie, House; see
Decker-Clough House

Clough House; see Decker-Clough House

Decker-Clough House (Clough House;
Antoinette, Marie, House)
(moved to Sheepscot River & State Rt. 27)
HABS ME-54 s p L

CUMBERLAND COUNTY

Brunswick

Bowdoin College, Massachusetts Hall
Bath St.
HABS ME-109 s pd L

Cape Elizabeth

Brown, C. A., House; see Brown-Donahue
House

Brown-Donahue House (Brown, C. A.,
House; Donahue, Helen, House)
Delano Park
HABS ME-119 s pd H

Donahue, Helen, House; see
Brown-Donahue House

Falmouth vic.

Merrill, James, House
Falmouth Rd.
HABS ME-115 pd L

Harpswell

Harpswell Neck Road Meetinghouse
(Harpswell Neck Road Townhouse)
State Rt. 123
HABS ME-58 s pd L

Harpswell Neck Road Townhouse; see
Harpswell Neck Road Meetinghouse

New Gloucester vic.

Shaker Church Family Barns
Sabbathday Lake, State Rt. 26
HABS ME-167 p L

Shaker Church Family Boys' Shop
Sabbathday Lake, State Rt. 26
HABS ME-166 p L

Shaker Church Family General View
Sabbathday Lake, State Rt. 26
HABS ME-165 p L

Shaker Church Family Washhouse
Sabbathday Lake, State Rt. 26
HABS ME-164 p L

Shaker Community Meetinghouse
Sabbathday Lake, State Rt. 26
HABS ME-107 s pd L

Shaker Ministry's Shop
Sabbathday Lake, State Rt. 26
HABS ME-163 p L

Portland

Bailey, Deacon John, House
1235 Congress St.
HABS ME-4 s pd L

Bethel Building; see Mariners' Church

Children's Hospital; see Storer-Mussey
House

Churchill House; see
Ingraham-Preble-Churchill House

Clapp, Charles, House (School of Fine &
Applied Art; Portland Art School)
97 Spring St.
HABS ME-62 s pd H

First Parish Church (Unitarian)
425 Congress St.
HABS ME-6 s pd L H

Fort Gorges
Hog Island Ledge, Portland Harbor
HABS ME-134 s pd H

Hunnewell-Shepley House; see Shepley
House

Ingraham-Preble-Churchill House
(Churchill House)
51 State St.
HABS ME-35 pd L

Longfellow, Henry W., House; see
Wadsworth-Longfellow House

Mariners' Church (Bethel Building)
Fore St.
HABS ME-135 pd H

McLellan-Sweat Mansion
111 High St.
HABS ME-121 s pd H

Mechanics' Hall
159 Congress St.
HABS ME-129 p L

Morse-Libby House (Victoria Mansion)
109 Danforth St.
HABS ME-53 s p L

Munjoy Hill Observatory; see Portland
Observatory

Mussey, John, House; see Storer-Mussey House

Park Street Block
between Spring & Gray Sts.
HABS ME-118   s p d   H

Portland Art School; see Clapp, Charles, House

Portland Club; see Shepley House

Portland Head Light
Portland Head
HABS ME-123   s p d   H

Portland Merchants' Exchange
Middle St.
HABS ME-133   p   L

Portland Observatory (Munjoy Hill Observatory)
138 Congress St.
HABS ME-1   s p d   L

School of Fine & Applied Art; see Clapp, Charles, House

Shepley House (Hunnewell-Shepley House; Portland Club)
156 State St.
HABS ME-127   s   H

Stevens, John Calvin, House
52 Bowdoin St.
HABS ME-137   pd   L H

Storer-Mussey House (Children's Hospital; Mussey, John, House)
91 Danforth St. NW
HABS ME-31   pd   L

Union Wharf Building (19-22)
Commercial St.
HABS ME-114   s pd   L H

U.S. Customs House
312 Fore St.
HABS ME-138   pd   H

U.S. Post Office & Courthouse, Old
169 Middle St.
HABS ME-120   pd   L

Victoria Mansion; see Morse-Libby House

Wadsworth-Longfellow House (Longfellow, Henry W., House)
487 Congress St.
HABS ME-2   s pd   L

Woodman Building
140 Middle St.
HABS ME-136   pd   H

South Portland

Portland Breakwater Lighthouse
Portland Harbor
HABS ME-112   s pd   L

South Windham vic.

Babbs Bridge; see Covered Bridge

Covered Bridge (Babbs Bridge)
Harry Cane Rd. spanning Presumpscot River
HABS ME-61   s   L

Stroudwater

Means, Capt. James, House
2 Waldo St.
HABS ME-5   s pd   L

Tate, George, House
1270 Westbrook St.
HABS ME-3   s pd   L

Windham Center vic.

Hanson, Ezekiel, House (Stencils)
Albion Rd.
HABS ME-69   s   L

HANCOCK COUNTY

Baker Island

Baker Island Light, Lightkeeper's House
HABS ME-172   s   H

Gilley, Elisha, House
HABS ME-171   s   H

Castine

Fort Pentagoet
Perkins St.
HABS ME-13   p   L

Ellsworth

Black, Col. John, House (Woodlawn)
W. Main St. (State Rt. 172)
HABS ME-25   pd   L H

Black House, Barn & Carriage House
W. Main St. (State Rt. 172)
HABS ME-25-A   p   H

City Library; see Jordan, Benjamin, House

Jordan, Benjamin, House (City Library)
46 State St.
HABS ME-24   pd   L

Woodlawn; see Black, Col. John, House

Little Cranberry Is.

Blue Duck Ships Store
Harborside on Hadlock Cove, Islesford
HABS ME-170   s   H

Southwest Harbor Vic

Carroll House
State Rt. 102
HABS ME-169   s   H

KENNEBEC COUNTY

Augusta

Fort Western, Main Building
Bowman St.
HABS ME-56   s pd   L

Maine State House
State & Capitol Sts.
HABS ME-130   s pd   H

Gardiner

Christ Church (Episcopal)
1 Dresden Ave.
HABS ME-143   pd   L

Oaklands
Dresden St. at Kennebec River
HABS ME-113   s pd   L

Hallowell

Bodwell, Gov. Joseph R., House
15 Middle St.
HABS ME-160   pd   L

Building, Granite-Fronted; see Sewall Warehouse

Emporium, The
154 Water St.
HABS ME-156   pd   L

Gage Block (106-114 Second Street (Row House))
HABS ME-145   pd   L

Hubbard Free Library
115 Second St.
HABS ME-158   pd   L

Hubbard, Gov. John, Barns
52 Winthrop St.
HABS ME-144-C   pd   L

Hubbard, Gov. John, Doctor's Office
52 Winthrop St.
HABS ME-144-B   pd   L

Hubbard, Gov. John, House
52 Winthrop St.
HABS ME-144-A   pd   L

106-114 Second Street (Row House); see Gage Block

Sewall Warehouse (Building, Granite-Fronted)
156 Water St.
HABS ME-150   pd   L

St. Matthew's Church (Episcopal)
20 Union St.
HABS ME-146   pd   L

Thing, Capt. Abraham, House
159 Second St.
HABS ME-147   pd   L

Hallowell Mill

Hallowell Mill
HAER ME-2   pd   L

Monmouth

Cumston Hall
Main St.
HABS ME-161   pd   L

Winslow

Fort Halifax, Blockhouse
U.S. Rt. 201
HABS ME-55   s pd   L

KNOX COUNTY

Camden

Cushing, Capt., House
31 Chestnut St.
HABS ME-88   pd   L

Rockland

Farnsworth, William A., Homestead
21 Elm St.
HABS ME-77   s pd   L

Snow, I., House
9 Water St.
HABS ME-96   pd   L

U.S. Customhouse & Post Office Building
17 School St.
HABS ME-139   pd   L

Rockport

Hanson-Cramer House
Sea St. (moved from Pascal's Ave.)
HABS ME-78   s p d   L

Shepard, H. L., Company, Lime Kiln
Rockport Harbor
HABS ME-095   p d   L

Tyler, Coburn, House Fence
Union St. (Old Camden Rd.)
HABS ME-100   p d   L

Rockport vic.

McCobb-Dodge House; see Spite House
Spite House (McCobb-Dodge House)
Calderwood Rd. (moved from ME,
   Phippsburg)
HABS ME-75   s p d   L

Thomaston

North Parish Meetinghouse
St. George Rd. (State Rt. 131)
HABS ME-105   p d   L

Ruggles, Judge John, House
29 Main St.
HABS ME-106   p d   L

Vinalhaven vic.

Saddleback Ledge Lighthouse
Penobscot Bay
HABS ME-79   s p d   L

Warren

Cobb, Miles, Farmhouse
Main St. & State Rt. 131 at Hinchley's
   Corner
HABS ME-76   s p d   L

LINCOLN COUNTY

Alna

Alna District School
State Rt. 218
HABS ME-33   s p d   L

Alna Meetinghouse
State Rt. 218
HABS ME-34   s p d   L

Jones-Hilton House
HABS ME-178   p   H

Bristol vic.

School House, Old Stone
State Rt. 130
HABS ME-47   s p d   L

Damariscotta

Cottrill, Matthew, House
Main St. (U.S. Rt. 1A)
HABS ME-93   p d   L

Day, Deacon Daniel, House
Bristol Rd. (State Rt. 129)
HABS ME-80   s p d   L

Damariscotta Mills

Kavanaugh, James, House
State Rt. 215 at Damariscotta Lake
HABS ME-22   s p d   L

St. Patrick's Roman Catholic Church
State Rt. 215
HABS ME-84   s p d   L

Dresden (Cedar Grove)

Bowman-Carney House
State Rt. 128
HABS ME-45   s p d   L

Pownalborough Courthouse
State Rt. 128
HABS ME-42   s p d   L

Head Tide

Carlton House
HABS ME-175   p   H

Head Tide Church
HABS ME-179   p   H

House, Center of town
HABS ME-176   p   H

Robinson, Edward Arlington, House
HABS ME-177   p   H

Jefferson vic.

Cattle Pound
State Rt. 126
HABS ME-60   s p d   L

Newcastle

Glidden, William T., Austin Block
Main St. (U.S. Rt. 1) & River Rd. (State
   Rt. 215)
HABS ME-81   s p d   L

Newcastle vic.

Perkins House
Main St.
HABS ME-83   s p d   L

North Edgecomb

Antoinette, Marie, House; see
   Decker-Clough House
Clough House; see Decker-Clough House
Decker-Clough House (Clough House;
   Antoinette, Marie, House)
State Rt. 27 (moved from Squam Island)
HABS ME-54   p d   L

Fort Edgecomb, Blockhouse
Davis Island
HABS ME-52   s p d   L

Waldoboro vic.

German Lutheran Church
State Rt. 32
HABS ME-44   s p d   L

Walpole vic.

Walpole Meetinghouse
State Rt. 129
HABS ME-50   s p d   L

Wiscasset

Academy, Old
Warren & Hodge Sts.
HABS ME-48   s p d   L

Clark-Wood House
High St.
HABS ME-87   p d   L

Hodge, Henry, House
Hodge & Main Sts.
HABS ME-49   s p d   L

Lee, Judge Silas, House
High St.
HABS ME-101   p d   L

Lincoln County Courthouse
High St.
HABS ME-97   p d   L

Lincoln County Jail, Old
Federal St. (State Rt. 218)
HABS ME-82   s p d   L

Nickels-Sortwell House
Main & Federal Sts.
HABS ME-102   p d   L

Page, Samuel, House
Lee St.
HABS ME-91   p d   L

Powder House, Old
Churchill St.
HABS ME-70   s   L

Scott, Capt. George, House
Federal St. (State Rt. 218)
HABS ME-85   s p d   L

OXFORD COUNTY

Paris (Paris Hill)

Hamlin Memorial Library; see Oxford
   Country Jail, Old
Hubbard House
Village Green
HABS ME-39   p d   L

Kimball House; see Rawson-Kimball House
Mallow House
Village Green
HABS ME-40   p d   L

Oxford Country Jail, Old (Hamlin
   Memorial Library)
Village Green
HABS ME-37   s p d   L

Parris, Gov. Albion K., Law Office
Village Green
HABS ME-38   p d   L

Rawson-Kimball House (Kimball House)
Village Green
HABS ME-41   p d   L

Porter

Porter Meetinghouse
Mill Brook
HABS ME-51   s p d   L

SAGADAHOC COUNTY

Bath

Central Church (Congregational)
804 Washington St.
HABS ME-148   p d   L

Church Block
44 Front St.
HABS ME-157   p d   L

Grace Episcopal Church
Oak & Middle Sts.
HABS ME-110   s pd   L

Patten, George F., House
118 Front St.
HABS ME-141   pd   L

Percy & Small Shipyard
451 Washington St.
HAER ME-1   pd   H

Richardson, Capt. John G., House
964 Washington St.
HABS ME-140   pd   L

Swedenborgian Church
876 Middle St.
HABS ME-151   pd   L

Tallman, Henry, House
982 High St.
HABS ME-152   pd   L

U.S. Custom House & Post Office
25 Front St.
HABS ME-153   pd   L

Winter Street Church (Congregational)
880 Washington St.
HABS ME-154   pd   L

Phippsburg

McCobb-Dodge House; see Spite House
McCobb-Hill-Minott House
Parker Head Rd.
HABS ME-117   s pd   L

Spite House (McCobb-Dodge House)
(moved to ME, Rockport vic., Calderwood Rd.)
HABS ME-75   s pd   L

Phippsburg vic.

Drummond Cemetery Wall
State Rts. 209 & 216
HABS ME-63   s   L

Phippsburg Congregational Church
Gun Hill at Kennebec River
HABS ME-108   s pd   L

Richmond

Richmond-Dresden Union Methodist Church
Pleasant St.
HABS ME-155   pd   L

Southard, Thomas Jefferson, Block
25 Front St.
HABS ME-159   pd   L

Southard, Thomas Jefferson, House
17 Church St.
HABS ME-149   pd   L

Stearns, Capt. David, House
3 Gardiner St.
HABS ME-142   pd   L

Robinhood

Riggs, Benjamin, House
Riggs Cove
HABS ME-46   s pd   L

Riggs, James, House
State Rt. 127
HABS ME-27   p   L

Riggs, Moses, House
Riggs Cove
HABS ME-28   p   L

Riggs Store Building
Riggs Cove
HABS ME-29   p   L

Riggs, Warner, Gravestone
Riggs Family Cemetery, Riggs Cove
HABS ME-59   s   L

Riggs Wharf Buildings
Riggs Cove
HABS ME-30   p   L

Topsham

Holden, Capt. Daniel, House
24 Elm St.
HABS ME-116   s pd   L

Topsham vic.

Hunter, John, Tavern
Topsham-Bowdoinham Rd. (State Rt. 24)
HABS ME-111   s pd   L

WALDO COUNTY

Belfast

Anderson, Gov. Hugh J., House; see Bishop-Anderson House

Avery-Stevens House (Stevens House)
38 Church St.
HABS ME-16   pd   L

Belfast National Bank
Main & Beaver Sts.
HABS ME-103   pd   L

Bishop-Anderson House (Anderson, Gov. Hugh J., House)
Church & Anderson Sts.
HABS ME-23   p   L

Burrill, William H., House
13 Church St.
HABS ME-89   pd   L

Field, Benjamin, House; see Field, Bohan Prentice, House

Field, Bohan Prentice, House (Field, Benjamin, House)
139 High St.
HABS ME-19   pd   L

First Church (Congregational Unitarian)
Church & Spring Sts.
HABS ME-86   s pd   L H

Johnson House; see Johnson-Pratt House

Johnson, Judge Alfred W., House; see Whittier, Thomas, House

Johnson, Ralph, House; see Johnson-Pratt House

Johnson-Pratt House (Johnson House; Johnson, Ralph, House)
100 High St.
HABS ME-20   s pd   L

Kimball-Salmon House (Salmon House)
46 Church St.
HABS ME-17   pd   L

Masonic Temple
Main & High (U.S. Rt. 1A) Sts.
HABS ME-104   pd   L

Salmon House; see Kimball-Salmon House

Shute, Captain William, House
10 Waldo Ave. (State Rt. 137)
HABS ME-99   pd   L

Stevens House; see Avery-Stevens House

Treadwell, Charles, House
26 Northport Ave. (moved from Miller & High Sts.)
HABS ME-94   pd   L

White, James P., House
1 Church St.
HABS ME-92   pd   L

Whittier, Thomas, House (Johnson, Judge Alfred W., House)
76 Church St.
HABS ME-21   pd   L

Belfast (east)

Black Horse Tavern
Searsport Ave. (U.S. Rt. 1)
HABS ME-18   pd   L

Belfast vic.

Miller, Joseph, House
Marsh Rd.
HABS ME-90   pd   L

Lincolnville

Bayshore Union Church
U.S. Rt. 1
HABS ME-98   pd   L

Searsport

Ward House
U.S. Rt. 1
HABS ME-73   p   L

WASHINGTON COUNTY

Columbia Falls

Ruggles, Judge Thomas, House
Pleasant River Bridge vic.
HABS ME-26   pd   L H

Machias

Burnham Tavern (Mason's Arms)
High St.
HABS ME-64   pd   L

Mason's Arms; see Burnham Tavern

St. Croix River

St. Croix Island National Monument; see St. Croix Isle. Nat'l Monument, Lighthouse & Res.

St. Croix Island National Monument, Barn
HABS ME168-D   s   H

St. Croix Island National Monument, Boathouse
HABS ME-168-E   s   H

St. Croix Island National Monument, Fog Bell Tower
HABS ME-168-B   s   H

St. Croix Island National Monument, Oil House
HABS ME-168-C   s   H

St. Croix Isle. Nat'l Monument, Lighthouse & Res. (St. Croix Island National Monument)
HABS ME-168-A   s   H

YORK COUNTY

Alfred

Holmes-Sayward House
U.S. Rt. 202 (State Rt. 4)
HABS ME-32   s p d   L

Biddeford

Haley, Benjamin, House
Pool Rd. (State Rt. 208)
HABS ME-36   p d   L

Lafayette House (Spring, Capt. Seth, Inn)
14 Elm St.
HABS ME-8   s p d   L

Spring, Capt. Seth, Inn; see Lafayette House

Boon Island

Boon Island Light Tower
HABS ME-122   p d   L

Kennebunk

Bourne, George W., House (Wedding Cake House)
104 Summer St. (State Rt. 35)
HABS ME-74   p d   L

Bourne, George W., House (Fence) (Wedding Cake House (Fence))
104 Summer St. (State Rt. 35)
HABS ME-71   s   L

Bourne House; see Parsons-Bourne House

First Parish Church (Unitarian)
U.S. Rt. 1 & State Rts. 35 & 9A
HABS ME-124   s p d   H

Kimball, James, House
2 Summer St.
HABS ME-14   p d   L

Lord, William, Building
U.S. Rt. 1 & State Rts. 35 & 9A
HABS ME-132   p d   H

Mousam House (Paneling)
U.S. Rt. 1
HABS ME-68   s   L

Parsons-Bourne House (Bourne House)
Bourne St.
HABS ME-15   p d   L

Wedding Cake House; see Bourne, George W., House

Wedding Cake House (Fence); see Bourne, George W., House (Fence)

Kennebunkport

Kennebunk River Club
Ocean Ave.
HABS ME-125   s p d   H

Larabee-Carl, House
North St.
HABS ME-72   s   L

Perkins Grist Mill
North St.
HABS ME-126   s p d   H

Kittery Point

Gerrish Warehouse
Pepperrell Cove
HABS ME-131   s p d   H

Pepperell, William, House
State Rt. 103 at Pepperrell Cove
HABS ME-128   s p d   H

New Berwick vic.

Maxwell, Alexander, Garrison House; see McIntire-Garrison House

McIntire-Garrison House (Maxwell, Alexander, Garrison House)
S. Berwick Rd. (State Rt. 91)
HABS ME-9   s p d   L

Saco

Cutts, Col. Thomas, House
Glen Haven Circle (moved from Factory Island)
HABS ME-7   s p d   L

Wells

Jefferds' Tavern
Harraseekit Rd. (moved to ME, York, U.S. Rt. 1A)
HABS ME-43   s p d

Storer-Garrison House
U.S. Rt. 1
HABS ME-12   p d   L

York

Jefferds' Tavern.
U.S. Rt. 1A (moved from ME, Wells vic.)
HABS ME-43   s p d   L

York (Ogunquit vic.)

Perkins, Isaiah, House
Shore Rd.
HABS ME-57   s   L

York (Scotland)

Junkins Garrison House
S. Berwick Rd. (State Rt. 91)
HABS ME-11   p   L

York (York Village)

King's Prison; see York County Gaol, Old

York County Gaol, Old (King's Prison)
4 Lindsay Rd.
HABS ME-10   s p d   L

Maryland

Baltimore

11 1/2 East Pleasant Street (House)
HABS MD-43-C   p d   L

Abell House; see North Charles Street (House, Cast-Iron Porches)

Aged Men's Home
1400 W. Lexington St.
HABS MD-182   p d   L

Aged Women's Home
1400 W. Lexington St.
HABS MD-183   p d   L

Albemarle & Granby Streets (Brick House)
HABS MD-360   p   L

102 Albermarle Street (Double House)
HABS MD-348   p   L

Aliceanna & South Dallas Streets (Brick Row House)
HABS MD-401   p   L

Archbishop's House (Roman Catholic Episcopal Residence)
408 N. Charles St.
HABS MD-400   p   L

Ashland Avenue, 100 Block (Brick Row Houses)
HABS MD-402   p   L

Athenaeum Club (Howard, William, House)
Charles & Franklin Sts.
HABS MD-68   p   L

Backus, Dr. John, House; see First Presbyterian Church Manse

Baltimore & Ohio Railroad, Camden Station
Camden St.
HABS MD-326
HAER MD-7   s p d   H

Baltimore & Ohio Railroad, Carrollton Viaduct
HAER MD-9   p d   H

Baltimore & Ohio Railroad, Howard Street Tunnel
HAER MD-11   p d   H

Baltimore & Ohio Railroad, Mount Clare Shops
HAER MD-6   s p   H

Baltimore & Ohio Railroad, Mount Clare Station
500 Block W. Pratt St.
HABS MD-852   p   L

Baltimore & Ohio Railroad, Mount Royal Station
Cathedral St. & Mt. Royal Ave.
HABS MD-193
HAER MD-10   p d   L

Baltimore & Ohio Railroad, Mt. Royal Sta.
   Trainshed
HAER MD-29   p   H
Baltimore & Ohio Railroad, Tobacco
   Warehouse
HAER MD-20   pd   H
Baltimore City Jail
801 Van Buren & E. Madison Sts.
HABS MD-184   p   L
Baltimore City Jail Gateway & Warden's
   House
400 E. Madison St.
HABS MD-184-A   p   L
Battle Monument
Calvert St.
HABS MD-185   pd   L
Belmont (d'Annenous, Chevalier Chas. F.
   A. Le P., House)
North & Harford Aves.
HABS MD-339   p   L
800 Block Wilmot Street (Houses)
HABS MD-389   p   L
Broadway & East Lombard Streets
   (House); see Cast-Iron Porches
Calvert & Lexington Streets (House)
NE Corner
HABS MD-67   p   L
Calvert & Lexington Streets (House)
HABS MD-64   p   L
Carroll, Charles Jr., Mansion; see
   Homewood
Carroll Mansion; see Caton House
Cast-Iron Balcony (Exeter & Watson
   Streets (House))
HABS MD-365   p   L
Cast-Iron Porches (Broadway & East
   Lombard Streets (House))
HABS MD-374   p   L
504-520 Cathedral Street (Houses)
HABS MD-376   p   L
505-517 Cathedral Street (Houses)
HABS MD-375   p   L
600-610 Cathedral Street (Houses)
HABS MD-377   p   L
607-609 Cathedral Street (Houses)
HABS MD-352   p   L
800-810 Cathedral Street (Row Houses)
Madison Ave.
HABS MD-379   p   L
Caton House (Carroll Mansion;
   Caton-Carroll House; Wilson, Henry,
   House)
Lombard & S. Front Sts.
HABS MD-5   s pd   L
Caton-Carroll House; see Caton House
Charles & Fayette Streets (Church)
HABS MD-66   p   L
Chestnut, William, House
Baltimore St.
HABS MD-345   p   L
Commercial & Farmers Bank; see Howard
   & Redwood Streets (Commercial
   Building)

Courtland Street (Houses)
St. Paul Place
HABS MD-65   p   L
Damon House, Old (Stewart, David,
   House; Upton; Damon-Stewart House)
811 W. Lanvale St.
HABS MD-347   p   L
Damon-Stewart House; see Damon House,
   Old
d'Annenous, Chevalier Chas. F. A. Le P.,
   House; see Belmont
1012 East Baltimore Street (House)
HABS MD-361   p   L
601-607 East Chase Street (Houses)
HABS MD-317   p   L
East Indian Restaurant; see 113 South
   Broadway Street (Second Story Porch)
East Lombard & South Front Streets
   (Brick House)
opposite Caton House
HABS MD-343   p   L
12 East Pleasant Street (Brick House)
HABS MD-373   p   L
11 East Pleasant Street (House)
HABS MD-43-B   pd   L
15 East Pleasant Street (House) (Smith, Dr.
   James, House)
HABS MD-43-D   pd   L
9 East Pleasant Street (House)
HABS MD-43-A   pd   L
Eutaw Place Baptist Church
Dolphin & Eutaw Sts.
HABS MD-194   p   L
Exeter & Watson Streets (House); see
   Cast-Iron Balcony
Fell House; see 1621 Thames Street (House)

Fell's Point Theatre; see 814 South
   Broadway (Brick Building)

Firehouse, Engine Company Number 15
Lombard St.
HABS MD-854   d   H

Firehouse, Engine Company Number 8
323 Mulberry St.
HABS MD-354   d   H

First Baptist Church (Round Top Church)
Sharp & Lombard Sts.
HABS MD-75   p   L

First Presbyterian Church
Madison St. & Park Ave.
HABS MD-195   pd   L

First Presbyterian Church
Guilford Ave. & Fayette St.
HABS MD-73   p   L

First Presbyterian Church Manse (Backus,
   Dr. John, House)
210 W. Madison St.
HABS MD-195-A   p   L

First Unitarian Church (Unitarian Church)
Franklin & Charles Sts.
HABS MD-229   p   L

Flag House (Pickersgill, Mary Young,
   House)
844 E. Pratt & Albemarle Sts.
HABS MD-356   p   L
1522 Fleet Street (House-Interior
   Stairway)
HABS MD-366   p   L
Forbes Houses; see 1626-1628 Thames
   Street (Row Houses)
Foreign Market; see 814 South Broadway
   (Brick Building)
Forrest & E. Monument Sts. (Row of Brick
   Houses)
HABS MD-404   p   L
Fort Hamilton
HABS MD-856   p   L
Fort Independence
HABS MD-857   p   L
Fort McHenry, Building A; see Fort
   McHenry, Commanding Officer's Office
   & Qtrs.
Fort McHenry, Building C; see Fort
   McHenry, Officers' Quarters
Fort McHenry, Commanding Officer's
   Office & Qtrs. (Fort McHenry, Building
   A)
Whetstone Point at Fort Ave.
HABS MD-196   p   L
Fort McHenry, Flag Pole Base
E. Fort Ave.
HABS MD-204   s   L
Fort McHenry National Monument &
   Historic Shrine (Fort Whetstone)
Whetstone Point at Fort Ave.
HABS MD-63   s pd   L
Fort McHenry, Officers' Quarters (Fort
   McHenry, Building C)
Whetstone Point at Fort Ave.
HABS MD-198   p   L
Fort McHenry, Powder Magazine
Fort Ave. at Whetstone Point
HABS MD-197   s pd   L
Fort McHenry, Soldiers' Barracks No. 1,
   Building D
Fort Ave. at Whetstone Point
HABS MD-199   s pd   L
Fort McHenry, Soldiers' Barracks No. 2,
   Building E
Fort Ave. at Whetstone Point
HABS MD-200   s pd   L
Fort Whetstone; see Fort McHenry
   National Monument & Historic Shrine
Franklin Square (Twin Houses)
100 Block N. Calhoun St., W. side
HABS MD-412   p   L
Franklin Street Presbyterian Church
Franklin & Cathedral Sts.
HABS MD-187   pd   L
Garrett Racing Stables (Montebello Estate
   Stables)
HABS MD-357   p   L

Garrett-Jacobs House
7, 9, 11, 13 W. Mount Vernon Place
HABS MD-188   pd   L

German Evangelical Reformed Church; see
Otterbein United Brethren Church

Gilman, Daniel C., House
614 Park Ave.
HABS MD-358   p   L

Gladding, Harry, House; see 1 West Mount
Vernon Place (House)

Harper, Robert Goodloe, Dairy &
Springhouse (Oaklands Springhouse)
(moved to Baltimore Museum of Art,
Charles St.)
HABS MD-394   p   L

Harper, Robert Goodloe, House
Cathedral St.
HABS MD-359   p   L

Hollingsworth-Steel House
931 Fell St.
HABS MD-189   pd   L

Homewood (Carroll, Charles Jr., Mansion)
N. Charles & Thirty-fourth Sts.
HABS MD-35   pd   L

Houses adjoining Caton House
802-804 E. Lombard St
HABS MD-350   p   L

Howard & Redwood Streets (Commercial
Building) (Commercial & Farmers Bank)
HABS MD-395   p   L

Howard, William, House; see Athenaeum
Club

Independent Fire Company, Engine House
Number 6
416 Gay St.
HABS MD-353   s d   H

Jencks, Francis, House; see 1 West Mount
Vernon Place (House)

Latrobe, J. H. B., House
Courtland (St. Paul Place) & Lexington Sts.
HABS MD-72   p   L

Lee & South Charles Street (Brick Row
Houses)
HABS MD-380   p   L

Lloyd Street Synagogue
Lloyd & Watson Sts.
HABS MD-190   pd   L

Lorman House
Charles & Lexington Sts.
HABS MD-69   p   L

Madison Avenue & Preston Street (Brick
House)
HABS MD-369   p   L

McKim Free School
1120 E. Baltimore St.
HABS MD-305   s p   L

McKim House
Park Ave. & Center St.
HABS MD-390   p   L

Mechanics Hall; see Watchman Fire
Company Firehouse

Mercantile Trust & Deposit Company
Redwood & Calvert Sts.
HABS MD-191   pd   L

Merchants' Shot Tower; see Phoenix Shot
Tower

Minor Basilica, Assumption of the Virgin
Mary; see Roman Catholic Cathedral of
Baltimore

Montebello Estate Stables; see Garrett
Racing Stables

36 Montgomery Street (House)
HABS MD-370   s p   L H

Morton, George C., House; see 107 West
Monument Street (House)

Mount Clare
Bayard & S. Monroe Sts., Carroll Park
HABS MD-192   pd   L

Mount Vernon Club; see Randall,
Blanchard, House

Municipal Museum; see Peale, Rembrandt,
Museum

National Union Bank Building
Fayette & Charles Sts.
HABS MD-393   L

606-628 North Calvert Street (Houses); see
Waterloo Row

608 North Calvert Street (Row House)
(Waterloo Row)
HABS MD-7-A   p   L

612 North Calvert Street (Row House)
(Waterloo Row)
HABS MD-7-B   p   L

616 North Calvert Street (Row House)
(Waterloo Row)
HABS MD-7-C   p   L

622 North Calvert Street (Row House)
(Waterloo Row)
HABS MD-7-E   p   L

620 North Calvert Street (Stable)
(Waterloo Row)
HABS MD-7-D   p   L

North Central Railroad, Freight Shed
HAER MD-38   pd   H

North Charles Street (House, Cast-Iron
Porches) (Schapiro, John D., House;
Peabody Conservatory of Music; Abell
House)
609 Washington Place (N. Charles St.)
HABS MD-363   p   L

417 North Charles Street (Town House)
HABS MD-411   p   L

608-614 North Paca Street (Brick Row
Houses)
HABS MD-405   p   L

508-522 North Paca Street (Houses)
HABS MD-382   p   L

Oaklands Springhouse; see Harper, Robert
Goodloe, Dairy & Springhouse

1734-1736 Orleans Street (Double House)
HABS MD-18   s pd   L

Otterbein United Brethren Church
(German Evangelical Reformed Church)
122 W. Conway St.
HABS MD-396   p   L

405-411 Park Avenue (Double Houses)
E. side between Mulberry & Franklin Sts.
HABS MD-351   p   L

Park Avenue (House Fronts)
400 Block (E. side)
HABS MD-383   p   L

Park Avenue (House Fronts)
400 Block & W. Centre St. (W. side)
HABS MD-384   p   L

833-837 Park Avenue (Houses)
HABS MD-385   p   L

Pascault Row
651-665 W. Lexington St.
HABS MD-397   pd   L

Peabody Conservatory of Music; see North
Charles Street (House, Cast-Iron
Porches)

Peale, Rembrandt, Museum (Municipal
Museum; Peale's Baltimore Museum &
Gallery of Fine Arts)
225 N. Holliday St.
HABS MD-398   pd   L

Peale's Baltimore Museum & Gallery of
Fine Arts; see Peale, Rembrandt,
Museum

Pennsylvania Railroad, Calvert Station
Calvert & Franklin Sts.
HABS MD-342   p   L

Pennsylvania Railroad, President Street
Station (Philadelphia, Wilmington &
Baltimore, Pres. St. Sta.)
Fleet St.
HABS MD-31
HAER MD-8   s pd   L H

Philadelphia, Wilmington & Baltimore,
Pres. St. Sta.; see Pennsylvania Railroad,
President Street Station

Phoenix Shot Tower (Merchants' Shot
Tower)
Front & Fayette Sts.
HABS MD-21   s pd   L

Pickersgill, Mary Young, House; see Flag
House

Pine Street, 400 Block (Brick Houses)
HABS MD-386   p   L

Pleasant Street (Houses)
9, 11, 11 1/2, 15 E. Pleasant St.
HABS MD-43   pd   L

Pratt & Paca Streets (Brick Building)
HABS MD-341   p   L

Randall, Blanchard, House (Tiffany-Fisher
House; Mount Vernon Club)
8 W. Mount Vernon Place
HABS MD-371   p   L

Residence Row (8-18 West Hamilton Street
(Houses))
HABS MD-399   p   L

Roman Catholic Cathedral of Baltimore
(Minor Basilica, Assumption of the
Virgin Mary)
Cathedral St.
HABS MD-186   pd   L

Roman Catholic Episcopal Residence; see
Archbishop's House

Round Top Church; see First Baptist
Church

Saint Paul & Saratoga Streets (House)
HABS MD-70   p   L

Sanders House; see 520-522 South Chapel
Street (Double House)

Schapiro, John D., House; see North
Charles Street (House, Cast-Iron
Porches)

Seven Store Fronts & Residences; see
635-647 West Pratt Street (Commercial
Buildings)

**Shakespeare Street, 1600 Block (Brick
Cottage)**
HABS MD-346   p   L

**1628-1630-1632 Shakespeare Street (Brick
Houses)**
HABS MD-387   p   L

Smith, Dr. James, House; see 15 East
Pleasant Street (House)

Somerset Street, 400 Block (Houses)
HABS MD-858   p   L

812 South Ann Street (House)
Fell's Point
HABS MD-853   s   H

814 South Broadway (Brick Building)
(Fell's Point Theatre; Foreign Market)
HABS MD-340   p   L

**122-128 South Broadway (Brick Row
Houses)**
HABS MD-403   p   L

**113 South Broadway Street (Second Story
Porch)** (East Indian Restaurant)
HABS MD-362   p   L

**520-522 South Chapel Street (Double
House)** (Sanders House)
Fell's Point
HABS MD-4   s pd L

**248-250 South Exeter Street (Double
House)**
HABS MD-349   p   L

104 South Exeter Street (House-Mantel)
HABS MD-364   p   L

832 South Hanover Street (Store Front)
HABS MD-6   s pd L

**104-106 South Paca Street (Double
Houses)**
HABS MD-17   s pd L

St. Francis Xavier Roman Catholic Church
Calvert & Pleasant Sts.
HABS MD-30   pd   L

St. Mary's Seminary Chapel
N. Paca St. & Druid Hill Ave.
HABS MD-13   s pd L

**St. Mary's Seminary, Mother Seton's
House**
600 N. Paca St.
HABS MD-391   p   L

St. Paul's Rectory
24 W. Saratoga & Cathedral Sts.
HABS MD-409   p   L

Steele-Taggart House; see Taggart-Steele
House

Stewart, David, House; see Damon House,
Old

Sugar House (Refinery)
Aliceanna & Chester Sts.
HABS MD-11   s pd L

Swan-Frick House
W. Franklin St.
HABS MD-74   p   L

Taggart-Steele House (Steele-Taggart
House)
Cathedral & Madison Sts.
HABS MD-410   p   L

1621 Thames Street (House) (Van Bidder
House; Fell House)
Fell's Point
HABS MD-22   s pd L

1626-1628 Thames Street (Row Houses)
(Forbes Houses)
HABS MD-406   p   L

Thomas-Jenks House; see 1 West Mount
Vernon Place (House)

Tiffany-Fisher House; see Randall,
Blanchard, House

Unitarian Church; see First Unitarian
Church

University of Maryland, Davidge Hall; see
University of Maryland, Medical
Building

University of Maryland, Medical Building
(University of Maryland, Davidge Hall)
Greene & Lombard Sts.
HABS MD-304   s p   L

Upton; see Damon House, Old

U.S. Appraisers Stores, Old (U.S. Public
Store Number 1)
Gay & Lombard Sts.
HABS MD-3   s pd L

U.S. Public Store Number 1; see U.S.
Appraisers Stores, Old

Van Bidder House; see 1621 Thames Street
(House)

Washington Monument
Mount Vernon Place & Washington Place
HABS MD-71   p   L

Watchman Fire Company Firehouse
(Mechanics Hall)
Montgomery St.
HABS MD-851   d   H

Waterloo Row (606-628 North Calvert
Street (Houses))
HABS MD-7   s pd L

Waterloo Row; see 608 North Calvert
Street (Row House)

Waterloo Row; see 622 North Calvert
Street (Row House)

Waterloo Row; see 612 North Calvert
Street (Row House)

Waterloo Row; see 616 North Calvert
Street (Row House)

Waterloo Row; see 620 North Calvert
Street (Stable)

922-924-926 Watson Street (Row Houses)
HABS MD-408   p   L

Waverly Terrace
N. Carey St. & Franklin Square
HABS MD-414   p   L

**341 West Franklin Street (House-Exterior
Stairway)**
HABS MD-367   p   L

8-18 West Hamilton Street (Houses); see
Residence Row

**837-843 West Lexington Street (Brick
Houses)**
HABS MD-381   p   L

742 West Lexington Street (House)
HABS MD-368   p   L

107 West Monument Street (House)
(Morton, George C., House)
HABS MD-1   s pd L

1 West Mount Vernon Place (House)
(Jencks, Francis, House; Thomas-Jenks
House; Gladding, Harry, House)
HABS MD-372   p   L

**635-647 West Pratt Street (Commercial
Buildings)** (Seven Store Fronts &
Residences)
HABS MD-16   s pd L

**23-47 West Preston Street (Brick Row
Houses)**
HABS MD-407   p   L

Wiessner (American) Brewery
Gay St.
HAER MD-25   p   H

Wilson, Henry, House; see Caton House

ALLEGANY COUNTY

Cumberland

**Baltimore & Ohio R. R., Queen City Hotel
& Station**
Park St.
HAER MD-4   pd   H

**Baltimore & Ohio Railroad, Bolt & Forge
Shop**
Spring St.
HAER MD-2-B   s pd   H

**Baltimore & Ohio Railroad, Cumberland
Shops**
S. of Williams St.
HAER MD-2   p   H

**Baltimore & Ohio Railroad, Rail Rolling
Mill**
Elm St.
HAER MD-2-A   s pd   H

Chesapeake & Ohio Canal, Aqueduct No. 10; see Chesapeake & Ohio Canal, Town Creek Aqueduct

Chesapeake & Ohio Canal, Lockhouse 75
W. of State Rt. 51
HAER MD-26   s   H

Chesapeake & Ohio Canal, Town Creek Aqueduct (Chesapeake & Ohio Canal, Aqueduct No. 10)
SW of State Rt. 51
HABS MD-813
HAER MD-31   s   H

Cumberland & Penn. R. R., Wills Creek Viaduct
Spanning Wills Creek at Braddock Run
HAER MD-5   pd   H

Cumberland vic.

Chesapeake & Ohio Canal, Aqueduct 11; see Chesapeake & Ohio Canal, Evitts Creek Aqueduct

Chesapeake & Ohio Canal, Evitts Creek Aqueduct (Chesapeake & Ohio Canal, Aqueduct 11)
State Rt. 51
HABS MD-824   p   H

Chesapeake & Ohio Canal, Lock 74
State Rt. 51
HABS MD-821   p   H

Chesapeake & Ohio Canal, Lock 75
HABS MD-822   p   H

Chesapeake & Ohio Canal, Lockhouse at Lock 74
State Rt. 51
HABS MD-820   p   H

Oldtown

Chesapeake & Ohio Canal, Lock 71
HABS MD-816   p   H

Chesapeake & Ohio Canal, Lockhouse at Lock 70 (Chesapeake & Ohio Canal, Lockhouse at Old Town Lock)
HABS MD-815   pd   H

Chesapeake & Ohio Canal, Lockhouse at Old Town Lock; see Chesapeake & Ohio Canal, Lockhouse at Lock 70

Oldtown vic.

Chesapeake & Ohio Canal, Busey Cabin (Chesapeake & Ohio Canal, Const. Office at Lock 60)
HABS MD-805   p   H

Chesapeake & Ohio Canal, Carpenters Shop at Lock 66 (Chesapeake & Ohio Canal, Woodwork Shop)
State Rt. 51
HABS MD-809   p   H

Chesapeake & Ohio Canal, Const. Office at Lock 60; see Chesapeake & Ohio Canal, Busey Cabin

Chesapeake & Ohio Canal, Lock 72 (Chesapeake & Ohio Canal, The Narrows)
State Rt. 51
HABS MD-819   p   H

Chesapeake & Ohio Canal, Lockhouse at Lock 68 (Chesapeake & Ohio Canal, Lockhouse, Crabtree's Lock)
HABS MD-814   pd   H

Chesapeake & Ohio Canal, Lockhouse at Lock 72 (Chesapeake & Ohio Canal, Lockhouse at The Narrows)
State Rt. 51
HABS MD-818   pd   H

Chesapeake & Ohio Canal, Lockhouse at The Narrows; see Chesapeake & Ohio Canal, Lockhouse at Lock 72

Chesapeake & Ohio Canal, Lockhouse, Crabtree's Lock; see Chesapeake & Ohio Canal, Lockhouse at Lock 68

Chesapeake & Ohio Canal, Paw-Paw Tunnel
HABS MD-810   p   H

Chesapeake & Ohio Canal, The Narrows; see Chesapeake & Ohio Canal, Lock 72

Chesapeake & Ohio Canal, Woodwork Shop; see Chesapeake & Ohio Canal, Carpenters Shop at Lock 66

Paw Paw

Chesapeake & Ohio Canal, Lock 63 1/3
N. of State Rt. 51
HAER MD-30-A   s   H

Chesapeake & Ohio Canal, Lock 64 2/3
N. of State Rt. 51
HAER MD-30-B   s   H

Chesapeake & Ohio Canal, Lock 66 (Chesapeake & Ohio Canal, Lock 66 Complex)
N. of State Rt. 51
HAER MD-30   s   H

Chesapeake & Ohio Canal, Lock 66 Complex; see Chesapeake & Ohio Canal, Lock 66

ANNE ARUNDEL COUNTY

House
HABS MD-890   p   L

Annapolis

Acton (Hammond's Plains; Murray Hill)
1 Acton Place
HABS MD-296   s pd   L H

Acton, Springhouse
11 Acton Place
HABS MD-296-A   pd   H

Adams-Kilty House
131 Charles St.
HABS MD-264   pd   H

Baer's Clothing Store; see Williams, James, House

Barber, George & John, Store
77-79 Main St.
HABS MD-266   s pd   H

Bladen's Folly; see St. John's College, McDowell Hall

Blue Ball Tavern; see Davis House

Brice, James III, House (Elks Club)
42 East St.
HABS MD-247   pd   L H

Brice, John II, House (Jennings House)
195 Prince George St.
HABS MD-282   pd   H

Brice, John III, House; see Dorsey, Maj. Edward, House

Brooksby-Shaw House (Shaw, John, House)
21 State Circle
HABS MD-250   pd   L H

Bryce, Frances, Boarding House (18 West Street (Building))
HABS MD-265   pd   H

Building, Three House Brick (Ridout, John, Tenant Houses)
110-112-114 Duke of Gloucester St.
HABS MD-252   pd   L H

Callahan, John, House; see Pinckney, William, House (Doorway)

Carroll, Charles, House
Duke of Gloucester St. & Spa Creek
HABS MD-293   pd   L H

Carroll, Charles, The Barrister, House; see Davis House

Carroll, Charles, The Settler, House
139 Market St.
HABS MD-285   pd   H

Carvel; see Scott, Dr. Upton, House

Carvel Hall Hotel; see Paca, William, House

Chase House, Annex
235 King George St.
HABS MD-244   pd   L H

Chase, Samuel, House; see Chase-Lloyd House

Chase-Lloyd House (Chase, Samuel, House)
22 Maryland Ave. & King George St.
HABS MD-243   s pd   L H

Creagh, Patrick, House; see Smith, Aunt Lucy, House

Custom House, Old; see Inn, Old

Davis House (Tydings House; Carroll, Charles, The Barrister, House; Blue Ball Tavern)
King George St. (moved from Main & Conduit Sts.)
HABS MD-258   pd   L H

Dockside Restaurant; see Williams, James, House

Donaldson-Steuart House; see King William's School (Interiors)

Dorsey, Maj. Edward, House (Brice, John III, House; Marchand House)
211 Prince George St.
HABS MD-107   p   L

Dulany, Lloyd, House
162 Conduit St.
HABS MD-277   pd   H

Elks Club; see Brice, James III, House

Franklin, James Shaw, Law Office
17 State Circle at Chancery Lane
HABS MD-280   d   H

Franklin Store
206 Main St. & Chancery Lane
HABS MD-281   pd   H

Gaver House; see Smith, Aunt Lucy, House

Ghiselin Boarding House (28 West Street (Building))
HABS MD-268   pd   H

Ghiselin Boarding House (30 West Street (Building))
HABS MD-269   pd   H

Golder, Archibald, Tavern (Greengold's Inc.; Hunter's Tavern)
50 West St.
HABS MD-233   d   H

Government House; see Governor's Mansion

Governor's Mansion (Government House)
State Circle at School St.
HABS MD-146   pd   L H

Grammer, Frederick, House; see Inn, Old

Great Hall; see St. John's College, McDowell Hall

Green, Jonas, House
124 Charles St.
HABS MD-259   pd   L H

Greengold's Inc.; see Golder, Archibald, Tavern

Hammond-Harwood House; see Harwood-Hammond House

Hammond's Plains; see Acton

Harwood-Hammond House (Hammond-Harwood House; Lockerman House)
19 Maryland Ave. & King George St.
HABS MD-251   pd   L H

Holland-Hohne House
45 Fleet St.
HABS MD-262   s pd   H

Hopkins, Walton H., House (Walton, Dr. Thomas O., House)
15 Maryland Ave. & King George St.
HABS MD-276   pd   H

Hunter's Tavern; see Golder, Archibald, Tavern

Inn, Old (Custom House, Old; Grammer, Frederick, House)
Main & Green Sts.
HABS MD-257   pd   L H

Inn, Old (Marx House; Middleton's Tavern)
Dock & Randall Sts.
HABS MD-256   pd   L H

Jennings House; see Brice, John II, House

Johnson, Reverdy, House
Saint John's College (moved from 9 Northwest St.)
HABS MD-273   pd   H

Kentish Inn; see King William's School (Interiors)

Key House; see Scott, Dr. Upton, House

King William's School (Interiors) (Workman, Anthony, Inn; Donaldson-Steuart House; Kentish Inn)
10 Francis St.
HABS MD-260   pd   L H

Lockerman House; see Harwood-Hammond House

Loockerman-Tilton House
9-11 Maryland Ave.
HABS MD-287   pd   H

160-166 Main Street (Building)
HABS MD-270   pd   H

Mann's Hotel Row Houses
150-160 Conduit St.
HABS MD-289   p   H

Marchand House; see Dorsey, Maj. Edward, House

Market House
Market Space, Main & Dock Sts.
HABS MD-234   s   L

Marx House; see Inn, Old

Middleton's Tavern; see Inn, Old

Monroe, James, Dry Goods Store
140 Main St.
HABS MD-261   s pd   H

Moss House; see Sands, John, House

Murray Hill; see Acton

Naval Academy Alumni Association House; see Ogle, Gov. Samuel, House

19-21 Northwest Street (Houses)
HABS MD-290   p   H

Ogle, Gov. Samuel, House (Ogle Hall; Naval Academy Alumni Association House; Stevenson, Dr. William, House)
33 College Ave.
HABS MD-242   pd   L H

Ogle Hall; see Ogle, Gov. Samuel, House

Paca, William, House (Carvel Hall Hotel)
186 Prince George St.
HABS MD-253   pd   L H

Pinckney, William, House (Doorway) (Pinckney-Callahan House; Callahan, John, House)
164 Conduit St. (moved from Bladen St.)
HABS MD-255   pd   L H

Pinckney-Callahan House; see Pinckney, William, House (Doorway)

Pinkney Street (Houses); see Taylor Street (Frame Houses)

4 Pinkney Street (Warehouse); see Tobacco Prize House

Randall, Alexander, Double House
88-90 State Circle
HABS MD-272   pd   H

Randall-Bordley House
9 Weems Place
HABS MD-232   d   H

Reynolds Tavern
4 Church Circle at Franklin St.
HABS MD-248   s pd   L H

Reynolds Tavern, Smokehouse
4 Church Circle
HABS MD-248-A   s pd   H

Ridout, John, House
120 Duke of Gloucester St.
HABS MD-91   pd   L H

Ridout, John, Tenant Houses; see Building, Three House Brick

Rutland, Thomas, House (Stewart, Peggy, House)
207 Hanover St.
HABS MD-278   pd   H

Sands, John, House (Moss House)
130 Prince George St.
HABS MD-254   pd   L H

Scott, Dr. Upton, House (Carvel; Key House)
4 Shipwright St.
HABS MD-246   s pd   L H

Scott, Upton, Stable
4 Shipwright St.
HABS MD-246-A   s pd   H

Shaw House; see Slicer-Shiplap House

Shaw, John, House; see Brooksby-Shaw House

Slicer-Shiplap House (Shaw House; Smith, Edward, House)
18 Pinkney St.
HABS MD-249   s pd   L H

Smith, Aunt Lucy, House (Creagh, Patrick, House; Gaver House)
160 Prince George St.
HABS MD-295   pd   L H

Smith, Edward, House; see Slicer-Shiplap House

St. Anne's Rectory, Old
215-217 Hanover St.
HABS MD-235   d   H

St. John's College, Brick Double House (St. John's College, Faculty Residence; St. John's College, Paca-Carroll Hall)
Saint John's St.
HABS MD-292   pd   L H

St. John's College, Chase-Stone House
235 King George St.
HABS MD-236   d   H

St. John's College, Faculty Residence; see St. John's College, Brick Double House

St. John's College, Humphreys Hall
College Ave.
HABS MD-274   pd   H

St. John's College, Key Memorial Hall
Saint John's St.
HABS MD-237   d   H

St. John's College, McDowell Hall (Great Hall; Bladen's Folly)
College Ave.
HABS MD-291   pd   L H

St. John's College, Paca-Carroll Hall; see St. John's College, Brick Double House

St. John's College, Pinkney Hall
College Ave.
HABS MD-275   pd   H

State House
State Circle
HABS MD-245   s pd   L H

Stevenson, Dr. William, House; see Ogle, Gov. Samuel, House

Stewart, Peggy, House; see Rutland, Thomas, House

Taylor Street (Frame Houses) (Pinkney Street (Houses))
HABS MD-271   pd   L H

Tobacco Prize House (4 Pinkney Street (Warehouse))
HABS MD-283   pd   H

Treasury Building, Old
State Circle
HABS MD-10   s pd   L H

Tydings House; see Davis House

Walton, Dr. Thomas O., House; see Hopkins, Walton H., House

18 West Street (Building); see Bryce, Frances, Boarding House

28 West Street (Building); see Ghiselin Boarding House

30 West Street (Building); see Ghiselin Boarding House

31-33 West Street (Commercial Building)
HABS MD-267   pd   H

Williams, James, House (Dockside Restaurant; Baer's Clothing Store)
22 Market Space
HABS MD-279   pd   H

Workman, Anthony, Inn; see King William's School (Interiors)

Annapolis vic.

Cheston House; see Ridge, The

Hawthorne Ridge; see Ridge, The

Ridge, The (Cheston House; Hawthorne Ridge)
Lankford Rd.
HABS MD-147   p   L

Sharpe, Gov. Horatio, House; see Whitehall

Whitehall (Sharpe, Gov. Horatio, House)
Whitehall Rd., U.S. Rt. 50 vic.
HABS MD-294   p   L

Butler vic.

Foxhall Farm; see McCeney, Dr., House

McCeney, Dr., House (Foxhall Farm)
Polling House Rd.
HABS MD-123   p   L

Collinsville vic.

Locust Grove
Chew's Inn vic.
HABS MD-121   p   L

Crownsville vic.

Rising Sun Tavern (Worthington, Charles, Tavern)
Generals Hwy. (State Rt. 178)
HABS MD-845   p   L

Worthington, Charles, Tavern; see Rising Sun Tavern

Cumberstone

Cedar Park (Galloway House; Ewen Upon Ewenton)
Cumberstone Rd. on West River
HABS MD-847   pd   L H

Ewen Upon Ewenton; see Cedar Park

Galloway House; see Cedar Park

Cumberstone vic.

Ivy Neck
Rhode & West Rivers
HABS MD-844   p   L

Davidsonville vic.

1556 Aberdeen Street (Old House near Doden) (Bridge Hill)
HABS MD-153   p   L

All Hallows Church
All Hallows Church Rd. & State Rt. 2
HABS MD-37   s pd   L

Bamford, Warren, House; see Friend's Choice

Bridge Hill; see 1556 Aberdeen Street (Old House near Doden)

Friend's Choice (Linden Grove; White Chimneys; Bamford, Warren, House)
Queen Anne Bridge Rd.
HABS MD-100   p   L

Hopkins-Iglehart House; see Mount Airy

Idlewilde; see Townsend House

Iglehart, James Alexis, House; see Mount Airy

Linden Grove; see Friend's Choice

Mount Airy (Iglehart, James Alexis, House; Hopkins-Iglehart House)
Mount Airy Rd., State Rt. 424 vic.
HABS MD-102   pd   L

Oakland
Ferry Rd.
HABS MD-101   p   L

Townsend House (Idlewilde; Townsend-Mackall Place)
Davidsonville Rd. (State Rt. 424)
HABS MD-103   p   L

Townsend-Mackall Place; see Townsend House

White Chimneys; see Friend's Choice

Edgewater

Castle, The (Worthington House; Larkin's Hundred)
Mill Swamp Rd.
HABS MD-152   p   L

Larkin's Hundred; see Castle, The

Worthington House; see Castle, The

Fairhaven vic.

Folly Farm (Larkin's Hill Farm; Larkin's Hills)
Mill Swamp Rd.
HABS MD-263   p   L

Larkin's Hill Farm; see Folly Farm

Larkin's Hills; see Folly Farm

Friendship vic.

Carr, Dr. Benjamin, House; see Trenton Hall

Harrison, Richard, House; see Holly Hill

Holland's Hills; see Holly Hill

Holly Hill (Rose Valley; Holland's Hills; Harrison, Richard, House)
Friendship Rd. (State Rt. 261)
HABS MD-284   pd   L

Rose Valley; see Holly Hill

Trenton Hall (Carr, Dr. Benjamin, House)
SW of Friendship Rd. (State Rt. 261)
HABS MD-155   p   L

Galesville vic.

Galloway Place, Old; see Tulip Hill

Galloway, Samuel, House; see Tulip Hill

Tulip Hill (Galloway Place, Old; Galloway, Samuel, House)
Cumberstone Rd.
HABS MD-286   p   L

Gambrills vic.

Anne Arundel County Free School; see First Free School

First Free School (Anne Arundel County Free School; Maryland Free School)
Rutland Rd. vic.
HABS MD-106   s p   L H

Maryland Free School; see First Free School

Harwood vic.

Bassford-Gardner House (Mount Pleasant)
HABS MD-144   pd   L

Mount Pleasant; see Bassford-Gardner House

Rawlings Tavern
State Rt. 2
HABS MD-112   p   L

Lothian

Hall, Sally, House; see Lothian

Lothian (Hall, Sally, House; Thomas, Philip, House)
Marlboro Rd. (State Rt. 408)
HABS MD-312   s   H

Thomas, Philip, House; see Lothian

Pindell

Neff, Benjamin C., House (Portland Manor)
Brooks Wood Rd.
HABS MD-130   p   L

Portland Manor; see Neff, Benjamin C., House

Robinson vic.

Old Annapolis Boulevard (Stone House)
HABS MD-288   p   L

Round Bay vic.

Belvoir (Scotts Plantation)
Generals Hwy. (State Rt. 178)
HABS MD-846   p   L

Scotts Plantation; see Belvoir

South River vic.
Almshouse at London Town (Town Hall, Old; London Town Publik House)
London Town Rd.
HABS MD-29   pd   L
Hopkins, Cadwalleder Edwards, House
Bell Branch Rd.
HABS MD-118   p   L
London Town Publik House; see Almshouse at London Town
Shadow Point; see Solomons Island Road (Frame House)
Solomons Island Road (Frame House) (Shadow Point)
HABS MD-298   p   L
South River Club
Solomons Island Rd. (State Rt. 2) vic.
HABS MD-843   p   L
Town Hall, Old; see Almshouse at London Town

Tracy's Landing vic.
Herring Creek Episcopal Church; see St. James Parish Episcopal Church
St. James Parish Episcopal Church (Herring Creek Episcopal Church)
Solomons Island Rd. (State Rt. 2)
HABS MD-850   p   L

BALTIMORE COUNTY

Baltimore vic.
Gaugh, Harry Dorsey, House; see Perry Hall
Linden
Belair Rd. (U.S. Rt. 1)
HABS MD-848   p   L
Perry Hall (Gaugh, Harry Dorsey, House)
Perry Hall Rd., U.S. Rt. 1 vic.
HABS MD-842   p   L

Cockeysville vic.
Balama Farms; see York Road (Stone House)
Hayfields Farm Buildings (Merryman, John, Farm Buildings)
Worthington Valley
HABS MD-15   s pd   L
Loveton
York Rd.
HABS MD-855   pd   H
Merryman, John, Farm Buildings; see Hayfields Farm Buildings
York Road (Stone House) (Balama Farms)
Marble Hill vic.
HABS MD-835   p   L

Ellicott City
Mill Houses
1209-1217 Oella Rd.
HABS MD-542   p   L

Fork vic.
Pork Forest
Harford Rd. (State Rt. 197)
HABS MD-832   p   L

Franklinville vic.
Orwell
Franklinville Rd.
HABS MD-28   pd   L

Hereford vic.
Barn, Stone & Brick; see Ednor & York Rds. (Stone Barn)
Ednor & York Rds. (Stone Barn) (Barn, Stone & Brick; Gorsuch, John M., Farm Barn; Glencoe Gardens)
HABS MD-61   L
Glencoe Gardens; see Ednor & York Rds. (Stone Barn)
Gorsuch, John M., Farm Barn; see Ednor & York Rds. (Stone Barn)

Ilchester
Mill Houses
River Rd.
HABS MD-830   p   L
Mill, Old
River Rd.
HABS MD-831   p   L

Ilchester vic.
Baltimore & Ohio Railroad, Patterson Viaduct; see Baltimore & Ohio Railroad, Viaduct
Baltimore & Ohio Railroad, Viaduct (Baltimore & Ohio Railroad, Patterson Viaduct)
Patapsco River
HABS MD-878
HAER MD-12   p   L H

Jerusalem vic.
Covered Bridge (Jericho Bridge)
Jericho Rd. spanning Little Gunpowder Falls
HABS MD-12   s pd   L
Jericho Bridge; see Covered Bridge

Kingsville
Kingsville Inn (Interiors) (Lassahn, E. F., Funeral Parlor)
11750 Belair Rd. (U.S. Rt. 1)
HABS MD-833   p   L
Lassahn, E. F., Funeral Parlor; see Kingsville Inn (Interiors)

Kingsville vic.
Bellevue Farm, Milk House (Milk House, Old)
Silver Spring Rd.
HABS MD-34   pd   L
Irish Lane (House) (7221 New Cut Road (House))
HABS MD-834   p   L

Milk House, Old; see Bellevue Farm, Milk House
7221 New Cut Road (House); see Irish Lane (House)

Long Green
Prospect Hill (Ringgold House)
Kanes Rd.
HABS MD-325   p   L
Ringgold House; see Prospect Hill

Monkton vic.
My Lady's Manor; see St. James' Church
St. James' Church (My Lady's Manor)
Monkton Rd.
HABS MD-836   p   L

Oella
Mill Houses
929-947 Oella Ave.
HABS MD-839   p   L
Mill, Old
Oella Ave.
HABS MD-837   p   L

Owings Mills
Cooperage Shop, Old
Reisterstown Rd.
HABS MD-840   p   L
Groff's Mill; see Mill Building
Mill Building (Groff's Mill; Owings Mill)
Bonita Ave.
HABS MD-841   p   L
Owings Mill; see Mill Building

Parkton vic.
Halfway House; see Weisburg Inn
Weisburg Inn (Halfway House)
York & Weisburg Rds.
HABS MD-332   p   L

Phoenix vic.
Phillpot House (Rockford)
Phillpot Rd.
HABS MD-333   p   L
Rockford; see Phillpot House

Pikesville
U.S. Arsenal
Reisterstown Rd.
HABS MD-14   s pd   L

Reisterstown vic.
Craddock House; see Ten Mile House
Ten Mile House (Craddock House)
Reisterstown Rd.
HABS MD-335   p   L

Relay
Baltimore & Ohio Railroad Bridge; see Thomas Viaduct
Latrobe's Folly; see Thomas Viaduct
Relay Viaduct; see Thomas Viaduct

Thomas Viaduct (Baltimore & Ohio
Railroad Bridge; Latrobe's Folly; Relay
Viaduct)
Spanning Patapsco River
HABS MD-535
HAER MD-3   p   L H

Sunnybrook

King's Tavern (Interior)
HABS MD-849   p   L

Sweet Air

Boyce, Roger, House; see Sweet Air
Clynmalira Manor; see Sweet Air
Sweet Air (Clynmalira Manor; Boyce,
Roger, House)
Manor Rd. & State Rt. 145
HABS MD-337   p   L

Towson

Baltimore County Courthouse
Washington Ave.
HABS MD-338   p   L
Hampton (Hampton National Historic Site;
Hampton Farm)
535 Hampton Lane; 537 1/2 St. Francis Rd.
HABS MD-226   s   L
Hampton, Blacksmith Shop; see Hampton,
Carpenter-Blacksmith Shop
Hampton, Burial Vault
535 Hampton Lane
HABS MD-226-W   d   L
Hampton, Carpenter-Blacksmith Shop
(Hampton, Blacksmith Shop)
537 1/2 St. Francis Rd.
HABS MD-226-I   s pd   L
Hampton, Carriage House
535 Hampton Lane
HABS MD-226-P   d   L
Hampton, Corn Crib
537 1/2 St. Francis Rd.
HABS MD-226-N   s pd   L
Hampton, Cow Barn
537 1/2 St. Francis Rd.
HABS MD-2226-H   s pd   L
Hampton, Dairy
537 1/2 St. Francis Rd.
HABS MD-226-F   s pd   L
Hampton Farm; see Hampton
Hampton, Farmhouse; see Hampton,
Overseer's House
Hampton, Gardener's House
535 Hampton Lane
HABS MD-226-V   d   L
Hampton, Granary; see Hampton, Long
Barn-Granary
Hampton, Greenhouse Number One
535 Hampton Lane
HABS MD-226-D   s pd   L
Hampton, Greenhouse Number Two
535 Hampton Lane
HABS MD-226-U   d   L
Hampton, Icehouse
535 Hampton Lane
HABS MD-226-E   s pd   L

Hampton, Long Barn-Granary (Hampton,
Granary)
537 1/2 St. Francis Rd.
HABS MD-226-G   s pd   L
Hampton Mansion
535 Hampton Lane
HABS MD-226-A   s pd   L
Hampton, Mule Barn
537 1/2 St. Francis Rd.
HABS MD-226-O   s pd   L
Hampton National Historic Site; see
Hampton
Hampton, Orangery
535 Hampton Lane
HABS MD-226-R   pd   L
Hampton, Overseer's House (Hampton,
Farmhouse)
537 1/2 St. Francis Rd.
HABS MD-226-J   s pd   L
Hampton, Privy
535 Hampton Lane
HABS MD-226-Q   d   L
Hampton, Quarters One
537 1/2 St. Francis Rd.
HABS MD-226-K   s   d   L
Hampton, Quarters Three
537 1/2 St. Francis Rd.
HABS MD-226-M   s pd   L
Hampton, Quarters Two
537 1/2 St. Francis Rd.
HABS MD-226-L   s pd   L
Hampton, Smokehouse
535 Hampton Lane
HABS MD-226-T   d   L
Hampton, Stable Number One
535 Hampton Lane
HABS MD-226-B   s pd   L
Hampton, Stable Number Two
535 Hampton Lane
HABS MD-226-C   s pd   L
Hampton, Woodshed
535 Hampton Lane
HABS MD-226-S   d   L

CALVERT COUNTY

Adelina

Berry; see Taney Place
Hance, Benjamin, House; see Taney Place
Taney Place (Berry; Hance, Benjamin,
House)
State Rt. 508
HABS MD-138   p   L

Barstow vic.

Cedar Hill (Gant House)
German Chapel Rd.
HABS MD-173   p   L
Gant House; see Cedar Hill

Chaneyville vic.

Caucaud, David, House; see Talbot, Dr.
Russell, House

Hampton; see Talbot, Dr. Russell, House
Talbot, Dr. Russell, House (Hampton;
Caucaud, David, House)
Flint Hill Rd.
HABS MD-145   p   L

Dare's Wharf vic.

Dare House
Dare's Rd. (State Rt. 402)
HABS MD-124   p   L

Huntingtown vic.

Huntingfields; see Stanforth, John, House
Lowery; see Stanforth, John, House
Lyon House; see Stanforth, John, House
Stanforth, John, House (Huntingfields;
Lowery; Lyon House)
Lowery Rd. vic.
HABS MD-105   L

Little Cove Point

Clark, Capt., House; see Eltonhead Manor
Eltonhead Manor (Clark, Capt., House;
Little Cove Point Road (Old House))
HABS MD-2   s pd   L
Little Cove Point Road (Old House); see
Eltonhead Manor

Lower Marlboro

Wilson House
(moved from MD, Upper Marlboro)
HABS MD-126   p   L

Lower Marlboro vic.

Building, Small
State Rt. 262
HABS MD-131   p   L
Graeme, Charles, House; see Graeme,
Malcolm, House
Graeme, Malcolm, House (Patuxent
Manor; Graeme, Charles, House)
State Rt. 262 vic.
HABS MD-122   p   L
Patuxent Manor; see Graeme, Malcolm,
House

Lusby vic.

Arminger's Bar; see Solomons Island Road
(Farmhouse)
Breedon-Day House & Farm Buildings
(Morgan Hill Farm Buildings; Day,
Robert, House; Day-Breedon Farm)
Sollers Rd.
HABS MD-175   s p   L
Charles' Gift (House on Calvert Cliffs;
Preston's Cliff)
State Rt. 2 & 4 vic.
HABS MD-416   s p   H
Christ Church Parish; see Middleham
Protestant Episcopal Chapel
Corn Crib on the Cliffs; see House, Old
Frame, & Log Corn Crib
Day, Robert, House; see Breedon-Day
House & Farm Buildings
Day-Breedon Farm; see Breedon-Day
House & Farm Buildings

Goldstein House (Parran's Park; Lusby
(House))
State Rts. 2 & 4
HABS MD-162   p   L

House, Old Frame, & Log Corn Crib (Corn
Crib on the Cliffs)
Calvert Cliffs
HABS MD-415   p   L

House on Calvert Cliffs; see Charles' Gift

Lusby (Frame House); see Solomons Island
Road (Farmhouse)

Lusby (House); see Goldstein House

Middleham Protestant Episcopal Chapel
(Christ Church Parish)
Solomons Island Rd. (State Rts. 2 & 4)
HABS MD-418   p   L

Morgan Hill Farm Buildings; see
Breedon-Day House & Farm Buildings

Parran's Park; see Goldstein House

Preston, Richard, House; see
Preston-on-the-Patuxent

Preston-on-the-Patuxent (Preston, Richard,
House)
Turner Rd.
HABS MD-419   p   L H

Preston's Cliff; see Charles' Gift

Solomons Island Road (Farmhouse)
(Arminger's Bar; Lusby (Frame House))
State Rts. 2 & 4
HABS MD-133   p   L

Solomons Island Road (Frame House)
HABS MD-889   p   L

Mackall

Mackall House (Mackall's Hill)
St. Leonard Creek
HABS MD-129   p   L

Mackall's Hill; see Mackall House

Prince Frederick vic.

Kitts Marsh Farm, Tobacco Barn; see
Tobacco Barn

Tobacco Barn (Kitts Marsh Farm, Tobacco
Barn)
Patuxent River, State Rt. 508
HABS MD-420   p   L

Solomons Island vic.

Tobacco Barn
Prince Frederick vic.
HABS MD-421   p   L

Stoakley

Solomons Island Road (Tobacco Barn)
State Rts. 2 & 4
HABS MD-422   p   L

Sunderland vic.

All Saints' Protestant Episcopal Church
State Rts. 2 & 4
HABS MD-423   p   L

Wallville vic.

Cage, The; see Parrott's Cage

Parran, Thomas, House; see Parrott's Cage

Parrott, William, House; see Parrott's Cage

Parrott's Cage (Parran, Thomas, House;
Cage, The; Parrott, William, House)
Cage Rd.
HABS MD-174   p   L

CAROLINE COUNTY

Federalsburg

Federalsburg Windmill
Oak Grove Rd.
HABS MD-425   p   L

Hillsboro

Main Street (Brick House) (Sellers, Francis,
House)
HABS MD-675   p   L

Sellers, Francis, House; see Main Street
(Brick House)

Old Town vic.

**Chesapeake & Ohio Canal, House,
Paw-Paw Tunnel**
State Rt. 51
HABS MD-811   p   H

Williston Landing

Philips Range; see Williston Road (Brick
House)

Potter Hall; see Williston Road (Brick
House)

Store, Old
HABS MD-427   p   L

Williston Road (Brick House) (Potter Hall;
Philips Range)
Choptank River vic.
HABS MD-426   p   L

CARROLL COUNTY

Keymar vic.

Keymar Bridge
Spanning Little Pipe Creek
HABS MD-20   s pd   L

Keysville-Frederick County Road Bridge
HAER MD-40   p   H

Randallstown vic.

Branton (Wyatt Place; Residence, Old)
Liberty Rd.
HABS MD-334   p   L

Residence, Old; see Branton

Wyatt Place; see Branton

CECIL COUNTY

Blue Ball

Blue Ball Tavern (Job, Andrew, House)
State Rt. 273 & Blue Ball Rd. (State Rt.
545)
HABS MD-428   p   L

Job, Andrew, House; see Blue Ball Tavern

Bohemia River

Bohemia (MacGregory Delight; Milligan
Hall; Milligan, George, House)
HABS MD-23   pd   L

MacGregory Delight; see Bohemia

Milligan, George, House; see Bohemia

Milligan Hall; see Bohemia

Calvert vic.

Meetinghouse, Brick
Calvert & Bayview Rds.
HABS MD-429   p   L

Cecilton

House, Old Frame
U.S. Rt. 213 & State Rt. 282
HABS MD-430   p   L

Cecilton vic.

Anchorage, The; see Fredericktown Road
(Brick Farmhouse)

Fredericktown Road (Brick Farmhouse)
(Anchorage, The)
U.S. Rt. 213
HABS MD-431   p   L

Greenfield Castle & Outbuildings
U.S. Rt. 213
HABS MD-432   p   L

Charlestown

**Bladen Street (Frame House with Gambrel
Roof)**
HABS MD-435   p   L

Indian Queen & Adjacent Houses (Indian
Queen Tavern; Red Lyon Inn's Indian
Queen Hotel)
Market St.
HABS MD-436   p   L

Indian Queen Tavern; see Indian Queen &
Adjacent Houses

Market Street (Brick House)
Indian Queen vic.
HABS MD-434   p   L

Red Lyon Inn's Indian Queen Hotel; see
Indian Queen & Adjacent Houses

Chesapeake City

**Chesapeake & Delaware Canal, Pump
House**
HAER MD-39   s   H

Conowingo vic.

Success
U.S. Rt. 222
HABS MD-437   p   L

Earleville vic.

Bellevue (Frisby's Prime Choice)
State Rt. 282
HABS MD-438   p   L

Frisby's Prime Choice; see Bellevue

Grove Neck; see Rich Neck Farm

Mount Harmon Plantation at World's End
HABS MD-861   p   H

Rich Neck Farm (Grove Neck)
Grove Neck Rd. vic.
HABS MD-457   p   L

Elk Mills

Elk Mills (Building)
State Rt. 277 vic.
HABS MD-439   p   L

Mill Houses (Mill Village, Row Houses)
State Rt. 277
HABS MD-440   p   L

Mill Village, Row Houses; see Mill Houses

Elk Mills vic.

House, Old Stone, with Frame Addition
State Rt. 316
HABS MD-441   p   L

Elkton

American Legion Cecil Post 15; see
Partridge Hall

Cast-Iron Grapevine Porch (226 Main
Street (House))
HABS MD-449   p   L

Elkton House; see 222 Main Street (Brick
House)

Elkton Landing (Stone House)
Landing Lane
HABS MD-444   p   L

Fountain Inn
HABS MD-442   p   L

Hollingsworth, Col. Henry, House; see
Partridge Hall

Hollingsworth Tavern
205 Main St.
HABS MD-443   p   L

222 Main Street (Brick House) (Elkton
House)
HABS MD-447   p   L

Main Street (House) (Mitchell, Dr.
Abraham, House)
E. of North St.
HABS MD-446   p   L

142 Main Street (House) (Wedding
Chapel)
HABS MD-450   p   L

205 Main Street (House)
HABS MD-448   p   L

226 Main Street (House); see Cast-Iron
Grapevine Porch

Main Street (House-Entrance Doorway)
E. of Bow St.
HABS MD-445   p   L

Mitchell, Dr. Abraham, House; see Main
Street (House)

Partridge Hall (Hollingsworth, Col. Henry,
House; American Legion Cecil Post 15)
129 Main St.
HABS MD-452   p   L

Pearce Store; see South Main Street (Brick
House)

South Main Street (Brick House) (Pearce
Store)
HABS MD-453   p   L

Wedding Chapel; see 142 Main Street
(House)

**West Main & North Bridge Streets (Brick
House)**
HABS MD-451   p   L

Elkton vic.

Brentwood; see West Williams Road (Brick
Farmhouse)

Cecil County Center & Red Cross; see
Holly Hall

Frenchtown Landing House
Frenchtown Rd.
HABS MD-454   p   L

Holly Hall (Cecil County Center & Red
Cross; Sewell, Gen. James, House)
U.S. Rt. 213
HABS MD-455   p   L

Sewell, Gen. James, House; see Holly Hall

West Williams Road (Brick Farmhouse)
(Brentwood)
HABS MD-456   p   L

North East

Green Hill, Slave Quarters & Woodhouse
(Russell, Thomas, House)
State Rt. 7
HABS MD-459   p   L

House, Frame
HABS MD-460   p   L

Inn, Old
HABS MD-461   p   L

Russell, Thomas, House; see Green Hill,
Slave Quarters & Woodhouse

St. Mary's Protestant Episcopal Church
State Rt. 272
HABS MD-462   p   L

Perryville vic.

Principio Furnace
Port Rd. (State Rt. 7)
HABS MD-467   p   L

Port Deposit

184-186 Conowingo Road (Row Houses);
see Main Street (Block of Houses)

Main Street (Block of Houses) (184-186
Conowingo Road (Row Houses))
U.S. Rt. 222
HABS MD-465   p   L

58 Main Street (Houses)
Conowingo Rd. (U.S. Rt. 222)
HABS MD-464   p   L

Main Street (Stone House)
Conowingo Rd. (U.S. Rt. 222)
HABS MD-463   p   L

Tome, Jacob, Mansion
U.S. Rt. 222
HABS MD-466   p   L

St. Augustine

Great House Farm; see Great House
Plantation

Great House Plantation (Great House
Farm)
Mitton Rd.
HABS MD-468   pd   L

Warwick

Old Bohemia; see St. Francis Xavier
Roman Catholic Church

St. Francis Xavier Roman Catholic Church
(Old Bohemia)
Warwick & Church Rds.
HABS MD-241   s pd   L

CHARLES COUNTY

Blossom Point

Ballast House
La Plata vic.
HABS MD-318   s pd   L

La Plata vic.

Locust Grove
HABS MD-240   s   H

Marbury vic.

Mattawoman; see Smallwood's Retreat

Smallwood, Gen. William, House; see
Smallwood's Retreat

Smallwood's Retreat (Mattawoman;
Smallwood, Gen. William, House)
State Rts. 224 & 484
HABS MD-38   s pd   L

Morgantown

Harris, Morgan, House; see Waverly

Waverly (Harris, Morgan, House)
State Rt. 229 vic.
HABS MD-177   p   L

Newport vic.

Sarum
HABS MD-860   p   H

Port Tobacco

Chapel Point Road (Gambrel Roof House)
(Stagg Hall; Parnham-Padgett House)
HABS MD-469   p   L

Parnham-Padgett House; see Chapel Point
Road (Gambrel Roof House)

Stagg Hall; see Chapel Point Road
(Gambrel Roof House)

Port Tobacco vic.

Brown, Dr. Gustavus, House; see Rose Hill

Habre de Venture (Stone, Thomas, House)
Rose Hill Rd.
HABS MD-470   p   L

Rose Hill (Brown, Dr. Gustavus, House)
Rose Hill Rd.
HABS MD-58   pd   L

Stone, Thomas, House; see Habre de
Venture

DORCHESTER COUNTY

Cambridge vic.

Farm Group
E. New Market vic.
HABS MD-471   p   L

Green Farm; see House, Brick end frame,
   with Gambrel roof

House, Brick end frame, with Gambrel roof
(Green Farm)
U.S. Rt. 50 vic.
HABS MD-474   p   L

House, Frame
E. New Market vic.
HABS MD-473   p   L

House, Haunted (Shoal Creek House)
U.S. Rt. 50 vic.
HABS MD-472   p   L

Shoal Creek House; see House, Haunted

Church Creek

Trinity Episcopal Church, Old
Church Creek Rd. (State Rt. 16)
HABS MD-201   pd   L

Eldorado vic.

Lee House; see Rehobeth
Rehobeth (Lee House)
Punkum Rd.
HABS MD-27   pd   L

New Market

Friendship Hall
State Rts. 16 & 14
HABS MD-475   p   L

House, Old, of the Hinges & Outbuildings
HABS MD-476   p   L

Rose Hill
HABS MD-859   s p   H

Secretary

Carthagena; see Sewall, Henry, House
My Lady Sewall's Manor House; see
   Sewall, Henry, House

Sewall, Henry, House (My Lady Sewall's
   Manor House; Carthagena; Tripp,
   Henry, House)
My Lady Sewall's Manor Rd. & State Rt.
14
HABS MD-60   pd   L

Tripp, Henry, House; see Sewall, Henry,
   House

Secretary vic.

Warwick Fort Manor House (Ruins)
Warwick Rd.
HABS MD-169   p   L

Vienna

Nanticoke River (Frame House)
HABS MD-477   L

FREDERICK COUNTY

Brunswick

Chesapeake & Ohio Canal, Lock 30
State Rt. 17 vic.
HABS MD-754   p   H

Catoctin vic.

Catoctin Furnace, Stack Number 2
(Isabella)
U.S. Rt. 15
HABS MD-478   p   L

Isabella; see Catoctin Furnace, Stack
   Number 2

Catoctin Village

Catoctin Manor (Iron Master's House)
U.S. Rt. 15
HABS MD-479   p   L

Iron Master's House; see Catoctin Manor

Main Street (Cottages) (Stone Workers'
   Cottages)
State Rt. 806
HABS MD-480   p   L

Stone Workers' Cottages; see Main Street
(Cottages)

Dickerson vic.

**Chesapeake & Ohio Canal, Monocacy
   Aqueduct**
Monocacy Rd.
HABS MD-19   s pd   L

Frederick

All Saints' Chapel; see All Saints' Parish
   Episcopal Church

All Saints' Parish Episcopal Church (All
   Saints' Chapel)
Lee Court
HABS MD-490   p   L

119-150 All Saints Street (Houses)
HABS MD-481   p   L

**Baltimore & Ohio RR, Frederick Passenger
   Station**
Market & All Saints' Sts.
HAER MD-18   p   H

Baltzell, Dr. John, House; see Loat's Female
   Orphan Home

Bentz Street (Houses)
HABS MD-484   p   L

314-322 Bentz Street (Houses)
HABS MD-483   p   L

Derange Street (Rusticated Wooden
   House) (West Patrick Street (House))
HABS MD-487   p   L

96-120 East Street (Houses)
HABS MD-485   p   L

Fifth Street (Double House)
HABS MD-482   p   L

Fourth Street (Row Cottages)
Fifth St.
HABS MD-494   p   L

**Frederick Academy of the Visitation
   Convent;** see St. John's Roman Catholic
   Church & Convent

Frederick County Historical Society; see
   Loat's Female Orphan Home

Hessian Barracks; see Revolutionary
   Barracks

Loat's Female Orphan Home (Frederick
   County Historical Society; Baltzell, Dr.
   John, House)
24 E. Church St.
HABS MD-489   p   L

407-411 North Market Street (Houses)
HABS MD-495   p   L

Revolutionary Barracks (Hessian Barracks)
242 S. Market St.
HABS MD-492   p   L

**St. John's Roman Catholic Church &
   Convent** (Frederick Academy of the
   Visitation Convent)
Second St.
HABS MD-496   pd   L

Taney, Roger Brook, House
121 S. Benzt St.
HABS MD-497   p   L

Trail & Ross Houses
Courthouse Square
HABS MD-498   p   L

West Patrick Street (House); see Derange
   Street (Rusticated Wooden House)

324-344 West Patrick Street (Houses)
HABS MD-486   p   L

Frederick vic.

Jug Bridge
Frederick Rd. spanning Monocacy River
HABS MD-488   p   L

Jug Bridge, Old Toll House
State Rt. 144
HABS MD-491   p   L

Rose Garden; see Rose Hill Manor

Rose Hill Manor (Rose Garden; Tasker's
   Chance)
1611 N. Market St.
HABS MD-493   p   L

Springfield
W. of U.S. Rt. 15
HABS MD-499   p   L

Tasker's Chance; see Rose Hill Manor

Keymar vic.

Keymar Bridge
Spanning Little Pipe Creek
HABS MD-20   s pd   L

Lander's Landing

Chesapeake & Ohio Canal, Lock 29
Catoctin Station vic.
HABS MD-752   p   H

**Chesapeake & Ohio Canal, Lockhouse at
   Lock 29**
Catoctin Station vic.
HABS MD-751   p   H

Liberty Town

Academy, Old
Liberty Rd. (State Rt. 26)
HABS MD-502   p   L

Coale, Richard, House; see Main Street
(Brick House)

Jones, Abraham, House; see
Jones-Sappington House

Jones-Sappington House (Jones, Abraham,
House; Sappington, Augustus, House)
Liberty Rd. (State Rt. 26)
HABS MD-501   L

Main Street (Brick House) (Sappington
House; Coale, Richard, House)
Liberty & Green Valley Rds. (State Rts. 26
& 75)
HABS MD-500   p   L

Sappington, Augustus, House; see
Jones-Sappington House

Sappington Farmhouse
Liberty Rd. (State Rt. 26)
HABS MD-503   p   L

Sappington House; see Main Street (Brick
House)

Wagner, Mary, House
Liberty Rd. (State Rt. 26)
HABS MD-504   p   L

Middletown

Stemble, Frederick, House
113-115 W. Main St.
HABS MD-331   s   L H

Point Of Rocks vic.

**Chesapeake & Ohio Canal, Catoctin Creek
Aqueduct** (Chesapeake & Ohio Canal,
Crooked Aqueduct)
Lock 29 vic.
HABS MD-753   p   H

**Chesapeake & Ohio Canal, Crooked
Aqueduct;** see Chesapeake & Ohio
Canal, Catoctin Creek Aqueduct

Chesapeake & Ohio Canal, Lock 28
U.S. Rt. 15
HABS MD-749   p   H

**Chesapeake & Ohio Canal, Lockhouse at
Lock 28**
U.S. Rt. 15 vic.
HABS MD-750   p   H

Union Bridge vic.

Hopewell
Pearre Rd.
HABS MD-328   p   L

Urbana

Amelung, John Frederick, House
Park Mills Rd.
HABS MD-32   pd L

GARRETT COUNTY

Granstville Vic

Casselman River Bridge
National Rd. at Little Crossings
HABS MD-139   p   L

HARFORD COUNTY

Bel Air

Harford National Bank
HABS MD-320   s   H

Liriodendron
502 W. Gordon St.
HABS MD-327   s p   L

Liriodendron, Barn
502 W. Gordon St.
HABS MD-327-A   s p   L

Masonic Lodge
Wall St.
HABS MD-319   s   H

Bel Air vic.

Booth House (Tudor Hill; Booth, Junius
Brutus, House; Tudor Hall)
Tudor Lane, RFD No. 1
HABS MD-510   p   L

Booth, Junius Brutus, House; see Booth
House

Dallam House (Dallams, The; Webster
House)
Wheel Rd.
HABS MD-507   p   L

Dallams, The; see Dallam House

Norris, Edward, House; see Olney

Olney (Shriver, J. Alexis, House; Norris,
Edward, House)
Hollingsworth Rd.
HABS MD-509   p   L

Shriver, J. Alexis, House; see Olney

Tudor Hall; see Booth House

Tudor Hill; see Booth House

Webster House; see Dallam House

Belcamp

Hall's Plains; see Sophia's Dairy

Simmon's Neglect; see Sophia's Dairy

Sophia's Dairy (Hall's Plains; Simmon's
Neglect)
Pulaski Hwy. vic.
HABS MD-8   s pd   L

Berkley vic.

Philip's Purchase; see Rigbie House

Rigbie, Col. James, House; see Rigbie
House

Rigbie House (Philip's Purchase; Rigbie,
Col. James, House)
Caselton Rd. (State Rt. 623)
HABS MD-24   pd L

Churchville vic.

Archer, Dr. John, House; see Medical Hall

Medical Hall (Archer, Dr. John, House)
Medical Hall Rd.
HABS MD-33   pd L

Snake Fence, Old, & Log House
HABS MD-511   p   L

Thomas Run House
Kalmia & Thomas Run Rds.
HABS MD-508   p   L

Creswell vic.

Mount Adams; see Mount, The

Mount, The (Mount Adams; Webster's
Mount; Webster, Capt., House; Webster,
D. L., House)
Fountain Green Rd. (State Rt. 543)
HABS MD-512   p   L

Webster, Capt., House; see Mount, The

Webster, D. L., House; see Mount, The

Webster's Mount; see Mount, The

Darlington

Kirk House
W. side Darlington Rd. (State Rt. 161)
HABS MD-513   p   L

Darlington vic.

Holloway House
Stafford Rd. (State Rt. 161)
HABS MD-515   p   L

Prospect Academy; see Schoolhouse, Stone
Hexagonal

Schoolhouse, Stone Hexagonal (Prospect
Academy)
3736 Green Spring Rd.
HABS MD-514   p   L

Fallston

Little Falls Friends' Meetinghouse; see
Quaker Meetinghouse

Quaker Meetinghouse (Little Falls Friends'
Meetinghouse)
E. side Mountain Rd.
HABS MD-516   p   L

Fallston vic.

Bon Air (Delaporte, Capt. Francis, House)
Laurel Brook Rd.
HABS MD-42   pd L

Delaporte, Capt. Francis, House; see Bon
Air

Forest Hill

St. Ignatius Catholic Church
533 E. Jarrettsville Rd.
HABS MD-522   p   L

Glenville

Paul, J. Gilman D., House (Proctor,
Thomas, House)
Deths Rd.
HABS MD-517   p   L

Proctor, Thomas, House; see Paul, J.
Gilman D., House

Havre De Grace

Angel Hill
Sego St.
HABS MD-520   p   L

**Congress & Saint John's Streets (Old
Ordinary)** (Ordinary on Waterfront)
HABS MD-519   p   L

Ordinary on Waterfront; see Congress &
Saint John's Streets (Old Ordinary)

Saint John's Street (Connected Frame Houses) (Swan's Inn)
Waterfront vic.
HABS MD-518   p   L
Swan's Inn; see Saint John's Street (Connected Frame Houses)

Havre De Grace vic.
Sion Hill School
2026 Level Rd.
HABS MD-521   p   L

Jerusalem
Grist Mill; see Jerusalem Grist Mill
Jerusalem Grist Mill (Grist Mill; Little Gunpowder)
Jerusalem Rd. vic., Little Gunpowder River
HABS MD-523   p   L
Little Gunpowder; see Jerusalem Grist Mill

Jerusalem vic.
Covered Bridge (Jericho Bridge)
Jericho Rd. spanning Little Gunpowder Falls
HABS MD-12   s pd   L
Jericho Bridge; see Covered Bridge

Joppatowne
Old Joppa; see Rumsey, Benjamin, House
Rumsey, Benjamin, House (Old Joppa)
Bridge Dr.
HABS MD-9   s pd   L

Lapidum
Carter, John, House; see Rock Run Mill, Outbuildings
Carter-Archec House; see Rock Run Mill, Outbuildings
Rock Run Grist Mill; see Rock Run Water Mill
Rock Run Mill, Outbuildings (Rock Run Miller's House; Carter-Archec House; Carter, John, House)
Susquehanna State Park, Rock Run Rd.
HABS MD-524   p   L
Rock Run Miller's House; see Rock Run Mill, Outbuildings
Rock Run Water Mill (Rock Run Grist Mill)
Susquehanna State Park, Stafford Rd.
HABS MD-525   p   L

Lapidum vic.
Land of Promise (Paul, Gilman, House)
Susquehanna State Park, 235 Quaker Bottom Rd.
HABS MD-526   p   L
Paul, Gilman, House; see Land of Promise

Level vic.
Royal Exchange; see 3850 West Chapel Road (Brick House Number 2)
3850 West Chapel Road (Brick House Number 2) (Royal Exchange)
HABS MD-528   p   L

3844 West Chapel Road (Brick House Number l)
HABS MD-527   p   L

Perryman
Spesutie Protestant Episcopal Church, Vestry
Perryman Rd. (State Rt. 159)
HABS MD-530   p   L

Stockton vic.
Mountain Road (Farmhouse)
HABS MD-531   p   L

Watervale
Gorsuch Mansion; see Joesting Farm
Joesting Farm (Gorsuch Mansion; Winters Run Golf Course)
Tollgate Rd.
HABS MD-532   p   L
Winters Run Golf Course; see Joesting Farm

Watervale vic.
Joshua's Meadows; see 300 North Tollgate Road (Old Brick Cottage)
300 North Tollgate Road (Old Brick Cottage) (Joshua's Meadows)
HABS MD-533   p   L

Wilna vic.
Prospect
Hollingsworth Rd. vic.
HABS MD-534   p   L

HOWARD COUNTY

Baltimore vic.
Folly Quarter
HABS MD-148   p   L

Ellicott City
Baltimore & Ohio Railroad, Ellicott's Mills (Ellicott City Station)
State Rt. 144 vic.
HAER MD-13   p   H
Berg Alnwick; see Patapsco Heights Girls' School
Columbia Pike (Stone Houses) (Tongue Row)
HABS MD-537   p   L
Columbia Pike (Stone Houses with Frame Additions)
HABS MD-538   p   L
3801 Columbia Pike(Connected Stone & Frame Houses)
HABS MD-539   p   L
Ellicott City Station; see Baltimore & Ohio Railroad, Ellicott's Mills
Ellicott, William, House; see Mount Ida
Hilltop Theatre; see Patapsco Heights Girls' School
House, Log
Merryman Rd.
HABS MD-321   s   L

Howard County Courthouse
Court Ave.
HABS MD-536   p   L
8133 Main Street (Shop Front)
HABS MD-544   p   L
8010-8046 Main Street (Stone House Facades) (Patapsco Hotel)
HABS MD-540   p   L
Maryland Women's War Relief Hospital; see Patapsco Heights Girls' School
Mill
Frederick Rd.
HABS MD-838   p   L
Mount Ida (Ellicott, William, House)
3691 Sarah's Lane
HABS MD-306   s p   L
Patapsco Female Institute; see Patapsco Heights Girls' School
Patapsco Heights Girls' School (Patapsco Female Institute; Hilltop Theatre; Maryland Women's War Relief Hospital; Berg Alnwick)
Church Rd.
HABS MD-543   p   L
Patapsco Hotel; see 8010-8046 Main Street (Stone House Facades)
Tongue Row; see Columbia Pike (Stone Houses)

Ellicott City vic.
Burleigh Manor
Centennial Lane
HABS MD-545   p   L
Doughoregan Manor
Manorhouse Rd.
HABS MD-230   p   L
Doughoregan Manor, Barn
Manorhouse Rd.
HABS MD-230-A   p   L

Ilchester vic.
Baltimore & Ohio Railroad, Ilchester Tunnel
E. side of Patapsco River
HAER MD-21   p   H

Relay
Baltimore & Ohio Railroad Bridge; see Thomas Viaduct
Latrobe's Folly; see Thomas Viaduct
Relay Viaduct; see Thomas Viaduct
Thomas Viaduct (Baltimore & Ohio Railroad Bridge; Latrobe's Folly; Relay Viaduct)
Spanning Patapsco River
HABS MD-535
HAER MD-3   p   L H

Savage
Baltimore & Ohio Railroad (Bollman's Iron Suspension & Trussed Bridge)
Savage Rd. vic.
HAER MD-1   s p   H
Bollman's Iron Suspension & Trussed Bridge; see Baltimore & Ohio Railroad

KENT COUNTY

Nicholson House; see 111 North Queen Street (House with Wood Porch)
111 North Queen Street (House with Wood Porch) (Nicholson House)
HABS MD-548   p   L

Chestertown

Abbey, The; see Pearce House
Catlin House; see Pearce House
101 Church Street (Brick House) (Geddes-Piper House)
Queen & Lawyer Sts. vic.
HABS MD-547   p   L
Custom House, Old
101-103 Water St.
HABS MD-549   p   L
Denton House; see Smyth-Letherbury House
Denton-Weeks House; see Smyth-Letherbury House
Geddes-Piper House; see 101 Church Street (Brick House)
Hubbard House; see Widehall
Pearce House (Abbey, The; Ringgold, Thomas, House; Catlin House)
106 Water St.
HABS MD-546   p   L
Ringgold, Thomas, House; see Pearce House
River House; see Smyth-Letherbury House
Smyth-Letherbury House (River House; Denton House; 107 Water Street (House); Denton-Weeks House)
HABS MD-231   s pd L
107 Water Street (House); see Smyth-Letherbury House
White Swan Tavern
233 High St.
HABS MD-239   s   L
Widehall (Hubbard House)
101 Water (Front) St.
HABS MD-550   p   L

Chestertown vic.

Airy Hill; see Wick's Place, Old
Godlington Manor
HABS MD-868   s p   H
Rose Hill
HABS MD-869   p   H
Wick's Place, Old (Airy Hill; Wick-Sterling House)
Airport Rd.
HABS MD-551   p   L
Wick-Sterling House; see Wick's Place, Old

Chesterville

Chesterville Store
HABS MD-866   s p   H
Gooding, Aaron L., Store; see Spencer, Isaac, House
Salter House; see Spencer, Isaac, House

Spencer, Isaac, House (Gooding, Aaron L., Store; Salter House)
Morgnec Rd. (Rt. 447) & Rt. 290
HABS MD-316   s p   L

Fairlee Creek

Carvill Hill
HABS MD-867   s p   H

Galena

Cottage, Frame
U.S. Rt. 213
HABS MD-552   p   L
Stephens House
U.S. Rt. 213
HABS MD-553   p   L

Georgetown

Knight, Kitty, House
U.S. Rt. 213
HABS MD-554   p   L
Valley Cottage; see Wallis House
Wallis House (Valley Cottage)
U.S. Rt. 213
HABS MD-555   p   L

Langford vic.

Farmhouse, Brick (Stephney Farm)
HABS MD-458   p   L
Stephney Farm; see Farmhouse, Brick

Locust Grove vic.

Farmhouse near Shrewsbury Church (Merritt Farmhouse)
U.S. Rt. 213
HABS MD-558   p   L
Merritt Farmhouse; see Farmhouse near Shrewsbury Church

Sandy Bottom

St. Paul's Episcopal Church
Sandy Bottom Rd.
HABS MD-556   p   L
St. Paul's Episcopal Church, Vestry House
Sandy Bottom Rd.
HABS MD-557   p   L

Still Pond

Harper, George, Store
MD. Rt. 292 & Main St.
HABS MD-324   s pd L

MONTGOMERY COUNTY

Chesapeake & Ohio Canal, Bridges, Aqueducts, etc.
HABS MD-57   s pd L
Chesapeake & Ohio Canal, Lockhouses
HABS MD-56   s pd L

Ashton

Brooke Manor; see Cherry Grove
Cherry Grove (Brooke Manor; Thomas, Richard, House)
17530 New Hampshire Ave. (State Rt. 650)
HABS MD-559   p   L

Clifton
17107 New Hampshire Ave.
HABS MD-54   s p   L
Thomas, Richard, House; see Cherry Grove

Beallsville

Charlene Manor (Griffith, Charles G., House)
State Rt. 28
HABS MD-560   p   L
Griffith, Charles G., House; see Charlene Manor
Inverness
State Rt. 28
HABS MD-561   p   L

Bethesda

Quarters, Old (Slave Quarters)
Wisconsin Ave. & State Rt. 193
HABS MD-84   L
Slave Quarters; see Quarters, Old

Brookeville

Brookeville Academy
Georgia Ave. (State Rt. 97)
HABS MD-563   p   L
Locust Grove (Thomas, John, House; Riggs, John Hammond, House)
3415 Brookeville Rd.
HABS MD-565   p   L
Riggs, John Hammond, House; see Locust Grove
Stone Lodge (Valley House)
318 Market St., Brookeville Center
HABS MD-566   p   L
Thomas, John, House; see Locust Grove
Valley House; see Stone Lodge

Brookeville vic.

Brewer House; see Greenwood
Davis, Ephraim, House; see Greenwood
Day House; see Greenwood
Greenwood (Hygham; Davis, Ephraim, House; Day House; Brewer House)
1721 Georgia Ave. (State Rt. 27)
HABS MD-564   L
Hygham; see Greenwood

Brookmont vic.

Chesapeake & Ohio Canal, Lockhouse at Lock 5 (Chesapeake & Ohio Canal, Lockhouse, Williard's Lock)
George Washington Pkwy. vic.
HABS MD-56-B   s   L
Chesapeake & Ohio Canal, Lockhouse at Lock 6
HABS MD-56-A   s d   L
Chesapeake & Ohio Canal, Lockhouse, Williard's Lock; see Chesapeake & Ohio Canal, Lockhouse at Lock 5

Burtonsville

Burton House
Birmingham Dr.
HABS MD-132   p   L

Cabin John vic.

Chesapeake & Ohio Canal, Lock 12
HABS MD-57-F   d   L
Chesapeake & Ohio Canal, Lockhouse at Lock 10
HABS MD-56-F   s   L
Chesapeake & Ohio Canal, Lockhouse at Lock 11
HABS MD-56-G   s   L
Chesapeake & Ohio Canal, Lockhouse at Lock 12
HABS MD-56-H   s   L
Chesapeake & Ohio Canal, Lockhouse at Lock 13
HABS MD-56-I   s   L
Chesapeake & Ohio Canal, Lockhouse at Lock 14
HABS MD-56-J   s   L
Chesapeake & Ohio Canal, Lockhouse at Lock 8
George Washington Pkwy. vic.
HABS MD-56-D   s   L
Chesapeake & Ohio Canal, Lockhouse at Lock 9
HABS MD-56-E   s   L
Chesapeake & Ohio Canal, Milestone, Lock 11 Vic.
HABS MD-57-G   s   L

Chevy Chase vic.

Hayes Manor (Williamson, Rev. Alexander, House)
4101 Manor Rd.
HABS MD-202   s p d   L
Williamson, Rev. Alexander, House; see Hayes Manor

Clarksburg

Dowden's Ordinary
State Rt. 355 & Stringtown Rd.
HABS MD-76   p   L

Colesville

Miller's House
E. Randolph Rd.
HABS MD-567   p   L
Valley Mill
E. Randolph Rd. (State Rt. 183)
HABS MD-568   p   L

Darnestown vic.

Kelley, John T., House; see Pleasant Hills
Pleasant Hills (Kelley, John T., House)
14800 Fisher Ave. (State Rt. 107)
HABS MD-141   p   L

Dawsonville

Aix La Chapelle (Brewer, Dr. William, House; Randles' Farm)
Darnestown Rd. (State Rt. 28)
HABS MD-569   p   L
Brewer, Dr. William, House; see Aix La Chapelle
Randles' Farm; see Aix La Chapelle

Dawsonville vic.

Darnall House
Whites Ferry Rd. (State Rt. 107)
HABS MD-570   p   L
Dawson, Robert Dayne, House
15200 Sugarland Rd.
HABS MD-55   s p   L

Dickerson

Gott, Richard Sr., House; see Mount Carmel
Locust Grove; see Mount Carmel
Mount Carmel (Gott, Richard Sr., House; Locust Grove)
State Rt. 28
HABS MD-571   p   L

Dickerson vic.

Chesapeake & Ohio Canal, Culvert 65
W. of Martinsburg Rd.
HAER MD-32   s p d   H
Rock Hall & Slave Quarters
HABS MD-572   p   L

Dickinson

Chesapeake & Ohio Canal, Campbell's Lock; see Chesapeake & Ohio Canal, Lock 27
Chesapeake & Ohio Canal, Lock 26 (Chesapeake & Ohio Canal, Wood's Lock)
Monocacy River Aqueduct vic.
HABS MD-744   p   H
Chesapeake & Ohio Canal, Lock 27 (Chesapeake & Ohio Canal, Campbell's Lock; Chesapeake & Ohio Canal, Spink's Ferry)
Monocacy River Aqueduct vic.
HABS MD-746   p   H
Chesapeake & Ohio Canal, Spink's Ferry; see Chesapeake & Ohio Canal, Lock 27
Chesapeake & Ohio Canal, Wood's Lock; see Chesapeake & Ohio Canal, Lock 26

Dickinson vic.

Chesapeake & Ohio Canal, Concrete Drainway (Chesapeake & Ohio Canal, Waste Weir, Lock 27)
Monocacy Aqueduct vic.
HABS MD-747   p   H
Chesapeake & OHio Canal, Lockhouse at Lock 26(Ruin) (Chesapeake & Ohio Canal, Lockhouse, Wood's Lock)
Monocacy River Aqueduct vic.
HABS MD-745   p   H
Chesapeake & Ohio Canal, Lockhouse at Lock 27
Monocacy River Aqueduct vic.
HABS MD-748   p   H
Chesapeake & Ohio Canal, Lockhouse, Wood's Lock; see Chesapeake & OHio Canal, Lockhouse at Lock 26(Ruin)
Chesapeake & Ohio Canal, Waste Weir, Lock 27; see Chesapeake & Ohio Canal, Concrete Drainway

Etchison

Etchison Cabin (Warfield Log Cabin; Etchison, Martha, House)
3111 Damascus Rd. (State Rt. 108)
HABS MD-573   p   L
Etchison, Martha, House; see Etchison Cabin
Warfield Log Cabin; see Etchison Cabin

Gaithersburg

Baltimore & Ohio Railroad, Waring Viaduct
Great Seneca Creek
HAER MD-22   p   H
Clopper's Mill, Miller's House; see Woodlands
Woodlands (Clopper's Mill, Miller's House)
State Rt. 117
HABS MD-575   p   L

Gaithersburg vic.

Magruder, Col. Zadok, House; see Mount Pleasant
Mount Pleasant (Magruder, Col. Zadok, House)
State Rt. 355 & Shady Grove Rd.
HABS MD-574   p   L

Glen Echo

Barton, Clara, House (Barton, Clara, National Historic Site)
5801 Oxford Rd.
HABS MD-300   s   H
Barton, Clara, National Historic Site; see Barton, Clara, House
Cabin John Aquaduct Bridge
MacArthur Blvd. spanning Cabin John Creek
HABS MD-180   p d   L

Glen Echo vic.

Chesapeake & Ohio Canal, Lockhouse & Lock 7 (Lockhouse & Shafer's Lock; Chesapeake & Ohio Canal, Shafer's Lock & Lockhouse)
George Washington Pkwy. vic.
HABS MD-56-C   s   L
Chesapeake & Ohio Canal, Shafer's Lock & Lockhouse; see Chesapeake & Ohio Canal, Lockhouse & Lock 7
Lockhouse & Shafer's Lock; see Chesapeake & Ohio Canal, Lockhouse & Lock 7

Great Falls

Chesapeake & Ohio Canal, Frame House Number 1
Lock 20 vic.
HABS MD-56-M   s   L
Chesapeake & Ohio Canal, Frame House Number 2
Lock 20 vic.
HABS MD-56-N   s   L

Chesapeake & Ohio Canal, Great Falls Tavern (Cromelin House)
Lock 20, MacArthur Blvd. vic.
HABS MD-56-R   s p   L

Chesapeake & Ohio Canal, Lock 20 (Chesapeake & Ohio Canal, Tavern Lock)
MacArthur Blvd.
HABS MD-57-E   s p   L

Chesapeake & Ohio Canal, Lockhouse (Ruins) , Lock 20
HABS MD-56-S   p   L

Chesapeake & Ohio Canal, Lockhouses & Tavern
HABS MD-56-L   s p   L

Chesapeake & Ohio Canal, Log House
Lock 20 vic.
HABS MD-56-0   s   L

Chesapeake & Ohio Canal, Repair Shop at Lock 20
HABS MD-57-D   s   L

Chesapeake & Ohio Canal, Tavern Lock; see Chesapeake & Ohio Canal, Lock 20

Cromelin House; see Chesapeake & Ohio Canal, Great Falls Tavern

Great Falls vic.

Chesapeake & Ohio Canal, Lockhouse at Lock 16
HABS MD-56-K   s   L

Chesapeake & Ohio Canal, Lockhouse at Lock 21 (Chesapeake & Ohio Canal, Swain's House, Lock 21; Chesapeake & Ohio Canal, Lockhouse at Oak Springs; Swain's Lockhouse at Lock 21)
Swain's Lock Rd., State Rt. 190 vic.
HABS MD-56-P   s   L

Chesapeake & Ohio Canal, Lockhouse at Oak Springs; see Chesapeake & Ohio Canal, Lockhouse at Lock 21

Chesapeake & Ohio Canal, Swain's House, Lock 21; see Chesapeake & Ohio Canal, Lockhouse at Lock 21

Swain's Lockhouse at Lock 21; see Chesapeake & Ohio Canal, Lockhouse at Lock 21

Laytonsville

Layton, John S., House
Sundown Rd. (State Rt. 420) & State Rt. 108
HABS MD-576   p   L

Laytonsville vic.

Four Chimney House; see Retirement

Ober, Robert, House; see Retirement

Retirement (Four Chimney House; Ober, Robert, House; Rolling Ridge)
7215 Sundown Rd. (State Rt. 420)
HABS MD-577   p   L

Rolling Ridge; see Retirement

Martinsburg vic.

Chesapeake & Ohio Canal, Broad Run Aqueduct; see Chesapeake & Ohio Canal, Culvert Number 44 1/2

Chesapeake & Ohio Canal, Broad Run Trunk; see Chesapeake & Ohio Canal, Culvert Number 44 1/2

Chesapeake & Ohio Canal, Culvert Number 44 1/2 (Chesapeake & Ohio Canal, Broad Run Aqueduct; Chesapeake & Ohio Canal, Broad Run Trunk)
Lock 25 vic.
HABS MD-741   s p   H

Chesapeake & Ohio Canal, Warehouse (Ruins) (Chesapeake & Ohio Canal, Warehouse, White's Ferry)
White's Ferry Rd. vic.
HABS MD-742   pd   H

Chesapeake & Ohio Canal, Warehouse, White's Ferry; see Chesapeake & Ohio Canal, Warehouse (Ruins)

Norbeck vic.

Elgar's Mill; see Muncaster Mill & Saw Mill

Milton's Mill; see Muncaster Mill & Saw Mill

Muncaster Mill & Saw Mill (Elgar's Mill; Milton's Mill)
State Rt. 115
HABS MD-94   p   L

Norwood

Thomas, Richard, House; see Woodlawn Manor

Woodlawn Manor (Thomas, Richard, House)
16501 Norwood Dr.
HABS MD-578   p   L

Olney

Barnsley, James F., House; see House, Small (Chimney)

Brooke, Col. Richard, House; see Fairhill

Fairhill (Brooke, Col. Richard, House)
3201 Sandy Spring Rd. (State Rt. 108)
HABS MD-581   p   L

House, Small (Chimney) (Barnsley, James F., House)
State Rt. 97
HABS MD-582   p   L

Olney House
HABS MD-583   p   L

Olney vic.

Belmont (Waters, Thomas, Place; Waters, William, House; Dorsey, Caleb, House)
Georgia Ave. (State Rt. 97) vic.
HABS MD-579   p   L

Birdsall, William, House; see Rockland

Brooke, Basil, House; see Falling Green

Dorsey, Caleb, House; see Belmont

Falling Green (Brooke, Basil, House)
4501 Laytonsville Rd. (State Rt. 108)
HABS MD-580   p   L

Rockland (Birdsall, William, House)
2701 Laytonsville Rd. (State Rt. 108)
HABS MD-584   p   L

Waters, Thomas, Place; see Belmont

Waters, William, House; see Belmont

Poolesville

Chiswell's Delight; see Grayhaven Manor

Chiswell's Inheritance; see Grayhaven Manor

Chiswell's Manor; see Grayhaven Manor

East Oaks Manor; see Little Oak Manor

Grayhaven Manor (Chiswell's Manor; Chiswell's Delight; Chiswell's Inheritance; Sara's Delight)
State Rt. 109 vic.
HABS MD-136   p   L

House, Stone (Valhalla; Rosedale)
107 Fisher Ave.
HABS MD-585   p   L

Irvine Farm; see Milford, Dr., House

Kilmain
Whites Ferry Rd. vic.
HABS MD-586   p   L

Kohloss Row; see Main Street (Houses)

Little Oak Manor (East Oaks Manor; Young, Henry, House)
21524 Whites Ferry Rd. (State Rt. 107)
HABS MD-587   p   L

Main Street (Houses) (Kohloss Row; Merchants Hotel)
Fisher Ave. & Jerusalem Rd. (State Rt. 109)
HABS MD-127   L

Merchants Hotel; see Main Street (Houses)

Milford, Dr., House (Poole's Hazard; Irvine Farm)
17610 Cattail Rd.
HABS MD-588   p   L

Poole, Dr. Sprig, House
HABS MD-591   p   L

Poole, Richard, House
HABS MD-590   p   L

Poole's Hazard; see Milford, Dr., House

Pyles House
HABS MD-592   p   L

Rosedale; see House, Stone

Sara's Delight; see Grayhaven Manor

Stoney Castle
State Rt. 109 vic.
HABS MD-119   p   L

Umstead House
HABS MD-593   p   L

Valhalla; see House, Stone

Young, Henry, House; see Little Oak Manor

Poolesville vic.

Mount Pleasant
HABS MD-589   p   L

Potomac vic.

Chesapeake & Ohio Canal, Lockhouse at Lock 18
HAER MD-33   s d   H

Chesapeake & Ohio Canal, Stop Gate, Lock 16
HABS MD-57-I   p   L

Redlands
Flower Hill
HABS MD-594   p   L

Redlands vic.
Magruder Place; see Ridge, The
Ridge, The (Magruder Place)
HABS MD-595   p   L

Riverside
Chesapeake & Ohio Canal, House at Lock 24
Tidewater vic.
HABS MD-56-T   s   H
Chesapeake & Ohio Canal, Lockhouse at Lock 22 (Chesapeake & Ohio Canal, Lockhouse, Pennyfield Lock)
Pennyfield Lock Rd., State Rt. 190 vic.
HABS MD-56-Q   s p   L
Chesapeake & Ohio Canal, Lockhouse, Pennyfield Lock; see Chesapeake & Ohio Canal, Lockhouse at Lock 22

Rockville
Baltimore & Ohio Railroad, Station & Freight House
98 Baltimore Rd.
HABS MD-238   s p d   L
Beallmont (Dawson House)
103 W. Montgomery Ave.
HABS MD-596   p   L
Dawson House; see Beallmont

Sandy Spring
Auburn Barn
HABS MD-597   p   L
Avelon
HABS MD-598   p   L
Cloverly
HABS MD-599   p   L
Friends Meetinghouse
Meetinghouse Lane
HABS MD-600   p   L
Harewood
HABS MD-601   p   L
Llewellyn Fields
HABS MD-602   p   L
Norwood
HABS MD-603   p   L

Seneca vic.
Chesapeake & Ohio Canal, Aqueduct Number 1 (Chesapeake & Ohio Canal, Seneca Creek Aqueduct)
Riley's Lock Rd. vic., State Rt. 190
HABS MD-57-B   s p   L
Chesapeake & Ohio Canal, Edward's Ferry; see Chesapeake & Ohio Canal, Lock 25
Chesapeake & Ohio Canal, Lock 25 (Chesapeake & Ohio Canal, Edward's Ferry)
Edward's Ferry Rd.
HABS MD-739   p   H

Chesapeake & Ohio Canal, Lockhouse & Lock at 24 (Chesapeake & Ohio Canal, Lockhouse & Riley's Lock)
Riley's Lock Rd.
HABS MD-57-C   s p   L
Chesapeake & Ohio Canal, Lockhouse & Riley's Lock; see Chesapeake & Ohio Canal, Lockhouse & Lock at 24
Chesapeake & Ohio Canal, Lockhouse at Lock 25 (Chesapeake & Ohio Canal, Lockhouse, Edward's Ferry)
Edward's Ferry Rd.
HABS MD-738   p d   H
Chesapeake & Ohio Canal, Lockhouse, Edward's Ferry; see Chesapeake & Ohio Canal, Lockhouse at Lock 25
Chesapeake & Ohio Canal, Seneca Creek Aqueduct; see Chesapeake & Ohio Canal, Aqueduct Number 1
Chesapeake & Ohio Canal, Swing Bridge, Lock 25
Edward's Ferry Rd. vic.
HABS MD-57-A   s   L
Kiplinger, Austin, House; see Montevideo
Montevideo (Peter, John Parke Custis, House; Kiplinger, Austin, House)
Montevideo Rd.
HABS MD-125   p   L
Peter, John Parke Custis, House; see Montevideo
River View
HABS MD-604   p   L
Stone Cutting Building
Tschiffeley Mill Rd.
HABS MD-299   s   L

Somerset vic.
Loughborough House; see Milton
Milton (Loughborough House)
River Rd.
HABS MD-10-1   s p d   L

Unity
Gaither-Brown House (Griffith, Henry II, House)
3801 Howard Chapel Rd.
HABS MD-113   p   L
Griffith, Henry II, House; see Gaither-Brown House

Unity vic.
Gaither, Samuel, Barn
3101 Mount Carmel Cemetery Rd.
HABS MD-108   p   L
Gaither, Samuel, House (Rolling Acres)
3101 Mount Carmel Cemetery Rd.
HABS MD-96   p   L
Rolling Acres; see Gaither, Samuel, House
Tridelphia Mill Group
Tridelphia Lake Rd.
HABS MD-114   p   L

PRINCE GEORGES COUNTY

Accokeek
Christ Church
Farmington Rd.
HABS MD-605   p   L

Aquasco
Cabin, Small
HABS MD-606   p   L
Grymes House
Aquasco Rd. (State Rt. 381)
HABS MD-607   p   L
House, Plank
HABS MD-608   p   L
Thomas House (Ruins)
HABS MD-880   p   L

Aquasco vic.
Poplar Hill
Croom (State Rt. 382) & Aquasco Rds.
HABS MD-609   p   L
Spring Hill
Aquasco Farm Rd.
HABS MD-610   p d   L

Ardmore vic.
Cottage, The
Ardwick-Ardmore & Lottsford Vista Rds.
HABS MD-632   p   L

Baden
Anchovie Hills (Cross Place; Magruder, Alexander, House)
Croom Rd. (State Rt. 382)
HABS MD-613   p d   L
Cross Place; see Anchovie Hills
Magruder, Alexander, House; see Anchovie Hills
St. Paul's Church
Baden-Westwood & Horsehead Rds.
HABS MD-110   p   L

Baden vic.
Connick's Folly
Aquasco Rd. (State Rt. 381)
HABS MD-614   p   L
Horsehead Tavern
Horsehead & Brandywine (State Rt. 381) Rds.
HABS MD-612   p   L

Bladensburg
Boatswick Hall (Lowndes, Christopher, House)
3901 Forty-eighth & Quincy Sts.
HABS MD-615   p   L
Cross House; see Parthenon Manor
Decatur Heights; see Parthenon Manor
Indian Queen Tavern, Old; see Washington, George, House
Inn, Old; see Washington, George, House
Lowndes, Christopher, House; see Boatswick Hall
Lowndes, Christopher, House; see Parthenon Manor

Magruder House
4703 Annapolis Rd. (State Rt. 450)
HABS MD-616   p   L

Parthenon Manor (Cross House; Decatur
    Heights; Lowndes, Christopher, House)
Edmonston Rd. (State Rt. 450 vic.)
HABS MD-313   s p   L H

Ross, Dr. David, House
Annapolis Rd. (moved to MD, Cockeysville)
HABS MD-120   s p   L

Washington, George, House (Indian Queen
    Tavern, Old; Inn, Old)
Baltimore Ave. & Upshur St.
HABS MD-617   p   L

Bowie

Belair (Bowie City Hall; Ogle, Samuel,
    House)
Tulip Grove Dr., Belair-at-Bowie
HABS MD-87   pd   L

Bowie City Hall; see Belair

Ogle, Samuel, House; see Belair

Bowie vic.

Duckett, Thomas, House; see Melford

Gladswood
Patuxent Wild Life Center, State Rt. 197
HABS MD-618   p   L

Melford (Duckett, Thomas, House;
    Slingluff House)
Crain Hwy. (U.S. Rt. 301)
HABS MD-627   p   L

Slingluff House; see Melford

Brown

Cleremont
HABS MD-669   p   L

Brown vic.

Dunblane (Magruder, John, House)
Westphalia Rd.
HABS MD-633   p   L

Magruder, John, House; see Dunblane

Buena Vista

Duvall, Benjamin, House; see Marietta

Marietta (Duvall, Benjamin, House)
5626 Bell Station Rd.
HABS MD-619   p   L

Buena Vista vic.

Duckett House; see Forest Hill

Forest Hill (Duckett House)
4310 Enterprise Rd. (State Rt. 556)
HABS MD-624   p   L

Cheltenham

Westwood
Westwood Dr.
HABS MD-621   p   L

Cheltenham vic.

Poplar Neck
U.S. Naval Research Station, Dangerfield
    Rd.
HABS MD-620   p   L

Clinton vic.

Griffin, Walter B., House; see Mudd, Dr.
    Sydney Emanuel, House

Mudd, Dr. Sydney Emanuel, House
    (Griffin, Walter B., House)
Grafton Lane & Colorado St.
HABS MD-622   p   L

Cockeysville

Ross, Dr. David, House
(moved to MD, Bladensburg, Annapolis
    Rd.)
HABS MD-120   s p   L

College Park

Inn, Old; see Rossburg House

Rossburg House (Inn, Old; University of
    Maryland, Faculty Club)
Baltimore Ave. (U.S. Rt. 1) vic.
HABS MD-623   p   L

University of Maryland, Faculty Club; see
    Rossburg House

Collington vic.

Bowie, Walter, House; see Willow Grove

Darnell's Grove; see Willow Grove

Duckett, Baruch, House; see Fairview

Fairview (Duckett, Baruch, House)
4410 Church Rd.
HABS MD-86   p   L

Holy Trinity Church
Annapolis Rd. (State Rt. 450)
HABS MD-625   p   L

Locust Grove; see Willow Grove

Trinity Parish House (Trinity Rectory)
Annapolis Rd. (State Rt. 450)
HABS MD-626   p   L

Trinity Rectory; see Trinity Parish House

Willow Grove (Bowie, Walter, House;
    Darnell's Grove; Locust Grove)
Annapolis Rd. (State Rt. 450)
HABS MD-628   p   L

Contee

Oaklands (Snowden, Richard, House)
Contee Rd.
HABS MD-109   p   L

Snowden, Richard, House; see Oaklands

Croom vic.

Bellefields (Sim, Col. Patrick, House; Sim's
    Delight)
3800 Duley Station Rd.
HABS MD-629   p   L

Claggett House; see Half Pone Farm

Half Pone Farm (Claggett House)
Patuxent River Park, Croom Airport Rd.
HABS MD-630   p   L

Sim, Col. Patrick, House; see Bellefields

Sim's Delight; see Bellefields

St. Thomas' Church
St. Thomas' Church & Croom Rds.
HABS MD-631   p   L

Fort Washington

Fort Washington National Park; see Fort
    Washington, Powder Magazine Number
    1

**Fort Washington, Powder Magazine
    Number 1** (Fort Washington National
    Park)
HABS MD-307   s   L

Fort Washington vic.

Hatton Mansion
HABS MD-111   p   L

Friendly vic.

Battersea; see Harmony Hall

Broad Creek Church (St. John's Church)
9801 Old Oxon Hill Rd.
HABS MD-49   pd   L

Harmony Hall (Battersea)
10500 Livingston Rd.
HABS MD-10-8   s pd   L H

Lyles House (Want Water)
Livingston Rd.
HABS MD-10-7   s pd   L H

St. John's Church; see Broad Creek Church

Want Water; see Lyles House

Landover vic.

Beall's Pleasure (Stoddert, Benjamin,
    House)
Landover Rd. vic.
HABS MD-635   p   L

Grovehurst
Brightseat Rd. & Hamlin St.
HABS MD-636   p   L

Stoddert, Benjamin, House; see Beall's
    Pleasure

Langley Park

Adelphi Mill (Riggs Mill; Adelphi Water
    Mill)
Adelphi Mill Recreation Center, State Rt.
    212
HABS MD-93   p   L

Adelphi Water Mill; see Adelphi Mill

Riggs Mill; see Adelphi Mill

Langley Park vic.

Adelphi Mill, Miller's House (Riggs Mill,
    Cottage)
Adelphi Mill Recreation Center, State Rt.
    212
HABS MD-93-A   p   L

Riggs Mill, Cottage; see Adelphi Mill,
    Miller's House

Largo vic.

Ellerslee; see Partnership

Friendship
Kolbies Corner, State Rts. 214 & 556
HABS MD-50   s p   L

Hall House; see Partnership

Largo
Big Chimney Branch Rd.
HABS MD-637   p   L

Magruder House; see Mount Lubentia
Mount Lubentia (Magruder House)
601 Largo Rd. & Kettering Dr.
HABS MD-638   p   L
Northampton
Northampton Way
HABS MD-639   p   L
Oakhill
Lochton Dr. & Prenton St.
HABS MD-640   p   L
Partnership (Hall House; Ellerslee)
Central Ave. (State Rt. 214)
HABS MD-641   p   L

Laurel vic.

Baltimore Road (House)
HABS MD-179   p   L
Montpelier (Snowden-Long House;
    Snowden, Thomas, House)
Montpelier Dr. & State Rt. 197
HABS MD-140   p   L
Rose Cottage; see Snowden Hill
Snow Hill (Snowden, Samuel, House)
Laurel-Bowie (State Rt. 197) & Contee Rds.
HABS MD-642   p   L
Snowden Hill (Rose Cottage)
Patuxent Wildlife Research Center
HABS MD-643   p   L
Snowden, Samuel, House; see Snow Hill
Snowden, Thomas, House; see Montpelier
Snowden-Long House; see Montpelier

Leeland

St. Barnabas Church
HABS MD-128   p   L

Leeland vic.

Bowie, Robert, House; see Bowieville
Bowieville (Bowie, Robert, House)
2300 Church Rd.
HABS MD-644   p   L

Mullikin

Elverton Hall
HABS MD-647   p   L
Essington Hall (Interiors)
Old Mount Oak Rd.
HABS MD-648   p   L

Nottingham

Bowie, John Jr., House; see Mattaponi
Cedars, The (House, Small; Smith, John,
    House)
HABS MD-51   s pd   L
Harmony Hall (Ruins)
Nottingham Rd.
HABS MD-650   p   L
House, Small; see Cedars, The
Mattaponi (Bowie, John Jr., House)
Mattaponi Rd.
HABS MD-651   p   L
Smith, John, House; see Cedars, The

Oxon Hill

Bain, Dr., House; see Salubria

Oxon Hill Manor
6701 Oxon Hill Rd.
HABS MD-301   pd   L
Salubria (Bain, Dr., House)
6900 Oxon Hill Rd. (State Rt. 414)
HABS MD-652   p   L

Oxon Hill vic.

Barnaby Manor
Wheeler & Wheeler Hills Rds.
HABS MD-314   s   L

Piscataway

Brent House (Hardy Tavern)
Piscataway Rd. (State Rt. 223)
HABS MD-653   p   L
Claggetts' Tavern; see Piscataway Tavern
Hardy Tavern; see Brent House
Piscataway Tavern (Claggetts' Tavern)
Piscataway Rd. (State Rt. 223) vic.
HABS MD-52   s p   L

Piscataway vic.

Belle Vue Farm; see Belview
Belview (Belle Vue Farm; Steed House)
3201 Steed Rd.
HABS MD-654   p   L
Hostetter House; see St. James
Marbury House; see Wyoming
St. James (Hostetter House; St. James Hill)
14200 Livingston Rd.
HABS MD-115   p   L
St. James Hill; see St. James
Steed House; see Belview
Wyoming (Marbury House)
330 Thrift St.
HABS MD-53   s p   L

Ritchie

Berry, Zechariah, House; see Concord
Concord (Berry, Zechariah, House)
8000 Walker Mill Rd.
HABS MD-656   p   L

Riverdale

Baltimore House (Riverdale; Calvert
    Mansion; de Stier, Baron, House)
4811 Riverdale Rd.
HABS MD-655   p   L
Calvert Mansion; see Baltimore House
de Stier, Baron, House; see Baltimore
    House
Riverdale; see Baltimore House

Rosaryville

Darnall, Henry II, House; see Poplar Hill
Dower House; see Mount Airy
His Lordship's Kindness; see Poplar Hill
Mount Airy (Dower House)
HABS MD-117   p   L
Poplar Hill (His Lordship's Kindness;
    Darnall, Henry II, House)
His Lordship's Kindness Rd.
HABS MD-315   s p   L

Seat Pleasant vic.

Berry, Zechariah, House; see Independence
Glenway (Hill, William H., House)
Rolling Ridge Dr.
HABS MD-657   p   L
Hill, William H., House; see Glenway
Independence (Berry, Zechariah, House)
Seventy-seventh St.
HABS MD-658   p   L

Thomas Brook vic.

Gwynn Park (Gwynn, William H., House)
296 Dyson Rd.
HABS MD-659   p   L
Gwynn, William H., House; see Gwynn
    Park

Townsend vic.

Pheasant's Thicket
HABS MD-879   p   H

Upper Marlboro

Billingsley (Weems House)
6900 Green Landing Rd.
HABS MD-660   p   L
Buck, Harry, House (Hill-Buck House)
N. of Main St.
HABS MD-661   p   L
Buck, Sarah, House
Main St. vic.
HABS MD-662   p   L
Carter, Bernard Moore, House; see
    Goodwood
Compton-Bassett Chapel
Marlboro Pike (State Rt. 408)
HABS MD-135   p   L
Compton-Bassett House (Hill, Clement V,
    House)
Old Marlboro Pike (State Rt. 408)
HABS MD-134   p   L
Content
14518 Church St.
HABS MD-663   p   L
Crawford, David, House; see Sasscer's
    House
Diggs, Ignatius, House; see Melwood Park
Goodwood (Carter, Bernard Moore, House)
HABS MD-664   p   L
Hill, Clement V, House; see
    Compton-Bassett House
Hill-Buck House; see Buck, Harry, House
Kingstead House; see Sasscer's House
Melwood Farms (Melwood House)
10200 Old Marlboro Pike (State Rt. 408)
HABS MD-670   p   L
Melwood House; see Melwood Farms
Melwood Park (Diggs, Ignatius, House)
Old Marlboro Pike (State Rt. 408)
HABS MD-142   p   L
Mount Pleasant
Mount Pleasant Rd.
HABS MD-665   pd   L

Sasscer's Green
1732 Crain Hwy. (U.S. Rt. 301)
HABS MD-666   p   L
Sasscer's House (Crawford, David, House;
  Kingstead House)
5415 Old Crain Hwy. (U.S. Rt. 301)
HABS MD-667   p   L
Upper Marlboro Tavern
Main St.
HABS MD-137   p   L
Weems House; see Billingsley
Wilson House
(moved to MD, Lower Marlboro)
HABS MD-126   p   L

Upper Marlboro vic.

Charleston; see Mount Calvert
Claggett, Thomas VI, House; see Weston
Mount Calvert (Charleston)
Mount Calvert Rd.
HABS MD-176   p   L
Overseer's House
5601 Old Crain Hwy.
HABS MD-645   p   L
Weston (Claggett, Thomas VI, House)
Old Crain Hwy. vic.
HABS MD-668   p   L
Woodstock
Crain Hwy. (U.S. Rt. 301)
HABS MD-646   p   L

Woodmore

Bermondsey (Hill, Charles, House)
Woodmore Rd.
HABS MD-671   p   L
Duckett, Isaac, House; see Pleasant
  Prospect
Hill, Charles, House; see Bermondsey
Mullikin, James, House; see Mullikin's
  Delight
Mullikin's Delight (Mullikin, James,
  House)
2307 Church Rd.
HABS MD-649   p   L
Pleasant Prospect (Duckett, Isaac, House)
13008 Woodmore Rd.
HABS MD-672   p   L

QUEEN ANNE COUNTY

Centreville vic.

Peace & Plenty (Wright House)
U.S. Rt. 213
HABS MD-673   p   L
Walnut Grove (Wright House)
Wright Neck Rd., Reed Creek vic.
HABS MD-228   s   L
Wright House; see Peace & Plenty
Wright House; see Walnut Grove

Church Hill vic.

Hollyday, James, House; see Readbourne
Readbourne (Hollyday, James, House)
Land's End Rd., Wilmer Neck
HABS MD-99   p   L

Kent Island

Fisherman's House
HABS MD-678   p   L

Romancoke

Kent Fort Manor
Kent Point Rd.
HABS MD-681   p   L

Ruthsburg vic.

Thomas House
State Rt. 304
HABS MD-25   pd   L

Stevensville

Kent Island (Brick House) (Steven's
  Adventure)
State Rt. 18 vic.
HABS MD-674   p   L
Steven's Adventure; see Kent Island (Brick
  House)

Stevensville vic.

Carvel House
Kent Point Rd. vic.
HABS MD-677   p   L
Friendship; see Stinton
House at Matapeake; see Stinton
Mattapex Farm; see Shippen Creek Road
  (Farm)
Shippen Creek Road (Farm) (Mattapex
  Farm)
HABS MD-680   p   L
Stinton (House at Matapeake; Friendship)
State Rt. 8
HABS MD-679   p   L

Wye Mills

Clover Fields (Forman House; Hemsley,
  William, House; Hopewell)
Forman's Lodge Rd.
HABS MD-178   p   L
Forman House; see Clover Fields
Hemsley, William, House; see Clover Fields
Hopewell; see Clover Fields

SOMERSET COUNTY

Crisfield

Make Peace (Roach-Gunby House)
Johnson Creek vic.
HABS MD-698   s pd   L
Roach-Gunby House; see Make Peace

Kingston vic.

Kingston Hall
Big Annemessex River vic., W. of Marion
Rd.
HABS MD-160   p   L
Waters House
State Rt. 413 vic.
HABS MD-161   p   L

Manokin

Almodington (Elzey, Col. Arnold, House)
Deal Island Rd.
HABS MD-699   L
Elzey, Col. Arnold, House; see
  Almodington

Manokin vic.

Sudler's Seclusion
HABS MD-865   s p   H

Millstone Landing

Catholic Church
Patuxent Naval Air Test Center
HABS MD-876   p   L

Princess Anne

Church Street (House)
HABS MD-151   p   L
Teackle, Littleton Dennis, House; see
  Teackle Mansion
Teackle Mansion (Teackle, Littleton
  Dennis, House)
Prince William & Mansion Sts.
HABS MD-164   p   L

ST. MARYS COUNTY

Bushwood

Ocean Hall
HABS MD-323   s p   H

Chaptico vic.

Bachelor's Hope (Hammersley, William,
  House; Manor Lodge)
Manor Rd.
HABS MD-59   d   L H
Hammersley, William, House; see
  Bachelor's Hope
Manor Lodge; see Bachelor's Hope

Charlotte Hall

Charlotte Hall Military Academy; see
  Charlotte Hall School
Charlotte Hall School (Charlotte Hall
  Military Academy)
State Rts. 5 & 236
HABS MD-682   p   L
Hatch-Dent House (White House)
State Rts. 236 & 5
HABS MD-683   p   L
House, Frame
HABS MD-684   p   L
White House; see Hatch-Dent House

Drayden vic.

Cherryfield; see Coad-Fenwick House
Coad-Fenwick House (Cherryfield; Porto
  Bello)
Cherryfield Point
HABS MD-685   p   L
McKay House; see West St. Mary's Manor
Porto Bello; see Coad-Fenwick House
West St. Mary's Manor (McKay House)
W. Saint Mary's Manor Rd.
HABS MD-97   pd   L

Great Mills

Allston, J. J., House; see Great Mills Road (House)

Great Mills Farmhouse; see Great Mills Road (House)

Great Mills Road (House) (Allston, J. J., House; Great Mills Farmhouse; Wolseley Manor)
Saint Mary's Creek vic.
HABS MD-158   p L

Wolseley Manor; see Great Mills Road (House)

Hollywood

Bowles, James, House; see Sotterly

Bowles Separation; see Sotterly

Industry
HABS MD-686   p L

Sotterly (Bowles Separation; Bowles, James, House)
State Rt. 245 & Vista Rd. vic.
HABS MD-181   s pd L

Sotterly, Slave Quarters
HABS MD-181-A   p H

Hollywood vic.

Cornwaleys, Thomas, House; see Resurrection Manor

Resurrection Manor (Scotch Neck; Cornwaleys, Thomas, House)
Old Hwy.
HABS MD-36   s p L

Scotch Neck; see Resurrection Manor

Laurel Grove vic.

Cremona
Sotterly vic.
HABS MD-694   p L

Dela Brooke House
Patuxent River vic.
HABS MD-695   p L

Leonardtown

Key House; see Tudor Hall

Tudor Hall (Key House)
Tudor Rd.
HABS MD-687   p L

Leonardtown vic.

Mulberry Fields
State Rt. 244
HABS MD-83   p L

Nevitt's St. Anne
HABS MD-873   s p H

St. Andrew's Episcopal Church
Saint Andrew's Church Rd.
HABS MD-45   pd L

Lexington Park

Halfhead Folly; see Long Lane Farm

Jarboe, Lt. Col. John, House; see Long Lane Farm

Long Lane Farm (Jarboe, Lt. Col. John, House; Halfhead Folly)
State Rt. 712 vic.
HABS MD-159   p L

Maddox vic.

Mill Point House
State Rt. 238 vic.
HABS MD-104   p L

Millstone Landing

Calvert House; see Mattapany

Mattapany (Calvert House)
Patuxent River vic.
HABS MD-688   p L

Susquehanna (Susquehanna Point)
HABS MD-689   p L

Susquehanna Point; see Susquehanna

Morganza

Little St. Thomas Barn
HABS MD-870   p H

New Market vic.

Barber, S. F., House
HABS MD-872   p H

Farmhouse
HABS MD-871   p H

Newton Neck

St. Francis Xavier Church
HABS MD-322   s H

Oakville vic.

Sandgates on Cat Creek
HABS MD-874   s p H

Ridge

Calvert, William, House; see Calvert's Rest

Calvert's Rest (Calvert, William, House; Scotland)
Curley Rd.
HABS MD-168   p L H

Scotland; see Calvert's Rest

Ridge vic.

Bard's Field
HABS MD-875   p H

St. Inigoes vic.

Jesuit Manor Farm, Old Tobacco Barn
HABS MD-167   p L

St. Ignatius Roman Catholic Church
Webster Field Rd.
HABS MD-166   p L

St. Mary's City

Trinity Protestant Episcopal Church
HABS MD-690   p L

St. Mary's City vic.

Clocker, Daniel, House; see Clocker's Fancy

Clocker's Fancy (Clocker, Daniel, House)
HABS MD-691   p L

Cornwallis Manor; see Cross Manor

Cross Manor (Cornwallis Manor)
HABS MD-692   p L

Farmhouse, Brick
HABS MD-877   p L

Valley Lee

St. George's Church
HABS MD-696   p L

Valley Lee vic.

House, Frame
HABS MD-697   p L

TALBOT COUNTY

Bethlehem

White Marsh Farm (White Marshes)
State Rt. 328
HABS MD-424   p L

White Marshes; see White Marsh Farm

Easton

House, Brick
Higgins or Locust St., S. of August St.
HABS MD-702   p L

North Washington Street (Brick Row Houses)
HABS MD-704   p L

Quaker Meetinghouse (Third Haven Meetinghouse, Old)
Washington St.
HABS MD-703   p L

107-109 South Washington Street (Brick Double Houses)
HABS MD-701   p L

18 South West Street (House)
HABS MD-302   s H

20 South West Street (House)
HABS MD-303   s H

Third Haven Meetinghouse, Old; see Quaker Meetinghouse

Washington Street (Brick Row Houses)
Opposite Courthouse
HABS MD-705   p L

Easton vic.

Bartlett-Dixon House; see Old Bloomfield

Dover Ferry Farm
Dover Rd. (State Rt. 331)
HABS MD-700   p L

Hollyday, Henry, House; see Ratcliffe Manor

Locust Grove
Villa Rd.
HABS MD-308   s pd L

Old Bloomfield (Bartlett-Dixon House)
Bloomfield Rd.
HABS MD-143   p L

Orchard Knob; see Troth's Fortune

Ratcliffe Manor (Hollyday, Henry, House)
Easton Pkwy. (State Rt. 322) vic.
HABS MD-89   p L

Troth, William, House; see Troth's Fortune

Troth's Fortune (Orchard Knob; Troth, William, House)
Dover Rd. (State Rt. 331)
HABS MD-98   p L

Matthews vic.

Beaver Neck Farm; see Cottage, Brick
Cottage, Brick (Beaver Neck Farm)
Easton-Denton Rd. (State Rt. 328)
HABS MD-710   p   L

Mc Daniel vic.

Indian Range Barn
State Rt. 33
HABS MD-310   s   L

Oxford vic.

Bingham House; see Jena
Gibson, Jacob, House; see Jena
Jena (Jenna; Bingham House; Gibson, Jacob, House)
Oxford Rd. (State Rt. 333)
HABS MD-163   p   L
Jenna; see Jena
Otwell
Otwell Rd.
HABS MD-706   p   L

Queen Anne

House, Gambrel Roof
HABS MD-887   p   L
Tavern, Old
HABS MD-708   p   L

St. Michaels vic.

Wye Town Farm, Corn Crib
Maritime Museum (moved from MD, Tunis Mills)
HABS MD-309   s p   L

Trappe

Dickinson House
Maple & S. Main Sts.
HABS MD-709   p   L

Tunis Mills

Wye House, Captain's House
Bruffs Island Rd.
HABS MD-88-D   p   L
Wye House, Corn Crib
Bruffs Island Rd.
HABS MD-88-E   p   L
Wye House, Mansion
Bruffs Island Rd.
HABS MD-88-C   p   L
Wye House, Orangery
Bruffs Island Rd.
HABS MD-88-A   s p   L
Wye House, Smokehouse
Bruffs Island Rd.
HABS MD-88-B   s p   L
Wye Town Farm, Corn Crib
Bruffs Island Rd. (moved to MD, St. Michaels vic.)
HABS MD-309   s p   L

Tunis Mills vic.

Fair View (Skinner House)
HABS MD-26   pd   L
Goldsborough, Robert, House; see Pleasant Valley

Hope House
Bruffs Island Rd. vic.
HABS MD-154   p   L
Lloyd, Edward IV, House; see Wye House
Pleasant Valley (Goldsborough, Robert, House)
Gross Coate Rd.
HABS MD-92   p   L
Skinner House; see Fair View
Wye House (Lloyd, Edward IV, House)
Bruffs Island Rd.
HABS MD-88   p   L

Wye Mills

Creamery, The; see Store Building, Old
House near Wye Oak; see House, Old & Wye Oak
House, Old & Wye Oak (House near Wye Oak)
Old Wye Mills-Easton Rd. (State Rt. 662)
HABS MD-712   p   L
St. Luke's Church (Wye Church, Old)
Old Wye Mills-Easton Rd. (State Rt. 662)
HABS MD-711   p   L
Store Building, Old (Creamery, The)
State Rts. 662 & 404
HABS MD-713   p   L
Wye Church, Old; see St. Luke's Church

WASHINGTON COUNTY

Antietam

Baltimore & Ohio Railroad, Long Bridge
HAER MD-37   p   H

Antietam vic.

Chesapeake & Ohio Canal, Antietam Creek Aqueduct (Chesapeake & Ohio Canal, Aqueduct 4)
Canal Rd.
HABS MD-205   s p   H
Chesapeake & Ohio Canal, Aqueduct 4; see Chesapeake & Ohio Canal, Antietam Creek Aqueduct
Chesapeake & Ohio Canal, Culvert 100; see Chesapeake & Ohio Canal, Culvert above Lock 37
Chesapeake & Ohio Canal, Culvert above Lock 37 (Chesapeake & Ohio Canal, Culvert 100)
HABS MD-206   s   H
Chesapeake & Ohio Canal, Lock 37 (Chesapeake & Ohio Canal, Mountain Lock)
Mountain Lock Rd.
HABS MD-207   s p   H
Chesapeake & Ohio Canal, Mountain Lock; see Chesapeake & Ohio Canal, Lock 37
Chesapeake & Ohio Canal, Waste Weir
Lift Lock 37 vic.
HABS MD-209   s   H
Poffenberger House & Barn
HABS MD-90   p   L

Roulette Farm Group
HABS MD-85   p   L

Antietam-Dargan vic.

Chesapeake & Ohio Canal, Lockhouse at Lock 37
Mountain Lock Rd.
HABS MD-208   s pd   H

Big Pool vic.

Fort Frederick
HABS MD-95   p   L

Clear Spring vic.

Chesapeake & Ohio Canal, Mule Barn
Lock 50 vic.
HAER MD-28   s   H

Fort Frederick vic.

Chesapeake & Ohio Canal, Culvert 39; see Chesapeake & Ohio Canal, Culvert above Lift Lock 48
Chesapeake & Ohio Canal, Culvert above Lift Lock 48 (Chesapeake & Ohio Canal, Culvert 39; Chesapeake & Ohio Canal, Neck Road Culvert; Chesapeake & Ohio Canal, Prather's Neck)
Four Locks Rd.
HABS MD-218   s   H
Chesapeake & Ohio Canal, Dam 5
Dam 5 Rd., above Lock 44
HABS MD-789   p   H
Chesapeake & Ohio Canal, Feeder Lock at Dam 5 (Chesapeake & Ohio Canal, Guard Lock at Dam 5; Chesapeake & Ohio Canal, Inlet Lock at Dam 5)
Dam 5 Rd., State Rt. 56 vic.
HABS MD-788   p   H
Chesapeake & Ohio Canal, First of the Four Locks; see Chesapeake & Ohio Canal, Lock 47
Chesapeake & Ohio Canal, Fourth of the Four Locks; see Chesapeake & Ohio Canal, Lock 50
Chesapeake & Ohio Canal, Guard Lock at Dam 5; see Chesapeake & Ohio Canal, Feeder Lock at Dam 5
Chesapeake & Ohio Canal, House at Lock 50
HABS MD-216   s p   H
Chesapeake & Ohio Canal, Inlet Lock at Dam 5; see Chesapeake & Ohio Canal, Feeder Lock at Dam 5
Chesapeake & Ohio Canal, Lock 46
Dam 5 vic.
HABS MD-793   s p   H
Chesapeake & Ohio Canal, Lock 47 (Chesapeake & Ohio Canal, First of the Four Locks)
HABS MD-211   s   H
Chesapeake & Ohio Canal, Lock 49 (Chesapeake & Ohio Canal, Third of the Four Locks)
HABS MD-213   s   H

Chesapeake & Ohio Canal, Lock 50
(Chesapeake & Ohio Canal, Fourth of
the Four Locks)
HABS MD-214   s   H

**Chesapeake & Ohio Canal, Lockhouse at
Dam 5**
Dam 5 Rd., State Rt. 56 vic.
HABS MD-790   pd   H

**Chesapeake & Ohio Canal, Lockhouse at
Lock 46**
Dam 5 vic.
HABS MD-792   pd   H

**Chesapeake & Ohio Canal, Lockhouse at
Lock 48**
Four Locks Rd.
HABS MD-215   s p   H

**Chesapeake & Ohio Canal, Neck Road
Culvert;** see Chesapeake & Ohio Canal,
Culvert above Lift Lock 48

Chesapeake & Ohio Canal, Prather's Neck;
see Chesapeake & Ohio Canal, Culvert
above Lift Lock 48

**Chesapeake & Ohio Canal, Roving Bridge
over Lock 46**
Dam 5 vic.
HABS MD-217   s   .   H

**Chesapeake & Ohio Canal, Third of the
Four Locks;** see Chesapeake & Ohio
Canal, Lock 49

Chesapeake & Ohio Canal, Tow Path
Locks 44 & 45 vic.
HABS MD-882   p   H

Chesapeake & Ohio Canal, Waste Weir 18;
see Chesapeake & Ohio Canal, Waste
Weir above Lock 50

**Chesapeake & Ohio Canal, Waste Weir
above Lock 50** (Chesapeake & Ohio
Canal, Waste Weir 18)
HABS MD-219   s   H

Chespeake & Ohio Canal, Lock 48
Four Locks Rd.
HABS MD-212   s   H

Hagerstown

Hager, Jonathan, House (Foundation)
HABS MD-39   s pd   L

Hagerstown Bank
HABS MD-44   pd   L

Hagerstown vic.

Bridge Spanning Conocheague River
Old National Trail
HABS MD-139-A   p   L

Hancock vic.

Chesapeake & Ohio Canal, Culvert 199
First Culvert above Lock 55
HABS MD-800   p   H

Chesapeake & Ohio Canal, Culvert 200
Second Culvert above Lock 55
HABS MD-801   p   H

**Chesapeake & Ohio Canal, Feeder Lock,
Lock 55**
Dam 6 vic.
HABS MD-881   p   H

Chesapeake & Ohio Canal, Lock 54
Deneen Rd.
HABS MD-796   p   H

Chesapeake & Ohio Canal, Lock 55
HABS MD-799   p   H

Chesapeake & Ohio Canal, Lock 56
(Chesapeake & Ohio Canal, Pearre
Lock)
Ziegler Rd.
HABS MD-802   p   H

**Chesapeake & Ohio Canal, Lockhouse at
Lock 54**
Deneen Rd.
HABS MD-797   pd   H

**Chesapeake & Ohio Canal, Lockhouse at
Lock 56** (Chesapeake & Ohio Canal,
Lockhouse at Pearre Lock)
Ziegler Rd.
HABS MD-803   pd   H

**Chesapeake & Ohio Canal, Lockhouse at
Pearre Lock;** see Chesapeake & Ohio
Canal, Lockhouse at Lock 56

Chesapeake & Ohio Canal, Pearre Lock;
see Chesapeake & Ohio Canal, Lock 56

Harpers Ferry

Chesapeake & Ohio Canal, Lock 32
HABS MD-759
HAER MD-27-A   s p   H

Chesapeake & Ohio Canal, Lock 33
Sandy Hook Rd. vic.
HABS MD-762
HAER MD-27-B   s p   H

**Chesapeake & Ohio Canal, Outlet above
Lock 32;** see Chesapeake & Ohio Canal,
Shenandoah River Lock

**Chesapeake & Ohio Canal, Shenandoah
River Lock** (Chesapeake & Ohio Canal,
Outlet above Lock 32)
HABS MD-760   p   H

Harpers Ferry vic.

**Chesapeake & Ohio Canal, Goodheart's
Lock;** see Chesapeake & Ohio Canal,
Lock 34

Chesapeake & Ohio Canal, Lock 34
(Chesapeake & Ohio Canal, Goodheart's
Lock)
Harpers Ferry Rd.
HABS MD-766   p   H

Chesapeake & Ohio Canal, Lock 35
HABS MD-773   s pd   H

Chesapeake & Ohio Canal, Lock 36
HABS MD-775   s pd   H

**Chesapeake & Ohio Canal, Lockhouse at
Feeder Lock**
Dam 3
HABS MD-768   s pd   H

Knoxville

**Chesapeake & Ohio Canal, Harpers Ferry
Complex**
Potomac River, Harpers Ferry vic.
HAER MD-27   s   H

**Chesapeake & Ohio Canal, Salty Dog
Tavern**
Lock 33 vic.
HAER MD-27-C   s   H

Knoxville vic.

**Baltimore & Ohio RR, Harpers Ferry
Bridge Piers**
Potomac River, Maryland Heights &
Harpers Ferry
HAER MD-16   pd   H

**Baltimore & Ohio RR, Harpers Ferry
Tunnel**
Potomac River vic.
HAER MD-17   p   H

Point Of Rocks

**Baltimore & Ohio Railroad, Point of Rocks
Station**
State Rt. 28 vic.
HABS MD-506
HAER MD-14   s p   H

Samples Manor

Brown, John, Farm; see Kennedy Farm

Kennedy Farm (Brown, John, Farm)
NE of Samples Manor (Dargan)
HABS MD-227   s pd   H

Sandy Hook vic.

**Chesapeake & Ohio Canal, Sea Wall, Lock
32**
Spanning Potomac River to Harper Ferry,
WV
HABS MD-886   p   H

Sharpsburg

Pry, Philip, House
State Rt. 34
HABS MD-864   s   H

Sharpsburg vic.

**Chesapeake & Ohio Canal, Co. Frame
Section House;** see Chesapeake & Ohio
Canal, Section House, Lock 39

Chesapeake & Ohio Canal, Culvert 100; see
Chesapeake & Ohio Canal, Culvert
above Lock 39

**Chesapeake & Ohio Canal, Culvert above
Lock 39** (Chesapeake & Ohio Canal,
Culvert 100)
Canal Rd., State Rt. 34 vic.
HABS MD-221   s   H

**Chesapeake & Ohio Canal, Feeder Lock
above Dam 4** (Chesapeake & Ohio
Canal, Guard Lock above Dam 4;
Chesapeake & Ohio Canal, Inlet Lock
above Dam 4)
HABS MD-222   s   H

**Chesapeake & Ohio Canal, Guard Lock
above Dam 4;** see Chesapeake & Ohio
Canal, Feeder Lock above Dam 4

**Chesapeake & Ohio Canal, Inlet Lock
above Dam 4;** see Chesapeake & Ohio
Canal, Feeder Lock above Dam 4

Chesapeake & Ohio Canal, Section House, Lock 39 (Chesapeake & Ohio Canal, Co. Frame Section House)
HABS MD-220   s   H

Chesapeake & Ohio Canal, Stop Gate at Dam 4
Downsville vic., Dam 4 Rd.
HABS MD-223   s   H

Chesapeake & Ohio Canal, Stop Gate at Dam 4; see Chesapeake & Ohio Canal, Stop Lock at Dam 4

Chesapeake & Ohio Canal, Stop Lock at Dam 4 (Chesapeake & Ohio Canal, Stop Gate at Dam 4; Chesapeake & Ohio Canal, Winch House at Dam 4)
Dam 4 Rd.
HABS MD-57-H   s   L

Chesapeake & Ohio Canal, Winch House at Dam 4; see Chesapeake & Ohio Canal, Stop Lock at Dam 4

Dunkard (Church of the Brethren) Church
Hagerstown & Smoketown Rds.
HABS MD-203   s p   L

Weverton vic.

Chesapeake & Ohio Canal, Dry Dock
HABS MD-885   s p d   H

Chesapeake & Ohio Canal, Feeder Lock, above Lock 35
Dam 3 vic., Harpers Ferry Vic.
HABS MD-883   s p d   H

Chesapeake & Ohio Canal, Israel Creek Aqueduct (Chesapeake & Ohio Canal, Israel Creek Culvert)
Lock 31 vic.
HABS MD-758   p   H

Chesapeake & Ohio Canal, Israel Creek Culvert; see Chesapeake & Ohio Canal, Israel Creek Aqueduct

Chesapeake & Ohio Canal, Lock 31
U.S. Rt. 340 vic.
HABS MD-755   p   H

Chesapeake & Ohio Canal, Lockhouse at Lock 31
U.S. Rt. 340 vic.
HABS MD-756   p   H

Chesapeake & Ohio Canal, Lockhouse, at Lock 36
Dam 3 vic.
HABS MD-884   s p d   H

Chesapeake & Ohio Canal, Waste Weir, Lock 31
U.S. Rt. 340 vic.
HABS MD-757   p   H

Williamsport

Chesapeake & Ohio Canal, Aqueduct 5; see Chesapeake & Ohio Canal, Conocheague Creek Aqueduct

Chesapeake & Ohio Canal, Conocheague Creek Aqueduct (Chesapeake & Ohio Canal, Aqueduct 5)
HABS MD-224   s p   H

Chesapeake & Ohio Canal, Lock 44 (Chesapeake & Ohio Canal, Williamsport Lock)
Canal St.
HABS MD-785   p   H

Chesapeake & Ohio Canal, Lockhouse at Lock 44 (Chesapeake & Ohio Canal, Lockhouse, Wmsport. Lock)
Canal St.
HABS MD-786   p d   H

Chesapeake & Ohio Canal, Lockhouse, Wmsport. Lock; see Chesapeake & Ohio Canal, Lockhouse at Lock 44

Chesapeake & Ohio Canal, Williamsport Lock; see Chesapeake & Ohio Canal, Lock 44

Potomac & Edison Company:C. & O. Canal Bridge
HAER MD-23   p   H

Salisbury Street, Pony Pratt Truss Bridge
Spanning Chesapeake & Ohio Canal
HAER MD-24   s p   H

Williamsport vic.

Chesapeake & Ohio Canal, Charles Mill (Chesapeake & Ohio Canal, Middlekauff's Mill)
Locks 44 & 45 vic.
HABS MD-210   s p d   H

Chesapeake & Ohio Canal, Middlekauff's Mill; see Chesapeake & Ohio Canal, Charles Mill

WICOMICO COUNTY

Allen vic.

Bounds Lott, House
HABS MD-862   s p   H

Hebron vic.

Chapel of Ease of Stephen Parish; see Spring Hill Church

Spring Hill Church (St. Paul's Episcopal Church; Chapel of Ease of Stephen Parish)
U.S. Rt. 50
HABS MD-715   p   L

St. Paul's Episcopal Church; see Spring Hill Church

Salisbury

Poplar Hill Mansion
117 Elizabeth St.
HABS MD-716   p   L

WORCESTER COUNTY

Beaverdam vic.

Schoolfield Farm, House
Hillman Rd.
HABS MD-225   s p d   L

Berlin

Burleigh Cottage; see Burley Cottage
Burley Cottage (Burleigh Cottage)
Main St.
HABS MD-149   p   L

Berlin vic.

Carey, Edward Lee, House; see Fassit House
Fassett, William, House; see Henry's Grove
Fassit House (Carey, Edward Lee, House)
Lewis Store Rd. (State Rt. 376)
HABS MD-170   p   L

Genesar House (Genezir House)
Stephen Decatur Memorial Rd. (State Rt. 611)
HABS MD-330   s p d   L H

Genezir House; see Genesar House
Henry, Julie, House; see Henry's Grove
Henry's Grove (Henry, Julie, House; Fassett, William, House)
Fassett Point, Stephen Decatur Memorial Rd. vic.
HABS MD-150   p   L

House, Gambrel (Ruins)
Sinapuxent Neck
HABS MD-171   p   L

Girdletree vic.

Barnes, Benjamin, House
Stockton Rd. (State Rt. 12)
HABS MD-156   p   L

Simperton
Watermelon Point, Bayside Rd.
HABS MD-157   p d   L

Pocomoke City vic.

Bishop Farm
McMaster Rd.
HABS MD-311   s   H

McKay, Sydney, House
HABS MD-863   s p   H

Snow Hill

Hall House (Olney, W. T., House)
Cherrix Rd.
HABS MD-62   p d   L

Olney, W. T., House; see Hall House

Snow Hill Landing

Devereaux House; see Mount Ephraim
Mount Ephraim (Devereaux House)
Bayside Rd., Chincoteague Bay vic.
HABS MD-165   p d   L

Snow Hill vic.

Dover
Public Landing Rd. (State Rt. 365)
HABS MD-172   p   L

Massachusetts

BARNSTABLE COUNTY

Barnstable

Barnstable Jail; see Jail, Old
Crocker Tavern
State Rt. 6A
HABS MA-694   s d   H
Gorham, Isaac, House
HABS MA-425   p   L
Jail, Old (Barnstable Jail)
State Rt. 6A & Old Jail Ln.
HABS MA-976   p   H
Lombard Farm, Barns (Poorhouse Barns)
Prospect St. (State Rt. 149)
HABS MA-964   s p d H
Lombard Farm, House (Poorhouse)
Prospect St. (State Rt. 149)
HABS MA-963   s p d H
Poorhouse; see Lombard Farm, House
Poorhouse Barns; see Lombard Farm,
  Barns
West Parish Congregational Church
State Rt. 149
HABS MA-779   p d H

Brewster

Brewster Mill (House)
HABS MA-439   p   L
Cobb, Capt. Elijah, House
Lower Rd.
HABS MA-732   p d H
Dillingham, Isaac, House
State Rt. 6A
HABS MA-733   p d H
Stony Brook Mill; see Water Mill, Old
Water Mill, Old (Stony Brook Mill)
Old Coach Rd.
HABS MA-179   s p d L H
Winslow House
HABS MA-344   p   L

Chatham

Atwood, Joseph, House
Atwood St.
HABS MA-161   s p   L
Chatham Windmill
Atwood St.
HABS MA-2-61   s p   L
Congregational Church
Old Harbor Rd. & Main St.
HABS MA-428   p   L
Howes, Capt. Solomon, House
Queen Anne Rd.
HABS MA-2-62   s p   L
Kimball-Ryder House
HABS MA-427   p   L

Chathamport

Ryder, Christopher, House
Ryder's Cove vic.
HABS MA-118   s p   L

Dennis

Howes-Jorgenson House
State Rt. 6A
HABS MA-731   p d H

East Sandwich

Nye House
King's Hwy.(U.S. Rt. 6)
HABS MA-206   s p   L

Eastham

Cape Cod Windmill (Eastham Windmill)
Samoset Rd. (moved from MA, Truro)
HABS MA-2-21   s p   L
Doane, Isaiah, House
Nauset Rd.
HABS MA-1125   p d H
Doane, John, House
Nauset Rd.
HABS MA-1127   p d H
Doane, Noah, House
Nauset Rd.
HABS MA-1126   p d H
Doane, Randall, House
Nauset Rd.
HABS MA-734   p d H
Doane, Simeon, House
Nauset Rd.
HABS MA-735   p d H
Doane, Sylvanus, House (Doane-Chase
  House)
Nauset Rd.
HABS MA-712   s p d H
Doane-Chase House; see Doane, Sylvanus,
  House
Eastham Windmill; see Cape Cod Windmill
Higgins House
HABS MA-433   p   L
Knowles, Seth, House (Nauset Moore
  Farm)
Fort Hill Rd.
HABS MA-1128   p d H
Knowles, Sylvanus, House
Fort Hill Rd.
HABS MA-1129   p d H
Nauset Moore Farm; see Knowles, Seth,
  House
Penniman, Capt. Edward, Barn
Fort Hill Rd.
HABS MA-699   s p d H
Penniman, Capt. Edward, House
Fort Hill Rd.
HABS MA-693   s p d H
Prence, Gov. Thomas, House
King's Hwy. (U.S. Rt. 6)
HABS MA-2-79   s p   L
Swift, Nathaniel, House
U.S. Rt. 6
HABS MA-736   p d H

Falmouth

Conent House
65 Palmer Ave.
HABS MA-977   p   H

Mashpee

Indian Church, Old
HABS MA-978   p   H

North Chatham

Nelson, Col. John, House; see Sampson,
  Jennie, House
Sampson, Jennie, House (Nelson, Col.
  John, House)
Cotchpinicutt Rd. (moved from MA,
  Lakeville)
HABS MA-297   p   L

Provincetown

Church of the Redeemer (Universalist
  Church)
Commercial St.
HABS MA-737   p d H
Pilgrim Monument
Bradford St.
HABS MA-738   p   H
Universalist Church; see Church of the
  Redeemer

Sandwich

Hoxie House
State Rt. 130
HABS MA-739   p d H

South Orleans

Kendrick, Jonathan, House
State Highway
HABS MA-119   s p   L

Truro

Adams, Zenas, House
N. Pamet Rd.
HABS MA-740   p d H
Atkins, Jonah, House (Kahn House)
S. Pamet Rd.
HABS MA-707   s p d H
Bog House, The
N. Pamet Rd.
HABS MA-1116   p d H
Cape Cod Windmill (Eastham Windmill)
(moved from MA, Plymouth)
HABS MA-2-21   s p   L
Cappers House; see Rich, Elisha, House
Cobb, Elisha, House (Collinson House)
Prince Valley Rd.
HABS MA-705   s p d H
Cobb, Elisha, Summer Kitchen (Collinson
  Summer Kitchen)
Prince Valley Rd.
HABS MA-706   s p d H
Cole, Joseph, House
Prince Valley Rd.
HABS MA-741   p d H

Collins, Benjamin, House
S. Pamet Rd.
HABS MA-711   s p d   H

Collins, Jonathan, House
S. Pamet Rd.
HABS MA-742   p d   H

Collinson House; see Cobb, Elisha, House

Collinson Summer Kitchen; see Cobb, Elisha, Summer Kitchen

Cooper House; see Rich, Thomas, House

Dyer, Benjamin, Barn
N. Pamet Rd.
HABS MA-698   s d   H

Dyer, Benjamin, House
N. Pamet Rd.
HABS MA-743   p d   H

Dyer, Ebenezer, House
Higgins Hollow Rd.
HABS MA-744   p d   H

Dyer, Joshua, House
N. Pamet Rd.
HABS MA-700   s p d   H

Dyer, Nathaniel, House
N. Pamet Rd.
HABS MA-713   s p d   H

Dyer, Thomas, House
Longnook Rd.
HABS MA-745   p d   H

Eastham Windmill; see Cape Cod Windmill

First Congregational Church
Truro Center
HABS MA-746   p d   H

Freeman, Edmund, House
Truro Rd.
HABS MA-702   s p d   H

Freeman, Edmund, Woodhouse
Truro Rd.
HABS MA-701   s p d   H

Harding, Ephraim, House
S. Pamet Rd.
HABS MA-714   s p d   H

Higgins, Daniel P., Barn
Higgins Hollow Rd.
HABS MA-696   s p d   H

Higgins, Daniel P., House
Higgins Hollow Rd.
HABS MA-747   p d   H

Higgins, Jedediah, House
Higgins Hollow Rd.
HABS MA-748   p d   H

Highland Hotel
Old King's Hwy. & Highland Rd.
HABS MA-749   p d   H

Highland Light; see Highland Lighthouse

Highland Lighthouse (Highland Light)
Highland Rd.
HABS MA-750   p d   H

Hopkins, Thomas, House
Holsbery Lane
HABS MA-751   p d   H

Kahn House; see Atkins, Jonah, House

Kelly, Benjamin S., House (Larsen House)
Higgins Hollow Rd.
HABS MA-716   s p d   H

Knowles, Paul, House
S. Pamet Rd.
HABS MA-752   p d   H

Larsen House; see Kelly, Benjamin S., House

Mayo, John, House
Old County Rd. vic.
HABS MA-1117   p d   H

Mayo, Nehemiah, House
Old County & Depot Rds.
HABS MA-753   p d   H

Mayo, Sally, House
Holsberry Ln.
HABS MA-1118   p d   H

Moynihan House; see Rich, Ephraim, House

Newcomb, William T., House
Pump Log Point Rd.
HABS MA-754   p d   H

Paine, Richard, House
Longnook & Higgins Hollow Rds.
HABS MA-755   p d   H

Paine, Samuel, House
Longnook & Higgins Hollow Rds.
HABS MA-756   p d   H

Paine-Atkins House
Longnook Rd.
HABS MA-757   p d   H

Rich, Atwood, House
Ryder Beach Rd.
HABS MA-719   s p d   H

Rich, Capt. Zoheth, House
Longnook Rd.
HABS MA-758   p d   H

Rich, Elisha, House (Cappers House)
Ryder Beach Rd.
HABS MA-710   s p d   H

Rich, Ephraim, House (Moynihan House)
Pump Log Point Rd.
HABS MA-717   s p d   H

Rich, Isaac, House
S. Pamet Rd.
HABS MA-759   p d   H

Rich, John C., House
Old County Rd. vic.
HABS MA-1119   p d   H

Rich, Joseph, House
S. Pamet Rd.
HABS MA-760   p d   H

Rich, Richard, House
S. Pamet Rd.
HABS MA-761   p d   H

Rich, Shebnah, House
Longnook Rd.
HABS MA-764   p d   H

Rich, Thomas, House (Cooper House)
Old County Rd.
HABS MA-762   p d   H

Rich, Thomas Jr., House
Old County Rd.
HABS MA-763   p d   H

Rich, Warren, House
Pump Log Point Rd.
HABS MA-765   p d   H

Rich-Cobb House
Prince Valley Rd.
HABS MA-766   p d   H

Rich-Higgins House
Longnook Rd.
HABS MA-718   s p d   H

Small, Isaac, House
Old King's Hwy. & Highland Rd.
HABS MA-695   s p d   H

Small, Thomas K., House
Old King's Hwy. & Highland Rd.
HABS MA-767   p d   H

Snow, Ambrose, House & Cobbler Shop
N. Pamet Rd.
HABS MA-768   p d   H

Snow, Ambrose, Privy
N. Pamet Rd.
HABS MA-697   s p d   H

Snow, Ephraim, House
N. Pamet Rd.
HABS MA-720   s p d   H

Snow, Joshua, House
N. Pamet Rd.
HABS MA-769   p d   H

Snow, Stephen, House
S. Pamet Rd.
HABS MA-770   p d   H

Snow, William P., House
S. Pamet Rd.
HABS MA-771   p d   H

Stocker, David, House
Holsberry Ln.
HABS MA-1120   p d   H

Wilson House
S. Pamet Rd.
HABS MA-1130   H

Woolley House
HABS MA-1121   s   H

Truro vic.

Harding, Lot, House
N. Pamet Rd.
HABS MA-715   s p d   H

Wellfleet

Atwood, Ebenezer L., House
Bound Brook Island Rd.
HABS MA-708   s p d   H

Atwood, Joel, House
Bound Brook Island Rd.
HABS MA-772   p d   H

Atwood-Higgins House
Bound Brook Island Rd.
HABS MA-1087   s p d   H

Baker, David, House
Bound Brook Island Rd.
HABS MA-709   s p d   H

Freeman, Joseph, House
Old Truro Rd.
HABS MA-773   p d   H

Gormley, Charles, House
Herring Pond Rd.
HABS MA-774 pd H

Grey, Henry, House
Pamet Point Rd.
HABS MA-1089 p H

Higgins, Elnathan, House
Pamet Point Rd.
HABS MA-775 pd H

Higgins, George K., Barn
Bound Brook Island Rd.
HABS MA-1122 p H

Higgins, Josiah, House
Gull & Higgins Ponds vic.
HABS MA-776 pd H

Newcomb, John, House (Wellfleet
Oysterman)
Williams Pond vic.
HABS MA-704 s pd H

Rich, Samuel, House
HABS MA-1123 pd H

Rowell House
Gull Pond Rd.
HABS MA-777 s pd H

Ryder-Paine House
Pamet Point Rd.
HABS MA-1124 p H

Wellfleet Oysterman; see Newcomb, John,
House

Williams, Justin, House
Pamet Point Rd.
HABS MA-703 s pd H

Young, B. S., House
U.S. Rt. 6
HABS MA-778 pd H

West Chatham

Buck House
Barn Hill Rd.
HABS MA-2-8 s p L

Harding, Enoch, Salt Works
Buck's Creek
HABS MA-172 s p L

Yarmouth

Kelly, Elizabeth, House
HABS MA-296 p L

BERKSHIRE COUNTY

Adams

Quaker Meetinghouse; see Society of
Friends Meetinghouse

Society of Friends Meetinghouse (Quaker
Meetinghouse)
West Rd. & Maple St.
HABS MA-2-44 s p L H

Clarksburg

Musterfield House
Middle Rd.
HABS MA-2-25 s p L

Egremont

Egremont Academy; see Town Hall

Town Hall (Egremont Academy)
State Rts. 41 & 17
HABS MA-220 s p L

Great Barrington

Bryant, William Cullen, House; see Dwight,
Gen. Joseph, House

Dwight, Gen. Joseph, House (Bryant,
William Cullen, House)
U.S. Rt. 7 & State Rt. 23
HABS MA-360 p L

Hancock

Shaker Building Number 4; see Shaker
Ministry's Washhouse

Shaker Church Family Brethren's Shop
U.S. Rt. 20
HABS MA-722 pd L

Shaker Church Family Concrete Barn
U.S. Rt. 20
HABS MA-1082 p L

**Shaker Church Family Dairy & Weave
Shop** (Shaker Church Family Sisters'
Shop (second))
U.S. Rt. 20
HABS MA-726 s pd L

Shaker Church Family Frame Barn (Shaker
Ministry's Barn & Wagon Shed)
U.S. Rt. 20
HABS MA-1083 p L

Shaker Church Family (General Views)
U.S. Rt. 20
HABS MA-721 p L

Shaker Church Family Icehouse
U.S. Rt. 20
HABS MA-1084 p L

**Shaker Church Family Main Dwelling
House**
U.S. Rt. 20
HABS MA-723 p L

Shaker Church Family Poultry House
U.S. Rt. 20
HABS MA-1093 p L

Shaker Church Family Round Barn
U.S. Rt. 20
HABS MA-674 s pd L

Shaker Church Family Seed Shop
U.S. Rt. 20
HABS MA-1095 p L

Shaker Church Family Sisters' Shop (first)
U.S. Rt. 20
HABS MA-1094 p L

**Shaker Church Family Sisters' Shop
(second);** see Shaker Church Family
Dairy & Weave Shop

Shaker Church Family Tannery
U.S. Rt. 20
HABS MA-727 pd L

Shaker Church Family Trustees' Office
U.S. Rt. 20
HABS MA-728 p L

**Shaker Church Family Washhouse &
Machine Shop**
U.S. Rt. 20
HABS MA-730 pd L

Shaker Meetinghouse (first)
U.S. Rt. 20
HABS MA-692 p L

Shaker Meetinghouse (second)
U.S. Rt. 20
HABS MA-724 pd L

Shaker Ministry's Barn & Wagon Shed; see
Shaker Church Family Frame Barn

Shaker Ministry's Shop
U.S. Rt. 20
HABS MA-725 p L

Shaker Ministry's Washhouse (Shaker
Building Number 4)
U.S. Rt. 20
HABS MA-729 p L

Lanesborough

First Baptist Church
HABS MA-463 p L

Registry of Deeds Building
HABS MA-372 p L

New Marlborough

Harmon, Lieutenant, House
HABS MA-386 p L

Pittsfield

Arrowhead (Bush-Melville House)
780 Holmes Rd.
HABS MA-2-23 s p L

Brattle, William Jr., House
626 Williams St.
HABS MA-2-54 s p L

Bulfinch Church
North St. & Maplewood Ave. (moved from
Park Row)
HABS MA-2-24 s p L

Bush-Melville House; see Arrowhead

Colt-Pingree House
HABS MA-477 p L

First Bank Building
800 East St. (moved from original Pittsfield
site)
HABS MA-2-46 s p L

Peace Party House
East St. & Wendell Ave.
HABS MA-478 p L

West Part School
West & Churchill Sts.
HABS MA-2-89 s p L

Richmond

Peirson House
HABS MA-396 p L

Sheffield

Ashley, Col. John, House
Cooper Rd. vic.
HABS MA-401 p L

Ashley, Gen. John, House (Doorway)
HABS MA-400 p L

Congregational Church
HABS MA-892 p H

Hall, Parker L., Law Office
State Rt. 7
HABS MA-233 s p L

South Lee

Merrell's Tavern
Main St.
HABS MA-622   s   L

South Williamstown

Deming, Titus, House
New Ashford Rd.
HABS MA-106   s p   L

Stockbridge

Congregational Church
Stockbridge Common
HABS MA-894   p   H

Hopkins, Mark, House
HABS MA-408   p   L

Housatonic National Bank
HABS MA-895   p   H

Yale-Duryea Mills
E. Main St.
HABS MA-107   s p   L

West Stockbridge

Bank Building, Old (House, Greek Temple)
HABS MA-496   p   L

Engine House (Ruins)
Mill St.
HABS MA-149   s p   L

House, Greek Temple; see Bank Building, Old

Marble House
HABS MA-415   p   L

Marble Mill
HABS MA-416   p   L

Williamstown

Smedley, Nehemiah, House
State Rt. 2
HABS MA-2-18   s p   L

Williamstown College, President's House
Williamstown College Campus
HABS MA-1164   p   H

Williamstown Railroad Station
N. Hoosac Rd. & Cole Ave.
HABS MA-1080   s d   H

BRISTOL COUNTY

Acoaxet

Richmond-Manchester House
Howland Rd.
HABS MA-160   s p   L

Attleboro

Robinson, Joel, House
HABS MA-437   p   L

Thatcher House
HABS MA-339   p   L

Well Sweep
HABS MA-438   p   L

Attleboro vic.

Daggett, John, House
480 N. Main St.
HABS MA-174   s p   L

Attleboro-Plainville

Angle Tree Stone
Town Line
HABS MA-181   s p   L

Dartmouth

Apponagansett Meetinghouse
HABS MA-441   p   L

Dighton

Baylies, Maj. Hadijah, House
HABS MA-431   p   L

Brick, The (Church)
HABS MA-355   p   L

Coram House
HABS MA-432   p   L

Delare Cottage
HABS MA-446   p   L

Ellery House
HABS MA-444   p   L

Tulip Tree House
HABS MA-445   p   L

East Taunton

Dean, Nathan, House
Old Colony Rd.
HABS MA-143   s p   L

Easton

Milestones P, Q, R & S
Bay St.
HABS MA-128   p   L

Fairhaven

Academy, Old
Main St.
HABS MA-690   pd   L

Bennett, Capt. Thomas, House
199 Main St.
HABS MA-608   s   L

Fish, Reuben, House
William & Union Sts.
HABS MA-136   s   L

Fall River

Academy Building (Borden Block; Academy of Music)
68-114 South Main St.
HABS MA-1000   s pd   L

Academy of Music; see Academy Building

American Print Works, Number 6 Mill; see Metacomet Mill, Number 6 Mill

Borden Block; see Academy Building

Borden, Richard, Manufacturing Co., Number 1 Mill
Rodman St. & Plymouth Ave.
HABS MA-984   s pd   L

Charlton Mill
Howe & Crawford Sts.
HABS MA-986   s pd   L

Davol Mills
Rodman St. & Plymouth Ave.
HABS MA-985   s pd   L

Durfee Mills
Plymouth Ave. & Pleasant St.
HABS MA-982   s pd   L

Metacomet Mill, Number 6 Mill (American Print Works, Number 6 Mill)
Davol & Anawan Sts.
HABS MA-983   s pd   L

Union Mills
Pleasant St. & Hwy. I-195, Interchange No. 12
HABS MA-981   s pd   L

Freetown

Barnaby, James, House
N. Main St.
HABS MA-2-27   s p   L

New Bedford

Baker Oil Works (Delano Oil Works)
South St.
HAER MA-10   p   H

Congregational Church (First Unitarian Church)
Union & Eighth Sts.
HABS MA-681   pd   L

Custom House
Second & William Sts.
HABS MA-682   pd   L

Delano Oil Works; see Baker Oil Works

First Unitarian Church; see Congregational Church

Friends Meetinghouse
Spring St.
HABS MA-467   pd   L

Grinell, Joseph, Mansion (St. John's Roman Catholic Convent & Academy)
379 County St.
HABS MA-675   pd   L

Harrison, John, Building
23 Centre St.
HABS MA-686   pd   L

Institution for Savings (Third District Courthouse)
Second & Williams Sts
HABS MA-684   pd   L

Merchants & Mechanics Bank Building
56-62 North Water St.
HABS MA-683   pd   L

North Front Street & Rose Alley (Warehouse)
HABS MA-688   pd   L

Rodman, Samuel Jr., House
Spring & County Sts.
HABS MA-466   pd   L

Rodman, William R., House
388 County St.
HABS MA-676   pd   L

Rotch, William J., House
19 Irving St. (moved from 103 Orchard St.)
HABS MA-678   pd   L

Rotch, William Jr., House
15 Johnny Cake Hill
HABS MA-679   pd   L

Russell, Charles, Building
Union & Water Sts.
HABS MA-687   pd   L

Seaman's Bethel
Johnny Cake Hill
HABS MA-680   pd   L

St. John's Roman Catholic Convent & Academy; see Grinell, Joseph, Mansion

Taber, Henry, House
115 Orchard St.
HABS MA-677   pd   L

Tallman, William, Warehouse
106 N. Front St.
HABS MA-685   pd   L

Third District Courthouse; see Institution for Savings

Union and Front Streets (Warehouse)
HABS MA-689   pd   L

Wamsutta Mill
Achushnet Ave.
HABS MA-987   p   L

North Attleboro

Daggett, Handel, House
HABS MA-390   p   L

Ellis, Jabez, House
HABS MA-391   p   L

Mann, Dr. Bezaleel, House
HABS MA-392   p   L

Powder House
Mount Hope St., Oldtown
HABS MA-148   s p   L

North Attleboro vic.

Congregational Church
Old Post Rd.
HABS MA-189   s p   L

Stanley-Mathewson House
Old Post Rd.
HABS MA-170   s p   L

Stearns, Capt. John, House
Old Post Rd., Oldtown
HABS MA-165   s p   L

North Dighton

Clouston, Capt. John, House
Somerset Ave.
HABS MA-164   s p   L

North Easton

New York, New Haven & Hartford Railroad Station; see Old Colony Railroad Station

Old Colony Railroad Station (New York, New Haven & Hartford Railroad Station)
HABS MA-663   pd   L

Norton

Avery, Rev. Joseph, House
Main St.
HABS MA-244   s p   L

Clark House; see Norton Cotton Mill House

Clark, Rev. Pitt, House
Mansfield Ave.
HABS MA-257   s p   L

Devoe House; see Norton Cotton Mill House

Milestones T & U
Bay St.
HABS MA-128   p   L

Newcomb, Jonathan, House
HABS MA-393   p   L

Norton Cotton Mill House (Clark House)
200 E. Main St.
HABS MA-997   p   L

Norton Cotton Mill House (Devoe House)
338 E. Main St. (moved from 198 E. Main St.)
HABS MA-998   p   L

Rehoboth

Carpenter, Col. Thomas, House
HABS MA-394   p   L

Seekonk

Martin, Lieut. Gov. Simeon, Blacksmith Shop
County St.
HABS MA-235   s   L

Martin, Lieut. Gov. Simeon, House
County St.
HABS MA-2-90   s p   L

Martin, Sylvanus, Barn
County St.
HABS MA-234   s   L

Somerset

Bowers, Jarathmael, House
55 Main St.
HABS MA-2-17   s p   L

Pettis, Henry, House
Main St. & Pierce Rd.
HABS MA-2-52   s p   L

South Somerset

Brayton, John, Homestead
Brayton Ave.
HABS MA-2-43   s p   L

South Westport

Waite-Potter House
Sanford Rd.
HABS MA-2-65   s p   L

Swansea

Luther, Joseph G., Store
Luther's Corner
HABS MA-134   s p   L

Tavern, Old
U.S. Rt. 6 & Milford Rd.
HABS MA-105   s p   L

DUKES COUNTY

Tisbury

Gray, Lucy, House
Indian Hill Rd.
HABS MA-2-88   s p   L

ESSEX COUNTY

Amesbury

Powder House
HABS MA-338   p   L

Rocky Hill Meetinghouse
Elm St. & Portsmouth Rd.
HABS MA-250   s p   L

Andover

Abbot, Benjamin, Farmhouse
Andover St. & Argilla Rd.
HABS MA-2-9   s p   L

Annisquam

Customs House, Old
River Rd.
HABS MA-2-12   s p   L

Hodgkins, William, Tide Mill
Washington St.
HABS MA-2-92   s p   L

Lobster Cove
HABS MA-115   s   L

Beverly

Balch, John, House
448 Cabot St.
HABS MA-584   p   L

Cabot, John, House & Garden
117 Cabot St.
HABS MA-282   s p   L

First Baptist Church (Pulpit)
HABS MA-619   s   L

Foster, George B., House & Fence
21 Bartlett St.
HABS MA-267   s p   L

Foster Warehouse
HABS MA-260   p   L

Kilham, Austin D., House (Garden)
8 Thorndike St.
HABS MA-266   s p   L

Pierce, Benjamin, House
305 Cabot St.
HABS MA-606   s   L

Powder House
Powder House Hill
HABS MA-583   p   L

Second Church
HABS MA-585   p   L

Boxford

Goodridge, Benjamin, House; see Gould, Daniel, House

Goodridge, Benjamin, Shoemaker's Shop; see Shoemaker's Shop

Gould, Daniel, House (Goodridge, Benjamin, House)
Georgetown Rd.
HABS MA-2-30   s p   L

Saw, Grist & Knife Mill Group
Middleton Rd.
HABS MA-2-15   s p   L

Shoemaker's Shop (Goodridge, Benjamin, Shoemaker's Shop)
Georgetown Rd.
HABS MA-2-58   s p   L

Danvers

Fowler, Samuel, House
166 High St.
HABS MA-586   p   L

Gage, General, House; see Lindens, The (House & Garden)

Holten, Judge Samuel, House
171 Holten St.
HABS MA-152   s p   L

Hooper, King, House & Garden; see Lindens, The (House & Garden)

Jacobs, George, House
Margin St.
HABS MA-243   s p   L

Lindens, The (House & Garden) (Hooper, King, House & Garden; Gage, General, House)
Sylvan St. (moved to Washington, D.C.)
HABS MA-2-33   s p   L

Nurse, Rebecca, House & Garden
149 Pine St.
HABS MA-239   s p   L

Oak Knoll (House & Garden)
Summer St.
HABS MA-205   s p   L

Porter, Elias Endicott, House & Farm Gates
Locust St.
HABS MA-289   s p   L

Putnam, Gen. Israel, Birthplace; see Putnam, Gen. Israel, House

Putnam, Gen. Israel, Birthplace (Garden); see Putnam, Gen. Israel, House (Garden)

Putnam, Gen. Israel, House (Putnam, Gen. Israel, Birthplace)
431 Maple St.
HABS MA-153   s p   L

Putnam, Gen. Israel, House (Garden) (Putnam, Gen. Israel, Birthplace (Garden))
431 Maple St.
HABS MA-153-A   s   L

Warren, Betsy K., Garden
124 High St.
HABS MA-290   s   L

Danvers vic.

Derby Summerhouse
Endicott Estate, Ingersoll St.
HABS MA-783   p   H

Georgetown

Brockelbank, Capt. Samuel, House (Fence); see White Horse Tavern (Fence)

36 East Main Street (House & Fence)
HABS MA-449   p   L

Nelson, Capt. Bill, House (Fence)
8 Elm St.
HABS MA-254   s p   L

White Horse Tavern (Fence) (Brockelbank, Capt. Samuel, House (Fence))
108 E. Main St.
HABS MA-253   s p   L

Gloucester

First Universalist Church (Independent Christian Church)
Middle St.
HABS MA-451   p   L

Independent Christian Church; see First Universalist Church

Schoolhouse
HABS MA-453   p   L

Hamilton-Ipswich

Warner's Bridge
Mill Rd., spanning Ipswich River
HABS MA-251   s p   L

Haverhill

Duston Garrison House (Duston, Thomas, House)
Hillsdale Ave.
HABS MA-273   p   L

Duston, Thomas, House; see Duston Garrison House

Ipswich

Appleton, William, House (Choate, Sally, House)
HABS MA-607   s   L

Caldwell, Waldo, House (Interiors)
High St.
HABS MA-462   p   L

Choate Bridge
State Rt. 1A, spanning Ipswich River
HABS MA-2-69   s p   L

Choate, Sally, House; see Appleton, William, House

Congregational Parsonage (Fencepost)
19 N. Main St.
HABS MA-255   s   L

Dane, Dr. Philemon, House & Fence
41 S. Main St.
HABS MA-256   s p   L

Heard, John, Estate
State Rt. 1A
HABS MA-321   p   L

Howard-Emerson House
Turkey Shore Rd.
HABS MA-423   p   L

Kimball, John, House
75 High St.
HABS MA-177   s p   L

Milestone TT; see Twenty-five-mile Stone

Morton-Corbett-House
8 East St.
HABS MA-457   p   L

40 North Main Street (House)
HABS MA-461   p   L

Post Office, Old
HABS MA-456   p   L

Proctor House
Jeffrey's Neck Rd. (moved from original location)
HABS MA-322   p   L

Renault-Foster House
Water St.
HABS MA-633   s   L

Saltonstall-Whipple House; see Whipple, John, House

Treadwell House
HABS MA-368   p   L

Twenty-five-mile Stone (Milestone TT)
Bay Rd.
HABS MA-128   p   L

Wade, Col. Nathaniel, House
HABS MA-458   p   L

Whipple, John, House (Saltonstall-Whipple House)
53 S. Main St.
HABS MA-460   p   L

Lawrence

Everett Mills; see Lawrence Machine Shop

Lawrence Machine Shop (Everett Mills)
Union St.
HABS MA-988   s p d   L

Pemberton Mill
Union St. vic.
HABS MA-989   p d   L H

Washington Mills, Gatehouse
North Canal
HABS MA-990   p d   L

Lynn

Lynn Realty Company, Building Number 28; see Lynn Realty Company, Building Number 3

Lynn Realty Company, Building Number 3 (Lynn Realty Company, Building Number 28)
696 Washington St.
HABS MA-1001   p d   L

Lynn Realty Company, Building Number 8
274 Broad St.
HABS MA-1002   p d   L

Manchester

Forster, Maj. Israel, House
State Rt. 127
HABS MA-373   p   L

Lee, Ma'm, Cottage
39 Forest St.
HABS MA-323   s p   L

Orthodox Congregational Church
Central & Church Sts.
HABS MA-268   p   L

Marblehead

Artillery House, Old; see Gun House, Old

Boardman House (Waters, William, House & Bakery)
Washington St.
HABS MA-2-31   s p   L

Gun House, Old (Artillery House, Old)
45 Elm St.
HABS MA-186   s p   L

Hooper, King, House; see Hooper, Robert, House

Hooper, Robert, House (Hooper, King, House)
8 Hooper St.
HABS MA-249   s p   L

Jayne, Peter, House
37 Mugford St.
HABS MA-374   p   L

Lee, Col. Jeremiah, Mansion
161 Washington St.
HABS MA-859   p   H

Powder House
Green St.
HABS MA-2-67   s p   L

Town House
Market Square
HABS MA-2-6   s p   L

Trevett, Capt. Samuel, House
65 Washington St.
HABS MA-104   s p   L

Waters, William, House & Bakery; see
Boardman House

Middleton

Bradstreet House
HABS MA-587   p   L

Newbury

Coffin, Tristram, House (Coffyn House)
14 High Rd.
HABS MA-472   p   L

Coffyn House; see Coffin, Tristram, House

Jackman, Richard, House; see
Jackman-Willett House

Jackman-Willett House (Jackman,
Richard, House)
Lower Green vic. (moved from original site)
HABS MA-471   p   L

Knight, Nathaniel, House; see
Knight-Short House

Knight-Short House (Knight, Nathaniel,
House; Short House)
6 High St.
HABS MA-468   p   L

Milestones UU, VV, WW, XX, YY & ZZ
Various Newbury locations
HABS MA-128   p   L

Short House; see Knight-Short House

Toppan, Dr. Peter, House
HABS MA-469   p   L

Newbury Old Town

Blue Anchor Tavern; see Swett-Ilsley House

Swett-Ilsley House (Blue Anchor Tavern)
4-6 High St.
HABS MA-472   s p   L

Newburyport

Cushing, John N., House & Garden
98 High St.
HABS MA-213   s p   L

Gaol, Gaoler's House & Barn
Auburn & Vernon Sts.
HABS MA-121   s p   L

Globe Steam Mills
Federal St.
HABS MA-295   s p   L

Hennessey House
2 Summer St.
HABS MA-2-82   s p d   L

Highway Cut-off Demolition Area
Summer, Winter, High & Merrimac Sts.
HABS MA-117   s p   L

Marden House
32 Summer St.
HABS MA-2-87   s p   L

Meetinghouse of First Religious Society
Pleasant St.
HABS MA-623   s p   L

Moulton, Joseph, House & Garden
89-91 High St.
HABS MA-216   s p   L

Pierce, Benjamin, House & Garden; see
Pierce-Knapp-Perry House & Garden

Pierce-Knapp-Perry House & Garden
(Pierce, Benjamin, House & Garden)
47 High St.
HABS MA-236   s p   L

Regan House
7 Birch St.
HABS MA-110   s p   L

Semple House
176 High St.
HABS MA-2-93   s   L

Stocker, Ebenezer, Garden; see
Stocker-Wheelwright Garden

Stocker-Wheelwright Garden
(Wheelwright, William, Garden; Stocker,
Ebenezer, Garden)
75 High St.
HABS MA-209   s   L

Stockman, Charles, House
31-33 Winter St.
HABS MA-140   s p   L

Stockman House
5 Birch St.
HABS MA-2-95   s p   L

Stonecutting Shop
2 Summer St.
HABS MA-2-97   s p   L

Thibault House
8 Summer St.
HABS MA-123   s p   L

Thurlow House
43 Winter St.
HABS MA-2-83   s p   L

Wheelwright, Abraham, House & Garden
(Wheelwright-Richardson House &
Garden)
77 High St.
HABS MA-780   p   L

Wheelwright, William, Garden; see
Stocker-Wheelwright Garden

Wheelwright-Richardson House & Garden;
see Wheelwright, Abraham, House &
Garden

North Andover

Bradstreet, Gov. Simon, House
(Parson-Barnard House)
159 Osgood St.
HABS MA-2-63   s p   L

Kittredge, Dr. Thomas, House & Fence
114 Academy Rd.
HABS MA-475   p   L

Parson-Barnard House; see Bradstreet, Gov.
Simon, House

Town Scales House
Andover St.
HABS MA-2-100   s p   L

Rockport

Bradley's Wharf (Motif Number One)
Bearskin Neck
HABS MA-227   s   L

Motif Number One; see Bradley's Wharf

Rowley

Billings, Elizabeth, House & Fence
Main St.
HABS MA-277   s p   L

Milestone BBB; see Twenty-seven-mile
Stone

Twenty-seven-mile Stone (Milestone BBB)
Newburyport Turnpike
HABS MA-128   p   L

Salem

Andrew, John, House & Garden; see
Andrew-Safford House & Garden

Andrew, John, Stable (Andrew-Safford
Stable)
13 Washington Square
HABS MA-281   s p   L

Andrew-Safford House & Garden (Andrew,
John, House & Garden)
13 Washington Sq.
HABS MA-281-A   s p   L

Andrew-Safford Stable; see Andrew, John,
Stable

Baldwin-Lyman, House (Fence)
92 Washington Sq.
HABS MA-485   p   L

Boardman-Bowen House (Fence)
1 Boardman St.
HABS MA-490   p   L

Bowker, Joel, Garden (Crombie, Benjamin,
Garden)
9 Crombie St.
HABS MA-262   s   L

Brooks House
260 Lafayette St.
HABS MA-796   p d   H

Cook-Oliver House
142 Federal St.
HABS MA-333   p   L

Corwin, Jonathan, House (Witch House,
The Old)
310 Essex St.
HABS MA-398   p   L

Crombie, Benjamin, Garden; see Bowker,
Joel, Garden

Crowninshield Warehouse
India St.
HABS MA-259   s p   L

Crowninshield-Devereaux House
74 Washington Sq.
HABS MA-582   p   L

Customs House & Public Stores
178 Derby St.
HABS MA-799   s pd   H

Daland, Benjamin, Garden; see Robinson,
John, Garden

Daland, Benjamin, Stable; see Robinson,
John, Stable

Daniel, Stephen, House
Daniels & Essex Sts.
HABS MA-116   s p   L

Derby, Richard, House
168 Derby St.
HABS MA-269   s pd   L H

Dodge, Pickering, House & Garden
40 Dearborn St.
HABS MA-184   s p   L

Dodge-Shreve House
29 Chestnut St.
HABS MA-795   pd   H

East India Marine Hall (Peabody Museum)
161 Essex St.
HABS MA-798   pd   H

Finnegan, Doctor, House (Fencepost)
HABS MA-487   p   L

First Universalist Meetinghouse
HABS MA-399   p   L

Forrester-Peabody House & Garden
29 Washington Sq.
HABS MA-264   s p   L

Forrester's Warehouse
187 Derby St. (Central Wharf)
HABS MA-572   s   L

Gardner-White-Pingree House & Garden
128 Essex St.
HABS MA-271   s p   L

Hamilton Hall
7 Cambridge St.
HABS MA-483   p   L H

Hawkes, Gen. Benjamin, House
4 Custom House Place
HABS MA-270   s p   L H

Hawthorne, Nathaniel, Birthplace
27 Union St.
HABS MA-581   p   L

Hodges, Capt. Jonathan, Summerhouse;
see Hodges-Peele-West Summerhouse

Hodges-Peele-West Summerhouse (Hodges,
Capt. Jonathan, Summerhouse)
12 Chestnut St.
HABS MA-265   s p   L

Hodges-Webb-Meek House
81 Essex St.
HABS MA-797   p   H

House of the Seven Gables; see Turner,
John, House

Lindall-Barnard-Andrews House (Fence)
393 Essex St.
HABS MA-484   p   L

Lindall-Gibbs-Osgood Garden
314 Essex St.
HABS MA-263   s   L

Loring-Emmerton House & Fence
Essex St.
HABS MA-480   p   L

Manning, Robert, Garden
33 Dearborn St.
HABS MA-187   s   L

Narbonne House
71 Essex St.
HABS MA-802   s pd   H

Oliver Primary School
HABS MA-329   p   L

Peabody Museum; see East India Marine
Hall

Phillips House & Fence
36 Chestnut St.
HABS MA-488   p   L

Phippen, Doctor, House & Fence
Chestnut St.
HABS MA-486   p   L

Pickering House & Fence
30 Chestnut St.
HABS MA-482   p   L

Pickering, John, House & Garden
18 Broad St.
HABS MA-212   s p   L

Pickman, Benjamin, House
165 Essex St.
HABS MA-332   p   L

Pierce, Jerathmeel, House & Garden
(Pierce-Nichols House & Garden)
80 Federal St.
HABS MA-224   s p   L

Pierce-Nichols House & Garden; see Pierce,
Jerathmeel, House & Garden

Public Library; see Waters-Bertram House

Robinson, John, Garden (Daland,
Benjamin, Garden)
18 Summer St.
HABS MA-208-A   s   L

Robinson, John, Stable (Daland, Benjamin,
Stable)
18 Summer St.
HABS MA-208   s p   L

Ropes Memorial
318 Essex St.
HABS MA-481   p   L

Rum Shop
Derby St. & Palfrey Court
HABS MA-801   s pd   H

Saltonstall, Leverett, Garden (Saunders,
Thomas, Garden)
41 Chestnut St.
HABS MA-228   s p   L

Saunders, Thomas, Garden; see Saltonstall,
Leverett, Garden

Scale House
178 Derby St.
HABS MA-800   s pd   H

Ship Chandler's Shop
Federal & North Sts.
HABS MA-291   s p   L

Turner, John, House (House of the Seven
Gables; Turner-Ingersoll House)
54 Turner St.
HABS MA-629   p   L H

Turner-Ingersoll House; see Turner, John,
House

Ward, Joshua, House (Washington House)
148 Washington St.
HABS MA-2-57   s p   L

Washington House; see Ward, Joshua,
House

Waters-Bertram House (Public Library)
370 Essex St.
HABS MA-803   pd   H

Witch House, The Old; see Corwin,
Jonathan, House

Saugus

Boardman House; see Scotch House

Scotch House (Boardman House)
7 Howard St.
HABS MA-492   s p   L

Swampscott

Humphrey, John, House
99 Paradise Rd.
HABS MA-580   p   L

Topsfield

Andrews House
HABS MA-621   s   L

Capen, Parson Joseph, House
Howlett St.
HABS MA-214   s pd   L H

Elmwood Mansion
HABS MA-524   p   L

Wenham

Milestones QQ, RR & SS
Bay Rd.
HABS MA-128   p   L

FRANKLIN COUNTY

Ashfield

Congregational Meetinghouse; see Town
Hall

St. John's Episcopal Church
Main St. & Baptist Corner Rd.
HABS MA-648   pd   L

Town Hall (Congregational Meetinghouse)
Main St.
HABS MA-436   pd   L

Buckland

Griswold, Maj. Joseph, House; see Lyon,
Mary, House

Lyon, Mary, House (Griswold, Maj. Joseph, House)
Upper St.
HABS MA-108   s p   L

Conway

Herrick, Joe, House (Old) (Parsons, Joel, House)
Poland Rd.
HABS MA-2-99   s p   L

Parsons, Joel, House; see Herrick, Joe, House (Old)

Deerfield

Frary-Barnard House
Old Deerfield St.
HABS MA-628   pd   L

Deerfield vic.

Allen House (Fuller Studio)
Bars Rd.
HABS MA-658   pd   L

Fuller Studio; see Allen House

Locke-Fuller House
Bars Rd.
HABS MA-645   s pd   L

Deerfield Village

Barnard-Willard House; see Manse, The Old

Church, Brick; see First Church of Deerfield

Dickinson, Capt. Thomas, House
Old Deerfield St.
HABS MA-641   s pd   L

Dickinson, David, House (Smith House)
Old Deerfield St.
HABS MA-640   s pd   L

First Church of Deerfield (Church, Brick)
Old Deerfield St.
HABS MA-639   s pd   L

First Deerfield Academy; see Memorial Hall

Indian House, Old (Fragments); see Sheldon, John, House (Fragments)

Lyman, Augustus, House (Williams, Bishop John, Birthplace)
Old Deerfield St.
HABS MA-625   pd   L

Manse, The Old (Barnard-Willard House)
Old Deerfield St.
HABS MA-626   pd   L

Memorial Hall (First Deerfield Academy)
Memorial Rd.
HABS MA-646   s pd   L

Nims, Godfrey, House
Old Deerfield St. & Memorial Rd.
HABS MA-647   s pd   L

Ray, Benjamin, House
Old Deerfield St.
HABS MA-624   pd   L

Sheldon, John, House (Fragments) (Indian House, Old (Fragments))
Memorial Hall Museum
HABS MA-649   s pd   L

Smith House; see Dickinson, David, House

Stebbins, Joseph, House
Old Deerfield St.
HABS MA-652   pd   L

Wells-Thorn House
Old Deerfield St. & Memorial Rd.
HABS MA-653   pd   L

Williams, Bishop John, Birthplace; see Lyman, Augustus, House

Williams, Parson John, House
Albany Rd.
HABS MA-627   s pd   L

East Northfield

Alexander, Simeon, House
188 Main St.
HABS MA-662   pd   L

Colton, Capt. Richard, House
Main St.
HABS MA-660   pd   L

Greenfield

Coleman-Hollister House
Bank Row
HABS MA-2-19   s p   L

Gould-Potter House
486 Main St.
HABS MA-642   s pd   L

Greenfield Public Library; see Leavitt-Hovey House

Leavitt-Hovey House (Greenfield Public Library)
402 Main St.
HABS MA-656   pd   L

Newton, Rev. Roger, House
Newton Place (moved from original location)
HABS MA-2-94   s p   L

Greenfield vic.

McHard House
U.S. Rt. 5
HABS MA-2-45   s p   L

Montague City

Covered Bridge
Spanning Connecticut River
HABS MA-101   s p   L

New Salem

Allen, Samuel C., House
S. Main St.
HABS MA-846   d   H

Northfield

Hall-Spring House
89 Main St.
HABS MA-643   pd   L

Lane, Capt. Samuel, House
33 Main St.
HABS MA-661   pd   L

Mattoon, Isaac, House
26 Main St.
HABS MA-659   pd   L

Pomery, William, House
Main St.
HABS MA-654   pd   L

Stratton House
HABS MA-476   p   L

White-Field House
Main & Maple Sts.
HABS MA-655   pd   L

Northfield vic.

Chalet Schell
HABS MA-1134   p   H

Riverside

Red House, The Old
French King Hwy. (Riverside)
HABS MA-2-60   s p   L

Shelburne

Arms House
Shelburne-Colrain Rd.
HABS MA-493   p   L

Bardwell, Daniel P., Ash House
Bardwell's Ferry Rd.
HABS MA-691   p   L

Bardwell, Daniel P., House
Bardwell's Ferry Rd.
HABS MA-657   pd   L

South Deerfield

Wapping School
Greenfield Rd.
HABS MA-2-81   s p   L

West Northfield

Belding, Elijah E., House
Mt. Hermon Station Rd.
HABS MA-635   pd   L

HAMPDEN COUNTY

Agawam

Colton-Cooley House; see Cooley, Isaac, House

Cooley, Isaac, House (Colton-Cooley House; King, Martin, Inn)
740 Elm St.
HABS MA-2-51   s p   L

King, Martin, Inn; see Cooley, Isaac, House

Leonard, Capt. Charles, House
663 Main St.
HABS MA-2-50   s p   L

Tobacco Barn
663 Main St.
HABS MA-151   s p   L

Brimfield

Chamberlain House
HABS MA-311   p   H

Chester

Bascom, Rev. Aaron, House
Middlefield Rd.
HABS MA-112   s p   L

Granville

Curtis Tavern
State Rt. 57
HABS MA-221   p   L H

Scott House
State Rt. 57
HABS MA-1135   p   H

Longmeadow

Colton, Capt. Gideon, House
1028 Longmeadow St.
HABS MA-2-36   s p   L

Field, Col. Alexander, House
280 Longmeadow St.
HABS MA-173   s p   L

Ludlow-Wilbraham

Covered Bridge
Spanning Chicopee River
HABS MA-497   p   L

North Brookfield

Potter, Capt. John, House
(moved to MA, Springfield vic.)
HABS MA-852   p   H

Palmer

Boston and Albany Railroad Station
HABS MA-664   pd   L

Springfield

Alexander House
HABS MA-406   p   L

Boston Road (Milestone)
HABS MA-407   p   L

Church of the Unity
207 State St.
HABS MA-637   pd   L

Mills-Stebbins House
3 Crescent Hill
HABS MA-973   s p   H

Springfield Armory
Hill Shop Area
HABS MA-1136   s   H

West Brookfield

Gilbert, Levi & Peletiah, House
(moved to MA, Springfield vic.)
HABS MA-850   p   H

West Springfield

Atkinson, John, Tavern
Exposition Grounds (moved from MA, Prescott)
HABS MA-844   p   H

Chesterfield Blacksmith Shop
Exposition Grnds. (moved from NH, Chesterfield)
HABS NH-41   s p   L H

Day, Josiah, House
Park Street Museum
HABS MA-634   s   L

Eddy, Zachariah, Law Office
Exposition Grounds (moved from MA, Middleboro)
HABS MA-851   p   H

Gilbert, Levi & Peletiah, House
Exposition Grnds (moved from MA, W. Brookfield)
HABS MA-850   p   H

Meetinghouse
HABS MA-630   p   L

Potter, Capt. John, House
Exposition Grnds. (moved from MA, N. Brookfield)
HABS MA-852   p   H

Salisbury Meetinghouse
Exposition Grounds (moved from NH, Salisbury)
HABS MA-843   p   H

Schoolhouse, Little Red
Eastern States Exposition Grounds
HABS MA-293   p   H

Westfield

Arnold House
140 Franklin St.
HABS MA-2-35   s p   L

Fowler, Albert, Tobacco Barn; see Tobacco Barn

Tobacco Barn (Fowler, Albert, Tobacco Barn)
South St. Ext.
HABS MA-103   s p   L

HAMPSHIRE COUNTY

Amherst

Boltwood-Stockbridge House
University of Massachusetts Campus
HABS MA-636   pd   L

Strong, Nehemiah, House
67 Amity St.
HABS MA-650   pd   L

Hadley

Huntington House
(Porter-Phelps-Huntington House)
State Rt. 47
HABS MA-361   p   L

Keefe, John, Tobacco Barns; see Tobacco Barns

Porter, Samuel, House
West St.
HABS MA-2-53   s p   L

Porter Store, Old
Old Hadley St.
HABS MA-158   s p   L

Porter-Phelps-Huntington House; see Huntington House

Tobacco Barns (Keefe, John, Tobacco Barns)
Old Hadley St.
HABS MA-113   s p   L

Hatfield

Billings, Cornelia, House
HABS MA-454   p   L

Billings, Lieut. David, House
77 Main St.
HABS MA-166   s p   L

Morton House (Partridge, Cotton, House)
Bridge Ln. & Lower Main St.
HABS MA-2-73   s p   L

Partridge, Cotton, House; see Morton House

Northampton

Allen House
HABS MA-474   p   L

Damons, Isaac, House
46 Bridge St.
HABS MA-638   pd   L

Hubbard House; see Parsons, Lieut. William, House

Hunt-Brewster House
18 Old South St.
HABS MA-644   pd   L

Parsons, Lieut. William, House (Hubbard House)
392 Bridge St. (moved to CT, Darien)
HABS MA-188   s d   L

Pelham

Charcoal Kilns
Valley Rd.
HABS MA-2-72   s p   L

Prescott

Atkinson, John, Tavern
(moved to MA, Springfield vic.)
HABS MA-844   p   H

Enfield Road (Schoolhouse)
HABS MA-2-98   s p   L

Schoolhouse, Old Red
Cooleyville Rd.
HABS MA-193   s p   L

South Hadley

Woodbridge, Col. Ruggles, House
26 Woodbridge St.
HABS MA-180   s p   L

Wright House
96 College St.
HABS MA-182   s p   L

Westhampton

Hunt, Capt. Jared, House
HABS MA-413   p   L

Worthington

Woodbridge, Jonathan, House
Four Corners
HABS MA-124   s   L

MIDDLESEX COUNTY

Acton

Faulkner House
High St.
HABS MA-543   p   L

Arlington

Calvary Methodist Episcopal Church, Tower
Mass. Ave. (moved from Boylston Market, Boston)
HABS MA-589   p   L

Russell, Jason, House
7 Jason St. (moved from original site)
HABS MA-588   p   L
Schwamb Mill
17 Mill Ln.
HAER MA-12   s pd   L

Ashby

Fitch, John, House; see Kendall, Asa,
House
Kendall, Asa, House (Fitch, John, House)
South Rd.
HABS MA-230   s p   L

Ashland

Frankland, Sir Henry, Garden
Old Bay Path
HABS MA-202   s   L

Auburndale

Boston and Albany Railroad Station
HABS MA-665   pd   L

Bedford

Meetinghouse of First Parish (Unitarian)
HABS MA-538   p   L
Penniman-Stearns House (Stearns House)
State Rt. 62
HABS MA-592   p   L
Pollard Tavern
Great Rd.
HABS MA-142   s p   L
Stearns House; see Penniman-Stearns
House

Bedford vic.

Garrison House, Old
Bedford Springs
HABS MA-539   p   L

Billerica

Allen Tavern
HABS MA-528   p   L
Bowers, Dr. William, House
HABS MA-530   p   L
First Parish Unitarian Church
HABS MA-529   p   L
Locke, Hon. Joseph, House
HABS MA-531   p   L
Manning, Ensign Samuel, Manse
Chelmsford Rd.
HABS MA-532   p   L
Schoolhouse, Little Red
HABS MA-591   p   L

Burlington

Winn, William H., House
New Bridge Ave. & Winn St.
HABS MA-199   s p   L
Wyman, Francis, House
Francis Wyman Rd.
HABS MA-298   s p   L

456

Cambridge

Abbot, Edwin H., House (Longy School of
Music)
1 Follen St.
HABS MA-1037   pd   H
22 Appian Way (House)
HABS MA-782   p   L
Batchelder, Francis, House
467 Cambridge St.
HABS MA-884   pd   H
Bates, Moses, House
69 Thorndike St.
HABS MA-876   pd   H
Boyd, Orman T., House (Wood, Charles P.,
House)
33 Linnaean St.
HABS MA-880   pd   H
Brattle, Gen. William, House
42 Brattle St.
HABS MA-274   p   L
Cambridge City Hall
795 Massachusetts Ave.
HABS MA-1038   pd   H
Cambridge Junior College; see Kelley,
Stillman F., House
1667 Cambridge Street (Apartment House)
HABS MA-879   pd   H
Carey, Arthur Astor, House
28 Fayerweather St.
HABS MA-1039   pd   L
Christ Church
Garden St.
HABS MA-2-3   s p   L
Coburn, Sara, House
7 Dana St.
HABS MA-871   pd   H
Deane, Ezra, House (Williams-Deane
House)
21-23 Fayette St.
HABS MA-864   pd   H
Dodge, Edward S., House
70 Sparks St.
HABS MA-1015   pd   L
Eight-mile Stones (Milestones JJ, KK)
Mass. Ave. & Garden St.
HABS MA-128   s p   L
**Episcopal Theo. School, St. John's Mem.
Chapel**
99 Brattle St.
HABS MA-1016   d   H
**Episcopal Theological School, Burnham
Hall** (Episcopal Theological School, Old
Refectory)
99 Brattle St.
HABS MA-1137   d   H
**Episcopal Theological School, Old
Refectory;** see Episcopal Theological
School, Burnham Hall
Episcopal Theological School, Quadrangle
99 Brattle St.
HABS MA-1079   d   H

Episcopal Theological School, Reed Hall
99 Brattle St.
HABS MA-863   d   H
First Baptist Church
5 Magazine St.
HABS MA-1017   pd   H
First Evangelical Congregational Church
(Prospect Congregational Church;
Prospect Street Church)
99 Prospect St.
HABS MA-1030   pd   L
Fiske, John, House
22 Berkeley St.
HABS MA-1018   pd   L
Flagstaff Park
Mass. Ave. & Kirkland St.
HABS MA-999   pd   L H
Fort Washington
Waverly St.
HABS MA-2-48   s p   L
Garden House (Gray, Asa, House)
88 Garden St.
HABS MA-1019   d   H
Gray, Asa, House; see Garden House
Greenough House
42 Quincy St.
HABS MA-1020   pd   L
Guyot-Horsford House & Stable
27 Craigie St.
HABS MA-1021   pd   L
Harvard College, Holden Chapel
Harvard Yard
HABS MA-2-1   s p   L
Harvard College, Hollis Hall
Harvard Yard
HABS MA-2-2   s p   L
Harvard University, Dudley Hall (Harvard
University, The Dunster)
Dunster St.
HABS MA-818   pd   H
Harvard University, Lawrence Hall
3 Kirkland St.
HABS MA-1022   pd   L
Harvard University, The Dunster; see
Harvard University, Dudley Hall
Higginson, Stephen Jr., House
7 Kirkland St.
HABS MA-840   p   L
Higginson, Thomas Wentworth, House
29 Buckingham St.
HABS MA-1023   pd   L
Houghton, Amory, House
61 Otis St.
HABS MA-865   pd   L
Hoyt, Benjamin, House
134 Otis St.
HABS MA-866   pd   H
Hyatt, Alpheus, House
19 Francis St.
HABS MA-883   pd   H
Ireland, Abraham, Gravestone (Stone LL)
Mass. Ave. & Garden St.
HABS MA-128   p   L

James, William, House
95 Irving St.
HABS MA-1024   pd   L

Kelley, Stillman F., House (Cambridge
     Junior College)
49 Washington Ave.
HABS MA-1025   pd   L H

Longfellow House & Garden; see
     Vassall-Craigie-Longfellow House &
     Garden

Longy School of Music; see Abbot, Edwin
     H., House

MacKay, Frances M., House
10 Follen St.
HABS MA-1026   pd   L

Melendy, Henry, House
81 Washington Ave.
HABS MA-1027   pd   L

Middlesex County Jailer's House
50 Thorndike St.
HABS MA-873   pd   H

Middlesex County Registry of Deeds
Third & Cambridge Sts.
HABS MA-877   pd   H

Middlesex County Superior Court Building
Third, Otis & Thorndike Sts.
HABS MA-1028   d   H

Milestones JJ, KK; see Eight-mile Stones

MIT, Ashdown House; see Riverbank
     Court

Norton-Burleigh House (Norton-Johnson
     House)
85 Brattle St.
HABS MA-886   pd   H

Norton-Johnson House; see
     Norton-Burleigh House

Parsons, Sabra, House; see Parsons-Warner
     House

Parsons-Warner House (Parsons, Sabra,
     House; Radcliffe College, Warner House)
63 Garden St.
HABS MA-1029   pd   L

Prospect Congregational Church; see First
     Evangelical Congregational Church

Prospect Street Church; see First
     Evangelical Congregational Church

Radcliffe College, Warner House; see
     Parsons-Warner House

Riverbank Court (MIT, Ashdown House)
305 Memorial Drive
HABS MA-1031   pd   L

Saunders, Charles, House
1627 Massachusetts Ave.
HABS MA-870   pd   H

Sewall, Stephen, House
13 DeWolfe St.
HABS MA-618   s   L

Sparks, Jared, House (Treadwell-Sparks
     House)
48 Quincy St. (moved to Kirkland St.)
HABS MA-869   pd   H

84-92 Spring Street (Row Houses)
HABS MA-867   pd   H

St. James Church
1991 Massachusetts Ave.
HABS MA-1032   pd   L

Stevens, Atherton, House; see
     Stevens-Hovey House

Stevens-Hovey House (Stevens, Atherton,
     House)
75 Winter St.
HABS MA-885   pd   H

Stone LL; see Ireland, Abraham,
     Gravestone

Stoughton, Mary Fiske, House
90 Brattle St.
HABS MA-1033   pd   H

Taylor, Charles, House & Stable
1105 Massachusetts Ave.
HABS MA-1034   pd   L

Thorpe, Annie Longfellow, House
115 Brattle St.
HABS MA-875   pd   H

Treadwell-Sparks House; see Sparks, Jared,
     House

Valentine-Fuller House & Garden
125 Prospect St.
HABS MA-283   s pd   L

Van Brunt, Henry, House
167 Brattle St.
HABS MA-874   pd   H

**Vassall-Craigie-Longfellow House &
     Garden** (Longfellow House & Garden)
105 Brattle St.
HABS MA-169   s p   L

Watson, Daniel, House
5 Russell St.
HABS MA-868   pd   H

Welch-Ross House
24 Craigie St.
HABS MA-1035   pd   L

Whittemore, George Washington, House
329 Harvard St.
HABS MA-881   pd   L

Williams-Deane House; see Deane, Ezra,
     House

Wood, Charles P., House; see Boyd, Orman
     T., House

Wyeth-Allyn House
5 Berkeley St.
HABS MA-1036   d   H

Carlisle

Unitarian Church
HABS MA-537   p   L

Chelmsford

First Congregational Church
HABS MA-601   p   L

Fiske House
Littleton St. & Billerica Rd.
HABS MA-318   p   L

Concord

Alcott House; see Orchard House

Ball, Caleb, House; see Wayside, The

Bank Building, Old
Main St.
HABS MA-2-4   s p   L

Brooks, Samuel, House
Great North Rd. (State Rt. 2A)
HABS MA-819   s pd   H

Brown, Reuben, House; see Bulkeley, Peter,
     House

Bulkeley, Peter, House (Brown, Reuben,
     House)
27 Lexington Rd.
HABS MA-791   pd   H

Bullethole House (Jones-Keyes House)
26 Monument St.
HABS MA-555   p   L H

Buttrick, Maj. John, House
HABS MA-1146   s   H

Emerson, Rev. William, House; see Manse,
     Old

Hunt-Hosmer Barn
Lowell Rd.
HABS MA-821   s pd   H

Hunt-Hosmer House
Lowell Rd.
HABS MA-820   s pd   H

Jones-Keyes House; see Bullethole House

Manse, Old (Emerson, Rev. William,
     House)
Monument St.
HABS MA-554   pd   L H

Meriam House
Meriam's Corner
HABS MA-822   p   H

Orchard House (Alcott House)
Lexington Rd.
HABS MA-552   p   L

Stowe, Widow, House
Lexington Rd.
HABS MA-794   p   H

Taylor, Jacob, House
663 Lexington Rd.
HABS MA-792   s p   H

Wayside, The (Ball, Caleb, House;
     Whitney, Samuel, House)
Lexington Rd.
HABS MA-551   s pd   L H

Whitney, Samuel, House; see Wayside, The

Wright Tavern
2 Lexington Rd.
HABS MA-553   s p   L H

East Lexington

Building, Stone (Cary Memorial Library)
1874 Massachusetts Ave.
HABS MA-605   p   L

Cary Memorial Library; see Building, Stone

Follen Church (Unitarian) (Octagon
     Church)
HABS MA-590   p   L

Octagon Church; see Follen Church (Unitarian)

Framingham

Boston and Albany Railroad Station
Waverly St.
HABS MA-666   p d   L

Eames, Jonathan, House (House, Old Red)
Union Ave.
HABS MA-324   p   L

First Baptist Church & Carriage Shed
HABS MA-320   p   L

Framingham Academy
Vernon & Grove Sts.
HABS MA-2-16   s p   L

Gates House & Elm
Gates St.
HABS MA-286   p   L

House, Old Red; see Eames, Jonathan, House

Kellogg House
Kellogg St.
HABS MA-359   p   L

Milestones PP & XXX
HABS MA-128   p   L

Nixon, Col. Thomas, House
881 Edmands Rd.
HABS MA-247   p   L

Pike-Haven-Foster House
Grove & Belknap Sts.
HABS MA-616   s p   L

Framingham vic.

Howe-Gregory House
Wayside Inn Rd.
HABS MA-238   p   L

Groton

Groton School
HABS MA-1148   p   H

Prescott, Dr. Oliver, Milestones
Farmers Row & Main St.
HABS MA-203   s p   L

Robbins, Andrew, House
HABS MA-603   p   L

Lawrence

South Canal Bridge
South Broadway vic.
HAER MA-11   p   H

Lexington

Buckman Tavern
Bedford St.
HABS MA-547   p d   L H

Fiske, Ebenezer, House
Massachusetts Ave.
HABS MA-1149   s   H

Hancock-Clarke House
35 Hancock St.
HABS MA-549   s p   L H

Hargrove Barn
Massachusetts Ave.
HABS MA-1150   s   H

Harrington, Jonathan Jr., House
Elm & Bedford Sts.
HABS MA-548   p   L

Munroe Tavern
1332 Massachusetts Ave.
HABS MA-550   s p   L H

Robbins-Stone House
699 Massachusetts Ave.
HABS MA-609   s   L

Whittemore, Jacob, House
21 Marrett St.
HABS MA-823   s p d   H

Lincoln

Brooks, Daniel, House (Brooks-Conary House)
Brooks Rd.
HABS MA-824   s p d   H

Brooks, Joshua, House
Great North Rd. (State Rt. 2A)
HABS MA-825   s p d   H

Brooks Tavern (Hartwell-Rogers House)
Great North Rd. (State Rt. 2A)
HABS MA-826   s p d   H

Brooks-Conary House; see Brooks, Daniel, House

Brown, Nathan, House (Brown-Carley House)
Tower Road Ln.
HABS MA-827   s p   H

Brown-Carley House; see Brown, Nathan, House

Hartwell, Sgt. Samuel, House
Virginia Rd.
HABS MA-828   s p d   H

Hartwell Tavern
Virginia Rd.
HABS MA-829   s p d   H

Hartwell-Rogers House; see Brooks Tavern

Milestone WWW; see Sixteen-mile Stone

Nelson, John, Barn
Great North Rd. (State Rt. 2A)
HABS MA-831   s p   H

Nelson, John, House
Great North Rd. (State Rt. 2A)
HABS MA-830   s p d   H

Nelson, Josiah, House
Nelson Rd.
HABS MA-832   s p d   H

Old Concord Road (Barn)
HABS MA-793   p   H

Sixteen-mile Stone (Milestone WWW)
HABS MA-128   p   L

Smith, Capt. William, House
Virginia Rd.
HABS MA-833   s p   H

Lowell

Boott & Massachusetts Cotton Mills, Agent's House (Child, Linus, House)
63-67 Kirk St.
HABS MA-996   p d   H

Bowers, Jarathmael, House & Barns
HABS MA-525   p   L

Brick Block
Dutton St.
HABS MA-1151   p   H

Child, Linus, House; see Boott & Massachusetts Cotton Mills, Agent's House

City Hall
HABS MA-1152   p   H

City Hall, Old
Merrimack St.
HABS MA-995   s d   H

Lowell Canal & Lock System
Merrimack & Concord Rivers
HAER MA-1   s p d   H

Lowell Canal System, Eastern Canal
Bridge & Armory Sts. vic.
HAER MA-7   p   H

Lowell Canal System, Hamilton Canal
Jackson St. vic.
HAER MA-4   p   H

Lowell Canal System, Lawrence Canal
HAER MA-6   p   H

Lowell Canal System, Moody Street Feeder
Moody St. vic.
HAER MA-9   p   H

Lowell Canal System, Northern Canal
Pawtucket & Ford Sts. vic.
HAER MA-8   s   H

Lowell Canal System, Pawtucket Canal
Pawtucket Falls vic.
HAER MA-2   p   H

Lowell Canal System, Pawtucket Canal, Swamp Locks
Revere St. vic.
HAER MA-2-B   s p   H

Lowell Canal System, Western Canal
Suffolk St. vic.
HAER MA-5   p   H

Middlesex Canal, Canal Office
Middlesex Village   •
HABS MA-380-A   p   L

New Block
Dutton St.
HABS MA-1153   p   H

Tenement House
Chelmsford Glass Works
HABS MA-327   p   L

Whistler, James Abbott McNeill, Birthplace
243 Worthen St.
HABS MA-526   p   L

Lowell-Somerville

Middlesex Canal
From Merrimack River to Boston Harbor
HABS MA-380   p   L

Malden

City Hall, Old; see Malden Town Hall

Five-mile Stone (Milestone AAA)
Newburyport Turnpike
HABS MA-128   p   L

Malden Town Hall (City Hall, Old)
Main & Pleasant Sts.
HABS MA-979   p d   L

Milestone AAA; see Five-mile Stone

Medford

Blanchard, George, House
18 Bradbury Ave.
HABS MA-2-5   s p   L
Hall, Andrew, House
45 High St.
HABS MA-159   s p   L
Hall, Benjamin Jr., House
57 High St.
HABS MA-2-56   s p   L
Hall, Ebenezer, House
49 High St.
HABS MA-261   s p   L
Lawrence Farmhouse
353 Lawrence Rd.
HABS MA-246   s   L
Magoun, Thatcher, House
117 High St.
HABS MA-194   s p   L
Middlesex Canal, Stone Bridge
HABS MA-380-B   p   L
Osgood, Rev. David, House
141 High St.
HABS MA-111   s p   L
Royal, Col. Isaac, House (Forecourt Fence)
    (Usher-Royall House (Forecourt Fence))
Main St.
HABS MA-130-A   s   L
Royall, Col. Isaac, Garden House
    (Usher-Royall Garden House)
Main St. vic.
HABS MA-129   s p   L
Royall, Col. Isaac, Slave Quarters
    (Usher-Royall Slave Quarters)
15 George St.
HABS MA-130   s p   L
Sawyer, Nathan, Cottage
306 Riverside Ave.
HABS MA-219   s p   L
Usher-Royall Garden House; see Royall,
    Col. Isaac, Garden House
Usher-Royall House (Forecourt Fence); see
    Royal, Col. Isaac, House (Forecourt
    Fence)
Usher-Royall Slave Quarters; see Royall,
    Col. Isaac, Slave Quarters

Melrose

Lynde, Ensign Thomas, House
HABS MA-464   p   L
Upham, Phineas, House
253 Upham St.
HABS MA-489   s p   L

Natick

Wilson, Henry, Shoe Shop
W. Central & Mill Sts.
HABS MA-176   s p   L

Newton

Boston & Albany Railroad Station
1897 Washington St.
HABS MA-667   pd   L

Crehore Paper Mill
375 Elliot St.
HABS MA-545   p   L
Jackson, Timothy, House & Garden
527 Washington St.
HABS MA-139   s p   L
Kenrick House
302 Waverly Ave.
HABS MA-387   p   L
Mill House Number 1
Chestnut St.
HABS MA-388-A   p   L
Mill House Number 2
Chestnut St.
HABS MA-388-B   p   L
Mill House Number 3
Sullivan Ave.
HABS MA-388-C   p   L
Mill House Number 4
Chestnut St.
HABS MA-388-D   p   L
Mill House Number 5
Chestnut St.
HABS MA-388-E   p   L
St. Mary's Episcopal Church
HABS MA-389   p   L
Three Mill Houses
Chestnut St. & Sullivan Ave.
HABS MA-388   p   L
Woodward, John, House
238 Woodward St.
HABS MA-146   s p   L
Wyman-Tower House
401 Woodward St.
HABS MA-147   s p   L

North Billerica

Middlesex Canal
HABS MA-380-C   p   L

North Pepperell

District School Number 4
North & Prescott Sts.
HABS MA-222   s   L

North Reading

Crosby, Guy M. Jr., House
HABS MA-523   p   L

North Woburn

Bartlett, Joseph, House; see
    Bartlett-Wheeler House
Bartlett-Wheeler House (Bartlett, Joseph,
    House)
827 Main St.
HABS MA-276   p   L
Middlesex Canal
School St.
HABS MA-380-D   p   L
Rumford, Count, Birthplace (House &
    Garden) (Thompson, Benjamin, House &
    Garden)
90 Elm St.
HABS MA-240   s p   L

Thompson, Benjamin, House & Garden;
    see Rumford, Count, Birthplace (House
    & Garden)

Pepperell

Jewett, Nehemiah, Bridge
Groton St., spanning Nashua River
HABS MA-225   s p   L
Prescott, Col. William, House
HABS MA-604   p   L

Reading

Bryant, Abram Jr., House; see Parker
    Tavern
Parker Tavern (Bryant, Abram Jr., House)
Washington St.
HABS MA-522   p   L

Sherborn

Leland, Deacon William, House
HABS MA-402   p   L

Shirley

First Parish Meetinghouse
HABS MA-540   p   L
Pound, Stone
HABS MA-541   p   L

Somerville

Lee, Maj. Gen., Headquarters; see Tufts,
    Oliver, House
Powder House, Old
Broadway & College Ave.
HABS MA-178   s p   L
Round House
HABS MA-501   p   L
Tufts, Francis, House
HABS MA-403   p   L
Tufts, Oliver, House (Lee, Maj. Gen.,
    Headquarters)
78 Sycamore St. (moved from original site)
HABS MA-404   p   L

South Pepperell vic.

Coburn's Tavern
State Rt. 119
HABS MA-226   s   L

South Sudbury

Howe's Tavern; see Wayside Inn
Red Horse Tavern; see Wayside Inn
Wayside Inn (Howe's Tavern; Red Horse
    Tavern)
Old Boston Post Rd. (U.S. Rt. 20)
HABS MA-632   p   L

Stoneham

First Congregational Church
HABS MA-593   p   L
Green, Jonathan, House
HABS MA-527   p   L

Townsend

Conant House
HABS MA-536   p   L
Methodist Episcopal Church
HABS MA-533   p   L

459

Spaulding Cooperage Shop
HABS MA-535   p   L
Spaulding Grist Mill
HABS MA-534   p   L

Tyngsborough
Brinley-O'Neill House
HABS MA-409   p   L
School Number 2
HABS MA-602   p   L
Tyng House
HABS MA-410   p   L

Wakefield
Hartshorne, Col. James, House
41 Church St.
HABS MA-521   p   L

Waltham
Gore, Gov. Christopher, Garden
Gore St.
HABS MA-210-A   s p   L
Gore, Gov. Christopher, Mansion
Gore St.
HABS MA-210   s   L
Lyman, Theodore, House (Garden & Summerhouse); see Vale, The (Garden & Summerhouse)
Mill, Stone
South St.
HABS MA-502   p   L
Vale, The (Garden & Summerhouse)
(Lyman, Theodore, House (Garden & Summerhouse))
Beaver St.
HABS MA-204   s p   L

Watertown
Bemis, John, House
425 Main St.
HABS MA-131   s p   L
Brown, Abraham, House
562 Main St.
HABS MA-781   p   L
Caldwell, Daniel, House
126 Main St.
HABS MA-132   s p   L
Conant House
HABS MA-494   p   L
Watertown Arsenal
Arsenal St.
HABS MA-974   p   H
Watertown Arsenal, Building Number 141
(Watertown Arsenal, Guardhouse; Watertown Redevelopment Authority Building)
463 Arsenal St.
HABS MA-1009   pd   L
Watertown Arsenal, Building Number 152
Arsenal St.
HABS MA-1010   p   H
Watertown Arsenal, Guardhouse; see Watertown Arsenal, Building Number 141

Watertown Redevelopment Authority Building; see Watertown Arsenal, Building Number 141

Wayland
Milestones MM, NN & OO
Various Wayland locations
HABS MA-128   p   L
Town Bridge, Old
Spanning Sudbury River
HABS MA-2-75   s p   L

West Medford
Brooks, Capt. Caleb, House; see Brooks Farmhouse
Brooks Farmhouse (Brooks, Capt. Caleb, House)
24 Woburn St.
HABS MA-229   s p   L
Brooks, Jonathan, House
Woburn & High Sts.
HABS MA-144   s p   L

Weston
Fiske, Isaac, Law Office (Lawyer's Office)
Central Ave.
HABS MA-2-34   s p   L
Golden Ball Tavern
662 Central Ave.
HABS MA-414   p   L
Lamson House
HABS MA-495   p   L
Lawyer's Office; see Fiske, Isaac, Law Office

Wilmington
Middlesex Canal, Lock-keeper's House
Gillis Lock, Shawsheen Ave.
HABS MA-380-F   p   L
Middlesex Canal, Lubber Brook Aqueduct
HABS MA-380-G   p   L
Middlesex Canal, Maple Meadow Brook Aqueduct
HABS MA-380-H   p   L
Middlesex Canal, Nichols Lock
Nichols St.
HABS MA-380-I   p   L

Wilmington-Billerica
Middlesex Canal, Shawsheen Aqueduct
HABS MA-380-E   p   L

Woburn
Baldwin, Col. Loammi, Mansion
Elm St.
HABS MA-419   p   L
Horn Pond Tavern
HABS MA-578   p   L

NANTUCKET COUNTY

Nantucket
African Society Baptist Church
York St.
HABS MA-909   s pd   L

Ayers, Lawrence, House; see Orange & Union Streets Neighborhood Study
Barker, Francis, House; see Orange & Union Streets Neighborhood Study
Barnard, John, House
84 Main St.
HABS MA-1105   s   L
Barrett, John Wendell, House (Wallace Hall)
72 Main St.
HABS MA-915   pd   L
Baxter, Capt. Reuben, House; see India Street Neighborhood Study
Beard, John, House; see Orange & Union Streets Neighborhood Study
Beard, Matthew, House; see Orange & Union Streets Neighborhood Study
Beebe, Nathan, House; see Orange & Union Streets Neighborhood Study
Big Shop, The; see Folger, Charles & Hiram, Shop
Blackburn, Elizabeth, House; see Orange & Union Streets Neighborhood Study
Breakers, The
HABS MA-970   p   H
Brock, Major, House; see India Street Neighborhood Study
Bunker, Andrew House; see India Street Neighborhood Study
Bunker, Joshua, House; see Orange & Union Streets Neighborhood Study
Bunker, Reuben R., House
Academy Hill
HABS MA-916   pd   L
Bunker, Tristram, House
3 Bear St.
HABS MA-900   s pd   L
Candle Factory; see Starbuck, Joseph, House
Carroll House; see India Street Neighborhood Study
Cary, Capt. Nathaniel, House; see Orange & Union Streets Neighborhood Study
Cary, Edward, House
117 Main St.
HABS MA-855   pd   L
Centre Street United Methodist Church
Centre & Main Sts.
HABS MA-1007   s pd   L
Chase, Abel, House; see Orange & Union Streets Neighborhood Study
Chase, Isaac, House; see Orange & Union Streets Neighborhood Study
Clapp, Timothy G., House; see Orange & Union Streets Neighborhood Study
Codd, James, House; see Orange & Union Streets Neighborhood Study
Coffin, Daniel, House; see India Street Neighborhood Study
Coffin, Henry, House
75 Main St.
HABS MA-811   s pd   L

Coffin, Jared, House (Ocean House)
29 Broad St.
HABS MA-918   pd   L
Coffin, Jared, House; see Moor's End
Coffin, Jethro, House (Oldest House)
Sunset Hill
HABS MA-919   pd   L
Coffin, Joshua, House
52 Centre St.
HABS MA-920   s pd   L
Coffin, Maj. Josiah, House
60 Cliff Rd.
HABS MA-911   s pd   L
Coffin, Thaddeus, House
89 Main St.
HABS MA-921   pd   L
Coffin-Athearn Stores
2 Union St.
HABS MA-906   s pd   L
Coffin-Gardner House
33 Milk St.
HABS MA-854   s pd   L
Coggeshall, Benjamin, House; see Orange
    & Union Streets Neighborhood Study
Coggeshall, Peleg, House; see Orange &
    Union Streets Neighborhood Study
Coleman, Elihu, House
Hawthorne Ln.
HABS MA-2-86   s pd   L
Coleman, Richard, House
21 Union St.
HABS MA-904   s pd   L
2nd Congregational Meetinghouse Society
    Church; see Orange & Union Streets
    Neighborhood Study
Daggett, Margaret Gardner, House
    (Sevenfires)
111 Main St.
HABS MA-922   pd   L
Dickie House; see McCleave-Dickie House
Dunham House; see India Street
    Neighborhood Study
East Mill; see Windmill, Old
Easton-Joy House (Joy, Obed, House)
4 N. Water St.
HABS MA-957   p   L
Easton-Wood House; see Wood, Charles,
    House
Eighteen-Hundred House
4 Mill St.
HABS MA-1102   s   L
Ewer, Silvanus, House; see Orange &
    Union Streets Neighborhood Study
First Congregational Church
62 Centre St.
HABS MA-902   s pd   L
First Congregational Church (North
    Vestry)
Beacon Hill
HABS MA-903   s pd   L
Fish Shanties
Old South Wharf
HABS MA-853   pd   L

Folger Block
56 & 58 Main St.
HABS MA-949   pd   L
Folger, Charles & Hiram, Shop (Big Shop,
    The)
35 Milk St.
HABS MA-923   pd   L
Folger, Peter, House
51 Centre St.
HABS MA-924   pd   L
Folger, Robert, House; see India Street
    Neighborhood Study
Folger, Seth, House; see Orange & Union
    Streets Neighborhood Study
Gaol, Old
Vestal St. (moved from original site)
HABS MA-120   s p   L
Gardner, Barnabas, House
153 Main St.
HABS MA-925   pd   L
Gardner, Benjamin, Store; see Holmes &
    Wyer Carpenters' Shop
Gardner, George, House
8 Pine St.
HABS MA-858   pd   L
Gardner, Grindell, House
30 Hussey St.
HABS MA-927   pd   L
Gardner, Richard, House
139 Main St.
HABS MA-955   pd   L
Gardner, Richard Jr., House
32 W. Chester St.
HABS MA-839   pd   L
Gardner, Sally Beard, House; see Orange &
    Union Streets Neighborhood Study
Gardner, Silas, House
21 Milk St.
HABS MA-928   pd   L
Gardner, Solomon & Paul, House; see
    Orange & Union Streets Neighborhood
    Study
Gorham, Josiah, House; see Orange &
    Union Streets Neighborhood Study
Great Point Lighthouse
Great Point
HABS MA-969   s pd   L
Green, Elisha, House; see Orange & Union
    Streets Neighborhood Study
Hadwen & Barney Candle House (Whaling
    Museum)
Broad & South Sts.
HABS MA-907   s pd   L
Hadwen, William, House (Satler
    Memorial)
96 Main St.
HABS MA-929   s pd   L
Hadwen-Wright House
94 Main St.
HABS MA-905   s pd   L
Holland House; see India Street
    Neighborhood Study

Holmes & Wyer Carpenters' Shop
    (Gardner, Benjamin, Store)
Straight Wharf
HABS MA-913   s pd   L
Hussey, Charles F., House; see India Street
    Neighborhood Study
Hussey, Christopher, House
12 Orange St.
HABS MA-1101   s   L
Hussey, Christopher, House; see Orange &
    Union Streets Neighborhood Study
Hussey, Eliab, House; see India Street
    Neighborhood Study
19 Hussey Street (House)
HABS MA-195   s p   L
Hussey, Zaccheus, House; see India Street
    Neighborhood Study
India House; see India Street Neighborhood
    Study
India Street Neighborhood Study (Folger,
    Robert, House)
27 India St.
HABS MA-1049   pd   L
India Street Neighborhood Study (Hussey,
    Eliab, House; Dunham House)
31 India St.
HABS MA-1047   pd   L
India Street Neighborhood Study (Baxter,
    Capt. Reuben, House)
23 India St.
HABS MA-1051   pd   L
India Street Neighborhood Study (Hussey,
    Zaccheus, House)
19 India St.
HABS MA-1053   pd   L
India Street Neighborhood Study (Macy,
    Gorham, House; Holland House)
39 India St.
HABS MA-1043   pd   L
India Street Neighborhood Study (Bunker,
    Andrew House)
41 India St.
HABS MA-1042   pd   L
India Street Neighborhood Study
15-45 India St.
HABS MA-1013   s pd   L
India Street Neighborhood Study (Swift,
    Benjamin, House)
29 India St.
HABS MA-1048   pd   L
India Street Neighborhood Study (Wood,
    Obediah, House)
17 India St.
HABS MA-1054   pd   L
India Street Neighborhood Study
    (Lawrence, George, House; Snow House)
35 India St.
HABS MA-1045   pd   L
India Street Neighborhood Study (Russell,
    John, House; Brock, Major, House)
33 India St.
HABS MA-1046   pd   L

India Street Neighborhood Study (Nye, Meletiah, House; Carroll House)
43 India St.
HABS MA-1041   pd   L

India Street Neighborhood Study (Stubbs, Capt. William, House)
15 India St.
HABS MA-1055   pd   L

India Street Neighborhood Study (Coffin, Daniel, House)
25 India St.
HABS MA-1050   pd   L

India Street Neighborhood Study (Hussey, Charles F., House; India House)
37 India St.
HABS MA-1044   pd   L

India Street Neighborhood Study (Swain, John Howland, House)
21 India St.
HABS MA-1052   pd   L

India Street Neighborhood Study (Taber, Rescom, House; Joy, Captain, House)
45 India St.
HABS MA-1040   pd   L

Jones, Capt. Silas, House
5 Orange St.
HABS MA-956   pd   L

Joy, Captain, House; see India Street Neighborhood Study

Joy, Obed, House; see Easton-Joy House

Joy, Reuben, House; see Macy, Zaccheus, House

Lawrence, George, House; see India Street Neighborhood Study

Leaded-Glass Fixed Window from a Nantucket House
Fair St. Museum
HABS MA-856   s   H

Lower Main Street, South Side (Buildings)
12 & 14 Main St.
HABS MA-954   pd   H

Macy, Francis, House
77 Main St.
HABS MA-931   pd   L

Macy, Gorham, House; see India Street Neighborhood Study

Macy, Job, House
11 Mill St.
HABS MA-932   s pd   L

Macy, Nathaniel, House
12 Liberty St.
HABS MA-1003   s pd   L

Macy, Thomas, Warehouse
Straight Wharf
HABS MA-914   s pd   L

Macy, William F., House; see Orange & Union Streets Neighborhood Study

Macy, Zaccheus, House (Joy, Reuben, House)
107 Main St.
HABS MA-934   pd   L

17-57 Main Street (Commercial Buildings)
HABS MA-952   pd   L

Main Street, South Side (Buildings)
18-54 Main St.
HABS MA-950   pd   L

Masonic Lodge; see Union Lodge, F. & A. M.

McCleave-Dickie House (Dickie House)
1 Weymouth St.
HABS MA-1099   s   L

Meridian Stones (Mitchell, William, Meridian Stones)
Main & Fair Sts.
HABS MA-183   s   L

Mitchell, Frederick, House
69 Main St.
HABS MA-936   pd   L

Mitchell, Maria, House; see Swain-Mitchell House

Mitchell, William, Meridian Stones; see Meridian Stones

Mooers, Lucinda, Homestead; see Orange & Union Streets Neighborhood Study

Moor's End (Coffin, Jared, House)
19 Pleasant St.
HABS MA-917   pd   L

Myrick, Andrew, House; see Orange & Union Streets Neighborhood Study

Nantucket Atheneum
Lower India & Federal Sts.
HABS MA-812   s pd   L

Nantucket Island, Aerial Views
HABS MA-1155   p   H

Nantucket Lodge No. 66, I. O. O. F.
7-21 Centre St.
HABS MA-908   s pd   L

Nantucket Looms, The
16 Main St.
HABS MA-951   pd   L

Nantucket Urban History Study
HABS MA-1157   p   H

Nichols, William, House; see Orange & Union Streets Neighborhood Study

Nye, Meletiah, House; see India Street Neighborhood Study

Ocean House; see Coffin, Jared, House

Oldest House; see Coffin, Jethro, House

Orange & Union Streets Neighborhood Study (Pierce, Easton, Russell, Bunker & Gardner Houses; Orange Street Block)
15, 17, 19, 21 & 23 Orange St.
HABS MA-947   s pd   L

Orange & Union Streets Neighborhood Study (Beebe, Nathan, House)
11 Union St.
HABS MA-1057   pd   L

Orange & Union Streets Neighborhood Study (Folger, Seth, House)
26 Orange St.
HABS MA-1072   pd   L

Orange & Union Streets Neighborhood Study (Gorham, Josiah, House; Blackburn, Elizabeth, House)
29 Orange St.
HABS MA-1074   pd   L

Orange & Union Streets Neighborhood Study (Coggeshall, Benjamin, House)
8 Orange St.
HABS MA-1062   pd   L

Orange & Union Streets Neighborhood Study (Bunker, Joshua, House; Snelling, Rev. Samuel, House)
25 Orange St.
HABS MA-1071   pd   L

Orange & Union Streets Neighborhood Study (Upton, George B., House)
2 Stone Alley
HABS MA-1077   pd   L

Orange & Union Streets Neighborhood Study (Gardner, Solomon & Paul, House)
1 & 3 Stone Alley
HABS MA-1076   pd   L

Orange & Union Streets Neighborhood Study (Green, Elisha, House)
9 Union St.
HABS MA-1056   pd   L

Orange & Union Streets Neighborhood Study (Macy, William F., House)
31 Orange St.
HABS MA-1075   pd   L

Orange & Union Streets Neighborhood Study (Coggeshall, Peleg, House; Cary, Capt. Nathaniel, House)
10 Orange St.
HABS MA-1063   pd   L

Orange & Union Streets Neighborhood Study (Tupper-Folger House; Tupper, Benjamin, House)
28 Orange St.
HABS MA-1073   pd   L

Orange & Union Streets Neighborhood Study (Barker, Francis, House)
13 Union St.
HABS MA-1058   pd   L

Orange & Union Streets Neighborhood Study (Beard, Matthew, House; Gardner, Sally Beard, House)
18 Orange St.
HABS MA-1068   pd   L

Orange & Union Streets Neighborhood Study (Chase, Isaac, House; Chase, Abel, House)
14 1/2 Orange St.
HABS MA-1066   pd   L

Orange & Union Streets Neighborhood Study (2nd Congregational Meetinghouse Society Church; Unitarian Church)
Orange St.
HABS MA-838   s pd   L

Orange & Union Streets Neighborhood Study (Hussey, Christopher, House)
12 Orange St.
HABS MA-1064   pd   L

Orange & Union Streets Neighborhood Study
8-31 Orange St., 9-21 Union St., Stone Alley
HABS MA-1014   s pd   L H

Orange & Union Streets Neighborhood Study (Beard, John, House; Mooers, Lucinda, Homestead)
20 Orange St.
HABS MA-1069   pd   L

Orange & Union Streets Neighborhood Study (Nichols, William, House; Clapp, Timothy G., House)
HABS MA-1059   pd   L

Orange & Union Streets Neighborhood Study (West, Joseph, House)
17 Union St.
HABS MA-1060   pd   L

Orange & Union Streets Neighborhood Study (Starbuck, Levi, House; Codd, James, House)
14 Orange St.
HABS MA-912   s pd   L

Orange & Union Streets Neighborhood Study (Myrick, Andrew, House)
16 Orange St.
HABS MA-1067   pd   L

Orange & Union Streets Neighborhood Study (Pinkham, Henry, House; Ayers, Lawrence, House)
13 Orange St.
HABS MA-1065   pd   L

Orange & Union Streets Neighborhood Study (Woodbury, Nathaniel, House)
22 Orange St.
HABS MA-1070   pd   L

Orange & Union Streets Neighborhood Study (Ewer, Silvanus, House)
19 Union St.
HABS MA-1061   pd   L

Orange Street Block; see Orange & Union Streets Neighborhood Study

Pacific Club; see Rotch, William, Warehouse

Pacific National Bank
Main, Centre & Liberty Sts.
HABS MA-938   pd   L

Pierce, Easton, Russell, Bunker & Gardner Houses; see Orange & Union Streets Neighborhood Study

Pinkham, Henry, House; see Orange & Union Streets Neighborhood Study

Raymond-Coleman House
53 Orange St.
HABS MA-837   pd   L

Rotch, William, Warehouse (Pacific Club)
Main & South Water Sts.
HABS MA-836   s pd   L

Russell, John, House; see India Street Neighborhood Study

Sandanwede
79 Hulbert Ave.
HABS MA-968   pd   L H

Sanford, Frederick C., Garden
Federal, Broad & Water Sts.
HABS MA-162   s   L

Satler Memorial; see Hadwen, William, House

Sea Cliff Inn
31 Cliff Rd.
HABS MA-967   pd   L

Sevenfires; see Daggett, Margaret Gardner, House

Snelling, Rev. Samuel, House; see Orange & Union Streets Neighborhood Study

Snow House; see India Street Neighborhood Study

Society of Friends Meetinghouse
Fair St.
HABS MA-966   s pd   L

Star of the Sea Youth Hostel
Western Ave.
HABS MA-1100   s   L

Starbuck, Christopher, House
105 Main St.
HABS MA-939   pd   L

Starbuck, Joseph, House (Candle Factory)
4 New Dollar Ln.
HABS MA-940   pd   L

Starbuck, Joseph, Houses (Three Bricks, The)
93, 95, & 97 Main St.
HABS MA-941   pd   L

Starbuck, Levi, House; see Orange & Union Streets Neighborhood Study

Starbuck, Thomas, Homestead
11 Milk St.
HABS MA-942   pd   L

Starbuck-Newhouse House
15 Liberty St.
HABS MA-1103   s   L

Stubbs, Capt. William, House; see India Street Neighborhood Study

Swain House
3 Weymouth St.
HABS MA-1098   s   L

Swain, John Howland, House; see India Street Neighborhood Study

Swain-Macy House (Valentine-Swain House)
99 Main St.
HABS MA-944   pd   L

Swain-Mitchell House (Mitchell, Maria, House)
1 Vestal St.
HABS MA-901   s pd   L

Swift, Benjamin, House; see India Street Neighborhood Study

Swift, Henry, House (Garden)
91 Main St.
HABS MA-167   s   L

Taber, Rescom, House; see India Street Neighborhood Study

Tashama Farm
Surfside Rd.
HABS MA-943   pd   L

Three Bricks, The; see Starbuck, Joseph, Houses

Tupper, Benjamin, House; see Orange & Union Streets Neighborhood Study

Tupper-Folger House; see Orange & Union Streets Neighborhood Study

Union Lodge, F. & A. M. (Masonic Lodge)
63 Main St.
HABS MA-899   pd   L

Unitarian Church; see Orange & Union Streets Neighborhood Study

Upton, George B., House; see Orange & Union Streets Neighborhood Study

U.S. Lifesaving Station
Surfside
HABS MA-930   pd   L

Valentine-Swain House; see Swain-Macy House

Wallace Hall; see Barrett, John Wendell, House

Wellington-Merrill House
27 Hulbert Ave.
HABS MA-1104   s   L

West, Joseph, House; see Orange & Union Streets Neighborhood Study

Whaling Museum; see Hadwen & Barney Candle House

Windmill, Old (East Mill)
N. Mill & S. Mill Sts.
HABS MA-141   s p   L

Wood, Charles, House (Easton-Wood House)
1 North Water St.
HABS MA-898   s pd   L

Wood, Obediah, House; see India Street Neighborhood Study

Woodbury, Nathaniel, House; see Orange & Union Streets Neighborhood Study

Wyer, Robert, House
33 Orange St.
HABS MA-946   pd   L

Yard Fences and Porch Newels
Nantucket County
HABS MA-614   s   L

Siasconset

Auld Lang Syne; see Coffin, Micah, House

Baxter, Capt. William, House; see Shanunga

Cary, Betsey, Cottage; see Shanunga

Coffin, Micah, House (Auld Lang Syne; Coleman, Capt. Henry, House)
Broadway
HABS MA-857   s pd   L

Coleman, Capt. Henry, House; see Coffin, Micah, House

Shanunga (Cary, Betsey, Cottage; Baxter, Capt. William, House)
Mitchell St. (moved from original location)
HABS MA-610   s pd   L

NORFOLK COUNTY

Attleboro-plainville

Angle Tree Stone
Town Line
HABS MA-181   s p   L

Braintree

Milestone J; see Twelve-mile Stone

Twelve-mile Stone (Milestone J)
Commercial St.
HABS MA-128   p   L

Brookline

John F. Kennedy National Historic Site;
    see Kennedy, John Fitzgerald, Birthplace

Kennedy, John Fitzgerald, Birthplace
    (John F. Kennedy National Historic Site)
83 Beals St.
HABS MA-897   s p   H

Milestones GG & OOO
Various Brookline locations
HABS MA-128   s p   L

O'Gorman, Lynch, House
41 Mason Terrace
HABS MA-959   p   H

Canton

Milestones L, M, N & O
Washington St.
HABS MA-128   p   L

Cohasset

Cushing-Nichols House
HABS MA-350   p   L

First Parish Meetinghouse
Cohasset Common
HABS MA-349   p   L

Fitch House
HABS MA-598   p   L

Hobart, Rev. Nehemiah, House
HABS MA-351   p   L

Shaw-Souther House
Highland Ave.
HABS MA-231   s   L

Dedham

Allin Congregational Church
High St.
HABS MA-568   p   L

Dedham Inn; see Richards, Edward M.,
    House

Fairbanks, Jonathan, House
511 East St.
HABS MA-223   s p d   L H

Fisher-Whiting House
218 Cedar St.
HABS MA-114   s p   L

Haven, Samuel, House
669 High St.
HABS MA-567   p   L

Lovell, John M., House; see Richards,
    Edward M., House

Powder House
162 Ames St.
HABS MA-2-66   s p   L

Richards, Edward M., House (Lovell, John
    M., House; Dedham Inn)
Highland Ave.
HABS MA-258   s p d   L

Dover

Caryl Parsonage
Dedham St.
HABS MA-357   p   L

Chickering House
HABS MA-566   p   L

First Parish Meetinghouse
Springdale Ave.
HABS MA-565   p   L

Wentworth, Col. Paul, House
(moved from NH, Salmon Falls)
HABS NH-35   s p d   L

Franklin

Schoolhouse, Little Red Brick
HABS MA-450   p   L

Medfield

Clark, Seth, House; see Peak House, The
Peak House, The (Clark, Seth, House)
Main St.
HABS MA-2-77   s p   L

Milton

Belcher, Gov. Jonathan, House & Garden
401 Adams St.
HABS MA-196   s p   L

Davenport, Isaac, House
HABS MA-465   p   L

Forbes, Capt. Robert Bennett, House
    (Forbes Museum)
215 Adams St.
HABS MA-975   p   H

Forbes Museum; see Forbes, Capt. Robert
    Bennett, House

Holbrook, Dr. Amos, Garden
203 Adams St.
HABS MA-232   s   L

Howe, Joseph N., House
597 Randolph Ave.
HABS MA-138   s p   L

**Hutchinson, Gov. Thomas, House &
    Garden**
195 Adams St.
HABS MA-168   s p   L

Hutchinson, Gov. Thomas, House (Wing)
195 Adams St.
HABS MA-168-A   s p   L

Milestones C, F, G, K, FFF & JJJ
Various Milton locations
HABS MA-128   s p   L

Powder House
781 Canton Ave.
HABS MA-2-66-A   s p   L

Shepard-Hinckley House
264 Brook Rd.
HABS MA-613   s   L

Suffolk Resolves House; see Vose, Daniel,
    House

Vose, Daniel, House (Suffolk Resolves
    House)
1370 Canton Ave. (moved from 38 Adams
    St.)
HABS MA-2-13   s p   L

Plainville

Slack, Benjamin, House
South St.
HABS MA-155   s p   L

Quincy

Adams, John, Birthplace
133 Franklin St.
HABS MA-596   s p   L H

Adams, John Quincy, Birthplace
141 Franklin St.
HABS MA-597   s p   L H

Adams Mansion (Adams National Historic
    Site; Vassal-Adams House; House, Old)
135 Adams St.
HABS MA-615   s p d   L H

Adams Mansion, Doghouse (Adams
    National Historic Site, Doghouse;
    Vassal-Adams House, Doghouse; House,
    Old-Doghouse)
135 Adams St.
HABS MA-994   s   H

Adams Mansion, Flower Garden (Adams
    National Historic Site, Flower Garden;
    Vassal-Adams House, Flower Garden;
    House, Old-Flower Garden)
135 Adams St.
HABS MA-1158   s   L H

Adams Mansion, Stone Library (Adams
    National Historic Site, Stone Library;
    Vassal-Adams House, Stone Library;
    House, Old-Stone Library)
135 Adams St.
HABS MA-841   s p   H

Adams Mansion, Woodshed (Adams
    National Historic Site, Woodshed;
    Vassal-Adams House, Woodshed; House,
    Old-Woodshed)
135 Adams St.
HABS MA-842   s   H

Adams National Historic Site; see Adams
    Mansion

Adams National Historic Site, Doghouse;
    see Adams Mansion, Doghouse

**Adams National Historic Site, Flower
    Garden;** see Adams Mansion, Flower
    Garden

**Adams National Historic Site, Stone
    Library;** see Adams Mansion, Stone
    Library

Adams National Historic Site, Woodshed;
    see Adams Mansion, Woodshed

Blue Bell Tavern; see Railroad House, Old

Church of the Presidents; see Stone Temple

Granite Railway
Pine Hill Quarry to Neponset River
HABS MA-150   s p   L

House, Old; see Adams Mansion

House, Old-Doghouse; see Adams Mansion,
    Doghouse

House, Old-Flower Garden; see Adams
    Mansion, Flower Garden

House, Old-Stone Library; see Adams
    Mansion, Stone Library

House, Old-Woodshed; see Adams
Mansion, Woodshed
Milestones H, I, CCC, DDD & EEE
Various Quincy locations
HABS MA-128   s p   L
Quincy, Col. Josiah, House
20 Muirhead St.
HABS MA-2-42   s p   L
Railroad House, Old (Blue Bell Tavern)
Granite Railway
HABS MA-150-A   s p   L
Stone, Temple (Unitarian Church; Church
of the Presidents)
1266 Hancock St.
HABS MA-599   p   L
Unitarian Church; see Stone Temple
Vassal-Adams House; see Adams Mansion
Vassal-Adams House, Doghouse; see
Adams Mansion, Doghouse
Vassal-Adams House, Flower Garden; see
Adams Mansion, Flower Garden
Vassal-Adams House, Stone Library; see
Adams Mansion, Stone Library
Vassal-Adams House, Woodshed; see
Adams Mansion, Woodshed

Randolph

Milestone GGG; see Twelve-mile Stone
Twelve-mile Stone (Milestone GGG)
Old St.
HABS MA-128   p   L

Sharon

Cobb's Tavern
36 Bay St.
HABS MA-336   pd   L

Stoughton

Atherton, Samuel, House
449 Central St.
HABS MA-200   s p   L
New Haven Railroad Station
HABS MA-972   pd   H
Washington Hotel
710 Turnpike St.
HABS MA-171   s p   L

Walpole

Milestone CC; see Twenty-mile Stone
Twenty-mile Stone (Milestone CC)
Town Hall vic.
HABS MA-128   p   L

Wellesley

Boston and Albany Railroad Station
HABS MA-668   pd   L
Deming, Capt. Asa, House
(moved from CT, Rocky Hill)
HABS CT-13   s pd   L
Ellis Stone Barn
Boylston St.
HABS MA-145   s p   L
Ware, Ruben, Mill
HABS MA-546   p   L

Westwood

Town Pound
Grove St.
HABS MA-2-32   s p   L

Weymouth

Adams, Abigail (Smith), House
450 Bridge St.
HABS MA-417   p   L
First Church
HABS MA-594   p   L
Wildes, Capt. William, House
872 Commercial St.
HABS MA-248   p   L

Wrentham

Fisher, David, House (Gray Door Inn)
HABS MA-420   p   L
Gray Door Inn; see Fisher, David, House
Guild-Kollock House
HABS MA-421   p   L

PLYMOUTH COUNTY

Bridgewater

Andrews House (Pratt, Betty, House)
38 Walnut St.
HABS MA-2-91   s p   L
Haywood House
HABS MA-343   p   L
Pratt, Betty, House; see Andrews House

Duxbury

King Caesar House
King Caesar Rd., Powder Point
HABS MA-326   p   L
U.S. Frigate Constitution, Cannon
HABS MA-2-84-B   p   L

Greenbush

Old Oaken Bucket House
Old Oaken Bucket Rd.
HABS MA-2-41   s p   L
Stedman, Isaac, Grist Mill
(Stedman-Russell-Stockbridge Grist Mill)
County Way
HABS MA-2-14   s p   L
Stedman-Russell-Stockbridge Grist Mill;
see Stedman, Isaac, Grist Mill

Halifax

Fence
HABS MA-328   p   L
Standish, Shadrach, House
Monponsett St.
HABS MA-2-70   s p   L
Wood, Timothy, House
HABS MA-362   p   L

Hanover Center

Stetson, Samuel, House
Hanover St.
HABS MA-611   s   L

Hingham

Beal, John, House
HABS MA-364   p   L
Cushing House
S. Pleasant St.
HABS MA-2-85   s p   L
First Parish Meetinghouse; see Old Ship
Church
Garrison House, Old; see Lincoln, Perez,
House
Lincoln, Gen. Benjamin, House
HABS MA-363   p   L
Lincoln, Perez, House (Garrison House,
Old)
123 North St. (moved from original
location)
HABS MA-600   p   L
Lincoln, Samuel, Cottage
182 North St.
HABS MA-620   s   L
Loring, Thomas, House
HABS MA-366   p   L
Old Ship Church (First Parish
Meetinghouse)
88 Main St.
HABS MA-595   s pd   L H
Pilgrim Cottage
HABS MA-455   p   L
Shute, Daniel, House
Main & S. Pleasant Sts.
HABS MA-197   s p   L

Kingston

Bradford, Maj. John, House (Jones River
Village Club)
Maple St. & Landing Rd.
HABS MA-2-78   s p   L
Holmes House
HABS MA-369   p   L
Jones River Village Club; see Bradford,
Maj. John, House
Sever, Squire William, House & Garden
2 Linden St.
HABS MA-135   s p   L
Willet, Capt. Thomas, House
HABS MA-370   p   L

Lakeville

Nelson, Col. John, House; see Sampson,
Jennie, House
Sampson, Jennie, House (Nelson, Col.
John, House)
Main St. (moved to MA, North Chatham)
HABS MA-297   p   L
Ward, George, House
Crooked Ln.
HABS MA-2-20   s p   L

Marion

First Universalist Church
Pleasant & Main Sts.
HABS MA-241   s   L

Marshfield

Hatch, Walter, House
HABS MA-375   p   L

Thomas, Anthony, House
HABS MA-376   p   L

Weatherbee, George H., House
HABS MA-377   p   L

Winslow House
HABS MA-815   p   L

Marshfield Hills

Clift House
Spring St.
HABS MA-207   s p   L

Middleborough

Central Methodist Church
Cherry St.
HABS MA-2-68   s p   L

Eddy, Zachariah, Law Office
(moved to MA, Springfield vic.)
HABS MA-851   p   H

First Congregational Church, Carriage Sheds
Plympton St.
HABS MA-2-39   s p   L

Mill Houses
24, 26 & 28 Jackson St.
HABS MA-379-B   p   L

Mill Houses
32 & 34 Jackson St.
HABS MA-379-D   p   L

Mill Houses
20 & 22 Jackson St.
HABS MA-379-A   p   L

Mill Houses
30 Jackson St.
HABS MA-379-C   p   L

Mill Houses
36 & 38 Jackson St.
HABS MA-379-E   p   L

Peirce, Col. P. H., Store
N. Main St.
HABS MA-2-7   s p   L

Peirce, L. T., Store
N. Main & Jackson Sts.
HABS MA-2-28   s p   L

Robinson, E., Store
N. Main & Jackson Sts.
HABS MA-2-29   s p   L

Sampson, Deborah, House
280 Wareham St.
HABS MA-2-49   s p   L

Sproat House
HABS MA-378   p   L

Tavern Inn, Old
Wareham St. (State Rt. 28)
HABS MA-2-40   s p   L

Thompson, Venus, House
Thompson St.
HABS MA-2-64   s p   L

Wood, Judge, Office
123 S. Main St.
HABS MA-198   s p   L

Wood, Silas, House
HABS MA-331   p   L

North Carver

Sturtevant House
N. Carver Green
HABS MA-2-96   s p   L

North Hingham

New North Meetinghouse
North & Lincoln Sts.
HABS MA-422   p   L

North Pembroke

Society of Friends Meetinghouse
State Rt. 3
HABS MA-2-59   s p   L

Norwell

Bryant-Cushing House
Cornet Stetson Rd.
HABS MA-109   s p   L

Plymouth

Cape Cod Windmill (Eastham Windmill)
(moved to MA, Truro)
HABS MA-2-21   s p   L

Eastham Windmill; see Cape Cod Windmill

Lord House (Garden); see Warren, David, House (Garden)

Warren, David, House (Garden) (Lord House (Garden))
24 North St.
HABS MA-185   s   L

Scituate vic.

Lighthouse & Keeper's House
Cedar Point Scituate Harbor
HABS MA-2-22   s p   L

South Hingham

Wilder, Jabez, House
Main St.
HABS MA-137   s p   L

Wareham

Fearing, Israel, House; see Fearing-Warr House

Fearing-Warr House (Fearing, Israel, House)
14 Elm St.
HABS MA-102   s p   L

SUFFOLK COUNTY

Boston

Abolition Church
Smith Court
HABS MA-2-74   s p   L

Amory-Ticknor House
9 Park St.
HABS MA-175   s p   L

Appleton, Nathan, House (Women's City Club)
40 Beacon St.
HABS MA-813   s pd   H

Arlington Street Church
Arlington & Boylston Sts.
HABS MA-817   p   H

B. F. Keith Memorial Theatre (Opera House)
539 Washington St.
HABS MA-1078   pd   L

Blake, James, House
735 Columbia Rd.
HABS MA-560   pd   L H

Boston City Hall
School St.
HABS MA-860   p   H

Boundary Stone TTT-Boston Stone; see Boundary Stones QQQ, RRR, SSS, & TTT

Boundary Stones QQQ, RRR, SSS, & TTT (Boundary Stone TTT-Boston Stone)
Various Boston locations
HABS MA-128   s p   L

68 Broad Street (Warehouse)
HABS MA-125   s p   L

Butler School
River St., Hyde Park
HABS MA-564   p   L

Capen House; see Union Oyster House (Restaurant)

Charles Street Meetinghouse; see Church of Third Baptist Society

Christ Church (Old North Church)
193 Salem St.
HABS MA-500   p   L

Church of Third Baptist Society (Charles Street Meetinghouse)
Charles St.
HABS MA-544   p   L

Clap, Bela & Caleb, House
44-46 Temple St.
HABS MA-2-80   s p   L

Clough, Ebenezer, House; see Clough-Langdon House

Clough-Langdon House (Clough, Ebenezer, House)
21 Unity St.
HABS MA-342   s pd   L

Clough-Langdon House; see Langdon House

Codman Building
30-48 Hanover St.
HABS MA-784   pd   H

Cornhill District (Houses)
Scollay Sq. & Brattle St.
HABS MA-790   p   H

Customs House
State St.
HABS MA-789   pd   H

15 Elm Street (Building)
HABS MA-788   pd   H

Faneuil Hall, Committee & Commandery Rooms
Dock Square
HABS MA-163   s p   L

Fort Independence
Castle Island
HABS MA-570   p   L

Fort Winthrop, Citadel
Governor's Island
HABS MA-617   s   L

Franklin, Benjamin, Birthplace Site; see 17
Milk Street (Building)

Franklin Park Zoo, Elephant House
Seaver St.
HABS MA-1097   p   L

Franklin Park Zoo, Feline House
Seaver St.
HABS MA-1096   p   L

Franklin Place & Tontine Crescent
Franklin St.
HABS MA-612   s   L

Gothic, The (Apartment House)
47 Allen St.
HABS MA-669   pd   L

91 Green Street (House)
HABS MA-671   pd   L

Hancock, Ebenezer, House; see
Marshall-Hancock House

Hancock, Ebenezer, House (Mantels); see
Marshall-Hancock House (Mantels)

Hancock House
Beacon St.
HABS MA-1159   p   H

Hollis Street Church
Hollis St.
HABS MA-156   s p   L

Hollis Street Theater
Hollis St.
HABS MA-157   s p   L

India Wharf Stores
306-308 Atlantic Ave.
HABS MA-2-76   s p   L

Iron Standard & Gate
Tremont Place
HABS MA-2-11-A   s p   L

King's Chapel
Tremont St.
HABS MA-1160   p   H

Langdon House (Clough-Langdon House)
21 Unity St.
HABS MA-342-A   s   L

Marshall House (Inn) (Mantels); see
Marshall-Hancock House (Mantels)

Marshall Inn; see Marshall-Hancock House

Marshall-Hancock House (Hancock,
Ebenezer, House; Marshall Inn)
10 Marshall St.
HABS MA-2-55   s p   L

Marshall-Hancock House (Mantels)
(Hancock, Ebenezer, House (Mantels);
Marshall House (Inn) (Mantels))
10 Marshall St.
HABS MA-2-55-A   s   L

Mass. Charitable Mechanics Assoc.,
Exhibition Hall
Huntington Ave. & West Newton St.
HABS MA-672   pd   L

Mass. General Hospital, Bulfinch Building
Fruit St.
HABS MA-556   p   L

Massachusetts State House, Gates & Steps
Beacon St.
HABS MA-245   s p   L

Mayhew School
Poplar & Chambers Sts.
HABS MA-673   pd   L

47 McLean Street (House)
HABS MA-670   pd   L

17 Milk Street (Building) (Franklin,
Benjamin, Birthplace Site)
HABS MA-1161   p   H

M.I.T., Rogers Building
491 Boylston St.
HABS MA-252   s p   L

New England Merchants Bank Building
State & Congress Sts.
HABS MA-1162   p   H

Nickerson, George A., House
303 Commonwealth Ave.
HABS MA-961   pd   H

Old North Church; see Christ Church

Old South Church; see Old South
Meetinghouse

Old South Meetinghouse (Old South
Church)
Washington & Milk Sts.
HABS MA-960   s p   H

Opera House; see B. F. Keith Memorial
Theatre

Otis, Harrison Gray, House (first) (Society
For the Preservation of N. E. Antiquities)
141 Cambridge St.
HABS MA-845   p   H

Otis, Harrison Gray, House (second)
85 Mount Vernon St.
HABS MA-962   s pd H

Painters' Arms
Hanover St.
HABS MA-128   p   L

Park Street Church
Tremont & Park Sts.
HABS MA-631   p   L

Parker, Daniel P., House (Women's City
Club)
39 Beacon St.
HABS MA-814   p   H

Parkman House (Tuckerman-Parkman
House)
33 Beacon St.
HABS MA-965   pd   H

Parkman Market
Cambridge & N. Grove Sts.
HABS MA-2-47   s p   L

Pierce, Moses, House (Pierce-Hichborn
House)
29 North Square
HABS MA-499   p   L

Pierce, Robert, House
24 Oakton Ave.
HABS MA-562   s pd L H

Pierce, Thomas, House
Adams & Minot Sts.
HABS MA-561   p   L H

Pierce-Hichborn House; see Pierce, Moses,
House

Province House, The; see Sergeant, Peter,
House

Quincy Market, North & South Buildings
Dock Sq.
HABS MA-1166   s   H

Reed, Reuben, Building
7-9 Elm St.
HABS MA-785   pd   H

Revere, Paul, House
19 North Square
HABS MA-491   p   L H

Savage House
30 Dock Square
HABS MA-503   s   L

Sears' Block
72 Cornhill St.
HABS MA-786   p   H

Sears' Convex Block (Sears' Crescent)
50-56 Cornhill St.
HABS MA-787   pd   H

Sears' Crescent; see Sears' Convex Block

Sergeant, Peter, House (Province House,
The)
Washington St.
HABS MA-816   p   L

Shirley, Governor, Mansion; see
Shirley-Eustis House

Shirley-Eustis House (Shirley, Governor,
Mansion)
33 Shirley St.
HABS MA-275   s p   L H

Society For the Preservation of N. E.
Antiquities; see Otis, Harrison Gray,
House (first)

St. Patrick's Church, Old
Northampton St.
HABS MA-154   s p   L

Steps between Brattle Street & Cornhill
HABS MA-1138   p   H

Three Examples of Ironwork
Various Boston locations
HABS MA-2-11   s p   L

Tool House
Copp's Hill Burial Ground
HABS MA-498   p   L

Transcript Building
Washington & Milk Sts.
HABS MA-1139   p   H

Tuckerman-Parkman House; see Parkman
House

Union Oyster House (Restaurant) (Capen
House)
41-43 Union St.
HABS MA-127   s p   L

Washington & Franklin Streets (Building)
HABS MA-1140   p   H

199 Washington Street (Building)
HABS MA-1141   p   H

258 Washington Street (Building)
HABS MA-1142   p   H
West Church
131 Cambridge St.
HABS MA-279   p   H
Whiting Building
Washington St.
HABS MA-1143   p   H
Women's City Club; see Appleton, Nathan, House
Women's City Club; see Parker, Daniel P., House
Wrought Iron Archway & Steps
Province & Bosworth Sts.
HABS MA-2-11-B   s   L

Boston vic.

Milestones
Various Boston vicinity locations
HABS MA-128   s p   L

Brighton

Milestones HH & II
Harvard St.
HABS MA-128   s p   L

Charlestown

Adams, Mayor, House
HABS MA-352   p   L
Andrews-Getchell House
21 Cordis Ave.
HABS MA-191   s p   L
Devens, Gen. Charles, House
30 Union St.
HABS MA-346   p   L
11 Devens Street (House)
HABS MA-348   p   L
Everett, Edward, House
16 Harvard St.
HABS MA-347   p   L
Hyde, George, House; see Hyde-Worthen House
Hyde-Lincoln House
32 Cordis Ave.
HABS MA-299   s p   L
Hyde-Worthen House (Hyde, George, House)
69 Rutherford Ave.
HABS MA-192   s p   L
U.S. Frigate Constitution, Cannon
(moved to NY, Schoharie)
HABS MA-2-84-C   p   L
U.S. Frigate Constitution, Commodore's Quarters
U.S. Navy Yard
HABS MA-2-84-A   s p   L
U.S. Navy Yard, Commandant's House
Chelsea St.
HABS MA-2-10   s p   L

Chelsea

Captains' Row
Marginal & Shurtleff Sts.
HABS MA-2-37   s p   L

Cary-Bellingham Mansion
34 Parker St.
HABS MA-576   p   L
Octagon House; see Tucker, Bevis, House
Tucker, Bevis, House (Octagon House)
HABS MA-579   p   L
Way-Ireland-Pratt House
481 Washington Ave.
HABS MA-211   s   L

Dorchester

Bird, Thomas, House; see Bird-Sawyer House
Bird-Sawyer House (Bird, Thomas, House)
41 Humphreys St.
HABS MA-278   s p   L
Clap, Roger, House
199 Boston St. (moved from 25 Willow Court)
HABS MA-190   s   L
Clapp, William, House
195 Boston St.
HABS MA-447   p   L
First Parish Church (Unitarian)
Church & Parish Sts.
HABS MA-569   p   L
Lyceum Hall
Meetinghouse Hill
HABS MA-571   p   L
Milestones A, B, E, HHH, III & PPP
Various Dorchester locations
HABS MA-128   s p   L
Second Church
Washington & Center Sts.
HABS MA-563   p   L

Jamaica Plain

Loring-Greenough House & Garden
12 South St.
HABS MA-272   s p   L

Medford

Royall, Col. Isaac, House (Usher-Royall House)
Main St.
HABS MA-577   p   L H
Usher-Royall House; see Royall, Col. Isaac, House

Revere vic.

Bennett, Samuel, House; see Bennett-Slade-Parsons House
Bennett-Slade-Parsons House (Bennett, Samuel, House; Rumney Hall)
50 Marshall St.
HABS MA-218   s   L
Rumney Hall; see Bennett-Slade-Parsons House

Roxbury

Curtis House
HABS MA-479   p   L
Dillaway-Thomas House
Eliot Square
HABS MA-558   p   L

First Church
Eliot Square
HABS MA-557   p   L
Hale, Edward Everett, House
39 Highland St.
HABS MA-559   p   L
Hayden, Judge, House & Garden
281 Heath St.
HABS MA-294   s p   L
Milestones D, Y, Z, AA, BB, FF & NN
Various Roxbury locations
HABS MA-128   s p   L
Milestones V, W & X; see Parting Stone, The
Parting Stone, The (Milestones V, W & X)
Roxbury & Center Sts.
HABS MA-128   s p   L
Puddingstone Building, Old
199 Ruggles St.
HABS MA-126   s p   L

South Boston

St. Augustine Chapel
St. Augustine Cemetery, Dorchester St.
HABS MA-2-26   s p   L

Waltham

Gore, Gov. Christopher, Coach House & Stable
HABS MA-834   p   H

Winthrop

Winthrop, Deane, House
40 Shirley St.
HABS MA-575   p   L

WORCESTER COUNTY

Athol

Meetinghouse
HABS MA-893   p   H

Auburn

Chapin, Thaddeus, House
HABS MA-340   p   L

Blackstone

Building, Old Stone
HABS MA-459   p   L

Bolton

Milestone YYY; see Thirty-one-mile Stone
Thirty-one-mile Stone (Milestone YYY)
HABS MA-128   p   L

Brookfield

Banister House
HABS MA-345   p   L
Crosby, Col. J., House
Main St.
HABS MA-133   s p   L

Charlton

Towne, Gen. Salem, House
Old County Rd. (moved to MA, Sturbridge)
HABS MA-2-38   s p   L

Fitchburg
Cushing Flour & Grain Mill
Laurel St. Bridge vic.
HABS MA-896   p   H

Harvard
Fruitlands
Fruitlands Museum, Prospect Hill Rd.
HABS MA-1005   s d   L
Ireland, Shadrach, House; see Shaker
     Church Family Square House
Shaker Church Family Barn (Ruins)
Shaker Rd. vic.
HABS MA-861   s p   L
**Shaker Church Family Dwelling House
     (second) (Shaker Church Family Second
     House)**
Shaker Rd.
HABS MA-810   s p d   L
Shaker Church Family, General Views
Shaker Rd.
HABS MA-862   p   H
Shaker Church Family Herb Drying House
Shaker Rd.
HABS MA-1091   s   L
Shaker Church Family Office Building; see
     Shaker Church Family Trustees' Office
     (second)
Shaker Church Family Second House; see
     Shaker Church Family Dwelling House
     (second)
Shaker Church Family Square House
     (Ireland, Shadrach, House)
Shaker Rd.
HABS MA-804   s p d   L
Shaker Church Family Tailors' Shop
Shaker Rd.
HABS MA-805   p d   L
**Shaker Church Family Trustees' Office
     (second) (Shaker Church Family Office
     Building)**
Shaker Rd.
HABS MA-809   p d   L
Shaker Holy Hill Outdoor Worship Area
Shaker Rd.
HABS MA-1092   s   L
Shaker House
Fruitlands Museum, Prospect Hill Rd.
HABS MA-1004   s d   L
Shaker Meetinghouse
Shaker Rd.
HABS MA-806   s p d   L
Shaker Ministry's House; see Shaker
     Ministry's Shop
**Shaker Ministry's Shop (Shaker Ministry's
     House)**
Shaker Rd.
HABS MA-807   s p d   L
Shaker North Family Dwelling House
Shaker Rd.
HABS MA-1090   s   L
Shaker South Family Applesauce Shop; see
     Shaker South Family Shop Number 1

Shaker South Family Barn
S. Shaker Rd.
HABS MA-808   s p d   L
Shaker South Family Dwelling House
S. Shaker Rd.
HABS MA-888   s p   L
Shaker South Family Laundry; see Shaker
     South Family Washhouse
Shaker South Family Privy
S. Shaker Rd.
HABS MA-1085   p   L
Shaker South Family Shop Number 1
     (Shaker South Family Applesauce Shop)
S. Shaker Rd.
HABS MA-890   p   L
Shaker South Family Shop Number 2
S. Shaker Rd.
HABS MA-891   p   L
**Shaker South Family Washhouse (Shaker
     South Family Laundry)**
S. Shaker Rd.
HABS MA-889   p   L

Lancaster
Fifth Meetinghouse; see First Parish
     Church
First Parish Church (Fifth Meetinghouse)
Lancaster Common
HABS MA-542   p   L

Mendon
**First Parish Church (Unitarian) &
     Carriage Shed**
Maple & Elm Sts.
HABS MA-242   s d   L
Milestones DD & EE
Hastings St.
HABS MA-128   p   L

Milford
Milestone VVV; see Thirty-four-mile Stone
Thirty-four-mile Stone (Milestone VVV)
HABS MA-128   p   L

Millville
Covered Bridge
HABS MA-440   p   L

Millville vic.
**Chestnut Hill Meetinghouse (South Parish
     Meetinghouse)**
Chestnut St.
HABS MA-122   s p   L
South Parish Meetinghouse; see Chestnut
     Hill Meetinghouse

North Uxbridge
Crown & Eagle Mills
123 Hartford Ave. East
HABS MA-991   s p d   L H

Oakham
Adams, Eli, House
HABS MA-284   p   L

Lincoln House
HABS MA-285   p   L
Saw Mill, Old
HABS MA-287   p   L

Rutland
Putnam, Gen. Rufus, House
Main St.
HABS MA-2-71   s p   L

Sturbridge
Towne, Gen. Salem, House
Sturbridge Village (moved from MA,
     Charlton)
HABS MA-2-38   s p   L
Wight, Oliver, House
State Rt. 131
HABS MA-217   s p   L

Templeton
Federated Church; see First Parish
     Congregational Church
First Parish Congregational Church
     (Federated Church)
Templeton Common
HABS MA-848   p   H
Lee, Col. Artemus, House
Templeton Common
HABS MA-849   p   H
Stiles, John W., House
Templeton Common
HABS MA-847   p   H

Uxbridge
Masonic Building & Courthouse
HABS MA-411   p   L
Wheelock, Lieut. Simeon, House
N. Main St.
HABS MA-412   p   L

Wilkinsonville
**Dudley, D. T. & Son Co., Machine Shop &
     Powerhouse**
Providence Rd.
HABS MA-1144   s   H
Dudley, D. T. & Son Company, Main Shop
Providence Rd.
HABS MA-1145   s   H

Worcester
Salisbury, Stephen, Mansion (first)
40 Highland St.
HABS MA-573   p   L
Salisbury, Stephen, Mansion (second)
HABS MA-574   p   L
**Worcester Cons. Street Railway, Admin.
     Building (Worcester Cons. Street
     Railway, Car Barn)**
99-109 Main St.
HABS MA-1106   p d   L
Worcester Cons. Street Railway, Car Barn;
     see Worcester Cons. Street Railway,
     Admin. Building

Michigan

ALGER COUNTY

East Munising

Becker Barn (Pictured Rocks National Lakeshore)
HABS MI-307   d   H
Pictured Rocks National Lakeshore; see Becker Barn

Grand Island

Log Building No. 4
Murray Bay, W. Shore
HABS MI-256   pd   H
Log Building Number 1
Murray Bay, W. Shore
HABS MI-253   pd   H
Log Building Number 2
Murray Bay, W. Shore
HABS MI-254   pd   H
Log Building Number 3
Murray Bay, W. Shore
HABS MI-255   pd   H
Log Building Number 8 (Stone Quarry Cottage)
Murray Bay, W. Shore
HABS MI-257   pd   H
Stone Quarry Cottage; see Log Building Number 8
Williams, Abraham, House (Hotel Annex)
Murray Bay, W. Shore
HABS MI-246   pd   H
Williams, Abraham, Log House
Murray Bay, W. Shore
HABS MI-252   pd   H
Williams Hotel
Murray Bay, W. Shore
HABS MI-258   p   H

BERRIEN COUNTY

Niles

Paine Bank
212 W. Third St.
HABS MI-220   s   L

CALHOUN COUNTY

Battle Creek

Michigan Central Railroad Station
Capitol Ave.
HABS MI-234   p   H

Marshall

Allcott House
302 W. Mansion St.
HABS MI-239   d   H
Baker, Abner, Carriage House
318 W. Mansion St.
HABS MI-237   pd   H

Baker, Abner, House
318 W. Mansion St.
HABS MI-236   s pd   H
Benedict-Joy House
224 N. Kalamazoo Ave.
HABS MI-240   pd   H
Brewer House (Oakhill)
Eagle St.
HABS MI-244   pd   H
Brooks, Craig Wright, House
High & Mansion Sts.
HABS MI-27-20   s pd   L
Brooks, Harold Craig, House (Fitch, Jabez, House)
N. Kalamazoo Ave. & Prospect St.
HABS MI-27-18   s pd   L
Capitol Hill School (Fourth Ward School)
Washington & Maple Sts.
HABS MI-227   pd   H
East Michigan Avenue (Commercial Building)
HABS MI-247   pd   H
117 East Michigan Avenue (Commercial Building)
HABS MI-245   pd   H
Fitch, Jabez, House; see Brooks, Harold Craig, House
Fourth Ward School; see Capitol Hill School
Honolulu House; see Pratt, Abner, House
Marshall Tavern
Michigan Ave. & Eagle St.
HABS MI-27-19   s pd   L
Oakhill; see Brewer House
Pratt, Abner, House (Honolulu House)
170 N. Kalamazoo Ave.
HABS MI-228   s pd   H
106 West Michigan Avenue (Commercial Building)
HABS MI-249   pd   H
136 West Michigan Avenue (Commercial Building)
HABS MI-248   pd   H

CHIPPEWA COUNTY

Sault Ste. Marie

Hydroelectric Plant & Canal; see Michigan Lake Superior Power Company
Michigan Lake Superior Power Company (Hydroelectric Plant & Canal)
Portage St.
HAER MI-1   s pd   L

CLINTON COUNTY

Ovid

Congregational Church (United Church)
N. Main & E. Pearl Sts.
HABS MI-250   pd   H

United Church; see Congregational Church

EATON COUNTY

Charlotte

Eaton County Courthouse
W. Lawrence Ave.
HABS MI-229   pd   H

Eaton Rapids

Gallery, John & William, Mill (Horner's Original Mill)
Canal & N. Main Sts.
HABS MI-226   s pd   H
Horner's Original Mill; see Gallery, John & William, Mill

Vermontville

First Congregational Church
W. Main & N. Main Sts.
HABS MI-225   s pd   H
First Congregational Church
S. Main & W. Main Sts.
HABS MI-224   s pd   H

HOUGHTON COUNTY

Calumet

Agassiz Park
Fourth St.
HABS MI-308   pd   H
Calumet & Hecla Bathhouse
Calumet & Depot Sts.
HABS MI-284   d   H
Calumet & Hecla Blacksmith Shop
HABS MI-291   d   H
Calumet & Hecla Gearhouse
77 Mine St.
HABS MI-290   d   H
Calumet & Hecla General Office
Red Jacket & Calumet Sts.
HABS MI-283   d   H
Calumet & Hecla Machine Shop
Mine & Depot Sts.
HABS MI-285   d   H
Calumet & Hecla Pattern Storage
HABS MI-293   d   H
Calumet & Hecla Public Library
101 Red Jacket Rd.
HABS MI-286   pd   H
Calumet & Hecla Roundhouse
Mine & Depot Sts.
HABS MI-287   pd   H
Calumet & Hecla Superior Boilerhouse & Stack
Mine & Depot Sts.
HABS MI-288   d   H
Calumet & Hecla Superior Engine House 5A
HABS MI-292   pd   H

Calumet Fire Station; see Red Jacket Fire Station

Calumet Theater & Town Hall; see Red Jacket Theater & Town Hall

Calumt & Hecla Warehouse Number 1 (North End Metal & Supply)
120 Red Jacket Rd.
HABS MI-289   pd   H

Curto's Place (Shute's Bar)
322 Sixth St.
HABS MI-281   d   H

Italian Hall
409 Seventh St.
HABS MI-282   d   H

North End Metal & Supply; see Calumt & Hecla Warehouse Number 1

Red Jacket Fire Station (Calumet Fire Station)
Sixth St.
HABS MI-277   d   H

Red Jacket Theater & Town Hall (Calumet Theater & Town Hall)
Elm & Sixth St.
HABS MI-278   d   H

Roman Catholic-French Canadian Church; see St. Anne's Church

Ryan Block
305-307 Sixth St.
HABS MI-279   d   H

Shute's Bar; see Curto's Place

St. Anne's Church (Roman Catholic-French Canadian Church)
Fifth & Scott Sts.
HABS MI-280   d   H

Hancock

Quincy Mining Company
HAER MI-2   s pd L

Jacobsville

Jacobsville Finnish Evangelical Lutheran Church
HABS MI-294   d   H

Lake Linden

Lindell Chocolate Shop
Calumet Ave.
HABS MI-295   d   H

INGHAM COUNTY

Lansing

Diamond Reo Motor Plant
2100 S. Washington St.
HAER MI-4   pd   L

Michigan State Capitol
Capitol St.
HABS MI-230   p   H

Olds, Ransom E., House
S. Washington Ave. & Main St.
HABS MI-231   pd   H

Mason vic.

516 Hogsback Road (House) (Sheehan House)
HABS MI-223   s pd   H

Sheehan House; see 516 Hogsback Road (House)

Williamston Twp.

St. Katherine's Episcopal Church
Meridian Rd.
HABS MI-232   s pd   H

IONIA COUNTY

Ionia

Hall, Frederick, House
126 E. Main St.
HABS MI-238   pd   H

JACKSON COUNTY

Grass Lake

Soper Residence (Village Farm)
971 Michigan Ave. (U.S. Rt. 12)
HABS MI-111   s pd   L

Village Farm; see Soper Residence

Grass Lake vic.

Smith, Hiram, House & Barn
Michigan & Wolf Lake Rds.
HABS MI-113   s pd   L

Smith, Sidney T., House
Michigan Ave. (U.S. Rt. 12)
HABS MI-115   s pd   L

KALAMAZOO COUNTY

Kalamazoo

Kalamazoo State Hospital
Oakland Dr.
HABS MI-251   pd   H

KENT COUNTY

East Grand Rapids

Lovett-Barnard House
2211 Lake Dr.
HABS MI-259   s pd   H

Grand Rapids

Amberg, David M., House
College Ave. & Logan St.
HABS MI-242   pd   H

Dikeman, Aaron B., House
302 Fulton St. SE
HABS MI-24   s pd   L

Grand Rapids Art Gallery; see Pike, Abraham, House

Grand Rapids City Hall
35 Lyon St. NW
HABS MI-243   pd   H

Hatch, Damon, House
445 Cherry St. SE
HABS MI-23   s pd   L

May, Meyer S., House
450 Madison Ave.
HABS MI-241   pd   H

Noble, Boardman, House
671 Front Ave. NW
HABS MI-22   s pd   L

Pike, Abraham, House (Grand Rapids Art Gallery)
230 E. Fulton St. SE
HABS MI-27-10   s pd   L H

Sanford, Samuel, House
540 Cherry St.
HABS MI-21   s pd   L

Turner, Eliphalet H., House
731 Front Ave. NW
HABS MI-27-12   s pd   L H

KEWEENAW COUNTY

Central Mine

Central Mine Methodist Episcopal Church
Main East-West Rd.
HABS MI-299   d   H

Central Mining Company Clerk's Office
Main East-West Rd.
HABS MI-300   d   H

LENAWEE COUNTY

Adrian

Civil War Monument
Monument Park
HABS MI-233   s pd   H

Tecumseh

Anderson, Elijah, House
401 Chicago Blvd. & N. Union St.
HABS MI-27-16   s pd   L

LIVINGSTON COUNTY

Brighton

Appleton, John D., House
325 S. Grand River Ave.
HABS MI-235   s pd   H

Rushton

Olds, Alonzo, House
10084 Rushton Rd.
HABS MI-15   s pd   L

MACKINAC COUNTY

Mackinac Island

American Fur Company Buildings
HABS MI-215   s pd   L

Biddle, Edward, House
HABS MI-216   s pd   L

Fort Mackinac, E. Blockhouse
HABS MI-213-B   s pd   L

Fort Mackinac, Guardhouse
HABS MI-28   s p d   L
Fort Mackinac, N. Blockhouse
HABS MI-213-C   s p d   L
Fort Mackinac, Officers Stone Quarters
HABS MI-25   s p d   L
Fort Mackinac, Officers Wood Quarters
HABS MI-26   s p d   L
Fort Mackinac, Post Headquarters
HABS MI-29   s p d   L
Fort Mackinac, Post Hospital
HABS MI-27   s p d   L
Fort Mackinac, Ramparts & Sally Ports
HABS MI-213-A   s p d   L
Fort Mackinac, West Blockhouse
HABS MI-213-D   s p d   L
Mission Church, Old
HABS MI-214   s p d   L
Mission Church, Old
HABS MI-214   s p   L

MARQUETTE COUNTY

Ishpeming
House, Reinforced-Concrete Shaft
HAER MI-3   pd   L

MONROE COUNTY

Monroe
McClelland, Gov. Robert B., House
47 E. Elm St.
HABS MI-17   s p d   L
Nims, Rudolph, House
206 W. Noble St.
HABS MI-18   s p d   L

WASHTENAW COUNTY

Ann Arbor
Anderson House
2301 Packard Rd.
HABS MI-27-22   s p d   L
Brown, Anson, Commercial Building
(Exchange & Ingalls Blacks)
1003-1005 Broadway
HABS MI-110   s p d   L
Colonial Inn
HABS MI-297   s   H
Covert, Norman B., House
1500 Dexter Ave.
HABS MI-118   s p   L
DeForest Barn
Dixboro & Geddes Rds.
HABS MI-301   s   H
Detroit Observatory (University
   Observatory)
E. Ann St.
HABS MI-302   s d   H
Exchange & Ingalls Blacks; see Brown,
   Anson, Commercial Building

Hall, Dr. Richard Neville, House
1330 Hill St.
HABS MI-305   s   H
Hoover House
2015 Washtenaw
HABS MI-303   s   H
Lloyd Residence
1734 Washtenaw
HABS MI-304   s   H
Perry House (Perry House, The Old)
1317 Pontiac St.
HABS MI-306   s   H
Perry House, The Old; see Perry House
Sinclair House
1223 Pontiac St.
HABS MI-27-3   s p d   L
Ticknor, Dr. Benajah, House
2781 Packard St.
HABS MI-19   s p d   L
University Observatory; see Detroit
   Observatory
Wilson, Judge R. S., House
E. Ann & N. Division Sts.
HABS MI-27-2   s p d   L

Dexter
Dexter, Judge Samuel W., House
W. Huron St.
HABS MI-116   s p d   L

Dexter vic.
Dexter, Judge Samuel, Country House
8401 Ann Arbor St.
HABS MI-27-21   s p d   L

Dixboro
Methodist Episcopal Church
Plymouth Rd.
HABS MI-16   s p d   L

Sharonville vic.
Porter, Squire Michael, House
Jacob & Kendall Rds.
HABS MI-114   s p d   L

Ypsilanti
Ballard, Arden H., House (Ladies Literary
   Club)
218 N. Washington St.
HABS MI-14   s p d   L
Ballard House
125 N. Huron St.
HABS MI-27-23   s p d   L
Ladies Literary Club; see Ballard, Arden
   H., House
U.S. Post Office
HABS MI-296   s   H

WAYNE COUNTY

Canton Township
Moore, Alfred, House
W. Warren & Ridge Rds.
HABS MI-112   s p d   L

Yost, William, House
6020 Sheldon Rd.
HABS MI-117   s p d   L

Dearborn
Detroit Arsenal
Michigan Ave. & Monroe Blvd.
HABS MI-27-7   s p d   L
Detroit Arsenal, Officers' Quarters
21950 Michigan Ave.
HABS MI-22-7-A   s p   L
Detroit Arsenal, Smith's& Carpenter's
   Shops
Garrison Ave.
HABS MI-27-7-B   s p   L
Detroit Arsenal, Sutler's Shop
Garrison Ave. & Monroe Blvd.
HABS MI-27-7-C   s p   L

Detroit
Beaver Realty Company; see Jones, James
   M., House
Christ Episcopal Church
976 E. Jefferson Ave.
HABS MI-260   p   L
City Hall, Old
HABS MI-221   p   L H
Customs House
Griswold & Larned Sts.
HABS MI-222   p   H
Detroit & Cleveland Navigation Company
   Warehouse
Wayne St.
HABS MI-119   s p d   L
1491 East Congress Street (House)
HABS MI-266   p   L
976-78 East Woodbridge Street (Double
   House)
HABS MI-263   p   L
First Bank in Detroit
Jefferson Ave. & Randolph St.
HABS MI-264   p   L
Fort Street Presbyterian Church
Fort & Third Sts.
HABS MI-265   p   L
Fort Wayne
W. Jefferson & Livernois Aves.
HABS MI-27-4   s p d   L
Fort Wayne, Old Barracks
W. Jefferson Ave.
HABS MI-27-4-A   s p   L
Fort Wayne, Powder House
W. Jefferson Ave.
HABS MI-27-4-B   s p   L
Fort Wayne, Sally Ports
W. Jefferson Ave.
HABS MI-27-4-C   s p   L
Grand Riviera Theatre
9222 Grand River Ave.
HABS MI-270   s p d   L
Guardian Building; see Union Trust
   Building

Jones, James M., House (Beaver Realty Company)
1460 E. Jefferson Ave.
HABS MI-13   s pd   L
Mariner's Church
Woodward Ave. 6 Woodbridge St.
HABS MI-11   s pd   L
Mercantile Building
554 W. Jefferson Ave.
HABS MI-267   p   L

Orchestra Hall (Paradise Theatre)
3711 Woodward Ave.
HABS MI-271   pd   L
Paradise Theatre; see Orchestra Hall
Seitz, Henry, Building (Wardwell House)
16109 E. Jefferson Ave., Grosse Pointe Park
HABS MI-12   s pd   L
Sibley House
976 E. Jefferson Ave.
HABS MI-269   p   L

St. John's Episcopal Church
Woodward Ave. & Vernor Hwy.
HABS MI-268   p   L
Sts. Peter & Paul's Jesuit Church
E. Jefferson Ave. & Saint Antoine St.
HABS MI-27-1   s pd   L
Union Trust Building (Guardian Building)
500 Griswold St.
HABS MI-273   p   H
Wardwell House; see Seitz, Henry, Building

Minnesota

ANOKA COUNTY

Anoka

Woodbury House
Main St. & Second Ave.
HABS MN-29-13   s   L

BLUE EARTH COUNTY

St. Clair

Indian Agency House
HABS MN-29-43   s pd   L

BROWN COUNTY

New Ulm

Berndt, Julius, House
HABS MN-1-6   p   L

CARLTON COUNTY

Sawyer

Church, Log
HABS MN-29-28   s pd   L

CHIPPEWA COUNTY

Montevideo

Wilkins, Daniel, Log House
Smith Park
HABS MN-1-1   pd   L

Watson vic.

Lac Qui Parle Mission Church (Ruins)
HABS MN-1-2   pd   L

CHISAGO COUNTY

Taylors Falls

Branch Street Library
HABS MN-29-17   s pd   L
First Methodist Church
Government St.
HABS MN-29-15   s pd   L
Folsom, W. H. C., House
HABS MN-29-16   s pd   L

DAKOTA COUNTY

Mendota

Faribault House
Minnesota River vic.
HABS MN-29-7   s pd   L
St. Peter's Catholic Church
HABS MN-29-4   s pd   L

GOODHUE COUNTY

Frontenac

St. Hubert's Lodge
Garrard Ave.
HABS MN-29-34   s pd   L

HENNEPIN COUNTY

Bloomington

Pond House
Nicollet Ave.
HABS MN-29-22   s pd   L

Excelsior

Trinity Chapel (Episcopal)
Second & Center Sts.
HABS MN-29-6   s pd   L

Minneapolis

Church of Minneapolis (New Church Society)
905 Fifth Ave.
HABS MN-29-9   s pd   L
Ferry Farm; see Stevens, Col. J. H., House
Godfrey, Ard, House
Ortman St.
HABS MN-29-2   s pd   L
Guaranty Loan Building; see Metropolitan Building
127 Main Street SE (Building)
HABS MN-29-8   s pd   L
425 Marshall Ave. (Commercial Building)
HABS MN-29-11   s pd   L
Metropolitan Building (Guaranty Loan Building)
308 S. Second Ave.
HABS MN-49   pd   H

New Church Society; see Church of Minneapolis
Our Lady of Lourdes Church
21 Prince St. SE
HABS MN-29-10   s pd   L
Pillsbury A Mill
Main St. & Third Ave. SE
HABS MN-29-5   s pd   L
Stevens, Col. J. H., House (Ferry Farm)
Minnehaha Park (moved from Ferry Farm, Miss. River)
HABS MN-29-1   s pd   L
West House
200 Second St. SE
HABS MN-29-14   s pd   L

St. Paul

Fort Snelling, Grandstand
HABS MN-56-E   p   L
Fort Snelling, Hexagon Tower
HABS MN-29-12   pd   L
Fort Snelling, Quarters
HABS MN-56-F-K   pd   L
Fort Snelling, Round Tower
HABS MN-29-3   pd   L
Fort Snelling, Stables
HABS MN-56-A-D   pd   L

ISANTI COUNTY

North Branch vic.

Dahl-Nordin House; see Nordin, John Mangus, House
Nordin, John Mangus, House (Dahl-Nordin House)
County Rd. 48
HABS MN-55   s p   L

LE SUEUR COUNTY

Le Sueur

Mayo House
HABS MN-29-44   pd   L

473

NICOLLET COUNTY

Fort Ridgeley

Fort Ridgeley, Commissary Building
HABS MN-1-5   p   L

Fort Ridgeley, Powder Magazine
HABS MN-1-4   p   L

RAMSEY COUNTY

St. Paul

Assumption School, Old
Eighth & Exchange Sts.
HABS MN-29-31   s pd   L

Burbank-Livingston-Griggs House; see
Griggs-Burbank House

Church of the Assumption (Roman Catholic)
51 W. Ninth St.
HABS MN-45   pd   L

Church of the Good Shepherd (Episcopal Church, Old)
Twelfth & Cedar Sts.
HABS MN-29-26   s pd   L

Custom House
Fifth & Wabasha Sts.
HABS MN-29-25   s pd   L

Episcopal Church, Old; see Church of the
Good Shepherd

German Presbyterian Church
Ramey & Pleasant Sts.
HABS MN-57   p   H

Griggs-Burbank House
(Burbank-Livingston-Griggs House)
432 Summit
HABS MN-53   pd   H

Hill, James J., House
240 Summit Ave.
HABS MN-52   p   L

Hunt, Daniel H., House
2478 Territorial Rd.
HABS MN-58   pd   H

Kellog, Frank B., House
633 Fairmont Ave.
HABS MN-51   p   L

Laurel Terrace; see Riley, Nina & Laurel
Row

Log Chapel (Muskego Church)
HABS MN-29-24   s pd   L

Mansion House; see Ramsey, Alexander,
House

Mattock School (Webster School)
Randolph St. & Snelling Ave.
HABS MN-29-27   s pd   L

McGrorty-Kittson House
603 Jackson St.
HABS MN-46   pd   L

Muskego Church; see Log Chapel

New York Building
6th & Minnesota Sts.
HABS MN-54   pd   H

Postelethwait House
Twelfth St.
HABS MN-29-30   s pd   L

Ramsey, Alexander, House (Mansion
House)
265 S. Exchange St.
HABS MN-48   pd   L

Ramsey, Justice Cornelius, House
252 W. Seventh St.
HABS MN-47   pd   L

Riley, Nina & Laurel, Row (Laurel
Terrace)
294-296 Laurel Ave.
HABS MN-61   p   H

Spangenberg House
375 Mt. Curve Ave.
HABS MN-60   p   H

Waldman, Anton, House
445 Smith St.
HABS MN-59   p   H

Webster School; see Mattock School

ST. LOUIS COUNTY

Duluth

Drug Store, First
E. Superior St.
HABS MN-29-21   s pd   L

Fire Hall, First
E. Second St.
HABS MN-29-20   s pd   L

Fire Tower
Rice Lake Rd.
HABS MN-29-39   s pd   L

Light House, Old
Minnesota Point
HABS MN-29-23   s pd   L

Post Office, First
First Alley
HABS MN-29-19   s pd   L

Duluth vic.

Krazszawaski Log House
Gnesen Rd.
HABS MN-29-36   s pd   L

Quaeva Log House
Rice Lake Rd.
HABS MN-29-29   s pd   L

Ely vic.

Logging Camp
HABS MN-29-37   s d   L

Shaft House; see Timber Headframe

Timber Headframe (Shaft House)
HABS MN-29-41   s d   L

TRAVERSE COUNTY

Brown's Valley

Brown, Joseph R., House
Sam Brown Mem. Park (moved from
Dakota Territory)
HABS MN-1-3   pd   L

WABASHA COUNTY

Lake City

Brown's Hotel
Lake Pepin
HABS MN-29-40   s pd   L

WASHINGTON COUNTY

Afton

Mackey House
Washington Ave.
HABS MN-29-38   s pd   L H

Octogonal House
Washington Ave.
HABS MN-29-32   s pd   L

Marine

Meeting Hall
HABS MN-29-18   s pd   L

Stillwater vic.

Bridge, Stone Highway
HABS MN-29-35   s pd   L

WINONA COUNTY

Troy vic.

Troy Mill
Saratoga Township
HABS MN-29-33   s pd   L

Mississippi

ADAMS COUNTY

Kingston

Greek Revival House (Church)
HABS MS-160   p   L

Natchez

Airlie (Buckner House)
Myrtle St.
HABS MS-43   pd   L

Arlington
Main St.
HABS MS-17-8   s pd   L

Arrighi
219-221 Main St.
HABS MS-17-9   s pd   L

Bahin House; see Williamsburg

Banachi, Mamye, House
821 Main St.
HABS MS-55   pd   L

Beltzhoover House; see Green Leaves

Bledsoe House; see Kings Tavern

Bontura House
Broadway & Market Sts.
HABS MS-161   p   L

Buckner House; see Airlie

Carpenter House; see Dunleith

Charity Hospital
HABS MS-148   pd   L

Connelly's Tavern; see Gilreath's Hill

Conti House (Holmes, Gov., House)
Wall St.
HABS MS-35   pd   L

Dunleith (Carpenter House)
Homochito St.
HABS MS-2   pd   L

Elward House
612 Washington St.
HABS MS-44   s pd   L

Feltus House; see Linden

First Church of Christ (Scientist)
206 Main St.
HABS MS-190   d   H

Gilreath's Hill (Connelly's Tavern)
Canal St.
HABS MS-17-4   s pd   L

Green Leaves (Beltzhoover House)
303 Rankin St.
HABS MS-8   pd   L

Holmes, Gov., House; see Conti House

Hope Farm (Villa) (Miller, Balfour, House)
Auburn Ave. & Homochitto St.
HABS MS-46   s pd   L

Kings Tavern (Bledsoe House)
Jefferson St.
HABS MS-37   pd   L

Lawyers' Row
State & Wall Sts.
HABS MS-10   pd   L

Linden (Feltus House)
HABS MS-17-10   s pd   L

Longwood (Ward House; Nutt's Folly)
HABS MS-1   pd   L

Main Street & Broadway (Building)
100 Main St.
HABS MS-193   d   H

Manse, The
Rankin St.
HABS MS-150   pd   L

311-313 Market Street (Parish House)
HABS MS-17-11   s pd   L

Marschalk Printing Office
Wall & Franklin Sts.
HABS MS-40   pd   L

Melrose
HABS MS-61   pd   L

Miller, Balfour, House; see Hope Farm (Villa)

Molasses Flats (Postlewaite Building)
200 Main St.
HABS MS-192   d   H

Monmouth
E. Franklin St. & Melrose Ave.
HABS MS-194   d   H

Natchez Bluffs & Under-the-Hill Historic District
Silver St.
HABS MS-212   d   H

Natchez City Map
HABS MS-17-12   s   L

Nutt's Folly; see Longwood

Postlewaite Building; see Molasses Flats

Railroad Terminal
200 Braodway St.
HABS MS-195   d   H

Rosalie
100 Orleans St.
HABS MS-17-1   s pd   L

Saint Catherine Street (House)
HABS MS-163   p   L

Slave Hospital
HABS MS-156   p   L

Spanish House, Old; see Washington & Wall Streets (House)

St. Mary's Cathedral
HABS MS-42   pd   L

Stanton Hall
Pearl & High Sts.
HABS MS-157   p   L

Stowers, Luther, House
107 S. Canal St.
HABS MS-196   d   H

Van Court House
510 Washington St.
HABS MS-17-7   s pd   L

Ward House; see Longwood

Washington & Wall Streets (House) (Spanish House, Old)
HABS MS-162   p   L

Williamsburg (Bahin House)
821 Main St.
HABS MS-197   d   H

Natchez vic.

Auburn (Duncan, Stephen, House)
Auburn Blvd. Duncan Memorial Park
HABS MS-9   pd   L

Bellevue; see Gloucester

Briars, The
HABS MS-41   pd   L

D'Evereux
HABS MS-17-6   s pd   L

Duncan, Stephen, House; see Auburn

Elmscourt
HABS MS-49   pd   L

Gardens, The (McConchie's House)
Cemetery Rd.
HABS MS-36   pd   L

Gloucester (Bellevue)
Lower Woodville Rd.
HABS MS-17-5   s pd   L

Homewood
HABS MS-149   s pd   L

McConchie's House; see Gardens, The

Saragosa
HABS MS-152   pd   L

Slave Quarters & Ruins, Concord
HABS MS-51   pd   L

Slave School
HABS MS-158   p   L

Springfield
U.S. Rt. 61
HABS MS-54   pd   L

Windy Hill Manor
Library Rd.
HABS MS-48   pd   L

Washington

Jefferson College
North St.
HABS MS-213   pd   H

Jefferson Military College
HABS MS-4   pd   L

Jefferson Military College, Kitchen
HABS MS-4-A   p   L

Jefferson Military College, President's House
HABS MS-5   pd   L

Meade, Cowles, House
HABS MS-7   pd   L

Methodist Church, Old
HABS MS-6   pd   L

Rawlings House
HABS MS-3   pd   L

Washington vic.

Brandon Hall
HABS MS-151   pd   L

Propinquity
U.S. Hwy. 61 N.
HABS MS-199   d   H

Selma
U.S. Hwy. 61 N.
HABS MS-198   d   H

Sweet Auburn
U.S. Hwy. 84 & 98 E.
HABS MS-200   d   H

AMITE COUNTY

Gloster vic.

Casselle House
HABS MS-62   pd   L

Liberty vic.

Chaffin House & Barn
HABS MS-57   pd   L

BOLIVAR COUNTY

Benoit

Burris House
HABS MS-140   pd   L

CARROLL COUNTY

Carrollton vic.

Cotesworth
HABS MS-111   pd   L
Malmaison
HABS MS-110   pd   L

Vaiden vic.

Vaiden, Dr. E. M., House
HABS MS-113   pd   L

CLAIBORNE COUNTY

Alcorn Station

**Alcorn State University, Literary Society
  Building**
HABS MS-201   d   H

Lorman vic.

Alcorn State University, Oakland Chapel
HABS MS-202   d   H

Port Gibson

Anchuka (Archer House)
HABS MS-28   pd   L
Archer House; see Anchuka
Catholic Church (St. Joseph's Catholic
  Church)
HABS MS-155   p   L
Christian Chapel Church
Church & Orange Sts.
HABS MS-203   d   H
Disharoon, G. L., House
Church St.
HABS MS-21   pd   L
Gage, R. D., House & Servants' House
HABS MS-24   pd   L
Jean, Dan, House
HABS MS-22   pd   L
Pope Building
625-27 Market St.
HABS MS-204   d   H
Port Gibson Bank
HABS MS-25   pd   L
Presbyterian Church
HABS MS-23   pd   L
Shreve House
HABS MS-27   pd   L
St. Joseph's Catholic Church; see Catholic
  Church
Van Dorn House
Van Dorn Dr.
HABS MS-205   d   H

Port Gibson vic.

Windson Plantation; see Windsor Castle
  Ruins
Windsor Castle Ruins (Windson
  Plantation)
HABS MS-26   pd   L

CLAY COUNTY

West Point

Cedar Oaks
Barton Ferry Rd.
HABS MS-182   s pd   L

HARRISON COUNTY

Biloxi

Fayard House, Old (Ruins)
HABS MS-13   pd   L
Filbrick (Philbrick House)
HABS MS-15   pd   L
Gillis House (Vance-Gillis House)
806 W. Beach
HABS MS-154   s pd   L H
Keller House (Wood, Ralph, House)
E. Beach
HABS MS-14   pd   L
Philbrick House; see Filbrick
Pleasant Reed House
928 Elmer St.
HABS MS-186   s d   H
Vance-Gillis House; see Gillis House
Wood, Ralph, House; see Keller House

Biloxi vic.

Beauvoir (Davis, Jefferson, House)
HABS MS-12   pd   L
Davis, Jefferson, House; see Beauvoir

Gulfport

Grass Lawn
720 E. Beach Blvd.
HABS MS-168   p   H

HINDS COUNTY

Clinton

Mississippi College, Chapel (Provine
  Chapel)
HABS MS-30   pd   L
Moss House, Old (Ruins)
HABS MS-31   pd   L
Provine Chapel; see Mississippi College,
  Chapel

Jackson

Bell, Joe, House
317 S. Congress St.
HABS MS-38   pd   L
Boyd House; see Oaks, The
Brame, Judge, House
HABS MS-80   pd   L
City Hall
HABS MS-147   pd   L
Governor's Mansion
316 E. Capitol St.
HABS MS-67   pd   L H
Julienne House
421 Yazoo St.
HABS MS-66   pd   L

Manship House
Northwest & Fortification Sts.
HABS MS-68   s pd   L H
Oaks, The (Boyd House)
823 N. Jefferson St.
HABS MS-211   d   H
Paramount Theater
115 E. Capitol St.
HABS MS-185   pd   L
Patton, John W., House
512 N. State St.
HABS MS-47   pd   L
Penney, J. C. (Building)
157 E. Capitol St.
HABS MS-184   pd   L
Powers, Col., House
Amite St.
HABS MS-65   pd   L
State Capitol, New
Mississippi St.
HABS MS-191   d   H
State Capitol, Old
100 N. State St.
HABS MS-56   pd   L H

Raymond

Hinds County Courthouse
HABS MS-32   pd   L

Raymond vic.

Peyton, John B., House (Waverly)
HABS MS-33   pd   L
Waverly; see Peyton, John B., House

HOLMES COUNTY

Lexington

Gwin House
HABS MS-109   pd   L

Lexington vic.

Dale House
HABS MS-108   pd   L

JACKSON COUNTY

Ocean Springs

Sullivan, Louis H., Summer House
HABS MS-166   s   L

Pascagoula

Bellevue; see Pollack House
De La Pointe-Krebs House; see French
  Fort, Old
Delmas, Valentine, House
Front St.
HABS MS-17   pd   L
French Fort, Old (De La Pointe-Krebs
  House; Spanish Fort, Old)
HABS MS-18   s   H
La Frederick de St. Ferol House
HABS MS-16   pd   L

476

Pollack House (Bellevue)
E. Beach Blvd.
HABS MS-20   pd   L
Spanish Fort, Old; see French Fort, Old
Warren, Frank, House
E. Beach
HABS MS-19   pd   L

JEFFERSON COUNTY

Cannonsburg vic.

Chamberlain House; see Mound Plantation
Mound Plantation (Mount Locust;
    Chamberlain House)
Natchez Trace National Pkwy.
HABS MS-159   s pd   L
Mount Locust; see Mound Plantation

Church Hill

Christ Episcopal Church; see Church Hill
    Chapel
Church Hill Chapel (Christ Episcopal
    Church)
HABS MS-34   pd   L

Fayette vic.

Springfield Plantation
Coles Creek vic.
HABS MS-206   d   H

Rodney

Presbyterian Church
HABS MS-29   pd   L
Sacred Heart Roman Catholic Church
Spring Branch Creek
HABS MS-208   d   H

Rodney vic.

Laurel Hill Plantation House
Rodney & Red Lick Rds.
HABS MS-207   d   H

LOWNDES COUNTY

Columbus

Banks House (White Arches)
HABS MS-104   pd   L
Billups, John, House (Snowden)
HABS MS-91   pd   L
Burris House (Riverview)
HABS MS-83   pd   L
Catholic Church (Church of the
    Annunciation)
HABS MS-101   pd   L
Cedars, The
HABS MS-84   pd   L
Church of the Annunciation; see Catholic
    Church
Errolton; see Weaver House
Flynn House
HABS MS-85   pd   L
Franklin Academy
HABS MS-89   pd   L
Franklin Square; see Pratt House

Hardy, J. W., Estate (Whitehall)
HABS MS-93   pd   L
Kinnebrew House (Temple Heights)
HABS MS-86   pd   L
Lee, Gen. Steven D., House
HABS MS-105   pd   L
Lowndes County Courthouse
HABS MS-81   pd   L
Magahy House (Shadow Lawn)
HABS MS-92   pd   L
Pratt House (Franklin Square)
HABS MS-102   pd   L
Riverview; see Burris House
Rosedale
HABS MS-82   pd   L
Shadow Lawn; see Magahy House
Snowden; see Billups, John, House
Temple Heights; see Kinnebrew House
Thomas, Pratt, House; see Woodward
    House
Weaver House (Errolton)
HABS MS-103   pd   L
White Arches; see Banks House
Whitehall; see Hardy, J. W., Estate
Woodward House (Thomas, Pratt, House)
HABS MS-88   pd   L

Columbus vic.

Sanders House
HABS MS-106   pd   L
Waverly
HABS MS-87   pd   L

Nashville Ferry

Gardner Farm; see Jeffries-Gardner Farm
Jeffries-Gardner Farm (Gardner Farm)
Carmen Church vic.
HABS MS-170   s pd L
Norwood-Williams House (Williams
    House)
Carmen Church vic.
HABS MS-171   pd   L
Williams House; see Norwood-Williams
    House

Steens vic.

Covered Bridge, Old
HABS MS-90   pd   L

MADISON COUNTY

Mannsdale

Chapel of the Cross
HABS MS-17-3   s pd L

MARION COUNTY

Columbia (South)

Ford House
HABS MS-11   pd   L

MONROE COUNTY

Aberdeen

Aberdeen Station (Frisco Railway Depot)
U.S. Rt. 45
HABS MS-169   s pd L
Barrett House
HABS MS-75   pd   L
Bradford Place
HABS MS-79   pd   L
Castle, The
HABS MS-76   pd   L
Davis, Col., House (Davis, Judge Reuben,
    House)
Commerce St.
HABS MS-74   pd   L
Davis, Judge Reuben, House; see Davis,
    Col., House
French House
HABS MS-71   pd   L
Frisco Railway Depot; see Aberdeen
    Station
Holiday Haven
Meridian St.
HABS MS-70   pd   L
Howard House
423 High St.
HABS MS-69   pd   L
Mann House
HABS MS-78   pd   L
Strong House
HABS MS-72   pd   L
Taylor's, Murff's, & Pickle's Stores
E. Bank of Tombigbee River
HABS MS-209   pd   H
Walker, W. B., House
HABS MS-73   pd   L
Woods House
HABS MS-77   pd   L

MONTGOMERY COUNTY

Winona

Moore, Col., House
HABS MS-112   pd   L

NOXUBEE COUNTY

Macon

Cline House
HABS MS-97   pd   L
Harrison House
HABS MS-96   pd   L
Pleasants, J. J., House
HABS MS-94   pd   L
Richardson House
HABS MS-95   pd   L
Scales House
HABS MS-98   pd   L
Yates House
HABS MS-99   pd   L

Macon vic.

Water Power Grist Mill, Old
HABS MS-100　　　　　pd　L

PRENTISS COUNTY

New Site

Searcy, Ezra, House
W. of Prentiss-Tishimingo County Line
HABS MS-172　　　　　pd　L

TISHOMINGO COUNTY

Bay Springs vic.

Bay Springs Bridge
Spanning Mackey's Creek
HAER MS-3　　　　s　　　H

Tishomingo

Adams, R. G., House
Mackeys Creek vic.
HABS MS-173　　　s pd　L
Allen Line Schoolteacher's House
Marietta & Jacinto Rd.
HABS MS-174　　　　pd　L
Butler Dogtrot
Old Natchez Trace
HABS MS-183　　　s pd　L
Butler, James T., House
Old Natchez Trace
HABS MS-175　　　　pd　L
Eaton, Billie, House
Old Natchez Trace
HABS MS-176　　　　pd　L
Eaton, John, House
Old Natchez Trace vic.
HABS MS-177　　　s p　　L
Holley, Nancy Belle, House
Old Natchez Trace vic.
HABS MS-178　　　　pd　L
Riddle, A. L., House
Old Natchez Trace vic.
HABS MS-179　　　　pd　L
Riddle, M. V., Barn
Old Natchez Trace vic.
HABS MS-180　　　s pd　L
Trimm, John R., Barn
Old Natchez Trace
HABS MS-181　　　s pd　L

WARREN COUNTY

Blakely

Blakely
HABS MS-137　　　　pd　L
Blakely Gin
HABS MS-138　　　　pd　L

Edwards vic.

Messinger House
HABS MS-135　　　　pd　L

Vicksburg

Balfour, Dr. William T., House
Crawford St.
HABS MS-116　　　　pd　L
Bodley House; see Plain Gables
Booth, Duncan, House
HABS MS-132　　　　pd　L
Bryan House; see Marshall, Rev. C. K.,
　House
Canizaro House; see McRae Bank
Confederate Avenue Bridge (Vicksburg
　National Military Park)
HABS MS-210　　　d　　H
Cook, Col. Edwin Grey, House
1104 Harrison St.
HABS MS-126　　　　pd　L
Floweree (Tuminello House)
2309 Pearl St.
HABS MS-167　　　s　　L
Green, Duff, House
Locust & First East St.
HABS MS-120　　　　pd　L
Hicks, Dr. John, House (Steigleman House)
Main St.
HABS MS-123　　　　pd　L
Hotel Washington
Washington & China Sts.
HABS MS-187　　　d　　H
Hyland House
HABS MS-136　　　　pd　L
Klein, John A., House
2200 Oak St.
HABS MS-129　　　　pd　L
Lake, William A., House
Main St.
HABS MS-122　　　　pd　L
Lane, John, House
Crawford St.
HABS MS-114　　　　pd　L
Luckett Group
1116 Crawford St.
HABS MS-117　　　　pd　L
Marshall, Rev. C. K., House (Bryan House)
1128 Grove St.
HABS MS-130　　　　pd　L
Masonic Temple
Grove & Washington Sts.
HABS MS-188　　　d　　H
McNutt, Gov. A. G., House
Monroe & First East Sts.
HABS MS-121　　　　pd　L
McRae Bank (Canizaro House; Planters
　Hall)
906 Monroe St.
HABS MS-118　　　　pd　L
Plain Gables (Bodley House)
805 Locust St.
HABS MS-127　　　　pd　L
Planters Hall; see McRae Bank
Porterfield House; see Shamrock
Shamrock (Porterfield House)
Oak St.
HABS MS-17-2　　　s pd　L

Shannon, Marmaduke, House
701 Adams St.
HABS MS-124　　　　pd　L
Shirley House; see Wexford Lodge
St. Francis Xavier Convent
Crawford St.
HABS MS-115　　　　pd　L
St. Paul's Catholic Church Rectory
Crawford St.
HABS MS-189　　　d　　H
Steele, Esther R., House
1202 Adams St.
HABS MS-128　　　　pd　L
Steigleman House; see Hicks, Dr. John,
　House
Tuminello House; see Floweree
Vicksburg National Military Park; see
　Confederate Avenue Bridge
Warren County Courthouse
Grove St.
HABS MS-119　　　s pd　L H
Wexford Lodge (Shirley House)
Vicksburg National Military Park
HABS MS-133　　　　pd　L
Wilson, Victor, House
1010 First East St.
HABS MS-125　　　　pd　L

Vicksburg vic.

Ferguson House
HABS MS-134　　　　pd　L
Fonsylvania; see Rummage House
Rummage House (Wale House;
　Fonsylvania)
HABS MS-131　　　　pd　L
Wale House; see Rummage House

WASHINGTON COUNTY

Chatham vic.

Everhope
HABS MS-145　　　　pd　L

Foote vic.

Erwin House (Mount Holly Plantation)
HABS MS-146　　　　pd　L
Mount Holly Plantation; see Erwin House

Greenville

McAlester House; see Wildwood
Wildwood (McAlester House)
HABS MS-141　　　　pd　L

Greenville vic.

Locust
HABS MS-142　　　　pd　L

Longwood

Longwood
HABS MS-144　　　　pd　L

Wayside

Belmont
HABS MS-143　　　　pd　L

WILKINSON COUNTY

Centreville vic.

Dixon House (Interior)
HABS MS-53   pd   L

Fort Adams

Curry House
HABS MS-63   pd   L
Murray House
HABS MS-64   pd   L

Fort Adams vic.

Desert Plantation; see Sample, Capt. Carmichael, House (Interior)

Sample, Capt. Carmichael, House (Interior) (Desert Plantation)
HABS MS-59   pd   L
Wall, Evans, House
HABS MS-52   pd   L

Woodville

Baptist Church
HABS MS-50   pd   L
Lewis House
HABS MS-58   pd   L
Right of Way & Track Map; see Yazoo & Mississippi Valley Railroad

Yazoo & Mississippi Valley Railroad (Right of Way & Track Map)
HAER MS-2   s   H

Woodville vic.

Saulsberry (Sheppard House)
HABS MS-60   pd   L
Sheppard House; see Saulsberry
West Feliciana Railroad Right-of-Way
HAER MS-1   pd   L

YAZOO COUNTY

Yazoo City vic.

Bleak House
HABS MS-139   pd   L

Missouri

Kansas City
Wornall House
146 West 61 Terrace
HABS MO-267   s   H

St. Louis
Allen-Collier Building
7-11 N. First St.
HABS MO-1160   s   L
Bacon House (Lace House)
1131 Morrison Ave.
HABS MO-110   pd   L
Bain, George, House
2115 Park Ave.
HABS MO-1157-A   pd   L
Bissell, Capt. Lewis, Mansion
Randall Pl.
HABS MO-16   s pd   L
Bissell, Gen. Daniel, House (Franklinville Farm)
10225 Bellefontaine Rd.
HABS MO-145   s pd   H
Blossom House
Union Blvd. & Enright Ave.
HABS MO-31-4   s pd   L
Booth-Papin Building
119-121 N. First St.
HABS MO-1162   s   L
Campbell, Robert, House
1508 Locust St.
HABS MO-12   pd   L
Castleman-Mackay Mansion
HABS MO-1161-A   pd   L
Cathedral, Old; see Church of St. Louis of France (Roman Catholic)
Cavender, Gen. John S., House
21 Benton Pl.
HABS MO-1162-A   pd   L
Chatillon-DeMenil House
3352 S. Thirteenth St.
HABS MO-14   pd   L
211-213 Chestnut Street (Commercial Building); see St. Louis River Front

Chinese Pavilion; see Tower Grove Park, Shelter Twenty-one
Chouteau, Auguste, Gravestone
Calvary Cemetery
HABS MO-124   pd   L
Chouteau Building
523-29 N. First St.
HABS MO-271   s   H
Church of St. Louis of France (Roman Catholic) (Cathedral, Old)
Third & Walnut Sts.
HABS MO-31-1   s pd   L
Church of St. Mary of Victory; see St. Mary's Roman Catholic Church
Church of the Messiah (Unitarian)
Garrison & Locust Sts.
HABS MO-1179   p   L
Clay, Col. Henry, House (Orchard Farm, Old)
HABS MO-118   pd   L
Clemens, James S., House
HABS MO-1163-A   pd   L
Cotton Belt Building
408 Pine
HABS MO-272   p   H
Eads Bridge
HABS MO-1190   p   L
Eliot House
4446 Westminster Place
HABS MO-1164-A   pd   L
Field, Eugene, House
634 S. Broadway
HABS MO-31-3   s pd   L
Franklinville Farm; see Bissell, Gen. Daniel, House
Gantt, Thomas, Building
219-221 Chestnut St.
HABS MO-1158   s   L
Gaty, Sam, Mansion
3408 N. Ninth St.
HABS MO-128   pd   L

Graham & Newman Building (Newman's Folly)
210-218-220 Olive St.
HABS MO-1177   p   L
Grant-Dent House
702 Fourth & Cerre Sts.
HABS MO-31-2   s pd   L
Hall Building
309 Market St.
HABS MO-1142   p   H
Johnson House
613 Market St.
HABS MO-1145   pd   L
Kulage-Backer House
1413 S. Tenth St.
HABS MO-115   d   L
Labadie Cottage
317 Poplar St.
HABS MO-127   pd   L
Labadie House
517-19 S. Third St.
HABS MO-119   s p   L
Lace House; see Bacon House
Lily Pond Summerhouse; see Tower Grove Park, Shelter Twenty-eight
Lindemann-Kahre House
6700 Robbins Mill Rd.
HABS MO-1191   p   L
Lionberger, Isaac H., House
HABS MO-1165   pd   L
Logan, Capt. Floyd, House
2825 Pine St.
HABS MO-1166   pd   L
Mallinckrodt House
3524 N. Ninth St.
HABS MO-129   pd   L
Marie & St. Joseph Church
8304 Minnesota Ave.
HABS MO-117   pd   L
Marine Hospital
Marine Ave.
HABS MO-1136   pd   L

Maury House
HABS MO-19   pd   L

McEwing-McManus House
3127 Laclede Ave.
HABS MO-1167   pd   L

Meier, Adolphus, House
Ninth & Bremen Ave.
HABS MO-130   pd   L

Merchants Bank Building
HABS MO-273   d   H

Merchants' Bank Building
First & Locust Sts.
HABS MO-1176   p   L

Michael Building
207 N. First St.
HABS MO-1157   s   L

Missouri Botanical Garden, Administration Building
2315 Tower Grove Ave.
HABS MO-1135-B   s pd   H

Missouri Botanical Garden, Gatehouse
Cleveland Ave.
HABS MO-1135-F   pd   H

Missouri Botanical Garden, Henry Shaw Mausoleum
2315 Tower Grove Ave.
HABS MO-1135-E   s d   H

Missouri Botanical Garden, Linnean House
2315 Tower Grove Ave.
HABS MO-1135-D   s pd   H

Missouri Botanical Garden, Museum
2315 Tower Grove Ave.
HABS MO-1135-C   s d   H

Missouri Botanical Gardens, Henry Shaw Townhouse
2315 Tower Grove Ave.
HABS MO-1135-A   s d   H

Missouri Botanical Garden
HABS MO-1135   s d   H

Musick's Ferry Rock House, Old
Hall Ferry Rd.
HABS MO-142   pd   L

New National Hotel; see St. Louis River Front

Newman's Folly; see Graham & Newman Building

119-121 North Main Street (Commercial Building); see St. Louis River Front

303 North Main Street (Commercial Building); see St. Louis River Front

305 North Main Street (Commercial Building); see St. Louis River Front

7-15 North Main Street (Commercial Building); see St. Louis River Front

Orchard Farm, Old; see Clay, Col. Henry, House

Papin Building
113-115 N. First St.
HABS MO-1161   s   L

Park Structure 29X; see Tower Grove Park, Superintendent's House

Park Structure 32X; see Tower Grove Park, West Gate House & Gate

Park Structure Fifteen; see Tower Grove Park, Music Stand

Parochial School, First in St. Louis
HABS MO-112   pd   L

Post Office Building, Old (Ruins)
22-26 N. Second St.
HABS MO-1139   s p   L H

Reller, F., House
821 Destreham St.
HABS MO-126   pd   L

Rice House; see St. Louis River Front

Rock House, Old
Wharf & Chestnut Sts.
HABS MO-31-5   s pd   L

Roy, Jean Baptiste, House (615 South Second Street (Old Stone House))
HABS MO-13   s pd   L

Scott's Hotel; see St. Louis River Front

Shaw, Henry, Country House (Tower Grove)
HABS MO-31-7   s pd   L

Sherman, Gen., House
912 Garrison Ave.
HABS MO-125   pd   L

Sherrick, George W., House
2618 S. Seventh St.
HABS MO-1168   pd   L

Sisters of St. Joseph Convent
HABS MO-123   pd   L

Soulard Mansion
1249 S. Ninth St.
HABS MO-113   pd   L

Soulard (Project)
HABS MO-275   p   H

615 South Second Street (Old Stone House); see Roy, Jean Baptiste, House

South Well; see Tower Grove Park, Shelter Eleven

St. John's Catholic Church
HABS MO-121   pd   L

St. Louis Arsenal, Building Number 3
Second & Arsenal Sts.
HABS MO-1158-A   p   L

St. Louis Arsenal, Building Number 6
Second & Arsenal Sts.
HABS MO-1159-A   p   L

St. Louis Arsenal, Old Barracks
Second & Arsenal Sts.
HABS MO-1160-A   pd   L

St. Louis Courthouse, Old
Fourth & Market Sts.
HABS MO-31-8   s pd   L

St. Louis Post Office & Customs House
Ninth & Locust vic.
HABS MO-1159   pd   L

St. Louis River Front (305 North Main Street (Commercial Building))
HABS MO-11-E   p   L

St. Louis River Front (115 Valentine Street (Brick House))
115 Valentine St.
HABS MO-11-F   p   L

St. Louis River Front (303 North Main Street (Commercial Building))
HABS MO-11-D   p   L

St. Louis River Front (New National Hotel; Scott's Hotel; U.S. Hotel; Rice House)
300 Market St.
HABS MO-1131   s pd   L

St. Louis River Front (211-213 Chestnut Street (Commercial Building))
HABS MO-11-C   p   L

St. Louis River Front (119-121 North Main Street (Commercial Building))
HABS MO-11-B   p   L

St. Louis River Front (7-15 North Main Street (Commercial Building))
HABS MO-11-A   p   L

St. Mary's Roman Catholic Church (Church of St. Mary of Victory)
748 S. Third St.
HABS MO-31-6   s pd   L

St. Nicholas Hotel; see Victoria Building

St. Patrick's Church
Sixth & Biddle Sts.
HABS MO-122   pd   L

St. Vincent de Paul Church
HABS MO-114   pd   L

200 Stein Street (Stone Row Houses)
HABS MO-17   pd   L

Steinkauler, Guido, House
HABS MO-1169   pd   L

Temple Israel (Union Memorial African Methodist Episcopal Church)
Leffingwell & Pine Sts.
HABS MO-1170   pd   L

Theilman, John G., House
1825 S. Ninth St.
HABS MO-1171   pd   L

Tower Grove; see Shaw, Henry, Country House

Tower Grove Park
HABS MO-1137   d   H

Tower Grove Park, Bridges
4274 Magnolia Ave.
HABS MO-1137-T   s d   H

Tower Grove Park, East Gate; see Tower Grove Park, Entrance Gates

Tower Grove Park, Entrance Gates (Tower Grove Park, East Gate)
Grand Ave. Entrance
HABS MO-1137-A   s pd   L H

Tower Grove Park, Music Stand (Park Structure Fifteen)
4274 Magnolia Ave.
HABS MO-1137-K   s d   H

Tower Grove Park, North Gate
4274 Magnolia Ave.
HABS MO-1137-C   s d   H

Tower Grove Park, Planthouse Range (Tower Grove Park, Structures 2 & 3)
4274 Magnolia Ave.
HABS MO-1137-U   d   H

Tower Grove Park, Sailboat Pond
4274 Magnolia Ave.
HABS MO-1137-H   d   H

Tower Grove Park, Shelter 16
4274 Magnolia Ave.
HABS MO-1137-L   s   H

Tower Grove Park, Shelter 19 & 20
4274 Magnolia Ave.
HABS MO-1137-0   s   H

Tower Grove Park, Shelter Eighteen
HABS MO-1137-N   s d   H

Tower Grove Park, Shelter Eleven (South Well)
4274 Magnolia Ave.
HABS MO-1137-J   s d   H

Tower Grove Park, Shelter Seventeen
4274 Magnolia Ave.
HABS MO-1137-M   s d   H

Tower Grove Park, Shelter Ten (Turkish Shelter)
4274 Magnolia Ave.
HABS MO-1137-I   s pd   H

Tower Grove Park, Shelter Twenty-eight (Lily Pond Summerhouse)
HABS MO-1137-S   s d   H

Tower Grove Park, Shelter Twenty-five
4274 Magnolia Ave.
HABS MO-1137-R   s pd   H

Tower Grove Park, Shelter Twenty-one (Chinese Pavilion)
4274 Magnolia Ave.
HABS MO-1137-P   s d   H

Tower Grove Park, Shelter Twenty-two
4274 Magnolia Ave.
HABS MO-1137-Q   s pd   H

Tower Grove Park, South Gate (Arsenal St.)
4274 Magnolia Ave.
HABS MO-1137-D   s d   H

Tower Grove Park, South Gate Lodge
4274 Magnolia Ave.
HABS MO-1137-E   s d   H

Tower Grove Park, Stone House & Stable Complex (Tower Grove Park, Structures, 31X, 7 & 6)
4274 Magnolia Ave.
HABS MO-1137-G   d   H

Tower Grove Park, Structures 2 & 3; see Tower Grove Park, Planthouse Range

Tower Grove Park, Structures, 31X, 7 & 6; see Tower Grove Park, Stone House & Stable Complex

Tower Grove Park, Superintendent's House (Park Structure 29X)
4274 Magnolia Ave.
HABS MO-1137-F   s pd   H

Tower Grove Park, West Gate House & Gate (Park Structure 32X)
4274 Magnolia Ave.
HABS MO-1137-B   s d   H

Turkish Shelter; see Tower Grove Park, Shelter Ten

Union Memorial African Methodist Episcopal Church; see Temple Israel

University Building
Sixteenth & Pine St.
HABS MO-120   pd   L

U.S. Hotel; see St. Louis River Front

115 Valentine Street (Brick House); see St. Louis River Front

Victoria Building (St. Nicholas Hotel)
Eighth & Locust Sts.
HABS MO-1138   pd   L

Wainwright Building
Seventh & Chestnut Sts.
HABS MO-1140   p   H

Walsh House
2721 Pine St.
HABS MO-15   pd   L

Washington Terrace
Union Blvd.
HABS MO-274   p   H

Water Tower, Red
Blair St.
HABS MO-1192   p   L

Whittemore, John, House
Garrison & Franklin Sts.
HABS MO-1178   p   L

BENTON COUNTY

Warsaw vic.

Heath, Calloway G., House
Rt. 7 & Rt. KK vic.
HABS MO-1248   s p   L

House
Rt. 7 & Rt. KK vic.
HABS MO-1239   pd   L

House
Rt. KK
HABS MO-1238   pd   L

House
Rt. O & Rt. 83 vic.
HABS MO-1240   pd   L

Kinkead, Samuel, House
S. Grand River & Little Tebo Creek vic.
HABS MO-1221   s pd   L

Lynn House
Hogles Creek School vic.
HABS MO-1241   pd   L

Peal Bend School
Rt. KK & Valley View vic.
HABS MO-1242   pd   L

BOONE COUNTY

Columbia

Boone County Courthouse, Old
HABS MO-1153   pd   L

University of Missouri, First Building (Columns)
HABS MO-1155   pd   L

University of Missouri, Jefferson, Thomas, Tombstone
HABS MO-1154   pd   L

Columbia vic.

Greenwood
HABS MO-1151   p   L

Shipley House
HABS MO-1149   p   L

Woodside
HABS MO-1152   p   L

CALLAWAY COUNTY

Auxvasse

Bennett House
HABS MO-185   pd   L

Auxvasse vic.

Curd, Gen., Mansion
HABS MO-184   pd   L

Swan, John, House
HABS MO-183   pd   L

Fulton

Courthouse
HABS MO-176   pd   L

Harris House
815 Court St.
HABS MO-173   pd   L

Henderson, Judge James S., House
703 Market St.
HABS MO-172   pd   L

Hockaday, Judge Irving, House
HABS MO-171   pd   L

McCradie House
Bluff & Fifth Sts.
HABS MO-174   pd   L

Nash-Hollman House
HABS MO-177   pd   L

Nesbeth Mansion
Old Fulton Rd.
HABS MO-175   pd   L

Mokane

Ferguson, Swan, House
HABS MO-181   pd   L

Moore, John B., House
HABS MO-182   pd   L

Ratekin, LeGrand, House
HABS MO-179   pd   L

Rogers Log Cabin
HABS MO-178   pd   L

Smith, Thomas, House
HABS MO-180   pd   L

CLAY COUNTY

Smithville vic.

Poff, James, House
Paradise Rd.
HABS MO-1225   pd   L

Rollins, Sophia, House
Farm Rt. F. vic.
HABS MO-1226   pd   L

Ross, Rueben, Barn
Clinton County Line vic.
HABS MO-1223   s pd   L

CLINTON COUNTY

Trimble

Waddell A Truss Bridge
Spanning Lin Branch Creek, State Rt. 4
HAER MO-1   s d   L

COLE COUNTY

Jefferson City vic.

Lohman's Landing Building
HABS MO-1194   pd   L

COOPER COUNTY

Boonville

Thespian Hall
Fifth & Vine Sts.
HABS MO-233   pd   L

FRANKLIN COUNTY

Detmold vic.

Pelster House & Barn
Cedar Fork Rd.
HABS MO-244   d   H

GASCONADE COUNTY

Bay

Bay Mercantile Company
County Rt. K
HABS MO-245   s d   H
Bay Mercantile Company, Barn
HABS MO-246   s   H
Bay Mercantile Company, Store
HABS MO-247   s   H

Gasconade vic.

Kotthoff-Weeks Farm
County Rt. J
HABS MO-248   s   H
Kotthoff-Weeks Farm, Barn
HABS MO-249   s p   H
Kotthoff-Weeks Farmhouse
HABS MO-250   s   H
Kotthoff-Weeks Farms, Smokehouse
County Rd. J
HABS MO-251   s   H

Hermann

Hermann Star Mills
238 E. First St.
HABS MO-252   s d   H
Pommer-Gentner House
108 Market St.
HABS MO-253   d   H
Rotunda, The
Eitzen Park (Fairgrounds)
HABS MO-254   d   H

Stone Hill Winery
401 W. Twelfth St.
HABS MO-255   s d   H
Strephly, C. P., House
130 W. Second St.
HABS MO-256   s d   H
White House Hotel
232 E. Wharf St.
HABS MO-257   d   L

Hermann vic.

Harrison Hill; see Poeschel, William, House
Poeschel, William, House (Harrison Hill)
W. Tenth St.
HABS MO-258   d   H

Owensville vic.

Krammer-Witte Barn
County Rt. P
HABS MO-259   s d   H

GREENE COUNTY

Ray House (Wilson's Creek Battlefield
National Park)
HABS MO-1201   s   H
Wilson's Creek Battlefield National Park;
see Ray House

HENRY COUNTY

Clinton vic.

Bethlehem Baptist Church
Rt. AA & 35 vic.
HABS MO-1227   pd   L
Bethlehem Baptist Church
Rt. AA & 35 vic.
HABS MO-1227   pd   L
Burkhart, Peter, Farm
Rt. EE
HABS MO-1228   pd   L
Chastain, Jeremiah, Farm
Tightwad vic.
HABS MO-1230   pd   L
French, George, Farm
Rt. AA & 35 vic.
HABS MO-1229   pd   L
House
HABS MO-1231   pd   L
Noble, Joseph, House
Rt. EE in LaDue
HABS MO-1249   s pd   L

Deepwater vic.

French, John, Barn
S. Grand River vic.
HABS MO-1245-A   s p   L
French, John, Farm
S. Grand River
HABS MO-1245   s pd   L
French, John, Outbuilding
S. Grand River vic.
HABS MO-1245-B   p   L

Gaskill, Moses, House
Rt. W vic.
HABS MO-1244   s pd   L
House
Rd. E
HABS MO-1232   pd   L
Lloyd, William C., House
Rd. E
HABS MO-1233   pd   L
Rickson House; see Stewart-Rickerson
House
Stewart-Rickerson House (Rickson House)
Rd. E. vic.
HABS MO-1234   pd   L

La Due

Batchelett House
HABS MO-260   s p   H

HOWARD COUNTY

Fayette vic.

Lilac Hill (Morrison House)
HABS MO-239   d   L
Morrison House; see Lilac Hill

Glasgow vic.

Jackson, John, House
HABS MO-241   pd   L
Sylvan Villa
Fayette Rd.
HABS MO-240   pd   L
Tarton-Turner House
HABS MO-242   p   L

New Franklin

Chilton House
Missouri Ave.
HABS MO-237   pd   L

New Franklin vic.

Burckhardt, Nicholas S., House
HABS MO-243   pd   L
Kingsbury House
HABS MO-238   p   L

JACKSON COUNTY

Independence

Adkins Cabin (Aiken Cabin)
107 W. Kansas Ave.
HABS MO-219   pd   L
Aiken Cabin; see Adkins Cabin
Jackson County Courthouse
107-109 W. Kansas Ave.
HABS MO-220   pd   L

Kansas City

Boley Building
1103 Walnut Jones St.
HABS MO-261   d   H
Emery Bird Thayer Building
1016 Grand Ave.
HABS MO-266   d   H

First Presbyterian Church
Pennyslvania St., Westport vic.
HABS MO-31-18   s p d   L

Folly Theatre; see Standard Theatre

Harris, John, House
4000 Baltimore Ave.
HABS MO-31-16   s p d   L

Muncipal Auditorum
1310 Wyandotte
HABS MO-262   d   H

New York Life Building
20 W. Ninth St.
HABS MO-263   d   H

Rockford School
Raytown & Longview Rd.
HABS MO-1224   s p d   L

Scarritt Building & Arcade
818 Grand Ave.
HABS MO-264   d   H

Standard Theatre (Folly Theatre)
300 W. Twelfth St.
HABS MO-265   d   H

Lees Summit

Farm Row; see Longview Farm, Workers'
   Cottages

Long, Robert A., House; see Longview
   Farm

Longview Farm (Long, Robert A., House)
Longview Rd.
HABS MO-1222   s p d   L

**Longview Farm, Assistant Manager's
   House**
HABS MO-1222-43   s p d   L

Longview Farm, Bandstand
Longview Rd.
HABS MO-1222-18   p   L

Longview Farm, Boarding House
   (Longview Farm, Hotel)
HABS MO-1222-33   s p d   L

Longview Farm, Brood Mare Barn
Longview Rd.
HABS MO-1222-38   p   L

**Longview Farm, Brood Mare Manager's
   House**
Longview Rd.
HABS MO-1222-39   p   L

Longview Farm, Chapel
Longview Rd.
HABS MO-1222-6   p   L

Longview Farm, Colt Barn
Longview Rd.
HABS MO-1222-34   p   L

Longview Farm, Dairy Manager's House
Longview Rd.
HABS MO-1222-23   p   L

Longview Farm, Duplex; see Longview
   Farm, Sunny Slope Farmhouse

Longview Farm, Entrance Gates
Longview Rd.
HABS MO-1222-5   p   L

**Longview Farm, Garage, Apartment &
   Powerhouse**
HABS MO-1222-26   s p d

Longview Farm, Gate Lodge Number 1
Longview Rd.
HABS MO-1222-46   p   L

Longview Farm, Gate Lodge Number 2
HABS MO-1222-47   s p d   L

Longview Farm, General Manager's House
HABS MO-1222-42   s p d   L

Longview Farm, Grandstand & Clubhouse
Longview Rd.
HABS MO-1222-17   p   L

**Longview Farm, Greenhouse Manager's
   House**
HABS MO-1222-27   s p d   L

Longview Farm, Greenhouses
HABS MO-1222-25   s p d   L

Longview Farm, Hog & Sale Barn
Longview Rd.
HABS MO-1222-35   p   L

Longview Farm, Hog Manager's House
Longview Rd.
HABS MO-1222-36   p   L

Longview Farm, Horse Trainer's House
Longview Rd.
HABS MO-1222-40   p   L

Longview Farm, Hospital Barn
Longview Rd.
HABS MO-1222-9   p   L

Longview Farm, Hotel; see Longview Farm,
   Boarding House

Longview Farm, Implement Shed
Longview Rd.
HABS MO-1222-30   p   L

Longview Farm, Main Residence
Longview Rd.
HABS MO-1222-1   p   L

Longview Farm, Manure Pit
Longview Rd.
HABS MO-1222-24   p   L

Longview Farm, North Dairy Barn
Longview Rd.
HABS MO-1222-21   p   L

Longview Farm, Office
Longview Rd.
HABS MO-1222-8   p   L

**Longview Farm, Paint, Carpentry &
   Blacksmith Shop**
Longview Rd.
HABS MO-1222-31   p   L

Longview Farm, Pump House
Longview Rd.
HABS MO-1222-11   p   L

Longview Farm, Saddle Horse Barn
Longview Rd.
HABS MO-1222-16   p   L

**Longview Farm, Saddle Horse Manager's
   House**
Longview Rd.
HABS MO-1222-19   p   L

Longview Farm, Show Horse Barn
Longview Rd.
HABS MO-1222-14   p   L

**Longview Farm, South Dairy
   Barn-Milkhouse**
Longview Rd.
HABS MO-1222-20   p   L

Longview Farm, Stallion Barn
Longview Rd.
HABS MO-1222-15   p   L

Longview Farm, Summer Camp
Longview Rd.
HABS MO-1222-13   p   L

Longview Farm, Sunny Slope Farmhouse
   (Longview Farm, Duplex)
Longview Rd.
HABS MO-1222-44   p   L

Longview Farm, Water Tank
Longview Rd.
HABS MO-1222-7   p   L

Longview Farm, Well House
Longview Rd.
HABS MO-1222-3   p   L

Longview Farm, Work Horse Barn
HABS MO-1222-29   s p d   L

Longview Farm, Workers' Cottages (Farm
   Row)
HABS MO-1222-41   s p d   L

Longview Farm, Worker's Residence
Longview Rd.
HABS MO-1222-45   p   L

Longview Farms, Pergola
Longview Rd.
HABS MO-1222-4   p   L H

JASPER COUNTY

Joplin

Conner Hotel, The
324 Main St.
HABS MO-1202   pd   L

JEFFERSON COUNTY

Barnhart

Cedars, The
HABS MO-198   pd   L

Cedars, The, Slave Cabin
HABS MO-198-A   pd   L

Beck

Pioneer Log House
HABS MO-194   pd   L

Danby

Brook, Capt., Farm
Rt. 25
HABS MO-1101   pd   L

Goldman vic.

Sandy Creek Bridge
HABS MO-1156   pd   L

Herculaneum

McMurray House
HABS MO-1100   pd   L

Kimmswick
Hermann-Oheim House
Fourth & Market Sts.
HABS MO-1132   s p d   L

Pevely
Harrington Log Cabin
HABS MO-196   p d   L
Moss, Milton, House
Pleasant Valley
HABS MO-197   p d   L
Ziegler, Capt., House
HABS MO-195   p d   L

Pevely vic.
Greystone
HABS MO-1133   s p d   L

LAFAYETTE COUNTY

Lexington
Anderson, Col. William Oliver, House
(Anderson House)
Civil War Battle of Lexington State Park
HABS MO-224   s p   L H
Anderson House; see Anderson, Col.
   William Oliver, House
Carr-O'Malley House
Highland Ave.
HABS MO-236   p   L
Chadwick House; see McCausland, W. G.,
   House
Christ Episcopal Church
HABS MO-235   p   L
Cumberland Presbyterian Church
HABS MO-227   p   L
Lafayette County Courthouse
HABS MO-228   p   L
McCausland, W. G., House (Chadwick
   House)
HABS MO-226   p   L
Pomeroy-Pristine House
1611 South St.
HABS MO-225   p   L

Lexington vic.
Aull House
HABS MO-234   p   L
Limerick's Folly
HABS MO-229   p   L

LINCOLN COUNTY

Moscow Mills
Drover's Inn
HABS MO-156   p d   L

LINN COUNTY

La Dede
Harris-Lamme House; see Pershing, Gen.
   John J., House

Pershing, Gen. John J., House
   (Harris-Lamme House)
State & Wahlow Sts.
HABS MO-268   s p   H

LIVINGSTON COUNTY

Lawson
Mount Vernon Church
Watkins Mill State Park
HABS MO-1185   s   L

MONROE COUNTY

Florida
Scobee, James W., Farm
Salt River vic.
HABS MO-1219   s p d   L
Violette, Merritt A., House
State Rt. 107 & County Rt. U vic.
HABS MO-1205   s p d   L

Goss
Eakin, Robert, Farm
County Rt. U vic.
HABS MO-1206   s p d   L
Mappin, Matthew, House
County Rt. U & U.S. Rt. 24 vic.
HABS MO-1207   s p d   L
Smith, Samuel H., House
Salt River vic.
HABS MO-1208   s p d   L

North Fork vic.
Fields, Charles, Granary
County Rt. P
HABS MO-1210   s p d   L

Paris vic.
Johnson, Daniel, House
State Rt. 154
HABS MO-1211   s p d   L

Stoutsville
Slee, Hugh C., House
Hill & Walnut Sts.
HABS MO-1213   s p d   L
Stoutsville, Town of
HABS MO-1212   s   L

Stoutsville vic.
Salt River Settlement
HABS MO-1203   s   L

Victor
Calhoon, A. Owen, House
Paris-to-Louisiana Rd. vic.
HABS MO-1215   p d   L
Hattersley, William, Store
Paris-to-Louisiana Rd. vic.
HABS MO-1216   s p d   L
Meeter, Mitchell, Barn
State Rt. 154 vic.
HABS MO-1218   s p d   L

Sinclair, James M., Farm
State Rt. 154 & County Rt. Z vic.
HABS MO-1220   s p d   L
Victor, Village of, General View
HABS MO-1214   s   L

Victor vic.
Crow, Basil, House
State Rt. 154
HABS MO-1217   s p d   L

PLATTE COUNTY

Noah's Arch Covered Bridge
County Rt. B over Little Platt River
HABS MO-270   s   H

RALLS COUNTY

Center vic.
Bell, Samuel F., House
County Rt. CC vic.
HABS MO-1204   s p d   L

Joanna
Peterson, John, House
HABS MO-1209   s p d   L

RAY COUNTY

Lawson
Franklin School
Watkins Mill State Park
HABS MO-1180   s   H

SALINE COUNTY

Arrow Rock
Bingham, George Caleb, House
Arrow Rock State Park
HABS MO-221   p d   L
City Jail, Old
Arrow Rock State Park
HABS MO-232   p d   L
Price House (Fence)
HABS MO-230   p   L
Seminary Building, Old
HABS MO-231   p d   L
Tavern, Old
Arrow Rock State Park
HABS MO-222   p d   L

Arrow Rock vic.
Sappington, William B., House
HABS MO-223   p d   L

SHELBY COUNTY

Bethel
Colony Tannery
HABS MO-1147   p   L

Bethel vic.

Elim House (Keil, Dr. William, House)
HABS MO-1146   p   L
Keil, Dr. William, House; see Elim House

ST. CHARLES COUNTY
Cottleville vic.

Campbell, Capt., House
HABS MO-157   pd   L

Dardenne

Mascheny, Dr., House
HABS MO-158   pd   L

Defiance

Parson's House
HABS MO-188   pd   L

Defiance vic.

Brien, Jonathan, House
HABS MO-160   pd   L
Fant, Buckner, House
HABS MO-189   pd   L
Hays, Daniel, Stone House
HABS MO-161   pd   L

Femme Osage

Boone, Nathan, House
HABS MO-159   pd   L

Flinthill vic.

Broadhead House
HABS MO-154   pd   L
Hubbart, Josiah, House
HABS MO-155   pd   L

Green Bottom

Flaugherty House
HABS MO-186   pd   L
Green House
HABS MO-187   pd   L

O'Fallon

Zumwalt, Jacob, Log Cabin
HABS MO-153   pd   L

Portage Des Sioux

Payne House
HABS MO-168   pd   L

St. Charles

Academy of the Sacred Heart; see Sacred
    Heart Convent
Chambers House; see Virginia Hotel
Chanter House
HABS MO-192   pd   L
Colier Methodist Episcopal Church
617 S. Main St.
HABS MO-166   pd   L
Coontz House
906 S. Main St.
HABS MO-164   pd   L
Flaugherty-McNair House
724 Main St.
HABS MO-169   pd   L

Griffith, Daniel D., House
HABS MO-152   pd   L
Keebe, Timothy, House
Main & Pike Sts.
HABS MO-191   pd   L
Kuhlmann House
HABS MO-163   pd   L
McElhiney Mansion
HABS MO-167   pd   L
Moore House
1017 S. Main St.
HABS MO-165   pd   L
Rock House
HABS MO-149   pd   L
Sacred Heart Convent (Academy of the
    Sacred Heart)
619 N. Second St.
HABS MO-147   pd   L H
Slave Cabin
HABS MO-170   pd   L
Slave House
HABS MO-151   pd   L
State Legislative Assembly Hall, First
208-214 S. Main St.
HABS MO-148   pd   L
Virginia Hotel (Chambers House)
234 S. Main St.
HABS MO-190   pd   L

St. Charles vic.

Potter House; see Shore House, Old
Shore House, Old (Potter House)
St. Charles Rd.
HABS MO-150   pd   L

Weldon Springs

Coonce, Jacob, Log Cabin
HABS MO-162   pd   L

ST. CLAIR COUNTY
Lowry City vic.

House
HABS MO-1235   pd   L
House
Rt. 22
HABS MO-1236   pd   L

Osceola

Aspass Dam; see Truman, Harry S., Dam
Flume; see Truman, Harry S., Dam
Truman, Harry S., Dam (Aspass Dam;
    Flume)
HAER MO-4   pd   H

Osceola vic.

Hooper, John M., House
HABS MO-1243   pd   L

Roscoe

Commercial Block (Jones Drug Block)
Main & First Sts.
HABS MO-1246   s pd   L

Jones Drug Block; see Commercial Block
Weinlig Store
Main St.
HABS MO-1247   s pd   L

Roscoe vic.

Pasley House
HABS MO-1237   pd   L

ST. LOUIS COUNTY
Affton

Benoist, Louis A., House; see Oakland
Oakland (Benoist, Louis A., House)
7801 Genesta St.
HABS MO-1182   s p   H

Affton vic.

Grant, Gen., Cabin; see Hardscrabble
Grant-Dent Country House (Whitehaven)
Grant Rd.
HABS MO-1150   s pd   L
Hardscrabble (Grant, Gen., Cabin)
Gravois Rd.
HABS MO-1134   pd   L
Whitehaven; see Grant-Dent Country
    House

Bellefontaine vic.

Bellefontaine Church
Bellefontaine Rd.
HABS MO-1144   pd   L

Carondelet

Marine Villa (Thul-Peters House)
3811 Kosciusko St.
HABS MO-1172   pd   L
Thul-Peters House; see Marine Villa

Chesterfield

Bates, Gov., House; see Thornhill
Bonhomme Church, Old (Presbyterian)
White & Conway Rds.
HABS MO-137   s pd   L H
Stuart Log Cabin
HABS MO-144   pd   L
Thornhill (Bates, Gov., House)
Arrowhead Lane
HABS MO-131   s pd   L H

Clayton

Hanley, Martin F., House
7600 Westmoreland Ave.
HABS MO-1193   s d   H

Crestwood

Long, William, Log House
9385 Pardee Rd.
HABS MO-1186   s p   L
Sappington House
Sappington Rd.
HABS MO-1173   pd   L

Ellisville

Ferris, Capt. Harvey, House
1362 Manchester Rd.
HABS MO-1184   s p   H

Florissant

Fort Bellefontaine
Bellefontaine Farms
HABS MO-146   pd   L
Myers, John B., House
180 W. Dunn Rd.
HABS MO-1183   s pd   H
Sisters of Loretto Convent
HABS MO-139   pd   L
St. Ferdinand Church
HABS MO-140   pd   L
St. Stanislaus Seminary
700 Howderschell Rd.
HABS MO-141   pd   L H

Florissant vic.

Mullanphy House; see Taille de Noyer
Taille de Noyer (Mullanphy House)
400 Taille de Noyer
HABS MO-1143   s pd   L

Fort Bellefontaine

Fort Bellefontaine, Powder Magazine
HABS MO-146-A   pd   L

Glendale

Armstrong House
700 E. Collins Ave.
HABS MO-143   pd   L

Kirkwood

Grace Episcopal Church
HABS MO-1187   p   H
Missouri-Pacific Railroad Station
HABS MO-1188   p   L
Mudd's Grove
302 W. Argonne Dr.
HABS MO-1189   p   H

Maplewood

Bartold Grove
Manchester & Hanley Sts.
HABS MO-193   pd   L

Overland

Ferguson Log Cabin
3631 Brown Rd.
HABS MO-132   pd   L
McKibben House
HABS MO-133   pd   L
Powers Mansion
National Bridge & Brown Rds.
HABS MO-134   pd   L

Pattonville

Fee Fee Church
Fee Fee Rd.
HABS MO-135   pd   L

Webster Groves

Peers Griffen House
224 College Ave.
HABS MO-1181   s p   H

Wellston

O'Brien, Dr., House
1232 Sutter Ave.
HABS MO-116   pd   L

STE. GENEVIEVE COUNTY

Bloomsdale

Drury House
HABS MO-1103   pd   L
Lee, Capt., House
Starr Rt.
HABS MO-1102   pd   L

Ste. Genevieve

Amoureaux House
HABS MO-1113   s pd   L
Baptiste, Jean, House; see Valle, Jean
     Baptiste, House
Beauvais, Joseph V., House
HABS MO-1121   s p   H
Bequet-Ribault House (Ribeau House)
St. Mary's (New Bourban) Rd.
HABS MO-1164   s   L
Bogy's House
HABS MO-1123   pd   L
Bolduc House, The
S. Main St.
HABS MO-1105   s   L
Courthouse, First (House, First Brick, West
     of Mississippi River)
Third & Market Sts.
HABS MO-1107   pd   L
Detchmendy House
Main & Market Sts.
HABS MO-1110   pd   L
Dufour House
HABS MO-1119   pd   L
Greentree Tavern; see Janis-Ziegler House
Guibourd, Jacques, House
HABS MO-1109   pd   L
**House, First Brick, West of Mississippi
     River;** see Courthouse, First
Indian Trading Post
Second & Merchant Sts.
HABS MO-31-13   s pd   L
Janis-Ziegler House (Greentree Tavern)
S. Main St.
HABS MO-1104   pd   L
Le Compte, Henry, House
HABS MO-1125   pd   L

Linn, Sen. Lewis, House
HABS MO-1117   pd   L
Loretto Convent, Old (Meillieur House)
Main St.
HABS MO-1111   pd   L
Meillieur House; see Loretto Convent, Old
Parochial School, First
HABS MO-1108   pd   L
Post Office, Old
HABS MO-1112   pd   L
Pratte, Joseph, House
HABS MO-1124   pd   L
Ribeau House; see Bequet-Ribault House
Rozier Bank
Second & Merchant Sts.
HABS MO-1116   pd   L
Second & Gabourie Streets (Old Stone
     House)
HABS MO-31-12   s pd   L
Shaw, Dr. Benjamin, House
HABS MO-1120   pd   L
Ste. Genevieve Academy
HABS MO-1118   pd   L
Ste. Genevieve Cemetery
Fifth St.
HABS MO-1130   pd   L
Valle, Felix & Odile Pratte, House
Merchant & Second Sts.
HABS MO-31-11   s pd   L
Valle, Francois B., House (Wilder House)
HABS MO-1122   pd   L
Valle, Jean Baptiste, House (Baptiste, Jean,
     House)
N. Main St.
HABS MO-1106   s p   H
Wilder House; see Valle, Francois B.,
     House
Wilder-Holt House
HABS MO-1174   s   L

WASHINGTON COUNTY

Old Mines

Murphy House
HABS MO-199   pd   L
St. Joachim's Church
HABS MO-1129   pd   L

Racola

Bequette Log House
HABS MO-1126   pd   L
Loomes San Soucie Log Cabin
HABS MO-1128   pd   L
Lucas Log Cabin
HABS MO-1127   pd   L

Montana

BEAVERHEAD COUNTY

Bannack

Beaverhead County Courthouse
Main St.
HABS MT-5   s p d   L

Methodist Church
Main St.
HABS MT-6   s p d   L

School and Masonic Temple
Main St.
HABS MT-4   s p d   L

BIG HORN COUNTY

Custer Battlefield

Custer Battlefield National Monument; see
    Superintendent's Lodge
Superintendent's Lodge (Custer Battlefield
    National Monument)
HABS MT-7   s p d   L

CASCADE COUNTY

Great Falls

108 Central (Commercial Building) (Park
    Hotel Annex)
HABS MT-36   s p d   H

Park Hotel Annex; see 108 Central
    (Commercial Building)

CUSTER COUNTY

Miles City

Miles, Gen., House
Hwy. 10
HABS MT-8   s p d   L

DEER LODGE COUNTY

Anaconda

Daly, Marcus, Hotel; see Montana Hotel
Montana Hotel (Daly, Marcus, Hotel)
Park St.
HABS MT-33   p d   H

GALLATIN COUNTY

Bozeman

City Hall & Opera House
Rouse Ave. & E. Main St.
HABS MT-18   s p d   L

Montana State University, Montana Hall
W. Garfield St.
HABS MT-25   p d   H

Tracy, William H., House
5 W. Mendenhall St.
HABS MT-29   p d   H

GOLDEN VALLEY COUNTY

Granite

Miners Union Hall
Main St.
HABS MT-15   s p d   L H

Superintendent's House
Magnolia Ave.
HABS MT-16   s p d   L H

JEFFERSON COUNTY

Elkhorn

Fraternity Hall
Main St.
HABS MT-9   s p d   L

LEWIS & CLARK COUNTY

Helena

Ashby, S. C., House
Dearborn St.
HABS MT-21   p d   H

Child, W. C., Ranch
State Hwy. 279
HABS MT-30   p d   H

Governor's Mansion, Old
304 N. Ewing St.
HABS MT-31   p d   H

Hauser, Samuel T., House
720 Madison Ave.
HABS MT-23   p d   H

Kluge House
540 W. Main St.
HABS MT-17   s p d   L H

Kohrs, Conrad, House
804 Dearborn Ave.
HABS MT-32   p d   H

Lewis & Clark County Courthouse
Broadway
HABS MT-27   p d   H

Masonic Temple, Second
Broadway & Jackson Sts.
HABS MT-34   p d   H

Neill, J. S. M., House
725 Madison Ave.
HABS MT-22   p d   H

Pover, T. C., Mansion
604 Harrison Ave.
HABS MT-28   p d   H

Seligman, A. J., House
802 Madison Ave.
HABS MT-24   p d   H

U.S. Assay Office
206 Broadway St.
HABS MT-26   p d   H

Helena vic.

Green Meadow Ranch
HABS MT-35   p d   H

MADISON COUNTY

Virginia City

Content Corner
Wallace & Jackson Sts.
HABS MT-2   s p d   L

Madison County Courthouse
Wallace St.
HABS MT-3   s p d   L

Sanders, Col. W. F., House
Idaho St.
HABS MT-1   s p d   L

MEAGHER COUNTY

White Sulphur Springs

Camp Baker; see Fort Logan, Blockhouse
Fort Logan, Blockhouse (Camp Baker)
HABS MT-19   s p d   L H

MISSOULA COUNTY

Fort Missoula

Fort Missoula, Laundry Building
HABS MT-20   p d   H

Missoula

Fort Missoula, N. C. O. Living Quarters
HABS MT-14   s p d   L

Fort Missoula, Powder Magazine
HABS MT-13   s p d   L H

POWELL COUNTY

Deer Lodge

Grant-Kohrs Ranch Complex
Hwy. 10
HABS MT-39   p d   H

Deer Lodge vic.

Chicago, Milwaukee, St. Paul & Pacific
    Railroad
Kentucky Ave.
HAER MT-5   p   H

RAVALLI COUNTY

Stevensville

Fort Owen
U.S. Rt. 93
HABS MT-12   s p d   L H

St. Mary's Mission (Roman Catholic)
HABS MT-10   s p d   L H

St. Mary's Pharmacy
HABS MT-11   s p d   L H

Nebraska

BUTLER COUNTY

Bellwood
Rohrich, Gustav, Sod House
HABS NE-35-10   s pd   L

DAKOTA COUNTY

Dakota City
Lutheran Church
Fourteenth & Hickory Sts.
HABS NE-35-19   s pd   L

DOUGLAS COUNTY

Florence
Mitchell House
Thirty-first & State Sts.
HABS NE-35-13   s pd   L

Omaha
Nash Building
901-911 Douglas St.
HABS NE-36   pd   L
Smith, M. E., Building
201 S. Tenth St.
HABS NE-35   pd   L

GAGE COUNTY

Beatrice
Freeman School
Homestead National Monument of America
HABS NE-22   s   H
Palmer-Epard Cabin
Homestead National Monument of America
HABS NE-21   s   H

KNOX COUNTY

Crofton
Chambers-Mayberry House
(moved from NE, Niobrara, Oak & Fifth Ave.)
HABS NE-23   s pd   L

Niobrara
American Legion Building (Dwight's, W. W., Jewelry Store)
Elm St.
HABS NE-24   s pd   L
Bonesteel, H. E., Company; see Koster's Theatre
Chambers-Mayberry House
Oak & Fifth Ave. (moved to NE, Crofton)
HABS NE-23   s pd   L
Dwight's, W. W., Jewelry Store; see American Legion Building

First Methodist Episcopal Church (Niobrara Public Library)
Fourth Ave.
HABS NE-25   s pd   L
First Presbyterian Church of Niobrara
Sixth & Maple Sts.
HABS NE-26   s pd   L
Independent Order of Odd Fellows Lodge Number 82; see Knox County Courthouse
Knox County Courthouse (Independent Order of Odd Fellows Lodge Number 82)
Fourth Ave. & Elm St.
HABS NE-27   s pd   L
Koster's Theatre (Niobrara, The; Bonesteel, H. E., Company; Olson's Market)
Elm St.
HABS NE-28   s pd   L
Masonic Temple; see Niobrara Valley Bank
Niobrara Public Library; see First Methodist Episcopal Church
Niobrara, The; see Koster's Theatre
Niobrara Tribune; see Swann's Drugstore
Niobrara Valley Bank (Masonic Temple; Palen Block)
Elm St.
HABS NE-29   s pd   L
Olson's Market; see Koster's Theatre
Opocensky, Frederick, House (Thierolf's Rest Home)
Sixth Ave.
HABS NE-30   s pd   L
Palen Block; see Niobrara Valley Bank
St. Paul's Episcopal Church
Fourth Ave. (moved to NE, Santee, Ind. Reserv.)
HABS NE-31   s pd   L
State Bank of Niobrara
Elm St.
HABS NE-32   s pd   L
Swann's Drugstore (Niobrara Tribune)
Elm St.
HABS NE-33   s pd   L
Thierolf's Rest Home; see Opocensky, Frederick, House
Zapadni Cesko-Bratreske Jednoty Hall Number 53
Fifth Ave.
HABS NE-34   s pd   L

Santee
St. Paul's Episcopal Church
Santee Indian Reservation (moved from NE, Niobra)
HABS NE-31   s pd   L

Santee Reservation
Chapel and Manse Congregational Mission
HABS NE-16   s pd   L

Santee vic.
Episcopal Church
Santee Indian Reservation
HABS NE-15   pd   L
Episcopal Mission
HABS NE-20   s   L

LANCASTER COUNTY

Lincoln
Bryan, William J., House
1625 D St.
HABS NE-35-8   s pd   L
Church of the Holy Trinity (Episcopal)
1200 J St.
HABS NE-35-6   s pd   L
Kennard, T. P., House
1627 H St.
HABS NE-35-4   s pd   L
McKinley High School
1500 M St.
HABS NE-35-2   s pd   L

NEMAHA COUNTY

Brownsville
Cogswell, A. P., House
HABS NE-38   p   L
Furnas, Gov. Robert W., House
Sixth St.
HABS NE-35-17   s pd   L
Methodist Church
Fifth St.
HABS NE-35-15   s pd   L

OTOE COUNTY

Nebraska City
Grant, S. L., House
Fourteenth St. & Third St.
HABS NE-35-3   s pd   L
Otoe County Courthouse
Tenth & Central Ave.
HABS NE-35-1   s pd   L
St. Benedict Parish Church & School
Clay & Fifth Sts.
HABS NE-35-5   s pd   L
Wessell House
Nebraska Ave. & Eighth St.
HABS NE-35-11   s pd   L

SARPY COUNTY

Bellevue
Presbyterian Church
Franklin & Twentieth Sts.
HABS NE-35-7   s pd   L
Town Hall
Main & Twenty-third Sts.
HABS NE-35-9   s pd   L

Nevada

DOUGLAS COUNTY

Genoa

Genoa, General View, 1890
Genoa vic.
HABS NV-3-12   p   L
Log Cabin, First
HABS NV-3-11   p   L

EUREKA COUNTY

Eureka

Eureka County Courthouse
Main St.
HABS NV-6-6   p   L
Eureka Sentinel Building
Monroe St.
HABS NV-6-7   p   L
First Methodist Church (Hooper Garage)
Spring St.
HABS NV-6-1   p   L
Hooper Garage; see First Methodist Church
Presbyterian Church
Edwards St.
HABS NV-6-5   p   L
St. Brendan's Roman Catholic Church
O'Neal Ave.
HABS NV-6-4   p   L

LINCOLN COUNTY

Pioche

Lincoln County Courthouse, Old
HABS NV-9-1   p   L

LYON COUNTY

Dayton

Bluestone Manufacturing Company
Main St. & Shady Ave.
HABS NV-13-20   s   L

Dayton vic.

Sutro Tunnel Entrance
Comstock Mines vic.
HABS NV-10-1   p   L

Weeks vic.

Fort Churchill (Ruins)
U.S. 95-A, Old Buckland Ranch
HABS NV-10-17   p   L

MINERAL COUNTY

Aurora

Main Street, General View
HABS NV-11-17   p   L

ORMSBY COUNTY

Carson City

Chartz, Alfred, House
412 Nevada St.
HABS NV-13-15   pd   L
Curry, Abraham, House
406 N. Nevada St.
HABS NV-13-13   pd   L
Ferris, G. W. G., House
311 W. Third St.
HABS NV-13-14   pd   L
First United Methodist Church
200 N. Division St.
HABS NV-13-10   pd   L
King Street, General View, 1880
HABS NV-13-20   p   L
Meder, Lew M., House
308 N. Nevada St.
HABS NV-13-27   s   L
Nevada State Capitol
Plaza at Carson St.
HABS NV-13-5   pd   L
Nevada State Orphanage
HABS NV-13-21   p   L
Nevada State Printing Office
S. Fall St.
HABS NV-13-9   pd   L
Rinckel, Mathias, Mansion
102 N. Curry St.
HABS NV-13-17   pd   L
Roberts, James D., House
1207 N. Carson St.
HABS NV-13-28   s   L
Second & Carson Streets, General View, 1860-70
HABS NV-13-23   p   L
Smail House
512 N. Curry St.
HABS NV-13-16   pd   L
Smaill, David, House
313 W. Ann St.
HABS NV-13-19   pd   L
St. Peter's Episcopal Church
312 N. Division St.
HABS NV-13-11   s pd   L
Stewart-Nye House
108 N. Minnesota St.
HABS NV-13-12   pd   L
Sweeney, E. D., Building
102 S. Curry St.
HABS NV-13-6   pd   L
Twain, Mark, House
Division & Spear Sts.
HABS NV-13-2   p   L
United States Mint
Carson St.
HABS NV-13-22   pd   L
U.S. Post Office
N. Carson St.
HABS NV-13-8   pd   L

Virginia & Truckee Railroad Shops
Between Plaza, Ann, Stewart & Sophia Sts.
HABS NV-13-7   s pd   L
Yerington, Henry Marvin, House
512 N. Division St.
HABS NV-13-18   pd   L

PERSHING COUNTY

Humboldt City

Bank (Ruins)
HABS NV-14-30   p   L
Humboldt City, General View, Ghost Town
HABS NV-14-29   p   L

STOREY COUNTY

Gold Hill

Liberty Fire House
HABS NV-15-13   p   L
Miner's Union Hall
B St.
HABS NV-15-14   p   L

Virginia

Fourth Ward School
S. C St. at Hwy. 17
HABS NV-15-21   s p   L

Virginia City

Bar, Old
C St.
HABS NV-15-33   p   L
Blaubelt Mansion
HABS NV-15-5   p   L
Brick Vaults, Office of Cons. Virginia Mining Co.
HABS NV-15-2   p   L
C Street Area Survey (Commercial Buildings)
HABS NV-15-1   p   L
Cemetery
HABS NV-15-79   p   L
Comstock House
C St.
HABS NV-15-35   p   L
Crystal Saloon
HABS NV-15-29   p   L
Episcopal Church
D St.
HABS NV-15-30   p   L
Evening Chronicle Building
C St.
HABS NV-15-39   p   L
Fire House
HABS NV-15-87   p   L
Fire Station
HABS NV-15-88   p   L

First Street (Commercial Buildings)
HABS NV-15-78   p   L

Frederick House
D St.
HABS NV-15-26   p   L

Hall of Records
B St.
HABS NV-15-89   p   L

Hardware & General Store
C St.
HABS NV-15-8   p   L

Harness Shop
HABS NV-15-81   p   L

Hose House
HABS NV-15-82   p   L

House, Frame
HABS NV-15-58   p   L

Jail
HABS NV-15-54   p   L

King House
HABS NV-15-31   p   L

Knights of Pythias Hall
W. side B St.
HABS NV-15-11   s p   L

Masonic Hall
C St.
HABS NV-15-18   p   L

Mine, General View
HABS NV-15-86   p   L

Miners' Union Hall
W. side B St.
HABS NV-15-20   s p   L

Molinelli's Hotel
C St.
HABS NV-15-38   p   L

Norcross Mining Office
HABS NV-15-41   p   L

Palace Ciothing Store Building
C St.
HABS NV-15-36   p   L

Piper's Opera House
B & Union Sts.
HABS NV-15-7   s p   L

Savage Mining Office
HABS NV-15-12   p   L

Shaft House, Active Mine
HABS NV-15-84   p   L

Shaft House, Consolidated CA & VA Mine
HABS NV-15-85   p   L

Silver Hotel
CSt.
HABS NV-15-40   p   L

St. Mary's in the Mountains
HABS NV-15-52   p   L

Store, Frame
HABS NV-15-80   p   L

Storey County Courthouse
HABS NV-15-19   p   L

Sutro Mansion
HABS NV-15-83   p   L

Twain, Mark, Enterprise Building
C St.
HABS NV-15-9   p   L

Union Brewery
HABS NV-15-37   p   L

Virginia City, General View Area Survey
HABS NV-15-77   p   L

Virginia City News Building
C St.
HABS NV-15-32   p   L

Virginia City Union Sunday School
C St.
HABS NV-15-4   p   L

Virginia Hotel
C St.
HABS NV-15-3   p   L

Wells Fargo Building
C St.
HABS NV-15-46   p   L

WHITE PINE COUNTY

Baker vic.

Lehman Caves National Monument; see
   Rhodes, C. T., Log Cabin
Rhodes, C. T., Log Cabin (Lehman Caves
   National Monument)
Lehman Caves entrance vic.
HABS NV-17-1   s pd   L

New Hampshire

CHESHIRE COUNTY

Chesterfield

Blacksmith Shop
(moved to MA, Storrowtown, West
   Springfield)
HABS NH-41   s   L

Exeter

Folsom, Simeon, House & Stores
Pleasant & High Sts.
HABS NH-8   s pd   L

Harrisville

Chesire Mill, Number One
Main & Grove Sts.
HABS NH-173   s pd   L

Chesire Mills Company Boarding House
Main St.
HABS NH-174   s pd   L

Harris Mill
Main & Prospect Sts.
HABS NH-171   s pd   L

Harris Mill Storehouse
Main & Prospect Sts.
HABS NH-172   s pd   L

Stoddard vic.

Bridge, Stone
Route 9
HABS NH-32   p   L

Walpole

Allen, Gen. Amasa, House
Main St.
HABS NH-53   pd   L

Bellows Falls Arch Bridge
HAER NH-6   s   H

Bellows-Grant House
Main St.
HABS NH-60   pd   L

Buffum House
Main & Middle Sts.
HABS NH-61   pd   L

Hooper Golf Club; see Watkins',
   Alexander, Tavern

Howland House (Interior)
Westminster St.
HABS NH-59   pd   L

Howland-Schofield House
Elm & Pleasant Sts.
HABS NH-65   pd   L

Knapp House
Wentworth Rd.
HABS NH-52   pd   L

Porter, Margaret, House
Main & Middle Sts.
HABS NH-63   pd   L

Walpole Academy (Walpole Historical
   Society)
Main St.
HABS NH-62   pd   L

Walpole Historical Society; see Walpole
   Academy

Watkins', Alexander, Tavern (Hooper Golf
   Club)
Prospect Hill
HABS NH-64   pd   L

Wing, Rodney, House
Westminster St.
HABS NH-58   pd   L

Westmoreland

Park Hill Meetinghouse
State Route 63
HABS NH-57   pd   L

GRAFTON COUNTY

Bath

Woods-Goodale Law Offices
U.S. Route 302
HABS NH-66   pd   L

Campton vic.

Pioneer Cabin
HABS NH-36   s pd   L

Enfield vic.

Shaker Church Family Cow Barn
State Route 4A
HABS NH-192   s pd   L

Shaker Church Family Dwelling House
(Shaker Great Stone House; Shaker
Enfield Center Second Dwelling)
State Route 4A
HABS NH-75   s pd   L

Shaker Church Family General Views
State Route 4A
HABS NH-190   s p   L

Shaker Church Family Laundry & Dairy
State Route 4A
HABS NH-193   p   L

Shaker Church Family Machine Shop
State Route 4A
HABS NH-175   p   L

Shaker Enfield Center Second Dwelling;
see Shaker Church Family Dwelling
House

Shaker Great Stone House; see Shaker
Church Family Dwelling House

Shaker Ministry's Shop
State Route 4A
HABS NH-194   p   L

Hanover

Choate House (Ripley, Sylvanus, House)
27 N. Main St.
HABS NH-72   pd   L

Dartmouth College Campus, Thorton Hall
HABS NH-70   pd   L

Dartmouth College, Reed hall
HABS NH-67   pd   L

Dartmouth College, Shattuck Observatory
HABS NH-69   pd   L

Dartmouth College, Webster Cottage
Main St.
HABS NH-68   pd   L

Dartmouth College, Wentworth Hall
HABS NH-71   pd   L

Delta Kappa Epsilon Fraternity House; see
Storrs, Capt. Aaron, House

Ripley, Sylvanus, House; see Choate House

Storrs, Capt. Aaron, House (Delta Kappa
Epsilon Fraternity House)
6 W. Wheelock St.
HABS NH-73   pd   L

Woodward-Lord House
41 College St.
HABS NH-74   pd   L

Lyme

Lyme Congregational Church
The Green
HABS NH-77   pd   L

Lyme Congregational Church, Horse Sheds
The Green
HABS NH-76   pd   L

Lyme vic.

Snow, Enos, Farm
River Rd.
HABS NH-78   pd   L

Wittenboro-Wagner House
HABS NH-79   pd   L

Orford

Covered Bridge
Spanning Connecticut River
HABS NH-29   s pd   L

Wheeler House
Orford St.
HABS NH-80   s pd   L

HILLSBOROUGH COUNTY

Antrim

Loomis House
HABS NH-49   s   L

Hillsboro

Bridge, Stone
Routes 32 & 9
HABS NH-32-C   p   L

Carr Bridge, Old
Spanning Beard Creek
HABS NH-32-B   s p   L

Dutton Twin Houses
W. Main St.
HABS NH-161   pd   H

Gleason Falls Bridge
Spanning Beard Brook
HABS NH-32-D   s p   L

Second New Hampshire Turnpike Bridge
Fullers Tannery
HABS NH-32-A   s p   L

Hillsborough

Bridges, Stone-Map of Locations
HABS NH-32-A   s d   L

Dutton Twin Houses
W. Main St.
HABS NH-162   pd   H

Hillsborough Center

Pierce Homestead
Routes 31 & 9
HABS NH-202   pd   H

Manchester

**Amoskeag Manufacturing Company, Mill
Number Nine**
Amoskeag Millyard
HABS NH-111   s   H

**Amoskeag Manufacturing Company, Paper
Mill**
Amoskeag Millyard
HABS NH-110   s   H

**Amoskeag Mills, River Dye House &
Bleach House**
Amoskeag Millyard
HABS NH-115   s   H

Amoskeag Millyard
Canal St.
HABS NH-109   s pd   L H

First Methodist Episcopal Church
Valley & Jewett Sts. (moved from NH,
Derryville)
HABS NH-28   s pd   L

**Manchester Mills, Counting Rooms &
Repair Shops**
HABS NH-119   s   H

Manchester Mills, Number One
HABS NH-116   s   H

Manchester Mills, Number Three
HABS NH-118   s   H

Manchester Mills, Number Two
HABS NH-117   s   H

Mills 2, 3, & 4; see Stark Mills

South Upper Canal Building
HABS NH-114   s   H

Stark Mills (Mills 2, 3, & 4)
HABS NH-113   s   H

Stark Mills, Number Four, South Half
HABS NH-112   s   H

MERRIMACK COUNTY

Blackwater River

Webster Meetinghouse
(moved to Webster-Corser Hill)
HABS NH-170   pd   H

Bow Mills vic.

Nicholas Saw Mill
HABS NH-31   s   H

Canterbury

Shaker Church Family Barn & Granary
Shaker Village Rd.
HABS NH-177   p   L

Shaker Church Family Boys' House
(Shaker Church Family Creamery)
Shaker Village Rd.
HABS NH-178   p   L

Shaker Church Family Brethen's Shop
Shaker Village Rd.
HABS NH-179   p   L

**Shaker Church Family Broom &
Carpenters' Shop**
Shaker Village Rd.
HABS NH-191   p   L

Shaker Church Family Children's House;
see Shaker Church Family East House

Shaker Church Family Creamery; see
Shaker Church Family Boys' House

Shaker Church Family Dwelling House
Shaker Village Rd.
HABS NH-180   p   L

Shaker Church Family East House (Shaker
    Church Family Girls' House; Shaker
    Church Family Children's House)
Shaker Village Rd.
HABS NH-184   d   L

Shaker Church Family Enfield House
    (Shaker Church Family Trustees' Office)
Shaker Village Rd.
HABS NH-181   d   L

**Shaker Church Family Firehouse and
    Powerhouse**
Shaker Village Rd.
HABS NH-182   p   L

Shaker Church Family General View
Shaker Rd.
HABS NH-183   p   L

Shaker Church Family Girls' House; see
    Shaker Church Family East House

Shaker Church Family Schoolhouse
Shaker Village Rd.
HABS NH-188   p   L

Shaker Church Family Syrup Shop
Shaker Village Rd.
HABS NH-189   p   L

Shaker Church Family Trustees' Office; see
    Shaker Church Family Enfield House

Shaker Church Family Washhouse
Shaker Village Rd.
HABS NH-185   p   L

Shaker Meetinghouse
Shaker Village Rd.
HABS NH-186   p   L

Shaker Ministry's Shop
Shaker Village Rd.
HABS NH-187   p   L

St. Andrew's Church (Episcopal)
Hopkinton Village
HABS NH-167   pd   H

Concord

Gothic Cottage; see Walker, Joseph, Estate

Merrimack County Bank
214 N. Main St.
HABS NH-164   p   H

**100-102 North Main Street, Stone
    Warehouse**
HABS NH-165   pd   H

Waker, Rev. Timothy, House
276 N. Main St.
HABS NH-166   pd   H

Walker, Joseph, Estate (Gothic Cottage)
278 N. Main St.
HABS NH-163   pd   H

Contoocook

Contoocook Covered Bridge
Spanning Contoocook River
HABS NH-21   s pd   L

Henniker

Ocean-Born-Mary House
Route 202
HABS NH-160   pd   H

Wilcoxen House
Route 9
HABS NH-203   pd   H

Hopkinton

Boulder Farm
HABS NH-42   s   L

Hopkinton vic.

Bridge, New; see Covered Bridge

Covered Bridge (Bridge, New; Henniker
    Bridge, New)
Spanning Contoocook River
HABS NH-30   s pd   L

Hennicker Bridge, New; see Covered
    Bridge

Penacock-Boscawen

Bonney Tavern
Daniel Webster Highway
HABS NH-25   H

Salisbury

Salisbury Meetinghouse
(moved to MA, Springfield vic.)
HABS NH-843   p   H

Salisbury Heights

Williams, Thomas & Eliphalet, House
Route 4
HABS NH-168   pd   H

Webster

Corser Hill Meetinghouse
Corser Hill
HABS NH-169   pd   H

Webster Meetinghouse
Corser Hill (moved from NH Blackwater
    River)
HABS NH-170   pd   H

ROCKINGHAM COUNTY

Derryville

First Methodist Episcopal Church
Mammoth & Huse Rds. (moved to NH,
    Manchester)
HABS NH-205   s pd   L

Exeter

Giddings Tavern
37 Park & Summers Sts.
HABS NH-2   s pd   L

Gilman Garrison
Water & Clifford Sts.
HABS NH-18   s pd   L

Liberty Emery House
41 Main St.
HABS NH-9   s pd   L

Powder House
HABS NH-13   s pd   L

Greenland

Weeks, Leonard, House
HABS NH-40   s p   H

Hampton

Moulton, Gen., House
HABS NH-50   s p   L

Hampton Falls

Cram, John, Farmstead
HABS NH-23   s pd   L

Weare Saw & Grist Mill
HABS NH-44   s pd   L

Kensington

Hardy, John, Small House
HABS NH-48   s   L

Lovering Farmhouse
HABS NH-46   s   L

Newington

Parsonage
HABS NH-19   s pd   L

Newmarket

Doe Garrison
Lamprey River & Great Bay
HABS NH-37   s pd   H

Northwood Narrows

James Saw Mill
Narrows Brook
HABS NH-45   s pd   L

Portsmouth

66 & 74 Jefferson Street, Twin Houses
HABS NH-107   p   H

Abbott House
82 Jefferson St.
HABS NH-81   p   H

90 Atkinson Street, L-Shaped House
HABS NH-93   p   H

Bailey, Daniel, House
139 Manning St.
HABS NH-82   p   H

Barnes, Capt., House
218 Islington St.
HABS NH-26   s pd   L

Blunt, Capt. Robert, House
144 Washington St.
HABS NH-83   pd   H

Boyd, Col. George, Tomb
Old North Cemetery
HABS NH-204   s p   L

Boyd-Raynes House (Meserve, Col.
    Nathaniel, House)
Maplewood Ave.
HABS NH-5   s pd   L

Chase, Reverend Stephen, House
358 Court St.
HABS NH-84   pd   H

Clark, John, House
95 Jefferson St.
HABS NH-85   s pd   H

Conant, Aaron, House
61 Washington St.
HABS NH-86   pd   H

Cullen House
186 Marcy St.
HABS NH-87   p   H

Custom House
Daniel & Penhallow Sts.
HABS NH-4   s pd   L H

33-35 Deer Street (House)
HABS NH-10   s pd   L

Drisco House
65-67 Charles St.
HABS NH-88   p   H

Goodwin House
55 Charles St.
HABS NH-89   p   H

Green House
167 Washington St.
HABS NH-90   p   H

Hough, Capt. Thomas, House
23-25 Liberty St.
HABS NH-91   p   H

Ingraham House
72 Atkinson St.
HABS NH-94   p   H

Kelley Property
454-456 Court St.
HABS NH-95   p   L

Langdon, Gov. John, House
143 Pleasant St.
HABS NH-51   s   L

Lowd, Peter, House
43 Charles St.
HABS NH-96   p   H

Meetinghouse, South
Marcy St., Meetinghouse Hill
HABS NH-105   pd   H

Meserve, Col. Nathaniel, House; see
Boyd-Raynes House

Odiorne, Augustus, House
46 Jefferson House
HABS NH-97   p   H

Peacock House
Atkinson & Jefferson Sts.
HABS NH-99   p   H

Penhallow, Deacon, House
95 Newton St.
HABS NH-100   p   H

Pierce House
153 Washington St.
HABS NH-101   p   H

Pitt Tavern
402-404 Court St.
HABS NH-102   pd   H

Ryder-Wood House
16 Jefferson St.
HABS NH-103   p   H

Shapley, Reuben, House
420 Court St.
HABS NH-104   pd   H

Sheafe Warehouse
Graves End St.
HABS NH-7   s pd   L

Shore, Christian, House; see Woodbury,
Gov. Levi, House

Smalley Estate
80 Atkinson St.
HABS NH-92   p   H

State House, Old
Court St.
HABS NH-98   p   H

Sunday School House
Washington St.
HABS NH-106   pd   H

Webster, Daniel, House
Junk Yard
HABS NH-108   p   H

Wentworth, Col. Joshua, House
121 Hanover St.
HABS NH-3   s pd   L

Wentworth-Collidge Mansion
Little Harbor Rd.
HABS NH-47   s   H

Whidden, Michael, House
117 Deer St.
HABS NH-11   s pd   L

Woodbury, Gov. Levi, House (Shore,
Christian, House)
Woodbury Ave. & Boyd Rd.
HABS NH-20   s p   L

Rockingham

Moody Parsonage
HABS NH-15   s pd   L

Rye

Seavey, Amos, House
Beach Blvd.
HABS NH-16   s pd   L

Sandown

Meetinghouse
HABS NH-17   s pd   L

Stratham

Winnicut Grist Mill
HABS NH-24   s pd   L

STRAFFORD COUNTY

Durham

Smith, Ebenezer, House
20 Main St.
HABS NH-14   s pd   L

Sullivan, Gen. John, House
New Market Rd.
HABS NH-1   s pd   L

Town Hall
Newmarket & Dover Rds.
HABS NH-6   s pd   L

Town Pound
Route 108
HABS NH-12   s   L

Woodman Garrison
Garrison Ave.
HABS NH-33   s pd   L

Durham vic.

Pendergast Garrison
Packer's Falls
HABS NH-22   s pd   L

Salmon Falls

Wentworth, Col. Paul, House
Dover St. (moved to MA, Dover)
HABS NH-35   s pd   L H

SULLIVAN COUNTY

Acworth

Acworth Meetinghouse
Town Green
HABS NH-54   pd   L

Grout, Nathaniel, House
HABS NH-55   pd   H

Charleston

Vryling-Lovell House
HABS NH-56   pd   L

Claremont

Claremont Rehabilatation Project; see
Monadnock Mills

Claremont Rehabilatation Project; see
Sugar River Grist Mill & Saw Mill

Claremont Rehabilatation Project; see
Sullivan Machinery Company

Claremont Rehabilitation Project
HAER NH-1   s pd   L H

Claremont Village Industrial District; see
River Street Historic District

Dexter, David, House (Dexter-Fitchburg
House)
HABS NH-195   pd   L

Dexter-Fitchburg House; see Dexter,
David, House

Monadnock Mills (Claremont
Rehabilatation Project)
HAER NH-2   s p   H

River Street Historic District (Claremont
Village Industrial District)
HAER NH-5   s   L H

Sugar River Grist Mill & Saw Mill
(Claremont Rehabilatation Project)
HAER NH-3   s   H

Sullivan Machinery Company (Claremont
Rehabilatation Project)
HAER NH-4   s p   L

Cornish

Ravine Studio
HABS NH-200-A   s   H

Saint-Gaudens, Augustus, Aspet House
(Saint-Gaudens, Augustus, National
Historic Site)
HABS NH-196   p   H

Saint-Gaudens, Augustus, Little Studio
(Saint-Gaudens, Augustus, National
Historic Site)
HABS NH-198   p   H
Saint-Gaudens, Augustus, National Historic
Site
State Route 12-A
HABS NH-200   s   H
Saint-Gaudens, Augustus, National Historic
Site; see Saint-Gaudens, Caretaker's
Cottage and Garden
Saint-Gaudens, Augustus, National Historic
Site; see Saint-Gaudens, Augustus, Aspet
House
Saint-Gaudens, Augustus, National Historic
Site; see Saint-Gaudens, Augustus, Little
Studio

Saint-Gaudens, Augustus, National Historic
Site; see Saint-Gaudens, Augustus,
Stables
Saint-Gaudens, Augustus, National Historic
Site; see Saint-Gaudens, Augustus, Studio
& Picture Gallery
Saint-Gaudens, Augustus, National Historic
Site; see Saint-Gaudens, Augustus,
Temple
Saint-Gaudens, Augustus, Ravine Studio
(Saint-Gaudens National Historic Site)
HABS NH-200-A   s   H
Saint-Gaudens, Augustus, Stables
(Saint-Gaudens, Augustus, National
Historic Site)
HABS NH-200-B   p   H

Saint-Gaudens, Augustus, Studio & Picture
Gallery (Saint-Gaudens, Augustus,
National Historic Site)
HABS NH-199   p   H

Saint-Gaudens, Augustus, Temple
(Saint-Gaudens, Augustus, National
Historic Site)
HABS NH-201   p   H

Saint-Gaudens, Caretaker's Cottage and
Garden (Saint-Gaudens, Augustus,
National Historic Site)
HABS NH-197   p   H

Saint-Gaudens National Historic Site; see
Saint-Gaudens, Augustus, Ravine Studio

New Jersey

ATLANTIC COUNTY

Absecon

Methodist Meetinghouse
50 W. Church st.
HABS NJ-662   s   L

Atlantic City

Absecon Lighthouse
Pacific Ave. bwt, Rhode Is. & Vermont
Aves.
HABS NJ-734   s pd   H
Blenheim Hotel
Ohio Ave. & Boardwalk
HABS NJ-864   s d   H
City Hall
Atlantic & Tennessee Aves.
HABS NJ-815   pd   H
Dennis Hotel
Michigan Ave. & Boardwalk
HABS NJ-862   s d   H
Marlbourough Hotel
Boardwalk at Park Place
HABS NJ-863   s d   H

Head-of-the-River

**Head-of-the-River Methodist Episcopal
Church**
Etna Rd.
HABS NJ-274   s pd   L

Leeds Point

Leeds, Japhet, House
Moss Mill Rd.
HABS NJ-399   s pd   L

Margate

Lucy; see Margate Elephant
Margate Elephant (Lucy)
Decatur & Atlantic Aves.
HABS NJ-816   s pd   H

Mays Landing

Forge, Walter, Mansion
HABS NJ-288   s pd   L
Mays Landing Presbyterian Church
HABS NJ-516   s pd   L

Port Republic

Clark, Adrial, House
Church Lane & Main Sts.
HABS NJ-645   s pd   L
Franklin Inn & Store
Mill Rd.
HABS NJ-663   s pd   L
Johnson, Joseph, House
New York Rd. (U.S. Rt. 9)
HABS NJ-728   pd   H

Smithville

Smith Homestead
1597 New York & Moss Hill Rds.
HABS NJ-280   s pd   L

Somers Point

Somers Mansion
Shore Rd. & Goll St.
HABS NJ-281   s pd   L

BERGEN COUNTY

Alpine

Cornwallis Headquarters
Palisade Interstate Park
HABS NJ-115   s pd   L

Alpine, Cresskill vic.

Huyler Dock House
Palisades Interstate Park
HABS NJ-167   s pd   L

Bergen

Lozier, Nicholas, House
393 Main St.
HABS NJ-177   s pd   L

Bergenfield

Kipp, Nicholas, House
221 N. Washington Ave.
HABS NJ-423   s pd   L

Closter

Doremus, David D., House
Piermont Rd.
HABS NJ-361   s pd   L
Durie, Nicholas, House
Schraalenburg Rd.
HABS NJ-472   s pd   L
Parcel, Walter, House; see Van der Beck
Slave House
Van der Beck Slave House (Parcel, Walter,
House)
Piermont Rd.
HABS NJ-363   s pd   L

Closter, Norwood vic.

De Clerque Farm Group
Piermont Rd.
HABS NJ-364   s pd   L

Cresskill

Huyler, Capt. John, Homestead
500 County Rd.
HABS NJ-168   s pd   L
Westervelt, Benjamin P., House
County Rd.
HABS NJ-422   s pd   L

Demarest

Bogert, Matthew P., Stone Well House
Orchard Rd.
HABS NJ-428   s pd   L

Dumont

**North Reformed Church of
Schraalenburgh**
Washington & Madison Aves.
HABS NJ-173   s pd   L

**North Reformed Church of
Schraalenburgh Parsonage**
191 Washington Ave.
HABS NJ-172   s p d   L
Zabriskie-Christie House
10 Colonial Court
HABS NJ-5   s p d   L

Dumont Borough

Demarest, Daniel, House
404 Washington Ave.
HABS NJ-657   s p d   L

East Rutherford

Kip-Outwater, Richard, House
231 Hackensack St.
HABS NJ-700   s p d   L

Emerson

Blauvelt House
Old Hook Rd.
HABS NJ-111   s p d   L

Englewood

Lydecker House
220 Grand Ave.
HABS NJ-162   s p d   L
Van Brunt, John, House
315 Grand Ave.
HABS NJ-392   s p d   L
Westervelt, Peter, House
290 Grand Ave.
HABS NJ-112   s p d   L

Fair Lawn

Ackerman, Maria Ann, House; see
Vanderbeck, Jacob, House
Hooper, Peter A., House
E. Fair Lawn Ave.
HABS NJ-174   s p d   L
Vanderbeck, Jacob, House (Ackerman,
Maria Ann, House)
Dunker Hook Rd.
HABS NJ-563   s p d   L
Vanderbeck, Jacob, House & Kitchen
Saddle River Rd. & Dunker Hook Lane
HABS NJ-45   s p d   L

Fair Lawn Borough

Alyea-Outwater House; see Lee, Maj.
Henry, Headquarters
Lee, Maj. Henry, Headquarters
(Alyea-Outwater House)
Wagaraw Rd.
HABS NJ-551   s p d   L

Fort Lee

Church of the Madonna
Church St.
HABS NJ-421   s p d   L

Franklin Lakes vic.

Packer House
600 Ewing Ave.
HABS NJ-528   s p d   L

Glen Rock

Berdan House
Lincoln Ave.
HABS NJ-299   s p d   L

Hackensack

Ackerman-Brinkerhoff House
184 Essex St.
HABS NJ-7   s p d   L
Demarest Homestead; see Van Giesen,
George, House
First Reformed Church of Hackensack
Church & Court Sts.
HABS NJ-4   s p d   L
Hopper, John, House
249 Polifly Rd.
HABS NJ-352   s p d   L
Terheun House
450 River & Anderson Sts.
HABS NJ-8   s p d   L
Van Giesen, George, House (Demarest
Homestead)
Terrace Ave. & Essex St.
HABS NJ-680   s p d   L
Washington Mansion House Tavern
(Zabriskie, Peter, House)
Main St. & Washington Pl.
HABS NJ-117   s p d   L
Zabriskie, Peter, House; see Washington
Mansion House Tavern

Hillsdale

Demarest, Samuel G., House
Demarest Ave.
HABS NJ-500   s p d   L

Hohokus

Hermitage, The (Provost, Col. Marc,
House)
335 N. Franklin Turnpike
HABS NJ-98   s p d   L
Provost, Col. Marc, House; see Hermitage,
The

Hohokus Twp.

Van Horn, Abram, House
Valley Rd.
HABS NJ-114   s p d   L

Leonia

Vreeland House
125 Lakeview Ave.
HABS NJ-158   s p d   L

Lyndhurst

Van Winkle, Jacob W., House
316 Riverside Ave.
HABS NJ-477   s p d   L

Maywood

Berdan, John D., House
465 Maywood Ave.
HABS NJ-640   s p d   L
Oldis-Brinckerhoff House
Maywood & Central Aves.
HABS NJ-697   s p d   L

Romine-Van Voorhis House; see Van
Voorhis, Henry A., House
Van Voorhis, Henry A., House
(Romine-Van Voorhis House)
306 Maywood Ave.
HABS NJ-667   s p d   L

Midland Park

Baldwin, David, House
60 Lake Ave.
HABS NJ-420   s p d   L
Lozier, Cornelius, House; see
Lozier-Wortendyke House
Lozier-Wortendyke House (Lozier,
Cornelius, House)
Paterson Ave. & Goffle Rd.
HABS NJ-375   s p d   L

Montvale Boro

Eckerson, Abram G., House
Chestnut Ridge Rd.
HABS NJ-175   s p d   L

New Milford

des Marest, David, House (Gurd House)
River Rd.
HABS NJ-11   s p d   L
des Marest, Samuel, House
River Rd.
HABS NJ-16   s p d   L
Gurd House; see des Marest, David, House

Nutley

Rutandt House, The
123 Prospect Ave.
HABS NJ-876   s d   H

Oakland

Church of Ponds
Oakland & Franklin Lakes Rd.
HABS NJ-116   s p d   L

Old Tappan

Haring, Cosyn, House; see Herring,
Dewerk Peter, House
Haring, David R., House
202 Old Tappan Rd.
HABS NJ-703   s p d   L
Haring, Frederick, House
Old Tappan & DeWolfe Rds.
HABS NJ-487   s p d   L
Haring, Gerrit J., House
W. Old Tappan Rd.
HABS NJ-459   s p d   L
Herring, Dewerk Peter, House (Haring,
Cosyn, House)
166 Pearl River Rd.
HABS NJ-154   s p d   L

Paramus

Banta House & Barn
Howland Ave.
HABS NJ-163   s p   L
Van Saun House
Howland Ave.
HABS NJ-343   s p d   L

Zabriskie, Albert J., House
Glen Ave.
HABS NJ-271   s p d   L
Zabriskie, Jacob, Farm Group
S. Paramus Rd.
HABS NJ-157   s p d   L

Park Ridge

Ackerson & Demarest Trading Post
Main St. & Mill Rd.
HABS NJ-176   s p d   L

Park Ridge vic.

Nortendyke Barn (Wortendyke Barn)
HABS NJ-735   p   L
Wortendyke Barn; see Nortendyke Barn

Ridgefield

De Groot, John, House
1008 De Groot Ave.
HABS NJ-170   s p d   L
**Reformed Church of English
    Neighborhood**
Edgewater Ave.
HABS NJ-552   s p d   L

Ridgefield Park

Brinkerhoff-Christie-Paulison Homestead
8 Homestead Place
HABS NJ-160   s p d   L

Ridgewood

Ackerman-Naugle, David, House
415 E. Saddle River Rd.
HABS NJ-155   s p d   L

River Edge

Des Marest, Samuel, House
E. Main St.
HABS NJ-733   s   H
Wilson, Peter, House
1027 Main St.
HABS NJ-655   s p d   L
Zabriskie-Steuben House
New Bridge Rd.
HABS NJ-47   s p d   L

Rivervale Twp.

Holdrom, William, House (Vanderbilt
    House)
Prospect & Rivervale Ave.
HABS NJ-686   s p d   L
**Vanderbilt House; see Holdrom, William,
    House**

Rochelle Park

Demarest, Samuel C., House
12 Rochelle Ave.
HABS NJ-90   s p d   L
Lutkins House
Passaic St.
HABS NJ-159   s p d   L

Rockleigh

Haring, Nicholas, House
Piermont Rd.
HABS NJ-169   s p d   L

Rutherford

Berry, John W., House (Jurianson, Juria,
    House)
Meadow Rd. & Crane Ave.
HABS NJ-468   s p d   L
**Jurianson, Juria, House; see Berry, John
    W., House**

Saddle River

Ackerman, Abram, House
199 E. Saddle River Rd.
HABS NJ-156   s p d   L
Ackerman-Washington Feed & Flour Mill;
    see Washington Feed & Flour Mill
**Bond Farm House; see Van Buskirk,
    Thomas, House**
Van Buskirk, Thomas, House (Bond Farm
    House)
E. Saddle River Rd.
HABS NJ-300   s p d   L
Van Buskirk-Arkerman House
E. Saddle River Rd.
HABS NJ-331   s p d   L
Washington Feed & Flour Mill
    (Ackerman-Washington Feed & Flour
    Mill)
E. Saddle River Rd.
HABS NJ-486   s p d   L
Zion Evangelical Lutheran Church
Allendale Ave.
HABS NJ-330   s p d   L

Saddle River Twp.

Demarest, Samuel C., House
511 Market St.
HABS NJ-542   s p d   L

Teaneck

Ackerman, John, House
1286 River Rd.
HABS NJ-298   s p d   L
Banta, Samuel, House
1485 Teaneck Rd.
HABS NJ-171   s p d   L
Brinkerhoff-Demarest (Homestead, Old)
493 Teaneck Rd.
HABS NJ-110   s p d   L
Homestead, Old; see Brinkerhoff-Demarest
Westervelt House
190 Teaneck Rd.
HABS NJ-113   s p d   L

Tenafly

Christie-Parsils House
195 Jefferson Ave.
HABS NJ-470   s p d   L
Westervelt House
256 Tenafly Rd.
HABS NJ-9   s p d   L

Upper Saddle River

Saddle River Reformed Church
E. Saddle River & Upper Saddle River Rds.
HABS NJ-255   s p d   L

Wyckoff

Branford, John, House (Van Blarcom-Van
    Horn House)
Lafayette & Wyckoff
HABS NJ-391   s p d   L
**Brown Stone Inn; see Quackenbush,
    Corines, House**
Quackenbush, Corines, House (Brown
    Stone Inn)
Wyckoff & Franklin Aves.
HABS NJ-702   s p d   L
**Van Blarcom-Van Horn House; see
    Branford, John, House**
Van Voorhis, Albert, House
Maple & Franklin Aves.
HABS NJ-161   s p d   L
Willis, Samuel & Abram, House
Main St.
HABS NJ-378   s p d   L
Wycoff Reformed Church
Main St.
HABS NJ-338   s p d   L

Wyckoff Twp.

Stagg, John C., House
Sicomac Rd. & Cedar Hill Ave.
HABS NJ-678   s p d   L

BURLINGTON COUNTY

Arneytown

Arneytown Tavern; see Lawrie House
Emley-Wildes House (Myrtlebank)
HABS NJ-303   s p d   L
Lawrie House (Arneytown Tavern)
HABS NJ-134   s p d   L
Myrtlebank; see Emley-Wildes House

Batsto

Atsion Stove & Pattern for stove casting
HABS NJ-40-A   p   L
**Babington, Rosanna Ireland, Cast Iron
    Gravestone**
Batsto Museum (moved from ME,
    Weymouth)
HABS NJ-882   p   L
Batso Village, Typical Worksman's Cottage
HABS NJ-40-D   s p   L
Batsto Village
HABS NJ-40-B   pd   L
General Store & Post Office
HABS NJ-366   s p d   L
Ironmaster's Mansion; see Manor House
Manor House (Ironmaster's Mansion;
    Richards Mansion)
Batsto Village
HABS NJ-40-C   p   L
Richards Grist Mill
HABS NJ-367   s p d   L
Richards, Jess, Burial Plot
Pleasant Mill Cemetery
HABS NJ-881   p   L

Richards Mansion; see Manor House
Richards Store House
HABS NJ-443   s p d   L
Slag Heap
Batsto Village
HABS NJ-879   p   L
Village, Old-General View
Batsto Village
HABS NJ-880   pd   L

Bordentown
Barton, Clara, School
142 Crosswicks & Burlington Sts.
HABS NJ-84   s p d   L
Friends Meetinghouse
HABS NJ-322   pd   L
Hopkinson, Francis, House
Park St. & Farnsworth Ave.
HABS NJ-64   s p d   L
Lovell-Maron, John, House
223 Farnsworth Ave.
HABS NJ-324   s p d   L
Sayre House
25 Farnsworth Ave.
HABS NJ-323   pd   L
Watson, Richard, House; see
   Watson-Gilder, Richard, House
Watson-Gilder, Richard, House (Watson,
   Richard, House)
HABS NJ-315   s p d   L
Wright, Joseph & Patience, House
100 Farnsworth Ave.
HABS NJ-314   pd   L

Burlington
Bishop's House; see Riverside
Burlington Library
23 W. Union St.
HABS NJ-319   pd   L
Chapel of the Holy Innocents (St. Mary's
   Hall)
HABS NJ-317   pd   L
Cooper-Lawrence House
457-459 High St.
HABS NJ-73   s p d   L
Doane House; see Riverside
Fleetwood, Joseph, Cottage (Toll House,
   Old)
Burlington Pike
HABS NJ-244   s p d   L
Grant, Gen., House
309 Wood St.
HABS NJ-320   pd   L
Hutchinson-Revell House
8 E. Pearl St.
HABS NJ-30   s p d   L
Neale-Collins, Issac, House
Broad & York Sts.
HABS NJ-312   s p d   L
Pearson-How, Hartshorn, House
453 High St.
HABS NJ-251   s p d   L

Riverside (Bishop's House; Doane House)
W. Delaware St.
HABS NJ-318   s p d   L
St. Mary's Church, New
HABS NJ-393   pd   L
St. Mary's Church, Old
W. Broad & Wood Sts.
HABS NJ-72   s p d   L
St. Mary's Hall; see Chapel of the Holy
   Innocents
Toll House, Old; see Fleetwood, Joseph,
   Cottage
Wright-Carey House
406 High St.
HABS NJ-321   pd   L

Charleston vic.
Rodman-Creely House
HABS NJ-369   s p d   L

Cinnaminson Twp.
Wright, Joseph, House
Taylor's Lane
HABS NJ-683   s p d   L

Columbus
Atkinson-Shinn, William R., House
Route 39
HABS NJ-313   s p d   L

Cookstown
Cookstown Tavern
Main St. & Bunting Bridge Rd.
HABS NJ-508   s p d   L

Cookstown vic.
Hockamick Log Cabin
HABS NJ-532   s   L

Crosswicks
Chesterfield Friends Meetinghouse
Front & Church Sts.
HABS NJ-25   s p d   L

Middletown-Braislin House
Main St.
HABS NJ-368   s p d   L

Eayrestown
Eayres-Githens Farm Buildings
HABS NJ-136   s p d   L

Eayrestown vic.
Black, John Jr., Barn
Newbold's Corner
HABS NJ-254   s p d   L

Evesboro vic.
Clinton, Gen., Headquarters
Evesboro Rd.
HABS NJ-504   s p d   L
Hewlings House
Mt. Laurel Rd.
HABS NJ-537   s p d   L

Evesham Twp.
Evans, Jacob, House
Marlton-Medford Rd.
HABS NJ-540   s p d   L
Wills, Jacob, House
HABS NJ-597   s p d   L

Ewansville
Woolston, John, House
Rt. 39
HABS NJ-365   s p d   L

Fieldsboro
Field-Stevens House (White Hill)
Delaware River
HABS NJ-203   s p d   L
White Hill; see Field-Stevens House

Jobstown
Black, John, Smokehouse
Monmouth Rd.
HABS NJ-263   s p d   L
Newbold-Hoffman House
Monmouth Rd.
HABS NJ-135   s p d   L

Jobstown vic.
Black, Thomas, Smokehouse (Ockanickon
   Farm)
Monmouth Rd.
HABS NJ-636   s p d   L
Ockanickon Farm; see Black, Thomas,
   Smokehouse

Kinkora
Biddle, William, House
HABS NJ-527   s p d   L

Lumberton
Haines-Budd House (Jones Farmhouse)
HABS NJ-438   s p d   L
Jones Farmhouse; see Haines-Budd House

Lumberton vic.
Moore-Stiles Farm
Bulls Head Rd.
HABS NJ-453   s p d   L

Maple Shade
Matlack, Reuben, Blacksmith &
   Wheelwright Shop
HABS NJ-264   s p d   L

Marlton vic.
Lippincott, Daniel, House
HABS NJ-596   pd   L

Moorestown
Tallman Smokehouse
Long Crossing Rd.
HABS NJ-137   s p d   L

Moorestown vic.
Cowperthwaite House
King's Hwy.
HABS NJ-471   s p d   L

Mount Holly

Ashhusrt Estate, Summer House
Garden St.
HABS NJ-448   s pd   L

Bispham Farmhouse
Rt. 138 & Madison Ave.
HABS NJ-400   s pd   L

Brainard, John, School
35 Brainard St.
HABS NJ-100   s pd   L

Burlington County Courthouse (Surrogate's Office)
High St.
HABS NJ-27   s pd   L

Burlington County Prison
128 High St.
HABS NJ-340   s pd   L H

Farmer's Trust Company Bank Building
21 Mill St.
HABS NJ-397   s pd   L

Fire Department Building, Old
S. Pine St.
HABS NJ-353   s pd   L

Girard, Stephen, House
HABS NJ-316   pd   L

Shinn-Curtis House
HABS NJ-890   p   H

Surrogate's Office; see Burlington County Courthouse

Three Tun Tavern
HABS NJ-230   pd   L

Woolman, John, Memorial
99 Branch St.
HABS NJ-71   s pd   L

Woolman, John, Shop
47 Mill St.
HABS NJ-457   s pd   L

Mount Laurel

Evesham Friends Meetinghouse
Mt. Laurel Rd.
HABS NJ-31   s pd   L

Mount Laurel vic.

Haines-Darnell House
Mt. Laurel Rd.
HABS NJ-589   pd   L

Hewlings, Joseph, House
HABS NJ-547   s pd   L

New Lisbon

Burlington County Almshouse
HABS NJ-290   pd   L

Rancocas

Friends Meetinghouse & School
HABS NJ-130   s pd   L

Friends School
Main St.
HABS NJ-250   s pd   L

Green-Grovatt House
HABS NJ-204   s pd   L

Haines, Ezre, House
Main St.
HABS NJ-246   s pd   L

Rancocas vic.

Buzby, Thomas, House
Rancocas River
HABS NJ-439   s pd   L

Rogers-Bitting House
HABS NJ-426   s pd   L

Red Lion

Sooy Place
HABS NJ-59   s pd   L

Sandtown

Prickett-Wilkins House
HABS NJ-456   s pd   L

South Pemberton

Burr, Hudson, Mansion
HABS NJ-238   s pd   L

Covered Bridge & Flood Gates, Old
HABS NJ-654   s   L

Springfield Twp.

Merritt, Jacob, House
HABS NJ-631   s pd   L

Ridgway, Job, House
HABS NJ-600   s pd   L

Springside vic.

Rogers, John, House
HABS NJ-241   s pd   L

Sykesville

Plattsburg Presbyterian Church
HABS NJ-382   s pd   L

Upper Mill

Bard, Peter, Log Cabin
Lebanon State Forest
HABS NJ-101   s pd   L

Vincetown

Hollingshead-Peacock House
Pemberton-Vincetown Rd.
HABS NJ-239   s pd   L

Woolston, John, House
51-53 Mill St.
HABS NJ-494   s pd   L

Washington Twp.

Quigley, John, House; see Wading River Tavern

Wading River Tavern (Quigley, John, House)
HABS NJ-444   s pd   L

Westhampton Twp.

Wills, Aaron, House
HABS NJ-541   s pd   L

CAMDEN COUNTY

Ancora

Spring Garden Inn
HABS NJ-534   s pd   L

Bellmawr

Hugg, Samuel, House
Big Timber Creek
HABS NJ-284   s pd   L

Hugg-Lippincott House; see Lippincott, Samuel B., House

Lippincott, Samuel B., House (Hugg-Lippincott House)
Creek Rd.
HABS NJ-283   pd   L

Bellmawr Borough

Kay House
HABS NJ-282   s pd   L

Bellmawr vic.

Dobbs House (Hugg-Brasilia-Crispin-Dobbs House)
HABS NJ-292   s pd   L

Glover House
Bellmawr Ave.
HABS NJ-380   s pd   L

Hugg-Brasilia-Crispin-Dobbs House; see Dobbs House

Blue Anchor

Blue Anchor Tavern
Folsom Rd.
HABS NJ-131   s pd   L

Camden

Camden Historical Society; see Pomona Hall

Cooper, Benjamin, House
Point & Erie Sts.
HABS NJ-304   s pd   L

Cooper, Joseph, House
Pyne Point Park
HABS NJ-70   s pd   L

Cooper, Samuel, House
1104 N. Twenty-second St.
HABS NJ-209   s pd   L

Grieveson House
1218 N. Thirty-second St.
HABS NJ-212   s pd   L

Newton Friends' Meetinghouse
Cooper St.
HABS NJ-843   p   H

Nicholson House
Admiral Wilson Blvd.
HABS NJ-102   s pd   L

Plummer, Frederick, House
1242 S. Front St.
HABS NJ-446   s pd   L

Pomona Hall (Camden Historical Society)
Park Blvd. & Euclid Ave.
HABS NJ-206   s pd   L

Taylor, Dr. H. Genet, House & Office
305 Cooper St.
HABS NJ-844   pd   H

Whitman, Walt, House
328 Mickle St.
HABS NJ-69   s pd   L

Chews Landing vic.

Hampton Hosptial House (Hillman House)
HABS NJ-285   s p d   L

Hillman House; see Hampton Hosptial House

Collingswood

Hopkins, Ebenezer, House; see Hopkins-Burr House

Hopkins-Burr House (Hopkins, Ebenezer, House)
King's Hwy.
HABS NJ-395   s p d   L

Delaware Twp.

Burrough-Wick Farm, Outbuildings
Church Rd.
HABS NJ-223   s p d   L

Fellowship-Del. Twp.

Childs-French Farm
Springdale Rd.
HABS NJ-211   s p d   L

Glendale

Kay-Cooper Tenant House
HABS NJ-210   s p d   L

Haddonfield

Boxwoods, The; see Gill, John, House
Dobbins-Eggman House
24 Potter St.
HABS NJ-103   s p d   L

Gill, John, House (Boxwoods, The)
343 Kings Highway East
HABS NJ-403   s p d   L

Haddon, Elizabeth, House; see Wood-Haddon House
Hip-Roof House; see Mickle House
Hopkins House
Birdwood-Hopkins Rd.
HABS NJ-133   s p d   L

Hopkins-Elkinton House
Haddon Ave. & Lake St.
HABS NJ-205   s p d   L

Indian King Tavern
233 King Highway E.
HABS NJ-99   s p d   L

Mickle House (Hip-Roof House)
23 Ellis St.
HABS NJ-132   s p d   L

Roberts, John, House
344 E. Kings Hwy.
HABS NJ-401   s p d   L

Wood-Haddon House (Haddon, Elizabeth, House)
201 Wood Lane & Hawthorne Ave.
HABS NJ-402   s p d   L

Haddonfield vic.

Gill Homestead at Tavistock
HABS NJ-207   s p d   L

Pennsauken

Burrough-Steelman House
Irving & Colonial Aves.
HABS NJ-301   s p d   L

Pennsauken Twp.

Burrough-Dover Farmhouse
HABS NJ-252   s p d   L

Wood-Phillips House
HABS NJ-208   s p d   L

Somerdale vic.

Warrick House
Warrick Rd.
HABS NJ-345   s p d   L

CAPE MAY COUNTY

Beesleys Point

Beesley House, Old
U.S. Hwy. 9
HABS NJ-482   s p d   L

Burnell House, Old
HABS NJ-495   s p d   L

Cape May

Allen, George, House
720 Washington St.
HABS NJ-845   s d   H

Atlantic Terrace House (Minnix House)
20 Jackson St.
HABS NJ-846   s d   H

Baronet, The; see Lewis, Joseph, House
Boyd, George W., House
1501 Beach Ave.
HABS NJ-847   s d   H

Cape Island Baptist Church (Franklin Street United Methodist Church)
Franklin & Lafayette Sts.
HABS NJ-848   s d   H

Cape Island Presbyterian Church (Community Center)
417 Lafayette St.
HABS NJ-742   s d   H

Cape May, Maps, Site & Floor Plans, & Details
HABS NJ-891   s   H

Carroll Villa
19 Jackson St.
HABS NJ-849   s d   H

Chalfonte Hotel
Howard & Sewell Sts.
HABS NJ-743   s p d   H

Church of the Advent; see St. John's Church
Colonial Hotel
Beach & Ocean Sts.
HABS NJ-850   s d   H

Community Center; see Cape Island Presbyterian Church
Congress Hall
Beach & Congress Sts.
HABS NJ-744   s p d   H

Cook's Villa; see Fryer's Cottage
Evans, Joseph R., Cottage
207 Congress Place
HABS NJ-893   s   H

Franklin Street United Methodist Church; see Cape Island Baptist Church
Fryer's Cottage (Cook's Villa)
9 Perry St.
HABS NJ-860   s d   H

Hall, Joseph, Cottage
645 Hughes St.
HABS NJ-894   s   H

Herzberg Family Cottage
8 Broadway
HABS NJ-895   s   H

Hildreth, George, House (Lyhano)
17 Jackson St.
HABS NJ-851   s d   L H

Hunt, Dr. Henry F., House
209 Congress Place
HABS NJ-898   s   H

Jackson's Clubhouse (Mainstay Inn)
635 Columbia Ave.
HABS NJ-748   s p d   H

Johnson, Eldridge, House (Pink House)
33 Perry St.
HABS NJ-853   s d   H

Knight, Edward C., Cottage
203 Congress Place
HABS NJ-892   s   H

Lafayette Hotel
Beach Dr. & Decatur St.
HABS NJ-745   p   H

Lewis, Joseph, House (Baronet, The)
819 Beach St.
HABS NJ-854   s d   H

Lyhano; see Hildreth, George, House
Macomber Hotel
Beach & Howard Sts.
HABS NJ-852   s   H

Mainstay Inn; see Jackson's Clubhouse

McConnell, John C., House
15 Jackson St.
HABS NJ-857   s   H

McCreary, John B., House
34 Gurney St.
HABS NJ-855   s d   H

Minnix House; see Atlantic Terrace House
Neafie-Levy House
28-30 Congress St.
HABS NJ-896   s   H

New Jersey Trust & Safe Deposit Company
526 Washington St.
HABS NJ-856   s d   H

Octagon Cottage; see Schellinger, Josiah, House

Physick, Dr. Emlen, House
1048 Washington St.
HABS NJ-746   s p d   H

Pink House; see Johnson, Eldridge, House

Schellinger, Josiah, House (Octagon
　Cottage)
1286 Lafayette St.
HABS NJ-747　　　　　pd　　H

St. John's Church (Church of the Advent)
Washington & Franklin Sts.
HABS NJ-858　　　s　d　　H

Stockton College
26 Gurney St.
HABS NJ-859　　　s　d　　H

Ware, J. Stratton, House
655 Hughes St.
HABS NJ-897　　　s　　　H

Windsor Hotel
Beach Dr. & Windsor St.
HABS NJ-749　　　　pd　　H

Cape May Courthouse

Holmes House; see Way, Judge, House
Holmes, Nathaniel, House
Main St. & Romney Pl.
HABS NJ-752　　s pd　　H

Stites, Benjamin, House
400 Shore Rd.
HABS NJ-750　　　pd　　H

Way, Judge, House (Holmes House)
U.S. Hwy. 9
HABS NJ-465　　s pd　L

Cape May Point

Coast Guard Station
Delaware Bay
HABS NJ-450　　s pd　L

Cold Spring

Cold Spring Presbyterian Church
HABS NJ-270　　　pd　L

Dennisville

Belle-Carroll House
Main St.
HABS NJ-751　　　pd　　H

Townsend, William, House
96 Delsea Dr.
HABS NJ-753　　　pd　　H

Goshen

Ludlam, James, House
Delsea Dr.
HABS NJ-754　　　p　　H

Ocean View

Rising Sun Tavern
158 Shore Rd.
HABS NJ-755　　　p　　H

Seaville Vicinity

Friends' Meetinghouse
Shore Rd.
HABS NJ-74　　s pd　L H

South Dennis

Falkenburg, Joseph, House
922 Delsea Dr.
HABS NJ-756　　　pd　　H

Woodbine

Woodbine Brotherhood Synagogue
612 Washington Ave.
HABS NJ-866　　　s pd　L

CUMBERLAND COUNTY

Bacon's Neck

Bacon House
HABS NJ-354　　s pd　L
Davis, Gabriel S., House
HABS NJ-267　　s pd　L

Bacon's Neck vic.

Maskell, Thomas, House (Vauxhall
　Gardens)
Bacon's Neck Rd.
HABS NJ-582　　s pd　L
**Vauxhall Gardens; see Maskell, Thomas,
　House**

Bayside vic.

Dennis, Philip, House
HABS NJ-583　　s pd　L

Bloomfield

First Presbyterian Church on-the-Green
HABS NJ-60　　s pd　L

Bridgeton

**Buck, Jeremiah, House; see Buck-Elmer
　House**
Buck-Elmer House (Buck, Jeremiah,
　House)
297 E. Commerce St.
HABS NJ-530　　s pd　L
Elmer, Robert, House
230 E. Commerce St.
HABS NJ-404　　s pd　L
First Presbyterian Church
W. Broad St.
HABS NJ-272　　s pd　L
Giles, James, House
143 W. Broad St.
HABS NJ-221　　s pd　L
Seeley House
274 E. Commerce St.
HABS NJ-497　　s pd　L
Woodruff-Lee House
330 Fayette St.
HABS NJ-670　　s pd　L

Deerfield vic.

Sneathen House
Deerfield St.
HABS NJ-344　　s pd　L

Dorchester vic.

Reeve-Marshall Log House
HABS NJ-215　　s pd　L

Dutch Neck

Brick, John III, House
County Rd. 50
HABS NJ-585　　s pd　L

Wheaton, William, House
County Rd. 50
HABS NJ-584　　s pd　L

Fairton

Fairfield Presbyterian Church
HABS NJ-273　　s pd　L

Greenwich

Ewing Homestead
Main St.
HABS NJ-138　　s pd　L
Ferry Tavern & Jail
HABS NJ-268　　s pd　L
Friends Meetinghouse, Old
Main St.
HABS NJ-105　　s pd　L
Gibbon, Leonard, Homestead
Main St.
HABS NJ-129　　s pd　L
School House, Old Stone
Greenwich St.
HABS NJ-222　　s pd　L
Sheppard, John, House
Main St.
HABS NJ-641　　s pd　L
Tavern, Old Stone
Main St.
HABS NJ-104　　s pd　L
Wood, Richard, House
Main St. & Bacon's Neck Rd.
HABS NJ-269　　s pd　L
Wood, Richard, Store
Main & Willow Sts.
HABS NJ-269-A　　s pd　L

Greenwich vic.

Ewing, Samuel, House
Main St.
HABS NJ-635　　s pd　L
Maskell, Thomas, Store
Main & Pine Sts.
HABS NJ-660　　s pd　L
Seeley-Davis Homestead
Davis Mill Rd.
HABS NJ-220-B　　s pd　L
Seeley-Davis Mill
Davis Mill Rd.
HABS NJ-220-A　　s pd　L

Mauricetown

**Maurice River Pratt Through-Truss Swing
　Bridge**
HAER NJ-20　　　p　　H

Roadstown

Cohansey Baptist Church
HABS NJ-463　　s pd　L
Gilman House; see Wood Tavern
Howell Homestead
Roadstown Rd.
HABS NJ-76　　s pd　L
Wood Tavern (Gilman House)
HABS NJ-44　　s pd　L

Sea Breeze

Sheppard, David, House
HABS NJ-554   s p d   L

Seeley

Seeley, Josiah, Homestead
Finley Station Rd.
HABS NJ-75   s p d   L

Seeley vic.

Loper, Uriah, House
Beebe Run Rd.
HABS NJ-514   s p d   L

ESSEX COUNTY

Belleville

Brandt House
205 Main St.
HABS NJ-387   s p d   L
Coeyman House
502 Belleville Ave.
HABS NJ-449   s p d   L
Lloyd House; see Rose Cottage
Macomb, Gen. Alexander, House
125 Main St.
HABS NJ-390   s p d   L
Rose Cottage (Lloyd House)
221 Main St.
HABS NJ-153   s p d   L
Speer House
319 Main St.
HABS NJ-389   s p d   L
Ward, Dr. Samuel L., House
191 Main St.
HABS NJ-388   s p d   L

Bloomfield

Davis House; see First Presbyterian Church on-the-Green, The Manse
Dodd, Daniel, House
339 Franklin St.
HABS NJ-688   p d   L
First Presbyt. Church on-the-Green, Parish House
HABS NJ-371   s p d   L
First Presbyterian Church on-the-Green, The Manse (Davis House)
HABS NJ-370   s p d   L

Boro Of N. Caldwell

Francisco, Henry, House
Allen Rd.
HABS NJ-653   s p d   L

Caldwell

Cleveland, Grover, Birthplace
207 Bloomfield Ave.
HABS NJ-179   s p d   L
Cory, John, House (House, Little)
485 Bloomfield Ave.
HABS NJ-143   s p d   L
House, Little; see Cory, John, House

Cedar Grove

Jacobus House
178 Grove Ave.
HABS NJ-475   s p d   L
Personett House
727 Pompton Ave.
HABS NJ-496   s p d   L

Fairfield vic.

Speer, Peter, House
Fairfield Rd.
HABS NJ-669   s p d   L
Van Ness, Peter, Farmhouse
Fairfield Rd.
HABS NJ-625   s p d   L

Irvington

Osborn, Henry, House
506 Stuyvesant Ave.
HABS NJ-618   s p d   L

Livingston

Force, William, House
343 S. Livingston Ave.
HABS NJ-556   s p d   L
Wade, Henry W., House
554 S. Livingston Ave.
HABS NJ-619   s p d   L

Maplewood

Ball, Timothy, House (Washington Inn)
425 Ridgewood Rd.
HABS NJ-50   s p d   L
Henderson, Robert, House; see Ogden, Montgomery, House
Ogden, Montgomery, House (Henderson, Robert, House)
22 Jefferson Ave.
HABS NJ-337   s p d   L
Washington Inn; see Ball, Timothy, House

Millburn

Parsil, William Jr., House
Parsonage Hill & White Oak Ridge Rds.
HABS NJ-627   s p d   L
Smith-Henderson Homestead
155 Millburn Ave.
HABS NJ-107   s p d   L

Montclair

Crane, King, House
159 Glenridge Ave.
HABS NJ-152   s p d   L
Munn Tavern (Swedish Church Parish House)
19 Valley Rd.
HABS NJ-372   s p d   L
Swedish Church Parish House; see Munn Tavern

Newark

Alling House
1012 Broad St.
HABS NJ-187   s p d   L
American Red Cross Chapterhouse; see Feigenspan House

Ballantine, John Holme, House and Stables
43 Washington St.
HABS NJ-757   p   H
Bascule Trunnion Lift Bridge; see Erie Railroad, New York Division Bridge
Beam, Anthony, House (Crane, Stephen, Birthplace)
14 Mulberry Place
HABS NJ-310   s p d   L
Broad Street, 900 Block (House)
HABS NJ-708   p   L
Carter, Anthony, House
3 Clay St.
HABS NJ-253   s p d   L
Chancellor Avenue School; see Lyons Farm Schoolhouse
Crane, Stephen, Birthplace; see Beam, Anthony, House
Davis-Agnew-Lloyd Houses
86-88 Plane St.
HABS NJ-180   s p d   L
Erie Railroad, New York Division Bridge (Bascule Trunnion Lift Bridge; Through-Truss Draw Bridge)
HAER NJ-25-A   p d   H
Essex County Jail
Newark, New & Wilsey Sts.
HABS NJ-758   p   H
Feigenspan House (American Red Cross Chapterhouse)
710 High St.
HABS NJ-759   p   H
First Baptist Peddie Memorial Church
Broad & Fulton Sts.
HABS NJ-760   p   H
First Presbyterian Church
820 Broad St.
HABS NJ-33   s p d   L
Gaddis, Elisha B., House
1016 Broad St.
HABS NJ-696   p d   L
Hobart, George S., House
599 Mount Prospect Ave.
HABS NJ-867   p d   L
House of Prayer, Rectory (Plume, Isaac, House)
407 Broad St.
HABS NJ-14   s p d   L
Kiersted, Aaron, House; see Pierson, Abraham, House
Kiersted, John, House; see Nichols, David, House
Lyons Farm Schoolhouse (Chancellor Avenue School)
Chancellor & Elizabeth Aves.
HABS NJ-3   s p d   L
Mount Pleasant Cemetery Gateway & Tombs
375 Broadway St.
HABS NJ-761   p   H
Newark Bay Bridge
HAER NJ-37   p   H

501

Nichols, David, House (Kiersted, John, House)
229 Mulberry
HABS NJ-242   s p d   L

Pierson, Abraham, House (Kiersted, Aaron, House)
231 Mulberry St.
HABS NJ-302   s p d   L

Plume, Isaac, House; see House of Prayer, Rectory

South Park Presbyterian Church
Broad St. & Clinton Ave.
HABS NJ-182   s p d   L

Sydenham, John, House
720 De Graw Ave.
HABS NJ-148   s p d   L H

Through-Truss Draw Bridge; see Erie Railroad, New York Division Bridge

Trinity Cathedral Church
Rector & Broad Sts.
HABS NJ-34   s p d   L

Nutley

Feland House
63 Enclosure
HABS NJ-373   s p d   L

Hay, James R., House
385 Passaic Ave.
HABS NJ-186   s p d   L

Kingsland House
3 Kingsland Rd.
HABS NJ-150   s p d   L

Vreeland Homestead
226 Chestnut St.
HABS NJ-6   s p d   L

Orange

Hillyer, Rev. Asa, Parsonage
59 Main St.
HABS NJ-656   s p d   L

Lighthipe House
548 Main St.
HABS NJ-245   s p d   L

Roseland

Williams-Harrison House
126 Eagle Rock Rd.
HABS NJ-109   s p d   L

Upper Montclair

Sigler-DeForest House
471 Valley Rd.
HABS NJ-308   s p d   L

West Caldwell

Bond House
Runnymeade Rd.
HABS NJ-184   s p d   L

Cory, Joseph, House; see Lane-Cory House

Crane, Nathaniel S., House
29 Clinton Rd.
HABS NJ-151   s p d   L

Harrison House
Orton Rd.
HABS NJ-183   s p d   L

Lane-Cory House (Cory, Joseph, House)
633 Bloomfield Ave.
HABS NJ-108   s p d   L

West Orange

Edison, Thomas A., House (Glenmont)
Park Way & Glen Ave.
HABS NJ-729   s p d   H

Edison, Thomas A., House, Outbuildings
Main St. & Lakeside Ave.
HABS NJ-808   p   H

Freeman House
61 S. Valley Rd.
HABS NJ-651   s p d   L

Glenmont; see Edison, Thomas A., House

Harrison, Caleb, House (Mountain Foot)
93 Northfield Ave.
HABS NJ-643   s p d   L

Mountain Foot; see Harrison, Caleb, House

Williams House
30 Ashwood Terrace
HABS NJ-624   s p d   L

GLOUCESTER COUNTY

Glassboro

St. Thomas' Episcopal Church
Main & Force Sts.
HABS NJ-376   s p d   L H

Malaga vic.

Zion Methodist Church
HABS NJ-665   s p d   L

Mantua

Carpenter, Thomas, House
(Eastlake-Carpenter House)
Main & Martel Sts.
HABS NJ-68   s p d   L

Eastlake-Carpenter House; see Carpenter, Thomas, House

Mantua vic.

Moffett, Archibald, House
HABS NJ-311   s p d   L

Mickleton

Mickleton Friends School
Democrat Rd.
HABS NJ-256   s p d   L

Otto-Tonkin House
Kings Highway
HABS NJ-46   s p d   L

Mount Royal

Death-of-the-Fox Inn
HABS NJ-231   p d   L

Mullica Hill

Mullica Hill Town Hall
S. Main St. (Bridgeton Pike) & Woodstown Rd.
HABS NJ-839   s p d   L

St. Stephen's Episcopal Church
51 N. Main St.
HABS NJ-889   p d   H

National Park

Fort Mercer Trenches
HABS NJ-878   p   L

Whitall House
Delaware River & Hessian Ave.
HABS NJ-79   s p d   L

Whitall, James Jr., House
HABS NJ-576   p d   L

Paulsboro

Paul House
HABS NJ-405   s p d   L

Swedesboro-Paulsboro Road (Log House)
HABS NJ-10   s p d   L

Paulsboro vic.

Francis, Tench, House & Barn
Manuta Creek
HABS NJ-410   s p d   L

Hopkins House (Paradise Farm)
HABS NJ-473   s p d   L

Paradise Farm; see Hopkins House

Rambo, John, House
Mantua Grove Rd.
HABS NJ-485   s p d   L

Pitman

Pitman Grave Camp Meeting
North, South, East, & West Aves.
HABS NJ-730   p d   L

Swedesboro

Stratton Mansion
HABS NJ-82-A   s p d   L

Trinity Church
Church & Main Sts.
HABS NJ-85   s p d   L

Vanleer Cedar Log Cabin
HABS NJ-92   s p d   L

Swedesboro vic.

Adams Methodist Episcopal Church
Road to Hendrickson's Mill
HABS NJ-83   s p d   L

Moravian Church
Sharptown Rd.
HABS NJ-81-A   s p d   L

Moravian Church, Rectory
HABS NJ-81-B   s p d   L

Stille, Peter, House
HABS NJ-82-B   s p d   L

Westville

West-Newbold House
HABS NJ-307   p   L

Woodbury

Friends Meetinghouse
120 N. Broad St.
HABS NJ-80   s p d   L

HUDSON COUNTY

Hoboken

Castle Stevens; see Stevens, Col. John, House

Erie-Lackawana Railroad Ferry Terminal & Warehouse
Hudson Place
HABS NJ-763   pd   H

Hoboken Fire Engine Company Number Two
1313 Washington St.
HABS NJ-764   pd   H

Stevens, Col. John, House (Castle Stevens)
Castle Point
HABS NJ-765   p   H

Stevens Gatehouse
Castle Point
HABS NJ-809   p   H

Jersey City

Apple Tree House; see Van Wagenen House

Bergen Church, Old
Bergen & Highland Aves.
HABS NJ-466   s pd   L

Central R. R. of N. J., Jersey City Ferry Terminal
HAER NJ-27   p   H

Erie Railroad, Bergen Hill Open Cut
HAER NJ-22   p   H

Erie Railroad, Ferryboat Susquehanna
HAER NJ-23   p   H

Erie Railroad, Pier 5 Immigrants Waiting Room
HAER NJ-24   p   H

Grace Episcopal Church (Van Vorst Episcopal Church)
Second & Erie Sts.
HABS NJ-766   pd   H

Gregory House
31 Erie St.
HABS NJ-503   s pd   L

Hudson County Courthouse
583 Newark Ave.
HABS NJ-841   pd   H

Montgomery Gateway East, One & Two
Montgomery & Monmouth St.
HABS NJ-868   pd   L H

Van Vorst Episcopal Church; see Grace Episcopal Church

Van Vorst House
531 Palisade Ave.
HABS NJ-501   s pd   L

Van Wagenen House (Apple Tree House)
298 Academy St.
HABS NJ-767   p   H

Union City

Alcorn, William, House
91 Palisade Ave.
HABS NJ-502   s pd   L

Browning, Cyrus S., House
161 Palisade Ave.
HABS NJ-506   s pd   L

HUNTERDON COUNTY

Califon vic.

Trimmer, William, House
HABS NJ-650   s pd   L

Clinton

Rariton River Fink Through-Truss Bridge
HAER NJ-18   pd   H

Rariton River Pony Pratt Truss Bridge
HAER NJ-19   p   H

Flemington

Emery, William E., House (Roselawn)
3 E. Main St.
HABS NJ-768   pd   H

Fisher, Mahlon, House
116 Main St.
HABS NJ-769   pd   H

Fleming Castle
5 Bonnel St.
HABS NJ-406   s pd   L

Hopewell, John C., House
55 E. Main St.
HABS NJ-770   pd   H

Hunterdon County Courthouse
Main & Court Sts.
HABS NJ-771   pd   H

Reading, John G., House
151-153 Main St.
HABS NJ-731   pd   L

Reading-Large House
119 Main St.
HABS NJ-396   s pd   L

Redding, Gov., House
HABS NJ-773   p   H

Roselawn; see Emery, William E., House

Union Hotel
76 Main St.
HABS NJ-732   pd   L

Wurts, Alexander, Law Office
59 Main St.
HABS NJ-772   pd   H

Lambertville

Holcombe House
HABS NJ-56   pd   L

Mountainville

Main Street (Commercial Building)
HABS NJ-887   p   H

Oldstone Barn (Philhower, C., Barn)
HABS NJ-888   p   H

Philhower, C., Barn; see Oldstone Barn

Oldwick

Alpaugh House (Illif House)
HABS NJ-886   p   H

Barnet, Dr. Oliver, House (Barnet House; Dillon House)
N. Vliettown Rd.
HABS NJ-774   p   H

Barnet House; see Barnet, Dr. Oliver, House

Barnett Hall Academy (Oldwick Commumity Center)
High St.
HABS NJ-775   p   H

Beaver's House
Main St. (Country Rt. 517)
HABS NJ-776   p   H

Clark House; see Dickerson, Charles E., House

Coughlin House; see Honeyman, Robert M., House

Crater-Slack House
High St.
HABS NJ-784   p   H

Dickerson, Charles E., House (Clark House)
Main St.
HABS NJ-777   p   H

Dillon House; see Barnet, Dr. Oliver, House

Durland, Garet, House (Johnson House)
Homestead Rd.
HABS NJ-778   p   H

Fisher, Jacob R., House
High St.
HABS NJ-779   p   H

Honeyman, Robert M., House (Coughlin House)
Joilet St.
HABS NJ-781   p   H

Illif House; see Alpaugh House

Johnson House; see Durland, Garet, House

Miller, Henry, House
Main St.
HABS NJ-782   p   H

Oldwick Commumity Center; see Barnett Hall Academy

Oldwick Methodist Church
Main St.
HABS NJ-783   p   H

Stryker House
High St.
HABS NJ-885   p   H

Van Doren House
Main St.
HABS NJ-785   p   H

Zion Lutheran Church
Main St.
HABS NJ-786   p   H

Pattenburg vic.

Clifford-Williamson House
HABS NJ-698   s pd   L

Raven Rock

Saxton, Quimby, House; see Saxtonville Tavern

Saxtonville Tavern (Saxton, Quimby, House)
HABS NJ-616   s pd   L

Ringoes

Amwell Academy
HABS NJ-513   s pd   L

Frame Grist Mill
Rt. 30
HABS NJ-451   s p d   L

Ringoes vic.
Williamson House
HABS NJ-235   s p d   L

Sergeantsville
Covered Bridge
Wickecheoke Creek
HABS NJ-442   s p d   L
Miller's House (Opdyke, John, Farm)
Rosemont Rd.
HABS NJ-455   s p d   L
Opdyke, John, Farm; see Miller's House

MERCER COUNTY

Hopewell
Brown's College
19 Broad St.
HABS NJ-232   p d   L
School Baptist Church, Old
Main St.
HABS NJ-199   s p d   L

Hopewell vic.
Weart-Hunt House
Stoutsburg-Amwell Rd.
HABS NJ-289   s p d   L

Hutchinson's Mill
Hutchinson House
HABS NJ-483   s p d   L

Lawrence Township
Spring Grove
Lewisville Rd.
HABS NJ-810   s p   H

Lawrenceville
Brearly House
HABS NJ-342   p d   L
Glencairn (Opdyke-Hunt House)
Lawrence Rd.
HABS NJ-296   s p d   L
Green House; see Harmony Hall
Harmony Hall (Green House)
Main St.
HABS NJ-52   s p d   L
Opdyke-Hunt House; see Glencairn
Presbyterian Church
Main St.
HABS NJ-53   s p d   L

Pennington
Hart, John D., House
Curlis Ave.
HABS NJ-454   s p d   L
Welling, John, House
Curlis Ave.
HABS NJ-409   s p d   L

Pennington vic.
Woolsey, Jeremiah M., House
HABS NJ-201   s p d   L

Princeton
Alexander Hall; see Princeton Theological
   Seminary
20 Alexander St. (House)
HABS NJ-795   p   L
29 Alexander St. (House)
HABS NJ-796   p   L
Bainbridge House
158 Nassau St.
HABS NJ-336   s p d   L
Beatty, Col. Jacob, House (Hyer, Col.
   Jacob, House)
19 Vandeventer St.
HABS NJ-789   p   L
Belgarde; see Princeton University,
   Borough Hall
Breckenridge, Professor John, House
   (Ridge, The)
72 Library Place
HABS NJ-790   p   L
Chancellor Green Library; see Princeton
   University, Library
Chancellor Green Student Center; see
   Princeton University, Library
Clarke, Thomas, House (Mercer, Gen.,
   House)
Mercer Rd.
HABS NJ-548   s p d   L
Dean's House (President's House, Old)
73 Nassau St.
HABS NJ-88   s p d   L
Field, Richard Stockton, House; see
   Princeton University, Guernsey Hall
Fieldwood; see Princeton University,
   Guernsey Hall
First Presbyterian Church
61 Nassau St.
HABS NJ-793   p   L
Gulick-Hudge-Scott House
Herrontown Rd.
HABS NJ-794   p   H
Hyer, Col. Jacob, House; see Beatty, Col.
   Jacob, House
Leonard, Judge Thomas, House; see
   Nassau Inn
Mercer, Gen., House; see Clarke, Thomas,
   House
Morven; see Stockton, Richard, House
Nassau Hall (Old North)
Nassau St.
HABS NJ-249   s p d   L
Nassau Inn (Leonard, Judge Thomas,
   House)
HABS NJ-434   p d   L
Old North; see Nassau Hall
Olden, Thomas, House
344 Stockton Rd.
HABS NJ-797   p   L

Potter, Thomas F., House
Princeton University Campus
HABS NJ-865   p   L
President's House, Old; see Dean's House
Princeton Bank & Trust
12-14 Nassau St.
HABS NJ-798   p   L
Princeton Theological Seminary
   (Alexander Hall; Seminary, Old)
Mercer St.
HABS NJ-787   p   L
Princeton University, Alexander Hall
Nassau St. & Palmer Sq.
HABS NJ-788   p   L
Princeton University, Borough Hall
   (Thomas, Senator John R., House;
   Belgarde)
50 Stockton St.
HABS NJ-799   pd   L
Princeton University, Guernsey Hall (Field,
   Richard Stockton, House; Fieldwood)
63 Lovers Lane
HABS NJ-792   pd   L
Princeton University, Library (Chancellor
   Green Library; Chancellor Green
   Student Center)
Nassau St. btw. Witherspoon & Tulane Sts.
HABS NJ-791   p   L
Ridge, The; see Breckenridge, Professor
   John, House
Seminary, Old; see Princeton Theological
   Seminary
Signer, The; see Stockton, Richard, House
Stockton, Richard, House (Morven; Signer,
   The)
63 Stockton St.
HABS NJ-408   pd   L
Stony Brook Bridge
Rt. 27
HABS NJ-29   s p d   L
Stony Brook Quaker Meetinghouse
Quaker Rd.
HABS NJ-140   s p d   L

Thomas, Senator John R., House; see
   Princeton University, Borough Hall

Tusculum; see Witherspoon, John, House

Tusculum Barn; see Witherspoon, John,
   Barn

Tusculum Springhouse; see Witherspoon,
   John, Springhouse

Witherspoon, John, Barn (Tusculum Barn)
166 Cherry Hill Rd.
HABS NJ-801   p   L

Witherspoon, John, House (Tusculum)
166 Cherry Hill Rd.
HABS NJ-800   p   L

Witherspoon, John, Springhouse
   (Tusculum Springhouse)
166 Cherry Hill Rd.
HABS NJ-802   p   L

Princeton vic.

Golden, John, House
Pretty Brook Rd.
HABS NJ-358   s pd   L

Trenton

Anchor (Stangl) Pottery Company
HAER NJ-26   p   H
Barracks, Old
S. Willow St.
HABS NJ-39   s pd   L
Bloomsbury Court; see Trent House
Bow Hill; see De Klyn House
Bright-Douglass House
Mahlon Stacy Park
HABS NJ-237   s pd   L
De Klyn House (Bow Hill)
Deutzville
HABS NJ-224   pd   L
Kingsbury Hall; see Trent House
Masonic Temple, Old
S. Willow & W. Lafayette Sts.
HABS NJ-141   s pd   L
Russell-Stokes House
HABS NJ-425   pd   L
Trent House (Kingsbury Hall; Bloomsbury
    Court; Woodlawn)
539 S. Warren St.
HABS NJ-200   s pd   L
Woodlawn; see Trent House

Washington Crossing

Johnson-McKonkey Ferry House
HABS NJ-19   s pd   L

MIDDLESEX COUNTY

Bonhamtown

Ford, Charles, House
Old Post Rd.
HABS NJ-467   s pd   L

Bound Brook vic.

Perry, Kenneth, Cottage
River Rd.
HABS NJ-710   pd   L
Perry, Kenneth, House
River Rd.
HABS NJ-709   pd   L

Carteret

Williams, Ichabod T., & Sons
HAER NJ-28   d   H

Highland Park vic.

Antill, Dr., House (Ross Hall)
River Rd.
HABS NJ-362   s pd   L
Ross Hall; see Antill, Dr., House

Kingston

Drawbridge, Lock & Tollhouse
Delaware & Raritan Canal
HABS NJ-359   s pd   L

Metuchen

Borough Improvement League House
    (Franklin School)
491 Middlesex Ave.
HABS NJ-226   s pd   L
Fairweather, Thomas, House
191 Middlesex Ave.
HABS NJ-216   s pd   L
Franklin School; see Borough Improvement
    League House
St. Luke's Episcopal Church
Middlesex & Oaks Aves.
HABS NJ-711   pd   L

Metuchen vic.

Shotwell-Runyon House
Happy Valley Lane
HABS NJ-55   s pd   L

Morristown

Abbett Avenue Bridge
HAER NJ-35   pd   H

N. Brunswick Twp.

Williamson House
Cozzens Lane
HABS NJ-89   s pd   L

New Brunswick

Bishop, James, House
College Ave. & Bartlett St.
HABS NJ-712   pd   L
Christ Episcopal Church
HABS NJ-38   pd   L
Delaware & Raritan Canal Lock
Raritan River btw. George & Hamilton Sts.
HABS NJ-713   pd   L
Doolittle-Demarest House; see Rutgers
    University
First Reformed Church of New Brunswick
Neilson St.
HABS NJ-716   pd   L
Hertzog, Peter, Theological Hall; see New
    Brunswick Theological Seminary
Indian Queen Tavern
Albany Ave. & Rt. 27
HABS NJ-875   p   H
Jarrad, Levi D., House; see Rutgers
    University
New Brunswick Theological Seminary
    (Hertzog, Peter, Theological Hall)
17 Seminary Place
HABS NJ-717   pd   L
**New Brunswick Theological Seminary,
    Library** (Sage, Gardener A., Library)
21 Seminary Place
HABS NJ-722   pd   L
**New Jersey Rubber Shoe Company
    Building No. 1**
Albany St.
HABS NJ-719   pd   L
**New Jersey Rubber Shoe Company
    Building No. 9**
Burnet St.
HABS NJ-720   pd   L

**Norfolk & New Brunswick Hosiery
    Company**
George & Hamilton Sts.
HABS NJ-721   pd   L
Queen's Building
Somerset St.
HABS NJ-119   s pd   L
Rutgers University (Doolittle-Demarest
    House)
George St. & Seminary Pl.
HABS NJ-714   pd   L
Rutgers University (Jarrad, Levi D.,
    House)
George St.
HABS NJ-718   pd   L
Rutgers University, Observatory (Schanck,
    Daniel S., Observatory)
George St.
HABS NJ-723   pd   L
Sage, Gardener A., Library; see New
    Brunswick Theological Seminary,
    Library
Schanck, Daniel S., Observatory; see
    Rutgers University, Observatory
Smith, Emily, House
29 Remson Ave.
HABS NJ-724   pd   L
Smith Stable & Carriage House
29 Remson Ave.
HABS NJ-725   pd   L
Strong, Judge Woodbridge, House
    (Stronghold)
272 Hamilton St.
HABS NJ-726   pd   L
Stronghold; see Strong, Judge Woodbridge,
    House
White-Buccleuch Mansion
River Rd.
HABS NJ-22   s pd   L

New Brunswick vic.

Farley Blacksmith Shop
82 Memorial Pky. (moved to Johnson Park)
HABS NJ-715   pd   L
Nevius House; see Smock, Matthias, House
Smock, Matthias, House (Nevius House)
River Rd.
HABS NJ-478   s pd   L

New Market

**Our Lady of Fatima R. C. Church,
    Rectory;** see Vail, William, House
Vail, William, House (Valmere; Our Lady
    of Fatima R. C. Church, Rectory)
501 New Market St.
HABS NJ-727   pd   L
Valmere; see Vail, William, House

North Stelton vic.

Dunn, Jeremiah, House
Stelton Rd.
HABS NJ-458   s pd   L

Perth Amboy

Anaconda Copper Works, Old (Records Storage Building)
Elm & Market Sts.
HAER NJ-32   p d   L

Governor's House
149 Kearny Ave.
HABS NJ-341   s p d   L

Kearny Cottage
Catalpa Ave.
HABS NJ-637   s p d   L

Parker Castle
Front & Water Sts.
HABS NJ-118   s p d   L

Records Storage Building; see Anaconda Copper Works, Old

Piscataway

St. James Episcopal Church
HABS NJ-197   s p d   L

Piscataway Twp.

Dunn, Walter G., Farmhouse
Hoe's Lane
HABS NJ-287   s p d   L

Fitz-Randolph, Ephraim, House
S. Randolphville Rd.
HABS NJ-277   s p d   L

Ivy Hall (Low, Cornelius, House)
1225 River Rd.
HABS NJ-360   s p d   L

Low, Cornelius, House; see Ivy Hall

Plainsboro vic.

Britton, Col. Dean, House
Dey Rd.
HABS NJ-225   s p d   L

Schalk Station

Groendyke House
HABS NJ-95   s p d   L

Woodbridge

Barron Library
HABS NJ-861   p   L H

MONMOUTH COUNTY

Allaire

Deserted Village, The; see Howell Iron Works

Howell Iron Works (Monmouth Blast Furnace; Deserted Village, The)
HABS NJ-28   s d   L

Howell Iron Works, Bakery
HABS NJ-28-A   s p   L

Howell Iron Works, Blacksmith Shop
HABS NJ-28-B   s   L

Howell Iron Works, Blast Furnace
HABS NJ-28-C   s p   L

Howell Iron Works, Carpenter Shop
HABS NJ-28-D   s   L

Howell Iron Works, Church
HABS NJ-28-E   s d   L

Howell Iron Works, Double House
HABS NJ-28-F   s d   L

Howell Iron Works, Enameling House
HABS NJ-28-G   s p   L

Howell Iron Works, Fuel Depot
HABS NJ-28-H   p   L

Howell Iron Works, Store
HABS NJ-28-I   s p   L

Howell Iron Works, Works Foreman's Cottage
HABS NJ-28-J   s p   L

Monmouth Blast Furnace; see Howell Iron Works

Allentown

Imlay, John, Mansion
28 S. Main St.
HABS NJ-24   s p d   L

Arneytown vic.

Mackenzie, Duncan, Place (Woodward, Thomas, Homestead)
Province Line Rd.
HABS NJ-202   s p d   L

Woodward, Thomas, Homestead; see Mackenzie, Duncan, Place

Chapel Hill

Conover Farm
Mountain Hill Rd.
HABS NJ-276   s p d   L

Creamridge vic.

Meirs, William, House
HABS NJ-509   s p d   L

Englishtown

Village Inn
Main & Water St.
HABS NJ-65   s p d   L

Everett vic.

Hendrickson, Denise, House
Everett Rd.
HABS NJ-679   s p d   L

Freehold vic.

Craig, John, House
HABS NJ-543   s p d   L

Highlands

Life Saving Station, Original
Spermacetti Cove (moved from Sandy Hook)
HABS NJ-42   s p d   L

Holland

Luyster, Johannes, House
Laurel Ave. & Middleton Rd.
HABS NJ-668   s p d   L

Holland-Holmdel Twp.

Hendrickson, Daniel, House
Holland Rd.
HABS NJ-498   s p d   L

Holmdel

Cooke, Dr. Robert W., Office
HABS NJ-666   s p d   L

Holmdel Twp.

Couwenhoven, Corneles, House
HABS NJ-646   s p d   L

Duncan, William J., House; see Longstreet House

Hendrickson, Hendrick, House
HABS NJ-544   s p d   L

Longstreet House (Duncan, William J., House)
HABS NJ-411   s p d   L

Lincroft vic.

North American Phalanx Phalanstery
Country Route 537
HABS NJ-842   p d   H

Long Branch

Grant, President U.S., Cottage (Potter, Howard, House)
995 Ocean Ave.
HABS NJ-884   p d   H

Potter, Howard, House; see Grant, President U.S., Cottage

Reservation Buildings 2 & 5
New Ocean Ave. & Joline Ave.
HABS NJ-883   s p   H

Matawan

Burrowes Mansion
94 Main St.
HABS NJ-198   s p d   L

Matawan Passenger Railroad Station & Freight House
RR Tracks bwt. Main St. & Atlantic Ave.
HABS NJ-873   p d   L

Middleton

Christ Episcopal Church
Church St. & King's Highway
HABS NJ-325   s p d   L

Franklin Academy
King's Highway
HABS NJ-424   s p d   L

Marlpit Hall; see Taylor, Edward I., House

Taylor, Edward I., House (Marlpit Hall)
King's Highway
HABS NJ-275   s p d   L

Phalanx vic.

Polhemus, Daniel, Farmhouse
HABS NJ-693   s p d   L

Prospertown vic.

Coward, John, House
HABS NJ-555   s p d   L

Sandy Hook

Life Saving Station, Original
Spermacetti Cove (moved to Highlands)
HABS NJ-42   s p d   L

Sandy Hook Lighthouse
HABS NJ-326   s p d   L

Shrewsbury

Allen Homestead
Broad St. & Sycamore Ave.
HABS NJ-228   s p d   L
Christ Episcopal Church
Broad St. & Sycamore Ave.
HABS NJ-37   s p d   L
Friends Meetinghouse
Sycamore Ave.
HABS NJ-568   s   L

Tennent

First Presbyterian Church (Tennent
    Church, Old)
HABS NJ-26   s p d   L
Tennent Church, Old; see First
    Presbyterian Church

Walnford vic.

Tilton House
HABS NJ-484   s p d   L

West Freehold

Clinton Gen., Headquarters
    (Conover-Hankinson House)
W. Main St.
HABS NJ-227   s p d   L
Conover-Hankinson House; see Clinton
    Gen., Headquarters

Wrightsville

Merino Hill; see Wright House
Wright House (Merino Hill)
Old Shrewsbury Rd.
HABS NJ-526   s p d   L

MORRIS COUNTY

Boonton vic.

Kingsland Homestead
Vreeland Ave.
HABS NJ-96   s p d   L
Miller, Adam, House at Powerville
HABS NJ-193   s p d   L
Scott, William, Mansion House
Powerville Rd.
HABS NJ-558   s p d   L

Chatham

Crane House (Pitt, William, Tavern)
HABS NJ-94   p d   L
Day, Stephen, House
62 Elmwood Rd.
HABS NJ-125   s p d   L
Day-Hamblen House
142 Main St.
HABS NJ-356   s p d   L
Day-Munn House
25 Main St.
HABS NJ-490   s p d   L
Pitt, William, Tavern; see Crane House

Chester

Chester House Hotel
HABS NJ-61   s p d   L

Corwin, Issac, House
HABS NJ-628   s p d   L
Drake, John, House
Main St.
HABS NJ-647   s p d   L

Denville vic.

Cook, Peter, House
Morris Rd.
HABS NJ-642   s p d   L

Dover vic.

Friends Meetinghouse of Randolph
HABS NJ-145   s p d   L
Washington Arms Tavern
HABS NJ-196   s p d   L

Florham Park

Campfield, James A., House
    (Cory-Campfield House)
HABS NJ-522   s p d   L
Cory-Campfield House; see Campfield,
    James A., House
Hopping, John, House
Ridgedale Ave. & Park Ave.
HABS NJ-692   s p d   L
Hopping, Silas, House
Park St.
HABS NJ-687   s p d   L

Hanover

Ball, Aaron, House
Mt. Pleasant Tpk.
HABS NJ-561   s p d   L
Green, Calvin, House
HABS NJ-517   s p d   L
Halfway House (Merry-Hopping House)
HABS NJ-676   s p d   L
Hopping, Daniel, House
Hanover Rd.
HABS NJ-195   s p d   L
Merry-Hopping House; see Halfway House
Woodruff, John, House
137 Mt. Pleasant Ave.
HABS NJ-681   s p d   L

Hanover Neck

Tuttle, John O., House
Eagle Rock Ave.
HABS NJ-511   s p d   L

Hanover Twp.

Pierson, Lewis, House
Horsehill Rd.
HABS NJ-689   s p d   L

Lincoln Park

Dey, Thomas, House
Lincoln Park Blvd.
HABS NJ-536   s p d   L
Dods, John, House
Highland St.
HABS NJ-93   s p d   L

Madison

Bottle Hill Tavern
127 Main St. & Alexander Ave.
HABS NJ-58   s p d   L
Bruen, Jonathan B., House
250 Main St.
HABS NJ-529   s p d   L
Miller, Andrew, House
105 Ridgedale Ave.
HABS NJ-124   s p d   L
Sayre, Daniel, House (Sayre, Ephrim,
    House)
31 Ridgedale Ave.
HABS NJ-146   s p d   L
Sayre, Ephrim, House; see Sayre, Daniel,
    House

Mendham

Hill Top Church
HABS NJ-63   s p d   L
Howell, Abraham, House; see Wolfe, Peter,
    House
Hudson, Aaron, House
Hilltop Rd.
HABS NJ-564   s p d   L
Ladies Seminary (Phoenix House)
HABS NJ-62   s p d   L
Phoenix House; see Ladies Seminary
Thompson House
HABS NJ-194   s p d   L
Wolfe, Peter, House (Howell, Abraham,
    House)
Hill Top Rd.
HABS NJ-623   s p d   L

Middle Valley

Miller, David, House
HABS NJ-519   s p d   L

Montville

Van Duyne, Abraham, House
State Rt. 32
HABS NJ-489   s p d   L

Montville vic.

Demarest Farmhouse
Changebridge Rd.
HABS NJ-309   s p d   L
Parlaman, Johannes, House
River Rd.
HABS NJ-49   s p d   L

Morristown

Abbett Avenue Bridge
HAER NJ-35   p d   H
Campfield, Dr. Jabez, House; see
    Schuyler-Hamilton House
Este, Capt. Moses, House
62 Water St. (moved to Speedwell Village)
HABS NJ-677   s p d   L
Ford, Colonel Jacob Jr., House
    (Washington's Headquarters)
230 Morris St.
HABS NJ-32   s p d   L

Guerin House
Jockey Hollow Rd.
HABS NJ-144   s p d   L

Hatfield, Moses, House
21 DeHart St.
HABS NJ-695   s p d   L

Kemble House
Mt. Kemble Ave.
HABS NJ-48   s p d   L

Liddell Mill
Jockey Hollow
HABS NJ-682   p   L

Macculloch, George P., Mansion
45 Macculloch Ave.
HABS NJ-658   p d   L

Mills, Timothy, House
27 Mills St.
HABS NJ-632   s p d   L

Russell, Sylvester D., House
89 Western Ave.
HABS NJ-659   s p d   L

Schuyler-Hamilton House (Campfield, Dr.
   Jabez, House)
5 Oliphant Pl.
HABS NJ-35   s p d   L

Washington's Headquarters; see Ford,
   Colonel Jacob Jr., House

Wick, Tempe, House
Mendham Rd., Jockey Hollow
HABS NJ-15   s p d   L

Mount Freedom vic.

Pool, Henry, House
County Rd. No. 20
HABS NJ-671   s p d   L

Mount Tabor vic.

Dickerson, Thomas, House
HABS NJ-644   s p d   L

Newfoundland

DeMouth-Snyder House
Green Pond Rd.
HABS NJ-217   s p d   L

Newfoundland vic.

Weaver-Hough House
HABS NJ-427   s p d   L

Parsipanny vic.

Parritt, Dr. Joseph, House
S. Beverwyck Rd.
HABS NJ-562   s p d   L

Parsippany vic.

Bowers-Benedict House; see Osborn,
   Thomas, House

Osborn, Thomas, House (Bowers-Benedict
   House)
Parsippany Rd.
HABS NJ-630   s p d   L

Pine Brook

Van Duyne, Simon, House
Maple Lane & Hook Mt. Rd.
HABS NJ-147   s p d   L

Pompton Plains

Berry, Martin, House
Jackson Ave. & Rt. 23
HABS NJ-546   s p d   L

Van Ness House
Jackson Ave. & Pompton Pine
HABS NJ-545   s p d   L

Ralston

Post Office (Ralston Manor House)
HABS NJ-357   s p d   L

Ralston, John, Mill
HABS NJ-339   s p d   L

Ralston Manor House; see Post Office

Rockaway

Jackson House
82 E. Main St.
HABS NJ-507   s p d   L

Speedwell Village

Este, Capt. Moses, House
(moved from Morristown, 62 Water St.)
HABS NJ-677   s p d   L

Split Rock

Split Rock Furnance
HABS NJ-553   s p d   L

Springtown vic.

Dernberger, Philip, House
HABS NJ-633   s p d   L

Sager, Adam, House
HABS NJ-626   s p d   L

Toms Point

Mead, Peter, House
Pine Brook Rd.
HABS NJ-87   p d   L

Towaco

Bott, Elmer E., House
State Highway No. 32
HABS NJ-452   s p d   L

Jacobus, Abram, Out Kitchen
U.S. 202
HABS NJ-492   s p d   L

Jacobus, John T., House
   (Mandeville-Jacobus House)
HABS NJ-474   s p d   L

Mandeville-Jacobus House; see Jacobus,
   John T., House

Vreeland, John H., Out Kitchen
HABS NJ-493   s p d   L

Towaco vic.

Doremus, Henry, House
State Route 32
HABS NJ-488   s p d   L

Washington Valley

Smith, John, House
HABS NJ-398   s p d   L

Whippany

Methodist Episcopal Church
Route 10, Troy Hills Rd.
HABS NJ-518   s p d   L

Tuttle, Joseph, House
Mount Pleasant Ave.
HABS NJ-469   s p d   L

Whippany vic.

Green-Cook House
Rt. 10
HABS NJ-639   s p d   L

OCEAN COUNTY

Barnegat

Barnegat Lighthouse
HABS NJ-43   p d   L

Cedar Bridge

Cedar Bridge Tavern
HABS NJ-41   s p d   L

Lakehurst vic.

Charcoal Pits
HABS NJ-291   s p d   L

Lanoka Harbor

Potter, Thomas, House
Murray Grove Rd.
HABS NJ-840   p   H

PASSAIC COUNTY

Clifton

Erie Railroad, Clifton Passenger Station
HAER NJ-21   p   H

Jacobus, Peter, House
Allwood Rd.
HABS NJ-559   s p d   L

Minett Varnish Kiln
Delawanna Ave.
HABS NJ-560   s p d   L

Speer, John Jacobus, House
   (Vreeland-Speer House)
Bloomfield Ave.
HABS NJ-149   s p d   L

Vanderhoof House
Weasel Brook Park
HABS NJ-328   s p d   L

Vreeland-Speer House; see Speer, John
   Jacobus, House

Haskell

Van Wagoner House
891 Ringwood Ave.
HABS NJ-520   s p d   L

Hawthorne

Doremus House; see Rea, John W., House

Knapik Inn; see Rea, John W., House

Lafayette Headquarters (Ryerson,
   Johannes, House)
Goffle Brook Park
HABS NJ-165   s p d   L

Marcellus-Vreeland House
Goffle Rd.
HABS NJ-258   s pd   L

Rea, John W., House (Doremus House;
    Knapik Inn)
675 Goffle Rd.
HABS NJ-178   s pd   L

Ryerson, Johannes, House; see Lafayette
    Headquarters

Van Winkle, Judge John S., House
868 Goffle Rd.
HABS NJ-531   s pd   L

Little Falls

Brower House
50 Paterson Ave.
HABS NJ-521   s pd   L

Matches, Robert, House
Browertown Rd.
HABS NJ-595   s pd   L

Matches-Beattie House
53-55 Main St.
HABS NJ-164   s pd   L

Lower Preakness

Bloomsbury Manor; see Dey Mansion

Dey Mansion (Bloomsbury Manor)
199 Totowa Rd.
HABS NJ-17   s pd   L

Mountain View

Van Duyne House
636 Fairfield Rd.
HABS NJ-464   s pd   L

Passaic

Anderson House; see Passaic Home &
    Orphan Asylum

Aycrigg Mansion (Masonic Temple)
Main Ave.
HABS NJ-413   s pd   L

Dutch Reformed Parsonage, Old; see Van
    Schott House

Masonic Temple; see Aycrigg Mansion

Passaic Home & Orphan Asylum
    (Anderson House)
River Rd. & Lafayette Ave.
HABS NJ-811   s   H

Van Schott House (Dutch Reformed
    Parsonage, Old)
125 Lexington Ave.
HABS NJ-121   s pd   L

Paterson

Allied Textile Printers
HAER NJ-17   pd   H

Barbour Flax Spinning Company
HAER NJ-11   pd   H

Barbour Flax Spinning Company, Granite
    Mill
HAER NJ-11-A   p   H

Barbour Flax Spinning Company, Machine
    Shop
HAER NJ-11-C   p   H

Barbour Flax Spinning Company, Spruce
    Street Mill
HAER NJ-11-B   p   H

Barkalow House
22 Van Houten St.
HABS NJ-327   s pd   L

Danforth (Cooke) Locomotive & Machine
    Company
HAER NJ-8   pd   H

Danforth Locomotive & Machine Shop,
    Erecting Shop
HAER NJ-8-A   p   H

Danforth Locomotive & Machine Shop,
    Blacksmith Shop
HAER NJ-8-B   p   H

Dolphin Manufacturing Company
HAER NJ-12   pd   H

Essex Mill
HAER NJ-6   s pd   H

Franklin Manufacturing Company,
    Waverly Mill
HAER NJ-7   pd   H

G. F. S. E. U. M. Power Canal System
HAER NJ-2   pd   H

Godwin (Hamil) Mill, Boiler & Engine
    House
HAER NJ-14   pd   H

Grant Locomotive
HAER NJ-9   pd   H

Great Falls S. U. M., Historic District
Oliver St.
HAER NJ-1   s pd   H

Hartley, Bernard, House
158-160 W. Broadway
HABS NJ-505   s pd   L

Industry Mill
HAER NJ-15   pd   H

Ivanhoe Mill, Wheelhouse
HAER NJ-10   pd   H

Passaic County Jail & Sheriff's House
Main St.
HABS NJ-381   s pd   L

Paterson Power Canal System
HAER NJ-36   pd   H

Phoenix Mill
HAER NJ-4   s pd   H

Rogers Locomotive & Machine Works
Oliver St.
HAER NJ-3   s pd   H

Rogers Locomotive & Machine Works,
    Admin. Building
Oliver St.
HAER NJ-3-D   s p   H

Rogers Locomotive & Machine Works,
    Erecting Shop
Oliver St.
HAER NJ-3-A   s p   H

Rogers Locomotive & Machine Works,
    Fitting Shop
Oliver St.
HAER NJ-3-B   s p   H

Rogers Locomotive & Machine Works,
    Millwright Shop
Oliver St.
HAER NJ-3-C   s p   L

Rosen Mill; see Union Works

South U. M. Hydrolic Plant
Oliver St.
HAER NJ-16   pd   H

Thompson, Daniel, House
11 Mill St.
HABS NJ-652   s pd   L

Todd & Rafferty Machine Company (Todd
    Mill)
HAER NJ-5   s pd   H

Todd Mill; see Todd & Rafferty Machine
    Company

Union Works (Rosen Mill)
Spruce & Market Sts.
HAER NJ-13   pd   H

Van Houten House
Totowa Ave.
HABS NJ-120   s pd   L

Paterson vic.

Van Riper House
HABS NJ-218   s pd   L

Pompton Falls vic.

Colfax-Dawes House
Paterson-Hamburg Turnpike
HABS NJ-123   s pd   L

Pompton Lakes vic.

Schuyler-Colfax House
Paterson-Hamburg Turnpike
HABS NJ-122   s pd   L

Preakness

Laruwe House; see Van Saun House

Van Saun House (Laruwe House)
Preakness Ave. & Singac Brook
HABS NJ-166   s   L

Ringwood

Ringwood Manor (Ryerson House)
HABS NJ-12-A   pd   L

Ringwood Manor, Smithy
HABS NJ-12   s pd   L

Ryerson House; see Ringwood Manor

Totowa

Van Allen-Garretson House
Totowa Rd.
HABS NJ-480   s pd   L

Upper Preakness

Merselis-Van Houten House
Paterson-Hamburg Pike
HABS NJ-257   s pd   L

Wanaque

Lines, Conrad House
Ringwood & Highland Aves.
HABS NJ-512   s pd   L

Wayne

Fosberg House
3 Edgemont Rd.
HABS NJ-870   pd   H

Jabobus Blacksmith Shop
110 Roonton Rd.
HABS NJ-871   pd   H

Sears House
958 Rt. 23
HABS NJ-872   pd   H

SALEM COUNTY

Alloway

Alloway Tavern
Main & Greenwich Sts.
HABS NJ-306   s pd   L

Evans House; see Holme-Reeves House

Fogg-Hopkins House
HABS NJ-262-D   s pd   L

Holme-Reeves House (Evans House)
HABS NJ-262-A   s pd   L

Alloway Twp.

Gamble Farmhouse; see Sinnickson, Thomas, House

Newkirk-Ballingers Mill & Houses
Tonard Rd.
HABS NJ-139   s pd   L

Sinnickson, Thomas, House (Gamble Farmhouse)
HABS NJ-638   s pd   L

Alloway vic.

Dickinson House (Oakland Station)
HABS NJ-243   s pd   L

Emmell Log Cabin
Elmer Rd.
HABS NJ-262-B   s pd   L

Oakford, William, House
Telegraph & Greenwich Rds.
HABS NJ-127   s pd   L H

Oakland Station; see Dickinson House

Auburn

Scull House
Auburn Rd.
HABS NJ-214   s pd   L

Daretown

Pittsgrove Presbyterian Church, Old
Aldine Rd.
HABS NJ-213   s pd   L

Elsinboro

Nicholson, Abel, House
HABS NJ-305   s pd   L

Elsinboro Twp.

Morris-Goodwin House
Fort Elfsboro Rd.
HABS NJ-690   s pd   L

Friesburg

Mench-Reall Log Cabin
HABS NJ-262-C   s pd   L

Hancocks Bridge

Cedar Plank House (Tyler, William, House)
Locust Island Rd. & Main St.
HABS NJ-106   s pd   L

Hancock House
Loucst Island Rd. & Main St.
HABS NJ-54   s pd   L

Tyler, William, House; see Cedar Plank House

Lower Alloways Creek

Denn, John Maddox, House
HABS NJ-260   s pd   L

Oakford, John & Hannah, House
HABS NJ-349   s pd   L

Stretch-Padgett House
HABS NJ-234   s pd   L

Lower Penns Neck

Goslin, Leon, House; see Johnson-Goslin House

Johnson-Goslin House (Goslin, Leon, House)
HABS NJ-347   s pd   L

Mannington Twp.

Brick, Richard, House; see Dolbow House

Dolbow House (Brick, Richard, House)
Compromise Rd.
HABS NJ-615   s pd   L H

Pledger House
HABS NJ-385   s pd   L

Mannington vic.

Fox, Jacob, House
HABS NJ-248   s pd   L

Pittsgrove vic.

Richman, Michael, House
HABS NJ-350   pd   L

Quinton vic.

Tyler, William, House
HABS NJ-128   s pd   L

Salem

Bradway House (Governor's House; Lighthouse)
32 W. Broadway
HABS NJ-379   pd   L

Clement-Redstrake House
West Broadway
HABS NJ-377   s pd   L

Friends Meetinghouse
E. Broadway & Walnut St.
HABS NJ-77   s pd   L

Governor's House; see Bradway House

Grant, Alexander, House
81-83 Market St.
HABS NJ-78   s pd   L

Hancock, Morris, House
314 E. Broadway
HABS NJ-591   pd   L

Johnson House
90 Market St.
HABS NJ-219   s pd   L

Jones, John, Law Office
W. Broadway & New Market St.
HABS NJ-261   s pd   L

Keasby
HABS NJ-804   p   L

Lighthouse; see Bradway House

Sinnickson House
HABS NJ-806   pd   L

Thompson, Hedge, House
HABS NJ-805   pd   L

Victorian Cottage
HABS NJ-803   pd   L

Worledge, John, House
323 E. Broadway
HABS NJ-383   s pd   L

Salem vic.

Holmeland; see Holmes, Benjamin, House

Holmes, Benjamin, House (Holmeland)
HABS NJ-481   s pd   L

Lambson Tavern
HABS NJ-384   pd   L

Mecum, William, House
HABS NJ-233   pd   L

Nicholson, Samuel, House
Oakwood Beach Rd.
HABS NJ-259   s pd   L

Smith, Richard, House
HABS NJ-348   pd   L

Sharptown vic.

Robinson-Kiger House
HABS NJ-445   s pd   L

Woodstown

Bassett, Samuel & Anne, House
HABS NJ-355   s pd   L

Clawson House (Shinn House)
68 N. Main St.
HABS NJ-461   s   L

Shinn House; see Clawson House

Woodstown vic.

Pissant House
HABS NJ-346   pd   L

Seven Star Tavern
HABS NJ-126   s pd   L

SOMERSET COUNTY

Basking Ridge

Presbyterian Church
Finley Ave.
HABS NJ-97   s pd   L

Washington Tavern
HABS NJ-707   p   L

Bernards Twp.

McMurtry's Saw Mill
Hardscrabble Rd.
HABS NJ-533   s pd   L

Bernardsville
Van Doren's Mill
HABS NJ-67   s p d   L

Bound Brook
Van Horn, Philip, House
Somerset Ave.
HABS NJ-523   s p d   L

Bound Brook vic.
Island Farm; see Smock-Hodge House
Kells Hall; see Smock-Hodge House
Schenck-Polhemus House
Easton Tpk. Rd.
HABS NJ-524   s p d   L
Smock-Hodge House (Kells Hall; Island
    Farm)
HABS NJ-525   s p d   L

East Millstone
Franklin House (Hotel); see Van Liew
    House
Van Liew House (Franklin House (Hotel))
Amwell Rd.
HABS NJ-648   s p d   L

Finderne vic.
Van Veghten House
HABS NJ-661   s p d   L

Frankfort
Du Bois, Abraham, House
HABS NJ-334   s p d   L

Franklin Park
Voorhees House; see Wyckoff, Jacobus,
    House
Wyckoff, Jacobus, House (Voorhees House)
Lincoln Hwy. (Countyline Rd.)
HABS NJ-447   s p d   L

Franklin Twp.
Suydam House; see Van Wickle, Symen,
    House
Van Wickle, Symen, House (Suydam
    House)
Easton Tpk.
HABS NJ-479   s p d   L

Liberty Corner
Compton House (House, Old Stone)
Valley Rd.
HABS NJ-247   s p d   L
Compton House; see De Mott, William F.,
    House
De Mott, William F., House (Compton
    House)
Valley Rd.
HABS NJ-185   s p d   L
House, Old Stone; see Compton House

Liberty Corner vic.
Annin-Smalley House
Valley Rd.
HABS NJ-240   s p d   L

Middlebush vic.
Hageman, Aaron, House
Cortelyou Lane
HABS NJ-620   s p d   L

Millstone
Dutch Reformed Church
Amwell Rd. & Main St.
HABS NJ-295   s p d   L
Van Doren, John, House (Washington's
    Headquarters)
HABS NJ-293   p d   L
Washington's Headquarters; see Van
    Doren, John, House

Pluckemin
Fenner, John, House
HABS NJ-188   s p d   L

Raritan
Cornell Homestead (Northwood)
Somerset St.
HABS NJ-333   s p d   L
Frelinghuysen, Gen. John, House
54 E. Somerset St.
HABS NJ-332   s p d   L
Northwood; see Cornell Homestead

Rocky Hill
Berrien, Judge John, House (Rockingham;
    Washington's Headquarters)
Rocky Hill Rd.
HABS NJ-18   s p d   L
Berrien, Peter, House
Old Rocky Hill Rd.
HABS NJ-91   s p d   L
Rockingham; see Berrien, Judge John,
    House
Washington's Headquarters; see Berrien,
    Judge John, House

S. Middlebush
Stoothoff, Cornelius, House (Suydam
    House)
County Rd. 31
HABS NJ-674   s p d   L
Suydam House; see Stoothoff, Cornelius,
    House

Somerville
Dutch Parsonage, Old; see Frelinghuysen
    Parsonage
Frelinghuysen Parsonage (Dutch
    Parsonage, Old)
Washington Place
HABS NJ-294   s p d   L
Lindsley, John, House
10 W. End Ave.
HABS NJ-374   s p d   L
Wallace House (Washington Headquarters)
Washington Place
HABS NJ-20   s p d   L
Washington Headquarters; see Wallace
    House

South Bound Brook
Staats, Abraham, House (Staats-Latourette;
    Von Steuben, Baron, Headquarters)
Canal Rd. (165 Main St.)
HABS NJ-57   s p d   L
Staats-Latourette; see Staats, Abraham,
    House
Von Steuben, Baron, Headquarters; see
    Staats, Abraham, House

South Middlebush
Nevius, David, House (Voorhees, Jacques,
    House)
HABS NJ-673   s p d   L
Voorhees, Jacques, House; see Nevius,
    David, House

SUSSEX COUNTY

Flatbrookville vic.
Smith-Rosenkrans House
Old Mine Rd.
HABS NJ-812   s p d   H

Hainesville
Nyce-Depue House
Old Mine Rd.
HABS NJ-737   s p   H

Hamburg
Haines, Gov., Mansion (Sharp House;
    Wheatsworth Inn)
HABS NJ-278   s p d   L
Sharp House; see Haines, Gov., Mansion
Wheatsworth Inn; see Haines, Gov.,
    Mansion

Millville
Shimer, Jacob, House
Old Mine Rd.
HABS NJ-818   s p d   H

Montague
Clark-Herman House (House, Brick; Hotel,
    Brick)
HABS NJ-437   p d   L
Ennis, William, House
Old Mine Rd.
HABS NJ-431   s p d   H
Foster-Armstrong Barn
Old Mine Rd.
HABS NJ-817-A   p   H
Hotel, Brick; see Clark-Herman House
House, Brick; see Clark-Herman House
Montague Ferry Keeper's House
HABS NJ-821   p d   H

Montague vic.
Ennes, William, House
Old Mine Rd.
HABS NJ-431   p d   L
Everitt House
Old Mine Rd.
HABS NJ-823   p d   H

Fort Namanock
HABS NJ-741 pd H
Foster-Armstrong House
Old Mine Rd.
HABS NJ-817 s pd H
Westbrook-Bell House
Old Mine Rd.
HABS NJ-435 s pd L H

Smith Ferry

Knight Corn Crib
HABS NJ-814 s pd H
Knight Hog House
Old Mine Rd.
HABS NJ-819 d H

Wallpack Center

Wallpack Center
HABS NJ-827 p H

Wallpack Center vic.

Hull, David R., House (Shoemaker, Daniel, House)
Wallpack Center
HABS NJ-820 s pd H
Hull, David R., Springhouse (Shoemaker, Daniel, Springhouse)
Wallpack Center
HABS NJ-820-A s pd H
Shoemaker, Daniel, House; see Hull, David R., House
Shoemaker, Daniel, Springhouse; see Hull, David R., Springhouse
Snable-Rundle House
Old Mine Rd.
HABS NJ-828 pd H
Van Campen Inn; see Van Campen, Isaac, House
Van Campen, Isaac, Barn; see Van Campen-Dewitt Barn
Van Campen, Isaac, House (Van Campen Inn)
Old Mine Rd.
HABS NJ-436 s pd L H
Van Campen-Dewitt Barn (Van Campen, Isaac, Barn)
HABS NJ-736 s pd H

Wantage

Titsworth House
State Hwy. 32
HABS NJ-433 s pd L

UNION COUNTY

Cranford

Crane House
124 Union Ave., N.
HABS NJ-189 s pd L

Elizabeth

Belcher, Gov., Mansion
1046 E. Jersey St.
HABS NJ-13 s pd L

Boudinot Mansion (Boxwood Hall)
1073 E. Jersey Ave.
HABS NJ-476 s pd L
Boxwood Hall; see Boudinot Mansion
Cartret Arms (Thomas, Robinson House)
16 S. Broad St.
HABS NJ-66 s pd L
Chateau, Old; see Jouet, Cavalier, Mansion
Crane, Nathaniel, House
HABS NJ-418 d L
First Presbyterian Church
Broad St.
HABS NJ-21 s pd L
Hampton House; see St. John's Church, Parsonage
Jouet, Cavalier, Mansion (Chateau, Old)
HABS NJ-2 s pd L
Magie House
330 Elmora Ave.
HABS NJ-351 s pd L
St. John's Church, Parsonage (Hampton House)
633 Pearl St.
HABS NJ-672 s pd L
Thomas, Robinson House; see Cartret Arms
Wilcox House
1000 Magie Ave.
HABS NJ-286 s pd L

Mountainside

Williams, Smith, House
Springfield Rd.
HABS NJ-86 s pd L

New Providence

Presbyterian Church
Springfield Ave. & Passaic St.
HABS NJ-297 s pd L

Plainfield

Plainfield Friend's Meetinghouse
Watchung Ave. & East Third St.
HABS NJ-142 s pd L H

Rahway

Lufberry Homestead
30 E. Grand Ave.
HABS NJ-329 s pd L
Merchant and Drovers Tavern (Von Tuyl Tavern)
Saint George's & Westfield Aves.
HABS NJ-36 s pd L
Von Tuyl Tavern; see Merchant and Drovers Tavern

Scotch Plains

Baker House
2511 Mountain Ave. & Jerusalem Rd.
HABS NJ-491 s pd L
Baptist Parsonage
347 Park Ave.
HABS NJ-419 pd L

Frazee House
Front St.
HABS NJ-415 pd L
Historic Inn, Old; see Stanberry, Recompense, Inn
Stanberry, Recompense, Inn (Historic Inn, Old)
E. Front St. & Park Ave.
HABS NJ-414 s pd L

Springfield

Bonnel House (Hemlocks, The)
504 Morris Ave.
HABS NJ-181 s pd L
Cannon Ball House; see Hutchings House
First Presbyterian Church
Main St. & Springfield Ave.
HABS NJ-1 s pd L
First Presbyterian Church, Parsonage
41 Main St.
HABS NJ-416 s pd L
Hemlocks, The; see Bonnel House
Hutchings House (Cannon Ball House)
126 Morris Ave.
HABS NJ-190 s pd L
Swain Homestead
S. Springfield Ave.
HABS NJ-191 s pd L

Union

Brandt-Headley Farm House
1827 Vauxhall Rd.
HABS NJ-266 s pd L
Connecticut Farms Presbyterian Church
Stuyvesant Ave.
HABS NJ-539 s pd L
Liberty Hall
Morris Ave.
HABS NJ-515 s pd L
Townley House
Morris & Potter Aves.
HABS NJ-192 s pd L
Townley, James, House
Morris Ave. & Green Lane
HABS NJ-535 s pd L
Townley, Richard, House
1407 Morris Ave.
HABS NJ-557 s pd L

Westfield

Varleth-Sip Manor
5 Cherry Lane
HABS NJ-265 s pd L

WARREN COUNTY

Asbury

Castner, Rev. Jacob R., Parsonage
Main St.
HABS NJ-699 s pd L

Calno

Van Campen, Abraham, House
Old Mine Rd.
HABS NJ-430 s pd L H

Delaware

Albertson House
HABS NJ-460   s   L

Hope

American House Hotel
Union St. & Moravian Alley
HABS NJ-704   s pd   L
Moravian Grist Mill Complex
High St. & Hackettstown Rd.
HABS NJ-569   pd   L H
Schenk, John, House (Swayze House)
Union St. & Moravian Alley
HABS NJ-580   pd   L
St. Luke's Episcopal Church
High St. & Hickory St.
HABS NJ-432   s pd   L
Swayze House; see Schenk, John, House

Hope vic.

Eight-Square Stone School, Old
HABS NJ-429   s pd   L
Moravian Farm House (Newton-Davis Farm)
HABS NJ-705   s pd   L
Newton-Davis Farm; see Moravian Farm House
Swayze, Israel, House & Kitchen
HABS NJ-706   s pd   L

Johnsonburg

Dennis Stone Barn (Storehouse)
Greendell Rd.
HABS NJ-441   s pd   L
Gibbs House (Octagon House)
Greendell Rd.
HABS NJ-440   s pd   L
Octagon House; see Gibbs House

Millbrook

Millbrook
HABS NJ-813   p   H

Millbrook vic.

Copper Mine Inn; see Union Hotel
Ferry, Dimmick, Farm; see Shoemaker, Moses, House
Ferry, Dimmick, Farm Barn; see Shoemaker, Moses, Barn
Ferry, Dimmick, Small House; see Shoemaker, Moses, Small House
Miller, E., House; see Van Campen, James, House
Shoemaker, Moses, Barn (Ferry, Dimmick, Farm Barn)
HABS NJ-824-B   p   H
Shoemaker, Moses, House (Ferry, Dimmick, Farm)
HABS NJ-824   pd   H
Shoemaker, Moses, Small House (Ferry, Dimmick, Small House)
HABS NJ-824-A   s pd   H

Union Hotel (Copper Mine Inn)
Old Mine Rd.
HABS NJ-740   pd   H
Van Campen, Abraham, House
HABS NJ-822   s pd   H
Van Campen, B. B., Farmhouse; see Van Campen, Moses, House
Van Campen, James, House (Miller, E., House)
HABS NJ-825   pd   H
Van Campen, Moses, House (Van Campen, B. B., Farmhouse)
HABS NJ-826   pd   H

Oxford

Oxford Furnace
HABS NJ-236   s pd   L

Pahaquarry Twp.

Millbrook Methodist Episcopal Church
HABS NJ-738   pd   H
Millbrook Schoolhouse
HABS NJ-739   pd   H

Phillipsburg

Morris Canal, Delaware River Portal
HAER NJ-29   p   H

Phillipsburg vic.

Morris Canal, Inclined Plane Ten West
HAER NJ-30   pd   H

New Mexico

BERNALILLO COUNTY

Albuquerque

Alvarada Hotel
First St.
HABS NM-123   p   H
Building
HABS NM-32   d   L
Charles Ilfeld Company Warehouse
200 First St. NW
HABS NM-105   pd   L
House
HABS NM-33   d   L

Isleta Pueblo

House, Adobe & Sod
HABS NM-79   d   L
House, Adobe (Walled Forecourt)
HABS NM-121   p   L
Houses, Row of, & Sod Wall
HABS NM-120   p   L

Isleto Pueblo

House, Adobe (Recessed Portal)
HABS NM-122   p   L

COLFAX COUNTY

Cimarron

Aztec Mill, Old
HABS NM-119   p   L
Blacksmith Shop
HABS NM-38   d   L
Cimarron Church
HABS NM-114   p   L
County Courthouse, Old
HABS NM-118   p   L
Diego, Don, Hotel; see St. James Hotel
Government Trading Store
HABS NM-116   p   L
Jail, Old Stone
HABS NM-117   p   L
St. James Hotel (Diego, Don, Hotel)
HABS NM-115   p   L

DONA ANA COUNTY

Las Cruces

Ascarate, Frank, House
HABS NM-80   d   L
House 127
HABS NM-81   d   L

Rodney

St. Francis de Sales Church
HABS NM-43   d   L

GUADALUPE COUNTY

Puerto De Luna

House
U.S. 84 vic.
HABS NM-138   s   H

MCKINLEY COUNTY

Gallup vic.

Pueblo of Zuni, Central & Original Portion
State Rd. 32 & 53 vic.
HABS NM-78   s   L

Zuni

Mission Nuestra Senora de Guadalpue de Zuni
Saint Johns vic.
HABS NM-124   s   H

MORA COUNTY

Tiptonville
Tipton House & Barn
HABS NM-19   s p d   L

Watrous vic.
Watrous House
HABS NM-18   s p d   L

OTERO COUNTY

Cienega
House, Double
HABS NM-82   d   L

QUAY COUNTY

Tucumcari
Baca-Goodman House
Third & Aber Sts.
HABS NM-108   s p   H

RIO ARRIBA COUNTY

Los Luceros Chapel
HABS NM-54   s   H
Los Luceros House
U.S. 64 vic.
HABS NM-53   s   H

Alcalde
Alcalde Village
Site of San Gabriel
HABS NM-83   d   L H
Church
HABS NM-84   d   L
Merrill House (Door)
HABS NM-34   d   L

Chamita
House
HABS NM-37   d   L

Espanola vic.
Pueblo of Santa Clara, Central Portion
State Rd. 30 vic.
HABS NM-98   s   L

SAN JUAN COUNTY

Bonito, Pueblo (Chaco Canyon National Monument)
HABS NM-30   s   L
Chaco Canyon National Monument; see Kin Klizhin
Chaco Canyon National Monument; see Bonito, Pueblo
Kin Klizhin (Chaco Canyon National Monument)
HABS NM-31   s   L

SAN MIGUEL COUNTY

Las Vegas vic.
Baco, Don Jose Albino, House
Old Santa Fe Trail
HABS NM-12   s pd   L

Pecos
Pecos Mission Church (Pecos National Monument)
HABS NM-77   s   H
Pecos National Monument; see Pecos Mission Church

Pecos vic.
Pecos Church (Ruins)
HABS NM-85   p   L

Romeroville
Houses on Plaza
HABS NM-87   p   L
Romero Barn
HABS NM-44   p   L
Romeroville Church
HABS NM-86   p   L

San Miguel
Territorial House
San Miguel del Vado St.
HABS NM-139   s   H
Warehouse & Stables
San Miguel del Vado
HABS NM-127   s   H

Villanueva vic.
El Cerrito, General View; see Pecos River Valley
Pecos River Valley (San Jose del Vado, General View)
HABS NM-131-B   s   H
Pecos River Valley (Spanish American Villages)
HABS NM-131   s d   H
Pecos River Valley (San Miguel del Vado, General View)
HABS NM-131-C   s   H
Pecos River Valley (El Cerrito, General View)
HABS NM-131-A   s   H
San Jose del Vado, General View; see Pecos River Valley
San Miguel del Vado, General View; see Pecos River Valley
Spanish American Villages; see Pecos River Valley

SANDOVAL COUNTY

Bland vic.
Bandelier National Monument; see Ceremonial Cave
Bandelier National Monument; see Kiva, Large

Ceremonial Cave (Bandelier National Monument)
HABS NM-17   s p d   L
Kiva, Large (Bandelier National Monument)
HABS NM-16   s p d   L

Santa Ana
Pueblo of Santa Ana
Jemez River vic.
HABS NM-106   s   H
Santa Ana Mission, Church
HABS NM-125   s   H

SANTA FE COUNTY

Canoncita
Church
HABS NM-36   p   L

Chimayo
El Santuario del Senor Esquipula
HABS NM-9   s p d   L
Plaza del Cerro
HABS NM-128   s d   H

Espanola vic.
Kiva
HABS NM-90   p   L
Pueblo of San Ildefonso
State Rd. 4 vic.
HABS NM-89   s p   L

Galisteo
House
HABS NM-39   p   L
Lucero House
HABS NM-129   s   H

Nambe (pueblo)
Kiva
HABS NM-8   s p d   L

Pojuaque vic.
Bouquet Ranch House
HABS NM-88   p   L

Santa Cruz
Santa Cruz Mission
HABS NM-45   p   L

Santa Fe
Applegate, Frank, House
Camino del Monte Sal
HABS NM-113   p   L
Borrego House (McCormick Prize House)
724 Canyon Rd.
HABS NM-14   s p d   L
El Palacio Real de Santa Fe (Palace of the Governors)
Palace Ave.
HABS NM-2   s p d   L
Garcia House
202 Closson St.
HABS NM-13   s p d   L

Loretto Academy & Grade School
HABS NM-134   s   H

McCormick Prize House; see Borrego
     House

Mignardot House
HABS NM-91   p   L

Nuestra Senora de Guadalupe
HABS NM-112   p   L

Palace of the Governors; see El Palacio
     Real de Santa Fe

Rael House
663, 667, 669 Canyon Rd.
HABS NM-15   s p d   L

Santa Fe vic.

Pueblo of Nambe
State Rd. 4 vic.
HABS NM-107   s   L

Pueblo of Tesuque, Central Portion
Tesque River vic.
HABS NM-103   s   L

San Miguel Church
HABS NM-1   s p d   L

SOCORRO COUNTY

Socorro

Baca Store
HABS NM-46   p   L

Opera House
HABS NM-47   p   L

Park Hotel
HABS NM-48   p   L

San Miguel Mission
HABS NM-49   p   L

TAOS COUNTY

Arroyo Hondo

Penitente Morada; see Upper Penitente
     Morada Chapel

Upper Penitente Morada Chapel
     (Penitente Morada)
HABS NM-60   s p d   L

Llano Quemado

Fernandez, Sofio, House
HABS NM-67   s   L

Penasco

Romero House
Embado Watershed vic.
HABS NM-73   s   L

Placita De Taos

La Capilla de Nuestra Senora de Dolores
HABS NM-93   p   L

Ranchito

Maritnez, Pascual, House
HABS NM-70   s   L

Martinez, Jose Maria, House
HABS NM-71   s   L

Martinez, Leandro, House
HABS NM-64   s   L

Ranchos De Taos

Caretaker's House
HABS NM-94   p   L

House, Adobe (Typical Roof Construction)
HABS NM-42   p   L

House (Recessed Portal)
HABS NM-95   p   L

House, Territorial Period
HABS NM-96   p   L

Long, Horace G., House
HABS NM-62   s   L

Mission Church of Ranchos de Taos
HABS NM-7   s p d   L

Talpa

La Capilla de Nuestra Senora de Talpa
HABS NM-10   s p d   L

La Morada de Talpa
SR. 3 vic.
HABS NM-130   s   H

Trujillo House
HABS NM-74   s   L

Taos

Adair House
Pueblo St.
HABS NM-50   p   L

Carson, Kit, House
Kit Carson Ave.
HABS NM-111   p   L

Chapel of Padre Antonio Jose Martinez
Garden of Irving Couse
HABS NM-110   p   L

Meyers, Ralph, House (Corbels)
HABS NM-51   d   L

Romero, Santiago, House
HABS NM-136   s   H

Valez, Don Antonio Jose, House
Santa Fe & Pueblo Rds. vic.
HABS NM-137   s   H

Taos Peublo

San Geronimo Mission
HABS NM-109   p   L

Taos vic.

Pueblo of Taos, Central Portion
HABS NM-102   s   L

Trampas

Atencio House
HABS NM-76   s   L

de Cruz, Jose, House
HABS NM-75   s   L

San Jose de Gracia Church
HABS NM-61   s p d   L H

Vadito

Casita Martinez
State Rt. 75
HABS NM-72   s   L

TORRANCE COUNTY

Manzano

Torreon, The
HABS NM-11   s p d   L

VALENCIA COUNTY

Acoma Pueblo

San Esteban del Rey Mission
HABS NM-5   s p d   L

Belen

Chavez House
Chihuahua, Santa Fe Trail
HABS NM-35   p   L

Casa Blanca vic.

Pueblo of Acoma (Sky City)
Casa Blanca vic.
HABS NM-6   s p d   L

Sky City; see Pueblo of Acoma

Laugna Pueblo

Houses (near Mission)
HABS NM-97   p   L

Old Laguna Pueblo

Meetinghouse
HABS NM-4   s p d   L

San Jose de Laguna Mission Church &
     Convento
HABS NM-3   s p d   L

Peralta

Alverete House (Door & Zaguan)
HABS NM-41   p   L

Church at Peralta
HABS NM-40   p   L

Our Lady of Guadalupe (Church)
HABS NM-132   s   H

Valencia vic.

Aragon, Don Simon, House
HABS NM-52   p   L

New York

ALBANY COUNTY

Albany

Bernstein Building (Entrance)
669 Broadway
HABS NY-3201 p L
922 Broadway (House)
HABS NY-378 s p L
Buel, Jesse, House
637 Western Ave.
HABS NY-5-A-6 s pd L
Church, Old Dutch
State, Market & Court Sts.
HABS NY-3129 p L
Church, Old Dutch (Pulpit)(Now in First Church)
Broadway & State Sts.
HABS NY-3129-A s H
Court of Appeals (Interiors)
(moved from State Capitol Building)
HABS NY-6001 p L
Doyle Building
Clinton Ave. & Broadway
HABS NY-3202 p L
Exchange, The; see Lansing-Pemberton House
First Church in Albany; see First Reformed Church
First Reformed Church (First Church in Albany; North Dutch Church; Reformed Protestant Dutch Church)
N. Pearl & Orange Sts.
HABS NY-3128 s pd L H
Flats, The; see Schuyler, Gen. Philip, House
Gable, Dutch
HABS NY-3111 p L
Hawk Street Bridge; see Hawk Street Viaduct
Hawk Street Viaduct (Hawk Street Bridge)
HABS NY-5528
HAER NY-10 pd L
Homeopathic Hospital, Old (Interiors)
123 N. Pearl St.
HABS NY-6002 pd L
House, Dutch Gable
674 Broadway
HABS NY-376 s p L
Hudson River Day Line Building
HABS NY-5710 s H
Hun House
149 Washington Ave.
HABS NY-5-A-12 s pd L
Lansing-Pemberton House (Exchange, The)
N. Pearl & Columbia Sts.
HABS NY-3203 pd L
Nipper; see RCA Building
North Dutch Church; see First Reformed Church

Pastures, The; see Schuyler Mansion (Ironwork)
Public School Number 15 (School Number 15)
75 Herkimer St.
HABS NY-5707 d L
RCA Building (Nipper)
Broadway & Loudonville Rd.
HABS NY-5711 p H
Reformed Protestant Dutch Church; see First Reformed Church
School Number 15; see Public School Number 15
Schuyler, Gen. Philip, House (Flats, The)
Troy Rd. vic. (see NY, Colonie)
HABS NY-3102 s p L H
Schuyler Mansion (Ironwork) (Pastures, The)
HABS NY-6256 p L
65 South Ferry Street (House)
HABS NY-6004 p L
Sturtevant, Widow, House
Pearl St.
HABS NY-6003 p L
Visscher, William, Building
100-102 N. Pearl St.
HABS NY-389 s p L
Whipple Cast & Wrought Iron Bowstring Truss Br.
Normans Kill vic.
HABS NY-5525
HAER NY-4 s pd L

Altamont

Severson, George, Inn
HABS NY-3205 p L
Severson House
HABS NY-3205 p L

Altamont vic.

Crounse Homestead
HABS NY-6005 p L

Berne vic.

Building, Old Stone
Old Indian Ladder Rd.
HABS NY-3164 p L
Livingston, Peter, House
Old Indian Ladder Rd.
HABS NY-5713 p L

Bethlehem

Bethlehem (Nicoll, Rensselaer, House)
HABS NY-5-A-4 s pd L
Nicoll, Rensselaer, House; see Bethlehem
Sunnybrook
HABS NY-5-A-13 s pd L
Van Wie, Hendrick, House
HABS NY-4204 p L

Clarksville

Chapman, W., House
HABS NY-6006 p L
Zeh House
HABS NY-6007 p L

Coeymans

Coeymans, Ariaantje, House
Coeymans Creek
HABS NY-333 s p L
Coyemans-Bronck House (Niles House)
State Rt. 144
HABS NY-390 s p L
Niles House; see Coyemans-Bronck House

Cohoes

Cohoes Co. Power Canal System (Head Gatehouse)
Mohawk River, Fonda Rd.
HABS NY-5527
HAER NY-8 pd L
Cohoes Company Power Canal System, Level 2
N. Mohawk St.
HABS NY-5527-A
HAER NY-9 pd L
Erie Canal (Enlarged), Double Lock; see Erie Canal (Enlarged), Lock Number 18
Erie Canal (Enlarged), Lock Number 18 (Erie Canal (Enlarged), Double Lock)
252 N. Mohawk St.
HABS NY-5530
HAER NY-11 pd L
Harmony Manufacturing Co., Mastodon Mill; see Harmony Manufacturing Co., Mill Number 3
Harmony Manufacturing Co., Mill Number 3 (Harmony Manufacturing Co., Mastodon Mill)
100 N. Mohawk St.
HABS NY-5526
HAER NY-5 pd L
Van Schaick, Wessel, House
Van Schaick Ave. & Delaware & Hudson R.R. Tracks
HABS NY-3121 s pd L

Colonie

Flats, The; see Schuyler, Gen. Philip, House
Flats, The, Kitchen; see Schuyler, Gen. Philip, Kitchen
Schuyler, Gen. Philip, House (Flats, The)
Troy Rd. vic. (see NY, Albany)
HABS NY-3102 p L
Schuyler, Gen. Philip, Kitchen (Flats, The, Kitchen)
(see NY, Albany)
HABS NY-3102-A s H

Dunnsville

Wemple Farm
HABS NY-3156 p L

Feura Bush

Bleeker House & Outbuildings (Vadney, John, House)
HABS NY-3163   p   L
Vadney House
HABS NY-3213   pd   L
Vadney, John, House; see Bleeker House & Outbuildings

Green Island

Rensselaer & Saratoga R.R., Green Island Shops
Tibbitts Ave. & Delaware & Hudson R.R. Tracks
HABS NY-5535
HAER NY-15   pd   L

Guilderland Center

Freeman House
HABS NY-6009   pd   L

Guilderland vic.

Case Homestead
HABS NY-6008   pd   L
Fort, Old Indian
HABS NY-3141   p   L

Houcks Corners

Houck Hall; see Tavern, Old
Tavern, Old (Houck Hall)
Feura Bush vic.
HABS NY-6000   pd   L

Kew Gardens

Bunche, Ralph, House
115-125 Grosvenor Rd.
HABS NY-5691   p   H

New Scotland Twp.

Bradt House
HABS NY-3225   p   L
Slingerland, Teunis Cornelius, House
HABS NY-3162   p   L
Van Rensselaer, Steven, House
HABS NY-3150   p   L

New Scotland vic.

Slingerlands Hill Farm
HABS NY-3232   p   L

Newtonville

Newton House
HABS NY-3234   p   L

Onesquethaw

Austin Homestead
HABS NY-3154   p   L
Mead, Judge Henry, House
HABS NY-3153   p   L
Onesquethaw Church
HABS NY-3152   p   L
Scott, John, House
HABS NY-3236   p   L
Van Dyke Homestead
HABS NY-3151   p   L

Rensselaerville

Conklin, Gurdon, House (Quaint Acres)
HABS NY-3224   p   L
Episcopal Church
HABS NY-3155   p   L
House, Old Stone
HABS NY-3143   p   L
Hutchinson, Eli, House (Rider, James, House)
HABS NY-6010   p   L
Quaint Acres; see Conklin, Gurdon, House
Rider, James, House; see Hutchinson, Eli, House

Unionville

McCullock House
Clipp Rd.
HABS NY-3149   p   L

Watervliet

Shaker Chruch Family Office; see Shaker Church Family Trustee's Office
Shaker Church Family Brethren's Workshop
Watervliet Shaker Rd., Colonie Township
HABS NY-3307   p   L
Shaker Church Family Dwelling House (second)
Watervliet Shaker Rd., Colonie Township
HABS NY-3308   p   L
Shaker Church Family (General Views)
Watervliet Shaker Rd., Colonie Township
HABS NY-3306   p   L
Shaker Church Family Herb House
Watervliet Shaker Rd., Colonie Twp.
HABS NY-3309   p   L
Shaker Church Family Laundry & Canning Factory; see Shaker Church Family Washhouse & Canning Factory
Shaker Church Family Main Dwelling House (first)
Watervliet Shaker Rd., Colonie Township
HABS NY-3310   p   L
Shaker Church Family Mill
Watervliet Shaker Rd., Colonie Township
HABS NY-3311   p   L
Shaker Church Family New Meetinghouse; see Shaker Meetinghouse (second)
Shaker Church Family Old Meetinghouse; see Shaker Meetinghouse (first)
Shaker Church Family School; see Shaker Schoolhouse
Shaker Church Family Seed House
Watervliet Shaker Rd., Colonie Township
HABS NY-3316   p   L
Shaker Church Family Sisters' Workshop
Watervliet Shaker Rd., Colonie Township
HABS NY-3277   p   L
Shaker Church Family Trustee's Office (Shaker Chruch Family Office)
Watervliet Shaker Rd., Colonie Township
HABS NY-3313   p   L

Shaker Church Family Washhouse & Canning Factory (Shaker Church Family Laundry & Canning Factory)
Watervliet Shaker Rd., Colonie Township
HABS NY-3275   p   L
Shaker Church Ministry's House; see Shaker Ministry's House
Shaker Meetinghouse (first) (Shaker Church Family Old Meetinghouse)
Watervliet Shaker Rd., Colonie Township
HABS NY-3314   p   L
Shaker Meetinghouse (second) (Shaker Church Family New Meetinghouse)
Watervliet Shaker Rd., Colonie Township
HABS NY-3276   p   L
Shaker Ministry's House (Shaker Church Ministry's House)
Watervliet Shaker Rd., Colonie Township
HABS NY-3312   p   L
Shaker North Family Dwelling House
Albany Shaker Rd., Colonie Township
HABS NY-3295   p   L
Shaker North Family (General Views)
Albany Shaker Rd., Colonie Township
HABS NY-3294   p   L
Shaker North Family Old Second House
Albany Shaker Rd., Colonie Township
HABS NY-3296   p   L
Shaker North Farm Barn
Albany Shaker Rd., Colonie Township
HABS NY-3318   p   L
Shaker Schoolhouse (Shaker Church Family School)
Watervliet Shaker Rd., Colonie Township
HABS NY-3315   p   L
Shaker South Family Ash House
Watervliet Shaker Rd., Colonie Township
HABS NY-3289   p   L
Shaker South Family Brothers' Dormitory (Shaker South Family Building Number 2)
Watervliet Shaker Rd., Colonie Township
HABS NY-3260   s pd   L
Shaker South Family Brothers' Workshop; see Shaker South Family Trustees' Office
Shaker South Family Building Number 1; see Shaker South Family Cottage
Shaker South Family Building Number 10; see Shaker South Family Horse & Wagon Barn
Shaker South Family Building Number 11; see Shaker South Family Icehouse
Shaker South Family Building Number 12; see Shaker South Family Cow & Hay Barn
Shaker South Family Building Number 15; see Shaker South Family Woodshed
Shaker South Family Building Number 2; see Shaker South Family Brothers' Dormitory
Shaker South Family Building Number 3; see Shaker South Family Dwelling House

Shaker South Family Building Number 4;
see Shaker South Family Trustees' Office

Shaker South Family Building Number 5;
see Shaker South Family Cottage

Shaker South Family Building Number 6;
see Shaker South Family Sisters'
Workshop

Shaker South Family Building Number 7;
see Shaker South Family Washhouse

Shaker South Family Building Number 8;
see Shaker South Family Cannery

Shaker South Family Cannery (Shaker
South Family Building Number 8)
Watervliet Shaker Rd., Colonie Township
HABS NY-3262   s p   L

Shaker South Family Cottage (Shaker
South Family Building Number 1)
Watervliet Shaker Rd., Colonie Township
HABS NY-3258   s pd   L

Shaker South Family Cottage (Shaker
South Family Building Number 5)
Watervielt Shaker Rd., Colonie Township
HABS NY-3242   s d   L

Shaker South Family Cow & Hay Barn
(Shaker South Family Building Number
12)
Watervliet Shaker Rd., Colonie Township
HABS NY-3245   s pd   L

Shaker South Family Dwelling House
(Shaker South Family Residence; Shaker
South Family Building Number 3)
Watervliet Shaker Rd., Colonie Township
HABS NY-3261   s pd   L

Shaker South Family (General Views)
Watervliet Shaker Rd., Colonie Township
HABS NY-3272   s pd   L

Shaker South Family Horse & Wagon Barn
(Shaker South Family Wagon Shed;
Shaker South Family Building Number
10)
Watervliet Shaker Rd., Colonie Township
HABS NY-3244   s   L

Shaker South Family Icehouse (Shaker
South Family Building Number 11)
Watervliet Shaker Rd., Colonie Township
HABS NY-3246   s   L

Shaker South Family Residence; see
Shaker South Family Dwelling House

Shaker South Family Sisters' Workshop
(Shaker South Family Building Number
6)
Watervliet Shaker Rd., Colonie Township
HABS NY-3290   p   L

Shaker South Family Trustees' Office
(Shaker South Family Brothers'
Workshop; Shaker South Family
Building Number 4)
Watervliet Shaker Rd., Colonie Township
HABS NY-3241   s pd   L

Shaker South Family Wagon Shed; see
Shaker South Family Horse & Wagon
Barn

Shaker South Family Washhouse (Shaker
South Family Building Number 7)
Watervliet Shaker Rd., Colonie Township
HABS NY-3243   s pd   L

Shaker South Family Woodshed (Shaker
South Family Building Number 15)
Watervliet Shaker Rd., Colonie Township
HABS NY-3247   s p   L

Shaker West Family Barn
Watervliet Shaker Rd., Colonie Township
HABS NY-3292   p   L

Shaker West Family Broom Shop (Shaker
West Family Workshop; Shaker West
Family Building Number 3)
Watervliet Shaker Rd., Colonie Township
HABS NY-3263   s p   L

Shaker West Family Building Number 1;
see Shaker West Family Main Dwelling
House

Shaker West Family Building Number 3;
see Shaker West Family Broom Shop

Shaker West Family Building Number 7;
see Shaker West Family Smokehouse

Shaker West Family Building Number 8;
see Shaker West Family Privy

Shaker West Family (General Views)
Watervliet Shaker Rd., Colonie Township
HABS NY-3274   p   L

Shaker West Family Main Dwelling House
(Shaker West Family Building Number
1)
Watervliet Shaker Rd., Colonie Township
HABS NY-3257   s p   L

Shaker West Family Privy (Shaker West
Family Building Number 8)
Watervliet Shaker Rd., Colonie Township
HABS NY-3265   s   L

Shaker West Family Smokehouse (Shaker
West Family Building Number 7)
Watervliet Shaker Rd., Colonie Township
HABS NY-3264   s   L

Shaker West Family Workshop; see Shaker
West Family Broom Shop

Watervliet Arsenal
S. Broadway
HAER NY-1-A   pd   H

Watervliet Arsenal, Cast Iron Storehouse
Westervelt Ave. & Gibson St.
HABS NY-5521
HAER NY-1   s pd   L

ALLEGANY COUNTY

Angelica

Belvidere
Genesee River
HABS NY-6011   pd   H

Church, Philip, House
Genesee River
HABS NY-6012   p   H

Belfast vic.

**Erie Railway, Allegany Division Bridge
375.41** (Genesee River Viaduct)
State Rt. 19
HAER NY-43   p   H

Genesee River Viaduct; see Erie Railway,
Allegany Division Bridge 375.41

Fillmore vic.

**Erie Railroad, Allegany Division Bridge
367.33** (Rush Creek Viaduct)
Botsford Hollow Rd.
HAER NY-42   p   H

Rush Creek Viaduct; see Erie Railroad,
Allegany Division Bridge 367.33

Wellsville

Erie Railroad, Wellsville Passenger Station
Pearl & Depot Sts.
HAER NY-103   p   H

BRONX COUNTY

Bronx

Bartow Mansion
Pelham Bay Park
HABS NY-456   p   L

Ferris Mansion
Ferris Ave.
HABS NY-432   s pd   L

Fordham Manor Reformed Church
71 Kingsbridge Rd. & Reservoir Ave.
HABS NY-4-22   s pd   L

Fort Schuyler
Throgg's Neck
HABS NY-4-30   s pd   L

Francis Mansion
Girard Ave. & E. 146th St.
HABS NY-457   s p   L

Hawkswood; see Marshall House

Hunter Island Mansion
Hunter Island
HABS NY-460   p   L

Lorillard Snuff Mill
Botanical Gardens, Bronx Park
HABS NY-462   s p   L

Marshall House (Hawkswood)
Rodman's Neck
HABS NY-467   p   L

Messiah Home for Children (Salvation
Army School for Officers' Training)
1771 Andrews Ave.
HABS NY-5699   pd   L

**Salvation Army School for Officers'
Training;** see Messiah Home for
Children

Van Cortlandt, Frederick, Mansion
Broadway & Two-hundred-forty-second St.
HABS NY-455   p   L

Varian, Isaac, House
277 Van Cortlandt Ave.
HABS NY-4-23   s pd   L

New York City

Croton Aqueduct, Old-Aqueduct Bridge
(Croton Aqueduct, Old-High Bridge)
Harlem River, Cross Bronx Expressway vic.
HAER NY-119   p   L

Croton Aqueduct, Old-High Bridge; see
Croton Aqueduct, Old-Aqueduct Bridge

Forty-eighth Police Precinct Building
1925 Bathgate Ave.
HABS NY-6013   p   H

**Interborough Rapid Transit, 149th Street
Kiosk**
Melrose Ave. & 149th St.
HAER NY-87   p   H

**Interborough Rapid Transit, Third Ave.
Elevated**
Third Ave.
HAER NY-68   p   H

BROOME COUNTY

Binghamton

Andrews, Doctor, House (Dobson Club)
272 Washington St.
HABS NY-5589   pd   L H

Binghamton City Hall
Collier St.
HABS NY-5568   pd   L

Broome County Courthouse
Court St.
HABS NY-5617   d   H

Christ Church
Washington & Henry Sts.
HABS NY-5566   pd   H

Church of the First Presbyterian Society
Chenago St.
HABS NY-5564   pd   H

City National Bank
49 Court St.
HABS NY-5635   p   H

**Delaware, Lackawana, & Western Railroad
Station**
Lewis & Chenago Sts.
HABS NY-5567
HAER NY-39   p   H

Dobson Club; see Andrews, Doctor, House

Dunk, Alfred, House
4 Pine St.
HABS NY-5565   pd   H

Ely-Hawley House; see Jones, Joseph R.,
House

Erie Railroad, Binghamton Freight Station
Lewis & Chenago Sts.
HAER NY-31   p   H

**Erie Railroad, Binghamton Passenger
Station**
Lewis & Chenago Sts.
HAER NY-30   p   H

Franklin-Whitney House
63 Front St.
HABS NY-5563   pd   H

**Hills, McLean & Haskins Department
Store;** see Perry Block

Jones, Joseph R., House (Ely-Hawley
House)
8 Riverside Dr.
HABS NY-5562   pd   L H

Monday Afternoon Club Clubhouse, The;
see Phelps, Sherman, House

New York State Inebriate Asylum
425 Robinson St.
HABS NY-5588   pd   L

Perry Block (Hills, McLean & Haskins
Department Store)
89 Court St.
HABS NY-5443   pd   L

Phelps, Sherman, House (Monday
Afternoon Club Clubhouse, The)
191 Court St.
HABS NY-5544   pd   L

Roberson Memorial
Front St.
HABS NY-5545   pd   H

U.S. Courthouse & Post Office
HABS NY-5587   p   H

Wells, J. Stuart, House
71 Main St.
HABS NY-5546   pd   L

Deposit

Deposit Lumber Company Mill
Borden St.
HAER NY-75   p   H

**Erie Railroad, Delaware Division Bridge
175.53**
Delaware River & Front St.
HAER NY-28   p   H

Erie Railroad, Deposit Station
Front St.
HAER NY-26   p   H

Erie Railroad, Oguaga Creek Bridge
State Rt. 17
HAER NY-27   p   H

Hyde, Sheldon, House (Hyde's Castle;
Pemberton, Doctor, House)
97 Second St.
HABS NY-5542   pd   L

Hyde's Castle; see Hyde, Sheldon, House

Pemberton, Doctor, House; see Hyde,
Sheldon, House

Endwell

Patterson, Amos, House (Washingtonian
Hall)
3725 River Rd.
HABS NY-5541   pd   L

Washingtonian Hall; see Patterson, Amos,
House

Maine vic.

Gates, Cyrus, House
Old Nanticoke Rd.
HABS NY-5540   pd   L

Vestal

**Delaware, Lackawana, & Western Railroad
Station**
N. Main St.
HAER NY-50   p   H

Whitney Point

Daniels, G. H., Clock Shop
Main St.
HABS NY-5539   pd   L

CATTARAUGUS COUNTY

Collins

Erie Railroad, Collins Passenger Station
HAER NY-135   p   H

Dayton

Erie Railroad, Dayton Tunnel
Allen St. vic.
HAER NY-46   p   H

East Randolph vic.

Gladden Wind Turbine
Pigeon Valley Rd.
HAER NY-82   s   H

Limestone vic.

**B & O & Erie R.R.s, Allegheny River
Bridges** (Parallel Pratt Through-Truss
Bridges)
Spanning Allegheny River
HAER NY-44   p   H

**B & O R.R., Riverside Junction
Interlocking Tower**
Allegheny River vic.
HAER NY-45   p   H

Parallel Pratt Through-Truss Bridges; see B
& O & Erie R.R.s, Allegheny River
Bridges

Salamanca

**B & O R.R., Downtown Salamanca
Passenger Station**
Main & Rochester Sts.
HAER NY-99   p   H

**B & O R.R., East Salamanca Passenger
Station**
Columbia Ave.
HAER NY-98   p   H

**Baltimore & Ohio R.R., Erie Railway
Bridge** (Baltimore Skewed
Through-Truss Bridge)
State Rt. 17 vic.
HAER NY-101   p   H

**Baltimore & Ohio R.R., Salamanca Repair
Shops**
Columbia Ave.
HAER NY-100   p   H

Baltimore Skewed Through-Truss Bridge;
see Baltimore & Ohio R.R., Erie Railway
Bridge

**Erie Railroad, Salamanca Passenger
Station**
Atlantic St.
HAER NY-37   p   H

Erie Railroad, Salamanca Turntable
Atlantic St.
HAER NY-38   p   H

CAYUGA COUNTY

Auburn

Flatiron Building
HABS NY-5702   s p d   H

Marshall, Capt. Alexander, House
Auburn-Aureling Rd.
HABS NY-219   s p d   L

Aurora

Scipio Lodge Number 110 (F. & A. M.)
Main St.
HABS NY-229   s p d   L

CHAUTAUQUA COUNTY

Ashville

Atherly House
406 W. Main St.
HABS NY-5607   p d   L

Bly, Smith, House
4 N. Maple St.
HABS NY-5462   p d   L

Chatauqua

Miller, Lewis, Cottage
Chatauqua Institute
HABS NY-6015   p   H

Dunkirk

Abel House
423 Central Ave.
HABS NY-6016   s   H

American Locomotive Company, Foundry
Roberts Rd.
HAER NY-40   p   H

Combined Railroad Right-of-Way
Middle & Brigham Rds.
HAER NY-77   p   H

Erie Railroad, Central Avenue Pier
Central Ave.
HAER NY-78   p   H

Jamestown

**Erie Railroad, Jamestown Passenger
   Station**
E. Second St.
HAER NY-59   p   H

Sinclairville

Copp House
Church, Joy, East & Okerlund Sts.
HABS NY-6017   p d   H

Westfield

Peck House
180 E. Main St.
HABS NY-6018   d   H

Rynd House
Washington & Pearl Sts.
HABS NY-6258   p d   H

CHEMUNG COUNTY

Elmira

Elmira Female College, Cowles Hall
Park Place & W. Washington Ave.
HABS NY-6019   p   H

Elmira Rolling Mill
Hatch & State Sts.
HAER NY-25   p   H

Erie Railroad, Elmira Passenger Station
Railroad Ave.
HAER NY-36   p   H

Horseheads

**Erie R.R. & Penn. R.R., Horseheads
   Tower**
State Rt. 328
HAER NY-32   p   H

COLUMBIA COUNTY

Blue Stores vic.

Hermitage, The (Livingston, Peter, House)
Linlithgo Hamlet vic.
HABS NY-362   s p d   L

Livingston, Peter, House; see Hermitage,
   The

Chatham Center

Van Walkenburg, John, House
State Rt. 66
HABS NY-5-A-20   s p d   L

Claverack

Miller, Clifford, House (Van Rensselaer,
   Jacob, House)
State Rt. 23
HABS NY-5-A-22   s p d   L

Van Rensselaer, Jacob, House; see Miller,
   Clifford, House

Copake

Miller's Tavern
HABS NY-354   p d   L

Copake vic.

House
HABS NY-3240   p   L

Cortland

Randall Summerhouse; see Randall, W. R.,
   Garden House

Randall, W. R., Garden House (Randall
   Summerhouse)
7 Reynolds Ave. (moved from 76 Main St.)
HABS NY-5596   p d   H

Germantown vic.

Lasher House
State Rt. 9G vic.
HABS NY-4358   s p   L

Greenport

Centre, Job, House; see Turtle House, Old
Turtle House, Old (Centre, Job, House)
Post Rd.
HABS NY-5-A-21   s p d   L

Hudson

Church, Frederick, Barn; see Olana, Barn
Church, Frederick, Coach House; see
   Olana, Coach House
Church, Frederick, Farmhouse; see Olana,
   Farmhouse
Church, Frederick, Horse Barn; see Olana,
   Horse Barn
Church, Frederick, House; see Olana
Church, Frederick, Pump House; see
   Olana, Pump House
Church, Frederick, Shed; see Olana, Shed
Olana (Church, Frederick, House)
State Rt. 9G
HABS NY-5501   s p   H
Olana, Barn (Church, Frederick, Barn)
State Rt. 9G
HABS NY-5501-B   s   H
Olana, Coach House (Church, Frederick,
   Coach House)
State Rt. 9G
HABS NY-5501-A   s   H
Olana, Farmhouse (Church, Frederick,
   Farmhouse)
State Rt. 9G
HABS NY-5501-F   s   H
Olana, Horse Barn (Church, Frederick,
   Horse Barn)
State Rt. 9G
HABS NY-5501-C   s   H
Olana, Pump House (Church, Frederick,
   Pump House)
State Rt. 9G
HABS NY-5501-E   s   H
Olana, Shed (Church, Frederick, Shed)
State Rt. 9G
HABS NY-5501-D   s   H
Worth, General, Hotel
213-215 Main St.
HABS NY-6023   p   H

Hudson vic.

Livingston House (Proper House)
State Rt. 9E, Livingston Township
HABS NY-3158   p d   L
Proper House; see Livingston House

Kinderhook

Spencer-Hinds House
HABS NY-3132   p   L
Van Alen, Adam, House (Van Tassell,
   Katrina, House)
Kinderhook Creek vic.
HABS NY-5-A-11   s p d   L
Van Tassell, Katrina, House; see Van Alen,
   Adam, House

Kinderhook vic.

Lindenwald (Van Buren, Martin, House)
Old Post Rd.
HABS NY-6021   p d   L
Van Buren, Martin, House; see Lindenwald

Livingston vic.

Callander House; see Ten Broeck House
Livingston, Mary, House
HABS NY-6022   p   L
Ten Broeck House (Callander House)
County Hwy. 82
HABS NY-357   s pd   L

Malden Bridge

Lippitt House
State Rts. 204 & 66
HABS NY-5-A-23   s pd   L

Mount Lebanon

Shaker Centre Family Ann Lee Cottage;
   see Shaker Centre Family Dwelling
   House (second)
**Shaker Centre Family Building Number
   13;** see Shaker Centre Family Southwest
   Work Cottage
**Shaker Centre Family Building Number
   15;** see Shaker Centre Family Smithy
**Shaker Centre Family Dwelling House
   (second)** (Shaker Centre Family Ann Lee
   Cottage)
Shaker Rd.
HABS NY-3339   p   L
Shaker Centre Family (General View)
Shaker Rd.
HABS NY-3337   p   L
Shaker Centre Family Medicine Factory
Shaker Rd.
HABS NY-3341   p   L
Shaker Centre Family Smithy (Shaker
   Centre Family Building Number 15)
Shaker Rd.
HABS NY-3256   s p   L
**Shaker Centre Family Southwest Work
   Cottage** (Shaker Centre Family Building
   Number 13)
Shaker Rd.
HABS NY-3266   s p   L
Shaker Centre Family Washhouse (Shaker
   Medicine Shop)
Shaker Rd.
HABS NY-3338   p   L
Shaker Church Family Apple Drying Kiln
Shaker Rd.
HABS NY-3304   p   L
**Shaker Church Family Brethren's
   Workshop** (Shaker Church Family
   Building Number 3)
Shaker Rd.
HABS NY-3293   p   L
Shaker Church Family Building Number 1;
   see Shaker Church Family Dwelling
   House
**Shaker Church Family Building Number
   12;** see Shaker Church Family Trustees'
   Office
**Shaker Church Family Building Number
   13;** see Shaker Church Family Nurse
   Shop

**Shaker Church Family Building Number
   18;** see Shaker Church Family Sisters'
   Workshop
Shaker Church Family Building Number 2;
   see Shaker Meetinghouse (second)
**Shaker Church Family Building Number
   20;** see Shaker Church Family
   Waterpower Building
Shaker Church Family Building Number 3;
   see Shaker Church Family Brethren's
   Workshop
Shaker Church Family Building Number 4;
   see Shaker Church Family Seed House
Shaker Church Family Building Number 5;
   see Shaker Ministry's Shop
Shaker Church Family Building Number 9;
   see Shaker Church Family Tannery
Shaker Church Family Building SS; see
   Shaker Schoolhouse
Shaker Church Family Dwelling House
   (Shaker Church Family Main Dwelling;
   Shaker Wickersham House; Shaker
   Church Family Building Number 1)
Shaker Rd.
HABS NY-3298   p   L
Shaker Church Family (General Views)
Shaker Rd.
HABS NY-3291   s pd   L
Shaker Church Family Herb House
Shaker Rd.
HABS NY-3305   p   L
Shaker Church Family Infirmary; see
   Shaker Church Family Nurse Shop
Shaker Church Family Main Dwelling; see
   Shaker Church Family Dwelling House
**Shaker Church Family Ministry's
   Residence;** see Shaker Ministry's Shop
Shaker Church Family Nurse Shop (Shaker
   Church Family Infirmary; Shaker
   Hinckley House; Shaker Church Family
   Building Number 13)
Shaker Rd.
HABS NY-3297   p   L
Shaker Church Family Office; see Shaker
   Church Family Trustees' Office
Shaker Church Family Reservoir
Shaker Rd.
HABS NY-3300   p   L
Shaker Church Family School; see Shaker
   Schoolhouse
Shaker Church Family Seed House (Shaker
   Whittaker House; Shaker Church Family
   Building Number 4)
Shaker Rd.
HABS NY-3301   p   L
Shaker Church Family Sisters' Workshop
   (Shaker Church Family Washhouse;
   Shaker Church Family Building Number
   18)
Shaker Rd.
HABS NY-3302   p   L

Shaker Church Family Tannery (Shaker
   Church Family Building Number 9)
Shaker Rd.
HABS NY-3303   p   L
Shaker Church Family Trustees' Office
   (Shaker Church Family Office; Shaker
   Church Family Building Number 12)
Shaker Rd.
HABS NY-3299   p   L
Shaker Church Family Washhouse; see
   Shaker Church Family Sisters' Workshop
**Shaker Church Family Waterpower
   Building** (Shaker Church Family
   Building Number 20)
Shaker Rd.
HABS NY-3267   s   L
Shaker Hinckley House; see Shaker Church
   Family Nurse Shop
Shaker Medicine Shop; see Shaker Centre
   Family Washhouse
Shaker Meetinghouse (second) (Shaker
   Church Family Building Number 2)
Shaker Rd.
HABS NY-3254   s pd   L
Shaker Ministry's Shop (Shaker Church
   Family Ministry's Residence; Shaker
   Church Family Building Number 5)
Shaker Rd.
HABS NY-3255   s p   L
Shaker North Family Building Number 6;
   see Shaker North Family Washhouse
   (second)
Shaker North Family Barn (Shaker North
   Family Stone Barn; Shaker North Family
   Building Number 14)
State Rt. 22 & U.S. Rt. 20
HABS NY-3251   s p   L
**Shaker North Family Brethren's Dwelling
   House;** see Shaker North Family
   Dwelling House (second)
Shaker North Family Brethren's Shop; see
   Shaker North Family Washhouse (first)
Shaker North Family Building Number 1;
   see Shaker North Family Dwelling House
   (first)
Shaker North Family Building Number 14;
   see Shaker North Family Barn
Shaker North Family Building Number 18;
   see Shaker North Family Washhouse
   (first)
Shaker North Family Building Number 19;
   see Shaker North Family Smithy
Shaker North Family Building Number 2;
   see Shaker North Family Office & Store
Shaker North Family Building Number 20;
   see Shaker North Family Lumber & Grist
   Mill
Shaker North Family Building Number 3;
   see Shaker North Family Icehouse
Shaker North Family Building Number 7;
   see Shaker North Family Dwelling House
   (second)

Shaker North Family Building Number 8;
see Shaker North Family Farm, Deacon's
Shop
**Shaker North Family Dwelling House
(first)** (Shaker North Family Residence;
Shaker North Family Building Number
1)
Shaker Rd.
HABS NY-3249   s p   L
**Shaker North Family Dwelling House
(second)** (Shaker North Family Second
House; Shaker North Family Brethren's
Dwelling House; Shaker North Family
Building Number 7)
State Rt. 22 & U.S. Rt. 20
HABS NY-3321   p   L
Shaker North Family Farm, Deacon's Shop
(Shaker North Family Men's Quarters &
Shop; Shaker North Family Building
Number 8)
Shaker Rd.
HABS NY-3325   p   L
Shaker North Family (General Views)
Shaker Rd.
HABS NY-3319   p   L
Shaker North Family Granary
Shaker Rd.
HABS NY-3320   p   L
Shaker North Family Icehouse (Shaker
North Family Building Number 3)
Shaker Rd.
HABS NY-3322   p   L
**Shaker North Family Laundry & Water
Power Bldg.;** see Shaker North Family
Washhouse (first)
**Shaker North Family Laundry &
Woodstore Building;** see Shaker North
Family Washhouse (second)
Shaker North Family Lumber & Grist Mill
(Shaker North Family Building Number
20)
Shaker Rd.
HABS NY-3253   s p   L
**Shaker North Family Men's Quarters &
Shop;** see Shaker North Family Farm,
Deacon's Shop
Shaker North Family Office & Store
(Shaker North Family Building Number
2)
Shaker Rd.
HABS NY-3323   p   L
Shaker North Family Residence; see
Shaker North Family Dwelling House
(first)
Shaker North Family Second House; see
Shaker North Family Dwelling House
(second)
Shaker North Family Smithy (Shaker
North Family Building Number 19)
Shaker Rd.
HABS NY-3268   s p   L
Shaker North Family Stone Barn; see
Shaker North Family Barn

Shaker North Family Washhouse (first)
(Shaker North Family Laundry & Water
Power Bldg.; Shaker North Family
Brethren's Shop; Shaker North Family
Building Number 18)
Shaker Rd.
HABS NY-3252   s p   L
Shaker North Family Washhouse (second)
(Shaker North Family Laundry &
Woodstore Building; Shaker North
Familly Building Number 6)
Shaker Rd.
HABS NY-3250   s p   L
Shaker Schoolhouse (Shaker Church
Family School; Shaker Church Family
Building SS)
Shaker Rd.
HABS NY-3259   s p   L
**Shaker Second Family Brethren's
Workshop** (Shaker Second Family
Building Number 2)
Shaker Rd.
HABS NY-3330   p   L
Shaker Second Family Building Number 2;
see Shaker Second Family Brethren's
Workshop
Shaker Second Family Chair Factory
Shaker Rd.
HABS NY-3328   p   L
Shaker Second Family Dwelling House
Shaker Rd.
HABS NY-3327   p   L
Shaker Second Family (General Views)
Shaker Rd.
HABS NY-3326   p   L
Shaker Second Family Herb House
Shaker Rd.
HABS NY-3329   p   L
**Shaker Second Family Sisters' Workshop &
Barn**
Shaker Rd.
HABS NY-3331   p   L
Shaker South Family Barn
Shaker Rd.
HABS NY-3342   p   L
Shaker South Family Building Number 1;
see Shaker South Family Dwelling House
(second)
Shaker South Family Building Number 2;
see Shaker South Family Dwelling House
(first)
Shaker South Family Building Number 6;
see Shaker South Family Washhouse
Shaker South Family Building Number 7;
see Shaker South Family Chair Factory
Shaker South Family Chair Factory
(Shaker South Family Chair Shop;
Shaker South Family Building Number
7)
Shaker Rd.
HABS NY-3335   p   L
Shaker South Family Chair Shop; see
Shaker South Family Chair Factory

**Shaker South Family Dwelling House
(first)** (Shaker South Family Office;
Shaker South Family Building Number
2)
Shaker Rd.
HABS NY-3334   p   L
**Shaker South Family Dwelling House
(second)** (Shaker South Family Building
Number 1)
Shaker Rd.
HABS NY-3333   s p   L
Shaker South Family (General Views)
Shaker Rd.
HABS NY-3332   p   L
Shaker South Family Infirmary; see Shaker
South Family Nurse Shop
**Shaker South Family Laundry &
Chairmaking Shop;** see Shaker South
Family Washhouse
Shaker South Family Nurse Shop (Shaker
South Family Infirmary)
Shaker Rd.
HABS NY-3336   p   L
Shaker South Family Office; see Shaker
South Family Dwelling House (first)
Shaker South Family Privy
Shaker Rd.
HABS NY-3248   s   L
Shaker South Family Washhouse (Shaker
South Family Laundry & Chairmaking
Shop; Shaker South Family Building
Number 6)
Shaker Rd.
HABS NY-3269   s p   L
Shaker Upper Canaan Family
Shaker Rd.
HABS NY-3340   p   L
Shaker Whittaker House; see Shaker
Church Family Seed House
Shaker Wickersham House; see Shaker
Church Family Dwelling House

New Concord
House, Gingerbread
HABS NY-3231   p   L
Pratt, Anson, House
HABS NY-355   s p d   L
Reformed Church
HABS NY-3218   p   L
Tompkins, Thomas L., House
HABS NY-3147   p   L

North Germantown
Hake's House
HABS NY-6020   p d   L

Old Chatham
Antinore Farm; see Van Walkenburg
House
Parsonage, Old
HABS NY-5493   p   L
Root-Harper House
HABS NY-5494   p   L
Run House (Porch)
HABS NY-5496   p   L

Van Walkenburg House (Antinore Farm)
HABS NY-5495   p   L
Wilbor, Samuel, House
HABS NY-5-A-24   s p d   L

Stockport

Lathrope House
HABS NY-6024   p d   L
Macy Woolen Mill, Old; see Print Works
Mill, Stone
HABS NY-6026   p   L
Print Works (Macy Woolen Mill, Old)
HABS NY-6025   p   L

CORTLAND COUNTY

Cincinnatus

Kingman, Col. John, House
Main St.
HABS NY-5600   p d   H

Cortland

Church, Cobblestone; see
    Unitarian-Universalist Church
Delaware, Lackawana & Western Railroad
    (Railroad Crossing Guard House;
    Railroad Crossing Watch Tower)
Central Ave. & Pendleton St.
HABS NY-5595   p d   H
Dibble, Horace A., House
90 N. Main St.
HABS NY-5591   p d   L
Hathaway Hall; see Hathaway, Samuel
    Gilbert, House
Hathaway, Samuel Gilbert, House
    (Hathaway Hall)
Solon Rd. (State Rt. 41)
HABS NY-5592   p d   H
Lehigh Valley Railroad Station
7 South Ave.
HABS NY-5594   p d   H
Railroad Crossing Guard House; see
    Delaware, Lackawana & Western
    Railroad
Railroad Crossing Watch Tower; see
    Delaware, Lackawana & Western
    Railroad
Randall, Henry Stephens, House
18 Tompkins St.
HABS NY-5593   p   H
Unitarian-Universalist Church (Church,
    Cobblestone)
3 Church St.
HABS NY-5590   p   H

Homer

Barber, Jedediah, House
18 N. Main St.
HABS NY-5597   p d   H
Calvary Episcopal Church
Park St.
HABS NY-5435   s p d   L

Donnelly, Augustus, House (Harum, David,
    House)
80 S. Main St.
HABS NY-5598   p d   H
Harum, David, House; see Donnelly,
    Augustus, House
Satterly, George, House; see Sautelle, Sig,
    Circus Training House
Sautelle, Sig, Circus Training House
    (Satterly, George, House)
S. Main St. (State Rt. 11)
HABS NY-5599   p d   L

Mc Graw

Lamont Library; see McGraw, Marcus,
    House
McGraw, Marcus, House (Lamont Library)
Main St.
HABS NY-5601   p d   L

DELAWARE COUNTY

Deposit

Edick, Conrad, House
1 River St.
HABS NY-5543   p d   L

Hancock

Erie Railroad, Hancock Freight Station
Front & Leonard Sts.
HAER NY-48   p   H
Erie Railroad, Hancock Passenger Station
Front St.
HAER NY-47   p d   H
NY, Ontario & Western R.R., Delaware
    River Bridge
Spanning Delaware River on W. Martin St.
HAER NY-66   p   H

Hancock vic.

Lordville Suspension Bridge
Spanning Delaware River on Warren Rd.
HAER NY-79   p   H

DUTCHESS COUNTY

Barrytown

Orlot
HABS NY-6027   s   H

Barrytown vic.

Edgewater
Station Rd.
HABS NY-5621   s p d   L
Edgewater, North Gatehouse
Station Rd.
HABS NY-5621-B   s p d   L
Edgewater, South Gatehouse
Station Rd.
HABS NY-5621-A   s p d   L
La Bergerie (Rokeby)
River Rd.
HABS NY-5623   s p d   L

Montgomery Place
Annandale Rd.
HABS NY-5625   s p d   L
Montgomery Place, Farmhouse
Annandale Rd.
HABS NY-5625-A   s p d   L
Montgomery Place, Swiss Cottage
Annandale Rd.
HABS NY-5625-B   s p d   L
Rokeby; see La Bergerie

Beacon

Brett House; see Teller House
Locust Grove; see Teller House
Mount Gulian; see Verplank House
Teller House (Brett House; Locust Grove)
De Windt St.
HABS NY-360   s   L
Verplank House (Mount Gulian)
HABS NY-4380   p   L

Brinckerhoff

Brinckerhoff, Col. John, House
State Rt. 82
HABS NY-4130   s p d   L

Dover Plains

Taber-Wing House
State Rt. 22
HABS NY-4117   s p d   L

Fishkill

Classic House
Brinkerhoff Rd.
HABS NY-3101   p   L
First Dutch Reformed Church
Main St.
HABS NY-4-202   s p d   L
Trinity Church
E. Main St.
HABS NY-4-201   s p d   L
Van Wyck House; see Wharton House
Wharton House (Van Wyck House)
U.S. Rt. 9
HABS NY-6028   d   H

Hyde Park

Bellefield Barn
Old Post Rd.
HABS NY-5665   s   L
Crumwold (Fencepost & Gate) (Rogers,
    Col. Archibald, House)
Fuller Ln.
HABS NY-4354   s   L
Eleanor Roosevelt National Historic Site;
    see Val-Kill
Eleanor Roosevelt National Historic Site;
    see Val-Kill, Factory
Franklin D. Roosevelt National Historic
    Site; see Roosevelt, Franklin D., House
Hyde Park; see Springwood
Milestone
Old Albany Post Rd.
HABS NY-4353   s   L

Rogers, Col. Archibald, House; see
   Crumwold (Fencepost & Gate)
Roosevelt, Franklin D., House (Franklin D.
   Roosevelt National Historic Site)
HABS NY-5618   p   H
Roosevelt House; see Springwood
Springwood (Roosevelt House; Hyde Park)
HABS NY-4355   s p   L
Stoutenburch, John, House (Porch)
HABS NY-4351   s   L
Tombstone of Bard Family
St. James' Churchyard, Albany Post Rd.
HABS NY-4352   s   L
Val-Kill (Eleanor Roosevelt National
   Historic Site)
State Rt. 9G
HABS NY-5666   s   L
Val-Kill, Factory (Eleanor Roosevelt
   National Historic Site)
State Rt. 9G
HABS NY-5666-B   s   L
Vanderbilt Boathouse (Vanderbilt Mansion
   National Historic Site)
HABS NY-3200   s   L
Vanderbilt Mansion National Historic Site;
   see Vanderbilt Boathouse

Millbrook
Nine Partners Meetinghouse
State Rt. 82 vic.
HABS NY-4129   s pd   L

Pleasant Valley
Dye House; see Mill & Office, Old Stone
Mill & Office, Old Stone (Dye House)
HABS NY-3238   p   L
Store Building, Old Stone
State Rt. 44
HABS NY-356   s pd   L

Poughkeepsie
Clinton, Gov. George, House; see Van
   Kleeck-Hay House
Glebe House
635 Main St.
HABS NY-5-A-203   s pd   L
Harmon Printing Building
207-209 Main St.
HABS NY-6029   pd   H
Springside, Barn & Stable
Academy St.
HABS NY-5500   pd   H
Springside, Cottage
Academy St.
HABS NY-5489   pd   H
Springside, Gatehouse
Academy St.
HABS NY-5499   pd   H
Van Kleeck-Hay House (Clinton, Gov.
   George, House)
549 Main St.
HABS NY-373   s   L
Winslow, James, Gatehouse
U.S. Rt. 9
HABS NY-4389   pd   L

Red Hook
House, Dutch (Interior)
HABS NY-3108   p   L
Mansion
HABS NY-3112   p   L
Martin Homestead
U.S. Rt. 9
HABS NY-341   s pd   L

Red Hook vic.
Rhinebeck Area Historic Survey
Hudson River (see NY, Rhinebeck)
HABS NY-5624   s   L

Rhinebeck
Delamater, Henry, House
44 Montgomery St.
HABS NY-5638   p   L
Rhinebeck Area Historic Survey
Hudson River (see NY, Red Hook vic.)
HABS NY-5624   s   L

Rhinebeck vic.
Leacote; see Meadows, The
Leacote, Stable Cottage; see Meadows,
   The, Stable Cottage
Leacote, Stables & Carriage House; see
   Meadows, The, Stables & Carriage
   House
Linden Grove; see Wyndcliffe
Meadows, The (Leacote)
River Rd.
HABS NY-5622   s pd   L
Meadows, The, Stable Cottage (Leacote,
   Stable Cottage)
River Rd.
HABS NY-5622-B   s pd   L
Meadows, The, Stables & Carriage House
   (Leacote, Stables & Carriage House)
River Rd.
HABS NY-5622-A   s pd   L
Wildercliff
Morton Rd.
HABS NY-5628   s pd   L
Wilderstein
Morton Rd.
HABS NY-5629   s pd   L
Wyndcliffe (Linden Grove)
Mill Rd.
HABS NY-5627   s pd   L

Staatsburg
Mills, Ogden, Mansion (Norrie-Mills
   Mansion)
HABS NY-6032   pd   H
Norrie-Mills Mansion; see Mills, Ogden,
   Mansion

Tioronda
De Peyster, Abraham, House (Newlin
   House)
Town of Fishkill
HABS NY-4-205   s   L
Newlin House; see De Peyster, Abraham,
   House

Tivoli
Clermont (Livingston, Little, House)
HABS NY-3159   p   L
Livingston, Little, House; see Clermont

Tivoli vic.
Rose Hill
Woods Rd.
HABS NY-5626   s pd   L

Tivoli-on-Hudson
Livingston, Clermont, Manor
HABS NY-3127   p   L

Upper Red Hook
Lyle House
HABS NY-6031   p   L

Wappingers Falls
Mesier House
Mesier Park, Mesier Ave.
HABS NY-372   s   L

ERIE COUNTY

Buffalo
Blessed Trinity Roman Catholic Church
317 Leroy Ave.
HABS NY-5709   pd   H
Buffalo City Hall
HABS NY-6033   p   H
Buffalo Gas Light Company Building
Genesee St.
HAER NY-64   p   H
Buffalo Lighthouse (Harbor Lighthouse)
Buffalo Harbor, Niagara River & Big
   Buffalo Cr.
HABS NY-60   s pd   H
Buffalo State Hospital; see State Lunatic
   Asylum
Cary House
184 Delaware Ave.
HABS NY-5613   pd   L
**D. L. & W. Railroad, Lackawanna
   Terminal**
Main St. & Buffalo River
HAER NY-63   s pd   L H
Dorsheimer, William, House
438 Delaware Ave.
HABS NY-5608   pd   L
Erie County Hall
HABS NY-6034   p   H
Erie County Savings Bank
16 Niagara St.
HABS NY-5615   pd   L H
Erie Railroad, East Buffalo Station
HAER NY-71   p   H
Erie Railroad, Kensington Avenue Station
Kensington Ave.
HAER NY-72   p   H
Erie Railroad, Main Street Station
Main St.
HAER NY-73   p   H

Erie Railroad, Walden Avenue Station
Walden Ave.
HAER NY-74   p   H
Guaranty Building; see Prudential Building
Harbor Lighthouse; see Buffalo Lighthouse
Heath, W. R., House
76 Soldiers Place
HABS NY-6035   p   H
Kremlin Building
Pearl & Eagle Sts.
HABS NY-5614   pd   L
Martin, Darwin, House
125 Jewett Parkway
HABS NY-5611   pd   L
Prudential Building (Guaranty Building)
28 Church St.
HABS NY-5487   pd   L
**Roosevelt, Theodore, Inaugural Nat. Hist.
  Site**; see Wilcox, Ansley, House
St. Louis Roman Catholic Church
Main & Edward Sts.
HABS NY-5488   pd   L
St. Paul's Episcopal Cathedral
Shelton Square
HABS NY-5612   pd   L
State Lunatic Asylum (Buffalo State
  Hospital)
400 Forest Ave.
HABS NY-5606   pd   L
U.S. Custom House
Washington & Seneca Sts.
HABS NY-5609   pd   L
U.S. Post Office
121 Ellicott St.
HABS NY-5605   pd   L
Wilcox, Ansley, House (Roosevelt,
  Theodore, Inaugural Nat. Hist. Site)
641 Delaware Ave.
HABS NY-5610   pd   L

Hyde Park
Eleanor Roosevelt National Historic Site;
  see Val-Kill, Stone Cottage
Val-Kill, Stone Cottage (Eleanor Roosevelt
  National Historic Site)
State Rt. 9G
HABS NY-5666-A   s   L

Lawtons vic.
Erie Railroad, Clear Creek Viaduct
U.S. Rt. 62
HAER NY-29   p   H

Poughkeepsie
150 Union Street (Commercial Building)
HABS NY-6030   p   H

ESSEX COUNTY

Fort Ticonderoga
Fort Ticonderoga
HABS NY-3212   p   L

Tahawus
**Adirondack Iron & Steel Company, New
  Furnace**
Hudson River
HAER NY-123   s pd L

FULTON COUNTY

Broadalbin
Hemlock Church
HABS NY-3210   p   L

Gloversville
Burr, Nathaniel, House
153 Kingsboro Ave.
HABS NY-6036   pd   L
Kingsboro Presbyterian Church
N. Kingsboro Ave.
HABS NY-381   pd   L

Johnstown
Black Horse Tavern
HABS NY-3126   p   L
Courthouse, Old
N. William St.
HABS NY-3139   pd   L
Drumm Homestead
W. State & Green Sts.
HABS NY-3233   p   L
Fort Johnstown, Old (Fulton County Jail)
Montgomery & S. Perry Sts.
HABS NY-394   p   L
Fulton County Jail; see Fort Johnstown,
  Old
Johnson Hall
HABS NY-3107   pd   L
Johnson Hall, Blockhouse
HABS NY-392   s p   L
Union Hall
E. Main St.
HABS NY-6259   pd   L

Mayfield
Rice Homestead
Rt. 30
HABS NY-365   pd   L

Perth
McIntyre, Duncan, House
HABS NY-3237   p   L
United Presbyterian Church
State Hwy. 30 vic.
HABS NY-363   s pd L
United Presbyterian Church, Parsonage
State Rt. 30 vic.
HABS NY-363-B   pd   L

GENESEE COUNTY

Batavia
Batavia Gas Light Co., Gasholder Houses
Evans St. vic.
HAER NY-41   p   H

Cary House
HABS NY-6037   p   H
Holland Land Office
W. Main St.
HABS NY-6038   p   H

Batavia vic.
Lehigh Valley R.R., Erie Railroad Bridge
State Rt. 5 vic.
HAER NY-51   p   H

GREENE COUNTY

Cairo
First Presbyterian Church
Main St.
HABS NY-4-25   s pd L

Catskill Mts.
Van Winkle, Rip, House
HABS NY-383   p   L

Leeds
Church, Stone
HABS NY-387   pd   L
Leeds Bridge
State Hwy. 23
HABS NY-4-8   s pd L

West Coxsackie
Bronck, Peter, House
HABS NY-3114   pd   L

HERKIMER COUNTY

Danube
Indian Castle Church
State Rt. 55
HABS NY-243   pd   L

Fort Herkimer
Schoolhouse, Old
HABS NY-3217   pd   L

Frankfort
Erie Canal, North Lock
Moyer Creek Crossing
HABS NY-231-C   p   L
Erie Canal, South Towpath Crossing
Moyer Creek Crossing
HABS NY-231-B   p   L
Erie Canal, Viaduct
Moyer Creek Crossing
HABS NY-231-A   p   L

Herkimer
Fort Herkimer Church
HABS NY-242   pd   L
Herkimer Jail
HABS NY-249   p   L
Reformed Church
HABS NY-6039   p   L

Ilion
Erie Canal Locks
HABS NY-6040   p   L

Indian Castle vic.

Van Wie House
HABS NY-3204   p   L

Little Falls

Fink, Major, House
HABS NY-248   p   L

Russia

Butler House
State Rd.
HABS NY-5-U-2   s pd   L

JEFFERSON COUNTY

Watertown

Jefferson County Courthouse, Old
Arsenal & Sherman Sts.
HABS NY-5438   p   H

New York State Armory (second)
Arsenal & Jackman St.
HABS NY-5437   p   H

125 Washington Street (Commercial Building)
HABS NY-5439   p   H

Watertown National Bank Building
Washington & Stone Sts.
HABS NY-5440   p   H

KINGS COUNTY

Brooklyn

Bennett House; see Wyckoff-Bennett House

Bergen House
HABS NY-6042   p   L

Cutting House; see Tillary, Dr. James, House

Ditmas House; see Van Nuyse, Johannes, House

Erasmus Hall (Academy)
Flatbush Ave.
HABS NY-519   s p   L

Fox Theatre
20 Flatbush Ave. & 1 Nevins St.
HABS NY-5554   pd   L

Gowanus; see Vechte-Cortelyou House

Lefferts House
Prospect Park (moved from 563 Flatbush Ave.)
HABS NY-511   s pd   L

Long Island Historical Society Building
128 Pierrepont St.
HABS NY-6100   d   H

Plymouth Church
Orange & Hicks Sts.
HABS NY-4-11   s pd   L

Port of New York, Grain Elevator Terminal
Columbia St.
HAER NY-69   p   H

Pratt Institute, Power Generating Plant
Hall St.
HAER NY-70   p   H

Robb House
Bedford Ave. & Clarkson
HABS NY-6043   s   H

Schenck House
Canarsie Park (fragments in Brooklyn Museum)
HABS NY-513   s pd   L

Schenck, Judge Teunis, House
Highland Park, Jamaica Ave.
HABS NY-517   s p   L

Schenck-Crooke House
21-23 E. Sixty-third St.
HABS NY-4-12   s pd   L

Szold, Harold J., House
57 Willow St.
HABS NY-4-34   s pd   L

Tillary, Dr. James, House (Cutting House)
15 Tillary St.
HABS NY-512   s pd   L

Van Nuyse, Johannes, House (Ditmas House)
150 Amersfort Place
HABS NY-4-15   s pd   L

Van Nuyse-Magaw House
1041 E. Twenty-second St
HABS NY-514   s p   L

Van Pelt Manor House
Eighty-first St. & Eighteenth Ave.
HABS NY-516   p   L

Vechte-Cortelyou House (Gowanus)
HABS NY-5112   p   L

Wyckoff Homestead
1325 Flushing Ave.
HABS NY-518   p   L

Wyckoff, Peter, House
5902 Canarsie Ln.
HABS NY-4-28   s pd   L

Wyckoff-Bennett House (Bennett House)
Kings Hwy. & 1669 E. Twenty-second St.
HABS NY-5110   s p   L

New York City

Brooklyn Bridge; see East River Bridge

East River Bridge (Brooklyn Bridge)
Park Row, Manhattan to Adams St., Brooklyn
HAER NY-18   p   H

Syracuse

Syracuse University, Hall of Languages
Syrcause University Campus
HABS NY-5446   p   H

LIVINGSTON COUNTY

Avon

Erie Railroad, Avon Freight Station
Rochester St.
HAER NY-53   p   H

Erie Railroad, Avon Station
Railroad Ave.
HAER NY-52   p   H

Caledonia

Clark, James R., House
Main St.
HABS NY-213   s pd   L

East Avon

Pearson, Joseph, House (Taintor House)
HABS NY-216   s pd   L

Taintor House; see Pearson, Joseph, House

Portageville vic.

Erie Railroad, Buffalo Division, Bridge 361.66 (Erie Railroad, Portage Viaduct)
State Rt. 436
HAER NY-54   p   H

Erie Railroad, Portage Viaduct; see Erie Railroad, Buffalo Division, Bridge 361.66

MADISON COUNTY

Canastota vic.

Roberts, Judge Nathan, House
State Hwy. 5
HABS NY-5-S-4   s pd   L

Cazenovia

Lincklaen, Col. John, House; see Lorenzo Mansion

Lorenzo Mansion (Lincklaen, Col. John, House)
HABS NY-5454   p   H

Chittenango

St. Paul's Episcopal Church
HABS NY-5453   p   H

Eaton Village

House, Stone; see Morse, Joseph, House

Morse, Joseph, House (House, Stone)
State Rt. 26 & Mill St.
HABS NY-5603   pd   L

Georgetown

Brown, Timothy, House (Brown's Temple; Spirit House)
S. Main St. & State Rt. 26
HABS NY-5602   pd   L

Brown's Temple; see Brown, Timothy, House

Spirit House; see Brown, Timothy, House

MONROE COUNTY

Brighton

Orringh Stone Tavern
2370 East Ave.
HABS NY-5-R-8   s pd   L

Clarkson

Jewett, Simeon B., House
Lake & Ridge Rds.
HABS NY-218   s pd   L

Henrietta

Kirby, Elihu, House
E. Henrietta & Lehigh Station Rds.
HABS NY-215   s pd   L

Rochester

Allison House
12 Vick Park-A
HABS NY-6044   pd   H

Anthony, Susan B., House
17 Madison St.
HABS NY-6045   p   H

Barry, Patrick, House
692 Mount Hope Ave.
HABS NY-5651   pd   L

Bates-Ryder House
1399 East Ave.
HABS NY-5639   pd   L

Bissell, Charles, House
666 East Ave.
HABS NY-5640   pd   L

Board of Education Building; see Rochester
Free Academy

Boynton, E. E., House
16 East Blvd.
HABS NY-5655   pd   L

Brewster, Henry A., House
Spring & Washington Sts., NW
HABS NY-220   s pd   L

Bronson, Amon, House
263 S. Plymouth Ave.
HABS NY-5662   pd   L

Campbell, Benjamin, House (Whittelsey
House)
Troup & S. Fitzhugh Sts.
HABS NY-5-R-6   s pd   L

Charlotte Lighthouse, Old; see Genessee
Lighthouse

Child, Jonathan, House
37 S. Washington St.
HABS NY-5-R-1   s pd   L

City Hall; see U.S. Post Office &
Courthouse

Crombie-Mathews House
135 Spring St.
HABS NY-5653   pd   L

Culver, Oliver, House
70 East Blvd.
HABS NY-5-R-5   s pd   L

D. A. R., Irondequoit Chapter House; see
Ely, Hervey, House

Danforth, George, House
200 West Ave.
HABS NY-5642   pd   L

Dann, Dr. Archibald, House
12 Vick Park
HABS NY-5657   pd   L

Ellwanger & Barry Nursery Office
668 Mt. Hope Ave.
HABS NY-5650   pd   L

Ely, Hervey, House (D. A. R., Irondequoit
Chapter House)
138 Troup St.
HABS NY-5661   pd   L

Federal Building
Fitzhugh St.
HABS NY-6046   pd   H

Female Academy of the Sacred Heart
8 Prince St.
HABS NY-5644   pd   L

First Presbyterian Church
101 Plymouth Ave South
HABS NY-5652   pd   L

First Universalist Church
S. Clinton Ave. & Court St.
HABS NY-5433   pd   L

Genessee Lighthouse (Charlotte
Lighthouse, Old)
Lake Ave.
HABS NY-228   s pd   L

Harris-Hollister-Spencer House
1005 East Ave.
HABS NY-5646   pd   L

Hills, Isaac, House
135 Plymouth Ave. South
HABS NY-5-R-10   s pd   L

Livingston Park Seminary
1 Livingston Park
HABS NY-5-R-9   s pd   L

Miner House
2 Argyle St.
HABS NY-6048   d   H

Monroe County Courthouse (Monroe
County Office Building)
39 W. Main St.
HABS NY-5641   pd   L

Monroe County Office Building; see
Monroe County Courthouse

Monroe County Penitentiary; see
Workhouse

Moore, Lindley M., House
22 Lake View Park
HABS NY-5432   s pd   L

Powers Building
16 Main St. West
HABS NY-5649   pd   L

Rochester Free Academy (Board of
Education Building)
13 Fitzhugh St.
HABS NY-5656   pd   L

Sibley, Hiram W., House
400 East Ave.
HABS NY-5648   pd   L

Smith, Silas O., House (Willard, Ernest R.,
House)
485 East Ave.
HABS NY-5-R-7   s pd   L

St. Luke's Church (Episcopal)
17 S. Fitzhugh St.
HABS NY-5654   pd   L

Thompson, George, House
546 East Ave.
HABS NY-5645   pd   L

Treat-Witherspoon House
25 Clarissa St.
HABS NY-5659   pd   L

U.S. Post Office & Courthouse (City Hall)
Fitzhugh & Church Sts.
HABS NY-5647   pd   L

Warehouse, Stone
1 Mt. Hope St.
HABS NY-5658   pd   L

Watts, Ebenezer, House
47 S. Fitzhugh St.
HABS NY-5660   pd   L

Whittelsey House; see Campbell, Benjamin,
House

Willard, Ernest R., House; see Smith, Silas
O., House

Workhouse (Monroe County Penitentiary)
1360 S. Ave.
HABS NY-5643   pd   L

MONTGOMERY COUNTY

Amsterdam

Allen, James, House
HABS NY-3206   p   L

Guy Park Manor
W. Main St.
HABS NY-369   pd   L

Canajoharie

Fort Rensselaer (Van Alstyne House)
HABS NY-3116   s pd   L H

Van Alstyne House; see Fort Rensselaer

Charleston

Baptist Church
State Rt. 148
HABS NY-385   pd   L

Fonda

House, Greek Revival
HABS NY-3115   p   L

Fort Hunter

Barn, Old Dutch
Wemple Farm
HABS NY-386   pd   L

Erie Canal, Empire Lock Number 29
HABS NY-5536
HAER NY-17   pd   L

Erie Canal, Schoharie Creek Aqueduct
Schoharie Creek
HABS NY-5533
HAER NY-6   s pd   L

Erie Canal, Yankee Hill Lock Number 28
Schoharie Creek Aqueduct vic.
HABS NY-5537
HAER NY-16   pd   L

Fort Johnson

Fort Johnson; see Johnson, Sir William,
House

Johnson, Sir William, House (Fort Johnson)
State Rts. 5 & 67
HABS NY-391   s pd   L

Fort Plain

Bleeker House; see Parris, Isaac, House &
  Trading Post
Bridge, Stone
HABS NY-3106   p   L
Parris, Isaac, House & Trading Post
  (Bleeker House)
HABS NY-3118   pd   L

Fultonville

Van Epps House
Franklin St.
HABS NY-377   s pd   L

Glen

Edwards House
HABS NY-3216   p   L

Minden

Widanka, Peter, House
HABS NY-6049   p   L

Nelliston vic.

Cochrane, General, House
State Rt. 5
HABS NY-384   pd   L
Palatine Church
State Rt. 5
HABS NY-364   s pd   L

Palatine Bridge

Fort Henrick Frey
State Rt. 5 vic. (Grand St.)
HABS NY-396   s pd   L
Frey House
State Rt. 5 (Grand St.)
HABS NY-367   pd   L
Lime Kiln
Fort Frey vic.
HABS NY-6047   p   L

Palatine Bridge vic.

Ehle House (Fort Ehle)
Old Kings Hwy. vic.
HABS NY-3104   pd   L
Fort Ehle; see Ehle House
Fort Wagner
HABS NY-368   pd   L

Pattersonville

Staley House
HABS NY-3148   p   L

St. Johnsville Vic

Fort Klock
U.S. Rt. 5
HABS NY-370   pd   L

Stone Arabia

Dutch Reformed Church
State Rt. 10
HABS NY-361   s pd   L
Trinity Lutheran Church
State Rt. 10
HABS NY-3161   pd   L

NASSAU COUNTY

East Rockaway

Hewlett, Oliver, House
86 Main St.
HABS NY-536   s pd   L

East Williston

Willis-Post House
Willis Ave.
HABS NY-533   s pd   L

Farmingdale

Old Maids' Home; see Powell House
Powell House (Old Maids' Home)
HABS NY-5311   p   L

Glen Cove

Pratt, Harold I., House
Crescent Beach Rd.
HABS NY-6242   pd   H

Great Neck

Eldridge Mill
HABS NY-539   p   L

Hempstead

Carman-Irish House
160 Marvin Ave.
HABS NY-4-408   s pd   L
Catholic Rectory
104 Greenwich St.
HABS NY-535   s pd   L
Harper House, Old
68 Washington St.
HABS NY-4-406   s   L
Snedecker, Isaac, House
359 Front St.
HABS NY-4-407   s pd   L
St. George's Church
Front St.
HABS NY-4-403   s   L
St. George's Rectory
Prospect & Greenwich Sts.
HABS NY-4-401   s pd   L
Wright, Constance, House
90 Greenwich St.
HABS NY-532   s pd   L

Lawrence

Rock Hall
Broadway
HABS NY-534   s pd   L

Manhasset

**Great Neck & Port Wash. RR, Cow's Neck
  Viaduct;** see Great Neck & Port Wash.
  RR, Manhasset Viaduct
**Great Neck & Port Wash. RR, Manhasset
  Viaduct** (Great Neck & Port Wash. RR,
  Cow's Neck Viaduct)
Manhasset Shore Rd. vic.
HAER NY-81   p   H
Onderdonk, Judge Horatio Gates, House
Strathmore Rd. & Rolling Hill Rd.
HABS NY-537   s pd   L

Massapequa

Fort Neck (House) (Tryon Hall)
HABS NY-4-402   s pd   L
Tryon Hall; see Fort Neck (House)

Matinecock

Matinecock Quaker Meetinghouse
HABS NY-6050   p   L

New Hyde Park

Kelsey House
Lakeville Rd.
HABS NY-531   s pd   L

Old Westbury

Turnpike House, Old
HABS NY-5310   p   L

Oyster Bay

Laurelton Hall (Tiffany Mansion)
Laurel Hollow & Ridge Rds.
HABS NY-5663   p   L
Roosevelt, Theodore, House; see Sagamore
  Hill
Sagamore Hill (Roosevelt, Theodore,
  House; Sagamore Hill National Historic
  Site)
HABS NY-6051   s p   H
Sagamore Hill National Historic Site; see
  Sagamore Hill
Tiffany Mansion; see Laurelton Hall

Roslyn

Montrose
HABS NY-6052   p   H
Robeson-Williams Grist Mill
HABS NY-6053   s p   H
Roslyn Presbyterian Church
33 E. Broadway
HABS NY-6054   s pd   H
Smith, James & William, Barn
106 Main St.
HABS NY-6055-A   s p   H
Smith, James & William, House
106 Main St.
HABS NY-6055   s pd   H
Wilkey, Warren, House
190 Main St.
HABS NY-6056   s pd   H

Sands Point

Sands Point Lighthouse
Middle Neck Rd.
HAER NY-93   p   H

Seaford

Verity, Stephen, Homestead
Montauk Hwy. & Washington Ave.
HABS NY-538   s p   L

Wantagh

Friends' Meetinghouse of Jerusalem
Wantagh Ave.
HABS NY-4-405   s d   L
Jones, Jackson, Homestead
Merrick Rd.
HABS NY-4-404   s   L

NEW YORK COUNTY

New York City
307-17 & 308-20 E. Forty-fourth St. (Apartments)
HABS NY-6059   s p d   H
48 & 50 King Street (Houses)
HABS NY-4-20   s p d   L
Albano Building
305-311 E. Forty-sixth St.
HABS NY-6057   p   H
All Saint's Church
286-290 Henry St.
HABS NY-4-10   s p d   L
Allied Arts Building
304-320 E. Forty-fifth St.
HABS NY-6058   p   H
Apothecary Shop (Interiors)
10 Greenwich St.
HABS NY-475-A   s p   L
Auchmuty Building; see South Street Seaport Museum

Bayard-Condict Building
65-69 Bleecker St.
HABS NY-5485   pd   L

Beekman, John, House
29-29 1/2 Cherry St.
HABS NY-452   s p d   L

Blackwell's Island Bridge (Queensboro Bridge)
Second Ave. to Northern Blvd., Long Island City
HAER NY-19   p   H

Block Houses (Numbers 1 & 2)
Central (110th St.) & Morningside Pks. (123rd St.)
HABS NY-443   s p d   L

165 Broadway (Building); see City Investing Building
Brooklyn Bridge; see East River Bridge

Carle Building
151-153 Water St., 134-136 Maiden Ln.
HABS NY-4390   pd   L

Charles & Company Building
335-341 E. Forty-fourth St.
HABS NY-6060   p   H

Church, Brick (Interiors)
Fifth Ave. & Thirty-seventh St.
HABS NY-468   p   L

Church of St. John the Evangelist
Eleventh St. & Wavery Place
HABS NY-437   s p d   L

Church of the Ascension
Fifth Ave. & Tenth St.
HABS NY-6061   s   H

Church of the Covenant
310 E. Forty-second St.
HABS NY-6062   p   H

Church of the Epiphany
Lexington Ave. & Thirty-fifth St.
HABS NY-454   p   L
Church of the Nativity
46-48 Second Ave.
HABS NY-5461   pd   H
City Investing Building (165 Broadway (Building))
HABS NY-5498   p   L
City Pier A
Battery Place
HAER NY-84   p   H
Colonnade Row; see La Grange Terrace
Cooper Union for the Advancement of Science & Art
Third & Fourth Aves., Astor Pl., Seventh St.
HAER NY-20   s p d   L
Crocheron, Jacob, House
47 Whitehall St.
HABS NY-5456   s   H
Croton Aqueduct, Old-Aqueduct Bridge (Croton Aqueduct, Old-High Bridge)
Harlem River, Cross Bronx Expressway vic.
HAER NY-119   p   L
Croton Aqueduct, Old-High Bridge; see Croton Aqueduct, Old-Aqueduct Bridge
Custom House, Old; see U.S. Sub-Treasury Building
Daily News Building
220-226 E. Forty-second St.
HABS NY-6063   p   H
Dakota, The (Apartments)
1 W. Seventy-second St., Central Park West
HABS NY-5467   pd   L
Dunbar Apartments; see Henson, Matthew, Apartment
Dyckman House
Broadway & Two-hundred-fourth St.
HABS NY-4-4   s p d   L
East River Bridge (Brooklyn Bridge)
Park Row, Manhattan to Adams St., Brooklyn
HAER NY-18   p   H
Eitel, John, Building; see South Street Seaport Museum
Ellington, Edward Kennedy (Duke), Apartment
935 St. Nicholas Ave., Apt. 4-A
HABS NY-5690   p   H
Erie Railroad, Chambers Street Ferry Terminal
Chambers St.
HAER NY-85   p   H
Erie Railroad, Twenty-third Street Ferry Terminal
HAER NY-86   p   H
Faile, Edward, Building; see South Street Seaport Museum
Federal Hall National Monument; see U.S. Sub-Treasury Building
Field's Building
168-170 John St. (formerly 32-38 Burling Slip)
HABS NY-4391   pd   L

Folies Bergere Theatre (Fulton Theatre; Hayes, Helen, Theatre)
210 W. Forty-sixth St.
HABS NY-5673   s pd   L
Fordham, George, House
329 Cherry St.
HABS NY-445   s p d   L
Forrest, Edwin, House
436 W. Twenty-second St.
HABS NY-4-14   s p d   L
Fort Jay
Governor's Island
HABS NY-4-6   s p d   L
Front & Whitehall Streets Study
HABS NY-6064   p   H
207 Front Street (Commercial Building); see South Street Seaport Museum
Front Street (Warehouse)
HABS NY-4378   s   L
Fulton Theatre; see Folies Bergere Theatre
Governor's Island Ferry Terminal; see Whitehall Street Ferry Terminal
Gracie Mansion
Carl Shurz Park, E. Sixty-eighth St.
HABS NY-461   p   L
Grant, General, National Memorial; see Grant's Monument
Grant's Monument (Grant's Tomb; Grant, General, National Memorial)
Riverside Drive & W. 122nd St.
HABS NY-5429   s p d   L H
Grant's Tomb; see Grant's Monument
10 Greenwich Street (House)
HABS NY-475   s p   L
14 Greenwich Street (House)
HABS NY-476   s p   L
16 Greenwich Street (House)
HABS NY-477   s p   L
18 Greenwich Street (House)
HABS NY-478   s p   L
20 Greenwich Street (House)
HABS NY-479   s p   L
4 Greenwich Street (House)
HABS NY-472   s   L
6 Greenwich Street (House)
HABS NY-473   s p   L
8 Greenwich Street (House)
HABS NY-474   s p   L
Greenwich Street Study (Plot plan)
HABS NY-472-A   s p   L
Gridley, John V., House
37 Charlton St.
HABS NY-441   s p d   L
4-10 Grove Street (Row Houses)
HABS NY-449   s p   L
Harlem Fire Watchtower
Madison Ave.
HAER NY-104   p   H
Harper, James, House
4 Gramercy Park
HABS NY-4-7   s p d   L
Hart-Carpenter-Havens Building; see South Street Seaport Museum

Hart-Havens-Lauderback Building; see
  South Street Seaport Museum
Haughwout, E. V. & Company, Building
488-492 Broadway
HABS NY-5459   s pd   L
Hayes, Helen, Theatre; see Folies Bergere
  Theatre
Hazlet, John, House
204-206 W. Thirteenth St.
HABS NY-444   s pd   L
48 Henry Street (Row House)
HABS NY-6065   d   H
Henson, Matthew, Apartment (Dunbar
  Apartments)
246 W. One-hundred-fiftieth St.
HABS NY-5697   p   H
Hotel Astor
1511-1515 Broadway
HABS NY-5464   pd   L
Houseman, Jacob, House & Office
2 Front St.
HABS NY-5458   s   H
Howell, Matthew, Building; see South
  Street Seaport Museum
India House
1 Hanover Square
HABS NY-4-2   s pd   L
Interborough Rapid Transit Subway
  (Original Line)
HAER NY-122   pd   L
Jefferson Market Courthouse; see Third
  Judicial District Courthouse
Jerome, Leonard W., Mansion
32 E. Twenty-sixth St.
HABS NY-5470   pd   L
John Street Methodist Episcopal Church,
  Old
44-46 John St.
HABS NY-4-27   s pd   L
Johnson, James Weldon, Apartment
187 W. One-hundred-thirty-fifth St.
HABS NY-5694   p   H
La Grange Terrace (Colonnade Row)
428-434 Lafayette Place
HABS NY-5604   s   L
Laing, Edgar, Stores
Washington & Murray Sts.
HABS NY-5469   s pd   L
Lawrence Building; see South Street
  Seaport Museum
Leake & Watts Orphanage, Old
Amsterdam Ave. & One-hundred-tenth St.
HABS NY-426   s pd   L
9 Lexington Avenue (House)

Livingston Building; see South Street
  Seaport Museum

Mantel, Derelict
HABS NY-4385   p   L

Mariners' Temple
Oliver & Henry Sts.
HABS NY-436   s pd   L

McKay, Claude, Apartment
180 W. One-hundred-thirty-fifth St.
HABS NY-5695   p   H
Metal Exchange Building
234 Pearl St.
HABS NY-431   s pd   L
Metropolitan Opera House
1423 Broadway
HABS NY-5486   pd   L
Meyer's Hotel; see South Street Seaport
  Museum
Mills, Florence, House
220 W. One hundred thirty-fifth St.
HABS NY-5696   p   H
Minnie Building
303 E. Forty-sixth St.
HABS NY-6066   p   H
Modernace Building
319 E. Forty-fourth St.
HABS NY-6067   p   H
Morris-Jumel Mansion
Edgecomb Ave. & 160th-162nd Sts.
HABS NY-469   p   L
Mott, Jordan L., House
2122 Fifth Ave.
HABS NY-450   s pd   L
Mount Vernon Coach House & Stable
  (Smith, Abigail Adams, Museum)
421 E. Sixty-first St.
HABS NY-5631   s   H
New York Amsterdam News Building
2293 Seventh Ave.
HABS NY-5693   p   H
New York Connecting RR, Hell Gate
  Bridge
Spanning East River, Wards Island &
  Astoria
HAER NY-88   p   H
New York Edison Company, Powerhouse
686-700 First Ave.
HABS NY-6068   p   H
New York Public Library, Jefferson
  Market Branch; see Third Judicial
  District Courthouse
New York Society Library
109 University Place
HABS NY-4-13   s pd   H
Northern Dispensary
165 Waverly Place
HABS NY-4-9   s pd   L
Olliffe Pharmacy
6 Bowery
HABS NY-4-17   s pd   L
Onderdonk, Harriet, Building; see South
  Street Seaport Museum
Panhellenic Tower
Mitchell Place
HABS NY-6069   p   H

Penn Station; see Pennsylvania Station

Pennsylvania Station (Penn Station)
370 Seventh Ave., W. 31st, 31st-33rd Sts.
HABS NY-5471   pd   L

Phoenix-Shaw Warehouse
68-70 Front St.
HABS NY-4394   pd   L
Queensboro Bridge; see Blackwell's Island
  Bridge
Queensboro Bridge Trolley Station
Second Ave., 49th-60th Sts.
HABS NY-6070   s   H
Racquet & Tennis Club
370 Park Ave., E. 52nd-53rd Sts.
HABS NY-5466   pd   L
Reeves Sound Studios
304 E. Forty-fourth St.
HABS NY-6071   p   H
Rhinelander Row
Seventh Ave., Twelfth-Thirteenth Sts.
HABS NY-463   p   L
Robeson, Paul, Apartment
555 Edgecomb Ave.
HABS NY-5692   p   H
Rogers, George P., Building; see South
  Street Seaport Museum
Rogers, Moses, House; see Watson, James,
  House
Roosevelt Island, Castle-Hospital; see
  Welfare Island, Castle-Hospital
Roosevelt Island, Church; see Welfare
  Island, Church
Roosevelt Island, Farmhouse; see Welfare
  Island, Farmhouse
Roosevelt Island, Insane Asylum; see
  Welfare Island, Insane Asylum
Roosevelt Island, Lighthouse; see Welfare
  Island, Lighthouse
Roosevelt Island, South Building; see
  Welfare Island, South Building
Roosevelt Island, Strecker Medical
  Laboratory; see Welfare Island, Strecker
  Medical Laboratory
Rose House; see South Street Seaport
  Museum
Schermerhorn Row
2-18 Fulton St., 92-93 South St.
HABS NY-6072   s d   H
Sea & Land Church
Henry & Market Sts.
HABS NY-446   s pd   L
Singer Tower
149 Broadway
HABS NY-5463   pd   L
Smith, Abigail Adams, Museum; see Mount
  Vernon Coach House & Stable
Smith, Gersom, Building; see South Street
  Seaport Museum
Society of Friends Meetinghouse
15 Rutherford Place
HABS NY-4-1   s pd   L
South Street Seaport
HABS NY-5632   s   H
South Street Seaport, Block 96W
Fulton, Front, Beekman & Water Sts.
HABS NY-5687   s   H

South Street Seaport Museum (Rogers, George P., Building)
21-25 Fulton St.
HABS NY-5633   s d   H

South Street Seaport Museum (Smith, Gersom, Building)
232-234 Front St.
HABS NY-5679   d   H

South Street Seaport Museum (Auchmuty Building)
142-144 Beekman St., 211 Front St.
HABS NY-5674   d   H

South Street Seaport Museum (Rose House)
273 Water St.
HABS NY-5686   d   H

South Street Seaport Museum (Lawrence Building)
205 Front St.
HABS NY-5676   s d   H

South Street Seaport Museum (Eitel, John, Building)
251 Water St. & 20 Peck Slip
HABS NY-5685   d   H

South Street Seaport Museum (Faile, Edward, Building)
236 Front St.
HABS NY-5680   d   H

South Street Seaport Museum (Howell, Matthew, Building)
206 Front St.
HABS NY-5677   s d   H

South Street Seaport Museum (Meyer's Hotel; Onderdonk, Harriet, Building)
116-119 South St.
HABS NY-5681   d   H

South Street Seaport Museum (Hart-Carpenter-Havens Building)
203-204 Front St.
HABS NY-5675   s d   H

South Street Seaport Museum (Ward, Jasper, Building)
45 Peck Slip, 151 South St.
HABS NY-5682   d   H

South Street Seaport Museum (Thompson, A. A. & Co., Building)
213-215 Water St.
HABS NY-5684   s d   H

South Street Seaport Museum (Livingston Building)
127-137 Beekman St.
HABS NY-5634   s d   H

South Street Seaport Museum (207 Front Street (Commercial Building))
HABS NY-5678   s d   H

South Street Seaport Museum (Hart-Havens-Lauderback Building)
207-211 Water St.
HABS NY-5683   s d   H

St. Ann's Church
295 Saint Ann's Ave. & E. 140th St.
HABS NY-433   s pd   L

St. James Roman Catholic Church
St. James Place
HABS NY-458   p   L

St. Luke's Chapel
447 Hudson St.
HABS NY-439   s pd   L

St. Mark's-in-the-Bouwerie
234 E. Eleventh St.
HABS NY-464   p   L

St. Paul's Chapel
Broadway & Fulton Sts.
HABS NY-453   p   L

St. Peter's Episcopal Church
436 W. Twentieth St.
HABS NY-438   pd   L

St. Peter's Roman Catholic Church
31 Barclay St.
HABS NY-4-3   s pd   L

St. Therese's Church
Henry & Rutgers Sts.
HABS NY-466   p   L

St. Vincent's Hospital Complex
153 W. Eleventh St.
HABS NY-5698   pd   L

St. Vincent's Hospital, Elizabeth Seton Building
151-167 W. Eleventh St.
HABS NY-5698-A   pd   L

St. Vincent's Hospital, Leon Lowenstein Clinic
7-15 Seventh Ave.
HABS NY-5698-B   pd   L

Streetlight
Second Ave. & E. Forty-ninth St.
HABS NY-6073   p   H

Stuyvesant Apartments
142 E. Eighteenth St.
HABS NY-435   s pd   L

Teller, Jane, Mansion
421 E. Sixty-first St.
HABS NY-459   p   L

Third Judicial District Courthouse (Jefferson Market Courthouse; New York Public Library, Jefferson Market Branch)
425 Ave. of the Americas
HABS NY-4392   pd   L

Thompson, A. A. & Co., Building; see South Street Seaport Museum

Tredwell, Seabury, House
29 E. Fourth St.
HABS NY-440   s p   L

Tribune Building
154 Printing House Sq., Nassau & Spruce Sts.
HABS NY-5468   pd   L

Trinity Church
Broadway & Wall St.
HABS NY-6074   s   H

Tudor City Complex
E. Forty-first St. & Tudor City Place
HABS NY-6075   p   H

Tweed Courthouse
52 Chambers St.
HABS NY-5688   p   H

United Nations Headquarters
U. N. Plaza
HABS NY-6076   p   H

United Nations Vicinity (Buildings)
Second Ave., 41, 43, 44, 46, 48 & 49 Sts.
HABS NY-6254   p   H

U.S. Sub-Treasury Building (Federal Hall National Monument; Custom House, Old)
Wall & Nassau Sts.
HABS NY-470   s pd   L H

Villard Houses
451-457 Madison Ave.
HABS NY-5636   s p   H

Walker, David, House & Office
45 Whitehall St.
HABS NY-5455   s   H

Ward, Jasper, Building; see South Street Seaport Museum

Washington Square North (House)
Washington Sq. North & Fifth Ave.
HABS NY-4-16-A   p   L

7 Washington Square North (House)
HABS NY-4-16-B   pd   L

8 Washington Square North (House)
HABS NY-4-16-C   s pd   L

61 Washington Square South (House)
HABS NY-447   s pd   L

71-77 Washington Street (House)
HABS NY-482   s p   L

15 Washington Street (Stairs)
HABS NY-482-A   p   L

13 Washington Street (Store Front)
HABS NY-481   s p   L

29 Washington Street (Store Front)
HABS NY-481-A   p   L

739 Washington Street (Town House)
HABS NY-4379   s   L

Watson, James, House (Rogers, Moses, House)
7 State St.
HABS NY-442   s pd   L H

Welfare Island, Castle-Hospital (Roosevelt Island, Castle-Hospital)
HABS NY-6077   p   H

Welfare Island, Church (Roosevelt Island, Church)
HABS NY-6078   p   H

Welfare Island, Farmhouse (Roosevelt Island, Farmhouse)
HABS NY-6079   p   H

Welfare Island, Insane Asylum (Roosevelt Island, Insane Asylum)
HABS NY-6080   p   H

Welfare Island, Lighthouse (Roosevelt Island, Lighthouse)
HABS NY-6081   p   H

Welfare Island, South Building (Roosevelt Island, South Building)
HABS NY-6082   p   H

Welfare Island, Strecker Medical
   Laboratory (Roosevelt Island, Strecker
   Medical Laboratory)
HABS NY-6083   p   H
116 West Eleventh Street (Building)
HABS NY-451   s pd   L
132 West Fourth Street (Building)
HABS NY-448   s pd   L
West Side Highway
HAER NY-133   p   L
Whitehall Street Ferry Terminal
   (Governor's Island Ferry Terminal)
Whitehall & Broad Sts.
HAER NY-90   p   H

NIAGARA COUNTY

Lewiston
Barton Hill
Center & River Sts.
HABS NY-6084   pd   H
Bates-Cook Law Office
755 Center St.
HABS NY-6085   pd   H
First Presbyterian Church
505 Cayuga St.
HABS NY-6086   pd   H
Frontier House
450 Center St.
HABS NY-6087   pd   H
Hennepin Hall
Center & Seventh Sts.
HABS NY-6088   pd   H
Kelsey Tavern
625 Center St.
HABS NY-6089   pd   H

Lockport
Bissell-Spaulding House
471 Market St.
HABS NY-6148   pd   H
Bond House
143 Ontario St.
HABS NY-6090   pd   H
Bouck, David, House (Merritt, Erricson,
   House)
532 Pine St.
HABS NY-6091   pd   H
Christ Episcopal Church
425 Market St.
HABS NY-6092   pd   H
Dayton, Nathan, House
499 Market St.
HABS NY-6093   pd   H
Erie Canal Locks, Barge Canal; see Erie
   Canal Locks, Second Set
Erie Canal Locks, Second Set (Erie Canal
   Locks, Barge Canal)
Cottage & Pine Sts.
HABS NY-6094   pd   H
Hitchings, Frances, House
Summitt St.
HABS NY-6095   pd   H

Hunt, Washington, House
363 Market St.
HABS NY-6096   pd   H
Jackson Block
1-9 Buffalo St.
HABS NY-6097   d   H
Lockport Bank Building
317-319 Market St.
HABS NY-6098   pd   H
Merritt, Erricson, House; see Bouck, David,
   House
New York Central R.R., Lockport Station
Washburn & Union Sts.
HAER NY-60   p   H
**New York State Barge Canal, Lockport
   Locks**
Lock St.
HAER NY-61   p   H
Second Presbyterian Church
71 Van Buren St.
HABS NY-6099   pd   H
Skinner, Josiah K., House
485 Market St.
HABS NY-6147   pd   H
Vine Street School
Vine & Garden Sts.
HABS NY-6149   pd   H

Niagara Falls
Adams, Edward D., Station Power Plant
Niagara River & Buffalo Ave.
HABS NY-6150   s p   H
Erie Railroad, La Salle Station
HAER NY-92   p   H
Erie Railroad, Niagara Falls Station
HAER NY-91   p   H
New York Central Railroad Station
Falls & Second Sts.
HABS NY-6151   d   H
University Club; see Whitney House
U.S. Custom House
Whirlpool St. at Lower Arch Bridge
HABS NY-6152   pd   H
Whitney House (University Club)
355 Buffalo Ave.
HABS NY-6153   pd   H

North Tonawanda
Erie Railroad, North Tonawanda Station
HAER NY-94   p   H

North Tonawanda vic.
Erie Railroad, Sawyer Creek Bridge
Spanning Sawyer Creek on U.S. Rt. 62
HAER NY-95   p   H

Somerset
Thirty-mile Point Lighthouse
Golden Hill Park, Lake Ontario
HABS NY-6154   pd   H

Youngstown
Fort Niagara
Fort Niagara State Park
HABS NY-6155   p   H

St. John's Episcopal Church
Main & Chestnut Sts.
HABS NY-6156   pd   H

ONEIDA COUNTY

Boonville vic.
Black River Canal, Locks 39-43
State Rt. 46
HAER NY-83   p   H

Oneida
Oneida Community's Mansion House; see
   Perfectionist Community Building
Perfectionist Community Building (Oneida
   Community's Mansion House)
Kenwood Ave.
HABS NY-5616   d   H

Rome
Barnes-Mudge House (Rome Club)
115 E. Dominick St.
HABS NY-5509   pd   L
Cole-Kingsley House (Women's
   Community Center)
110 E. Liberty St.
HABS NY-5512   pd   L
Draper, Virgil, House
121 E. Dominick St.
HABS NY-5510   pd   L
Empire House
111-113 E. Dominick St.
HABS NY-5508   pd   L
Floyd, Gen. William, House
Westernville
HABS NY-5513   p   H
Liberty Hall (Stryker, John, House)
112 E. Liberty St.
HABS NY-5511   pd   L
Liberty Hall (1851 Hot Air Furnace)
   (Stryker, John, House (1851 Hot Air
   Furnace))
112 E. Liberty St.
HABS NY-5511-A   pd   L
Oneida County Courthouse
HABS NY-6111   p   H
Rome Club; see Barnes-Mudge House
Stryker, John, House; see Liberty Hall
**Stryker, John, House (1851 Hot Air
   Furnace);** see Liberty Hall (1851 Hot Air
   Furnace)
Women's Community Center; see
   Cole-Kingsley House

Utica
City Hall
Genesee & Pearl Sts.
HABS NY-5444   p   H

Vernon Center
Tuttle, Hiram, House
HABS NY-5-S-9   pd   L

Whitesboro
Town Hall
Park Ave.
HABS NY-5-U-1   s pd   L

ONONDAGA COUNTY

Kempster House
HABS NY-6157   p   H

000
Sabine House
HABS NY-6158   p   H

Camillus
Camillus Baptist Church
Genesee St.
HABS NY-6159   p   H

Delphi Falls
Meetinghouse of the First Baptist Society
Town of Pompey
HABS NY-5431   s p   H

Elbridge Vic
Munro, John, House
State Rt. 5
HABS NY-6160   p   H

Fabius
Benson House
Ride Rd.
HABS NY-6161   p   H

Fayetteville
Collin, Charles, House
7860 E. Genesee St.
HABS NY-6163   p   H
McViciar, John, House
315 Genesee St.
HABS NY-6164   p   H

Jamesville
St. Mark's Episcopal Church
HABS NY-6165   p   H

Jamesville vic.
Izes, Doctor, House
E. Seneca Turnpike
HABS NY-6118   p   H

Jordan
Junod House
150 N. Main St.
HABS NY-6166   p   H
15 Main Street (Commercial Building)
HABS NY-6167   p   H
Rogers, W. C., Block
Main & Mechanics Sts.
HABS NY-6168   p   H
Tanner, Doctor, House
HABS NY-6169   p   H

Liverpool
Gleason, Lucius, House
Sycamore & Second Sts.
HABS NY-6171   p   H

Hicks, J. P., Building; see Hotel, Cobblestone
Hicks, Jonathan, House
609 Vine St.
HABS NY-6172   p   H
Hotel, Cobblestone (Hicks, J. P., Building)
HABS NY-6170   p   H

Manlius
Smith Hall
Seneca Turnpike
HABS NY-6173   p   H

Marcellus
Bradley, Dan, House
HABS NY-6174   p   H
Marcellus Presbyterian Church
Seneca Turnpike & North St.
HABS NY-6175   p   H

Marcellus vic.
District School Number 9
HABS NY-227   s pd   L

Martisco
Martisco Station
Marcellus & Otisco Sts.
HABS NY-6176   p   H

Onondaga Hill
Easton Storehouse
Seneca Turnpike
HABS NY-223   s pd   L
Hutchinson, General George, House
4311 W. Seneca Turnpike
HABS NY-6177   p   L H
Onondaga County Poorhouse
Onondaga Rd.
HABS NY-6162   p   H

Oran
Travelers' & Drovers' Tavern
Cherry Valley Turnpike
HABS NY-5-S-6   s pd   L

Plainville vic.
Voorhees, Colonel, House; see Whig Hall
Whig Hall (Voorhees, Colonel, House)
State Rt. 370 & Gates Rd.
HABS NY-6178   p   H

Pompey
Beard-Conan Store
HABS NY-225   s pd   L
Marsh, Moses Seymour, Store
HABS NY-224   s pd   L
Pompey Presbyterian Church
Fabius Pompey Rd.
HABS NY-5-S-5   s pd   L

Skaneateles
Benedict, Doctor, House
43 State St.
HABS NY-6179   p   H
Community Place
HABS NY-6180   p   H

Dezeng, Richard, House (Roosevelt Hall)
W. Lake Rd.
HABS NY-6181   p   H
Jewett, Freeborn, Mansion
11 Genesee St.
HABS NY-6183   p   H
Jewett House, Small
81 Genesee St.
HABS NY-6182   p   H
Lamb, Alfred, House
Franklin St.
HABS NY-6184   p   H
Lee, Benoit, Law Office (Sphinx, The)
Skaneateles Public Library
HABS NY-6185   p   H
Legg Hall
Genesee St.
HABS NY-6186   p   H
Loveless House, The
77 Jordan St.
HABS NY-6187   p   H
Meetinghouse of the Skaneateles Baptist Society
State St.
HABS NY-6188   p   H
Merriam House
W. Genesee St.
HABS NY-5-S-3   s pd   L
Roosevelt Hall; see Dezeng, Richard, House
Smith, Reuel, House
W. Lake Rd.
HABS NY-5452   p   H
Sphinx, The; see Lee, Benoit, Law Office

Skaneateles vic.
District School Number 17
W. Lake Rd.
HABS NY-226   s pd   L

Syracuse
Andrew Block
W. Fayette & Clinton Sts.
HABS NY-6190   p   H
Botanic Infirmary, Old (Thomson, Dr. Cyrus, Block)
W. Genesee St.
HABS NY-5447   p   H
Brown, Alexander, House
726 W. Onondaga St.
HABS NY-6191   p   H
Brown-Lipe-Chaplin Division; see General Motors Factory
Church of St. John the Baptist
Park & Court Sts.
HABS NY-6193   p   H
Church of St. John the Evangelist
214 N. State St.
HABS NY-6194   p   H
City Bank Building; see Kirk Fireproof Building
Dutch Reformed Church
HABS NY-6196   p   H

Forman, Samuel, House
409 W. Seneca St.
HABS NY-5-S-2   s pd   L

General Motors Factory
   (Brown-Lipe-Chaplin Division)
Marcellus St.
HABS NY-6192   p   H

Gere, Robert, Bank Building
1212 E. Water St.
HABS NY-6197   p   H

Grace Episcopal Church
819 Madison St.
HABS NY-6198   p   H

Greenway Place
Hawley Ave. & McBride St.
HABS NY-6199   p   H

Gridley, John, House
205 E. Seneca Turnpike
HABS NY-222   s pd   L H

Kellogg House
Lancaster & Euclid Ave.
HABS NY-6200   p   H

Kirk Fireproof Building (City Bank
   Building)
HABS NY-6202   p   H

Leavenworth, General, House
607 James St.
HABS NY-5-S-1   s pd   L

McCarthy Warehouse, Edwards Annex
W. Washington & S. Clinton Sts.
HABS NY-6203   p   H

**Onondaga County Savings Bank Building,
   Old**
Erie Blvd. & Salina St.
HABS NY-5450   p   H

Park Avenue Methodist Church (St. Paul's
   Armenian Apostolic Church)
312 N. Geddes St.
HABS NY-6204   p   H

Searle, Nathaniel, House
5323 S. Salina St.
HABS NY-6207   p   H

Sedgewick House
742 James St.
HABS NY-5445   p   H

1622 South Salina Street (House)
HABS NY-6206   p   H

St. Paul's Armenian Apostolic Church; see
   Park Avenue Methodist Church

St. Paul's Episcopal Church
Fayette St. & Montgomery St.
HABS NY-6205   p   H

Syracuse Savings Bank
102 N. Salina St.
HABS NY-5449   p   H

Syracuse State School, State Idiot Asylum
Burnet Park
HABS NY-6208   p   H

**Syracuse University, John R. Crouse
   Building**
HABS NY-6195   p   H

Teall, Oliver, House
105 S. Beeck St.
HABS NY-6209   p   H

Third Onondaga County Courthouse
Clinton Sq.
HABS NY-5430   s p   H

Thomson, Dr. Cyrus, Block; see Botanic
   Infirmary, Old

Tolman, Hawey, House
5516 S. Salina St.
HABS NY-6210   p   H

Weighlock Building
Erie Blvd. East & Montgomery St.
HABS NY-5451   p   H

Wesleyan Methodist Church
304 E. Onondaga St.
HABS NY-6211   p   H

111 West Kennedy Street (House)
HABS NY-6201   p   H

White, Hamilton, House
S. Townsend & E. Genesee St.
HABS NY-6212   p   H

White Memorial Building
E. Washington & S. Salina Sts.
HABS NY-5448   p   H

Wilkinson, Horace, House
703 Walnut Ave.
HABS NY-6213   p   H

ONTARIO COUNTY

Bristol Center

Presbyterian Church
HABS NY-235   p   L

Canandaigua

Carr-Hayes House
Gibson & Hubbell Sts.
HABS NY-214   s pd   L

First Congregational Church
N. Main St.
HABS NY-5-R-11   s pd   L

Granger, Gideon, House
295 N. Main St.
HABS NY-5-R-2   s pd   L

Lansing, Henry, House
72 E. Gibson St.
HABS NY-212   s pd   L

Geneva

Burns, Andrew, House
859 S. Main St.
HABS NY-230   s p   L

Chapman, Jebidiah, House
562 S. Main St.
HABS NY-232   s p   L

Chew House (Entrance)
600 S. Main St.
HABS NY-239   p   L

Hotel Geneva; see Nester Hotel

Jacobs Building
523 Exchange St.
HABS NY-5705   pd   L

Nester Hotel (Hotel Geneva)
529-533 Exchange St.
HABS NY-5706   pd   L

Truslow House
606 S. Main St.
HABS NY-238   p   L

Wheat House, The
584 S. Main St.
HABS NY-237   p   L

Williamson, Col. Charles, House
839 S. Main St.
HABS NY-233   s p   L

Naples

Cleveland, Ephraim, House
HABS NY-236   p   L

ORANGE COUNTY

Goshen

Erie Railroad, Goshen Station
Grand St.
HAER NY-55   p   H

Harriman

Harriman Passenger Station
HAER NY-136   p   H

Middletown

Erie Railroad, Middletown Station
James St.
HAER NY-56   p   H

New Windsor

Haskell House
State Rt. 32
HABS NY-5664   pd   H

Newburgh

71 Ann Street (House)
HABS NY-6214   p   H

Anthony House
201 Montgomery St.
HABS NY-6215   p   H

55 Broad Street (House)
HABS NY-6216   p   H

City Club; see Culbert, Dr. William A. M.,
   House

City Library
Grand St.
HABS NY-6217   p   H

Clinton, George, Statue
Clinton's Square, Water St.
HABS NY-6231   p   H

Colden Street (Houses)
HABS NY-6218   p   H

Crawford House
189 Montgomery St.
HABS NY-6219   pd   H

Culbert, Dr. William A. M., House (City
   Club)
120 Grand St.
HABS NY-6220   pd   H

Dutch Reformed Church
Third & Grant Sts.
HABS NY-6221   pd   H

Egyptian-style Tomb
Calvary Cemetery
HABS NY-6222　　　p　　H

288 Grand Street (House)
HABS NY-6224　　　p　　H

78-86 Grand Street (Houses)
HABS NY-6223　　　p　　H

Hasbrouck House (Washington's Headquarters)
Washington, Liberty, Lafayette, Colden Sts.
HABS NY-4131　　s p　L

Hasbrouck, William C., House
99 Montgomery St.
HABS NY-6255　　p d　H

Hodges Funeral Home; see Warren, W. E., House

Leonard, C. M., Company Firehouse
HABS NY-6225　　p　H

Newburgh Savings Bank (Soul-Saving Church of God)
Smith & Second Sts.
HABS NY-6226　　p　H

Orange County Courthouse
Second & Grand Sts.
HABS NY-6227　　p　H

Reeve House
129 Montgomery St.
HABS NY-6228　　s p　H

Ringgold Fire Company Firehouse
63 Golden St.
HABS NY-6229　　p　H

Roe, William, House
160 Grand St.
HABS NY-6230　　p d　H

Soul-Saving Church of God; see Newburgh Savings Bank

Stevens, Halsey, House
182 Grand St.
HABS NY-6232　　p d　H

Sunflower House
195 Montgomery St.
HABS NY-6233　　p　H

Walker-Marvel House
53 Ann St.
HABS NY-6234　　p d　H

Warren, W. E., House (Hodges Funeral Home)
196 Grand St.
HABS NY-6235　　p　H

Washington's Headquarters; see Hasbrouck House

Wright, William, House
Interstate Hwy. 84
HABS NY-5689　　p　L

Otisville

Erie Railroad, Otisville Tunnel
Sanitarium Rd. to Otisville Rd.
HAER NY-21　　p　H

Port Jervis

Erie Railroad, Port Jervis Roundhouse
Pike St.
HAER NY-23　　p　H

Erie Railroad, Port Jervis Station
Jersey Ave.
HAER NY-22　　p　L

Port Jervis vic.

Erie Railroad, Port Jervis Rock Cut
Neversink & Shinhollow Rds. vic.
HAER NY-24　　p　H

Salisbury Mills vic.

Erie Railroad, Moodna Creek Viaduct
Orrs Mill Rd.
HAER NY-62　　p　H

ORLEANS COUNTY

Albion

Bartlett House
135 W. Bank St.
HABS NY-6236　　p d　H

D. A. R. House
N. Main St.
HABS NY-6237　　p d　H

First Presbyterian Church
E. State St.
HABS NY-6238　　p d　H

Lanson House
HABS NY-2　　p　L

Pratt Opera House
114-120 N. Main St.
HABS NY-6239　　p d　H

Childs

Church, Cobblestone
Ridge Rd. (U.S. Rt. 104)
HABS NY-6240　　p d　H

Schoolhouse, Cobblestone
Ridge Rd. (U.S. Rt. 104)
HABS NY-6241　　p d　H

Gaines

Whipple House
Ridge Rd.
HABS NY-1　　p　L

Murray

Hunn, John, House
Ridge & E. Holley Rds.
HABS NY-217　　s p d　L

Orangeburg vic.

Saunders, I. V., House
Ridge Rd.
HABS NY-3　　p　L

OSWEGO COUNTY

Oswego

Oswego City Library
E. Second & E. Oneida Sts.
HABS NY-5434　　s p　H

Public Market Building, Old
Bridge St. vic.
HABS NY-5436　　p　H

Port Ontario vic.

Salmon River Lighthouse
Lake Ontario
HABS NY-6112　　p　L

OTSEGO COUNTY

Cherry Valley

House
State Rt. 20
HABS NY-241　　p　L

Cooperstown

Building, Iron-clad
92 Main St., Otsego Township
HABS NY-253　　p d　L

Byberry Cottage
River St., Otsego Township
HABS NY-250　　p d　L

Clark Real Estate Office; see Otsego County Bank

Cory, Ellery, House
24 Pioneer St., Otsego Township
HABS NY-252　　p d　L

Edgewater
Lake St., Otsego Township
HABS NY-251　　p d　L

Lakelands
Main St., Middlefield Township
HABS NY-254　　p d　L

Main Street (House)
HABS NY-247　　p　L

Otsego County Bank (Clark Real Estate Office)
19 Main St., Otsego Township
HABS NY-255　　p d　L

Pomeroy House
Main & River Sts., Otsego Township
HABS NY-256　　p d　L

Presbyterian Church
Pioneer & Elm Sts., Otsego Township
HABS NY-257　　p d　L

Smithy, The
55 Pioneer St., Otsego Township
HABS NY-258　　p d　L

Woodside Hall
Main St., Middlefield Township
HABS NY-259　　p d　L

Woodside Hall, Gate Tower
Main St., Middlefield Township
HABS NY-262　　p d　L

East Springfield

Hyde Hall
E. Lake Rd. vic.
HABS NY-260　　p d　L

Hyde Hall, Covered Bridge
E. Lake Rd. vic.
HABS NY-263　　p d　L

Hyde Hall, Gatehouse
E. Lake Rd.
HABS NY-264　　p d　L

Middlefield Cen. vic.
Hop Barn & Kiln
HABS NY-265   pd   L

Oaksville
Williams-Childs House
State Rt. 28, Otsego Township
HABS NY-266   pd   L

Westville vic.
Cottage, Gothic
State Rt. 166 vic., Middlefield Township
HABS NY-261   pd   L

PUTNAM COUNTY

Garrison
Boscobel
State Rt. 9D
HABS NY-5667   s   H
Galloway Farmhouse
Manitou Rd.
HABS NY-4-107   s pd   L
Grist Mill
Manitou Rd.
HABS NY-4-108   s pd   L

QUEENS COUNTY

Bowery Bay
Riker Homestead
Eightieth St.
HABS NY-4-29   s pd   L

Flushing
Bowne House
37-01 Bowne St.
HABS NY-523   s p   L
Prince House
Northern Blvd. & Lawrence St.
HABS NY-4-19   s pd   L
Society of Friends Meetinghouse
Northern Blvd.
HABS NY-521   s p   L

Jackson Heights
LaGuardia Airport, Marine Air Terminal;
see New York Municipal Airport, Marine
Air Terminal
New York Municipal Airport, Marine Air Terminal (LaGuardia Airport, Marine
Air Terminal)
Bowery Bay, Grand Central Pkwy.
HAER NY-89   p   H

Long Island City
American Chicle Company Factory
Thomson Ave.
HAER NY-80   p   H
Bodine Castle
43-16 Vernon Blvd.
HABS NY-5465   pd   L

Maspeth
Hubb Estate
52-15 Flushing Ave.
HABS NY-522   s p   L
Woodward House
1891 Flushing Ave.
HABS NY-527   p   L

New York City
Blackwell's Island Bridge (Queensboro
Bridge)
Second Ave. to Northern Blvd., Long Island
City
HAER NY-19   p   H
Queensboro Bridge; see Blackwell's Island
Bridge

Queens
Mel's Diner
3046 College Point Blvd.
HABS NY-6113   s   H

Ridgewood
Covert House
1410 Flushing Ave.
HABS NY-525   p   L
Van Anda House (Vander
Ende-Onderdonk House)
1416 Flushing Ave.
HABS NY-524   s p   L
Vander Ende-Onderdonk House; see Van
Anda House
Wyckoff Farmhand House
1306 Flushing Ave.
HABS NY-526   p   L

RENSSELAER COUNTY

East Greenbush
Breese, Jan, House (De Bries, Hendrick,
House)
Castleton Rd.
HABS NY-5-A-2   s pd   L
De Bries, Hendrick, House; see Breese, Jan,
House

Melrose vic.
Greens, Richard, House
HABS NY-3142   p   L

Petersburg
Baptist Church
State Rt. 22
HABS NY-6114   p   L
Gardner House
State Rt. 22
HABS NY-3136   pd   L

Petersburg vic.
Reynolds, Elijah, House
State Rt. 22
HABS NY-6243   pd   L

Rensselaer
Beverwyck (Van Rensselaer, William
Patterson, House)
Washinghton Ave. ext.
HABS NY-5-A-10   s pd   L
Crailo, The (Fort Crailo; Van Rensselaer
House)
10 Riverside Dr.
HABS NY-3105   pd   L
Fort Crailo; see Crailo, The
Genet, Citizen, House (Prospect Hill)
HABS NY-3160   p   L
Prospect Hill; see Genet, Citizen, House
Van Rensselaer House; see Crailo, The
Van Rensselaer, William Patterson, House;
see Beverwyck

Schaghticoke vic.
Banker House
HABS NY-3130   p   L

Troy
Burden Iron Company; see Burden Iron
Works
**Burden Iron Company, Lower (Steam)
Works;** see Burden Iron Works, Lower
(Steam) Works
Burden Iron Company, Office Building;
see Burden Iron Works, Office Building
**Burden Iron Company, Upper (Water)
Works;** see Burden Iron Works, Upper
(Water) Works
Burden Iron Company, Water Wheel; see
Burden Iron Works, Water Wheel
Burden Iron Works (Burden Iron
Company)
Wynants Kill & Burden St.
HAER NY-7   pd   L
Burden Iron Works, Lower (Steam) Works
(Burden Iron Company, Lower (Steam)
Works)
Hudson River, Wynants Kill vic.
HAER NY-7-C   p   L
Burden Iron Works, Office Building
(Burden Iron Company, Office Building)
Polk St.
HABS NY-5524
HAER NY-7-D   pd   L
Burden Iron Works, Upper (Water) Works
(Burden Iron Company, Upper (Water)
Works)
Burden St. & Wynants Kill
HAER NY-7-A   p   L
Burden Iron Works, Water Wheel (Burden
Iron Company, Water Wheel)
U.S. Rt. 4
HAER NY-7-B   p   L
Church of the Holy Cross
Eighth & Grand Sts.
HABS NY-6257   s pd   H

Cluett, Albert, House (Howard House;
Hart House)
59 Second St.
HABS NY-5-A-3   s pd   L

District School Number 1
N. Greenbush Rd.
HABS NY-329   s p d   L
Gurley, W. & L. E., Building
514 Fulton St.
HABS NY-5532
HAER NY-13   p d   L
Hart House; see Cluett, Albert, House
House, Gothic Revival
HABS NY-3239   p   L
Howard House; see Cluett, Albert, House
Rensselaer Iron Works, Rail Mill
Adams St. & Hudson River
HABS NY-5523
HAER NY-3   s p d   L
St. John's Rectory (Balcony)
First & Liberty Sts.
HABS NY-358   s p d   L
Troy Gas Light Company, Gasholder House
Jefferson St. & Fifth Ave.
HABS NY-5522
HAER NY-2   s p d   L
Vail, Thomas Samuel, House
46 First St.
HABS NY-5-A-7   s p d   L
Warren Family Chapel
Oakwood Cemetery
HABS NY-6253   s   H

RICHMOND COUNTY

Dongan Hills; see Perine House
Perine House (Dongan Hills)
1476 Richmond Rd.
HABS NY-4371   p   L

000

Tysen, Jacob, House
355 Fillmore St.
HABS NY-6117   s   H

New Brighton

Sailors' Snug Harbor
Richmond Terrace, Tysen Ave. & Delafield Place
HABS NY-5473   s p d   L H
Sailors' Snug Harbor, Building A; see Sailors' Snug Harbor, Dormitory
Sailors' Snug Harbor, Building B; see Sailors' Snug Harbor, Dormitory
Sailors' Snug Harbor, Building C; see Sailors' Snug Harbor, Dormitory & Admin. Building
Sailors' Snug Harbor, Building D; see Sailors' Snug Harbor, Dormitory
Sailors' Snug Harbor, Building E; see Sailors' Snug Harbor, Dormitory
Sailors' Snug Harbor, Captain's Cottage No. 2
Richmond Terrace
HABS NY-6244   s   H

Sailors' Snug Harbor, Chapel
Richmond Terrace
HABS NY-5480   s p d   L H
Sailors' Snug Harbor, Dining Hall (Sailors' Snug Harbor, Infirmary)
Richmond Terrace
HABS NY-5479   p d   L
Sailors' Snug Harbor, Dormitory (Sailors' Snug Harbor, Building B)
Richmond Terrace
HABS NY-5475   d   L
Sailors' Snug Harbor, Dormitory (Sailors' Snug Harbor, Building E)
Richmond Terrace
HABS NY-5478   s d   L H
Sailors' Snug Harbor, Dormitory (Sailors' Snug Harbor, Building A)
Richmond Terrace
HABS NY-5474   d   L
Sailors' Snug Harbor, Dormitory (Sailors' Snug Harbor, Building D)
Richmond Terrace
HABS NY-5477   s p d   L H
Sailors' Snug Harbor, Dormitory & Admin. Building (Sailors' Snug Harbor, Building C)
Richmond Terrace
HABS NY-5476   s p d   L H
Sailors' Snug Harbor, East Gatehouse
Richmond Terrace
HABS NY-5484   p d   L
Sailors' Snug Harbor, Governor's House
Richmond Terrace
HABS NY-6115   s   H
Sailors' Snug Harbor, Infirmary; see Sailors' Snug Harbor, Dining Hall
Sailors' Snug Harbor, Main Gatehouse (Sailors' Snug Harbor, North Gatehouse)
Richmond Terrace
HABS NY-5482   s p d   L H
Sailors' Snug Harbor, Music Hall
Richmond Terrace
HABS NY-6116   s   H
Sailors' Snug Harbor, North Gatehouse; see Sailors' Snug Harbor, Main Gatehouse
Sailors' Snug Harbor, Recreation Building
Richmond Terrace
HABS NY-6245   s   H
Sailors' Snug Harbor, Residences
Richmond Terrace
HABS NY-5481   p d   L
Sailors' Snug Harbor, West Gatehouse
Richmond Terrace
HABS NY-5483   s p d   L H

New Dorp

Britton-Cubberly House
New Dorp Ln.
HABS NY-4-5   s p d   L

Clausen House
291 New Dorp Ln.
HABS NY-4374   p   L

Lake-Tysen House
Cobbs Ave.
HABS NY-4373   p   L
Miller Field, Seaplane Hangar
New Dorp Ln.
HABS NY-5671   s   H

Richmond

Cortelyou House
HABS NY-4372   p   L

Rosebank

Austen, Elizabeth Alice, House
2 Hyland Blvd.
HABS NY-5472   p d   L

Tottenville

Billop House (Conference House)
Hylan Blvd.
HABS NY-4370   p   L
Conference House; see Billop House

ROCKLAND COUNTY

Germonds

Barn, The Old
HABS NY-4121   s p   L

Nyack

Erie Railroad, Nyack Station
Railroad Ave.
HAER NY-96   p   H

Orangeburg vic.

Van Houten House
HABS NY-4120   s p   L

Palisades

House, the Big
State Rt. 9W vic.
HABS NY-4122   s p d   L

Pearl River vic.

Sickles House
HABS NY-4119   s p   L

Sparkill

Sparkill Passenger Station
HAER NY-137   p   H

Tappan

Andre, Major, House (Prison) ('Seventy-six House)
Main St.
HABS NY-4-18   s p d   L
Bake House, Old
HABS NY-4362   p   L
De Windt House
Livingston Ave. & Oak Tree Rd.
HABS NY-4123   s p   L
Dutch Reformed Church
Main St.
HABS NY-4357   p   L
'Seventy-six House; see Andre, Major, House (Prison)

Tompkins Cove
Boulderburg
HABS NY-6119   s   H

SARATOGA COUNTY

Ballston Lake
Hawkwood Mansion
HABS NY-6246   p   L

Ballston Lake vic.
Buell House; see Palmer House
Palmer House (Buell House)
HABS NY-6247   p   L

Ballston Spa
First Presbyterian Church
High & Bath Sts.
HABS NY-3207   p   L

Burnt Hills
Kingsley, William, Tavern
Saratoga & Charlton Rds.
HABS NY-3209   p   L

Charlton
Methodist Episcopal & Freehold Presbyt. Church
Charleston Rd.
HABS NY-3211   pd   L

Grooms Corners
Best, Robert, House
HABS NY-3215   p   L

High Bridge vic.
Pashley House
HABS NY-3137   p   L

Malta
Round Lake Association
HABS NY-6120   s   H

Rexford
Erie Canal (Enlarged), Rexford Aqueduct;
see Erie Canal (Enlarged), Upper
Mohawk River Aqueduct
Erie Canal (Enlarged), Upper Mohawk River Aqueduct (Erie Canal (Enlarged), Rexford Aqueduct)
Mohawk River, State Rt. 146
HABS NY-5531
HAER NY-12   pd   L

Saratoga
Bryan Inn
High Rock Spring
HABS NY-3131   p   L
Champlain & Hudson Canal
HABS NY-6121   p   H
Schuyler House
Saratoga National Historic Park
HABS NY-6122   p   H

Saratoga vic.
Bridge, Old
HABS NY-3157-C   p   L

Main Mill Building
HABS NY-3157-A   p   L
Mill Group, Old
HABS NY-3157   p   L
Mill Owner's House
HABS NY-3157-B   p   L
Original Church (Ruins)
HABS NY-3157-D   p   L

Stillwater
Neilson, John, House
Bemis Heights, Saratoga National Historic Park
HABS NY-3317   s pd   H

Vischers Ferry
Amity
HABS NY-3146   p   L

Waterford
Champlain Canal, Waterford Locks
U.S. Rt. 4
HABS NY-5534
HAER NY-14   pd   L

SCHENECTADY COUNTY

Alplaus
Alplaus School, Old
Maple Ave.
HABS NY-380   pd   L
Governor's Inn; see Yates, Governor, Summer Home
Stevens, Alex, Barn
HABS NY-3145   p   L
Stevens House
Alplaus Rd.
HABS NY-366   s pd   L H
Yates, Governor, Summer Home (Governor's Inn)
Maple Ave.
HABS NY-3138   p   L

Duanesburg
Christ Episcopal Church
State Rt. 20 & Church Rd.
HABS NY-331   pd   L
Duane House; see Featherstonhaugh Mansion
Featherstonhaugh Mansion (Duane House)
State Rt. 20
HABS NY-330   pd   L
North, Gen. William, House
N. Mansion Rd.
HABS NY-346   pd   L

Giffords
Cheeseman's Tavern
Western Turnpike
HABS NY-339   p   L

Glenville
Glenville Centre Reformed Church
Bolt Rd.
HABS NY-3219   p   L

Sanders, Joseph, House
HABS NY-6124   p   L
Van Epps Hotel
HABS NY-3214   p   L

Glenville Center
Syman House
HABS NY-3140   p   L

Niskayuna
Erie Canal (Enlarged), Rexford Aqueduct;
see Erie Canal (Enlarged), Upper
Mohawk River Aqueduct
Erie Canal (Enlarged), Upper Mohawk River Aqueduct (Erie Canal (Enlarged), Rexford Aqueduct)
(see NY, Rexford)
HABS NY-5531
HAER NY-12   pd   L
Niskayuna Reformed Church
State Rt. 7 (Troy Rd.)
HABS NY-351   pd   L
Tymeson House
HABS NY-6125   p   L

Pattersonville
Staley House
HABS NY-3148   p   L

Princetown
Liddle House
State Rt. 7 vic.
HABS NY-352   pd   L

Quaker Street Vil.
Society of Friends Meetinghouse
State Rt. 7
HABS NY-347   s pd   L

Rotterdam
Bradt House
Schermerhorn Rd. (State Rt. 5S)
HABS NY-353   pd   L
Schermerhorn House
Schermerhorn Rd. & State Rt. 5S
HABS NY-371   pd   L

Rotterdam Jct.
Mabie, John, House
River Rd. (State Rt. 55)
HABS NY-337   s pd   L
Van Slyck House
State Rt. 5S
HABS NY-5712   p   L

Rotterdam Twp.
Veeder Farm
Wescott Rd.
HABS NY-3123   p   L

Schenectady
Brandt, Capt. Arent, House
HABS NY-3223   pd   L
Brouwer-Rosa House (Rosa House)
14 N. Church St.
HABS NY-345   s pd   L

Courthouse, Old; see Schenectady County Courthouse
DeGraaf, Jeremiah, House
25-27 Front St.
HABS NY-3271 pd L
First Presbyterian Church
215 Union St.
HABS NY-3288 pd L
Forrest, David P., House
39 Front St.
HABS NY-3278 pd L
121 Front Street (House)
HABS NY-6126 p L
29 Front Street (House)
HABS NY-3221 p L
31 Front Street (House)
HABS NY-3222 p L
Glen, John, House
58 Washington Ave.
HABS NY-340 pd L
Kendall, Widow, House
10 N. Ferry St.
HABS NY-3282 pd L
Miller Farm, Old
Consaul Rd.
HABS NY-3124 p L
Mohawk Bank, Old
1 N. Church St.
HABS NY-349 p L
10-12 North Street (House)
HABS NY-6249 p L
13 North Street (House)
HABS NY-6248 p L
Peck, Jan, House
27 N. Ferry St.
HABS NY-3285 pd L
Rosa House; see Brouwer-Rosa House
Sanders, Robert, House
43-45 Washington Ave.
HABS NY-335 s pd L H
Schenectady County Courthouse
(Courthouse, Old)
108 Union St.
HABS NY-334 s pd L H
Schnectady County Clerk's Office
13 Union St.
HABS NY-6127 s H
9 South Church Street (Mantels)
HABS NY-3226 p L
St. George's Church
20-30 N. Ferry St.
HABS NY-344 s pd L H
Tenant Houses
Cottage Row
HABS NY-3283 pd L
Union College, North & South College, Old
Union St.
HABS NY-348 p L
Union College, Nott Memorial Library
HABS NY-3270 pd L
201 Union Street (House)
HABS NY-3284 pd L

Van Guysling House
HABS NY-374 pd L
Van Slyck, Adrian, House
114 Front St.
HABS NY-3273 pd L
Veeder Farmhouse
2201 Rosendale Rd.
HABS NY-3279 pd L
Veeder, Nicholas, House
104-106 Front St.
HABS NY-3281 pd L
Veeder, Nicholas, Slave House
205 Green St.
HABS NY-3280 pd L
Vrooman, Adam, House
119 Front St.
HABS NY-3286 pd L
Vrooman, Adam, Kitchen
119 Front St.
HABS NY-3287 pd L
Yates, Abraham, House
109 Union St.
HABS NY-336 s pd L
Yates, Governor, House
17 Front St.
HABS NY-6250 p L
Yates, Joseph, House
26 Front St.
HABS NY-6128 p L

Scotia
Glen, Abraham, House
Mohawk Ave.
HABS NY-338 pd L
Glen-Sanders House
2 Sanders Ave.
HABS NY-5-A-1 s pd L

SCHOHARIE COUNTY

Berne vic.
House, Stone
Old Schoharie Turnpike
HABS NY-6101 p L

Breadabeen
Chichester, L. H., House
HABS NY-3208 p L

Esperance
Presbyterian Church
HABS NY-3135 p L

Middleburg
Reformed Church
HABS NY-3133 p L

North Blenheim
Blenheim Covered Bridge
Spanning Schoharie River
HABS NY-359 s pd L
Dutch Reformed Church
HABS NY-3235 p L

Schoharie
Fort, Old Stone; see Reformed Dutch Church
Lutheran Church, Old
HABS NY-3144 p L
Lutheran Parsonage
HABS NY-5490 p L
Reformed Dutch Church (Fort, Old Stone)
HABS NY-5491 p L
Swart's Tavern
HABS NY-5492 p L
U.S. Frigate Constitution, Cannon
(moved from MA, Charlestown)
HABS NY-5497 p L
Van Vrooman, Col. Peter, House
HABS NY-3125 p L

Schoharie vic.
Log Cabin
HABS NY-388 pd L

SCHUYLER COUNTY

Mecklenburg
Methodist Church
HABS NY-240 p L

SENECA COUNTY

Geneva
Rose Hill
HABS NY-6102 p H

Seneca Falls
Sackett, Garry V., House
W. Bayard & Sackett Sts.
HABS NY-2-21 s pd L
Stanton, Elizabeth Cady, House
32 Washington St.
HABS NY-6103 p H

STEUBEN COUNTY

Atlanta
Delaware, Lackawana & Western RR, Atlanta Station
Main & Beecher Sts.
HAER NY-58 p H

Corning
Erie Railroad, Corning Station
Erie Ave. & Pine St.
HAER NY-76 p H

Corning vic.
Erie Railroad, Corning Side Hill Cut
Chemung River
HAER NY-35 p H

Hornell
Erie Railroad, Hornell Erecting Shop
Canisteo River, Cedar St.
HAER NY-34 p H

Erie Railroad, Hornell Station
Loder St.
HAER NY-33　　　　　　　p　　H
Merrill Silk Mill
HAER NY-126　　　　　　pd　　L

Painted Post

Erie RR, Painted Post Passenger & Freight Station
Water St.
HAER NY-97　　　　　　　p　　H

SUFFOLK COUNTY

Amagansett

Conklin, Ananias, House
Main St.
HABS NY-5416　　　　s　　　L

Aqueboque

Corwin House
HABS NY-5422　　　　　p　　L

Babylon

Conklin, Nat, House
280 Deer Park Ave.
HABS NY-542　　　s pd　　L
Merrick Road (House)
HABS NY-6104　　　　s　　　H

Bridgehampton

Beebe Windmill
Atlantic Ocean Rd.
HAER NY-67　　　　s　　　H
Bull's Head Tavern; see Wick's Tavern
Hampton House
HABS NY-6105　　　　p　　L
Sayrelands
Montauk Hwy.
HABS NY-5619　　　　s　　　H
Wick's Tavern (Bull's Head Tavern)
Montauk Hwy.
HABS NY-5419　　　　s　　　L

Brookhaven

Town Clerk's Office
HABS NY-5423　　　　p　　L

Centereach

First Congregational Church
HABS NY-5425　　　　p　　H

Centerport

Suydam House
HABS NY-5420　　　　p　　L

Commack

Smith, Caleb, House & Slave House
HABS NY-5411　　　　p　　L

Cutchogue

Fleet-Goldsmith-Kendrick House
New Suffolk Ln.
HABS NY-5714　　　　p　　L
Horton-Wickham-Landon Barn
Kings Hwy.
HABS NY-5417　　　　s　　　L

Horton-Wickham-Landon House
Kings Hwy. (moved from NY, Southhold)
HABS NY-546　　　s p　　L

East Hampton

Clinton Academy
Main St.
HABS NY-4-24　　s pd　　L
Dominy House
N. Main St.
HABS NY-5418　　　s p　　L
Gardiner Windmill
Main St.
HABS NY-4-21　　s pd　　L
Home Sweet Home; see Payne, John Howard, Memorial
Hook Windmill
Main St. & State Rt. 27
HAER NY-105　　　s　　　H
House
HABS NY-6106　　　　p　　L
Mulford Farm House
James Lane
HABS NY-5412　　　　p　　L
Payne, John Howard, Memorial (Home Sweet Home)
James Ln.
HABS NY-547　　　s p　　L
Payne, John Howard, Memorial, Windmill
James Ln. (moved from Mill Hill & NY, Pantigo)
HABS NY-547-A　　　　p　　L

Gardner's Island

Gardner's Island Windmill
HAER NY-125　　　s　　　H

Greenlawn

Cedarcroft; see Laurel Lodge
Cedarcroft, Apartments; see Laurel Lodge, Apartments
Cedarcroft, Log Cabin; see Laurel Lodge, Log Cabin
Cedarcroft, Studio; see Laurel Lodge, Studio
Laurel Lodge (Cedarcroft)
Arbutus Rd.
HABS NY-5703　　　　pd　　L
Laurel Lodge, Apartments (Cedarcroft, Apartments)
Arbutus Rd.
HABS NY-5703-A　　　pd　　L
Laurel Lodge, Log Cabin (Cedarcroft, Log Cabin)
Arbutus Rd.
HABS NY-5703-C　　　pd　　L
Laurel Lodge, Studio (Cedarcroft, Studio)
Arbutus Rd.
HABS NY-5703-B　　　pd　　L

Hauppauge

Smith, Joshua Brewster, House
HABS NY-5414　　　　p　　L

Huntington

First Presbyterian Church
125 E. Main St.
HABS NY-5410　　　s p　　L H
Sammis, Silas, House
W. Neck Ave. & Sammis Rd.
HABS NY-544　　　s p　　L

Huntington, South

Barker Estate; see Carll Homestead
Carll Homestead (Barker Estate)
Melville Blvd.
HABS NY-543　　　s p　　L

Huntington vic.

Caumsett Manor
Lloyd Neck
HABS NY-6107　　　　pd　　H

Lloyd Harbor

Lefferts Tide Mills; see Van Wyck Tide Mills
Lloyd, Joseph, Manor House
Lloyd Harbor Rd. & Lloyd Ln.
HABS NY-5670　　　s p　　L
Van Wyck Tide Mills (Lefferts Tide Mills)
Huntington Harbor, Southdown Rd.
HAER NY-106　　　s p　　H

Lloyd Neck

Fort Hill
Cold Spring Harbor vic.
HABS NY-6108　　　　pd　　H

Mastic Beach

Floyd, Gen. William, House
Washington Ave. & Wavecrest Dr.
HABS NY-5427　　　s pd　　L

Melville

Smith, Isaac, Farmhouse
Upper Hollow & Pine Lawn Rds.
HABS NY-545　　　s p　　L

Pantigo

Payne, John Howard, Memorial, Windmill
Amagansett Rd. (moved to NY, East Hampton)
HABS NY-547-A　　　　p　　L

Sag Harbor

First Presbyterian Church (Whalers' Church)
HABS NY-548　　　　p　　L
House
HABS NY-5426　　　　p　　L
Whalers' Church; see First Presbyterian Church

Selden vic.

Lake Grove (House)
HABS NY-5424　　　　p　　L

Setauket

Castelma House
HABS NY-5413　　　　p　　L
Thompson, Benjamin, House
HABS NY-549　　　　p　　L

Smithtown

Mills, Moses, House
HABS NY-5421   p   L

Presbyterian Church
HABS NY-6109   p   H

Smith, Obediah, House
853 Saint Johnland Rd., San Remo
HABS NY-6110   s pd   H

St. James vic.

Mills Pond House
660 N. Country Rd. (State Rt. 25A)
HABS NY-5668   s pd   L

Wainscott

Osborne, Thomas, House
Wainscott Rd.
HABS NY-5415   s   L

Watermill vic.

Windmill
HAER NY-134   s   H

West Hills

Whitman, Walt, Birthplace
Amityville Rd. (State Rt. 110)
HABS NY-541   s pd   L

SULLIVAN COUNTY

Callicoon

**Erie Railroad, Callicoon Passenger &
    Freight Sta.**
Main St.
HAER NY-65   p   H

Minisink Ford

**Delaware & Hudson Canal, Delaware
    Aqueduct**
(see PA, Lackawaxen)
HABS NY-5529
HAER PA-1   s pd   L

Philippsport

Store, Old
HABS NY-6129   p   L

TIOGA COUNTY

Owego

Lovejoy, Doctor, House
100 Front St.
HABS NY-5428   s pd   L H

Pumpelly, Harmon, House
    (Pumpelly-Parker House)
113 Front St.
HABS NY-5460   pd   L

Pumpelly-Parker House; see Pumpelly,
    Harmon, House

TOMPKINS COUNTY

Ithaca

Congregational Church
N. Geneva & W. Seneca Sts.
HABS NY-5441   p   H

Lehigh Valley Railroad Station
W. Buffalo St. & Taughannock Blvd.
HABS NY-5630   p   H

Tompkins County Courthouse (second)
E. Court St.
HABS NY-5442   pd   H

ULSTER COUNTY

Ellenville

Reformed Church
HABS NY-4381   p   L

Gardiner

Deyo-Bevier House
Ireland's Corners
HABS NY-4365   p   L

Le Fevre, Matthew, House
HABS NY-4366   p   L

High Falls

Canal Locks & Dupuy House
HABS NY-4375   p   L

De Motte House
Delaware & Hudson Canal
HABS NY-4383   p   L

Hurley

DuMond House (Spy House; Guard House,
    Old)
Main St. (State Hwy. 6)
HABS NY-4-302   s pd   L

Guard House, Old; see DuMond House

Hasbrouck House
HABS NY-4382   p   L

Hurley Street (House)
HABS NY-4376   p   L

Spy House; see DuMond House

Van Deusen, Capt. Jan, House
Hurley St.
HABS NY-4369   p   L

Hurley vic.

Well Head Cover
HABS NY-4377   p   L

Kerhonkson

Hardenbergh, Johannes, House
HABS NY-4125   s p   L

Kingston

Clinton Avenue Historic District (Nichols,
    Albert G., House)
296-300 Clinton Ave.
HABS NY-5561-D   pd   L

Clinton Avenue Historic District
HABS NY-5561   s pd   L

Clinton Avenue Historic District (Smith
    House, South)
290 Clinton Ave.
HABS NY-5561-B   pd   L

Clinton Avenue Historic District
    (Newcomb House)
304 Clinton Ave.
HABS NY-5561-E   pd   L

Clinton Avenue Historic District (Van
    Gaasbeek, Thomas, House)
308 Clinton Ave.
HABS NY-5561-G   pd   L

Clinton Avenue Historic District (Smith
    House, North)
294 Clinton Ave.
HABS NY-5561-C   pd   L

Clinton Avenue Historic District (Peters
    House)
306 Clinton Ave.
HABS NY-5561-F   pd   L

Clinton Avenue Historic Distrtict
    (Westbrook, Frederick L., House)
286 Clinton Ave.
HABS NY-5561-A   pd   L

Dutch Church, Old; see Reformed
    Protestant Dutch Church

Fair Street Reformed Dutch Church; see
    Second Reformed Dutch Church

Fireman's Hall
267 Fair St.
HABS NY-5672   p   L

First Post Office; see
    Vandenburgh-Hasbrouck House

Jansen House
HABS NY-3230   p   L

Kiersted, Dr. Luke, House
93 John St.
HABS NY-5559   s pd   L

Kingston Bank (Kingston Trust Company)
27 Main St.
HABS NY-5571   pd   L

Kingston City Hall
408 Broadway
HABS NY-5570   pd   L

Kingston Trust Company; see Kingston
    Bank

Loughran, Dr. Robert, House
296 Fair St.
HABS NY-5560   s pd   L

Newcomb House; see Clinton Avenue
    Historic District

Nichols, Albert G., House; see Clinton
    Avenue Historic District

Pearl & Wall Streets (House)
HABS NY-3229   p   L

Peters House; see Clinton Avenue Historic
    District

Philips, Christian F., House
120 Saint James St.
HABS NY-5572   s pd   L

Reformed Protestant Dutch Church (Dutch
    Church, Old)
Main St.
HABS NY-5573   pd   L

Second Reformed Dutch Church (Fair
    Street Reformed Dutch Church)
209 Fair St.
HABS NY-5569   pd   L

Senate House (Ten Broeck House)
HABS NY-4360   p   L

Slight, Henry, House
Green & Crown Sts.
HABS NY-3228   p   L

Smith House, North; see Clinton Avenue
    Historic District

Smith House, South; see Clinton Avenue
    Historic District

Sudam, John, House
Wall & Main Sts.
HABS NY-4-301   s pd   L

Ten Broeck House; see Senate House

Tompkins, Edward, Well House
Grove St.
HABS NY-5574   s   L

Tremper, John, House
3 N. Front St.
HABS NY-5557   s pd   L

Van Gaasbeek, Thomas, House; see Clinton
    Avenue Historic District

Van Weye-Van Keuren House
138 Green St.
HABS NY-5575   pd   L

Vandenburgh-Hasbrouck House (First Post
    Office; Weels, Jacobus, Cabinet Shop)
10 Crown St.
HABS NY-3227   s pd   L

Weeks, James B., House
26 Pearl St.
HABS NY-3103   s pd   L

Weels, Jacobus, Cabinet Shop; see
    Vandenburgh-Hasbrouck House

Wells, George & Solomen, House
106 Saint James St.
HABS NY-5576   pd   L

Westbrook, Frederick L., House; see
    Clinton Avenue Historic Distrtict

Whittaker-Hoffman House
N. Front & Green Sts.
HABS NY-5556   s pd   L

Kingston vic.

Fitch, S. & W. B., Depot & Office Building
Abeel St.
HABS NY-5558   s pd   L

Ten Broeck, Benjamin, House
Flatbush
HABS NY-6131   p   L

Marbletown

Bevier, Louis, House
State Rt. 213 vic.
HABS NY-4361   s p   L

Napanoch

Bevier, Cornelius, House
HABS NY-4132   p   L

Conrad-Bevier House (Ruins)
HABS NY-4126   p   L

New Paltz

Bevier-Elting House
Hugenot St. & Broadhead Ave.
HABS NY-4-304   s pd   L

Fort Dubois
81 Hugenot St.
HABS NY-6132   s d   H

Freer, Hughes, House
32 Hugenot St.
HABS NY-4-303   s pd   L

Hasbrouck, Abraham, House
Hugenot St.
HABS NY-4363   p   L

Hasbrouck, Jean, House
Hugenot St.
HABS NY-471   s pd   L

Hasbrouck, Oscar, House
Rt. 299 vic.
HABS NY-4364   p   L

New Paltz vic.

Hasbrouck, Col. Josiah, House; see Locust
    Lawn

Hasbrouck, Col. Josiah, Well House; see
    Locust Lawn, Well House

House
HABS NY-4368   p   L

LeFevre House, Old
Wallkill River
HABS NY-4386   p   L

Locust Lawn (Hasbrouck, Col. Josiah,
    House)
State Rt. 32
HABS NY-4388   s pd   L

Locust Lawn, Well House (Hasbrouck, Col.
    Josiah, Well House)
State Rt. 32
HABS NY-4367   pd   L

Mohonk Mountain House
Mountain Rest Rd.
HABS NY-5700   pd   L

Rifton

Perrine's Bridge
Spanning Wallkill River
HABS NY-4-204   s pd   L

Shawangunk

Decker, Johannes, Barn
HABS NY-6133   s   H

Decker, Johannes, Coach House
HABS NY-6134   s   H

Decker, Johannes, House
HABS NY-6135   s pd   H

Decker, Johannes, Icehouse
HABS NY-6136   s   H

Stone Ridge

Lounsberry House; see
    Wynkoop-Lounsberry House

Sally Tock Tavern; see Sally Tock's Inn

Sally Tock's Inn (Sally Tock Tavern)
HABS NY-4384   p   L

Wynkoop-Lounsberry House (Lounsberry
    House)
HABS NY-4387   p   L

Wawarsing

Bruin House
HABS NY-4128   p   L

DePuy House
HABS NY-4127   p   L

WASHINGTON COUNTY

Fort Ann

House, Old Stone (Library)
HABS NY-6139   p   L

House, Oldest
HABS NY-6137   p   L

House, Stone
HABS NY-6138   p   L

Kingsbury

Schoolhouse, Stone
HABS NY-6140   p   L

WESTCHESTER COUNTY

Croton Aqueduct, Old
HAER NY-120   p   H

New Croton Dam & Reservoir
Croton River
HAER NY-132   pd   L

Bedford

Baylis House
Bedford Green
HABS NY-4112   s pd   L

Schoolhouse & Post Office
Bedford Green
HABS NY-4111-A   s pd   L

Chappaqua

Greely, Horace, House; see Rehoboth

Rehoboth (Greely, Horace, House)
HABS NY-4124   p   L

Chappaqua vic.

Society of Friends Meetinghouse
Pine's Bridge Rd.
HABS NY-4-102   s pd   L

Dobbs Ferry

**Croton Aqueduct, Old-Maintenance
    Building**
Walnut St.
HAER NY-116   s   L

Croton Aqueduct, Old-Overseer's House
Walnut St.
HAER NY-115   s   L

Kendall, Messmore, House (Livingston
    House)
Albany Post Rd.
HABS NY-4-105   s pd   L

Livingston House; see Kendall, Messmore,
    House

Greenburgh

Odell House (Rochambeau Headquarters)
425 Ridge Rd.
HABS NY-6141   d   H

Rochambeau Headquarters; see Odell
    House

Hastings-on-Hudson

**Croton Aqueduct, Old-Quarry Railroad
    Bridge**
Warburton Ave.
HAER NY-117   s   L

Irvington

Armour-Stiner House
45 W. Clinton Ave.
HABS NY-5620   s p d   H

**Croton Aqueduct, Old-Jewell's Brook
    Culvert**
Station Rd.
HAER NY-114   s   L

Odell Inn
S. Broadway
HABS NY-4109   pd   L

Katonah

Jay, John, House
State Rt. 22
HABS NY-4393   p   H

Mamaroneck

Town Hall, Old
Prospect Ave.
HABS NY-4114   s p d   L

Mount Vernon

St. Paul's Church (St. Paul's Church
    National Historic Site)
Boston Post Rd., Eastchester
HABS NY-4121   s d   L H

St. Paul's Church National Historic Site;
    see St. Paul's Church

New Rochelle

Paine, Thomas, House
Paine & North Aves.
HABS NY-4120   p   L

Parcot-Drake House (Door)
75 Eastchester Rd.
HABS NY-6142   p   L

North Salem

June House, Outhouse
HABS NY-4116   s p d   L

North Tarrytown

Croton Aqueduct, Old-Mill River Culvert
Sleepy Hollow Cemetery, U.S. Rt. 9 vic.
HAER NY-112   s   L

**Croton Aqueduct, Old-Mill River Waste
    Weir**
Sleepy Hollow Cemetery, U.S. Rt. 9 vic.
HAER NY-113   s   L

First Dutch Reformed Church; see Old
    Dutch Reformed Church

Old Dutch Reformed Church (Sleepy
    Hollow Church; First Dutch Reformed
    Church)
Albany Post Rd. (U.S. Rt. 9)
HABS NY-6143   s p   H

Sleepy Hollow Church; see Old Dutch
    Reformed Church

Ossining

Croton Aqueduct, Old-North Waste Weir
Snowden Ave.
HAER NY-109   s   L

**Croton Aqueduct, Old-Sing Sing Kill
    Bridge**
Aqueduct Rd. & Broadway
HAER NY-110   s   L

**Croton Aqueduct, Old-Ventilator Number
9**
Spring St. & Everett Ave.
HAER NY-111   s   L

Main Street Crescent
209-217 Main St.
HABS NY-5704   pd   L

Ossining vic.

**Croton Aqueduct, Old-Indian Creek
    Culvert**
Reservoir Rd.
HAER NY-108   s   L

Pleasantville

Earle House; see St. John's Church, Rectory
St. John's Church, Rectory (Earle House)
Bedford Rd.
HABS NY-4110   s p   L

Rye

Kirby Mill; see Tide Mill Yacht Basin
Parsons-Lounsbury House
Boston Post Rd.
HABS NY-4115   s p d   L

Square House
Purchase St.
HABS NY-6144   s d   H

Tide Mill Yacht Basin (Kirby Mill)
Kirby Ln.
HABS NY-6145   s d   H

Salem Center

Town Hall
HABS NY-4118   s p d   L

Scarsdale

Drovers' Tavern, Old; see Wayside Inn
Popham House
1015 Post Rd.
HABS NY-4-103   s p d   L

Scarsdale Library; see Wayside Inn
Wayside Inn (Drovers' Tavern, Old;
    Scarsdale Library)
Post Rd. & Wayside Ln.
HABS NY-4-104   s p d   L

Somers

Elephant Hotel
State Rt. 116 vic.
HABS NY-4-101   s p d   L

Tarrytown

Lyndhurst, Boat Landing
635 S. Broadway
HABS NY-5538-F   p   L

Lyndhurst, Greenhouse
635 S. Broadway
HABS NY-5538-B   p   L

Lyndhurst, Main House
635 S. Broadway
HABS NY-5538-A   s p d   L

Lyndhurst, Outbuildings
635 S. Broadway
HABS NY-5538-C   p   L

Lyndhurst, Stables
635 S. Broadway
HABS NY-5538-D   p   L

Lyndhurst, Swimming Pool
635 S. Broadway
HABS NY-5538-E   p   L

Requa House
575 S. Broadway
HABS NY-5552   s   H

Tarrytown vic.

Irving, Washington, House; see Sunnyside
Sunnyside (Irving, Washington, House)
U.S. Rt. 9
HABS NY-5637   s p   L

Valhalla vic.

Miller, Elijah, House
W. Lake Dr.
HABS NY-4113   s p d   L

Vancortlandville

St. Peter's Church
Hillside Cemetery
HABS NY-4-106   s p d   L

White Plains

Westchester County Courthouse
Main, Court, Grand Sts. & Martine Ave.
HABS NY-5701   s p   H

Yonkers

Croton Aqueduct, Old-Sawmill River Culvert
Nepperhan Ave.
HAER NY-118   s   L

Yorktown

Croton Aqueduct, Old-Entrance Entablature

Old Croton Dam Bridge vic.
HAER NY-107   s   L

WYOMING COUNTY

Portageville vic.

Erie Railroad, Buffalo Division, Bridge 361.66 (Erie Railroad, Portage Viaduct)
State Rt. 436
HAER NY-54   p   H

Erie Railroad, Portage Viaduct; see Erie Railroad, Buffalo Division, Bridge 361.66

Warsaw

Erie Railroad, Warsaw Passenger & Freight Station
Alt. U.S. Rt. 20
HAER NY-49   p   H

North Carolina

ALAMANCE COUNTY

Glencoe

Glencoe Cotton Mills
State Rts. 1598 & 1600
HAER NC-6   s pd   L

ANSON COUNTY

Morven vic.

Flower's Farm Cottage Press
State Rt. 1826
HAER NC-1   s pd   L

BEAUFORT COUNTY

Bath

Bonner, Capt. Joseph, House
Front & Main Sts.
HABS NC-206   s pd   H
Glebe House; see Williams House
Lucas-Tompkins House; see Williams House
Marsh House; see Palmer-Marsh House
Palmer-Marsh House (Marsh House)
Main St.
HABS NC-310   pd   L H
Palmer-Marsh Smokehouse
Main St.
HABS NC-311   pd   L
St. Thomas' Episcopal Church
Craven St.
HABS NC-274   p   L
Williams House (Lucas-Tompkins House; Glebe House)
Main & Craven Sts.
HABS NC-275   p   L

Washington

Fowle Warehouse
Respass & Main Sts.
HABS NC-210   s pd   H
Haven Warehouse
Van North & Main Sts.
HABS NC-209   s pd   H

BLADEN COUNTY

Elizabethtown

Greek Revival House (McDowell House)
State Rt. 1198 & NC Rt. 87
HABS NC-173   p   L
McDowell House; see Greek Revival House

Elizabethtown vic.

Neal-Brissom House; see Oakland
Oakland (Neal-Brissom House)
Cape Fear River & Rt. 21
HABS NC-135   pd   L

BRUNSWICK COUNTY

Brunswick Town

St. Philip's Church (Ruins)
State Rt. 1533
HABS NC-109   d   L

Southport

Bellamy House (Williamson House)
HABS NC-316   p   L
Fort Johnson
HABS NC-317   p   L
Williamson House; see Bellamy House

BUNCOMBE COUNTY

Asheville

Chateau Nollman; see Raven Cross Inn
Henrietta House (White House Inn)
78 Biltmore St.
HABS NC-276   p   L
Raven Cross Inn (Ravenscroft Inn; Chateau Nollman)
29 Ravenscroft Dr.
HABS NC-277   p   L
Ravenscroft Inn; see Raven Cross Inn
White House Inn; see Henrietta House

Fairview vic.

Sherrill's Inn
Lake Lure, U.S. Rt. 74
HABS NC-226   s   L

Old Trap vic.

Cartwright House (Williams House)
NC Rt. 343
HABS NC-51   pd   L
Williams House; see Cartwright House

Ridgecrest vic.

Swannanoa Tunnel
U.S. Rt. 70
HAER NC-12   d   L

CALDWELL COUNTY

Lenoir vic.

Fort Defiance (Lenoir, Gen. William, House)
State Rt. 268, Yadkin Valley
HABS NC-106   p   L
Lenoir, Gen. William, House; see Fort Defiance

Patterson

Clover Hill (Jones, Col. Edmond, House)
State Rt. 1514
HABS NC-142   p   L
Jones, Col. Edmond, House; see Clover Hill

Patterson vic.

Davenport, Col., House; see Walnut Fountain
Walnut Fountain (Davenport, Col., House)
NC Rt. 268
HABS NC-143   p   L

CAMDEN COUNTY

Camden

Camden County Courthouse
NC Rt. 343
HABS NC-69   pd   L

Camden vic.

Fairfield Hall; see Gregory, Gen. Isaac, House
Gregory, Gen. Isaac, House (Fairfield Hall)
State Rt. 1121
HABS NC-48   pd   L

Grice House (Grist House; Milford; Relfe-Grice-Sawyer House)
Ship Yard Ferry Rd.
HABS NC-16   pd   L
Grist House; see Grice House
Milford; see Grice House
Relfe-Grice-Sawyer House; see Grice House

South Mills vic.

Abbott House; see Gordon House
Gordon House (Hinton House; Abbott House)
State Rt. 1224
HABS NC-56   pd   L
Hinton House; see Gordon House
Morgan House
U.S. Rt. 17
HABS NC-27   pd   L

CARTERET COUNTY

Beaufort

Beaufort High School
Broad St. (moved from Courthouse Sq.)
HABS NC-225   s   L
Beaufort Jail, Old
Courthouse Sq. on Cedar St.
HABS NC-228   s   L
135 Craven Street (House) (Langdon House)
HABS NC-42   pd   L
Davis House (Inn, Old; Davis House Hotel)
121-123-125 Front St.
HABS NC-20   pd   L
Davis House Hotel; see Davis House
Duncan House
107 Front St.
HABS NC-28   pd   L
Easton House; see Thomas House
Henry, Jacob, House; see Thomas House
House, Joe, House (Nelson House)
205 Front St.
HABS NC-90   pd   L
Inn, Old; see Davis House
Langdon House; see 135 Craven Street (House)
Mace House
619 Ann St.
HABS NC-84   pd   L
Nelson House; see House, Joe, House
St. Paul's Episcopal Church
209 Ann St.
HABS NC-204   s   d   L H
Thomas House (Henry, Jacob, House; Easton House)
229 Front St.
HABS NC-87   pd   L

Beaufort vic.

Fort Macon
Bogue Point on Fort Macon Rd.
HABS NC-79   s pd   L

CASWELL COUNTY

Hamer vic.

Melrose; see Williams House
Williams House (Melrose)
NC Rt. 62 & State Rt. 1596
HABS NC-119   p   L

Locust Hill vic.

Moore House; see Stamp's Quarter
Stamp's Quarter (Moore House)
U.S. Rt. 158 vic.
HABS NC-118   p   L

Milton

Baptist Meetinghouse; see Milton Church
Clay House; see Irwin House
Irvine House; see Irwin House
Irwin House (Irvine House; Clay House)
High & Broad Sts.
HABS NC-114   p   L
Milton Church (Baptist Meetinghouse)
Warehouse St.
HABS NC-113   p   L
Row Houses (Union Tavern; Yellow Tavern)
Broad St.
HABS NC-110   p   L
Shops, Old
Broad St.
HABS NC-111   p   L
Stores, Old
Broad St.
HABS NC-112   p   L
Union Tavern; see Row Houses
Yellow Tavern; see Row Houses

Yanceyville

Caswell County Courthouse
Main St.
HABS NC-192   s pd   L H
Caswell News Building (Store, Brick)
W. Main St.
HABS NC-117   p   L
Dongola; see Graves, Jeremiah, House
Forest House; see Poteat Inn
Graves, Jeremiah, House (Dongola)
Main St.
HABS NC-115   p   L
Poteat Inn (Forest House)
N. Main & N. First Sts.
HABS NC-116   p   L
Store, Brick; see Caswell News Building
Womack's Mill
HAER NC-14   s pd   L

Yanceyville vic.

Graves House; see Pediment House
Pediment House (Graves House)
U.S. Rt. 158 & NC Rt. 86
HABS NC-120   p   L

CATAWBA COUNTY

Hickory

Wilson, Joe, House
Old Robinson Cemetery (moved from Startown Rd.)
HABS NC-216   s   L H

CHOWAN COUNTY

Edenton

Bandon
HABS NC-319   p   L
Beverley Hall (State Bank, Old)
114 W. King St.
HABS NC-190   p   L
Bockover House; see Everett House
Bond House; see Courthouse Green (House)
Booth House (William House; Burton House)
133 E. Church St. (moved to N. Granville St.)
HABS NC-77   pd   L
Burton House; see Booth House
Charlton House; see Sawyer House
Chowan County Courthouse
E. King St.
HABS NC-12-G-3   s pd   L
Courthouse Green (House) (Bond House)
405 Court St.
HABS NC-146   p   L
Cupola House (Eden, Gov., House)
408 S. Broad St.
HABS NC-2   s pd   L
Custom House, East; see Custom House, Old
Custom House, Old (Custom House, East)
403 Court St.
HABS NC-151   p   L
Eden, Gov., House; see Cupola House
Everett House (Wool House; Bockover House; Leigh House)
120 W. Queen St.
HABS NC-152   p   L
Hewes House; see Jones House
Iredell, James, House
107 E. Church St.
HABS NC-150   p   L
Jones House (Hewes House)
105 King St.
HABS NC-145   p   L
Leigh House; see Everett House
Page House (Pembroke Hall)
W. King St.
HABS NC-47   pd   L
Pembroke Hall; see Page House
Sawyer House (Charlton House)
206 W. Eden St.
HABS NC-147   p   L

State Bank, Old; see Beverley Hall
Warren, Dr., House; see Wessington
Wessington (Warren, Dr., House)
120 W. King St.
HABS NC-171   pd L
William House; see Booth House
Wool House; see Everett House

Edenton vic.
Athol (Benbury Hall; Skinner, Joshua, House)
State Rt. 1114
HABS NC-45   pd L
Benbury Hall; see Athol
Blount House; see Mulberry Hill
Coffield House
HABS NC-64   pd L
Coke Farm; see Hoskins Place
Dillard's Mill
HABS NC-318   p L
Hayes Manor (Hayes Plantation)
E. Water St. vic.
HABS NC-3   s pd L
Hayes Plantation; see Hayes Manor
Hoskins Place (Coke Farm)
U.S. Rt. 17 (moved to NC, Somerset vic.)
HABS NC-62   pd L
Mulberry Hill (Blount House)
Sound Shore Rd.
HABS NC-81   pd L
Sandy Point Plantation
Sound Shore Rd.
HABS NC-54   pd L
Skinner, Joshua, House; see Athol

Somerset vic.
Coke Farm; see Hoskins Place
Hoskins Place (Coke Farm)
Locust Grove Rd. vic. (moved from NC, Edenton Vic.)
HABS NC-62   p L

CRAVEN COUNTY

Edenton
St. Paul's Episcopal Church
W. Church & N. Broad Sts.
HABS NC-12-G-1   s pd L
St. Paul's Episcopal Church, Wall & Fence
W. Church & N. Broad Sts.
HABS NC-12-G-2   s L

New Bern
Academy, First (Central Elementary School)
New St. at Hancock
HABS NC-280   p L
108 Broad Street (House) (Hollister House; Swert-Shields House)
614 Broad St.
HABS NC-290   p L
109 Broad Street (House) (Hollister House)
613 Broad St.
HABS NC-70   pd L

Bryan, James Washington, House; see Bryan, Washington, House & Office
Bryan, Washington, House & Office (Bryan, James Washington, House)
603 & 605 Pollack St.
HABS NC-12-F-2   s pd L
45 Burn Street (House) (Gill, James, House; Burns House)
823 Pollock St.
HABS NC-279   p L
Burns House; see 45 Burn Street (House)
Burnside's Headquarters; see Slover House
Central Elementary School; see Academy, First
Clark House; see Davis House
Coor, James, House; see Gaston, Judge William, House
Coor-Gaston House; see Gaston, Judge William, House
130 Craven Street (House) (Jerkins-Dufy House)
301 Johnson St.
HABS NC-291   p L
120 Craven Street (Office); see Smallwood, Dr., Office
Craven-Nixon House; see Taylor-Ward House
Davis House (Clark House)
419 Metcalf St.
HABS NC-281   p L
Davis, Maj. James, House; see Hanff House
Donald, Judge, Law Office & House (Donnell, Judge, Law Office & House)
163 Craven St.
HABS NC-12-F-3   s pd L
Donnell, Judge, Law Office & House; see Donald, Judge, Law Office & House
First Presbyterian Church
New & Middle Sts.
HABS NC-12-F-1   s pd L
Gaston, Judge William, House (Coor, James, House; Coor-Gaston House)
421 Craven St.
HABS NC-125   p L
Gill, James, House; see 45 Burn Street (House)
Hancock House; see Lee House
Hanff House (Davis, Maj. James, House; Hanff-Metz House; Metz House)
313 George St.
HABS NC-278   p L
Hanff-Metz House; see Hanff House
Harvey House (Harvey Mansion)
219 Tryon Palace Dr.
HABS NC-282   p L
Harvey Mansion; see Harvey House
Hollister House; see 109 Broad Street (House)
Hollister House; see 108 Broad Street (House)
Ives, Allen, House (Mitchell-Bryan House)
211 Johnson St.
HABS NC-283   p L

Jarvis-Hand House; see Jarvis-Slover House
Jarvis-Slover House (Jones House; Jarvis-Hand House; Jones-Jarvis House)
528 E. Front St.
HABS NC-284   p L
Jerkins-Dufy House; see 130 Craven Street (House)
Jones House; see Jarvis-Slover House
Jones-Jarvis House; see Jarvis-Slover House
Lee House (Hancock House; McLin House)
507 Middle St.
HABS NC-52   pd L
Leech, Col., House; see Louisiana House
Louisiana House (Moulton-Clark House; Vail-Moulton House; Leech, Col., House)
515 E. Front St.
HABS NC-285   p L
Masonic Opera House; see Masonic Temple
Masonic Temple (St. John's Lodge Number 3, A. F. & A. M.; Masonic Opera House)
Hancock & Johnson Sts.
HABS NC-286   p L
McLin House; see Lee House
Metz House; see Hanff House
Mitchell-Bryan House; see Ives, Allen, House
Moulton-Clark House; see Louisiana House
New Bern City Schools Administration Building; see Roberts House
Nixon-Ward House; see Taylor-Ward House
Oaksmith House; see Simpson-Duffy House
O'Hara, R., House (Oliver House)
185 Pollack St. (moved to 512 E. Front St.)
HABS NC-166   pd L
Oliver House; see O'Hara, R., House
Roberts House (Tisdale-Jones House; New Bern City Schools Administration Building)
New & Metcalf Sts.
HABS NC-287   p L
Simpson-Duffy House (Oaksmith House; Simpson-Oaksmith-Patterson House)
E. Front & Pollack Sts.
HABS NC-288   p L
Simpson-Oaksmith-Patterson House; see Simpson-Duffy House
Slover House (Burnside's Headquarters; Slover-Bradham House; Slover-Guinon House)
E. Front & Johnson Sts.
HABS NC-289   p L
Slover-Bradham House; see Slover House
Slover-Guinon House; see Slover House

Smallwood, Dr., Office (120 Craven Street (Office))
505 Craven St.
HABS NC-247   p L

Smallwood, Eli, House; see Smallwood-Jones House

Smallwood-Jones House (Ward House; Smallwood, Eli, House)
524 E. Front St.
HABS NC-12-F-4   s pd   L
St. John's Lodge Number 3, A. F. & A. M.; see Masonic Temple
St. Paul's Catholic Church
510 Middle St.
HABS NC-53   pd   L
Stanly, John Wright, House
New St. (moved to 307 George St.)
HABS NC-67   pd   L
Swert-Shields House; see 108 Broad Street (House)
Taylor, Isaac, House; see Taylor-Ward House
Taylor-Ward House (Craven-Nixon House; Taylor, Isaac, House; Nixon-Ward House)
228 Craven St.
HABS NC-172   pd   L
Tisdale-Jones House; see Roberts House
Vail-Moulton House; see Louisiana House
Ward House; see Smallwood-Jones House

CUMBERLAND COUNTY

Fayetteville
Cool Spring Inn (Davis Inn, Old; MacKethan House)
Cool Spring St.
HABS NC-292   p   L
Davis Inn, Old; see Cool Spring Inn
309 Dick Street (House) (Nimocks House)
225 Dick St.
HABS NC-298   p   L
First Presbyterian Church
Bow & Ann Sts.
HABS NC-294   p   L
Hotel, Old (Ironwork)
HABS NC-296   p   L
Liberty Point Store (Liberty Row)
Bow St. & Cool Spring Ln.
HABS NC-295   p   L
Liberty Row; see Liberty Point Store
MacKethan House; see Cool Spring Inn
Market House, Old
Hay, Green, Person & Gillespie Sts.
HABS NC-194   s p   L
McLaughlin House; see 456 Person Street (House)
445 Moore Street (House)
HABS NC-299   p   L
Nimocks House; see 309 Dick Street (House)
456 Person Street (House) (McLaughlin House)
HABS NC-293   p   L
Thorton House
219 Maiden Ln.
HABS NC-297   p   L

CURRITUCK COUNTY

Shawboro vic.
Culong; see Forbes House
Ferebee House; see Forbes House
Forbes House (Culong; Ferebee House)
State Rt. 1147
HABS NC-82   pd

DARE COUNTY

Duck vic.
Caffey's Inlet, Life-Saving Station
State Rt. 1200
HABS NC-207   s   d   H

DAVIDSON COUNTY

Lexington
Davidson County Courthouse, Old
Main & Center Sts.
HABS NC-300   p   L
Lexington vic.
Caldcleuch House
HABS NC-123   pd   L

DAVIE COUNTY

Mocksville vic.
Cooleemee Plantation (Hairston House)
U.S. Rt. 64
HABS NC-212   s   d   L
Hairston House; see Cooleemee Plantation

DUPLIN COUNTY

Faison vic.
Hill, Buckner, House; see Taylor-Hill House
Taylor-Hill House (Hill, Buckner, House)
State Rt. 1354
HABS NC-174   p   L

DURHAM COUNTY

Durham
American Tobacco Company
HAER NC-10   pd   L
Watts, George W., Liggett & Myers Tobacco Company
HAER NC-5   s   L

EDGECOMBE COUNTY

Tarboro
Cotton Press
Albermarle St. (moved from Norfleet Plantation)
HABS NC-60   s pd   L H

Lanier House (Pender-Lanier House)
1002 Main St.
HABS NC-26   pd   L
Pender-Lanier House; see Lanier House
Taylor, Brinson, & Aycock Law Offices; see Williams, Dr. Don, House
Williams, Dr. Don, House (Taylor, Brinson, & Aycock Law Offices)
Saint James St.
HABS NC-100   p   L
Tarboro vic.
Coolmore (Powell House)
U.S. Rt. 64
HABS NC-59   pd   L
Powell House; see Coolmore

FORSYTH COUNTY

Bethabara
Bethabara Parsonage (Brewers House; Mucke House; Mickey House)
U.S. Rt. 421
HABS NC-193   s pd   L
Brewers House; see Bethabara Parsonage
Mickey House; see Bethabara Parsonage
Mucke House; see Bethabara Parsonage
Bethania
Jones Livestock Barn; see Salem Tavern Barn
Jones Plantation Barn; see Salem Tavern Barn
Salem Tavern Barn (Jones Plantation Barn; Jones Livestock Barn)
Tobaccoville Rd. (moved to NC, Winston-Salem)
HABS NC-240   s   H
Clemmons
Fries Manaufacturing & Power Company, Idols Station
Yadkin River
HAER NC-9   pd   L
Kernersville
Korner's Folly
271 S. Main St.
HABS NC-208   s pd   H
Korner's Folly, Brick Privy
271 S. Main St.
HABS NC-239   p   H
Old Town
Bethabara Moravian Church
2147 Bethabara Rd. (State Rt. 1681)
HABS NC-12-C-4   s pd   L
Winston-Salem
Anstalt; see Salem Boys School
Arista Mill, Rehabilitation Center
HAER NC-17   s   L
Belo House
455 S. Main St.
HABS NC-103   pd   L

547

Bishop's House; see 519 Church Street
(House)

Boner, John Henry, House; see Lick-Boner
House

Cape Fear Bank; see Loesch, Israel, Bank &
House

Chimney House
113 W. Walnut (moved to E. Tennessee)
HABS NC-242   p L

519 Church Street (House) (Bishop's
House; Minister's House)
HABS NC-301   p L

Ebert-Reich House; see Reich, Christian,
House

Girls Boarding School Annex; see Salem
College, Old Chapel Annex

Gothic Revival House (Steiner House;
Home Church Parsonage)
513 S. Church St.
HABS NC-246   p L

Home Church Parsonage; see Gothic
Revival House

Home Moravian Church
529 S. Church St.
HABS NC-134   p L

House of the Community Physician
(Vierling House)
463 S. Church St.
HABS NC-162   p L

Jones Livestock Barn; see Salem Tavern
Barn

Jones Plantation Barn; see Salem Tavern
Barn

Land Office Building, Old (Vorsteher
House; Warden House; Moravian
Archives & Music Foundation)
501 S. Main St.
HABS NC-104   p L

Leinbach, Henry, House
508 S. Main St.
HABS NC-12-C-2 s p d L

Lick-Boner House (Boner, John Henry,
House)
512 Salt St.
HABS NC-241   p L

Loesch, Israel, Bank & House (Cape Fear
Bank)
500 S. Main St.
HABS NC-243   p L

Minister's House; see 519 Church Street
(House)

Moravian Archives & Music Foundation;
see Land Office Building, Old

Reich, Christian, House (Ebert-Reich
House)
731 S. Main St.
HABS NC-244   p L

Salem Boys School (Wachovia Historical
Society Museum; Anstalt)
Main & Academy Sts.
HABS NC-12-C-1 s p d L

Salem College, Administration Building;
see Salem College, Office Building

Salem College, Alumnae House; see Salem
College, Old Chapel Annex

Salem College, Brothers House (Single
Brothers House; Single Brethren's House)
600 S. Main St.
HABS NC-102   p d L

Salem College, General View
Salem Square
HABS NC-141   p L

Salem College, Office Building (Salem
College, Administration Building)
9-11 Academy St.
HABS NC-158   p L

Salem College, Old Chapel Annex (Girls
Boarding School Annex; Salem College,
Alumnae House)
601 S. Church St.
HABS NC-95   p L

Salem College, Sisters House (Single Sisters
House)
619-621 S. Church St.
HABS NC-101   p d L

Salem Manufacturing Company, Arista
Cotton Mill
HAER NC-3   s p d L

Salem Tavern Barn (Jones Plantation Barn;
Jones Livestock Barn)
Old Salem, S. Main St. (moved from NC,
Bethania)
HABS NC-240   s H

Schulz House & Shoe Shop; see Turner
House

Single Brethren's House; see Salem College,
Brothers House

Single Brothers House; see Salem College,
Brothers House

Single Sisters House; see Salem College,
Sisters House

Steiner House; see Gothic Revival House

Tavern, The
800 S. Main St.
HABS NC-12-C-3 s p d L

Turner House (Schulz House & Shoe Shop)
712-714 S. Main St.
HABS NC-245   p L

Vierling House; see House of the
Community Physician

Vogler, Christoph, House
700 S. Main St.
HABS NC-105   p L

Vorsteher House; see Land Office Building,
Old

Wachovia Historical Society Museum; see
Salem Boys School

Warden House; see Land Office Building,
Old

Winston-Salem vic.

Rock, Adam Spach, House; see Spach,
Adam, House

Spach, Adam, House (Rock, Adam Spach,
House)
HABS NC-94   p L

FRANKLIN COUNTY

Jacksonville

Collins Place, Old
Warrenton Way (moved from NC,
Louisburg vic.)
HABS NC-224   s L

Louisburg

Person, Prudence, House
603 N. Main St.
HABS NC-180   p L

Shaw House
114 Main St.
HABS NC-181   p L

Louisburg vic.

Bunn Road; see Green Hill Place

Cascine (Perry House)
State Rt. 1702
HABS NC-6   s p d L

Cascine Mill; see Perry Mill

Collins Place, Old
State Rt. 561 (moved to NC, Jacksonville)
HABS NC-224   s L

Green Hill Place (Bunn Road)
State Rts. 1760 & 1761
HABS NC-183   p L

House, Early
HABS NC-182   p L

Perry House; see Cascine

Perry Mill (Cascine Mill)
U.S. Rt. 401
HABS NC-184   p L

Pearces

Las Perry Apple Mill & Press
HAER NC-13   d L

GASTON COUNTY

Mc Adenville

McAden Mill, Number 2
Main St.
HABS NC-199 s d H

GATES COUNTY

Buckland

Buckland; see Smith House

Smith House (Buckland)
NC Rt. 37
HABS NC-73   p d L

Gates vic.

Riddick House
U.S. Rt. 13
HABS NC-71   p d L

Riddick House, Little (Riddick House, Old)
U.S. Rt. 13
HABS NC-80   p d L

Riddick House, Old; see Riddick House,
Little

Gatesville vic.
Carter Farmhouse
State Rt. 1100
HABS NC-32 pd L
Carter Farms, Barns
State Rt. 1100
HABS NC-33 pd L
Hinton House
Main St.
HABS NC-50 pd L
Roberts, John, House
(moved to Carter Farm, State Rt. 1100)
HABS NC-34 pd L

Hobbsville vic.
Sumner-Winslow House; see Winslow House
Winslow House (Sumner-Winslow House)
NC Rt. 32
HABS NC-36 pd L

Mintonsville vic.
Walton House
State Rt. 1101
HABS NC-140 p L

Sandy Cross
Huffheimer House
HABS NC-88 pd L

Trotville vic.
Stallings, Whitmer, House (Whitstallings House)
State Rt. 1415
HABS NC-248 p L
Whitstallings House; see Stallings, Whitmer, House

GUILFORD COUNTY

Greensboro
Buick Motor Co. & Greensboro Motor Co. Dealerships
309 & 315 N. Elm St.
HABS NC-232 pd L
Dick, Judge, House; see Dunleith
Dunleith (Dick, Judge, House)
677 Chestnut St.
HABS NC-231 s L
Henry, O., Hotel
N. Elm & Bellemeade Sts.
HABS NC-233 pd L
Pomona Terra Cotta Company
HAER NC-2 s L

Jamestown
Friends School & Meetinghouse
(Jamestown Friends Meetinghouse; Quaker Meetinghouse)
High Point City Park
HABS NC-92 p L
Jamestown Friends Meetinghouse; see Friends School & Meetinghouse

McCulloch Gold Mill
Copper Branch, N. of State Rt. 1153
HAER NC-7 s pd L
Mendenhall House (Mendenhall, Richard, Plantation House)
U.S. Rt. 29-70A
HABS NC-37 pd L
Mendenhall, Richard, Plantation House; see Mendenhall House
Quaker Meetinghouse; see Friends School & Meetinghouse

Jamestown vic.
Mendenhall Counting House
HABS NC-97 p L

Oak Ridge
Benbow House
HABS NC-96 p L

HALIFAX COUNTY

Airlie vic.
Prospect Hill
HABS NC-157 pd L

Enfield vic.
Cedar Grove (Whitaker, Jack, House; Strawberry Hill)
Scotland Neck Rd.
HABS NC-227 s L
Strawberry Hill; see Cedar Grove
Whitaker, Jack, House; see Cedar Grove

Halifax
Clerk's Office, Old; see Halifax County Clerk's Office
Constitution House (Constitution-Burgess House)
E. of Market Sq.
HABS NC-29 pd L
Constitution-Burgess House; see Constitution House
Ferrell, Michael, Counting House (McMahon, Michael, Store)
Main St.
HABS NC-13 pd L
Gaol, Old; see Halifax County Jail
Grove, The
HABS NC-177 d L
Halifax County Clerk's Office (Clerk's Office, Old)
King & Market Sts.
HABS NC-15 s pd L
Halifax County Jail (Gaol, Old)
King St.
HABS NC-200 s L
House, Dutch Roof (Owens House)
Saint David St.
HABS NC-176 p L
McMahon, Michael, Store; see Ferrell, Michael, Counting House
Owens House; see House, Dutch Roof

Pope House (Sally-Billy House)
Saint Andrew's St. (moved from NC, Scotland Neck)
HABS NC-76 pd L
Sally-Billy House; see Pope House

Roanoke Rapids
Roanoke Navigational Canal
Weldon vic.
HABS NC-320 s H

Scotland Neck vic.
Durham Farm; see Smith House
Kelvin Grove; see Smith House
Pope House (Sally-Billy House)
State Rt. 1117 (moved to NC, Halifax)
HABS NC-76 pd L
Sally-Billy House; see Pope House
Smith House (Durham Farm; Kelvin Grove)
State Rt. 1118
HABS NC-66 pd L

Tillery vic.
Glen Burne; see Tillery, Junius, House
Hermitage, The; see Tillery, Junius, House
Tillery, Junius, House (Hermitage, The; Glen Burne)
NC Rt. 481
HABS NC-17 pd L

HAYWOOD COUNTY

Cataloochee
Tyne, Woody, Cabin
Great Smoky Mountains National Park
HABS NC-5 s pd L

Cataloochee vic.
Conrad, Jim, Smokehouse; see Pioneer Farmstead, Meat House
Pioneer Farmstead, Meat House (Conrad, Jim, Smokehouse)
(moved to NC, Newfound Gap vic.)
HABS NC-202 s L

HENDERSON COUNTY

Flat Rock
Buck House; see Memminger House
Church of St. John-in-the-Wilderness
U.S. Rt. 25
HABS NC-12-A-1 s pd L
Memminger House (Sandburg Estate; Buck House; Sandburg, Carl, National Historic Site)
State Rt. 1123
HABS NC-305 s H
Sandburg, Carl, National Historic Site; see Memminger House
Sandburg Estate; see Memminger House

Fletcher
Calvery Episcopal Church
U.S. Rt. 25
HABS NC-12-A-3 p L

Hendersonville
Dixon's Sanitorium; see Judson College
Fletcher House
NC Rt. 69
HABS NC-264 p L
Judson College (Western North Carolina Female College; Dixon's Sanitorium)
Third Ave. & W. Flemming St.
HABS NC-12-A-2 s pd L
St. James Episcopal Church
766 N. Main St.
HABS NC-249 p L
Western North Carolina Female College; see Judson College

Murfreesboro
Melrose; see Murfree House
Murfree House (Melrose)
100 E. Broad St.
HABS NC-14 pd L

HERTFORD COUNTY

Britton House
Main St.
HABS NC-12 pd L
Chowan College (Columns, The; McDowell Columns Building)
Jones Dr.
HABS NC-30 pd L
Columns, The; see Chowan College
Freeman House (Hertford Academy Building)
200 E. Broad St.
HABS NC-19 pd L
Harrell House (Pipkin, Dr. Isaac, House)
207 Wynne St.
HABS NC-11 pd L
Hertford Academy Building; see Freeman House
Hotel, Old (Lassiter Hotel)
417 W. Main St.
HABS NC-31 pd L
Lassiter Hotel; see Hotel, Old
McDowell Columns Building; see Chowan College
Methodist Church
HABS NC-98 p L
Murfree Law Office; see Post Office, Old
Pipkin, Dr. Isaac, House; see Harrell House
Post Office, Old (Murfree Law Office)
318 Williams St.
HABS NC-129 p L
Rea, William, Store; see White & Britton Store
Smith House
Williams & Fourth Sts.
HABS NC-74 pd L

Trader House (Wheeler House)
403 E. Broad St.
HABS NC-57 pd L
Vaughn, Uriah, House (Yeates-Myrick-Vaughn House)
415 W. Main St.
HABS NC-21 pd L
Wheeler House; see Trader House
White & Britton Store (Rea, William, Store)
Williams & Fifth Sts.
HABS NC-89 pd L
Williams House(Doorway)
320 Williams St.
HABS NC-130 p L
Yeates-Myrick-Vaughn House; see Vaughn, Uriah, House

IREDELL COUNTY

Mount Mourne
Houston Farmhouse
State Rt. 1102
HABS NC-155 p L
Morrison House; see Mount Mourne
Mount Mourne (Morrison House)
State Rts. 1170 & 1189
HABS NC-154 p L

JOHNSTON COUNTY

Smithfield
Hastings House
Johnston St. (moved to First St.)
HABS NC-303 s H

LINCOLN COUNTY

Iron Station vic.
Forney, David, Mansion; see Ingleside
Ingleside (Forney, David, Mansion)
State Rt. 1383
HABS NC-250 p L

Lincolnton vic.
Brevard House (Mount Tisgah; Mount Tirzah)
State Rt. 1360 vic.
HABS NC-251 p L
Mount Tirzah; see Brevard House
Mount Tisgah; see Brevard House

Maiden vic.
St. Matthew's Arbor (St. Matthew's Reformed Church Meeting Shed; St. Matthew's Reformed Church)
State Rt. 321
HABS NC-217 s L
St. Matthew's Reformed Church; see St. Matthew's Arbor
St. Matthew's Reformed Church Meeting Shed; see St. Matthew's Arbor

MCDOWELL COUNTY

Marion vic.
Carson House (Tavern, Old)
U.S. Rt. 70
HABS NC-144 p L
Tavern, Old; see Carson House

MECKLENBURG COUNTY

Caldwell vic.
Hickory Grove; see Wilson House
Wilson House (Hickory Grove)
NC Rt. 115
HABS NC-12-B-3 s p L

Charlotte
Sugaw Creek Presbyterian Church
101 Sugaw Creek Rd.
HABS NC-12-B-5 s pd L

Charlotte vic.
McIntyre Cabin; see McIntyre Log House
McIntyre Log House (McIntyre Cabin)
NC Rt. 271
HABS NC-12-B-4 s pd L
Wallis, Ezekial, Rock House
NC Rt. 27
HABS NC-12-B-1 s pd L
Whitley's Mill
State Rt. 2074
HABS NC-12-B-2 s pd L

Davidson
Davidson College, Chambers, Maxwell, Building
HABS NC-61 pd L
Davidson College, Eumanean Hall
HABS NC-12-B-7 s pd L
Davidson College, Philanthropic Hall
HABS NC-12-B-8 s pd L

MONTGOMERY COUNTY

Albemarle
Coggins Gold Mine, Rich-Cog Mining Company
HAER NC-4 s pd L

NASH COUNTY

Dortches
Dortch House
State Rt. 1527
HABS NC-68 pd L

Rocky Mount
Battle House
NC Rt. 43-48 (Falls Rd.)
HABS NC-201 s L

Rocky Mount Mills
Bunn House; see Lewis House
House, The Brick; see Lewis House

Lewis House (Stonewall; Bunn House; House, The Brick)
HABS NC-58   pd L
Stonewall; see Lewis House

NEW HANOVER COUNTY

Wilmington

Bellamy Mansion
503 Market St.
HABS NC-198   s d L H
Cassidey-Harper House; see Harper House
Dudley, Gov., House; see Dudley Mansion House
Dudley Mansion House (Dudley, Gov., House)
S. Front & Nun Sts.
HABS NC-307   p   L
Harper House (Cassidey-Harper House)
1-5 Church St.
HABS NC-252   p   L

NORTHAMPTON COUNTY

Jackson Vic

Ransom, Matt Whittaker, House; see Verona
Verona (Ransom, Matt Whittaker, House)
U.S. Rt. 158
HABS NC-214   s   L

ORANGE COUNTY

Chapel Hill

Chapel of the Cross
304 E. Franklin St.
HABS NC-195   s pd   L

Hillsborough

Berry Brick House
208 W. Queen St.
HABS NC-315   pd   H
Burke House (Heartsease; Burke-Heartt House)
113 E. Queen St.
HABS NC-159   pd   L H
Burke-Heartt House; see Burke House
Cottage, Frame, opposite Burke-Heartt House (Webb House)
E. Queen St.
HABS NC-267   p   L
Eagle Hall; see Masonic Lodge
Forrest, R. O., House; see Twin Chimneys
Hassell-Nash House (Nash House)
116 W. Queen St.
HABS NC-160   pd   L H
Heartsease; see Burke House
Hillsborough Presbyterian Church
Churton & W. Tryon Sts.
HABS NC-238   pd   H
King Street Opera House; see Masonic Lodge

Little Hawfields
HABS NC-164   L
Lloyd, T. E., House; see Nash Law Office
Masonic Hall; see Masonic Lodge
Masonic Lodge (Masonic Hall; Eagle Hall; King Street Opera House)
142 W. King St.
HABS NC-268   pd   L H
Moorefields
State Rt. 1135
HABS NC-271   pd   H
Murphy, Dr. Robert, House; see Seven Hearths
Nash House; see Hassell-Nash House
Nash Law Office (Lloyd, T. E., House)
143 W. Margaret Ln.
HABS NC-314   pd   H
Nash-Hooper House
118 W. Tryon St.
HABS NC-272   pd   H
Orange County Courthouse
King & Churton Sts.
HABS NC-191   s pd   L H
Palmer House (Patterson-Palmer House)
173 W. Margaret Lane
HABS NC-222   s pd   H
Patterson-Palmer House; see Palmer House
Ruffin, Chief Justice Thomas, Law Office
Burnside, Cameron Park
HABS NC-270   pd   H
Ruffin House (Ruffin-Roulhac House)
Churton & Orange Sts.
HABS NC-312   p   L
Ruffin-Roulhac House; see Ruffin House
Sans Souci Plantation
E. Corbin St. (Old North St.)
HABS NC-221   pd   H
Seven Hearths (Murphy, Dr. Robert, House)
157 E. King St.
HABS NC-223   s pd   H
St. Matthew's Episcopal Church
St. Mary's Rd.
HABS NC-273   pd   H
Twin Chimneys (Forrest, R. O., House)
168 W. King St.
HABS NC-313   p   H
Webb House; see Cottage, Frame, opposite Burke-Heartt House

Hillsborough vic.

Ayr Mount (Kirkland Place)
Saint Mary's Rd.
HABS NC-220   s pd   L H
Barracks, The (Hillsborough Military Academy)
Barracks Rd.
HABS NC-269   p   L
Hillsborough Military Academy; see Barracks, The
Kirkland Place; see Ayr Mount

PASQUOTANK COUNTY

Elizabeth City

Charles House
710 W. Colonial Ave.
HABS NC-170   pd   L
Christ Church
Church & McMorine Sts.
HABS NC-46   pd   L
Fearing House; see Grice-Fearing House
Grice-Fearing House (Fearing House)
200 S. Road St.
HABS NC-169   pd   L
Smithson House (Whitehurst-Temple House)
Newland Hwy.
HABS NC-168   pd   L
Whitehurst-Temple House; see Smithson House

Elizabeth City vic.

Blackbeard House; see House, Brick
House, Brick (House, Old Brick; Teach, Edward, House; Blackbeard House; Jackson House)
182 Brick House Ln.
HABS NC-65   pd   L
House, Old Brick; see House, Brick
Jackson House; see House, Brick
Teach, Edward, House; see House, Brick

Nixonton

Customs House; see Lane House
Lane House (Customs House)
State Rt. 1137
HABS NC-44   pd   L

PENDER COUNTY

Topsail Sound

Ashe's Neck; see Sloop Point Plantation
MacMillan House; see Sloop Point Plantation
Sloop Point Plantation (MacMillan House; Ashe's Neck)
U.S. Rt. 17, Holly Ridge vic.
HABS NC-219   s   L

PERQUIMANS COUNTY

Bethel vic.

Ashland (Skinner, John, House)
Harvey Point
HABS NC-25   pd   L
Bateman House
HABS NC-43   pd   L
Cedar Vale (Gatting House)
State Rt. 1339
HABS NC-49   pd   L
Felton, Elisha, House; see Pender House
Gatting House; see Cedar Vale
Harrell House
State Rt. 1347
HABS NC-253   p   L

Myers House (Myers-White House)
State Rt. 1347
HABS NC-22   pd   L
Myers-White House; see Myers House
Pender House (Felton, Elisha, House)
State Rt. 1339
HABS NC-99   p   L
Road Landing
State Rts. 1340 & 1339
HABS NC-86   pd   L
Skinner, John, House; see Ashland
White, Isaac, House; see White, Thomas, House
White, Thomas, House (White, Isaac, House)
State Rt. 1339
HABS NC-127   p   L

Hertford vic.
Cove Grove
State Rt. 1301
HABS NC-40   pd   L
Davenport House (Sanders House)
State Rt. 1336
HABS NC-78   pd   L
Fletcher-Skinner House; see Skinner House
Jones House; see Riverside
Newbold-White House; see White-Newbold House
Newby, David, House
State Rt. 1336 (moved from State Rt. 1300)
HABS NC-41   pd   L
Nixon House (Nixon-Fleetwood House)
State Rt. 1341
HABS NC-126   p   L
Nixon-Fleetwood House; see Nixon House
Riverside (Jones House; Winslow House)
State Rt. 1301
HABS NC-308   p   L
Sanders House; see Davenport House
Skinner House (Fletcher-Skinner House)
State Rt. 1301
HABS NC-55   pd   L
Sumner House (Sumnerville)
State Rt. 1300
HABS NC-63   pd   L
Sumnerville; see Sumner House
White House
State Rt. 1336
HABS NC-254   p   L
White House
State Rt. 1336
HABS NC-75-A   p   L
White-Newbold House (Newbold-White House)
State Rt. 1336
HABS NC-75   pd   L
Winslow House; see Riverside

New Hope vic.
Davis House (Sutton-Newby House)
State Rt. 1300
HABS NC-85   pd   L

Land's End; see Leigh House
Leigh House (Land's End)
State Rt. 1300
HABS NC-18   pd   L
Perry House
State Rt. 1300
HABS NC-133   pd   L
Stockton
State Rt. 1329
HABS NC-83   pd   L
Sutton-Newby House; see Davis House
Whedbee House
State Rt. 1316
HABS NC-39   pd   L

Winfall vic.
Belvidere; see Newby, Exum, House
Newby, Exum, House (Belvidere)
NC Rt. 37
HABS NC-38   pd   L

PERSON COUNTY

Woodsdale
Woodsdale Station
State Rt. 1322
HABS NC-304   s   H

POLK COUNTY

Columbus
Baptist Church (Columbus Baptist Church)
Main St. & Huston Rd.
HABS NC-255   p   L
Columbus Baptist Church; see Baptist Church
Polk County Courthouse
Courthouse St.
HABS NC-256   p   L
Polk County Jail, Old
Walker St.
HABS NC-257   p   L

RICHMOND COUNTY

Rockingham
Great Falls Mill (Richmond Manufacturing Company)
W. Washington & Broad Ave.
HABS NC-205   s   L
Richmond Manufacturing Company; see Great Falls Mill

ROBESON COUNTY

Lumber Bridge
Presbyterian Church
HABS NC-165   p   L

ROCKINGHAM COUNTY

Wentworth
Wright Tavern
NC Rt. 65
HABS NC-161   p   L

ROWAN COUNTY

Granite Quarry vic.
Braun, Michael, House (House, Old Stone)
State Rt. 2308
HABS NC-149   p   L
House, Old Stone; see Braun, Michael, House

Rockwell vic.
Grace Evangelical & Reformed Church; see Grace Lower Stone Church
Grace Lower Stone Church (Grace Evangelical & Reformed Church)
State Rts. 1221 & 2335
HABS NC-258   p   L
Organ Evangelical Lutheran Church (Zion Evangelical Lutheran Church)
State Rt. 1006
HABS NC-259   p   L
Zion Evangelical Lutheran Church; see Organ Evangelical Lutheran Church

Salisbury
Beacham's Seafoods Complex; see Yadkin Railway Headquarters Building
Davis House
303 S. Main St.
HABS NC-260   p   L
Eames, Richard, Building (Salisbury Supply & Commission Company Building)
220-222 N. Depot St.
HABS NC-234   pd   L
First Presbyterian Church
W. Innis & Jackson Sts.
HABS NC-218   s   L
Rowan County Courthouse
200 N. Main St.
HABS NC-12-B-6   s pd   L
Salisbury Supply & Commission Company Building; see Eames, Richard, Building
Swaringen Wholesale Grocery
210-216 N. Lee St.
HABS NC-235   pd   L
Toll House
Cardwell St.
HABS NC-261   p   L
Whitehead, Marcellus, House
223 N. Fulton St.
HABS NC-262   p   L
Yadkin Railway Headquarters Building (Beacham's Seafoods Complex)
120-132 E. Council St.
HABS NC-236   pd   L

Spencer
Southern Railway Spencer Shops
HAER NC-8   s pd   L

RUTHERFORD COUNTY

Spindale
Cox House; see Spindale Recreation House
Spindale Recreation House (Tavern, Old;
    Cox House)
101 Main St.
HABS NC-263   p   L
Tavern, Old; see Spindale Recreation
    House

SAMPSON COUNTY

Harrells vic.
Log Cabin
HABS NC-178   p   L
Seavy House
HABS NC-179   p   L

STANLEY COUNTY

Albemarle
Freeman-Marks House
112 N. Third St.
HABS NC-237   s   H

SURRY COUNTY

Mount Airy
Mount Airy Furniture Company
HAER NC-11   d   L

SWAIN COUNTY

Newfound Gap vic.
Conrad, Jim, Smokehouse; see Pioneer
    Farmstead Meat House
Pioneer Farmstead, Corn Crib (Queen, Joe,
    Place, Corn Crib)
U.S. 441 (moved from Thomas Divide)
HABS NC-302   s   H
Pioneer Farmstead Meat House (Conrad,
    Jim, Smokehouse)
U.S. Rt. 441 (moved from NC, Cataloochee
    vic.)
HABS NC-202   s   H
Pounding Mill
Pioneer Museum, Rt. 441 (moved from
    Deep Creek)
HABS NC-4   s pd   L H
Queen, Joe, Place, Corn Crib; see Pioneer
    Farmstead, Corn Crib

TYRRELL COUNTY

Creswell vic.
Magnolia
State Rt. 1118
HABS NC-72   pd   L

VANCE COUNTY

Henderson vic.
Ashland Plantation House
Satterwhite Rd.
HABS NC-213   s   L

Williamsboro
Burnside (Hunt-Hamilton House)
State Rt. 1335
HABS NC-167   p   L
House
HABS NC-187   p   L
Hunt-Hamilton House; see Burnside
St. John's Episcopal Church
State Rt. 1329
HABS NC-136   pd   L

WAKE COUNTY

Cary
Hines, Ambassador Walter, Birthplace; see
    Page, A. T. House
Page, A. T. House (Hines, Ambassador
    Walter, Birthplace)
Wilkenson St.
HABS NC-306   s   H

Falls
Falls of the Neuse Manufacturing Plant
HAER NC-18   pd   L

Raleigh
Bank of the State of North Carolina; see
    Christ Church Rectory
Christ Church Rectory (Bank of the State
    of North Carolina)
Wilmington St. & New Bern Ave.
HABS NC-196   s pd   L H
Christ Episcopal Church
120 E. Edenton St.
HABS NC-12-D-4 & 215 s pd   L
Haywood Hall
211 New Bern Ave.
HABS NC-229   s   L
Heck-Lee House; see Lee, Capt., House
Johnson, Andrew, Birthplace
Mordecai Place (moved from 123
    Fayetteville St.)
HABS NC-12-D-1   s   L
Lane, Joel, House (Wakefield Plantation)
728 Hargatt St.
HABS NC-12-D-2   s d L

Lee, Capt., House (Heck-Lee House)
503 E. Jones St.
HABS NC-230   s   L
Merriman-Wynne House; see Wynne
    House
State Capitol
Capitol Sq.
HABS NC-265   p   L
Vass, William, House
501 N. Halifax St.
HABS NC-12-D-3   s   L
Wakefield Plantation; see Lane, Joel, House
Wynne House (Merriman-Wynne House)
209 Ashe Ave.
HABS NC-197   s pd   L H

Raleigh vic.
Midway Plantation
U.S. Rt. 64
HABS NC-211   s   L

WARREN COUNTY

Henderson vic.
Montmorenci
HABS NC-93   p   L

Littleton
Little Manor; see Mosby Hall
Mosby Hall (Little Manor)
Mosby Ave.
HABS NC-156   p   L

Warrenton
Davis, Peter, Store
Front St.
HABS NC-1   s pd   L
Fitts-Palmer House; see Palmer House
Green, Otis, House (Green Tavern)
HABS NC-266   p   L
Green Tavern; see Green, Otis, House
Mordecai House; see Palmer House
Palmer House (Fitts-Palmer House;
    Mordecai House)
210 Plummer St.
HABS NC-185   p   L

Warrenton vic.
Buck Springs; see Macon, Nathaniel, House
Elgin
State Rt. 1509
HABS NC-121   p   L
House
HABS NC-186   p   L
Hudgins House (Johnston-Plummer House)
Rt. 401
HABS NC-108   p   L

Johnston-Plummer House; see Hudgins
   House
Macon, Nathaniel, House (Buck Springs;
   Williams-Reid-Macon House)
HABS NC-107   p   L
Williams-Reid-Macon House; see Macon,
   Nathaniel, House

WASHINGTON COUNTY

Creswell vic.

Belgrade; see Pettigrew House

Collins, Josiah, House; see Somerset Place

Pettigrew House (Belgrade)
State Rt. 1158
HABS NC-35   pd   L

Somerset Place (Collins, Josiah, House)
Lake Phelps, Pettigrew State Park
HABS NC-23   pd   L

Somerset Place, Granary
Lake Phelps, Pettigrew State Park
HABS NC-24   pd   L

WAYNE COUNTY

Fremont vic.

Exum House
HABS NC-175   p   L

WILKES COUNTY

Sparta vic.

Brinegar Cabin
Blue Ridge Pkwy.
HABS NC-188   s pd   L

North Dakota

BENSON COUNTY

Devils Lake vic.

Fort Totten (Fort Totten, State Historic
   Site)
HABS ND-17   s pd   L
Fort Totten, Adjutant's Office
HABS ND-5   s pd   L
Fort Totten, Bake House; see Fort Totten,
   Bakery Shop
Fort Totten, Bakery Shop (Fort Totten,
   Bake House)
HABS ND-14   s pd   L
**Fort Totten, Capt. & First Lt. Qtrs., Bldgs.
   2 & 4**
HABS ND-7   s pd   L
**Fort Totten, Commanding Officers'
   Quarters**
HABS ND-6   s pd   L
Fort Totten, Commissary (Fort Totten,
   Commissary Storehouse)
HABS ND-16   pd   L
Fort Totten, Commissary Storehouse; see
   Fort Totten, Commissary
**Fort Totten, Company Barracks, Building
   11, 12 & 14** (Fort Totten, Company
   Quarters)
HABS ND-13   s pd   L
Fort Totten, Company Quarters; see Fort
   Totten, Company Barracks, Building 11,
   12 & 14
Fort Totten, Hospital
HABS ND-10   s pd   L
Fort Totten, Magazine
HABS ND-11   s pd   L
Fort Totten, Quartermaster's Storehouse
   (Fort Totten, Quartermasters's
   Warehouse)
HABS ND-12   s pd   L

Fort Totten, Quartermasters's Warehouse;
   see Fort Totten, Quartermaster's
   Storehouse
**Fort Totten, Second Lt.'s Quarters, Bldgs. 1
   & 5**
HABS ND-8   s pd   L
Fort Totten, State Historic Site; see Fort
   Totten
**Fort Totten, Surgeon & Chaplain's
   Quarters**
HABS ND-9   s pd   L

BURLEIGH COUNTY

Bismarck

Roosevelt, Theodore, Cabin; see Roosevelt,
   Theodore, Maltese Cross-Ranch Cabin
**Roosevelt, Theodore, Maltese Cross-Ranch
   Cabin** (Roosevelt, Theodore, Cabin;
   Roosevelt, Theodore, National
   Monument Park)
Roosevelt State Park (moved from ND,
   Medora vic.)
HABS ND-1   s pd   L
**Roosevelt, Theodore, National Monument
   Park;** see Roosevelt, Theodore, Maltese
   Cross-Ranch Cabin

HETTINGER COUNTY

Mott

Mott Rainbow Arch Bridge
Cannonball River
HAER ND-1   p   H

MCKENZIE COUNTY

Grassy Butte

Grassy Butte Post Office
Hwy. 85
HABS ND-19   pd   H

MCLEAN COUNTY

Elbowoods

Congregational Mission
Fort Berthold Indian Reservation
HABS ND-2   s pd   L H

Elbowoods vic.

Indian Dance Lodge
Fort Berthold Indian Reservation
HABS ND-3   s pd   L

TRAILL COUNTY

Mayville

Grinager, Inga, B., House; see Robinson,
   William, H., House
Robinson, William, H., House (Grinager,
   Inga, B., House)
127 Fourth Ave. NE
HABS ND-15   s   H

WILLIAMS COUNTY

Fort Buford

**Regimental Headquarters, Stable &
   Powder Magazine**
HABS ND-4   s pd   L

Ohio

ADAMS COUNTY

Manchester

Massie, Gen. Nathaniel, House
Buckeye Station Bluff, Rt. 52
HABS OH-632   s p d   L H

ASHLAND COUNTY

Ashland vic.

Freer House
Wooster Rd.
HABS OH-22-21   s p d   L

ASHTABULA COUNTY

Colebrook

Freewill Baptist Church
HABS OH-249   pd   L

Jefferson

Giddings, Joshua R., Law Office
Chestnut & Walnut Sts.
HABS OH-268   s p d   L
Talcott House
Walnut St.
HABS OH-256   s d   L
Wade, Benjamin, House
22 Jefferson St.
HABS OH-2236   p   H

Unionville vic.

Harper, Col. Robert, House
HABS OH-22-26   s p d   L

BELMONT COUNTY

Blaine

Bridge on Old National Road
U.S. Hwy. 40 & Wheeling Creek
HABS OH-2107   d   L H

Blaine vic.

Bridge & Milestone
HABS OH-2108   p   L
Milestone on Old S Bridge
HABS OH-2109   p   L

Morristown vic.

Bridge on Old National Road
N. of U.S. Hwy. 40 at Barkcamp Creek
HABS OH-2146   d   H
Bridge on Old National Road
U.S. Hwy. 40, E. of Stillwater Creek
HABS OH-2147   d   H

St. Clairsville

Tavern
HABS OH-2111   p   L

St. Clairsville vic.

Arch Culvert
HABS OH-2110   p   L

Zanesville

Bridge
Between Cambridge, OH & Wheeling, W.
VA
HABS OH-2106-F   p   L

Zanesville vic.

Bridge
Between St. Clairsville & Zanesville
HABS OH-2106-E   p   L
Culvert
Between Cambridge & St. Clairsville
HABS OH-2106-B   p   L
House, Stone
HABS OH-2106-A   p   L
S Bridge
Between St. Clairsville & Zanesville
HABS OH-2106-D   p   L
Structures on Old National Trail
Between Batlimore, MD & Zanesville, OH
HABS OH-2106   d   L

BROWN COUNTY

Georgetown

Schoolhouse
Water St.
HABS OH-629   s p d   L
Thompson, John, House
HABS OH-2218   p   L
Thompson, Nettie, House
W. on State Rd. 125
HABS OH-628   pd   L

Ripley

Rankin, Dr. John, House
Liberty Hill
HABS OH-630   s p d   L H

BUTLER COUNTY

Collinsville vic.

Covered Bridge
Spanning Seven Mile Creek
HABS OH-623   s   L

Darrtown vic.

Krebs, Charles, Place
S. of Morning Sun, State Rt. 224
HABS OH-2225   p   L

Hamilton vic.

New London Pike Covered Bridge
Spanning Indian Creek
HABS OH-624   s   L

Monroe vic.

Harkrader House
HABS OH-2234   p   L

Oxford

Guest House (Rodger's Place)
300 E. High St.
HABS OH-6-21   s p d   L
Oxford Female College, Fisher Hall)
Miami University Campus
HABS OH-2140   pd   H
Presbyterian Parsonage
E. High St.
HABS OH-622   pd   L
Rodger's Place; see Guest House

West Chester

Blue Shutters Residence
Rt. 25
HABS OH-2235   p   L

CARROLL COUNTY

Carrollton

McCook, Daniel, House
Public Square
HABS OH-2153   d   H

CLARK COUNTY

Harmony

Tavern, Old; see Warren, Reuben, House
Warren, Reuben, House (Tavern, Old)
Rt. 40
HABS OH-635   p   L

CLERMONT COUNTY

Bantam vic.

Pinkham House & Farm
Ohio State Rt. 125, Amelia-Bantam Rd.
HABS OH-2204   s p d   L

CLINTON COUNTY

Clarksville

Covered Bridge
Rt. 3
HABS OH-2224   p   L

New Vienna vic.

Harris, E., House (Snow Hill)
State Rt. No. 73
HABS OH-2250   s p d   H
Snow Hill; see Harris, E., House

COSHOCTON COUNTY

Isleta vic.

Fort, Old Stone
N. of Isleta
HABS OH-410   pd   L

CUYAHOGA COUNTY

Bentleyville

Bentley House
N. Miles Rd.
HABS OH-25   s pd   L

Brecksville

Brecksville Inn
Brecksville Rd.
HABS OH-234   s pd   L

Congregational Church
Highland Drive
HABS OH-22-30   s pd   L

Chagrin Falls

Crawford, W. J., House
170 Cleveland St.
HABS OH-225   s pd   L

March, H. W., House
E. Washington St.
HABS OH-219   s pd   L

Warren-Hollis House
43 E. Orange St.
HABS OH-22-1   s pd   L

Chagrin Falls vic.

Sykes House
Rt. 232
HABS OH-253   s pd   L

Cleveland

**(Republic Steel Company);
(REPUBLIC STEEL COMPANY);** see
   Corrigan, McKinney, Steel Company

Abbey Avenue Viaduct
HAER OH-5   pd   L

B & O Railroad Bridge Number 464
   (Scherzer Rolling Lift Bridge)
Spanning Old Ship Canal & Cuyahoga
   River
HAER OH-15   p   L

Baker, R. & L., Company; see Rauch &
   Lang Carriage Company

Baldwin Filtration Plant & Reservoir; see
   Division Avenue Pumping Station &
   Filtration Plant

Brookside Park Bridge
Spanning Big Creek & Cleveland
   Metroparks
HAER OH-14   p   L

Carling Brewing Company Building; see
   Peerless Motor Company Plant Number
   1

Carnegie-Lorain Bridge
HAER OH-16   p   H

Case, Leonard, Homestead
1295 E. Twentieth St.
HABS OH-22   s pd   L

Center Street Swing Bridge
SW of Public Square
HAER OH-10   pd   L

Central Furnaces
2650 Broadway
HAER OH-12   pd   L

Church, Old Stone; see First Presbyterian
   Church

Cleveland Arcade
401 Euclid Ave.
HABS OH-2119   s pd   L

Cleveland Automobile Industry
HAER OH-11   d   L

Cleveland Breakwater at Cleveland Harbor
HAER OH-1   pd   L

Cleveland Municpal Airport
HAER OH-2   pd   L

Cleveland-Chandler Motors Corporation
HAER OH-11-G   pd   L

Corrigan, McKinney, Steel Company
   ((Republic Steel Company))
3100 W. Forty-fifth St.
HAER OH-13   pd   L

Detroit Street Bridge, Old
HAER OH-8   d   L

Detroit Superior High Level Bridge
HAER OH-6   pd   L

Diebolt Brewing Company Stable
2695 Pittsburgh Ave.
HAER OH-20   p   L

**Division Avenue Pumping Station &
   Filtration Plant** (Baldwin Filtration Plant
   & Reservoir)
HAER OH-3   pd   L

Dunham, Rufus, Tavern
6709 Euclid Ave.
HABS OH-22-29   s pd   L H

First Presbyterian Church (Church, Old
   Stone)
91 Public Square
HABS OH-2124   pd   L

Fisher Body Ohio Company
HAER OH-11-H   pd   L

**Ford Motor Company Branch Assembly
   Plant**
HAER OH-11-E   pd   L

Garfield, Pres. James Abram, Monument
12316 Euclid Ave.
HABS OH-2122   pd   L

May, T. P., Residence
1458 E. Twelfth St.
HABS OH-24   s d   L

Mould, H., House
2637 Cedar Ave.
HABS OH-21   s p   L

Peerless Motor Car Company
Quincy Ave. & E. Ninety-third St.
HAER OH-11-D   pd   L H

Peerless Motor Company Plant Number 1
   (Carling Brewing Company Building)
Quincy Ave. & E. Ninety-third St.
HABS OH-2123   pd   L

Pennsylvania Railway Ore Dock
HAER OH-18   pd   L

Rauch & Lang Carriage Company (Baker,
   R. & L., Company)
W. Twenty-fifth St. & Monroe Ave.
HAER OH-11-B   pd   L

Rockefeller Building
614 Superior Ave.
HABS OH-2125   pd   L

Scherzer Rolling Lift Bridge; see B & O
   Railroad Bridge Number 464

Shaker Heights Rapid Transit Line
HAER OH-4   pd   L

Sidaway Avenue Footbridge (Suspension
   Bridge)
Jackowo & Garden Valley neighborhood
   vic.
HAER OH-9   pd   L

Society National Bank Building
127-45 Public Square
HABS OH-2128   pd   L

St. John's Episcopal Church
2600 Church Ave.
HABS OH-2126   pd   L

**St. Michael the Archangel Roman Catholic
   Church**
3114 Scranton Rd.
HABS OH-2127   pd   L

Stearns, F. B., Company
HAER OH-11-F   pd   L

Superior Avenue Viaduct
Cleveland E. & W. side, Cuyahoga Valley
   vic.
HAER OH-7   pd   L

Suspension Bridge; see Sidaway Avenue
   Footbridge

Trinity Episcopal Church
Euclid Ave. & E. Twenty-Second St.
HABS OH-2129   pd   L

**U.S. Post Office, Customs House &
   Courthouse**
Public Square
HABS OH-2121   pd   L

Wade Park Avenue Bridge
Liberty Blvd., Rockefeller Park
HABS OH-2130   pd   L

Weddell, Peter, House
W. Sixth St. & Frankfort Ave.
HABS OH-23   s p   L

White Company (White Motor Company)
HAER OH-11-C   pd   L

Winton Motor Carriage Company
Berea Rd. & Madison Ave.
HAER OH-11-A   pd   L

Cleveland Heights

Tremaine-Gallagher House
3001 Fairmount Blvd.
HABS OH-2131   pd   L

Cleveland vic.

Fosdick House
Canal Rd.
HABS OH-228 s pd L

Dover

Hurst, Thomas, Residence
31156 Detroit Rd.
HABS OH-231 s pd L

Gates Mills

Chagrin Valley Hunt Club (Doorway)
Mayfield & River Rds.
HABS OH-215 s pd L

St. Christopher's-By-The-River
Mayfield Rd.
HABS OH-212 s pd L H

Lakewood

Honam, John, House
1396 St. Charles Ave. (moved to Lakewood
Park)
HABS OH-27 s pd L

Nicholson, Ezra, House
1335 Detroit Ave.
HABS OH-210 s pd L

Warren House
Warren & Fisher Rds.
HABS OH-28 s pd L

North Olmsted

Carpenter, F. D., House
Lorain Rd.
HABS OH-213 s pd L

Universalist Church
Lorain & Butternut Ridge Rds.
HABS OH-222 s pd L

Parma

Gilchrist House
6515 York Rd.
HABS OH-214 s pd L

Parma Heights

Fay Homestead
Wooster Pike
HABS OH-22-23 s pd L

Rocky River

Rocky River Bridge
Spanning Rocky River Gorge at Detroit
Ave.
HAER OH-21 pd H

Solon vic.

Blackman House
Pettibone Rd.
HABS OH-233 s pd L

Strongsville

Pomeroy, Alanson, House
Pearl & Westwood Rds.
HABS OH-2132 pd H

Whitesburg

White House at Whitesburg
High St.
HABS OH-224 s pd L

DELAWARE COUNTY

Delaware

Mansion House; see Ohio Wesleyan
University, Elliott Hall

Ohio Wesleyan University, Elliott Hall
(Mansion House)
E. of Sandusky St., Ohio Wesleyan
University
HABS OH-2134 pd H

Ohio Wesleyan University, Sturges Library
(Sturges Hall)
E. of Sandusky St., Ohio Wesleyan
University
HABS OH-2135 pd H

Sturges Hall; see Ohio Wesleyan
University, Sturges Library

ERIE COUNTY

Milan

Edison, Thomas A., Birthplace
Front St. & Choate Ave.
HABS OH-22-22 s pd L

Vermilion vic.

Rosedale; see Swift, Joseph, House
Swift Hollow; see Swift, Joseph, House
Swift, Joseph, House (Rosedale; Swift
Hollow)
S. of Vermillion, on Vermillion River
HABS OH-26 s pd L

FAIRFIELD COUNTY

Lancaster

Devol-Dallow House
HABS OH-413 s H

Duplar, E., House
Rt. 22
HABS OH-2232 p L

Effinger, Samuel, House (Reber Tavern)
HABS OH-41 pd L H

Giani-Mumaugh Memorial
Main & High Sts.
HABS OH-419 s L

MacCracken-Hoffman House
105 E. Wheeling St.
HABS OH-414 s H

Reber Tavern; see Effinger, Samuel, House
Stanberry-Rising House
HABS OH-415 s H

FRANKLIN COUNTY

Columbus

American Savings Bank; see Central
National Bank Building
Baker Art Gallery
232 S. High St.
HABS OH-2213 pd L

Central National Bank Building (American
Savings Bank)
152-156 S. High St.
HABS OH-2214 pd L

Commercial & Apartment Building, Brick
82-86 E. Town St.
HABS OH-2210 pd L

Empress Theater; see Knickerbocker
Theater
Gayety Theater; see Knickerbocker Theater
Greene, Thurman, Building (La Salle Wine
Shop)
242-244 S. High St.
HABS OH-2211 pd L

Hartman Building & Theater
73-87 E. State St.
HABS OH-2215 pd L

Kelley, Alfred, House
282 E. Broad St.
HABS OH-47 s pd L H

Knickerbocker Theater (Empress Theater;
Gayety Theater)
246-254 S. High St.
HABS OH-2212 pd L

La Salle Wine Shop; see Greene, Thurman,
Building
Loew's & United Artists Ohio Theatre
39 E. State St.
HABS OH-2148 pd L

Worthington

St. John's Episcopal Church
High St. & Granville Rd.
HABS OH-2238 s H

GALLIA COUNTY

Gallipolis

432 First Avenue (House); see Our House
Gallipolis Post Office
First Ave.
HABS OH-633 s pd L

Our House (432 First Avenue (House))
HABS OH-631 s pd L

GEAUGA COUNTY

Aurora

Treat House
Rt. 43
HABS OH-230 s pd L

Burton

Cook, Meriman, House
Claridon & Burton Rds.
HABS OH-278 s d L

Lawyer, Lew, Residence
HABS OH-258 s pd L

Claridon

Congregational Church
Rt. 85
HABS OH-237 s pd L

Claridon vic.

Moffett, Chester, House
HABS OH-279   s d   L

Taylor, Corydon, House
Taylor Rd.
HABS OH-274   s p d   L

GREENE COUNTY

Clifton

Clifton Hotel (Tavern)
Water & Main Sts.
HABS OH-2154   d   H

Clifton vic.

Whiteman, Benjamin, House
N. side of N. River Rd.
HABS OH-2155   d   H

Yellow Springs

Antioch College, Main Hall
Livermore St. & N. College Ave.
HABS OH-644   s p d   L H

GUERNSEY COUNTY

Cambridge

Bridge on Old National Road
N. of U.S. Hwy. 40 at Saltfork
HABS OH-2113   p d   L H

Cambridge vic.

Bridge on Old National Road
N. branch of Leatherwood Creek
HABS OH-2144   p d   H

Bridge on Old National Road
W. Cambridge on U.S. Hwy. 40
HABS OH-2112   d   L H

S Bridge
W. of Cambridge
HABS OH-2114   p   L

Middlebourne vic.

Bridge
HABS OH-2115   p   L

S Bridge
HABS OH-2116   p   L

Old Washington vic.

Bridge on Old National Road
U.S. Hwy. 40-A and Saltfork
HABS OH-2145   d   H

Zanesville vic.

Bridge
Between Zanesville & Cambridge
HABS OH-2106-C   p   L

Culvert
Between Cambridge & St. Clairsville
HABS OH-2106-B   p   L

HAMILTON COUNTY

Cincinnati

Cathedral of St. Peter in Chains (St. Peter's Cathedral)
Eighth & Plum Sts.
HABS OH-638   p d   L

Cincinnati Union Terminal
1301 Western Ave.
HABS OH-630   p d   L

Cooksey House
856 Lincoln Ave.
HABS OH-2206   p d   L

46 Court (House)
Raleigh Alley vic.
HABS OH-641   p   L

807-850 Dayton Street; see Dayton Street Historic District

816 Dayton Street (Entrance Detail); see Dayton Street Historic District

Dayton Street Historic District (Law, James, House)
818 Dayton St.
HABS OH-2200-S   d   L H

Dayton Street Historic District (Hauck, Louis, House)
842 Dayton St.
HABS OH-2200-M   s d   L H

Dayton Street Historic District (Hatch, George, House)
830 Dayton St.
HABS OH-2200-L   s d   L H

Dayton Street Historic District (807-850 Dayton Street)
HABS OH-2200   s   L H

Dayton Street Historic District (938 Dayton Street (House))
HABS OH-2200-I   d   L H

Dayton Street Historic District (936 Dayton Street (House))
HABS OH-2200-H   d   L H

Dayton Street Historic District (837 Dayton Street (House))
HABS OH-2200-E   s d   L H

Dayton Street Historic District (932 Dayton Street (House))
HABS OH-2200-G   d   L

Dayton Street Historic District (Skaats-Hauck House)
812 Dayton St.
HABS OH-2200-U   d   L H

Dayton Street Historic District (Hauck & Hickenlooper (House))
HABS OH-2200-N   s   L H

Dayton Street Historic District (816 Dayton Street (Entrance Detail))
HABS OH-2200-C   s   L H

Dayton Street Historic District (808-824 Dayton Street (Houses))
HABS OH-2200-P   s   L H

Dayton Street Historic District (808 Dayton Street (House))
HABS OH-2200-A   d   H

Dayton Street Historic District (Gazley House)
824 Dayton St.
HABS OH-2200-K   d   L H

Dayton Street Historic District (Hickenlooper, Andrew, House)
838 Dayton St.
HABS OH-2200-O   s d   L H

Dayton Street Historic District (816-812 Dayton Street (Houses))
HABS OH-2200-Q   s   L H

Dayton Street Historic District (829 Dayton Street (House))
HABS OH-2200-D   s d   L H

Dayton Street Historic District (850 Dayton Street (House))
HABS OH-2200-F   d   L H

Dayton Street Historic District (850-846 Dayton Street (Houses))
HABS OH-2200-R   s   L H

Dayton Street Historic District (816 Dayton Street (House))
HABS OH-2200-B   d   H

Dayton Street Historic District (Earnshaw, Joseph, House)
846 Dayton St.
HABS OH-2200-J   d   L H

Dayton Street Historic District (St. Augustine School)
923 Bank St.
HABS OH-2200-T   p d   L H

808 Dayton Street (House); see Dayton Street Historic District

816 Dayton Street (House); see Dayton Street Historic District

829 Dayton Street (House); see Dayton Street Historic District

837 Dayton Street (House); see Dayton Street Historic District

850 Dayton Street (House); see Dayton Street Historic District

932 Dayton Street (House); see Dayton Street Historic District

936 Dayton Street (House); see Dayton Street Historic District

938 Dayton Street (House); see Dayton Street Historic District

808-824 Dayton Street (Houses); see Dayton Street Historic District

816-812 Dayton Street (Houses); see Dayton Street Historic District

850-846 Dayton Street (Houses); see Dayton Street Historic District

Earnshaw, Joseph, House; see Dayton Street Historic District

629-31 East Third St. (House)
HABS OH-2199   p   L

Eighth Street District (Queensgate II)
W. Eighth, John & W. Seventh Sts.
HABS OH-2208   p d   L

Farmers College
5553 Belmont Ave.
HABS OH-23-3   s p d   L

Fourth & Laurence Streets (House)
HABS OH-640   p   L
Gazley House; see Dayton Street Historic
    District
2935 Gilbert Avenue (House)
HABS OH-2207   pd   L
Hatch, George, House; see Dayton Street
    Historic District
Hauck & Hickenlooper (House); see
    Dayton Street Historic District
Hauck, Louis, House; see Dayton Street
    Historic District
Hickenlooper, Andrew, House; see Dayton
    Street Historic District
Jordon House
857 Beecher St.
HABS OH-2205   pd   L
Kemper, James, Log Cabin
Zoological Gardens
HABS OH-23-2   s pd   L
Law, James, House; see Dayton Street
    Historic District
Magrue, Joseph, House
1413 Western Ave.
HABS OH-2216   pd   L
Marine Hospital
Third & Kilgour Sts.
HABS OH-23-10   s pd   L
Methodist Episcopal Church (Wesley
    Chapel)
322 E. Fifth St.
HABS OH-23-1   s pd   L
National Theater
312 Sycamore St.
HABS OH-23-7   s pd   L
Plum Street Temple; see Wise, Isaac M.,
    Temple
Queensgate II; see Eighth Street District
Sinton, David, Home (Taft, Charles P.,
    Museum)
316 Pike St.
HABS OH-23-9   s pd   L
Skaats-Hauck House; see Dayton Street
    Historic District
St. Augustine School; see Dayton Street
    Historic District
St. Heinrich's Roman Catholic Church
1057 Flint St.
HABS OH-2203   pd   L
St. Peter's Cathedral; see Cathedral of St.
    Peter in Chains
Taft, Charles P., Museum; see Sinton,
    David, Home
Thomson, John, House; see Willowburn
Wesley Chapel; see Methodist Episcopal
    Church
Willowburn (Thomson, John, House)
1562 Hobart Ave.
HABS OH-6-16   s pd   L
Wise, Isaac M., Temple (Plum Street
    Temple)
Eighth & Plum Sts.
HABS OH-643   s pd   L

Cincinnati vic.
Baxter, William, House
Ridge Ave.
HABS OH-23-12   s   d   L
Elizabethtown
Presbyterian Church
HABS OH-23-11   s pd   L
Harrison
Looker, Othniel, House
New Haven Rd.
HABS OH-23-5   s pd   L
Harrison vic.
Eighteen Mile House
E. on U.S. Rt. 52
HABS OH-23-4   s pd   L
Mariemont
Ferris, Elithalet, House (Mariemont
    Historical Museum)
3905 Plainville Rd.
HABS OH-23-15   s pd   L
Mariemont Historical Museum; see Ferris,
    Elithalet, House
Mariemont vic.
Ferris, Joseph, House
5801 Wooster Pike
HABS OH-23-8   s pd   L
Milford
Camp Dennison, Officers' Quarters &
    Guard House
Rt. 50, NW of Milford
HABS OH-6-18   s pd   L
Montgomery vic.
Barn, Frame
U.S. Rt. 3
HABS OH-2221   p   L
Mt. Carmel vic.
Campbell, John, Residence
Mt. Carmel Rd.
HABS OH-23-13   s pd   L
Mt. Healthy vic.
Whallon, James, Residence
Winton Rd., Rt. 5, Lockland
HABS OH-6-17   s pd   L
Newtown
Harrison House (Landers' House)
Newtown Rd.
HABS OH-620   pd   L
Landers' House; see Harrison House
North Bend vic.
Harrison, Scott, House
Brower Rd.
HABS OH-23-6   s pd   L

Whitewater
Shaker Centre Family, Broom Shop
E. side of Oxford Rd.
HABS OH-2190   p   L H

Shaker Centre Family, Trustees' Office
Oxford Rd.
HABS OH-2191   p   L
Shaker Centre Family, Washhouse
Oxford Rd.
HABS OH-2192   p   L
Shaker Meetinghouse
Oxford Rd.
HABS OH-2189   p   L
Shaker North Family, Dwelling House
Oxford Rd.
HABS OH-2196   p   L
Shaker North Family, General View
Oxford Rd.
HABS OH-2197   p   L
Shaker North Family, Seed House
Oxford Rd.
HABS OH-2195   p   L
Shaker North Family, Smokehouse
Oxford Rd.
HABS OH-2198   p   L
Shaker North Family, Woodshed
Oxford Rd.
HABS OH-2193   p   L

HANCOCK COUNTY

Findlay vic.
Ewing, P. W., House
Rt. 68
HABS OH-22-11   s pd   L

HARRISON COUNTY

Cadiz
Harrison National Bank Building
Market & Main Sts.
HABS OH-2150   d   H

HIGHLAND COUNTY

Sinking Spring
Octagonal Schoolhouse
HABS OH-2233   p   L

HOCKING COUNTY

Adelphi vic.
Spencer, Jesse, House
HABS OH-46   pd   L

HURON COUNTY

Monroeville
Schug, Albert F., House
29 Brown St.
HABS OH-22-19   s pd   L
Norwalk
Fulstow, Dr. P. H., House
99 W. Main St.
HABS OH-211   s pd   L

Martin, E. G., House
54 W. Main St.
HABS OH-22-20   s p d   L

KNOX COUNTY

Gambrier

Kenyon College, Neff, Peter, Cottage
Wiggin St.
HABS OH-49   s p d   L H

Mt. Vernon

Curtis-Devin House
101 N. Main St.
HABS OH-22-18   s p d   L

LAKE COUNTY

Kirtland Village

Kirtland Temple (Mormon)
HABS OH-22-25   s p d   L H

Mentor

Bolton, Thomas, House
Euclid Rd. & E. Seventy-first St.
HABS OH-22-28   s p d   L
White, Florence Graves, House
HABS OH-2239   s   H

Painesville

City Hall; see Courthouse, Old
Courthouse, Old (City Hall)
Richmond & Mentor Aves.
HABS OH-235   s p d   L
Lockwood House
S. Park Place
HABS OH-255   s d   L
Malin House
30 S. Park Place
HABS OH-240   s p d   L
Marshall, Seth, Residence
375 Bank St.
HABS OH-236   s p d   L
Mathews, Dr. John H., House
N. State St.
HABS OH-22-24   s p d   L
Rider Tavern
HABS OH-269   p d   L

Unionville

Unionville Tavern
County Line Rd.
HABS OH-246   s p d   L

Willoughby

Elwell House; see Robinson, William P., House
Robinson, William P., House (Elwell House)
3742 Erie St.
HABS OH-2120   p d   H

LAWRENCE COUNTY

Burlington

Lawrence County Jail
Burlington Rd. & U.S. Hwy. 52
HABS OH-2149   d   H

LICKING COUNTY

Granville

St. Luke's Episcopal Church
200 E. Broadway
HABS OH-400   p d   L H

LOGAN COUNTY

N. Lewisburg vic.

Gray, Matt, House
HABS OH-22-14   s p   L

LORAIN COUNTY

Avon Township

Baldauf, William, House
Avon Center Rd.
HABS OH-238   s p d   L
Hardwick House
Detroit Rd.
HABS OH-226   s p d   L
Hurst, W. & L. E., House
Detroit Rd.
HABS OH-221   s p d   L

Avon vic.

Sweet House
Detroit Rd.
HABS OH-229   s p d   L

Avon Village

Lewis House
Avon Center Rd.
HABS OH-245   s p d   L
Robinson-Fitch House
Avon Center Rd.
HABS OH-241   s p d   L
Wilson-Riegelsberger House
Rieglsberger Rd.
HABS OH-239   s p d   L

Huntington vic.

Clark-Pratt-Kemery Residence
Rt. 58
HABS OH-277   s p d   L
Dirlam-Allen House
State Rt. 58
HABS OH-266   s p d   L
Roice-Tipton House
Bursley Rd.
HABS OH-273   s p d   L

Oberlin

First Church in Oberlin (Congregational)
N. Main & W. Lorain Sts.
HABS OH-2117   s p d   L

Wellington

Gillette, H. M., Residence
Rt. 18, Blue Goose Corners
HABS OH-276   s p d   L
Warner House
370 S. Main St.
HABS OH-2118   p d   L

LUCAS COUNTY

Maumee

St. Paul's Episcopal Church
E. Wayne & Elizabeth Sts.
HABS OH-19   d   L H

Toledo

First National Bank (Securities Bank)
312 Summit St.
HABS OH-2201   p   L
Oliver House (Hotel)
27 Broadway & Ottawa Sts.
HABS OH-2242   p   H
Securities Bank; see First National Bank

Waterville

Columbian House (Tavern)
River Rd.
HABS OH-22-17   s p d   L

MADISON COUNTY

Lafayette

Tavern, Red Brick
U.S. Rt. 40
HABS OH-2246   p   L

MEDINA COUNTY

Seville

Maukee Inn; see St. John House
St. John House (Wallick & Whiteside Residence; Maukee Inn)
HABS OH-217   s p d   L
Wallick & Whiteside Residence; see St. John House
Welday House
HABS OH-216   s p d   L

Weymouth

First Congregational Church
State Rt. 3
HABS OH-257   s d   L

MEIGS COUNTY

Chester

Meigs County Courthouse, Old
HABS OH-642   p d   L

MONTGOMERY COUNTY

Dayton

Log Cabin, Old; see Newcom Tavern
Montgomery County Courthouse, Old
Third & Main Sts.
HABS OH-51   s pd   L H
Newcom Tavern (Log Cabin, Old)
Van Cleve Park, E. Monument Ave.
HABS OH-627   s pd   L

MUSKINGUM COUNTY

Hopewell vic.

Bridge on Old National Road; see Covered
   Bridge, Old
Covered Bridge, Old (Bridge on Old
   National Road)
W. of Zanesville P. O., U.S. Hwy. 40
HABS OH-44   p   L H

Zanesville

Bridge
Between Cambridge, OH & Wheeling, W.
   VA
HABS OH-2106-F   p   L
Bridge, Stone
Rt. 40
HABS OH-43   p   L
Buckingham, Alvah, House
405 Moxahala Ave.
HABS OH-420   s   H
Nye-Potts House
Adams St.
HABS OH-421   s   H
Welles House
209 Muskingum Ave.
HABS OH-422   s   H

Zanesville vic.

Bridge
Between Zanesville & Cambridge
HABS OH-2106-C   p   L
Bridge
HABS OH-43-A   p   L
Bridge
Between St. Clairsville & Zanesville
HABS OH-2106-E   p   L
Bridge on Old National Road
N. of U.S. Hwy. 40, branch of Timber Run
HABS OH-2143   d   H
Covered Bridge, Old
HABS OH-45   p   L
Headley, Usual, Inn
Rt. 40
HABS OH-2217   p   L
House, Stone
HABS OH-2106-A   p   L
S Bridge
Between St. Clairsville & Zanesville
HABS OH-2106-D   p   L
Structures on Old National Trail
Between Batlimore, MD & Zanesville, OH
HABS OH-2106   d   L

NOBLE COUNTY

Caldwell

I. O. O. F. Block
North & West Sts.
HABS OH-2151   d   H

OTTAWA COUNTY

Limestone vic.

Bridge
HABS OH-18   p   L

PERRY COUNTY

Somerset

Perry County Courthouse, Old
Town Square
HABS OH-412   s pd   L H

PICKAWAY COUNTY

Circleville vic.

Mount Oval Farm; see Renwick, William,
   House
Renwick, William, House (Mount Oval
   Farm)
U.S. Rt. 23, Emerson Rd. & Congo Creek
   vic.
HABS OH-2142   d   H

Kinderhook vic.

Milestone of Zane's Trace
Rt. 22
HABS OH-42   p   L

PIKE COUNTY

Jasper

Jones House (Stone)
State Hwy. 24
HABS OH-634   s pd   L

Piketon vic.

Lucas, Gov., House
HABS OH-636   s   L

PORTAGE COUNTY

Atwater

Congregational Church
HABS OH-22-7   s pd   L

Aurora

Egglestone, Chauncey, House; see
   Hopwood House
Hopwood House (Egglestone, Chauncey,
   House)
Egglestone Rd.
HABS OH-243   s pd   L
Howard, C. R., House
Rt. 17
HABS OH-244   s pd   L

Root, Emery, House
Chillicothe Rd.
HABS OH-242   s pd   L
Willard, Archibald M., Residence
Rt. 82
HABS OH-232   s pd   L

Deerfield

Day, Judge Alva, House; see Shively, Lois,
   House (Entrance Doorway)
Shively, Lois, House (Entrance Doorway)
   (Day, Judge Alva, House)
HABS OH-22-10   s pd   L

Freedom

Freedom Congregational Church
HABS OH-2236   s   H

Rootstown

Rootstown Town Hall
HABS OH-2243   s   H

Streetsboro

Baptist Church, Old (Methodist Church)
Rt. 43 & 14
HABS OH-251   s pd   L
Methodist Church; see Baptist Church, Old

PUTNAM COUNTY

Ottawa

Putnam County Courthouse
Hickory St.
HABS OH-2133   d   H

ROSS COUNTY

Chillicothe

Barret, Vernon, House (Greene, Judge,
   House)
HABS OH-2230   p   L
Greene, Judge, House; see Barret, Vernon,
   House

Chillicothe vic.

Adena (Mount Prospect Hall; Worthington,
   Gov. Thomas, House)
St. Margaret's Cemetery vic.
HABS OH-645   s pd   L
Mount Prospect Hall; see Adena
Worthington, Gov. Thomas, House; see
   Adena

SANDUSKY COUNTY

Fremont

Edgerton House
Buckland Ave.
HABS OH-22-16   s pd   L
Sandusky County Courthouse
S. Park St.
HABS OH-22-15   s pd   L

SHELBY COUNTY

Lockington
Miami & Erie Canal Locks
Loramie Portage site vic.
HABS OH-411   pd   L

STARK COUNTY

Canton
Church of the Savior (United Methodist);
see First Methodist Church
First Methodist Church (Church of the Savior (United Methodist))
Cleveland Ave. & W. Tuscarawas St.
HABS OH-2152   d   H

Limaville
Baldwin, Alonzo, House (Entrance Doorway)
State Rt. 225
HABS OH-22-9   s pd   L

SUMMIT COUNTY

Akron
Perkins, Col. Simon, House (Perkins Hill)
Maple St.
HABS OH-22-8   s pd   L
Perkins Hill; see Perkins, Col. Simon, House
Quaker Oats Cereal Factory
HAER OH-17   pd   L

Bath
Hopkins House (Entrance)
Rt.21
HABS OH-262   s pd   L

Copley
Arnold House
HABS OH-220   s pd   L

Hudson
Baldwin-Buss House
Main St. & Streetsboro Rd.
HABS OH-22-4   s pd   L
Chapel; see Western Reserve Academy, Chapel
Dormitory, Dining Hall (Doorway); see Western Reserve Academy, Bliss-Slaughter House
First National Bank of Hudson
HABS OH-2240   s   H
Hudson Library & Historical Society
HABS OH-2241   s   H
Loomis Observatory; see Western Reserve Academy, Loomis Observatory
North Hall; see Western Reserve Academy, North Hall
President's House; see Western Reserve Academy, President's House

Western Reserve Academy, Bliss-Slaughter House (Dormitory, Dining Hall (Doorway))
Hudson & College Sts.
HABS OH-271   s pd   L
Western Reserve Academy, Chapel (Chapel)
Western Reserve Academy
HABS OH-22-2   s pd   L
Western Reserve Academy, Loomis Observatory (Loomis Observatory)
Western Reserve Academy
HABS OH-22-5   s pd   H
Western Reserve Academy, North Hall (North Hall)
Western Reserve Academy
HABS OH-22-3   s pd   L
Western Reserve Academy, President's House (President's House)
Hudson & College Sts.
HABS OH-275   s pd   L

Ira (Village) vic.
Hale, Jonathan, House
Oak Hill Rd.
HABS OH-250   s pd   L

Kent
First Universalist Church
HABS OH-2244   s   H
Franklin Township Hall
218 Gougler Ave.
HABS OH-2245   s   H

Northfield vic.
French House
Town Line Rd., Rt. 8 vic.
HABS OH-252   s d   L

Peninsula
Bronson, H. V., House
Rt. 303
HABS OH-267   s pd   L

Tallmadge
Congregational Church
HABS OH-22-6   s pd   L

Twinsburg
Elliott Building
Rt. 14
HABS OH-227   s pd   L
Twinsburg Congregational Church
Rt. 14
HABS OH-29   s pd   L

Twinsburg vic.
Herrick House
Rt. 91
HABS OH-223   s pd   L

TRUMBULL COUNTY

Bristolville
Congregational Church
State Rt. 45 & 88
HABS OH-263   s pd   L

Methodist Church, Old
HABS OH-260   pd   L

Kinsman
Congregational-Presbyterian Church
Rt. 5
HABS OH-247   s pd   L

Kinsman vic.
Allen, Peter, House
State Rt. 7
HABS OH-248   s pd   L

Newton Falls
Covered Bridge
Spanning Mahoney River
HABS OH-270   s pd   L

North Bloomfield
Brownwood Farm
HABS OH-261   pd   L

North Bristol
White House
State Rt. 45
HABS OH-259   s pd   L

Warren
Edwards-Webb House (Iddings, Dr. Warren, House)
259 South St.
HABS OH-272   s pd   L
Iddings, Dr. Warren, House; see Edwards-Webb House
Kinsman, F., Office
303 Mahoning Ave.
HABS OH-265   s d   L
Kinsman, Judge Frederick, House
303 Mahoning Ave.
HABS OH-264   s pd   L

TUSCARAWAS COUNTY

Zoar
Beiter House Number 3
Fourth & Main Sts.
HABS OH-284   s pd   L
Blacksmith Shop
HABS OH-298   s pd   L
Brewery
Fifth & Park Sts.
HABS OH-291   s pd   L
Cider Mill, Planing Mill & Cabinet Shop
Second & Foltz Sts.
HABS OH-293   s pd   L
Cobbler Shop
Main St.
HABS OH-2103   s pd   L
Cow Barn
Second St.
HABS OH-283   s pd   L
Dormitory
Third St.
HABS OH-2101   s pd   L

Epsicopal Church
Main St.
HABS OH-281   s p d   L
First & Main Streets (House)
HABS OH-2105   p d   L
First Meetinghouse
Fourth St., between Park & Main
HABS OH-286   s p d   L
Garden (Tree of Life)
HABS OH-286   p   L
Gardener's Cottage
Fourth St.
HABS OH-282   s p d   L
General Store & Post Office
HABS OH-2100   s p d   L
Grist Mill
First St.
HABS OH-288   s p d   L
Gunn, Alexander, Cottage; see Hermitage
  (Log Cabin)
Hermitage (Log Cabin) (Gunn, Alexander,
  Cottage)
Third St.
HABS OH-296   s p d   L
House on Hill
Planing Mill vic.
HABS OH-294-A   p d   L
Jebenhauschen (Log Cabin)
Fourth St.
HABS OH-287   s p d   L
Kappel House
Third & Main Sts.
HABS OH-289   s p d   L
Keucherer House
Third & Main Sts.
HABS OH-290   s p d   L
Number One (King's Palace)
Main & Third Sts.
HABS OH-297   s p d   L
Planing Mill, Old
HABS OH-294   p d   L

Rieker Residence
Third St.
HABS OH-2104   p d   L
Saddler Shop
Second St.
HABS OH-299   s p d   L
Sewing House
Second & Park Sts.
HABS OH-285   s p d   L
Woolen Water Mill
HABS OH-2102   s d   L
Zeeb House (Log Cabin)
Fourth & Park Sts.
HABS OH-295   s p d   L
Zoar Hotel
Second & Main Sts.
HABS OH-280   s p d   L
Zoar Jail
Foltz St.
HABS OH-292   s p d   L
Zoar-Maps & General History
HABS OH-297   p d   L

UNION COUNTY

North Lewisburg vic.
Covered Bridge
Spanning Spain's Creek
HABS OH-22-12   s p d   L
Covered Bridge
Spanning Darby Creek
HABS OH-22-13   s p d   L

WARREN COUNTY

Corwin vic.
McKay, Moses, House
New Burlington Rd.
HABS OH-2202   s p d   L

Foster
Morrow, Gov., House
HABS OH-2248   s p   L
Harveysburg
Lukins, Levi, House
Middletown Rd., R. R. 3
HABS OH-2209   s p d   L
Lebanon
Golden Lamb Hotel
Main St.
HABS OH-625   s p d   L
Lebanon vic.
Scott, Thomas P., House
HABS OH-637   s   L
Union Village
Shaker South Family, Dwelling House
State Rts. 63 & 741 intersection
HABS OH-639   s p   L
Waynesville
Quaker Meetinghouse
HABS OH-426   s p d   H

WAYNE COUNTY

Wooster
Moore-Brewster House
202 Market St.
HABS OH-254   s p d   L

WYANDOT COUNTY

Mc Cutchenville
Greek Revival House (Shoemaker House)
HABS OH-22-27   s p d   L
Shoemaker House; see Greek Revival
  House

Oklahoma

ADAIR COUNTY

Stillwell
Adair County Courthouse
Public Square
HABS OK-32   d   H

CHEROKEE COUNTY

Park Hill
Hunter's Home; see Murrell, George M.,
  House
Murrell, George M., House (Hunter's
  Home)
Murrell Rd.
HABS OK-28   s d   H
Three Columns at Tsa-La-Gi
HABS OK-34   p d   H

Tahlequah
Cherokee County Court Building; see
  Cherokee National Capitol Building
Cherokee County Jail; see Cherokee
  National Penitentiary
Cherokee Female Seminary (Seminary
  Hall)
Northeastern Oklahoma State Univ.
  Campus
HABS OK-23   s d   H
Cherokee National Capitol Building
  (Cherokee County Court Building)
100 S. Muskogee Ave.
HABS OK-24   s p d   H

Cherokee National Penitentiary (Cherokee
  County Jail)
124 E. Choctaw St.
HABS OK-25   s d   H
Cherokee Supreme Court Building
130 E. Keetoowah St.
HABS OK-26   s d   H
Loeser, Dr. Irvin D., Log Cabin (Loeser's
  Cabin)
121 E. Smith St.
HABS OK-27   d   H
Loeser's Cabin; see Loeser, Dr. Irvin D.,
  Log Cabin
Seminary Hall; see Cherokee Female
  Seminary

COMANCHE COUNTY

Fort Sill

Commanding Officer's Quarters; see Sherman House

Post Headquarters, Old
Quanah Rd.
HABS OK-35   s d   H

Sherman House (Commanding Officer's Quarters)
HABS OK-36   d   H

DELAWARE COUNTY

Flint vic.

Beck's Mill; see Hildebrand's Mill
Hildebrand's Mill (Beck's Mill)
HABS OK-29   d   H

Rose vic.

Saline Courthouse
HABS OK-33   d   H

LOGAN COUNTY

Guthrie

Carnegie Library
402 E. Oklahoma Ave.
HABS OK-14   s pd   L

Cooperative Publishing Company Building; see State Capitol Company Building

Ferd-Heim Brewing Company (Heim Brewing Company)
424 W. Oklahoma Ave.
HABS OK-19   pd   L

Gray Brothers Block
101 W. Oklahoma Ave.
HABS OK-12   s pd   L

Guthrie Historic District; see Guthrie, Town of

Guthrie, Town of (Guthrie Historic District)
U.S. Rt. 77 & State Rd. 33
HABS OK-10   pd   L H

Guthrie Waterworks
S. Division St.
HABS OK-20   pd   L

Heilman, P. J., House
401 E. Cleveland Ave.
HABS OK-15   s pd   L

Heim Brewing Company; see Ferd-Heim Brewing Company

Logan County Courthouse; see Oklahoma State Capitol

Oklahoma State Capitol (Logan County Courthouse)
301 E. Harrison Ave.
HABS OK-21   pd   L H

Stapleton Block
114 N. Division St.
HABS OK-16   s d   L

State Capitol Company Building (Cooperative Publishing Company Building)
301 W. Harrison Ave.
HABS OK-17   s pd   L

Trinity Episcopal Church
310 E. Noble Ave.
HABS OK-11   s pd   L

Union Station
W. Oklahoma & Railroad Aves.
HABS OK-18   pd   L

Victor Block
202 W. Harrison Ave.
HABS OK-13   s pd   L

MUSKOGEE COUNTY

Fort Gibson

Dragoon Headquarters; see Howard House
Fort Gibson, Bake Oven
Garrison Ave.
HABS OK-34-7   s pd   L

Fort Gibson, Barracks Building
Garrison Ave.
HABS OK-34-1   s pd   L

Fort Gibson, Blacksmith Shop
Garrison Ave.
HABS OK-34-8   s pd   L

Fort Gibson, Commanding Officer's Quarters
Coppinger Ave.
HABS OK-34-2   s pd   L

Fort Gibson, Commissary Building
Garrison Ave.
HABS OK-34-5   s pd   L

Fort Gibson, Headquarters Building
Garrison Ave.
HABS OK-34-4   s pd   L

Fort Gibson, Powder House; see Fort Gibson, Powder Magazine

Fort Gibson, Powder Magazine (Fort Gibson, Powder House)
Garrison Ave.
HABS OK-34-6   s pd   L

Houston, Sam, Cabin
HABS OK-9   s pd   L

Howard House (Dragoon Headquarters)
Creek St.
HABS OK-34-3   s pd   L

NOBLE COUNTY

Perry

Atchison, Topeka, Santa Fe Railroad Station
HABS OK-37   p   H

St. Louis, San Francisco Railroad Station
HABS OK-38   p   H

OKFUSKEE COUNTY

Okemah vic.

Guthrie, Woodie, Birthplace
HABS OK-22   p   H

SEQUOYAH COUNTY

Marble City

Citizen's State Bank
Seminole & Main Sts.
HABS OK-30   d   H

Marble City vic.

Dwight Mission, Administration Building
Rural Rt.
HABS OK-31   d   H

WAGONER COUNTY

Fort Gibson

Houston, Sam, Cabin
HABS OK-9   s pd   L

Oregon

BENTON COUNTY

Hoskins

Watson, James, House
HABS OR-30   s pd   L

CLACKAMAS COUNTY

Canby

Canby Railroad Depot
HABS OR-131   pd   L

Milwaukie

Lewelling, Seth, House
Lot 5
HABS OR-1   pd   L

Molalla vic.

Dibble House
HABS OR-7   s pd   L

Dickey, John K., House
HABS OR-6   s pd   L

Mt. Pleasant

Ainsworth, John C., House
HABS OR-4   pd   L

Holmes, William, House (Rose Farm)
HABS OR-3   s pd   L

Locust Farm; see McCarver, Morton, House

McCarver, Morton, House (Locust Farm)
HABS OR-5   s pd   L

Rose Farm; see Holmes, William, House

Oregon City

McLoughlin House National Historic Site;
  see McLoughlin, John, House
McLoughlin, John, House (McLoughlin
  House National Historic Site)
McLoughlin Park (moved from Second &
  Third Sts.)
HABS OR-2   pd L

West Linn

Willamette Falls Lock Chamber
HAER OR-1   pd H

Wilsonville vic.

Curry, George L., House
HABS OR-8   s pd L

DOUGLAS COUNTY

Oakland

Powell, Louis, House
Second Ave. & Maple St.
HABS OR-36   s pd L
Young, Edward G., House
Second Ave. & Maple St.
HABS OR-37   s pd L

Yoncalla vic.

Ambrose, Alfred T., House
HABS OR-35   pd L
Applegate, Charles, House
HABS OR-34   s pd L

JACKSON COUNTY

Ashland vic.

Tolman, James C., House
Pacific Hwy.
HABS OR-42   s pd L

Central Point

McCredie, William, House
2606 Old Stage Rd.
HABS OR-128   pd L

Gold Hill vic.

Rock Point Tavern
HABS OR-40   pd L

Jacksonville

Anderson & Glenn Store
125 W. California St.
HABS OR-61   pd L
Applegate House
750 S. Third St.
HABS OR-56   p L
Applegate, Mark, House
655 S. Third St.
HABS OR-57   p L
Armstrong, Minerva, House; see Cool
  House
Barn, B. & B.
N. Third & D Sts.
HABS OR-58   p L

Beekman Bank
110 W. California St.
HABS OR-59   pd L
Beekman House
E. California St.
HABS OR-60   p L
Bilger House
540 Blackstone Alley
HABS OR-62   p L
Briethbarth House
180 Oregon St.
HABS OR-63   p L
Britt House
201 S. First St.
HABS OR-49   s pd L
Brunner Brothers Store
170 S. Oregon St.
HABS OR-64   pd L
Building, Brick (Dowell's, B. F., Law
  Office)
125 S. Third St.
HABS OR-73   pd L
Colvig House
410 S. Oregon St.
HABS OR-67   p L
Cool House (Armstrong, Minerva, House)
E. California St. & Sixth St.
HABS OR-68   p L
Davidson House
503 N. Sixth St.
HABS OR-70   p L
Davis-Kubli House
HABS OR-101   p L
Deroboam House
390 E. California St.
HABS OR-71   p L
Dowell, B. F., House
470 N. Fifth St.
HABS OR-72   p L
Dowell's, B. F., Law Office; see Building,
  Brick
Drew, Ben, Commission House
160 E. California St.
HABS OR-74   pd L
Duncan, Judge, House
285 S. First St.
HABS OR-75   p L
**Fisher Brothers Store & Bella Union
  Saloon**
180 & 170 W. California St.
HABS OR-76   pd L
Greenman-Jackson House
E. California & Fifth Sts.
HABS OR-77   p L
Greer, Dr. G. W., House (Reed House)
250 N. Oregon St.
HABS OR-43   s pd L
Gwinn House
415 E. C St. (moved from Courthouse Lot)
HABS OR-78   p L
Haines Brothers House, Brick
110 S. Oregon St.
HABS OR-79   pd L

Harbaugh House
425 Huener Lane
HABS OR-81   p L
Harris-Chambers House
210 N. Third St.
HABS OR-82   p L
Helms House
320 S. Oregon St.
HABS OR-83   p L
I. O. O. F. Lodge; see McCully Building
Jackson County Courthouse (Jacksonville
  Museum)
N. Fifth St.
HABS OR-69   pd L
Jacksonville City Hall
205 W. Main St.
HABS OR-66   pd L
Jacksonville Historic District
HABS OR-127   pd L
Jacksonville Inn; see Ryan's, P. J., First
  Brick Store Building
Jacksonville Museum; see Jackson County
  Courthouse
Judge & Nunan's Saddlery
165 E. California St.
HABS OR-87   pd L
Kahler, C. W., Law Office
105 N. Third St.
HABS OR-90   pd L
Kahler, William, House
310 N. Sixth St.
HABS OR-89   p L
Kahler-Reuter House
410 E. E St.
HABS OR-91   p L
Kahler's Drugstore
120 W. California St.
HABS OR-88   pd L
Keegan, Chris, House
105 E. D St.
HABS OR-92   p L
Keegan, Owen, House
455 Huener Lane
HABS OR-93   p L
Klippel House
220 Eighth St.
HABS OR-94   p L
Langell House (Catholic Rectory)
210 N. Fourth St.
HABS OR-96   p L
Love & Bilger Tin Shop
150 W. California St.
HABS OR-97   pd L
Love House
175 N. Third St.
HABS OR-98   pd L
Magruder House
455 E. California St.
HABS OR-99   p L
Masonic Building
California & Oregon Sts.
HABS OR-100   pd L

McCully Building (I. O. O. F. Lodge)
175 S. Oregon St.
HABS OR-102   pd   L

McCully House
240 E. California St.
HABS OR-103   p   L

Methodist Episcopal Church
Fifth & D Sts.
HABS OR-104   pd   L

Moore House
635 S. Third St.
HABS OR-106   p   L

Muller, Max, House
465 E. California St.
HABS OR-107   p   L

Neuber's Jewelry Store
130 W. California St.
HABS OR-108   pd   L

305 North Fourth Street (House)
HABS OR-110   p   L

525 North Sixth Street (House)
HABS OR-84   p   L

Nunan, Jeremiah, House
635 Oregon St.
HABS OR-109   pd   L

Orth Building
140 S. Oregon St.
HABS OR-111   pd   L

Orth House
425 S. Third St. (moved from 105 S. Third St.)
HABS OR-85   p   L

Orth House
Main & Third St.
HABS OR-112   p   L

Presbyterian Church
California & Sixth Sts.
HABS OR-113   pd   L

Reames, Thomas G., House
540 E. California St.
HABS OR-114   p   L

Redmen's Lodge & Kubli Building
105 & 115 W. California St.
HABS OR-95   pd   L

Reed House; see Greer, Dr. G. W., House

Rogue River Valley, Electric Power Substation
225 W. California St.
HABS OR-116   p   L

Rogue River Valley, Railroad Station
Oregon & W. C. Sts.
HABS OR-117   pd   L

Ryan's, P. J., First Brick Store Building
(Jacksonville Inn)
175 E. California St.
HABS OR-118   pd   L

Ryan's, P. J., Store
135 W. California St.
HABS OR-119   pd   L

Sachs Brothers Store
140 W. California St.
HABS OR-120   pd   L

Schumpf & Miller Stores
155 & 157 W. California St.
HABS OR-122   pd   L

Sifers-Savage House
160 W. C St.
HABS OR-44   s pd   L

325 Sixth Street (House)
HABS OR-86   p   L

St. Joseph's Roman Catholic Church
Fourth & D Sts.
HABS OR-121   pd   L

Table Rock Billiard Saloon (Facade)
S. Oregon St.
HABS OR-123   pd   L

U.S. Hotel
California & Third Sts.
HABS OR-124   pd   L

Jacksonville vic.

Bybee, William, House
HABS OR-45   s pd   L

Hanley House
1053 Hanley Rd.
HABS OR-80   p   L

Miller, J. N. T., House
Old Stage Rd.
HABS OR-105   p   L

Phoenix

Colver, Hiram, House
Pacific Hwy.
HABS OR-41   s pd   L

Rogue River vic.

Birdseye, David N., House
HABS OR-39   pd   L

JOSEPHINE COUNTY

Wolf Creek

Wolf Creek Tavern
Pacific Hwy.
HABS OR-38   s pd   L

LANE COUNTY

Eugene

University of Oregon, Deady Hall
University of Oregon Campus
HABS OR-53   pd   L

University of Oregon, Villard Hall
Uiversity of Oregon Campus
HABS OR-50   pd   L

Lorane vic.

Cartwright, Darius B., House
HABS OR-33   s pd   L

LINN COUNTY

Jefferson vic.

Baber, Granville H., House
HABS OR-32   s pd   L

MARION COUNTY

Aurora

Keil, Elias, House
HABS OR-9   s pd   L

Gervais vic.

Brown, Samuel, House
HABS OR-10   s pd   L

Howell Prairie

McCorkle, George F., House
HABS OR-11   pd   L

Jefferson

Conser, Jacob, House
HABS OR-31   s pd   L

Parkersville

Parker, William, House
HABS OR-46   s pd   L

Salem

Chemawa Indian School
5495 Chugach Ave.
HABS OR-129   p   L

Chemawa Indian School, Electrical Shop
5495 Chugach St. NE
HABS OR-129-M   pd   L

Chemawa Indian School, Hawley Hall
5495 Chugach St. NE
HABS OR-129-L   pd   L

Chemawa Indian School, House
2994 Misty St.
HABS OR-129-H   p   L

Chemawa Indian School, House
2984 Misty St.
HABS OR-129-I   p   L

Chemawa Indian School, House
2974 Misty St.
HABS OR-129-J   p   L

Chemawa Indian School, House
3005 Misty St.
HABS OR-129-A   pd   L

Chemawa Indian School, House
3004 Misty St.
HABS OR-129-B   pd   L

Chemawa Indian School, House
3014 Misty St.
HABS OR-129-D   pd   L

Chemawa Indian School, House
2995 Misty St.
HABS OR-129-G   p   L

Chemawa Indian School, Industrial Shops
5495 Chugach St. NE
HABS OR-129-F   pd   L

Chemawa Indian School, McBride Hall
5495 Chugach St. NE
HABS OR-129-C   pd   L

Chemawa Indian School, McNary Hall
5495 Chugach St. NE
HABS OR-129-K   pd   L

Chemawa Indian School, Winowa Hall
5495 Chugach St. NE
HABS OR-129-E   pd   L

Kay, Thomas, Woolen Mill Company
(Mission Mill Museum)
Twelfth St.
HABS OR-54   s   H
Mission Mill Museum; see Kay, Thomas,
Woolen Mill Company

Silverton

Brown, James, House
Fifth & Main Sts.
HABS OR-12   s p d   L

MULTNOMAH COUNTY

Portland

Hotel Lenox (Lenox Hotel, New)
1100-1116 SW Third St.
HABS OR-130   p d   L
Lenox Hotel, New; see Hotel Lenox
Market Block, New & Theatre
1035 SW Second Ave.
HABS OR-51   p d   L
Oriental Theatre
828 SE Grand Ave.
HABS OR-55   p d   L
Pioneer Post Office
Fifth St. between Yamhill & Morrison Sts.
HABS OR-52   p d   L

Sauvie's Island

Bybee, James F., House
HABS OR-47   s p d   L

POLK COUNTY

Dallas

Lyle, John E., House
State Hwy. 22
HABS OR-27   p d   L

Ellendale

Boarding House
HABS OR-28   s p d   L

Pedee

Johnson, John, House
HABS OR-29   s p d   L

Perrydale

Richmond, T. G., House
HABS OR-26   s p d   L

Rickreall

Nesmith, James W., House
HABS OR-25   s p d   L

WASHINGTON COUNTY

Forest Grove

Pacific University, Old College Hall
HABS OR-15   s p d   L
Smith, Alvin T., House
HABS OR-16   p d   L

Reedville

Reed, Simeon G., House
HABS OR-13   p d   L

West Union

West Union Baptist Church
HABS OR-14   s p d   L

YAMHILL COUNTY

Dayton

Fort Yamhill
U.S. Hwy. 99
HABS OR-21   s p d   L

Dundee

Hagey, Levi, House
HABS OR-20   s p d   L

Hopewell vic.

Gay, George K., House
HABS OR-24   s p d   L

Lafayette

Cook, Amos T., House
HABS OR-22   s p d   L

Lafayette vic.

Fletcher, Francis, House
HABS OR-23   s p d   L

Yamhill

Bedwell, Elisha, House
HABS OR-18   s p d   L

Yamhill vic.

Merchant, Robert, House
HABS OR-19   s p d   L
Morris, Eliam Small, House
HABS OR-17   s p d   L

Pennsylvania

ADAMS COUNTY

Bermudian vic.

Christ Evangelical Lutheran Church
(Latimore Township)
HABS PA-348   p d   L

Fairfield Bor.

Fairfield Inn; see Miller, William, House
Miller, William, House (Fairfield Inn)
HABS PA-350   p d   L

Floradale vic.

Peters, George, House (Peters, John,
House)
(Menallen Township)
HABS PA-362   p d   L
Peters, John, House; see Peters, George,
House

Gettysburg Bor.

Adams County Courthouse
HABS PA-265   p d   H
Bushman House
HABS PA-365   p   L

Culp House
HABS PA-354   s p d   L H
Gettysburg College, Old Dorm; see
Pennsylvania College, Pennsylvania Hall
Gettysburg National Military Park; see
McPherson Barn
**Lutheran Theological Seminary, Main
Building**
HABS PA-359   p d   L
McPherson Barn (Gettysburg National
Military Park)
HABS PA-5139   s   L
Pennsylvania College, Pennsylvania Hall
(Gettysburg College, Old Dorm)
HABS PA-360   p d   L

Gettysburg vic.

Black Horse Tavern
(Cumberland Township)
HABS PA-361   p d   L
Bricker Outdoor Bake Oven (Fox Outdoor
Bake Oven)
Taneytown Rd. (Cumberland Township)
HABS PA-355   s p d   L H

Brien House (Bryan House; Gettysburg
National Military Park)
(Cumberland Township)
HABS PA-342   s p d   L H
Bryan House; see Brien House
**Conewago (Huntingtown) Presbyterian
Church, doorway**
HABS PA-345   p   L
Fox Outdoor Bake Oven; see Bricker
Outdoor Bake Oven
Gettysburg National Military Park; see
Brien House
Leister, Lydia, House
Taneytown Rd.
HABS PA-341   s p   L
McClean House
Mummasburg Rd. (Cumberland Township)
HABS PA-1187   s   H

Slyder Farm, Summer Kitchen
Plum Run Rd. (Cumberland Township)
HABS PA-356-A   s   H

Slyder Farmhouse
Plum Run Rd. (Cumberland Township)
HABS PA-356   s p d   L H

Spangler Barn; see Spangler Carriage House

Spangler Carriage House (Spangler Barn) (Cumberland Township)
HABS PA-357   pd   L

Weikert Barn (Cumberland Township)
HABS PA-358   pd   L

Weikert House (Cumberland Township)
HABS PA-363   pd   L

Weikert Summer Kitchen (Cumberland Township)
HABS PA-353   pd   L

Heidlersburg vic.

Rock Chapel (Methodist) (Huntington Township)
HABS PA-352   pd   L

Hunterstown vic.

Covered Bridge over Conewago Creek; see Snyder's Fording Covered Bridge

Snyder's Fording Covered Bridge (Covered Bridge over Conewago Creek) (Straban-Tyrone Township)
HABS PA-351   pd   L

Iron Springs vic.

Stevens Furnace (Ruins) (Hamiltonban Township)
HABS PA-346   pd   L

Stevens Viaduct Spanning Tom's Creek (Hamiltonban Township)
HABS PA-347   pd   L

Littlestown vic.

St. John's Lutheran Church State Rt. 194 (Germany Township)
HABS PA-269   pd   H

Zora

Mason-Dixon Line Marker
HABS PA-349   pd   L

ALLEGHENY COUNTY

Ben Avon Bor.

Dalzell House 228 Dalzell Ave.
HABS PA-605   s   L

Churchill Bor.

Beulah Presbyterian Church Beulah Rd. (State Rt. 130)
HABS PA-602   s   L

Clairton

Clairton Works, 14 Inch Mill Engines 1 & 2 State St. vic.
HAER PA-49-B   p   H

Clairton Works, 22 Inch Number 2 Mill Engine State St.
HAER PA-49-C   p   H

Clairton Works, Blast Furn. Blowing Eng. Bldg. State St. vic.
HAER PA-49-A   p   H

U.S. Steel Corporation, Clairton Works
HAER PA-49   p   H

Dravosburg vic.

Rhodes, A. S., Springhouse Bull Run Rd.
HABS PA-413   s pd   L

Evergreen Hamlet

Hampton, Wade, House (Hampton-Kelly House; Kelly House) Evergreen Hamlet Rd. (Ross Twp.)
HABS PA-606   s   L

Hampton-Kelly House; see Hampton, Wade, House

Kelly House; see Hampton, Wade, House

Mc Keesport

McConnell House; see Muse, John J., House

Muse, John J., House (McConnell House) Muse's Lane
HABS PA-603   s   L

Pittsburgh

Allegheny County Courthouse & Jail 436 Grant St. (Courthouse)., 420 Ross St. (Jail)
HABS PA-610   s pd   L H

Allegheny County Jail Fifth St. & Ross Ave.
HABS PA-1157   pd   H

Allegheny Post Office, Old; see U.S. Allegheny Post Office

Beau Brummell Club 954 Liberty Ave.
HABS PA-625   s   L

Bedford, Dr. Nathaniel, Monument Trinity Cathedral Churchyard
HABS PA-44   s pd   L

Bouquet's Redoubt; see Fort Pitt Blockhouse

Brady Street Bridge (South Twenty-Second Street Bridge) Spanning Monongahela River
HABS PA-614
HAER PA-3   s pd   L

Brewer, Charles, House 1131 Western Ave.
HABS PA-41   s pd   L

Byers-Lyons House 901 Ridge St.
HABS PA-1158   p   H

Carnegie Inst. of Techology, Machinery Hall Tower (Carnegie Mellon University, Machinery Hall Tower) Carnegie Mellon University Campus
HABS PA-1174   s   L

Carnegie Institute of Technology, Adim. Building (Carnegie Mellon University, Baker Hall) Frew St.
HABS PA-1172   s p   L H

Carnegie Mellon University, Baker Hall; see Carnegie Institute of Technology, Adim. Building

Carnegie Mellon University, Machinery Hall Tower; see Carnegie Inst. of Techology, Machinery Hall Tower

Chatham College, Berry Hall; see Wilson House

Coltart, Joseph, House 3431 Forbes St.
HABS PA-47   s pd   L

Croghan House (Schenley House; Picnic Place) Stanton Heights
HABS PA-8-8   s pd   L

Emmanuel Protestant Episcopal Church North & Allegheny Sts.
HABS PA-426   s pd   L

English-Oliver House (Oliver House) 845 Ridge Ave.
HABS PA-425   s pd   L

Fahnestock, Benjamin A., House 408 Penn Ave.
HABS PA-45   s pd   L

124 Fancourt St. (Brick Cornices); see 442 Third Avenue (Brick Cornices)

Forks of the Ohio; see Fort Pitt Blockhouse

Fort Pitt Blockhouse (Bouquet's Redoubt; Forks of the Ohio) Point State Park
HABS PA-430   s pd   L

Fulton Theater 101 Sixth St.
HABS PA-1180   s   L

Garden Theater, The 10-12-14 W. North Ave.
HABS PA-1278   s pd   L

101 Grant Street (Brick Cornices); see 442 Third Avenue (Brick Cornices)

Harter, Eva, House 2557 Beechwood Blvd.
HABS PA-622   s   L

Heathside Cottage 416 Catoma St.
HABS PA-623   s   L

Heidelberg Apartments & Cottages Braddock Ave. & Waverly St. vic.
HABS PA-431   s pd   L

Hogg-Brunot House 216 Stockton Ave.
HABS PA-428   s pd   L

Jones & Laughlin Steel Corporation (Morgan Billet Mill Engine)
HAER PA-48   p   L

Karns, John, House 900 N. Canal St.
HABS PA-424   s pd   L

Klages, Allen M., House
5525 Beverly Pl.
HABS PA-621   s   L

334 Liberty Avenue (Brick Cornices); see
442 Third Avenue (Brick Cornices)

Manchester Bridge; see North Side Point
Bridge

Miller, James, House
HABS PA-410   s pd   L

Mitchell, John M., House
524 Third Ave.
HABS PA-42   s pd   L

Morgan Billet Mill Engine; see Jones &
Laughlin Steel Corporation

Neal, Robert, Cabin
Schenley Park
HABS PA-46   s pd   L

**North Side Point Bridge (Manchester
Bridge)**
HAER PA-4   s pd   L

North Side Post Office; see U.S. Allegheny
Post Office

Oliver House; see English-Oliver House

Pennsylvania Railroad Station Rotunda
(Union Railroad Station Rotunda)
Liberty, Grant & Eleventh Sts.
HABS PA-1175   s pd   L H

Picnic Place; see Croghan House

Pittsburgh & Lake Erie Station
HABS PA-1231   p   H

Point Bridge
Spanning Monongahela River
HABS PA-604
HAER PA-5   s   L

Post Office Museum, Old; see U.S.
Allegheny Post Office

Schenley House; see Croghan House

132 Second Avenue (Brick Cornices); see
442 Third Avenue (Brick Cornices)

Shadyside Presbyterian Church
Amberson Ave. & Westminister Pl. vic.
HABS PA-432   pd   L

Shoenberger, John H., House
425 Penn Ave.
HABS PA-43   s pd   L

Singer, John F., House
1318 Singer Pl.
HABS PA-433   s pd   L

Smithfield Street Bridge
HAER PA-2   pd   L

South Twenty-Second Street Bridge; see
Brady Street Bridge

St. Peter's Protestant Episcopal Church
Forbes St. & Craft Ave. (moved from Grant
St.)
HABS PA-48   s pd   L

442 Third Avenue (Brick Cornices) (132
Second Avenue (Brick Cornices); 124
Fancourt St. (Brick Cornices); 334
Liberty Avenue (Brick Cornices); 101
Grant Street (Brick Cornices))
HABS PA-49   s d   L

Union Railroad Station Rotunda; see
Pennsylvania Railroad Station Rotunda

U.S. Allegheny Arsenal
Fortieth & Butler Sts.
HABS PA-8-1   s d   L

U.S. Allegheny Arsenal, Armory
HABS PA-8-1-F   s p   L

U.S. Allegheny Arsenal, Barracks Building
Thirty-ninth St.
HABS PA-8-1-C   s p   L

U.S. Allegheny Arsenal, Boiler House
HABS PA-8-1-G   s p   L

U.S. Allegheny Arsenal, Carriage House
HABS PA-8-1-L   p   L

**U.S. Allegheny Arsenal, Commandants'
Quarters**
Fortieth St.
HABS PA-8-1-A   s p   L

U.S. Allegheny Arsenal, Entrance Gates
Thirty-ninth St.
HABS PA-8-1-J   s p   L

U.S. Allegheny Arsenal, Guardhouse
Butler St.
HABS PA-8-1-K   s p   L

U.S. Allegheny Arsenal, Machine Shop
HABS PA-8-1-H   s p   L

U.S. Allegheny Arsenal, N. C. O. Quarters
Thirty-ninth St.
HABS PA-8-1-D   s p   L

U.S. Allegheny Arsenal, Officers' Quarters
Thirty-ninth St.
HABS PA-8-1-B   s p   L

**U.S. Allegheny Arsenal, Storehouse
Number 2**
HABS PA-8-1-E   s p   L

U.S. Allegheny Post Office (Allegheny Post
Office, Old; North Side Post Office; Post
Office Museum, Old)
Ohio St.
HABS PA-1178   s   L

**U.S. Bureau of Mines, Experimentation
Station**
Forbes Ave.
HABS PA-1166   s   H

Washington Crossing Bridge
Fortieth St.
HABS PA-1179   s   L

815-817 Western Avenue (House)
HABS PA-1247   p   H

Wilson House (Chatham College, Berry
· Hall)
HABS PA-1250   p   H

Sewickley

Sewickley Bridge
HAER PA-53   s pd   L

Sewickley Hts. Bor.

Fairacres (Jones, B. F., House)
Blackburn Rd.
HABS PA-607   s   L

Jones, B. F., House; see Fairacres

Sewickley Valley

Bridge Number One Ohio River (Sewickley
Bridge)
HAER PA-56   s   H

Sewickley Bridge; see Bridge Number One
Ohio River

Sharpsburg vic.

Ferry House
403 Dorseyville Rd. (O'Hara Twp.)
HABS PA-616   s   L

Swissvale Bor.

Trevanion Avenue (House)
HABS PA-626   s   L

BEAVER COUNTY

Ambridge Bor.

Economy Feast Hall
Church St.
HABS PA-612   s   L

Economy Meetinghouse (St. John's
Lutheran Church)
Church St.
HABS PA-627   s   L

Economy Tailor Shop & Wine Cellar
Church St.
HABS PA-613   s   L

Economy Town Plan
HABS PA-1176   s   L

St. John's Lutheran Church; see Economy
Meetinghouse

BERKS COUNTY

Baumstown vic.

Boone, Daniel, Birthplace
State Rt. 422 vic. (Exeter Twp.)
HABS PA-149   pd   L

Bernville

Conrad's Warehouse
HAER PA-57   s pd   H

Gruber Wagon Works
HAER PA-14   p   H

Lamm's Mill
HAER PA-58   p   H

Pleasant Valley Roller Mill
HAER PA-59   pd   H

Speicher Bridge
HAER PA-60   s pd   H

Union Canal Locks
HAER PA-61   pd   H

Bernville vic.

Haag-Haak Log House
State RT. 183 (Penn Twp.)
HABS PA-254   pd   L

House, Log
Host Rd. vic. (N. Heidelberg Township)
HABS PA-255   pd   L

South Bernville Hotel
Bernville-Robesonia & Host Rds. vic.
HABS PA-257   pd   L

Birdsboro

Bird, William, Mansion
Mill & Main Sts.
HABS PA-1024   pd   L

Brooke Manor
Furnace St.
HABS PA-1075   s pd   L

Brownsville vic.

Dundore Farm (Hottenstein Farm)
(moved from Mt. Pleasant vic.)
HABS PA-261   s pd   L

Hottenstein Farm; see Dundore Farm

Douglasville

Building, Old; see St. Gabriel's Church
Jones, Mouns, House (Ruins)
U.S. Rt. 422 (Amity Township)
HABS PA-1032   s pd   L

St. Gabriel's Church (Building, Old)
U.S. Rt. 422 (Amity Township)
HABS PA-1038   pd   L

Hay Creek

Hay Creek Forge
Birdsboro, Pa.
HAER PA-62   pd   H

Jacksonwald

Hock, C., Farmhouse
HABS PA-150   p   L

Kutztown vic.

Le Van Mill
Kutztown Rd. vic.
HABS PA-1030   s pd   L

Lenhartsville

Berger Farm; see Konig-Speicher Farm
Konig-Speicher Farm (Berger Farm)
(moved from Mt. Pleasant vic.)
HABS PA-258   s pd   L

Limekiln vic.

Bertolet-Herbein Cabin
(Oley Township)
HABS PA-1047   s pd   L

Ha Penny Farm; see Knabb, Abraham,
  Barn

Ha Penny Farm; see Knabb, Abraham,
  House

Knabb, Abraham, Barn (Ha Penny Farm)
Oley Line Rd. vic. (Exeter Township)
HABS PA-1043   pd   L

Knabb, Abraham, House (Ha Penny Farm)
Oley Line Rd. vic. (Exeter Township)
HABS PA-1045   pd   L

Knabb-Bieber Mill
Monocacy Creek (Exeter Township)
HABS PA-1031   pd   L

Schneider, David, House
(Oley Township)
HABS PA-1044   pd   L

Lobachsville vic.

Keim House
(Pike Township)
HABS PA-1039   pd   L

Keim Stone Cabin
(Pike Township)
HABS PA-1041   pd   L

Yoder Barn
(Pike Township)
HABS PA-1060   pd   L

Yoder, Jacob, House
(Pike Township)
HABS PA-1036   pd   L

Yoder Stone Cabin
(Pike Township)
HABS PA-1040   pd   L

Mt. Pleasant vic.

Berger Farm; see Konig-Speicher Farm
Berger Farm; see Konig-Speicher Farm
Conrad, John, House (Sheidy House)
Sheidy Rd. (Penn Township)
HABS PA-259   s pd   L

Conrad, Joseph, Farm (Miller's Farm)
State Rt. 183 & Bright School Rd. (Penn
  Twp.)
HABS PA-260   s d   L

Conrad, Joseph, Farm, Barn
St. Rt. 183 & Bright School Rd. (Penn
  Twp.)
HABS PA-260-B   s p   L

Conrad, Joseph, Farm, House
State Rt. 83 & Bright School Rd. (Penn
  Twp.)
HABS PA-260-A   s p   L

Conrad, Joseph, Farm, Pig House
St. Rt. 183 & Bright School Rd. (Penn
  Twp.)
HABS PA-260-C   p   L

Conrad, Joseph, Farm, Springhouse
St. Rt. 183 & Bright School Rd. (Penn
  Twp.)
HABS PA-260-D   p   L

Dundore Farm (Hottenstein Farm)
(moved to Brownsville vic.)
HABS PA-261   s pd   L

Dundore Farm (Hottenstein Farm)
State Rt. 183 (moved to Brownsville vic.)
HABS PA-261   s pd   L

Dundore Farm, Barn
State Rt. 183 vic. (Penn Township)
HABS PA-261-B   s p   L

Dundore Farm, Corn Crib & Wagon Shed
State Rt. 183 vic. (Penn Township)
HABS PA-261-C   s p   L

Dundore Farm, Granary
State Rt. 183 vic. (Penn Township)
HABS PA-261-D   s p   L

Dundore Farm, House
State Rt. 183 (Penn Township)
HABS PA-261-A   s p   L

Dundore Farm, Milk Shed
State Rt. 183 vic. (Penn Township)
HABS PA-261-E   s p   L

Dundore Farm, Root Cellar
State Rt. 183 vic. (Penn Township)
HABS PA-261-F   s p   L

Dundore Farm, Smokehouse
State Rt. 183 vic. (Penn Township)
HABS PA-261-G   s p   L

Dundore Farm, Springhouse
State Rt. 183 (Penn Township)
HABS PA-261-H   s p   L

Dundore Farm, Wheat Barn
State Rt. 183 vic. (Penn Township)
HABS PA-261-I   p   L

Gruber House; see Penn, William, Tavern
Gruber, Jacob, House (Speicher House)
Mt. Pleasant Rd. (Penn Township)
HABS PA-262   pd   L

Heck-Stamm-Unger Farm; see Stamm
  Farm

Hottenstein Farm; see Dundore Farm
Hottenstein Farm; see Dundore Farm
Konig-Speicher Farm (Berger Farm)
Church Rd. (moved to Lenhartsville)
HABS PA-258   s pd   L

Konig-Speicher Farm (Berger Farm)
(moved to Lenhartsville)
HABS PA-258   s pd   L

Konig-Speicher Farm, Log House
Church Rd., (N. Heidelberg Township)
HABS PA-258-A   p   L

Konig-Speicher Farm, Outdoor Bake Oven
Church Rd. (N. Heidelberg Township)
HABS PA-258-D   p   L

Konig-Speicher Farm, Smokehouse
Church Rd. (N. Heidelberg Township)
HABS PA-258-E   s p   L

Konig-Speicher Farm-Barn
Church Rd. (N. Heidelberg Township)
HABS PA-258-C   p   L

Konig-Speicher Farm-House
Church Rd. (N. Heidelberg Township)
HABS PA-258-B   p   L

Miller's Farm; see Conrad, Joseph, Farm
Moorehead House; see Stamm, Eliza,
  House

Octagon House; see Stoudt, George, House
Penn, William, Tavern (Gruber House)
Gruber Rd. & State Rt. 183 (Penn Twp.)
HABS PA-263   pd   L

Penn, William, Tavern, Privy
Gruber Rd. & State Rt. 183 (Penn Twp.)
HABS PA-263-A   p   L

Penn, William, Tavern, Smokehouse
Gruber Rd. & State Rt. 183 (Penn Twp.)
HABS PA-263-B   p   L

Penn, William, Tavern, Washhouse &
  Butcher Shop
Gruber Rd. & State Rt. 183 (Penn Twp.)
HABS PA-263-C   p   L

Querean House; see Stamm, Isaac, House

Reber Farm
Gruber Rd. vic. (Bern Township)
HABS PA-256   d   L

Reber Farm, Barn
Gruber Rd. vic. (Bern Township)
HABS PA-256-B   p   L

Reber Farm, Canal Store
Gruber Rd. vic. (Bern Township)
HABS PA-256-C   p   L

Reber Farm, House
Gruber Rd. vic. (Bern Township)
HABS PA-256-A   pd   L

Reifsnyder Farm; see
  Riem-Schmidt-Deppen Farm

Riem-Schmidt-Deppen Farm (Reifsnyder Farm)
State Rt. 183 & Church Rd. (Penn Twp.)
HABS PA-264   d   L

Riem-Schmidt-Deppen Farm, Barn
State Rt. 183 & Church Rd. (Penn Twp.)
HABS PA-264-A   p   L

Sheidy House; see Conrad, John, House
Speicher House; see Gruber, Jacob, House
Stamm, Eliza, House (Moorehead House)
Gruber Rd. (Penn Township)
HABS PA-113   s pd   L

Stamm Farm (Heck-Stamm-Unger Farm)
Gruber Rd. vic. (Penn Township)
HABS PA-266   pd   L

Stamm Farm, Barn
Gruber Rd. (Penn Township)
HABS PA-266-B   p   L

Stamm Farm, Butcher Shed, Wash House, Root Cellar
Gruber Rd. (Penn Township)
HABS PA-266-E   p   L

Stamm Farm, Chicken & Brooder Houses
Gruber Rd. (Penn Township)
HABS PA-266-C   p   L

Stamm Farm, Corn Crib & Wagon Shed
Gruber Rd. (Penn Township)
HABS PA-266-D   p   L

Stamm Farm, House
Gruber Rd. vic. (Penn Township)
HABS PA-266-A   p   L

Stamm Farm, Summer Kitchen, Smokehouse
Gruber Rd. (Penn Township)
HABS PA-266-F   p   L

Stamm, Isaac, House (Querean House)
Gruber Rd. (Penn Township)
HABS PA-112   s pd   L

Stoudt, George, House (Octagon House)
Eight Cornered House Rd. (Penn Twp.)
HABS PA-267   pd   L

Oley vic.

DeTurk House
State Rt. 622 vic. (Oley Township)
HABS PA-1023   s pd   L

Kaufman Barns
State Rt. 662 vic. (Oley Township)
HABS PA-1059   pd   L

Kaufman House
State Rt. 662 vic. (Oley Township)
HABS PA-1042   pd   L

Kaufman House, Small
State Rt. 662 vic. (Oley Township)
HABS PA-1046   pd   L

Philadelphia

312 South Front Street (House)
HABS PA-5180   p   H

Reading

12 North Fifth Street (House)
HABS PA-5143   pd   L

16-20 North Fifth Street (House)
HABS PA-5144   pd   L

26 North Fifth Street (House)
HABS PA-5146   pd   L

401 Penn Street (House)
HABS PA-5147   pd   L

Reading Friends Meeting
N. Sixth St.
HABS PA-1048   pd   L

Reading News Building (Sharp Building)
22-24 N. Fifth St.
HABS PA-5145   pd   L

Rennas Hotel, The (State Store Building)
403 Penn St.
HABS PA-5148   pd   L

Sharp Building; see Reading News Building
Skew Arch Bridge
N. Sixth St.
HABS PA-1025   pd   L

State Store Building; see Rennas Hotel, The

Robesonia

Ege, George, Mansion
U.S. Rt. 422 vic.
HABS PA-1026   pd   L

Spangsville vic.

Griesemer Mill
State Rt. 562 (Oley Township)
HABS PA-1019   pd   L

Griesemer Mill Covered Bridge
State Rt. 662 vic. (Oley Twp.)
HABS PA-1020   pd   L

Hunter House
State Rt. 662 vic. (Oley Twp.)
HABS PA-1034   pd   L

Spang House
State Rt. 662 vic. (Oley Twp.)
HABS PA-1033   pd   L

St. Peters vic.

Hopewell Village, Bethesda Baptist Church (Hopewell Village National Historic Site)
HABS PA-5167   s   H

Hopewell Village, Boarding House Number Twenty-four (Hopewell Village National Historic Site)
HABS PA-5158   s   H

Hopewell Village, Charcoal House, Number Nine (Hopewell Village National Historic Site)
HABS PA-5159   s   H

Hopewell Village, Employees Quarters, Number 71 (Hopewell Village National Historic Site; Lloyd House; Lucas House)
HABS PA-5160   s p   H

Hopewell Village, Furnace Office-Store, Number Three (Hopewell Village National Historic Site)
HABS PA-5161   s p   H

Hopewell Village, Ironmaster's Mansion (Hopewell Village National Historic Site)
HABS PA-5162   p   H

Hopewell Village, Lloyd Harrison House (Hopewell Villlage National Historic Site)
HABS PA-5168   p   H

Hopewell Village National Historic Site
HABS PA-5157   p   H

Hopewell Village National Historic Site; see Hopewell Village, Bethesda Baptist Church

Hopewell Village National Historic Site; see Hopewell Village, Boarding House Number Twenty-four

Hopewell Village National Historic Site; see Hopewell Village, Charcoal House, Number Nine

Hopewell Village National Historic Site; see Hopewell Village, Employees Quarters, Number 71

Hopewell Village National Historic Site; see Hopewell Village, Furnace Office-Store, Number Three

Hopewell Village National Historic Site; see Hopewell Village, Ironmaster's Mansion

Hopewell Village National Historic Site; see Hopewell Village, Tenant House, Number One

Hopewell Village National Historic Site; see Hopewell Village, Tenant House, Number Three

Hopewell Village National Historic Site; see Hopewell Village, Village Barn

Hopewell Village, Tenant House, Number One (Hopewell Village National Historic Site)
HABS PA-5163   s   H

Hopewell Village, Tenant House, Number Three (Hopewell Village National Historic Site)
HABS PA-5165   s   H

Hopewell Village, Tenant House, Number Two (Hopewwell Village National Historic Site)
HABS PA-5164   s   H

Hopewell Village, Village Barn (Hopewell Village National Historic Site)
HABS PA-5166   s p   H

Hopewell Villlage National Historic Site; see Hopewell Village, Lloyd Harrison House

Hopewwell Village National Historic Site; see Hopewell Village, Tenant House, Number Two

Lloyd House; see Hopewell Village, Employees Quarters, Number 71
Lucas House; see Hopewell Village, Employees Quarters, Number 71

Stonersville

Blacksmith Shop, Log
HABS PA-148   p   L

Stonersville vic.

Exeter Friends Meetinghouse
State Rt. 662 (Exeter Twp.)
HABS PA-1021   s pd   L
Mill Tract Farm
Mill Rd. (Exeter Township)
HABS PA-1037   s pd   L

Womelsdorf vic.

Brown House
U.S. Rt. 422 vic. (Marion Township)
HABS PA-1049   pd   L
Charming Forge, Ironmaster's House
Tulpehocken Creek (Marion Township)
HABS PA-1022   pd   L
Lime Kilns
State Rt. 419
HABS PA-142   p   L

Yellow House

Yellow House Hotel
Rts. 662 & 562 (Amity Twp.)
HABS PA-1035   pd   L

Yellow House vic.

De Benneville, Dr. George, House
State Rt. 662 vic. (Oley Township)
HABS PA-1029   pd   L
Fisher, Henry, House
State Rt. 622 (Oley Twp.)
HABS PA-1027   pd   L

BLAIR COUNTY

Cresson vic.

Allegheny Portage Railroad, Skew Arch Bridge
HABS PA-1232   s   H

BRADFORD COUNTY

Athens Township

Franklin, Col. John, House
HABS PA-226   pd   L

Sayre

Lehigh Valley Railroad, Sayre Repair Shops
HAER PA-33   p   L
Lehigh Valley Railroad, Sayre Station
HAER PA-32   p   L

Terrytown

Log Cabin
HABS PA-227   s pd   L

Wysox

Presbyterian Church, Brick
State Rt. 187
HABS PA-222   s pd   L

BUCKS COUNTY

Andalusia

Andalusia (Biddle, Nicholas, Estate)
Cornwells Hts. vic.
HABS PA-1248   s pd   H
Biddle, Nicholas, Estate; see Andalusia

Bristol

Lenox-Keene House
710 Radcliffe St.
HABS PA-1234   p   H

Doylestown

Bucks County Historical Society; see Mercer Museum
Harvey House
15 E. State St.
HABS PA-1006   p   L
Mercer Museum (Bucks County Historical Society)
Pine & Ashland Sts.
HABS PA-1007   pd   L H

Doylestown vic.

Fonthill (Mercer, H. C., House)
E. Court St. (Buckingham Twp.)
HABS PA-1140   pd   H
Mercer, H. C., House; see Fonthill
Mercer, H. C., Tile Works; see Moravian Pottery and Tile Works
Moravian Pottery and Tile Works (Mercer, H. C., Tile Works)
State Rt. 313 (Buckingham Twp.)
HABS PA-1139   pd   H

Newton vic.

Jenks' Hall
Ellis Rd. (Middletown Township)
HABS PA-1235   d   H

Riegelsville

Delaware River Bridge
HAER PA-31   p   L

BUTLER COUNTY

Harmony vic.

Stauffer, David, Farm Buildings
HABS PA-414   s pd   L

CAMBRIA COUNTY

Cresson vic.

Lemon, Samuel, House
(Cresson Township)
HABS PA-1236   s   H

Geistown vic.

Allegheny Portage Railroad, Staple Bend Tunnel
(Conemaugh Township)
HABS PA-1233   s   H

CENTRE COUNTY

Bellefonte

Brockerhoff House
Bishop & Springs Sts.
HABS PA-333   s pd   L
Harris, James, House (Willowbank)
S. Potter St.
HABS PA-331   s pd   L
Linn, Henry S., House
N. Allegheny St.
HABS PA-8-5   s pd   L
Willowbank; see Harris, James, House

Boalsburg

Boalsburg Tavern
HABS PA-8-7   s pd   L

Centre Hall vic.

Fort Tavern
HABS PA-336   s pd   L

Nittany

Schaeffer House
HABS PA-8-6   s pd   L

Philipsburg

Halehurst; see Philips, Hardman, House
Philips, Hardman, House (Halehurst)
E. Presqueisle St.
HABS PA-332   s pd   L
Union Church
E. Presqueisle St.
HABS PA-334   s pd   L

Rock Forge

Benner House
HABS PA-335   s p   L

CHESTER COUNTY

Avondale Bor.

Avondale; see Miller, William, House
Miller, William, Barn
Elliott Rd.
HABS PA-5137-A   p   L
Miller, William, House (Avondale)
Elliott Rd.
HABS PA-5137   pd   L
Miller, William, Tenant House
Elliot Rd.
HABS PA-5137-B   p   L

Bacton

Hopper, Margaret, Log House; see Jacobs, John, House
House
(moved from Concordville)
HABS PA-174   p   L

Jacobs, John, Barn
Conestoga Rd. (East Whiteland Township)
HABS PA-1209-A   p   L
Jacobs, John, House (Hopper, Margaret,
    Log House)
Conestoga Rd. (East Whiteland Township)
HABS PA-1209   pd   L

Bacton vic.
Gunkle, Michael, Spring, Mill
Moore Rd. (East Whiteland Township)
HABS PA-1113   pd   L

Berwyn vic.
Bair, Mary A., House (Hunter-Bair House)
Conestoga Rd. & Cassatt Ave. (Tredyffrin
    Twp.)
HABS PA-117   pd   L
Hunter-Bair House; see Bair, Mary A.,
    House

Birmingham
Birmingham Friends Meetinghouse
Birmingham & Meetinghouse Rds.
HABS PA-1193   s pd   L
Birmingham Octagonal Schoolhouse
Birmingham & Meetinghouse Rds.
HABS PA-5138   p   L

Birmingham vic.
Darlington, Thomas, House (Spackman
    Corner Chimney House)
228 W. Street Rd. (Thornbury Township)
HABS PA-1110   pd   L
Sharpless House (Walker House)
Birmingham Rd. (Birmingham Township)
HABS PA-118   pd   L
Spackman Corner Chimney House; see
    Darlington, Thomas, House
Walker House; see Sharpless House

Bulltown
Bull, Thomas, House; see Mount Pleasant
Mount Pleasant (Bull, Thomas, House;
    Roberts' Plantation)
Bulltown Rd. (East Nantmeal Twp.)
HABS PA-248   p   L
Roberts' Plantation; see Mount Pleasant

Chadds Ford vic.
Barnes-Brinton House
U.S. Rt. 1 (Pennsbury Township)
HABS PA-173   pd   L
Harvey, William, House
Brinton Bridge Rd. (Pennsbury Twp.)
HABS PA-1204   pd   L

Charlestown
Charlestown Village Historic District; see
    Harvey, Job, House
Charlestown Village House; see Harvey,
    Job, House
Harvey, Job, House (Charlestown Village
    House; Charlestown Village Historic
    District)
Church Rd. (Charlestown Township)
HABS PA-1196   pd   L

Chatham
Center Chimney House; see Half-Way
    House Tavern, New
Half-Way House Tavern, New (Center
    Chimney House)
State Rts. 41 & 841 (London Grove Twp.)
HABS PA-119   pd   L

Chatham vic.
Morriseianna
State Rt. 41 (London Grove Twp.)
HABS PA-146   pd   L
Pusey House
Woodview Rd. (London Grove Township)
HABS PA-158   pd   L

Chester Springs
Chester Springs Hotel; see Yellow Springs
    Tavern
Good News Building; see Yellow Springs
    Tavern
Yellow Springs Bathhouse
Yellow Springs & Art School Rds.
HABS PA-1197   pd   L
Yellow Springs Summerhouse
Yellow Springs & Art School Rds.
HABS PA-1198   pd   L
Yellow Springs Tavern (Chester Springs
    Hotel; Good News Building)
Yellow Springs & Art School Rds.
HABS PA-1131   pd   L

Chester Springs vic.
Up-and-Down Sawmill
(moved to Smithsonian Inst., Wash., D. C.)
HABS PA-116   pd   L

Chrome
Chrome Hotel; see Cross Keys Tavern
Cross Keys Tavern (Chrome Hotel)
State Rts. 272 & 42 vic. (East Nottingham
    Twp.)
HABS PA-1200   pd   L

Clonmell vic.
Pennock, Joseph House; see Primitive Hall
Primitive Hall (Pennock, Joseph House)
State Rt. 841 (W. Marlborough Twp.)
HABS PA-167   pd   L

Coatesville vic.
Romansville Friends Meetinghouse Sheds
(moved from PA, Romansville)
HABS PA-1101   pd   L
Stoltzfus House
U.S. Rt. 30 vic. (Valley Township)
HABS PA-159   pd   L

Concordville
House
(moved to Bacton)
HABS PA-174   p   L

Copesville
Brandywine Bridge; see Cope's Bridge
Cope's Bridge (Brandywine Bridge)
State Rt. 162 (East Bradford Twp.)
HABS PA-206   pd   L

Copesville vic.
Taylor, Abiah, House
Brandywine Creek Rd. (East Bradford Twp.
)
HABS PA-204   pd   L
Taylor-Parke House
St. Rt. 162 (East Bradford Twp.)
HABS PA-205   p   L

Coventryville
Coventry Forge Inn (Nutt, Samuel, House)
Nantmeal Rd. (South Coventry Township)
HABS PA-1133   pd   L
Nutt, Samuel, House; see Coventry Forge
    Inn

Devault vic.
Bones, William & Rebecca, House
White Horse Rd. vic. (Charlestown
    Township)
HABS PA-1189   pd   L
Bones, William & Rebecca, Springhouse
White Horse Rd. vic. (Charlestown
    Township)
HABS PA-1189-A   pd   L
Church of St. Peter-in-the-Great Valley (St.
    Peter's Protestant Episcopal Church)
Saint Peter's Rd. (East Whiteland
    Township)
HABS PA-1106   pd   L
St. Peter's Protestant Episcopal Church; see
    Church of St. Peter-in-the-Great Valley
William Barn
Mine Rd. (Charlestown Township)
HABS PA-1216   pd   L

Downingtown Bor.
Downingtown Public Library; see Todd,
    William A., House
Hunt-Pollock Mill
Race St.
HABS PA-170   pd   L
Todd, William A., House (Downingtown
    Public Library)
330 E. Lancaster Ave.
HABS PA-169   p   L

Downingtown vic.
Ashbridge House; see Baldwin-Sharpless
    House
Baldwin-Sharpless House (Ashbridge
    House)
U.S. Rt. 30 (East Caln Township)
HABS PA-1309   pd   L
Belle School
(East Caln Township)
HABS PA-168   p   L
Downing House
Bell Tavern Rd. (East Caln Township)
HABS PA-171   pd   L

Hoopes Currying Shop
U.S. Rt. 322 (Caln Township)
HABS PA-1222   pd   L
Mendenhall-Valentine-Edge House
State Rt. 40 (Caln Twp.)
HABS PA-1201   pd   L
Parke House
Rock Raymond Rd. (Caln Twp.)
HABS PA-1211   pd   L
Valentine-Edge Mill
State Rt. 340
HABS PA-1202   pd   L

Glenloch
Loch Aerie (Lockwood, William E., House)
U.S. Rt. 30 (E. Whiteland Twp.)
HABS PA-181   pd   L
Lockwood, William E., House; see Loch Aerie
Zook Barn
King Rd. (East Whiteland Township)
HABS PA-1218   pd   L

Green Lawn vic.
Marlboro Plank House; see Sharity Road (House)
Sharity Road (House) (Marlboro Plank House)
(West Marlborogh Township)
HABS PA-160   pd   L

Grubbs Mill
Ivy House; see Wollerton, Charles, House
Log House; see Wollerton, Charles, House
Wollerton, Charles, House (Ivy House; Log House)
Valley Creek & Sunset Hollow Rds.
HABS PA-1208   pd   L

Hopewell
Hopewell Academy
Hopewell Rd. (East Nottingham Twp.)
HABS PA-1311   pd   L

Kennett Sq. vic.
Cedarcroft (Taylor, Bayard, House)
Bayard Dr. (East Marlborough Twp.)
HABS PA-172   p   L
Taylor, Bayard, House; see Cedarcroft

Knauertown
Halley House; see Rogers, Phillip, House
Penn Wick; see Rogers, Phillip, House
Rogers, Philip, Barn
State Rt. 23 (Warwick Twp.)
HABS PA-114-A   p   L
Rogers, Phillip, House (Penn Wick; Halley House)
State Rt. 83 (Warwick Twp.)
HABS PA-114   p   L

Knauertown vic.
Branson, William, House; see Warrenpoint
Templin House; see Warrenpoint

Warrenpoint (Branson, William, House; Templin House)
State Rt. 83 (Warwick Twp.)
HABS PA-115   pd   L

Landenberg vic.
Miller-Pusey Mill
Broad Run Rd. (New Garden Township)
HABS PA-252   s   L

Ludwigs Cor. vic.
Buckwalter, John, House
State Rt. 401 (East Nantmeal Twp.)
HABS PA-1195   pd   H

Marsh
Hause Smokehouse
State Rt. 401 (East Nantmeal Twp.)
HABS PA-1206   pd   L
Hause Store
State Rt. 401 (East Nantmeal Twp.)
HABS PA-1205   pd   L

Marshallton
Bradford Friends Meetinghouse; see Marshallton Friends Meetinghouse
Cunningham Blacksmith Shop; see Marshallton Blacksmith Shop
Marshall, Humphry, House
State Rt. 162 (West Bradford Twp.)
HABS PA-203   pd   L
Marshallton Blacksmith Shop (Cunningham Blacksmith Shop)
State Rt. 162 (West Bradford Twp.)
HABS PA-1102   pd   L
Marshallton Friends Meetinghouse (Bradford Friends Meetinghouse)
Northbrook Rd. (West Bradford Twp.)
HABS PA-1105   pd   L

Marshallton vic.
Arnold-Temple House (Temple-Webster-Stoner House)
Broad Run Rd. (West Bradfort Twp.)
HABS PA-1109   pd   L
Temple-Webster-Stoner House; see Arnold-Temple House

Martins's Corner
Martin's Corner House
Cedar Knoll Rd. (West Caln Township)
HABS PA-209   pd   L

Milltown
Hickman House (Milltown Plank House)
St. Rt. 3 (East Goshen Township)
HABS PA-166   p   L
Milltown Plank House; see Hickman House

Mount Rocky
Ankrim, Samuel, Shop (Brick Shop)
Chrome Rd. (Elk Township)
HABS PA-1194   pd   L
Brick Shop; see Ankrim, Samuel, Shop
Mount Rocky Methodist Church
Chrome & Chrome-New London Rds.
HABS PA-1210   pd   L

Northbrook vic.
Allen House
Northbrook Rd. (Pocopson Township)
HABS PA-1190   pd   L

Paoli vic.
Cedar Hollow Railroad Station
Cedar Hollow Rd. (Tredyffrin Twp.)
HABS PA-1199   pd   L
Diamond Rock Schoolhouse
Yellow Springs Rd. (Tredyffrin Twp.)
HABS PA-207   pd   L
Jerman-Walker Springhouse (Wilson Springhouse)
N. Valley Rd. (Tredyffrin Township)
HABS PA-1217   pd   L
Waynesborough
2049 Waynesborough Rd. (Easttown Township)
HABS PA-208   pd   L
Wilson Springhouse; see Jerman-Walker Springhouse

Parkesburg Bor.
Parke, David, House
40 E. Main St.
HABS PA-200   pd   L
Parke, John, House
345 Main St.
HABS PA-1310   pd   L

Parkesburg vic.
Upper Octoraro Presbyterian Church Session House
State Rt. 10 & Octoraro Rd.
HABS PA-201   pd   L

Phoenixville vic.
Moore Hall; see Moore, William, House
Moore, William, House (Moore Hall)
State Rt. 23 & Reading Railroad Tracks vic.
HABS PA-1135   pd   L

Pittsburgh
North Side Market
Federal & E. Ohio Sts.
HABS PA-601   s   L

Pughtown vic.
Lundale Farm, House (Townsend, Samuel House)
State Rt. 100
HABS PA-1308   s   L
Lundale Farm, Springhouse
State Rt. 100
HABS PA-1308-A   s   L
Townsend, Samuel House; see Lundale Farm, House

Romansville
Barn, 1804; see Romans, John, Barn
Romans, John, Barn (Barn, 1804)
Star Gazer Rd. (West Bradford Twp.)
HABS PA-165   pd   L

Romansville Friends Meetinghouse
(moved to PA, Coatsville vic.)
HABS PA-1101   pd   L

Romansville Friends Meetinghouse Sheds
Shadyside Rd. (moved to Coatesville vic.)
HABS PA-1101   pd   L

Sconnelltown

Sconnelltown House
Birmingham Rd. (East Bradford Twp.)
HABS PA-202   pd   L

Sconnelltown vic.

Strode's Grist Mill
Lenape & Birmingham Rds.
HABS PA-251   pd   L

St. Peters vic.

Hopewell Village National Historic Site
HABS PA-5157   p   H

Strafford

Eagle School
Old Eagle School Rd. (Tredyffrin Twp.)
HABS PA-1129   pd   L

Strafford Railroad Station
Old Eagle School Rd. (Tredyffrin Twp.)
HABS PA-268   pd   L

Tanguy vic.

Hoopes, Daniel, House
State Rt. 926 (Westtown Twp.)
HABS PA-161   pd   L

Thorndale

Pim Hexagonal School (Six-Sided School)
Caln Twp. Municipal Park (moved from
   Bailey Rd.)
HABS PA-5136   pd   L

Six-Sided School; see Pim Hexagonal
   School

Towerville

Fallowfield Octagonal House; see Pierce,
   Lukens, House

Pierce, Lukens, House (Fallowfield
   Octagonal House)
Wilmington Rd. (East Fallowfield Twp.)
HABS PA-1139   p   L

West Chester Bor.

Bank of Chester County (National Bank of
   Chester County; Southeast National
   Bank)
17 N. High St.
HABS PA-1126   pd   L

Baptist Church of West Chester
221 S. High St.
HABS PA-1191   pd   L

Brinton Serpentine House; see Brinton,
   Sibyla, House

Brinton, Sibyla, House (Brinton Serpentine
   House)
311 S. Church St.
HABS PA-249   p   L

Chester County Courthouse
10 N. High St.
HABS PA-1119   pd   L

Chester County Historical Society; see
   Chester County Horticultural Hall

Chester County Horticultural Hall (Chester
   County Historical Society)
225 N. High St.
HABS PA-1121   pd   L

Chester County Hotel (Mansion House
   Hotel)
36 W. Market St.
HABS PA-1112   pd   L

Chester County Prison
235 W. Market St.
HABS PA-1134   pd   L

136 East Gay Street (Bakery) (Sorber Brick
   Store)
HABS PA-244   p   L

Ebbs, William, House; see Mayfield

Everhart, William, Building (Highley
   Building)
28 W. Market St.
HABS PA-1207   pd   L

First Presbyterian Church
130 W. Miner St.
HABS PA-1115   pd   L

Hickman Fountain
225 N. Matlack St. (moved from Chester
   Courthouse)
HABS PA-247   p   L

Highley Building; see Everhart, William,
   Building

Holy Trinity Protestant Episcopal Church
238 S. High St.
HABS PA-1223   pd   L

Mansion House Hotel; see Chester County
   Hotel

Matlack-Townsend House (Townsend,
   David, House)
225 N. Matlack St.
HABS PA-243   pd   L

Mayfield (Ebbs, William, House)
600 N. New St.
HABS PA-1104   pd   L

National Bank of Chester County; see Bank
   of Chester County

Pennsylvania Railroad Station
Market St.
HABS PA-246   p   L

Sharples, Philip, House
400 S. Church St.
HABS PA-164   pd   L

Sorber Brick Store; see 136 East Gay Street
   (Bakery)

Southeast National Bank; see Bank of
   Chester County

Townsend, David, House; see
   Matlack-Townsend House

Villa Maria Convent; see West Chester
   Young Ladies Seminary (School)

West Chester State College; see West
   Chester State Normal School

West Chester State Normal School (West
   Chester State College)
S. High St.
HABS PA-250   p   L

**West Chester Young Ladies Seminary
   (School)** (Villa Maria Convent)
300 Maple Ave.
HABS PA-1215   pd   L

West Chester vic.

Collins, Joseph, House
633 Goshen Rd.
HABS PA-1114   pd   L

Matlack, George, House
409 Westtown Rd.
HABS PA-1221   pd   L

Rogers, William & Mary, House; see
   Rogers-Hoopes House

Rogers-Hoopes House (Rogers, William &
   Mary, House)
1121 Fernhill Rd.
HABS PA-1212   pd   L

Taylor, Lowndes, Barn
937 Pottstown Pike
HABS PA-1100   pd   L

Taylor, Lowndes, Carriage House
937 Pottstown Pike
HABS PA-1100-A   p   L

Taylor, Lowndes, Smokehouse
937 Pottstown Pike
HABS PA-1100-B   p   L

West Grove vic.

Jackson, Joseph, House
Old Baltimore Pike (London Grove Twp.)
HABS PA-1224   pd   L

Westtown vic.

Beehive, The; see Woodward, Richard,
   House

Woodward, Richard, House (Beehive, The)
Concord Rd. (Thornbury Township)
HABS PA-1192   pd   L

Whitehorse vic.

Bartram's Covered Bridge
Spanning Crum Creek
   (Willistown-Newtown Townships)
HABS PA-1108   pd   L

Plumsock; see Yarnall-Hibberd House

Thomas Mill
Crum Creek (Willistown Township)
HABS PA-1214   pd   L

Vogdes, Jacob, House
Providence Rd. (Willistown Township)
HABS PA-1219   pd   L

Yarnall-Hibberd House (Plumsock)
Plumsock Rd. (Willistown Township)
HABS PA-182   pd   L

Willistown vic.

Yarnall-Garrett House
West Chester Pike (Willistown Township)
HABS PA-1203   pd   L

Willowdale

Pyle House
State Rt. 926 (East Marlborough Twp.)
HABS PA-162   p   L

Wyebrooke vic.

Isabella Furnace
Bollinger Dr. (West Nantmeal Twp.)
HABS PA-163   pd   L

CLINTON COUNTY

Lock Haven

Frank-Harvey House
229 N. Jay St.
HABS PA-1304   s pd   H
McCormick, John F., House
234 E. Church St.
HABS PA-1305   s pd   H
Mussina, Lyons, House
123 N. Jay St.
HABS PA-1306   s pd   H
Vosburg, Andrew, House
302 E. Church St.
HABS PA-1303   s pd   H

COLUMBIA COUNTY

Briar Creek

Methodist Episcopal Church
HABS PA-213   s pd   L

Catawissa

Quaker Meetinghouse
Third & South Sts.
HABS PA-212   s pd   L

Millville

Friends Meetinghouse
HABS PA-218   s pd   L

CRAWFORD COUNTY

Cambridge Spr. vic.

**Erie Railroad, Diverging French Creek
    Bridges**
State Rt. 408 vic.
HAER PA-27-A & 27-B   p   H
**Erie Railroad, Parallel French Creek
    Bridge**
State Rt. 408 vic.
HAER PA-28-A & 28-B   p   H

Cambridge Springs

Erie Railroad Cambridge Springs Station
Railroad St. vic.
HAER PA-26   p   H

Cochranton

**Erie Railroad, Cochranton Passenger &
    Freight Sta.**
St. Rt. 173
HAER PA-29   p   H

Conneautville

Conneautville Baptist Church; see Trinity
    Protestant Episcopal Church
Trinity Protestant Episcopal Church
    (Conneautville Baptist Church)
1301 Water St.
HABS PA-609   s   L

East Titusville vic.

Chase House
Old Enterprise-Titusville Rd.
HABS PA-1237   p   H

Hydetown

Ridgeway, Charles, House
HABS PA-5130   p   L
Ridgeway House
HABS PA-543   p   L

Meadville

Allegheny College, Bentley Hall
HABS PA-525   p   L
Atlanta & Great Western Railroad
    (Meadville Blacksmith Shop; Erie
    Railroad)
HAER PA-11-B   s p   H
Atlanta & Great Western Railroad
    (Meadville Repair Shops; Erie Railroad)
HAER PA-11   p   H
Atlanta & Great Western Railroad
    (Meadville Storehouse; Erie Railroad)
HAER PA-11-C   s p   H
Atlanta & Great Western Railroad
    (Meadville Machine & Erecting Shop;
    Erie Railroad)
HAER PA-11-A   s p   L
Erie Railroad; see Atlanta & Great Western
    Railroad
Erie Railroad; see Atlanta & Great Western
    Railroad
Erie Railroad; see Atlanta & Great Western
    Railroad
Erie Railroad; see Atlanta & Great Western
    Railroad
Erie Railroad, Meadville Station
U.S. Rt. 6-19
HAER PA-13   p   H
Erie Railway, Meadville Station
McHenry St.
HAER PA-12   p   H
Independent Congregational Church
HABS PA-524   p   L
Mead Avenue Bridge
HAER PA-19   p   L
Meadville Blacksmith Shop; see Atlanta &
    Great Western Railroad
Meadville Machine & Erecting Shop; see
    Atlanta & Great Western Railroad
Meadville Repair Shops; see Atlanta &
    Great Western Railroad
Meadville Storehouse; see Atlanta & Great
    Western Railroad
Reynolds House
HABS PA-548   p   L

Meadville vic.

**Erie Railroad, Buchanan Junction
    Interlocking Tower**
HAER PA-20   p   H
Thomas, Albert, Summerhouse
Rt. 98
HABS PA-563   p   L

New Richmond vic.

Flint House
HABS PA-576   p   L

Riceville

Congregational Church
State Rt. 77
HABS PA-514   s pd   L
Grist Mill
Oil Creek
HABS PA-532   pd   L
Hendryx House
State Rt. 77
HABS PA-520   s pd   L
Westgate-Bruner House
State Rt. 77
HABS PA-519   s pd   L

Saegertown

Saeger, Edward, House
HABS PA-523   p   L

Titusville

Drake, Col., House
HABS PA-5108   p   L
Kelly, William, Homestead
HABS PA-5115   p   L

Townville

Stevens House
HABS PA-5126   p   L

Woodcock

McPheeter House
HABS PA-546   p   L
Methodist Church
HABS PA-5135   p   L

DAUPHIN COUNTY

Fort Hunter

Fort Hunter Mansion
HABS PA-38   s pd   L

Harrisburg

Broad Street Market, Frame Wing
Verbeke St.
HABS PA-1156   s p   H
First Capitol Buildings
HABS PA-37   s pd   L
Maclay, William, Mansion
Front & South Sts.
HABS PA-310   s pd   L
**St. Stephen's P. E. Church, Residence of
    Dean**
215 N. Front St.
HABS PA-39   s pd   L

U.S. Post Office & Courthouse
Third & Walnut Sts.
HABS PA-1255   pd   H

Lingelestown vic.
Mackey, Capt. James, House
HABS PA-312   s   L

Middletown
St. Peter's Church, United Lutheran
N. Union St.
HABS PA-36   s pd   L

Paxtang
Elder, John, House & Barn
Twenty-fourth & Ellerslie Sts.
HABS PA-32   s pd   L
Paxton Presbyterian Church
Sharon St.
HABS PA-31   s pd   L
Rutherford Stone House (Springhouse)
HABS PA-33   s pd   L
Springhouse; see Rutherford Stone House

Paxtang vic.
Willow Dale Farm, Brick House
HABS PA-35   s pd   L

DELAWARE COUNTY

Broomall vic.
Massey, Thomas, House
Lawrence & Springhouse Rds. (Marple Twp.)
HABS PA-1257   pd   H

Chadds Ford
Chadds, John, House
State Rt. 100 (Birmingham Township)
HABS PA-1256   pd   H
Gilpin, Joseph, Cart House
U.S. Rt. 1 (Birmingham Township)
HABS PA-1116-A   pd   H
Gilpin, Joseph, House (Lafayette Quarters)
U.S. Rt. 1 (Birmingham Township)
HABS PA-1116   pd   L
Gilpin, Joseph, Root House
U.S. Rt. 1 (Birmingham Township)
HABS PA-1116-B   p   H
Gilpin, Joseph, Springhouse
U.S. Rt. 1 (Birmingham Township)
HABS PA-1116-C   p   H
Lafayette Quarters; see Gilpin, Joseph, House

Concordville
House
U.S. Rt. 1 vic. (moved to Bacton)
HABS PA-174   p   L

Darby
Bonsall House
1009 Main St.
HABS PA-127   p   L

Darby vic.
Blue Bell Tavern
7303 Woodland Ave.
HABS PA-131   pd   L
Swedish Log Cabin, Lower
Darby Creek vic.
HABS PA-135   s pd   L
Swedish Log Cabin, Upper
Darby Creek vic.
HABS PA-136   s pd   L

Dilworthtown vic.
Brinton 1704 House
Oakland Rd. (Birmingham Township)
HABS PA-1258   pd   H

Essington
Lazaretto, The
Delaware River vic.
HABS PA-125   pd   L H

Havertown vic.
Flintlock (Reese, Joseph, House)
Lawrence Rd. (Haverford Township)
HABS PA-1230   p   H
Lawrence Cabin
(Haverford Township)
HABS PA-1238   p   H
Nitre Hall Powder Magazine
(Haverford Township)
HABS PA-1279   s   H
Pont Reading House
2713 Havertown Rd. (Haverford Township)
HABS PA-1239   p   H
Reese, Joseph, House; see Flintlock

Ithan
Academy of Notre Dame de Namur; see Godfrey, Lincoln, House
Godfrey, Lincoln, House (Academy of Notre Dame de Namur)
Sproul & Godfrey Rds. (Radnor Twp.)
HABS PA-1241   p   H

Media vic.
Quaker Meetinghouse
HABS PA-180   p   L

Norwood
Mortensen, Morton, House
Winona Ave. & Amosland Rd.
HABS PA-1240   s   H

Radnor
Bel Orme
County Line Rd. (Radnor Township)
HABS PA-1001   pd   L
Bolingbroke
King of Prussia Rd.(Radnor Twp.)
HABS PA-1000   pd   L
Gaybrook; see Hillside
Hillside (Gaybrook)
King of Prussia Rd. (Radnor Township)
HABS PA-1002   pd   L

Morgan Barn
Matsons Ford Rd. (Radnor Township)
HABS PA-1003   pd   L
Morgan Farmhouse
Matsons Ford Rd. (Radnor Township)
HABS PA-1004   pd   L
St. Martin's Church (Episcopal)
King of Prussia Rd. (Radnor Township)
HABS PA-1242   p   H
Vanor
Lancaster Ave. & Radnor Railroad Station vic.
HABS PA-193   pd   L

St. Davids
Nantmell Hall
Lancaster Ave., Radnor-Chester Rd. vic.
HABS PA-192   pd   L
Nantmell Hall, Tenant House
Lancaster Ave. & Radnor-Chester Rd.
HABS PA-1066   pd   L

Swarthmore
Pennock, William, House
Swarthmore Ave. (moved to PA, Upland)
HABS PA-1243   p   H

Upland
Pennock, William, House
Race St. (moved from Swarthmore)
HABS PA-1243   p   H
Pusey, Caleb, House
Race St.
HABS PA-1079   s p   H

Villanova
Ashwood
208 Ashwood Rd. (Radnor Township)
HABS PA-194   pd   L
Chuckswood (House, Brick)
Spring Mill Rd. (Radnor Township)
HABS PA-195   pd   L
House, Brick; see Chuckswood
Woodstock
South Spring Mill Rd. (Radnor Township)
HABS PA-196   pd   L
Woodstock, Barn
South Spring Mill Rd. (Radnor Township)
HABS PA-197   pd   L

Wallingford
Avondale; see Leiper, Thomas, House
Furness, Horace H., Estate; see Lindenshade
Horace, Jayne House; see Subrosa
Leiper, Thomas, House (Avondale)
519 Avondale Rd. (Nether Providence Twp.)
HABS PA-1244   p   H
Lindenshade (Furness, Horace H., Estate)
Furness La. (Nether Providence Twp.)
HABS PA-1245   pd   H
Subrosa (Horace, Jayne House)
Turner Rd. (Nether Providence Twp.)
HABS PA-1213   p   H

Wayne

Jones Farm, Springhouse
Lancaster Pike & Farm Rd. (Radnor Twp.)
HABS PA-199   pd   L

Jones Farmhouse
Lancaster Pike (Radnor Township)
HABS PA-198   pd   L

St. David's Church, Old (Episcopal)
Valley Forge Rd.
HABS PA-176   pd   L H

Whitehorse vic.

Bartram's Covered Bridge
Spanning Crum Creek
   (Willistown-Newtown Townships)
HABS PA-1108   pd   L

ERIE COUNTY

Corry

Hatch School
HABS PA-515   pd   L

Corry vic.

Penna. Railroad, Erie Railroad Bridge
State Rt. 89
HAER PA-34   p   L

Edinboro

First Constitutional Presbyterian Church
HABS PA-5114   p   L

Hencke House
HABS PA-5113   p   L

Erie

Customs House, Old
415 State St.
HABS PA-53   s pd   L

Empire Stores (Gage Hotel)
501-505 State St.
HABS PA-5142   pd   L

Gage Hotel; see Empire Stores

Hughes Log House
136 E. Third St.
HABS PA-5117   p   L

Land Lighthouse
Front St.
HABS PA-517   s pd   L

Perry Memorial Building (Tavern, Old)
Second & French Sts.
HABS PA-52   s pd   L

Presque Isle Lighthouse
Peninsula Dr., Presque Isle State Park
HABS PA-624   s   L

Reed Mansion
Sixth & Peach Sts.
HABS PA-57   pd   L

Tavern, Old; see Perry Memorial Building

Tracy Building
532-527 French St.
HABS PA-5154   pd   L

Whitman, Benjamin, House
Ninth & Peach Sts.
HABS PA-542   p   L

Woodruff House
417 State St.
HABS PA-56   s pd   L

Erie vic.

Strong House
Perry Highway
HABS PA-559   p   L

Girard

Hutchinson House
155 E. Main St.
HABS PA-59   s pd   L

Girard vic.

Blair Cabin
Blair Rd.
HABS PA-510   s pd   L

Thompson, Denman, House
Blair Rd.
HABS PA-58   s pd   L

Harborcreek

Davidson House
HABS PA-5110   p   L

Dodge House
HABS PA-5121   p   L

Moorheadville

Backus House
HABS PA-5120   p   L

Moorhead House
HABS PA-51   s pd   L

North East

First Baptist Church
Railroad St.
HABS PA-513   s pd   L

Octagon Barn
HABS PA-574   p   L

Sillman-Phillips House
HABS PA-512   pd   L

North Springfield

Stevenson House
Lake Rd.
HABS PA-55   s pd   L

Sterrettania

Sterrett Cabin (Interiors)
Conneaut Rd.
HABS PA-511   s pd   L

Summit

Summit Stone School
HABS PA-5122   p   L

Union City

Erie Railroad, Crossing Gate Tower
Lincoln St.
HAER PA-47   p   H

Erie Railroad, Union City Freight Station
HAER PA-46   p   H

Erie Railway, Union City Station
Lincoln St.
HAER PA-45   p   H

Rockwell House
HABS PA-5124   p   L

Waterford

Brotherton House
HABS PA-5102   p   L

Doctor's Office
HABS PA-5134   p   L

Eagle Hotel
HABS PA-521   p   L

Judson, Amos, House
HABS PA-522   p   L

St. Peter's Episcopal Church
Cherry St.
HABS PA-544   p   L

Waterford Academy
Fourth & Cherry Sts.
HABS PA-54   s pd   L

Waterford Covered Bridge
Spanning Le Boeuf Creek
HABS PA-535   pd   L

Wattsburg

Chaffe House
HABS PA-590   p   L

Howard Double House
HABS PA-5116   p   L

FAYETTE COUNTY

Brownsville Bor.

Bowman's Castle (Nemacolin Castle)
Front & Second Sts.
HABS PA-429   s pd   L H

Nemacolin Castle; see Bowman's Castle

Fairchance

Nixon Tavern
Fairchance Rd.
HABS PA-8-3   s pd   L

Fayette City vic.

Cook, Col. Edward, House
HABS PA-412   s pd   L

Hopwood

Hayden, Ben, House
HABS PA-8-4   s pd   L

Uniontown vic.

Mount Washington Tavern
HABS PA-417   p   L

FRANKLIN COUNTY

Chambersburg Bor.

Brand Stable, The; see Fisher, Rev. Samuel
   R., Stable

Fisher, Rev. Samuel R., Stable (Brand
   Stable, The)
123-125 S. Main St.
HABS PA-5155   pd   L

59 West Queen Street (House)
HABS PA-5156   pd   L

GREENE COUNTY

Brock

Valley Methodist Manse
(Wayne Township)
HABS PA-619   s   L

Ruff Creek vic.

Covered Bridge
Spanning Ruff Creek (Washington Twp.)
HABS PA-618   s   L

HUNTINGTON COUNTY

Franklinville vic.

Colerain Forge House
State Rt. 45 vic. (Franklin Twp.)
HABS PA-615   s   L

Penna. Furnace

Lyons, John, House (Mansion House)
Penna. Furnace Rd. (Franklin Twp.)
HABS PA-611   s   L
Mansion House; see Lyons, John, House

LACKAWANNA COUNTY

Carbondale

Miners & Mechanics Bank Building
13 N. Main St.
HABS PA-5153   s p d   H

Clarks Green

Clark, William, House
Abington Rd.
HABS PA-231   s p d   L
Stone, Lemuel, House
HABS PA-220   s p d   L

Scranton

Silkman House
2006 N. Main Ave.
HABS PA-217   s p d   L
U.S. Post Office
HABS PA-1251   p   H

Waverly

Main Street School, One Room
HABS PA-214   s p d   L

LANCASTER COUNTY

Brickerville

Emanuel Evangelical Lutheran Church
HABS PA-364   p   L

Cocalico

Cook House, Outdoor Stone
HABS PA-155   p   L
Cotton Mill, Old
HABS PA-156   p   L
Farm Group & Mill Pond
HABS PA-154   p   L

Drumore vic.

Cider Press at Hesses' Mill
(Drumore Township)
HABS PA-367   p   H

Ephrata

Cloisters, Bake House Oven
HABS PA-320-C   s p   L
Cloisters, Cabin Number 3
HABS PA-320-E   s   L
Cloisters, Clockmaker's Cottage
HABS PA-320-F   s p   L
Cloisters, Graveyard
HABS PA-320-G   p   L
Cloisters, House on Hill
HABS PA-320-H   p   L
Cloisters, Mill
HABS PA-320-I   p   L
Cloisters, The
HABS PA-320   s p d   L
Cloisters, The Academy
HABS PA-320-A   p   L
Cloisters, The Almonry
HABS PA-320-B   s p   L
Cloisters, The Bethania
HABS PA-320-D   p   L
Cloisters, The Saal
HABS PA-320-J   s p   L
Cloisters, The Saron
HABS PA-320-K   s p   L
Cloisters, Whitehaus & Summer Kitchen
(Community Physicians House)
HABS PA-320-L   s p   L
Community Physicians House; see
     Cloisters, Whitehaus & Summer Kitchen

Hinkletown

Red Barn, Old
HABS PA-157   p   L

Lancaster

City Hall
Penn Sq.
HABS PA-1343   pd   H
125 Howard Avenue (House)
HABS PA-1355   pd   H
Lutheran Church of the Holy Trinity
31 S. Duke St.
HABS PA-575   pd   L H
Montgomery, William, House
21 S. Queen St.
HABS PA-1061   pd   H
Musser-Reigart House (Proctor-Bowman
     House)
323 W. King St.
HABS PA-373   pd   H
Proctor-Bowman House; see
     Musser-Reigart House
Sehner-Ellicott House
123 N. Prince St.
HABS PA-372   s p d   H
Smith, Judge Charles, House
22 S. Queen St.
HABS PA-369   pd   H

U.S. Post Office & Courthouse
120 N. Duke St.
HABS PA-370   p   H

Lancaster vic.

Rockford
U.S. Rt. 222 (West Lampeter Twp.)
HABS PA-368   s p d   H
Wheatland
1120 Marietta Ave.
HABS PA-1265   s   H

Landisville

Bachman-Landis-Kauffman House
Kauffman Rd. (East Hempfield Twp.)
HABS PA-1246   s   L

Maple Grove vic.

Stoneroads Mill Bridge
Spanning Little Conestoga Creek
HABS PA-321   s   L

Marietta vic.

Johnson's Mill Bridge
(East Donegal-Rapho Township)
HABS PA-1173   s   L

Pinetown

Leaman Rifle Works Bridge
Spanning Conestoga Creek
HABS PA-319   s   L

Willow Street vic.

Herr, Hans, House
1851 Hans Herr Dr. (West Lampeter Twp.)
HABS PA-371   pd   H

LEBANON COUNTY

Kleinfeltersville

Barn, Brick End
HABS PA-153   p   L

Millbach

Illig's Mill; see Miller House & Mill
Miller House & Mill (Mueller House; Illig's
     Mill)
Newmanstown-Klienfeltersville Rd.
HABS PA-151   pd   L
Mueller House; see Miller House & Mill

Newmanstown vic.

Fort Zeller; see Zeller, Heinrich, House
Zeller, Heinrich, House (Fort Zeller)
Mill Creek (Millcreek Twp.)
HABS PA-141   s p d   L H

LEHIGH COUNTY

Allentown

Newhorter, Thomas, House
     (Nunnemacher, Daniel, House)
Lehigh & Lawrence Sts.
HABS PA-1271   s d   H
Nunnemacher, Daniel, House; see
     Newhorter, Thomas, House

LUZERNE COUNTY

Exeter

Coray, Elisha Atherton, House
HABS PA-27   s p d   L
Coray, Elisha Atherton, Mill
Sutton's Creek
HABS PA-216   s p d   L

Forty Fort Bor.

Culver, William, House
278 River St.
HABS PA-240   s p d   L
Denison House
Wyoming Ave.
HABS PA-25   s p d   L
Elm Lawn; see Shoemaker House
Forty Fort Meetinghouse
River St.
HABS PA-21   s p d   L
Perkins House
HABS PA-232   p d   H
Real, Benjamin, Homestead
318 River St.
HABS PA-233   s p d   L
Shoemaker House (Elm Lawn)
1577 Wyoming Ave.
HABS PA-22   s p d   L
Snowden, Father, House
991 Wyoming Ave.
HABS PA-223   s p d   L
Tripp House, The
1086 Wyoming House
HABS PA-236   s p d   L

Hanover Green

Hanover Green Meetinghouse
Nanticoke vic.
HABS PA-26   s p d   L

Kingston

Helme Tavern, The
238 Wyoming Ave.
HABS PA-235   s p d   L
Meyers, Lawrence, House
98 Main St.
HABS PA-245   s p d   L

Nanticoke

Mill, Samantha, House
493 E. Main St.
HABS PA-24   s p d   L

Nanticoke vic.

Harvey House
72-74 McDonald St.
HABS PA-237   s p d   L

Plymouth

Gaylord, Henderson, House
135 W. Main St.
HABS PA-28   s p d   L
Wright, Col. H. B., House
843-845 W. Main St.
HABS PA-224   s p d   L

Wapwallopen

Union Reformed & Lutheran Church
HABS PA-219   p d   L

Wilkes Barre

Bowman, Capt. Samuel, House
220 N. Main St.
HABS PA-241   s p d   L
Butler, Col. Zebulon, Homestead
313 S. River St.
HABS PA-239   s p d   L
McLean, Alexander, House
156 Carey Ave.
HABS PA-242   s p d   L
Pickering, Timothy, House
130 S. Main St.
HABS PA-230   s p d   L

Wyoming

Crawford House
482 Wyoming Ave.
HABS PA-234   s p d   L
Swetland House
885 Wyoming Ave.
HABS PA-23   s p d   L
Swetland Store
828 Wyoming Ave.
HABS PA-211   s p d   L
Wyoming Institute
Institute St.
HABS PA-29   s p d   L

LYCOMING COUNTY

Muncy vic.

Reading-Halls Station Bridge
U.S. Rt. 220
HAER PA-55   s   H

Williamsport

Parson, Judge A. V., Mansion
5 E. Fourth St.
HABS PA-326   s p   L
Updegraff, Thomas, House
Reach Rd.
HABS PA-327   s   L
Updegraff, Thomas, Log Granary
Reach Rd.
HABS PA-327-A   s   L

MCKEAN COUNTY

Betula

Shattuck, Richard, Lodge
HABS PA-5106   p   L

Crosby vic.

Marsh Stone House
State Rt. 46
HABS PA-5105   s p d   L

Eldred

Chrisman House
HABS PA-551   p   L

King's Run Road

Chevalier House
HABS PA-5104   s p d   L

Mt. Jewett vic.

Erie Railroad, Bradford Division, Bridge
   (Kinzua Viaduct)
Spanning Kinzua Creek
HAER PA-7   p   H
Erie Railroad, Mt. Jewett Station
U.S. Rt. 6, at S. Kushequa Rd. vic.
HAER PA-21   p   H
Kinzua Viaduct; see Erie Railroad,
   Bradford Division, Bridge

Port Allegany vic.

Coleman House
HABS PA-557   p   L

Smethport

Backus House
HABS PA-533   s p d   L
Medbury Place
604 Main St.
HABS PA-5103   s p   L

West Eldred vic.

Lamphier House
HABS PA-552   p d   L

MERCER COUNTY

Greenville

Goodwin House
36 S. Mercer St.
HABS PA-567   p   L
Penn High School
Penn. Ave. at Main St.
HABS PA-547   p d   L
Stewart, Vance, House
HABS PA-568   p   L

Mercer

Bell House
HABS PA-564   p   L
Garrett Cenotaph
HABS PA-534   p d   L
Jail, Old Stone
HABS PA-560   p   L
Magoffin, Dr. Beriah, House
116 Venago St.
HABS PA-561   p   L
Magoffin House
119 S. Pitt St.
HABS PA-565   p   L
Robinson, W. J., House
HABS PA-562   p   L

Mercer vic.

Johnson House
Springfield Falls
HABS PA-581   p   L

Sheakleyville

Scrivens House
HABS PA-558   p   L

Scrivens Store
Main St.
HABS PA-537   s p d   L

MONROE COUNTY

Bushkill vic.

Clark-Heller Mill
(Middle Smithfield Township)
HABS PA-1159   p d   H

Delaware Water Gap

Delaware Water Gap Railroad Station
(Delaware-Lackawanna-Western
Railroad Station)
HABS PA-1168   p d   H

**Delaware-Lackawanna-Western Railroad
Station;** see Delaware Water Gap
Railroad Station

Shawnee-on-del. vic.

Camp Ministerium; see Turn, John, Farm
Coldspring Farm; see Dewitt Farm, House
Dewitt Farm, House (Coldspring Farm)
(Middle Smithfield Township)
HABS PA-1165   s p d   H

Dewitt Farm, Springhouse
(Middle Smithfield Township)
HABS PA-1165-B   s p d   H

Dewitt Farm, Woodshed
(Middle Smithfield Township)
HABS PA-1165-C   s p d   H

Farrington House; see Michael, Samuel,
House
Michael Barn, The
River Rd. (Middle Smithfield Twp.)
HABS PA-1259   s p d   H

Michael, George, House (Theune House)
(Middle Smithfield Township)
HABS PA-1160   p d   H

Michael, Samuel, House (Farrington
House)
River Rd. (Middle Smithfield Twp.)
HABS PA-1170   p d   H

Robacker House; see Valentine-Weaver
House
Rouch House; see Treible, Peter, House
Schoolhouse, River (Schoolhouse, Stone)
(Smithfield Township)
HABS PA-1167   s p d   H

Schoolhouse, Stone; see Schoolhouse, River
Theune House; see Michael, George, House
Treible, Peter, House (Rouch House)
River Rd. (Smithfield Twp.)
HABS PA-1161   s p d   H

Turn, John, Farm (Camp Ministerium)
River Rd. (Middle Smithfield Twp.)
HABS PA-1274   s p d   H

Turn, John, Farm, Barn
River Rd.
HABS PA-1274-A   p d   H

Turn, John, Farm, Lime Kiln
River Rd.
HABS PA-1274-B   s p d   H

Turn, John, Farm, Smokehouse
River Rd.
HABS PA-1274-D   s p d   H

Turn, John, Farm, Weavehouse
River Rd.
HABS PA-1274-E   s p d   H

Turn, John, Farm, Weavehouse
River Rd.
HABS PA-1274-E   s p   H

Valentine-Weaver House (Robacker
House)
River Rd. (Smithfield Twp.)
HABS PA-1164   s p d   H

Walter-Kautz Farm
(Smithfield Township)
HABS PA-1169   s p d   H

Walter-Kautz Farm, Barn
(Smithfield Township)
HABS PA-1169-B   s p d   H

**Walter-Kautz Farm, Corn Crib & Wagon
Shed**
(Smithfield Township)
HABS PA-1169-C   s p d   H

Walter-Kautz Farm, Icehouse
(Smithfield Township)
HABS PA-1169-D   s p d   H

Walter-Kautz Farm, Icehouse
(Smithfield Township)
HABS PA-1169-D   s p   H

**Walter-Kautz Farm, Washhouse &
Woodshed**
(Smithfield Township)
HABS PA-1169-E   p   H

Zion Evangelical Lutheran Church
HABS PA-1136   s p d   H

Shawnee-on-Deleware vic.

Dewitt Farm, Barn
(Middle Smithfield Township)
HABS PA-1165-A   s p d   H

MONTGOMERY COUNTY

Ambler vic.

Mathers Mill
Mathers Lane
HABS PA-126   p d   L

Bala-Cynwyd

Pencoyd Farm (Roberts Estate)
355 E. City Ave. (Lower Merion Twp.)
HABS PA-1087   p d   L

Pencoyd Farm, Barn (Roberts Estate)
355 E. City Ave. (Lower Merion Twp.)
HABS PA-1090   p   L

Pencoyd Farm, Smokehouse (Roberts
Estate)
355 E. City Ave. (Lower Merion Twp.)
HABS PA-1089   p   L

Roberts Estate; see Pencoyd Farm, Barn
Roberts Estate; see Pencoyd Farm,
Smokehouse
Roberts Estate; see Pencoyd Farm

Bryn Mawr

Bryn Mawr Hospital Thrift Shop; see
Whitehall Railroad Station
First Bryn Mawr Railroad Station; see
Whitehall Railroad Station
Pennsylvania Railroad Bryn Mawr Station
Bryn Mawr & Morris Aves.
HABS PA-1081   p d   L

Whitehall Railroad Station (Bryn Mawr
Hospital Thrift Shop; First Bryn Mawr
Railroad Station)
Glenbrook Ave. & Haverford Rd.
HABS PA-577   p   H

Haverford

Quaker Meetinghouse
HABS PA-179   p   L

Horsham vic.

Graeme Park, House & Barn
Keith Valley Rd. (Horsham Twp.)
HABS PA-579   p   H

Jenkintown

Alvethorpe
HABS PA-130   p d   L

King Of Prussia

King of Prussia Inn
U.S. Rt. 202 (Upper Merion Twp.)
HABS PA-1009   s p d   L

Lederach

Bay Pony Inn; see Lederach, Henry,
Tavern
Farmhouse, Old Stone; see Kolb-Ziegler
House
Kolb-Ziegler House (Farmhouse, Old
Stone)
State Rt. 113
HABS PA-580   d   H

Lederach, Andrew, Homestead
St. Rt. 113
HABS PA-582   d   H

Lederach Corner Store; see Ziegler,
Dilman, Store
Lederach, Henry, Tavern (Bay Pony Inn;
Tavern, Large Stone)
State Rt. 113 & Salford Rd.
HABS PA-583   d   H

Tavern, Large Stone; see Lederach, Henry,
Tavern
Ziegler, Dilman, Store (Lederach Corner
Store)
Cross & Salfordville Rds.
HABS PA-584   d   H

Merion

Wayne, Gen. Anthony, Inn
625 Montgomery Ave.
HABS PA-144   p   L

Narberth vic.

**Lower Merion Friends Meetinghouse &
Carriage House**
Montgomery Ave. & Meetinghouse Lane
HABS PA-145   p   L H

Norristown

West Marshall Street Bridge
HAER PA-54   pd   L

Trappe

Augustus Lutheran Church; see Trappe
  Church, Old
Trappe Church, Old (Augustus Lutheran
  Church)
HABS PA-175   p   L

Valley Forge vic.

Potts, Isaac, House (Washington's
  Headquarters; Valley Forge National
  Historic Park)
HABS PA-1171   p   L
Valley Forge National Historic Park; see
  Potts, Isaac, House
Washington's Headquarters; see Potts,
  Isaac, House

Whitemarsh

Hope Lodge
Bethehem & Skippack Pikes
HABS PA-18   s pd   L

NORTHAMPTON COUNTY

Belfast vic.

Henry Gun Factory
HABS PA-122   s pd   L
Henry Gun Factory, Workman's House
HABS PA-123   s pd   L

Bethlehem

Bell House (Moravian Seminary, Bell
  House)
56 W. Church St.
HABS PA-1152   p   L
Central Moravian Church (Moravian
  Seminary, Church)
406 Main St.
HABS PA-1147   p   L
Central Railroad Station of New Jersey
Lehigh St.
HABS PA-1149   p   L
**Eighteenth Century Moravian Industrial
  Area**
Monocacy Creek vic.
HABS PA-1151   p   L
Gemein Haus
62-66 W. Church St.
HABS PA-1142   s pd   L
Goundie House
501 Main St.
HABS PA-1145   s pd   L
Grist Miller's House
459 Old York Rd.
HABS PA-1144   pd   L
Lester House
HABS PA-1005   p   L
Luckenbach Flour Mill
Monocacy Creek vic.
HAER PA-50   s pd   L

Luckenbach Grist Mill
Ohio Rd., Monocacy Creek vic.
HABS PA-1148   pd   L
Moravian Seminary, Bell House; see Bell
  House
Moravian Seminary, Church; see Central
  Moravian Church
Schnitz House
38 W. Church St.
HABS PA-1154   pd   L
Single Brethren's House
89 W. Church St.
HABS PA-1141   s pd   L
Single Sisters' House
44 W. Church St.
HABS PA-1153   p   L
Sun Inn
564 Main St.
HABS PA-1150   s   L
Tannery
Monocacy Creek vic.
HABS PA-1143   s pd   L
Waterworks
Monocacy Creek vic.
HABS PA-1146   pd   L
Widows' House
53 W. Church St.
HABS PA-1155   p   L

Easton

Cinruss Building; see 31 North Fourth
  Street (Commercial Building)
**31 North Fourth Street (Commercial
  Building)** (Cinruss Building)
HABS PA-5140   pd   L
**33-35 North Fourth Street (Commercial
  Building)** (Patio Club Building)
HABS PA-5141   pd   L
Parsons-Taylor House
S. Fourth & Ferry Sts.
HABS PA-1008   pd   L
Patio Club Building; see 33-35 North
  Fourth Street (Commercial Building)

Portland vic.

Munsch House; see Slateford Farm, House
Slateford Farm, House (Munsch House)
(Upper Mt. Bethel Township)
HABS PA-1249   s pd   H
Slateford Farm, Springhouse
(Upper Mt. Bethel Township)
HABS PA-1249-B   s p   H
Slateform Farm, Small Dwelling
(Upper Mt. Bethel Township)
HABS PA-1249-A   s p   H

Wind Gap vic.

Ross-Common Manor
HABS PA-177   p   L

PHILADELPHIA COUNTY

Frankford

Lardner House; see Lynfield House
Lynfield House (Lardner House)
HABS PA-132   pd   L

Germantown

Johnson House
6306 Germantown Ave.
HABS PA-7-7   s pd   L H
Keyser House
6205 Germantown Ave.
HABS PA-11   s d   L

Philadelphia

2225 & 2227 Green Street (Houses); see
  Green Street Area Study
2229 & 2231 Green Street (Houses); see
  Green Street Area Study
113-117 1/2 South Street (Apartments)
HABS PA-1316   d   H
Abercombie, Capt. James, House
  (Perelman Antique Toy Museum)
268-270 S. Second St.
HABS PA-1316   s pd   H
Academy of Music; see American Academy
  of Music
Academy of Notre Dame (Rittenhouse
  Square)
208 S. Nineteenth St., Rittenhouse Sq.
HABS PA-1492   p   H
American Academy of Music (Academy of
  Music)
232-246 S. Broad St.
HABS PA-1491   pd   L
American Fire Insurance Company
308-310 Walnut St.
HABS PA-1386   pd   H
**American Life Insurance Company
  Building** (Manhattan Building)
330-336 Walnut St.
HABS PA-1064   pd   L
American Philosophical Society
104 S. Fifth St.
HABS PA-1464   p   H
Arbour, William, House
HABS PA-1051   s pd   L
Arcade Building (Commercial Trust
  Building)
1428-1434 Market St.
HABS PA-1493   pd   H
Arch Street Friends Meetinghouse
330 Arch St.
HABS PA-1388   pd   L
620 Arch Street (House)
HABS PA-1423   pd   H
628-630 Arch Street (House)
HABS PA-1424   pd   H
501-527 Arch Street (Houses)
HABS PA-1387   pd   H
Arch Street Methodist Episcopal Church
Broad & Arch Sts.
HABS PA-1494   pd   L

Arch Street Opera House (Troc, The)
1003-1005 Arch St.
HABS PA-1495   pd   H

Arch Street Presbyterian Church; see West
Arch Street Presbyterian Church

Armat, Thomas, House
5450 Germantown Ave.
HABS PA-1671   d   H

Ashmead, William, House
5334 Germantown Ave.
HABS PA-1673   d   H

Askins-Jones House; see 720-724 South
Front Street (House)

Atwater Kent Museum; see Franklin
Institute

Ayer, N. W. & Company Building
204-212 S. Seventh St.
HABS PA-1390   pd   H

Ayres-Lamb House; see Lamb, Peter,
House

Baird, Donald L., Company Warehouse
327-329 S. Water St.
HABS PA-1378   p   H

Bake House & Oven
423 S. Second St.
HABS PA-1317   pd   L

Baltimore & Ohio Railroad Station
Twenty-fourth & Chestnut Sts.
HABS PA-1220   s pd   H

Bank of North America
305-307 Chestnut St.
HABS PA-1391   pd   H

Bank of Pennsylvania (Philadelphia Bank)
421 Chestnut St.
HABS PA-1392   pd   H

Bartram, John, Hotel; see Hotel Walton

Bartram, John, House
Fifty-fourth St.
HABS PA-1132   s pd   L

Baugh Warehouse; see Beck-Care
Warehouse

Baynton House; see Germantown Historical
Society Area Study

Beck Street, 200 Block; see Beck Street
Area Study

Beck Street Area Study (Court of Homes;
Beck Street, 200 Block)
HABS PA-1542   p   H

111-113 Beck Street (Buildings)
HABS PA-1581   p   H

Beck-Care Warehouse (Baugh Warehouse)
20 S. Delaware St.
HABS PA-1188   s pd   H

Beggarstown School
6669 Germantown Ave.
HABS PA-1675   pd   L

Bel Air (Belleaire; Singley House; Lasse
Cock's Manor House)
League Island Park (Passyunk Twp.)
HABS PA-1124   s p   L

Belfield; see Peale, Charles Wilson, House

Belleaire; see Bel Air

Bellevue-Stratford Hotel
Broad & Walnut Sts.
HABS PA-1226   pd   H

Belmont Mansion
Belmont Mansion Dr.   •
HABS PA-1649   pd   L

Berry-Blair House
415 Locust St.
HABS PA-1063   pd   H

Berry-Coxe House
413 Locust St.
HABS PA-1062   s pd   L

**Bethal African Methodist Episcopal
Church** (Mother Bethal African
Methodist Espiscopal Church)
419 S. Sixth St.
HABS PA-1318   pd   L

Bethel Christian Center; see Mariners'
Bethel Church

Billmeyer, Michael, House; see 6505-6507
Germantown Avenue (House)

Binney, H. Esq., House
HABS PA-1903   p   H

Bird, Joseph, Houses
813-815 S. Hancock St.
HABS PA-1543   p   H

Birely House
313 Richmond St.
HABS PA-1743   d   H

Blackwell, Rev. Robert , House; see St.
Peter's Protestant Episcopal Church

Blackwell, Reverend Robert, House (St.
Peter's Church House (Episcopal))
313 Pine St.
HABS PA-1319   pd   L

Blair, Samuel Jr., House
6105 Germantown Ave.
HABS PA-7-5   s pd   L

Bleakley House; see Cannonball Farm

Blight Warehouse
101-103 S. Front St.
HABS PA-1393   p   H

Boat House Row
E. River Drive
HABS PA-1650   pd   H

Bonsall, John, House
706 Locust St. (Washington Sq.)
HABS PA-1394   pd   L

Bridges, Robert, House; see 507 South
Front Street (House)

Bridges-LaTour House
509 S. Front St.
HABS PA-1321   p   H

Bringhurst Houses
5448 Germantown Ave.
HABS PA-1679   d   H

British Building; see Internat'l Exhibition of
1876, St. George's House

Brock, John & Sons, Warehouse
242-244 Delaware Ave.
HABS PA-1395   pd   L

Bromley, John & Sons, Building
201-263 Lehigh Ave.
HABS PA-1744   pd   H

Brown, Anna S., House & Store
408 Richmond St.
HABS PA-1745   d   H

Bulletin Building
Juniper & Filbert Sts.
HABS PA-1496   pd   H

Burden, Joseph, House
132 S. Fourth St.
HABS PA-1949   p   H

Burholme
Burholme Park
HABS PA-186   s p   L

Burk, Alfred E., House
1500 N. Broad St.
HABS PA-1722   pd   L

Burnham, George, House
3401 Powelton Ave.
HABS PA-1627   pd   L

Burnside; see Hamilton-Hoffman House

Bussey-Poulson House
320 S. Fourth St.
HABS PA-1323   s p   H

Busti, Paul, Mansion
Forty-fourth St. & Haverford Ave.
HABS PA-1628   s pd   H

Butcher & Brother Warehouse
142-144 N. Front St.
HABS PA-1396   d   H

Butler, Anthony, House
132-134 Olive St.
HABS PA-1747   d   H

Byrne-Cavenaugh House
130-132 Queen St.
HABS PA-1545   pd   L

Callowhill Street Bridge; see Spring Garden
Street Bridge

Cannonball Farm (Bleakley House)
HABS PA-134   pd   L

Carpenter, Joshua, House (Carpenters'
Mansion)
615-619 Chestnut St.
HABS PA-1397   d   H

Carpenters' Company, Front Store
Carpenters Ct. & 322 Chestnut St.
HABS PA-1398-A   s pd   H

Carpenter's Company Hall
Carpenters Ct. & 320 Chestnut St.
HABS PA-1398   s pd   H

Carpenters' Company, New Hall
Carpenters Ct. & 322 Chestnut St.
HABS PA-1398-B   pd   H

Carpenters' Mansion; see Carpenter,
Joshua, House

Cast Iron Sidewalk
1907 N. Seventh St.
HABS PA-1723   pd   L

Cathedral of Saints Peter & Paul
Eighteenth & Race Sts.
HABS PA-1497   p   H

29-31 Catherine Street (Alley)
HABS PA-5181   p   H

Catherine Street Area Study (33 Catherine
  Street (House))
HABS PA-1069   s p d   H

Catherine Street Area Study
HABS PA-5182   p d   H

Catherine Street Area Study (27 Catherine
  Street (House); Edwards, William,
  House)
HABS PA-1928   p   H

Catherine Street Area Study (31 Catherine
  Street (House))
HABS PA-1573   p   H

27 Catherine Street (House); see Catherine
  Street Area Study

31 Catherine Street (House); see Catherine
  Street Area Study

33 Catherine Street (House); see Catherine
  Street Area Study

Cedar Grove
Landsdowne Dr.
HABS PA-1651   p d   H

Centennial Guard Box
Traffic Triangle, Benjamin Franklin Pky.
  vic.
HABS PA-1652   p   L

Centennial National Bank
Thirty-second & Market Sts.
HABS PA-1095   s p d   H

Chalkey Hall
3869 Sepviva St.
HABS PA-110   s p d   L

Chamounix Mansion
Chamounix Dr.
HABS PA-1653   p d   L

Chestnut Hill Academy; see Wissachickon
  Inn

Chestnut Street Area Study (213-243
  Chestnut Street (Commercial Buildings))
HABS PA-1402   p d   H

Chestnut Street Bridge
Schuykill River, Chestnut St. vic.
HABS PA-1054   p d   L

**213-243 Chestnut Street (Commercial
  Buildings); see** Chestnut Street Area
  Study

Chew Mansion; see Cliveden

Chinatown YMCA (Chinese Cultural &
  Community Center)
125 N. Tenth St.
HABS PA-1498   p d   L

**Chinese Cultural & Community Center;
  see** Chinatown YMCA

Christ Church
22-26 N. Second St.
HABS PA-1071   s p   L

Church of St. James the Less
3200 W. Clearfield St.
HABS PA-1725   p d   L

Church of St. Luke (Church of St. Luke &
  Epiphany)
330 S. Thirteenth St.
HABS PA-1499   p d   L

Church of St. Luke & Epiphany; see
  Church of St. Luke

Church of St. Phillips de Neri
220-228 Queen St.
HABS PA-1547   p d   H

Church of St. Vincent de Paul
101-107 E. Price St.
HABS PA-1680   d   H

Church of the Gesu
Eighteenth & Thompson Sts.
HABS PA-1724   p d   L

Church of the Holy Trinity
Nineteenth & Walnut Sts.
HABS PA-1085   s p d   H

Church of the Immaculate Conception
1020 N. Front St.
HABS PA-1901   p d   H

Church of the Redeemer
101-107 Queen St.
HABS PA-1077   p d   L

Clarkson-Watson House
5275-5277 Germantown Ave.
HABS PA-1681   p d   H

Cliffs, The
Columbia Ave., Fairmount Park
HABS PA-185   s p d   L

Clifton House
852 S. Front St.
HABS PA-1548   d   H

Cliveden (Chew Mansion)
6401 Germantown Ave.
HABS PA-1184   s p d   H

Clunie; see Mount Pleasant

Clymers Alley (Clymers Court)
770 S. Front St.
HABS PA-1582   p   H

Clymers Court; see Clymers Alley

Collins, Samuel, House; see 783 South
  Front Street (House)

Columbia Engine Company
3420 Market St.
HABS PA-1629   d   H

Commercial Exchange
135 S. Second St.
HABS PA-1406   p d   L

Commercial Trust Building; see Arcade
  Building

**Commercial Union Assurance Company
  Building**
416-420 Walnut St.
HABS PA-1076   p d   L

Compton (Morris House)
Meadowbrook Ave.
HABS PA-1682   p d   H

Concord School
6309 Germantown Ave.
HABS PA-12   s p d   L

Conyngham-Hacker House; see
  Germantown Historical Society Area
  Study

Coombes Alley; see Harrison, Henry,
  Houses

Cooper, Jacob, House
118 Cuthbert St.
HABS PA-1407   p   H

Cope, Caleb & Company Store
429 Market St.
HABS PA-1408   p   H

Cope, Edward Drinker, Houses
2100-2102 Pine St.
HABS PA-1500   d   H

Court of Homes; see Beck Street Area Study

Cove Cornice House; see Stafford's
  Tavern-Paschall House

Covered Bridge
Thomas Mill Rd. (Spanning Wissahickon
  Creek)
HABS PA-19   s p   L

Currie, Dr. William, House
271 S. Fifth St.
HABS PA-191   p d   L

Curtis Publishing Company
Sixth & Walnut Sts.
HABS PA-1902   p   H

Customs House, Old; see Second Bank of
  the United States

Davis-Lenox House
217 Spruce St.
HABS PA-1324   p d   L

Delancey Street Area Study
2301-2323 Delancey St.
HABS PA-1502   p d   H

307 Delancey Street (House)
HABS PA-1927   p   L

105 Delancey Street (Warehouse)
HABS PA-1377   p   H

Department for Males; see Pennsylvania
  Hospital for the Insane

Deshler-Morris House
5442 Germantown Ave.
HABS PA-1683   p   H

Detweiler House
8226 Germantown Ave.
HABS PA-1684   d   H

Diamond Street Area Study
1601-1643 Diamond St.
HABS PA-1726   p d   H

Dilworth-Todd-Moylan House
Fourth & Walnut Sts.
HABS PA-1409   p d   H

Disston, Henry & Sons, Building
Front & Laurel Sts.
HABS PA-1757   d   H

Dock Street Sewer
Dock & Third Sts. vic.
HABS PA-1072   s   H

Donaldson, William, Houses
14-16 Queen St.
HABS PA-1551   p   H

Dorfenille House
5139 Germantown Ave.
HABS PA-1685   d   H

Dowers-Okill House
115 N. Water St.
HABS PA-1410   pd   H

Drexel & Company
135-143 S. Fifteenth St.
HABS PA-1503   pd   L

Drexel Institute (Drexel University)
Thirty-second & Chestnut Sts.
HABS PA-1630   pd   L

Drexel University; see Drexel Institute

Drinker, John, House (Krider Gun Shop)
133-135 Walnut St.
HABS PA-1055   s pd   L

Drinker, John, House
241 Pine St.
HABS PA-1325   pd   L

Drinker's Court
236-238 Delancey St.
HABS PA-1326   pd   L

Duche House
24 Catherine St.
HABS PA-1552   pd   H

Duche-Walker House
26 Catherine St.
HABS PA-1553   pd   H

Duncannon Iron Company, Warehouse & Office
122-124 Race St.
HABS PA-1412   d   H

Dunlap-Eyre House
1003 Spruce St.
HABS PA-1504   pd   L

Eagle Hotel
Sixth & Girard Ave.
HABS PA-1727   pd   H

Eakins, Thomas, House
1729 Mt. Vernon St.
HABS PA-1728   pd   H

Eastburn Mariner's Bethel Church
Front & Delancey Sts.
HABS PA-1327   p   H

Eastern State Penitentiary
Corinthian Ave., Brown & Twenty-second
Sts. vic.
HABS PA-1729   pd   H

Eckert-Tarrant House
38 Catherine St.
HABS PA-1554   pd   H

Eden, Beth, House; see Shunk School

Edwards, William, House; see Catherine
Street Area Study

Elfreth, Jeremiah, House
126 Elfreth's Alley
HABS PA-1413   p   H

Elfreth's Alley Area Study
HABS PA-1103   s   L

Elliot, John, House
37 Queen St.
HABS PA-1555   p   H

Elliot, John, House; see Marshall's Court
Area Study

Ellison, John B. & Sons, Building
22-26 S. Sixth St.
HABS PA-1414   pd   L

Ely-Osbourne Houses & Stores
136-138 South St.
HABS PA-1557   d   H

Endt, Theobald, House
5222-5224 Germantown Ave.
HABS PA-1686   d   H

Episcopal Hospital (Hospital of the P. E.
Church in Philadelphia)
Front St. & Lehigh Ave.
HABS PA-1764   p   H

Estlack, Thomas, House
413 Lombard St.
HABS PA-1328   pd   H

Fairmount Waterworks
Fairmount Park
HABS PA-1654
HAER PA-51   s p   H

Fairmount Waterworks Rehabilitation Project
HAER PA-52   s   L

Falls Bridge
E. River Dr. & Calumet St.
HABS PA-1655   s d   H

Far East Chinese Restaurant; see 907-909
Race Street (Commercial Buildings)

Farmers & Mechanics Bank
427 Chestnut St.
HABS PA-1415   pd   H

Federal Reserve Bank (Federal Reserve
Bank of Philadelphia)
921-939 Chestnut St.
HABS PA-1506   pd   L

Federal Reserve Bank of Philadelphia; see
Federal Reserve Bank

Fell-Van Rensselaer House (Pennsylvania
Athletic Club)
Eighteenth & Walnut Sts.
HABS PA-1507   pd   H

Fielding, Mantle, House
28 W. Walnut Lane
HABS PA-1687   pd   L

Finlow-Nichell House
770 S. Front St.
HABS PA-1558   p   H

Fire Association Building (Irvin Building)
401-403 Walnut St.
HABS PA-1434   d   H

Fireman's Hall; see Philadelphia Fire
Department, Engine Co. Number 8

First Bank of the United States (Girard's,
Stephen, Bank)
120 S. Third St.
HABS PA-1417   s p   L

First Baptist Church of Germantown
36-42 E. Price St.
HABS PA-1688   pd   L

First German Reformed Church
322-330 Race St.
HABS PA-1910   p   H

**First German Reformed Church Area
Study**
129-151 N. Fourth St.
HABS PA-1418   pd   H

First National Bank (First Pennsylvania
Banking & Trust Company)
315 Chestnut St.
HABS PA-1011   pd   L

**First Pennsylvania Banking & Trust
Company;** see First National Bank

**First Pennsylvania Banking & Trust
Company;** see Kensington National Bank

First Polish Baptist Church; see Mariners'
Bethel Church

First Presbyterian Church
Seventh St. & Washington Sq. vic.
HABS PA-1117   s   L

First Unitarian Church
2121 Chestnut St.
HABS PA-1508   pd   L

Fitzgerald, Thomas, House; see 437
Lombard Street (House)

Fitzwater Street Area Study (24-32
Fitzwater Street (Buildings))
HABS PA-1560   p   H

Fitzwater Street Area Study (11-23
Fitzwater Street (Buildings))
HABS PA-1559   pd   H

11-23 Fitzwater Street (Buildings); see
Fitzwater Street Area Study

24-32 Fitzwater Street (Buildings); see
Fitzwater Street Area Study

Fleisher, Samuel S., Art Memorial
711-721 Catharine St.
HABS PA-1229   s   H

Flickwer-Williamson Houses
809-811 S. Hancock St.
HABS PA-1561   p   H

Flickwir-Nugent Houses; see 731-733 South
Front Street (Houses)

Fort Mifflin
Mud Island, Marine & Penrose Ferry Rds.
HABS PA-1225   s pd   L

Fort Mifflin Arsenal; see Fort Mifflin,
Guard House

Fort Mifflin, Artillery Shed
Mud Island, Marine & Penrose Ferry Rds.
HABS PA-1225-B   s pd   L

**Fort Mifflin, Commandant's House
(Headquarters)**
Mud Island, Marine & Penrose Ferry Rds.
HABS PA-1225-C   s pd   L

Fort Mifflin, Commissary; see Fort Mifflin,
Storehouse

Fort Mifflin, Frame Guard House
Mud Island, Marine & Penrose Ferry Rds.
HABS PA-1225-J   p   L

Fort Mifflin, Guard House (Fort Mifflin
Arsenal)
Mud Island, Marine & Penrose Ferry Rds.
HABS PA-1225-A   s pd   L

Fort Mifflin, Hospital (Fort Mifflin, Mess
House)
Mud Island, Marine & Penrose Ferry Rds.
HABS PA-1225-I   s pd   L

Fort Mifflin, Mess House; see Fort Mifflin,
Hospital

Fort Mifflin Officers' Quarters
Mud Island, Marine & Penrose Ferry Rds.
HABS PA-1225-F   s pd   L

Fort Mifflin, Powder Magazine
Mud Island, Marine & Penrose Ferry Rds.
HABS PA-1225-G   s pd   L

Fort Mifflin, Smith's Shop
Mud Island, Marine & Penrose Ferry Rds.
HABS PA-1225-H   s pd   L

Fort Mifflin, Soldiers' Barracks
Mud Island, Marine & Penrose Ferry Rds.
HABS PA-1225-E   s pd   L

Fort Mifflin, Storehouse (Fort Mifflin,
Commissary)
Mud Island, Marine & Penrose Ferry Rds.
HABS PA-1225-D   s pd   L

Fountain of the Sea Horses
Aquarium Lane
HABS PA-1656   p   L

Frankford Town Hall
4255 Frankford Ave.
HABS PA-1758   pd   L

**Franklin Hose Company, Number
Twenty-eight** (Harmony Engine
Company, Number Six)
730-732 S. Broad St.
HABS PA-1566   pd   H

Franklin Institute (Atwater Kent Museum)
15 S. Seventh St.
HABS PA-121   s pd   L H

Franklin Row; see Sims, Joseph, House

Franklin Sugar Refinery (Merchants
Warehouse)
701-715 S. Front St.
HABS PA-1562   pd   H

Free Quakers Meetinghouse
500 Arch St.
HABS PA-1120   s pd   L H

Friends Select School, Log Cabin
Sixteenth & Race Sts.
HABS PA-143   p   L

**Friendship Engine Company, Number
Fifteen**
2200-2204 E. Norris St.
HABS PA-1759   pd   H

Fromberger, John, Houses (Germantown
Insurance Company)
5501 Germantown Ave.
HABS PA-1690   pd   L H

Fullerton, John, Houses; see 606-608 South
Front Street (Houses)

Garden, C. H., & Company, Building
606 Market St.
HABS PA-1419   pd   H

Garrett-Buchanan Building; see Megargee
Brothers Building

Gaul-Forrest House
1326 N. Broad St.
HABS PA-1730   pd   L

Gentilhommiere; see Girard, Stephen,
Country House

George, Henry, House
413 S. Tenth St.
HABS PA-1509   pd   L

Germantown Academy
110 Schoolhouse Lane
HABS PA-7-4   s pd   L H

6377 Germantown Avenue (House)
HABS PA-1699   pd   H

6505-6507 Germantown Avenue (House)
(Billmeyer, Michael, House)
HABS PA-1677   s pd   L H

Germantown Cricket Club (Manheim
Club)
5140 Morris St.
HABS PA-1693   pd   L H

Germantown Historic District (Green Tree
Tavern; Pastorius House)
6023 Germantown Ave.
HABS PA-1695   d   L

Germantown Historical Society Area Study
(Howell House)
5218 Germantown Ave.
HABS PA-1164-C   p   H

Germantown Historical Society Area Study
(Baynton House)
5208 Germantown Ave.
HABS PA-1164-A   p   H

Germantown Historical Society Area Study
(Conyngham-Hacker House)
5214 Germantown Ave.
HABS PA-1164-B   p   H

Germantown Historical Society Area Study
5208-5214-5218-5226 Germantown Ave.
HABS PA-1694   p   H

Germantown Insurance Company; see
Fromberger, John, Houses

Girard Avenue Bridge
Girard Ave. spanning Schuykill River
HABS PA-1657   pd   H

Girard Bank; see Girard Trust Corn
Exchange Bank

Girard College, Founders Hall
Girard Ave. & Corinthian St.
HABS PA-1731   pd   H

Girard Row
326-334 Spruce St.
HABS PA-1330   s pd   H

Girard, Stephen, Country House
(Gentilhommiere)
Shunk & Twenty-first Sts.
HABS PA-140   s pd   L

Girard, Stephen, Country House (Utility
Building)
Shunk & Twenty-first Sts.
HABS PA-1082   s pd   L

Girard Trust Corn Exchange Bank (Girard
Bank)
34-36 S. Broad St.
HABS PA-1510   pd   L H

Girard's, Stephen, Bank; see First Bank of
the United States

Gladstone Hotel (Greystone Apartments)
Eleventh & Pine Sts.
HABS PA-1511   d   H

Glen Fern; see Livezey House

Gloria Dei (Church) (Swedes Church, Old)
929 S. Water St.
HABS PA-120   s pd   L H

Godley, Jesse, Warehouse
19-27 Queen St.
HABS PA-1564   p   H

Goodwin Building
317-319 N. Second St.
HABS PA-1760   d   H

Gordon, George, Building
300 Arch St.
HABS PA-1065   s pd   L

Granite Street Vaults
100-112 & 101-127 Granite St.
HABS PA-1420   p   H

Green Street Area Study (2225 & 2227
Green Street (Houses))
HABS PA-1732-G   p   H

Green Street Area Study (2219 Green
Street (House))
HABS PA-1732-D   p   H

Green Street Area Study (2221 Green
Street (House))
HABS PA-1732-E   p   H

Green Street Area Study (2201 Green
Street (House))
HABS PA-1732-A   p   H

Green Street Area Study (2205 Green
Street (House))
HABS PA-1732-B   p   H

Green Street Area Study (2229 & 2231
Green Street (Houses))
HABS PA-1732-H   p   H

Green Street Area Study (2223 Green
Street (House))
HABS PA-1732-F   p   H

Green Street Area Study (2213-2215 Green
Street (House))
HABS PA-1732-C   p   H

Green Street Area Study
2201-2231 Green St.
HABS PA-1732   d   H

2201 Green Street (House); see Green
Street Area Study

2205 Green Street (House); see Green
Street Area Study

2213-2215 Green Street (House); see Green
Street Area Study

2219 Green Street (House); see Green
Street Area Study

2221 Green Street (House); see Green
Street Area Study

2223 Green Street (House); see Green
Street Area Study

Green Tree Tavern; see Germantown
Historic District

Greystone Apartments; see Gladstone Hotel

Griffith-Peale House
8100 Frankford Ave.
HABS PA-1761   pd   H

Grumblethorpe (Wister's Big House)
5267 Germantown Ave.
HABS PA-7-1   s pd   L H

Grumblethorpe Tenant House (Wister's
    Tenant House)
5269 Germantown Ave.
HABS PA-7-6   s pd   L H

Haines House; see Wyck

Hall, John, House
327 S. Third St.
HABS PA-1331   s p   H

Hall-Wister House
330 S. Third St.
HABS PA-1332   pd   H

Hamilton, Andrew, House; see Woodlands

Hamilton Village; see Woodlands

Hamilton-Hoffman House (Burnside)
Coggs Creek Parkway
HABS PA-1053   pd   L

Hansell, John, House
153 N. Sixth St.
HABS PA-1012   pd   L

Harmony Engine Company, Number Six;
    see Franklin Hose Company, Number
    Twenty-eight

Harper, William Jr., House
621-623 S. American St.
HABS PA-1567   d   H

Harrison Building
4 S. Fifteenth St.
HABS PA-1088   pd   L

Harrison, Charles C., Building
1001-1005 Market St.
HABS PA-550   pd   H

Harrison, Henry, Houses (Coombes Alley)
112-116 Cuthbert St.
HABS PA-1421   s p   H

Harrison House, Old
Point No Point (Richmond Ave.)
HABS PA-1458   pd   L H

Hart-Patterson House; see 603 South Front
    Street (House)

Hatfield House
E. Fairmount Park (moved from Pulaski
    Ave.)
HABS PA-1658   pd   L H

Hazelton & Company Building
Filbert Ave.
HABS PA-5178   pd   H

Henderson House; see 602 South Front
    Street (House)

Hensel, Colladay & Company Factory
45-51 N. Seventh St.
HABS PA-1422   pd   L H

Hill, David, House
309 S. Third St.
HABS PA-1333   pd   L

Hill-Physick House
321 S. Fourth St.
HABS PA-1334   pd   H

Hilyard, Eber, House; see 427 Lombard
    Street (House)

Hockley, Thomas, House
235 S. Twenty-first St.
HABS PA-1512   pd   L

Holloway, Thomas, Houses
125-131 Ellen St.
HABS PA-1763   d   H

Holy Redeemer Chinese Catholic Church
    & School
Vine St. & Ridge Ave.
HABS PA-1513   p   H

Holy Trinity Roman Catholic Church
    (German)
601-609 Spruce St.
HABS PA-1336   pd   H

Homestead, The; see Parry, Charles T.,
    House

Hood Cemetery, Entrance
4901 Germantown Ave.
HABS PA-1697   p   L

Hope Engine Company Number Seventeen
733-735 S. Sixth St.
HABS PA-1572   pd   H

Hope Hose Company & Fellowship Engine
    Co. No. 29
New Market, Head House
HABS PA-1351   p   H

Hospital of the P. E. Church in
    Philadelphia; see Episcopal Hospital

Hotel Walton (Bartram, John, Hotel)
Broad & Locust Sts.
HABS PA-1091   pd   L

Houston-Sauveur House
8205 Seminole Ave.
HABS PA-1700   p   H

Howell & Brothers Building
12-14 S. Sixth St.
HABS PA-1428   pd   H

Howell House; see Germantown Historical
    Society Area Study

Hutton, Nathaniel, House; see 814 South
    Front Street (House)

Independence Hall, Assembly Room
Chestnut St.
HABS PA-1430-B   p   H

Independence Hall Complex, City Hall
Chestnut St.
HABS PA-1432   s p   L H

Independence Hall Complex, Congress
    Hall (Philadelphia County Court House)
Chestnut St.
HABS PA-1431   p   L H

Independence Hall Complex,
    Independence Hall (State House of
    Pennsylvania)
Chestnut St.
HABS PA-1430   p   L H

Independence Hall, First Floor Hall
Chestnut St.
HABS PA-1430-A   p   H

Independence Hall, Garret
Chestnut St.
HABS PA-1430-G   p   H

Independence Hall, Second Floor
Chestnut St.
HABS PA-1430-D   p   H

Independence Hall, Supreme Court Room
Chestnut St.
HABS PA-1430-C   p   H

Independence Hall, Tower
Chestnut St.
HABS PA-1430-E   p   H

Independence Hall, Tower Stairhall
Chestnut St.
HABS PA-1430-F   p   H

Independence National Historic Park
HABS PA-1951   p   H

Independence National Historical Park,
    Stable
422 Walnut St.
HABS PA-1401   pd   H

Independent Order of Odd Fellows
Third & Brown Sts.
HABS PA-1771   p   H

Institute of the Pennsylvania Hospital; see
    Pennsylvania Hospital for the Insane

Insurance Patrol
509 Arch St.
HABS PA-1433   pd   H

Internat'l Exhibition of 1876, Memorial
    Hall
North Concourse Fairmount Park
HABS PA-1659   pd   H

Internat'l Exhibition of 1876, Ohio
    Building
Belmont Ave., Fairmount Park
HABS PA-1660   p   H

Internat'l Exhibition of 1876, St. George's
    House (British Building)
State's Dr.
HABS PA-1080   pd   L

Irish, Nathaniel, House
704 S. Front St.
HABS PA-1013   s p   L H

Irvin Building; see Fire Association
    Building

Italian Villa; see Lea, Henry Charles, House

Iungerich Warehouse
147 S. Front St.
HABS PA-1403   p   H

Ivy Lodge
29 E. Penn St.
HABS PA-1701   p   H

Jacoby, Wigard, House
8327 Germantown Ave.
HABS PA-1702   d   H

Jayne Building (Jayne, Dr., Granite
    Building)
242-244 Chestnut St.
HABS PA-188   s pd   L H

Jayne, Dr., Granite Building; see Jayne
    Building

Jefferson Fire Insurance Company
423 Walnut St.
HABS PA-1435   pd   H

Jefferson, Joseph, House
Sixth & Spruce Sts.
HABS PA-1340   p   H

Jordan-Stoddart House
404 S. Fifth St.
HABS PA-1341   p   H

Justi, Henry D., House
3401 Baring St.
HABS PA-1632   pd   H

Kenilworth Street Area Study
109-123 Kenilworth St.
HABS PA-1588   pd   H

Kensington National Bank (First
Pennsylvania Banking & Trust
Company)
2-8 W. Girard Ave.
HABS PA-1773   pd   H

Keyser Brothers Iron Works
HAER PA-40   pd   L

Kid-Chandler House
323 Walnut St.
HABS PA-1436   pd   H

Kid-Physick House
325 Walnut St.
HABS PA-1437   pd   H

Kirkbride's Hospital; see Pennsylvania
Hospital, Dept. of Mental Diseases

Knight Building
301-303 N. Second St.
HABS PA-1775   d   H

Kosciuszko House; see 301 Pine Street
(House)

Krider Gun Shop; see Drinker, John, House

Lamb, Peter, House (Ayres-Lamb House)
28 Catherine St.
HABS PA-1590   pd   H

**Land Title Bank & Trust Company
Building** (Land Title Building)
S. Broad St.
HABS PA-1514   pd   H

Land Title Building; see Land Title Bank
& Trust Company Building

Lasse Cock's Manor House; see Bel Air

Latour Warehouse
508 S. Water St.
HABS PA-1056   s pd   L

Laurel Hill (Rawle, Randolph, House)
Farimount Park
HABS PA-13   s pd   L

Laurel Hill Cemetery
Fairmount Park
HABS PA-1811   p   H

Laurel Hill Cemetery Gatehouse
3820 Ridge Ave.
HABS PA-1811-A   pd   H

Lea, Henry Charles, House (Italian Villa)
3903 Spruce St.
HABS PA-1633   pd   H

123-125 League Street (Houses)
HABS PA-1583   p   H

Lee, Robert M., House & Law Office
109-111 N. Sixth St.
HABS PA-1052   s pd   L

Leidy, Joseph Jr., House (Poor Richard
Club)
1319 Locust St.
HABS PA-1515   pd   H

Leland Building
37-39 S. Third St.
HABS PA-1086   pd   L

Lemon Hill
Lemon Hill Dr., Fairmount Park
HABS PA-1010   s pd   L H

Letitia Street (House) (Penn, William,
House)
Lansdowne Dr., W. Fairmount Park
HABS PA-184   s p   L H

**Library Company of Philadelphia,
Ridgeway Branch**
900 S. Broad St.
HABS PA-1616   pd   H

Library, Old; see University of
Pennsylvania, Furness Building

Lippincott, Joshua B., House
204 S. Nineteenth St.
HABS PA-1516   pd   H

Lit Brothers Store
701-739 Market St.
HABS PA-1438   pd   H

Livezey House (Glen Fern)
Livezey Lane & Wissahickon Creek
HABS PA-14   s pd   L H

1314-1320 Locust Street (Buildings)
HABS PA-1917   p   H

404-406-408 Locust Street (Houses)
HABS PA-1915   p   H

Lombard Street Area Study
323-333 Lombard St.
HABS PA-1678   pd   H

117 Lombard Street (House) (Palmer,
John, House)
HABS PA-1353   p   H

427 Lombard Street (House) (Hilyard,
Eber, House)
HABS PA-1335   p   H

437 Lombard Street (House) (Fitzgerald,
Thomas, House)
HABS PA-1329   p   H

Loudoun
4650 Germantown Ave.
HABS PA-1705   p   H

Mack, Connie, Stadium; see Shibe Park

Mackley, Carl, Apartments
Bristol, M, Cayuga Sts. & Castor Ave.
HABS PA-1779   d   H

Maloby, Thomas, House & Tavern
700 S. Front St.
HABS PA-1595   p   H

Man Full of Trouble Tavern; see Stafford's
Tavern-Paschall House

Manhattan Building; see American Life
Insurance Company Building

Manheim Club; see Germantown Cricket
Club

Manning Street Area Study; see Marshall's
Court Area Study

Mariners' Bethel Church (First Polish
Baptist Church; Bethel Christian Center)
923 S. Front St.
HABS PA-1596   pd   L H

Market Street Area Study
617-637 Market St.
HABS PA-1441   pd   H

Market Street National Bank Building
(One East Penn Square Building)
Market & Juniper Sts. Centre Square
HABS PA-1517   pd   H

Marks-Dunbar House
849 S. Front St.
HABS PA-1597   p   H

Marshall's Court Area Study (Elliot, John,
House)
407 Marshall's Court
HABS PA-1345-B   p   H

Marshall's Court Area Study (Manning
Street Area Study)
HABS PA-1345   p   H

Marshall's Court Area Study (Simpson,
David, House)
411 Marshall's Court
HABS PA-1345-C   p   H

Marshall's Court Area Study (Shinn,
Samuel, House)
Marshall's Court
HABS PA-1345-A   p   H

Mask & Wig Club; see 310 South Quince
Street (Coach House & Stable)

Mason, James S. & Company Store
138-140 N. Front St.
HABS PA-1442   d   H

Maxfield-Elliott House
35 Queen St.
HABS PA-1600   p   H

Maxwell, Ebenezer, House
Tulpehocken & Greene Sts., Germantown
HABS PA-1098   s pd   H

**McClare-Hutchinson Building
(Commercial)**
20 S. Third St.
HABS PA-1439   pd   H

McCrea, James, House
108-110 Sansom St.
HABS PA-1440   p   H

McGee, Ann, Houses
128-130 Brown St.
HABS PA-1778   d   H

McKean, Thomas Jr., House
269 S. Fifth St.
HABS PA-190   s pd   L

McMullin, Robert, House; see 411 Pine
Street (House)

Mears-Heaton House
240 Delancey St.
HABS PA-1070   s   H

Mechanics' Bank (Norwegian Seamen's
Church)
22 S. Third St.
HABS PA-1443   pd   H

Megargee Brothers Building
(Garrett-Buchanan Building)
18-20 S. Sixth St.
HABS PA-1444   pd   H

Mellon, Thomas, House; see 716 Spruce
Street (House)

Mellor & Meigs Architectural Office
205 S. Juniper St.
HABS PA-1519   pd   H

Mennonite Meeting House
6119 Germantown Ave.
HABS PA-15   s pd   L H

Mercer, Thomas, Houses
2-12 Christian St.
HABS PA-1601   pd   H

Merchant's Exchange; see Philadelphia
Exchange Company

Merchant's Hotel (Washington Hotel)
40-50 N. Fourth St.
HABS PA-1445   pd   H

Merchants Warehouse; see Franklin Sugar
Refinery

Mifflin, John, House
523 S. Front St.
HABS PA-1347   d   H

Mikyeh-Israel Cemetery Gatehouse
1100 Block, Federal St.
HABS PA-1602   pd   H

Mitchell, Thomas, House
276 S. Third St.
HABS PA-1348   pd   H

Moffert, Robert, House (Moffert-Urquhart
House)
35 Catherine St.
HABS PA-1603   d   H

Moffert-Urquhart House; see Moffert,
Robert, House

Monastery
Kitchen's Lane & Wissahickon Creek,
Fairmount Park
HABS PA-183   s pd   L H

Moore, Clarence B., House
1321 Locust St.
HABS PA-1521   pd   H

Moore, John, House; see 734 South Front
Street (House)

Morris Brewery
Chancellor & S. American Sts.
HABS PA-1446   p   H

Morris House; see Compton

**Mother Bethal African Methodist
Espiscopal Church;** see Bethal African
Methodist Episcopal Church

Mount Moriah Cemetery Gatehouse
6299 Kingsessing Ave.
HABS PA-1634   p   L

Mount Pleasant (Clunie)
East Fairmount Park
HABS PA-1130   s p   L H

Mount Sinai Cemetery, Chapel
Bridge & Cottage Sts.
HABS PA-1783   pd   H

Moyamensing Prison; see Philadelphia
County Prison

Moyamensing Prison, Debtors' Wing; see
Philadelphia County Prison

Murphy-Johnson House
42 Catherine St.
HABS PA-1606   pd   H

Musical Fund Hall (Musical Fund Society
Hall)
808 Locust St.
HABS PA-1447   pd   H

Musical Fund Society Hall; see Musical
Fund Hall

Mutual Fire Insurance Company Building
Germantown Ave. & School House Lane
HABS PA-1014   pd   L

National Bank of Northern Liberties
Third & Vine Sts.
HABS PA-1784   pd   H

National Guard's Hall
518-20 Race St.
HABS PA-1015   pd   L

Navigator Statue
310 Market St.
HABS PA-1466   d   H

Neave, Samuel, House & Store
272-274 S. Second St.
HABS PA-1349   s pd   H

142-150 Nectarine Street (Houses)
HABS PA-1769   d   H

Nevel, Thomas, House
338 S. Fourth St.
HABS PA-1350   p   H

New Century Club
214 S. Twelfth St.
HABS PA-1522   pd   H

**New York Mutual Life Insurance
Company Building** (Victory Building)
1001-1005 Chestnut St.
HABS PA-1523   p   H

39-43 Norfolk Street (Houses)
HABS PA-1584   p   H

Norris-Cadwalader House
240 S. Fourth St.
HABS PA-1352   pd   H

**114 North Eleventh Street (Commercial
Building)**
HABS PA-1929   p   H

North Front Street Area Study
2-66 N. Front St.
HABS PA-1448   pd   H

**110 North Ninth Street (Restaurant & Apt.
Bldg.)**
HABS PA-1536   d   H

**305-307 North Second Street (Commercial
Bldgs.)**
HABS PA-1751   d   H

**405-407 North Second Street (Commercial
Bldgs.)**
HABS PA-1752   d   H

North Seventh Street Area Study (21-33
North Seventh Street (Commercial
Buildings))
HABS PA-1449   p   H

**9 North Seventh Street (Commercial
Building)**
HABS PA-1939   pd   H

**21-33 North Seventh Street (Commercial
Buildings);** see North Seventh Street
Area Study

North Third Street Area Study
HABS PA-1450   pd   H

113 North Water Street (House)
HABS PA-1425   p   H

**Northern Liberty Hose Company Number
Four** (Snappers; Philadelphia Fire
Department, Engine Co. No. 21)
714 New Market St.
HABS PA-1785   pd   H

**Northern Saving Fund, Safe Deposit &
Trust Co.**
600 Spring Garden St.
HABS PA-1733   s pd   L H

Norwegian Seamen's Church; see
Mechanics' Bank

One East Penn Square Building; see
Market Street National Bank Building

Ormiston House
Reservoir Dr., Fairmount Park
HABS PA-187   s p   L H

Overbrook School for the Blind; see
Pennsylvania Institution for the Blind

Palmer, John, House; see 117 Lombard
Street (House)

Pancake, Phillip, House
333 S. Fifth St.
HABS PA-1354   pd   H

Pancoast-Lewis-Wharton House
336 Spruce St.
HABS PA-1083   s pd   L H

Parry, Charles T., House (Homestead, The)
1921 Arch St.
HABS PA-1524   p   H

Paschall, Jonathan, House
36 Christian St.
HABS PA-1607   p   H

Pastorius House; see Germantown Historic
District

Peale, Charles Wilson, House (Belfield)
5500 N. Twentieth St.
HABS PA-1676   p   H

Penn. Mutual Building; see Penn. Mutual
Life Insurance Company Building

**Penn. Mutual Life Insurance Company
Building** (Penn. Mutual Building)
Third & Dock Sts.
HABS PA-1451   pd   H

Penn, William, House; see Letitia Street
(House)

Pennsylvania Academy of Fine Arts
Broad & Cherry Sts.
HABS PA-1525   pd   H

Pennsylvania Athletic Club; see Fell-Van
  Rensselaer House
Pennsylvania Company for Insurances on
  Lives
431 Chestnut St.
HABS PA-1452   d   H
Pennsylvania Company for Insurances on
  Lives
304 Walnut St.
HABS PA-1453   pd   H
Pennsylvania Fire Insurance Company
508-510 Walnut St.
HABS PA-1454   pd   H
Pennsylvania Historical Society
Thirteenth & Locust Sts.
HABS PA-1942   p   H
Pennsylvania Hospital
Ninth & Pine Sts.
HABS PA-1123   s pd   L H
Pennsylvania Hospital, Dept. of Mental
  Diseases (Kirkbride's Hospital)
Forty-fourth & Market Sts.
HABS PA-1636   pd   H
Pennsylvania Hospital for the Insane
  (Department for Males; Institute of the
  Pennsylvania Hospital)
111 N. Forty-ninth St.
HABS PA-1635   p   H
Pennsylvania Institute for Deaf & Dumb
  (Philadelphia College of Art)
320 S. Broad St.
HABS PA-1526   pd   H
Pennsylvania Institution for the Blind
  (Overbrook School for the Blind)
Sixty-fourth St. & Malvern Ave.
HABS PA-1637   p   H
Pennsylvania Railroad, Chestnut Hill Line
Chelton Ave.
HABS PA-1943   p   H
Pennsylvania Railroad, Germantown
  Junction
HABS PA-1941   p   H
Pennsylvania Railroad Station, Broad
  Street Station
Broad & Market Sts.
HABS PA-1527   pd   H
Pennypack Creek Bridge
8300 Frankford Ave.
HABS PA-1786   p   H
Perelman Antique Toy Museum; see
  Abercombie, Capt. James, House
Perseverance Hose Company, Number Five
314 Race St.
HABS PA-1455   d   H
Phil., Germantown & Norristown RR,
  Germantown Depot
5731-5735 Germantown Ave.
HABS PA-1707   pd   H
Phil., Wilmington & Balt. R. R. Freight
  Sta. Shed (Semple Company Warehouse)
Fifteenth & Carpenter Sts.
HABS PA-1611   pd   H

Phila. Fire Department, Number 3 & Patrol
  House; see Weccacoe Engine Company,
  Number 9
Philadelphia & Reading Railroad Terminal
  Station
Twelth & Market Sts.
HABS PA-1528   pd   H
Philadelphia Art Club
220 S. Broad St.
HABS PA-1529   pd   H
Philadelphia Athenaeum
219 S. Sixth St. (E. Washington Sq.)
HABS PA-1389   s pd   H
Philadelphia Athenaeum, Brick Privy
219 S. Sixth St. (E. Washington Sq.)
HABS PA-1389-A   s pd   H
Philadelphia Bank; see Bank of
  Pennsylvania
Philadelphia Bourse
Market & Chestnut Sts.
HABS PA-1456   pd   H
Philadelphia City Hall
Broad & Market Sts., Penn Square
HABS PA-1530   pd   H
Philadelphia College of Art; see
  Pennsylvania Institute for Deaf & Dumb
Philadelphia Contributionship, House Fire
  Insurance
212 S. Fourth St.
HABS PA-1457   pd   H
Philadelphia County Court House; see
  Independence Hall Complex, Congress
  Hall
Philadelphia County Prison (Moyamensing
  Prison)
1400 S. Tenth St.
HABS PA-1096   pd   H
Philadelphia County Prison (Moyamensing
  Prison, Debtors' Wing)
Tenth St.
HABS PA-1097   s p   H
Philadelphia Exchange Company
  (Merchant's Exchange)
Dock, Third & Walnut Sts.
HABS PA-1028   p   L
Philadelphia Fire Department, Engine Co.
  No. 21; see Northern Liberty Hose
  Company Number Four
Philadelphia Fire Department, Engine Co.
  Number 2
826-828 New Market St.
HABS PA-1787   pd   H
Philadelphia Fire Department, Engine Co.
  Number 8 (Fireman's Hall)
149 N. Second St.
HABS PA-1459   s p   H
Philadelphia Gas Works, Point Breeze
  Meter House
Passyunk Ave.
HAER PA-41   s   H
Philadelphia Hose Company, Number One
33 N. Seventh St.
HABS PA-1460   pd   H

Philadelphia Masonic Temple
HABS PA-1532   pd   H
Philadelphia Museum of Art
Benjamin Franklin Pkwy.
HABS PA-1661   pd   H
Philadelphia National Bank; see
  Philadelphia Trust, Safe Deposit &
  Insurance Co.
Philadelphia Opera House
1400-1418 Poplar St.
HABS PA-1734   pd   H
Philadelphia Saving Fund Society
700 Walnut St., Washington Sq.
HABS PA-1462   pd   H
Philadelphia Saving Fund Society
306 Walnut St.
HABS PA-1461   pd   H
Philadelphia Saving Fund Society Building
Twelth & Market Sts.
HABS PA-1533   pd   H
Philadelphia Trust, Safe Deposit &
  Insurance Co. (Philadelphia National
  Bank)
415 Chestnut St.
HABS PA-1181   s pd   H
Philadelphia Zoo, Bear Pits
Fairmount Park
HABS PA-1662   p   H
Philadelphia Zoo, Entrance Pavilions
Girard Ave. & 34th St., Fairmount Park
HABS PA-1663   p   H
Physick-Conner House
240 Pine St.
HABS PA-1356   d   H
Picklands, Thomas, House
307 S. Third St.
HABS PA-1357   p   H
Piles, John, House
328 S. Third St.
HABS PA-1358   p   H
301 Pine Street (House) (Kosciuszko
  House)
HABS PA-1342   pd   H
411 Pine Street (House) (McMullin,
  Robert, House)
HABS PA-1344   p   H
Poe, Edgar Allen, House
530 N. Seventh St.
HABS PA-1735   pd   H
Poor Richard Club; see Leidy, Joseph Jr.,
  House
Port Royal (Stiles-Lukens House)
Tacony St.
HABS PA-111   s pd   L
Porter, Sedgeley, House (Sedgeley Guard
  House)
Girard Ave. & Sedgeley Dr.
HABS PA-1665   p   H
Portico Row; see Portico Square
Portico Square (Portico Row)
900-930 Spruce St.
HABS PA-1534   pd   H

Potts, Horace T. & Company Warehouse
316-320 N. Third St.
HABS PA-1789   s p d   H

Potts, Joseph P., House; see 3905 Spruce
  Street (House)

Powder Magazine
Magazine Lane
HABS PA-124   s p d   L

Powel, Samuel, House
244 S. Third St.
HABS PA-1359   p d   H

Preisendanz, Christian A., Wagon Works
520-526 New Market St.
HABS PA-1791   d   H

Preston Retreat
500-518 N. Twentieth St.
HABS PA-1736   p d   H

Protestant Episcopal City Mission; see St.
  Paul's Prostestant Episcopal Church

Provident Life & Trust Company Bank
409 Chestnut St.
HABS PA-1058   s p d   L

Pugh, Isaac, Paper Hangings Factory
440 New Market St.
HABS PA-1792   d   H

Purres, Hugh, Store
626 S. Second St.
HABS PA-1612   d   H

523-525 Quarry Street (House)
HABS PA-1426   p   H

Quarters A; see U.S. Naval Base,
  Commandants' Quarters

Queen Street Area Study
26-28 Queen St.
HABS PA-1613   p   H

**907-909 Race Street (Commercial
  Buildings) (Far East Chinese Restaurant)**
HABS PA-1505   p d   L H

Ralston, Robert, House
521 Arch St.
HABS PA-1016   p d   L H

Ralston School
625 S. American St.
HABS PA-1614   p d   H

Rawle, Randolph, House; see Laurel Hill

Reed, Jacob, Sons, Building
1424 Chestnut St.
HABS PA-1535   d   H

Reed, Samuel & Joseph, Houses
518-520 S. Front St.
HABS PA-1615   p d   H

**Reliance Insurance Company of
  Philadelphia Bldg.**
429 Walnut St.
HABS PA-1465   p d   H

Reynolds-Morris House
225 S. Eighth St.
HABS PA-1107   s p d   L H

Rhoads-Barclay House
217 Delancey St.
HABS PA-1057   s p d   L H

Richardson, Nathaniel, House; see 524
  South Front Street (House)

Rich-Comly House
4276 Orchard St.
HABS PA-1794   s p d   L H

Rich-Truman House
320 Delancey St.
HABS PA-1074   s p d   L

Ridge Avenue Farmers Market Company
1810 Ridge Ave.
HABS PA-1737   p d   H

Ridgeland
Chamounix Dr., Fairmount Park
HABS PA-1664   p   L

Rittenhouse House
Lincoln Dr. & Rittenhouse St.
HABS PA-16   s p d   L H

Rittenhouse Square; see Academy of Notre
  Dame

Robeson House; see Shoomac Park

Robinson, William, House
23 Clymer St.
HABS PA-1361   p   H

Rogers-Cassatt House
202 S. Nineteenth St., Rittenhouse Sq.
HABS PA-1537   p d   H

Roney, John, House
117 N. Sixth St.
HABS PA-1017   s d   L

Rooming House
115 Bainbridge St.
HABS PA-1617   d   H

Rowley-Pullman House
238 S. Third St.
HABS PA-1467   p d   H

Royal House
5011 Germantown Ave.
HABS PA-1709   d   H

Royal Insurance Company Building
212 S. Third St.
HABS PA-1468   p d   H

Rumpp, C. F. & Sons, Inc., Factory
114-130 N. Fifth St. at Cherry St.
HABS PA-1469   p d   H

Rush, Benjamin, Birthplace
Red Lion Rd.
HABS PA-1796   p d   H

Russell Building
152-154 N. Front St.
HABS PA-1797   d   H

Saint James Street Area Study (202-206
  Saint James Street (Building))
HABS PA-1474   H

202-206 Saint James Street (Building); see
  Saint James Street Area Study

Sansom, William, House
707 Walnut St.
HABS PA-1476   p   H

Schaeffer, Harriet, House
433 W. Stafford St.
HABS PA-1712   p   H

Schenck Building
535-537 Arch St.
HABS PA-1078   p d   L

Schiable, Charles, Store & House
104 Fairmount Ave.
HABS PA-1798   d   H

Schirely, Henry, House; see 329 South
  Third Street (House)

Schuykill Arsenal
2620 Gray's Ferry Ave.
HABS PA-1540   p d   H

Schuykill Hose, Hook & Ladder Company
1227 Locust St., No. 24
HABS PA-1577   p d   H

Scott-Wanamaker House
3032 Walnut St.
HABS PA-1578   p d   H

Second Bank of the United States (Customs
  House, Old)
420 Chestnut St.
HABS PA-137   s p d   L H

Sedgeley Guard House; see Porter,
  Sedgeley, House

Semple Company Warehouse; see Phil.,
  Wilmington & Balt. R. R. Freight Sta.
  Shed

Shibe Park (Mack, Connie, Stadium)
2701 N. Twenty-first St.
HABS PA-1738   p d   H

Shinn, Samuel, House; see Marshall's Court
  Area Study

Shippen-Wistar House
238 S. Fourth St.
HABS PA-1365   p d   H

Shoomac Park (Robeson House)
Ridge Ave. & Wissahickon Dr.
HABS PA-1067   s p d   L

Shunk School (Eden, Beth, House)
807 New Market St.
HABS PA-1800   d   H

Shur's Lane Mills
428 Shur's Lane
HABS PA-1713   p d   H

Siddons, William, House
851-53 S. Front St.
HABS PA-1618   d   H

Simpson, David, House; see Marshall's
  Court Area Study

Sims, Joseph, House (Franklin Row)
228 S. Ninth St.
HABS PA-1186   s p d   H

Singer, John, Warehouse
319 1/2 Market St.
HABS PA-1478   p d   H

Singley House; see Bel Air

Sink-Burgin House; see 331 South Fifth
  Street (House)

Sisk Houses; see Stafford's Tavern-Paschall
  House

Smith, Daniel Jr., House; see 505 South
  Front Street (House)

Smith Memorial Arch
N. Concourse & Lansdowne Dr.
HABS PA-1666   p d   H

Smythe Building
101-105 Arch St.
HABS PA-1479   d   H

Snappers; see Northern Liberty Hose
Company Number Four

Society Hill Synagogue; see Spruce Street
Baptist Church

Solitude
Fairmount Park, Zoo grounds
HABS PA-1127   s pd   L

Somerton; see Strawberry Mansion

Sons of Temperance Fountain
Independence Sq. (moved from Belmont &
Fount.)
HABS PA-1480   pd   H

Souder, Charles F., House
514 Race St.
HABS PA-1018   pd   L

331 South Fifth Street (House)
(Sink-Burgin House)
HABS PA-1366   pd   H

315-317-319 South Fifth Street
(Townhouses)
HABS PA-1322   pd   H

South Front Street Area Study
W. side Front St. btw. South & Catherine
Sts.
HABS PA-1812   pd   H

312 South Front Street (House)
HABS PA-1950   p   H

505 South Front Street (House) (Smith,
Daniel Jr., House)
HABS PA-1367   p   H

507 South Front Street (House) (Bridges,
Robert, House)
HABS PA-1320   p   H

510 South Front Street (House) (Wharton,
Isaac, House)
HABS PA-1381   p   H

524 South Front Street (House)
(Richardson, Nathaniel, House)
HABS PA-1360   d   H

602 South Front Street (House) (Henderson
House)
HABS PA-1571   d   H

603 South Front Street (House)
(Hart-Patterson House)
HABS PA-1569   p   H

626 South Front Street (House) (Spafford,
William, House)
HABS PA-1620   pd   H

720-724 South Front Street (House)
(Askins-Jones House)
HABS PA-1541   p   H

734 South Front Street (House) (Moore,
John, House)
HABS PA-1605   p   H

783 South Front Street (House) (Collins,
Samuel, House)
HABS PA-1549   p   H

814 South Front Street (House) (Hutton,
Nathaniel, House)
HABS PA-1586   p   H

836 South Front Street (House)
HABS PA-1952   pd   H

919 South Front Street (House) (Wharton,
John, House)
HABS PA-1624   p   H

319-321 South Front Street (Houses)
HABS PA-1337   p   H

606-608 South Front Street (Houses)
(Fullerton, John, Houses)
HABS PA-1563   p   H

731-733 South Front Street (Houses)
(Flickwir-Nugent Houses)
HABS PA-1585   d   H

806-808 South Front Street (Houses)
HABS PA-1594   p   H

310 South Quince Street (Coach House &
Stable) (Mask & Wig Club)
HABS PA-1518   pd   H

125-127 South Second Street (Commercial
Bldgs.)
HABS PA-1405   s   d   H

252 South Second Street (House)
HABS PA-1934   p   H

600 South Second Street (House)
HABS PA-1575   d   H

252 South Third Street (House)
HABS PA-1945   p   H

259 South Third Street (House) (Waln,
Isaac, House)
HABS PA-1376   p   H

266-276 South Third Street (House)
HABS PA-1936   p   H

329 South Third Street (House) (Schirely,
Henry, House)
HABS PA-1364   p   H

South Water Street Area Study (Houses)
516-26 S. Water St.
HABS PA-1619   d   H

South Water Street Area Study
(Warehouses)
100-50 S. Water St.
HABS PA-1810   p   H

532 South Water Street (House)
HABS PA-1809   p   H

South Water Street (Houses)
S. Water & Fitzwater Sts.
HABS PA-1953   p   H

Southern Loan Company of Philadelphia
(Tradesmen's National Bank of
Philadelphia)
300 S. Second St.
HABS PA-1368   pd   H

Southwark Hose Company, Number Nine
512 S. Third St.
HABS PA-1369   pd   H

Spafford, William, House; see 626 South
Front Street (House)

Sparks Shot Tower
129-131 Carpenter St.
HABS PA-1621   pd   H

Spring Garden Fire Insurance Company
431 Walnut St.
HABS PA-1481   pd   H

Spring Garden Institute
523-525 N. Broad St.
HABS PA-1739   pd   H

Spring Garden Street Bridge (Callowhill
Street Bridge)
Spring Garden & Callowhill Sts.
HABS PA-1667   pd   H

Spruce Street Area Study
2009-2045 Spruce St.
HABS PA-1579   pd   H

Spruce Street Baptist Church (Society Hill
Synagogue)
426 Spruce St.
HABS PA-1370   d   H

3905 Spruce Street (House) (Potts, Joseph
P., House)
HABS PA-1638   pd   H

716 Spruce Street (House) (Mellon,
Thomas, House)
HABS PA-1346   p   H

700-714 Spruce Street (Houses)
HABS PA-253   s pd   L

722-730 Spruce Street (Houses)
HABS PA-1339   pd   H

St. Agatha's Roman Catholic Church
3801 Spring Garden St.
HABS PA-1639   pd   H

St. Andrew's Church (Episcopal) (St.
George's Greek Orthodox Cathedral)
250-254 S. Eighth St.
HABS PA-1362   pd   H

St. Augustine's Roman Catholic Church
Fourth & New Sts.
HABS PA-1471   pd   H

St. Charles Borromeo Roman Catholic
Church
Twentieth & Christian Sts.
HABS PA-1546   pd   H

St. Charles Hotel
60-66 N. Third St.
HABS PA-1472   pd   H

St. Clement's Protestant Episcopal Church
128 N. Twentieth St.
HABS PA-1538   p   H

St. Elizabeth Roman Catholic Church
1845 N. Twenty-third St.
HABS PA-1940   p   H

St. Francis DeSales Roman Catholic
Church
4629-4635 Springfield Ave.
HABS PA-1640   p   H

St. Francis Xavier's Church (Roman
Catholic)
2321 Green St.
HABS PA-1933   p   H

St. George's Greek Orthodox Cathedral;
see St. Andrew's Church (Episcopal)

St. George's Methodist Episcopal Church
235 N. Fourth St.
HABS PA-1473   pd   H

St. James Roman Catholic Church
3728 Chestnut St.
HABS PA-1641   pd   H

St. John's Lutheran Church
511-523 Race St.
HABS PA-1935   p   H

St. Mark's Church (Episcopal)
1625 Locust St.
HABS PA-1093   pd   L H

St. Mary's Protestant Episcopl Church
3916 Locust St., Hamilton Village
HABS PA-1642   pd   H

St. Mary's Roman Catholic Church
244 S. Fourth St.
HABS PA-1363   p   H

St. Paul's Prostestant Episcopal Church
(Protestant Episcopal City Mission)
225 S. Third St.
HABS PA-1475   s pd   H

**St. Peter's Church House (Episcopal); see
Blackwell, Reverend Robert, House**

St. Peter's Protestant Episcopal Church
(Blackwell, Rev. Robert , House)
Third & Pine Sts.
HABS PA-1118   pd   H

St. Stephan's Protestant Episcopal Church
19 S. Tenth St.
HABS PA-1576   pd   H

St. Timothy's Protestant Episcopal Church
5720 Ridge Ave.
HABS PA-1710   p   H

**St. Timothy's Working Men's Club &
Institute**
5164 Ridge Ave.
HABS PA-1711   p   H

Stafford's Tavern-Paschall House (Man
Full of Trouble Tavern; Cove Cornice
House; Sisk Houses)
127-129 Spruce St.
HABS PA-128   s pd   L H

**Stanfield House; see Woods, Capt. John,
House**

**State House of Pennsylvania; see
Independence Hall Complex,
Independence Hall**

Stenton
Courtland & Eighteenth Sts.
HABS PA-1714   pd   H

Stenton Barn
4685 N. Eighteenth St.
HABS PA-1715   d   H

**Stetson Hat Factory; see Stetson, John B.,
Company**

Stetson, John B., Company (Stetson Hat
Factory)
Germantown & Columbia Aves.
HABS PA-1227   pd   L

Stewart, Thomas, House
410 Locust St.
HABS PA-189   s pd   L H

Stiles, Edward, House
128 N. Front St.
HABS PA-1482   d   H

Stiles, William, House
310 Cypress St.
HABS PA-1371   p   H

Stiles-Lukens House; see Port Royal

Stocker, John Clement, House
402 S. Front St.
HABS PA-1068   s pd   L

Stone-Penrose House
700 Locust St.
HABS PA-1483   pd   H

Stortz, John & Sons, Store
210 Vine St.
HABS PA-1484   d   H

Strawberry Mansion (Somerton)
Fairmount Park
HABS PA-1668   pd   L

Strawberry Mansion Bridge
Ford Rd. & E. River Dr.
HABS PA-1669   pd   H

Stride-Madison House
429 Spruce St.
HABS PA-1073   s pd   L

Sully, Thomas, House
530 Spruce St.
HABS PA-1372   p   H

Summers-Worrell House
505 Delancey St.
HABS PA-1373   p   H

**Swedes Church, Old; see Gloria Dei
(Church)**

Sweetbrier
Fairmount Park
HABS PA-1670   pd   H

Tabernacle Presbyterian Church
3700 Chestnut St.
HABS PA-1099   pd   L

Tanner, Henry O., House
2908 W. Diamond St.
HABS PA-1740   d   H

Third Presbyterian Church
422 Pine St.
HABS PA-1379   p   H

Toby-Shaw House
12 Queen St.
HABS PA-1937   p   H

**Tradesmen's National Bank of
Philadelphia; see Southern Loan
Company of Philadelphia**

Trinity Church, Oxford
6900 Oxford Ave.
HABS PA-17   s pd   L

Trinity Lutheran Church
19 N. Queen Lane
HABS PA-1716   pd   H

Trinity Luthern Church, Sower House
5300 Germantown Ave.
HABS PA-1717   d   H

Troc, The; see Arch Street Opera House

Tuttleman Brothers & Faggen Building
56-60 N. Second St.
HABS PA-1485   p   H

Union League of Philadelphia
140 S. Broad St.
HABS PA-1626   pd   H

University of Pennsylvania, College Hall
Woodland Ave.
HABS PA-1643   pd   H

**University of Pennsylvania, Furness
Building** (Library, Old)
HABS PA-1644   pd   H

**University of Pennsylvania, Men's
Dormitories**
Spruce St.
HABS PA-1645   pd   H

**University of Pennsylvania, University
Museum**
3620 South St.
HABS PA-1646   pd   H

Upper Ferry Bridge
Spring Garden St.
HABS PA-1946   p   H

Upsula
6430 Germantown Ave.
HABS PA-1718   p   H

U.S. Bonded Warehouse
Lombard & Front Sts.
HABS PA-1375   p   H

U.S. Hose Company, Number Fourteen
423 Buttonwood St.
HABS PA-1804   pd   H

U.S. Mint
Sixteenth & Garden Sts.
HABS PA-1741   p   H

U.S. Mint, Old
Chestnut & Juniper Sts.
HABS PA-1938   p   H

U.S. Naval Asylum, Biddle Hall (U.S.
Naval Home)
Gray's Ferry Ave.
HABS PA-1622-A   pd   H

U.S. Naval Asylum, Governor's House
Gray's Ferry Ave.
HABS PA-1622-B   pd   H

U.S. Naval Asylum, Laning Hall
Gray's Ferry Ave.
HABS PA-1622-C   pd   H

U.S. Naval Asylum, Surgeon's House
Gray's Ferry Ave.
HABS PA-1622-D   pd   H

U.S. Naval Asylum, Surgeon's House
Gray's Ferry Ave.
HABS PA-1622-D   p   H

U.S. Naval Base, Commandants' Quarters
(Quarters A)
Davis Ave.
HABS PA-1623   d   H

**U.S. Naval Home; see U.S. Naval Asylum,
Biddle Hall**

U.S. Post Office & Courthouse
Fifth & Chestnut Sts.
HABS PA-1954   p   H

Valley Green Inn
Wissahickon Dr.
HABS PA-1719   s p   L

Vernon
Germantown Ave., Vernon Park
HABS PA-7-2   s pd   L

Victory Building; see New York Mutual
Life Insurance Company Building
123-127 Vine Street (Commercial Bldgs.)
HABS PA-1754   d   H
Waln, Isaac, House; see 259 South Third
Street (House)
131 Walnut Street (Casement Window)
HABS PA-1948   s   H
329 Walnut Street (House)
HABS PA-1947   p   H
Walnut Street Theater
Ninth & Walnut Sts.
HABS PA-1487   pd   H
Wanamaker, John, Store
Thirteenth & Chestnut Sts.
HABS PA-1692   pd   H
Washington Hose Company, Number Ten
35 N. Ninth St.
HABS PA-1488   d   H
Washington Hotel; see Merchant's Hotel
Washington Square Area Study
Sixth, Seventh, Walnut & Locust Sts.
HABS PA-1489   p   H
Water Trough and Fountain
Ninth St.
HABS PA-1379   p   H
Weccacoe Engine Company, Number 9
(Phila. Fire Department, Number 3 &
Patrol House)
117-21 Queen St.
HABS PA-1610   pd   H
Weidersum, George, House
405 Richmond Ave.
HABS PA-1807   p   H
West Arch Street Presbyterian Church
(Arch Street Presbyterian Church)
1726-32 Arch St.
HABS PA-1696   pd   L H
Western Saving Fund Society
1000-08 Walnut St.
HABS PA-1703   pd   H
Wetherill, Joseph, House
233 Delancey St.
HABS PA-1380   pd   H
Wharton, Isaac, House; see 510 South Front
Street (House)
Wharton, John, House; see 919 South Front
Street (House)
Wharton, Joseph, House
119 Lombard St.
HABS PA-1382   p   H
Wharton-Stewart House
27 Christian St.
HABS PA-1185   s pd   H
White, Bishop William, House
309 Walnut St.
HABS PA-1490   pd   H
White Tower
159 N. Broad St.
HABS PA-1721   d   H
Widener, Peter A. B., House
1200 N. Broad St.
HABS PA-1742   pd   H

Wildes-Sonder Houses
455-57 N. Second St.
HABS PA-1808   d   H
Williams-Hopkinson House
338 Spruce St.
HABS PA-1084   s pd   L H
Williams-Mathurin House
427 Spruce St.
HABS PA-1383   pd   H
Winder, William, Houses
234-34 S. Third St.
HABS PA-1384   pd   H
Winemore, Phillip, House
220 Spruce St.
HABS PA-1050   s pd   L
Wissachickon Inn (Chestnut Hill Academy)
500 W. Willow Grove Ave.
HABS PA-1720   pd   H
Wister's Big House; see Grumblethorpe
Wister's Tenant House; see Grumblethorpe
Tenant House
Wood, George, Houses
325-37 S. Fifth St.
HABS PA-1385   pd   H
Woodford
Ford Rd. & Greenland Dr.
HABS PA-1307   pd   H
5901 Woodland Avenue (Cottage)
HABS PA-138   s p   L
Woodland Terrace Area Study
501-19 & 500-20 Woodland Terrace
HABS PA-1647   p   H
Woodlands (Hamilton, Andrew, House;
Hamilton Village)
Thirty-ninth St. & Woodland Ave.
HABS PA-1125   s pd   L H
Woods, Capt. John, House (Stanfield
House)
Front & Lombard Sts.
HABS PA-1111   s   d L
Woolfall-Huddel House
9 Queen St.
HABS PA-1625   p   H
Workman Place
742-46 S. Front St.
HABS PA-133   pd   L H
Wyck (Haines House)
6026 Germantown Ave.
HABS PA-7-3   s pd   L H
Wynnestay
Fifty-second St. & Woodbine Ave.
HABS PA-1648   p   H

PIKE COUNTY

Bushkill

Bushkill Gristmill (Peters Mill)
Lehman Twp.
HABS PA-1137   s pd   H
Bushkill Hotel; see Peter House Hotel
Corner House; see Peter House Hotel

Peter House Hotel (Bushkill Hotel; Corner
House)
Lehman Twp.
HABS PA-1138   pd   H
Peters Mill; see Bushkill Gristmill

Dingman's Ferry

Delaware House Hotel
HABS PA-1162   p   H
Delaware River Bridge
HAER PA-15   s p   L H
Dutch Reformed Church
HABS PA-1273   pd   H
St. John the Evangelist Episcopal Church
HABS PA-1254   s pd   H

Egypt Mills vic.

Eshback House; see Nyce, William, House
Eshback Tenant House; see Van Gorden,
Jacobus, House
Nyce, William, House (Eshback House)
HABS PA-1163   p   H
Van Gorden, Jacobus, House (Eshback
Tenant House)
HABS PA-5180   s pd   H

Lackawaxen

**Delaware & Hudson Canal, Delaware
Aqueduct**
Spanning Delaware River, State Rt. 590
HAER PA-1   s pd   L
Erie Railroad, Delaware Division, Bridge
Spanning Lackawaxen River
HAER PA-24   p   H

Milford

Milford Jail
Broad & High Sts.
HABS PA-221   s pd   L

Milford vic.

Callahan House; see Helm, Jacob, House
Helm, Jacob, House (Callahan House)
Rt. 209, Dingman Twp.
HABS PA-1275   pd   H

Millrift

Erie Railroad, Delaware River Bridge
Spanning Delaware River
HAER PA-23   p   H

Shohola

Erie Railroad, Shohola Creek Bridge
State Rt. 434
HAER PA-43   p   H
Erie Railroad, Shohola Passenger Station
Rohman Ave. & Richardson St.
HAER PA-42   p   H

Shohola vic.

**Erie Railroad, Shohola Side Hill Cut &
Revetment**
Delaware River
HAER PA-44   p   H

POTTER COUNTY

Coudersport

Barn, Log
Rt. 6 (Lyman Run Rd.)
HABS PA-5127   s pd   L

Coudersport Jail
HABS PA-5132   p   L

Ives House
Third & East Sts.
HABS PA-528   s pd   L

Lillibridge House
HABS PA-5107   p   L

Presbyterian Church
HABS PA-529   p   L

Roulette

Wiedrich House
HABS PA-5129   p   L

SNYDER COUNTY

Selinsgrove

Academy, Old
Market & W. Snyder Sts.
HABS PA-325   s pd   L

SOMERSET COUNTY

Addison

Toll House
U.S. Rt. 40 (Cumberland Rd.)
HABS PA-5177   p   L

Rockwood vic.

Shaulis, W. L., House
HABS PA-416   p   L

SULLIVAN COUNTY

Ganoga Lake

Ricketts, William R., House
North Mountain Colley
HABS PA-210   s pd   L

SUSQUEHANNA COUNTY

Lanesboro

Erie Railroad, Delaware Division, Bridge
State Rt. 171
HAER PA-16   p   H

Erie Railroad, Delaware Division, Bridge
(Starrucca Viaduct)
Starruca Creek
HAER PA-6   p   H

Erie Railroad, Delaware Division, Culvert
State Rt. 171, Canawacta Creek
HAER PA-17   p   H

Starrucca Viaduct; see Erie Railroad,
Delaware Division, Bridge

Lanesboro vic.

Erie Railroad, Cascade Bridge Site
Cascade Creek
HAER PA-18   p   H

Milford vic.

**Erie Railroad, Pond Eddy Side Hill Cut &
Fill**
Delaware River, South Bank
HAER PA-30   p   H

Montrose

Lyons, John, House; see Mulford, Sylvanus,
House

Mulford, Sylvanus, House (Lyons, John,
House)
65 Church St.
HABS PA-215   s pd   L

Susquehanna

**Erie Railroad, Susquehanna Blacksmith
Shop**
Main St.
HAER PA-10-C   p   H

Erie Railroad, Susquehanna Boiler Shop
Main St. vic.
HAER PA-10-D   p   H

Erie Railroad, Susquehanna Boiler Shop
Main St. vic.
HAER PA-10-E   p   H

**Erie Railroad, Susquehanna Carpenter
Shop**
Exchange St.
HAER PA-10-B   p   H

**Erie Railroad, Susquehanna Freight
Station**
Front St.
HAER PA-9   p   H

**Erie Railroad, Susquehanna Machine &
Erecting Shop** (Long Shop)
Main St.
HAER PA-10-A   p   H

Erie Railroad, Susquehanna Repair Shops
Main St.
HAER PA-10   s p   H

**Erie Railroad, Susquehanna Transfer
Table**
Main St.
HAER PA-10-G   p   H

**Erie RR, Susquehanna Passenger Station
& Hotel** (Starracca House)
Front St.
HAER PA-8   s p   H

**Erie RR, Susquehanna Repair Shops
Office Bldg.**
Main St.
HAER PA-10-F   p   H

Long Shop; see Erie Railroad,
Susquehanna Machine & Erecting Shop

Starracca House; see Erie RR,
Susquehanna Passenger Station & Hotel

VENANGO COUNTY

Cherry Tree

Cherry Tree Presbyterian Church
HABS PA-530   s pd   L

Public School
HABS PA-539   p   L

Franklin

Ridgeway Log House
HABS PA-578   p   L

Oil City

**Pennsylvania Railroad, Allegheny River
Bridge**
River St. vic.
HAER PA-22   p   L

Pleasantville

Free Methodist Church
HABS PA-531   s pd   L

Quinn House
HABS PA-518   s pd   L

WARREN COUNTY

Garland

Mill, Old (Interior)
HABS PA-540   p   L

Irvine

Irvine Estate, House by the Pines
HABS PA-522   pd   L

Irvine Estate, Irvine Farmhouse
HABS PA-525   s pd   L

Irvine Estate, Miller's House
HABS PA-526   s pd   L

Irvine Estate, Tenant House
HABS PA-527   s pd   L

Irvine Presbyterian Church
HABS PA-516   s pd   L

Pittsfield

Acock House
HABS PA-554   p   L

Hotel, Old
HABS PA-553   p   L

Rhodes House
HABS PA-556   p   L

Terry House
HABS PA-555   p   L

Tidioute

Hotel, Old (Ryan House)
HABS PA-585   p   L

Ryan House; see Hotel, Old

WASHINGTON COUNTY

Canonsburg

Roberts, John, Stone House
225 N. Central Ave.
HABS PA-1177   s   L

Finleyville vic.

Methodist Church, James Chapel
Gill Hall Rd., Union Twp.
HABS PA-600   s   L

Meadow Lands vic.

Wylie-Miller Barn
U.S. Rt. 19 (North Strabane Twp.)
HABS PA-427   s pd   L

Washington

**Washington & Jefferson College, Admin.
  Building**
HABS PA-8-2   s pd   L

West Brownsville Vic

Dorsey House
HABS PA-5176   p   H

WAYNE COUNTY

Bethany

Wilmot, David, House
Wayne St.
HABS PA-225   s pd   L

Hawley

Erie Railroad, Hawley Coaling Station
HAER PA-25   p   H

Honesdale

House, Italian Villa
HABS PA-5175   p   L
Thompson, Andrew, House
HABS PA-229   s pd   L

Whites Valley

Octagon School House
HABS PA-228   s pd   L

WESTMORELAND COUNTY

Fellsburg

Fellsburg Methodist Episcopal Church
Webster Rd. & State Rt. 201 (Rostraver
  Twp.)
HABS PA-608   s   L

Laughlintown vic.

Penguin Court; see Scaife, Alan M., House
Scaife, Alan M., House (Penguin Court)
U.S. Rt. 30 (Ligonier Twp.)
HABS PA-620   s   L

New Kensington vic.

Milligan, Samuel, Mill (Water Power Grist
  Mill)
Little Pucketos Creek
HABS PA-411   s pd   L
**Water Power Grist Mill; see Milligan,
  Samuel, Mill**

West Newton Borough

Plumer, John C., House
131 S. Water St.
HABS PA-617   s   L

West Newton vic.

Bells Mill Bridge
Sewickley Creek
HABS PA-415   s pd   L

WYOMING COUNTY

North Mehoopany

Kintner Mill
HABS PA-238   s pd   L

YORK COUNTY

Davidsburg vic.

**Kleister Log House; see Wertz-Lashee
  House**
Wertz-Lashee House (Kleister Log House)
R. D. 2, Washington Twp.
HABS PA-5183   pd   H

Detters Mill

Detter's Mill Covered Bridge (Picketts
  Covered Bridge)
Warrington-Dover Twp.
HABS PA-5184   pd   H
**Picketts Covered Bridge; see Detter's Mill
  Covered Bridge**

Hallam Borough

Shultz, Martin, House
Emig St.
HABS PA-5185   pd   H

Laurel vic.

Guinston United Presbyterian Church
R. D. 1, Chanceford Twp.
HABS PA-5187   pd   H

Oil City

**Pennsylvania Railroad, Allegheny River
  Bridge**
HAER PA-22   p   L

Pittsfield

Church
HABS PA-5133   p   L

York

**American Chain & Cable Company
  Factory**
HAER PA-52   pd   L
Billmeyer House
225 E. Market St.
HABS PA-5188   pd   H
Chambers, Joseph, House (Gates House)
W. Market St.
HABS PA-5189   pd   H
Christ Lutheran Church
S. George St.
HABS PA-366   p   L

Cookes House
Codorus St. & Mill Lane
HABS PA-5190   pd   H
**Direct Hotel; see North George Street
  Historic District**
Gates House; see Chambers, Joseph, House
Golden Plough Tavern
W. Market St.
HABS PA-5169   pd   H
**105 North George Street (Commercial
  Building); see North George Street
  Historic District**
**109-111 North George Street (Commercial
  Building); see North George Street
  Historic District**
**107 North George Street (Commerical
  Building); see North George Street
  Historic District**
North George Street Historic District
  (101-103 North George Street (Hotel);
  Direct Hotel)
HABS PA-569   pd   L
North George Street Historic District
  (109-111 North George Street
  (Commercial Building))
HABS PA-572   pd   L
North George Street Historic District (107
  North George Street (Commerical
  Building))
HABS PA-571   pd   L
North George Street Historic District
HABS PA-573   pd   L
North George Street Historic District (105
  North George Street (Commercial
  Building))
HABS PA-570   pd   L
101-103 North George Street (Hotel); see
  North George Street Historic District
**21-23 West Market Street (Commercial
  Building)**
HABS PA-1313   pd   L
Willis House
190 Williss Rd.
HABS PA-5170   pd   H
York County Courthouse (Doorway)
250 E. Market St.
HABS PA-5171   pd   H

York vic.

Barn, Log; see Wolff Barn
Beard Tavern (Valley Inn)
2805 E. Market St.
HABS PA-5172   pd   H
Dietz House (Hermit's House)
R. D. 7 (Pleasant Valley Rd.)
HABS PA-5173   pd   H
Hermit's House; see Dietz House
Valley Inn; see Beard Tavern
Wolff Barn (Barn, Log)
Roosevelt Rd. Ext. (Bull Rd.)
HABS PA-5174   pd   H

Puerto Rico

Hacienda Azucarera Las Fuentes:Sugar Mill
HAER PR-25   p   H

Aguadilla
Punta Beringuen Lighthouse
HAER PR-19   p   H

Arecibo
Arecibo Lighthouse
HAER PR-13   p   H

Arroyo
Punta de las Figuras Lighthouse
HAER PR-10   p   H

Cabo Rojo
Morrillos de Cabo Rojo Lighthouse
HAER PR-11   p   H

Culbritas
Culbrita Island Lighthouse
HAER PR-12   p   H

Fajardo
Cebezas San Juan Lighthouse
HAER PR-18   p   H

Guancia
Puerto Guanico Lighthouse
HAER PR-14   p   H

Guanica
Hacienda Azucarera La Igualdad:Sugar Mill
HAER PR-7   s   H

Manati
Hacienda Azucarera La Esperanza:Cane Crushing Mill (Hacienda La Esperanza, Sugar Plantation & Mill)
HAER PR-1   s   L
Hacienda Azucarera La Esperanza:House
HAER PR-1-C   s p   L
Hacienda Azucarera La Esperanza:Intermediate Gears
HAER PR-1-F   p   H
Hacienda Azucarera La Esperanza:Lime Kiln
HAER PR-1-D   s   L
Hacienda Azucarera La Esperanza:Mill (Ruins)
HAER PR-1-B   s p   L
Hacienda Azucarera La Esperanza:Steam Engines
HAER PR-1-E   p   H
Hacienda la Esperanza, Steam Engine & Mill
HAER PR-1-A   s p   L
Hacienda La Esperanza, Sugar Plantation & Mill; see Hacienda Azucarera La Esperanza:Cane Crushing Mill

Maunabo
Punta Tuna Lighthouse
HAER PR-9   p   H

Mayaguez
Hacienda Azucarera Buena Vista:Sugar Mill (Hacienda Vives)
HAER PR-4   s   H
Hacienda Vives; see Hacienda Azucarera Buena Vista:Sugar Mill

Ponce
Armstrong, Carlos, Casa
9 Plaza Munoz Rivera
HABS PR-74   s   d   H
Bestard, Margarita, Casa
118 Calle Reina
HABS PR-69   s   d   H
Caja de Muertos Lighthouse
HAER PR-17   p   H
Cardona Lighthouse
HAER PR-16   p   H
Font, Fredrico, Casa
34 Calle Castillo
HABS PR-71   s   d   H
Historic Zone
HABS PR-75   s   H
Irizarry, Ramon, Casa
Calle Torre & Calle Reina
HABS PR-70   s   d   H
Lara, Rita, Casa
Calle Virtud & Calle Estrella
HABS PR-73   s   d   H
Vendrell, Fernando, Casa
3 Calle Amor
HABS PR-72   s   d   H

Punta Ferro Vieques
Lighthouse
HAER PR-22   p   H

Punta Giguero
Punta Giguero Lighthouse
HAER PR-24   p   H

Punta Mulas, Vieques
Punta Mulas Lighthouse
HAER PR-15   p   H

Rincon
Punta Jiguero Lighthouse
HAER PR-21   p   H

San German
El Coto:Sugar Mill (Ruins); see Hacienda Azucarera El Coto:Sugar Mill
Hacienda Azucarera El Coto:Sugar Mill (El Coto:Sugar Mill (Ruins))
HAER PR-3   s   L
Templo de Porta Coeli
HABS PR-45   s p d   L

San Juan
Arsenal, Chapel
Calle Puntilla & Arsenal
HABS PR-99-A   s   L H
Arsenal, Entrance Portico
Calle Puntilla & Arsenal
HABS PR-99-B   s   H
Arsenal, Naval Storehouses (Spanish Naval Headquarters)
Calle Puntilla & Arsenal
HABS PR-99   s p d   H
Block Study
Plaza de Armas & the Alcadia vic.
HABS PR-120   d   H
102 Calle de la Cruz (House)
HABS PR-113   p   H
104 Calle de la Cruz (House)
HABS PR-64   s p d   H
106 Calle de la Cruz (House)
HABS PR-103   s p   H
108 Calle de la Cruz (House)
HABS PR-119   p   H
151 Calle de la Luna (House)
HABS PR-114   p   H
153 Calle de la Luna (House)
HABS PR-118   p   H
155 Calle de la Luna (House)
HABS PR-115   p   H
150 Calle del Sol (House)
HABS PR-117   p   H
152 Calle del Sol (House)
HABS PR-108   p   H
154 Calle del Sol (House)
HABS PR-107   p   H
156 Calle del Sol (House)
HABS PR-111   p   H
101 Calle Fortaleza (House)
HABS PR-104   s   H
101 Calle San Jose (Casa de los Azuleiox; Palacio Berrocal)
HABS PR-62   s p d   H
103 Calle San Jose (House)
HABS PR-63   s p d   H
105 Calle San Jose (House)
HABS PR-68   p d   H
107 Calle San Jose (House)
HABS PR-116   p d   H
109 Calle San Jose (House)
HABS PR-67   s p d   H
Capilla del Cristo
Cristo & Tetuan Sts.
HABS PR-42   s p d   L
Casa Blanca & Adjacent Buildings
HABS PR-106   s   H
Casa de los Azuleiox; see 101 Calle San Jose
Casa de Ratones
251 Calle de Cristo
HABS PR-105   s   H

597

Castillo de San Cristobal
Fuerta Le Princesa
HABS PR-95   s   H

Castillo de San Cristobal, Cistern Heads
HABS PR-102   s d   H

Castillo de San Cristobal, Entrance
Blvd. Norzagaray
HABS PR-56   s   H

Castillo de San Cristobal, Fuerte El Albanico
Blvd. Norzagaray
HABS PR-94   s   H

Castillo de San Cristobal, Guardhouse
Fuerte El Abanico
HABS PR-59   s   H

Castillo de San Cristobal, Northeast Gate
Blvd. Norzagaray
HABS PR-58   s   H

Castillo de San Cristobal, Officer's Quarters
Blvd. Norzagaray
HABS PR-98   s   H

Castillo de San Cristobal, Quarters Number 210
Blvd. Norezagaray
HABS PR-96   s d   H

Castillo de San Cristobal, Quarters Number 211
Blvd. Norzagaray
HABS PR-97   s d   H

Castillo de San Cristobal, Quarters Number 9
Blvd. Norzagaray
HABS PR-60   s   H

Castillo de San Cristobel, South Gate
Blvd. Norzagaray
HABS PR-57   s   H

Castillo de San Felipe del Morro (El Morro)
HABS PR-48   s pd   L H

Defenses, Outer
HABS PR-53   s pd   L

El Morro; see Castillo de San Felipe del Morro

El Polvorin (Powder House)
HABS PR-46   s pd   L

Escambron Battery (Puerta de Tierra)
HABS PR-50   s pd   L

Fort of El Canvelo (San Juan de la Cruz)
Cabras Island
HABS PR-52   s p   L

Fort of San Geronimo (Puerta de Tierra)
HABS PR-49   s pd   L

Fort San Cristobal
HABS PR-47   s pd   L

Giorgetti, Eduardo, House
Ponce de Leon Ave.
HABS PR-65   s pd   H

Governor's Palace; see La Fortaleza

Historic Zone, Block Study
Calle de las Cruz, Sol, Luna & San Jose
HABS PR-61   s p   H

Iglesia de San Jose (Plaza San Jose)
HABS PR-41   s pd   L

Iglesia San Mateo de Cangrejos
HABS PR-66   s pd   H

Korber, William, House
903 Ponce de Leon Ave.
HABS PR-109   pd   H

La Fortaleza (Governor's Palace)
Calle Fortaleza
HABS PR-54   p   L

Palacio Berrocal; see 101 Calle San Jose

Plaza San Jose; see Iglesia de San Jose

Porto Rico Hotel & Chalet
HABS PR-110   p   H

Powder House; see El Polvorin

Puerta de San Juan (Door)
HABS PR-43   s pd   L

Puerta de Tierra; see Escambron Battery
Puerta de Tierra; see Fort of San Geronimo
Puerta de Tierra; see Ravelin Second Line of Defense

Railroad Terminal Building
Calle Commercio & Calle Harding
HABS PR-112   pd   H

Ravelin Second Line of Defense (Puerta de Tierra)
HABS PR-51   s pd   L

Sally Port & Chapel; see San Felipe Del Morro

San Felipe Del Morro (Sally Port & Chapel)
HABS PR-55   s   L

San Juan de la Cruz; see Fort of El Canvelo

Spanish Naval Headquarters; see Arsenal, Naval Storehouses

Superintendent's Dwelling-QSI
HAER PR-20   p   H

St. John

Castillo del Morro Lighthouse
HAER PR-23   p   H

Toa Baja

Hacienda Azucarera Santa Elena: Sugar Mill (Ruins)
HAER PR-6   s   L

Victoria

Hacienda Azucarera La Concepcion: Sugar Mill
HAER PR-2   s p   H

Vieques Island

Fort of Vieques
HABS PR-44   s pd   L H

Rhode Island

BRISTOL COUNTY

Bristol

Borden, Capt. Parker, House
736 Hope St.
HABS RI-265   p   L

Bosworth, Nathaniel, House
814 Hope St.
HABS RI-109   d   L

Bourn, John, House
417 Hope St.
HABS RI-260   p   L

Bradford, Deputy Gov. William, House; see Royall, Isaac, House

Bristol Congregational Church
HABS RI-375   p   L

DeWolf, Gen. George, House
501 Hope St.
HABS RI-263   p   L

DeWolf, Mark Anthony, House
Poppasquash Neck
HABS RI-262   p   L

DeWolf-Middleton House (Hey Bonnie Hall)
Poppasquash Rd.
HABS RI-3-12   s pd   L

Herreshoff House
Pleasant Point
HABS RI-126   p   L

Hey Bonnie Hall; see DeWolf-Middleton House

Howe, John, House
341 Hope St.
HABS RI-131   p   L

Low, William G., House
3 Low Ln.
HABS RI-346   p   L

Morice-Babbitt House
328 Hope St.
HABS RI-264   p   L

Reynolds, Joseph, House
956 Hope St.
HABS RI-70   pd   L

Royall, Isaac, House (Bradford, Deputy Gov. William, House)
Metacom Ave.
HABS RI-261   p   L

Warren, Russell, House
86 State St.
HABS RI-259   p   L

Warren

Bliss-Ruisden House
606 Main St.
HABS RI-266   p   L

Warren Ladies Seminary
HABS RI-267   p   L
Waterman House
392 S. Water St.
HABS RI-268   p   L

KENT COUNTY

Anthony
Greene, Gen. Nathaniel, House
Greene St.
HABS RI-269   p   L

Buttonwoods
Greene, James, House
698 Buttonwoods Ave.
HABS RI-270   p   L

East Greenwich
Eldredge, James, House
40 Division St.
HABS RI-58   p   L
Gorton, Samuel Jr., House
777 Love Ln.
HABS RI-271   p   L
Kent County Courthouse
Main St. (Post Rd.)
HABS RI-57   p   L
Union Mill
Main St.
HABS RI-59   p   L
Varnum, Gen. James M., House
57 Pierce St.
HABS RI-56   p   L
Weaver, Clement, House
125 Howland Rd.
HABS RI-46   s p   L

Spring Green
Greene, John, House
Spring Green Rd.
HABS RI-54   p d   L

Warwick
Greene, Job, House
W. Shore Rd. (Hoxie)
HABS RI-20   s p d   L

West Greenwich
Grist Mill
State Rt. 3
HABS RI-376   p   H
Hopkins Mill
State Rt. 3 & Nooseneck River
HABS RI-303   p d   L

West Warwick
Lippitt Mill
825 Main St.
HABS RI-338
HAER RI-4   s p d   L H

NEWPORT COUNTY

Jamestown
Cajacet; see Paine, Capt. Thomas, House
Carr, Gov. Caleb, House
Conanicut Island
HABS RI-272   p   L
Paine, Capt. Thomas, House (Cajacet)
E. Shore Rd.
HABS RI-273   p   L

Middleton
Berkeley, Bishop George, House; see Whitehall
Whitehall (Berkeley, Bishop George, House)
Berkeley Ave.
HABS RI-52   p   L

Middletown
Bannister, John, House
Broadway (Parts in Winterthur Museum)
HABS RI-141   p d   L
Elam, Gervais, House; see Vaucluse
Vaucluse (Elam, Gervais, House)
Wapping Rd. (Parts in Metropolitan Museum, NY)
HABS RI-16   s p d   L

Newport
Art Association of Newport, The; see Griswold, John N. A., House
Audrain Building
220-230 Bellevue Ave.
HABS RI-333   p d   L
Ayrault, Daniel, House (Doorway)
Thames & Ann Sts. (moved to Newport Hist. Soc.)
HABS RI-275   p   L
Baldwin, Charles H., House (Gamir Doon)
Bellevue Ave.
HABS RI-334   p d   L
Banister, John, House (Sayer-Banister House)
56 Pelham St.
HABS RI-139   p   L
Barney, Jonathan, House (Maxon-Jeffers House; Maxon House)
Spring & Barney Sts.
HABS RI-140   s   L
Bell, Isaac, House (Edna Villa)
70 Perry St.
HABS RI-308   s p d   L
Berwind, Edward J., House; see Elms, The
Bliss, Elder John, House (House, Stone End)
2 Wilbur Ave.
HABS RI-104   p   L
Bowen's Wharf, General Views
HABS RI-377   p   H
Bowen's Wharf, Warehouse Number 1
(Cowley's Wharf, Ship Chandler's; Stevens Wharf, Ship Chandler's)
HABS RI-304   s p   H

Bowen's Wharf, Warehouse Number 2
(Cowley's Wharf, Warehouse; Stevens' Wharf, Warehouse)
HABS RI-305   s p   H
Breakers, The (Vanderbilt, Cornelius, House)
Ochre Point Ave.
HABS RI-339   p   H
Brenton, Jahleel, House
Thames St. (Mantels at Mill St. & Prospect St.)
HABS RI-36   p   L
Bull, Jireh, House; see Maudsley, Capt. John, House
Challoner, Ninyon, House
HABS RI-105   p   L
Chateau-sur-Mer (Wetmore House)
Bellevue Ave.
HABS RI-313   s p   H
Clagget, Caleb, House
22 Bridge St.
HABS RI-348   p   L
Clarke, John, House; see Pitt's Head Tavern
Coddington, Gov. Williams, House
Marlborough St. (Parts in R.I. Hist. Society)
HABS RI-101   p   L
Colony House (State House, Old)
Washington Square
HABS RI-33   p   L H
Covell House; see Sanford-Covell House
Cowley's Wharf, Ship Chandler's; see Bowen's Wharf, Warehouse Number 1
Cowley's Wharf, Warehouse; see Bowen's Wharf, Warehouse Number 2
Dennis House; see Grafton, William, House
Edgar, Commodore William, House
29 Old Beach Rd.
HABS RI-318   p d   L
Edna Villa; see Bell, Isaac, House
Elms, The (Berwind, Edward J., House)
HABS RI-344   p   H
Fort Adams
Newport Neck
HABS RI-347   s p d   L H
Fort Adams, Battery Bankhead
Brenton Point
HABS RI-347-H   s   H
Fort Adams, Battery Belton
Brenton Point
HABS RI-347-E   s   H
Fort Adams, Battery Reilly
Brenton Point
HABS RI-347-F   s   H
Fort Adams, Battery Talbot
Brenton Point
HABS RI-347-G   s   H
Fort Adams, Redoubt
Brenton Point
HABS RI-347-D   s d   H

Fort Adams, Stables
Brenton Point
HABS RI-347-J   s   H

Friends Meetinghouse
Farewell St.
HABS RI-310   p   H

Gale, Levi, House (Jewish Community
   Center)
89 Touro St. (moved from Washington
   Square)
HABS RI-328   pd   L

Gamir Doon; see Baldwin, Charles H.,
   House

Gibbs-Gardner-Bowler House; see Vernon
   House

Grafton, William, House (Dennis House)
65 Poplar St.
HABS RI-349   p   L

Greene, Amanda, House (Mantel)
Spring & Bridge Sts.
HABS RI-277   p   L

Griswold, John N. A., House (Art
   Association of Newport, The)
76 Bellevue Ave.
HABS RI-322   s pd   L H

House, Stone End; see Bliss, Elder John,
   House

Hunt, Richard Morris, House; see
   Hypotenuse

Hypotenuse (Hunt, Richard Morris, House)
33 Catherine St.
HABS RI-315   pd   L

Izard, Ralph S., House
10 Pell St.
HABS RI-319   p   H

Jewish Community Center; see Gale, Levi,
   House

King Block
204-214 Bellevue Ave.
HABS RI-332   pd   L

King, David, House
20 Catherine St.
HABS RI-317   pd   L

King, William, House; see Sanford-Covell
   House

Kingscote
Bellevue & Bowery Sts.
HABS RI-307   s p   H

Lillibridge House; see Pitt's Head Tavern

Linden Gate (Marquand, Henry G., House)
Old Beach Rd.
HABS RI-335   p   H

Lucas, Augustus, House
40 Division St.
HABS RI-336   p   L

Malbone, Francis, House
Malbone Rd.
HABS RI-340   p   H

Marble House
HABS RI-378   p   H

Market, Brick (Public Granary)
127 Thames St.
HABS RI-276   p   L

Marquand, Henry G., House; see Linden
   Gate

23 Mary Street (Doorway)
HABS RI-137   p   L

Mason, Gen. George Champlin, House
31 Old Beach Rd.
HABS RI-341   p   H

Maudsley, Capt. John, House (Bull, Jireh,
   House)
228 Spring St.
HABS RI-35   p   L

Maxon House; see Barney, Jonathan,
   House

Maxon-Jeffers House; see Barney,
   Jonathan, House

Mill, Stone (Viking Tower)
Touro Park
HABS RI-103   p   L

41 Mill Street (Doorway)
HABS RI-136   p   L

Mumford, Stephen, House; see
   Wanton-Lyman-Hazard House

Newport Casino
186-202 Bellevue Ave.
HABS RI-331   pd   L

Newport Steam Factory
Thames & Howard Sts.
HABS RI-324   s pd   H

Nichols-Wanton-Hunter House
   (Wanton-Hunter House)
54 Washington St.
HABS RI-7   s pd   L

Olmsted, A. H., House; see Wildacre

Peckham Coal & Oil Company
HABS RI-379   p   H

10 Pelham Street (House)
HABS RI-138   p   L

Perry Mill
HABS RI-380   p   H

Pitt's Head Tavern (Clarke, John, House;
   Lillibridge House)
Bridge St. (moved from Clarke St. & 5
   Charles St.)
HABS RI-279   p   L

Porter, Mary T., House
25 Greenough Pl.
HABS RI-314   pd   L

Powel, James C., House
28 Greenough Pl.
HABS RI-320   pd   L

Public Granary; see Market, Brick

Redwood, Abraham, Garden House
   (Redwood, Abraham, Summerhouse)
50 Bellevue Rd. (moved from original
   location)
HABS RI-274   p   L

Redwood, Abraham, Summerhouse; see
   Redwood, Abraham, Garden House

Redwood Library
50 Bellevue Ave.
HABS RI-100   s pd   L

Richardson, Thomas, House; see Spencer,
   Micah, House

Richardson-Blatchford House
37 Catherine St.
HABS RI-316   pd   L

Robinson, Thomas, House
64 Washington St.
HABS RI-280   pd   L

Sabbatarian Meetinghouse
82 Touro St. (moved from Spring & Barney
   Sts.)
HABS RI-113   s p   L H

Sanford, Milton H., House; see
   Sanford-Covell House

Sanford-Covell House (Covell House;
   Sanford, Milton H., House; King,
   William, House; Villa Marina)
72 Washington St.
HABS RI-345   p   H

Sayer-Banister House; see Banister, John,
   House

Second Congregational Church
13-17 Clarke St.
HABS RI-325   p   H

Sherman, William Watts, House
Shepard Ave.
HABS RI-342   p   H

Spencer, Micah, House (Richardson,
   Thomas, House)
85-87 Thames St.
HABS RI-3   s pd   L

State House, Old; see Colony House

Stevens Building (Stevens, Robert,
   Warehouse)
Bowen's Wharf, 261 Thames St.
HABS RI-306   s p   H

Stevens, Robert, Warehouse; see Stevens
   Building

Stevens Wharf, Ship Chandler's; see
   Bowen's Wharf, Warehouse Number 1

Stevens' Wharf, Warehouse; see Bowen's
   Wharf, Warehouse Number 2

Swinburne, Daniel T., House
6 Greenough Pl.
HABS RI-312   pd   L

Thames Street Business District
Thames St., between Wash. Sq. &
   Memorial Blvd.
HABS RI-337   pd   H

Tilton, Samuel, House
12 Sunnyside Place
HABS RI-309   s pd   L

Tompkins, Tillinghast, House
11 Redwood St.
HABS RI-311   s pd   L H

**Touro Synagogue, Congregation Jeshuat
   Israel**
85 Touro St.
HABS RI-278   s pd   L

Travers Block
166-184 Bellevue Ave.
HABS RI-330   pd   L

Trinity Church
141 Spring St.
HABS RI-102   pd   L

Tripp, John, House
88 Washington St. (moved from RI, Manton)
HABS RI-23   s pd   L

United Congregational Church
Spring & Pelham Sts.
HABS RI-326   pd   L

Vanderbilt, Cornelius, House; see Breakers, The

Vernon House (Gibbs-Gardner-Bowler House)
46 Clarke St.
HABS RI-34   s pd   L

Viking Tower; see Mill, Stone

Villa Marina; see Sanford-Covell House

Wanton-Hunter House; see Nichols-Wanton-Hunter House

Wanton-Lyman-Hazard House (Mumford, Stephen, House)
17 Broadway
HABS RI-13   s p   L

Warren, Capt. John, House
62 Washington St.
HABS RI-350   p   L

Wetmore House; see Chateau-sur-Mer

White, Isaac P., House
66 Ayrault St.
HABS RI-321   p   H

Whitehorne, Samuel, House
414 Thames St.
HABS RI-323   p   L

Wildacre (Olmsted, A. H., House)
Ocean Dr.
HABS RI-343   p   H

Williams, John W., House
33 S. Baptist St.
HABS RI-327   p   L

PROVIDENCE COUNTY

Gran's Grist & Saw Mill
HAER RI-13   s   H

Albion

Blackstone Canal
School St.
HAER RI-11   p   H

Ashton vic.

Blackstone Canal
Blackstone River & Washington Hwy. (Quinnville)
HAER RI-10   p   H

Blackstone Canal, Tender's House
Blackstone River, Washington Hwy. vic.
HAER RI-10-A   p   H

Centerdale

Allendale Mill
494 Woonasquatucket Ave.
HABS RI-302   s pd   L

Olney, Epenetus, House
370 Woonasquatucket Ave.
HABS RI-89   p   L

Central Falls

Blackstone Canal
State Rt. 126
HAER RI-8   p   H

Central Falls vic.

Blackstone Canal
Front St. & Lonsdale Ave. (Lonsdale)
HAER RI-9   p   H

Chepachet vic.

Plante Grist Mill
U.S. Rt. 44
HAER RI-5   s p   H

Cumberland Hill

Ballou, Elder, Meetinghouse
Ballou Meetinghouse Rd. & W. Wrentham Rd.
HABS RI-14   s pd   L

Cooke, Cyrus, House
W. Wrentham Rd.
HABS RI-281   p   L

Greenville

Windsor, Daniel, House
Austin Ave.
HABS RI-282   p   L

Johnston

Clemence, Thomas, House
38 George Waterman Rd.
HABS RI-6   s pd   L H

Thornton Homestead
Atwood Ave. & Memorial Ave.
HABS RI-80   p   L

Limerock

Manton, T. H., House
Wilbur Rd.
HABS RI-93   p   L

Masonic Temple
Great Rd. & Anna Sayles Rd.
HABS RI-94   p   L

Whitman, Valentine Jr., House
Great Rd. & Meetinghouse Rd.
HABS RI-8   s pd   L

Limerock vic.

Whipple, Eleazer, House
Great Rd.
HABS RI-95   p   L

Lincoln

Angell, Widow Anthony, House
Louisquisset Pike (State Rt. 146)
HABS RI-96   p   L

Arnold, Benjamin, House
Entrance A Rd. to Lincoln Woods Reservation
HABS RI-86   p   L

Arnold, Eleazer, House
Great Rd.
HABS RI-87   p   L H

Arnold, Israel, House
Great Rd.
HABS RI-91   p   L

Butterfly Factory
Great Rd.
HABS RI-48   pd   L

Croade Tavern
Great Rd. (moved from RI, Pawtucket)
HABS RI-88   p   L

Fireplace House
Entrance A Rd. to Lincoln Woods Reservation
HABS RI-85   p   L

Friends Meetinghouse
Great Rd.
HABS RI-17   s pd   L

Hearthside (Smith, Stephen H., House)
Great Rd.
HABS RI-47   p   L

Jenks, Capt. John, House
Great Rd.
HABS RI-92   p   L

Millstone
Barneys Pond Bridge vic.
HABS RI-84   p   L

Moffatt Mill; see Olney, George, Machine Shop

Olney, George, Machine Shop (Moffatt Mill)
Great Rd.
HABS RI-90   p   L

Smith, Stephen H., House; see Hearthside

Manton

Tripp, John, House
953 1/2 Manton Ave. (moved to RI, Newport)
HABS RI-23   s pd   L

Tripp, John, House
981 Manton Ave.
HABS RI-79   p   L

North Providence

Olney, Capt. Stephen, House
138 Smithfield Rd.
HABS RI-77   p   L

Smith, Joseph, House
109 Cushing St.
HABS RI-76   p   L

North Scituate

Lapham Institute (Smithfield Seminary)
Seminary Ln.
HABS RI-291   p   L

Smithfield Seminary; see Lapham Institute

Oaklawn

Searle, Edward, House
107 Wilbur Ave.
HABS RI-11   s pd   L

Pawtucket

Croade Tavern
13-15 Dexter St. (moved to RI, Lincoln)
HABS RI-88   p   L

Dagget, John, House
Slater Park
HABS RI-83   p   L

Pidge Tavern
586 Pawtucket Ave.
HABS RI-29   s p   L

Slater Mill
Slater St.
HABS RI-82
HAER RI-1   p   L H

Starkweather-Stearns House
60 Summit Ave. (moved from 57 Summit Ave.)
HABS RI-81   p   L

Wilkinson Mill
Roosevelt Ave.
HAER RI-2   p   H

Providence

Adams, Seth, House
26 Benevolent St.
HABS RI-168   pd   L

Allen, Amos, House
62 Benefit St.
HABS RI-148   pd   L

Allen, Candace, Coach House
12 Benevolent St.
HABS RI-170   p   L

Allen, Candace, House
12 Benevolent St.
HABS RI-169   pd   L

American Screw Company
Stevens St.
HAER RI-6   s p   H

Ammadon's, Alpheus, Inn; see Golden Ball Inn

Antram, William, House
953 1/2 Smith St.
HABS RI-381   s   H

Arcade, The
130 Westminster St.
HABS RI-206   pd   L

Arnold, Christopher, House
7 Arnold St.
HABS RI-171   pd   L

Ashton, William Jr., House
368 Benefit St.
HABS RI-26   s pd   L

Bailey, William M., House
189 Eaton St.
HABS RI-382   pd   H

Baker, Josiah, House
23 Arnold St.
HABS RI-190   pd   L

Barker, William C., Building
266-268 S. Main St.
HABS RI-209   pd   L

Barnes, Joanna, House
49 Benefit St.
HABS RI-144   pd   L

Barney, Cromwell, House
91 Williams St.
HABS RI-252   pd   L

Beckwith, Truman, House (Handicraft Club)
42 College St.
HABS RI-21   s pd   L

Beneficent Congregational Church (Round Top)
300 Weybosset St.
HABS RI-210   pd   L

Benson, George, House
64 Angell St.
HABS RI-172   pd   L

Binney, William, House
72 Prospect St.
HABS RI-224   pd   L

Bishop's House; see Ives, Moses B., House

Blackstone Canal
Charles & Randall Sts., Canal & Haymarket Sts.
HAER RI-7   p   H

Blanding, Shubael, House
20 Cooke St.
HABS RI-211   pd   L

Block, Granite (Hotel Bristol)
6-18 Market Sq.
HABS RI-30   s p   L

Bowen, Isaac Jr., House
312 Benefit St.
HABS RI-161   pd   L

Bowen, Jabez, House
39 Bowen St.
HABS RI-173   pd   L

Bowen, Tully, House
389 Benefit St.
HABS RI-167   pd   L

Bradley, George M., House
189 Eaton St.
HABS RI-383   pd   H

Brown, Gov. Elisha, House
537 N. Main St.
HABS RI-9   s pd   L

Brown, James, Warehouse
142-152 S. Water St.
HABS RI-246   pd   L

Brown, John, House
52 Power St.
HABS RI-75   pd   L

Brown, Joseph, House
50 S. Main St.
HABS RI-53   pd   L

Brown, Moses, School; see Friends' School

Brown, Nicholas, House
29 S. Main St.
HABS RI-99   p   L

Brown, Richard, House
587 Rochambeau Ave.
HABS RI-31   s p   L

Brown, Riley, House
2 Thayer St.
HABS RI-174   pd   L

Brown University, Brown Library; see Brown University, Robinson Hall

Brown University, Manning Hall
Prospect St.
HABS RI-181   pd   L

Brown University, Robinson Hall (Brown University, Brown Library)
Waterman & Prospect Sts.
HABS RI-185   pd   L

Brown University, University Hall
Prospect St.
HABS RI-283   p   L

Brown, William L., House
23 John St.
HABS RI-225   pd   L

Bucklin, George, House
10 Arnold St.
HABS RI-175   pd   L

Bucklin-Eddy Building
283-297 S. Main St.
HABS RI-254   pd   L

Bullock, Richmond, House
288-292 S. Main St.
HABS RI-248   d   L

Buonanno Garage, Old
Crockett St.
HABS RI-372   p   L

Burnside, Gen. Ambrose, House
314 Benefit St.
HABS RI-162   pd   L

Burrough, James, House
160 Power St.
HABS RI-226   pd   L

Burroughs, Robert S., House
6 Cooke St.
HABS RI-212   pd   L

Burroughs, Robert S., House; see Tobey, Dr. S. B., House

Carlile, Samuel, House
87 Williams St.
HABS RI-251   pd   L

Carpenter, Zachariah, House
20 Arnold St.
HABS RI-176   pd   L

Carrington, Edward, House
66 Williams St.
HABS RI-19   s pd   L

Carter, John, House (Shakespeare's Head)
21 Meeting St.
HABS RI-1   s pd   L

Cathedral of St. John; see St. John's Church

Church, John, House (Pearce, Levi, House)
25-27 John St.
HABS RI-240   pd   L

Church, William, House
22 Arnold St.
HABS RI-177   pd   L

City Hall
Exchange Place
HABS RI-192   pd   L

City Poor Farm; see Dexter Asylum

Clark & Nightingale Block
247-259 S. Main St.
HABS RI-253   pd   L

Colony House; see State House, Old

Comstock Block
265-277 S. Main St.
HABS RI-228   pd   L

Cooke, Benoni, House
110 S. Main St.
HABS RI-213   pd   L

Corliss, George H., House
45 Prospect St.
HABS RI-229   pd   L

Cushing, Benjamin, House
38 1/2 N. Court St.
HABS RI-193   pd   L

Daggett's Tavern; see Golden Ball Inn

Dexter Asylum (City Poor Farm)
Hope St. & Lloyd Ave.
HABS RI-231   pd   L

Dexter, Ebenezer Knight, House
300 Angell St.
HABS RI-178   pd   L

Dexter, Edward, House
72 Waterman St. (moved from George St.)
HABS RI-15   s pd   L

Dexter, Jeremiah, House
957 N. Main St.
HABS RI-5   s pd   L

Dike, Henry A., House
101 Prospect St.
HABS RI-250   pd   L

Dodge, Seril, House
10 Thomas St.
HABS RI-3-7   s pd   L

Dorr, Sullivan, House
109 Benefit St.
HABS RI-284   p   L

Ellis, Cyrus, House
31 John St.
HABS RI-232   pd   L

Exchange Coffee House
1-5 Market Square
HABS RI-98   p   L

Fenner, Gov. James, House
41 Waterman St.
HABS RI-55   pd   L

First Baptist Meetinghouse
75 N. Main St.
HABS RI-38   pd   L

First Congregational Church (First
   Unitarian Church)
301 Benefit St.
HABS RI-159   pd   L

**First Unitarian Church; see First
   Congregational Church**

Franklin House Hotel
32 Market Sq.
HABS RI-22   s p   L

**Franklin Institute Building; see Williams,
   Roger, Bank**

Friends' School (Brown, Moses, School)
257 Hope St.
HABS RI-255   pd   L

Glove Tavern; see Golden Ball Inn

Goddard, Francis W., House
71 George St.
HABS RI-194   pd   L

Goddard, William, House
38 Brown St.
HABS RI-195   pd   L

Golden Ball Inn (Daggett's Tavern;
   Williams, Roger, Hotel; Ammadon's,
   Alpheus, Inn; Glove Tavern)
159 Benefit St.
HABS RI-73   pd   L

Gorham, Jabez, House
56 Benefit St.
HABS RI-146   pd   L

Greene, John Holden, House
150 Power St.
HABS RI-196   pd   L

Greenman, William, House
24 Thayer St.
HABS RI-179   pd   L

Guild, Samuel, House (Pearce, Daniel,
   House; Lightning Splitter House)
53 Transit St.
HABS RI-258   pd   L

Hale, Joseph, House
106 George St.
HABS RI-197   pd   L

Hall, Abner, House
116 Hope St.
HABS RI-198   pd   L

Halsey, Thomas L., House
140 Prospect St.
HABS RI-233   pd   L

Hamilton Building
Westminster & Exchange Sts.
HABS RI-285   p   L

**Handicraft Club; see Beckwith, Truman,
   House**

Harding, William, House
278-282 S. Main St.
HABS RI-234   pd   L

Harris, Stephen, House
135 Benefit St.
HABS RI-151   pd   L

Holden, Thomas R., House (Humphrey,
   Josiah, House)
118 Benefit St.
HABS RI-150   pd   L

Holroyd, William, House
106 Angell St.
HABS RI-180   pd   L

Hopkins, Stephen, House
12 Hopkins St.
HABS RI-28   s pd   L

Hoppin, Benjamin, Homestead
Snow & Westminster Sts.
HABS RI-286   p   L

Hoppin, Thomas F., House
383 Benefit St.
HABS RI-166   pd   L

Hotel Bristol; see Block, Granite

**Humphrey, Josiah, House; see Holden,
   Thomas R., House**

Ives, Moses B., House (Bishop's House)
10 Brown St.
HABS RI-199   pd   L

Ives, Thomas P., Block
270-276 Benefit St.
HABS RI-158   pd   L

Ives, Thomas P., House
66 Power St.
HABS RI-235   pd   L

Ives, Thomas P., Stable & Coach House
66 Power St.
HABS RI-236   pd   L

Jastram, Mawney, House
61 Benefit St.
HABS RI-147   pd   L

Jenckes, John, House (Jenckes, Joseph,
   House)
43 Benefit St.
HABS RI-12   s pd   L

**Jenckes, Joseph, House; see Jenckes, John,
   House**

Jenckes, Thomas A., House
2 Angell St.
HABS RI-214   pd   L

Kilton-Wilkinson House
201 S. Main St.
HABS RI-230   pd   L

Kimball, James M., House
108 Prospect St.
HABS RI-237   pd   L

King, Dr. William J., House
48 College St.
HABS RI-200   pd   L

Larcher, John, House
282 Benefit St.
HABS RI-32   s pd   L

**Lightning Splitter House; see Guild,
   Samuel, House**

Lippitt, Gov. Henry, House
199 Hope St.
HABS RI-239   pd   L

Lippitt-Green House
14 John St.
HABS RI-223   pd   L

Market House
Market Sq.
HABS RI-74   pd   L

Mason, John B., House (Tockwotten Hall
   Hotel)
Tockwotten & East Sts.
HABS RI-288   p   L

Mason, John, House (Mantel)
Weybosset St. (moved to R.I. School of
   Design)
HABS RI-287   p   L

Mason, Nathan, House
33 Arnold St.
HABS RI-182   pd   L

Mason, Nathan, House (Sweet, Menzies,
   House)
34 Arnold St.
HABS RI-215   pd   L

Merchants Cold Storage Warehouse
160 Kingsley Ave.
HAER RI-12   pd   L

Metcalf, Stephen O., House
132 Bowen St.
HABS RI-216   pd   L

Nightingale, Col. Joseph, House
357 Benefit St.
HABS RI-164   pd   L

Owen, George & Smith, Building
9 Steeple St.
HABS RI-256   pd   L

Pearce, Daniel, House; see Guild, Samuel,
   House

Pearce, Earle D., House
225-227 Benefit St.
HABS RI-154   pd   L

Pearce, Edward, House
2 Benevolent St.
HABS RI-201   pd   L

Pearce, Levi, House; see Church, John,
   House

Pearce, Nathaniel, House
305 Brook St. (moved from 41 George St.)
HABS RI-184   pd   L

Pearson, Luther, House
6 Thayer St.
HABS RI-183   pd   L

Pine Street (House, Interior)
(Fragments in Plantations Club, Weybosset
   St.)
HABS RI-289   p   L

Pioneer Fire Company Building
296-302 S. Main St.
HABS RI-247   d   L

Pope, West, House
97 Williams St.
HABS RI-249   pd   L

Potter, Charles, House
154 Waterman St.
HABS RI-217   pd   L

Potter, Russell, House
26 John St.
HABS RI-241   pd   L

Providence & Worcester RR, Freight
   House (Providence & Worcester RR,
   South Freight House; Providence &
   Worcester RR, Merchandise House)
Canal St.
HAER RI-3   s p   H

Providence & Worcester RR, Merchandise
   House; see Providence & Worcester RR,
   Freight House

Providence & Worcester RR, South
   Freight House; see Providence &
   Worcester RR, Freight House

Providence Athenaeum
251 Benefit St.
HABS RI-156   pd   L

Providence Marine Corps Arsenal
176 Benefit St.
HABS RI-152   pd   L

Purkis, Robert, House
37 Charles Field St.
HABS RI-202   pd   L

Reynolds, Benjamin & John, House
88 Benefit St.
HABS RI-149   pd   L

Reynolds, John, House
81 Power St. (moved from 31 Benevolent
   St.)
HABS RI-71   s p   L

Rhodes, James T., House
367 Benefit St.
HABS RI-165   pd   L

Richmond, Samuel, House
36 Bowen St.
HABS RI-203   pd   L

Roffee, Caleb, House
92 Williams St.
HABS RI-257   pd   L

Round Top; see Beneficent Congregational
   Church

Russell, Joseph, House
118 N. Main St. (fragments in Brooklyn
   Museum)
HABS RI-242   pd   L

Schoolhouse, Brick
24 Meeting St.
HABS RI-191   pd   L

Seamans, Nathan, House
15 Arnold St.
HABS RI-186   pd   L

Shakespeare's Head; see Carter, John,
   House

Sheldon, Christopher, Warehouse
369-371 S. Main St.
HABS RI-218   pd   L

Sheldon House
336 Benefit St.
HABS RI-163   pd   L

Sheldon, Remington, Business Building
379-381 S. Main St.
HABS RI-219   pd   L

Smith, C. Morris, House
112 Benevolent St.
HABS RI-187   pd   L

Smith, Franklin, House
9 Hidden St.
HABS RI-220   pd   L

Smith, Martha, House; see Smith, Rev.
   Francis, House

Smith, Rev. Francis, House (Smith,
   Martha, House)
35 Benefit St.
HABS RI-143   pd   L

Snow, Peter W., House
104 Benevolent St.
HABS RI-188   pd   L

St. John's Church (Cathedral of St. John)
271 N. Main St.
HABS RI-204   pd   L

St. Stephen's Church
114 George St.
HABS RI-189   pd   L

Staples, Samuel, House
52 Benefit St.
HABS RI-145   pd   L

State House, Old (Colony House)
155 N. Main St.
HABS RI-18   s pd   L

Sweet, Menzies, House; see Mason,
   Nathan, House

Taft, Robert W., House
154 Hope St.
HABS RI-205   pd   L

Taylor, Deacon Edward, House
9 Thomas St.
HABS RI-243   pd   L

Tillinghast, Capt. Joseph, House
403 S. Main St.
HABS RI-4   s pd   L

Tobey, Dr. S. B., House (Burroughs, Robert
   S., House)
110 Benevolent St.
HABS RI-227   pd   L

Tockwotten Hall Hotel; see Mason, John
   B., House

Townsend, Solomon, House
35 Charles Field St.
HABS RI-221   pd   L

Underwood, Edward S., House
28 John St.
HABS RI-244   pd   L

Ward, Eliza, House
2 George St.
HABS RI-207   pd   L

Warner, Samuel, House
362 S. Main St.
HABS RI-10   s d   L

Waterman, Richard, House
219 Benefit St.
HABS RI-153   pd   L

Watson, William, House; see Wilkinson,
   William, House

Wells, Elisha, House
30 John St.
HABS RI-245   pd   L

Westcott, Samuel, House
240 Benefit St.
HABS RI-25   s   L

Westminster Congregational Church
119 Mathewson St.
HABS RI-290   p   L

Whipple, John, House
54 College St.
HABS RI-208   pd   L

Wilkinson, William, House (Watson,
   William, House)
69 College St.
HABS RI-24   s pd   L

Williams, Betsy, Cottage
Roger Williams Park
HABS RI-69   pd   L

Williams, Roger, Bank (Franklin Institute
   Building)
27 Market Sq.
HABS RI-37   p   L

Williams, Roger, Hotel; see Golden Ball
   Inn

Woods, Marshall, House
62 Prospect St.
HABS RI-222   pd   L
Woodward, William, House
22 James St.
HABS RI-27   pd   L

Slatersville
Mill House K; see Slater Mill, House K
Slater Mill, House K (Mill House K)
20 School St.
HABS RI-293   p   L
Slatersville Green
Green & School Sts.
HABS RI-292   p   L

Smithfield
Arnold, Capt. Daniel, House
71 Great Rd. (State Rt. 146)
HABS RI-294   p   L
St. Michael's Catholic Church
15 Homestead Ave.
HABS RI-110   pd   L

Thornton
Fenner, Thomas, House
1538 Plainfield St.
HABS RI-72   p   L

Woonsocket
Clinton Mill
93 Clinton St.
HABS RI-299   s pd   L
Club Marquette; see St. Anne's Gymnasium
Holbrook, Capt., House
383 S. Main St.
HABS RI-295   p   L
Providence & Worcester Railroad Station
HABS RI-373   p   H
St. Anne's Gymnasium (Club Marquette)
74 Cumberland St.
HABS RI-374   pd   L
Woonsocket Company, Number 1 Mill
100 Front St.
HABS RI-300   s pd   L
Woonsocket Company, Number 2 Mill
115 Front St.
HABS RI-301   s pd   L

WASHINGTON COUNTY

Belleville
Mobra Castle; see Phillips, Samuel, House
Phillips, Samuel, House (Mobra Castle)
Tower Hill Rd. (U.S. Rt. 1)
HABS RI-50   s p   L

Kenyon
Clarke, Samuel, House
Lewiston Ave.
HABS RI-296   p   L

Kingston
Carpenter, Solomon, House (Indian Acres)
144 South Rd.
HABS RI-61   p   L
Congregational Church (Kingston Congregational Church)
Kingstown Rd. (State Rt. 138)
HABS RI-64   p   L
Douglas House
Kingstown Rd. (State Rt. 138)
HABS RI-60   p   L
Fayerweather House
Mooresfield Rd. (State Rt. 138) & Kingston Rd.
HABS RI-62   p   L
French, Gen. Cyrus, House
Kingstown Rd. (State Rt. 138) & College Rd.
HABS RI-51   s pd   L
Hagadorn House; see Taylor, Thomas Stafford, House
Indian Acres; see Carpenter, Solomon, House
Kingston Congregational Church; see Congregational Church
Taylor, Thomas Stafford, House (Hagadorn House)
1305 Kingstown Rd. (State Rt. 138)
HABS RI-297   p   L

Kingston Hill
Kingston Inn (Kingstown Hill)
HABS RI-44   pd   L
Kingstown Hill; see Kingston Inn

North Kingston
Northrup, Palmer, House
7919 Post Rd. (U.S. Rt. Alt. 1)
HABS RI-40   s p   L
Reynolds, Joseph, House (Reynolds-Lawrence House)
Forge Rd.
HABS RI-3-8   s pd   L
Reynolds-Lawrence House; see Reynolds, Joseph, House
Smith, Richard Jr., House
Post Rd. (U.S. Rt. Alt. 1)
HABS RI-39   p   L
Stuart, Gilbert, Birthplace; see Stuart, Gilbert, House
Stuart, Gilbert, House (Stuart, Gilbert, Birthplace)
Hammond Hill Rd.
HABS RI-120   p   L

North Kingstown
Hammond, Benjamin, Grist Mill
Hammond Hill Rd.
HABS RI-2   s pd   L
Quonset Point Naval Air Station
HAER RI-15   pd   L

Saunderstown
Casey, Edward P., House
Boston Neck Rd. (State Rt. 138)
HABS RI-41   p   L

South Kingston
Glebe, The
Tower Hill Rd.
HABS RI-42   p   L

Wakefield
Dockray, John, House
Dockray St.
HABS RI-43   p   L

Westerly
Babcock, Dr. Joshua, House
124 Granite St.
HABS RI-142   pd   L

Wickford
Bailey, George, House (Wall, Daniel, House)
79 Main St.
HABS RI-68   p   L
Barney, Capt. Richard, House
115 Main St.
HABS RI-67   p   L
Case, Immanuel, House (Gardiner House)
41 Main St.
HABS RI-3-13   s pd   L
Cooper, Thomas, House (Doorway)
75 Main St.
HABS RI-66   p   L
Gardiner House; see Case, Immanuel, House
Narragansett Church, Old; see St. Paul's Episcopal Church
Northrup, Cyrus, House
90 Main St.
HABS RI-298   p   L
Reynolds, Jonathan, House
85 Main St.
HABS RI-65   p   L
Smith, John, House
4 Gold St.
HABS RI-63   p   L
St. Paul's Episcopal Church (Narragansett Church, Old)
Church Lane (moved from Tower Hill)
HABS RI-45   p   L
Wall, Daniel, House; see Bailey, George, House

South Carolina

Clemson

de St. Julien, Paul, Plantation House; see
Hanover
Hanover (de St. Julien, Paul, Plantation
House)
(moved from SC, Pinopolis)
HABS SC-36   s pd   L H

ABBEVILLE COUNTY

Abbeville

Trinity Episcopal Church
Church St.
HABS SC-38   pd   L

Lowndesville vic.

Caldwell-Hutchison Farm
County Rd. 93
HABS SC-382   s pd   H
**Caldwell-Hutchison Farm, Blacksmith
Shop**
County Rd. 93
HABS SC-382-A   s p   H
Featherstone Tenant Farm
County Rd. 81
HABS SC-381   s pd   H
Harper-Featherstone Farm, Well House
County Rd. 81
HABS SC-379-A   s pd   H
Harper-Featherstone Tenant Farm
County Rd. 81
HABS SC-380   s pd   H
Long-Hutchison Farm
County Rd. 123
HABS SC-383   pd   H
Long-Hutchison Farm, Tenant Barn
County Rd. 123
HABS SC-383-B   s pd   L

Rocky River

Abbeville Hydroelectric Power Plant
State Hwy. 284
HAER SC-5   pd   L

Savannah River

Georgia-Carolina Memorial Bridge
HAER SC-3   pd   L
Seaboard Coast Line Railroad Bridge
Calhoun Falls vic., Spanning Savannah
River
HAER SC-6   pd   L

AIKEN COUNTY

Charleston

Robinson-Aiken House
48 Elizabeth St.
HABS SC-269   s pd   L
Robinson-Aiken Service Building & Stable
48 Elizabeth St.
HABS SC-275   s pd   L

ANDERSON COUNTY

Anderson

Maxwell, Jeff, House
1109 W. Whitner St. & Maxwell Ave.
HABS SC-322   pd   L
Morris House
220 E. Morris & S. Manning Sts.
HABS SC-323   pd   L
Orange Grove (Silcox House)
1092 N. Main St. & N. Blvd.
HABS SC-120   s pd   L H
Poppy House
805 S. McDuffie St.
HABS SC-324   pd   H
Prevost, Nick, House
105 N. Prevost St.
HABS SC-325   pd   H
Silcox House; see Orange Grove
Sullivan House
E. Franklin St.
HABS SC-123   p   L

Anderson vic.

Varennes Tavern
HABS SC-5   s p   L

Lowndesville vic.

Gregg Shoals Dam & Power Plant
Spanning Savannah River
HAER SC-7   pd   L

Pendleton

Ashtabula (Gibbes, Lewis Ladson,
Plantation House)
Old Greenville Hwy.
HABS SC-328   pd   H
Farmers' Hall
Village Green
HABS SC-13-12   s pd   L
Gibbes, Lewis Ladson, Plantation House;
see Ashtabula
Maverick, Samuel, Plantation House; see
Montpelier
Mont Pelier; see Montpelier
Montpelier (Maverick, Samuel, Plantation
House; Mont Pelier)
Old Greenville Hwy.
HABS SC-329   s pd   H
Pendleton Presbyterian Church
Broad & S. Mechanic Sts.
HABS SC-326   pd   H
St. Paul's Episcopal Church
Queen's St.
HABS SC-327   pd   H
Sycamore Ave.
HABS SC-283   s   H

Pendleton vic.

Altamont
HABS SC-282   s   H
Burt, Frank, House; see Oaklawn

Oaklawn (Burt, Frank, House)
HABS SC-279   s   L
Woodburn
U.S. Rts. 76 & 123
HABS SC-285   pd   H

Savannah River

Sanders Ferry Bridge
State Hwy. 184, Spanning Savannah River
HAER SC-2   pd   L
Smith-McGee Bridge
Georgia Rt. 181, spanning Savannah River
HAER SC-4   pd   L

BAMBERG COUNTY

Bamberg vic.

Simms, William Gilmore, House; see
Woodlands (Ruins)
Woodlands (Ruins) (Simms, William
Gilmore, House)
U.S. Rt. 78
HABS SC-219   p   L

Ehrhardt

Civil War Memorial Shed
Rivers Bridge State Park
HABS SC-389   s   H

Ehrhardt vic.

Confederate Memorial Pavilion
Rivers Bridge State Park
HABS SC-388   d   H
Murdock House
HABS SC-231   p   L

BEAUFORT COUNTY

Beaufort

Baptist Church
Charles St.
HABS SC-290   pd   L
Barnwell House; see Hepworth, Thomas,
House
Danner, Porter, House; see Johnson, Dr.
Joseph, House
Fuller, Thomas, House (Tabby Manse)
1211 Bay & Harrington Sts.
HABS SC-287   pd   L
Hepworth, Thomas, House (Barnwell
House)
214 New St.
HABS SC-16   s pd   L
Hext House
207 Handcock St.
HABS SC-289   pd   L
House
HABS SC-221   p   L

Johnson, Dr. Joseph, House (Danner, Porter, House)
Craven St.
HABS SC-187   p   L
Lafayette House; see Verdier, John Mark, House
Maxcy-Rhett House
1111 Craven & Church Sts.
HABS SC-288   pd   H
McLeod House; see Smith, John Joyner, House
Means, Col. Edward, House
804 Pinckney St.
HABS SC-220   p   L
Smith, John Joyner, House (McLeod House)
400 Wilmington & Bay Sts.
HABS SC-291   pd   L
Tabby Manse; see Fuller, Thomas, House
Talbird House (Ruins); see Tolbert House (Ruins)
Tolbert House (Ruins) (Talbird House (Ruins))
Hamilton & Hancock Sts.
HABS SC-138   p   L
Verdier, John Mark, House (Lafayette House)
801 Bay & Scott Sts.
HABS SC-139   pd   L
Whitehall (Ruins)
Whitehall Point
HABS SC-222   p   L

Hunting Island
Hunting Island Lighthouse Complex
Hunting Island State Park
HABS SC-385   s   d   H

Sheldon vic.
Prince William's Parish Church (Ruins)
HABS SC-137   pd   L

BERKELEY COUNTY

Cordesville
Ball, Elias, Plantation House; see Comingtee
Comingtee (Ball, Elias, Plantation House)
Cooper River
HABS SC-132   pd   L

Cordesville vic.
Limerick (Mahon, Michael, Plantation)
Cooper River, E. Branch
HABS SC-8   s pd   L
Mahon, Michael, Plantation; see Limerick
North Chachan Plantation, Stable
Cooper River, W. Branch
HABS SC-119   pd   L
Pogson, Rev. Milward, Plantation House; see Wappaola
Strawberry Chapel
Cooper River, W. Branch
HABS SC-37   pd   L

Wappahola; see Wappaola
Wappaola (Pogson, Rev. Milward, Plantation House; Wappahola; Wappoola)
Cooper River, W. Branch
HABS SC-82   pd   L
Wappoola; see Wappaola

Cross
Cabin
HABS SC-35   pd   L

Cross vic.
Cabin
HABS SC-230   p   L

Eutaville vic.
Loch Dhu
HABS SC-56   pd   L

Eutaw Springs vic.
Lawson's Pond (Porcher, Charles Cordes, Plantation House)
HABS SC-57   pd   L
Palmer, Joseph, Plantation House; see Springfield
Porcher, Charles Cordes, Plantation House; see Lawson's Pond
Springfield (Palmer, Joseph, Plantation House)
HABS SC-55   pd   L

Goose Creek
Parish of St. James (formerly); see St. James' Protestant Episcopal Church
St. James' Protestant Episcopal Church (Parish of St. James (formerly))
HABS SC-79   pd   L H

Goose Creek vic.
Crowfield Ruins (Middleton, William, Plantation House)
HABS SC-6   s pd   L
Elms, The (Ruins) (Izard, Henry, Plantation House)
University Blvd. (U.S. Rt. 78)
HABS SC-167   pd   L
Izard, Henry, Plantation House; see Elms, The (Ruins)
Middleton, William, Plantation House; see Crowfield Ruins

Huger vic.
Middleburg (Simons, Benjamin, Plantation House)
Cooper River, E. Branch
HABS SC-13   s pd   L
Pompion Hill Chapel
Cooper River, S. Side
HABS SC-34   pd   L
Simons, Benjamin, Plantation House; see Middleburg

Lake Moultrie vic.
Santee Canal Structures (Area Survey)
HABS SC-240   p   L

Moncks Corner vic.
Berkeley Country Club; see Exeter
Biggin Church (Ruins)
Cooper River, W. Branch
HABS SC-30   pd   L
Broughton, Thomas, Plantation House; see Mulberry
Butler, Hugh, Plantation House; see Exeter
Exeter (Butler, Hugh, Plantation House; Berkeley Country Club)
Cooper River, W. Branch
HABS SC-12   s pd   L
Gippy (White, John Sims, Plantation House)
Cooper River, W. Branch
HABS SC-169   pd   L
Mulberry (Broughton, Thomas, Plantation House)
Cooper River, W. Branch
HABS SC-393   p   L
White, John Sims, Plantation House; see Gippy

Pine Grove vic.
Carson, William Augustus, Plantation House; see Dean Hall
Dean Hall (Carson, William Augustus, Plantation House)
Cooper River, W. Side
HABS SC-40   pd   L
Medway Plantation
U.S. Rt. 52
HABS SC-140   pd   L

Pineville
Blueford Plantation (Oakland Club)
State Rt. 45
HABS SC-236   p   L
Oakland Club; see Blueford Plantation

Pineville vic.
Belle Isle Plantation, Washhouse
Upper Santee
HABS SC-241   p   L
House
State Rt. 45 & U.S. Rt. 52
HABS SC-237   p   L

Pinopolis
de St. Julien, Paul, Plantation; see Hanover
Hanover (de St. Julien, Paul, Plantation)
(moved to SC, Clemson, Clemson University Campus)
HABS SC-36   s pd   L H

Pinopolis vic.
Black Oak Church
HABS SC-33   p   L
Bunker Hill Plantation House
HABS SC-27   pd   L
Cain, William, Plantation House; see Somerset
Cedar Spring Plantation House
HABS SC-23   pd   L

Indianfield Plantation House
HABS SC-26   pd   L
North Hampton Plantation House
   (Northampton Plantation House)
HABS SC-17   pd   L
North Hampton Plantation Outbuildings
   (Northampton Plantation Outbuildings)
HABS SC-18   pd   L
Northampton Plantation House; see North
   Hampton Plantation House
Northampton Plantation Outbuildings; see
   North Hampton Plantation Outbuildings
Ophir (Porcher, Col. Thomas, Plantation
   House)
HABS SC-19   pd   L
Pooshee Plantation House
HABS SC-22   pd   L
Porcher, Col. Thomas, Plantation House;
   see Ophir
Porcher, Thomas, Plantation House; see
   White Hall
Somerset (Cain, William, Plantation
   House)
HABS SC-20   pd   L
Wampee Plantation House
HABS SC-24   pd   L
White Hall (Porcher, Thomas, Plantation
   House)
HABS SC-28   pd   L
Woodlawn Plantation House
Dover Plantation (moved from SC, Lake
   Moultrie)
HABS SC-25   pd   L

St. Stephens

House
E. of Railroad Tracks
HABS SC-239   p   L
St. Stephen's Church
HABS SC-74   pd   L

Wando River

St. Thomas' & St. Dennis' Church
Clements Ferry Rd. vic.
HABS SC-29   pd   L

CHARLESTON COUNTY

Charleston

Aiken, Joseph, House
20 Charlotte St.
HABS SC-91   pd   L
Aiken, William, House; see South Carolina
   Railroad-Southern Railway Co.
Ashe, Col. John, House
32 S. Battery
HABS SC-321   p   L
Axson, Samuel Edward, House
4 Greenhill St.
HABS SC-197   s   L
Bank of South Carolina (Chamber of
   Commerce)
50 Broad St.
HABS SC-116   pd   L

Bank of United States (Charleston City
   Hall)
Broad & Meeting Sts.
HABS SC-76   pd   L
56 Beaufain Street (House) (St. Michael's
   Church, Rectory)
HABS SC-134   p   L
Belser, Christopher, House
2 Amherst St.
HABS SC-203   s pd   L
Bennett, Gov. Thomas, House
1 Lucas St.
HABS SC-101   pd   L
Bennett, Thomas, House
89 Smith St.
HABS SC-267   pd   L
Bennett's Rice Mill
E. Bay, Hasell, Concord & Laurens Sts.
HABS SC-13-7   s pd   L
Beth Elohim Synagogue; see Kahal Kadosh
   Beth Elohim Synagogue
Bethel Methodist Church
57 Pitt St.
HABS SC-153   pd   L
Blacklock, William, Carriage House
18 Bull St.
HABS SC-272   pd   L
Blacklock, William, Gazebo
18 Bull St.
HABS SC-273   pd   L
Blacklock, William, House
18 Bull St.
HABS SC-109   pd   L
Blake, Daniel, Tenements
2-4 Courthouse Square
HABS SC-128   p   L
Bocquet, Maj. Peter Jr., House
95 Broad St.
HABS SC-264   pd   L
Brewton, Miles, House
27 King St.
HABS SC-78   pd   L H
Brewton, Robert, House
71 Church St.
HABS SC-370   pd   H
Brewton-Sawter House (Century Antiques
   House)
77 Church St.
HABS SC-191   p   L
Bull, Lt. Gov. William, House
43 Meeting St.
HABS SC-155   p   L
Calhoun & East Bay Streets (House)
HABS SC-375   p   H
85 Calhoun Street (Building)
HABS SC-265   pd   L
Capers, Richard, House
69 Church St.
HABS SC-215   p   L
Castle Pickney
Charleston Harbor
HABS SC-195   pd   L

Century Antiques House; see
   Brewton-Sawter House
17 Chalmers Street (House) (Pink House)
HABS SC-127   pd   L
36 Chalmers Street (House)
HABS SC-71   p   L
Chamber of Commerce; see Bank of South
   Carolina
Charleston City Hall; see Bank of United
   States
Charleston County Courthouse
Broad & Meeting Sts.
HABS SC-131   pd   L
Charleston Hotel
Meeting St.
HABS SC-77   pd   L
Charleston Orphan House, Chapel
13 Vanderhorst St.
HABS SC-146   p   L
10 Charlotte Street (House)
HABS SC-85   pd   L
32 Charlotte Street (House)
HABS SC-96   p   L
33 Charlotte Street (House)
HABS SC-159   p   L
43 Charlotte Street (House)
HABS SC-93   pd   L
Chisolm, Alexander Robert, House
6 Montague St.
HABS SC-260   pd   L
143-145 Church Street (House) (Pirate
   House)
HABS SC-164   p   L
92 Church Street (House) (St. Philip's
   Church, Rectory)
HABS SC-90   pd   L
**Circular Congregational Church, Parish
   House;** see Lance Hall
Citadel, Old; see South Carolina State
   Arsenal
College of Charleston
66 George St.
HABS SC-175   pd   L
County Records Building (Mesne
   Conveyance Office; Fireproof Building)
100 Meeting St. at Chalmers St.
HABS SC-154   s pd   L
de Saussure, Chancellor, House
18 Montague St.
HABS SC-94   pd   L
de Saussure, Louis, House
1 E. Battery
HABS SC-98   pd   L
Dictator; see Rutledge, John, House
East Bay & Reid Streets (House)
HABS SC-205   p   L
East Bay & Tradd Street (House)
HABS SC-226   p   L
Edmonston, Charles, House
21 E. Battery
HABS SC-54   pd   L
Edwards, George, Gates; see Simmons,
   Francis, House

Elfe, Thomas, Workshop; see 54 Queen
Street (House)

Eliot, Charles, House; see 43 Legare Street
(House)

Exchange Building & Custom House
122-26 E. Bay St.
HABS SC-45   pd   L H

Faber House (Ward Mansion)
631 E. Bay St.
HABS SC-204   p   L

Farmers' & Exchange Bank
141 E. Bay St.
HABS SC-268   pd   L

Fickin House; see Mikell, I. Jenkins, House

Fireproof Building; see County Records
Building

First Baptist Church
61-67 Church St.
HABS SC-121   pd   L

First Scots Presbyterian Church
57 Meeting St.
HABS SC-80   pd   L

Fort Moultrie (Fort Sumter National
Monument)
W. Fort St. & Central Ave.
HABS SC-196   s pd   L H

Fort Sumter (Fort Sumter National
Monument)
HABS SC-194   pd   L

Fort Sumter National Monument; see Fort
Moultrie

Fort Sumter National Monument; see Fort
Sumter

Fraser, Charles, House
55 King St.
HABS SC-147   p   L

French Protestant Huguenot Church
136 Church St.
HABS SC-105   pd   L

Gate
96 Ashley Ave.
HABS SC-108   p   L

Glebe House (Smith, Bishop Robert,
House)
6 Glebe St.
HABS SC-261   s pd   L

Glebe Street Presbyterian Church (Mount
Zion A.M.E. Church)
7 Glebe St.
HABS SC-266   pd   L

Glover, Dr. Joseph, House
81 Rutledge Ave.
HABS SC-320   pd   L

Harvey, William, House
110 Broad St.
HABS SC-65   pd   L

Harvey-Lining House & Pharmacy
Broad & Kings Sts.
HABS SC-106   pd   L

86 Hasell Street (House)
HABS SC-52   p   L

33 Hayne Street (Commercial Building)
HABS SC-308   pd   L

Heyward, Thomas, House (Manigault,
Henry, House)
18 Meeting St.
HABS SC-160   p   L

Heyward, Thomas Jr., House
(Heyward-Washington House)
87 Church St.
HABS SC-64   pd   L

Heyward-Washington House; see Heyward,
Thomas Jr., House

Hibernian Hall
105 Meeting St.
HABS SC-136   pd   L

House, Jerkinhead Roof; see 392-394
Meeting Street (House)

Islington Manor
135 Cannon St.
HABS SC-278   pd   L

Izard-Pinckney House
114 Broad St.
HABS SC-100   pd   L

Jewish Orphanage, Old
88 Broad St.
HABS SC-13-15   s pd   L

Kahal Kadosh Beth Elohim Synagogue
(Beth Elohim Synagogue)
90 Hasell St.
HABS SC-81   s pd   L

**183-185 King Street (Commercial
Building)**
HABS SC-301   pd   L

191 King Street (Commercial Building)
HABS SC-302   pd   L

**211-213 King Street (Commercial
Building)**
HABS SC-303   pd   L

237 King Street (Commercial Building)
HABS SC-304   pd   L

Ladson House
8 Meeting St.
HABS SC-95   pd   L

Lance Hall (Circular Congregational
Church, Parish House)
138 Meeting St.
HABS SC-50   p   L

10 Legare Street (House)
HABS SC-212   p   L

43 Legare Street (House) (Eliot, Charles,
House)
HABS SC-162   p   L

**32 Legare Street (House, Drawing Room
Wing);** see Swordgate House

Levy, Moses C., House
301 E. Bay St.
HABS SC-99   s pd   L

Lowndes Grove (Lowndes, William, House)
Saint Margaret St. & Sixth Ave.
HABS SC-178   p   L

Lowndes, William, House; see Lowndes
Grove

Lucas, Jonathan, House
286 Calhoun St.
HABS SC-41   pd   L

4 Magazine Street (House)
HABS SC-103   pd   L

Manigault, Henry, House; see Heyward,
Thomas, House

Manigault, Joseph, House
350 Meeting St. & Ashmead Place
HABS SC-67   pd   L

Marine Hospital, Old
20 Franklin St.
HABS SC-13-10   s pd   L

Market Hall
188 Meeting St.
HABS SC-135   pd   L

Martin, Robert, House
16 Charlotte St.
HABS SC-150   p   L

226 Meeting Street (Commercial Building)
HABS SC-307   pd   L

227 Meeting Street (Commercial Building)
HABS SC-305   pd   L

229 Meeting Street (Commercial Building)
HABS SC-306   pd   L

392-394 Meeting Street (House) (House,
Jerkinhead Roof)
HABS SC-42   p   L

Melcher-Enston House
105 Drake ST.
HABS SC-202   p   L

Mesne Conveyance Office; see County
Records Building

Middleton-Pinckney House
14 George St.
HABS SC-51   pd   L

Mikell, I. Jenkins, House (Fickin House)
Rutledge Ave. & Montague St.
HABS SC-43   p   L

Mikell, I. Jenkins, Servants' Quarters
Rutledge Ave. & Montague St.
HABS SC-44   p   L

Mills, Clark, Studio
51 Broad St.
HABS SC-371   p   H

Mixson's Seed & Garden Supplies
217 E. Bay
HABS SC-372   p   L

Morris-Gadsden House
329 E. Bay St.
HABS SC-14   s pd   L

Motte, Col. Issac, House
30 Meeting St.
HABS SC-263   pd   L

Moultrie, Dr. James, House
20 Montague St.
HABS SC-209   p   L

Mount Zion A.M.E. Church; see Glebe
Street Presbyterian Church

Parker-Drayton House
6 Gibbes St.
HABS SC-70   pd   L

Payne, Commodore, House
64 Vanderhorst St.
HABS SC-68   pd   L

Pelzer House
107 Ashley Ave.
HABS SC-104   p   L

Petigru, James Louis, Law Office
8 St. Michael's Place
HABS SC-148   p   L

Pink House; see 17 Chalmers Street (House)

Pirate House; see 143-145 Church Street (House)

Porcher, Philip, House
19 Archdale St.
HABS SC-165   p   L

Porter Academy; see U.S. Arsenal, Main Building

Porter Academy, Armory; see U.S. Arsenal, Powder Magazine

Porter Academy, Chapel; see U.S. Arsenal, Artillery Shed

Porter Academy, Colcock Hall; see U.S. Arsenal, Foundry Building

Porter Academy, Officers' Dwellings; see U.S. Arsenal, Building

Porter Academy, President's House; see U.S. Arsenal, Building

Powder Magazine, Old City
21 Cumberland St.
HABS SC-88   pd   L

Primrose House
332 E. Bay & Vernon Sts.
HABS SC-107   p   L

Pringle, Judge Robert, House
70 Tradd St.
HABS SC-166   p   L

54 Queen Street (House) (Elfe, Thomas, Workshop)
HABS SC-286   s pd   L

Radcliffe, Thomas, House; see Ratcliffe, Thomas, House

Ramsey, Dr. David, House
92 Broad St.
HABS SC-13-1   s pd   L

Ratcliffe, Thomas, House (Radcliffe, Thomas, House)
24 George St.
HABS SC-53   pd   L

Ravenal, Daniel, House
68 Broad St.
HABS SC-133   pd   L

Ravenal, William, House
13 E. Bay St.
HABS SC-161   pd   L

Rhett, Col. William, House
54 Hasell St.
HABS SC-171   pd   L

Robinson-Aiken Cow House
48 Elizabeth St.
HABS SC-274   s pd   L

Robinson-Aiken House
48 Elizabeth St.
HABS SC-269   s pd   L

Robinson-Aiken Necessary Building
48 Elizabeth St.
HABS SC-277   s pd   L

Robinson-Aiken Service Building & Stable
48 Elizabeth St.
HABS SC-275   s pd   L

Robinson-Aiken Slave Building & Kitchens
48 Elizabeth St.
HABS SC-276   s pd   L

Roper, Robert William, House
9 E. Battery
HABS SC-173   p   L

Russell, Nathaniel, House
51 Meeting St.
HABS SC-145   pd   L

74 Rutledge Avenue (House)
HABS SC-210   p   L

95 Rutledge Avenue (House)
HABS SC-216   p   L

Rutledge, John, House (Dictator)
116 Broad St.
HABS SC-394   d   L

Savage, Thomas, House
8 S. Battery
HABS SC-115   pd   L

Seabrook, William, House
Steamboat Creek
HABS SC-124   pd   L

Second Presbyterian Church
342 Meeting St.
HABS SC-92   pd   L

Shingler, William Pinckney, House
9 Limehouse St.
HABS SC-300   pd   L

Shirras, Alexander, House
271 Meeting St.
HABS SC-217   p   L

Shrewsbury, Stephen, House
311 E. Bay
HABS SC-258   pd   L

Simmons, Francis, House (Edwards, George, Gates)
14 Legare St.
HABS SC-47   pd   L

Smith, Bishop Robert, House; see Glebe House

Smith, Josiah, House
7 Meeting St.
HABS SC-225   p   L

59 Smith Street (House)
HABS SC-84   pd   L

Smith, William Mason, House
26 Meeting St.
HABS SC-149   p   L

So. Carolina RR-Southern Railway Co., Camden Depot
Anne St.
HABS SC-373-B   p   H

4 South Battery (House) (Villa Margherita)
HABS SC-174   p   L

South Carolina Railroad-Southern Railway Co. (Aiken, William, House)
456 King St.
HABS SC-373-A   p   H

South Carolina RR-Southern Railway Co., Warehouse
42 John St.
HABS SC-373-C   p   H

South Carolina State Arsenal (Citadel, Old)
Marion Square
HABS SC-184   pd   L

47 South Meeting Street (House)
HABS SC-46   p   L

St. John's Lutheran Church
10 Archdale St.
HABS SC-168   pd   L

St. Mary's Roman Catholic Church
89 Hasell St.
HABS SC-48   pd   L

St. Michael's Church, Rectory; see 56 Beaufain Street (House)

St. Michael's Episcopal Church
80 Meeting St.
HABS SC-62   s pd   L

St. Philip's Church, Rectory; see 92 Church Street (House)

St. Philip's Protestant Episcopal Church
146 Church St.
HABS SC-75   pd   L

State Powder Magazines & Administration Bldgs.
Charleston Neck
HABS SC-13-13   s pd   L

Steele, William, House
89 Beaufain St.
HABS SC-86   pd   L

Stuart, Col. John, House
106 Tradd St.
HABS SC-156   pd   L

Swordgate House (32 Legare Street (House, Drawing Room Wing))
109 Tradd St. (moved from 32 Legare St.)
HABS SC-271   pd   L

Three Sisters (Building)
Calhoun & E. Bay St.
HABS SC-384   p   H

46 Tradd Street (House)
HABS SC-66   pd   L

72 Tradd Street (House)
HABS SC-122   pd   L

Trinity Methodist Church; see Westminster Presbyterian Church

U.S. Arsenal, Artillery Shed (Porter Academy, Chapel)
167 Ashley Ave.
HABS SC-296   pd   L

U.S. Arsenal, Building (Porter Academy, Officers' Dwellings)
167 Ashley Ave.
HABS SC-295   pd   L

U.S. Arsenal, Building (Porter Academy, President's House)
167 Ashley Ave.
HABS SC-299   pd   L

U.S. Arsenal, Foundry Building (Porter
  Academy, Colcock Hall)
167 Ashley Ave.
HABS SC-297   pd   L

U.S. Arsenal, Main Building (Porter
  Academy)
167 Ashley Ave.
HABS SC-294   pd   L

U.S. Arsenal, Powder Magazine (Porter
  Academy, Armory)
167 Ashley Ave.
HABS SC-298   pd   L

U.S. Customs House
E. Bay & Market Sts.
HABS SC-39   pd   L H

U.S. Post Office Building
Broad & Meeting Sts.
HABS SC-293   pd   L

14 Vanderhorst Street (House)
HABS SC-163   p   L

67 Vanderhorst Street (House)
HABS SC-181   p   L

Villa Margherita; see 4 South Battery
  (House)

Walker, John Falls, House
344 E. Bay St.
HABS SC-262   pd   L

Ward Mansion; see Faber House

Warren & Smith Streets (House)
HABS SC-208   p   L

West Point Rice Mill
Ashley River, Calhoun St. vic.
HABS SC-214   p   L

Westminster Presbyterian Church (Trinity
  Methodist Church)
273 Meeting St.
HABS SC-292   s pd   L

Charleston vic.

Ball, John, House; see Marshlands

Drayton Hall
State Rt. 61
HABS SC-377   s p   L H

Drayton Hall, Brick Office
State Rt. 61
HABS SC-377-A   s   L

Fort Johnson, Powder Magazine
James Island, Charleston Harbor
HABS SC-387   s d   H

Marshlands (Ball, John, House)
College of Charleston (moved from Cooper
  River)
HABS SC-259   pd   L

St. Andrew's Episcopal Church
State Rt. 61
HABS SC-4   s pd   L

Edisto Island

Brookland
HABS SC-141   p   L

Hamilton, Paul, House (Ruins) (House,
  Brick)
Russell Creek
HABS SC-1   s pd   L

House, Brick; see Hamilton, Paul, House
  (Ruins)

Presbyterian Church
HABS SC-125   p   L

Goose Creek vic.

Elms, The (Ruins) (Izard, Henry,
  Plantation House)
University Blvd. (U.S. Rt. 78)
HABS SC-167   pd   L

Izard, Henry, Plantation House; see Elms,
  The (Ruins)

Mc Clellanville

Lucas, William, House (Wedge, The)
U.S. Rts. 17 & 701
HABS SC-144   p   L

Wedge, The; see Lucas, William, House

Mc Clellanville vic.

Fairfield; see Lynch House

Hampton Plantation
Wambaw Creek, S. side
HABS SC-72   pd   L

Harrietta Plantation
U.S. Rts. 17 & 701
HABS SC-143   pd   L

Lynch House (Fairfield)
U.S. Rts. 17 & 701
HABS SC-10   s pd   L

St. James' Episcopal Church
Wambaw Creek, S. side
HABS SC-69   pd   L

Mount Pleasant vic.

Boone Hall Quarters
HABS SC-102   pd   L

Oakland Plantation
HABS SC-9   s pd   L

Snee Farm
HABS SC-87   pd   L

Sullivans Island

**Fort Moultrie, Cable Tank Storage
  Building** (Fort Sumter National
  Monument)
HABS SC-196-A   s   H

Fort Sumter National Monument; see Fort
  Moultrie, Cable Tank Storage Building

CHESTER COUNTY

Chester vic.

Sealy, Obadiah, House
State Rt. 9
HABS SC-130   p   L

Great Falls

Rock House (Ruins)
Catawba River
HABS SC-158   p   L

Great Falls vic.

Rocky Mount Canal, Lock Keeper's House
HABS SC-386   s d   H

CHESTERFIELD COUNTY

Cheraw

Cheraw Lyceum; see Equity Court, Old

Duvall House
226 Third St.
HABS SC-227   p   L

Equity Court, Old (Cheraw Lyceum)
Market & Seaboard Sts.
HABS SC-179   pd   L

Lafayette House; see Pegues-McKay House

Lane House; see St. David's Episcopal
  Church, Rectory

Masonic Hall
Market & Second Sts.
HABS SC-180   p   L

Pegues-McKay House (Lafayette House)
Kershaw & Third Sts.
HABS SC-172   p   L

Police Station; see Town Hall

St. David's Episcopal Church
First & Church Sts.
HABS SC-112   pd   L

St. David's Episcopal Church, Rectory
  (Lane House)
515 Market St.
HABS SC-378   pd   L

Town Hall (Police Station)
Market & Second Sts.
HABS SC-151   p   L

Cheraw vic.

McLaurin, Tom, House
State Rt. 382
HABS SC-229   p   L

Sessions, H. E., House
State Rt. 9
HABS SC-228   p   L

Chesterfield

Craig, John, House
Courthouse vic.
HABS SC-188   pd   L

CLARENDON COUNTY

Manning

Oakland (Wyndham, William, House)
HABS SC-235   p   L

Wyndham, William, House; see Oakland

COLLETON COUNTY

Walterboro

Library
Wichman St. & N. Miller (moved from
  Fishburne St.)
HABS SC-2   pd   L

Mansion
HABS SC-192   p   L

Walterboro vic.

Cabin
HABS SC-249   p   L

DARLINGTON COUNTY

Mechanicsville vic.

Flowers, B. C., House (Fountain, Wilson, House)
Cash's Ferry Rd.
HABS SC-111 pd L

Fountain, Wilson, House; see Flowers, B. C., House

Society Hill vic.

Cedar Grove (Gandy, Lila, House)
Rt. 2
HABS SC-113 pd L

Gandy, Lila, House; see Cedar Grove

DORCHESTER COUNTY

Ashley River

Middleton Place
Ashley River Rd.
HABS SC-218 d L

Ashley River, North Bank

Dorchester Church Tower
Dorchester Creek Junction
HABS SC-189 p L

Fort Dorchester
Dorchester Creek Junction
HABS SC-185 p L

FAIRFIELD COUNTY

Monticello vic.

Church, Old Brick; see First Associate Reformed Presbyterian Church

Ebenezer Church; see First Associate Reformed Presbyterian Church

First Associate Reformed Presbyterian Church (Ebenezer Church; Church, Old Brick)
State Rt. 213
HABS SC-157 p L

Winnsboro

Fairfield County Courthouse
Congress & Washington Sts.
HABS SC-213 pd L

Fire Station & Municipal Offices
Congress & Washington Sts.
HABS SC-182 p L

FLORENCE COUNTY

Mars Bluff vic.

Columns, The (Johnson, Dr. William R., Plantation House)
U.S. Rts. 76 & 301
HABS SC-117 pd L

Johnson, Dr. William R., Plantation House; see Columns, The

GEORGETOWN COUNTY

Georgetown

Allston House
405 Front St.
HABS SC-310 pd L

Church of Prince George Winyah
Broad & Highmarket Sts.
HABS SC-49 pd L

Crowley Store
936 Front St.
HABS SC-313 pd L

Georgetown County Courthouse
Screven & Prince Sts.
HABS SC-142 p L

Henning-Ward House
614 Prince St.
HABS SC-309 pd L

Man, Mary, House
528 Front St.
HABS SC-317 pd L

Market Building (Police Department Building)
Front & Screven Sts.
HABS SC-198 p L

Middleton House
15 Cannon St.
HABS SC-314 pd L

Pawley, George, House
1019 Front St.
HABS SC-312 pd L

Police Department Building; see Market Building

Pyatt, John S., House
630 Highmarket St.
HABS SC-311 pd L

Winyah Indigo Society Hall
Prince & Cannon Sts.
HABS SC-199 p L

Withers, Frances, House
202 Cannon St.
HABS SC-316 pd L

Withers House
622 Highmarket St.
HABS SC-315 pd L

Withers House
316 Screven St.
HABS SC-318 pd L

Georgetown vic.

House
Annandale Plantation vic.
HABS SC-232 p L

Negro Baptist Church
Friendfield Estate
HABS SC-89 pd L

Silver Hill Plantation
Friendfield Estate, Sampit River
HABS SC-89 p L

Santee River, North

Hopsewee
U.S. Rts. 17 & 701
HABS SC-200 p L

GREENVILLE COUNTY

Greenville

Christ Episcopal Church
N. Church St.
HABS SC-13-6 s pd L

Greenville vic.

Poinsett, Joel, House
HABS SC-183 p L

KERSHAW COUNTY

Camden

Alberta Team House; see Mathis, Samuel, House

Alexander, Elizabeth G., House
612 Laurens St.
HABS SC-330 pd H

Bethesda Presbyterian Church
Dekalb & Market Sts.
HABS SC-331 pd H

Bloomsbury (Chesnut, James, House)
1707 Lyttleton St.
HABS SC-332 pd H

Chesnut, James, House; see Bloomsbury

Chestnut, Gen. James, House; see Kamchatka

Davis, Bishop, House
Broad & Walnut Sts.
HABS SC-333 pd H

Dekalb, Baron, Monument
N. Dekalb & Market Sts.
HABS SC-13-8 s pd L

Douglas, James K., House
York St.
HABS SC-334 pd H

Flake, Samuel, House; see Greenleaf Villa

Greenleaf Villa (Flake, Samuel, House)
1307 Broad St.
HABS SC-335 pd H

Holly Hedge (Johnson, William E., House)
302 Greene St.
HABS SC-336 pd H

Horsebranch Hall (McRae House)
Kirkwood Ln.
HABS SC-337 pd H

Johnson, William E., House; see Holly Hedge

Kamchatka (Chestnut, Gen. James, House)
Kirkwood Ln.
HABS SC-338 pd H

Kershaw County Courthouse (Masonic Hall)
Broad & King Sts.
HABS SC-13-9 s pd L

Masonic Hall; see Kershaw County Courthouse

Mathis, Samuel, House (Alberta Team House)
1409 Broad St.
HABS SC-339 pd H

McRae House; see Horsebranch Hall
Price, Fanny, House & Store
Broad & York
HABS SC-340   p d   H
Shannon, Charles John, House
1502 Broad St.
HABS SC-341   p d   H

Camden vic.
Boykin, John, Plantation House; see
    Coolspring
Chestnut, James, Plantation House; see
    Mulberry
Coolspring (Boykin, John, Plantation
    House)
U.S. Rts. 521 & 601
HABS SC-342   p d   H
Mulberry (Chestnut, James, Plantation
    House)
U.S. Rt. 521
HABS SC-343   p d   H

MARLBORO COUNTY

Bennettsville
Courthouse (Entrance)
HABS SC-223   p   L
Ruins
Adjoining Golf Club
HABS SC-224   p   L

OCONEE COUNTY

Clemson
Calhoun, John C., Law Office; see Fort
    Hill, Dependency
Fort Hill (McElhenny-Calhoun-Clemson
    Plantation House)
Clemson University Campus
HABS SC-344   p d   H
Fort Hill, Dependency (Calhoun, John C.,
    Law Office)
Clemson University Campus
HABS SC-345   p d   H
Fort Hill Dependency, Kitchen
Clemson University Campus
HABS SC-346   p d   H
**McElhenny-Calhoun-Clemson Plantation
    House;** see Fort Hill

Clemson vic.
Church, Old Stone; see Hopewell
    Meetinghouse
Hopewell Meetinghouse (Church, Old
    Stone)
Anderson-Seneca Rd., U.S. Rt. 76 vic.
HABS SC-347   p d   H

Oconee Station
Fort of Indian Trading Station, Old; see
    Oconee Station
Oconee Station (Fort of Indian Trading
    Station, Old)
Walhalla vic.
HABS SC-348   p d   H
Richards, William, House
Walhalla vic.
HABS SC-349   p d   H

Tamassee
Sharpe, Elam Jr., Plantation; see Tamassee
Tamassee (Sharpe, Elam Jr., Plantation;
    Tomassee)
HABS SC-284   s p d   H
Tomassee; see Tamassee

West Union
Strother, J. R., House
State Rts. 28 & 11 (Old Georgian Rd.)
HABS SC-351   p d   L

Westminster
Horseshoe; see Robinson, Galbraith, House
Robinson, Galbraith, House (Horseshoe)
Horseshoe Bridge Rd.
HABS SC-350   p d   H

ORANGEBURG COUNTY

Eutaw Springs vic.
Belvidere (Sinkler, James, Plantation
    House)
HABS SC-21   p d   L
Eutaw
HABS SC-61   p   L
Gaillard, Capt. Peter, Plantation House; see
    Rocks, The
Numertia Plantation House
HABS SC-32   p   L
Pond Bluff (Simons, Keating, Plantation
    House)
HABS SC-59   p d   L
Pond Bluff, Outbuildings
HABS SC-60   p d   L
Rocks, The (Gaillard, Capt. Peter,
    Plantation House)
HABS SC-58   p d   L
Simons, Keating, Plantation House; see
    Pond Bluff
Sinkler, James, Plantation House; see
    Belvidere
Walworth Plantation House
State Rt. 6
HABS SC-31   p   L

PICKENS COUNTY

Gowensville vic.
Chapmans Bridge
Hwy. 414
HABS SC-391   s d   H

RICHLAND COUNTY

Columbia
Central National Bank (Sylvan Building)
Hampton & Main Sts.
HABS SC-255   p d   L
Crawford-Clarkson House
Bull & Blanding Sts.
HABS SC-250   p d   L
DeBruhl-Marshall House
1401 Laurel St.
HABS SC-13-3   s p d   L
First Baptist Church
Hampton St.
HABS SC-251   p d   L
First Presbyterian Church
Marion & Lady Sts.
HABS SC-352   p d   H
Fisher-Bachman House
1615 Hampton St.
HABS SC-353   p d   H
Hall, Ainsley, Mansion
Blanding St.
HABS SC-13-16   s p d   L
Hall-Hampton-Preston House
1615 Blanding St.
HABS SC-354   p d   H
Lunatic Asylum (South Carolina State
    Hospital, Mills Building)
Bull St. & Elmwood Ave.
HABS SC-253   p d   L
O'Neal, Richard Jr., House
1028 Elmwood Ave.
HABS SC-252   p d   L
**South Carolina State Hospital, Mills
    Building;** see Lunatic Asylum
South Carolina State House
Capitol Sq.
HABS SC-319   p d   L
South Caroliniana Library; see University
    of South Carolina, Library
Sylvan Building; see Central National Bank
Trinity Episcopal Church
Sumter & Gervais Sts.
HABS SC-355   p d   H
University of South Carolina, Library
    (South Caroliniana Library)
S. Sumter St.
HABS SC-13-11   s p d   L
**University of South Carolina, President's
    House**
Sumter St.
HABS SC-110   p   L

Columbia vic.
Hampton, Wade, Mansion (Ruins); see
    Millwood (Ruins)
Millwood (Ruins) (Hampton, Wade,
    Mansion (Ruins))
U.S. Rt. 76 (Garners Ferry Rd.)
HABS SC-256   p d   L

SUMTER COUNTY

Pinewood vic.

Manning, Gov. John Lawrence, Plantation;
see Milford

Milford (Manning, Gov. John Lawrence,
Plantation)
Wedgefield-Rimini Rd.
HABS SC-257   s p d   L

Milford Plantation, Accessory Building
Wedgefield-Rimini Rd.
HABS SC-356   p d   L

Milford Plantation, Entrance Gateway
Wedgefield-Rimini Rd.
HABS SC-357   p d   L

Milford Plantation, Porter's Lodge
Wedgefield-Rimini Rd.
HABS SC-358   p d   L

Milford Plantation, Spring House
Wedgefield-Rimini Rd.
HABS SC-359   p d   L

Milford Plantation, Stables
Wedgefield-Rimini Rd.
HABS SC-360   p d   L

Milford Plantation, Water Tower
Wedgefield-Rimini Rd.
HABS SC-361   p d   L

Poinsett State Park

Ramsey House
HABS SC-238   p   L

Stateburg

Anderson, Gen., Plantation House; see
Oaks, The

Borough House (Hill Crest)
State Rt. 261 & Garners Ferry Rd.
HABS SC-362   p d   L

Borough House, Dependency
State Rt. 261 & Garners Ferry Rd.
HABS SC-363   p   L

Borough House, Dry Well Shelter
State Rt. 261 & Garners Ferry Rd.
HABS SC-364   p   L

Borough House, Hooper Tombs
State Rt. 261 & Garners Ferry Rd.
HABS SC-365   p   L

Borough House, Kitchen-Storehouse
State Rt. 261 & Garners Ferry Rd.
HABS SC-366   p   L

Borough House, School
State Rt. 261 & Gardners Ferry Rd.
HABS SC-367   p   L

Borough House School Road (Cabin)
HABS SC-244   p   L

Borough House, Weaving House
State Rt. 261 & Garners Ferry Rd.
HABS SC-368   p   L

Brookland Plantation House
Old Charleston Rd. (State Rt. 261)
HABS SC-243   p   L

Carson Plantation House; see Homefield

DeLage Chapel; see Sumter, Gen. Thomas,
Tomb

Episcopal Church of the Holy Cross
State Hwy. 261
HABS SC-13-14   p   H

High Hills Baptist Church
Kings Hwy. (State Rt. 261)
HABS SC-13-5   s p d   L

Hill Crest; see Borough House

Homefield (Carson Plantation House)
HABS SC-245   p   L

Marshton Plantation House
Camden Rd.
HABS SC-246   p   L

Needwood Plantation House
HABS SC-247   p   L

Oaks, The (Anderson, Gen., Plantation
House)
Stateburg-Wedgefield Rd.
HABS SC-248   p   L

Sumter, Gen. Thomas, Tomb (DeLage
Chapel)
HABS SC-13-4   s p d   L

Sumter vic.

Cabin
HABS SC-63   p   L

Wedgefield vic.

Melrose (Singleton, Capt. Matthew,
Plantation)
Kings Hwy. (State Rt. 261)
HABS SC-7   s p d   L

Singleton, Capt. Matthew, Plantation; see
Melrose

UNION COUNTY

Union vic.

Gist, William H., House
U.S. Rt. 176
HABS SC-390   s d   H

WILLIAMSBURG COUNTY

Kingstree

Nelson House
HABS SC-233   p   L

Williamsburg County Courthouse
Main St.
HABS SC-234   p   L

YORK COUNTY

Clover vic.

Hawthorne House
Catawba River
HABS SC-193   s p   L

House, Henry, House (Kings Mountain
National Military Park)
HABS SC-15   s p   L

Kings Mountain National Military Park;
see House, Henry, House

Sandy Hook vic.

Ford, John, House
HABS SC-392   p   H

York vic.

McElwee, William, House
Kings Mountain Recreational Area
HABS SC-11   s p d   L

South Dakota

BON HOMME COUNTY

Tabor

Bon Homme Mill
Gavins Point Reservoir vic.
HABS SD-6   s p d   L

CLAY COUNTY

Vermillion

Austin-Whittemore House (Clay County
Historic Society)

15 Austin St.
HABS SD-12   p   H

Clay County Historic Society; see
Austin-Whittemore House

Inman House
415 E. Main St.
HABS SD-13   p   H

**University of South Dakota, Main
Building, Old**
HABS SD-11   p   H

CUSTER COUNTY

Custer vic.

Wind Cave National Park, Visitors Center
U.S. Rt. 385 vic.
HABS SD-9   p   L

DEWEY COUNTY

Cheyenne River Agcy.

**St. John's Episcopal Mission, Chapel &
Rectory**
Fort Bennett vic.
HABS SD-5   s p d   L

GREGORY COUNTY

Pickston vic.

Fort Randall Church, Old
Right Bank, Missouri River
HABS SD-4   s pd   L

HUGHES COUNTY

Pierre vic.

Fort Bennett, Blacksmith Shop & Barracks, Old
Fort Bennett
HABS SD-8   s pd   L
Oahe Congregational Mission
Oahe Reservior vic.
HABS SD-7   s pd   L

PENNINGTON COUNTY

Rapid City

614-632 Main Street
HABS SD-10   p   H

ROBERTS COUNTY

Fort Sisseton

Fort Sisseton, Commandant's Quarters
HABS SD-1   pd   L
Fort Sisseton, North Barracks
HABS SD-2   pd   L
Fort Sisseton, Powder Magazine
HABS SD-3   pd   L

UNION COUNTY

Elk Point

Union County Courthouse
Courthouse Square
HABS SD-17   p   H

YANKTON COUNTY

Yankton

Gurney Seed Plant
Second & Capitol Sts.
HABS SD-15   p   H
Yankton College, Conservatory
HABS SD-14   p   H

Tennessee

BLOUNT COUNTY

Cades Cove

Forge Creek Dam, John Cable Mill
Great Smoky Mountains National Park
HABS TN-159   s p   L H
Forge Creek Dam-John Cable Mill
Great Smoky Mountains National Park
HABS TN-159   s p   L H
Shields, Witt, Barn
HABS TN-160   s p   H

Cades Cove vic.

Whitehead, Henry, Place
HABS TN-161   s pd   L H
Whitehead, Henry, Smokehouse
Great Smoky Mountains National Park
HABS TN-162   s pd   L H

BRADLEY COUNTY

Cleveland

Hughes, U. J., House (Wilson, C. J., House)
3202 Ocoee St.
HABS TN-204   s d   H
Wilson, C. J., House; see Hughes, U. J., House

CANNON COUNTY

Cades Cove

Greenbriar School
Great Smokey Mountains National Park
HABS TN-116   s pd   L H

CARTER COUNTY

Elizabethton

Carter, John & Landon, House
HABS TN-231   s   H

Elizabethton Covered Bridge
Hattie Ave.
HABS TN-224   pd   H

Elizabethton vic.

Taylor, Gen. Nathaniel, House
State Hwy. 67
HABS TN-94   pd   L

CLAIBORNE COUNTY

Harragate

Huff, Daniel, Mill
HABS TN-195   s   H

COCKE COUNTY

Jenkins, Chandler, Cabin
Indian Camp Rd.
HABS TN-120   s   H

DAVIDSON COUNTY

Antioch

Hays, Charles, House (Hays-Kiser House)
834 Reeves Rd.
HABS TN-65   pd   L
Hays-Kiser House; see Hays, Charles, House

Donelson

McGavok, David, House; see Two Rivers
Two Rivers (McGavok, David, House)
3130 McGavok Pike
HABS TN-15   s pd   H

Donelson vic.

Blue Brick, Old
Stewart's Ferry Pike
HABS TN-129   pd   L
Ridley, James, House
Stewart Ferry Rd.
HABS TN-140   pd   L

Hermitage

Hermitage, The (Jackson, Andrew, House)
HABS TN-52   s pd   L
Jackson, Andrew, House; see Hermitage, The
Tulip Grove
HABS TN-127   pd   L

Hermitage vic.

Cleveland Hall
HABS TN-130   pd   L
Hermitage Church
HABS TN-136   pd   L

Nashville

Acklin, Col. J. A. S., House; see Belmont
Belmont (Acklin, Col. J. A. S., House)
S. Sixteenth Ave.
HABS TN-56   pd   L
Children's Museum; see University of Nashville, Main Building
Fine Arts Building; see Vanderbilt University, Gym
First Baptist Church
Seventh & Broadway
HABS TN-42   p   H
First Presbyterian Church; see Presbyterian Church (Downtown)
Fisk University (Jubilee Hall)
Seventeenth Ave., North
HABS TN-19   pd   H
Grand Ole Opry House; see Ryman Auditorium
Heiman, Adolphus, House
900 Jefferson St., NW
HABS TN-25   pd   L
Holy Trinity Episcopal Church
615 Sixth Ave., South
HABS TN-135   s pd   L H

Jubilee Hall; see Fisk University
Morgan, S. D., & Co. Building
208-210 Public Square
HABS TN-16   s pd   H
Overton, Judge John, House; see
  Traveller's Rest
Presbyterian Church (Downtown) (First
  Presbyterian Church)
154 Fifth Ave.
HABS TN-17   s pd   H
Public Arcade
Fourth & Fifth Sts.
HABS TN-24   p   H
Public Square Commercial Area
216 Public Sq.
HABS TN-57   p   H
Riverwood
HABS TN-128   pd   L
Ryman Auditorium (Grand Ole Opry
  House)
118 Opry Pl.
HABS TN-23   p   H
**Second Avenue North, Commercial
  District**
HABS TN-20   pd   H
St. Mary's Cathedral
328 Fifth Ave., North
HABS TN-13   s pd   H
State Capitol
State Capitol Blvd. & Cedar St.
HABS TN-51   s pd   L H
Tennessee State Penitentiary, Main Prison
West End Centennial Blvd.
HABS TN-33   pd   H
Traveller's Rest (Overton, Judge John,
  House)
Farrell Pky.
HABS TN-14   s pd   H
Union Station
1001 Broadway
HABS TN-21   pd   H
University of Nashville, Main Building
  (Children's Museum)
724 Second Ave., South
HABS TN-18   s pd   H
Vanderbilt University, Gym (Fine Arts
  Building)
Twenty-third Ave., South & West End Blvd.
HABS TN-11   s pd   H
Vanderbilt Universiyt, West Side Row
West End Ave. & Twenty-fourth Ave.,
  South
HABS TN-34   pd   L H
Werthen Bag Company
HABS TN-22   p   H
Windsor
HABS TN-133   pd   L
Worker's House
1724 N. Jefferson St.
HABS TN-26   pd   L

Nashville vic.
Belair
HABS TN-134   pd   L

Belle Meade
HABS TN-132   pd   L
Harding, John, Cabin-Belle Meade Estate
HABS TN-139   p   L
Spence House
Lebanon Pike
HABS TN-138   pd   L

FAYETTE COUNTY

Lagrange
Hancock Hall
Hwy. 57 (Third St.)
HABS TN-174   d   H
Immanuel Episcopal Church
Second St.
HABS TN-173   s d   H

FRANKLIN COUNTY

Winchester
Hundred Oaks
Oak St.
HABS TN-221   d   H

GILES COUNTY

Gatlinburg vic.
Garland, Townsend, Place-Corn Crib
Great Smoky Mountains National Park
HABS TN-119   s   H

GREENE COUNTY

Chuckey vic.
Earnest House
HABS TN-143   pd   L
Earnest Log House
HABS TN-144   pd   L

Greeneville
Brown-Milligan House
HABS TN-145   pd   L
Cumberland Presbyterian Church
N. Main & W. Church Sts.
HABS TN-146   pd   L
Davis House
Maple Ave.
HABS TN-147   pd   L
Dickson-Williams Mansion
N. Irish & W. Church Sts.
HABS TN-148   pd   L
First Presbyterian Church
N. Main St.
HABS TN-149   pd   L
Johnson, Andrew, First House; see
  Kerbaugh
Johnson, Andrew, House
217 S. Main St.
HABS TN-142   s   L
Kerbaugh (Johnson, Andrew, First House)
Depot & College Sts.
HABS TN-227   s p   H

Law Office
McKee & S. Irish Sts.
HABS TN-150   pd   L
Rumbough-Doughty House
215 S. Irish St.
HABS TN-151   pd   L
Sevier-Coles House
214 N. Main St.
HABS TN-153   pd   L
Sevier-Coles House, Outbuildings
HABS TN-223   p   H
Sevier-Coles Law Offices
214 N. Main St.
HABS TN-223   d   H
Sevier-Johnson-Susong-House
S. Main St.
HABS TN-154   pd   L
St. James Episcopal Church
W. Church St.
HABS TN-152   pd   L

Greeneville vic.
Reaves-Crislip House
HABS TN-155   pd   L

Tusculum
College, Old (Tusculum College)
HABS TN-157   pd   L
Doak House
HABS TN-156   pd   L
Tusculum College; see College, Old
Tusculum College, McCormick Hall
HABS TN-196   s   H
Tusculum College, Springhouse
HABS TN-222   p   H

GRUNDY COUNTY

Beersheba Springs
Beersheba Inn, Old (Beersheba Springs
  Hotel)
HABS TN-54   s pd   L H
Beersheba Springs Hotel; see Beersheba
  Inn, Old

HAMBLEN COUNTY

Morristown
Crosby, Caleb, Threshing Barn
Noeton
HABS TN-118   s p   H
Deadrick-Taylor House (Taylor, Frank W.,
  House)
U.S. Hwy. 11-E
HABS TN-97   pd   L
Rural Mount
St. Rt. 160
HABS TN-203   s d   H
Taylor, Frank W., House; see
  Deadrick-Taylor House

HAMILTON COUNTY

Chattanooga

Brown Furniture Co. Warehouse; see Trigg, Dobbs & Co. Warehouse

Etheridge, D. S., Automobile Showroom & Tire Store
329 Market St.
HABS TN-206   d   H

Orange Grove Housing for Industrial Workers
1131-1209 E. Thirteenth St.
HABS TN-205   s   d   H

Times Building
HABS TN-199   s   H

Tivoli Theater
709-713 Broad St.
HABS TN-207   d   H

Trigg, Dobbs & Co. Warehouse (Brown Furniture Co. Warehouse)
1152 Market St.
HABS TN-229   pd   L

Union Depot
W. Ninth St., btw. Chestnut & Broad Sts.
HABS TN-233   pd   H

Warner, John H., House
800 Vine St.
HABS TN-208   d   H

HARDEMAN COUNTY

Bolivar

McNeal, Col., House
Union & Bills Streets
HABS TN-10   s pd   L H

HARDIN COUNTY

Hohenwald vic.

Log Cabin, Early
Meriwether Lewis National Monument Hwy. 48
HABS TN-158   p   L

Savannah (Pittsburg)

Cherry Mansion
101 Main St.
HABS TN-141   s pd   L H

HAWKINS COUNTY

Rogersville

Bynom-Clay Home
265 E. Main St.
HABS TN-220   d   H

HENRY COUNTY

Paris

Atkins-Jackson House
Dresden Hwy. (State Hwy. 54)
HABS TN-180   d   H

Crawford-Governor Porter House
407 Dunlap St.
HABS TN-176   s   d   H

JEFFERSON COUNTY

White Pine

Fairfax; see Franklin, Isaac, House
Franklin, Isaac, House (Fairfax)
HABS TN-197   s   H

KNOX COUNTY

Knoxville

Blount, William, Mansion
State St. & Hill Ave.
HABS TN-101   s pd   L

Campbell House
Cumberland Ave. & Central St.
HABS TN-103   s pd   L

Chisholm Tavern
Front & Gay Sts.
HABS TN-111   s pd   L

Commerce Avenue Fire Hall
201-205 Commerce Ave.
HABS TN-211   d   H

Jackson Avenue Warehouse District
101-103, 122 & 124 Jackson Ave., 105-107 E. Jackson
HABS TN-212   d   H

Jackson, Dr. George, House
State St. & Hill Ave.
HABS TN-102   s pd   L

McGhee, Lawson, Library
217 Market St.
HABS TN-213   d   H

Ziegler, Issac B., House
712 N. Fourth Ave.
HABS TN-216   d   H

Knoxville vic.

Ramsey House (Swan Pond; Ramsey, J. G. M., House)
Thorngrove Pike
HABS TN-104   s pd   L H

Ramsey, J. G. M., House; see Ramsey House

Swan Pond; see Ramsey House

LOUDON COUNTY

Lenoir City

Lenoir Cotton Mill
HABS TN-198   s   H

Loudon

Blair's Ferry Storehouse
800 Main St.
HABS TN-41   d   H

MADISON COUNTY

Jackson

Southern Engine & Boiler Works
342 N. Royal St.
HABS TN-185   d   H

Union Station
N. Royal St.
HABS TN-184   d   H

Wisdom, John L., House
535 E. Main St.
HABS TN-177   s   d   H

MARION COUNTY

South Pittsburgh

Christ Episcopal Church & Parish House
Third & Holly Sts.
HABS TN-45   d   H

MAURY COUNTY

Columbia

Mercer Hall (Otey, Bishop James Hervey, Hall)
HABS TN-61   pd   L

Otey, Bishop James Hervey, Hall; see Mercer Hall

Columbia vic.

Clifton Place (Pillow, Gen. Gideon J., House)
State Hwy. 6
HABS TN-62   pd   L

Pillow, Gen. Gideon J., House; see Clifton Place

Polk-Cranberry House; see Rattle & Snap

Rattle & Snap (Polk-Cranberry House)
Hwy. 43
HABS TN-63   pd   L H

Zion Church (Presbyterian)
St. Rt. 1
HABS TN-64   pd   L

MCMINN COUNTY

Athens vic.

Cleage, Samuel, House
Lee Hwy. at Business Rt. II
HABS TN-201   s   d   H

MONTGOMERY COUNTY

Clarksville

Clarksville Dept. of Electricity; see U.S. Post Office

Federal Building; see U.S. Post Office

Grange Warehouse
Riverside St.
HABS TN-39   pd   L

Poston Block
126, 128 & 130 Public Square
HABS TN-35   pd   L

617

U.S. Post Office (Clarksville Dept. of
   Electricity; Federal Building)
Commerce & S. Second Sts.
HABS TN-38   pd   L

MORGAN COUNTY

Rugby
Hughes, Thomas, Public Library
HABS TN-200   s   H

OVERTON COUNTY

Livingston
Roberts, Gov. Albert H., Law Office
114 E. Main St.
HABS TN-218   d   H

ROANE COUNTY

Kingston
Roane County Courthouse
Public Square
HABS TN-202   s   d   H

ROBERTSON COUNTY

Cedar Hill vic.
Washington, Joseph, House; see
   Wessyngton
Wessyngton (Washington, Joseph, House)
HABS TN-32   pd   L H

RUTHERFORD COUNTY

Murfreesboro
Oaklands
N. Maney Ave.
HABS TN-31   pd   H

SEVIER COUNTY

Elkmont vic.
Great Smokey Mountain National Park; see
   Little Greenbriar School & Church
   House
Little Greenbriar School & Church House
   (Great Smokey Mountain National Park)
HABS TN-116   s pd

Gatlinburg
Mingus Mill
Great Smoky Mountains National Park
HABS TN-225   s p   H
Walker Sisters Place
Great Smoky Mountains National Park
HABS TN-121   p   H

Gatlinburg vic.
Bales, Ephraim, Place
Roaring Fork Trail, Great Smoky
   Mountains N. P.
HABS TN-117   s pd   L
Junglebrook Cabin Group, Barn
HABS TN-123   p   H
Junglebrook Cabin Group, House
HABS TN-122   p   H
Junglebrook Tub Mill
Cherokee Orchard Rd., Great Smoky
   Mountains N. P.
HABS TN-163   s   L
McCarter, Tyson, Place
Great Smoky Mountains National Park
HABS TN-226   s   H
Reagan, Alfred, House
Roaring Fork Trail, Great Smoky Moutains
   N. P.
HABS TN-164   s   L
Reagan, Alfred, Tub Mill
Roaring Fork Trail, Great Smoky
   Mountains N. P.
HABS TN-165   s   L

Knoxville vic.
Buckingham House
Sevierville Pike
HABS TN-110   s pd   L

SHELBY COUNTY

Brunswick
Davies Manor
Davies Plantation Rd.
HABS TN-183   d   H

Memphis
Allenburg Cotton Company
104-106 S. Front St.
HABS TN-188   d   H
Annesdale
1325 Lamar Ave.
HABS TN-178   d   H
Brinkley Female College, Ghost House
683 S. Fifth St.
HABS TN-189   d   H
Calvary Episcopal Church
102 N. Second St.
HABS TN-182   d   H
Claiborn Temple; see Second Presbyterian
   Church
Cotton Brokerage House
45-47 Union Ave.
HABS TN-187   d   H
Dunscomb House
584 S. Front St.
HABS TN-1   s pd   L
First Baptist Church
379 Beale Street
HABS TN-181   d   H
Goyer-Lee House
690 E. Adams St.
HABS TN-171   s d   H

Handwerker Gingerbread Playhouse
865 N. Thomas St.
HABS TN-169   s d   H
Hunt-Phelan House
533 Beale Ave.
HABS TN-3   s pd   L H
Littleton-Pettit House
496 Beale Ave.
HABS TN-7   pd   L
North Memphis Driving Park
1450 N. Thomas St.
HABS TN-170   d   H
Second Presbyterian Church (Claiborn
   Temple)
Hernando St. & Pototoe Ave.
HABS TN-186   pd   H
Titus Block
Third & Market Sts.
HABS TN-4   s pd   L
Topp, Robertson, House
565 Beale Ave.
HABS TN-2   s pd   L
Turnage-Young House
196 E. Court St.
HABS TN-172   s d   H
Watkins, J. R., Building
70 W. E. H. Crump Blvd.
HABS TN-179   d   H

STEWART COUNTY

Dover vic.
Bear Spring Furance
HABS TN-36   pd   L

SULLIVAN COUNTY

Blountville
Deery Inn, Old
Old 4 South 11-W
HABS TN-167   s pd   H
Fain, John, Barn
HABS TN-194   s   H

Kingsport
Netherland Inn
2144 Knoxville Highway
HABS TN-166   s pd   H

SUMNER COUNTY

Castalian Springs
Castalian Springs; see Wynnewood
Wynne House; see Wynnewood
Wynnewood (Wynne House; Castalian
   Springs)
HABS TN-81   pd   L

Gallatin
Blythe, Sam, House
Hartsman Pike
HABS TN-137   pd   L

Fairvue (Franklin, Issac, House)
U.S. Hwy. 31-E
HABS TN-80   pd   L H
Franklin, Issac, House; see Fairvue

Gallatin vic.
Bridge, Stone at Bowling Green
HABS TN-236   p   L
Cragfont (Winchester, Gen. James, House)
Hwy. 25
HABS TN-82   pd   L
Winchester, Gen. James, House; see
  Cragfont

Hendersonville vic.
Priestly-Bradford House
Gellatin Pike
HABS TN-126   pd   L
Rock Castle
Indian Lake Rd. (Berry Lane)
HABS TN-131   s pd   L H

TROUSDALE COUNTY

Dixon Springs
McGee, John, House
HABS TN-230   s p   H

WARREN COUNTY

Mcminnville
Northcut Plantation (Wheeler Place)
Wheeler Lane
HABS TN-219   d   H
Wheeler Place; see Northcut Plantation

WASHINGTON COUNTY

Johnson City
Cobb House
U.S. Hwy. 41
HABS TN-92   pd   L
Mountain Home V. A.Medical Center
HAER TN-19-1   pd   L H
Tipton-Hayes House
U.S. Hwy. 19
HABS TN-93   pd   L

Johnson City vic.
Hammer, Issac, House
HABS TN-40   p   H

Jonesboro
Hecker-Kennedy House
400 W. Main St.
HABS TN-210   s d   H
Sulphur Springs Methodist Campground
Sulphur Spring Rd., North
HABS TN-209   d   H

Leesburg
Devault Tavern
North Tennessee Rt. 81
HABS TN-217   d   H

Limestone
Stone House, Old
HABS TN-96   pd   L

WAYNE COUNTY

Clifton vic.
Stencil House
HABS TN-190   d   H

WHITE COUNTY

Sparta
Lincoln, Jesse, House
Rt. 5
HABS TN-193   s   H

WILLIAMSON COUNTY

Franklin
Carter House
1140 Columbia Ave.
HABS TN-37   pd   L

Texas

ANDERSON COUNTY

Palestine
Dorsett House
HABS TX-127   pd   L
Egan House; see Schoolhouse, Red Brick
Gathright House; see Pessony, George,
  House
Mallard-Alexander-McNaughton House
407 E. Kolstad St.
HABS TX-128   pd   L
Pessony, George, House (Gathright House)
HABS TX-126   pd   L
Schoolhouse, Red Brick (Egan House)
HABS TX-129   pd   L
Schwirter House
HABS TX-130   pd   L

ANGELINA COUNTY

Lufkin vic.
Gann, John, House
Rt. 94 vic.
HABS TX-285   pd   L

ARANSAS COUNTY

Fulton
Fulton, George W., House
S. Beach St.
HABS TX-3116   pd   L

Rockport
Mathis, T. H., House
612 S. Church St.
HABS TX-3115   pd   L

ARMSTRONG COUNTY

Claude
J. A. Milk & Meat Cooler
TX Rt. 207 & Farm Rd. 2272 (moved from
  TX, Lubbock)
HABS TX-3236   s   L

BASTROP COUNTY

Bastrop vic.
Crocheron, Henry, House
1502 Wilson St.
HABS TX-335   s pd   L

Hill, A. Wiley, House
Rt. 304, Hill's Prairie vic.
HABS TX-336   s pd   L
Jung-Pearcy House
909 Pecan St.
HABS TX-3127   pd   L
Sayers, Gov. Joseph D., House
1903 Wilson St.
HABS TX-33-C-5   s pd   L
Wilbarger House
1403 N. Main St.
HABS TX-33-C-6   s pd   L

Webberville vic.
Burleson, Aaron, House
HABS TX-3126   pd   L
Dog-Run House; see Ireland, Tom, House
Ireland, Tom, House (Dog-Run House)
HABS TX-337   pd   L

BELL COUNTY

Salado vic.
Robertson, E. Sterling C., Plantation
  House
W. access Rd. I-35 vic.
HABS TX-394   s pd   L

Shady Villa (Stagecoach Inn)
E. access Rd. I-35
HABS TX-395   pd   L

Stagecoach Inn; see Shady Villa

BEXAR COUNTY

San Antonio

Alamo Madre Acequia
E. of Alamo St., N. of Durango Blvd.
HAER TX-1-A   p   H

**Alamo Roman & Portland Cement
   Company Factory**
N. Saint Mary's St. in Brackenridge Park
HABS TX-3173   s pd   H

Alamo, The; see Mission San Antonio de
   Valero

Alamo, The; see Mission San Antonio de
   Valero, Church

Alamo, The; see Mission San Antonio de
   Valero, Convent

Altgelt, Ernst H., House (Isbell, George P.,
   House)
226 King William St.
HABS TX-3147   pd   L

Argyle House
924 Patterson & Argyle-Alamo Heights
HABS TX-36   pd   L

Ball, John, House
120 King William St.
HABS TX-3151   pd   L

Bexar County Courthouse
Main Plaza, 20 Dolorosa St.
HABS TX-3174   s pd   H

Boelhauwe, Joseph, House
321 N. Alamo
HABS TX-3153   pd   L

Concepcion Mission; see Mission Nuestra
   Senora de la Purisima Concepcion

Cos House
513 Paseo de la Villita
HABS TX-33-A-6   s pd   L

Dashiell, Col. Jeremiah Y., House
511 Paseo de la Villita
HABS TX-3169   s pd   H

Denman House; see Lewis, Nat., House

**Des Mazieres, Francis Louis, Store
   Building & House**
Martinez & S. Alamo Sts.
HABS TX-33-A-2   s pd   L

Devine, Judge Thomas J., House
HABS TX-332   pd   L

Espada Acequia:Diversion Dam
SW of Military Dr. & S. Presa St., Southton
HAER TX-1-B   H

Espada Acequia:Piedras Creek Aqueduct
   (Espada Aqueduct)
Espada Rd. & Piedra Creek
HABS TX-322
HAER TX-1-C   pd   L H

Espada Aqueduct; see Espada
   Acequia:Piedras Creek Aqueduct

Espada Mission; see Mission San Francisco
   de la Espada

French Mansard House; see Kingsley, Dr.
   D. B. F., House

Henry, O., House (Porter, William Sydney,
   House)
Lone Star Brewery, 600 Lane Star Blvd.
HABS TX-325   pd   L

Isbell, George P., House; see Altgelt, Ernst
   H., House

Kampmann, John R., House
HABS TX-396   pd   L

Kingsley, Dr. D. B. F., House (French
   Mansard House)
408 Elm St.
HABS TX-33-A-3   s pd   L

Lege, Charles L., House (Santleben House)
533 Elmira St.
HABS TX-3172   s pd   H

Lewis, Nat., House (Denman House)
112 Lexington
HABS TX-393   pd   L

Menger Hotel
Alamo Plaza
HABS TX-35   pd   L

**Mission Nuestra Senora de la Purisima
   Concepcion** (Concepcion Mission)
807 Mission Rd.
HABS TX-319   s pd   L H

Mission San Antonio de Valero (Alamo,
   The)
Alamo Plaza
HABS TX-318   s pd   L H

Mission San Antonio de Valero, Church
   (Alamo, The)
Alamo Plaza
HABS TX-318-A   s pd   L H

Mission San Antonio de Valero, Convent
   (Alamo, The)
Alamo Plaza
HABS TX-318-B   s pd   L H

Mission San Francisco de la Espada
   (Espada Mission)
Espada Rd.
HABS TX-320   s pd   L H

Mission San Jose y San Miguel de Aguayo
   (San Jose Mission)
6539 San Jose
HABS TX-333   s pd   L H

**Mission San Jose y San Miguel de Aguayo,
   Chapel**
6539 San Jose
HABS TX-333-B   s pd   L H

**Mission San Jose y San Miguel de Aguayo,
   Church**
6539 San Jose
HABS TX-333-A   s pd   L H

**Mission San Jose y San Miguel de Aguayo,
   Convent**
6539 San Jose
HABS TX-333-C   s pd   L H

**Mission San Jose y San Miguel de Aguayo,
   Granary**
6539 San Jose
HABS TX-333-D   s pd   L H

**Mission San Jose y San Miguel de Aguayo,
   Ramparts**
6539 San Jose
HABS TX-333-E   s pd   L H

Mission San Juan Capistrano
Berg's Mill-Graf Rd.
HABS TX-321   s pd   L H

Mission San Juan Capistrano, Chapel
Berg's Mill-Graf Rd.
HABS TX-321-A   s pd   L H

Mission San Juan Capistrano, Habitation A
Berg's Mill-Graf Rd.
HABS TX-321-C   s pd   L H

Mission San Juan Capistrano, Habitation B
Berg's Mill-Graf Rd.
HABS TX-321-D   s pd   L H

Mission San Juan de Capistrano, Convent
Berg's Mill-Graf Rd.
HABS TX-321-B   s pd   L H

**Mission Senora de la Purisima Concepcion,
   Church**
807 Mission Rd.
HABS TX-319-A   s pd   L H

**Mission Senora de la Purisima Concepcion,
   Convent**
807 Mission Rd.
HABS TX-319-B   s pd   L H

Mitchell-Oge' House
209 Washington St.
HABS TX-3171   s pd   H

Navarro, Jose Antonio, House
228 S. Laredo St.
HABS TX-3148   pd   L

Navarro, Jose Antonio, Store
232 S. Laredo St.
HABS TX-317   s pd   L

Norton-Polk-Mathis House
401 King William St.
HABS TX-3225   s   H

Porter, William Sydney, House; see Henry,
   O., House

Ruiz, Francisco, House
Witte Museum, 3801 Broadway,
   Brackenridge Park
HABS TX-3117   pd   L

San Antonio Acequias
Hildebrand Ave. & Minita Creek
HAER TX-1   s d   H

San Fernando Cathedral
Main Plaza, 115 Main Ave.
HABS TX-34   pd   L H

San Jose Grist Mill
SW of San Jose Dr., E. of Espada Rd.
HAER TX-2   s p   H

San Jose Mission; see Mission San Jose y
   San Miguel de Aguayo

Santleben House; see Lege, Charles L.,
   House

Seng, Magnus, House
HABS TX-33-A-15   s pd   L

St. Mark's Episcopal Church
307 E. Pecan St.
HABS TX-33   pd   L

Steves, Eduard, House (Steves Homestead)
509 King William St.
HABS TX-3150   pd   L

Steves Homestead; see Steves, Eduard, House

Twohig, John, House
Witte Museum, 3801 Broadway, Brackenridge Park
HABS TX-31   pd   L

Uhl, Gustave, House
HABS TX-316   pd   L

Ursuline Academy
300 Augusta St.
HABS TX-32   s pd   L H

Ursuline Academy, 1872 House
HABS TX-32-F   pd   L H

Ursuline Academy, Academy Building
300 Augusta St.
HABS TX-32-A   pd   L H

Ursuline Academy, Academy Building Addition
300 Augusta St.
HABS TX-32-B   pd   L H

Ursuline Academy, Chapel
HABS TX-32-C   pd   L H

Ursuline Academy, Dormitory
HABS TX-32-D   pd   L H

Ursuline Academy, Laundry Building
HABS TX-32-G   pd   L H

Ursuline Academy, Priest's House
HABS TX-32-E   pd   L H

U.S. San Antonio Arsenal Complex
Bounded by Flores & Arsenal Sts.
HABS TX-3175   d   H

U.S. San Antonio Arsenal, Depot
Arsenal Grounds
HABS TX-3175-B   d   H

U.S. San Antonio Arsenal, Magazine
Arsenal Grounds
HABS TX-3175-F   s pd   H

U.S. San Antonio Arsenal, Office Building
Arsenal Grounds
HABS TX-3175-C   pd   H

U.S. San Antonio Arsenal, Officer's Quarters
Arsenal Grounds
HABS TX-3175-A   pd   H

U.S. San Antonio Arsenal, Servants' Quarters
Arsenal Grounds
HABS TX-3175-D   pd   H

U.S. San Antonio Arsenal, Stable & Grounds
Arsenal Grounds
HABS TX-3175-E   d   H

U.S. San Antonio Arsenal, Storehouse
Arsenal Grounds
HABS TX-3175-G   s pd   H

Vance, James, House
HABS TX-33-A-1   s pd   L

Veramendi, Don Fernando, Palace; see Veramendi Palace

Veramendi Palace (Veramendi, Don Fernando, Palace)
130 Soledad St.
HABS TX-3128   pd   L

Vollrath House & Store
712 S. Alamo St.
HABS TX-3152   pd   L

Wulff, Anton, House
107 King William St.
HABS TX-3149   pd   L

San Antonio vic.

Casa Vieja (Old House)
Blue Wing Rd.
HABS TX-323   s pd   L

Casa Vieja Lime Kiln & Arch
Blue Wing Rd.
HABS TX-324   pd   L

Old House; see Casa Vieja

Somerset vic.

Cowan, I. M., House
HABS TX-382   pd   L

BOSQUE COUNTY

Kimball

Kimball Academy
Rt. 174, Brazos River vic.
HABS TX-139   pd   L

BRAZORIA COUNTY

Angleton vic.

Chenango Sugar Mill
Chenango vic.
HABS TX-283   s pd   L

Brazoria

McCormick House (McCormick-Ashcomb House)
HABS TX-249   pd   L

McCormick-Ashcomb House; see McCormick House

West Columbia vic.

Varner-Hogg Plantation House
Varner Hogg State Park Museum
HABS TX-251   pd   L

CALDWELL COUNTY

Lockhart vic.

Blackwell, James, House
HABS TX-391   pd   L

Lane, Dr. Pleasant, House
HABS TX-392   pd   L

CAMERON COUNTY

Brownsville

Alonso Building
510-514 E. Saint Charles St.
HABS TX-3270   pd   L

Browne-Wagner House
245 E. Saint Charles St.
HABS TX-3271   pd   L

Cameron County Courthouse
1150 E. Madison St.
HABS TX-3272   pd   L

Cross Family House
911 E. Madison St.
HABS TX-3273   pd   L

Douglas Drug Store
1201 E. Elizabeth St.
HABS TX-3274   pd   L

El Globo Chiquito (Laiseca Store)
1054 E. Monroe St.
HABS TX-3275   s pd   L

El Globo Nuevo
1502 E. Madison St.
HABS TX-3276   s pd   L

Field-Pacheco Complex
1049 E. Monroe St.
HABS TX-3277   s pd   L

Fort Brown Commissary & Guard House (Building 88) (Texas Southmost College)
May St. & Gorgas Dr. vic.
HABS TX-3278   pd   L

Fort Brown Medical Laboratory (Building 84) (Texas Southmost College)
May St. & Gorgas Dr. vic.
HABS TX-3279   pd   L

Garza House
1009 E. Thirteenth St.
HABS TX-3280   pd   L

La Madrilena (Ortiz, Adrian, House)
1002 E. Madison St.
HABS TX-3281   s pd   L

Laiseca Store; see El Globo Chiquito

Neale House
230 Neale Rd. (moved from 625 E. Fourteenth St.)
HABS TX-3282   pd   L

Ortiz, Adrian, House; see La Madrilena

Sacred Heart Roman Catholic Church
E. Sixth & E. Elizabeth Sts.
HABS TX-3283   pd   L

Southern Pacific Railroad Passenger Station
601 E. Madison St.
HABS TX-3284   pd   L

Stillman House
1305 E. Washington St.
HABS TX-3285   pd   L

Texas Southmost College; see Fort Brown Commissary & Guard House (Building 88)

Texas Southmost College; see Fort Brown Medical Laboratory (Building 84)

Tijerina, Tomas, House
333 E. Adams St.
HABS TX-3286   s p d   L

Trevino House
1405 E. Jefferson St.
HABS TX-3287   s p d   L

Valdez House
815 E. Fourteenth St.
HABS TX-3288   p d   L

Brownsville vic.

Carmen Ranch House (Cortina, Juan,
    Headquarters)
Rio Grande vic.
HABS TX-33-AB-3   s p d   L

Church of the Immaculate Conception
Twelfth & Jefferson Sts.
HABS TX-3139   p d   L

Cortina, Juan, Headquarters; see Carmen
    Ranch House

Port Isabel

Point Isabel Lighthouse
NE of Brownsville
HABS TX-33-AB   s p d   L

CHAMBERS COUNTY

Anahuac

Chambers, Gen. Thomas Jefferson, House
Cummings St.
HABS TX-281   s p d   L

COLORADO COUNTY

Columbus vic.

Tait, Dr. Charles W., Plantation House
Rt. 71 vic.
HABS TX-282   s p d   L

Tait, Dr. Charles W., Town House
526 Wallace St.
HABS TX-250   p d   L

COMAL COUNTY

New Braunfels

Evandberg Orphanage (Waisenhaus; West
    Texas Orphan Asylum)
Evandberg Ave. & Guadalupe River vic.
HABS TX-3145   p d   L

First Protestant Church
HABS TX-3314   p   H

Forke, J. L., House
593 Seguin St.
HABS TX-373   p d   L

Hinman, Heinrich, House
Castell Ave.
HABS TX-3253   s p d   L

**Homann, Friedrich, Saddlery &
    Residence** (New Braunfels Coffee
    Company)
136 Seguin St.
HABS TX-33-A-11   s p d   L

Klein-Naegelin House (Naegelin House)
511 S. Seguin Ave.
HABS TX-33-A-10   s p d   L

Landa Rock Mill
Landa St., Landa Park vic.
HABS TX-3251   p d   L

Lindheimer, Ferdinand, House
491 S. Comal Ave.
HABS TX-374   s p d   L

Naegelin House; see Klein-Naegelin House

New Braunfels Coffee Company; see
    Homann, Friedrich, Saddlery &
    Residence

Schmidt, Phillip, House
354 Bridge St.
HABS TX-372   p d   L

Waisenhaus; see Evandberg Orphanage

West Texas Orphan Asylum; see
    Evandberg Orphanage

CROCKETT COUNTY

Ozona vic.

Picket & Sotol House
SW of Howard's Creek (moved to TX,
    Lubbock)
HABS TX-3316   s   H

DALLAS COUNTY

Dallas

Morehead-Gano Log House
Old City Park (moved from TX, Grapevine
    vic.)
HABS TX-3269   s   d   L H

DE WITT COUNTY

Thomastown vic.

Murphree, Thomas, House
HABS TX-279   p d   L

DEAF SMITH COUNTY

Bovina vic.

Las Escarbadas Ranch House
Tierra Blanca Draw
HABS TX-3229   s   L

DICKENS COUNTY

Dickens

Matador Half-Dugout
Dickens vic. (moved to TX, Lubbock)
HABS TX-3232   s   L

Spur-Swenson Granary
Dickens vic. (moved to TX, Lubbock)
HABS TX-3230   s   L

DONLEY COUNTY

Clarendon

Bairfield School
Farm Rd. 262 (Moved to TX, Lubbock)
HABS TX-3243   s   L

EL PASO COUNTY

El Paso

County Jail, Old
San Elizario Plaza
HABS TX-3304   p d   L

First National Bank Building (Star Jewelry)
100-102 E. San Antonio Ave.
HABS TX-3308   s p d   L

Hart, Simeon, Grist Mill
HABS TX-3109   p d   L

Hollywood Cafe; see Merrick Building

Merrick Building (St. Charles Hotel;
    Hollywood Cafe)
301-303 S. El Paso St.
HABS TX-3309   s p d   L

San Elizario Plaza Gazebo
San Elizario Plaza
HABS TX-3305   p d   L

South El Paso Street Historic District
S. El Paso, S. Oregon & S. Santa Fe Sts.
HABS TX-3307   s p d   L

St. Charles Hotel; see Merrick Building

Star Jewelry; see First National Bank
    Building

San Elizario

Casa Ronquillo; see Viceregal House

El Palacio; see Viceregal House

El Paso County Courthouse, First; see Los
    Portales

Garcia, Gregorio, House; see Los Portales

Iglesia de San Elceario (San Elizario
    Chapel)
San Elizario Plaza
HABS TX-3106   s p d   L

Los Portales (El Paso County Courthouse,
    First; Garcia, Gregorio, House)
San Elizario Plaza
HABS TX-3107   s p d   L

Lujan, Jesus, House
San Elizario Plaza
HABS TX-3108   p d   L

San Elizario Chapel; see Iglesia de San
    Elceario

Viceregal House (El Palacio; Casa
    Ronquillo; Viceroy's Palace)
SE of San Elizario Plaza
HABS TX-3110   s p d   L

Viceroy's Palace; see Viceregal House

Socorro

Mission Nuestra Senora del Socorro
Moon Rd. at Farm Rd. 258
HABS TX-3105   s p d   L

Ysleta

Mission de San Antonio de la Isleta del Sur
(Our Lady of Mount Carmel Church;
Mission Nuestra Senora del Carmen)
Alameda Ave. & Zaragosa Drive
HABS TX-3104   s pd   L

Mission Nuestra Senora del Carmen; see
Mission de San Antonio de la Isleta del
Sur

Our Lady of Mount Carmel Church; see
Mission de San Antonio de la Isleta del
Sur

Ysleta-San Elizario

El Camino de las Misiones
Ysleta, Socorro, San Elizario vic.
HABS TX-3306   s d   L

FAYETTE COUNTY

La Grange

Etario Club; see Steihl, Judge J. C., House
Frede, Francis, House (Kaulbach House)
LaFayette St.
HABS TX-3120   pd   L
Kaulbach House; see Frede, Francis, House
Kirsch, Anton, House
HABS TX-3122   pd   L
Steihl, Judge J. C., House (Etario Club)
Fannin at Franklin Sts.
HABS TX-3121   pd   L

Round Top

(Texas Pioneer Arts Foundation);
(TEXAS PIONEER ARTS
FOUNDATION); see Schumann House
II
Bethlehem Lutheran Church
White St.
HABS TX-3124   s pd   L
Henkel, Edward, House
Henkel Square, Live Oak & First Sts.
HABS TX-3196   s pd   L
Kneip, Ferdinand, House
HABS TX-3123   pd   L
Rummel, Carl Wilhelm, House
First St.
HABS TX-3200   s pd   L
Schumann House II ((Texas Pioneer Arts
Foundation))
Henkel Square
HABS TX-3197   s   H
Wantke-Pochmann House
White & Third Sts.
HABS TX-3188   s pd   L
Zapp-Von Rosenberg House
Henkel Square, Live Oak & First Sts.
HABS TX-3252   pd   L

Warrenton

Neese Homestead, Old
HABS TX-3313   s   H

FORT BEND COUNTY

Galveston

Hutchings, John Henry, House
2816 Ave. O
HABS TX-154   pd   H

GALVESTON COUNTY

Albert, J. T., House; see Turner Hall
Ashton Villa; see Brown, James Mareau,
House
Austin, Edward T., House
1502 Market St. (Ave. D)
HABS TX-261   pd   L
Ball, George, House
1405 Twenty-fourth St.
HABS TX-27   s pd   L H
Ballinger Building
2201 Post Office St.
HABS TX-3297   p   H
Berlocher, John, Building; see Strand
Historic District
Bishop's Palace; see Gresham, Col. Walter,
House
Blum, Leon & H., Building; see Strand
Historic District
B'Nai Israel Synagogue
707 Twenty-second St.
HABS TX-3298   pd   H
Bolton Estate Building; see Strand Historic
District
Brown, James Mareau, House (Ashton
Villa; El Mina Shrine Temple)
2328 Broadway
HABS TX-33-B-3   s pd   L H
Brown-Denison-Moore House (Moore,
Bartlett, House)
3112 Ave. O
HABS TX-257   pd   L
Cherry, Wilbur F., House
1602 Church St.
HABS TX-252   pd   L H
Darragh, Mrs. John L., House
519 Fifteenth St.
HABS TX-2104   pd   H
Eaton Memorial Chapel of Trinity
Episcopal Church
710 Twenty-second St.
HABS TX-295   pd   H
El Mina Shrine Temple; see Brown, James
Mareau, House
Federal Building; see U.S. Custom House
First National Bank Building; see Strand
Historic District
First Presbyterian Church
Church & Nineteenth Sts.
HABS TX-2106   pd   H
Galveston Bagging & Cordage Factory
Winnie St.
HABS TX-3319   s pd   H

Galveston News Building
2108 Mechanic St.
HABS TX-289   pd   H
Goldbeck College; see Marwitz, Herman,
House
Grace Episcopal Church
1115 Thirty-sixth St.
HABS TX-3299   p   H
Greenleve, Block & Company, Building;
see Strand Historic District
Gresham, Col. Walter, House (Bishop's
Palace)
1402 Broadway
HABS TX-2103   s pd   H
Grover, George Washington, House
1520 Market St.
HABS TX-296   pd   H
Heidenheimer Building; see Strand Historic
District
Heidenheimer Castle; see
Sydnor-Heidenheimer House
Hendley Building
2000-2016 Strand
HABS TX-290   s pd   H
Hutchings, Sealy & Company, Building;
see Strand Historic District
Jefferson, Thomas, League Building; see
Strand Historic District
Kauffman & Runge Building; see Strand
Historic District
Landes, Henry A., House
1604 Post Office St.
HABS TX-2102   pd   H
Lasker, Morris, House
1718-1726 Broadway
HABS TX-2100   pd   H
Lewis, Allen, House
2328 Ave. G (moved from Ave. J &
Twenty-fifth St.)
HABS TX-256   pd   L
Marwitz, Herman, House (Goldbeck
College)
801 Twenty-second St.
HABS TX-2105   pd   H
2014 Mechanic Street (Commercial
Building); see Strand Historic District
Menard, Michel B., House
1603 Thirty-third St.
HABS TX-26   s pd   L H
Merchants Mutual Insurance Company
Building; see Strand Historic District
Moody, M. L., House
Ave. M & Twenty-third St.
HABS TX-254   pd   L
Moody, W. L., Building; see Strand
Historic District
Moore, Bartlett, House; see
Brown-Denison-Moore House
Palmetto House-Hotel; see Strand Historic
District
Pix Building
2126 Post Office St.
HABS TX-3300   p   H

Powhatan House
3427 Ave. O
HABS TX-28   s p d   L H

Rice, Baulard & Company, Building
200 Block of Tremont
HABS TX-3301   p   H

Rosenberg Building; see Strand Historic
District

Rosenberg, Henry, House
1306 Market St.
HABS TX-260   s p d   L H

Sealy, George, House
2424 Broadway
HABS TX-298   p d   H

Smith, J. F. & Brothers, Building; see
Strand Historic District

St. Mary's Cathedral
Twenty-first St. & Church Ave.
HABS TX-293   s p d   H

St. Patrick's Catholic Church
Thirty-fourth & K Sts.
HABS TX-3302   p   H

Strand Historic District (Washington
Hotel)
23 (Tremont) & Mechanic Sts.
HABS TX-3296-P   p   H

Strand Historic District (Merchants
Mutual Insurance Company Building)
2317-2319 Strand
HABS TX-3296-K   p d   H

Strand Historic District (First National
Bank Building)
2127 Strand
HABS TX-3296-E   p   H

Strand Historic District
Strand & Mechanic Sts.
HABS TX-3296   p   H

Strand Historic District (Rosenberg
Building)
2309-2311 Strand
HABS TX-3296-M   p   H

Strand Historic District (2014 Mechanic
Street (Commercial Building))
HABS TX-3296-A   p   H

Strand Historic District (Bolton Estate
Building; Smith, J. F. & Brothers,
Building)
2321-23 Strand
HABS TX-3296-N   p d   H

Strand Historic District (Greenleve, Block
& Company, Building)
2310-2314 Strand
HABS TX-3296-G   p d   H

Strand Historic District (Hutchings, Sealy
& Company, Building)
2326-2328 Strand
HABS TX-3296-I   p   H

Strand Historic District
(Wood-Rosenfield-House-Berlocher
Buildings)
2213-2223 Strand
HABS TX-3296-B   p   H

Strand Historic District (Ufford, E. L.,
Building)
303-309 Twenty-third St.
HABS TX-3296-O   p d   H

Strand Historic District (Heidenheimer
Building)
2127 Mechanic St.
HABS TX-3296-H   p   H

Strand Historic District (Moody, W. L.,
Building)
2202-2206 Strand
HABS TX-3296-Q   p   H

Strand Historic District (Kauffman &
Runge Building)
222 Twenty-second St.
HABS TX-3296-J   p d   H

Strand Historic District (Blum, Leon & H.,
Building)
2310-2328 Mechanic St.
HABS TX-3296-D   p   H

Strand Historic District (Palmetto
House-Hotel)
2302 Mechanic St.
HABS TX-3296-L   p   H

Strand Historic District (Berlocher, John,
Building)
2315 Mechanic St.
HABS TX-3296-C   p   H

Strand Historic District (Jefferson, Thomas,
League Building)
2301-2307 Strand
HABS TX-3296-F   p d   H

Sydnor-Heidenheimer House
(Heidenheimer Castle)
1602 Sealy St.
HABS TX-2101   p d   H

Trinity Episcopal Church
708 Twenty-second St.
HABS TX-294   s p d   H

Trube, John C., House
1621-27 Sealy Ave.
HABS TX-299   p d   H

Trueheart-Adriance Building
212 Twenty-second St.
HABS TX-291   s p d   H

Turner Hall (Albert, J. T., House)
2015 Ave. I
HABS TX-21   s p d   L

Twenty-seventh Avenue H (Part of
Powhatan House)
HABS TX-28-A   p d   L

Ufford, E. L., Building; see Strand Historic
District

**University of Texas, Medical School
Building**
914-916 Strand
HABS TX-292   p d   H

Ursuline Convent
Ave. N & Twenty-fifth St.
HABS TX-3227   p d   H

U.S. Custom House (Federal Building)
Twentieth & Post Office Sts.
HABS TX-259   s p d   L H

Washington Hotel; see Strand Historic
District

Williams, Samuel May, House; see
Williams-Tucker House

Williams-Tucker House (Williams, Samuel
May, House)
3601 Ave. P
HABS TX-297   s p d   H

Wolston, John, House
1705 Thirty-fifth St.
HABS TX-258   p d   L

**Wood-Rosenfield-House-Berlocher
Buildings;** see Strand Historic District

GARZA COUNTY

Post

U Lazy S Carriage, Saddle & Harness Shop
W. Farm Rd. 669, S. of Post (moved to TX,
Lubbock)
HABS TX-3242   s   L

GILLESPIE COUNTY

Cherry Spring

Rode-Kothe House
E. of U.S. 87 at Cherry Spring
HABS TX-378   p d   L

Rode-Kothe Sheep Barn
E. of U.S. 87 at Cherry Spring
HABS TX-33-A-14   p d   L

Fredericksburg

Dietz, Heinrich G., House
Creek & Bowie Sts.
HABS TX-380   p d   L

First Courthouse (Post Office, Old)
Main & Crockett Sts.
HABS TX-33-A-7   s p d   L

Kammlah, Heinrich, House
309 W. Main St.
HABS TX-379   p d   L

Kiehne-Foerster House
405 E. Main St.
HABS TX-381   p d   L

Pfeil House
125 W. San Antonio St.
HABS TX-33-A-13   s p d   L

Post Office, Old; see First Courthouse

St. Mary's Catholic Church, Old
San Antonio St.
HABS TX-33-C-2   s p d   L

Staudt, Sunday, House
512 W. Creek St.
HABS TX-33-A-8   s p d   L

Tatsch, John Peter, House
210 N. Bowie St.
HABS TX-33-A-12   s p d   L

GOLIAD COUNTY

Goliad

Davis House (McCampbell, John S.,
   House)
HABS TX-385   pd   L
McCampbell, John S., House; see Davis
   House

Goliad vic.

Boyd, William H., House
HABS TX-303   pd   L
La Bahia Presidio Chapel
S. on U.S. Rt. 183
HABS TX-387   pd   L
Peck, Capt. Barton, House
S. of U.S. 59
HABS TX-384   pd   L

GONZALES COUNTY

Belmont vic.

King, Tom, House
HABS TX-352   pd   L

GRIMES COUNTY

Anderson vic.

Baptist Church
Main St.
HABS TX-276   pd   L
Barnes, Gen. James W., Plantation House
   (Prairie Woods)
Farm Rd. 1774 vic.
HABS TX-287   s pd   L
Black-Schroder Springhouse (Neblett
   Springhouse)
HABS TX-220   pd   L
Boggess, H. H., House
Fanthorp St., Farm Rd. 1774 vic.
HABS TX-221   pd   L
Bowman, John, House
   (Bowman-Clarke-Kelley House; Clarke
   House, Old)
W. of Anderson
HABS TX-272   pd   L
Bowman-Clarke-Kelley House; see
   Bowman, John, House
Buchanan, Dr. J. E., House
HABS TX-223   pd   L
Cawthorn, E. W., House (Womack House)
Farm Rd. 149 vic.
HABS TX-274   pd   L
Clarke House, Old; see Bowman, John,
   House
Dickson, David C., House
Farm Rd. 1774
HABS TX-273   pd   L
Fanthorp Tavern
S. Main St.
HABS TX-217   pd   L
Fuqua, Ephraim, House
La Bahia Rd.
HABS TX-275   pd   L

Green, Allen, House
HABS TX-218   pd   L
Neblett Springhouse; see Black-Schroder
   Springhouse
Pahl, Henry, House
HABS TX-219   pd   L
Prairie Woods; see Barnes, Gen. James W.,
   Plantation House
Womack House; see Cawthorn, E. W.,
   House

Navasota vic.

Bechtol House (Navasota Beauty Shop)
HABS TX-216   pd   L
Collins-Camp House (Foster House; Felder,
   Alfred, House)
HABS TX-215   pd   L
Felder, Alfred, House; see Collins-Camp
   House
Foster House; see Collins-Camp House
Freeman, Ira M., House
HABS TX-271   pd   L
Gibbs-Foster House
TX Rt. 90 vic.
HABS TX-214   pd   L
Navosota Beauty Shop; see Bechtol House

Plantersville vic.

Baker, Capt. Isaac, House; see Cedaar Hall
Cedaar Hall (Baker, Capt. Isaac, House)
HABS TX-225   pd   L
College Dormitory, Old; see Markey's
   Seminary Dormitory
Easley, A. B., House
HABS TX-227   pd   L
Markey's Seminary Dormitory (College
   Dormitory, Old)
W. edge of Plantersville
HABS TX-277   pd   L
Walton, Maj. Peter, House
HABS TX-226   pd   L

Roans Prairie vic.

Kennard, Anthony D., House
HABS TX-229   pd   L
Kennard, Mark, House
HABS TX-228   pd   L

Stoneham vic.

Sanders-McIntyre House
HABS TX-224   pd   L

GUADALUPE COUNTY

Seguin

Aunt Margaret's House
HABS TX-348   pd   L
Baxter-Fennell House (Fennell, Dr. J. D.,
   House)
202 E. Walnut St.
HABS TX-347   pd   L
Campbell, Mosey, House
HABS TX-329   pd   L
Coopender, Luke, House
HABS TX-344   pd   L

Erskine House I; see Humphrey-Erskine
   House
Erskine House II
513 E. Nolte St.
HABS TX-343   pd   L
Fennell, Dr. J. D., House; see
   Baxter-Fennell House
Flores, Manuel, House
HABS TX-340   pd   L
Herron, Parson Andrew, House
906 W. Court St.
HABS TX-345   pd   L
Herron-Vaughn House (Vaughn, Tom,
   House)
S. Goodrich St.
HABS TX-346   pd   L
Hollomon House
315 Glen Cove Dr.
HABS TX-350   pd   L
Humphrey-Erskine House (Erskine House
   I)
902 N. Austin St.
HABS TX-328   s pd   L
Isom's House
HABS TX-349   pd   L
Johnson-LeGette-Miller House (Miller,
   Thad B., House)
Johnson Ave.
HABS TX-341   pd   L
Magnolia Hotel
203 S. Crockett St.
HABS TX-327   pd   L
McCulloch, Ben, House
Kingsbury vic.
HABS TX-353   pd   L
Miller, Thad B., House; see
   Johnson-LeGette-Miller House
Sebastopol; see Young, Col. Joshua, House
Vaughn, Tom, House; see Herron-Vaughn
   House
White, Judge John P., House
HABS TX-351   pd   L
Young, Col. Joshua, House (Sebastopol;
   Zorn, Joseph, House)
704 Mill Ave.
HABS TX-33-A-9   s pd   L
Zorn, Joseph, House; see Young, Col.
   Joshua, House

Seguin vic.

Baume, Jose, de la, Cabin; see El Capote
   Cabin
El Capote Cabin (Baume, Jose, de la,
   Cabin)
S. of Guadalupe River (moved to TX,
   Lubbock)
HABS TX-3317   s   H

HALE COUNTY

Abernathy vic.

Barton, Joseph J., House
Bartonsite (moved to TX, Lubbock)
HABS TX-3315   s   H

HARRIS COUNTY

Houston

Carrington, Dr., House
Crawford St. & Rusk Ave.
HABS TX-33-B-2   s pd   L

Kellum-Noble House (Shelter House)
Sam Houston Park, 212 Dallas Ave.
HABS TX-23   s pd   L

Longcope, E., House
102 Chenevert St.
HABS TX-22   s pd   L

Nichols-Rice-Cherry House
Sam Houston Park (moved from San
    Jacinto St.)
HABS TX-33-B-1   s pd   L

Shelter House; see Kellum-Noble House

HARRISON COUNTY

Karnack vic.

Andrews-Taylor House
State Rt. 43, Farm Rd. 2862 vic.
HABS TX-147   s pd   L

Marshall vic.

Alexander House
HABS TX-124   pd   L

Carter House
HABS TX-121   pd   L

First Methodist Church South
300 E. Houston St.
HABS TX-122   pd   L

Henderson, J. B., House (Stage Coach
    Stop)
U.S. Rt. 59
HABS TX-120   pd   L

Holcombe, Beverly Lafayette, House; see
    Wyalucing

Munce House
HABS TX-123   pd   L

Stage Coach Stop; see Henderson, J. B.,
    House

Whetstone House
HABS TX-125   pd   L

Wyalucing (Holcombe, Beverly Lafayette,
    House)
Bishop & W. Bush Sts.
HABS TX-33-D-4   pd   L

HAYS COUNTY

Driftwood vic.

Camp Ben McCulloch; see Johnson's
    Institute

Friday Mountain Camp; see Johnson's
    Institute

Johnson's Institute (Camp Ben McCulloch;
    Friday Mountain Camp)
Farm Rd. 1826
HABS TX-398   pd   L

HILL COUNTY

Hillsboro

Hill County Courthouse
Public Squre, Waco, Elm, Covington &
    Franklin Sts.
HABS TX-138   pd   L

Itasca vic.

Randle-Turner House
Farm Rd. 934
HABS TX-136   s pd   L

HOCKLEY COUNTY

Levelland

Slaughter Two-Story Dugout
Levelland vic. (moved to TX, Lubbock)
HABS TX-3228   s   L

HOUSTON COUNTY

Crockett vic.

Collin, Tom, House; see Park Hill

Monroe-Coleman House
707 E. Houston St.
HABS TX-232   pd   L

Park Hill (Collin, Tom, House)
Between Farm Rds. 229 & 2076
HABS TX-233   pd   L

JEFFERSON DAVIS COUNTY

Fort Davis

Fort Davis
TX Rt. 17
HABS TX-3102   pd   L

Fort Davis, Barracks
TX Rt. 17
HABS TX-3102-A   p   L

Fort Davis, Chapel
TX Rt. 17
HABS TX-3102-B   p   L

Fort Davis, Hospital
TX Rt. 17
HABS TX-3158   s   L

Fort Davis, Magazine
TX Rt. 17
HABS TX-3159   s   L

Fort Davis, Officer's Quarters
TX Rt. 17
HABS TX-3102-C   p   L

Fort Davis, Quarters, HB-14
TX Rt. 17
HABS TX-3156   s p   L

JIM HOGG COUNTY

Cuevitas

Roderiguez, Eugenio, House & Post Office
Farm Rd. 649
HABS TX-3138   pd   L

KARNES COUNTY

Csestochowa

**Nativity of the Blessed Virgin Mary
    Church**
W. of Rt. 123
HABS TX-3261   s d   H

Panna Maria vic.

Moscygamba Houses
Off Farm Rd. 81, TX Rt. 123 vic.
HABS TX-312   pd   L

Urbanczyk House
Farm Rd. 81 vic.
HABS TX-311   pd   L

Whetstone Ranch House
Farm Rd. 81 vic.
HABS TX-388   pd   L

Pawelekville

Pawelek, Machie, House
TX. 123 at Farm Rd. 887
HABS TX-314   s pd   L

KENDALL COUNTY

Boerne vic.

Becker House; see Schertz House

Schertz House (Becker House)
Farm Rd. 474 & Spring Creek Rd.
HABS TX-375   pd   L

Comfort

Faltin House
Seventh St.
HABS TX-376   s pd   L

KERR COUNTY

Center Point vic.

Ganahl, Dr. Charles, House (Zanzenburg)
Historic marker at site on TX Rt. 27
HABS TX-377   s pd   L

Zanzenburg; see Ganahl, Dr. Charles,
    House

KING COUNTY

Truscott

Masterson Rock Bunkhouse
Truscott vic. (moved to TX, Lubbock)
HABS TX-3231   s   L

LUBBOCK COUNTY

Lubbock

Bairfield School
The Ranch Headquarters (moved from TX,
    Clarendon)
HABS TX-3243   s   L

Barton, Joseph J., House
Ranching Heritage Center (moved from
    TX, Abernathy)
HABS TX-3315   s   H

Baume, Jose, de la, Cabin; see El Capote Cabin

El Capote Cabin (Baume, Jose, de la, Cabin)
Ranching Heritage Center (moved from TX, Seguin)
HABS TX-3317   s   H

Hedwigs Hill Cabin
The Ranch Headquarters (moved from TX, Mason)
HABS TX-3233   s   L

J. A. Milk & Meat Cooler
The Ranch Headquarters (moved from TX, Claude)
HABS TX-3236   s   L

Jowell Ranch House
The Ranch Headquarters (moved from TX, Palo Pinto)
HABS TX-3237   s   L

Long S Box & Strip House
The Ranch Headquarters (moved from TX, Patricia)
HABS TX-3241   s   L

Masterson Rock Bunkhouse
The Ranch Headquarters (moved from TX, Truscott)
HABS TX-3231   s   L

Matador Guest House & Office
The Ranch Headquarters (moved from TX, Matador)
HABS TX-3262   s   L

Matador Half-Dugout
The Ranch Headquarters (moved from TX, Dickens)
HABS TX-3232   s   L

Picket & Sotol House
Ranching Heritage Center (moved from TX, Ozona)
HABS TX-3316   s   H

Renderbrook-Spade Blacksmith Shop
Ranching Heritage Center (moved from Tx, Co. City)
HABS TX-3238   s   H

Reynolds-Gentry Barn
Ranching Heritage Center (moved from TX, Albany)
HABS TX-3318   s   H

Slaughter Two-Story Dugout
The Ranch Headquarters (moved from TX, Levelland)
HABS TX-3228   s   L

Smith-Harrell House
The Ranch Headquarters (moved from TX, Snyder)
HABS TX-3235   s   L

Spur-Swenson Granary
The Ranch Headquarters (moved from TX, Dickens)
HABS TX-3230   s   L

U Lazy S Carriage, Saddle & Harness House
The Ranch Headquarters (moved from TX, Post)
HABS TX-3242   s   L

MARION COUNTY

Jefferson

Christ Episcopal Church
Main & Taylor Sts.
HABS TX-143   s pd   L

Cockell House; see Cutrer-Key House

Cutrer-Key House (Cockell House)
State Rt. 59
HABS TX-116   s pd   L

DeWare House
202 E. Dixon St.
HABS TX-149   pd   L

Epperson, Benjamin H., House; see House of the Seasons

House of the Seasons (Epperson, Benjamin H., House)
409 S. Alley St.
HABS TX-142   s pd   L

Jefferson Historical Society Museum; see U.S. Courthouse & Post Office

Murphy-Dannelly House
410 Delte St.
HABS TX-148   s pd   L

Planters Bank Building & Warehouse
224 E. Austin St.
HABS TX-144   s pd   L

Presbyterian Church
600 E. Jefferson St.
HABS TX-150   pd   L

Sedberry House
211 N. Market St.
HABS TX-151   pd   L

St. Mary's Catholic School-Sinai Hebrew Synagogue
209 N. Henderson St.
HABS TX-141   s pd   L

U.S. Courthouse & Post Office (Jefferson Historical Society Museum)
224 W. Austin St.
HABS TX-140   s pd   L

Wibler-Woods House
502 E. Walker St.
HABS TX-153   pd   L

Wright-Lester House
301 S. Friou St.
HABS TX-145   s pd   L

Jefferson vic.

Abernathy-Singleton House
204 N. Soda St.
HABS TX-146   s pd   L

Alley, D. N., Sr., House (Ward House)
209 E. Broadway
HABS TX-117   pd   L

Alley House; see Duke, W. S., House

Alley-Carlson House
501 E. Walker St.
HABS TX-152   pd   L

Beard House; see Birge, Noble A., House

Birge, Noble A., House (Beard House)
212 N. Vale St.
HABS TX-113   s pd   L

Camp, J., Building (Jefferson Journal Building)
112 N. Vale St.
HABS TX-111   pd   L

Culberson House
403 N. Walnut St.
HABS TX-114   pd   L

Duke, W. S., House (Keese House; Alley House)
112 S. Friou St.
HABS TX-119   pd   L

Excelsior Hotel (Irvine House)
Austin St.
HABS TX-112   s pd   L

Freeman, Willamson M., House
Rt. 49
HABS TX-33-D-3   s pd   L

Immaculate Conception Roman Catholic Church
201 N. Vale St.
HABS TX-13   s pd   L

Irvine House; see Excelsior Hotel

Jefferson Courthouse, Old
304 W. Broadway
HABS TX-118   pd   L

Jefferson Journal Building; see Camp, J., Building

Kahn Saloon Building
123 W. Austin St.
HABS TX-110   pd   L

Keese House; see Duke, W. S., House

Presbyterian Manse (Rogers, Gen. James Harrison, House)
221 Delta St.
HABS TX-14   s pd   L

Rogers, Gen. James Harrison, House; see Presbyterian Manse

Spellings, Solomon A., House
107 E. Clarkesville St.
HABS TX-115   pd   L

Ward House; see Alley, D. N., Sr., House

MARTIN COUNTY

Patricia

Long S Box & Strip House
Patricia vic. (moved to TX, Lubbock)
HABS TX-3241   s   L

MASON COUNTY

Mason

Hedgewigs Hill Cabin
U.S. 87 vic. (moved to TX, Lubbock)
HABS TX-3233   s   L

MEDINA COUNTY

Castroville

Landmark Inn; see Vance Hotel Complex

Simon Cabin; see Simon House

Simon House (Simon Cabin; Vance Hotel, Bathhouse)
Florence & Florella Sts.
HABS TX-3-54   pd L
Vance Hotel, Bathhouse; see Simon House
Vance Hotel Complex (Landmark Inn)
Florence & Fiorella Sts.
HABS TX-33-A-4   s p d L

Castroville vic.
Bendele, Joe, House
Angelo St.
HABS TX-357   pd L
Carle, Andrew, House
Main & Lafayette Sts.
HABS TX-33-A-5   s p d L
Carle, Joseph, House & Store
Madird & Angelo Sts. (Houston Square)
HABS TX-390   s p d L
Castro, Henry, Storehouse
HABS TX-356   pd L
Courthouse, Old
On former site of present City Hall
HABS TX-364   pd L
de Mentel, Charles, House
NW of Castroville
HABS TX-369   pd L
First Catholic Church
Angelo St.
HABS TX-359   pd L
First Lutheran Church
HABS TX-363   pd L
Goldberg, C. F., House
HABS TX-358   pd L
Haass, Louis, House
Florence St.
HABS TX-367   pd L
Hoog, Peter, House; see Tondre, Nicholas, House
Ihnken, Gerhard, House & Store
HABS TX-365   pd L
Merian, John, House
London & Angelo Sts.
HABS TX-368   pd L
Pingenot, P. F., House
Petersburg St.
HABS TX-360   pd L
Quintle & Haas Mill
Millrace, Medina River, S. of Florella St.
HABS TX-355   pd L
Quintle, Laurent, House & Store
Medina River off Hwy. 90
HABS TX-362   s p d L
Tarde Hotel
Florella & Madrid Sts.
HABS TX-389   pd L
Tondre, Nicholas, House (Hoog, Peter, House)
Florence & Amelia Sts.
HABS TX-366   pd L
Vance, John, House
Florella St.
HABS TX-361   pd L

D'hanis
Ney, Joseph, House
Parker's Creek, E. of Farm Rd. 2200
HABS TX-3100   pd L

Quihi vic.
Boehle, Louis, House
Quihi Rd.
HABS TX-33-A-18   s p d L
Von Schorobiny, Rudolph, Houses I & II
S. of Quihi
HABS TX-371   pd L

MENARD COUNTY

Fort Mc Kavet
Fort McKavett
W. of Menard on Farm Rd. 864
HABS TX-3111   pd L

MITCHELL COUNTY

Colorado City vic.
Renderbrook-Spade Blacksmith Shop
SW of Colorado River (moved to Tx, Lubbock)
HABS TX-3238   s   H

MOTLEY COUNTY

Matador
Matador Guest House & Office
TX Rt. 70 vic. (moved to TX, Lubbock)
HABS TX-3262   s   L

NACOGDOCHES COUNTY

Chireno vic.
Old Half-Way Inn
W. of Chireno on TX Rt. 21
HABS TX-33-D-5   s p d L

Nacogdoches vic.
Bean, Peter Ellis, House
Melrose Rd.
HABS TX-236   pd L
Church of the Divine Infant (Sacred Heart Church)
Cotton Ford Rd.
HABS TX-266   pd L
Hoya Library; see Sterne, Adolphus, House
Nacogdoches University
High School Grounds, Washington Square
HABS TX-235   pd L
Sacred Heart Church; see Church of the Divine Infant
Sterne, Adolphus, House (Hoya Library)
211 LaNana St.
HABS TX-234   pd L
Ybarbo Ranch House
Stephen F. Austin College Grounds
HABS TX-268   pd L

NUECES COUNTY

Corpus Christi
Muely, Conrad, House & Store
210 Chaparral St.
HABS TX-3114   s pd L

PALO PINTO COUNTY

Palo Pinto
Jowell Ranch House
Possum Kingdom Lake (moved to TX, Lubbock)
HABS TX-3237   s   L

PANOLA COUNTY

Carthage vic.
Collins, Jasper, House
HABS TX-15   pd L
Morris, Dempsey, House
HABS TX-17   pd L
Parker, J. B., House
201 W. Sabine
HABS TX-18   pd L
Snow House
HABS TX-16   pd L

PRESIDIO COUNTY

Presidio vic.
Fort Leaton
SE of Presidio between Farm Rd. 170 & Rio Grande
HABS TX-3103   s pd L

Shafter vic.
Fortin de Cibolo (Little Fort of Cibolo)
Cibolo Creek
HABS TX-3118   pd L
Fortin de Cienega
Cienega Creek
HABS TX-3119   s pd L
Little Fort of Cibolo; see Fortin de Cibolo

SABINE COUNTY

Milam vic.
Gaines-McGowan House
Toledo Bend Reservoir site
HABS TX-267   pd L

SAN AUGUSTINE COUNTY

San Augustine
Blount, Col. Stephen W., House
501 E. Columbia St.
HABS TX-33-D-1   s p d L
Cartwright, Columbus, House
Sharp St.
HABS TX-239   pd L

Cartwright, Matthew, House
505 E. Main St.
HABS TX-238   s p d   L

Cullen-Roberts House
Congress & Market Sts.
HABS TX-237   p d   L

Johnson, C. C., House
Congress St.
HABS TX-242   p d   L

San Augustine vic.

Garrett, William, Plantation House
TX Rt. 21
HABS TX-33-D-2   s p d   L

Hale-Blount House
TX Rt. 21
HABS TX-240   p d   L

Sublett, Col. Phillip A., House
TX Rt. 21
HABS TX-241   p d   L

SCURRY COUNTY

Snyder

Smith-Harrell House
N. of Snyder (moved to TX, Lubbock)
HABS TX-3235   s   L

SHELBY COUNTY

Center vic.

Jones, Louis, House
HABS TX-12   p d   L

Smith, Emzy C., House
N. of Farm Rd. 2026
HABS TX-11   p d   L

SMITH COUNTY

Bullard vic.

Dewberry, Col. John, Plantation House
Farm Rd. 346
HABS TX-133   p d   L

Douglas House
HABS TX-134   p d   L

Loftin, Pitt, House
Farm Rd. 344
HABS TX-132   p d   L

Loftkin, Alf, House
HABS TX-135   p d   L

STARR COUNTY

Rio Grande City

Courthouse, Old
Water St. at Texas Ave.
HABS TX-33-AB-2   s p d   L

Davis, Henry Clay, House
Britton Ave.
HABS TX-33-AB-4   s p d   L

Pena, Silverio De La, Drugstore & Post Office
Main & Lopez Sts.
HABS TX-3136   p d   L

Ramirez, Jose, House
Corpus & Third Sts.
HABS TX-3133   p d   L

Roma

Church of our Lady of Refuge of Sinners
N. end of Main Plaza on Estrella St.
HABS TX-3135   p d   L

Garcia, Leocadia Leandro, House
SW corner of Main Plaza
HABS TX-3131   p d   L

Guerra, Manuel, Residence & Store
W. side of Main Plaza at Hidalgo St.
HABS TX-3146   p d   L

Ramirez, Rafael Garcia, House
E. side of Main Plaza at Hidalgo St.
HABS TX-3134   p d   L

Saens, Nextor, Store
Hidalgo St. & Juarez Alley
HABS TX-3129   s p d   L

TARRANT COUNTY

Fort Worth

Pollock-Capps House
1120 Penn St.
HABS TX-3240   s p d   H

Wharton-Scott House
1509 Pennsylvania St.
HABS TX-3289   s   H

Grapevine vic.

Morehead-Gano Log House
Rt. 121, NW of Bethel Rd. (moved to TX, Dallas)
HABS TX-3269   s d   L H

THROCKMORTON COUNTY

Alvany vic.

Reynolds-Gentry Barn
Clearfork at Brazos River (moved to TX, Lubbock)
HABS TX-3318   s   H

TRAVIS COUNTY

Austin

Bremond, Eugene, House
404 W. Seventh St.
HABS TX-3143   p d   L

Bremond, John, House
W. Seventh & Guadalupe Sts.
HABS TX-3140   p d   L

Carrington-Covert House
1511 Colorado St.
HABS TX-3311   p d   L

French Legation to Republic of Texas
Seventh & San Marcos Sts.
HABS TX-33-C-1   s p d   L

General Land Office; see Land Office

Gethsemane Lutheran Church
Sixteenth St. & Congress Ave.
HABS TX-3137   s p d   L

Goodman Building
202 W. Thirteenth St.
HABS TX-3263   s p d   L

Governor's Mansion
1010 Colorado St.
HABS TX-33-C-4   s p d   L

Houghton Carriage House
1111 Guadalupe St., rear of 307 W. Twelfth St.
HABS TX-3624-A   s p d   L

Houghton, John H., House
307 W. Twelfth St.
HABS TX-3264   s p d   L

Land Office (General Land Office; Land Office, Old)
108 E. Eleventh St.
HABS TX-397   s p d   L

Land Office, Old; see Land Office

Lundberg Bakery
1006 Congress Ave.
HABS TX-3267   s p d   L

Millett, C. F., Mansion
Ninth & Brazos Sts.
HABS TX-3142   p d   L

Neill-Cochran Residence
2310 San Gabriel St.
HABS TX-3239   s d   H

Orsay Tenant House
310 E. Fourteenth St.
HABS TX-3265   s p d   L

Pease, Gov. Elisha M., Mansion (Woodlawn)
6 Niles Rd.
HABS TX-330   p d   L

Raymond, Nathaniel, House
204 E. Twenty-fourth St.
HABS TX-331   p d   L

Simms-Vance House
1802 San Gabriel St.
HABS TX-33-C-3   s p d   L

Smith House
502 W. Thirteenth St.
HABS TX-3312   p   H

Taylor-Hunnicutt House
405 W. Twelfth St. (moved from Guadalupe St.)
HABS TX-3268   s p d   L

Texas State Capitol
Congress & Eleventh Sts.
HABS TX-3326   p d   L

Townsend, Angela, House
1802 West Ave.
HABS TX-3141   p d   L

504 West Fourteenth Street (House)
HABS TX-3266   s p d   L

502 West Thirteenth Street (House)
HABS TX-3295   p d   L

Woodlawn; see Pease, Gov. Elisha M., Mansion

Austin vic.

Sneed, Judge Sebron G., House
Rt. I-35 & Bluff Springs Rd.
HABS TX-399   s p d   L

VAL VERDE COUNTY

Langtry

Bean, Judge Roy, Saloon & Justice Court
(Jersey Lilly Saloon)
HABS TX-3101   p d   L
Jersey Lilly Saloon; see Bean, Judge Roy,
Saloon & Justice Court

VICTORIA COUNTY

Mission Valley vic.

Davidson, Quincy, House
HABS TX-248   p d   L
De Leon, Patricio, Ranch House
HABS TX-278   p d   L
Rives, James, House
HABS TX-246   p d   L

Victoria

Callender, William L., House
404 W. Guadalupe St.
HABS TX-247   s p d   L
Goldman, A., House
HABS TX-245   p d   L
Rupley Building
HABS TX-280   p d   L

WALKER COUNTY

Huntsville vic.

Yoakum, Henderson, House
HABS TX-231   p d   L

WALLER COUNTY

Hempstead vic.

Croce, Leonard, Plantation House; see
Liendo
Liendo (Croce, Leonard, Plantation House)
Farm Rd. 1488 & Wyatt Chapel Rd. vic.
HABS TX-33-B-4   s p d   L

WASHINGTON COUNTY

Chappell Hill

Stage Coach Tavern
Farm Rd. 1155 at Farm Rd. 2447
HABS TX-24   s p d   L H

Chappell Hill vic.

Browning, Col. William W., House
Farm Rds. 1155 & 1371
HABS TX-265   p d   L
Sledge, Col. William Madison, House
(Smith, John, House)
W. of Chappell Hill
HABS TX-25   s p d   L
Smith, John, House; see Sledge, Col.
William Madison, House

Independence

Blue, J. M., House
HABS TX-210   p d   L

Independence vic.

Baptist Church
Farm Rds. 390 & 50
HABS TX-29   p d   L
Clark House; see Holmes, Willett, House
Holmes, Willett, House (Clark House)
HABS TX-211   p d   L
Houston, Sam, House
Farm Rd. 390
HABS TX-264   p d   L
Mexican Jail (Toalson House)
Farm Rds. 390 & 50 vic.
HABS TX-263   p d   L
Robertson, Gen. Jerome B., House
Farm Rds. 50 & 390
HABS TX-33-B-9   s p d   L
Seward, John H., House
Farm Rd. 390
HABS TX-33-B-8   s p d   L
Seward, Samuel, House
NE of Independence
HABS TX-262   p d   L
Toalson House; see Mexican Jail

Washington vic.

Barrington (House); see Jones, Anson,
House
Brown, John M., House
Farm Rd. 912
HABS TX-213   s p d   L
Jones, Anson, House (Barrington (House))
Brazos State Park vic.
HABS TX-212   p d   L

WEBB COUNTY

Laredo

Bertani, Paul Prevost, House
604 Iturbide St.
HABS TX-3293   s p d   L

de la Garza, Zoila, House
509 Iturbide St.
HABS TX-3291   s p d   L
**Leyendecker, Jo Emma, & Salinas, Dr.
Guillermo, House**
702 Iturbide St.
HABS TX-3290   s p d   L
Montemayor, Jose A., House (Vela, Carlos,
House)
601 Zaragosa St.
HABS TX-3292   s p d   L
Vela, Carlos, House; see Montemayor, Jose
A., House
Viscaya de Leal, Rosario, House
620 Zaragosa St.
HABS TX-3294   s p d   L

WILLIAMSON COUNTY

Round Rock vic.

Anderson, Washington, House (El Milagro)
TX Rt. 79 at NE edge of Round Rock
HABS TX-2106   p d   L
Cole, Dr. J. T., House (Stage Shop, Old)
W. of I-35 access Rd.
HABS TX-3144   p d   L
El Milagro; see Anderson, Washington,
House
Merrell, Capt. Nelson, House
E. of I-35 on TX Rt. 79
HABS TX-3132   p d   L
Stage Shop, Old; see Cole, Dr. J. T., House

Taylor vic.

McFadin, D. H., House
Farm Rd. 1331, E. of TX Rt. 95
HABS TX-339   p d   L

WILSON COUNTY

Floresville vic.

Seguin, Juan N., Ranch House
NW of Floresville
HABS TX-39   s p d   L
Yndo, Miguel, House
Farm Rd. 1303
HABS TX-37   p d   L

Labatt

Flores, Francisco, Ranch House
HABS TX-38   p d   L

Poth vic.

Beauregard Ranch Buildings
S. of Poth
HABS TX-310   pd   L

Sutherland Springs

Polley, Col. Joseph H., House; see
    Whitehall
Whitehall (Polley, Col. Joseph H., House)
Farm Rd. 539
HABS TX-326   s pd   L

YOUNG COUNTY

Newcastle vic.

Fort Belknap
S. on TX Rt. 251
HABS TX-33-D-7   s pd   L

ZAPATA COUNTY

Falcon vic.

Ramirez, Jose, House
Falcon Reservoir Site
HABS TX-3130   s   L

San Ygnacio

San Ygnacio Ranch Buildings (Trevino,
    Jesus, House)
Uribe & Trevino Sts.
HABS TX-3112   s pd   L
Trevino, Jesus, House; see San Ygnacio
    Ranch Buildings

Zapata vic.

San Bartolo Ranch Buildings
Falcon Reservoir Site
HABS TX-3113   pd   L

Utah

BEAVER COUNTY

Beaver

Beaver County Courthouse
Center & First East Sts.
HABS UT-61   s pd   L

BOX ELDER COUNTY

Brigham City

Mercantile & Manufacturing Association
    Tannery
First East St.
HABS UT-46   pd   L
Snow, Lorenzo, House
Forest St.
HABS UT-45   pd   L
Southern Pacific RR, Ogden-Lucin Cutoff
    Trestle
HAER UT-13   s pd   L

Collinston vic.

Bear River Hotel; see Hampton's Ford
    Stage Station
Hampton's Ford Stage Station (Bear River
    Hotel)
State Rt. 154
HABS UT-42   s pd   L
Hampton's Ford Stage Station, Barn
State Rt. 154
HABS UT-43   pd   L

Corinne

Methodist Episcopal Church
Colorado & S. Sixth Sts.
HABS UT-40   pd   L

Fielding vic.

Irrigation Diversion Canal
Bear River
HAER UT-9   p   L
Utah Sugar Company, Wheelon
    Hydoelectric Plant
Bear River
HAER UT-8   s pd   L

Garland vic.

Utah Sugar Company
Factory St.
HAER UT-19   s pd   L

Willard

Baird, Robert Bell, House
195 W. Central St.
HABS UT-89   s   d   H
Edwards, John, Granary
55 S. Second St.
HABS UT-90-A   s   H
Edwards, John, House
55 S. Second St.
HABS UT-90   s   d   H
Jones, Shadrach, House
101 W. Second St.
HABS UT-86   s   d   H
Mason, George, Granary
150 N. Second West St.
HABS UT-92-A   s   H
Mason, George, House
150 N. Second West St.
HABS UT-92   s   d   H

CACHE COUNTY

Cache Junction

Cache Junction Depot
HABS UT-92   s   d   H

Logan

Oregon Short Line Railroad Station
    (Union Pacific Railroad Station)
Sixth West St.
HABS UT-44   s pd   L
Temple Barn
368 E. Second North
HABS UT-84   s   d   H
Union Pacific Railroad Station; see Oregon
    Short Line Railroad Station

EMERY COUNTY

Emery

Emery Latter-Day Saints Church
Block 23
HABS UT-96   s   d   H

GARFIELD COUNTY

Panguitch

Bishop's Storehouse
Center St. & First East
HABS UT-95   s   d   H

GRAND COUNTY

Green River

Irrigation Water Wheel
Hastings Ranch
HAER UT-18   p   L

IRON COUNTY

Cedar City

Bladen, Mary, House
200 West St.
HABS UT-6   p   L
Haight, Isaac C., House
200 North & 100 East Sts.
HABS UT-5   p   L
Hunter, Joseph S., House
86 E. Center St.
HABS UT-7   p   L
Pioneer Cabin; see Wood, George Lamar,
    Cabin
Wood, George Lamar, Cabin (Pioneer
    Cabin)
City Park (moved from original location)
HABS UT-4   p   L

Old Irontown

Coke Oven
State Rt. 56 vic.
HABS UT-59   s pd   L

MILLARD COUNTY

Cove Fort
Cove Fort
State Rts. 4 & 161
HABS UT-57   s pd   L

Fillmore
Callister, Bishop Thomas, House
30 W. Center St.
HABS UT-75   p   L
Rock Schoolhouse
First West & First South Sts.
HABS UT-32   s pd   L
Territorial Capital
Main, Center, First South & First West Sts.
HABS UT-33   pd   L

SALT LAKE COUNTY

Bingham Canyon
International Smelting & Refining Company (Tooele Smelter, Roaster Ore Bins)
Bingham Canyon
HAER UT-20-E   pd   L
International Smelting & Refining Company (Tooele Smelter; Reverberatory, Converter & Casting Building)
Bingham Canyon
HAER UT-20-G   pd   L
Reverberatory, Converter & Casting Building; see International Smelting & Refining Company
Tooele Smelter; see International Smelting & Refining Company
Tooele Smelter, Roaster Ore Bins; see International Smelting & Refining Company
Utah Copper Company, Bingham Canyon Mine
State Rt. 48
HAER UT-21   s pd   L

Holladay
Big Cottonwood Power Co., Hydro. Plant (Stairs); see Utah Power Co., Hydroelectric Plant (Stairs)
Big Cottonwood Power Co., Hydroelectric Plant; see Utah Power Company, Granite Hydroelectric Plant
Big Cottonwood Power Company; see Utah Power Company
Utah Power Co., Hydroelectric Plant (Stairs) (Big Cottonwood Power Co., Hydro. Plant (Stairs))
HAER UT-3   pd   L
Utah Power Company (Big Cottonwood Power Company; Wooden Flume, Stairs)
HAER UT-3A   pd   L
Utah Power Company, Granite Hydroelectric Plant (Big Cottonwood Power Co., Hydroelectric Plant)
HAER UT-4   pd   L

Wooden Flume, Stairs; see Utah Power Company

Magna
Kennecott Copper Company, Magna Concentrator; see Utah Copper Company, Magna Concentrator
Utah Copper Company, Magna Concentrator (Kennecott Copper Company, Magna Concentrator)
HAER UT-24   s pd   L

Riverton
Jordan Narrows Hydroelectric Plant; see Salt Lake City Water & Electrical Power Co.
Salt Lake City Water & Electrical Power Co. (Jordan Narrows Hydroelectric Plant)
Jordan River
HAER UT-15   pd   L

Salt Lake City
Beehive House (Young, Brigham, House)
E. South Temple St.
HABS UT-36-U-1   s pd   L
Chase, Isaac Mill
Sixth East St.
HABS UT-49   s pd   L
Church of Jesus Christ of Latter-Day Saints; see Salt Lake Tabernacle
Church of Jesus Christ of Latter-Day Saints; see Salt Lake Temple
Church of Jesus Christ of Latter-Day Saints; see Seventh Ward Chapel
Conklin-Dern Mansion
711 E. South Temple St.
HABS UT-73   pd   L
Culmer, William H., House
33 C St.
HABS UT-85   s d   H
Deuel, Osmyn, Log Cabin
Temple Square (moved from original site)
HABS UT-36-U-3   pd   L
Devereaux; see Staines-Jennings Mansion
Dooly Building
109 W. Second South St.
HABS UT-91   pd   L
Eico Overhead Loader
HAER UT-29   pd   L
Fisher, Albert, Carriage House
1206 W. Second South St.
HABS UT-50   s pd   L
Fort Douglas, Building Number 55; see Fort Douglas, Commander's Residence
Fort Douglas, Commander's Residence (Fort Douglas, Building Number 55)
HABS UT-68   p   L
Fort Douglas, Officers' Duplexes
Officers' Circle
HABS UT-67   s pd   L
Fourteenth District School; see Fremont School

Fremont School (Fourteenth District School)
139 S. Second West St.
HABS UT-24   s pd   L
Granite Paper Mill
6900 Big Cottonwood Canyon Rd.
HABS UT-39   pd   L
Interstate Pressed Brick Company; see Salt Lake Pressed Brick Company
Keith-Brown Mansion
529 E. South Temple
HABS UT-97   s d   H
McCune, Alfred W., Mansion
200 N. Main St.
HABS UT-87   s d   H
Meyer, Frederick A. E., House
929 E. Second South St.
HABS UT-51   s pd   L H
Mormon Temple; see Salt Lake Temple
Moutain Dell Dam
Interstate Hwy. 80
HAER UT-16   s pd   L
Nelson-Wheeler-Whipple House
564 W. 400 North
HABS UT-100   s pd   H
Perkins, Francis H., House
77 S St.
HABS UT-98   pd   L
Salt Lake Pressed Brick Company (Interstate Pressed Brick Company)
1100 East St.
HAER UT-7   pd   L
Salt Lake Tabernacle (Church of Jesus Christ of Latter-Day Saints)
Temple Square
HABS UT-36-U-2
HAER UT-1   s pd   L
Salt Lake Temple (Church of Jesus Christ of Latter-Day Saints; Mormon Temple)
Temple Square
HABS UT-2   p   L
Seventh Ward Chapel (Church of Jesus Christ of Latter-Day Saints)
116 W. Fifth South St.
HABS UT-22   s pd   L
Seventh Ward Recreation Hall; see Whittier School
St. Mark's Episcopal Cathedral
231 E. First South St.
HABS UT-41   s pd   L
Staines-Jennings Mansion (Devereaux)
334 W. South Temple St.
HABS UT-37   s pd   L
Union Pacific Railroad Station
400 East St.
HABS UT-88   s d   H

Utah Commercial & Savings Bank
22 E. First South St.
HABS UT-72   s pd   L

Whittier School (Seventh Ward Recreation Hall)
120 W. Fifth South St.
HABS UT-23   pd   L

Young, Brigham, House; see Beehive House

Z. C. M. I.; see Zion's Cooperative Mercantile Institution

Zion's Cooperative Mercantile Institution (Z. C. M. I.)
15 S. Main St.
HABS UT-47   s p d   L

Zion's First National Bank Clock
First South & Main sts.
HABS UT-48   p   L

SANPETE COUNTY

Ephraim

Ephraim Co-op Building; see Ephraim United Order Mercantile Institution

Ephraim United Order Mercantile Institution (Ephraim Co-op Building)
Main & First North
HABS UT-106   d   H

Peterson, Canute, House
10 N. Main St.
HABS UT-64   s p d   L

Gunnison

Casino Theater (Star Theater)
Main St. (U.S. Rt. 89)
HABS UT-76   p   L

Star Theater; see Casino Theater

Manti

Church of Jesus Christ of Latter-Day Saints; see Manti Temple

Manti Temple (Church of Jesus Christ of Latter-Day Saints)
Main St. (U.S. Rt. 89)
HABS UT-71   pd   L

Spring City

Bishop's Storehouse; see Spring City Area Study

Church of Jesus Christ of Latter-day Saints; see Spring City Area Study

City Hall; see Spring City Area Study

Hons, Peter, House; see Spring City Area Study

House, Adobe; see Spring City Area Study

House, Frame; see Spring City Area Study

House, Stone; see Spring City Area Study

Hyde, Orson, House; see Spring City Area Study

Log Cabin; see Spring City Area Study

Log Cabin; see Spring City Area Study

Masonic Lodge; see Spring City Area Study

Public School; see Spring City Area Study

Spring City Area Study (Log Cabin)
HABS UT-70-H   p   L

Spring City Area Study (Masonic Lodge)
B St.
HABS UT-70-I   p   L

Spring City Area Study (Hyde, Orson, House)
Main & C Sts.
HABS UT-70-F   p   L

Spring City Area Study (Bishop's Storehouse)
Fourth & E Sts.
HABS UT-70-B   p   L

Spring City Area Study (House, Frame)
Second & B Sts.
HABS UT-70-D   p   L

Spring City Area Study (Log Cabin)
First & B Sts.
HABS UT-70-G   p   L

Spring City Area Study (City Hall)
Main St.
HABS UT-70-C   p   L

Spring City Area Study (Hons, Peter, House)
Fourth & F Sts.
HABS UT-70-E   p   L

Spring City Area Study
HABS UT-70   s p d   L

Spring City Area Study (Tithing Office)
Second St.
HABS UT-70-M   p   L

Spring City Area Study (House, Stone)
Main & F Sts.
HABS UT-70-K   p   L

Spring City Area Study (House, Adobe)
First St.
HABS UT-70-A   p   L

Spring City Area Study (Tithing Barn)
Second St.
HABS UT-70-L   p   L

Spring City Area Study (Ward Chapel; Church of Jesus Christ of Latter-day Saints)
Main St.
HABS UT-70-N   p   L

Spring City Area Study (Public School)
Fourth & E Sts.
HABS UT-70-J   p   L

Tithing Barn; see Spring City Area Study

Tithing Office; see Spring City Area Study

Ward Chapel; see Spring City Area Study

SUMMIT COUNTY

Hoytsville

Hoyt, Samuel Pierce, House
U.S. Rt. 189 vic.
HABS UT-62   s pd   L

Hoyt, Samuel Pierce, Mill
U.S. Rt. 189 vic.
HABS UT-63   pd   L

Park City

New Deal Market
204 Main St.
HABS UT-99   pd   L

Silver King Mining Co., Ore Loading Station
HAER UT-11   s pd   L

St. Mary of the Assumption Church
Park Ave.
HABS UT-35   pd   L

St. Mary of the Assumption School
Park Ave.
HABS UT-34   s pd   L

Park City vic.

Calfornia Comstock Mill
HAER UT-26   pd   L

Keystone Mill
HAER UT-28   pd   L

Silver King Mining Co., Covered Tramway
Park City West
HAER UT-22-C   pd   L

Silver King Mining Co., Main Shaft & Hoist
Park City West
HAER UT-22-A   s pd   L

Silver King Mining Company, Ore Mill
Park City West
HAER UT-22-B   pd   L

Silver King Mining Company, Silver King Mine
Woodside Gulch
HAER UT-22   s p   H

Silver King Mining Company, Warehouse
Park City West
HAER UT-22-D   p   L

Silver King Mining Company, Water Tanks
Park City West
HAER UT-22-E   p   L

Silver Creek Jct.

Kimball Hotel
U.S. Rt. 40
HABS UT-53   s pd   L

TOOELE COUNTY

Knolls/Wendover vic.

Lincoln Highway, Wendover Cutoff
Great Salt Lake Desert
HAER UT-23   s pd   L

Ophir

DeLamar Mercur Mines Co., Golden Gate Mill
HAER UT-10   pd   L

Town Hall
43 Main St.
HABS UT-38   s pd   L

Tooele

International Smelting & Refining Company (Tooele Smelter)
State Rt. 178
HAER UT-20   s pd   L

Tooele County Courthouse & City Hall
Vine St.
HABS UT-52   s pd   L

Tooele Smelter; see International Smelting & Refining Company

Tooele vic.

International Smelting & Refining Company (Tooele Smelter, Miscellaneous Ore Bins)
Bingham Canyon
HAER UT-20-H   p d   L

International Smelting & Refining Company (Tooele Smelter, Charge Bins)
Bingham Canyon
HAER UT-20-J   p d   L

International Smelting & Refining Company (Tooele Smelter, Powerhouse)
Bingham Canyon
HAER UT-20-A   s p d   L

International Smelting & Refining Company (Tooele Smelter, Office Building)
Bingham Canyon
HAER UT-20-B   p   L

International Smelting & Refining Company (Tooele Smelter, Drossing Plant)
Bingham Canyon
HAER UT-20-L   p d   L

International Smelting & Refining Company (Tooele Smelter, Sample Mill)
Bingham Canyon
HAER UT-20-D   p   L

International Smelting & Refining Company (Tooele Smelter, Receiving Bins)
Bingham Canyon
HAER UT-20-C   p d   L

International Smelting & Refining Company (Tooele Smelter, Sinter Plant)
Bingham Canyon
HAER UT-20-I   p   H

International Smelting & Refining Company (Tooele Smelter, Blast Furnace Building)
Bingham Canyon
HAER UT-20-K   p d   L

International Smelting & Refining Company (Tooele Smelter, Roaster Building)
Bingham Canyon
HAER UT-20-F   p d   L

Tooele Smelter, Blast Furnace Building; see International Smelting & Refining Company

Tooele Smelter, Charge Bins; see International Smelting & Refining Company

Tooele Smelter, Drossing Plant; see International Smelting & Refining Company

Tooele Smelter, Miscellaneous Ore Bins; see International Smelting & Refining Company

Tooele Smelter, Office Building; see International Smelting & Refining Company

Tooele Smelter, Powerhouse; see International Smelting & Refining Company

Tooele Smelter, Receiving Bins; see International Smelting & Refining Company

Tooele Smelter, Roaster Building; see International Smelting & Refining Company

Tooele Smelter, Sample Mill; see International Smelting & Refining Company

Tooele Smelter, Sinter Plant; see International Smelting & Refining Company

UINTAH COUNTY

Vernal

Ashley Post Office
1335 W. 2000 North
HABS UT-94   s d   H

UTAH COUNTY

Fairfield

Carson, John, House (Stagecoach Inn)
Main St.
HABS UT-31   p d   L

District School
N. Church St.
HABS UT-29   s p d   L

District School Gymnasium
N. Church St.
HABS UT-30   p   L

Stagecoach Inn; see Carson, John, House

Goshen vic.

Tintic Standard Reduction Mill
Warm Springs Mtn.
HAER UT-12   s p d   L

Olmstead

Denver & Rio Grande Western RR, Provo River Bridge
Spanning Provo River
HAER UT-14   p d   L

Orem vic.

Telluride Power Co., Nunn Hydroelectric Plant
Provo River
HAER UT-2   p d   L

Telluride Power Co., Olmstead Hydroelectric Plant
Provo River
HAER UT-5   s p d   L

Telluride Power Company, Provo River Bridge
Spanning Provo River
HAER UT-2A   p d   L

Pleasant Grove

Fugal Blacksmith Shop
650 N. Fourth East St.
HABS UT-56   s p d   L

Halliday, John R., House
90 E. Second North
HABS UT-93   s d   H

Provo

Provo Brickyard, Turbine House
1620 N. 200 West St.
HABS UT-36   s p d   L

WASATCH COUNTY

Heber City

Church of Jesus Christ of Latter-Day Saints; see Wasatch Stake Tabernacle

Hatch, Abram, House
81 E. Center St.
HABS UT-83   s p d   L

Heber Amusement Hall
100 North & 100 West Sts.
HABS UT-28   s p d   L

Heber Light & Power Company
HAER UT-6   s p d   L

Wasatch County Courthouse
Main St.
HABS UT-25   s p d   L

Wasatch County Jail
Center St.
HABS UT-26   s p d   L

Wasatch Stake Tabernacle (Church of Jesus Christ of Latter-Day Saints)
Main St.
HABS UT-27   s p d   L

Midway

Watkins-Coleman House
5 E. Main St.
HABS UT-54   s p d   L

WASHINGTON COUNTY

Hurricane

Hurricane Irrigation Canal
State Rt. 15 vic.
HAER UT-17   s p d   L

Leeds

Angell, George E. House; see Wilkinson, Charles, House

Stirling, William, House
HABS UT-77   p   L

Wilkinson, Charles, House (Angell, George E. House)
HABS UT-78   p   L

Middleton

McDonald, Alexander F., House
HABS UT-79   p   L

Pine Valley

Church of Jesus Christ of Latter-Day Saints; see Pine Valley Ward Chapel

Pine Valley Tithing Office
Main St.
HABS UT-69   pd   L

Pine Valley Ward Chapel (Church of Jesus Christ of Latter-Day Saints)
Main & Grass Valley Sts.
HABS UT-60   s pd   L

Rockville

Deseret Telegraph & Post Office Building
State Rt. 15
HABS UT-36-U-4   s pd   L

Silver Reef

Wells, Fargo & Company Express Building
Main St.
HABS UT-58   s pd   L

St. George

Blake, B. F., House
141 S. 100 East St.
HABS UT-80   p   L

Burgess, Melancthon W., House
HABS UT-12   p   L

Cannon, David H., House
49 E. 100 South St.
HABS UT-9   p   L

Chamber of Commerce; see Washington County Courthouse

Church of Jesus Christ of Latter-Day Saints; see St. George Tabernacle

Ivins, Anthony W., House (Ivins, Israel, House)
157 N. 100 West St.
HABS UT-18   p   L

Ivins, Israel, House; see Ivins, Anthony W., House

Lund, Robert, House
100 West & 200 North Sts.
HABS UT-15   p   L

McArthur, Daniel D., House
159 W. Tabernacle St.
HABS UT-11   p   L

Saigmiller House
HABS UT-19   p   L

Snow, Erastus, House
150 N. Main St.
HABS UT-13   p   L

162 South 300 West Street (House)
HABS UT-81   p   L

St. George Tabernacle (Church of Jesus Christ of Latter-Day Saints)
Main St.
HABS UT-16   s pd   L

St. George Tithing Office
Main & Tabernacle Sts.
HABS UT-8   p   L

Washington County Courthouse (Chamber of Commerce)
100 North St.
HABS UT-10   p   L

Woolley, Edwin G., House
217 N. 100 West St.
HABS UT-14   p   L

Young, Brigham, Office
200 North St.
HABS UT-20   pd   L

Young, Brigham, Winter House
200 North & 100 West Sts.
HABS UT-66   pd   L

Toquerville

Naegle Winery
Spring St. (State Rt. 15)
HABS UT-65   pd   L

Spilsbury, David, House
Spring St. (State Rt. 15)
HABS UT-82   p   L

Washington

Chapel of Jesus Christ of Latter-Day Saints; see Washington Ward Chapel

Covington, Bishop Robert D., House
HABS UT-3   p   L

Pioneer Cotton Mill; see Washington Cotton Mill

Washington Cotton Mill (Pioneer Cotton Mill)
Mill Creek
HABS UT-1   s pd   L

Washington Ward Chapel (Chapel of Jesus Christ of Latter-Day Saints)
HABS UT-17   p   L

WAYNE COUNTY

Fruita

Capitol Reef National Monument; see Fruita School House

Fruita School House (Capitol Reef National Monument)
State Rt. 24
HABS UT-21   s pd   L

WEBER COUNTY

Ogden

Goodyear, Miles, Cabin
Tabernacle Park
HABS UT-55   s d   L

Union Pacific Railroad, Gateway Bridge
Spanning Weber Canyon
HAER UT-27   s pd   L

Vermont

ADDISON COUNTY

Middlebury

Congregational Church
Main & Seymour Sts.
HABS VT-11   pd   L

Middlebury College, Administration Building; see Middlebury College, Old Chapel

Middlebury College, Old Chapel (Middlebury College, Administration Building)
Rt. 30
HABS VT-89   p   L

Middlebury College, Painter Hall
Rt. 30
HABS VT-88   p   L

Middlebury Community House; see Seymour, Horatio, House

Painter, Gamaliel, House
Court & S. Pleasant Sts.
HABS VT-84   p   L

Seymour, Horatio, House (Middlebury Community House)
Main & Seymour Sts.
HABS VT-85   p   L

Orwell

Baptist Church (Community Hall)
Rt. 73
HABS VT-74   p   L

Benson-Orwell Parish; see Congregational Church

Community Hall; see Baptist Church

Congregational Church (Benson-Orwell Parish; United Church of Christ)
Rt. 73
HABS VT-75   p   L

United Church of Christ; see Congregational Church

Orwell vic.

Willcox-Cutts Mansion
Rt. 22A
HABS VT-72   p   L

Vergennes

Strong, Gen. Samuel, House
W. Main St.
HABS VT-12   s pd   L

BENNINGTON COUNTY

Arlington

Canfield, Martha, Library; see Smith-Canfield House

Smith-Canfield House (Canfield, Martha, Library)
Rt. 7 vic.
HABS VT-83 p L

Bennington

First Church, Old; see First Congregational Church

First Congregational Church (First Church, Old)
Monument Ave.
HABS VT-90 pd L

Robinson, Gen. David, House
HABS VT-21 pd L

North Bennington

Church, Old Stone; see Hindillville Methodist Episcopal Church

Hindillville Methodist Episcopal Church (Church, Old Stone)
Hillside St. & River Rd.
HABS VT-80 p L

Orwell House
Bennington Rd.
HABS VT-81 p L

Shaftsbury Center

Galusha, Gov., House
HABS VT-20 pd L

South Shaftsbury

Hawkins House (Monroe House)
HABS VT-19 pd L

Monroe House; see Hawkins House

South Shaftsbury vic.

White Pillar
State Rt. 7
HABS VT-82 p L

CALEDONIA COUNTY

Barnet Center

Jack, Alexander, Dye & Print Works; see Thresher, Ben, Mill

Judkins Wagon & Woodworking Shop; see Thresher, Ben, Mill

Thresher, Ben, Mill (Jack, Alexander, Dye & Print Works; Judkins Wagon & Woodworking Shop)
HAER VT-10 s pd H

St. Johnsbury

Fairbanks, E. & T., & Co., Two Story Covered Bridge
HAER VT-1-A s p H

Fairbanks, E. & T., & Company
HAER VT-1 p H

Mt. Vernon Street Bridge (Sleepers River Lenticular Semi-deck Truss Bridge)
HAER VT-2 p H

Sleepers River Lenticular Semi-deck Truss Bridge; see Mt. Vernon Street Bridge

CHITTENDEN COUNTY

Burlington

First Church (First Congregational Church)
Winooski & Buell Sts.
HABS VT-73 p L

First Congregational Church; see First Church

First Congregational Society Church (Unitarian Church)
Pearl St. & Elmwood Ave.
HABS VT-24 s pd L

Isham, Deming, House
308 Pearl St.
HABS VT-71 p L

Unitarian Church; see First Congregational Society Church

Jericho Center vic.

Chittenden, Gov. Martin, House
Rt. 117
HABS VT-69 p L

Richmond

Round Church, Old; see Round Meetinghouse

Round Meetinghouse (Round Church, Old; Town Hall)
Town Common
HABS VT-70 p L

Town Hall; see Round Meetinghouse

Winooski

Porter Screen Warehouse & Dist. Co., Warehouse 11
E. Spring St.
HABS VT-101-A pd L

Porter Screen Warehouse & Distributing Co. Complex
Spring St.
HABS VT-101 p L H

FRANKLIN COUNTY

Highgate Falls

St. John's Church (Protestant Episcopal)
Highgate Falls Common
HABS VT-87 p L

Store
Highgate Falls Common
HABS VT-86 p L

GRAND ISLE COUNTY

Grand Isle

Hyde-Jackson Log Cabin
Rt. 2 vic.
HABS VT-66 p L

South Hero

Inn, Old Stone; see Island House

Island House (Inn, Old Stone)
Rt. 2
HABS VT-65 p L

ORANGE COUNTY

Randolph

Chase-Redfield Barn
Main St.
HABS VT-54 pd L

Chase-Redfield House
Main St.
HABS VT-39 pd L

Randolph Center

Edgerton, Lebbeus, House
Main St.
HABS VT-38 pd L

Strafford

Morrill, Sen. Justin Smith, House
HABS VT-55 pd L

Strafford Meetinghouse
On the Green
HABS VT-36 pd L

Thetford vic.

Latham House
HABS VT-56 pd L

ORLEANS COUNTY

Brownington

Brownington Congregational Church
HABS VT-95 s H

Eaton, Cyrus House
HABS VT-96 s H

House, Old Stone
HABS VT-97 d H

RUTLAND COUNTY

Castleton

Congregational Church of Christ in Castleton (Federated Church)
Main St.
HABS VT-17 s pd L

Dake, Thomas Royal, House
South St.
HABS VT-77 p L

Federated Church; see Congregational Church of Christ in Castleton

Gridley, Selah, House
Main St.
HABS VT-79 p L

Harris, Josiah, House
Main & Mill Sts.
HABS VT-14 s pd L

1810 House; see Meecham-Ainsworth House

Langdon, B. F., House
Main & North Sts.
HABS VT-76 p L

Mallory, Rollin C., House
Main St.
HABS VT-78 p L

Meecham-Ainsworth House (1810 House)
Main St.
HABS VT-15   pd   L

Ransom House (Stairway)
South St.
HABS VT-18   pd   L

Ransom, Justus, House
Main St.
HABS VT-91   p   L

Watters House
Main & South Sts.
HABS VT-16   s pd   L

Rutland

Googan House
HABS VT-13   s pd   L

WASHINGTON COUNTY

Montpelier

Pavilion Hotel
HABS VT-93   s pd   H

Reed, Hezekiah, House (Vermont Mutual
    Fire Insurance Company Building)
89 Brick St.
HABS VT-67   p   L

**Vermont Mutual Fire Insurance Company
    Building;** see Reed, Hezekiah, House

Vermont State House
State St. at Western Ave.
HABS VT-68   p   L

WINDHAM COUNTY

Grafton

Congregational Church
HABS VT-23   s pd   L

Rockingham

Meetinghouse
HABS VT-22   pd   L

Pulsifer, David, Inn
Rt. 103
HABS VT-41   pd   L

Windham

Olcott, Elias, House
Upper Meadows Settlement
HABS VT-42   pd   L

WINDSOR COUNTY

Bethel

Paige, Dr. Alfred, House
Main St.
HABS VT-40   pd   H

Cavendish

Dutton, Salmon, House
HABS VT-25   s   L

Chester

Congregational Church
Church & Main Sts.
HABS VT-49   pd   L

Chester Depot

Edson, Dr., House (Stone Village Inn)
North St.
HABS VT-44   pd   L

Spaulding, Granville, House
North St.
HABS VT-45   pd   L

Stone Village Inn; see Edson, Dr., House

Chester vic.

Earl House (Red House)
State Rt. 103
HABS VT-43   pd   L

Red House; see Earl House

Norwich

Hatch-Peisch House
Main St.
HABS VT-52   pd   L

Norwich Congregational Church (South
    Church)
Norwich Green
HABS VT-53   pd   L

South Church; see Norwich Congregational
    Church

Norwich vic.

Olcott-Johnson House
Old Norwich Center
HABS VT-51   s pd   L

Perkinsville

Foster, Rev. Dan, House
Weathersfield Center
HABS VT-60   pd   L

**Weathersfield Congregational Church &
    Town Hall**
Weathersfield Center
HABS VT-57   s pd   L

Perkinsville vic.

Stoughton Farmstead
Black River vic. (moved to VT, Amsden
    Vic.)
HABS VT-59   s pd   L

Warren-Child House
Old Crown Point Rd.
HABS VT-58   s pd   L

Royalton vic.

Fox Stand Inn
Rts. 14 & 107
HABS VT-37   pd   L

Simonsville

Rowell's Inn
State Rt. 11
HABS VT-50   pd   L

Springfield

Gould House
Parker Hill Rd.
HABS VT-46   pd   L

Weston

Farrar, Capt., Inn; see Farrar-Mansur
    House

Farrar-Mansur House (Farrar, Capt., Inn)
Weston Green
HABS VT-48   pd   L

Vermont Country Store
Weston Common
HABS VT-47   pd   L

Windsor

Conant-Hubbard House
52 Main St.
HABS VT-63   s pd   L

Constitution House, The Old
15 N. Main St.
HABS VT-35   pd   L

Courthouse & Post Office
Main St.
HABS VT-62   pd   L

South Congregational Church, Old
Main St.
HABS VT-64   s pd   L

St. Paul's Episcopal Church
State & Court Sts.
HABS VT-61
HAER   pd   L

Townsend House
5 Courthouse St.
HABS VT-34   pd   L

Trask, Nahum, House
25 N. Main St.
HABS VT-33   pd   L

Woodstock

Aylwin House
48 Elm St.
HABS VT-32   pd   L

D. A. R. Historic Museum; see Parker,
    Tille, Tavern

Dana, Charles, House
26 Elm St.
HABS VT-31   pd   L

Elm Street Bridge
HAER VT-3   pd   H

Lyman, Job, House
30 Elm St.
HABS VT-26   pd   L

Mower, Gen. Lyman, House
16 The Green
HABS VT-27   pd   L

Parker, Tille, Tavern (D. A. R. Historic
    Museum)
26 The Green
HABS VT-28   pd   L

Richardson, Capt. Israel, Tavern
9 The Green
HABS VT-29   pd   L

Swan, Benjamin, House
37 Elm St.
HABS VT-30   pd   L

Virgin Islands

British West Indies
Estate Clay Gut, Windmill
HABS VI-95   s   H

ST. JOHN ISLAND COUNTY

Caneel Bay
Caneel Bay Plantation Sugar Factory
HABS VI-69   p d   H

Coral Bay
Frederiks Fort
Fortberg Hill
HABS VI-74   p d   H

Cruz Bay
Christians Fort
Cruz Bay vic.
HABS VI-70   p   H

Estate Annaberg
Bake Oven
Maho Bay Quarter vic.
HABS VI-135-A   s p   H
Cookhouse
Maho Bay Quarter vic.
HABS VI-135-B   s   H
Estate Annaberg, Windmill, Sugar Factory (Ruins)
HABS VI-20   s p   H
Sugar Factory
Maho Bay Quarter vic.
HABS VI-18   s p d   H

Estate Carolina
Estate Carolina, Windmill
HABS VI-136   s   H

Estate Denis Bay
Estate Denis Bay, Windmill
HABS VI-160   s   H

Estate Hammer
Mill Tower (Ruins)
Estate Hammer Farms
HABS VI-75   s p   H

Estate Mary Point
Estate Mary Point, Great House
HABS VI-159   s   H

Estate Susannaberg
Estate Susannaberg
HABS VI-78   s p   H

May Point
May Point Estate, Great House
HABS VI-77   p   H

Reef Bay
Estate Reef Bay
HAER VI-2   s p   H
Estate Reef Bay, Wattle House
HABS VI-73   p   H

Reef Bay Great House, Service Building
HABS VI-71   s p   H
Reef Bay Indian Petroglyphs
HABS VI-76   p   H
Reef Bay Sugar Factory
HABS VI-2   s p   L

Whistling Cay
Customs House
St. Johns vic.
HABS VI-87   s   H

ST. THOMAS ISLAND COUNTY

Charlotte Amalie
Berg, Gov. Hans Hendrik, House; see Catharineberg
Bethania; see Frederick Lutheran Church, Parish Hall
Bluebeard's Castle (Bluebeard's Hill; Frederiksfort)
HABS VI-16   p d   L H
Bluebeard's Hill; see Bluebeard's Castle
Catharineberg (Berg, Gov. Hans Hendrik, House; Denmark Hill; Estate Number 8, Store Nordside Quarter)
HABS VI-12   p d   L
Catharineberg Porter's House & Cookhouse (Estate Number 8, Store Nordside Quarter)
HABS VI-13   p   L
Christiansfort
Waterfront
HABS VI-137   p   H
Commercial Hotel & Coffee House (Grand Hotel)
Morre Gade 44-45
HABS VI-8   p d   L
Denmark Hill; see Catharineberg
Dronningensgade 10 (House)
HABS VI-141   p   H
Dronningensgade 11-15 (House)
HABS VI-142   p   H
Dronningensgade 16-18 (House)
HABS VI-143   p   H
Dronningensgade 2 (House)
HABS VI-138   p   H
Dronningensgade 22 (House)
HABS VI-144   p   H
Dronningensgade 25B (House)
HABS VI-145   p   H
Dronningensgade 30-31 (House)
HABS VI-146   p   H
Dronningensgade 32 (House)
HABS VI-153   p   H
Dronningensgade 8B (House)
HABS VI-139   p   H
Dronningensgade 8B-18 (House)
HABS VI-140   p   H

Dronningensgade Area Study (Ninty-nine Steps)
HABS VI-83-A   p   H
Estate Number 8, Store Nordside Quarter; see Catharineberg
Estate Number 8, Store Nordside Quarter; see Catharineberg Porter's House & Cookhouse
Frederick Lutheran Church, Parish Hall (Lind, Jacob H. S., House; Bethania)
Norre Gade 6
HABS VI-15   p   L
Frederiksfort; see Bluebeard's Castle
Government House
Kongensgade 21-22
HABS VI-17   p d   L
Grand Hotel; see Commercial Hotel & Coffee House
Hotel 1829 (Lavalette, A., (House))
Kongensgade 30A
HABS VI-11   p d   H
Kongensgade 1B (House)
HABS VI-154   p   H
Kronprinsensgade 11(House); see Kronprinsensgade Area Study
Kronprinsensgade 22 (House); see Kronprinsensgade Area Study
Kronprinsensgade 5 (House); see Kronprinsensgade Area Study
Kronprinsensgade 76 (House); see Kronprinsensgade Area Study
Kronprinsensgade 78 (House); see Kronprinsensgade Area Study
Kronprinsensgade 80 (House); see Kronprinsensgade Area Study
Kronprinsensgade Area Study (Kronprinsensgade 11(House))
HABS VI-155   p   H
Kronprinsensgade Area Study (Kronprinsensgade 76 (House))
HABS VI-152   p   H
Kronprinsensgade Area Study (Kronprinsensgade 5 (House))
HABS VI-84-A   p   H
Kronprinsensgade Area Study
Kronprinsensgade
HABS VI-84   p   H
Kronprinsensgade Area Study (Kronprinsensgade 22 (House))
HABS VI-156   p   H
Kronprinsensgade Area Study (Kronprinsensgade 78 (House))
HABS VI-157   p   H
Kronprinsensgade Area Study (Kronprinsensgade 80 (House))
HABS VI-158   p   H
Lavalette, A., (House); see Hotel 1829
Lind, Jacob H. S., House; see Frederick Lutheran Church, Parish Hall

Lutheran Cemetary, Hospital Grounds
Nord Gade vic.
HABS VI-147   p   H

Lutheran Church
North St.
HABS VI-80   pd   H

Lutheran Parsonage
Kongensgade 23
HABS VI-81   pd   H

Ninty-nine Steps; see Dronningensgade Area Study

Nisky Moravian Mission & Church
Harwood Hwy. vic.
HABS VI-86   p   H

Norregade Estate
HABS VI-148   p   H

Quarters B
Kongensgade 32-33
HABS VI-82   pd   H

Raadetsgade I, II, III, IV, V, Area Study
HABS VI-85   p   H

St. Thomas Reformed Church
Nye Gade 4B
HABS VI-9   pd   L

Synagogue of Beracha Veshalom Vegemiluth Hasidim (Synagogue of Blessing & Peace & Acts of Piety)
Krystalgade 16A & B
HABS VI-10   pd   L H

Synagogue of Blessing & Peace & Acts of Piety; see Synagogue of Beracha Veshalom Vegemiluth Hasidim

Charlotte Amalie vic.

Beth Ha-Chaim (House of Life; Jewish Cemetery Chapel)
Kronprindsensgade vic.
HABS VI-14   pd   L

House of Life; see Beth Ha-Chaim

Jewish Cemetery Chapel; see Beth Ha-Chaim

Christiansted

Christiansted Library; see Customhouse & Post Office

Customhouse & Post Office (Christiansted Library)
Christiansted Warf Square vic.
HABS VI-4   s pd   L

Estate Contant

Estate Contant, Windmill
HABS VI-149   s   H

Estate Solberg

Estate Solberg, Windmill
HABS VI-150   s   H

Hassel Island

Creque Marine Railway
HAER VI-1   s   L H

St. Thomas Marine Slip
HAER VI-10   p   H

Raphune

Windmill Tower
HABS VI-151   s   H

VIRGIN ISLANDS COUNTY

Bulows Minde

Bulows Minde Estate House
Bulows Minde
HABS VI-7   s p   H

Christiansted

Anglican Church
27 King St.
HABS VI-21   pd   H

Cavanaughs Butik; see Kongensgade 54

Christiansted Warf Area
HABS VI-90   p   H

Customhouse, Old (Scalehouse)
Christiansted Warf Square vic.
HABS VI-3   s pd   L

Drewes House
Kongens Gade 46 & 47
HABS VI-22   pd   H

Dronningens Tvaergade 42 (House)
HABS VI-39   p   H

Dutch Reformed Church; see Lutheran Church

67 East Street (House)
HABS VI-34   pd   H

Estate Annaly
HAER VI-8   p   H

Estate Clifton Hill
S. Central St.
HAER VI-4   s p   H

Estate Mount Stewart
Centerline Rd. vic.
HAER VI-9   p   H

Estate Rust op Twist
HAER VI-3   s   H

Fort Christiansuaern
Company St. vic.
HABS VI-5   s pd   L H

Friedensberg; see Friedensfeld

Friedensfeld (Friedensberg; Friedensthal; Nioky)
HABS VI-91   p   H

Friedensthal
HABS VI-24   p   H

Friedensthal; see Friedensfeld

Government House
2-3 King St.
HABS VI-42   p   H

Hamilton House
Kongensgade 56-57
HABS VI-92   p   H

Hendrick's Butchery
Company & Queen Sts. vic.
HABS VI-25   p   H

4-5 Hill Street (House)
HABS VI-35   pd   H

56-58 Hill Street (House)
HABS VI-36   pd   H

Hospitalsgade 21-22 (House)
HABS VI-93   p   H

Hospitalsgade 23 (House)
HABS VI-94   p   H

Hospitalsgade 25 (House)
HABS VI-104   p   H

Hospitalsgade 27 (House)
HABS VI-105   p   H

Hospitalsgade 28 (House) (Rosendale Quest House)
HABS VI-106   p   H

Hospital-Street Plan
HABS VI-32   p   H

King Christian Hotel
Kongensgade 59
HABS VI-118   p   H

King Street Study Area
Kongensgade 1, 78, 45-49 & Customs House
HABS VI-44   p   H

7 King's Cross Street (House)
HABS VI-40   pd   H

Kirkegade 10 (House)
HABS VI-109   p   H

Kirkegade 15, Kopagnigade 1, Kirkegade 16A (Houses)
HABS VI-110   p   H

Kirkegade 16B & 17 (Houses)
HABS VI-111   p   H

Kirkegade, General Views
Church St.
HABS VI-108   p   H

Kompagnigade 1A (House)
HABS VI-112   p   H

Kompagnigade 39 (House)
HABS VI-37   p   H

Kompagnigade 51 (House)
HABS VI-38   p   H

Kongensgade 21 (House)
HABS VI-113   p   H

Kongensgade 53
HABS VI-115   p   H

Kongensgade 54 (Cavanaughs Butik)
HABS VI-89   p   H

Kongensgade 58 (House)
HABS VI-117   p   H

La Princesse Public School
King St.
HABS VI-99   p   H

Lutheran Church (Dutch Reformed Church)
Kongensgade & Dronningens Tvaer Gade
HABS VI-23   pd   H

Lutheran Church of the Lord (Steeple Building)
Company St.
HABS VI-1   s pd   L H

Lutheran Church of the Lord of Zebaoth; see Weathervane, Steeple Building

Lutheran Church Parsonage
Kongensgade 51
HABS VI-26   pd   H

Markoe House
16B Church St.
HABS VI-27 pd H

Moravian Church
Western Suburbs, King St. vic.
HABS VI-28 pd H

Moravian Mission House, Parsonage
King St. vic.
HABS VI-29 p H

Newton House
Company St. 56
HABS VI-30 pd H

Nioky; see Friedensfeld

Pentheney Hotel
Kongensgade 45A & 46B
HABS VI-31 pd H

Post Office
Church & Company Sts.
HABS VI-43 p H

Rosendale Quest House; see Hospitalsgade
28 (House)

Scalehouse; see Customshouse, Old

Steeple Building; see Lutheran Church of
the Lord

Strade & Danish House
Kongensgade 55
HABS VI-116 p H

33-35 Strand Gade (House)
HABS VI-41 pd H

Virgin Islands Bank
Kongensgade 52
HABS VI-114 p H

Weathervane, Steeple Building (Lutheran
Church of the Lord of Zebaoth)
Company Building
HABS VI-1-A s H

Christiansted vic.

Castle Coakley
HABS VI-96 p H

Little La Grange Estate
HABS VI-100 p H

Little Princess
HABS VI-101 p H

Northside
HABS VI-102 p H

Plantation Hope
HABS VI-97 p L

Plantation Jerusalem
HABS VI-98 p H

Prosperity
HABS VI-103 p H

St. Johns
HABS VI-161 p H

Company's Quarter

Richmond
HABS VI-119 p H

Richmond Prison
HABS VI-163 p H

Fredensfeld

Moravian Church
HABS VI-57 pd H

Moravian Parsonage
HABS VI-58 pd H

Frederiksted

Benjamin House (Peterson, Judge Reuban,
House)
Dronningengens Gade 48
HABS VI-45 pd H

Customs House
Strande Gade
HABS VI-46 pd H

Dronningengsgade 13 (House)
HABS VI-52 p H

Dronningengsgade 44 (House)
HABS VI-53 p H

Dronningengsgade 45 (House)
HABS VI-120 p H

Dronningengsgade 64 (House)
HABS VI-122 p H

Dronningsgade 49-50 (House)
HABS VI-121 p H

Frederiksfort
King St. vic.
HABS VI-47 pd H

**Glasgow Overhead Crank Steam Engine &
Cane Mill** (McOnie Steam Engine)
Estate Whim
HAER VI-5 s H

King Street Area Study
Kongensgade 6, 8, 9, 17, 56, 57, 36, 53, 54,
55, 58
HABS VI-50 p H

Kongensgade 10-13 (House)
HABS VI-125 p H

Kongensgade 14-17 (House)
HABS VI-126 p H

Kongensgade 18 (House)
HABS VI-127 p H

Kongensgade 37B (House)
HABS VI-128 p H

Kongensgade 5-7 (House)
HABS VI-123 p H

Kongensgade 8-9 (House)
HABS VI-124 p H

Market Street (House)
HABS VI-54 p H

McOnie Steam Engine; see Glasgow
Overhead Crank Steam Engine & Cane
Mill

Milltower Sugar Factory
HABS VI-6 s H

Peterson, Judge Reuban, House; see
Benjamin House

Strandgade 10-13 (House)
HABS VI-129 p H

Strandgade 14-17 (House)
HABS VI-130 p H

Whim Great House
HABS VI-49 d H

King's Quarter

Orange Grove
HABS VI-55 p H

Slob Great House
Centerline Rd. vic.
HABS VI-56 pd H

Peter's Rest

Peters's Rest Estate
HABS VI-131 p H

Peter's Rest vic.

Letterbox
Peter's Rest Estate
HABS VI-132 p H

Prince's Quarter

Mount Pleasant
HABS VI-59 p H

Princess Quarter

School at Diamond, The
HABS VI-133 p H

Queen's Quarter

Gateway (Ruins)
Centerline Rd.
HABS VI-134 p H

Sion Farm, Great House
Centerline Rd. vic.
HABS VI-60 p H

Sion Hill Estate, Cook House
Centerline Rd. vic.
HABS VI-62 pd H

Sion Hill Estate, Factory (Ruin)
Centerline Rd. vic.
HABS VI-63 pd H

Sion Hill Estate, Great House
Centerline Rd. vic.
HABS VI-64 pd H

Sion Hill Estate, Mill
Centerline Rd. vic.
HABS VI-65 pd H

Sion Hill Estate, Privy
Centerline Rd. vic.
HABS VI-66 p H

Sion Hill Estate, Retaining Wall
Centerline Rd. vic.
HABS VI-67 p H

Sion Hill Estate, Stable
Centerline Rd. vic.
HABS VI-68 pd H

Sion Hill, General Estate
HABS VI-61 p H

Virginia

Adam, Robert, House; see
  Fairfax-Adam-Hodgson House

Adam Silver Shop
318 King St.
HABS VA-667   pd   L

Alfriend Building; see Gordon, John, House

Alley House; see Queen Street Area Survey

Appich Buildings
408-414 King St.
HABS VA-677   pd   L

Arch Hall; see Lewis, Lawrence, House

Atheneum, The; see Old Dominion Bank

Ayres Gun Shop
324 King St.
HABS VA-456   pd   L

Bank of Alexandria
133 N. Fairfax St.
HABS VA-449   pd   L

Bank of Potomac (Capitol, Northern &
  West Virginia (Civil War))
415 Prince St.
HABS VA-458   pd   L

Barrett, Kate Waller, House; see
  Dick-Janney House

Bayne-Moore-House
  (Bayne-Moore-Mourot House)
811 Prince St.
HABS VA-453   p   L

Bayne-Moore-Mourot House; see
  Bayne-Moore-House

Bird House; see Dalton House

Black, Justice Hugo L., House; see
  Vowell-Snowden-Black House

Black, Justice Hugo L., Stable; see
  Vowell-Snowden-Black Stable

Blue Door, The, Antique Shop; see Lynch,
  Captain, House

Braddock's Headquarters; see Carlyle,
  John, House

Brown, Bedford, Building
113-115 S. Fairfax St.
HABS VA-669   pd   L

Brown, Dr. William, House
212 S. Fairfax St.
HABS VA-466   pd   L

Bunch of Grapes Tavern; see
  Dalton-Herbert Houses

Burson House; see Wilson-Hopkins House

**Capitol, Northern & West Virginia (Civil
  War);** see Bank of Potomac

Carlin House; see Washington Street Area
  Survey

Carlyle, John, House (Braddock's
  Headquarters)
123 N. Fairfax St.
HABS VA-101   s pd   L H

Carne School; see St. John's Academy

Caton, James R., House
111 S. Fairfax St.
HABS VA-668   pd   L

Chatham, Henry, House
106-108 Pitt St.
HABS VA-680   pd   L

Chequire, Bernard, House
202 King St.
HABS VA-455   pd   L

Christ Church (Episcopal Church)
Columbus & Cameron Sts.
HABS VA-479   s pd   L

City Hotel; see Mason's Ordinary (Coffee
  House)

City Tavern; see Mason's Ordinary (Coffee
  House)

Coryton, Catharine, House
522-524 King St.
HABS VA-686   pd   L

Craddock House; see
  DeNeale-Craddock-Crocker House

Craik, Dr. James, House (Murry-Craik
  House)
210 Duke St.
HABS VA-583   p   L

Crocker House; see
  DeNeale-Craddock-Crocker House

Dalton House (Bird House)
209 N. Fairfax St.
HABS VA-460   pd   L

Dalton-Herbert Houses (Lee, Anne,
  Memorial Home for the Aged; Wise's
  Tavern; Bunch of Grapes Tavern)
201 N. Fairfax St.
HABS VA-934   pd   L

DeNeale-Craddock-Crocker House
  (Craddock House; Crocker House)
323 S. Fairfax St.
HABS VA-229   p   L

Devaughan, James H., House (Shuman's)
516 King St.
HABS VA-679   pd   L

Dick-Janney House (Barrett, Kate Waller,
  House)
408 Duke St.
HABS VA-696   pd   L

Duffey House
203 S. Fairfax St.
HABS VA-454   pd   L

Duke Street Area Survey (700 Duke Street
  (House))
HABS VA-1051   p   H

Duke Street Area Survey (200 Duke Street
  (House))
HABS VA-1050   p   H

200 Duke Street (House); see Duke Street
  Area Survey

201 Duke Street (House); see McConnell,
  Alexander, House

700 Duke Street (House); see Duke Street
  Area Survey

Dulany, Benjamin, House
601 Duke St.
HABS VA-697   pd   L

Dulany, Benjamin, Stable
601 Duke St.
HABS VA-447   pd   L

Episcopal Church; see Christ Church

Evans, John T., Building
320 King St.
HABS VA-666   pd   L

Fairfax, George William, House; see
  Fairfax-Adam-Hodgson House

Fairfax, Lord, House (Yeaton-Fairfax
  House; Yeaton-Crilly House)
607 Cameron St.
HABS VA-211   pd   L

Fairfax-Adam-Hodgson House (Fairfax,
  George William, House; Adam, Robert,
  House)
207 Prince St.
HABS VA-230   p   L

Farmer's Bank of Alexandria; see 200
  Prince & 201 South Lee Streets (House)

Fawcett House; see Murray-Dick-Fawcett
  House

Fendall House
611 Oronoco St.
HABS VA-1049   p   H

First National Bank
503-507 King St.
HABS VA-672   pd   L

Fitzgerald, John, Warehouse; see
  Patterson-Fitzgerald Warehouse

Flounder House
317 S. SaintAsaph St.
HABS VA-462   pd   L

Flounder House (Number 403 only); see
  South Fairfax Street Area Survey

Flounder Tavern Building; see Warehouse
  Area Survey

Flounder Warehouse (Little Theater
  Workshop)
207 Ramsay's Alley
HABS VA-474   pd   L

Fortney, Jacob, House; see Royal Street
  Area Survey

Fowle, William, House (Fowle-Taylor
  House)
711 Prince St.
HABS VA-574   p   L

Fowle-Taylor House; see Fowle, William,
  House

Free Methodist Church; see Old Dominion
  Bank

Friendship Fire Company (Friendship
  Veteran's Fire Engine Company)
107 S. Alfred St.
HABS VA-463   s pd   L

Friendship Veteran's Fire Engine Company; see Friendship Fire Company

Gadsby's Tavern; see Mason's Ordinary (Coffee House)

Gordon, John, House (Alfriend Building)
631 King St.
HABS VA-938   pd   L

Greene Funeral Home; see Jockey Club, The

Gregory, William, Building (first)
400-402 King St.
HABS VA-674   pd   L

Gregory, William, Building (second)
404-406 King St.
HABS VA-690   pd   L

Gregory, William, House (Leadbeater House, Old)
329 N. Washington St.
HABS VA-416   pd   L

Hallowell, James, School For Young Ladies; see 213-215 North Fairfax Street (Houses)

Hallowell School; see Wilson-Hopkins House

Hallowell-Carlin House; see Washington Street Area Survey

Hampson, Bryan, House (Wales House)
120 S. Fairfax St.
HABS VA-468   pd   L

Harper-Buckingham-Berry Building
312 King St.
HABS VA-664   pd   L

Harper-Vowell House
213 Prince St.
HABS VA-939   p   L

Hollinsbury, John, House; see Queen Street Area Survey

House, Greek Revival
801 Duke St.
HABS VA-461   p   L

House, Little; see Queen Street Area Survey

House of the Smiling Face; see Ladd House

Howard House; see Washington Street Area Survey

Jacobs-Miner House
113 S. Royal St.
HABS VA-673   pd   L

Janney, Elisha, House
404 Duke St.
HABS VA-703   pd   L

Jefferson Street Area Survey (222 Jefferson Street (Building))
HABS VA-1053   p   H

Jefferson Street Area Survey (215 Jefferson Street (Building))
HABS VA-1052   p   H

215 Jefferson Street (Building); see Jefferson Street Area Survey

222 Jefferson Street (Building); see Jefferson Street Area Survey

Jockey Club, The (Greene Funeral Home)
814 Franklin St.
HABS VA-102   s p   L

Johnston, George, Homesite; see Old Dominion Bank

Johnston, Reuben, House; see South Fairfax Street Area Survey

Johnston-Vowell House
224 S. Lee St.
HABS VA-451   pd   L

Kennedy Buildings
416-418 King St.
HABS VA-670   pd   L

King Street, 300 Block (General Views); see 300-320 King Street (Buildings)

King Street, 400 Block (General View); see 400-430 King Street (Buildings)

King Street, 500 Block (General View); see 500-532 King Street (Buildings)

300-320 King Street (Buildings) (King Street, 300 Block (General Views))
HABS VA-920   p   L

400-430 King Street (Buildings) (King Street, 400 Block (General View))
HABS VA-921   p   L

500-532 King Street (Buildings) (King Street, 500 Block (General View))
HABS VA-922   p   L

Korn & Wisemiller Building
202 S. Saint Asaph & 502 Prince Sts.
HABS VA-704   pd   L

Ladd House (House of the Smiling Face)
320 N. Fairfax St.
HABS VA-212   p   L

LaFayette-Lawrason-Cazenove House; see Lawrason, Thomas, House

Lannon's Opera House
500-508 King St.
HABS VA-675   pd   L

Lawrason, Thomas, House (LaFayette-Lawrason-Cazenove House)
301 S. Saint Asaph St.
HABS VA-467   pd   L

Leadbeater Drug Store; see Stabler-Leadbeater Drug Corporation

Leadbeater House
414 N. Washington St.
HABS VA-457   pd   L

Leadbeater House, Old; see Gregory, William, House

Leadbeater, James, House (Leadbeater-Barrett House)
213 S. Pitt St.
HABS VA-641   s   H

Leadbeater-Barrett House; see Leadbeater, James, House

Leadbeater-Stabler Apothecary Shop; see Stabler-Leadbeater Apothecary Shop

Lee, Anne, Memorial Home for the Aged; see Dalton-Herbert Houses

Lee, Charles, House; see Washington Street Area Survey

Lee, Edmund Jennings, House
428 N. Washington St.
HABS VA-452   pd   L

Lee, Robert E., House; see Potts-Fitzhugh House

Lee Street Area Survey (601 South Lee Street (House))
HABS VA-620-B   p   L

Lee Street Area Survey (605 South Lee Street (House))
HABS VA-620-C   p   L

Lee Street Area Survey (615 South Lee Street (House))
HABS VA-620-D   p   L

Lee Street Area Survey (403 South Lee Street (House))
HABS VA-620-A   p   L

Lewis, Lawrence, House (Arch Hall)
815 Franklin St. (moved to VA, Lorton)
HABS VA-109   s pd   L

Little Theater Workshop; see Flounder Warehouse

Lloyd House; see Wise-Hooe-Lloyd House

Lockwood-Cross Building
314 King St.
HABS VA-665   pd   L

Longden, John, House
111 S. Royal St.
HABS VA-689   pd   L

Longden, John, Houses
105-107 S. Royal St.
HABS VA-685   pd   L

Lyceum, The (McGuire House)
201 S. Washington St.
HABS VA-185   s pd   L H

Lynch, Captain, House (Blue Door, The, Antique Shop)
708 Wolfe St.
HABS VA-476   pd   L

Lynn, Adam, House (first)
518-520 King St.
HABS VA-676   pd   L

Lynn, Adam, House (second)
532 King St.
HABS VA-687   pd   L

Lynn, Adam, House (third)
104 S. Saint Asaph St.
HABS VA-688   pd   L

Married Houses; see Thompson, Jonah, Houses

Mason's Ordinary (Coffee House) (Gadsby's Tavern; City Hotel; City Tavern)
128 N. Royal St.
HABS VA-100   s pd   L

McConnell, Alexander, House (201 Duke Street (House))
HABS VA-459   pd   L

McConnell, Alexander, Tenement Houses
223-225 S. Lee St.
HABS VA-475-A   pd   L

McGuire House; see Lyceum, The

Miller, Mordecai, House; see South Fairfax Street Area Survey

Miller, Samuel, Building
420 King St.
HABS VA-671   p d   L

Murray-Dick-Fawcett House (Fawcett House)
517 Prince St.
HABS VA-104   s p   L

Murry-Craik House; see Craik, Dr. James, House

213-215 North Fairfax Street (Houses) (Hallowell, James, School For Young Ladies; St. Mary's Academy)
HABS VA-448   p   L

310 North Lee Street (Doorway)
HABS VA-940   p   L

110-112 North Pitt Street (Houses)
HABS VA-683   p   L

109 North Royal Street (Building); see Royal Street Area Survey

207 North Royal Street (House); see Royal Street Area Survey

217 North Royal Street (House); see Royal Street Area Survey

219 North Royal Street (House)
HABS VA-293   p   L

221 North Royal Street (House); see Royal Street Area Survey

215 North Washington Street (House); see Washington Street Area Survey

407 North Washington Street (House); see Washington Street Area Survey

Old Dominion Bank (Free Methodist Church; Atheneum, The; Johnston, George, Homesite)
201 Prince St.
HABS VA-428   p   L

Orange & Alexandria RR, Wilkes Street Tunnel (Southern Railway, Wilkes Street Tunnel)
Wilkes Street vic.
HAER VA-18   s d   L

Patterson-Fitzgerald Warehouse (Fitzgerald, John, Warehouse)
101-105 S. Union St.
HABS VA-132   s p d   L

Pharmaceutical Museum; see Stabler-Leadbeater Apothecary Shop

Plain, George, House; see South Fairfax Street Area Survey

Potts-Fitzhugh House (Lee, Robert E., House)
607 Oronoco St.
HABS VA-707   p d   L

Presbyterian Church; see Presbyterian Meetinghouse

Presbyterian Meetinghouse (Presbyterian Church)
321 S. Fairfax St.
HABS VA-231   p   L

200 Prince & 201 South Lee Streets (House) (Farmer's Bank of Alexandria)
HABS VA-937   p   L

605 Prince Street (House)
HABS VA-964   p   L

607 Prince Street (House)
HABS VA-965   p   L

103-133 Prince Street (Row Houses, General View)
HABS VA-924   p   L

Pythian Temple
319 Cameron St.
HABS VA-252   p   L

Queen Street Area Survey (519 Queen Street (House))
HABS VA-600-K   p   L

Queen Street Area Survey (517 Queen Street (House))
HABS VA-600-J   p   L

Queen Street Area Survey (308 Queen Street (House))
HABS VA-600-C   p   L

Queen Street Area Survey (525 Queen Street (House); Hollinsbury, John, House)
HABS VA-600-M   p   L

Queen Street Area Survey (301-303 Queen Street (Row Houses))
HABS VA-600-A   p   L

Queen Street Area Survey (312 Queen Street (House); Summers-Scott House)
HABS VA-600-D   p   L

Queen Street Area Survey (513-515 Queen Street (Houses))
HABS VA-600-I   p   L

Queen Street Area Survey (305-307 Queen Street (Row Houses))
HABS VA-600-B   p   L

Queen Street Area Survey (319-325 Queen Street (Row Houses))
HABS VA-600-F   p   L

Queen Street Area Survey (511 Queen Street (House))
HABS VA-600-H   p   L

Queen Street Area Survey (317 Queen Street (House))
HABS VA-600-E   p   L

Queen Street Area Survey (523 Queen Street (House); House, Little; Alley House)
HABS VA-600-L   p   L

Queen Street Area Survey (510 Queen Street (House))
HABS VA-600-G   p   L

214 Queen Street (House)
HABS VA-446   p d   L

308 Queen Street (House); see Queen Street Area Survey

312 Queen Street (House); see Queen Street Area Survey

317 Queen Street (House); see Queen Street Area Survey

510 Queen Street (House); see Queen Street Area Survey

511 Queen Street (House); see Queen Street Area Survey

517 Queen Street (House); see Queen Street Area Survey

519 Queen Street (House); see Queen Street Area Survey

523 Queen Street (House); see Queen Street Area Survey

525 Queen Street (House); see Queen Street Area Survey

513-515 Queen Street (Houses); see Queen Street Area Survey

301-303 Queen Street (Row Houses); see Queen Street Area Survey

305-307 Queen Street (Row Houses); see Queen Street Area Survey

319-325 Queen Street (Row Houses); see Queen Street Area Survey

Ramsay, Dennis, House
221 S. Lee St.
HABS VA-475-B   p d   L

Ramsay, William, House
221 King St.
HABS VA-103   s p   L

Ramsay-Atkinson House
113 N. Fairfax St.
HABS VA-464   p d   L

Roberdeau, Gen. Daniel, House
418 S. Lee St.
HABS VA-469   p d   L

Royal Street Area Survey (103-107 Royal Street (Commercial Building))
HABS VA-619-A   p   L

Royal Street Area Survey (109 North Royal Street (Building))
HABS VA-619-B   p   L

Royal Street Area Survey (217 North Royal Street (House))
HABS VA-619-G   p   L

Royal Street Area Survey (122 South Royal Street (House))
HABS VA-619-E   p   L

Royal Street Area Survey (112 South Royal Street (House))
HABS VA-619-C   p   L

Royal Street Area Survey (221 North Royal Street (House))
HABS VA-619-H   p   L

Royal Street Area Survey (207 North Royal Street (House); Fortney, Jacob, House)
HABS VA-619-F   p   L

Royal Street Area Survey (120 South Royal Street (House))
HABS VA-619-D   p   L

103-107 Royal Street (Commercial Building); see Royal Street Area Survey

Second Presbyterian Church, Westminster Bldg.
521-523 Prince St.
HABS VA-682   p d   L

Shuman's; see Devaughan, James H., House

Simmonds, Samuel, House
109 S. Royal St.
HABS VA-684   p d   L

Snowden House; see
  Vowell-Snowden-Black House
Snowden Stable; see
  Vowell-Snowden-Black Stable
South Fairfax Street, 100 Block (General
  View)
HABS VA-919   p   L
South Fairfax Street Area Survey (117
  South Fairfax Street (House))
HABS VA-618-B   p   L
South Fairfax Street Area Survey (124
  South Fairfax Street (House); Wilson,
  James, House)
HABS VA-618-D   p   L
South Fairfax Street Area Survey (118
  South Fairfax Street (House))
HABS VA-618-C   p   L
South Fairfax Street Area Survey (131-137
  South Fairfax Street (Row Houses))
HABS VA-618-E   p   L
South Fairfax Street Area Survey (207-209
  South Fairfax Street (Double House))
HABS VA-618-F   p   L
South Fairfax Street Area Survey (213
  South Fairfax Street (House); Johnston,
  Reuben, House)
HABS VA-618-G   p   L
South Fairfax Street Area Survey (511-517
  South Fairfax Street (Row Houses))
HABS VA-618-J   p   L
South Fairfax Street Area Survey (227
  South Fairfax Street (House); Plain,
  George, House)
HABS VA-618-H   p   L
South Fairfax Street Area Survey (109
  South Fairfax Street (House); Miller,
  Mordecai, House)
HABS VA-618-A   pd   L
South Fairfax Street Area Survey (403-405
  South Fairfax Street (Houses); Flounder
  House (Number 403 only))
HABS VA-618-I   p   L
207-209 South Fairfax Street (Double
  House); see South Fairfax Street Area
  Survey
109 South Fairfax Street (House); see
  South Fairfax Street Area Survey
117 South Fairfax Street (House); see
  South Fairfax Street Area Survey
118 South Fairfax Street (House); see
  South Fairfax Street Area Survey
124 South Fairfax Street (House); see
  South Fairfax Street Area Survey
213 South Fairfax Street (House); see
  South Fairfax Street Area Survey
227 South Fairfax Street (House); see
  South Fairfax Street Area Survey
403-405 South Fairfax Street (Houses); see
  South Fairfax Street Area Survey
131-137 South Fairfax Street (Row
  Houses); see South Fairfax Street Area
  Survey

511-517 South Fairfax Street (Row
  Houses); see South Fairfax Street Area
  Survey
106 South Lee Street (House)
HABS VA-465   pd   L
310 South Lee Street (House)
HABS VA-584   p   L
403 South Lee Street (House); see Lee
  Street Area Survey
601 South Lee Street (House); see Lee
  Street Area Survey
605 South Lee Street (House); see Lee
  Street Area Survey
615 South Lee Street (House); see Lee
  Street Area Survey
221-225 South Lee Street (Houses)
HABS VA-475   pd   L
South Pitt Street Area Survey (110 South
  Pitt Street (Building))
HABS VA-1054   p   H
110 South Pitt Street (Building); see South
  Pitt Street Area Survey
112 South Royal Street (House); see Royal
  Street Area Survey
120 South Royal Street (House); see Royal
  Street Area Survey
122 South Royal Street (House); see Royal
  Street Area Survey
308 South Union Street (House)
HABS VA-267   p   L
415-417 South Washington Street (Double
  House); see Washington Street Area
  Survey
207 South Washington Street (House); see
  Washington Street Area Survey
209 South Washington Street (House); see
  Washington Street Area Study
411 South Washington Street (Row
  House); see Washington Street Area
  Survey
Southern Railway, Wilkes Street Tunnel;
  see Orange & Alexandria RR, Wilkes
  Street Tunnel
St. John's Academy (Carne School)
Duke & S. Columbus Sts.
HABS VA-450   pd   L
St. Mary's Academy; see 213-215 North
  Fairfax Street (Houses)
St. Paul's Episcopal Church
216 S. Pitt St.
HABS VA-340   pd   L
St. Paul's Episcopal Church, Rectory
417 Duke St.
HABS VA-708   pd   L
Stabler-Leadbeater Apothecary Shop
  (Leadbeater-Stabler Apothecary Shop;
  Pharmaceutical Museum)
107 S. Fairfax St.
HABS VA-175   s pd L
Stabler-Leadbeater Drug Corporation
  (Leadbeater Drug Store)
King & S. Fairfax Sts.
HABS VA-948   p   L

Stockton House; see
  Vowell-Snowden-Black House
Stockton Stable; see Vowell-Snowden-Black
  Stable
Summers-Scott House; see Queen Street
  Area Survey
Swope, Col. Michael, House
210 Prince St.
HABS VA-292   p   L
Taylor-Fraser House
414 Franklin St. (moved from 109 S. Pitt
  St.)
HABS VA-678   pd   L
Thompson, Jonah, Houses (Twin Houses;
  Married Houses)
211 N. Fairfax St.
HABS VA-251   pd   L
Twin Houses; see Thompson, Jonah,
  Houses
Van Havre-Daingerfield House
608 Cameron St.
HABS VA-710   pd   L
Vowell-Snowden-Black House (Snowden
  House; Black, Justice Hugo L., House;
  Stockton House)
619 S. Lee St.
HABS VA-709   pd   L
Vowell-Snowden-Black Stable (Snowden
  Stable; Black, Justice Hugo L., Stable;
  Stockton Stable)
Franklin St.
HABS VA-711   pd   L
Wales House; see Hampson, Bryan, House
Warehouse Area Survey (Flounder Tavern
  Building)
Gazette (Sharpshin) & Market Square
  Alleys
HABS VA-621 & VA-637 s pd   L
Warehouse, Small; see Water Street
  (Warehouse)
Warfield Building
501 King St.
HABS VA-681   pd   L
Washington, George, Town House
  (reconstructed)
508 Cameron St.
HABS VA-597   pd   L
Washington Street Area Study (209 South
  Washington Street (House))
HABS VA-617-B   p   L
Washington Street Area Survey (215 North
  Washington Street (House);
  Hallowell-Carlin House; Carlin House)
HABS VA-617-C   p   L
Washington Street Area Survey (411 South
  Washington Street (Row House))
HABS VA-617-E   p   L
Washington Street Area Survey (207 South
  Washington Street (House); Howard
  House)
HABS VA-617-A   p   L

Washington Street Area Survey (407 North Washington Street (House); Lee, Charles, House)
HABS VA-617-D   p   L

Washington Street Area Survey (415-417 South Washington Street (Double House))
HABS VA-617-F   p   L

Water Street (Warehouse) (Warehouse, Small)
HABS VA-133   s p   L

Wilson, James, House; see South Fairfax Street Area Survey

Wilson-Hopkins House (Hallowell School; Burson House)
609 Oronoco St.
HABS VA-933   p   L

Wise-Hooe-Lloyd House (Lloyd House)
220 N. Washington St.
HABS VA-582   s pd   L

Wise's Tavern; see Dalton-Herbert Houses

Yeaton-Crilly House; see Fairfax, Lord, House

Yeaton-Fairfax House; see Fairfax, Lord, House

Alexandria vic.

Jones Point Lighthouse
Jones Point, Potomac River
HABS VA-1067   s pd   L

Bedford vic.

Bowstring Truss Bridge; see Roaring Run Bridge

Roaring Run Bridge (Bowstring Truss Bridge)
State Rt. 637, spanning Roaring Run
HAER VA-7   s p   L H

Blossom Hill

Ackiss, Francis, House
Pungo Ridge Rd.
HABS VA-226   p   L

Charlottesville

Albemarle County Courthouse
Court Square
HABS VA-970   s   L

Blenheim Library
State Rt. 727
HABS VA-1004   s   L H

Calvary Baptist Church; see Woolen Mills Chapel

1 Cottage Lane (House)
HABS VA-1005   s   L H

117 Cream Street (House)
HABS VA-1007   s   H

1901 East Market Street (Building)
HABS VA-989   s   H

Fry's Spring Filling Station
2115 Jefferson Park Ave.
HABS VA-1021   s d   H

Garth Chapel (St. James Church)
State Rt. 676
HABS VA-1023   s   H

Inge's Store
331-333 Main St.
HABS VA-1015   s d   H

Locust Grove, Kitchen
810 Locust Ave.
HABS VA-1022   s d   H

Monroe Hill Law Office
McCormick Rd.
HABS VA-1027   s d   H

Norris-McCue House
HABS VA-1003   s   L

St. James Church; see Garth Chapel

University of Virginia
University Ave. & Rugby Rd.
HABS VA-193   p   L

104 Twelfth Street (Outbuilding)
HABS VA-1006   s   H

Union Chapel; see Woolen Mills Chapel

University of Virginia, Buckingham Palace
Carr's Hill, University of Virginia Campus
HABS VA-979   s   L

University of Virginia, Pavilions
University Ave. & Rugby Rd.
HABS VA-193-A   p   L

University of Virginia, Rotunda
University Ave. & Rugby Rd.
HABS VA-193-B   p   L

University of Virginia, The Row
University Ave. & Rugby Rd.
HABS VA-193-C   p   L

University of Virginia, Serpentine Wall
University Ave. & Rugby Rd.
HABS VA-193-D   p   L

Woolen Mills Chapel (Union Chapel; Calvary Baptist Church)
HABS VA-1068   s d   H

Chesapeake vic.

Powers House
U.S. Rt. 17
HABS VA-228   p   L

Chuckatuck

Gateposts, Wood
State Rt. 125
HABS VA-800   p   L

Quarters, The
State Rt. 125
HABS VA-199   p   L

Colonial Heights

Archer's Hill; see Oak Hill

Dunn Hill; see Oak Hill

Hector's Hill; see Oak Hill

Oak Hill (Dunn Hill; Hector's Hill; Archer's Hill)
151 Carroll Ave.
HABS VA-135   pd   L

Violet Bank
U.S. Rt. 1 vic.
HABS VA-322   pd   L

Fairfax

Earp's Ordinary
Main St.
HABS VA-963   s   L

Falls Church

Bartlett-Lawton House; see Lawton House

Biggs House
Great Falls & Little Falls Sts.
HABS VA-735   pd   H

Cherry Hill (Harvey-Riley House)
312 Park Ave.
HABS VA-733   p   H

Crossman, Charles, House
421 N. Washington St.
HABS VA-734   pd   H

Dulin House
Graham Rd.
HABS VA-278   p   L

170 East Broad Street (House)
HABS VA-736   p   H

Falls Church (Episcopal)
115 E. Fairfax St.
HABS VA-288   p   L

Harvey-Riley House; see Cherry Hill

Home Hill; see Lawton House

Lawton House (Bartlett-Lawton House; Home Hill)
HABS VA-732   p   H

Pond-Copeland House
407 E. Columbia St.
HABS VA-737   pd   H

Pope, Loren B., House; see Pope-Leighey House

Pope-Leighey House (Pope, Loren B., House)
1005 Locust St. (moved to VA, Mt. Vernon vic.)
HABS VA-638   s pd   L H

Rollins, George F., House
109 E. Columbia St.
HABS VA-738   pd   H

Fredericksburg

Brompton
Sunken Rd. & Hanover St.
HABS VA-569   p   L

Federal Hill, Summerhouse
510 Hanover St.
HABS VA-11-4   s pd   L

100 Hanover Street (House)
HABS VA-204   p   L

House (Long House, Old)
607 Sophia St.
HABS VA-263   p   L

Jail, Old; see Warehouse, Stone

Kenmore
1201 Washington Ave.
HABS VA-305   pd   L

Long House, Old; see House

Mercer, Gen. Hugh, Apothecary Shop
1020 Caroline St.
HABS VA-1030   s   H

Rising Sun Tavern
1306 Caroline St.
HABS VA-11-1   s p d L

Sentry Box House
133 Caroline St.
HABS VA-300   p L

511-519 Sophia Street (Houses)
HABS VA-205   p L

710-716 Sophia Street (Houses)
HABS VA-207   p L

Warehouse & Miscellaneous Buildings
307-313 Sophia St.
HABS VA-206   p L

Warehouse, Stone (Jail, Old)
915 Sophia St.
HABS VA-262   p L

Washington, Mary, House
1200 Charles St.
HABS VA-11-2   s p d L

Hampton

Campbellton Smokehouse
HABS VA-480   p L

Eagle Point
HABS VA-481   p L

Fortress Monroe, Main Gate (Fortress Monroe, Main Sally Port)
U.S. Rts. 60 & 258
HABS VA-595   s L

Fortress Monroe, Main Sally Port; see Fortress Monroe, Main Gate

Harrisonburg

106 North Liberty Street (House)
HABS VA-907   p L

Hickory vic.

Academy, Old
State Rts. 625 & 170
HABS VA-227   p L

Kempsville

Lovett, Reuben, House
State Rt. 627 vic.
HABS VA-560   p L

Pleasant Hall; see Singleton House

Princess Anne County Courthouse
State Rt. 165
HABS VA-556   p L

Singleton House (Pleasant Hall)
State Rt. 165
HABS VA-238   pd L

Kempsville vic.

Cornick, Henry T., House
Potters & Colonial Rds. vic.
HABS VA-558   p L

Fairfield Plantation, Dependency (White House, The; Walke House)
State Rt. 190 vic.
HABS VA-557   p L

Walke House; see Fairfield Plantation, Dependency

White House, The; see Fairfield Plantation, Dependency

Lexington

Alexander, Withrow, House & Store
Main & Washington Sts.
HABS VA-905   s p d H

Chesapeake & Ohio Railroad Station; see Valley Railroad Station

Jordan's Point (Stono)
State Rt. 303 & U.S. Rt. 11
HABS VA-900   s p d H

Lee-Jackson House
4 University Place
HABS VA-903   d H

Main Street Area Survey
HABS VA-897   p H

Pendleton-Coles House
319 Letcher Ave.
HABS VA-898   pd H

Reid-White House
208 W. Nelson St.
HABS VA-955   s H

Stono; see Jordan's Point

Valley Railroad Station (Chesapeake & Ohio Railroad Station)
HABS VA-904   pd H

Virginia Military Inst., Superintendent's House
V.M.I. Post Parade Grounds
HABS VA-901   pd H

Virginia Military Institute, Barracks
V.M.I. Post Parade Grounds
HABS VA-902   pd H

Washington & Lee University
HABS VA-568   p L

Washington & Lee University, Lee Chapel
HABS VA-906   pd H

Washington & Lee University, Washington Hall
HABS VA-568-A   pd H

London Bridge vic.

Eastwood
Great Neck Lake
HABS VA-242   pd L

Hudgins House (Huggins House)
U.S. Rt. 58
HABS VA-243   pd L

Huggins House; see Hudgins House

Keeling, Adam, House
Keeling Rd.
HABS VA-11-17   s p d L

Lynchburg

Atlantic, Miss. & Ohio RR, Jefferson Street Tunnel (Norfolk & Western RR, Jefferson Street Tunnel)
HAER VA-9   p L

Lynchburg Rehabilitation Project
HAER VA-30   s L

Norfolk & Western RR, Jefferson Street Tunnel; see Atlantic, Miss. & Ohio RR, Jefferson Street Tunnel

Point of Honor
112 Cabell St.
HABS VA-311   pd L

Sixth Street Bridge
Spanning Blackwater Creek
HAER VA-6   p H

Lynnhaven vic.

Boush House; see Wishart, James, House

Thoroughgood, Adam, House
Thoroughgood Ln.
HABS VA-209   pd L H

Wishart, James, House (Boush House)
State Rt. 649 vic.
HABS VA-11-16   s p d L

Manassas

Tudor Hall
Tudor Lane
HABS VA-835   p L

Mclean vic.

Maplewood (Villa Nuova)
7676 Old Springhouse Rd.
HABS VA-739   p H

Villa Nuova; see Maplewood

Newport News

Denbigh Plantation
HABS VA-1046   p H

Jones, Matthew, House
HABS VA-163   s p d L

Nimmo vic.

Brock Farm Quarters (Brook Farm Quarters)
State Rt. 615 vic.
HABS VA-400   pd L

Brook Farm Quarters; see Brock Farm Quarters

Woodhouse, Jonathan, House
State Rt. 632 vic.
HABS VA-239   pd L

Norfolk

Purdy-Whittle House; see Whittle House

Whittle House (Purdy-Whittle House)
225 W. Freemason St.
HABS VA-11-15   s p d L

Oceana vic.

Salisbury Plains
State Rt. 1002
HABS VA-559   p L

Petersburg

Appomattox Iron Works
Old St.
HAER VA-25   s p H

Battersea
793 Appomattox St.
HABS VA-136   s p d L

Bolling House; see Bollingbrook

Bolling, Robert, House; see Lawn, The

Bollingbrook (East Hill; Bolling House)
Franklin, Madison & Jefferson Sts. vic.
HABS VA-79   s d L

208-208A Bollingbrook Street (Double House) (Dunlop House)
HABS VA-816   p L

Bowers, William H., House (Southworth's Drug Store)
254 N. Sycamore St.
HABS VA-68   s pd   L
Center Hill
Franklin St.
HABS VA-815   p   L
City Hall; see U.S. Customs House & Post Office, Old
Clerk's House; see House, Stone
Dunlop, David, Tobacco Factory
45-127 Old St.
HABS VA-663
HAER VA-29   pd   L
Dunlop House; see 208-208A Bollingbrook Street (Double House)
Dunn House & Outbuildings
105 S. Sycamore St.
HABS VA-130   s pd   L
East Hill; see Bollingbrook
Elliot House
269 High St.
HABS VA-662   pd   L
Exchange, The
15-19 W. Bank St.
HABS VA-647   s pd   L
Farmers' Market, Old
W. Old & Rock Sts.
HABS VA-649   s pd   L
Friend, Nathaniel Jr., House
27-29 Bollingbrook St.
HABS VA-651   pd   L
Gill, Erasmus, House
53 S. Market St.
HABS VA-650   pd   L
Gilliam Rowhouses; see Read's, John B., Row
Golden Ball Tavern
Grove Ave. & N. Market St.
HABS VA-818   p   L
706 Grove Avenue (House & Store); see Pig Alley Block Study
Harrison House; see Strachan, Dr. Alexander Glass, House
Hinton House
416 High St.
HABS VA-426   p   L
House, Brick
Wills St., Blandford
HABS VA-819   p   L
House, Stone (Lloyd House; Clerk's House)
Crater Rd. & E. Washington St. (Blandford)
HABS VA-96   s pd   L
406-408 Hurt Street (Double House); see Pig Alley Block Study
411-413 Hurt Street (Double House); see Pig Alley Block Study
412 Hurt Street (Store); see Pig Alley Block Study
Hustings Courthouse
Courthouse Ave. & N. Sycamore St.
HABS VA-657   pd   L

Jackson, John, House
410 High St.
HABS VA-661   pd   L
Lawn, The (Bolling, Robert, House)
224 S. Sycamore St.
HABS VA-814   p   L
Lloyd House; see House, Stone
May's, David, Row
217 -223 High St.
HABS VA-660   pd   L
Norfolk & Western RR, Petersburg Freight Station; see Southside Virginia RR, Petersburg Freight Station
O'Hara, Charles, House (Rat Castle; Trapezium House)
244 N. Market St.
HABS VA-820   p   L
Petersburg Gas Light Company, Gasholder
Bank & Madison Sts. vic.
HAER VA-14   s p   H
Pig Alley Block Study (412 Hurt Street (Store))
HABS VA-644   s pd   L
Pig Alley Block Study (411-413 Hurt Street (Double House))
HABS VA-645   s pd   L
Pig Alley Block Study (706 Grove Avenue (House & Store))
HABS VA-653   pd   L
Pig Alley Block Study
Hurt St., Plum St. & Grove Ave.
HABS VA-930   p   L
Pig Alley Block Study (702-704 Plum Street (Double House))
HABS VA-656   pd   L
Pig Alley Block Study (703-713 Plum Street (Row Houses))
HABS VA-655   pd   L
Pig Alley Block Study (406-408 Hurt Street (Double House))
HABS VA-654   pd   L
702-704 Plum Street (Double House); see Pig Alley Block Study
703-713 Plum Street (Row Houses); see Pig Alley Block Study
Pride's Tavern
N. West & McKenzie Sts.
HABS VA-821   p   L
Rat Castle; see O'Hara, Charles, House
Read's, John B., Row (Gilliam Rowhouses)
102-104 W. Old St.
HABS VA-643   s pd   L
Romaine House; see Scott, Albert L., House
Scott, Albert L., House (Romaine House)
29 S. Market St.
HABS VA-648   s pd   L
Smith's, John H., Row
209-215 High St.
HABS VA-646   s pd   L
Southside Virginia RR, Petersburg Freight Station (Norfolk & Western RR, Petersburg Freight Station)
River St.
HAER VA-28   p   L

Southworth's Drug Store; see Bowers, William H., House
Spottswood House; see Stirling Castle
Stirling Castle (Spottswood House)
320 W. High St. (moved from original site)
HABS VA-822   p   L
Strachan, Dr. Alexander Glass, House (Harrison House; Strachan-Harrison House)
302 Cross St.
HABS VA-642   s pd   L
Strachan-Harrison House; see Strachan, Dr. Alexander Glass, House
Tabb Street Presbyterian Church
21 W. Tabb St.
HABS VA-658   pd   L
Trapezium House; see O'Hara, Charles, House
U.S. Customs House & Post Office, Old (City Hall)
121-141 N. Union St.
HABS VA-659   pd   L
Warehouse, Stone
Market St.
HABS VA-823   p   L
Washington Street Methodist Church
Washington & Adams St.
HABS VA-299   p   L

Reids Ferry vic.

Pembroke
State Rt. 603
HABS VA-181   s pd   L

Richmond

Adams, Dr. John, Double House
2501-2503 E. Grace St.
HABS VA-865   p   L
Allen, William C., Double House
4-6 E. Main St.
HABS VA-869   p   L
Allen-Ellet House; see Ellet, Andrew, House
Allison-Moore-Crump Building
1309 E. Main St.
HABS VA-846   pd   L
Ampthill
211 Ampthill Rd. (moved from Va, Richmond vic.)
HABS VA-159   s pd   L
Ballard Street & Tobacco Alley (House)
HABS VA-879   p   L
Barret, William, House
Fifth & Cary Sts.
HABS VA-425   p   L
Bell Tower, The
Capitol Square
HABS VA-116   s pd   L
Belvin House (William, William C., House)
412 N. Eighth St.
HABS VA-111   s pd   L
Bott, Miles, House
216 Cowardin Ave.
HABS VA-119   s pd   L

Bowser, Rosa D., Branch Library; see Dill, Adolph, House

Branch-Glasgow House (Glasgow, Ellen, House)
1 W. Main St.
HABS VA-857   p   L

Bransford, Frederick Cecil, House; see Bransford House

Bransford House (Bransford, Frederick Cecil, House; Bransford-Cecil House; Cecil Memorial)
1005 Clay St. (moved from 13 N. Fifth St.)
HABS VA-161   p   L

Bransford-Cecil House; see Bransford House

Brockenbrough, Dr. John, House (White House of the Confederacy)
1201 E. Clay St.
HABS VA-861   p   L

Call, Daniel, House
217 W. Grace St.
HABS VA-866   p   L

Cameron, Alexander, House
519 E. Franklin St.
HABS VA-876   p   L

Carter, Curtis, House (Carter-Crozet House; Crozet House)
100 E. Main St.
HABS VA-1070   p   L

Carter-Crozet House; see Carter, Curtis, House

Caskie, Mrs. James, House (Hancock-Palmer-Caskie House; Hancock, Michael, House; Hancock-Wirt-Caskie House)
2 N. Fifth St.
HABS VA-113   s pd   L

Cecil Memorial; see Bransford House

Chamberlayne Avenue & Saint Peter Street (House) (Mann, William, House)
HABS VA-856   p   L

311-313 College Street (Double House)
HABS VA-875   p   L

Columbian Block
1301-1307 E. Cary St.
HABS VA-842   pd   L

Crozet House; see Carter, Curtis, House

De Saussure House (Freeman, Samuel, House)
316 E. Main St.
HABS VA-114   s pd   L

Dill, Adolph, House (Bowser, Rosa D., Branch Library)
00 Clay St.
HABS VA-862   p   L

Donnan-Asher Iron Front Building
1207-1211 E. Main St.
HABS VA-853   pd   L

107 East Cary Street (House)
HABS VA-859   p   L

402 East Cary Street (House)
HABS VA-891   p   L

1008 East Clay Street (House)
HABS VA-1061   p   L

804 East Clay Street (House) (Wiseham House)
HABS VA-889   p   L

206 East Leigh Street (House)
HABS VA-890   p   L

2216-2218 East Main Street (Double House)
HABS VA-118   s pd   L

2416 East Main Street (House)
HABS VA-864   p   L

1909 East Main Street (Store)
HABS VA-1064   p   L

1010 East Marshall Street (House)
HABS VA-1066   p   L

2600 East Marshall Street (House)
HABS VA-854   p   L

Eighteenth & Main Streets (House) (Hampton-McCurdy House)
HABS VA-851   p   L

Ellet, Andrew, House (Allen-Ellet House)
2702 E. Grace St.
HABS VA-850   p   L

Ellet-Todd-Lawrence Building
1019-1021 E. Cary St.
HABS VA-844   pd   L

Fifth & Leigh Streets (House)
HABS VA-888   p   L

Freeman, Samuel, House; see De Saussure House

Gentry-Stokes-Crew House; see Twenty-eighth & E. Franklin Streets (House)

George, William O., House; see 116 South Third Street (House)

Gill House; see Grey House

Glasgow, Ellen, House; see Branch-Glasgow House

Gosden House (Tucker House)
Third & Leigh Sts.
HABS VA-852   p   L

6 Granby Street (Cottage)
HABS VA-881   p   L

Greenhow House
403 E. Grace St.
HABS VA-112   s pd   L

Grey House (Gill House)
1007 McDonough St.
HABS VA-131   s pd   L

Hampton-McCurdy House; see Eighteenth & Main Streets (House)

Hancock, Michael, House; see Caskie, Mrs. James, House

Hancock-Palmer-Caskie House; see Caskie, Mrs. James, House

Hancock-Wirt-Caskie House; see Caskie, Mrs. James, House

Hawes House (Mann-Hawes House)
506 E. Leigh St.
HABS VA-115   s pd   L

Haxall, Bolling W., House (Women's Club)
211 E. Franklin St.
HABS VA-1057   p   L

Hickock House; see Ritter-Hickock House

Hobson-Nolting House (Nolting House)
409 E. Main St.
HABS VA-160   s pd   L

Howard-Palmer House; see Palmer House

James River & Kanawha Canal, Locks 1-5 (Kanawha Canal, Tidewater Connection Locks)
HAER VA-23   pd   H

James River & Kanawha Canal, Three Mile Locks; see Kanawha Canal, 1st Grand Division Locks 1 & 2

Jefferson Hotel
Main, Jefferson, Franklin & Adams Sts.
HABS VA-840   pd   L

Kanawha Canal, 1st Grand Division Locks 1 & 2 (James River & Kanawha Canal, Three Mile Locks)
Pump House Dr.
HAER VA-24   s   H

Kanawha Canal, Tidewater Connection Locks; see James River & Kanawha Canal, Locks 1-5

Kent, Horace, House (Kent-Valentine House)
First & Franklin Sts.
HABS VA-858   p   L

Kent-Valentine House; see Kent, Horace, House

Lee, General, House; see Stewart, Norman, House

531 Leigh Street (House)
HABS VA-885   p   L

Linden Row
100-118 E. Franklin St.
HABS VA-247   p   L

Main Street Station
1520 E. Main St.
HABS VA-848   pd   L

Malone, James, Row; see Twenty-third & Franklin Streets (Houses)

Mann, William, House; see Chamberlayne Avenue & Saint Peter Street (House)

Mann-Hawes House; see Hawes House

Marshall, John, House
402 N. Ninth St.
HABS VA-309   pd   L

Masonic Hall; see Mason's Hall

Mason's Hall (Masonic Hall)
1805 E. Franklin St.
HABS VA-11-21   s pd   L

Monroe, James, Tomb
Hollywood Cemetery
HABS VA-843   pd   L

Morris, John, Cottage
2500 E. Grace St.
HABS VA-860   p   L

Nolting House; see Hobson-Nolting House

706 North Eighteenth Street (House)
HABS VA-887   p   L

778 North Ninth Street (Cottage)
HABS VA-877   p   L

616 North Ninth Street (House)
HABS VA-1065   p   L

1200-1202 North Seventeenth Street
    (Double House)
HABS VA-886   p   L

516 North Third Street (House)
HABS VA-894   p   L

9 North Twenty-Third Street (House)
HABS VA-884   p   L

Oaks, The
307 Stockton Ln. (moved from VA, Mattoax
    vic.)
HABS VA-157   pd   L

Old Stone House (Poe Museum; Poe
    Shrine)
1916 E. Main St.
HABS VA-120   s pd   L

Palmer House (Howard-Palmer House)
211 W. Franklin St.
HABS VA-867   p   L

Parsons, Samuel, House (Virginia Division
    of Youth Services)
601 Spring St.
HABS VA-434   p   L

Phillip Morris Leaf Storage Warehouse
1717-1721 E. Cary St.
HABS VA-849   pd   L

Poe Museum; see Old Stone House

Poe Shrine; see Old Stone House

Pohlig Paper Box Factory
    (Yarbrough-Turpin Tobacco Factory)
Twenty-fifth & Franklin Sts.
HABS VA-863   p   L

Pratt's Castle
324 S. Fourth St.
HABS VA-162   pd   L

Quarles, John D., House
1 E. Main St.
HABS VA-871   p   L

Ritter-Hickock House (Hickock House)
821 W. Franklin St.
HABS VA-855   p   L

Rutherfoord-Hobson House
2 W. Franklin St.
HABS VA-423   p   L

Scott-Clarke House
9 S. Fifth St.
HABS VA-421   p   L

Seventeenth & Venable Streets (House)
HABS VA-883   p   L

Sixth & Franklin Streets (House)
HABS VA-1060   p   L

Smith, John D., House
2617 E. Franklin St.
HABS VA-872   p   L

212-214 South First Street (Double House)
HABS VA-892   p   L

South Fourth & Byrd Streets (House)
HABS VA-1063   p   L

102 South Third Street (House)
HABS VA-893   p   L

116 South Third Street (House) (George,
    William O., House)
HABS VA-868   p   L

St. John's Church (Episcopal)
E. Grace & Broad Sts.
HABS VA-11-22   s pd   L

Stearns Iron Front Building
1007-1013 E. Main St.
HABS VA-847   pd   L

Stewart, Norman, House (Stewart-Lee
    House; Lee, General, House)
707 E. Franklin St.
HABS VA-895   p   L

Stewart-Lee House; see Stewart, Norman,
    House

Tenth & Clay Streets (House)
HABS VA-1062   p   L

Third & East Main Streets (House)
HABS VA-420   p   L

Third & Leigh Streets (House)
HABS VA-1059   p   L

Tomlinson, A. M., House; see Twenty-fifth
    & Venable Streets (House)

Tucker Cottage
612 N. Third St.
HABS VA-959   s   H

Tucker House; see Gosden House

Twenty-eighth & E. Franklin Streets
    (House) (Gentry-Stokes-Crew House)
HABS VA-873   p   L

Twenty-fifth & Venable Streets (House)
    (Tomlinson, A. M., House)
HABS VA-926   p   L

Twenty-first & Venable Streets (House)
HABS VA-880   p   L

Twenty-third & Franklin Streets (Houses)
    (Malone, James, Row)
HABS VA-870   p   L

Union Station Train Shed
Main St.
HAER VA-4   s   H

Valentine Museum; see Wickham House

Venable & Tulip Streets (House)
HABS VA-878   p   L

Virginia Division of Youth Services; see
    Parsons, Samuel, House

Virginia Fire & Marine Insurance Building
1015 E. Main St.
HABS VA-845   s pd   L

21 West Clay Street (House)
HABS VA-882   p   L

400 West Franklin Street (House)
HABS VA-422   p   L

White House of the Confederacy; see
    Brockenbrough, Dr. John, House

Whitlock Double House
628-630 N. Seventeenth St.
HABS VA-874   p   L

Wickham House (Wickham-Valentine
    House; Valentine Museum)
1015 E. Clay St.
HABS VA-310   pd   L

Wickham-Valentine House; see Wickham
    House

William, William C., House; see Belvin
    House

Wilton
Wilton Rd. (moved from Va, Richmond
    vic.)
HABS VA-158   pd   L

Wiseham House; see 804 East Clay Street
    (House)

Women's Club; see Haxall, Bolling W.,
    House

Yarbrough-Turpin Tobacco Factory; see
    Pohlig Paper Box Factory

Saint Brides vic.
House (Ruins)
HABS VA-249   p   L

South Richmond
Dunlop Mills
HABS VA-925   p   L

Staunton
Baltimore & Ohio RR, Folly Mills Creek
    Viaduct; see Valley Railroad, Folly Mills
    Creek Viaduct

Manse, The (Wilson, Woodrow, Birthplace)
Frederick & Coalter Sts.
HABS VA-11-9   s pd   L

Stuart-Robertson House (Entrance Gates)
120 Church St.
HABS VA-11-7   s pd   L

Valley Railroad, Folly Mills Creek Viaduct
    (Baltimore & Ohio RR, Folly Mills
    Creek Viaduct)
Folly Mills Creek
HAER VA-8   s   L H

Wilson, Woodrow, Birthplace; see Manse,
    The

Suffolk
Dairy, Old
HABS VA-1043   p   H

Suffolk vic.
Joiner Farmhouse
HABS VA-324   pd   L

Waynesboro
Blue Ridge Railroad, Culvert (Chesapeake
    & Ohio Railroad, Culvert)
U.S. Rt. 250 vic.
HAER VA-12-1   pd   L

Chesapeake & Ohio Railroad, Culvert; see
    Blue Ridge Railroad, Culvert

Williamsburg
Audrey House; see Page, Gov. John, House

Barlow House; see De Neufville House

Barraud, Dr. Philip, House (Mercer House)
Francis & Botetourt Sts.
HABS VA-234   p   L

Belle Farm
(moved from VA, Ordinary vic.)
HABS VA-69   p   L

Blair, Archibald, House
Nicholson St.
HABS VA-196   pd L

Blair, John, House
Duke of Gloucester St.
HABS VA-910   pd L

Bland, Richard, House (Bland-Wetherburn House; Wetherburn's Tavern)
Duke of Gloucester St.
HABS VA-403   pd L

Bland-Wetherburn House; see Bland, Richard, House

Bowden-Armstead House
HABS VA-1026 s p H

Bracken House; see Braken House

Braken House (Bracken House)
HABS VA-523   p L

Bruton Parish Church
Duke of Gloucester St.
HABS VA-191 s p L H

Camm-Blair Apothecary Shop (Prentis Store)
Duke of Gloucester & Colonial Sts.
HABS VA-316 s pd L H

Capitol, The (reconstructed)
Duke of Gloucester St.
HABS VA-365   pd L

Chiswell, Col. Charles, House (Interiors)
Francis St.
HABS VA-404   pd L

Coke-Garrett House
Nicholson St.
HABS VA-527   p L

Colonial Hotel; see Spencer's Hotel

Courthouse, Old
Courthouse Green
HABS VA-528 s p L H

De Neufville House (Orr, Capt. Hugh, House; Barlow House)
Duke of Gloucester & Colonial Sts.
HABS VA-245   pd L

Foundation of Early Church
Bruton Parish Churchyard
HABS VA-176 s L

Galt, Anne, House; see Nelson-Galt House

Gaol, Old (Public Gaol)
Nicholson St.
HABS VA-530   p L

Golden Ball Shop; see Hunter, Margaret, Shop

Governor's Palace (reconstructed)
Palace Green
HABS VA-327   pd L

Greenhow-Repiton Office; see Prison, Old

Griffin House
410 W. Francis St.
HABS VA-1008 s H

Hunter, Margaret, Shop (Golden Ball Shop)
Duke of Gloucester St.
HABS VA-526   p L

Jackson, George, House & Store (Lamb, Lucy, House)
York St.
HABS VA-524   p L

Kerr House; see Palmer House

Lamb, Lucy, House; see Jackson, George, House & Store

Little Christian House; see Timson, William, House

Ludwell-Paradise House (Paradise House)
Duke of Gloucester St.
HABS VA-189   pd L

Magazine, The (Powder Horn)
Duke of Gloucester St.
HABS VA-529 s p L H

McClandish House (Orrell, John, House)
Francis St.
HABS VA-328   pd L

Mercer House; see Barraud, Dr. Philip, House

Moody House (Roper House)
Francis St.
HABS VA-237   pd L

Nelson-Galt House (Galt, Anne, House)
Francis St.
HABS VA-522   p L

Nicholson, Robert, House
York St.
HABS VA-188   p L

Orr, Capt. Hugh, House; see De Neufville House

Orrell, John, House; see McClandish House

Page, Gov. John, House (Audrey House)
Palace Green vic.
HABS VA-273   pd L

Palmer House (Kerr House)
Duke of Gloucester St.
HABS VA-525   p L

Paradise House; see Ludwell-Paradise House

Peachy House; see Randolph, Peyton, House

Peachy-Randolph House; see Randolph, Peyton, House

Powder Horn; see Magazine, The

Prentis Store; see Camm-Blair Apothecary Shop

Prison, Old (Greenhow-Repiton Office)
Duke of Gloucester St.
HABS VA-406   pd L

Public Gaol; see Gaol, Old

Public Records Office (Treasurer's House)
Duke of Gloucester St.
HABS VA-195 s p L H

Randolph, Peyton, House (Peachy-Randolph House; Peachy House)
Nicholson & N. England Sts.
HABS VA-197   pd L

Randolph-Semple House; see Semple House

Reid, George, Wellhead
209 E. Duke of Gloucester St.
HABS VA-1011 s H

Roper House; see Moody House

Semple House (Randolph-Semple House)
Francis St.
HABS VA-911   p L

Spencer's Hotel (Colonial Hotel)
Duke of Gloucester & Queen Sts.
HABS VA-356   pd L

Taliaferro-Cole Shop
Duke of Gloucester St.
HABS VA-531   p L

Tayloe Office
112 E. Nicholson St.
HABS VA-1010 s H

Timson, William, House (Little Christian House)
Prince George & Nassau Sts.
HABS VA-383   pd L

Treasurer's House; see Public Records Office

Tucker, St. George, House
106 W. Nicholson St.
HABS VA-1012 s H

Wetherburn's Tavern; see Bland, Richard, House

William & Mary College, Brafferton Hall (William & Mary College, First Indian School)
College Yard
HABS VA-346 s pd L H

William & Mary College, First Indian School; see William & Mary College, Brafferton Hall

William & Mary College, Main Building (William & Mary College, Wren Building)
College Yard
HABS VA-401 s pd L H

William & Mary College, President's House
College Yard
HABS VA-913   p L

William & Mary College, Wren Building; see William & Mary College, Main Building

Wythe, George, House
101 Palace Green St.
HABS VA-1009 s H

Williamsburg vic.

Carter's Grove
U.S. Rt. 60 vic.
HABS VA-351 s pd L H

Winchester

Abram's Delight; see Hollingsworth, Isaac, House

Amherst Street Area Survey
HABS VA-694 s d H

Glen Burnie
801 Amherst St.
HABS VA-698   d H

Holliday Office Building; see Lawyer's Row
Hollingsworth, Isaac, House (Abram's
    Delight)
Rouss Spring Rd.
HABS VA-692   s d   H
Kurtz, Adam, House (Washington, George,
    Headquarters)
S. Braddock & W. Cork Sts.
HABS VA-699   pd   H
Lawyer's Row (Holliday Office Building)
30, 32, 34 & 36 Rouss Ave.
HABS VA-691   s pd   H
Logan, Lloyd, House
135 N. Braddock St.
HABS VA-700   d   H
Washington, George, Headquarters; see
    Kurtz, Adam, House

ACCOMAC COUNTY

Accomac

Bayly, Richard D., House (St. James
    Rectory; Episcopal Rectory)
Back St.
HABS VA-622   pd   L
Debtor's Prison (Jailor's House)
State Rt. 764
HABS VA-623   pd   L
Episcopal Rectory; see Bayly, Richard D.,
    House
Fisher-Seymour House
State Rt. 13
HABS VA-624   pd   L
Fisher-Seymour Icehouse
State Rt. 13
HABS VA-636   pd   L
Jailor's House; see Debtor's Prison
St. James Rectory; see Bayly, Richard D.,
    House

Accomac vic.

Bowman's Folly (Cropper, Gen. John,
    House)
Folly Creek
HABS VA-625   pd   L
Bowman's Folly, Dovecote (Cropper, Gen.
    John, Dovecote)
Folly Creek
HABS VA-634   pd   L
Bowman's Folly, Privy (Cropper, Gen.
    John, Privy)
Folly Creek
HABS VA-635   pd   L
Cropper, Gen. John, Dovecote; see
    Bowman's Folly, Dovecote
Cropper, Gen. John, House; see Bowman's
    Folly
Cropper, Gen. John, Privy; see Bowman's
    Folly, Privy
Cropper, Thomas, House; see Runnymede
Folly Farm; see Folly, The
Folly Farm Dovecote; see Folly, The,
    Dovecote

Folly Farm Icehouse; see Folly, The,
    Icehouse
Folly, The (Smith-Custis House; Folly
    Farm; Nock Farm)
Folly Creek
HABS VA-626   pd   L
Folly, The, Dovecote (Smith-Custis
    Dovecote; Folly Farm Dovecote; Nock
    Farm Dovecote)
Folly Creek
HABS VA-633   pd   L
Folly, The, Icehouse (Smith-Custis
    Icehouse; Folly Farm Icehouse; Nock
    Farm Icehouse)
Folly Creek
HABS VA-632   pd   L
Mount Custis
State Rt. 662
HABS VA-627   pd   L
Nock Farm; see Folly, The
Nock Farm Dovecote; see Folly, The,
    Dovecote
Nock Farm Icehouse; see Folly, The,
    Icehouse
Runnymede (Cropper, Thomas, House)
Walston Creek
HABS VA-628   pd   L
Smith-Custis Dovecote; see Folly, The,
    Dovecote
Smith-Custis House; see Folly, The
Smith-Custis Icehouse; see Folly, The,
    Icehouse

Atlantic vic.

Mount Wharton
Wishart Point
HABS VA-551   p   L

Cashville vic.

Topping House
Dahl Swamp
HABS VA-482   pd   L

Chesconessex vic.

Ohio; see Wise House
West, Revell, House
Deep Creek
HABS VA-931   pd   L
Wise House (Ohio)
Deep Creek
HABS VA-486   p   L H

Craddockville

Hermitage (Rogers House; Nealy Place)
Craddock Creek
HABS VA-483   pd   L
Nealy Place; see Hermitage
Rogers House; see Hermitage

Craddockville vic.

Hedra Cottage (Farm) (Hedrick Cottage
    (Farm))
Scarborough Cut
HABS VA-484   p   L

Hedrick Cottage (Farm); see Hedra
    Cottage (Farm)

Greenbush vic.

Bull House (Bull-Coard House; Slave
    Trader's House)
State Rt. 764
HABS VA-493   p   L
Bull-Coard House; see Bull House
Slave Trader's House; see Bull House

Guilford

Clayton, George, House
State Rt. 73 vic.
HABS VA-629   pd   L
Hinman-Mason House
HABS VA-630   pd   L
Mason House (Thoroughgood House)
HABS VA-952   s   H
Thoroughgood House; see Mason House

Hallwood

Wessel's Root Cellar
State Rts. 701 & 692 vic.
HABS VA-953   s   H

Horntown vic.

Chincoteague Farm (Corbin Hall; Corbin)
Chincoteague Bay
HABS VA-489   L
Corbin; see Chincoteague Farm
Corbin Hall; see Chincoteague Farm
Douglas Hall; see Poplar Grove
Poplar Grove (Wallop House; Douglas
    Hall)
Mosquito Creek
HABS VA-932   pd   L
Wallop House; see Poplar Grove

Lee Mont vic.

Drummond House
Drummond Pond
HABS VA-487   p   L
Drummond Store
Drummond Pond
HABS VA-488   p   L

Locustville vic.

Mount Hope House
HABS VA-1030   p   H

Mappsville vic.

Wharton Place
Assawaman Creek vic.
HABS VA-490   pd   L

Modest Town vic.

Long Place, The; see Saltbox House
Saltbox House (Long Place, The)
State Rts. 679 & 772
HABS VA-491   p   L H

New Church vic.

Pitts Neck Farm
State Rt. 709
HABS VA-492   p   L

Onancock

Kerr Place
Crockett Ave & Market St.
HABS VA-494   p   L

Painter vic.

Thunder Castle (Thunder Cottage)
State Rt. 607 vic.
HABS VA-496   p   L
Thunder Cottage; see Thunder Castle

Pungoteague

Siamese Twin House
HABS VA-1031   p   H
St. George's Church
State Rt. 178
HABS VA-497   p   L

Pungoteague vic.

Ker, Edward, House; see Shepherd's Plain
Melrose; see Shepherd's Plain
Shepherd's Plain (Melrose; Ker, Edward, House)
State Rt. 178
HABS VA-631   pd   L

Quinby vic.

Warwick
Upshur Bay vic.
HABS VA-495   p   L

Tasley vic.

Custis House
Deep Creek vic.
HABS VA-485   pd   L

ALBEMARLE COUNTY

Alberene

Alberene Company House
HABS VA-1032   s   H

Batesville

Mount Ed Baptist Church
State Rt. 635
HABS VA-999   s   L
Walters-Page House
HABS VA-1033   s d   H

Charlottesville vic.

Carrsbrook
South Fork River vic.
HABS VA-150   pd   L
D. S. Tavern
HABS VA-1019   s d   H
Darby's Folly
Barracks Rd (State Rt. 658)
HABS VA-981   s   L
Farmington (Farmington Country Club)
U.S. Rt. 250 vic.
HABS VA-253   p   L
Farmington Country Club; see Farmington
Fry, Col. Joshua, House; see Viewmont
Monticello
State Rt. 53 vic.
HABS VA-241   pd   L H

Viewmont (Fry, Col. Joshua, House)
Carter's Bridge vic.
HABS VA-11-12   s p d   L

Covesville

Cove Presbyterian Church
U.S. Rt. 29
HABS VA-982   s d   H

Crozet

Brown-Parrott House
State Rt. 680
HABS VA-992   s   L

Earlysville vic.

Buck Mountain Episcopal Church
State Rt. 743
HABS VA-971   s   L

Glendower

Christ Church (Episcopal Church)
State Rt. 713
HABS VA-972   s   L
Episcopal Church; see Christ Church

Greenwood

Blue Ridge Railroad, Greenwood Tunnel
(Chesapeake & Ohio Railroad, Greenwood Tunnel)
HAER VA-3   s p   L H
Chesapeake & Ohio Railroad, Greenwood Tunnel; see Blue Ridge Railroad, Greenwood Tunnel

Hatton

Hatton Grange Mill
HABS VA-990   s   H

Howardsville

George Lodge Number 32 (Masonic Lodge Number 32)
State Rt. 602
HABS VA-975   s   L
Masonic Lodge Number 32; see George Lodge Number 32

Ivy

Spring Hill Farm, Claim House
State Rt. 637
HABS VA-980   s d   H

Keswick

Monroe Law Office
U.S. Rt. 250 vic.
HABS VA-988   s   L

North Garden

Crossroads Tavern
State Rt. 692
HABS VA-993   s   L H
Old Zion Baptist Church
U.S. Rt. 29
HABS VA-995   s   L

North Garden vic.

Sunny Bank
HABS VA-996   s   H

Scottsville

Chesapeake & Ohio Railroad Station
Main St. (State Rt. 6)
HABS VA-977   s   L
Disciples of Christ Church
Main St. (State Rt. 6)
HABS VA-974   s   H
Mount Walla; see Scott, John, House
Scott, Daniel, House (Valmont)
State Rt. 726
HABS VA-1001   s   L H
Scott, John, House (Mount Walla)
Jackson St.
HABS VA-986   s   L
Sowell House
State Rt. 20
HABS VA-1016   s d   H
St. John's Episcopal Church
Harrison & Bird Sts.
HABS VA-973   s   L
Valmont; see Scott, Daniel, House

Shadwell

Chesapeake & Ohio Railroad Station
HABS VA-1013   s d   H

Simeon

Ashlawn
HABS VA-1017   s d   H
St. Luke's Chapel
State Rts. 53 & 732
HABS VA-1025   s d   H

Simeon vic.

Springdale Farm
Buck Island Creek vic.
HABS VA-1024   s d   H

ALLEGHANY COUNTY

Covington vic.

Humpback Covered Bridge
Spanning Dunlap Creek
HAER VA-1   s p d   L H

Sweet Chalybeate

Red Sweet Springs; see Sweet Chalybeate
Sweet Chalybeate (Red Sweet Springs)
State Rt. 311
HABS VA-1035   p   H

AMELIA COUNTY

Amelia vic.

Archer-Hindle House; see Woodlands
Hindle House; see Woodlands
Woodlands (Hindle House; Archer-Hindle House)
Amelia Courthouse vic.
HABS VA-269   s d   L

Mattoax vic.

Oaks, The
(moved to VA, Richmond)
HABS VA-157   pd   L

Oaks, The
(moved to VA, Richmond)
HABS VA-157   pd   L

AMHERST COUNTY

Clifford
House, Brick
State Rt. 151
HABS VA-54   pd   L

Dillwyn vic.
Bellmont
State Rt. 667 vic.
HABS VA-11-14   s pd   L

APPOMATTOX COUNTY

Appomattox
Appomattox Courthouse
Appomattox Courthouse National Historic
  Park
HABS VA-716   p   H
Appomattox National Historic Site
HABS VA-1036   s   H
Clover Hill Tavern; see Tavern
Jail, The
Appomattox Courthouse National Historic
  Park
HABS VA-436   p   L
Kelly House
Appomattox Courthouse National Historic
  Park
HABS VA-1037   s   H
Legrand House
Appomattox Courthouse National Historic
  Park
HABS VA-715   p   H
McDearmon-Tibbs House
State Rt. 24 vic.
HABS VA-714   p   H
McLean House (Raine-McLean House;
  Surrender House)
Appomattox Courthouse National Historic
  Park
HABS VA-240   s pd   L
Patterson House; see Tavern
Plunkett-Meeks Store & House
Appomattox Courthouse National Historic
  Park
HABS VA-432   p   L
Raine-McLean House; see McLean House
Sears, J., House
State Rt. 631
HABS VA-713   p   H
Store, Old
Appomattox Courthouse National Historic
  Park
HABS VA-435   p   L
Surrender House; see McLean House

Tavern (Clover Hill Tavern; Patterson
  House)
Appomattox Courthouse National Historic
  Park
HABS VA-439   p   L
Wright, Maria, House
Appomattox Courthouse National Historic
  Park
HABS VA-947   s   H

ARLINGTON COUNTY

Arlington
Arlington House (Custis-Lee Mansion; Lee,
  Robert E., House)
Arlington National Cemetery Grounds
HABS VA-443   s   L
Custis-Lee Mansion; see Arlington House
Lee, Robert E., House; see Arlington House

AUGUSTA COUNTY

Afton vic.
Blue Ridge Railroad, Blue Ridge Tunnel
  (Chesapeake & Ohio Railroad, Blue
  Ridge Tunnel)
Rockfish Gap
HAER VA-5   p   L
Blue Ridge Railroad, Blue Ridge Tunnel;
  see Blue Ridge Railroad, Crozet Tunnel
Blue Ridge Railroad, Crozet Tunnel (Blue
  Ridge Railroad, Blue Ridge Tunnel)
Rockfish Gap
HAER VA-2   s p   L H
**Chesapeake & Ohio Railroad, Blue Ridge
  Tunnel; see Blue Ridge Railroad, Blue
  Ridge Tunnel**

Crimora vic.
South River Bridge
State Rt. 612, spanning South River
HAER VA-19   p   L

Fishersville vic.
Tinkling Spring Church
State Rt. 608
HABS VA-717   s   H

Fort Defiance
Church, Old Stone
U.S. Rt. 11
HABS VA-11-10   s pd   L

Staunton vic.
Folly Farm
Folly Mills Creek
HABS VA-11-8   s pd   L H

Waynesboro vic.
Rockfish Service Station
Station Rt. 865
HABS VA-962   s   H

Weyers Cave vic.
Middle River Bridge
State Rt. 256, spanning Middle River
HAER VA-26   p   L

BATH COUNTY

Bacova vic.
Buckhorn Manor (McClintic House)
State Rt. 603
HABS VA-966   s pd   L
Buckhorn Manor, Housekeeping Cabin;
  see Buckhorn Manor, Log Dwelling
Buckhorn Manor, Kitchen (McClintic
  House, Kitchen)
State Rt. 603
HABS VA-966-A   s p   L
Buckhorn Manor, Log Dwelling (Buckhorn
  Manor, Housekeeping Cabin; McClintic
  House, Log Dwelling; McClintic House,
  Housekeeping Cabin)
State Rt. 603
HABS VA-966-C   p   L
Buckhorn Manor, Log Outbuilding
  (McClintic House, Log Outbuilding)
State Rt. 603
HABS VA-966-D   p   L
Buckhorn Manor, Springhouse (McClintic
  House, Springhouse)
State Rt. 603
HABS VA-966-B   s p   L
McClintic House; see Buckhorn Manor
**McClintic House, Housekeeping Cabin; see
  Buckhorn Manor, Log Dwelling**
**McClintic House, Kitchen; see Buckhorn
  Manor, Kitchen**
**McClintic House, Log Dwelling; see
  Buckhorn Manor, Log Dwelling**
**McClintic House, Log Outbuilding; see
  Buckhorn Manor, Log Outbuilding**
**McClintic House, Springhouse; see
  Buckhorn Manor, Springhouse**

BEDFORD COUNTY

Forest vic.
Poplar Forest
State Rt. 1 vic.
HABS VA-303   s pd   L H

BOTETOURT COUNTY

Buchanan
Buchanan Foot Bridge (James River
  Suspension Bridge)
Spanning James River
HAER VA-17   p   L
**James River Suspension Bridge; see
  Buchanan Foot Bridge**

CAMPBELL COUNTY

Gladys vic.
Marysville Covered Bridge
Spanning Seneca Creek
HAER VA-20   p   L

Long Island vic.
Green Hill Plantation & Main House
State Rt. 728
HABS VA-419   pd   L
Green Hill Plantation, Brick Dependency
State Rt. 728
HABS VA-604   pd   L
Green Hill Plantation, Cobblestone Walks & Drives
State Rt. 728
HABS VA-615   pd   L
Green Hill Plantation, Duck House
State Rt. 728
HABS VA-608   pd   L
Green Hill Plantation, Frame Barn
State Rt. 728
HABS VA-610   pd   L
Green Hill Plantation, Frame Dependency
State Rt. 728
HABS VA-602   pd   L
Green Hill Plantation, Gateposts
State Rt. 728
HABS VA-616   pd   L
Green Hill Plantation, Granary
State Rt. 728
HABS VA-613   pd   L
Green Hill Plantation, Icehouse
State Rt. 728
HABS VA-603   pd   L
Green Hill Plantation, Kitchen
State Rt. 728
HABS VA-606   pd   L
Green Hill Plantation, Laundry
State Rt. 728
HABS VA-609   pd   L
Green Hill Plantation, Log Barn
State Rt. 728
HABS VA-611   pd   L
Green Hill Plantation, Log Quarters (Detail)
HABS VA-419-A   p   L
Green Hill Plantation, Slave Auction Block
State Rt. 728
HABS VA-605   pd   L
Green Hill Plantation, Slave Quarters
State Rt. 728
HABS VA-607   pd   L
Green Hill Plantation, Stable (Ruins)
State Rt. 728
HABS VA-612   pd   L
Green Hill Plantation, Tobacco Barn
State Rt. 728
HABS VA-614   pd   L

Lynchburg vic.
Johnson, Christopher, Cottage
State Rt. 126
HABS VA-11-11   s pd   L

Rustburg vic.
White Hall
State Rt. 637
HABS VA-66   pd   L

CAROLINE COUNTY

Bowling Green
Caroline County Courthouse
U.S. Rt. 301 & Courthouse Ln.
HABS VA-718   p   L
Mansion, The Old
State Rt. 2 vic.
HABS VA-128   s pd   L

Bowling Green vic.
Mulberry Place
Tanyard Swamp vic.
HABS VA-719   p   L
Oak Ridge
Elliot's Pond vic.
HABS VA-720   p   L

Port Royal
Roy House
HABS VA-721   p   L
St. Peter's Episcopal Church & Bell Tower
Water St. (State Rt. 1006)
HABS VA-261   p   L
St. Peter's Episcopal Church, Rectory
Water St. (State Rt. 1006)
HABS VA-260   p   L

Port Royal vic.
Camden
Rappahannock River
HABS VA-184   pd   L
Catlett House; see Gaymont
Gaymont (Rose Hill; Catlett House)
U.S. Rt. 17 vic.
HABS VA-306   pd   L
Rose Hill; see Gaymont

Woodford
Flippo House (Sycamore Tavern, Old)
HABS VA-344   pd   L
Sycamore Tavern, Old; see Flippo House

CHARLES CITY COUNTY

Charles City
Charles City County Courthouse
State Rt. 5
HABS VA-60   pd   L

Charles City vic.
Berkeley (Harrison Family Home)
State Rt. 633 vic.
HABS VA-363   pd   L
Farmington
Morris Creek vic.
HABS VA-95   s   L
Glebe House
State Rt. 615 vic.
HABS VA-723   p   L

Greenway (Marlee; Tyler, President John, Birthplace)
State Rt. 5 vic.
HABS VA-11-23   s pd   L
Harrison Family Home; see Berkeley
Indian Field
State Rt. 5
HABS VA-376   p   L
Lower Weyanoke; see Weyanoke
Marlee; see Greenway
Sherwood Forest (Walnut Grove; Tyler, John, House)
State Rt. 5 vic.
HABS VA-722   p   L H
Shirley
State Rt. 608 vic.
HABS VA-388   pd   L H
Shirley, Dependencies
State Rt. 608 vic.
HABS VA-364   p   L
Tyler, John, House; see Sherwood Forest
Tyler, President John, Birthplace; see Greenway
Walnut Grove; see Sherwood Forest
Westover
State Rt. 633
HABS VA-402   s pd   L
Weyanoke (Lower Weyanoke)
Weyanoke Rd.
HABS VA-290   pd   L

Tettington vic.
Rowe, The
James River vic.
HABS VA-142   pd   L

CHARLOTTE COUNTY

Brookneal
Staunton Hill
State Rt. 619
HABS VA-1020   s   H

Red Hill
Henry, Patrick, Law Offices; see Red Hill
Red Hill (Henry, Patrick, Law Offices)
HABS VA-1034   p   H

CHESTERFIELD COUNTY

Richmond vic.
Ampthill
(moved to VA, Richmond)
HABS VA-159   s pd   L
Bellona Arsenal, Workshops
State Rt. 673 vic.
HABS VA-139   pd   L

Skinquarter
Skinquarter House
U.S. Rt. 360
HABS VA-724   p   L

South Richmond
Dunlop Mills
HABS VA-925   p   L

CLARKE COUNTY

Berryville vic.
Clifton
State Rt. 610 vic.
HABS VA-725   p   L

Boyce
Summerville
Page Run
HABS VA-180   s pd   L

Boyce vic.
Annefield
State Rt. 633 vic.
HABS VA-256   pd   L
Lee Headquarters; see Saratoga, Main
   House & Outbuildings
Saratoga, Main House & Outbuildings (Lee
   Headquarters)
Roseville Run
HABS VA-246   pd   L

Millwood
Burwell Mill (Millwood Mill)
State Rt. 723
HABS VA-354   p   L
Carter Hall
State Rt. 723 vic.
HABS VA-358   pd   L
Millwood Mill; see Burwell Mill

Millwood vic.
Chapel, Old
HABS VA-352   pd   L

White Post vic.
Greenway Court
HABS VA-108   s pd   L
Greenway Court, Estate Office
State Rt. 658 vic.
HABS VA-332   pd   L
Greenway Court, Outbuilding
State Rt. 658 vic.
HABS VA-108   p   L
Greenway Court, Powder House
State Rt. 658 vic.
HABS VA-108-B   s pd   L
Tuleyries, The
State Rt. 628 vic.
HABS VA-353   pd   L

CULPEPER COUNTY

Brandy Station vic.
Little Fork Church
State Rts. 624 & 627
HABS VA-147   s   L

Jeffersonton vic.
Greenfield
State Rt. 621 vic.
HABS VA-433   p   L

CUMBERLAND COUNTY

Caira
Grace Episcopal Church
State Rt. 632
HABS VA-970   s   L

Cartersville
Cartersville Bridge
Spanning James River
HAER VA-11   p   H

Cumberland
Cumberland County Courthouse
U.S. Rt. 60
HABS VA-192   pd   L
**Cumberland County Courthouse, Clerk's
   Office**
U.S. Rt. 60
HABS VA-192-A   p   L

Cumberland vic.
Covered Bridge (Trent's Bridge)
Spanning Willis River
HABS VA-11-13   s pd   L
Trent's Bridge; see Covered Bridge

DINWIDDIE COUNTY

Dinwiddie vic.
Burnt Quarter
State Rt. 613 vic.
HABS VA-386   pd   L
Kingston
State Rt. 619 vic.
HABS VA-384   pd   L
Plank House
State Rt. 647
HABS VA-314   pd   L

Ford vic.
Roseberry, House & Outbuildings
State Rt. 640 & U.S. Rt. 460 vic.
HABS VA-727   p   L

Hebron vic.
Harris House
U.S. Rt. 460
HABS VA-726   p   L

Petersburg vic.
Mayfield
U.S. Rt. 460 (moved from original location)
HABS VA-958   s   H
Wales
U.S. Rt. 460 vic.
HABS VA-152   s pd   L

ESSEX COUNTY

Center Cross vic.
Bowlers, Frame House & Kitchen
State Rt. 684
HABS VA-728   p   L
Mount Verde (Omnium Hill)
State Rt. 660
HABS VA-729   p   L
Omnium Hill; see Mount Verde

Champlain vic.
Cloverfield; see St. Anne's Parish Glebe
   House
Fonthill
State Rt. 631 vic.
HABS VA-330   pd   L
St. Anne's Parish Glebe House (Cloverfield)
U.S. Rt. 17
HABS VA-232   pd   L

Dunnsville vic.
Bathurst
Piscataway Creek
HABS VA-129   s pd   L
Ben Lomond
U.S. Rt. 17 vic.
HABS VA-730   p   L

Loretto vic.
Brooke's Bank
U.S. Rt. 17 vic.
HABS VA-731   s   H
Elmwood
State Rt. 640 vic.
HABS VA-323   pd   L
Kinloch
State Rt. 41 vic.
HABS VA-387   pd   L
Vauter's Episcopal Church
U.S. Rt. 17
HABS VA-410   pd   L

Paul's Crossroads
Woodlawn
HABS VA-991   s   H

Tappahannock
Customs House, Old
109 Prince St.
HABS VA-499   p   L
Debtor's Prison; see Lawyer's Office, Old
Emerson's Ordinary (House Number 2;
   Henly House)
314 Water Ln.
HABS VA-573   p   L
Emerson's Ordinary; see House Number
   One
Glebe House
HABS VA-961   s   L
Henly House; see Emerson's Ordinary
House Number 2; see Emerson's Ordinary
House Number One (Emerson's Ordinary)
314 Water Ln.
HABS VA-498   p   L

Lawyer's Office, Old (Debtor's Prison)
321 Prince St.
HABS VA-500   p   L
Ritchie House
227 Prince St.
HABS VA-501   s p   L H

FAIRFAX COUNTY

Accotink vic.
Belvoir (Fairfax House)
HABS VA-179   s p   L
Fairfax House; see Belvoir

Annandale
Ossian Hall
5001 Regina Dr.
HABS VA-598   s p   L

Annandale vic.
Green Spring Farm (Moss House)
4601 Green Spring Rd.
HABS VA-277   p   L
Moss House; see Green Spring Farm

Bush Hill
Bush Hill (Gunnell House)
HABS VA-507   p   L
Gunnell House; see Bush Hill

Centreville
Jamesson, Malcom, House (Mount Gilead)
5634 Mt. Gilead Rd.
HABS VA-280   p   L
Mount Gilead; see Jamesson, Malcom, House
Newgate Tavern (Spread Eagle Tavern)
HABS VA-1038   p   L
Plank Meat House
HABS VA-282   p   L
Spread Eagle Tavern; see Newgate Tavern

Chantilly vic.
Leeton
4619 Centreville Rd.
HABS VA-599   pd   L
Sully (Sully Plantation)
3601 Sully Rd.
HABS VA-250   s pd   L
Sully Plantation; see Sully

Colchester
Metzer House
HABS VA-580   pd   L

Fairfax vic.
Hope Park
11807 Pope's Head Rd.
HABS VA-107   s p   L
Hope Park Mill; see Piney Branch Mill
House, Stone (Innisfail)
11800 Fairfax Station Rd.
HABS VA-279   p   L

Innisfail; see House, Stone
Piney Branch Mill (Hope Park Mill; Robey's Mill)
1212 Pope's Head Rd.
HABS VA-741   s p   L H
Robey's Mill; see Piney Branch Mill

Great Falls
Great Falls Canal (Potowmack Canal)
Potomac River
HAER VA-13   s p   H
Great Falls Canal, Lock Number 1 (Potowmack Canal, Lock Number 1)
Old Dominion Dr. vic.
HAER VA-13-A   s p   H
Great Falls Canal, Lock Number 2 (Potowmack Canal, Lock Number 2)
Old Dominion Dr. vic.
HAER VA-13-B   s p   H
Great Falls Canal, Locks Number 3-5 (Potowmack Canal, Locks Number 3-5)
Old Dominion Dr. vic.
HAER VA-13-C   p   H
Potowmack Canal; see Great Falls Canal
Potowmack Canal, Lock Number 1; see Great Falls Canal, Lock Number 1
Potowmack Canal, Lock Number 2; see Great Falls Canal, Lock Number 2
Potowmack Canal, Locks Number 3-5; see Great Falls Canal, Locks Number 3-5

Great Falls vic.
Colvin Run Mill
10017 Colvin Run Rd.
HABS VA-502   p   L

Herndon vic.
Dranesville Tavern; see Tavern, Old
Tavern, Old (Dranesville Tavern)
119119 Leesburg Pike (moved from orig. location)
HABS VA-503   s p   L H

Lorton
Arch Hall; see Lewis, Lawrence, House
Lewis, Lawrence, House (Arch Hall)
11701 River Dr. (moved from VA, Alexandria)
HABS VA-109   s pd   L

Lorton vic.
Belmont; see Washington, Edward, House
Cocke-Washington House; see Washington, Edward, House
Colchester Inn (Fairfax Arms Tavern)
10712 Old Colchester Rd.
HABS VA-413   pd   L
Fairfax Arms Tavern; see Colchester Inn
Gunston Hall
10719 Gunston Rd.
HABS VA-141   pd   L
Pohick Church
9301 Richmond Hwy.
HABS VA-190   pd   L H

Washington, Edward, House (Belmont; Cocke-Washington House)
10913 Belmont Blvd.
HABS VA-578   pd   L

Manassas
Groveton Monument
Manassas National Battlefield Park
HABS VA-1039   s   H

Mount Vernon vic.
Washington's Grist Mill
55414 Mt. Vernon Memorial Hwy.
HABS VA-506   p   L

Mt. Vernon
Mount Vernon
Mt. Vernon Memorial Hwy.
HABS VA-505   p   L H

Mt. Vernon vic.
Pope, Loren B., House; see Pope-Leighey House
Pope-Leighey House (Pope, Loren B., House)
9000 Richmond Hwy. (moved from VA, Falls Church)
HABS VA-638   s pd   L H
Woodlawn Plantation
9000 Richmond Hwy.
HABS VA-337   s p   L H

Ravensworth vic.
Lee Estate, House & Stable; see Ravensworth, House & Stable
Ravensworth, House & Stable (Lee Estate, House & Stable)
5200 Port Royal Rd.
HABS VA-105   s p   L

Vienna vic.
Ash Grove
8900 Ash Grove Ln.
HABS VA-504   s pd   L

FAUQUIER COUNTY

Delaplane
Delaplane, John, House
HABS VA-967   s p   H
Delaplane, John, Stone House
HABS VA-967-A   p   H
Delaplane Post Office
HABS VA-968   p   H
Delaplane Store
HABS VA-969   p   H

Marshall vic.
Marshall, John, House (Oak Hill)
U.S. Rt. 17 vic.
HABS VA-11-5   s pd   L
Oak Hill; see Marshall, John, House

Paris
Watts Ashby Tavern
State Rts. 759 & 701
HABS VA-743   p   L

The Plains vic.

Gordonsdale Cabin; see Log House
Log Cabin; see Log House
Log House (Gordonsdale Cabin; Log
  Cabin)
State Rt. 750 vic.
HABS VA-11-6   s p d   L

Upperville

House, Old
U.S. Rt. 50
HABS VA-478   s   L

FLOYD COUNTY

Willis vic.

Mabry Mill
Blue Ridge Pkwy.
HABS VA-165   s p d   L

FLUVANNA COUNTY

Bremo Bluff vic.

Bremo
State Rt. 656 vic.
HABS VA-302   p d   L

Cohasset

Fork Union Depot
State Rt. 6
HABS VA-978   s   L

FREDERICK COUNTY

Clearbrook vic.

Hopewell Friends Meetinghouse
State Rt. 672
HABS VA-693   s p d   H

Middletown vic.

Belle Grove
State Rt. 727
HABS VA-259   s p d   L H
Fort, Old Stone; see House, Stone
House, Stone (Fort, Old Stone)
Middle Marsh Brook
HABS VA-210   p d   L

Winchester vic.

Red Lion Tavern; see Tavern Number
  One, Old
Tavern Number One, Old (Red Lion
  Tavern)
204-208 S. Loudoun St.
HABS VA-508   p   L
Tavern Number Two, Old
HABS VA-509   p   L

GLOUCESTER COUNTY

Bellamy vic.

Baytop (Capahosic House; York River
  Lodge)
State Rt. 618
HABS VA-744   p   L
Capahosic House; see Baytop
York River Lodge; see Baytop

Bena vic.

Little England (Sara's Creek House)
State Rt. 672 vic.
HABS VA-515   p   L
Sara's Creek House; see Little England

Gloucester

Botetourt Hotel; see Botetourt Inn & Barn
  (Ruins)
Botetourt Inn & Barn (Ruins) (Botetourt
  Hotel)
Main St.
HABS VA-513   p   L
Gloucester County Courthouse
U.S. Rt. 17
HABS VA-511   p   L
Gloucester Women's Club; see Longbridge
  Ordinary
Hay's Store
HABS VA-1040   p   H
Longbridge Ordinary (Gloucester Women's
  Club)
U.S. Rt. 17 & State Rt. 14
HABS VA-512   p   L

Gloucester vic.

Abingdon Glebe House
U.S. Rt. 17 vic.
HABS VA-746   p   L
Belroi; see Reed, Dr. Walter, House
Reed, Dr. Walter, House (Belroi)
State Rts. 614 & 616
HABS VA-57   p d   L
Roaring Springs
State Rt. 616 vic.
HABS VA-983   s   L
Ware Church
State Rt. 3
HABS VA-408   p d   L

James Store vic.

Toddsbury
North River
HABS VA-417   p d   L

Naxera vic.

Land's End
Severn River
HABS VA-518   p d   L

Ordinary

House, Old (Sewall's Ordinary)
U.S. Rt. 17 (moved from original location)
HABS VA-519   p   L
Sewall's Ordinary; see House, Old

Ordinary vic.

Belle Farm
State Rt. 656 (moved to VA.Williamsburg)
HABS VA-69   p d   L

Ware Neck

Belleville
HABS VA-994   s   H

White Marsh

White Marsh Store
U.S. Rt. 17
HABS VA-520   p   L

White Marsh vic.

Abingdon Church
U.S. Rt. 17
HABS VA-182   s p d   L
Carter's Creek House; see Fairfield
Fairfield (Carter's Creek House)
HABS VA-272   p d   L
Rosewell
Carter Creek
HABS VA-61   p d   L

Woods Crossroads Vic

Marlfield
State Rt. 612 vic.
HABS VA-514   p   L
Mount Prodigal (Roane House)
U.S. Rt. 17 vic.
HABS VA-510   p   L
Roane House; see Mount Prodigal

GOOCHLAND COUNTY

Ashland vic.

Fork Church
State Rt. 738
HABS VA-409   p d   L

Goochland

Goochland County Courthouse
State Rt. 6 vic.
HABS VA-224   p   L
Lawyer's Office
U.S. Rt. 522
HABS VA-225   p   L

Goochland vic.

James River & Kanawha Canal
  (Lickinghole Creek Aqueduct)
Lickinghole Creek vic.
HAER VA-10   s   L
Lickinghole Creek Aqueduct; see James
  River & Kanawha Canal

Manakin

House, Old
State Rt. 21
HABS VA-315   p   L
Manakin Village
State Rts. 6 & 621
HABS VA-218   p d   L

Manakin Village, Structure Number 1
State Rt. 621
HABS VA-219   p   L

Manakin Village, Structure Number 2
State Rt. 621
HABS VA-220   p   L

Manakin Village, Structure Number 3
State Rt. 621
HABS VA-221   p   L

Manakin vic.

Powell's Tavern
State Rt. 650
HABS VA-748   p   L

Richmond vic.

Tuckahoe Plantation
River Rd.
HABS VA-712   s   L H

Sabot

Saddlebag House
State Rt. 6
HABS VA-215   p   L

HALIFAX COUNTY

South Boston vic.

Berry Hill Plantation
State Rt. 659 vic.
HABS VA-304   pd   L

HANOVER COUNTY

Ashland vic.

Church Quarter
State Rt. 738
HABS VA-751   p   L

Fairfield; see Rocky Mills Mansion
Rocky Mills Mansion (Fairfield)
(moved to Va, Richmond vic.)
HABS VA-146   s pd   L

Beaver Dam

Scotchtown
State Rt. 685 vic.
HABS VA-117   s pd   L

Beaver Dam vic.

Edgewood
Newfound River
HABS VA-749   p   L

Mount Olivet Church
State Rt. 671
HABS VA-750   p   L

Cold Harbor

Gathwright House
State Rt. 156 vic.
HABS VA-76   s p   L H

Watt, Hugh, House
Richmond National Battlefield Park
HABS VA-477   s pd   L

Gumtree vic.

Dewberry
Little River vic.
HABS VA-752   p   L

Hanover

Barksdale Theater; see Tavern at Hanover
Courthouse
Hall of Justice; see Tavern at Hanover
Courthouse
Hanover County Courthouse
U.S. Rt. 301
HABS VA-429   p   L

Hanover Tavern; see Tavern at Hanover
Courthouse
Tavern at Hanover Courthouse (Hanover
Tavern; Barksdale Theater; Hall of
Justice)
State Rt. 1002
HABS VA-521   p   L

Mechanicsville vic.

Fairfield Farm; see Gaines, William, House
(Quarters)
Gaines, Doctor, House; see Powhite
Gaines, William, House (Quarters)
(Fairfield Farm)
State Rt. 615 vic.
HABS VA-78   s pd   L H

Pollard House (Williamsville)
Studley Rd.
HABS VA-343   pd   L

Powhite (Gaines, Doctor, House)
Richmond National Battlefield Park
HABS VA-335   p   L

Rural Plains
State Rt. 606
HABS VA-753   p   L

Williamsville; see Pollard House

Zion's Crossroads

Beaver Dam Baptist Church
HABS VA-1058   s   H

HENRICO COUNTY

Glen Allen vic.

Quarters Cabin
Gayton Rd. vic.
HABS VA-222   p   L

Richmond vic.

Cox House
Richmond National Battlefield Park
HABS VA-396   p   L

Fairfield; see Rocky Mills Mansion
Malvern Hill
State Rt. 156 vic.
HABS VA-89   s pd   L

Rocky Mills Mansion (Fairfield)
211 Ross Rd. (moved from Va, Ashland
vic.)
HABS VA-146   s pd   L

Wilton
Wilton Rd. (moved to VA, Richmond)
HABS VA-158   pd   L

ISLE OF WIGHT COUNTY

Smithfield

Barrett House
S. Church St.
HABS VA-140   pd   L

Clerk's Office; see Office, Small Brick
Grove Hotel (Pierce, Thomas, House)
Mason St.
HABS VA-301   p   L

Isle of Wight County Courthouse
Main & Mason Sts.
HABS VA-294   p   L

Mason's Hall
Mason St.
HABS VA-424   p   L

Office, Small Brick (Clerk's Office)
Mason & Main Sts.
HABS VA-754   p   L

Pierce, Thomas, House; see Grove Hotel

Smithfield vic.

St. Luke's Church
State Rt. 10 vic.
HABS VA-11-20   s pd   L

JAMES CITY COUNTY

Croaker vic.

Richardson House
HABS VA-88   s pd   L

Jamestown Island

Architectural Remains (Unit B, Sub-units
89 & 97)
HABS VA-25   s pd   L

Architectural Remains (Unit A, Sub-unit
39)
HABS VA-26   s pd   L

Architectural Remains (Unit B, Sub-unit
101)
HABS VA-31   s   L

Architectural Remains (Unit B, Structure
112)
HABS VA-445   s p   L

Architectural Remains (Project 194,
Structure 117)
HABS VA-471   s   L

Architectural Remains (Unit B, Sub-unit
86)
HABS VA-29   s   L

Architectural Remains (Unit B, Sub-units
59 & 73)
HABS VA-27   s pd   L

Architectural Remains (Unit B, Structure
110)
HABS VA-444   s p   L

Architectural Remains (Project 194, Structure 115)
HABS VA-470   s L

Architectural Remains (Project 103, Structure 125)
HABS VA-473   s L

Architectural Remains (Project 103, Structure 123)
HABS VA-472   s L

Architectural Remains (Unit B, Sub-unit 76)
HABS VA-30   s L

Architectural Remains (Unit B, Sub-unit 62)
HABS VA-28   s pd L

Project 103, Structure 123; see Architectural Remains

Project 103, Structure 125; see Architectural Remains

Project 194, Structure 115; see Architectural Remains

Project 194, Structure 117; see Architectural Remains

Unit A, Sub-unit 39; see Architectural Remains

Unit B, Structure 110; see Architectural Remains

Unit B, Structure 112; see Architectural Remains

Unit B, Sub-unit 101; see Architectural Remains

Unit B, Sub-unit 62; see Architectural Remains

Unit B, Sub-unit 76; see Architectural Remains

Unit B, Sub-unit 86; see Architectural Remains

Unit B, Sub-units 59 & 73; see Architectural Remains

Unit B, Sub-units 89 & 97; see Architectural Remains

Lightfoot vic.

Pinewoods; see Warburton House
Warburton House (Pinewoods)
Pinewoods Pond vic.
HABS VA-532   p L

Toano

Marston House (Chimney)
HABS VA-319   pd L

Toano vic.

Hickory Neck Church
U.S. Rt. 60
HABS VA-214   p L
MartinFarmhouse; see Martin's Farm
Martin's Farm (MartinFarmhouse)
U.S. Rt. 60
HABS VA-756   p L
Windsor Castle
State Rt. 610
HABS VA-254   pd L

Williamsburg vic.

Berkeley, Gov. William, House; see Greenspring
Greenspring (Berkeley, Gov. William, House)
State Rt. 614 vic.
HABS VA-440   s L
Keith's Creek House; see Skiff's Creek House
Kingsmill Plantation, Dependencies
Kingsmill Pond vic.
HABS VA-208   pd L
Maine Farm
State Rt. 614 vic.
HABS VA-71   pd L
Poplar Hall
Skiff's Creek vic.
HABS VA-755   p L
Powhatan (Powhatan Farm)
Powhatan Creek
HABS VA-177   s pd L
Powhatan Farm; see Powhatan
Skiff's Creek House (Keith's Creek House)
Skiff's Creek vic.
HABS VA-407   pd L

KING AND QUEEN COUNTY

Newtown vic.

Ballentine House (Dewsville)
(moved to VA, Yorktown)
HABS VA-596   pd L
Dewsville; see Ballentine House
Drysdale Glebe House
HABS VA-398   pd L
Jackson Farm (Buildings)
HABS VA-361   p L
Southworth House
HABS VA-313   pd L

KING GEORGE COUNTY

Comorn vic.

Lamb's Creek Church (Episcopal)
State Rt. 694
HABS VA-98   s L H
Marmion
State Rt. 649 vic.
HABS VA-145   s p L

Owens vic.

St. Paul's Church (Episcopal)
State Rts. 206 & 218
HABS VA-266   d L

Port Royal vic.

Belle Grove
Rappahannock River
HABS VA-274   pd L
Woodlawn
Rappahannock River
HABS VA-213   pd L

KING WILLIAM COUNTY

Aylett vic.

Cherry Grove, Servants' Quarters
State Rt. 30 vic.
HABS VA-762   p L
Moeser House
State Rt. 30 vic.
HABS VA-154   s pd L
Rumford Academy
State Rt. 600 vic.
HABS VA-258   d L

King William

King William County Courthouse & Stable
State Rt. 619
HABS VA-123   s pd L

King William vic.

Green Level
State Rt. 621 vic.
HABS VA-759   p L
Winterham
State Rt. 629
HABS VA-761   p L

Lester Manor vic.

Elsing Green
State Rt. 632 vic.
HABS VA-67   pd L

Mangohick

Cottage (House)
State Rt. 604
HABS VA-534   p L
House; see Cottage
Mooklar House
State Rts. 604 & 30
HABS VA-764   p L

Mangohick vic.

Hornquarter Farm
State Rt. 614 vic.
HABS VA-149   pd L
Mangohick Baptist Church
State Rt. 638
HABS VA-763   p L
Palestine
State Rt. 604 vic.
HABS VA-765   p L
Retreat
State Rt. 604 vic.
HABS VA-767   p L
Roseville
State Rt. 604 vic.
HABS VA-766   p L

Manquin vic.

Dabney House; see Seven Springs
Fontainebleu
State Rt. 618
HABS VA-379   p L
Seven Springs (Dabney House)
State Rt. 605 vic.
HABS VA-244   pd L

Rumford vic.

Acquinton Church (Upper Church of St. John's Parish)
State Rt. 629
HABS VA-760   p   L

Upper Church of St. John's Parish; see Acquinton Church

Sweet Hall

Sweet Hall
Pamunkey River
HABS VA-385   pd   L

Sweet Hall vic.

House, Old (Seaton House)
State Rt. 634
HABS VA-533   p   L

Seaton House; see House, Old

St. John's Church, Old
State Rt. 30 vic.
HABS VA-758   p   L

Waterville; see Windsor Shade

Windsor Shade (Waterville)
Pamunkey River
HABS VA-257   p   L

West Point vic.

Chelsea
Mattaponi River
HABS VA-399   pd   L

LANCASTER COUNTY

Bertrand vic.

Towles House
Rappahannock River
HABS VA-62   s pd   L

Farnham

Edgehill
State Rt. 354 vic.
HABS VA-431   p   L

Kilmarnock vic.

Christ Church
State Rt. 646
HABS VA-70   pd   L

Lancaster

Clerk's Office
State Rt. 3
HABS VA-360   pd   L

Hughlett House
State Rt. 3
HABS VA-412   pd   L

Lively vic.

St. Mary's Whitechapel Church
State Rts. 354 & 201
HABS VA-59   pd   L

Merry Point

Verville
State Rt. 611
HABS VA-151   pd   L

Merry Point vic.

Home of the Blind Preacher; see Waddel, James, House

Waddel, James, House (Home of the Blind Preacher)
State Rt. 604
HABS VA-297   p   L

Morattico

Morattico
Rappahannock River
HABS VA-73   pd   L

Nuttsville vic.

Oakley
State Rt. 622
HABS VA-535   p   L

Ottoman vic.

Belmont
State Rt. 662
HABS VA-296   p   L

Oak Hill
State Rt. 604 vic.
HABS VA-298   p   L

Somers vic.

Belle Isle
State Rt. 683
HABS VA-64   s pd   L

Weems

Corotoman (Spinster's House)
Rappahannock River
HABS VA-153   s pd   L

Spinster's House; see Corotoman

LOUDOUN COUNTY

Leesburg

Bank, Old (Valley Bank)
1 N. Church St.
HABS VA-378   p   L

House
HABS VA-1041   p   H

1-5 North King Street (Commercial Building); see 1-5 North King Street (Drug Store)

1-5 North King Street (Drug Store) (1-5 North King Street (Commercial Building))
HABS VA-375   p   L

13 South King Street (Commercial Building); see 13 South King Street (Nichols Law Office)

13 South King Street (Nichols Law Office) (13 South King Street (Commercial Building))
HABS VA-438   p   L

Valley Bank; see Bank, Old

Leesburg vic.

Cabin
Goose Creek vic.
HABS VA-536   p   L

Church of Our Savior; see Oatlands Historic District

Little Oatlands; see Oatlands Historic District

Mountain Gap School; see Oatlands Historic District

Oatlands, Bachelor Cottage; see Oatlands Historic District

Oatlands, Carter Barn; see Oatlands Historic District

Oatlands, Greenhouse; see Oatlands Historic District

Oatlands Historic District (Oatlands, Outbuildings)
U.S. Rt. 15 vic.
HABS VA-949-H   d   H

Oatlands Historic District (Oatlands, Greenhouse)
U.S. Rt. 15 vic.
HABS VA-949-C   s   L

Oatlands Historic District (Oatlands, Servants' Quarters)
U.S. Rt. 15 vic.
HABS VA-949-E   s   L

Oatlands Historic District (Little Oatlands)
U.S. Rt. 15 vic.
HABS VA-949-G   s   L

Oatlands Historic District (Oatlands, Main House)
U.S. Rt. 15 vic.
HABS VA-949-A   s   L

Oatlands Historic District (Oatlands, Studio)
U.S. Rt. 15 vic.
HABS VA-949-D   s   L

Oatlands Historic District (Church of Our Savior)
U.S. Rt. 15
HABS VA-949-L   d   H

Oatlands Historic District (Oatlands, Carter Barn)
U.S. Rt. 15 vic.
HABS VA-949-F   s   L

Oatlands Historic District (Mountain Gap School)
U.S. Rt. 15
HABS VA-949-K   s   L

Oatlands Historic District (Oatlands, Bachelor Cottage)
U.S. Rt. 15 vic.
HABS VA-949-B   s   L

Oatlands Historic District
U.S. Rt. 15
HABS VA-949   s pd   L H

Oatlands, Main House; see Oatlands Historic District

Oatlands, Outbuildings; see Oatlands Historic District

Oatlands, Servants' Quarters; see Oatlands Historic District

Oatlands, Studio; see Oatlands Historic District

Lenah Post Office

Cottage, The
HABS VA-537　　　　p　L

Waterford

Apothecary Shop (Haines-Shuey House)
Main & Water Sts.
HABS VA-777　　　　p　L

Arch House; see Gover, Miriam, House

Atley-Huff House (Hough-Haines House)
Main St. Hill
HABS VA-779　　　　p　L

Bank Building, Old (Bank House)
Main St.
HABS VA-378-A　　　p　L

Bank House; see Bank Building, Old

Baptist Church
High & Church Sts.
HABS VA-796　　　　p　L

Braden-Binker House; see Morland, Charles, House

Clockmaker's House & Shop (Nettle, W. & Sarah, House)
Second St.
HABS VA-787　　　　p　L

Cottage, Brick (Gover-Phillips Cottage)
Main St.
HABS VA-776　　　　p　L

Curtis, Lloyd, House (Myers, Mahlon, House)
Main St. Hill
HABS VA-785　　　　p　L

Divine, Charles W., House; see Loudoun Hotel

Dorsey, Edward, House; see Middle Huff House

Dutton, John B., House; see Steer House

Edwards Barn (Hough, William, Barn)
John Brown's Rdwy.
HABS VA-782　　　　p　L

Edwards, Doctor, House (Edwards-Hough House)
Main St. Hill & Butcher's Row
HABS VA-772　　　　p　L

Edwards House (Hough, William, House)
John Brown's Rdwy.
HABS VA-781　　　　p　L

Edwards-Hough House; see Edwards, Doctor, House

Fairfax Meetinghouse
State Rts. 665 & 698
HABS VA-773　　　　p　L

French-Atlee House; see Sidewell House

Gover, Miriam, House (Arch House)
Main St.
HABS VA-380　　　　p　L

Gover, Samuel A., House; see Gover-James House

Gover-James House (Gover, Samuel A., House)
Main St.
HABS VA-382　　　　p　L

Gover-Matthews Log House
Main St.
HABS VA-775　　　　p　L

Gover-Phillips Cottage; see Cottage, Brick

Haines-Shuey House; see Apothecary Shop

Hampier-Robinson House (Robinson, Nancy, Log House)
Water St.
HABS VA-778　　　　p　L

Hough, Hector, House (Moore, James, House)
Main St. Hill
HABS VA-784　　　　p　L

Hough, John & Samuel, House; see Huff, Robert, House

Hough, William, Barn; see Edwards Barn

Hough, William, House; see Edwards House

Hough-Haines House; see Atley-Huff House

House, Stuccoed Brick (Schooley, Ephraim, House)
Second St.
HABS VA-790　　　　p　L

House, Yellow Brick (Nettle, William, House)
Second St.
HABS VA-786　　　　p　L

Huff, Robert, House (Hough, John & Samuel, House)
Main St. Hill
HABS VA-780　　　　p　L

Loudoun Hotel (Divine, Charles W., House)
Main St.
HABS VA-769　　　　p　L

Main Street (Log Cabin)
(moved from original location)
HABS VA-783　　　　p　L

Main Street (Shop) (Mount-Silcott House)
Main St.
HABS VA-381　　　　p　L

Mansfield, Virginia, House (Walker-Phillips House)
Second St.
HABS VA-795　　　　p　L

Middle Huff House (Dorsey, Edward, House)
Main St. Hill
HABS VA-770　　　　p　L

Mill Wheel
Catoctin Creek
HABS VA-788　　　　p　L

Mock House; see Shawen-Schooley House

Moore, James, House; see Hough, Hector, House

Morland, Charles, House (Braden-Binker House)
Main St. Hill
HABS VA-768　　　　p　L

Mount-Silcott House; see Main Street (Shop)

Myers, Mahlon, House; see Curtis, Lloyd, House

Nettle, W. & Sarah, House; see Clockmaker's House & Shop

Nettle, William, House; see House, Yellow Brick

Noland Ferry House
Big Spring Rd.
HABS VA-538　　　pd　L

Patton House; see Steer, James M., House

Robinson, Nancy, Log House; see Hampier-Robinson House

Schooley, Elizabeth Hough, House (Walker, Nathan, House)
Main St. & John Brown's Rdwy.
HABS VA-789　　　　p　L

Schooley, Ephraim, House; see House, Stuccoed Brick

Schooley, John, House
Second St.
HABS VA-791　　　　p　L

Schoolhouse; see Williams Warehouse

Shawen-Schooley House (Mock House)
Main St. Hill
HABS VA-793　　　　p　L

Sidewell House (French-Atlee House)
Second & Church Sts.
HABS VA-774　　　　p　L

Steer House (Dutton, John B., House)
Second & Mahlon Sts.
HABS VA-771　　　　p　L

Steer, James M., House (Patton House)
Second & Factory Sts.
HABS VA-794　　　　p　L

Walker, Nathan, House; see Schooley, Elizabeth Hough, House

Walker-Phillips House; see Mansfield, Virginia, House

Waterford School
HABS VA-1014　　　s　d　L

Williams, John B., House (Williams, William, House)
Second & Janney Sts.
HABS VA-797　　　　p　L

Williams Warehouse (Schoolhouse)
Second & Janney Sts.
HABS VA-798　　　　p　L

Williams, William, House; see Williams, John B., House

LOUISA COUNTY

Green Springs

Ionia Barn
HABS VA-1000　　　s　　H

MADISON COUNTY

Madison

Madison County Courthouse
U.S. Rt. 29
HABS VA-325　　　pd　L

Madison vic.

Hebron Lutheran Church (Fence, Gate & Stile)
State Rts. 638 & 653
HABS VA-411   pd   L

MECKLENBURG COUNTY

Buffalo Springs

Hotel Cottages
State Rt. 767 vic.
HABS VA-186   p   L

Clarksville vic.

Prestwould Plantation
U.S. Rt. 15 vic.
HABS VA-320   pd   L

South Hill

624 Mecklenburg Avenue (Tavern, Old)
HABS VA-312   p   L

MIDDLESEX COUNTY

Christ Church vic.

Christ Church
State Rt. 638
HABS VA-539   p   L

Churchview vic.

House
La Grange Creek vic.
HABS VA-517   p   L
House, Old; see La Grange
La Grange (House, Old)
La Grange Creek vic.
HABS VA-516   p   L

Urbanna

Customs House; see House, Old
House, Old (Customs House)
State Rt. 1002
HABS VA-799   p   L
Mills, James & Co., Storehouse; see Tobacco Warehouse
Tobacco Warehouse (Mills, James & Co., Storehouse)
State Rt. 1002
HABS VA-589   pd   L

Urbanna vic.

Hewick House
State Rts. 615 & 602 vic.
HABS VA-540   p   L

MONTGOMERY COUNTY

Elliston vic.

Fotheringay
U.S. Rt. 11 vic.
HABS VA-348   pd   L

NELSON COUNTY

Afton vic.

Blue Ridge Railroad, Blue Ridge Tunnel (Chesapeake & Ohio Railroad, Blue Ridge Tunnel)
Rockfish Gap
HAER VA-5   p   L
Blue Ridge Railroad, Blue Ridge Tunnel; see Blue Ridge Railroad, Crozet Tunnel
Blue Ridge Railroad, Crozet Tunnel (Blue Ridge Railroad, Blue Ridge Tunnel)
Rockfish Gap
HAER VA-2   s p   L H
Chesapeake & Ohio Railroad, Blue Ridge Tunnel; see Blue Ridge Railroad, Blue Ridge Tunnel

Lovingston

Nelson County Courthouse
U.S. Rt.29
HABS VA-336   pd   L

NEW KENT COUNTY

Barhamsville

Union Level
State Rt. 633 vic.
HABS VA-442   pd   L

Barhamsville vic.

Smokehouse
State Rt. 30 vic.
HABS VA-541   p   L

New Kent vic.

Criss-Cross (Poindexter House)
State Rt. 617 vic.
HABS VA-126   s pd   L
Poindexter House; see Criss-Cross
Woodland
HABS VA-803   p   L

Providence

Potts, Doctor, House; see Providence Forge House
Providence Forge House (Providence Hall; Potts, Doctor, House)
U.S. Rt. 60 (moved to VA, Williamsburg)
HABS VA-912   p   L
Providence Hall; see Providence Forge House

Providence Forge Vic

Cedar Grove
State Rt. 609
HABS VA-802   p   L
Grist Mill; see Providence Forge
Providence Forge (Grist Mill)
Old Forge Pond
HABS VA-110   s pd   L

Quinton vic.

Lucas, Doctor, House
State Rt. 33
HABS VA-121   s   L

Tunstall vic.

Castle, The
State Rt. 608 vic.
HABS VA-124   s pd   L
Ferry, The; see Poplar Grove
Poplar Grove (Ferry, The)
Pamunkey River
HABS VA-801   p   L
Road View Farm, Kitchen
State Rt. 609 vic.
HABS VA-97   s pd   L
St. Peter's Church
State Rt. 642
HABS VA-127   s pd   L

NORTHAMPTON COUNTY

Bridgetown vic.

Belote; see West House
Hungar's Church
State Rt. 619
HABS VA-542   p   L
Vaucluse
State Rt. 619
HABS VA-437   p   L
West House (Belote; Wester House)
Wester House Creek
HABS VA-544   s p   L H
Wester House; see West House
Winonah
Hungar Creek
HABS VA-543   s p   L H

Capeville vic.

Arlington, John Custis Tomb
Old Plantation Creek
HABS VA-811   p   H

Cheriton vic.

Eyre Hall
U.S. Rt. 13 & State Rt. 636 vic.
HABS VA-809   p   H
Stratton Manor
State Rt. 642 vic.
HABS VA-545   p   L

Eastville

Cessford
U.S. Rt. 13
HABS VA-808   p   H
Courthouse Group Area Survey
U.S. Rt. 13
HABS VA-594   pd   L

Eastville vic.

Caserta
Mattawoman Creek vic.
HABS VA-591   pd   L
Cherry Grove
State Rt. 634 vic.
HABS VA-592   pd   L
Holly Brook
U.S. Rt. 13 vic.
HABS VA-593   pd   L

Kendall Grove
State Rt. 674
HABS VA-807   p   H

Hadlock P.O. vic.
Tankard's Rest
State Rts. 618 & 604 vic.
HABS VA-806   p   L

Jamesville vic.
Mattissippi; see Sturges House
Sommers House
State Rt. 183 vic.
HABS VA-546   s p   L H

Sturges House (Mattissippi)
Occohannock Creek
HABS VA-547   s p   L H

Nassawadox
Happy Union
Holly Grove Cove
HABS VA-805   p   H

Holly Grove
Holly Grove Cove
HABS VA-804   p   H

Nassawadox vic.
Brownsville
State Rt. 608 vic.
HABS VA-810   p   H

Woodlands
State Rt. 600 vic.
HABS VA-590   pd   L

Old Town Neck
Westover
State Rt. 630 vic.
HABS VA-957   s   H

Shadyside vic.
Pear Valley
State Rt. 628 vic.
HABS VA-960   s   H

Townsend vic.
Fitchett House (Point Pleasant)
State Rt. 600
HABS VA-548   p   L

Point Pleasant; see Fitchett House

Wardtown vic.
Christian House; see Locust Grove
Fisher House
Holly Grove Cove
HABS VA-549   p   L

Locust Grove (Christian House)
Nassawadox Creek
HABS VA-550   p   L

NORTHUMBERLAND COUNTY

Ditchley
Ditchley
State Rt. 607
HABS VA-308   pd   L

NOTTOWAY COUNTY

Blackstone
Anderson House; see Schwartz Tavern
Schwartz Tavern (Anderson House)
111 Tavern St.
HABS VA-813   p   L

Nottoway
Nottoway County Courthouse
State Rt. 625
HABS VA-812   p   L

ORANGE COUNTY

Gordonsville
Taylor, Zachary, Birthplace
HABS VA-1044   p   H

Montpelier Sta. vic.
Piedmont Log House
HABS VA-987   s   H

Montpelier Station
Monteplier Depot
HABS VA-997   s   H

Orange vic.
Howard Place (Mayhurst)
U.S. Rt. 15
HABS VA-1029   s   H

Mayhurst; see Howard Place

PAGE COUNTY

Luray vic.
Fort Egypt
State Rt. 615
HABS VA-200   s pd   L

Fort Massanutten
State Rt. 615 vic.
HABS VA-341   pd   L

Fort Stover
State Rt. 660 vic.
HABS VA-194   s pd   L

PITTSYLVANIA COUNTY

Chatham
Pittsylvania County Courthouse
State Rt. 57 & U.S. Rt. 29
HABS VA-271   pd   L

Danville
Tobacco District Rehabilitation Project
HAER VA-31   s   L

Danville vic.
Dan's Hill
State Rt. 1011 vic.
HABS VA-11-24   s pd   L

Gretna
Yancy Cabin (Yates Tavern)
U.S. Rt. 29 vic.
HABS VA-270   pd   L

POWHATAN COUNTY

Huguenot vic.
Keswick, Brick House (first)
State Rt. 711 vic.
HABS VA-85-A   s pd   L

Keswick, Guest House
State Rt. 711 vic.
HABS VA-85-C   p   L

Keswick, House & Quarters
State Rt. 711 vic.
HABS VA-85   s pd   L

Keswick, Kitchen
State Rt. 711 vic.
HABS VA-85-D   p   L

Keswick, Main House (second)
State Rt. 711 vic.
HABS VA-164   p   L

Keswick, Smokehouse
State Rt. 711 vic.
HABS VA-85-E   p   L

Keswick, The Quarters
State Rt. 711 vic.
HABS VA-85-B   s pd   L

Malvern
State Rt. 711 vic.
HABS VA-338   pd   L

Powhatan
Tavern, Old
State Rt. 30
HABS VA-441   p   L

Powhatan vic.
Belnemus
U.S. Rt. 60 vic.
HABS VA-86   pd   L

Woodberry Mill (Numbers One & Two)
State Rt. 614 vic.
HABS VA-201   p   L

Wyndham vic.
Norwood
State Rt. 711 vic.
HABS VA-148   pd   L

PRINCE EDWARD COUNTY

Worsham
Jail
U.S. Rt. 15
HABS VA-552   p   L

PRINCE GEORGE COUNTY

Hopewell
Appomattox Manor
Cedar Lane
HABS VA-824   pd   H

Hopewell vic.

Flowerdew Hundred
State Rt. 639
HABS VA-295   p   L

Prince George vic.

Brandon
State Rt. 611
HABS VA-143   pd   L

Merchants Hope Church
State Rt. 641
HABS VA-405   pd   L

PRINCE WILLIAM COUNTY

Aden

House, Green
State Rt. 646
HABS VA-825   p   L

Pilgrim's Rest
State Rt. 607 vic.
HABS VA-837   p   L

Aden vic.

Effingham
State Rt. 646 vic.
HABS VA-575   pd   L

Brentsville vic.

Fleetwood (Gibson House)
State Rt. 611
HABS VA-275   p   L
Gibson House; see Fleetwood
House, Old; see Moor Green
Lee House; see Park Gate
Moor Green (House, Old)
State Rt. 692
HABS VA-554   p   L
Park Gate (Lee House)
State Rt. 653
HABS VA-555   p   L

Bull Run

Sudley
Sudley Rd.
HABS VA-427   p   L

Bull Run vic.

Carter House; see Mountain View
Mountain View (Carter House)
6421 Bull Run Post Office Rd.
HABS VA-291   p   L

Cathardin vic.

Log Cabin
State Rt. 701
HABS VA-287   p   L

St. John's Church (Ruins)
HABS VA-286   p   L

Dumfries

Dumfries House; see Williams' Ordinary
Hotel, Old; see Williams' Ordinary
Love's Tavern; see Williams' Ordinary
Main Street (Frame House)
HABS VA-827   p   L

Merchent House
Main St.
HABS VA-91   s pd L
Tebbs House; see Tebbs-Mundy House
Tebbs-Mundy House (Tebbs House)
Main St.
HABS VA-178   s pd L
Williams' Ordinary (Hotel, Old; Dumfries
   House; Love's Tavern)
Main St.
HABS VA-826   p   L

Dumfries vic.

Leesylvania (Ruins)
State Rt. 610
HABS VA-281   p   L

Gainesville vic.

Dogan House
U.S. Rt. 29 & State Rt. 622
HABS VA-581   s pd L

Groveton

Chinn House (Remains)
Manassas National Battlefield Park
HABS VA-138   s pd L

Haymarket

McCormack Cabin; see McCormack House
McCormack House (McCormack Cabin)
Fayette St.
HABS VA-283   p   L

Haymarket vic.

Hagley (Tyler House)
State Rt. 601
HABS VA-276   p   L
Harrison House; see La Grange
Hutchison House; see Prospect Hill
La Grange (Harrison House)
State Rt. 681
HABS VA-289   p   L
Poplar Hill (Tyler House)
State Rt. 601 vic.
HABS VA-830   p   L
Prospect Hill (Hutchison House)
State Rt. 624
HABS VA-832   p   L
Retreat, The (Woolsey; Shelter, The)
State Rts. 601 & 234 vic.
HABS VA-285   p   L
Shelter, The; see Retreat, The
Tyler House; see Hagley
Tyler House; see Poplar Hill
Waverly Mills
State Rt. 679
HABS VA-284   p   L
Woolsey; see Retreat, The

Manassas

Beauregard, General, Headquarters; see
   Liberia

Liberia (Weir House; Beauregard, General,
   Headquarters)
627 Centreville Rd.
HABS VA-834   p   L
Weir House; see Liberia

Manassas vic.

Ben Lomond (House, Stone)
State Rt. 234
HABS VA-836   p   L
Brent House; see White House, The
House, Stone (Mathews House)
Manassas National Battlefield Park
HABS VA-144   s pd L
House, Stone; see Ben Lomond
Mathews House; see House, Stone
White House, The (Brent House)
State Rt. 619
HABS VA-553   p   L

Minnieville

Bel Air (Belle Air; Ewell House)
State Rt. 640 vic.
HABS VA-99   s p   L
Belle Air; see Bel Air
Ewell House; see Bel Air

Occoquan

Den, The; see Rockledge
Merchant's Grist Mill & Mill House
   (Ruins)
Mill St.
HABS VA-576   pd   L
Rockledge (Den, The)
Mill St.
HABS VA-577   s pd L

Thoroughfare

Beverley's Mill
State Rt. 55
HABS VA-828   p   L
House (Ruins) (Meadowland (Ruins))
Beverley's Mill vic. (State Rt. 55)
HABS VA-829   p   L
Meadowland (Ruins); see House (Ruins)

Waterfall

Evergreen
State Rt. 630 vic.
HABS VA-833   p   L
Mount Atlas
State Rt. 731 vic.
HABS VA-831   p   L

Woodbridge vic.

Blackburn House; see Rippon Lodge
King's Highway (Remains)
Parallel to U.S. Rt. 1
HABS VA-579   pd   L
Rippon Lodge (Blackburn House)
State Rt. 638
HABS VA-106   s p   L
Scarlit, Martin, Gravestone
Belmont Bay
HABS VA-838   p   L

RAPPAHANNOCK COUNTY

Sperryville vic.
Estes Mill
U.S. Rt. 211 & State Rt. 667
HABS VA-374   pd   L
Sawmill
U.S. Rt. 11
HABS VA-839   p   L

Washington
Court Green Area Survey (Street Scene)
   (Courthouse & Lawyer's Office)
HABS VA-561   p   L
Courthouse & Lawyer's Office; see Court
   Green Area Survey (Street Scene)

RICHMOND COUNTY

Farnham
Farnham Church (Episcopal)
State Rts. 602 & 607
HABS VA-562   p   L

Tidewater vic.
Indian Banks
State Rt. 606
HABS VA-74   pd   L

Warsaw
Clerk's Office
U.S. Rt. 360
HABS VA-331   pd   L
Lawyer's Office
U.S. Rt. 360 & State Rt. 3
HABS VA-563   p   L
Richmond County Courthouse
U.S. Rt. 360
HABS VA-896   p   L
St. John's Episcopal Church
U.S. Rt. 360
HABS VA-564   p   L

Warsaw vic.
Elmore House
State Rt. 3
HABS VA-63   s p   L
Farmhouse
HABS VA-565   p   L
Linden Farm
Lancaster Rd.
HABS VA-566   p   L
Menokin
Menokin Bay
HABS VA-156   s pd   L
Mount Airy (Tayloe, John, Plantation)
State Rt. 646 vic.
HABS VA-72   pd   L H
Sabine Hall
State Rt. 624 vic.
HABS VA-155   s pd   L
Tayloe, John, Plantation; see Mount Airy

ROANOKE COUNTY

Salem
Moravian House (Williams-Brown House &
   Store)
423 E. Main St.
HABS VA-347   p   L
Williams-Brown House & Store; see
   Moravian House

ROCKBRIDGE COUNTY

Lexington vic.
Covered Bridge
Spanning Maury River
HABS VA-567   p   L
James River & Kanawha Canal (South
   River Dam & Lock)
Maury River
HAER VA-22   p   H
**James River & Kanawha Canal, Ben Salem
   Lock**
Maury River
HAER VA-21   p   H
Log Cabin; see Winterview Farm
South River Dam & Lock; see James River
   & Kanawha Canal
Stone House
Ross Rd.
HABS VA-899   pd   H
Winterview Farm (Log Cabin)
Interstate Hwy. 81
HABS VA-956   s   H

SCOTT COUNTY

Clinchport
Clinchport Masonic Lodge No. 267
Second Ave.
HABS VA-984   s pd   L
Flanary, Kathleen S., House
Second Ave.
HABS VA-985   s pd   L

SHENENDOAH COUNTY

Birdhaven
Barb Mill
Elks Run
HABS VA-137   pd   L

Strasburg
Fort Bowman (Harmony Hall)
Frontage Rd.
HABS VA-909   s p   L H
Frontier Fort (Hupp House)
HABS VA-908   p   L
Harmony Hall; see Fort Bowman
Hupp House; see Frontier Fort

SMYTH COUNTY

Marion vic.
Thomas, Abijah, House
Thomas Bridge Rd.
HABS VA-639   s   H

SPOTSYLVANIA COUNTY

Chancellorsville
Chancellorsville (Ruins)
State Rts. 3 & 610
HABS VA-77   s pd   L

Fredericksburg vic.
Fredericksburg Country Club; see
   Smithfield Hall
Haley Farmhouse; see Todd House
Haney Farmhouse; see Todd House
Mannsfield
Rappahannock River
HABS VA-122   s pd   L
Salem Church
State Rt. 3
HABS VA-640   s   H
Smithfield Hall (Fredericksburg Country
   Club)
Rappahannock River
HABS VA-570   p   L
Todd House (Haley Farmhouse; Haney
   Farmhouse)
HABS VA-367   p   L

Guinea vic.
Jackson Shrine (Thornton, John, House)
Fredericksburg National Military Park
HABS VA-637   H
Thornton, John, House; see Jackson Shrine

Salem Church
Steiger House
State Rt. 3
HABS VA-369   p   L

Spotsylvania
Harrison House (Ruins)
State Rt. 208
HABS VA-392   p   L
Spotsylvania County Jail (Spotsylvania
   County Offices)
HABS VA-265   p   L
Spotsylvania County Offices; see
   Spotsylvania County Jail

Spotsylvania vic.
Danby Farm, Outbuildings
State Rt. 208
HABS VA-391   p   L
Herndon House
State Rt. 612
HABS VA-372   p   L
Whig Hill (Wigg Hill)
State Rt. 208
HABS VA-373   p   L
Wigg Hill; see Whig Hill

STAFFORD COUNTY

Falmouth

Barrett, Kate Waller, Birthplace; see 121
Prince Street (House)
Clifton; see 121 Prince Street (House)
Falmouth Baptist Church (Facade); see
Union Church (Facade)
121 Prince Street (House) (Clifton; Barrett,
Kate Waller, Birthplace)
HABS VA-264   p   L
Union Church (Facade) (Falmouth Baptist
Church (Facade))
Carter St.
HABS VA-203   p   L

Falmouth vic.

Chatham (Fitzhugh House)
State Rts. 3 & 607 vic.
HABS VA-339   pd   L
Ferry Farm Surveying Office; see
Washington, George, Surveying Office
Fitzhugh House; see Chatham
Washington, George, Surveying Office
(Ferry Farm Surveying Office)
712 King's Hwy.
HABS VA-90   s pd   L

Fredericksburg vic.

Lansdown, Smokehouse (Reynolds House,
Smokehouse)
571 Lansdown Rd.
HABS VA-368   p   L
Reynolds House, Smokehouse; see
Lansdown, Smokehouse

Stafford

Stafford Co. Courthouse Complex, Clerk's
Office
U.S. Rt. 1 & State Rt. 630
HABS VA-56-B   p   L
Stafford County Courthouse Complex
U.S. Rt. 1 & State Rt. 630
HABS VA-56   pd   L
Stafford County Courthouse Complex,
Courthouse
U.S. Rt. 1 & State Rt. 630
HABS VA-56-A   pd   L
Stafford County Courthouse Complex, Jail
U.S. Rt. 1 & State Rt. 630
HABS VA-56-C   p   L

Stafford vic.

Aquia Church
U.S. Rt. 1 & State Rt. 676
HABS VA-415   pd   L

SURRY COUNTY

Bacon's Castle vic.

Allen's Brick House; see Bacon's Castle
Bacon's Castle (Allen's Brick House)
State Rt. 617
HABS VA-75   s pd   L H

Crump House
State Rt. 617 vic.
HABS VA-233   p   L

Cabin Point

House (Dutch Brickwork Detail)
State Rt. 10
HABS VA-390   p   L
Ordinary, The
State Rts. 10 & 613
HABS VA-236   p   L

Claremont

Claremont, Manor Office
State Rt. 609 vic.
HABS VA-430   p   L

Otterdam vic.

Boats, Samuel, House; see Snow Hill
Snow Hill (Boats, Samuel, House)
HABS VA-1045   s   H

Surry vic.

Clerestory House
State Rt. 31
HABS VA-248   p   L
Four-Mile Tree Plantation, Servants'
Quarters
James River vic.
HABS VA-55   pd   L
Point Pleasant
Surry County Courthouse vic.
HABS VA-94   s p   L
Smith's Fort Plantation; see Warren House
Warren House (Smith's Fort Plantation)
Surry County Courthouse vic.
HABS VA-397   pd   L

SUSSEX COUNTY

Sussex

Windsor Farm (Winsor)
State Rt. 602
HABS VA-255   p   L
Winsor; see Windsor Farm

WARREN COUNTY

Front Royal vic.

Mount Zion
State Rt. 624
HABS VA-357   pd   L

WESTMORELAND COUNTY

Hague

Wilton
HABS VA-1047   p   L

Oak Grove

Blenheim
State Rt. 204 vic.
HABS VA-571   s p   L H

Wakefield (Washington, George,
Birthplace)
State Rt. 204
HABS VA-393   p   L H
Washington, George, Birthplace; see
Wakefield

Stratford

Stratford (Stratford Hall)
State Rt. 214
HABS VA-307   s pd   L
Stratford Hall; see Stratford

Tucker Hill vic.

Yeocomico Church
State Rt. 606
HABS VA-268   pd   L

Westmoreland

Nomoni Hall
HABS VA-1048   p   L

YORK COUNTY

Grafton vic.

Dairy House
York County Poor Farm (U.S. Rt. 17)
HABS VA-84   s p   L

Yorktown

Archer House
Water St.
HABS VA-914   s   H
Architectural Remains (Bake Oven)
117 Water St.
HABS VA-915   s   H
Architectural Remains (Foundations)
Lot 30, Main & Church Sts.
HABS VA-93   s   L
Architectural Remains (Foundations)
Lot 30, Main & Church Sts.
HABS VA-92   s   L
Architectural Remains (Structures L & M)
Lot 77, Main St.
HABS VA-917   s   H
Ballentine House (Dewsville)
Main St. (moved from VA, Newtown vic.)
HABS VA-596   pd   L
Blow, Capt. George P., House; see York
Hall
Customs House
Main & Read Sts.
HABS VA-202   p   L
Dewsville; see Ballentine House
Digges, Dudley, House; see West House
Lightfoot House (Somerwell House;
Yorktown Hotel)
Church & Main Sts.
HABS VA-87   s pd   L
Main Street (Medical Shop) (Main Street
(Post Office))
HABS VA-395   p   L
Main Street (Post Office); see Main Street
(Medical Shop)

Moore House (Temple Farm)
State Rt. 676
HABS VA-80   s pd   L
Nelson House; see York Hall
Powder Horn, Engraved
HABS VA-394   p   L
Sessions-Sheild House; see Sheild House
Sheild House (Sessions-Sheild House)
Pearl & Main Sts.
HABS VA-81   s pd   L
Somerwell House; see Lightfoot House
Swan Tavern
Main St.
HABS VA-83   s pd   L

Temple Farm; see Moore House
West House (Digges, Dudley, House)
77 Main St.
HABS VA-82   s pd   L H
Wharf Buildings
State Rt. 238
HABS VA-371   p   L
York Hall (Nelson House; Blow, Capt.
   George P., House)
Pearl & Main Sts.
HABS VA-58   pd   L H
Yorktown Hotel; see Lightfoot House

Yorktown vic.
Bellfield Cemetery (Digges Family
   Cemetery)
Digges Rd. vic.
HABS VA-918   p   L
Digges Family Cemetery; see Bellfield
   Cemetery
End View
HABS VA-572   p   L
Kiskiack (Naval Mine Depot)
State Rt. 238 vic.
HABS VA-183   s   L
Ringfield
King Creek
HABS VA-318   pd   L

Washington

ASOTIN COUNTY

Mission Orchard
Silcott House
HABS WA-114   pd   L

CLALLAM COUNTY

Dungeness vic.
Clallam County Courthouse (Weekly
   Farm)
HABS WA-70   pd   L
Jail, First (Pettit Place)
Pettit Farm
HABS WA-71   pd   L
Pettit Place; see Jail, First
Weekly Farm; see Clallam County
   Courthouse

CLARK COUNTY

Vancouver
Fort Vancouver, Barracks
HABS WA-41-C   p   L
Fort Vancouver, Barracks, Officers' Club
HABS WA-39-W-14   p   L
Fort Vancouver, Gen. Grant's
   Headquarters
HABS WA-41-B   s p   L
Fort Vancouver, Post Library
HABS WA-41-D   s p   L
Providence Academy
Tenth St.
HABS WA-99   pd   L
Slocum House
Fifth & Daniel Sts.
HABS WA-81   pd   L

Vancouver vic.
Covington, Richard, Cabin
Loverich Park
HABS WA-38   s pd   L

FRANKLIN COUNTY

White Bluffs vic.
Hudson Bay Post
Columbia River vic.
HABS WA-110   pd   L

GARFIELD COUNTY

Stember Creek
Lee, Andrew E., Barn
Alpowa Ridge vic.
HABS WA-115   pd   L

GRAYS HARBOR COUNTY

Montesano
Byles, C. M., House
Main & Spruce Sts.
HABS WA-101   pd   L
Methodist Episcopal Church
Church & Spruce Sts.
HABS WA-108   pd   L

South Montesano
Scammon, Isaiah, House
Chehalis River vic.
HABS WA-20   s pd   L

Stimson vic.
Hicklin House
State Hwy. 110
HABS WA-105   pd   L

ISLAND COUNTY

Coupeville
Alexander Blockhouse
Island Hwy., Main St., Whidby Island
HABS WA-39-W-8   s p   L
Cook Blockhouse; see Davis Blockhouse

Coupe, Capt. Thomas, House
Whidby Island
HABS WA-140   pd   L
Davis Blockhouse (Cook Blockhouse)
Cemetery Grounds vic., Whidby Island
HABS WA-39-W-11   s p   L
Dow, Thomas J., House
Front St.
HABS WA-39-W-12   s p   L
Ebey, Jacob, Homestead (original)
Whidby Island
HABS WA-104   pd   L
Haller, Maj. Granville O., House (second)
Whidby Island
HABS WA-121   pd   L
Masonic Hall
Whidby Island
HABS WA-143   pd   L
Robertson, Capt. John, House (Rosenfield
   House)
Front St., Whidby Island
HABS WA-135   pd   L
Rosenfield House; see Robertson, Capt.
   John, House
Swift, Capt. James Henry, House
Front & Colbert Sts.
HABS WA-120   pd   L

Coupeville vic.

Doyle, R. L., House
Whidby Island
HABS WA-141   pd   L
Ebey House
Ebey's Landing, Whidby Island
HABS WA-39-W-13   s p   L
Ebey, Jacob, Blockhouse
Sunnyside Cemetery vic., Whidby Island
HABS WA-39-W-16   s p   L
Engle, William B., House
Ebey's Prairie, Whidby Island
HABS WA-39-W-15   s p   L

Island Courthouse (first)
Whidby Island
HABS WA-39-W-7   s p   L

Kineth, John, House
Snakelumt Point, Whidby Island
HABS WA-39-W-19   s p   L

Terry, Charles T., House
Ebey's Landing, Whidby Island
HABS WA-102   pd   L

Fort Casey vic.

Robertson, Capt. John, House (Sergeant
   House)
Whidby Island
HABS WA-119   pd   L

Sergeant House; see Robertson, Capt. John,
   House

Oak Harbor vic.

Busby House
Whidby Island
HABS WA-118   pd   L

Gould House
Whidby Island
HABS WA-142   pd   L

Haller, Maj. Granville O., House (first)
Whidby Island
HABS WA-130   pd   L

Izett, Capt. John M., House
Whidby Island
HABS WA-39-W-23   s p   L

San De Fuca

Crockett, Walter, Blockhouse
Whidby Island
HABS WA-97   pd   L

Power, I. B., House
Whidby Island
HABS WA-76   pd   L

San De Fuca vic.

Hathaway, Capt. Eli, House
Penn Cove, Whidby Island
HABS WA-124   pd   L

JEFFERSON COUNTY

Chimacum

Bishop, Steven, House (son)
HABS WA-73   pd   L

Nisbet Barn
Valley Rd.
HABS WA-72   pd   L

Westergard House
West Valley Rd.
HABS WA-131   pd   L

Chimacum vic.

Glendale House
HABS WA-74   pd   L

Peterson Place
HABS WA-75   pd   L

Port Townsend

Buckley Jewelry Shop
Water & Quincy Sts.
HABS WA-125   pd   L

Clinger, J. G., House
Water & Monroe Sts.
HABS WA-137   pd   L

Eisenbeis House
Franklin & Clay Sts.
HABS WA-138   pd   L

Fowler, E. S., House; see Fowler House, Big
Fowler, E. S., House; see Fowler House,
   Little

Fowler House, Big (Fowler, E. S., House)
Water & Quincy Sts.
HABS WA-136   pd   L

Fowler House, Little (Fowler, E. S., House)
Jefferson & Polks Sts.
HABS WA-123   pd   L

Jefferson County Courthouse; see Leader
   Building

Leader Building (Jefferson County
   Courthouse)
HABS WA-128   pd   L

Rothschild House
Jefferson & Taylor Sts.
HABS WA-127   pd   L

St. Paul's Episcopal Church
Jefferson & Tyler Sts.
HABS WA-69   pd   L

Starrett Building
Adams & Washington Sts.
HABS WA-126   pd   L

Tucker, A. H., House
Quincy & Franklin Sts.
HABS WA-129   pd   L

KING COUNTY

Seattle

Alaska-Yukon-Pacific Exposition Grounds,
   Building; see Hoo Hoo House
Hoo Hoo House (University of Washington,
   Faculty Club; Alaska-Yukon-Pacific
   Exposition Grounds, Building)
University of Washington Campus
HABS WA-148   L

University of Washington, Faculty Club;
   see Hoo Hoo House

KLICKITAT COUNTY

Goldendale

Goldendale Blockhouse
Courthouse Park (moved from original
   location)
HABS WA-89   pd   L

Goldendale vic.

Alexander House
HABS WA-86   pd   L

Hopkins House & Barn
HABS WA-95   pd   L

Potter, Myron, Cabin
HABS WA-88   pd   L

LEWIS COUNTY

Centralia

Borst Blockhouse
Borst Park
HABS WA-39-W-9   s p   L

Chehalis

McFadden, O. B., House
1639 Chehalis Ave.
HABS WA-83   pd   L

Chehalis vic.

Jackson Prairie Courthouse
U.S. Hwy. 99
HABS WA-39-W-10   s p   L

Claquato

Claquato Church, Old (Protestant
   Episcopal Church)
HABS WA-39-W-6   s p   L

Protestant Episcopal Church; see Claquato
   Church, Old

Mossy Rock vic.

Riley, James, House
HABS WA-132   pd   L

LINCOLN COUNTY

Lincoln vic.

Fort Spokane, Hospital
HABS WA-111-B   p   L

Fort Spokane, Indian School & Officers'
   Quarters
HABS WA-111-C   p   L

Fort Spokane, Jail
HABS WA-111-D   p   L

Fort Spokane, New Guardhouse
Miles
HABS WA-144   s   L

Fort Spokane, Officers' Quarters
HABS WA-111-E   p   L

Fort Spokane, Old Guardhouse
HABS WA-111-A   p   L

Fort Spokane, Powder Magazine
Miles
HABS WA-147   s p   L

Fort Spokane, Quartermaster Building
Miles
HABS WA-146   s   L

Fort Spokane, Stable Barn
Miles
HABS WA-145   s p   L

OKANOGAN COUNTY

Omak vic.

St. Mary's Mission (Wayfarer's Cabin)
Colville Indian Reservation
HABS WA-35   s pd   L

Wayfarer's Cabin; see St. Mary's Mission

PACIFIC COUNTY

Oysterville

County Jail
HABS WA-109   pd   L
Crellen, John, House (Heckes Hotel)
HABS WA-103   pd   L
Crellen, Tom, House
HABS WA-106   pd   L
Espey Estate House
HABS WA-100   pd   L
Heckes Hotel; see Crellen, John, House
Nelson, Tom, House
HABS WA-107   pd   L
Wirt House
HABS WA-98   pd   L

PEND OREILLE COUNTY

Usk

Kalispel Indian Log Cabin
HABS WA-77   pd   L

PIERCE COUNTY

Fort Steilacoom

Officers' Houses
HABS WA-39-W-18   s p   L

Puyallup

Meeker, Ezra, House
Third & E. Meeker Sts.
HABS WA-96   pd   L

Steilacoom

Black, Capt., House
Seventh & Stevens Sts.
HABS WA-117   pd   L
Catholic Church
Nisqually & Main Sts.
HABS WA-39-W-2   s p   L
Gales House
Seventh & Stevens Sts.
HABS WA-134   pd   L
Jail, Old Brick
HABS WA-39-W-1   p   L
Judson, Stephen, House
Main St.
HABS WA-122   pd   L
Keach, Philip, House
HABS WA-39-W-5   s p   L
Wallus, Fred, House
Seventh St.
HABS WA-139   pd   L

Tacoma

Fort Nisqually
Point Defiance Park
HABS WA-37   s   d   L
Fort Nisqually, Corner Bastion
Point Defiance Park
HABS WA-37-A   s p   L

Fort Nisqually, Factor's House
Point Defiance Park
HABS WA-37-B   s p   L
Fort Nisqually, Granary
Point Defiance Park
HABS WA-37-C   s p   L
Post Office, First
Point Defiance Park
HABS WA-116   pd   L

SAN JUAN COUNTY

Friday Harbor

English Camp (Remains)
Garrison Bay, San Juan Island
HABS WA-39-W-17   s p   L

SKAMANIA COUNTY

Fort Rains

Fort Rains, Blockhouse
N. Bonnerville vic.
HABS WA-90   pd   L

SPOKANE COUNTY

Deer Park vic.

Hazard Post Office
Wild Rose Prairie
HABS WA-28   s pd   L

Hillyard

St. Michael's Mission Church
Mount St. Michaels
HABS WA-113   pd   L

Spokane

West 1624 Pacific Avenue (House)
HABS WA-149   s   L

STEVENS COUNTY

Arden vic.

Ayers Barn
HABS WA-94   pd   L

Chewelah

Douglas Cabin
HABS WA-26   s pd   L
Indian Agency Building; see McPherson,
   Dr. F. P., Cabin
McCrea, George, Cabin
HABS WA-80   pd   L
McPherson, Dr. F. P., Cabin (Indian
   Agency Building)
Third St. East
HABS WA-27   s pd   L

Chewelah vic.

King, Peter, Cabin
HABS WA-78   pd   L
Regenary Cabin
HABS WA-30   s pd   L

Waitt, George, Cabin
HABS WA-79   pd   L

Colville vic.

Clugston, John, Barn
Clugston Rd.
HABS WA-34   s pd   L
Harbaugh, Dan, Homestead
HABS WA-36   s pd   L
Holst, John, Homestead (Stevens County
   Courthouse)
HABS WA-32   s pd   L
Stagecoach Station, Barn
HABS WA-33   s pd   L
Stevens County Courthouse; see Holst,
   John, Homestead

Ford vic.

Haines, Guy, Cottage
HABS WA-92   pd   L
Haines, Guy, House
HABS WA-93   pd   L
Tshimakain Mission
HABS WA-91   pd   L

Kettle Falls vic.

St. Paul's Mission
HABS WA-31   s pd   L

THURSTON COUNTY

Chambers Prairie

Chambers, David, House
HABS WA-21   s pd   L

Olympia

Evans, Elwood, House (McMicken House)
Douglas St.
HABS WA-39-W-22   s   L
McMicken House; see Evans, Elwood,
   House

Stimson vic.

Hicklin House
State Hwy. 110
HABS WA-105   pd   L

WALLA WALLA COUNTY

Walla Walla vic.

Clark, Ransom, Cabin
HABS WA-39   s pd   L

WHATCOM COUNTY

Bellingham

Courthouse, Old
1106 E St.
HABS WA-39-W-3   s p   L
Pickett, Capt. George E., House
910 Bancroft St.
HABS WA-39-W-4   s p   L

WHITMAN COUNTY

Cashup
Stagecoach Station
HABS WA-29   s p d   L

Pullman Junction vic.
Collins, O. M., House
HABS WA-112   p d   L

YAKIMA COUNTY

Cowiche vic.
Splawn, A. J., House
HABS WA-84   p d   L

Naches vic.
Burge, Andy, Cabin
Reservoir vic.
HABS WA-82   p d   L

Sawyer vic.
Sawyer, W. P., Cabin
HABS WA-24   s p d   L

Tampico vic.
St. Joseph's Mission
Ahtanum Valley
HABS WA-40   s p d   L

Union Gap
Garvis, P. T., Store
HABS WA-85   p d   L

Wenas
Longmire, David, House
HABS WA-87   p d   L

White Swan
Indian Methodist Episcopal Church
   (Indian Mission)
HABS WA-133   p d   L
Indian Mission; see Indian Methodist
   Episcopal Church

White Swan vic.
Fort Simcoe, Commandant's House &
   Blockhhouse
HABS WA-25   s p d   L

West Virginia

BERKELEY COUNTY

Gerrardstown
Hollis, Trammell, House (Prospect Hill
   Farm)
HABS WV-153   p   L
Prospect Hill Farm; see Hollis, Trammell,
   House

Martinsburg
Martinsburg East & West Roundhouses,
   Machine Shops
HAER WV-1   s p   L H
Martinsburg Station & Hotel
HAER WV-17   p   L

BROOKE COUNTY

Bethany
Bethany Church of Christ
HABS WV-213   p   H
Bethany College, Old Main Building
Rt. 67
HABS WV-118   s p d   L
Campbell, Alexander, Mansion
Rt. 67
HABS WV-212   s p d   L
Campbell, Alexander, Study
Rt. 67
HABS WV-119   s p d   L

CABELL COUNTY

Huntington
Baltimore & Ohio Railroad: Passenger
   Station, Old
Heritage Village
HABS WV-176   s   H
Band, Old
Heritage Village
HABS WV-175   H

FAYETTE COUNTY

Gauley Bridge
Miller Tavern, Old
HABS WV-21-11   d   L

GREENBRIER COUNTY

Alderson
Federal Reformatory for Women
Rt. 3, S. of Greenbriar River
HABS WV-113   p d   H

Lewisburg
Church, Old Stone (Presbyterian)
Church St.
HABS WV-21-1   s p d   L
Greenbrier County Courthouse
Randolph & Market Sts.
HABS WV-115   p   L

Rainelle
Meadow River Lumber Company
HAER WV-24   s   L
Meadow River Lumber
   Company: Powerhouse
HAER WV-24-B   s   L
Meadow River Lumber Company: Sawmill
HAER WV-24-A   s   L
Meadow River Lumber Company: Shops
HAER WV-24-C   s   L

Renick
Renick House
U.S. Rt. 219
HABS WV-116   p d   L

Ronceverte
Church of the Incarnation (Episcopal)
Rt. 219
HABS WV-110   p   L
Edgar House
Rt. 63 vic.
HABS WV-111   p   L

White Sulphur Spring
Greenbrier; see White Sulphur Springs
White Sulphur Springs (Greenbrier)
Rt. 60
HABS WV-131   p   H

HAMPSHIRE COUNTY

Romney
Valley Bank Building
HABS WV-44   p   L

HARDY COUNTY

Moorefield
Willow Wall
HABS WV-220   s   H

HARRISON COUNTY

Bridgeport
Bridgeport Lamp Chimney Co: Simpson
   Creek Bridge
State Rt. 58
HAER WV-23   d   L H

JEFFERSON COUNTY

Charles Town
Courthouse
George & Washington Sts.
HABS WV-21-4   p d   L
Happy Retreat (Mordington)
HABS WV-10   p   L
Log Cabin
212 Lawrence St.
HABS WV-16   p   L
Mordington; see Happy Retreat
236 Washington Street (House, Doorway)
HABS WV-147   p   L

Charles Town vic.

Baptist Church, Old (Jones, C. W., House)
Shepherdstown Rd.
HABS WV-35   p   L

Brick Mansion-Locust Hill
HABS WV-145   p   L

Cassilis; see Manning, Vinton, House

Cedar Lawn (Poplar Hill)
Summit Point Rd.
HABS WV-15   p   L

Claymont Court
Summit Point Rd.
HABS WV-13   p   L

Flowing Spring
Shepherdstown Rd.
HABS WV-149   p   L

Gap View Farm
HABS WV-11   p   L

Harewood
HABS WV-2   s pd   L

Henderson, Henry, House
HABS WV-143   p   L

Jones, C. W., House; see Baptist Church, Old

Kennedy, Andrew, House; see Manning, Vinton, House

Level Green
HABS WV-22   p   L

Manning, Vinton, House (Cassilis; Kennedy, Andrew, House)
Berryville Rd.
HABS WV-144   p   L

Piedmont (Quarry Banks)
HABS WV-50   p   L

Poplar Hill; see Cedar Lawn

Quarry Banks; see Piedmont

St. George's Chapel (Ruins)
HABS WV-3   s pd   L

Vestal House (Outbuildings)
HABS WV-17   p   L

Darke

Darke, Gen., House
HABS WV-5   p   L

Darke vic.

Hilliard Farm-Framing from Shepherdstown House
HABS WV-38-A   p   L

Hilliard's Farm Barn
HABS WV-38   p   L

Lucas, Robert, House
HABS WV-24   p   L

Halltown

Walnut Hill
HABS WV-29   p   L

Harpers Ferry

Anderson, William, Building (Harpers Ferry National Historical Park)
HABS WV-173   s   H

Anderson, William, House (Kitchen) (Harpers Ferry National Historical Park)
HABS WV-173-A   s   H

Annin, Samuel, House (Harpers Ferry National Historical Park; Master Armorer's House, Building Number 34-35)
HABS WV-19   s   H

Bank of Harpers Ferry & Bank Annex (Harpers Ferry National Historical Park; Stephenson, Ann G., House, Building Number 12)
HABS WV-152   s   H

Brown's Fort, Armory Fire Engine House; see Brown's, John, Fort

Brown's, John, Fort (Harpers Ferry National Historical Park; Brown's Fort, Armory Fire Engine House)
HABS WV-21-5   pd   L

Downey, Susan, House, Building Number 15 (Harpers Ferry National Historical Park)
High St.
HABS WV-23   s pd   L

Harper House (Harpers Ferry National Historical Park)
Marmion Row
HABS WV-168   s   H

Harpers Ferry National Historic Park; see Tearney Building

Harpers Ferry National Historic Park; see Unseld, John C., Building

Harpers Ferry National Historic Park; see Wager, Gerard B., Building

Harpers Ferry National Historic Park; see White Hall

Harpers Ferry National Historical Park; see Anderson, William, Building

Harpers Ferry National Historical Park; see Anderson, William, House (Kitchen)

Harpers Ferry National Historical Park; see Annin, Samuel, House

Harpers Ferry National Historical Park; see Bank of Harpers Ferry & Bank Annex

Harpers Ferry National Historical Park; see Brown's, John, Fort

Harpers Ferry National Historical Park; see Downey, Susan, House, Building Number 15

Harpers Ferry National Historical Park; see Harper House

Harpers Ferry National Historical Park; see Jewelry Store, Building Number 14

Harpers Ferry National Historical Park; see Morrell House

Harpers Ferry National Historical Park; see Paymaster's Quarters

Harpers Ferry National Historical Park; see Richards, William, Building

Harpers Ferry National Historical Park; see Roeder House

Harpers Ferry National Historical Park; see Roeder Store

Jewelry Store, Building Number 14 (Harpers Ferry National Historical Park)
HABS WV-226   s   H

Lockwood House; see Paymaster's Quarters

Master Armorer's House, Building Number 34-35; see Annin, Samuel, House

Morrell House (Harpers Ferry National Historical Park; Paymaster Clerk's Quarters)
HABS WV-171   s   H

Paymaster Clerk's Quarters; see Morrell House

Paymaster's Quarters (Harpers Ferry National Historical Park; Lockwood House)
HABS WV-179   s   H

Richards, William, Building (Harpers Ferry National Historical Park)
HABS WV-32   s   H

Roeder House (Harpers Ferry National Historical Park)
High St.
HABS WV-174   s   H

Roeder Store (Harpers Ferry National Historical Park)
HABS WV-223   s   H

Stephenson, Ann G., House, Building Number 12; see Bank of Harpers Ferry & Bank Annex

Tearney Building (Harpers Ferry National Historic Park)
HABS WV-172   s   H

Unseld, John C., Building (Harpers Ferry National Historic Park)
HABS WV-170   s   H

Wager, Gerard B., Building (Harpers Ferry National Historic Park)
HABS WV-155   s   H

White Hall (Harpers Ferry National Historic Park)
HABS WV-156   s   H

Kearneyville

McIntyre, Effie, House
HABS WV-27   p   L

Southwood
HABS WV-28   p   L

Leetown

Hut; see Lee Barn & Outbuildings

Lee Barn & Outbuildings (Hut)
HABS WV-4   s pd   L

Woodberry
HABS WV-158   p   L

Leetown vic.

Royer House (Mantel)
HABS WV-21   p   L

Traveler's Rest
HABS WV-1   s pd   L

Middleway

Grantham House
HABS WV-51   p   L

Stone, Gilbert, House
HABS WV-160   p   L

Myerstown vic.

Lewis, Anne, House; see Rocks, The
Rocks, The (Lewis, Anne, House)
Shenandoah River
HABS WV-159   p   L

Ranson

Ranson House
HABS WV-48   p   L

Rippon vic.

Beverly (Burns, Marshall, House)
Berryville Rd.
HABS WV-36   p   L

Briscoe House (Bullskin Farm)
Berryville Rd.
HABS WV-39   p   L

Bullskin Farm; see Briscoe House
Burns, Marshall, House; see Beverly
Mason House; see Rock Hall
Rock Hall (Mason House)
HABS WV-40   p   L

Wheatland
Berryville Pike
HABS WV-49   p   L

Shenandoah Junction

Burr-McGarry House
Warm Springs Rd.
HABS WV-42   p   L

Clearland
Shepherdstown Rd.
HABS WV-31   p   L

Elmwood (Lucas, Rion, House)
HABS WV-25   p   L

Lucas, Rion, House; see Elmwood
Osborne House
Sandy Ridge Rd.
HABS WV-26   p   L

Vickers, Newton, House
Shepherdstown Rd.
HABS WV-37   p   L

Shepherdstown

Hilliard Farmhouse
HABS WV-221   p   L

**Market House, Old (Shepherdstown Public
    Library)**
HABS WV-161   s   H

Morgan, Richard, House
High St.
HABS WV-166   p   L

Shepherd, Thomas, Gristmill
HAER WV-5   s pd   L H

**Shepherdstown Public Library; see Market
    House, Old**

Shepherdstown vic.

Dandridge House; see Grove, The
Falling Spring; see Morgan, Jacob, House
Grove, The (Rose Break; Dandridge House)
HABS WV-34   p   L

Morgan, Jacob, House (Falling Spring)
HABS WV-33   p   L

Rose Break; see Grove, The
Springdale
HABS WV-30   p   L

Summit Point

Thompson, Dr., House
HABS WV-18   p   L

White House
HABS WV-12   p   L

Wheatland

Locust Hill
HABS WV-9   p   L

KANAWHA COUNTY

Cedar Grove

Church, Old Brick
HABS WV-21-12   d   L

Charles Town

Littlepage; see Mansion, Old Stone
Mansion, Old Stone (Littlepage)
HABS WV-21-10   d   H

Charleston

Craik-Patton House (Elm Grove)
Daniel Boone Park, U.S. Rt. 60
HABS WV-214   pd   L

Elm Grove; see Craik-Patton House
Gates Building
108 Capitol St.
HABS WV-218   s p   L

**Glenwood (Laidley-Summers-Quarrier
    House)**
800 Orchard St.
HABS WV-211   s pd   L

**Laidley-Summers-Quarrier House; see
    Glenwood**
MacCorkle Mansion; see Sunrise
Ruffner Cabin
Daniel Boone Park, U.S. Rt. 60
HABS WV-219   pd   L

St. John's Episcopal Church
1105 Quarrier St.
HABS WV-215   pd   L

Sunrise (MacCorkle Mansion)
746 Myrtle Rd.
HABS WV-216   pd   L

West Virginia Capitol
1800 Washington St. E.
HABS WV-217   pd   L

Harpers Ferry

Building Number 11A (Harpers Ferry
    National Historical Park)
HABS WV-222   s   H

**Harpers Ferry National Historical Park; see
    Building Number 11A**

Malden

**African Zion Baptist Church; see Malden
    Historic District**

**Dickinson, J. Q. & Company, Office
    Building**; see Malden Historic District
4212 Fallam Drive; see Malden Historic
    District
Kanawha-Salines Presbyterian Church; see
    Malden Historic District
4001 Malden Drive; see Malden Historic
    District
4003 Malden Drive; see Malden Historic
    District
4004 Malden Drive; see Malden Historic
    District
4006 Malden Drive; see Malden Historic
    District
4007 Malden Drive; see Malden Historic
    District
4008 Malden Drive; see Malden Historic
    District
4011 Malden Drive; see Malden Historic
    District
4012 Malden Drive; see Malden Historic
    District
4102 Malden Drive; see Malden Historic
    District
4103 Malden Drive; see Malden Historic
    District
4105 Malden Drive; see Malden Historic
    District
4112 Malden Drive; see Malden Historic
    District
4200 Malden Drive; see Malden Historic
    District
4202 Malden Drive; see Malden Historic
    District
4203 Malden Drive; see Malden Historic
    District
4205 Malden Drive; see Malden Historic
    District
4207 Malden Drive; see Malden Historic
    District
4208 Malden Drive; see Malden Historic
    District
4300 Malden Drive; see Malden Historic
    District
4301 Fallam Drive; see Malden Historic
    District
4304 Malden Drive; see Malden Historic
    District
4305 Malden Drive; see Malden Historic
    District
4306 Malden Drive; see Malden Historic
    District
4309 Malden Drive; see Malden Historic
    District
4312 Malden Drive; see Malden Historic
    District
4401 Malden Drive; see Malden Historic
    District
4402 Malden Drive; see Malden Historic
    District
4412 Malden Drive; see Malden Historic
    District

4414 Malden Drive; see Malden Historic District

4416 Malden Drive; see Malden Historic District

4502 Malden Drive; see Malden Historic District

Malden Historic District (African Zion Baptist Church)
4104 Malden Drive
HABS WV-210-6   s pd   L

Malden Historic District (4203 Malden Drive)
HABS WV-210-28   pd   L

Malden Historic District (4414 Malden Drive)
HABS WV-210-19   pd   L

Malden Historic District (4008 Malden Drive)
HABS WV-210-3   pd   L

Malden Historic District (4102 Malden Drive)
HABS WV-210-5   pd   L

Malden Historic District (4205 Malden Drive)
HABS WV-210-27   pd   L

Malden Historic District (4412 Malden Drive)
HABS WV-210-18   pd   L

Malden Historic District (4200 Malden Drive)
HABS WV-210-8   pd   L

Malden Historic District (4207 Malden Drive)
HABS WV-210-26   pd   L

Malden Historic District (Putney, Richard E., House)
4406 Malden Dr.
HABS WV-210-17   s pd   L

Malden Historic District (4112 Malden Drive)
HABS WV-210-7   pd   L

Malden Historic District (4309 Malden Drive)
HABS WV-210-23   pd   L

Malden Historic District (4301 Malden Drive)
HABS WV-210-25   d   L

Malden Historic District (4401 Malden Drive)
HABS WV-210-22   s pd   L

Malden Historic District (4305 Malden Drive)
HABS WV-210-24   pd   L

Malden Historic District (4003 Malden Drive)
HABS WV-210-33   pd   L

Malden Historic District (4103 Salines Drive)
HABS WV-210-36   s pd   L

Malden Historic District (4202 Malden Drive)
HABS WV-210-9   d   L

Malden Historic District (4304 Malden Drive)
HABS WV-210-12   pd   L

Malden Historic District (Malden Methodist Church)
4308 Malden Dr.
HABS WV-210-14   s pd   L

Malden Historic District (Kanawha-Salines Presbyterian Church)
4305 Salines Dr.
HABS WV-210-35   s pd   L

Malden Historic District (4103 Malden Drive)
HABS WV-210-30   s pd   L

Malden Historic District (4300 Malden Drive)
HABS WV-210-11   pd   L

Malden Historic District (4402 Malden Drive)
HABS WV-210-16   s pd   L

Malden Historic District (4502 Malden Drive)
HABS WV-210-21   s pd   L

Malden Historic District (4007 Malden Drive)
HABS WV-210-32   pd   L

Malden Historic District (Dickinson, J. Q. & Company, Office Building)
Malden Dr.
HABS WV-210-40   s p   L

Malden Historic District (4004 Malden Drive)
HABS WV-210-1   s pd   L

Malden Historic District (4208 Malden Drive)
HABS WV-210-10   s pd   L

Malden Historic District (4001 Malden Drive)
HABS WV-210-34   s pd   L

Malden Historic District (4306 Malden Drive)
HABS WV-210-13   pd   L

Malden Historic District (4312 Malden Drive)
HABS WV-210-15   s d   L

Malden Historic District (4212 Fallam Drive)
HABS WV-210-39   s pd   L

Malden Historic District (4105 Malden Drive)
HABS WV-210-29   s pd   L

Malden Historic District (Malden Missionary Baptist Church)
202 Wise Dr.
HABS WV-210-38   s pd   L

Malden Historic District (4101 Salines Drive)
HABS WV-210-37   s pd   L

Malden Historic District (4416 Malden Drive)
HABS WV-210-20   pd   L

Malden Historic District (4011 Malden Drive)
HABS WV-210-31   pd   L

Malden Historic District (4006 Malden Drive)
HABS WV-210-2   s pd   L

Malden Historic District
Georges, Malden, Planters Drs. & U.S. Rt. 60
HABS WV-210   s pd   L

Malden Historic District (4012 Malden Drive)
HABS WV-210-4   s pd   L

Malden Methodist Church; see Malden Historic District

Malden Missionary Baptist Church; see Malden Historic District

Putney, Richard E., House; see Malden Historic District

4101 Salines Drive; see Malden Historic District

4103 Salines Drive; see Malden Historic District

MARION COUNTY

Barracksville

Barracksville Covered Bridge
Spanning Buffalo Creek on Pike St.
HAER WV-8   s pd   H

MARSHALL COUNTY

Benwood

Baltimore & Ohio Railroad:Benwood Bridge
HAER WV-15   p   L H

MASON COUNTY

Point Pleasant

Mansion House, Old
First & Main Sts.
HABS WV-21-2   s   L

MINERAL COUNTY

Keyser

Baltimore & Ohio Railroad:Keyser Machine Shop
Spring St.
HAER WV-22   pd   L H

New Creek vic.

House, Stone; see Tavern, Old Stone
Tavern, Old Stone (House, Stone)
Rt. 50
HABS WV-45   p   L

MONONGALIA COUNTY

Dellslow vic.

Elkins Coal & Coke Company:Richard Ovens
Deckers Creek, State Rt. 7-92
HAER WV-21   s   L

Morgantown

Easton Roller Mill
West Run Rd.
HAER WV-4   s pd   L

Seneca Glass Company Factory
Beechurst Ave.
HAER WV-6   s   L

Morgantown vic.

Arnett, Carl, House
HABS WV-47   p   L

MONROE COUNTY

Red Sulphur Springs

Route 12 (House)
HABS WV-120   p   H

Salt Sulphur Springs

Salt Sulpher Springs, General Views
HABS WV-117   pd   H

Sweet Springs

Lewis House; see Lynnside
Lynnside (Lewis House)
State Rts. 3 & 311
HABS WV-59   p   L
Rowan, Andrew S., Memorial Home; see
    Sweet Springs, General View
**St. John the Evangelist Church (Roman
    Catholic)**
State Rts. 3 & 311
HABS WV-60   p   L
Sweet Springs Bath House
State Rt. 311
HABS WV-56   p   L
Sweet Springs Cottages
State Rt. 311
HABS WV-57   p   L
Sweet Springs, General View (Rowan,
    Andrew S., Memorial Home)
State Rt. 311
HABS WV-55   p   L
Sweet Springs Hotel
State Rt. 311
HABS WV-58   pd   L

Union

Church
HABS WV-121   p   H
House
HABS WV-122   p   H
Rehoboth Church
State Rt. 3
HABS WV-112   p   L

MORGAN COUNTY

Berkeley Springs

Strother, David Hunter, House
HABS WV-43   p   L

Great Cacapon

**Baltimore & Ohio Railroad:Cacapon River
    Viaduct**
HAER WV-20   p   L H

Paw Paw

Construction Office
Tunnel on Canal
HABS WV-224   p   H

OHIO COUNTY

Elm Grove

Monument Place (Shepherd Hall)
HABS WV-21-8   pd   L
Shepherd Hall; see Monument Place

Wheeling

Ackermann, Gregor, House; see Webster
    Historic District
**Baltimore & Ohio Railroad:Wheeling
    Freight Station**
HAER WV-3   s p   L H
Bank of Wheeling
1229 Main St., Clay District
HABS WV-182   s d   H
Bridge on Old National Trail
HABS WV-14   p   L
Bridgeport Bridge
HAER WV-25   s   L
Brues House
201 N. Front St., Wheeling Island
HABS WV-183   d   H
Centre Market Historic District (Reed
    Building)
2125 Market St.
HABS WV-184-A   s d   H
Centre Market Historic District (Thoner,
    John, House)
2238 Market St.
HABS WV-184-B   s d   H
Centre Market Historic District (Zink,
    William T., Double House)
2206-2208 Market St.
HABS WV-184-C   s d   H
Centre Market Historic District
HABS WV-184
HAER WV-26   s p   L H
East Wheeling (Frissell, Dr. John, House)
54 Fourteenth St.
HABS WV-196-A   s d   H
East Wheeling (Paxton-Reed House)
100 Twelfth St.
HABS WV-196-D   d   H
East Wheeling (Paull, George, House)
57 Fourteenth St.
HABS WV-196-B   s d   H
East Wheeling (Ridgeley, Absalom, House)
58 Fourteenth St., South Side
HABS WV-196-E   s d   H
East Wheeling (Paull, Thomas, House)
1314 Chapline St.
HABS WV-196-C   s d   H

East Wheeling (First Presbyterian Church)
1301 Chapline St., East Wheeling
HABS WV-196-F   d   H
East Wheeling
HABS WV-196   s   H
East Wheeling (McColloch Street
    (Cottages))
HABS WV-196-G   d   H
First Presbyterian Church; see East
    Wheeling
Frissell, Dr. John, House; see East Wheeling
Goering, William, House; see Upper Main
    Street
Hess, Christian, House; see Upper Main
    Street
Holliday, John A., House; see Webster
    Historic District
Independence Hall; see U.S. Custom House
Klieves, Bernard, House; see Webster
    Historic District
Klieves, Theodore, House; see Webster
    Historic District
List, Henry K., House; see Upper Main
    Street
McColloch Street (Cottages); see East
    Wheeling
Moore, Nancy, House; see Webster Historic
    District
Paull, George, House; see East Wheeling
Paull, Thomas, House; see East Wheeling
Paxton-Reed House; see East Wheeling
Reed Building; see Centre Market Historic
    District
Ridgeley, Absalom, House; see East
    Wheeling
Schmulbach, Henry, House; see Webster
    Historic District
Speidel, Joseph & Company, Building
1417 Main St.
HABS WV-204   s d   H
Thoner, John, House; see Centre Market
    Historic District
Upper Main Street (Vigilant Engine
    House)
648-650 Main St., Washington District
HABS WV-205-D   s d   H
Upper Main Street (List, Henry K., House)
827 Main St., North Wheeling
HABS WV-205-C   d   H

Upper Main Street (Hess, Christian, House)
811 Main St., Washington District
HABS WV-205-B   s d   H

Upper Main Street (Goering, William,
    House)
701 Main St., North Wheeling
HABS WV-205-A   d   H

Upper Main Street
HABS WV-205   s   H

U.S. Custom House (Independence Hall)
Market & Sixteenth Sts.
HABS WV-53   p   L

Vigilant Engine House; see Upper Main Street
Webster Historic District (Wells, Edgar, House)
2301 & 2303 Chapline St.
HABS WV-188-G   s   d   H
Webster Historic District (Ackermann, Gregor, House)
2319 Chapline St.
HABS WV-188-A   s   d   H
Webster Historic District (Klieves, Bernard, House)
2315 Chapline St.
HABS WV-188-C   s   d   H
Webster Historic District
2301-2319 Chapline St.
HABS WV-188   s   H
Webster Historic District (Moore, Nancy, House)
2305 Chapline St.
HABS WV-188-E   s   d   H
Webster Historic District (Schmulbach, Henry, House)
2311 Chapline St.
HABS WV-188-F   s   d   H
Webster Historic District (Holliday, John A., House)
2307 Chapline St.
HABS WV-188-B   d   H
Webster Historic District (Klieves, Theodore, House)
2313 Chapline St.
HABS WV-188-D   d   H
Wells, Edgar, House; see Webster Historic District
Wheeling
HABS WV-181   s   H
Wheeling Suspension Bridge
HAER WV-2   s   H
Zink, William T., Double House; see Centre Market Historic District

PENDLETON COUNTY

Parkersburg vic.
Hammer Mill
Monogahela National Forest
HABS WV-8   pd   L

POCAHONTAS COUNTY

Dunmore

Dunmore Methodist Church
State Rt. 28
HABS WV-54   p   L

Hillsboro vic.

Buck, Pearl S., Birthplace; see Stulting Place
Stulting Place (Buck, Pearl S., Birthplace)
U.S. Rt. 219
HABS WV-20   s   L

PRESTON COUNTY

Bretz
Elkins Coal & Coke Company: Bretz Ovens, 1904
Deckers Creek
HAER WV-7   d   H

Tunnelton
Baltimore & Ohio Railroad: Kingwood Tunnel
HAER WV-16   d   H
Baltimore & Ohio Railroad: Rowlesburg Bridge
Cheat River
HAER WV-13   d   H
Baltimore & Ohio Railroad: Tray Run Viaduct
Tray Run
HAER WV-18   d   H

RITCHIE COUNTY

Petroleum
West Oil Company: Endless Wire Pumping Station

U.S. Rt. 50
HAER WV-9   s pd   L H
West Oil Company: Machine Shop
U.S. Rt. 50
HAER WV-9-C   s   L
West Oil Company: Oil Rigs
U.S. Rt. 50
HAER WV-9-B   s   L
West Oil Company: Powerhouse
HAER WV-9-A   s   L

SUMMERS COUNTY

Talcott vic.
Graham House
State Rt. 3
HABS WV-114   p   L

TAYLOR COUNTY

Grafton
B. & O. Railroad, Northwest Virginia: Grafton Bridge
Tygart Valley River
HAER WV-11   pd   H
Grafton Machine Shop & Factory
HAER WV-10   s   L

WOOD COUNTY

Parkersburg
Baltimore & Ohio Railroad: Parkersburg Bridge
Ohio River
HAER WV-12   pd   L
Stephenson House
1131 Seventh St.
HABS WV-46   p   L
Wood County Jail
HABS WV-225   s   H

Wisconsin

BROWN COUNTY

De Pere
Wilcox, Randall, House
N. Broadway
HABS WI-28-20   s   L

Green Bay
Fort Howard Hospital
Chestnut Ave. & Kellogg St.
HABS WI-28-6   s pd   L

Moravian Church
Moravian St.
HABS WI-28-3   s pd   L
Tank Cottage
S. Tenth Ave.
HABS WI-165   s pd   L

COLUMBIA COUNTY
Portage
Indian Agency House
HABS WI-16   s pd   L

CRAWFORD COUNTY

Prairie Du Chien

Benedict, Alonzo, House
HABS WI-244   pd   L
Brisbois, Michael, House
HABS WI-28-18   s pd   L
Brisbois Warehouse
HABS WI-245   pd   L

DANE COUNTY

Daleyville vic.

Hauge Norwegian Evangelical Lutheran Church
State Rt. 78
HABS WI-240　　　s p d　L

Madison

Dudley House
508 N. Francis St.
HABS WI-234　　　s　d　L

DODGE COUNTY

Iron Ridge vic.

Mueller House
County Trunk AP
HABS WI-150　　　s p d　L

Lebanon Township

Christian Barn
State Rt. 109
HABS WI-148　　　s p d　L

Lowell

Sock Road Bridge
HAER WI-2　　　　　p d　H

Watertown vic.

Kuenzi Barn
County Trunk EM
HABS WI-151　　　s p d　L
Langholff House & Barn
State Rt. 109
HABS WI-149　　　s p d　L

FOND DU LAC COUNTY

Ripon

Republican Schoolhouse
Second & Elm Sts.
HABS WI-15　　　s p d　L

GRANT COUNTY

Platteville

Mitchell-Roundtree House
HABS WI-28-4　　　s p d　L

IOWA COUNTY

Dodgerville

Iowa County Courthouse
Main St.
HABS WI-28-15　　　s p d　L

Mineral Point

Cornish Miner's House, No. 1
114 Shakerag Alley
HABS WI-28-17　　　s p d　L
Cornish Miner's House, No. 2
HABS WI-28-14　　　s p d　L

Harris Cottage
425 Church St.
HABS WI-239　　　s p d　L
Odd Fellows Hall
Front & Vine Sts.
HABS WI-237　　　s p d　L

JEFFERSON COUNTY

Palmyra

Enterprise Building, The
Main St.
HABS WI-17　　　s p d　L

Watertown

German Methodist Episcopal Church; see
Wesley Methodist Church
Octagon House
HABS WI-135　　　s p d　L
Wesley Methodist Church (German
Methodist Episcopal Church)
201 N. Fifth St.
HABS WI-278　　　p d　L
Wesley Methodist Church, Parsonage
207 N. Fifth St.
HABS WI-279　　　p d　L

LA CROSSE COUNTY

La Crosse

U.S. Courthouse & Post Office
Fourth & State Sts.
HABS WI-277　　　s p d　L

LAFAYETTE COUNTY

New Diggings

St. Augustine's Church
HABS WI-236　　　s　d　L

MARATHON COUNTY

Wausau

Northern Hotel
428 Jackson St.
HABS WI-282　　　p d　L
Washington House
329 Washington St.
HABS WI-281　　　p d　L

MILWAUKEE COUNTY

Hales Corners

Curtin, Jeremiah, House
Grange Rd.
HABS WI-120　　　s p d　L

Milwaukee

All Saints' Episcopal Cathedral
828 E. Juneau Ave.
HABS WI-265　　　p d　L

Basilica of St. Josaphat
601 W. Lincoln Ave.
HABS WI-258　　　p d　L
Bogk, F. C., House
2420 N. Terrace Ave.
HABS WI-252　　　s p d　L
Brandt House
1205 N. Eighth St.
HAER .　　　　　s p d　L
Calvary Presbyterian Church
935 W. Wisconsin Ave.
HABS WI-264　　　p d　L
Chamber of Commerce (Mackie Building)
611 N. Broadway
HABS WI-158　　　p d　L
Church, Benjamin, House
1533 N. Fourth St.
HABS WI-13　　　s p d　L
City Hall
200 E. Wells St.
HABS WI-254　　　p d　L
Diederichs, Edward, House
1241 N. Franklin Place
HABS WI-262　　　p d　L
Downer, Jason, House
1201 N. Prospect Ave.
HABS WI-260　　　p d　L
First Unitarian Church
1009 E. Ogden Ave.
HABS WI-267　　　p d　L
Fitzgerald, Robert P., House
1119 N. Marshall St.
HABS WI-266　　　p d　L
Gipfel Brewery
423-427 W. Juneau Ave.
HABS WI-248　　　s p d　L
Holy Trinity Church
S. Fourth & W. Bruce Sts.
HABS WI-161　　　p d　L
Immanuel Presbyterian Church
1100 N. Astor St.
HABS WI-263　　　p d　L
Insurance Exchange Building (State Bank
of Wisconsin)
210 E. Michigan Ave.
HABS WI-157　　　p d　L
Iron Block
205 E. Wisconsin Ave.
HABS WI-251　　　s p d　L
Machek, Robert, House
1305 N. Nineteenth St.
HABS WI-250　　　s p d　L
Mackie Building; see Chamber of
Commerce
Miller, George P., House
1060 E. Juneau Ave.
HABS WI-276　　　p d　L

Milwaukee County Historical Center; see
Second Ward Savings Bank

Mitchell Building
N. Water & E. Michigan Sts.
HABS WI-156　　　p d　L

676

North Point Water Tower
E. North Ave.
HABS WI-249   s p d   L

Northwestern Mutual Life Insurance Co. Home Office
605-623 N. Broadway
HABS WI-268   pd   L

Pabst Theater
144 E. Wells St.
HABS WI-269   pd   L

Plankinton, Elizabeth, House
1492 W. Wisconsin Ave.
HABS WI-280   s p d   L

Public Library & Museum
814 W. Wisconsin Ave.
HABS WI-270   pd   L

Public Service Building
231 W. Michigan St.
HABS WI-275   pd   L

Second Ward Savings Bank (Milwaukee County Historical Center)
HABS WI-256   pd   L

Small Block
704 N. Milwaukee St.
HABS WI-259   pd   L

Smith, Lloyd R., House
2220 N. Terrace Ave.
HABS WI-272   pd   L

St. James Episcopal Church
833 W. Wiconsin Ave.
HABS WI-255   pd   L

St. Mary's Church
836 N. Broadway
HABS WI-160   pd   L

St. Paul's Episcopal Church & Parish House
904 E. Knapp St.
HABS WI-271   pd   L

St. Peter's Church
2469 N. Murray Ave.
HABS WI-28-10   s p d   L

St. Stanislaus Church
524 W. Mitchell St.
HABS WI-159   pd   L

State Bank of Wisconsin; see Insurance Exchange Building

Stevens Block
724-728 N. Milwaukee
HABS WI-257   pd   L

Stewart, Alexander, House
2030 S. Kinnickinnic St.
HABS WI-28-9   s p d   L

Trinity Evangelical Lutheran Church
1046 N. Ninth St.
HABS WI-273   pd   L

Uihlein, Alfred, House
1639 N. Fifth St.
HABS WI-253   s p d   L

Wisconsin Club Gazebo
900 W. Wisconsin Ave.
HABS WI-274   p   L

Paynesville

Paynesville Cemetery Chapel
Rock Creek vic.
HABS WI-114   s p d   L

Wauwatosa

Damon, Lowell, House
2107 Wauwatosa Ave. & Rogers St.
HABS WI-121   s p d   L

OCONTO COUNTY

Lena

Wood Block Masonry Barn, No. 1
HABS WI-286   p   H
Wood Block Masonry Barn Number 2
HABS WI-285   p   H

OUTGAMIE COUNTY

Kaukauna

Grignon House
Augustin Rd.
HABS WI-28-13   s p d   L

OZAUKEE COUNTY

Cedarburg

Cedarburg Mill
215 E. Columbia Ave.
HABS WI-154   s p d   L

Cedarburg vic.

Covered Bridge
Spanning Cedar Creek vic.
HABS WI-28-12   s p d   L

Freistadt

Hilgendorf House
State Rt. 167
HABS WI-146   s p d   L

Hamilton

Concordia Mills
HABS WI-28-23   s p d   L

Port Washington

Blake House
511 Grand Ave.
HABS WI-125   s p d   L

Thiensville vic.

Bonniwell, William T., House
Wauwatosa Ave.
HABS WI-28-7   s p d   L

Peuschel, Max E., House
County Trunk M
HABS WI-155   s p d   L

Peushel, Max E., Barn & Shed
State Rt. 167
HABS WI-164   pd   L

RACINE COUNTY

Burlington

Immaculate Conception Church
HABS WI-126   s p d   L

Luther Hall
Jefferson & Dyer Sts.
HABS WI-127   s p d   L

Meinhardt Bank
Chestnut & Pine Sts.
HABS WI-131   s p d   L

Burlington vic.

Mormon House
Hwy. 20
HABS WI-130   s p d   L

Honey Creek vic.

Fraser, James, House
HABS WI-140   s p d   L

Racine

First Presbyterian Church
Seventh St. & College Ave.
HABS WI-28-8   s p d   L

Fratt House, The
HABS WI-124   s p d   L

Hunt House
1247 Main St.
HABS WI-28-1   s p d   L

Johnson Wax Corporation Building
HABS WI-284   p   H

Kuehneman, William F., House
1135 S. Main St.
HABS WI-153   s p d   L

Rochester vic.

Russell, Henry, House
Old Hoyt Rd.
HABS WI-138   s p d   L

ROCK COUNTY

Milton

Inn, Old; see Milton House
Milton House (Inn, Old)
Fort Atkinson St.
HABS WI-119   s p d   L

Pioneer Log Cabin
Public Square vic.
HABS WI-18   s p d   L

SAUK COUNTY

Baraboo

Ringling, AL. Theatre
136 Fourth St.
HABS WI-261   pd   L

SHEBOYGAN COUNTY

Greenbush

Wade House
HABS WI-122   s p d   L

WALWORTH COUNTY

East Troy vic.
School, Stone
HABS WI-19   s d   L

Elkhorn
Octagonal House
E. South St.
HABS WI-14   s p d   L

Lake Geneva
Geneva Hotel
HABS WI-283   p   H

WASHINGTON COUNTY

Ackerville vic.
Lehner, Phillip, House
U.S. 41 vic.
HABS WI-144   s   L

Jackson
Koepsel House
HABS WI-147   s   L

Jackson vic.
Krueger House
State Rt. 60
HABS WI-142   s   L
Rusch Cottage
W. of Kirchhayn
HABS WI-143   s   L

Kirchhayn vic.
Turck, Christian, House
HABS WI-28-5   s p d   L

Krichhayn
Krause House
Spring Valley & Maple Rds.
HABS WI-145   s   L

Richfield
Lehmann House
HABS WI-141   s   L

West Bend vic.
Maxon Farmhouse
HABS WI-112   s p d   L

WAUKESHA COUNTY

Big Bend vic.
Smith, Jesse, Cobblestone Inn
HABS WI-28-16   s p d   L

Chamberlain
Martin Inn
HABS WI-113   s d   L

Delafield
Hawk's Inn
Main & Genesee Sts.
HABS WI-110   s p d   L
St. John Chrysostom Church
Church St.
HABS WI-162   p d   L

Menomonee Falls vic.
Miller, Charles, House
County Line Rd.
HABS WI-28-11   s p d   L

Merton
First Baptist Church; see Merton Baptist
  Church
Merton Baptist Church (First Baptist
  Church)
HABS WI-28-19   s p d   L

Milwaukee vic.
Dunkel, Robert, Inn
Bluemound Rd.
HABS WI-28-2   s p d   L

Nashotah vic.
Chapel of St. Mary the Virgin
Upper Nashotah Lake
HABS WI-163   s p d   L

Okauchee
Okauchee House (Okauchee Inn)
U.S. Hwys. 16 & 19
HABS WI-11   s p d   L
Okauchee Inn; see Okauchee House

Prospect
Baptist Church
State Hwy. 15
HABS WI-12   s p d   L
Smith, William, Farmhouse
HABS WI-116   s p d   L
Vanderpool Farmhouse
HABS WI-115   s p d   L

Saylesville
Booth House
HABS WI-132   s p d   L

Waukesha
Lain-Estberg House
299 Wisconsin Ave.
HABS WI-133   s p d   L
Town Hall
Wisconsin Ave.
HABS WI-111   s p d   L

WAUPACA COUNTY

Waupaca
Fisher-Fallgatter Mill
HAER WI-1   p d   L

WINNEBAGO COUNTY

Neenah
Doty Loggery; see Grand Loggery
Grand Loggery (Doty Loggery)
E. Lincoln Ave.
HABS WI-118   s p d   L

Neenha
Doty Loggery; see Grand Loggery
Grand Loggery (Doty Loggery)
E. Lincoln Ave.
HABS WI-118   s p d   L

Wyoming

ALBANY COUNTY

Centennial
Knight, S. H. Science Camp
State Rt. 130
HABS WY-75   p   L

Laramie
Ames Monument
Interstate 80
HABS WY-72   p d   L

Ivinson Mansion (Laramie Plains Museum)
603 Ivinson Ave.
HABS WY-74   p   L
Laramie Plains Museum; see Ivinson
  Mansion

Rock River vic.
Rock Creek Water Tower
Junction of Rock Creek & Union Pacific
  Railroad
HABS WY-55-A   s p d   L

Rock River vic.
Rock Creek Water Tower
Junction of Rock Creek & Union Pacific
  Railroad
HABS WY-55-A   s p   L

W. Laramie
Wyoming Territorial Penitentiary
N. side of State Rt. 130
HABS WY-76   p   L

Wheatland vic.

Padgett, William H., House
Flying X Ranch
HABS WY-84   s   H

Woods Landing vic.

Boswell, N. K. Ranch
State Hwy. 10
HABS WY-85   s   H

CARBON COUNTY

Fort Fred Steele

Fort Fred Steele
HABS WY-86   s   H

FREMONT COUNTY

Atlantic City

Atlantic City
Southpass Rd.
HABS WY-60   d   L

Carpenter's Hall
HABS WY-61   p   L

Hyde's Hall
HABS WY-62   p   L

Mercantile Bar
HABS WY-63   p   L

St. Andrew's Episcopal Church
HABS WY-64   p   L

Fort Washakie

Boarding School & Roberts Residence; see
Shoshone Episcopal Mission

Church of the Redeemer; see Shoshone
Episcopal Mission

Holy Saints John Chapel; see Shoshone
Episcopal Mission

Mission House; see Shoshone Episcopal
Mission

Roberts' Mission; see Shoshone Episcopal
Mission

Shoshone Episcopal Mission (Boarding
School & Roberts Residence; Mission
House)
Wind River Indian Reservation
HABS WY-54-A   s p d   L

Shoshone Episcopal Mission (St. David's
Church)
Wind River Indian Reservation
HABS WY-54-D   p d   L

Shoshone Episcopal Mission (Church of the
Redeemer)
Wind River Indian Reservation
HABS WY-54-C   p d   L

Shoshone Episcopal Mission (Roberts'
Mission; Shoshone School for Indian
Girls)
Wind River Indian Reservation
HABS WY-54   s p d   L

Shoshone Episcopal Mission (Holy Saints
John Chapel)
Wind River Indian Reservation
HABS WY-54-B   s p d   L

Shoshone Indian Cemetary
Wind River Indian Reservation
HABS WY-52   p d   L

Shoshone School for Indian Girls; see
Shoshone Episcopal Mission

St. David's Church; see Shoshone Episcopal
Mission

Miner's Delight

Hamilton City; see Miner's Delight

Miner's Delight (Hamilton City)
Atlantic City vic.
HABS WY-59   p d   L

Moneta

Sheep Shearing Shed
Moneta Access Rd.
HABS WY-53   s p d   L

South Pass Ave.

Sweetwater County Jail
Grant St.
HABS WY-50   s p d   L

South Pass City

B & H Mine, The
South Pass City vic.
HABS WY-56   p   L

Barney Tibbals Cabin
Price St. & South Pass Ave.
HABS WY-34   s p d   L

Black Horse Livery Stable
Grant St.
HABS WY-29   s p d   L

Carissa Mine, The
South Pass City vic.
HABS WY-30   p d   L

Carissa Saloon
South Pass Ave.
HABS WY-31   s p d   L

Cave, The (Fort Bourbon)
South Pass Ave.
HABS WY-32   s p d   L

Chipp, Jean, Cabin; see Dakota Street
(Cabin)

Dakota Street (Cabin) (Chipp, Jean,
Cabin)
HABS WY-33   s p d   L

Dance Hall
South Pass Ave. & Dakota St.
HABS WY-35   s p d   L

Duncan Mine
South Pass City vic.
HABS WY-57   p   L

Exchange Bank & Recorder's Office
South Pass Ave. & Price St.
HABS WY-36   s p d   L

Fort Bourbon; see Cave, The

**Grant & Price Streets (Commercial
Building)** (Morris, Esther, Hat Shop)
Grant & Price Sts.
HABS WY-41   s p d   L

Grecian Bend Saloon
South Pass Ave.
HABS WY-37   s p d   L

Houghton-Colter General Store
South Pass Ave.
HABS WY-38   s p d   L

Idaho House (South Pass Hotel; Sherlock
Hotel)
South Pass Ave.
HABS WY-48   s p d   L

Libby Cabin (Pest House)
State Route 28, (moved from South Pass
City vic.)
HABS WY-39   s p d   L

Masonic Lodge
South Pass Ave.
HABS WY-40   p d   L

Morris, Esther, Hat Shop; see Grant &
Price Streets (Commercial Building)

Palmetto Gulch Stamp Mill
Willow Creek, Palmetto Gulch vic.
HABS WY-42   p d   L

Pest House; see Libby Cabin

Privy I & II
South Pass Ave.
HABS WY-44   s p d   L

Roberts-Payne House
Dakota St.
HABS WY-43   s p d   L

Schoolhouse
South Pass Ave.
HABS WY-46   s p d   L

Sherlock Hotel; see Idaho House

Sherlock House
South Pass Ave.
HABS WY-47   s p d   L

Shields, Carrie, Mine
South Pass City vic.
HABS WY-58   p   L

Smith-Sherlock Store
South Pass Ave.
HABS WY-49   s p d   L

South Pass City, General View
HABS WY-27   s p d   L

South Pass Hotel; see Idaho House

Tibbals-Sager Cabin
South Pass Ave.
HABS WY-45   s p d   L

GOSHEN COUNTY

Cheyenne

Union Pacific Passenger Station
121 W. Fifteenth St.
HABS WY-80   p   L

Fort Laramie

Fort Laramie, Administration Building
HABS WY-14   s   H

Fort Laramie, Calvary Barracks
HABS WY-5   s p d   L

Fort Laramie, Commissary Storehouse
HABS WY-9   s p d   L

Fort Laramie, Hospital (Ruins)
HABS WY-13   s p d   L

Fort Laramie, Magazine
HABS WY-11   s p d   L

Fort Laramie National Monument
HABS WY-89   s p d   L
Fort Laramie, N.C.O. Quarters
HABS WY-16   s   H
Fort Laramie, New Bakery
HABS WY-15   s   H
Fort Laramie, Officer's Quarters A
HABS WY-7   s p d   L
Fort Laramie, Officer's Quarters F
HABS WY-4   s p d   L
Fort Laramie, Old Bakery
HABS WY-10   s p d   L
Fort Laramie, Old Bedlam
HABS WY-1   s p d   L H
Fort Laramie, Old Guard House
HABS WY-8   s p d   L
Fort Laramie, Pit Toilet
HABS WY-3   s p d   L
Fort Laramie, Stable
HABS WY-12   s p d   L
Fort Larmie, Officer's Ouarters E
HABS WY-6   s p d   L

Fort Laramie vic.

Fort Laramie, Sutler's Store
HABS WY-2   s p d   L
**North Platte River Bowstring Truss Bridge,
1875**
Spanning North Platte River
HAER WY-1   p   H

LARAMIE COUNTY

Cheyenne

Atlas Theatre
213 W. Sixteenth St.
HABS WY-77   p   L
Fort David A. Russell, N. C. O. Quarters
   (Warren, Francis E., Air Force Base
   Building 74)
First Ave. & Eight St.
HABS WY-65   s p d   L
Fort David A. Russell Veterinary Hospital
   (Warren, Francis E., Air Force Base,
   Building 29)
Third St. & Second Ave.
HABS WY-66   s p d   L
St. Mark's Episcopal Church
1908 Central Ave.
HABS WY-78   p   L
State Capitol Building
Twenty-fourth St. & Capitol Ave.
HABS WY-79   p   L
**Warren, Francis E., Air Force Base,
   Building 29; see Fort David A. Russell
   Veterinary Hospital**
**Warren, Francis E., Air Force Base
   Building 74; see Fort David A. Russell,
   N. C. O. Quarters**

PARK COUNTY

Cody vic.

**Buffalo Bill Dam; see Shoshone Dam,
1905-1910**
**Shoshone Dam, 1905-1910 (Buffalo Bill
   Dam)**
HAER WY-2   p   H

PLATTE COUNTY

Chugwater

**Swan Land & Cattle Company (Two Bar
   Ranch)**
State Rt. 313
HABS WY-71   s p   L
Swan Land & Cattle Company, Barn
State Rt. 313
HABS WY-71-A   p   L
**Swan Land & Cattle Company, Main
   Office**
State Rt. 313
HABS WY-71-B   p   L
**Swan Land & Cattle Company, Manager's
   House**
State Rt. 313
HABS WY-71-C   s p d   L
**Swan Land & Cattle Company, Mercantile
   Store**
State Rt. 313
HABS WY-71-D   s p d   L
**Two Bar Ranch; see Swan Land & Cattle
   Company**

Guernsey

Guernsey State Park Museum
Highway 317
HABS WY-81   p   L

Pepperville

Watertower
N. side of U.S. Rt. 26
HABS WY-82   p   L

SHERIDAN COUNTY

Sheridan

Sheridan Inn
HABS WY-28   s p d   L H

SWEETWATER COUNTY

Granger

Granger Stage Station
Old Rt. 30 N.
HABS WY-67   s p d   L

Point Of Rocks

Point of Rocks Stage Station
Rock Springs vic.
HABS WY-69   s p d   L
Point of Rocks Stage Station, Stable
Rock Springs vic.
HABS WY-69-A   s p d   L H

TETON COUNTY

Kell vic.

Chambers', Andy, Ranch House
Mormon Row Rd.
HABS WY-83   s p d   L
Kelly vic.
Moulton, T. A., Ranch
Mormon Row Rd.
HABS WY-26   s p d   L

Moose

Menor's Ferry (Museum)
Snake River
HABS WY-24   s p d   L
Noble, Maud, Cabin
Menor's Ferry, Snake River, moved from
   Cottonwood Cr
HABS WY-23   s p d   L

Moose vic.

Cunningham Cabin
Btw. Snake River & US Route 89
HABS WY-25   s p d   L
Mangus Cabin
Park Highway vic.
HABS WY-22   s p d   L

Norris Junciton

Norris Soldiers Station
Norris Campgrounds & Gibbon River vic.
HABS WY-21   s p d   L

Yellowstone Nat'l Pk

Golden Gate Viaduct, 1885
HAER WY-3   p   H
Old Faithful Inn
Yellowstone National Park
HABS WY-87   p   H

UINTA COUNTY

Piedmont

Piedmont Charcoal Kilns
Fort Bridger vic.
HABS WY-68   s p d   L

Index to County by City

The arrangement of cities and towns within the checklist is alphabetical by county. This index lists all cities and towns in the checklist by state and indicates the county in which they are located. Independent cities—those cities that are legally separate from any county— precede county listings in the checklist. They appear in the index without a reference to a county name.

Alabama

Abbeville, HENRY COUNTY
Alexandria, CALHOUN COUNTY
Aliceville, PICKENS COUNTY
Aliceville vic., PICKENS COUNTY
Allenton, WILCOX COUNTY
Allsboro vic., COLBERT COUNTY
Alpine, TALLADEGA COUNTY
Alpine vic., TALLADEGA COUNTY
Andalusia vic., COVINGTON COUNTY
Anniston vic., CALHOUN COUNTY
Athens, LIMESTONE COUNTY
Athens vic., LIMESTONE COUNTY
Auburn, LEE COUNTY
Auburn vic., LEE COUNTY

Belle Mina, LIMESTONE COUNTY
Benton, LOWNDES COUNTY
Bexar, MARION COUNTY
Birmingham, JEFFERSON COUNTY
Blakely, BALDWIN COUNTY
Boligee, GREENE COUNTY
Boligee vic., GREENE COUNTY
Brewersville, SUMTER COUNTY
Brick vic., COLBERT COUNTY
Bridgeport, JACKSON COUNTY
Bucksville, TUSCALOOSA COUNTY

Burkville vic., LOWNDES COUNTY
Burnt Corn vic., MONROE COUNTY

Cahaba, DALLAS COUNTY
Camden, WILCOX COUNTY
Camden vic., WILCOX COUNTY
Canton Bend, WILCOX COUNTY
Canton Bend vic., WILCOX COUNTY
Capell, WILCOX COUNTY
Carrollton, PICKENS COUNTY
Center Star vic., LAUDERDALE COUNTY
Chastang, MOBILE COUNTY
Cherokee vic., COLBERT COUNTY
Chewacla, LEE COUNTY
Citronelle, MOBILE COUNTY
Claiborne, MONROE COUNTY
Clifton Ferry, WILCOX COUNTY
Clinton, GREENE COUNTY
Coatopa vic., SUMTER COUNTY
Columbia, HOUSTON COUNTY
Columbia vic., HENRY COUNTY
Cottonton, RUSSELL COUNTY
Courtland, LAWRENCE COUNTY
Courtland vic., LAWRENCE COUNTY
Coy vic., WILCOX COUNTY
Crawford, RUSSELL COUNTY
Crews Depot, LAMAR COUNTY

Dadeville, TALLAPOOSA COUNTY
Dadeville vic., TALLAPOOSA COUNTY

Dauphin Island, MOBILE COUNTY
Dawes, MOBILE COUNTY
Dayton, MARENGO COUNTY
Decatur, MORGAN COUNTY
Demopolis, MARENGO COUNTY
Dixon Mills vic., MARENGO COUNTY
Dudleyville vic., TALLAPOOSA COUNTY

Eastaboga vic., TALLADEGA COUNTY
Edwardsville, CLEBURNE COUNTY
Elmore vic., ELMORE COUNTY
Erie, GREENE COUNTY
Eufaula, BARBOUR COUNTY
Eutaw, GREENE COUNTY
Eutaw vic., GREENE COUNTY

Faunsdale vic., MARENGO COUNTY
Fayette vic., FAYETTE COUNTY
Florence, LAUDERDALE COUNTY
Florence vic., LAUDERDALE COUNTY
Forkland, GREENE COUNTY
Forkland vic., GREENE COUNTY
Forkland vic., HOUSTON COUNTY
Fort Mitchell, RUSSELL COUNTY
Franklin vic., MONROE COUNTY

Gallion, HALE COUNTY
Glenville, RUSSELL COUNTY
Gold Hill, LEE COUNTY

Gordon, HOUSTON COUNTY
Gordon vic., HOUSTON COUNTY
Greensboro, HALE COUNTY
Greensboro vic., HALE COUNTY
Greenville, BUTLER COUNTY
Greenville vic., BUTLER COUNTY
Grove Hill vic., CLARKE COUNTY
Gulf Shores vic., BALDWIN COUNTY

Haleburg vic., HENRY COUNTY
Harpersville vic., SHELBY COUNTY
Helena vic., SHELBY COUNTY
Herrick, FAYETTE COUNTY
High Ridge vic., BULLOCK COUNTY
Huntsville, MADISON COUNTY

Jacksonville, CALHOUN COUNTY
Jacksonville vic., CALHOUN COUNTY
Jefferson, MARENGO COUNTY
Jefferson vic., MARENGO COUNTY

Lafayette, CHAMBERS COUNTY
Leighton, COLBERT COUNTY
Leighton vic., COLBERT COUNTY
Linden, MARENGO COUNTY
Livingston, SUMTER COUNTY
Livingston vic., SUMTER COUNTY
Loachapoka, LEE COUNTY
Loachapoka vic., LEE COUNTY
Lowndesboro, LOWNDES COUNTY
Lowndesboro vic., LOWNDES COUNTY
Luverne vic., CRENSHAW COUNTY

Manningham vic., BUTLER COUNTY
Marion, PERRY COUNTY
Marion vic., PERRY COUNTY
Martin's Station, DALLAS COUNTY
Mc Intosh, WASHINGTON COUNTY
Memphis, PICKENS COUNTY
Millers Ferry, WILCOX COUNTY
Millers Ferry vic., WILCOX COUNTY
Mobile, MOBILE COUNTY
Mon Louis Island, MOBILE COUNTY
Monroeville vic., MONROE COUNTY
Montevallo, SHELBY COUNTY
Montgomery, MONTGOMERY COUNTY
Mooresville, LIMESTONE COUNTY
Moulton, LAWRENCE COUNTY
Moundville vic., HALE COUNTY
Mount Ida vic., CRENSHAW COUNTY
Mount Jefferson, LEE COUNTY
Mount Pleasant, MONROE COUNTY
Mount Vernon, MOBILE COUNTY
Mulberry vic., AUTAUGA COUNTY
Munford, TALLADEGA COUNTY

New Market, MADISON COUNTY
Newbern, HALE COUNTY
Notasulga vic., LEE COUNTY

Oak Bowery, CHAMBERS COUNTY
Oak Hill, WILCOX COUNTY
Opelika vic., LEE COUNTY
Orion, PIKE COUNTY
Orion vic., PIKE COUNTY
Orrville, DALLAS COUNTY
Orrville vic., DALLAS COUNTY
Oxford, CALHOUN COUNTY
Oxford vic., CALHOUN COUNTY

Peachburg, BULLOCK COUNTY
Peachburg vic., BULLOCK COUNTY
Perdue Hill, MONROE COUNTY
Pickensville, PICKENS COUNTY
Pine Apple, WILCOX COUNTY
Pittsview vic., RUSSELL COUNTY
Point Clear, BALDWIN COUNTY
Prairieville, HALE COUNTY
Prattville, AUTAUGA COUNTY
Prattville vic., AUTAUGA COUNTY

Ridgeville, BUTLER COUNTY
Robinson Springs, ELMORE COUNTY
Rogersville vic., LAUDERDALE COUNTY

Sawyerville vic., HALE COUNTY
Seale, RUSSELL COUNTY
Seale vic., RUSSELL COUNTY
Selma, DALLAS COUNTY
Selma vic., DALLAS COUNTY
Sheffield, COLBERT COUNTY
Sheffield vic., COLBERT COUNTY
Shorterville, HENRY COUNTY
Shorterville vic., HENRY COUNTY
Somerville, MORGAN COUNTY
Spring Hill, MOBILE COUNTY
Spring Valley vic., COLBERT COUNTY
St. Stephens, WASHINGTON COUNTY
Stockton, BALDWIN COUNTY
Suggsville, CLARKE COUNTY
Sulligent, LAMAR COUNTY
Summerfield, DALLAS COUNTY
Sylacauga, TALLADEGA COUNTY
Sylacauga vic., TALLADEGA COUNTY

Talladega, TALLADEGA COUNTY
Talladega vic., TALLADEGA COUNTY
Tensaw, BALDWIN COUNTY
Toulminville, MOBILE COUNTY
Town Creek vic., LAWRENCE COUNTY
Tuscaloosa, TUSCALOOSA COUNTY
Tuscumbia, COLBERT COUNTY
Tuscumbia vic., COLBERT COUNTY
Tuskegee, MACON COUNTY
Tuskegee vic., MACON COUNTY

Union Springs, BULLOCK COUNTY
Union Springs vic., BULLOCK COUNTY
Uniontown, PERRY COUNTY

Vilula, RUSSELL COUNTY

Watsonia, GREENE COUNTY
Weaver, CALHOUN COUNTY
Weaver vic., CALHOUN COUNTY
Wetumpka, ELMORE COUNTY
Wetumpka vic., ELMORE COUNTY
Wheeler Station, LAWRENCE COUNTY
White Plains, CALHOUN COUNTY
Winterboro, TALLADEGA COUNTY
Woodland, RANDOLPH COUNTY
Woodward, JEFFERSON COUNTY

Alaska

Haines vic., HAINES COUNTY

Ketchikan vic., KETCHIKAN GATEWAY COUNTY
Kodiak, KODIAK ISLAND COUNTY

Mc Carthy, CORDOVA-MC CARTHY COUNTY

Sitka, SITKA COUNTY

Arizona

Arivaca, PIMA COUNTY

Bowie vic., COCHISE COUNTY

Camp Verde, YAVAPAI COUNTY
Chinle vic., APACHE COUNTY
Coolidge vic., PINAL COUNTY

Fairbank, COCHISE COUNTY
Fairbank vic., COCHISE COUNTY
Florence, PINAL COUNTY

Ganado, APACHE COUNTY
Grand Canyon N. P., COCONINO COUNTY

Kayenta vic., NAVAJO COUNTY

Moccasin vic., MOHAVE COUNTY

Nogales vic., SANTA CRUZ COUNTY

Page vic., COCONINO COUNTY
Patagonia, SANTA CRUZ COUNTY
Patagonia vic., SANTA CRUZ COUNTY
Phoenix, MARICOPA COUNTY
Poston vic., PINAL COUNTY
Prescott, YAVAPAI COUNTY
Prescott vic., YAVAPAI COUNTY

Sacaton, PINAL COUNTY
Sacaton vic., PINAL COUNTY

Tombstone, COCHISE COUNTY
Tubac, SANTA CRUZ COUNTY
Tubac vic., SANTA CRUZ COUNTY
Tucson, PIMA COUNTY
Tucson vic., PIMA COUNTY

Walpi, COCONINO COUNTY
Wickenburg, MARICOPA COUNTY
Willcox, COCHISE COUNTY

Arkansas

Blevins, HEMPSTEAD COUNTY

Clarksville vic., JOHNSON COUNTY

Fayetteville vic., WASHINGTON COUNTY
Fort Smith, SEBASTIAN COUNTY

Little Rock, PULASKI COUNTY

Pea Ridge vic., BENTON COUNTY

Van Buren, CRAWFORD COUNTY

Washington, HEMPSTEAD COUNTY
Washington vic., HEMPSTEAD COUNTY
Wilson, MISSISSIPPI COUNTY

California

Agua Fria, MARIPOSA COUNTY
Alamo, CONTRA COSTA COUNTY
Alba, SAN JOAQUIN COUNTY

Albany Flat, CALAVERAS COUNTY
Albion, MENDOCINO COUNTY
Altaville, CALAVERAS COUNTY
Amador City, AMADOR COUNTY
Anaheim, ORANGE COUNTY
Angel Island, MARIN COUNTY
Angels Camp, CALAVERAS COUNTY
Angels Camp vic., CALAVERAS COUNTY
Arcata, HUMBOLDT COUNTY
Atherton, SAN MATEO COUNTY
Auburn, PLACER COUNTY

Bagby, MARIPOSA COUNTY
Baldwin Park, LOS ANGELES COUNTY
Bear River, YUBA COUNTY
Bear Valley, MARIPOSA COUNTY
Bell, LOS ANGELES COUNTY
Belmont, SAN MATEO COUNTY
Benicia, SOLANO COUNTY
Berkeley, ALAMEDA COUNTY
Beverly Hills, LOS ANGELES COUNTY
Bidwell Bar, BUTTE COUNTY
Big Oak Flat, TUOLUMNE COUNTY
Bodie, MONO COUNTY
Bolinas, MARIN COUNTY
Brentwood vic., CONTRA COSTA COUNTY
Bridgeport, NEVADA COUNTY
Bridgeville, HUMBOLDT COUNTY
Brown's Valley vic., YUBA COUNTY
Buellton, SANTA BARBARA COUNTY
Buellton vic., SANTA BARBARA COUNTY
Buena Vista, AMADOR COUNTY
Burlingame, SAN MATEO COUNTY
Butte City, AMADOR COUNTY

Calabasas, LOS ANGELES COUNTY
Calabasas vic., LOS ANGELES COUNTY
Calistoga vic., NAPA COUNTY
Callahan, SISKIYOU COUNTY
Campo Seco, CALAVERAS COUNTY
Carlsbad vic., SAN DIEGO COUNTY
Carmel, MONTEREY COUNTY
Carrville, TRINITY COUNTY
Carson Hill, CALAVERAS COUNTY
Cherokee, BUTTE COUNTY
Chico, BUTTE COUNTY
Chinese Camp, TUOLUMNE COUNTY
Chino vic., SAN BERNARDINO COUNTY
Clear View, CALAVERAS COUNTY
Coloma, EL DORADO COUNTY
Coloma vic., EL DORADO COUNTY
Columbia, TUOLUMNE COUNTY
Colusa, COLUSA COUNTY
Concord, CONTRA COSTA COUNTY
Copperopolis, CALAVERAS COUNTY
Copperopolis vic., CALAVERAS COUNTY
Coronado, SAN DIEGO COUNTY
Corral Hollows, SAN JOAQUIN COUNTY
Coulterville, MARIPOSA COUNTY
Coyote, SANTA BARBARA COUNTY
Coyote, SANTA CLARA COUNTY
Coyote vic., SANTA CLARA COUNTY
Cupertino, SANTA CLARA COUNTY

Danville, CONTRA COSTA COUNTY
Dobbins, YUBA COUNTY

Downieville, SIERRA COUNTY
Downieville vic., SIERRA COUNTY
Dragon Gulch, TUOLUMNE COUNTY
Drytown, AMADOR COUNTY

El Dorado, EL DORADO COUNTY
Eldoradotown, CALAVERAS COUNTY
Elizabeth Lake vic., LOS ANGELES COUNTY
Elk, MENDOCINO COUNTY
Escalon, SAN JOAQUIN COUNTY
Eureka, HUMBOLDT COUNTY

Felix, CALAVERAS COUNTY
Felix vic., CALAVERAS COUNTY
Fiddletown, AMADOR COUNTY
Folsom, SACRAMENTO COUNTY
Fort Bragg vic., MENDOCINO COUNTY
Fort Mason, SAN FRANCISCO COUNTY
Fort Ross, SONOMA COUNTY
Fourth Crossing, CALAVERAS COUNTY
Fremont, ALAMEDA COUNTY
Fremont (Niles), ALAMEDA COUNTY
Fremont (Warm Spring), ALAMEDA COUNTY
French Camp, SAN JOAQUIN COUNTY

Garberville vic., HUMBOLDT COUNTY
Gilroy, SANTA CLARA COUNTY
Gilroy vic., SANTA CLARA COUNTY
Glen Canyon, SANTA CRUZ COUNTY
Glencoe, CALAVERAS COUNTY
Glendale, LOS ANGELES COUNTY
Goodyear's Bar, SIERRA COUNTY
Grass Valley, NEVADA COUNTY
Groveland vic., TUOLUMNE COUNTY
Guadalupe, SANTA BARBARA COUNTY

Half Moon Bay, SAN MATEO COUNTY
Happy Valley, CALAVERAS COUNTY
Hayward, ALAMEDA COUNTY
Hillsborough, SAN MATEO COUNTY
Hornitos, MARIPOSA COUNTY

Indian Gulch, MARIPOSA COUNTY
Inglewood, LOS ANGELES COUNTY

Jackass Hill, TUOLUMNE COUNTY
Jackson, AMADOR COUNTY
Jackson Gate, AMADOR COUNTY
Jesus Maria, CALAVERAS COUNTY
Jolon vic., MONTEREY COUNTY
Julian, SAN DIEGO COUNTY

Keeler, INYO COUNTY
Kelsey, EL DORADO COUNTY
Knights Ferry, STANISLAUS COUNTY
Kyburz, EL DORADO COUNTY

La Jolla, SAN DIEGO COUNTY
Lassen Volcanic vic., SHASTA COUNTY
Lathrop, SAN JOAQUIN COUNTY
Lebec vic., KERN COUNTY
Locke, SACRAMENTO COUNTY
Lockeford, SAN JOAQUIN COUNTY
Lodi, SAN JOAQUIN COUNTY
Lompoc vic., SANTA BARBARA COUNTY
Long Beach, LOS ANGELES COUNTY
Los Altos, SANTA CLARA COUNTY
Los Altos Hills, SANTA CLARA COUNTY
Los Angeles, LOS ANGELES COUNTY

Los Banos vic., MERCED COUNTY
Los Gatos, SANTA CLARA COUNTY
Lynwood, LOS ANGELES COUNTY

Mad River, HUMBOLDT COUNTY
Mare Island, SOLANO COUNTY
Mariposa, MARIPOSA COUNTY
Martinez, CONTRA COSTA COUNTY
Marysville, VENTURA COUNTY
Marysville, YUBA COUNTY
Melones vic., CALAVERAS COUNTY
Mendocino, MENDOCINO COUNTY
Menlo Park, SAN MATEO COUNTY
Menlo Park, SANTA CLARA COUNTY
Michigan Bar, AMADOR COUNTY
Millbrae, SAN MATEO COUNTY
Millerton, EL DORADO COUNTY
Millerton, FRESNO COUNTY
Millerton vic., FRESNO COUNTY
Milpitas, SANTA BARBARA COUNTY
Milpitas vic., SANTA CLARA COUNTY
Mokelumne Hill, CALAVERAS COUNTY
Monta Vista vic., SANTA CLARA COUNTY
Montecito, SANTA BARBARA COUNTY
Monterey, MONTEREY COUNTY
Monterey vic., MONTEREY COUNTY
Montezuma, TUOLUMNE COUNTY
Moraga Valley, CONTRA COSTA COUNTY
Morgan Hill, SANTA CLARA COUNTY
Morgan Hill vic., SANTA CLARA COUNTY
Mormon Bar, MARIPOSA COUNTY
Mount Bullion, MARIPOSA COUNTY
Mount Ophir, MARIPOSA COUNTY
Murphy's, CALAVERAS COUNTY

Napa, NAPA COUNTY
Nashville, EL DORADO COUNTY
National City, SAN DIEGO COUNTY
Navaro River, MENDOCINO COUNTY
Nevada City, NEVADA COUNTY
New Almaden, SANTA CLARA COUNTY
Newport Beach, ORANGE COUNTY
Nipomo vic., SAN LUIS OBISPO COUNTY
North Bloomfield, NEVADA COUNTY

Oak Grove, SAN DIEGO COUNTY
Oakland, ALAMEDA COUNTY
Oceanside, SAN DIEGO COUNTY
Olema vic., MARIN COUNTY
Oleta, AMADOR COUNTY

Pala, SAN DIEGO COUNTY
Palo Alto, SANTA CLARA COUNTY
Pasadena, ALPINE COUNTY
Pasadena, LOS ANGELES COUNTY
Pescadero, SAN MATEO COUNTY
Pescadero vic., SAN MATEO COUNTY
Petaluma vic., SONOMA COUNTY
Pilot Hill, CALAVERAS COUNTY
Pilot Hill, EL DORADO COUNTY
Pine Grove, AMADOR COUNTY
Piru vic., VENTURA COUNTY
Placerville, EL DORADO COUNTY
Pleasanton, ALAMEDA COUNTY
Plymouth, AMADOR COUNTY
Point Loma, SAN DIEGO COUNTY
Pomona, LOS ANGELES COUNTY
Portola Valley, SAN MATEO COUNTY

Poverty Flat, CALAVERAS COUNTY
Prado vic., RIVERSIDE COUNTY
Priests, TUOLUMNE COUNTY

Quartz Mountain, TUOLUMNE COUNTY

Red Bluff vic., SHASTA COUNTY
Red Bluff vic., TEHAMA COUNTY
Red Dog, NEVADA COUNTY
Redwood City, SAN MATEO COUNTY
Roaring Camp, CALAVERAS COUNTY
Rough And Ready, NEVADA COUNTY
Round Top, AMADOR COUNTY

Sacramento, SACRAMENTO COUNTY
Salinas, MONTEREY COUNTY
Salinas vic., MONTEREY COUNTY
San Andreas, CALAVERAS COUNTY
San Diego, SAN DIEGO COUNTY
San Diego (Old Town), SAN DIEGO COUNTY
San Dimas vic., LOS ANGELES COUNTY
San Fernando, LOS ANGELES COUNTY
San Francisco, SAN FRANCISCO COUNTY
San Fransisco, SAN FRANCISCO COUNTY
San Gabriel, LOS ANGELES COUNTY
San Gregorio, SAN MATEO COUNTY
San Jose, SANTA CLARA COUNTY
San Juan, NEVADA COUNTY
San Juan Bautista, SAN BENITO COUNTY
San Juan Capistrano, NEVADA COUNTY
San Juan Capistrano, ORANGE COUNTY
San Leandro, ALAMEDA COUNTY
San Luis Obispo, SAN LUIS OBISPO COUNTY
San Luis Rey (Vista), SAN DIEGO COUNTY
San Marino, LOS ANGELES COUNTY
San Martin, SANTA CLARA COUNTY
San Mateo, SAN MATEO COUNTY
San Miguel vic., SAN LUIS OBISPO COUNTY
San Pablo, CONTRA COSTA COUNTY
San Pedro Valley, MONO COUNTY
San Rafael, MARIN COUNTY
Santa Barbara, SANTA BARBARA COUNTY
Santa Catalina Isl., LOS ANGELES COUNTY
Santa Clara, SANTA CLARA COUNTY
Santa Clara vic., SANTA CLARA COUNTY
Santa Cruz, SANTA CRUZ COUNTY
Santa Margarita vic., SAN LUIS OBISPO COUNTY
Santa Monica, LOS ANGELES COUNTY
Santa Rosa, SONOMA COUNTY
Santa Rosa vic., SONOMA COUNTY
Saratoga, SANTA CLARA COUNTY
Saratoga vic., SANTA CLARA COUNTY
Sawyers Bar, SISKIYOU COUNTY
Shasta, SHASTA COUNTY
Shaw's Flat, TUOLUMNE COUNTY
Shingle Springs, EL DORADO COUNTY
Sierra City, SIERRA COUNTY
Sierraville, SIERRA COUNTY
Soledad, MONTEREY COUNTY
Solvang, SANTA BARBARA COUNTY
Sonoma, SONOMA COUNTY
Sonora, TUOLUMNE COUNTY
Sonora vic., TUOLUMNE COUNTY
Soquel, SANTA CRUZ COUNTY
South Pasadena, LOS ANGELES COUNTY
Spring Valley, SAN DIEGO COUNTY

Springfield, TUOLUMNE COUNTY
Stanford, SANTA CLARA COUNTY
Stent, TUOLUMNE COUNTY
Stockton, SAN JOAQUIN COUNTY
Stockton vic., SAN JOAQUIN COUNTY
Strawberry, EL DORADO COUNTY
Susanville vic., LASSEN COUNTY
Sweetland, NEVADA COUNTY

Timbuctoo, YUBA COUNTY
Tracy vic., ALAMEDA COUNTY
Tragedy Springs, EL DORADO COUNTY
Tulare, TULARE COUNTY
Tuttletown, TUOLUMNE COUNTY
Tuttletown vic., TUOLUMNE COUNTY

Union City, ALAMEDA COUNTY

Vacaville, SOLANO COUNTY
Ventura, VENTURA COUNTY
Volcano, AMADOR COUNTY

Warner Springs, SAN DIEGO COUNTY
Warner Springs vic., SAN DIEGO COUNTY
Wawona, MARIPOSA COUNTY
Weaverville, TRINITY COUNTY
Westport, MENDOCINO COUNTY
Whittier, LOS ANGELES COUNTY
Willows, GLENN COUNTY
Winterhaven, IMPERIAL COUNTY
Woodbridge, SAN JOAQUIN COUNTY
Woods Crossing, TUOLUMNE COUNTY
Woodside, SAN MATEO COUNTY

Yosemite Natl. Park, MARIPOSA COUNTY

Canal Zone

Colon vic.,

Colorado

Central City, GILPIN COUNTY

Denver, DENVER COUNTY
Denver vic., DENVER COUNTY

Glenwood Springs, GARFIELD COUNTY
Greeley, WELD COUNTY
Gunnison vic., GUNNISON COUNTY

Kokomo, SUMMIT COUNTY

La Junta, BENT COUNTY

Mount Vernon, JEFFERSON COUNTY

Ophir vic., SAN MIGUEL COUNTY

Rifle vic., GARFIELD COUNTY

Segundo, LAS ANIMAS COUNTY
Silver Plume, CLEAR CREEK COUNTY
Silverton, SAN JUAN COUNTY

Tijeras, LAS ANIMAS COUNTY
Trinidad, LAS ANIMAS COUNTY

Waterton, JEFFERSON COUNTY
Weston vic., LAS ANIMAS COUNTY
Wolcott, EAGLE COUNTY

Connecticut

Barkhamsted, LITCHFIELD COUNTY
Bethany, NEW HAVEN COUNTY
Bolton (center), TOLLAND COUNTY
Branford, NEW HAVEN COUNTY
Bridgeport, FAIRFIELD COUNTY
Brooklyn, WINDHAM COUNTY

Canterbury, WINDHAM COUNTY
Cheshire, NEW HAVEN COUNTY
Chester, MIDDLESEX COUNTY
Clinton, MIDDLESEX COUNTY
Colchester, NEW LONDON COUNTY
Colebrook, LITCHFIELD COUNTY
Cornwall, LITCHFIELD COUNTY
Cos Cob, FAIRFIELD COUNTY

Darien, FAIRFIELD COUNTY
Durham, MIDDLESEX COUNTY

East Canaan, LITCHFIELD COUNTY
East Granby, HARTFORD COUNTY
East Haddam, MIDDLESEX COUNTY
East Hartford, HARTFORD COUNTY
East Hartland, HARTFORD COUNTY
East Haven, NEW HAVEN COUNTY
East Windsor Hill, HARTFORD COUNTY
Eastford vic., WINDHAM COUNTY
Easton, FAIRFIELD COUNTY
Essex, MIDDLESEX COUNTY

Fairfield, FAIRFIELD COUNTY
Falls Village, LITCHFIELD COUNTY
Farmington, HARTFORD COUNTY
Fitchville, NEW LONDON COUNTY

Gaylordsville, LITCHFIELD COUNTY
Glastonbury, HARTFORD COUNTY
Goshen, LITCHFIELD COUNTY
Greenwich, FAIRFIELD COUNTY
Guilford, NEW HAVEN COUNTY

Hadlyme, NEW LONDON COUNTY
Hamburg Cove, NEW LONDON COUNTY
Hamden, NEW HAVEN COUNTY
Hampton, WINDHAM COUNTY
Hartford, HARTFORD COUNTY
Harwinton, LITCHFIELD COUNTY

Kent, LITCHFIELD COUNTY
Killingworth, MIDDLESEX COUNTY

Lakeville, LITCHFIELD COUNTY
Lebanon, NEW LONDON COUNTY
Litchfield, LITCHFIELD COUNTY
Lyme, NEW LONDON COUNTY

Madison, NEW HAVEN COUNTY
Meriden, NEW HAVEN COUNTY
Middlefield, MIDDLESEX COUNTY
Middletown, MIDDLESEX COUNTY
Milford, NEW HAVEN COUNTY
Montowese, NEW HAVEN COUNTY
Moodus, MIDDLESEX COUNTY

New Canaan, FAIRFIELD COUNTY
New Canaan vic., FAIRFIELD COUNTY
New Haven, NEW HAVEN COUNTY
New London, NEW LONDON COUNTY

New Preston, LITCHFIELD COUNTY
Norfolk, LITCHFIELD COUNTY
North Branford, NEW HAVEN COUNTY
North Branford vic., NEW HAVEN COUNTY
North Canaan, LITCHFIELD COUNTY
North Cornwall, LITCHFIELD COUNTY
North Greenwich, FAIRFIELD COUNTY
North Guilford, NEW HAVEN COUNTY
North Plain, MIDDLESEX COUNTY
North Stonington, NEW LONDON COUNTY
North Woodbury, LITCHFIELD COUNTY
Northford Center, NEW HAVEN COUNTY
Norwalk, FAIRFIELD COUNTY
Norwich, NEW HAVEN COUNTY
Norwich, NEW LONDON COUNTY
Norwichtown, NEW LONDON COUNTY

Old Lyme, NEW LONDON COUNTY
Old Saybrook, MIDDLESEX COUNTY

Pawcatuck, NEW LONDON COUNTY
Plainfield, WINDHAM COUNTY
Portland, MIDDLESEX COUNTY
Preston City, NEW LONDON COUNTY

Redding, FAIRFIELD COUNTY
Ridgefield, FAIRFIELD COUNTY
Rocky Hill, HARTFORD COUNTY

Scantic, HARTFORD COUNTY
Sharon, LITCHFIELD COUNTY
Silvermine, FAIRFIELD COUNTY
South Canaan, LITCHFIELD COUNTY
South Canterbury, WINDHAM COUNTY
South Glastonbury, HARTFORD COUNTY
South Norwalk, FAIRFIELD COUNTY
Southbury, NEW HAVEN COUNTY
Southport, FAIRFIELD COUNTY
Stamford, FAIRFIELD COUNTY
Stanwich vic., FAIRFIELD COUNTY
Sterling Hill, WINDHAM COUNTY
Stonington, NEW LONDON COUNTY
Straitsville, NEW HAVEN COUNTY
Stratford, FAIRFIELD COUNTY
Suffield, HARTFORD COUNTY
Suffield Center, HARTFORD COUNTY

Taftville, NEW LONDON COUNTY
Torrington, LITCHFIELD COUNTY
Trumbull, FAIRFIELD COUNTY

W. Stafford Springs, TOLLAND COUNTY
Wallingford, NEW HAVEN COUNTY
Waterbury, NEW HAVEN COUNTY
Watertown, LITCHFIELD COUNTY
West Goshen, LITCHFIELD COUNTY
West Hartford, HARTFORD COUNTY
West Haven, NEW HAVEN COUNTY
West Suffield, HARTFORD COUNTY
Westport, FAIRFIELD COUNTY
Wethersfield, HARTFORD COUNTY
Whitneyville, NEW HAVEN COUNTY
Willimantic, WINDHAM COUNTY
Wilton, FAIRFIELD COUNTY
Winchester Center, LITCHFIELD COUNTY
Windsor, HARTFORD COUNTY
Windsor Hill, HARTFORD COUNTY
Winsted, LITCHFIELD COUNTY
Woodbridge, NEW HAVEN COUNTY

Woodbury, LITCHFIELD COUNTY
Woodbury vic., LITCHFIELD COUNTY
Woodstock, WINDHAM COUNTY

Delaware

Ashland, NEW CASTLE COUNTY

Bethel, SUSSEX COUNTY
Biddles Corner vic., NEW CASTLE COUNTY
Bridgeville, SUSSEX COUNTY

Camden, KENT COUNTY
Camden vic., KENT COUNTY
Centerville vic., NEW CASTLE COUNTY
Christiana, NEW CASTLE COUNTY
Christiana vic., NEW CASTLE COUNTY
Claymont, NEW CASTLE COUNTY
Claymont vic., NEW CASTLE COUNTY
Clayton vic., KENT COUNTY
Collins Beach vic., NEW CASTLE COUNTY
Cool Spring vic., SUSSEX COUNTY
Corner Ketch vic., NEW CASTLE COUNTY
Cowgill Corner, KENT COUNTY

Dagsboro, SUSSEX COUNTY
Dover, KENT COUNTY
Dover vic., KENT COUNTY

Frederica, KENT COUNTY
Frederica vic., KENT COUNTY

Georgetown, SUSSEX COUNTY
Glasgow, NEW CASTLE COUNTY
Granogue vic., NEW CASTLE COUNTY
Greenville vic., NEW CASTLE COUNTY
Greenwood vic., SUSSEX COUNTY

Harrington vic., KENT COUNTY
Hockessin vic., NEW CASTLE COUNTY

Kenton vic., KENT COUNTY
Kirkwood vic., NEW CASTLE COUNTY

Laurel, SUSSEX COUNTY
Laurel vic., SUSSEX COUNTY
Lebanon vic., KENT COUNTY
Leipsic, KENT COUNTY
Leipsic vic., KENT COUNTY
Lewes, SUSSEX COUNTY
Little Creek vic., KENT COUNTY

Magnolia, KENT COUNTY
Mermaid vic., NEW CASTLE COUNTY
Middletown vic., NEW CASTLE COUNTY
Milford, SUSSEX COUNTY
Milford vic., KENT COUNTY
Millsboro, SUSSEX COUNTY
Milltown vic., NEW CASTLE COUNTY
Montchanin vic., NEW CASTLE COUNTY

New Castle, NEW CASTLE COUNTY
New Castle vic., NEW CASTLE COUNTY
Newark, NEW CASTLE COUNTY
Newark vic., NEW CASTLE COUNTY
Newport, NEW CASTLE COUNTY

Oak Orchard vic., SUSSEX COUNTY
Odessa, NEW CASTLE COUNTY

Odessa vic., NEW CASTLE COUNTY
Ogletown vic., NEW CASTLE COUNTY

Pea Patch Island, NEW CASTLE COUNTY
Price's Corner vic., NEW CASTLE COUNTY

Rehoboth Beach vic., SUSSEX COUNTY
Rockland vic., NEW CASTLE COUNTY

Seaford vic., SUSSEX COUNTY
Smyrna, KENT COUNTY
Smyrna vic., KENT COUNTY
Smyrna vic., NEW CASTLE COUNTY
Stanton, NEW CASTLE COUNTY
Stanton vic., NEW CASTLE COUNTY

Taylor's Bridge, NEW CASTLE COUNTY
Taylor's Bridge vic., NEW CASTLE COUNTY

Wilmington, NEW CASTLE COUNTY
Wilmington vic., NEW CASTLE COUNTY
Woodland, SUSSEX COUNTY
Woodland vic., SUSSEX COUNTY

Yorklyn, NEW CASTLE COUNTY

District of Columbia

Washington

Florida

Altamonte Springs, SEMINOLE COUNTY
Apalachicola, FRANKLIN COUNTY
Auburndale, POLK COUNTY

Capps, JEFFERSON COUNTY
Coral Gables, DADE COUNTY
Cross Creek, ALACHUA COUNTY

Dry Tortugas, MONROE COUNTY

Ellenton, MANATEE COUNTY

Fernandina Beach, NASSAU COUNTY
Fort George Island, DUVAL COUNTY

Gainesville, ALACHUA COUNTY

Hampton Springs vic., TAYLOR COUNTY

Jacksonville, DUVAL COUNTY

Key West, MONROE COUNTY

Lakeland, POLK COUNTY

Madison, MADISON COUNTY
Manalapan, PALM BEACH COUNTY
Marianna, JACKSON COUNTY
Miami, DADE COUNTY
Monticello, JEFFERSON COUNTY

Orlando, ORANGE COUNTY

Palm Beach, PALM BEACH COUNTY
Pensacola, ESCAMBIA COUNTY

Quincy, GADSDEN COUNTY

Rattlesnake Island, ST. JOHNS COUNTY

St. Augustine, POLK COUNTY
St. Augustine, ST. JOHNS COUNTY

St. Augustine vic., FLAGLER COUNTY
St. Johns Bluff, DUVAL COUNTY
Starke, BRADFORD COUNTY

Tallahassee, LEON COUNTY
Tallahassee vic., LEON COUNTY
Tampa, HILLSBOROUGH COUNTY
Tampa, Ybor City, HILLSBOROUGH COUNTY

White Springs, HAMILTON COUNTY

Georgia

Arnoldsville vic., OGLETHORPE COUNTY
Athens, CLARKE COUNTY
Atlanta, FULTON COUNTY
Atlanta vic., COBB COUNTY
Augusta, RICHMOND COUNTY
Augusta vic., RICHMOND COUNTY

Barnesville vic., PIKE COUNTY
Bibb, MUSCOGEE COUNTY
Broadfield vic., GLYNN COUNTY

Clinton, JONES COUNTY
Cobbham, MC DUFFIE COUNTY
Columbus, MUSCOGEE COUNTY
Columbus vic., MUSCOGEE COUNTY
Covington, NEWTON COUNTY
Covington vic., NEWTON COUNTY
Crawfordville, TALIAFERRO COUNTY
Cumberland Island, CAMDEN COUNTY

Dahlenega, LUMPKIN COUNTY
Darien, MC INTOSH COUNTY
Darien vic., MC INTOSH COUNTY

Elbert, ELBERT COUNTY
Elberton vic., ELBERT COUNTY

Fairburn vic., FULTON COUNTY

Gainesville, HALL COUNTY
Glenwood vic., WHEELER COUNTY
Griffen, SPALDING COUNTY

Haddock vic., JONES COUNTY
Heardmont vic., ELBERT COUNTY
High Shoals, WALTON COUNTY
Hoschton vic., BARROW COUNTY

Jefferson, JACKSON COUNTY
Jekyll Island, GLYNN COUNTY

Kennesaw Mnt., COBB COUNTY
Knoxville, CRAWFORD COUNTY

La Fayette, WALKER COUNTY
La Grange, TROUP COUNTY
La Grange vic., TROUP COUNTY
Lexington, OGLETHORPE COUNTY
Louisville, JEFFERSON COUNTY

Macon, BIBB COUNTY
Madison, MORGAN COUNTY
Marietta, COBB COUNTY
Marshallville, MACON COUNTY
Marshallville vic., MACON COUNTY
Mc Donough, HENRY COUNTY
Middleton, ELBERT COUNTY
Midway, LIBERTY COUNTY

Milledgeville, BALDWIN COUNTY
Milledgeville vic., BALDWIN COUNTY
Monroe, WALTON COUNTY

Newnan vic., COWETA COUNTY

Oxford, NEWTON COUNTY

Panola vic., DE KALB COUNTY
Pearl vic., ELBERT COUNTY

Rincon, EFFINGHAM COUNTY
Rock Spring., WALKER COUNTY
Rome, FLOYD COUNTY
Roswell, FULTON COUNTY
Ruckersville, ELBERT COUNTY
Ruckersville vic., ELBERT COUNTY

Sapelo Island, MC INTOSH COUNTY
Savannah, CHATHAM COUNTY
Savannah, ELBERT COUNTY
Savannah vic., CHATHAM COUNTY
Savannah vic., ELBERT COUNTY
Sparta, HANCOCK COUNTY
Spring Place, MURRAY COUNTY
St. Mary's, CAMDEN COUNTY
St. Mary's vic., CAMDEN COUNTY
St. Simons Island, GLYNN COUNTY

Talbotton, TALBOT COUNTY
Thomasville, THOMAS COUNTY
Toccoa vic., STEPHENS COUNTY

Washington, WILKES COUNTY
Watkinsville, OCONEE COUNTY
Waynesboro, BURKE COUNTY
West Point, TROUP COUNTY
Whitesville vic., HARRIS COUNTY
Woodbine vic., CAMDEN COUNTY

Hawaii

Hanalei, KAUAI COUNTY
Honolulu, HONOLULU COUNTY

Kailua Kona, HAWAII COUNTY
Kohala, HAWAII COUNTY
Kualapuu,

Lahaina, MAUI COUNTY
Lahainaluna, MAUI COUNTY

Olowalu, MAUI COUNTY

Paia, MAUI COUNTY
Pearl Harbor, HONOLULU COUNTY
Puako, HAWAII COUNTY
Pukoo, MAUI COUNTY

Spreckelsville, MAUI COUNTY

Ulupalakua, MAUI COUNTY

Waiakoa, MAUI COUNTY
Wailuku, MAUI COUNTY

Idaho

American Falls, POWER COUNTY
Avery, SHOSHONE COUNTY

Boise, ADA COUNTY

Cataldo, KOOTENAI COUNTY

Idaho City, BOISE COUNTY

Kamiah vic., IDAHO COUNTY

Snake River Plateau, ADA COUNTY

Twin Falls, TWIN FALLS COUNTY

Illinois

Addison, DU PAGE COUNTY
Albion, EDWARDS COUNTY
Alton, MADISON COUNTY
Anna, UNION COUNTY
Aurora, KANE COUNTY

Batavia, KANE COUNTY
Beardstown, CASS COUNTY
Belleville, ST. CLAIR COUNTY
Belvidere, BOONE COUNTY
Belvidere vic., BOONE COUNTY
Bement, PIATT COUNTY
Bement vic., PIATT COUNTY
Bishop Hill, HENRY COUNTY
Bloomingdale vic., DU PAGE COUNTY
Bloomington, MC LEAN COUNTY
Brookfield, COOK COUNTY

Cahokia, ST. CLAIR COUNTY
Cairo, ALEXANDER COUNTY
Carbondale vic., JACKSON COUNTY
Carlyle, CLINTON COUNTY
Channahon vic., WILL COUNTY
Cherry Valley, BOONE COUNTY
Chicago, COOK COUNTY
Columbia, MONROE COUNTY

Decatur, MACON COUNTY
Depue, BUREAU COUNTY

Eden vic., RANDOLPH COUNTY
Edwardsville, MADISON COUNTY
Edwardsville vic., MADISON COUNTY
Elgin, BROWN COUNTY
Elmhurst, DU PAGE COUNTY
Evanston, COOK COUNTY

Fall Creek vic., ADAMS COUNTY
Fayville, KANE COUNTY
Fort Gage, RANDOLPH COUNTY
Fort Sheridan, LAKE COUNTY
Fullersburg, DU PAGE COUNTY
Fullersburg vic., DU PAGE COUNTY

Galena, JO DAVIESS COUNTY
Galena vic., JO DAVIESS COUNTY
Geneva, KANE COUNTY
Geneva vic., KANE COUNTY
Genoa vic., DOUGLAS COUNTY
Glencoe, COOK COUNTY
Godfrey, MADISON COUNTY
Grand Detour, OGLE COUNTY

Halfday, LAKE COUNTY
Homer vic., CHAMPAIGN COUNTY
Jacksonville, MORGAN COUNTY
Jonesboro, UNION COUNTY
Jubilee, PEORIA COUNTY

Kaskaskia, RANDOLPH COUNTY
Kenilworth, COOK COUNTY
Knoxville, KNOX COUNTY

La Moille vic., BUREAU COUNTY
Lebanon, ST. CLAIR COUNTY
Lee Center, LEE COUNTY
Lena vic., STEPHENSON COUNTY
Lewiston, FULTON COUNTY
Lisbon, KENDALL COUNTY

Mackinaw, TAZEWELL COUNTY
Marengo, MC HENRY COUNTY
Mendota, LA SALLE COUNTY
Monmouth, WARREN COUNTY
Monticello, PIATT COUNTY
Mossville, PEORIA COUNTY
Mount Vernon, JEFFERSON COUNTY
Mundelein, LAKE COUNTY

Naderville, DU PAGE COUNTY
Naperville, DU PAGE COUNTY
Naperville vic., DU PAGE COUNTY
Nauvoo, HANCOCK COUNTY
New Baden vic., ST. CLAIR COUNTY
New Haven, GALLATIN COUNTY
Normal, MC LEAN COUNTY

Oak Park, COOK COUNTY
Onarga vic., IROQUOIS COUNTY
Oquawka, HENDERSON COUNTY
Oquawka vic., HENDERSON COUNTY
Ottawa, LA SALLE COUNTY

Paris, EDGAR COUNTY
Payson, ADAMS COUNTY
Petersburg, MENARD COUNTY
Pittsfield, PIKE COUNTY
Plainsfield, WILL COUNTY
Plano vic., KENDALL COUNTY
Pleasant Plains, SANGAMON COUNTY
Prairie Du Rocher, RANDOLPH COUNTY

Quincy, ADAMS COUNTY

Redbud, RANDOLPH COUNTY
River Forest, COOK COUNTY
Riverside, COOK COUNTY
Rock Island, ROCK ISLAND COUNTY
Rockford, WINNEBAGO COUNTY
Rockton, WINNEBAGO COUNTY

Shawneetown, GALLATIN COUNTY
Sparta vic., RANDOLPH COUNTY
Springfield, SANGAMON COUNTY
St. Charles, KANE COUNTY
Sublette, LEE COUNTY

Thebes, ALEXANDER COUNTY
Tilden vic., RANDOLPH COUNTY
Toulon, STARK COUNTY
Tremont, TAZEWELL COUNTY

Virginia vic., CASS COUNTY

Warrenville, DU PAGE COUNTY
Warsaw, HANCOCK COUNTY
Waterloo vic., MONROE COUNTY
Waukegan, LAKE COUNTY
Waukegan vic., LAKE COUNTY
Wilmette, COOK COUNTY

Winchester, SCOTT COUNTY
Woodstock, MC HENRY COUNTY

Indiana

Alamo vic., MONTGOMERY COUNTY
Alton vic., CRAWFORD COUNTY
Anderson, MADISON COUNTY
Aurora vic., DEARBORN COUNTY

Bloomington, MONROE COUNTY
Brownsville, UNION COUNTY

Cambridge City, WAYNE COUNTY
Cannelton, PERRY COUNTY
Centerville, WAYNE COUNTY
Centerville vic., FAYETTE COUNTY
Chesterton, PORTER COUNTY
Chesterton vic., PORTER COUNTY
Clay City, CLAY COUNTY
Columbus, BARTHOLOMEW COUNTY
Connersville, FAYETTE COUNTY
Connersville vic., FAYETTE COUNTY
Corydon, HARRISON COUNTY
Crawfordsville, MONTGOMERY COUNTY
Cutler vic., CARROLL COUNTY

Evansville, VANDERBURG COUNTY

Fairfield, FRANKLIN COUNTY
Fort Wayne, ALLEN COUNTY
Fountain City, WAYNE COUNTY

Geneva, ADAMS COUNTY
Gosport, OWEN COUNTY
Greensburg vic., DECATUR COUNTY

Huntington, HUNTINGTON COUNTY

Indianapolis, MARION COUNTY

Jeffersonville, CLARK COUNTY

Kokomo, HOWARD COUNTY

Lafayette, TIPPECANOE COUNTY
Liberty vic., UNION COUNTY

Madison, JEFFERSON COUNTY
Madison vic., JEFFERSON COUNTY
Matthews, GRANT COUNTY
Metamora, FRANKLIN COUNTY
Michigan City, LA PORTE COUNTY
Milton vic., WAYNE COUNTY
Mishawaka, ST. JOSEPH COUNTY
Mitchell, LAWRENCE COUNTY
Mongo, LAGRANGE COUNTY
Montezuma, PARKE COUNTY
Morris, RIPLEY COUNTY
Mount Auburn, WAYNE COUNTY
Muncie, DELAWARE COUNTY
Muncie vic., DELAWARE COUNTY

New Albany, FLOYD COUNTY
New Carlisle, LA PORTE COUNTY
New Harmony, POSEY COUNTY
Newburgh, WARRICK COUNTY
Noblesville, HAMILTON COUNTY
Noblesville vic., HAMILTON COUNTY

North Manchester, WABASH COUNTY

Paoli, ORANGE COUNTY
Pendleton vic., MADISON COUNTY
Pennville, WAYNE COUNTY
Pinola, LA PORTE COUNTY
Pleasant Township, ALLEN COUNTY

Richmond, WAYNE COUNTY
Ridgeville, RANDOLPH COUNTY
Rochester vic., FULTON COUNTY
Rushville, RUSH COUNTY
Rushville vic., RUSH COUNTY

Salem, WASHINGTON COUNTY
South Bend, ST. JOSEPH COUNTY

Turkey Run St. Park, PARKE COUNTY

Vera Cruz vic., WELLS COUNTY
Vernon, JENNINGS COUNTY
Versailles vic., RIPLEY COUNTY
Vevay, SWITZERLAND COUNTY
Vincennes, KNOX COUNTY

Washington, DAVIESS COUNTY
West Baden, ORANGE COUNTY

Yountsville, MONTGOMERY COUNTY

Iowa

Agency City, WAPELLO COUNTY
Amana, IOWA COUNTY
Amana vic., IOWA COUNTY
Ames, BUCHANAN COUNTY
Ames, STORY COUNTY

Bentonsport, VAN BUREN COUNTY
Boone, BOONE COUNTY
Burlington, DES MOINES COUNTY

Carlisle vic., WARREN COUNTY
Cedar Rapids, LINN COUNTY
Cherokee, CHEROKEE COUNTY
Clarinda, PAGE COUNTY
Clermont vic., FAYETTE COUNTY
Clinton, CLINTON COUNTY
Council Bluffs, POTTAWATTAMIE COUNTY

Davenport, SCOTT COUNTY
Decorah, WINNESHIEK COUNTY
Des Moines, POLK COUNTY
Dow City, CRAWFORD COUNTY
Dubuque, DUBUQUE COUNTY
Dubuque vic., DUBUQUE COUNTY

Elkader, CLAYTON COUNTY

Fairfield, JEFFERSON COUNTY
Festina vic., WINNESHIEK COUNTY
Fort Dodge, WEBSTER COUNTY
Fort Madison, LEE COUNTY

Gilbert vic., STORY COUNTY

Hampton, FRANKLIN COUNTY
Holy Cross vic., DUBUQUE COUNTY

Independence, BUCHANAN COUNTY
Iowa City, JOHNSON COUNTY

Keosauqua, VAN BUREN COUNTY
Knoxville vic., MARION COUNTY

Le Claire, SCOTT COUNTY

Marietta, MARSHALL COUNTY
Marshalltown, MARSHALL COUNTY
Mason City, CERRO GORDO COUNTY
Monroe, JASPER COUNTY
Mount Pleasant, HENRY COUNTY
Muscatine, MUSCATINE COUNTY

Nashua vic., CHICKASAW COUNTY
Newton, JASPER COUNTY

Oskaloosa vic., MASHAKA COUNTY

Pella, MARION COUNTY

Quasqueton, BUCHANAN COUNTY

Red Oak, MONTGOMERY COUNTY
Rock Rapids, LYON COUNTY

Sheldahl, STORY COUNTY
Sioux City, WOODBURY COUNTY
Spirit Lake, DICKINSON COUNTY
Springdale vic., CEDAR COUNTY
St. Donatus, JACKSON COUNTY

Valley Junction vic., POLK COUNTY
Vandalia, JASPER COUNTY
Vinton, BENTON COUNTY

Waterloo, BLACK HAWK COUNTY
Webster City, HAMILTON COUNTY
West Branch, CEDAR COUNTY
Winterset, MADISON COUNTY

Kansas

Abilene, DICKINSON COUNTY
Albany, NEMAHA COUNTY

Baldwin, DOUGLAS COUNTY

Catherine, ELLIS COUNTY
Clinton vic., DOUGLAS COUNTY
Council Grove, MORRIS COUNTY

Fort Leavenworth, LEAVENWORTH COUNTY
Fort Riley, RILEY COUNTY

Highland, DONIPHAN COUNTY

Kansas City vic., JOHNSON COUNTY

Larned, PAWNEE COUNTY
Lawrence, DOUGLAS COUNTY
Liebenthal, RUSH COUNTY

Manhattan, RILEY COUNTY
Miller vic., LYON COUNTY
Muncie, WYANDOTTE COUNTY
Munjor, ELLIS COUNTY

Osawatomie, MIAMI COUNTY
Oskaloosa, JEFFERSON COUNTY
Overland Park, JOHNSON COUNTY

Schoenchen, ELLIS COUNTY
Silver Lake vic., SHAWNEE COUNTY
Springdale vic., LEAVENWORTH COUNTY
Stull vic., DOUGLAS COUNTY

Vinland, DOUGLAS COUNTY

Wabaunsee, WABAUNSEE COUNTY

Kentucky

Bardstown, NELSON COUNTY
Bardstown vic., NELSON COUNTY
Beattyville, LEE COUNTY
Brandenburg, MEADE COUNTY
Buechel vic., JEFFERSON COUNTY
Burlington vic., BOONE COUNTY
Butler, PENDLETON COUNTY

Cynthiana, HARRISON COUNTY

Danville, BOYLE COUNTY
Danville vic., BOYLE COUNTY

Fishtrap vic., JOHNSON COUNTY
Frankfort, FRANKLIN COUNTY

Geneva vic., HENDERSON COUNTY
Grahamton, MEADE COUNTY
Greensburg, GREEN COUNTY

Harrodsburg, MERCER COUNTY
Harrodsburg vic., MERCER COUNTY
Henderson, HENDERSON COUNTY
Hodgenville, LARUE COUNTY

Lexington, FAYETTE COUNTY
Lexington vic., FAYETTE COUNTY
Louisville, JEFFERSON COUNTY
Louisville vic., JEFFERSON COUNTY
Ludlow, KENTON COUNTY

Maysville, MASON COUNTY
Munfordville vic., HART COUNTY

Paris, BOURBON COUNTY
Pisgah, WOODFORD COUNTY
Pleasant Hill, MERCER COUNTY

Richmond, MADISON COUNTY

Shelbyville, SHELBY COUNTY
Shelbyville vic., SHELBY COUNTY
South Union, LOGAN COUNTY
Springfield, WASHINGTON COUNTY
St. Matthews, JEFFERSON COUNTY
Stanford, LINCOLN COUNTY
Stanton, POWELL COUNTY

Talmage, MERCER COUNTY
Tompkinsville vic., MONROE COUNTY

Washington, MASON COUNTY
White Hall, MADISON COUNTY

Louisiana

Alexandria vic., RAPIDES COUNTY

Bains, WEST FELICIANA COUNTY
Baton Rouge, EAST BATON ROUGE COUNTY
Bermuda, NATCHITOCHES COUNTY
Burnside, ASCENSION COUNTY

Clinton, EAST FELICIANA COUNTY
Convent vic., ST. JAMES COUNTY

Geismar vic., ASCENSION COUNTY
Grand Coteau, ST. LANDRY COUNTY

Hahnville, ST. CHARLES COUNTY

Lucy, ST. JOHN THE BAPTIST COUNTY

Melrose, NATCHITOCHES COUNTY
Mississippi River, ST. BERNARD COUNTY

Napoleonville vic., ASSUMPTION COUNTY
Natchitoches, NATCHITOCHES COUNTY
New Iberia, IBERIA COUNTY
New Orleans, ORLEANS COUNTY
New Orleans vic., ORLEANS COUNTY
New Roads vic., POINTE COUPEE COUNTY

Opelousas, ST. LANDRY COUNTY
Opelousas vic., ST. LANDRY COUNTY

Plaquemine, IBERVILLE COUNTY

Saint Francisville, WEST FELICIANA COUNTY
Saint Rose, ST. CHARLES COUNTY
Saint Rose vic., ST. CHARLES COUNTY
Shreveport, CADDO COUNTY
Sunset vic., ST. LANDRY COUNTY

Thibadoux, LAFOURCHE COUNTY

Union vic., ST. JAMES COUNTY

Washington, ST. LANDRY COUNTY
Weyanoke vic., WEST FELICIANA COUNTY
White Castle vic., IBERVILLE COUNTY

Maine

Alfred, YORK COUNTY
Alna, LINCOLN COUNTY
Augusta, KENNEBEC COUNTY

Baker Island, HANCOCK COUNTY
Bath, SAGADAHOC COUNTY
Belfast, WALDO COUNTY
Belfast (east), WALDO COUNTY
Belfast vic., WALDO COUNTY
Biddeford, YORK COUNTY
Boon Island, YORK COUNTY
Bristol vic., LINCOLN COUNTY
Brunswick, CUMBERLAND COUNTY

Camden, KNOX COUNTY
Cape Elizabeth, CUMBERLAND COUNTY
Castine, HANCOCK COUNTY
Columbia Falls, WASHINGTON COUNTY

Damariscotta, LINCOLN COUNTY
Damariscotta Mills, LINCOLN COUNTY
Dresden (Cedar Grove), LINCOLN COUNTY

Ellsworth, HANCOCK COUNTY

Factory Island,
Falmouth vic., CUMBERLAND COUNTY

Gardiner, KENNEBEC COUNTY

Hallowell, KENNEBEC COUNTY
Hallowell Mill, KENNEBEC COUNTY

Harpswell, CUMBERLAND COUNTY
Head Tide, LINCOLN COUNTY

Jefferson vic., LINCOLN COUNTY

Kennebunk, YORK COUNTY
Kennebunkport, YORK COUNTY
Kittery Point, YORK COUNTY

Lincolnville, WALDO COUNTY
Little Cranberry Is., HANCOCK COUNTY

Machias, WASHINGTON COUNTY
Monmouth, KENNEBEC COUNTY

New Berwick vic., YORK COUNTY
New Gloucester vic., CUMBERLAND COUNTY
Newcastle, LINCOLN COUNTY
Newcastle vic., LINCOLN COUNTY
North Edgecomb, LINCOLN COUNTY

Paris (Paris Hill), OXFORD COUNTY
Phippsburg, SAGADAHOC COUNTY
Phippsburg vic., SAGADAHOC COUNTY
Porter, OXFORD COUNTY
Portland, CUMBERLAND COUNTY

Richmond, SAGADAHOC COUNTY
Robinhood, SAGADAHOC COUNTY
Rockland, KNOX COUNTY
Rockport, KNOX COUNTY
Rockport vic., KNOX COUNTY

Saco, YORK COUNTY
Searsport, WALDO COUNTY
South Portland, CUMBERLAND COUNTY
South Windham vic., CUMBERLAND COUNTY
Southwest Harbor Vic, HANCOCK COUNTY
Squam Island,
St. Croix River, WASHINGTON COUNTY
Stroudwater, CUMBERLAND COUNTY

Thomaston, KNOX COUNTY
Topsham, SAGADAHOC COUNTY
Topsham vic., SAGADAHOC COUNTY

Vinalhaven vic., KNOX COUNTY

Waldoboro vic., LINCOLN COUNTY
Walpole vic., LINCOLN COUNTY
Warren, KNOX COUNTY
Wells, YORK COUNTY
Windham Center vic., CUMBERLAND COUNTY
Winslow, KENNEBEC COUNTY
Wiscasset, LINCOLN COUNTY

York, YORK COUNTY
York (Ogunquit vic.), YORK COUNTY
York (Scotland), YORK COUNTY
York (York Village), YORK COUNTY

Maryland

Accokeek, PRINCE GEORGES COUNTY
Adelina, CALVERT COUNTY
Allen vic., WICOMICO COUNTY
Annapolis, ANNE ARUNDEL COUNTY
Annapolis vic., ANNE ARUNDEL COUNTY
Antietam, WASHINGTON COUNTY
Antietam vic., WASHINGTON COUNTY

Antietam-Dargan vic., WASHINGTON COUNTY
Aquasco, PRINCE GEORGES COUNTY
Aquasco vic., PRINCE GEORGES COUNTY
Ardmore vic., PRINCE GEORGES COUNTY
Ashton, MONTGOMERY COUNTY

Baden, PRINCE GEORGES COUNTY
Baden vic., PRINCE GEORGES COUNTY
Baltimore
Baltimore vic., BALTIMORE COUNTY
Baltimore vic., HOWARD COUNTY
Barstow vic., CALVERT COUNTY
Beallsville, MONTGOMERY COUNTY
Beaverdam vic., WORCESTER COUNTY
Bel Air, HARFORD COUNTY
Bel Air vic., HARFORD COUNTY
Belcamp, HARFORD COUNTY
Berkley vic., HARFORD COUNTY
Berlin, WORCESTER COUNTY
Berlin vic., WORCESTER COUNTY
Bethesda, MONTGOMERY COUNTY
Bethlehem, TALBOT COUNTY
Big Pool vic., WASHINGTON COUNTY
Bladensburg, PRINCE GEORGES COUNTY
Blossom Point, CHARLES COUNTY
Blue Ball, CECIL COUNTY
Bohemia River, CECIL COUNTY
Bowie, PRINCE GEORGES COUNTY
Bowie vic., PRINCE GEORGES COUNTY
Brookeville, MONTGOMERY COUNTY
Brookeville vic., MONTGOMERY COUNTY
Brookmont vic., MONTGOMERY COUNTY
Brown, PRINCE GEORGES COUNTY
Brown vic., PRINCE GEORGES COUNTY
Brunswick, FREDERICK COUNTY
Buena Vista, PRINCE GEORGES COUNTY
Buena Vista vic., PRINCE GEORGES COUNTY
Burtonsville, MONTGOMERY COUNTY
Bushwood, ST. MARYS COUNTY
Butler vic., ANNE ARUNDEL COUNTY

Cabin John vic., MONTGOMERY COUNTY
Calvert vic., CECIL COUNTY
Cambridge vic., DORCHESTER COUNTY
Catoctin vic., FREDERICK COUNTY
Catoctin Village, FREDERICK COUNTY
Cecilton, CECIL COUNTY
Cecilton vic., CECIL COUNTY
Centreville vic., QUEEN ANNE COUNTY
Chaneyville vic., CALVERT COUNTY
Chaptico vic., ST. MARYS COUNTY
Charlestown, CECIL COUNTY
Charlotte Hall, ST. MARYS COUNTY
Cheltenham, PRINCE GEORGES COUNTY
Cheltenham vic., PRINCE GEORGES COUNTY
Chesapeake City, CECIL COUNTY
Chestertown, KENT COUNTY
Chestertown vic., KENT COUNTY
Chesterville, KENT COUNTY
Chevy Chase vic., MONTGOMERY COUNTY
Church Creek, DORCHESTER COUNTY
Church Hill vic., QUEEN ANNE COUNTY
Churchville vic., HARFORD COUNTY
Clarksburg, MONTGOMERY COUNTY
Clear Spring vic., WASHINGTON COUNTY
Clinton vic., PRINCE GEORGES COUNTY
Cockeysville, PRINCE GEORGES COUNTY

Cockeysville vic., BALTIMORE COUNTY
Colesville, MONTGOMERY COUNTY
College Park, PRINCE GEORGES COUNTY
Collington vic., PRINCE GEORGES COUNTY
Collinsville vic., ANNE ARUNDEL COUNTY
Conowingo vic., CECIL COUNTY
Contee, PRINCE GEORGES COUNTY
Creswell vic., HARFORD COUNTY
Crisfield, SOMERSET COUNTY
Croom vic., PRINCE GEORGES COUNTY
Crownsville vic., ANNE ARUNDEL COUNTY
Cumberland, ALLEGANY COUNTY
Cumberland vic., ALLEGANY COUNTY
Cumberstone, ANNE ARUNDEL COUNTY
Cumberstone vic., ANNE ARUNDEL COUNTY

Dare's Wharf vic., CALVERT COUNTY
Darlington, HARFORD COUNTY
Darlington vic., HARFORD COUNTY
Darnestown vic., MONTGOMERY COUNTY
Davidsonville vic., ANNE ARUNDEL COUNTY
Dawsonville, MONTGOMERY COUNTY
Dawsonville vic., MONTGOMERY COUNTY
Dickerson, MONTGOMERY COUNTY
Dickerson vic., FREDERICK COUNTY
Dickerson vic., MONTGOMERY COUNTY
Dickinson, MONTGOMERY COUNTY
Dickinson vic., MONTGOMERY COUNTY
Drayden vic., ST. MARYS COUNTY

Earleville vic., CECIL COUNTY
Easton, TALBOT COUNTY
Easton vic., TALBOT COUNTY
Edgewater, ANNE ARUNDEL COUNTY
Eldorado vic., DORCHESTER COUNTY
Elk Mills, CECIL COUNTY
Elk Mills vic., CECIL COUNTY
Elkton, CECIL COUNTY
Elkton vic., CECIL COUNTY
Ellicott City, BALTIMORE COUNTY
Ellicott City, HOWARD COUNTY
Ellicott City vic., HOWARD COUNTY
Etchison, MONTGOMERY COUNTY

Fairhaven vic., ANNE ARUNDEL COUNTY
Fairlee Creek, KENT COUNTY
Fallston, HARFORD COUNTY
Fallston vic., HARFORD COUNTY
Federalsburg, CAROLINE COUNTY
Forest Hill, HARFORD COUNTY
Fork vic., BALTIMORE COUNTY
Fort Frederick vic., WASHINGTON COUNTY
Fort Washington, PRINCE GEORGES COUNTY
Fort Washington vic., PRINCE GEORGES
  COUNTY
Franklinville vic., BALTIMORE COUNTY
Frederick, FREDERICK COUNTY
Frederick vic., FREDERICK COUNTY
Friendly vic., PRINCE GEORGES COUNTY
Friendship vic., ANNE ARUNDEL COUNTY

Gaithersburg, MONTGOMERY COUNTY
Gaithersburg vic., MONTGOMERY COUNTY
Galena, KENT COUNTY
Galesville vic., ANNE ARUNDEL COUNTY
Gambrills vic., ANNE ARUNDEL COUNTY
Georgetown, KENT COUNTY
Girdletree vic., WORCESTER COUNTY

Glen Echo, MONTGOMERY COUNTY
Glen Echo vic., MONTGOMERY COUNTY
Glenville, HARFORD COUNTY
Granstville Vic, GARRETT COUNTY
Great Falls, MONTGOMERY COUNTY
Great Falls vic., MONTGOMERY COUNTY
Great Mills, ST. MARYS COUNTY

Hagerstown, WASHINGTON COUNTY
Hagerstown vic., WASHINGTON COUNTY
Hancock vic., WASHINGTON COUNTY
Harpers Ferry, WASHINGTON COUNTY
Harpers Ferry vic., WASHINGTON COUNTY
Harwood vic., ANNE ARUNDEL COUNTY
Havre De Grace, HARFORD COUNTY
Havre De Grace vic., HARFORD COUNTY
Hebron vic., WICOMICO COUNTY
Hereford vic., BALTIMORE COUNTY
Hillsboro, CAROLINE COUNTY
Hollywood, ST. MARYS COUNTY
Hollywood vic., ST. MARYS COUNTY
Huntingtown vic., CALVERT COUNTY

Ilchester, BALTIMORE COUNTY
Ilchester vic., BALTIMORE COUNTY
Ilchester vic., HOWARD COUNTY

Jerusalem, HARFORD COUNTY
Jerusalem vic., BALTIMORE COUNTY
Jerusalem vic., HARFORD COUNTY
Joppatowne, HARFORD COUNTY

Kent Island, QUEEN ANNE COUNTY
Keymar vic., CARROLL COUNTY
Keymar vic., FREDERICK COUNTY
Kingston vic., SOMERSET COUNTY
Kingsville, BALTIMORE COUNTY
Kingsville vic., BALTIMORE COUNTY
Knoxville, WASHINGTON COUNTY
Knoxville vic., WASHINGTON COUNTY

La Plata vic., CHARLES COUNTY
Lander's Landing, FREDERICK COUNTY
Landover vic., PRINCE GEORGES COUNTY
Langford vic., KENT COUNTY
Langley Park, PRINCE GEORGES COUNTY
Langley Park vic., PRINCE GEORGES COUNTY
Lapidum, HARFORD COUNTY
Lapidum vic., HARFORD COUNTY
Largo vic., PRINCE GEORGES COUNTY
Laurel Grove vic., ST. MARYS COUNTY
Laurel vic., PRINCE GEORGES COUNTY
Laytonsville, MONTGOMERY COUNTY
Laytonsville vic., MONTGOMERY COUNTY
Leeland, PRINCE GEORGES COUNTY
Leeland vic., PRINCE GEORGES COUNTY
Leonardtown, ST. MARYS COUNTY
Leonardtown vic., ST. MARYS COUNTY
Level vic., HARFORD COUNTY
Lexington Park, ST. MARYS COUNTY
Liberty Town, FREDERICK COUNTY
Little Cove Point, CALVERT COUNTY
Locust Grove vic., KENT COUNTY
Long Green, BALTIMORE COUNTY
Lothian, ANNE ARUNDEL COUNTY
Lower Marlboro, CALVERT COUNTY
Lower Marlboro vic., CALVERT COUNTY
Lusby vic., CALVERT COUNTY

Mackall, CALVERT COUNTY
Maddox vic., ST. MARYS COUNTY
Manokin, SOMERSET COUNTY
Manokin vic., SOMERSET COUNTY
Marbury vic., CHARLES COUNTY
Martinsburg vic., MONTGOMERY COUNTY
Matthews vic., TALBOT COUNTY
Mc Daniel vic., TALBOT COUNTY
Middletown, FREDERICK COUNTY
Millstone Landing, SOMERSET COUNTY
Millstone Landing, ST. MARYS COUNTY
Monkton vic., BALTIMORE COUNTY
Morgantown, CHARLES COUNTY
Morganza, ST. MARYS COUNTY
Mullikin, PRINCE GEORGES COUNTY

New Market, DORCHESTER COUNTY
New Market vic., ST. MARYS COUNTY
Newport vic., CHARLES COUNTY
Newton Neck, ST. MARYS COUNTY
Norbeck vic., MONTGOMERY COUNTY
North East, CECIL COUNTY
Norwood, MONTGOMERY COUNTY
Nottingham, PRINCE GEORGES COUNTY

Oakville vic., ST. MARYS COUNTY
Oella, BALTIMORE COUNTY
Old Town vic., CAROLINE COUNTY
Oldtown, ALLEGANY COUNTY
Oldtown vic., ALLEGANY COUNTY
Olney, MONTGOMERY COUNTY
Olney vic., MONTGOMERY COUNTY
Owings Mills, BALTIMORE COUNTY
Oxford vic., TALBOT COUNTY
Oxon Hill, PRINCE GEORGES COUNTY
Oxon Hill vic., PRINCE GEORGES COUNTY

Parkton vic., BALTIMORE COUNTY
Paw Paw, ALLEGANY COUNTY
Perryman, HARFORD COUNTY
Perryville vic., CECIL COUNTY
Phoenix vic., BALTIMORE COUNTY
Pikesville, BALTIMORE COUNTY
Pindell, ANNE ARUNDEL COUNTY
Piscataway, PRINCE GEORGES COUNTY
Piscataway vic., PRINCE GEORGES COUNTY
Pocomoke City vic., WORCESTER COUNTY
Point Of Rocks, WASHINGTON COUNTY
Point Of Rocks vic., FREDERICK COUNTY
Poolesville, MONTGOMERY COUNTY
Poolesville vic., MONTGOMERY COUNTY
Port Deposit, CECIL COUNTY
Port Tobacco, CHARLES COUNTY
Port Tobacco vic., CHARLES COUNTY
Potomac vic., MONTGOMERY COUNTY
Prince Frederick vic., CALVERT COUNTY
Princess Anne, SOMERSET COUNTY

Queen Anne, TALBOT COUNTY

Randallstown vic., CARROLL COUNTY
Redlands, MONTGOMERY COUNTY
Redlands vic., MONTGOMERY COUNTY
Reisterstown vic., BALTIMORE COUNTY
Relay, BALTIMORE COUNTY
Relay, HOWARD COUNTY
Ridge, ST. MARYS COUNTY
Ridge vic., ST. MARYS COUNTY

Ritchie, PRINCE GEORGES COUNTY
Riverdale, PRINCE GEORGES COUNTY
Riverside, MONTGOMERY COUNTY
Robinson vic., ANNE ARUNDEL COUNTY
Rockville, MONTGOMERY COUNTY
Romancoke, QUEEN ANNE COUNTY
Rosaryville, PRINCE GEORGES COUNTY
Round Bay vic., ANNE ARUNDEL COUNTY
Ruthsburg vic., QUEEN ANNE COUNTY

Salisbury, WICOMICO COUNTY
Samples Manor, WASHINGTON COUNTY
Sandy Bottom, KENT COUNTY
Sandy Hook vic., WASHINGTON COUNTY
Sandy Spring, MONTGOMERY COUNTY
Savage, HOWARD COUNTY
Seat Pleasant vic., PRINCE GEORGES COUNTY
Secretary, DORCHESTER COUNTY
Secretary vic., DORCHESTER COUNTY
Seneca vic., MONTGOMERY COUNTY
Sharpsburg, WASHINGTON COUNTY
Sharpsburg vic., WASHINGTON COUNTY
Snow Hill, WORCESTER COUNTY
Snow Hill Landing, WORCESTER COUNTY
Snow Hill vic., WORCESTER COUNTY
Solomons Island vic., CALVERT COUNTY
Somerset vic., MONTGOMERY COUNTY
South River vic., ANNE ARUNDEL COUNTY
St. Augustine, CECIL COUNTY
St. Inigoes vic., ST. MARYS COUNTY
St. Mary's City, ST. MARYS COUNTY
St. Mary's City vic., ST. MARYS COUNTY
St. Michaels vic., TALBOT COUNTY
Stevensville, QUEEN ANNE COUNTY
Stevensville vic., QUEEN ANNE COUNTY
Still Pond, KENT COUNTY
Stoakley, CALVERT COUNTY
Stockton vic., HARFORD COUNTY
Sunderland vic., CALVERT COUNTY
Sunnybrook, BALTIMORE COUNTY
Sweet Air, BALTIMORE COUNTY

Thomas Brook vic., PRINCE GEORGES COUNTY
Townsend vic., PRINCE GEORGES COUNTY
Towson, BALTIMORE COUNTY
Tracy's Landing vic., ANNE ARUNDEL COUNTY
Trappe, TALBOT COUNTY
Tunis Mills, TALBOT COUNTY
Tunis Mills vic., TALBOT COUNTY

Union Bridge vic., FREDERICK COUNTY
Unity, MONTGOMERY COUNTY
Unity vic., MONTGOMERY COUNTY
Upper Marlboro, PRINCE GEORGES COUNTY
Upper Marlboro vic., PRINCE GEORGES COUNTY
Urbana, FREDERICK COUNTY

Valley Lee, ST. MARYS COUNTY
Valley Lee vic., ST. MARYS COUNTY
Vienna, DORCHESTER COUNTY

Wallville vic., CALVERT COUNTY
Warwick, CECIL COUNTY
Watervale, HARFORD COUNTY
Watervale vic., HARFORD COUNTY
Weverton vic., WASHINGTON COUNTY
Williamsport, WASHINGTON COUNTY

Williamsport vic., WASHINGTON COUNTY
Williston Landing, CAROLINE COUNTY
Wilna vic., HARFORD COUNTY
Woodmore, PRINCE GEORGES COUNTY
Wye Mills, QUEEN ANNE COUNTY
Wye Mills, TALBOT COUNTY

Massachusetts

Acoaxet, BRISTOL COUNTY
Acton, MIDDLESEX COUNTY
Adams, BERKSHIRE COUNTY
Agawam, HAMPDEN COUNTY
Amesbury, ESSEX COUNTY
Amherst, HAMPSHIRE COUNTY
Andover, ESSEX COUNTY
Annisquam, ESSEX COUNTY
Arlington, MIDDLESEX COUNTY
Ashby, MIDDLESEX COUNTY
Ashfield, FRANKLIN COUNTY
Ashland, MIDDLESEX COUNTY
Athol, WORCESTER COUNTY
Attleboro, BRISTOL COUNTY
Attleboro vic., BRISTOL COUNTY
Attleboro-Plainville, BRISTOL COUNTY
Attleboro-plainville, NORFOLK COUNTY
Auburn, WORCESTER COUNTY
Auburndale, MIDDLESEX COUNTY

Barnstable, BARNSTABLE COUNTY
Bedford, MIDDLESEX COUNTY
Bedford vic., MIDDLESEX COUNTY
Beverly, ESSEX COUNTY
Billerica, MIDDLESEX COUNTY
Blackstone, WORCESTER COUNTY
Bolton, WORCESTER COUNTY
Boston, SUFFOLK COUNTY
Boston vic., SUFFOLK COUNTY
Boxford, ESSEX COUNTY
Braintree, NORFOLK COUNTY
Brewster, BARNSTABLE COUNTY
Bridgewater, PLYMOUTH COUNTY
Brighton, SUFFOLK COUNTY
Brimfield, HAMPDEN COUNTY
Brookfield, WORCESTER COUNTY
Brookline, NORFOLK COUNTY
Buckland, FRANKLIN COUNTY
Burlington, MIDDLESEX COUNTY

Cambridge, MIDDLESEX COUNTY
Canton, NORFOLK COUNTY
Carlisle, MIDDLESEX COUNTY
Charlestown, SUFFOLK COUNTY
Charlton, WORCESTER COUNTY
Chatham, BARNSTABLE COUNTY
Chathamport, BARNSTABLE COUNTY
Chelmsford, MIDDLESEX COUNTY
Chelsea, SUFFOLK COUNTY
Chester, HAMPDEN COUNTY
Clarksburg, BERKSHIRE COUNTY
Cohasset, NORFOLK COUNTY
Concord, MIDDLESEX COUNTY
Conway, FRANKLIN COUNTY

Danvers, ESSEX COUNTY
Danvers vic., ESSEX COUNTY

Dartmouth, BRISTOL COUNTY
Dedham, NORFOLK COUNTY
Deerfield, FRANKLIN COUNTY
Deerfield vic., FRANKLIN COUNTY
Deerfield Village, FRANKLIN COUNTY
Dennis, BARNSTABLE COUNTY
Dighton, BRISTOL COUNTY
Dorchester, SUFFOLK COUNTY
Dover, NORFOLK COUNTY
Duxbury, PLYMOUTH COUNTY

East Lexington, MIDDLESEX COUNTY
East Northfield, FRANKLIN COUNTY
East Sandwich, BARNSTABLE COUNTY
East Taunton, BRISTOL COUNTY
Eastham, BARNSTABLE COUNTY
Easton, BRISTOL COUNTY
Egremont, BERKSHIRE COUNTY

Fairhaven, BRISTOL COUNTY
Fall River, BRISTOL COUNTY
Falmouth, BARNSTABLE COUNTY
Fitchburg, WORCESTER COUNTY
Framingham, MIDDLESEX COUNTY
Framingham vic., MIDDLESEX COUNTY
Franklin, NORFOLK COUNTY
Freetown, BRISTOL COUNTY

Georgetown, ESSEX COUNTY
Gloucester, ESSEX COUNTY
Granville, HAMPDEN COUNTY
Great Barrington, BERKSHIRE COUNTY
Greenbush, PLYMOUTH COUNTY
Greenfield, FRANKLIN COUNTY
Greenfield vic., FRANKLIN COUNTY
Groton, MIDDLESEX COUNTY

Hadley, HAMPSHIRE COUNTY
Halifax, PLYMOUTH COUNTY
Hamilton-Ipswich, ESSEX COUNTY
Hancock, BERKSHIRE COUNTY
Hanover Center, PLYMOUTH COUNTY
Harvard, WORCESTER COUNTY
Hatfield, HAMPSHIRE COUNTY
Haverhill, ESSEX COUNTY
Hingham, PLYMOUTH COUNTY

Ipswich, ESSEX COUNTY

Jamaica Plain, SUFFOLK COUNTY

Kingston, PLYMOUTH COUNTY

Lakeville, PLYMOUTH COUNTY
Lancaster, WORCESTER COUNTY
Lanesborough, BERKSHIRE COUNTY
Lawrence, ESSEX COUNTY
Lawrence, MIDDLESEX COUNTY
Lexington, MIDDLESEX COUNTY
Lincoln, MIDDLESEX COUNTY
Longmeadow, HAMPDEN COUNTY
Lowell, MIDDLESEX COUNTY
Lowell-Somerville, MIDDLESEX COUNTY
Ludlow-Wilbraham, HAMPDEN COUNTY
Lynn, ESSEX COUNTY

Malden, MIDDLESEX COUNTY
Manchester, ESSEX COUNTY
Marblehead, ESSEX COUNTY
Marion, PLYMOUTH COUNTY

Marshfield, PLYMOUTH COUNTY
Marshfield Hills, PLYMOUTH COUNTY
Mashpee, BARNSTABLE COUNTY
Medfield, NORFOLK COUNTY
Medford, MIDDLESEX COUNTY
Medford, SUFFOLK COUNTY
Melrose, MIDDLESEX COUNTY
Mendon, WORCESTER COUNTY
Middleborough, PLYMOUTH COUNTY
Middleton, ESSEX COUNTY
Milford, WORCESTER COUNTY
Millville, WORCESTER COUNTY
Millville vic., WORCESTER COUNTY
Milton, NORFOLK COUNTY
Montague City, FRANKLIN COUNTY

Nantucket, NANTUCKET COUNTY
Natick, MIDDLESEX COUNTY
New Bedford, BRISTOL COUNTY
New Marlborough, BERKSHIRE COUNTY
New Salem, FRANKLIN COUNTY
Newbury, ESSEX COUNTY
Newbury Old Town, ESSEX COUNTY
Newburyport, ESSEX COUNTY
Newton, MIDDLESEX COUNTY
North Andover, ESSEX COUNTY
North Attleboro, BRISTOL COUNTY
North Attleboro vic., BRISTOL COUNTY
North Billerica, MIDDLESEX COUNTY
North Brookfield, HAMPDEN COUNTY
North Carver, PLYMOUTH COUNTY
North Chatham, BARNSTABLE COUNTY
North Dighton, BRISTOL COUNTY
North Easton, BRISTOL COUNTY
North Hingham, PLYMOUTH COUNTY
North Pembroke, PLYMOUTH COUNTY
North Pepperell, MIDDLESEX COUNTY
North Reading, MIDDLESEX COUNTY
North Uxbridge, WORCESTER COUNTY
North Woburn, MIDDLESEX COUNTY
Northampton, HAMPSHIRE COUNTY
Northfield, FRANKLIN COUNTY
Northfield vic., FRANKLIN COUNTY
Norton, BRISTOL COUNTY
Norwell, PLYMOUTH COUNTY

Oakham, WORCESTER COUNTY

Palmer, HAMPDEN COUNTY
Pelham, HAMPSHIRE COUNTY
Pepperell, MIDDLESEX COUNTY
Pittsfield, BERKSHIRE COUNTY
Plainville, NORFOLK COUNTY
Plymouth, PLYMOUTH COUNTY
Prescott, HAMPSHIRE COUNTY
Provincetown, BARNSTABLE COUNTY

Quincy, NORFOLK COUNTY

Randolph, NORFOLK COUNTY
Reading, MIDDLESEX COUNTY
Rehoboth, BRISTOL COUNTY
Revere vic., SUFFOLK COUNTY
Richmond, BERKSHIRE COUNTY
Riverside, FRANKLIN COUNTY
Rockport, ESSEX COUNTY
Rowley, ESSEX COUNTY

Roxbury, SUFFOLK COUNTY
Rutland, WORCESTER COUNTY

Salem, ESSEX COUNTY
Sandwich, BARNSTABLE COUNTY
Saugus, ESSEX COUNTY
Scituate vic., PLYMOUTH COUNTY
Seekonk, BRISTOL COUNTY
Sharon, NORFOLK COUNTY
Sheffield, BERKSHIRE COUNTY
Shelburne, FRANKLIN COUNTY
Sherborn, MIDDLESEX COUNTY
Shirley, MIDDLESEX COUNTY
Siasconset, NANTUCKET COUNTY
Somerset, BRISTOL COUNTY
Somerville, MIDDLESEX COUNTY
South Boston, SUFFOLK COUNTY
South Deerfield, FRANKLIN COUNTY
South Hadley, HAMPSHIRE COUNTY
South Hingham, PLYMOUTH COUNTY
South Lee, BERKSHIRE COUNTY
South Orleans, BARNSTABLE COUNTY
South Pepperell vic., MIDDLESEX COUNTY
South Somerset, BRISTOL COUNTY
South Sudbury, MIDDLESEX COUNTY
South Westport, BRISTOL COUNTY
South Williamstown, BERKSHIRE COUNTY
Springfield, HAMPDEN COUNTY
Stockbridge, BERKSHIRE COUNTY
Stoneham, MIDDLESEX COUNTY
Stoughton, NORFOLK COUNTY
Sturbridge, WORCESTER COUNTY
Swampscott, ESSEX COUNTY
Swansea, BRISTOL COUNTY

Templeton, WORCESTER COUNTY
Tisbury, DUKES COUNTY
Topsfield, ESSEX COUNTY
Townsend, MIDDLESEX COUNTY
Truro, BARNSTABLE COUNTY
Truro vic., BARNSTABLE COUNTY
Tyngsborough, MIDDLESEX COUNTY

Uxbridge, WORCESTER COUNTY

Wakefield, MIDDLESEX COUNTY
Walpole, NORFOLK COUNTY
Waltham, MIDDLESEX COUNTY
Waltham, SUFFOLK COUNTY
Wareham, PLYMOUTH COUNTY
Watertown, MIDDLESEX COUNTY
Wayland, MIDDLESEX COUNTY
Wellesley, NORFOLK COUNTY
Wellfleet, BARNSTABLE COUNTY
Wenham, ESSEX COUNTY
West Brookfield, HAMPDEN COUNTY
West Chatham, BARNSTABLE COUNTY
West Medford, MIDDLESEX COUNTY
West Northfield, FRANKLIN COUNTY
West Springfield, HAMPDEN COUNTY
West Stockbridge, BERKSHIRE COUNTY
Westfield, HAMPDEN COUNTY
Westhampton, HAMPSHIRE COUNTY
Weston, MIDDLESEX COUNTY
Westwood, NORFOLK COUNTY
Weymouth, NORFOLK COUNTY

Wilkinsonville, WORCESTER COUNTY
Williamstown, BERKSHIRE COUNTY
Wilmington, MIDDLESEX COUNTY
Wilmington-Billerica, MIDDLESEX COUNTY
Winthrop, SUFFOLK COUNTY
Woburn, MIDDLESEX COUNTY
Worcester, WORCESTER COUNTY
Worthington, HAMPSHIRE COUNTY
Wrentham, NORFOLK COUNTY

Yarmouth, BARNSTABLE COUNTY

Michigan

Adrian, LENAWEE COUNTY
Ann Arbor, WASHTENAW COUNTY

Battle Creek, CALHOUN COUNTY
Brighton, LIVINGSTON COUNTY

Calumet, HOUGHTON COUNTY
Canton Township, WAYNE COUNTY
Central Mine, KEWEENAW COUNTY
Charlotte, EATON COUNTY

Dearborn, WAYNE COUNTY
Detroit, WAYNE COUNTY
Dexter, WASHTENAW COUNTY
Dexter vic., WASHTENAW COUNTY
Dixboro, WASHTENAW COUNTY

East Grand Rapids, KENT COUNTY
East Munising, ALGER COUNTY
Eaton Rapids, EATON COUNTY

Grand Island, ALGER COUNTY
Grand Rapids, KENT COUNTY
Grass Lake, JACKSON COUNTY
Grass Lake vic., JACKSON COUNTY

Hancock, HOUGHTON COUNTY

Ionia, IONIA COUNTY
Ishpeming, MARQUETTE COUNTY

Jacobsville, HOUGHTON COUNTY

Kalamazoo, KALAMAZOO COUNTY

Lake Linden, HOUGHTON COUNTY
Lansing, INGHAM COUNTY

Mackinac Island, MACKINAC COUNTY
Marshall, CALHOUN COUNTY
Mason vic., INGHAM COUNTY
Monroe, MONROE COUNTY

Niles, BERRIEN COUNTY

Ovid, CLINTON COUNTY

Rushton, LIVINGSTON COUNTY

Sault Ste. Marie, CHIPPEWA COUNTY
Sharonville vic., WASHTENAW COUNTY

Tecumseh, LENAWEE COUNTY

Vermontville, EATON COUNTY

Williamston Twp., INGHAM COUNTY

Ypsilanti, WASHTENAW COUNTY

Minnesota

Afton, WASHINGTON COUNTY
Anoka, ANOKA COUNTY

Bloomington, HENNEPIN COUNTY
Brown's Valley, TRAVERSE COUNTY

Duluth, ST. LOUIS COUNTY
Duluth vic., ST. LOUIS COUNTY

Ely vic., ST. LOUIS COUNTY
Excelsior, HENNEPIN COUNTY

Fort Ridgeley, NICOLLET COUNTY
Frontenac, GOODHUE COUNTY

Lake City, WABASHA COUNTY
Le Sueur, LE SUEUR COUNTY

Marine, WASHINGTON COUNTY
Mendota, DAKOTA COUNTY
Minneapolis, HENNEPIN COUNTY
Montevideo, CHIPPEWA COUNTY

New Ulm, BROWN COUNTY
North Branch vic., ISANTI COUNTY

Sawyer, CARLTON COUNTY
St. Clair, BLUE EARTH COUNTY
St. Paul, HENNEPIN COUNTY
St. Paul, RAMSEY COUNTY
Stillwater vic., WASHINGTON COUNTY

Taylors Falls, CHISAGO COUNTY
Troy vic., WINONA COUNTY

Watson vic., CHIPPEWA COUNTY

Mississippi

Aberdeen, MONROE COUNTY
Alcorn Station, CLAIBORNE COUNTY

Bay Springs vic., TISHOMINGO COUNTY
Benoit, BOLIVAR COUNTY
Biloxi, HARRISON COUNTY
Biloxi vic., HARRISON COUNTY
Blakely, WARREN COUNTY

Cannonsburg vic., JEFFERSON COUNTY
Carrollton vic., CARROLL COUNTY
Centreville vic., WILKINSON COUNTY
Chatham vic., WASHINGTON COUNTY
Church Hill, JEFFERSON COUNTY
Clinton, HINDS COUNTY
Columbia (South), MARION COUNTY
Columbus, LOWNDES COUNTY
Columbus vic., LOWNDES COUNTY

Edwards vic., WARREN COUNTY

Fayette vic., JEFFERSON COUNTY
Foote vic., WASHINGTON COUNTY
Fort Adams, WILKINSON COUNTY
Fort Adams vic., WILKINSON COUNTY

Gloster vic., AMITE COUNTY
Greenville, WASHINGTON COUNTY
Greenville vic., WASHINGTON COUNTY
Gulfport, HARRISON COUNTY

Jackson, HINDS COUNTY

Kingston, ADAMS COUNTY

Lexington, HOLMES COUNTY
Lexington vic., HOLMES COUNTY
Liberty vic., AMITE COUNTY
Longwood, WASHINGTON COUNTY
Lorman vic., CLAIBORNE COUNTY

Macon, NOXUBEE COUNTY
Macon vic., NOXUBEE COUNTY
Mannsdale, MADISON COUNTY

Nashville Ferry, LOWNDES COUNTY
Natchez, ADAMS COUNTY
Natchez vic., ADAMS COUNTY
New Site, PRENTISS COUNTY

Ocean Springs, JACKSON COUNTY

Pascagoula, JACKSON COUNTY
Port Gibson, CLAIBORNE COUNTY
Port Gibson vic., CLAIBORNE COUNTY

Raymond, HINDS COUNTY
Raymond vic., HINDS COUNTY
Rodney, JEFFERSON COUNTY
Rodney vic., JEFFERSON COUNTY

Steens vic., LOWNDES COUNTY

Tishomingo, TISHOMINGO COUNTY

Vaiden vic., CARROLL COUNTY
Vicksburg, WARREN COUNTY
Vicksburg vic., WARREN COUNTY

Washington, ADAMS COUNTY
Washington vic., ADAMS COUNTY
Wayside, WASHINGTON COUNTY
West Point, CLAY COUNTY
Winona, MONTGOMERY COUNTY
Woodville, WILKINSON COUNTY
Woodville vic., WILKINSON COUNTY

Yazoo City vic., YAZOO COUNTY

Missouri

Affton, ST. LOUIS COUNTY
Affton vic., ST. LOUIS COUNTY
Arrow Rock, SALINE COUNTY
Arrow Rock vic., SALINE COUNTY
Auxvasse, CALLAWAY COUNTY
Auxvasse vic., CALLAWAY COUNTY

Barnhart, JEFFERSON COUNTY
Bay, GASCONADE COUNTY
Beck, JEFFERSON COUNTY
Bellefontaine vic., ST. LOUIS COUNTY
Bethel, SHELBY COUNTY
Bethel vic., SHELBY COUNTY
Bloomsdale, STE. GENEVIEVE COUNTY
Boonville, COOPER COUNTY

Carondelet, ST. LOUIS COUNTY
Center vic., RALLS COUNTY
Chesterfield, ST. LOUIS COUNTY
Clayton, ST. LOUIS COUNTY
Clinton vic., HENRY COUNTY

Columbia, BOONE COUNTY
Columbia vic., BOONE COUNTY
Cottleville vic., ST. CHARLES COUNTY
Crestwood, ST. LOUIS COUNTY

Danby, JEFFERSON COUNTY
Dardenne, ST. CHARLES COUNTY
Deepwater vic., HENRY COUNTY
Defiance, ST. CHARLES COUNTY
Defiance vic., ST. CHARLES COUNTY
Detmold vic., FRANKLIN COUNTY

Ellisville, ST. LOUIS COUNTY

Fayette vic., HOWARD COUNTY
Femme Osage, ST. CHARLES COUNTY
Flinthill vic., ST. CHARLES COUNTY
Florida, MONROE COUNTY
Florissant, ST. LOUIS COUNTY
Florissant vic., ST. LOUIS COUNTY
Fort Bellefontaine, ST. LOUIS COUNTY
Fulton, CALLAWAY COUNTY

Gasconade vic., GASCONADE COUNTY
Glasgow vic., HOWARD COUNTY
Glendale, ST. LOUIS COUNTY
Goldman vic., JEFFERSON COUNTY
Goss, MONROE COUNTY
Green Bottom, ST. CHARLES COUNTY

Herculaneum, JEFFERSON COUNTY
Hermann, GASCONADE COUNTY
Hermann vic., GASCONADE COUNTY

Independence, JACKSON COUNTY

Jefferson City vic., COLE COUNTY
Joanna, RALLS COUNTY
Joplin, JASPER COUNTY

Kansas City,
Kansas City, JACKSON COUNTY
Kimmswick, JEFFERSON COUNTY
Kirkwood, ST. LOUIS COUNTY

La Dede, LINN COUNTY
La Due, HENRY COUNTY
Lawson, LIVINGSTON COUNTY
Lawson, RAY COUNTY
Lees Summit, JACKSON COUNTY
Lexington, LAFAYETTE COUNTY
Lexington vic., LAFAYETTE COUNTY
Lowry City vic., ST. CLAIR COUNTY

Maplewood, ST. LOUIS COUNTY
Mokane, CALLAWAY COUNTY
Moscow Mills, LINCOLN COUNTY

New Franklin, HOWARD COUNTY
New Franklin vic., HOWARD COUNTY
North Fork vic., MONROE COUNTY

O'Fallon, ST. CHARLES COUNTY
Old Mines, WASHINGTON COUNTY
Osceola, ST. CLAIR COUNTY
Osceola vic., ST. CLAIR COUNTY
Overland, ST. LOUIS COUNTY
Owensville vic., GASCONADE COUNTY

Paris vic., MONROE COUNTY
Pattonville, ST. LOUIS COUNTY
Pevely, JEFFERSON COUNTY

Pevely vic., JEFFERSON COUNTY
Portage Des Sioux, ST. CHARLES COUNTY

Racola, WASHINGTON COUNTY
Roscoe, ST. CLAIR COUNTY
Roscoe vic., ST. CLAIR COUNTY

Smithville vic., CLAY COUNTY
St. Charles, ST. CHARLES COUNTY
St. Charles vic., ST. CHARLES COUNTY
St. Louis,
Ste. Genevieve, STE. GENEVIEVE COUNTY
Stoutsville, MONROE COUNTY
Stoutsville vic., MONROE COUNTY

Trimble, CLINTON COUNTY

Victor, MONROE COUNTY
Victor vic., MONROE COUNTY

Warsaw vic., BENTON COUNTY
Webster Groves, ST. LOUIS COUNTY
Weldon Springs, ST. CHARLES COUNTY
Wellston, ST. LOUIS COUNTY

Montana

Anaconda, DEER LODGE COUNTY

Bannack, BEAVERHEAD COUNTY
Bozeman, GALLATIN COUNTY

Custer Battlefield, BIG HORN COUNTY

Deer Lodge, POWELL COUNTY
Deer Lodge vic., POWELL COUNTY

Elkhorn, JEFFERSON COUNTY

Fort Missoula, MISSOULA COUNTY

Granite, GOLDEN VALLEY COUNTY
Great Falls, CASCADE COUNTY

Helena, LEWIS & CLARK COUNTY
Helena vic., LEWIS & CLARK COUNTY

Miles City, CUSTER COUNTY
Missoula, MISSOULA COUNTY

Stevensville, RAVALLI COUNTY

Virginia City, MADISON COUNTY

White Sulphur Springs, MEAGHER COUNTY

Nebraska

Beatrice, GAGE COUNTY
Bellevue, SARPY COUNTY
Bellwood, BUTLER COUNTY
Brownsville, NEMAHA COUNTY

Crofton, KNOX COUNTY

Dakota City, DAKOTA COUNTY

Florence, DOUGLAS COUNTY

Lincoln, LANCASTER COUNTY

Nebraska City, OTOE COUNTY
Niobrara, KNOX COUNTY

Omaha, DOUGLAS COUNTY

Santee, KNOX COUNTY
Santee Reservation, KNOX COUNTY
Santee vic., KNOX COUNTY

Nevada

Aurora, MINERAL COUNTY

Baker vic., WHITE PINE COUNTY

Carson City, ORMSBY COUNTY

Dayton, LYON COUNTY
Dayton vic., LYON COUNTY

Eureka, EUREKA COUNTY

Genoa, DOUGLAS COUNTY
Gold Hill, STOREY COUNTY

Humboldt City, PERSHING COUNTY

Pioche, LINCOLN COUNTY

Virginia, STOREY COUNTY
Virginia City, STOREY COUNTY

Weeks vic., LYON COUNTY

New Hampshire

Acworth, SULLIVAN COUNTY
Antrim, HILLSBOROUGH COUNTY

Bath, GRAFTON COUNTY
Blackwater River, MERRIMACK COUNTY
Bow Mills vic., MERRIMACK COUNTY

Campton vic., GRAFTON COUNTY
Canterbury, MERRIMACK COUNTY
Charleston, SULLIVAN COUNTY
Chesterfield, CHESHIRE COUNTY
Claremont, SULLIVAN COUNTY
Concord, MERRIMACK COUNTY
Contoocook, MERRIMACK COUNTY
Cornish, SULLIVAN COUNTY

Derryville, ROCKINGHAM COUNTY
Durham, STRAFFORD COUNTY
Durham vic., STRAFFORD COUNTY

Enfield vic., GRAFTON COUNTY
Exeter, CHESHIRE COUNTY
Exeter, ROCKINGHAM COUNTY

Greenland, ROCKINGHAM COUNTY

Hampton, ROCKINGHAM COUNTY
Hampton Falls, ROCKINGHAM COUNTY
Hanover, GRAFTON COUNTY
Harrisville, CHESHIRE COUNTY
Henniker, MERRIMACK COUNTY
Hillsboro, HILLSBOROUGH COUNTY

Hillsborough, HILLSBOROUGH COUNTY
Hillsborough Center, HILLSBOROUGH COUNTY
Hopkinton, MERRIMACK COUNTY
Hopkinton vic., MERRIMACK COUNTY

Kensington, ROCKINGHAM COUNTY

Lyme, GRAFTON COUNTY
Lyme vic., GRAFTON COUNTY

Manchester, HILLSBOROUGH COUNTY

Newington, ROCKINGHAM COUNTY
Newmarket, ROCKINGHAM COUNTY
Northwood Narrows, ROCKINGHAM COUNTY

Orford, GRAFTON COUNTY

Penacock-Boscawen, MERRIMACK COUNTY
Portsmouth, ROCKINGHAM COUNTY

Rockingham, ROCKINGHAM COUNTY
Rye, ROCKINGHAM COUNTY

Salisbury, MERRIMACK COUNTY
Salisbury Heights, MERRIMACK COUNTY
Salmon Falls, STRAFFORD COUNTY
Sandown, ROCKINGHAM COUNTY
Stoddard vic., CHESHIRE COUNTY
Stratham, ROCKINGHAM COUNTY

Walpole, CHESHIRE COUNTY
Webster, MERRIMACK COUNTY
Westmoreland, CHESHIRE COUNTY

New Jersey

Absecon, ATLANTIC COUNTY
Allaire, MONMOUTH COUNTY
Allentown, MONMOUTH COUNTY
Alloway, SALEM COUNTY
Alloway Twp., SALEM COUNTY
Alloway vic., SALEM COUNTY
Alpine, BERGEN COUNTY
Alpine, Cresskill vic., BERGEN COUNTY
Ancora, CAMDEN COUNTY
Arneytown, BURLINGTON COUNTY
Arneytown vic., MONMOUTH COUNTY
Asbury, WARREN COUNTY
Atlantic City, ATLANTIC COUNTY
Auburn, SALEM COUNTY

Bacon's Neck, CUMBERLAND COUNTY
Bacon's Neck vic., CUMBERLAND COUNTY
Barnegat, OCEAN COUNTY
Basking Ridge, SOMERSET COUNTY
Batsto, BURLINGTON COUNTY
Bayside vic., CUMBERLAND COUNTY
Beesleys Point, CAPE MAY COUNTY
Belleville, ESSEX COUNTY
Bellmawr, CAMDEN COUNTY
Bellmawr Borough, CAMDEN COUNTY
Bellmawr vic., CAMDEN COUNTY
Bergen, BERGEN COUNTY
Bergenfield, BERGEN COUNTY
Bernards Twp., SOMERSET COUNTY
Bernardsville, SOMERSET COUNTY
Bloomfield, CUMBERLAND COUNTY

Bloomfield, ESSEX COUNTY
Blue Anchor, CAMDEN COUNTY
Bonhamtown, MIDDLESEX COUNTY
Boonton vic., MORRIS COUNTY
Bordentown, BURLINGTON COUNTY
Boro Of N. Caldwell, ESSEX COUNTY
Bound Brook, SOMERSET COUNTY
Bound Brook vic., MIDDLESEX COUNTY
Bound Brook vic., SOMERSET COUNTY
Bridgeton, CUMBERLAND COUNTY
Burlington, BURLINGTON COUNTY

Caldwell, ESSEX COUNTY
Califon vic., HUNTERDON COUNTY
Calno, WARREN COUNTY
Camden, CAMDEN COUNTY
Cape May, CAPE MAY COUNTY
Cape May Courthouse, CAPE MAY COUNTY
Cape May Point, CAPE MAY COUNTY
Carteret, MIDDLESEX COUNTY
Cedar Bridge, OCEAN COUNTY
Cedar Grove, ESSEX COUNTY
Chapel Hill, MONMOUTH COUNTY
Charleston vic., BURLINGTON COUNTY
Chatham, MORRIS COUNTY
Chester, MORRIS COUNTY
Chews Landing vic., CAMDEN COUNTY
Cinnaminson Twp., BURLINGTON COUNTY
Clifton, PASSAIC COUNTY
Clinton, HUNTERDON COUNTY
Closter, BERGEN COUNTY
Closter, Norwood vic., BERGEN COUNTY
Cold Spring, CAPE MAY COUNTY
Collingswood, CAMDEN COUNTY
Columbus, BURLINGTON COUNTY
Cookstown, BURLINGTON COUNTY
Cookstown vic., BURLINGTON COUNTY
Cranford, UNION COUNTY
Creamridge vic., MONMOUTH COUNTY
Cresskill, BERGEN COUNTY
Crosswicks, BURLINGTON COUNTY

Daretown, SALEM COUNTY
Deerfield vic., CUMBERLAND COUNTY
Delaware, WARREN COUNTY
Delaware Twp., CAMDEN COUNTY
Demarest, BERGEN COUNTY
Dennisville, CAPE MAY COUNTY
Denville vic., MORRIS COUNTY
Dorchester vic., CUMBERLAND COUNTY
Dover vic., MORRIS COUNTY
Dumont, BERGEN COUNTY
Dumont Borough, BERGEN COUNTY
Dutch Neck, CUMBERLAND COUNTY

East Millstone, SOMERSET COUNTY
East Rutherford, BERGEN COUNTY
Eayrestown, BURLINGTON COUNTY
Eayrestown vic., BURLINGTON COUNTY
Elizabeth, UNION COUNTY
Elsinboro, SALEM COUNTY
Elsinboro Twp., SALEM COUNTY
Emerson, BERGEN COUNTY
Englewood, BERGEN COUNTY
Englishtown, MONMOUTH COUNTY
Everett vic., MONMOUTH COUNTY
Evesboro vic., BURLINGTON COUNTY

Evesham Twp., BURLINGTON COUNTY
Ewansville, BURLINGTON COUNTY

Fair Lawn, BERGEN COUNTY
Fair Lawn Borough, BERGEN COUNTY
Fairfield vic., ESSEX COUNTY
Fairton, CUMBERLAND COUNTY
Fellowship-Del. Twp., CAMDEN COUNTY
Fieldsboro, BURLINGTON COUNTY
Finderne vic., SOMERSET COUNTY
Flatbrookville vic., SUSSEX COUNTY
Flemington, HUNTERDON COUNTY
Florham Park, MORRIS COUNTY
Fort Lee, BERGEN COUNTY
Frankfort, SOMERSET COUNTY
Franklin Lakes vic., BERGEN COUNTY
Franklin Park, SOMERSET COUNTY
Franklin Twp., SOMERSET COUNTY
Freehold vic., MONMOUTH COUNTY
Friesburg, SALEM COUNTY

Glassboro, GLOUCESTER COUNTY
Glen Rock, BERGEN COUNTY
Glendale, CAMDEN COUNTY
Goshen, CAPE MAY COUNTY
Greenwich, CUMBERLAND COUNTY
Greenwich vic., CUMBERLAND COUNTY

Hackensack, BERGEN COUNTY
Haddonfield, CAMDEN COUNTY
Haddonfield vic., CAMDEN COUNTY
Hainesville, SUSSEX COUNTY
Hamburg, SUSSEX COUNTY
Hancocks Bridge, SALEM COUNTY
Hanover, MORRIS COUNTY
Hanover Neck, MORRIS COUNTY
Hanover Twp., MORRIS COUNTY
Haskell, PASSAIC COUNTY
Hawthorne, PASSAIC COUNTY
Head-of-the-River, ATLANTIC COUNTY
Highland Park vic., MIDDLESEX COUNTY
Highlands, MONMOUTH COUNTY
Hillsdale, BERGEN COUNTY
Hoboken, HUDSON COUNTY
Hohokus, BERGEN COUNTY
Hohokus Twp., BERGEN COUNTY
Holland, MONMOUTH COUNTY
Holland-Holmdel Twp., MONMOUTH COUNTY
Holmdel, MONMOUTH COUNTY
Holmdel Twp., MONMOUTH COUNTY
Hope, WARREN COUNTY
Hope vic., WARREN COUNTY
Hopewell, MERCER COUNTY
Hopewell vic., MERCER COUNTY
Hutchinson's Mill, MERCER COUNTY

Irvington, ESSEX COUNTY

Jersey City, HUDSON COUNTY
Jobstown, BURLINGTON COUNTY
Jobstown vic., BURLINGTON COUNTY
Johnsonburg, WARREN COUNTY

Kingston, MIDDLESEX COUNTY
Kinkora, BURLINGTON COUNTY

Lakehurst vic., OCEAN COUNTY
Lambertville, HUNTERDON COUNTY

Lanoka Harbor, OCEAN COUNTY
Lawrence Township, MERCER COUNTY
Lawrenceville, MERCER COUNTY
Leeds Point, ATLANTIC COUNTY
Leonia, BERGEN COUNTY
Liberty Corner, SOMERSET COUNTY
Liberty Corner vic., SOMERSET COUNTY
Lincoln Park, MORRIS COUNTY
Lincroft vic., MONMOUTH COUNTY
Little Falls, PASSAIC COUNTY
Livingston, ESSEX COUNTY
Long Branch, MONMOUTH COUNTY
Lower Alloways Creek, SALEM COUNTY
Lower Penns Neck, SALEM COUNTY
Lower Preakness, PASSAIC COUNTY
Lumberton, BURLINGTON COUNTY
Lumberton vic., BURLINGTON COUNTY
Lyndhurst, BERGEN COUNTY

Madison, MORRIS COUNTY
Malaga vic., GLOUCESTER COUNTY
Mannington Twp., SALEM COUNTY
Mannington vic., SALEM COUNTY
Mantua, GLOUCESTER COUNTY
Mantua vic., GLOUCESTER COUNTY
Maple Shade, BURLINGTON COUNTY
Maplewood, ESSEX COUNTY
Margate, ATLANTIC COUNTY
Marlton vic., BURLINGTON COUNTY
Matawan, MONMOUTH COUNTY
Mauricetown, CUMBERLAND COUNTY
Mays Landing, ATLANTIC COUNTY
Maywood, BERGEN COUNTY
Mendham, MORRIS COUNTY
Metuchen, MIDDLESEX COUNTY
Metuchen vic., MIDDLESEX COUNTY
Mickleton, GLOUCESTER COUNTY
Middle Valley, MORRIS COUNTY
Middlebush vic., SOMERSET COUNTY
Middleton, MONMOUTH COUNTY
Midland Park, BERGEN COUNTY
Millbrook, WARREN COUNTY
Millbrook vic., WARREN COUNTY
Millburn, ESSEX COUNTY
Millstone, SOMERSET COUNTY
Millville, SUSSEX COUNTY
Montague, SUSSEX COUNTY
Montague vic., SUSSEX COUNTY
Montclair, ESSEX COUNTY
Montvale Boro, BERGEN COUNTY
Montville, MORRIS COUNTY
Montville vic., MORRIS COUNTY
Moorestown, BURLINGTON COUNTY
Moorestown vic., BURLINGTON COUNTY
Morristown, MIDDLESEX COUNTY
Morristown, MORRIS COUNTY
Mount Freedom vic., MORRIS COUNTY
Mount Holly, BURLINGTON COUNTY
Mount Laurel, BURLINGTON COUNTY
Mount Laurel vic., BURLINGTON COUNTY
Mount Royal, GLOUCESTER COUNTY
Mount Tabor vic., MORRIS COUNTY
Mountain View, PASSAIC COUNTY
Mountainside, UNION COUNTY
Mountainville, HUNTERDON COUNTY
Mullica Hill, GLOUCESTER COUNTY

N. Brunswick Twp., MIDDLESEX COUNTY
National Park, GLOUCESTER COUNTY
New Brunswick, MIDDLESEX COUNTY
New Brunswick vic., MIDDLESEX COUNTY
New Lisbon, BURLINGTON COUNTY
New Market, MIDDLESEX COUNTY
New Milford, BERGEN COUNTY
New Providence, UNION COUNTY
Newark, ESSEX COUNTY
Newfoundland, MORRIS COUNTY
Newfoundland vic., MORRIS COUNTY
North Stelton vic., MIDDLESEX COUNTY
Nutley, BERGEN COUNTY
Nutley, ESSEX COUNTY

Oakland, BERGEN COUNTY
Ocean View, CAPE MAY COUNTY
Old Tappan, BERGEN COUNTY
Oldwick, HUNTERDON COUNTY
Orange, ESSEX COUNTY
Oxford, WARREN COUNTY

Pahaquarry Twp., WARREN COUNTY
Paramus, BERGEN COUNTY
Park Ridge, BERGEN COUNTY
Park Ridge vic., BERGEN COUNTY
Parsipanny vic., MORRIS COUNTY
Parsippany vic., MORRIS COUNTY
Passaic, PASSAIC COUNTY
Paterson, PASSAIC COUNTY
Paterson vic., PASSAIC COUNTY
Pattenburg vic., HUNTERDON COUNTY
Paulsboro, GLOUCESTER COUNTY
Paulsboro vic., GLOUCESTER COUNTY
Pennington, MERCER COUNTY
Pennington vic., MERCER COUNTY
Pennsauken, CAMDEN COUNTY
Pennsauken Twp., CAMDEN COUNTY
Perth Amboy, MIDDLESEX COUNTY
Phalanx vic., MONMOUTH COUNTY
Phillipsburg, WARREN COUNTY
Phillipsburg vic., WARREN COUNTY
Pine Brook, MORRIS COUNTY
Piscataway, MIDDLESEX COUNTY
Piscataway Twp., MIDDLESEX COUNTY
Pitman, GLOUCESTER COUNTY
Pittsgrove vic., SALEM COUNTY
Plainfield, UNION COUNTY
Plainsboro vic., MIDDLESEX COUNTY
Pluckemin, SOMERSET COUNTY
Pompton Falls vic., PASSAIC COUNTY
Pompton Lakes vic., PASSAIC COUNTY
Pompton Plains, MORRIS COUNTY
Port Republic, ATLANTIC COUNTY
Preakness, PASSAIC COUNTY
Princeton, MERCER COUNTY
Princeton vic., MERCER COUNTY
Prospertown vic., MONMOUTH COUNTY

Quinton vic., SALEM COUNTY

Rahway, UNION COUNTY
Ralston, MORRIS COUNTY
Rancocas, BURLINGTON COUNTY
Rancocas vic., BURLINGTON COUNTY
Raritan, SOMERSET COUNTY
Raven Rock, HUNTERDON COUNTY
Red Lion, BURLINGTON COUNTY

Ridgefield, BERGEN COUNTY
Ridgefield Park, BERGEN COUNTY
Ridgewood, BERGEN COUNTY
Ringoes, HUNTERDON COUNTY
Ringoes vic., HUNTERDON COUNTY
Ringwood, PASSAIC COUNTY
River Edge, BERGEN COUNTY
Rivervale Twp., BERGEN COUNTY
Roadstown, CUMBERLAND COUNTY
Rochelle Park, BERGEN COUNTY
Rockaway, MORRIS COUNTY
Rockleigh, BERGEN COUNTY
Rocky Hill, SOMERSET COUNTY
Roseland, ESSEX COUNTY
Rutherford, BERGEN COUNTY

S. Middlebush, SOMERSET COUNTY
Saddle River, BERGEN COUNTY
Saddle River Twp., BERGEN COUNTY
Salem, SALEM COUNTY
Salem vic., SALEM COUNTY
Sandtown, BURLINGTON COUNTY
Sandy Hook, MONMOUTH COUNTY
Schalk Station, MIDDLESEX COUNTY
Scotch Plains, UNION COUNTY
Sea Breeze, CUMBERLAND COUNTY
Seaville Vicinity, CAPE MAY COUNTY
Seeley, CUMBERLAND COUNTY
Seeley vic., CUMBERLAND COUNTY
Sergeantsville, HUNTERDON COUNTY
Sharptown vic., SALEM COUNTY
Shrewsbury, MONMOUTH COUNTY
Smith Ferry, SUSSEX COUNTY
Smithville, ATLANTIC COUNTY
Somerdale vic., CAMDEN COUNTY
Somers Point, ATLANTIC COUNTY
Somerville, SOMERSET COUNTY
South Bound Brook, SOMERSET COUNTY
South Dennis, CAPE MAY COUNTY
South Middlebush, SOMERSET COUNTY
South Pemberton, BURLINGTON COUNTY
Speedwell Village, MORRIS COUNTY
Split Rock, MORRIS COUNTY
Springfield, UNION COUNTY
Springfield Twp., BURLINGTON COUNTY
Springside vic., BURLINGTON COUNTY
Springtown vic., MORRIS COUNTY
Swedesboro, GLOUCESTER COUNTY
Swedesboro vic., GLOUCESTER COUNTY
Sykesville, BURLINGTON COUNTY

Teaneck, BERGEN COUNTY
Tenafly, BERGEN COUNTY
Tennent, MONMOUTH COUNTY
Toms Point, MORRIS COUNTY
Totowa, PASSAIC COUNTY
Towaco, MORRIS COUNTY
Towaco vic., MORRIS COUNTY
Trenton, MERCER COUNTY

Union, UNION COUNTY
Union City, HUDSON COUNTY
Upper Mill, BURLINGTON COUNTY
Upper Montclair, ESSEX COUNTY
Upper Preakness, PASSAIC COUNTY
Upper Saddle River, BERGEN COUNTY

Vincetown, BURLINGTON COUNTY

Wallpack Center, SUSSEX COUNTY
Wallpack Center vic., SUSSEX COUNTY
Walnford vic., MONMOUTH COUNTY
Wanaque, PASSAIC COUNTY
Wantage, SUSSEX COUNTY
Washington Crossing, MERCER COUNTY
Washington Twp., BURLINGTON COUNTY
Washington Valley, MORRIS COUNTY
Wayne, PASSAIC COUNTY
West Caldwell, ESSEX COUNTY
West Freehold, MONMOUTH COUNTY
West Orange, ESSEX COUNTY
Westfield, UNION COUNTY
Westhampton Twp., BURLINGTON COUNTY
Westville, GLOUCESTER COUNTY
Whippany, MORRIS COUNTY
Whippany vic., MORRIS COUNTY
Woodbine, CAPE MAY COUNTY
Woodbridge, MIDDLESEX COUNTY
Woodbury, GLOUCESTER COUNTY
Woodstown, SALEM COUNTY
Woodstown vic., SALEM COUNTY
Wrightsville, MONMOUTH COUNTY
Wyckoff, BERGEN COUNTY
Wyckoff Twp., BERGEN COUNTY

New Mexico

Acoma Pueblo, VALENCIA COUNTY
Albuquerque, BERNALILLO COUNTY
Alcalde, RIO ARRIBA COUNTY
Arroyo Hondo, TAOS COUNTY

Belen, VALENCIA COUNTY
Bland vic., SANDOVAL COUNTY

Canoncita, SANTA FE COUNTY
Casa Blanca vic., VALENCIA COUNTY
Chamita, RIO ARRIBA COUNTY
Chimayo, SANTA FE COUNTY
Cienega, OTERO COUNTY
Cimarron, COLFAX COUNTY

Espanola vic., RIO ARRIBA COUNTY
Espanola vic., SANTA FE COUNTY

Galisteo, SANTA FE COUNTY
Gallup vic., MCKINLEY COUNTY

Isleta Pueblo, BERNALILLO COUNTY
Isleto Pueblo, BERNALILLO COUNTY

Las Cruces, DONA ANA COUNTY
Las Vegas vic., SAN MIGUEL COUNTY
Laugna Pueblo, VALENCIA COUNTY
Llano Quemado, TAOS COUNTY

Manzano, TORRANCE COUNTY

Nambe (pueblo), SANTA FE COUNTY

Old Laguna Pueblo, VALENCIA COUNTY

Pecos, SAN MIGUEL COUNTY
Pecos vic., SAN MIGUEL COUNTY
Penasco, TAOS COUNTY
Peralta, VALENCIA COUNTY

Placita De Taos, TAOS COUNTY
Pojuaque vic., SANTA FE COUNTY
Puerto De Luna, GUADALUPE COUNTY

Ranchito, TAOS COUNTY
Ranchos De Taos, TAOS COUNTY
Rodney, DONA ANA COUNTY
Romeroville, SAN MIGUEL COUNTY

San Miguel, SAN MIGUEL COUNTY
Santa Ana, SANDOVAL COUNTY
Santa Cruz, SANTA FE COUNTY
Santa Fe, SANTA FE COUNTY
Santa Fe vic., SANTA FE COUNTY
Socorro, SOCORRO COUNTY

Talpa, TAOS COUNTY
Taos, TAOS COUNTY
Taos Peublo, TAOS COUNTY
Taos vic., TAOS COUNTY
Tiptonville, MORA COUNTY
Trampas, TAOS COUNTY
Tucumcari, QUAY COUNTY

Vadito, TAOS COUNTY
Valencia vic., VALENCIA COUNTY
Villanueva vic., SAN MIGUEL COUNTY

Watrous vic., MORA COUNTY

Zuni, MCKINLEY COUNTY

New York

Albany, ALBANY COUNTY
Albion, ORLEANS COUNTY
Alplaus, SCHENECTADY COUNTY
Altamont, ALBANY COUNTY
Altamont vic., ALBANY COUNTY
Amagansett, SUFFOLK COUNTY
Amsterdam, MONTGOMERY COUNTY
Angelica, ALLEGANY COUNTY
Aqueboque, SUFFOLK COUNTY
Ashville, CHAUTAUQUA COUNTY
Atlanta, STEUBEN COUNTY
Auburn, CAYUGA COUNTY
Aurora, CAYUGA COUNTY
Avon, LIVINGSTON COUNTY

Babylon, SUFFOLK COUNTY
Ballston Lake, SARATOGA COUNTY
Ballston Lake vic., SARATOGA COUNTY
Ballston Spa, SARATOGA COUNTY
Barrytown, DUTCHESS COUNTY
Barrytown vic., DUTCHESS COUNTY
Batavia, GENESEE COUNTY
Batavia vic., GENESEE COUNTY
Beacon, DUTCHESS COUNTY
Bedford, WESTCHESTER COUNTY
Belfast vic., ALLEGANY COUNTY
Berne vic., ALBANY COUNTY
Berne vic., SCHOHARIE COUNTY
Bethlehem, ALBANY COUNTY
Binghamton, BROOME COUNTY
Blue Stores vic., COLUMBIA COUNTY
Boonville vic., ONEIDA COUNTY

Bowery Bay, QUEENS COUNTY
Breadabeen, SCHOHARIE COUNTY
Bridgehampton, SUFFOLK COUNTY
Brighton, MONROE COUNTY
Brinckerhoff, DUTCHESS COUNTY
Bristol Center, ONTARIO COUNTY
Broadalbin, FULTON COUNTY
Bronx, BRONX COUNTY
Brookhaven, SUFFOLK COUNTY
Brooklyn, KINGS COUNTY
Buffalo, ERIE COUNTY
Burnt Hills, SARATOGA COUNTY

Cairo, GREENE COUNTY
Caledonia, LIVINGSTON COUNTY
Callicoon, SULLIVAN COUNTY
Camillus, ONONDAGA COUNTY
Canajoharie, MONTGOMERY COUNTY
Canandaigua, ONTARIO COUNTY
Canastota vic., MADISON COUNTY
Catskill Mts., GREENE COUNTY
Cazenovia, MADISON COUNTY
Centereach, SUFFOLK COUNTY
Centerport, SUFFOLK COUNTY
Chappaqua, WESTCHESTER COUNTY
Chappaqua vic., WESTCHESTER COUNTY
Charleston, MONTGOMERY COUNTY
Charlton, SARATOGA COUNTY
Chatauqua, CHAUTAUQUA COUNTY
Chatham Center, COLUMBIA COUNTY
Cherry Valley, OTSEGO COUNTY
Childs, ORLEANS COUNTY
Chittenango, MADISON COUNTY
Cincinnatus, CORTLAND COUNTY
Clarkson, MONROE COUNTY
Clarksville, ALBANY COUNTY
Claverack, COLUMBIA COUNTY
Coeymans, ALBANY COUNTY
Cohoes, ALBANY COUNTY
Collins, CATTARAUGUS COUNTY
Colonie, ALBANY COUNTY
Commack, SUFFOLK COUNTY
Cooperstown, OTSEGO COUNTY
Copake, COLUMBIA COUNTY
Copake vic., COLUMBIA COUNTY
Corning, STEUBEN COUNTY
Corning vic., STEUBEN COUNTY
Cortland, COLUMBIA COUNTY
Cortland, CORTLAND COUNTY
Cutchogue, SUFFOLK COUNTY

Danube, HERKIMER COUNTY
Dayton, CATTARAUGUS COUNTY
Delphi Falls, ONONDAGA COUNTY
Deposit, BROOME COUNTY
Deposit, DELAWARE COUNTY
Dobbs Ferry, WESTCHESTER COUNTY
Dover Plains, DUTCHESS COUNTY
Duanesburg, SCHENECTADY COUNTY
Dunkirk, CHAUTAUQUA COUNTY
Dunnsville, ALBANY COUNTY

East Avon, LIVINGSTON COUNTY
East Greenbush, RENSSELAER COUNTY
East Hampton, SUFFOLK COUNTY
East Randolph vic., CATTARAUGUS COUNTY
East Rockaway, NASSAU COUNTY

East Springfield, OTSEGO COUNTY
East Williston, NASSAU COUNTY
Eaton Village, MADISON COUNTY
Elbridge Vic, ONONDAGA COUNTY
Ellenville, ULSTER COUNTY
Elmira, CHEMUNG COUNTY
Endwell, BROOME COUNTY
Esperance, SCHOHARIE COUNTY

Fabius, ONONDAGA COUNTY
Farmingdale, NASSAU COUNTY
Fayetteville, ONONDAGA COUNTY
Feura Bush, ALBANY COUNTY
Fillmore vic., ALLEGANY COUNTY
Fishkill, DUTCHESS COUNTY
Flushing, QUEENS COUNTY
Fonda, MONTGOMERY COUNTY
Fort Ann, WASHINGTON COUNTY
Fort Herkimer, HERKIMER COUNTY
Fort Hunter, MONTGOMERY COUNTY
Fort Johnson, MONTGOMERY COUNTY
Fort Plain, MONTGOMERY COUNTY
Fort Ticonderoga, ESSEX COUNTY
Frankfort, HERKIMER COUNTY
Fultonville, MONTGOMERY COUNTY

Gaines, ORLEANS COUNTY
Gardiner, ULSTER COUNTY
Gardner's Island, SUFFOLK COUNTY
Garrison, PUTNAM COUNTY
Geneva, SENECA COUNTY
Geneva, ONTARIO COUNTY
Georgetown, MADISON COUNTY
Germantown vic., COLUMBIA COUNTY
Germonds, ROCKLAND COUNTY
Giffords, SCHENECTADY COUNTY
Glen, MONTGOMERY COUNTY
Glen Cove, NASSAU COUNTY
Glenville, SCHENECTADY COUNTY
Glenville Center, SCHENECTADY COUNTY
Gloversville, FULTON COUNTY
Goshen, ORANGE COUNTY
Great Neck, NASSAU COUNTY
Green Island, ALBANY COUNTY
Greenburgh, WESTCHESTER COUNTY
Greenlawn, SUFFOLK COUNTY
Greenport, COLUMBIA COUNTY
Grooms Corners, SARATOGA COUNTY
Guilderland Center, ALBANY COUNTY
Guilderland vic., ALBANY COUNTY

Hancock, DELAWARE COUNTY
Hancock vic., DELAWARE COUNTY
Harriman, ORANGE COUNTY
Hastings-on-Hudson, WESTCHESTER COUNTY
Hauppauge, SUFFOLK COUNTY
Hempstead, NASSAU COUNTY
Henrietta, MONROE COUNTY
Herkimer, HERKIMER COUNTY
High Bridge vic., SARATOGA COUNTY
High Falls, ULSTER COUNTY
Homer, CORTLAND COUNTY
Hornell, STEUBEN COUNTY
Horseheads, CHEMUNG COUNTY
Houcks Corners, ALBANY COUNTY
Hudson, COLUMBIA COUNTY
Hudson vic., COLUMBIA COUNTY

Huntington, SUFFOLK COUNTY
Huntington vic., SUFFOLK COUNTY
Huntington, South, SUFFOLK COUNTY
Hurley, ULSTER COUNTY
Hurley vic., ULSTER COUNTY
Hyde Park, DUTCHESS COUNTY
Hyde Park, ERIE COUNTY

Ilion, HERKIMER COUNTY
Indian Castle vic., HERKIMER COUNTY
Irvington, WESTCHESTER COUNTY
Ithaca, TOMPKINS COUNTY

Jackson Heights, QUEENS COUNTY
Jamestown, CHAUTAUQUA COUNTY
Jamesville, ONONDAGA COUNTY
Jamesville vic., ONONDAGA COUNTY
Johnstown, FULTON COUNTY
Jordan, ONONDAGA COUNTY

Katonah, WESTCHESTER COUNTY
Kerhonkson, ULSTER COUNTY
Kew Gardens, ALBANY COUNTY
Kinderhook, COLUMBIA COUNTY
Kinderhook vic., COLUMBIA COUNTY
Kingsbury, WASHINGTON COUNTY
Kingston, ULSTER COUNTY
Kingston vic., ULSTER COUNTY

Lawrence, NASSAU COUNTY
Lawtons vic., ERIE COUNTY
Leeds, GREENE COUNTY
Lewiston, NIAGARA COUNTY
Limestone vic., CATTARAUGUS COUNTY
Little Falls, HERKIMER COUNTY
Liverpool, ONONDAGA COUNTY
Livingston vic., COLUMBIA COUNTY
Lloyd Harbor, SUFFOLK COUNTY
Lloyd Neck, SUFFOLK COUNTY
Lockport, NIAGARA COUNTY
Long Island City, QUEENS COUNTY

Maine vic., BROOME COUNTY
Malden Bridge, COLUMBIA COUNTY
Malta, SARATOGA COUNTY
Mamaroneck, WESTCHESTER COUNTY
Manhasset, NASSAU COUNTY
Manlius, ONONDAGA COUNTY
Marbletown, ULSTER COUNTY
Marcellus, ONONDAGA COUNTY
Marcellus vic., ONONDAGA COUNTY
Martisco, ONONDAGA COUNTY
Maspeth, QUEENS COUNTY
Massapequa, NASSAU COUNTY
Mastic Beach, SUFFOLK COUNTY
Matinecock, NASSAU COUNTY
Mayfield, FULTON COUNTY
Mc Graw, CORTLAND COUNTY
Mecklenburg, SCHUYLER COUNTY
Melrose vic., RENSSELAER COUNTY
Melville, SUFFOLK COUNTY
Middleburg, SCHOHARIE COUNTY
Middlefield Cen. vic., OTSEGO COUNTY
Middletown, ORANGE COUNTY
Millbrook, DUTCHESS COUNTY
Minden, MONTGOMERY COUNTY
Minisink Ford, SULLIVAN COUNTY
Mount Lebanon, COLUMBIA COUNTY

Mount Vernon, WESTCHESTER COUNTY
Murray, ORLEANS COUNTY

Napanoch, ULSTER COUNTY
Naples, ONTARIO COUNTY
Nelliston vic., MONTGOMERY COUNTY
New Brighton, RICHMOND COUNTY
New Concord, COLUMBIA COUNTY
New Dorp, RICHMOND COUNTY
New Hyde Park, NASSAU COUNTY
New Paltz, ULSTER COUNTY
New Paltz vic., ULSTER COUNTY
New Rochelle, WESTCHESTER COUNTY
New Scotland Twp., ALBANY COUNTY
New Scotland vic., ALBANY COUNTY
New Windsor, ORANGE COUNTY
New York City, BRONX COUNTY
New York City, KINGS COUNTY
New York City, NEW YORK COUNTY
New York City, QUEENS COUNTY
Newburgh, ORANGE COUNTY
Newtonville, ALBANY COUNTY
Niagara Falls, NIAGARA COUNTY
Niskayuna, SCHENECTADY COUNTY
North Blenheim, SCHOHARIE COUNTY
North Germantown, COLUMBIA COUNTY
North Salem, WESTCHESTER COUNTY
North Tarrytown, WESTCHESTER COUNTY
North Tonawanda, NIAGARA COUNTY
North Tonawanda vic., NIAGARA COUNTY
Nyack, ROCKLAND COUNTY

Oaksville, OTSEGO COUNTY
Old Chatham, COLUMBIA COUNTY
Old Westbury, NASSAU COUNTY
Oneida, ONEIDA COUNTY
Onesquethaw, ALBANY COUNTY
Onondaga Hill, ONONDAGA COUNTY
Oran, ONONDAGA COUNTY
Orangeburg vic., ORLEANS COUNTY
Orangeburg vic., ROCKLAND COUNTY
Ossining, WESTCHESTER COUNTY
Ossining vic., WESTCHESTER COUNTY
Oswego, OSWEGO COUNTY
Otisville, ORANGE COUNTY
Owego, TIOGA COUNTY
Oyster Bay, NASSAU COUNTY

Painted Post, STEUBEN COUNTY
Palatine Bridge, MONTGOMERY COUNTY
Palatine Bridge vic., MONTGOMERY COUNTY
Palisades, ROCKLAND COUNTY
Pantigo, SUFFOLK COUNTY
Pattersonville, MONTGOMERY COUNTY
Pattersonville, SCHENECTADY COUNTY
Pearl River vic., ROCKLAND COUNTY
Perth, FULTON COUNTY
Petersburg, RENSSELAER COUNTY
Petersburg vic., RENSSELAER COUNTY
Philippsport, SULLIVAN COUNTY
Plainville vic., ONONDAGA COUNTY
Pleasant Valley, DUTCHESS COUNTY
Pleasantville, WESTCHESTER COUNTY
Pompey, ONONDAGA COUNTY
Port Jervis, ORANGE COUNTY
Port Jervis vic., ORANGE COUNTY
Port Ontario vic., OSWEGO COUNTY

Portageville vic., LIVINGSTON COUNTY
Portageville vic., WYOMING COUNTY
Poughkeepsie, DUTCHESS COUNTY
Poughkeepsie, ERIE COUNTY
Princetown, SCHENECTADY COUNTY

Quaker Street Vil., SCHENECTADY COUNTY
Queens, QUEENS COUNTY

Red Hook, DUTCHESS COUNTY
Red Hook vic., DUTCHESS COUNTY
Rensselaer, RENSSELAER COUNTY
Rensselaerville, ALBANY COUNTY
Rexford, SARATOGA COUNTY
Rhinebeck, DUTCHESS COUNTY
Rhinebeck vic., DUTCHESS COUNTY
Richmond, RICHMOND COUNTY
Ridgewood, QUEENS COUNTY
Rifton, ULSTER COUNTY
Rochester, MONROE COUNTY
Rome, ONEIDA COUNTY
Rosebank, RICHMOND COUNTY
Roslyn, NASSAU COUNTY
Rotterdam, SCHENECTADY COUNTY
Rotterdam Jct., SCHENECTADY COUNTY
Rotterdam Twp., SCHENECTADY COUNTY
Russia, HERKIMER COUNTY
Rye, WESTCHESTER COUNTY

Sag Harbor, SUFFOLK COUNTY
Salamanca, CATTARAUGUS COUNTY
Salem Center, WESTCHESTER COUNTY
Salisbury Mills vic., ORANGE COUNTY
Sands Point, NASSAU COUNTY
Saratoga, SARATOGA COUNTY
Saratoga vic., SARATOGA COUNTY
Scarsdale, WESTCHESTER COUNTY
Schaghticoke vic., RENSSELAER COUNTY
Schenectady, SCHENECTADY COUNTY
Schoharie, SCHOHARIE COUNTY
Schoharie vic., SCHOHARIE COUNTY
Scotia, SCHENECTADY COUNTY
Seaford, NASSAU COUNTY
Selden vic., SUFFOLK COUNTY
Seneca Falls, SENECA COUNTY
Setauket, SUFFOLK COUNTY
Shawangunk, ULSTER COUNTY
Sinclairville, CHAUTAUQUA COUNTY
Skaneateles, ONONDAGA COUNTY
Skaneateles vic., ONONDAGA COUNTY
Smithtown, SUFFOLK COUNTY
Somers, WESTCHESTER COUNTY
Somerset, NIAGARA COUNTY
Sparkill, ROCKLAND COUNTY
St. James vic., SUFFOLK COUNTY
St. Johnsville Vic, MONTGOMERY COUNTY
Staatsburg, DUTCHESS COUNTY
Stillwater, SARATOGA COUNTY
Stockport, COLUMBIA COUNTY
Stone Arabia, MONTGOMERY COUNTY
Stone Ridge, ULSTER COUNTY
Syracuse, KINGS COUNTY
Syracuse, ONONDAGA COUNTY

Tahawus, ESSEX COUNTY
Tappan, ROCKLAND COUNTY
Tarrytown, WESTCHESTER COUNTY
Tarrytown vic., WESTCHESTER COUNTY

Tioronda, DUTCHESS COUNTY
Tivoli, DUTCHESS COUNTY
Tivoli vic., DUTCHESS COUNTY
Tivoli-on-Hudson, DUTCHESS COUNTY
Tompkins Cove, ROCKLAND COUNTY
Tottenville, RICHMOND COUNTY
Troy, RENSSELAER COUNTY

Unionville, ALBANY COUNTY
Upper Red Hook, DUTCHESS COUNTY
Utica, ONEIDA COUNTY

Valhalla vic., WESTCHESTER COUNTY
Vancortlandville, WESTCHESTER COUNTY
Vernon Center, ONEIDA COUNTY
Vestal, BROOME COUNTY
Vischers Ferry, SARATOGA COUNTY

Wainscott, SUFFOLK COUNTY
Wantagh, NASSAU COUNTY
Wappingers Falls, DUTCHESS COUNTY
Warsaw, WYOMING COUNTY
Waterford, SARATOGA COUNTY
Watermill vic., SUFFOLK COUNTY
Watertown, JEFFERSON COUNTY
Watervliet, ALBANY COUNTY
Wawarsing, ULSTER COUNTY
Wellsville, ALLEGANY COUNTY
West Coxsackie, GREENE COUNTY
West Hills, SUFFOLK COUNTY
Westfield, CHAUTAUQUA COUNTY
Westville vic., OTSEGO COUNTY
White Plains, WESTCHESTER COUNTY
Whitesboro, ONEIDA COUNTY
Whitney Point, BROOME COUNTY

Yonkers, WESTCHESTER COUNTY
Yorktown, WESTCHESTER COUNTY
Youngstown, NIAGARA COUNTY

North Carolina

Airlie vic., HALIFAX COUNTY
Albemarle, MONTGOMERY COUNTY
Albemarle, STANLEY COUNTY
Asheville, BUNCOMBE COUNTY

Bath, BEAUFORT COUNTY
Beaufort, CARTERET COUNTY
Beaufort vic., CARTERET COUNTY
Bethabara, FORSYTH COUNTY
Bethania, FORSYTH COUNTY
Bethel vic., PERQUIMANS COUNTY
Brunswick Town, BRUNSWICK COUNTY
Buckland, GATES COUNTY

Caldwell vic., MECKLENBURG COUNTY
Camden, CAMDEN COUNTY
Camden vic., CAMDEN COUNTY
Cary, WAKE COUNTY
Cataloochee, HAYWOOD COUNTY
Cataloochee vic., HAYWOOD COUNTY
Chapel Hill, ORANGE COUNTY
Charlotte, MECKLENBURG COUNTY
Charlotte vic., MECKLENBURG COUNTY
Clemmons, FORSYTH COUNTY

Columbus, POLK COUNTY
Creswell vic., TYRRELL COUNTY
Creswell vic., WASHINGTON COUNTY

Davidson, MECKLENBURG COUNTY
Dortches, NASH COUNTY
Duck vic., DARE COUNTY
Durham, DURHAM COUNTY

Edenton, CHOWAN COUNTY
Edenton, CRAVEN COUNTY
Edenton vic., CHOWAN COUNTY
Elizabeth City, PASQUOTANK COUNTY
Elizabeth City vic., PASQUOTANK COUNTY
Elizabethtown, BLADEN COUNTY
Elizabethtown vic., BLADEN COUNTY
Enfield vic., HALIFAX COUNTY

Fairview vic., BUNCOMBE COUNTY
Faison vic., DUPLIN COUNTY
Falls, WAKE COUNTY
Fayetteville, CUMBERLAND COUNTY
Flat Rock, HENDERSON COUNTY
Fletcher, HENDERSON COUNTY
Fremont vic., WAYNE COUNTY

Gates vic., GATES COUNTY
Gatesville vic., GATES COUNTY
Glencoe, ALAMANCE COUNTY
Granite Quarry vic., ROWAN COUNTY
Greensboro, GUILFORD COUNTY

Halifax, HALIFAX COUNTY
Hamer vic., CASWELL COUNTY
Harrells vic., SAMPSON COUNTY
Henderson vic., VANCE COUNTY
Henderson vic., WARREN COUNTY
Hendersonville, HENDERSON COUNTY
Hertford vic., PERQUIMANS COUNTY
Hickory, CATAWBA COUNTY
Hillsborough, ORANGE COUNTY
Hillsborough vic., ORANGE COUNTY
Hobbsville vic., GATES COUNTY

Iron Station vic., LINCOLN COUNTY

Jackson Vic, NORTHAMPTON COUNTY
Jacksonville, FRANKLIN COUNTY
Jamestown, GUILFORD COUNTY
Jamestown vic., GUILFORD COUNTY

Kernersville, FORSYTH COUNTY

Lenoir vic., CALDWELL COUNTY
Lexington, DAVIDSON COUNTY
Lexington vic., DAVIDSON COUNTY
Lincolnton vic., LINCOLN COUNTY
Littleton, WARREN COUNTY
Locust Hill vic., CASWELL COUNTY
Louisburg, FRANKLIN COUNTY
Louisburg vic., FRANKLIN COUNTY
Lumber Bridge, ROBESON COUNTY

Maiden vic., LINCOLN COUNTY
Marion vic., MCDOWELL COUNTY
Mc Adenville, GASTON COUNTY
Milton, CASWELL COUNTY
Mintonsville vic., GATES COUNTY
Mocksville vic., DAVIE COUNTY
Morven vic., ANSON COUNTY
Mount Airy, SURRY COUNTY

Mount Mourne, IREDELL COUNTY
Murfreesboro, HENDERSON COUNTY
Murfreesboro, HERTFORD COUNTY

New Bern, CRAVEN COUNTY
New Hope vic., PERQUIMANS COUNTY
Newfound Gap vic., SWAIN COUNTY
Nixonton, PASQUOTANK COUNTY

Oak Ridge, GUILFORD COUNTY
Old Town, FORSYTH COUNTY
Old Trap vic., BUNCOMBE COUNTY

Patterson, CALDWELL COUNTY
Patterson vic., CALDWELL COUNTY
Pearces, FRANKLIN COUNTY

Raleigh, WAKE COUNTY
Raleigh vic., WAKE COUNTY
Ridgecrest vic., BUNCOMBE COUNTY
Roanoke Rapids, HALIFAX COUNTY
Rockingham, RICHMOND COUNTY
Rockwell vic., ROWAN COUNTY
Rocky Mount, NASH COUNTY
Rocky Mount Mills, NASH COUNTY

Salisbury, ROWAN COUNTY
Sandy Cross, GATES COUNTY
Scotland Neck vic., HALIFAX COUNTY
Shawboro vic., CURRITUCK COUNTY
Smithfield, JOHNSTON COUNTY
Somerset vic., CHOWAN COUNTY
South Mills vic., CAMDEN COUNTY
Southport, BRUNSWICK COUNTY
Sparta vic., WILKES COUNTY
Spencer, ROWAN COUNTY
Spindale, RUTHERFORD COUNTY

Tarboro, EDGECOMBE COUNTY
Tarboro vic., EDGECOMBE COUNTY
Tillery vic., HALIFAX COUNTY
Topsail Sound, PENDER COUNTY
Trotville vic., GATES COUNTY

Warrenton, WARREN COUNTY
Warrenton vic., WARREN COUNTY
Washington, BEAUFORT COUNTY
Wentworth, ROCKINGHAM COUNTY
Williamsboro, VANCE COUNTY
Wilmington, NEW HANOVER COUNTY
Winfall vic., PERQUIMANS COUNTY
Winston-Salem, FORSYTH COUNTY
Winston-Salem vic., FORSYTH COUNTY
Woodsdale, PERSON COUNTY

Yanceyville, CASWELL COUNTY
Yanceyville vic., CASWELL COUNTY

North Dakota

Bismarck, BURLEIGH COUNTY

Devils Lake vic., BENSON COUNTY

Elbowoods, MCLEAN COUNTY
Elbowoods vic., MCLEAN COUNTY

Fort Buford, WILLIAMS COUNTY

Grassy Butte, MCKENZIE COUNTY

Mayville, TRAILL COUNTY
Mott, HETTINGER COUNTY

Ohio

Adelphi vic., HOCKING COUNTY
Akron, SUMMIT COUNTY
Ashland vic., ASHLAND COUNTY
Atwater, PORTAGE COUNTY
Aurora, GEAUGA COUNTY
Aurora, PORTAGE COUNTY
Avon Township, LORAIN COUNTY
Avon vic., LORAIN COUNTY
Avon Village, LORAIN COUNTY

Bantam vic., CLERMONT COUNTY
Bath, SUMMIT COUNTY
Bentleyville, CUYAHOGA COUNTY
Blaine, BELMONT COUNTY
Blaine vic., BELMONT COUNTY
Brecksville, CUYAHOGA COUNTY
Bristolville, TRUMBULL COUNTY
Burlington, LAWRENCE COUNTY
Burton, GEAUGA COUNTY

Cadiz, HARRISON COUNTY
Caldwell, NOBLE COUNTY
Cambridge, GUERNSEY COUNTY
Cambridge vic., GUERNSEY COUNTY
Canton, STARK COUNTY
Carrollton, CARROLL COUNTY
Chagrin Falls, CUYAHOGA COUNTY
Chagrin Falls vic., CUYAHOGA COUNTY
Chester, MEIGS COUNTY
Chillicothe, ROSS COUNTY
Chillicothe vic., ROSS COUNTY
Cincinnati, HAMILTON COUNTY
Cincinnati vic., HAMILTON COUNTY
Circleville vic., PICKAWAY COUNTY
Claridon, GEAUGA COUNTY
Claridon vic., GEAUGA COUNTY
Clarksville, CLINTON COUNTY
Cleveland, CUYAHOGA COUNTY
Cleveland Heights, CUYAHOGA COUNTY
Cleveland vic., CUYAHOGA COUNTY
Clifton, GREENE COUNTY
Clifton vic., GREENE COUNTY
Colebrook, ASHTABULA COUNTY
Collinsville vic., BUTLER COUNTY
Columbus, FRANKLIN COUNTY
Copley, SUMMIT COUNTY
Corwin vic., WARREN COUNTY

Darrtown vic., BUTLER COUNTY
Dayton, MONTGOMERY COUNTY
Deerfield, PORTAGE COUNTY
Delaware, DELAWARE COUNTY
Dover, CUYAHOGA COUNTY

Elizabethtown, HAMILTON COUNTY

Findlay vic., HANCOCK COUNTY
Foster, WARREN COUNTY
Freedom, PORTAGE COUNTY
Fremont, SANDUSKY COUNTY

Gallipolis, GALLIA COUNTY
Gambrier, KNOX COUNTY
Gates Mills, CUYAHOGA COUNTY
Georgetown, BROWN COUNTY
Granville, LICKING COUNTY

Hamilton vic., BUTLER COUNTY
Harmony, CLARK COUNTY
Harrison, HAMILTON COUNTY
Harrison vic., HAMILTON COUNTY
Harveysburg, WARREN COUNTY
Hopewell vic., MUSKINGUM COUNTY
Hudson, SUMMIT COUNTY
Huntington vic., LORAIN COUNTY

Ira (Village) vic., SUMMIT COUNTY
Isleta vic., COSHOCTON COUNTY

Jasper, PIKE COUNTY
Jefferson, ASHTABULA COUNTY

Kent, SUMMIT COUNTY
Kinderhook vic., PICKAWAY COUNTY
Kinsman, TRUMBULL COUNTY
Kinsman vic., TRUMBULL COUNTY
Kirtland Village, LAKE COUNTY

Lafayette, MADISON COUNTY
Lakewood, CUYAHOGA COUNTY
Lancaster, FAIRFIELD COUNTY
Lebanon, WARREN COUNTY
Lebanon vic., WARREN COUNTY
Limaville, STARK COUNTY
Limestone vic., OTTAWA COUNTY
Lockington, SHELBY COUNTY

Manchester, ADAMS COUNTY
Mariemont, HAMILTON COUNTY
Mariemont vic., HAMILTON COUNTY
Maumee, LUCAS COUNTY
Mc Cutchenville, WYANDOT COUNTY
Mentor, LAKE COUNTY
Middlebourne vic., GUERNSEY COUNTY
Milan, ERIE COUNTY
Milford, HAMILTON COUNTY
Monroe vic., BUTLER COUNTY
Monroeville, HURON COUNTY
Montgomery vic., HAMILTON COUNTY
Morristown vic., BELMONT COUNTY
Mt. Carmel vic., HAMILTON COUNTY
Mt. Healthy vic., HAMILTON COUNTY
Mt. Vernon, KNOX COUNTY

N. Lewisburg vic., LOGAN COUNTY
New Vienna vic., CLINTON COUNTY
Newton Falls, TRUMBULL COUNTY
Newtown, HAMILTON COUNTY
North Bend vic., HAMILTON COUNTY
North Bloomfield, TRUMBULL COUNTY
North Bristol, TRUMBULL COUNTY
North Lewisburg vic., UNION COUNTY
North Olmsted, CUYAHOGA COUNTY
Northfield vic., SUMMIT COUNTY
Norwalk, HURON COUNTY

Oberlin, LORAIN COUNTY
Old Washington vic., GUERNSEY COUNTY
Ottawa, PUTNAM COUNTY
Oxford, BUTLER COUNTY

Painesville, LAKE COUNTY
Parma, CUYAHOGA COUNTY
Parma Heights, CUYAHOGA COUNTY
Peninsula, SUMMIT COUNTY
Piketon vic., PIKE COUNTY

Ripley, BROWN COUNTY
Rocky River, CUYAHOGA COUNTY
Rootstown, PORTAGE COUNTY

Seville, MEDINA COUNTY
Sinking Spring, HIGHLAND COUNTY
Solon vic., CUYAHOGA COUNTY
Somerset, PERRY COUNTY
St. Clairsville, BELMONT COUNTY
St. Clairsville vic., BELMONT COUNTY
Streetsboro, PORTAGE COUNTY
Strongsville, CUYAHOGA COUNTY

Tallmadge, SUMMIT COUNTY
Toledo, LUCAS COUNTY
Twinsburg, SUMMIT COUNTY
Twinsburg vic., SUMMIT COUNTY

Union Village, WARREN COUNTY
Unionville, LAKE COUNTY
Unionville vic., ASHTABULA COUNTY

Vermilion vic., ERIE COUNTY

Warren, TRUMBULL COUNTY
Waterville, LUCAS COUNTY
Waynesville, WARREN COUNTY
Wellington, LORAIN COUNTY
West Chester, BUTLER COUNTY
Weymouth, MEDINA COUNTY
Whitesburg, CUYAHOGA COUNTY
Whitewater, HAMILTON COUNTY
Willoughby, LAKE COUNTY
Wooster, WAYNE COUNTY
Worthington, FRANKLIN COUNTY

Yellow Springs, GREENE COUNTY

Zanesville, BELMONT COUNTY
Zanesville, MUSKINGUM COUNTY
Zanesville vic., BELMONT COUNTY
Zanesville vic., GUERNSEY COUNTY
Zanesville vic., MUSKINGUM COUNTY
Zoar, TUSCARAWAS COUNTY

Oklahoma

Flint vic., DELAWARE COUNTY
Fort Gibson, MUSKOGEE COUNTY
Fort Gibson, WAGONER COUNTY
Fort Sill, COMANCHE COUNTY

Guthrie, LOGAN COUNTY

Marble City, SEQUOYAH COUNTY
Marble City vic., SEQUOYAH COUNTY

Okemah vic., OKFUSKEE COUNTY

Park Hill, CHEROKEE COUNTY
Perry, NOBLE COUNTY

Rose vic., DELAWARE COUNTY

Stillwell, ADAIR COUNTY

Tahlequah, CHEROKEE COUNTY

Oregon

Ashland vic., JACKSON COUNTY
Aurora, MARION COUNTY

Canby, CLACKAMAS COUNTY
Central Point, JACKSON COUNTY

Dallas, POLK COUNTY
Dayton, YAMHILL COUNTY
Dundee, YAMHILL COUNTY

Ellendale, POLK COUNTY
Eugene, LANE COUNTY

Forest Grove, WASHINGTON COUNTY

Gervais vic., MARION COUNTY
Gold Hill vic., JACKSON COUNTY

Hopewell vic., YAMHILL COUNTY
Hoskins, BENTON COUNTY
Howell Prairie, MARION COUNTY

Jacksonville, JACKSON COUNTY
Jacksonville vic., JACKSON COUNTY
Jefferson, MARION COUNTY
Jefferson vic., LINN COUNTY

Lafayette, YAMHILL COUNTY
Lafayette vic., YAMHILL COUNTY
Lorane vic., LANE COUNTY

Milwaukie, CLACKAMAS COUNTY
Molalla vic., CLACKAMAS COUNTY
Mt. Pleasant, CLACKAMAS COUNTY

Oakland, DOUGLAS COUNTY
Oregon City, CLACKAMAS COUNTY

Parkersville, MARION COUNTY
Pedee, POLK COUNTY
Perrydale, POLK COUNTY
Phoenix, JACKSON COUNTY
Portland, MULTNOMAH COUNTY

Reedville, WASHINGTON COUNTY
Rickreall, POLK COUNTY
Rogue River vic., JACKSON COUNTY

Salem, MARION COUNTY
Sauvie's Island, MULTNOMAH COUNTY
Silverton, MARION COUNTY

West Linn, CLACKAMAS COUNTY
West Union, WASHINGTON COUNTY
Wilsonville vic., CLACKAMAS COUNTY
Wolf Creek, JOSEPHINE COUNTY

Yamhill, YAMHILL COUNTY
Yamhill vic., YAMHILL COUNTY
Yoncalla vic., DOUGLAS COUNTY

Pennsylvania

Addison, SOMERSET COUNTY
Allentown, LEHIGH COUNTY

Ambler vic., MONTGOMERY COUNTY
Ambridge Bor., BEAVER COUNTY
Andalusia, BUCKS COUNTY
Athens Township, BRADFORD COUNTY
Avondale Bor., CHESTER COUNTY

Bacton, CHESTER COUNTY
Bacton vic., CHESTER COUNTY
Bala-Cynwyd, MONTGOMERY COUNTY
Baumstown vic., BERKS COUNTY
Belfast vic., NORTHAMPTON COUNTY
Bellefonte, CENTRE COUNTY
Ben Avon Bor., ALLEGHENY COUNTY
Bermudian vic., ADAMS COUNTY
Bernville, BERKS COUNTY
Bernville vic., BERKS COUNTY
Berwyn vic., CHESTER COUNTY
Bethany, WAYNE COUNTY
Bethlehem, NORTHAMPTON COUNTY
Betula, MCKEAN COUNTY
Birdsboro, BERKS COUNTY
Birmingham, CHESTER COUNTY
Birmingham vic., CHESTER COUNTY
Boalsburg, CENTRE COUNTY
Briar Creek, COLUMBIA COUNTY
Brickerville, LANCASTER COUNTY
Bristol, BUCKS COUNTY
Brock, GREENE COUNTY
Broomall vic., DELAWARE COUNTY
Brownsville Bor., FAYETTE COUNTY
Brownsville vic., BERKS COUNTY
Bryn Mawr, MONTGOMERY COUNTY
Bulltown, CHESTER COUNTY
Bushkill, PIKE COUNTY
Bushkill vic., MONROE COUNTY

Cambridge Spr. vic., CRAWFORD COUNTY
Cambridge Springs, CRAWFORD COUNTY
Canonsburg, WASHINGTON COUNTY
Carbondale, LACKAWANNA COUNTY
Catawissa, COLUMBIA COUNTY
Centre Hall vic., CENTRE COUNTY
Chadds Ford, DELAWARE COUNTY
Chadds Ford vic., CHESTER COUNTY
Chambersburg Bor., FRANKLIN COUNTY
Charlestown, CHESTER COUNTY
Chatham, CHESTER COUNTY
Chatham vic., CHESTER COUNTY
Cherry Tree, VENANGO COUNTY
Chester Springs, CHESTER COUNTY
Chester Springs vic., CHESTER COUNTY
Chrome, CHESTER COUNTY
Churchill Bor., ALLEGHENY COUNTY
Clairton, ALLEGHENY COUNTY
Clarks Green, LACKAWANNA COUNTY
Clonmell vic., CHESTER COUNTY
Coatesville vic., CHESTER COUNTY
Cocalico, LANCASTER COUNTY
Cochranton, CRAWFORD COUNTY
Concordville, CHESTER COUNTY
Concordville, DELAWARE COUNTY
Conneautville, CRAWFORD COUNTY
Copesville, CHESTER COUNTY
Copesville vic., CHESTER COUNTY
Corry, ERIE COUNTY
Corry vic., ERIE COUNTY

Coudersport, POTTER COUNTY
Coventryville, CHESTER COUNTY
Cresson vic., BLAIR COUNTY
Cresson vic., CAMBRIA COUNTY
Crosby vic., MCKEAN COUNTY

Darby, DELAWARE COUNTY
Darby vic., DELAWARE COUNTY
Davidsburg vic., YORK COUNTY
Delaware Water Gap, MONROE COUNTY
Detters Mill, YORK COUNTY
Devault vic., CHESTER COUNTY
Dilworthtown vic., DELAWARE COUNTY
Dingman's Ferry, PIKE COUNTY
Douglasville, BERKS COUNTY
Downingtown Bor., CHESTER COUNTY
Downingtown vic., CHESTER COUNTY
Doylestown, BUCKS COUNTY
Doylestown vic., BUCKS COUNTY
Dravosburg vic., ALLEGHENY COUNTY
Drumore vic., LANCASTER COUNTY

East Titusville vic., CRAWFORD COUNTY
Easton, NORTHAMPTON COUNTY
Edinboro, ERIE COUNTY
Egypt Mills vic., PIKE COUNTY
Eldred, MCKEAN COUNTY
Ephrata, LANCASTER COUNTY
Erie, ERIE COUNTY
Erie vic., ERIE COUNTY
Essington, DELAWARE COUNTY
Evergreen Hamlet, ALLEGHENY COUNTY
Exeter, LUZERNE COUNTY

Fairchance, FAYETTE COUNTY
Fairfield Bor., ADAMS COUNTY
Fayette City vic., FAYETTE COUNTY
Fellsburg, WESTMORELAND COUNTY
Finleyville vic., WASHINGTON COUNTY
Floradale vic., ADAMS COUNTY
Fort Hunter, DAUPHIN COUNTY
Forty Fort Bor., LUZERNE COUNTY
Frankford, PHILADELPHIA COUNTY
Franklin, VENANGO COUNTY
Franklinville vic., HUNTINGTON COUNTY

Ganoga Lake, SULLIVAN COUNTY
Garland, WARREN COUNTY
Geistown vic., CAMBRIA COUNTY
Germantown, PHILADELPHIA COUNTY
Gettysburg Bor., ADAMS COUNTY
Gettysburg vic., ADAMS COUNTY
Girard, ERIE COUNTY
Girard vic., ERIE COUNTY
Glenloch, CHESTER COUNTY
Green Lawn vic., CHESTER COUNTY
Greenville, MERCER COUNTY
Grubbs Mill, CHESTER COUNTY

Hallam Borough, YORK COUNTY
Hanover Green, LUZERNE COUNTY
Harborcreek, ERIE COUNTY
Harmony vic., BUTLER COUNTY
Harrisburg, DAUPHIN COUNTY
Haverford, MONTGOMERY COUNTY
Havertown vic., DELAWARE COUNTY
Hawley, WAYNE COUNTY
Hay Creek, BERKS COUNTY

Heidlersburg vic., ADAMS COUNTY
Hinkletown, LANCASTER COUNTY
Honesdale, WAYNE COUNTY
Hopewell, CHESTER COUNTY
Hopwood, FAYETTE COUNTY
Horsham vic., MONTGOMERY COUNTY
Hunterstown vic., ADAMS COUNTY
Hydetown, CRAWFORD COUNTY

Iron Springs vic., ADAMS COUNTY
Irvine, WARREN COUNTY
Ithan, DELAWARE COUNTY

Jacksonwald, BERKS COUNTY
Jenkintown, MONTGOMERY COUNTY

Kennett Sq. vic., CHESTER COUNTY
King Of Prussia, MONTGOMERY COUNTY
King's Run Road, MCKEAN COUNTY
Kingston, LUZERNE COUNTY
Kleinfeltersville, LEBANON COUNTY
Knauertown, CHESTER COUNTY
Knauertown vic., CHESTER COUNTY
Kutztown vic., BERKS COUNTY

Lackawaxen, PIKE COUNTY
Lancaster, LANCASTER COUNTY
Lancaster vic., LANCASTER COUNTY
Landenberg vic., CHESTER COUNTY
Landisville, LANCASTER COUNTY
Lanesboro, SUSQUEHANNA COUNTY
Lanesboro vic., SUSQUEHANNA COUNTY
Laughlintown vic., WESTMORELAND COUNTY
Laurel vic., YORK COUNTY
Lederach, MONTGOMERY COUNTY
Lenhartsville, BERKS COUNTY
Limekiln vic., BERKS COUNTY
Lingelestown vic., DAUPHIN COUNTY
Littlestown vic., ADAMS COUNTY
Lobachsville vic., BERKS COUNTY
Lock Haven, CLINTON COUNTY
Ludwigs Cor. vic., CHESTER COUNTY

Maple Grove vic., LANCASTER COUNTY
Marietta vic., LANCASTER COUNTY
Marsh, CHESTER COUNTY
Marshallton, CHESTER COUNTY
Marshallton vic., CHESTER COUNTY
Martins's Corner, CHESTER COUNTY
Mc Keesport, ALLEGHENY COUNTY
Meadow Lands vic., WASHINGTON COUNTY
Meadville, CRAWFORD COUNTY
Meadville vic., CRAWFORD COUNTY
Media vic., DELAWARE COUNTY
Mercer, MERCER COUNTY
Mercer vic., MERCER COUNTY
Merion, MONTGOMERY COUNTY
Middletown, DAUPHIN COUNTY
Milford, PIKE COUNTY
Milford vic., PIKE COUNTY
Milford vic., SUSQUEHANNA COUNTY
Millbach, LEBANON COUNTY
Millrift, PIKE COUNTY
Milltown, CHESTER COUNTY
Millville, COLUMBIA COUNTY
Montrose, SUSQUEHANNA COUNTY
Moorheadville, ERIE COUNTY
Mount Rocky, CHESTER COUNTY

Mt. Jewett vic., MCKEAN COUNTY
Mt. Pleasant vic., BERKS COUNTY
Muncy vic., LYCOMING COUNTY

Nanticoke, LUZERNE COUNTY
Nanticoke vic., LUZERNE COUNTY
Narberth vic., MONTGOMERY COUNTY
New Kensington vic., WESTMORELAND COUNTY
New Richmond vic., CRAWFORD COUNTY
Newmanstown vic., LEBANON COUNTY
Newton vic., BUCKS COUNTY
Nittany, CENTRE COUNTY
Norristown, MONTGOMERY COUNTY
North East, ERIE COUNTY
North Mehoopany, WYOMING COUNTY
North Springfield, ERIE COUNTY
Northbrook vic., CHESTER COUNTY
Norwood, DELAWARE COUNTY

Oil City, VENANGO COUNTY
Oil City, YORK COUNTY
Oley vic., BERKS COUNTY

Paoli vic., CHESTER COUNTY
Parkesburg Bor., CHESTER COUNTY
Parkesburg vic., CHESTER COUNTY
Paxtang, DAUPHIN COUNTY
Paxtang vic., DAUPHIN COUNTY
Penna. Furnace, HUNTINGTON COUNTY
Philadelphia, BERKS COUNTY
Philadelphia, PHILADELPHIA COUNTY
Philipsburg, CENTRE COUNTY
Phoenixville vic., CHESTER COUNTY
Pinetown, LANCASTER COUNTY
Pittsburgh, ALLEGHENY COUNTY
Pittsburgh, CHESTER COUNTY
Pittsfield, WARREN COUNTY
Pittsfield, YORK COUNTY
Pleasantville, VENANGO COUNTY
Plymouth, LUZERNE COUNTY
Port Allegany vic., MCKEAN COUNTY
Portland vic., NORTHAMPTON COUNTY
Pughtown vic., CHESTER COUNTY

Radnor, DELAWARE COUNTY
Reading, BERKS COUNTY
Riceville, CRAWFORD COUNTY
Riegelsville, BUCKS COUNTY
Robesonia, BERKS COUNTY
Rock Forge, CENTRE COUNTY
Rockwood vic., SOMERSET COUNTY
Romansville, CHESTER COUNTY
Roulette, POTTER COUNTY
Ruff Creek vic., GREENE COUNTY

Saegertown, CRAWFORD COUNTY
Sayre, BRADFORD COUNTY
Sconnelltown, CHESTER COUNTY
Sconnelltown vic., CHESTER COUNTY
Scranton, LACKAWANNA COUNTY
Selinsgrove, SNYDER COUNTY
Sewickley, ALLEGHENY COUNTY
Sewickley Hts. Bor., ALLEGHENY COUNTY
Sewickley Valley, ALLEGHENY COUNTY
Sharpsburg vic., ALLEGHENY COUNTY
Shawnee-on-Deleware vic., MONROE COUNTY
Sheakleyville, MERCER COUNTY

Shohola, PIKE COUNTY
Shohola vic., PIKE COUNTY
Smethport, MCKEAN COUNTY
Spangsville vic., BERKS COUNTY
St. Davids, DELAWARE COUNTY
St. Peters vic., BERKS COUNTY
St. Peters vic., CHESTER COUNTY
Sterrettania, ERIE COUNTY
Stonersville, BERKS COUNTY
Stonersville vic., BERKS COUNTY
Strafford, CHESTER COUNTY
Summit, ERIE COUNTY
Susquehanna, SUSQUEHANNA COUNTY
Swarthmore, DELAWARE COUNTY
Swissvale Bor., ALLEGHENY COUNTY

Tanguy vic., CHESTER COUNTY
Terrytown, BRADFORD COUNTY
Thorndale, CHESTER COUNTY
Tidioute, WARREN COUNTY
Titusville, CRAWFORD COUNTY
Towerville, CHESTER COUNTY
Townville, CRAWFORD COUNTY
Trappe, MONTGOMERY COUNTY

Union City, ERIE COUNTY
Uniontown vic., FAYETTE COUNTY
Upland, DELAWARE COUNTY

Valley Forge vic., MONTGOMERY COUNTY
Villanova, DELAWARE COUNTY

Wallingford, DELAWARE COUNTY
Wapwallopen, LUZERNE COUNTY
Washington, WASHINGTON COUNTY
Waterford, ERIE COUNTY
Wattsburg, ERIE COUNTY
Waverly, LACKAWANNA COUNTY
Wayne, DELAWARE COUNTY
West Brownsville Vic, WASHINGTON COUNTY
West Chester Bor., CHESTER COUNTY
West Chester vic., CHESTER COUNTY
West Eldred vic., MCKEAN COUNTY
West Grove vic., CHESTER COUNTY
West Newton Borough, WESTMORELAND COUNTY
West Newton vic., WESTMORELAND COUNTY
Westtown vic., CHESTER COUNTY
Whitehorse vic., CHESTER COUNTY
Whitehorse vic., DELAWARE COUNTY
Whitemarsh, MONTGOMERY COUNTY
Whites Valley, WAYNE COUNTY
Wilkes Barre, LUZERNE COUNTY
Williamsport, LYCOMING COUNTY
Willistown vic., CHESTER COUNTY
Willow Street vic., LANCASTER COUNTY
Willowdale, CHESTER COUNTY
Wind Gap vic., NORTHAMPTON COUNTY
Womelsdorf vic., BERKS COUNTY
Woodcock, CRAWFORD COUNTY
Wyebrooke vic., CHESTER COUNTY
Wyoming, LUZERNE COUNTY
Wysox, BRADFORD COUNTY

Yellow House, BERKS COUNTY
Yellow House vic., BERKS COUNTY

York, YORK COUNTY
York vic., YORK COUNTY

Zora, ADAMS COUNTY

Puerto Rico

Aguadilla
Arecibo
Arroyo

Cabo Rojo
Culbritas

Fajardo

Guancia
Guanica

Manati
Maunabo
Mayaguez

Ponce
Punta Ferro Vieques
Punta Giguero
Punta Mulas, Vieques

Rincon

San German
San Juan
St. John

Toa Baja

Victoria
Vieques Island

Rhode Island

Albion, PROVIDENCE COUNTY
Anthony, KENT COUNTY
Ashton vic., PROVIDENCE COUNTY

Belleville, WASHINGTON COUNTY
Bristol, BRISTOL COUNTY
Buttonwoods, KENT COUNTY

Centerdale, PROVIDENCE COUNTY
Central Falls, PROVIDENCE COUNTY
Central Falls vic., PROVIDENCE COUNTY
Chepachet vic., PROVIDENCE COUNTY
Cumberland Hill, PROVIDENCE COUNTY

East Greenwich, KENT COUNTY

Greenville, PROVIDENCE COUNTY

Jamestown, NEWPORT COUNTY
Johnston, PROVIDENCE COUNTY

Kenyon, WASHINGTON COUNTY
Kingston, WASHINGTON COUNTY
Kingston Hill, WASHINGTON COUNTY

Limerock, PROVIDENCE COUNTY
Limerock vic., PROVIDENCE COUNTY
Lincoln, PROVIDENCE COUNTY

Manton, PROVIDENCE COUNTY
Middleton, NEWPORT COUNTY
Middletown, NEWPORT COUNTY

Newport, NEWPORT COUNTY
North Kingston, WASHINGTON COUNTY
North Kingston, WASHINGTON COUNTY
North Providence, PROVIDENCE COUNTY
North Scituate, PROVIDENCE COUNTY

Oaklawn, PROVIDENCE COUNTY

Pawtucket, PROVIDENCE COUNTY
Providence, PROVIDENCE COUNTY

Saunderstown, WASHINGTON COUNTY
Slatersville, PROVIDENCE COUNTY
Smithfield, PROVIDENCE COUNTY
South Kingston, WASHINGTON COUNTY
Spring Green, KENT COUNTY

Thornton, PROVIDENCE COUNTY

Wakefield, WASHINGTON COUNTY
Warren, BRISTOL COUNTY
Warwick, KENT COUNTY
West Greenwich, KENT COUNTY
West Warwick, KENT COUNTY
Westerly, WASHINGTON COUNTY
Wickford, WASHINGTON COUNTY
Woonsocket, PROVIDENCE COUNTY

South Carolina

Abbeville, ABBEVILLE COUNTY
Anderson, ANDERSON COUNTY
Anderson vic., ANDERSON COUNTY
Ashley River, DORCHESTER COUNTY
Ashley River, North Bank, DORCHESTER COUNTY

Bamberg vic., BAMBERG COUNTY
Beaufort, BEAUFORT COUNTY
Bennettsville, MARLBORO COUNTY

Camden, KERSHAW COUNTY
Camden vic., KERSHAW COUNTY
Charleston, CHARLESTON COUNTY
Charleston, AIKEN COUNTY
Charleston, CHARLESTON COUNTY
Charleston vic., CHARLESTON COUNTY
Cheraw, CHESTERFIELD COUNTY
Cheraw vic., CHESTERFIELD COUNTY
Chester vic., CHESTER COUNTY
Chesterfield, CHESTERFIELD COUNTY
Clemson
Clemson, OCONEE COUNTY
Clemson vic., OCONEE COUNTY
Clover vic., YORK COUNTY
Columbia, RICHLAND COUNTY
Columbia vic., RICHLAND COUNTY
Cordesville, BERKELEY COUNTY
Cordesville vic., BERKELEY COUNTY
Cross, BERKELEY COUNTY
Cross vic., BERKELEY COUNTY

Edisto Island, CHARLESTON COUNTY
Ehrhardt, BAMBERG COUNTY

Ehrhardt vic., BAMBERG COUNTY
Eutaville vic., BERKELEY COUNTY
Eutaw Springs vic., BERKELEY COUNTY
Eutaw Springs vic., ORANGEBURG COUNTY

Georgetown, GEORGETOWN COUNTY
Georgetown vic., GEORGETOWN COUNTY
Goose Creek, BERKELEY COUNTY
Goose Creek vic., BERKELEY COUNTY
Goose Creek vic., CHARLESTON COUNTY
Gowensville vic., PICKENS COUNTY
Great Falls, CHESTER COUNTY
Great Falls vic., CHESTER COUNTY
Greenville, GREENVILLE COUNTY
Greenville vic., GREENVILLE COUNTY

Huger vic., BERKELEY COUNTY
Hunting Island, BEAUFORT COUNTY

Kingstree, WILLIAMSBURG COUNTY

Lake Moultrie vic., BERKELEY COUNTY
Lowndesville vic., ABBEVILLE COUNTY
Lowndesville vic., ANDERSON COUNTY

Manning, CLARENDON COUNTY
Mars Bluff vic., FLORENCE COUNTY
Mc Clellanville, CHARLESTON COUNTY
Mc Clellanville vic., CHARLESTON COUNTY
Mechanicsville vic., DARLINGTON COUNTY
Moncks Corner vic., BERKELEY COUNTY
Monticello vic., FAIRFIELD COUNTY
Mount Pleasant vic., CHARLESTON COUNTY

Oconee Station, OCONEE COUNTY

Pendleton, ANDERSON COUNTY
Pendleton vic., ANDERSON COUNTY
Pine Grove vic., BERKELEY COUNTY
Pineville, BERKELEY COUNTY
Pineville vic., BERKELEY COUNTY
Pinewood vic., SUMTER COUNTY
Pinopolis, BERKELEY COUNTY
Pinopolis vic., BERKELEY COUNTY
Poinsett State Park, SUMTER COUNTY

Rocky River, ABBEVILLE COUNTY

Sandy Hook vic., YORK COUNTY
Santee River, North, GEORGETOWN COUNTY
Savannah River, ABBEVILLE COUNTY
Savannah River, ANDERSON COUNTY
Sheldon vic., BEAUFORT COUNTY
Society Hill vic., DARLINGTON COUNTY
St. Stephens, BERKELEY COUNTY
Stateburg, SUMTER COUNTY
Sullivans Island, CHARLESTON COUNTY
Sumter vic., SUMTER COUNTY

Tamassee, OCONEE COUNTY

Union vic., UNION COUNTY

Walterboro, COLLETON COUNTY
Walterboro vic., COLLETON COUNTY
Wando River, BERKELEY COUNTY
Wedgefield vic., SUMTER COUNTY
West Union, OCONEE COUNTY
Westminster, OCONEE COUNTY
Winnsboro, FAIRFIELD COUNTY

York vic., YORK COUNTY

South Dakota

Cheyenne River Agcy., DEWEY COUNTY
Custer vic., CUSTER COUNTY

Elk Point, UNION COUNTY

Fort Sisseton, ROBERTS COUNTY

Pickston vic., GREGORY COUNTY
Pierre vic., HUGHES COUNTY

Rapid City, PENNINGTON COUNTY

Tabor, BON HOMME COUNTY

Vermillion, CLAY COUNTY

Yankton, YANKTON COUNTY

Tennessee

Antioch, DAVIDSON COUNTY
Athens vic., MCMINN COUNTY

Beersheba Springs, GRUNDY COUNTY
Blountville, SULLIVAN COUNTY
Bolivar, HARDEMAN COUNTY
Brunswick, SHELBY COUNTY

Cades Cove, BLOUNT COUNTY
Cades Cove, CANNON COUNTY
Cades Cove vic., BLOUNT COUNTY
Castalian Springs, SUMNER COUNTY
Cedar Hill vic., ROBERTSON COUNTY
Chattanooga, HAMILTON COUNTY
Chuckey vic., GREENE COUNTY
Clarksville, MONTGOMERY COUNTY
Cleveland, BRADLEY COUNTY
Clifton vic., WAYNE COUNTY
Columbia, MAURY COUNTY
Columbia vic., MAURY COUNTY

Dixon Springs, TROUSDALE COUNTY
Donelson, DAVIDSON COUNTY
Donelson vic., DAVIDSON COUNTY
Dover vic., STEWART COUNTY

Elizabethton, CARTER COUNTY
Elizabethton vic., CARTER COUNTY
Elkmont vic., SEVIER COUNTY

Franklin, WILLIAMSON COUNTY

Gallatin, SUMNER COUNTY
Gallatin vic., SUMNER COUNTY
Gatlinburg, SEVIER COUNTY
Gatlinburg vic., GILES COUNTY
Gatlinburg vic., SEVIER COUNTY
Greeneville, GREENE COUNTY
Greeneville vic., GREENE COUNTY

Harrogate, CLAIBORNE COUNTY
Hendersonville vic., SUMNER COUNTY
Hermitage, DAVIDSON COUNTY
Hermitage vic., DAVIDSON COUNTY
Hohenwald vic., HARDIN COUNTY

Jackson, MADISON COUNTY
Johnson City, WASHINGTON COUNTY

Johnson City vic., WASHINGTON COUNTY
Jonesboro, WASHINGTON COUNTY

Kingsport, SULLIVAN COUNTY
Kingston, ROANE COUNTY
Knoxville, KNOX COUNTY
Knoxville vic., KNOX COUNTY
Knoxville vic., SEVIER COUNTY

Lagrange, FAYETTE COUNTY
Leesburg, WASHINGTON COUNTY
Lenoir City, LOUDON COUNTY
Limestone, WASHINGTON COUNTY
Livingston, OVERTON COUNTY
Loudon, LOUDON COUNTY

Mcminnville, WARREN COUNTY
Memphis, SHELBY COUNTY
Morristown, HAMBLEN COUNTY
Murfreesboro, RUTHERFORD COUNTY

Nashville, DAVIDSON COUNTY
Nashville vic., DAVIDSON COUNTY

Paris, HENRY COUNTY

Rogersville, HAWKINS COUNTY
Rugby, MORGAN COUNTY

Savannah (Pittsburg), HARDIN COUNTY
South Pittsburgh, MARION COUNTY
Sparta, WHITE COUNTY

Tusculum, GREENE COUNTY

White Pine, JEFFERSON COUNTY
Winchester, FRANKLIN COUNTY

Texas

Abernathy vic., HALE COUNTY
Alvany vic., THROCKMORTON COUNTY
Anahuac, CHAMBERS COUNTY
Anderson vic., GRIMES COUNTY
Angleton vic., BRAZORIA COUNTY
Austin, TRAVIS COUNTY
Austin vic., TRAVIS COUNTY

Bastrop vic., BASTROP COUNTY
Belmont vic., GONZALES COUNTY
Boerne vic., KENDALL COUNTY
Bovina vic., DEAF SMITH COUNTY
Brazoria, BRAZORIA COUNTY
Brownsville, CAMERON COUNTY
Brownsville vic., CAMERON COUNTY
Bullard vic., SMITH COUNTY

Carthage vic., PANOLA COUNTY
Castroville, MEDINA COUNTY
Castroville vic., MEDINA COUNTY
Center Point vic., KERR COUNTY
Center vic., SHELBY COUNTY
Chappell Hill, WASHINGTON COUNTY
Chappell Hill vic., WASHINGTON COUNTY
Cherry Spring, GILLESPIE COUNTY
Chireno vic., NACOGDOCHES COUNTY
Clarendon, DONLEY COUNTY
Claude, ARMSTRONG COUNTY

Colorado City vic., MITCHELL COUNTY
Columbus vic., COLORADO COUNTY
Comfort, KENDALL COUNTY
Corpus Christi, NUECES COUNTY
Crockett vic., HOUSTON COUNTY
Csestochowa, KARNES COUNTY
Cuevitas, JIM HOGG COUNTY

D'hanis, MEDINA COUNTY
Dallas, DALLAS COUNTY
Dickens, DICKENS COUNTY
Driftwood vic., HAYS COUNTY

El Paso, EL PASO COUNTY

Falcon vic., ZAPATA COUNTY
Floresville vic., WILSON COUNTY
Fort Davis, JEFFERSON DAVIS COUNTY
Fort Mc Kavet, MENARD COUNTY
Fort Worth, TARRANT COUNTY
Fredericksburg, GILLESPIE COUNTY
Fulton, ARANSAS COUNTY

Galveston, FORT BEND COUNTY
Galveston, GALVESTON COUNTY
Goliad, GOLIAD COUNTY
Goliad vic., GOLIAD COUNTY
Grapevine vic., TARRANT COUNTY

Hempstead vic., WALLER COUNTY
Hillsboro, HILL COUNTY
Houston, HARRIS COUNTY
Huntsville vic., WALKER COUNTY

Independence, WASHINGTON COUNTY
Independence vic., WASHINGTON COUNTY
Itasca vic., HILL COUNTY

Jefferson, MARION COUNTY
Jefferson vic., MARION COUNTY

Karnack vic., HARRISON COUNTY
Kimball, BOSQUE COUNTY

La Grange, FAYETTE COUNTY
Labatt, WILSON COUNTY
Langtry, VAL VERDE COUNTY
Laredo, WEBB COUNTY
Levelland, HOCKLEY COUNTY
Lockhart vic., CALDWELL COUNTY
Lubbock, LUBBOCK COUNTY
Lufkin vic., ANGELINA COUNTY

Marshall vic., HARRISON COUNTY
Mason, MASON COUNTY
Matador, MOTLEY COUNTY
Milam vic., SABINE COUNTY
Mission Valley vic., VICTORIA COUNTY

Nacogdoches vic., NACOGDOCHES COUNTY
Navasota vic., GRIMES COUNTY
New Braunfels, COMAL COUNTY
Newcastle vic., YOUNG COUNTY

Ozona vic., CROCKETT COUNTY

Palestine, ANDERSON COUNTY
Palo Pinto, PALO PINTO COUNTY
Panna Maria vic., KARNES COUNTY
Patricia, MARTIN COUNTY
Pawelekville, KARNES COUNTY
Plantersville vic., GRIMES COUNTY

Port Isabel, CAMERON COUNTY
Post, GARZA COUNTY
Poth vic., WILSON COUNTY
Presidio vic., PRESIDIO COUNTY

Quihi vic., MEDINA COUNTY

Rio Grande City, STARR COUNTY
Roans Prairie vic., GRIMES COUNTY
Rockport, ARANSAS COUNTY
Roma, STARR COUNTY
Round Rock vic., WILLIAMSON COUNTY
Round Top, FAYETTE COUNTY

Salado vic., BELL COUNTY
San Antonio, BEXAR COUNTY
San Antonio vic., BEXAR COUNTY
San Augustine, SAN AUGUSTINE COUNTY
San Augustine vic., SAN AUGUSTINE COUNTY
San Elizario, EL PASO COUNTY
San Ygnacio, ZAPATA COUNTY
Seguin, GUADALUPE COUNTY
Seguin vic., GUADALUPE COUNTY
Shafter vic., PRESIDIO COUNTY
Snyder, SCURRY COUNTY
Socorro, EL PASO COUNTY
Somerset vic., BEXAR COUNTY
Stoneham vic., GRIMES COUNTY
Sutherland Springs, WILSON COUNTY

Taylor vic., WILLIAMSON COUNTY
Thomastown vic., DE WITT COUNTY
Truscott, KING COUNTY

Victoria, VICTORIA COUNTY

Warrenton, FAYETTE COUNTY
Washington vic., WASHINGTON COUNTY
Webberville vic., BASTROP COUNTY
West Columbia vic., BRAZORIA COUNTY

Ysleta, EL PASO COUNTY
Ysleta-San Elizario, EL PASO COUNTY

Zapata vic., ZAPATA COUNTY

Utah

Beaver, BEAVER COUNTY
Bingham Canyon, SALT LAKE COUNTY
Brigham City, BOX ELDER COUNTY

Cache Junction, CACHE COUNTY
Cedar City, IRON COUNTY
Collinston vic., BOX ELDER COUNTY
Corinne, BOX ELDER COUNTY
Cove Fort, MILLARD COUNTY

Emery, EMERY COUNTY
Ephraim, SANPETE COUNTY

Fairfield, UTAH COUNTY
Fielding vic., BOX ELDER COUNTY
Fillmore, MILLARD COUNTY
Fruita, WAYNE COUNTY

Garland vic., BOX ELDER COUNTY
Goshen vic., UTAH COUNTY
Green River, GRAND COUNTY
Gunnison, SANPETE COUNTY

Heber City, WASATCH COUNTY
Holladay, SALT LAKE COUNTY
Hoytsville, SUMMIT COUNTY
Hurricane, WASHINGTON COUNTY

Knolls/Wendover vic., TOOELE COUNTY

Leeds, WASHINGTON COUNTY
Logan, CACHE COUNTY

Magna, SALT LAKE COUNTY
Manti, SANPETE COUNTY
Middleton, WASHINGTON COUNTY
Midway, WASATCH COUNTY

Ogden, WEBER COUNTY
Old Irontown, IRON COUNTY
Olmstead, UTAH COUNTY
Ophir, TOOELE COUNTY
Orem vic., UTAH COUNTY

Panguitch, GARFIELD COUNTY
Park City, SUMMIT COUNTY
Park City vic., SUMMIT COUNTY
Pine Valley, WASHINGTON COUNTY
Pleasant Grove, UTAH COUNTY
Provo, UTAH COUNTY

Riverton, SALT LAKE COUNTY
Rockville, WASHINGTON COUNTY

Salt Lake City, SALT LAKE COUNTY
Silver Creek Jct., SUMMIT COUNTY
Silver Reef, WASHINGTON COUNTY
Spring City, SANPETE COUNTY
St. George, WASHINGTON COUNTY

Tooele, TOOELE COUNTY
Tooele vic., TOOELE COUNTY
Toquerville, WASHINGTON COUNTY

Vernal, UINTAH COUNTY

Washington, WASHINGTON COUNTY
Willard, BOX ELDER COUNTY

Vermont

Arlington, BENNINGTON COUNTY

Barnet Center, CALEDONIA COUNTY
Bennington, BENNINGTON COUNTY
Bethel, WINDSOR COUNTY
Brownington, ORLEANS COUNTY
Burlington, CHITTENDEN COUNTY

Castleton, RUTLAND COUNTY
Cavendish, WINDSOR COUNTY
Chester, WINDSOR COUNTY
Chester Depot, WINDSOR COUNTY
Chester vic., WINDSOR COUNTY

Grafton, WINDHAM COUNTY
Grand Isle, GRAND ISLE COUNTY

Highgate Falls, FRANKLIN COUNTY

Jericho Center vic., CHITTENDEN COUNTY

Middlebury, ADDISON COUNTY
Montpelier, WASHINGTON COUNTY

North Bennington, BENNINGTON COUNTY
Norwich, WINDSOR COUNTY
Norwich vic., WINDSOR COUNTY

Orwell, ADDISON COUNTY
Orwell vic., ADDISON COUNTY

Perkinsville, WINDSOR COUNTY
Perkinsville vic., WINDSOR COUNTY

Randolph, ORANGE COUNTY
Randolph Center, ORANGE COUNTY
Richmond, CHITTENDEN COUNTY
Rockingham, WINDHAM COUNTY
Royalton vic., WINDSOR COUNTY
Rutland, RUTLAND COUNTY

Shaftsbury Center, BENNINGTON COUNTY
Simonsville, WINDSOR COUNTY
South Hero, GRAND ISLE COUNTY
South Shaftsbury, BENNINGTON COUNTY
South Shaftsbury vic., BENNINGTON COUNTY
Springfield, WINDSOR COUNTY
St. Johnsbury, CALEDONIA COUNTY
Strafford, ORANGE COUNTY

Thetford vic., ORANGE COUNTY

Vergennes, ADDISON COUNTY

Weston, WINDSOR COUNTY
Windham, WINDHAM COUNTY
Windsor, WINDSOR COUNTY
Winooski, CHITTENDEN COUNTY
Woodstock, WINDSOR COUNTY

Virgin Islands

British West Indies
Bulows Minde, VIRGIN ISLANDS COUNTY

Caneel Bay, ST. JOHN ISLAND COUNTY
Charlotte Amalie, ST. THOMAS ISLAND COUNTY
Charlotte Amalie vic., ST. THOMAS ISLAND COUNTY
Christiansted, ST. THOMAS ISLAND COUNTY
Christiansted, VIRGIN ISLANDS COUNTY
Christiansted vic., VIRGIN ISLANDS COUNTY
Company's Quarter, VIRGIN ISLANDS COUNTY
Coral Bay, ST. JOHN ISLAND COUNTY
Cruz Bay, ST. JOHN ISLAND COUNTY

Estate Annaberg, ST. JOHN ISLAND COUNTY
Estate Carolina, ST. JOHN ISLAND COUNTY
Estate Contant, ST. THOMAS ISLAND COUNTY
Estate Denis Bay, ST. JOHN ISLAND COUNTY
Estate Hammer, ST. JOHN ISLAND COUNTY
Estate Mary Point, ST. JOHN ISLAND COUNTY
Estate Solberg, ST. THOMAS ISLAND COUNTY
Estate Susannaberg, ST. JOHN ISLAND COUNTY

Fredensfeld, VIRGIN ISLANDS COUNTY
Frederiksted, VIRGIN ISLANDS COUNTY

Hassel Island, ST. THOMAS ISLAND COUNTY

King's Quarter, VIRGIN ISLANDS COUNTY

May Point, ST. JOHN ISLAND COUNTY

Peter's Rest, VIRGIN ISLANDS COUNTY
Peter's Rest vic., VIRGIN ISLANDS COUNTY
Prince's Quarter, VIRGIN ISLANDS COUNTY
Princess Quarter, VIRGIN ISLANDS COUNTY

Queen's Quarter, VIRGIN ISLANDS COUNTY

Raphune, ST. THOMAS ISLAND COUNTY
Reef Bay, ST. JOHN ISLAND COUNTY

Whistling Cay, ST. JOHN ISLAND COUNTY

Virginia

Accomac, ACCOMAC COUNTY
Accomac vic., ACCOMAC COUNTY
Accotink vic., FAIRFAX COUNTY
Aden, PRINCE WILLIAM COUNTY
Aden vic., PRINCE WILLIAM COUNTY
Afton vic., AUGUSTA COUNTY
Afton vic., NELSON COUNTY
Alberene, ALBEMARLE COUNTY
Alexandria
Alexandria vic.
Amelia vic., AMELIA COUNTY
Annandale, FAIRFAX COUNTY
Annandale vic., FAIRFAX COUNTY
Appomattox, APPOMATTOX COUNTY
Arlington, ARLINGTON COUNTY
Ashland vic., GOOCHLAND COUNTY
Ashland vic., HANOVER COUNTY
Atlantic vic., ACCOMAC COUNTY
Aylett vic., KING WILLIAM COUNTY

Bacon's Castle vic., SURRY COUNTY
Bacova vic., BATH COUNTY
Barhamsville, NEW KENT COUNTY
Barhamsville vic., NEW KENT COUNTY
Batesville, ALBEMARLE COUNTY
Beaver Dam, HANOVER COUNTY
Beaver Dam vic., HANOVER COUNTY
Bedford vic.
Bellamy vic., GLOUCESTER COUNTY
Bena vic., GLOUCESTER COUNTY
Berryville vic., CLARKE COUNTY
Bertrand vic., LANCASTER COUNTY
Birdhaven, SHENENDOAH COUNTY
Blackstone, NOTTOWAY COUNTY
Blossom Hill
Bowling Green, CAROLINE COUNTY
Bowling Green vic., CAROLINE COUNTY
Boyce, CLARKE COUNTY
Boyce vic., CLARKE COUNTY
Brandy Station vic., CULPEPER COUNTY
Bremo Bluff vic., FLUVANNA COUNTY
Brentsville vic., PRINCE WILLIAM COUNTY
Bridgetown vic., NORTHAMPTON COUNTY
Brookneal, CHARLOTTE COUNTY
Buchanan, BOTETOURT COUNTY
Buffalo Springs, MECKLENBURG COUNTY
Bull Run, PRINCE WILLIAM COUNTY
Bull Run vic., PRINCE WILLIAM COUNTY
Bush Hill, FAIRFAX COUNTY

Cabin Point, SURRY COUNTY
Caira, CUMBERLAND COUNTY

705

Capeville vic., NORTHAMPTON COUNTY
Cartersville, CUMBERLAND COUNTY
Cashville vic., ACCOMAC COUNTY
Cathardin vic., PRINCE WILLIAM COUNTY
Center Cross vic., ESSEX COUNTY
Centreville, FAIRFAX COUNTY
Champlain vic., ESSEX COUNTY
Chancellorsville, SPOTSYLVANIA COUNTY
Chantilly vic., FAIRFAX COUNTY
Charles City, CHARLES CITY COUNTY
Charles City vic., CHARLES CITY COUNTY
Charlottesville
Charlottesville vic., ALBEMARLE COUNTY
Chatham, PITTSYLVANIA COUNTY
Cheriton vic., NORTHAMPTON COUNTY
Chesapeake vic.
Chesconessex vic., ACCOMAC COUNTY
Christ Church vic., MIDDLESEX COUNTY
Chuckatuck
Churchview vic., MIDDLESEX COUNTY
Claremont, SURRY COUNTY
Clarksville vic., MECKLENBURG COUNTY
Clearbrook vic., FREDERICK COUNTY
Clifford, AMHERST COUNTY
Clinchport, SCOTT COUNTY
Cohasset, FLUVANNA COUNTY
Colchester, FAIRFAX COUNTY
Cold Harbor, HANOVER COUNTY
Colonial Heights
Comorn vic., KING GEORGE COUNTY
Covesville, ALBEMARLE COUNTY
Covington vic., ALLEGHANY COUNTY
Craddockville, ACCOMAC COUNTY
Craddockville vic., ACCOMAC COUNTY
Crimora vic., AUGUSTA COUNTY
Croaker vic., JAMES CITY COUNTY
Crozet, ALBEMARLE COUNTY
Cumberland, CUMBERLAND COUNTY
Cumberland vic., CUMBERLAND COUNTY

Danville, PITTSYLVANIA COUNTY
Danville vic., PITTSYLVANIA COUNTY
Delaplane, FAUQUIER COUNTY
Dillwyn vic., AMHERST COUNTY
Dinwiddie vic., DINWIDDIE COUNTY
Ditchley, NORTHUMBERLAND COUNTY
Dumfries, PRINCE WILLIAM COUNTY
Dumfries vic., PRINCE WILLIAM COUNTY
Dunnsville vic., ESSEX COUNTY

Earlysville vic., ALBEMARLE COUNTY
Eastville, NORTHAMPTON COUNTY
Eastville vic., NORTHAMPTON COUNTY
Elliston vic., MONTGOMERY COUNTY

Fairfax
Fairfax vic., FAIRFAX COUNTY
Falls Church
Falmouth, STAFFORD COUNTY
Falmouth vic., STAFFORD COUNTY
Farnham, LANCASTER COUNTY
Farnham, RICHMOND COUNTY
Fishersville vic., AUGUSTA COUNTY
Ford vic., DINWIDDIE COUNTY
Forest vic., BEDFORD COUNTY
Fort Defiance, AUGUSTA COUNTY
Fredericksburg

Fredericksburg vic., SPOTSYLVANIA COUNTY
Fredericksburg vic., STAFFORD COUNTY
Front Royal vic., WARREN COUNTY

Gainesville vic., PRINCE WILLIAM COUNTY
Gladys vic., CAMPBELL COUNTY
Glen Allen vic., HENRICO COUNTY
Glendower, ALBEMARLE COUNTY
Gloucester, GLOUCESTER COUNTY
Gloucester vic., GLOUCESTER COUNTY
Goochland, GOOCHLAND COUNTY
Goochland vic., GOOCHLAND COUNTY
Gordonsville, ORANGE COUNTY
Grafton vic., YORK COUNTY
Great Falls, FAIRFAX COUNTY
Great Falls vic., FAIRFAX COUNTY
Green Springs, LOUISA COUNTY
Greenbush vic., ACCOMAC COUNTY
Greenwood, ALBEMARLE COUNTY
Gretna, PITTSYLVANIA COUNTY
Groveton, PRINCE WILLIAM COUNTY
Guilford, ACCOMAC COUNTY
Guinea vic., SPOTSYLVANIA COUNTY
Gumtree vic., HANOVER COUNTY

Hadlock P.O. vic., NORTHAMPTON COUNTY
Hague, WESTMORELAND COUNTY
Hallwood, ACCOMAC COUNTY
Hampton
Hanover, HANOVER COUNTY
Harrisonburg
Hatton, ALBEMARLE COUNTY
Haymarket, PRINCE WILLIAM COUNTY
Haymarket vic., PRINCE WILLIAM COUNTY
Hebron vic., DINWIDDIE COUNTY
Herndon vic., FAIRFAX COUNTY
Hickory vic.
Hopewell, PRINCE GEORGE COUNTY
Hopewell vic., PRINCE GEORGE COUNTY
Horntown vic., ACCOMAC COUNTY
Howardsville, ALBEMARLE COUNTY
Huguenot vic., POWHATAN COUNTY

Ivy, ALBEMARLE COUNTY

James Store vic., GLOUCESTER COUNTY
Jamestown Island, JAMES CITY COUNTY
Jamesville vic., NORTHAMPTON COUNTY
Jeffersonton vic., CULPEPER COUNTY

Kempsville
Kempsville vic.
Keswick, ALBEMARLE COUNTY
Kilmarnock vic., LANCASTER COUNTY
King William, KING WILLIAM COUNTY
King William vic., KING WILLIAM COUNTY

Lancaster, LANCASTER COUNTY
Lee Mont vic., ACCOMAC COUNTY
Leesburg, LOUDOUN COUNTY
Leesburg vic., LOUDOUN COUNTY
Lenah Post Office, LOUDOUN COUNTY
Lester Manor vic., KING WILLIAM COUNTY
Lexington
Lexington vic., ROCKBRIDGE COUNTY
Lightfoot vic., JAMES CITY COUNTY
Lively vic., LANCASTER COUNTY
Locustville vic., ACCOMAC COUNTY
London Bridge vic.

Long Island vic., CAMPBELL COUNTY
Loretto vic., ESSEX COUNTY
Lorton, FAIRFAX COUNTY
Lorton vic., FAIRFAX COUNTY
Lovingston, NELSON COUNTY
Luray vic., PAGE COUNTY
Lynchburg
Lynchburg vic., CAMPBELL COUNTY
Lynnhaven vic.

Madison, MADISON COUNTY
Madison vic., MADISON COUNTY
Manakin, GOOCHLAND COUNTY
Manakin vic., GOOCHLAND COUNTY
Manassas
Manassas, FAIRFAX COUNTY
Manassas, PRINCE WILLIAM COUNTY
Manassas vic., PRINCE WILLIAM COUNTY
Mangohick, KING WILLIAM COUNTY
Mangohick vic., KING WILLIAM COUNTY
Manquin vic., KING WILLIAM COUNTY
Mappsville vic., ACCOMAC COUNTY
Marion vic., SMYTH COUNTY
Marshall vic., FAUQUIER COUNTY
Mattoax vic., AMELIA COUNTY
Mclean vic.
Mechanicsville vic., HANOVER COUNTY
Merry Point, LANCASTER COUNTY
Merry Point vic., LANCASTER COUNTY
Middletown vic., FREDERICK COUNTY
Millwood, CLARKE COUNTY
Millwood vic., CLARKE COUNTY
Minnieville, PRINCE WILLIAM COUNTY
Modest Town vic., ACCOMAC COUNTY
Montpelier Sta. vic., ORANGE COUNTY
Montpelier Station, ORANGE COUNTY
Morattico, LANCASTER COUNTY
Mount Vernon vic., FAIRFAX COUNTY
Mt. Vernon, FAIRFAX COUNTY

Nassawadox, NORTHAMPTON COUNTY
Nassawadox vic., NORTHAMPTON COUNTY
Naxera vic., GLOUCESTER COUNTY
New Church vic., ACCOMAC COUNTY
New Kent vic., NEW KENT COUNTY
Newport News
Newtown vic., KING AND QUEEN COUNTY
Nimmo vic.
Norfolk
North Garden, ALBEMARLE COUNTY
North Garden vic., ALBEMARLE COUNTY
Nottoway, NOTTOWAY COUNTY
Nuttsville vic., LANCASTER COUNTY

Oak Grove, WESTMORELAND COUNTY
Occoquan, PRINCE WILLIAM COUNTY
Oceana vic.
Old Town Neck, NORTHAMPTON COUNTY
Onancock, ACCOMAC COUNTY
Orange vic., ORANGE COUNTY
Ordinary, GLOUCESTER COUNTY
Ordinary vic., GLOUCESTER COUNTY
Otterdam vic., SURRY COUNTY
Ottoman vic., LANCASTER COUNTY
Owens vic., KING GEORGE COUNTY

Painter vic., ACCOMAC COUNTY
Paris, FAUQUIER COUNTY
Paul's Crossroads, ESSEX COUNTY
Petersburg
Petersburg vic., DINWIDDIE COUNTY
Port Royal, CAROLINE COUNTY
Port Royal vic., CAROLINE COUNTY
Port Royal vic., KING GEORGE COUNTY
Powhatan, POWHATAN COUNTY
Powhatan vic., POWHATAN COUNTY
Prince George vic., PRINCE GEORGE COUNTY
Providence, NEW KENT COUNTY
Providence Forge Vic, NEW KENT COUNTY
Pungoteague, ACCOMAC COUNTY
Pungoteague vic., ACCOMAC COUNTY

Quinby vic., ACCOMAC COUNTY
Quinton vic., NEW KENT COUNTY

Ravensworth vic., FAIRFAX COUNTY
Red Hill, CHARLOTTE COUNTY
Reids Ferry vic.
Richmond
Richmond vic., CHESTERFIELD COUNTY
Richmond vic., GOOCHLAND COUNTY
Richmond vic., HENRICO COUNTY
Rumford vic., KING WILLIAM COUNTY
Rustburg vic., CAMPBELL COUNTY

Sabot, GOOCHLAND COUNTY
Saint Brides vic.
Salem, ROANOKE COUNTY
Salem Church, SPOTSYLVANIA COUNTY
Scottsville, ALBEMARLE COUNTY
Shadwell, ALBEMARLE COUNTY
Shadyside vic., NORTHAMPTON COUNTY
Simeon, ALBEMARLE COUNTY
Simeon vic., ALBEMARLE COUNTY
Skinquarter, CHESTERFIELD COUNTY
Smithfield, ISLE OF WIGHT COUNTY
Smithfield vic., ISLE OF WIGHT COUNTY
Somers vic., LANCASTER COUNTY
South Boston vic., HALIFAX COUNTY
South Hill, MECKLENBURG COUNTY
South Richmond
South Richmond, CHESTERFIELD COUNTY
Sperryville vic., RAPPAHANNOCK COUNTY
Spotsylvania, SPOTSYLVANIA COUNTY
Spotsylvania vic., SPOTSYLVANIA COUNTY
Stafford, STAFFORD COUNTY
Stafford vic., STAFFORD COUNTY
Staunton
Staunton vic., AUGUSTA COUNTY
Strasburg, SHENENDOAH COUNTY
Stratford, WESTMORELAND COUNTY
Suffolk
Suffolk vic.
Surry vic., SURRY COUNTY
Sussex, SUSSEX COUNTY
Sweet Chalybeate, ALLEGHANY COUNTY
Sweet Hall, KING WILLIAM COUNTY
Sweet Hall vic., KING WILLIAM COUNTY

Tappahannock, ESSEX COUNTY
Tasley vic., ACCOMAC COUNTY
Tettington vic., CHARLES CITY COUNTY
The Plains vic., FAUQUIER COUNTY
Thoroughfare, PRINCE WILLIAM COUNTY

Tidewater vic., RICHMOND COUNTY
Toano, JAMES CITY COUNTY
Toano vic., JAMES CITY COUNTY
Townsend vic., NORTHAMPTON COUNTY
Tucker Hill vic., WESTMORELAND COUNTY
Tunstall vic., NEW KENT COUNTY

Upperville, FAUQUIER COUNTY
Urbanna, MIDDLESEX COUNTY
Urbanna vic., MIDDLESEX COUNTY

Vienna vic., FAIRFAX COUNTY

Wardtown vic., NORTHAMPTON COUNTY
Ware Neck, GLOUCESTER COUNTY
Warsaw, RICHMOND COUNTY
Warsaw vic., RICHMOND COUNTY
Washington, RAPPAHANNOCK COUNTY
Waterfall, PRINCE WILLIAM COUNTY
Waterford, LOUDOUN COUNTY
Waynesboro
Waynesboro vic., AUGUSTA COUNTY
Weems, LANCASTER COUNTY
West Point vic., KING WILLIAM COUNTY
Westmoreland, WESTMORELAND COUNTY
Weyers Cave vic., AUGUSTA COUNTY
White Marsh, GLOUCESTER COUNTY
White Marsh vic., GLOUCESTER COUNTY
White Post vic., CLARKE COUNTY
Williamsburg
Williamsburg vic.
Williamsburg vic., JAMES CITY COUNTY
Willis vic., FLOYD COUNTY
Winchester
Winchester vic., FREDERICK COUNTY
Woodbridge vic., PRINCE WILLIAM COUNTY
Woodford, CAROLINE COUNTY
Woods Crossroads Vic, GLOUCESTER COUNTY
Worsham, PRINCE EDWARD COUNTY
Wyndham vic., POWHATAN COUNTY

Yorktown, YORK COUNTY
Yorktown vic., YORK COUNTY

Zion's Crossroads, HANOVER COUNTY

Washington

Arden vic., STEVENS COUNTY

Bellingham, WHATCOM COUNTY

Cashup, WHITMAN COUNTY
Centralia, LEWIS COUNTY
Chambers Prairie, THURSTON COUNTY
Chehalis, LEWIS COUNTY
Chehalis vic., LEWIS COUNTY
Chewelah, STEVENS COUNTY
Chewelah vic., STEVENS COUNTY
Chimacum, JEFFERSON COUNTY
Chimacum vic., JEFFERSON COUNTY
Claquato, LEWIS COUNTY
Colville vic., STEVENS COUNTY
Coupeville, ISLAND COUNTY
Coupeville vic., ISLAND COUNTY
Cowiche vic., YAKIMA COUNTY

Deer Park vic., SPOKANE COUNTY
Dungeness vic., CLALLAM COUNTY

Ford vic., STEVENS COUNTY
Fort Casey vic., ISLAND COUNTY
Fort Rains, SKAMANIA COUNTY
Fort Steilacoom, PIERCE COUNTY
Friday Harbor, SAN JUAN COUNTY

Goldendale, KLICKITAT COUNTY
Goldendale vic., KLICKITAT COUNTY

Hillyard, SPOKANE COUNTY

Kettle Falls vic., STEVENS COUNTY

Lincoln vic., LINCOLN COUNTY

Mission Orchard, ASOTIN COUNTY
Montesano, GRAYS HARBOR COUNTY
Mossy Rock vic., LEWIS COUNTY

Naches vic., YAKIMA COUNTY

Oak Harbor vic., ISLAND COUNTY
Olympia, THURSTON COUNTY
Omak vic., OKANOGAN COUNTY
Oysterville, PACIFIC COUNTY

Port Townsend, JEFFERSON COUNTY
Pullman Junction vic., WHITMAN COUNTY
Puyallup, PIERCE COUNTY

San De Fuca, ISLAND COUNTY
San De Fuca vic., ISLAND COUNTY
Sawyer vic., YAKIMA COUNTY
Seattle, KING COUNTY
South Montesano, GRAYS HARBOR COUNTY
Spokane, SPOKANE COUNTY
Steilacoom, PIERCE COUNTY
Stember Creek, GARFIELD COUNTY
Stimson vic., GRAYS HARBOR COUNTY
Stimson vic., THURSTON COUNTY

Tacoma, PIERCE COUNTY
Tampico vic., YAKIMA COUNTY

Union Gap, YAKIMA COUNTY
Usk, PEND OREILLE COUNTY

Vancouver, CLARK COUNTY
Vancouver vic., CLARK COUNTY

Walla Walla vic., WALLA WALLA COUNTY
Wenas, YAKIMA COUNTY
White Bluffs vic., FRANKLIN COUNTY
White Swan, YAKIMA COUNTY
White Swan vic., YAKIMA COUNTY

West Virginia

Alderson, GREENBRIER COUNTY

Barracksville, MARION COUNTY
Benwood, MARSHALL COUNTY
Berkeley Springs, MORGAN COUNTY
Bethany, BROOKE COUNTY
Bretz, PRESTON COUNTY
Bridgeport, HARRISON COUNTY

Cedar Grove, KANAWHA COUNTY
Charles Town, JEFFERSON COUNTY

Charles Town, KANAWHA COUNTY
Charles Town vic., JEFFERSON COUNTY
Charleston, KANAWHA COUNTY

Darke, JEFFERSON COUNTY
Darke vic., JEFFERSON COUNTY
Dellslow vic., MONONGALIA COUNTY
Dunmore, POCAHONTAS COUNTY

Elm Grove, OHIO COUNTY

Gauley Bridge, FAYETTE COUNTY
Gerrardstown, BERKELEY COUNTY
Grafton, TAYLOR COUNTY
Great Cacapon, MORGAN COUNTY

Halltown, JEFFERSON COUNTY
Harpers Ferry, JEFFERSON COUNTY
Harpers Ferry, KANAWHA COUNTY
Hillsboro vic., POCAHONTAS COUNTY
Huntington, CABELL COUNTY

Kearneyville, JEFFERSON COUNTY
Keyser, MINERAL COUNTY

Leetown, JEFFERSON COUNTY
Leetown vic., JEFFERSON COUNTY
Lewisburg, GREENBRIER COUNTY

Malden, KANAWHA COUNTY
Martinsburg, BERKELEY COUNTY
Middleway, JEFFERSON COUNTY
Moorefield, HARDY COUNTY
Morgantown, MONONGALIA COUNTY
Morgantown vic., MONONGALIA COUNTY
Myerstown vic., JEFFERSON COUNTY

New Creek vic., MINERAL COUNTY

Parkersburg, WOOD COUNTY
Parkersburg vic., PENDLETON COUNTY
Paw Paw, MORGAN COUNTY
Petroleum, RITCHIE COUNTY
Point Pleasant, MASON COUNTY

Rainelle, GREENBRIER COUNTY
Ranson, JEFFERSON COUNTY
Red Sulphur Springs, MONROE COUNTY
Renick, GREENBRIER COUNTY
Rippon vic., JEFFERSON COUNTY
Romney, HAMPSHIRE COUNTY
Ronceverte, GREENBRIER COUNTY

Salt Sulphur Springs, MONROE COUNTY
Shenandoah Junction, JEFFERSON COUNTY
Shepherdstown, JEFFERSON COUNTY
Shepherdstown vic., JEFFERSON COUNTY
Summit Point, JEFFERSON COUNTY
Sweet Springs, MONROE COUNTY

Talcott vic., SUMMERS COUNTY
Tunnelton, PRESTON COUNTY

Union, MONROE COUNTY

Wheatland, JEFFERSON COUNTY
Wheeling, OHIO COUNTY
White Sulphur Spring, GREENBRIER COUNTY

Wisconsin

Ackerville vic., WASHINGTON COUNTY

Baraboo, SAUK COUNTY
Big Bend vic., WAUKESHA COUNTY
Burlington, RACINE COUNTY
Burlington vic., RACINE COUNTY

Cedarburg, OZAUKEE COUNTY
Cedarburg vic., OZAUKEE COUNTY
Chamberlain, WAUKESHA COUNTY

Daleyville vic., DANE COUNTY
De Pere, BROWN COUNTY
Delafield, WAUKESHA COUNTY
Dodgerville, IOWA COUNTY

East Troy vic., WALWORTH COUNTY
Elkhorn, WALWORTH COUNTY

Freistadt, OZAUKEE COUNTY

Green Bay, BROWN COUNTY
Greenbush, SHEBOYGAN COUNTY

Hales Corners, MILWAUKEE COUNTY
Hamilton, OZAUKEE COUNTY
Honey Creek vic., RACINE COUNTY

Iron Ridge vic., DODGE COUNTY

Jackson, WASHINGTON COUNTY
Jackson vic., WASHINGTON COUNTY

Kaukauna, OUTGAMIE COUNTY
Kirchhayn vic., WASHINGTON COUNTY
Krichhayn, WASHINGTON COUNTY

La Crosse, LA CROSSE COUNTY
Lake Geneva, WALWORTH COUNTY
Lebanon Township, DODGE COUNTY
Lena, OCONTO COUNTY
Lowell, DODGE COUNTY

Madison, DANE COUNTY
Menomonee Falls vic., WAUKESHA COUNTY
Merton, WAUKESHA COUNTY
Milton, ROCK COUNTY
Milwaukee, MILWAUKEE COUNTY
Milwaukee vic., WAUKESHA COUNTY
Mineral Point, IOWA COUNTY

Nashotah vic., WAUKESHA COUNTY
Neenah, WINNEBAGO COUNTY
Neenha, WINNEBAGO COUNTY
New Diggings, LAFAYETTE COUNTY

Okauchee, WAUKESHA COUNTY

Palmyra, JEFFERSON COUNTY
Paynesville, MILWAUKEE COUNTY
Platteville, GRANT COUNTY
Port Washington, OZAUKEE COUNTY
Portage, COLUMBIA COUNTY

Prairie Du Chien, CRAWFORD COUNTY
Prospect, WAUKESHA COUNTY

Racine, RACINE COUNTY
Richfield, WASHINGTON COUNTY
Ripon, FOND DU LAC COUNTY
Rochester vic., RACINE COUNTY

Saylesville, WAUKESHA COUNTY

Thiensville vic., OZAUKEE COUNTY

Watertown, JEFFERSON COUNTY
Watertown vic., DODGE COUNTY
Waukesha, WAUKESHA COUNTY
Waupaca, WAUPACA COUNTY
Wausau, MARATHON COUNTY
Wauwatosa, MILWAUKEE COUNTY
West Bend vic., WASHINGTON COUNTY

Wyoming

Atlantic City, FREMONT COUNTY

Centennial, ALBANY COUNTY
Cheyenne, GOSHEN COUNTY
Cheyenne, LARAMIE COUNTY
Chugwater, PLATTE COUNTY
Cody vic., PARK COUNTY

Fort Fred Steele, CARBON COUNTY
Fort Laramie, GOSHEN COUNTY
Fort Laramie vic., GOSHEN COUNTY
Fort Washakie, FREMONT COUNTY

Granger, SWEETWATER COUNTY
Guernsey, PLATTE COUNTY

Kell vic., TETON COUNTY
Kelly vic., TETON COUNTY

Laramie, ALBANY COUNTY

Miner's Delight, FREMONT COUNTY
Moneta, FREMONT COUNTY
Moose, TETON COUNTY
Moose vic., TETON COUNTY

Norris Junciton, TETON COUNTY

Pepperville, PLATTE COUNTY
Piedmont, UINTA COUNTY
Point Of Rocks, SWEETWATER COUNTY

Rock River, ALBANY COUNTY
Rock River vic., ALBANY COUNTY

Sheridan, SHERIDAN COUNTY
South Pass City, FREMONT COUNTY

W. Laramie, ALBANY COUNTY
Wheatland vic., ALBANY COUNTY
Woods Landing vic., ALBANY COUNTY

Yellowstone Nat'l Pk, TETON COUNTY

View of the main church of the San Xavier del Bac Mission, near Tucson, Pima County, Arizona. (HABS ARIZ–13, LC HABS ARIZ, 10–TUSCO.V, 3–1)